Tort La

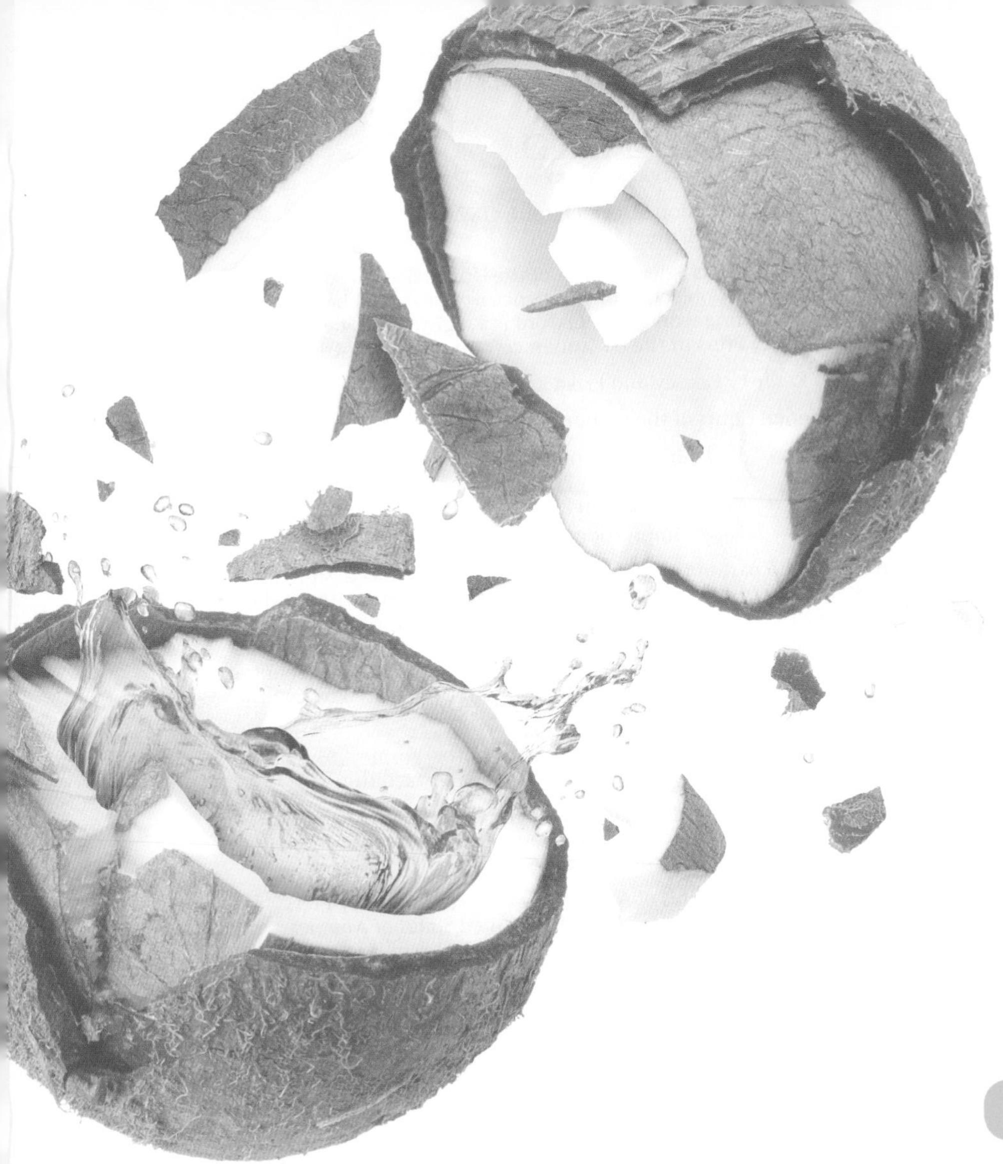

7th Edition

TORT LAW

Kirsty Horsey & Erika Rackley

OXFORD
UNIVERSITY PRESS

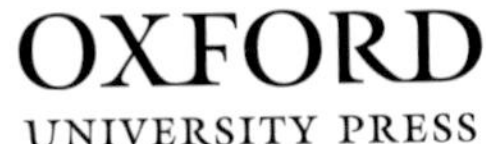

OXFORD
UNIVERSITY PRESS

Great Clarendon Street, Oxford, OX2 6DP,
United Kingdom

Oxford University Press is a department of the University of Oxford. It furthers the University's objective of excellence in research, scholarship, and education by publishing worldwide. Oxford is a registered trade mark of Oxford University Press in the UK and in certain other countries

Fourth edition 2015
Fifth edition 2017
Sixth edition 2019

Impression: 1

Published in the United States of America by Oxford University Press
198 Madison Avenue, New York, NY 10016, United States of America

British Library Cataloguing in Publication Data
Data available

Library of Congress Control Number: 2021941601

ISBN 978–0–19–886776–0

Printed in Great Britain by
Bell & Bain Ltd., Glasgow

About the authors

Kirsty Horsey

Kirsty Horsey is a Reader in Law at the University of Kent, teaching tort law to undergraduate students across all years. Her research interests lie in the overlap of medical, family and tort law. She has written widely on the regulation of assisted reproduction and in particular surrogacy, and is the editor of a number of related edited collections including, most recently, *Revisiting the Regulation of Human Fertilisation and Embryology* (Routledge, 2015)). She is co-author (with Erika Rackley) of *Casebook on Tort Law* (16th edn, OUP, 2021). She tweets at @khorsey.

Erika Rackley

Erika Rackley is a Professor in the Law School at the University of Kent. She has taught tort law at a number of universities in the UK. Her research interests are broadly in the field of feminism, gender and law, particularly in relation to judicial diversity. She is author of *Women, Judging and the Judiciary: From Difference to Diversity* (Routledge, 2012), co-author (with Kirsty Horsey) of *Casebook on Tort Law* (16th edn, OUP, 2021) and co-editor of *Feminist Perspectives on Tort Law* (Routledge, 2012) and *Women's Legal Landmarks: Celebrating the History of Women and Law in the UK and Ireland* (Hart, 2018). She occasionally tweets at @erikarackley.

Keep up to date with changes and developments in this fast-moving area of law with updates at **@horseyrackley**. Section references enable you to easily identify the relevant material in the book.

Preface

It has been an eventful couple of years since our last edition. As always, this edition includes a number of new cases. These are listed, with others, at the front of this book.

This edition of *Tort Law* and our companion casebook *Casebook on Tort Law* (previously *Kidner's Casebook on Torts*) have been updated during the UK lockdown in response to the ongoing global Coronavirus pandemic. Inevitably, this has brought with it a number of unique challenges. We are extremely grateful for the patience and support of our editor, Sarah Stephenson, and everyone at OUP as excuses have been made and deadlines missed. We are also indebted to our much trusted and hugely respected copy-editor, Joy Ruskin-Tompkins, who we're sure had to correct even more typos and formatting errors than usual. We remain extremely grateful to our colleagues and students—both at our own institution and elsewhere, anonymous and known—who continue to take the time to comment on earlier editions and whose knowledge and insights inform this one. Particular thanks are due to Charlie Webb for his help with revisions to Chapter 3. Thank you for your time and collegiality.

Finally, as always, thanks to Mike, Frank, Billy, Charlie, Enyo and Kasper—you rock!

We have done our best to state the law as of 31 March 2021.

Kirsty Horsey
Erika Rackley

New to this edition

The seventh edition has been thoroughly revised to reflect all recent developments in the law of torts since publication of the last edition, including new cases:

- *Henderson* v *Dorset Healthcare University NHS Foundation Trust* [2020] UKSC 43 (illegality defence)
- *Serafin* v *Malkiewicz and others* [2020] UKSC 23 (defamation)
- *WM Morrison Supermarkets plc* v *Various Claimants* [2020] UKSC 12 (vicarious liability)
- *Barclays Bank plc* v *Various Claimants* [2020] UKSC 13 (vicarious liability)
- *R (on the application of Jalloh (formerly Jollah))* v *Secretary of State for the Home Department* [2020] UKSC 4 (false imprisonment)
- *ZXC* v *Bloomberg LP* [2020] 3 WLR 838 (privacy)
- *Lachaux* v *Independent Print* [2019] UKSC 27 (defamation)
- *Poole Borough Council* v *GN* [2019] UKSC 25 (liability of public bodies)
- *Equitas Insurance Ltd* v *Municipal Mutual Insurance Ltd* [2019] EWCA Civ 718 (causation)
- *Khan* v *Meadows* [2019] EWCA Civ 152 (wrongful birth; damages)
- *Fearn and others* v *The Board of Trustees of the Tate Gallery* [2020] EWCA Civ 104 (nuisance; privacy)

Guided tour of learning features

Tort Law is a pedagogically rich learning resource. This guided tour will show you how to make the most of your text.

Problem-focused approach to learning

Problem question

Read this problem question carefully, and keep it through the chapter that follows. At the end of the c what you have learnt to the problem question and a

Margaret, who is 75, is in the supermarket on a busy Satur in her chest. It transpires she is having a heart attack and the supermarket is crowded, no one comes to help her.

Brian, the store manager, puts a call out over the PA present, but otherwise offers no assistance. Hearing th comes forward and tries to help Margaret, but fails to

At the beginning of each chapter you will find a **problem question** of the type you might expect to see in an exam. Don't worry about answering this question right away—it's just to give you a taste of the kind of topics and issues covered.

Keep the question in mind while you read the chapter, and at the end of the chapter you will be asked to try to answer it, and given some ideas about how you might begin to approach it.

If you need some more pointers in thinking about how to tackle this question:

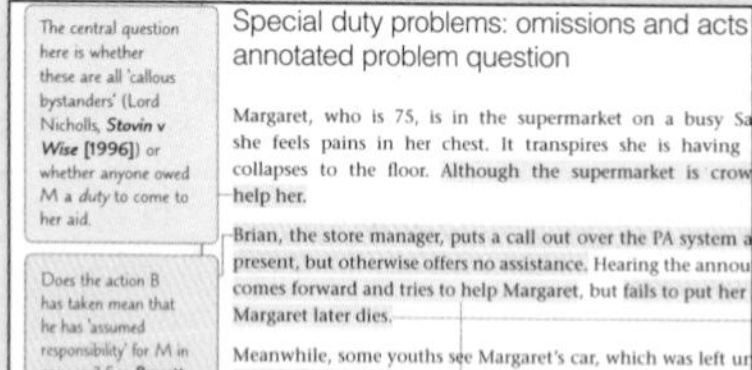
The central question here is whether these are all 'callous bystanders' (Lord Nicholls, ***Stovin v Wise* [1996]**) or whether anyone owed M a *duty* to come to her aid.

Does the action B has taken mean that he has 'assumed responsibility' for M in

Special duty problems: omissions and acts
annotated problem question

Margaret, who is 75, is in the supermarket on a busy Sa she feels pains in her chest. It transpires she is having collapses to the floor. Although the supermarket is crow help her.

Brian, the store manager, puts a call out over the PA system a present, but otherwise offers no assistance. Hearing the annou comes forward and tries to help Margaret, but fails to put her Margaret later dies.

Meanwhile, some youths see Margaret's car, which was left ur

An **annotated version of the problem with issues and cases to consider** can be found in the Appendix.

A **suggested outline answer** to check your ideas against can be found in the **online resources** that accompany the book.

Considering these problem questions is a way of enhancing your skills and there is not necessarily one way to approach an answer. You should ensure that you take on board the specific guidance from your institutions on answering such questions.

In each chapter you will also find included

List of brief scenarios After the problem question, each chapter opens with a bullet-pointed list of scenarios to get you thinking about the issues at stake. The likely outcomes are outlined in the chapter.

Pause for reflection boxes These are placed to help you stop, reflect on and question what you have been reading. They help you to consider how the law works in practice, its policy ramifications and how it relates to other key issues.

Counterpoint boxes These boxes highlight critiques of the law, identify areas of controversy or problems with the current law, and/or suggest possible options for reform.

Annotated statutes and judgments These explain the more difficult points of law and help you to develop the invaluable skills of reading, interpreting and analysing—essential for your study.

End-of-chapter questions To test your understanding and prepare for seminars and exams.

Tort Law is also accompanied by **online resources** providing students and lecturers with ready-to-use teaching and learning resources. **www.oup.com/he/horsey7e**

Student resources can be used to consolidate your learning after each lecture, to prepare for seminars, as a starting point to research a coursework essay, and of course during your revision. The resources available include:

- **Additional content** 'Introduction to the tort of negligence: putting it together', 'A basic overview of product liability in contract law' and 'The "McLibel" litigation'.
- **Annotated web links** video clips of news reports and direct links to key cases.
- **Outline answers to chapter opening problem questions** check the answer you have drafted and gain pointers on how to improve your grade.
- **Hints on answering end-of-chapter questions, and the questions posed in the 'Counterpoint' and 'Pause for reflection' boxes** check you're on the right track.
- **General guidance on how to answer problem questions and essays**
- **Further annotated judgments with explanatory notes and points for you to consider** help you to develop the skills of reading and analysing judgments.
- **Electronic versions of annotated judgments and statutes from the book** so that you can refer to them quickly while reading the relevant chapters.

Lecture resources include a fully customisable test bank containing ready-made assessments with which to test your students and aid their learning. Each answer is accompanied by feedback to explain to the student why their answer is correct or incorrect, and where in this book they can find further information.

Contents in brief

TABLE OF CASES xxiv
TABLE OF LEGISLATION xlvii
LIST OF ABBREVIATIONS OF COMMONLY CITED WORKS lii

1 Introduction 1

PART I The tort of negligence 25

2 Introduction to the tort of negligence 29
3 Duty of care: basic principles 58
4 Special duty problems: omissions and acts of third parties 78
5 Special duty problems: psychiatric harm 102
6 Special duty problems: public bodies 138
7 Special duty problems: economic loss 188
8 Breach of duty: the standard of care 217
9 Causation and remoteness of damage 251
10 Defences to negligence 290

PART II Special liability regimes 315

11 Occupiers' liability 319
12 Product liability 353
13 Employers' liability 386
14 Breach of statutory duty 397

PART III The personal torts 407

15 Intentional interferences with the person 410
16 Invasion of privacy 449
17 Defamation 485

PART IV The land torts 535

18 Trespass to land and nuisance 537
19 Actions under the rule of *Rylands* v *Fletcher* 583

PART V Liability, damages and limitations 605

20 Vicarious liability 607
21 Damages for death and personal injuries 625

APPENDIX: ANNOTATED PROBLEM QUESTIONS 665
INDEX 683

Contents in full

TABLE OF CASES xxiv
TABLE OF LEGISLATION xlvii
LIST OF ABBREVIATIONS OF COMMONLY CITED WORKS lii

1 Introduction **1**
1.1 Introduction 1
1.2 What is tort law? 2
1.2.1 What interests does tort law protect? 3
1.3 The disparate aims of tort law: a case study on *Woodroffe-Hedley* v *Cuthbertson* 8
1.3.1 Doing (corrective) justice 9
1.3.2 Compensation 11
1.3.3 Deterrence 18
1.3.4 Vindication 19
1.4 Tort law and the Human Rights Act 1998 20
1.5 A note on terminology 22
1.6 Conclusion 22
End-of-chapter questions 23
Further reading 23

PART I The tort of negligence 25

2 Introduction to the tort of negligence **29**
2.1 Introduction 29
2.2 Mapping the historical development of the tort of negligence 32
2.3 Explaining the historical development of the tort of negligence 37
2.3.1 The influence of social and political thinking in an age of principles 38
2.3.2 A positive response to victims of workplace injuries 39
2.3.3 Supporting infant industries 39
2.4 The role of the modern law of negligence 40
2.5 The elements of the tort of negligence 41
2.5.1 Duty 42
2.5.2 Breach 43
2.5.3 Causation and remoteness 44
2.5.4 Putting it all together 44
2.6 Case example: *X & Y* v *London Borough of Hounslow* 47

2.7 Conclusion 56
End-of-chapter questions 56
Further reading 56

3 Duty of care: basic principles 58
3.1 Introduction 58
3.2 From *Donoghue* to *Caparo*—a brief history of the duty of care 61
3.3 Establishing a duty of care: *Caparo Industries* v *Dickman* 65
3.3.1 The myth of the *Caparo* three-stage test 65
3.3.2 Debunking the three-stage 'test' 68
3.3.3 The incremental approach 69
3.4 Where does this leave us? 74
3.5 Conclusion 76
End-of-chapter questions 76
Further reading 77

4 Special duty problems: omissions and acts of third parties 78
4.1 Introduction 78
4.2 Acts and omissions 79
4.2.1 Control 84
4.2.2 Assumption of responsibility 86
4.2.3 Creating or adopting risks 88
4.3 Summary of when a duty of care may be found in respect of omissions 89
4.4 Liability for acts of third parties: the general rule 89
4.5 When is there liability for the acts of third parties? 89
4.5.1 A special relationship between defendant and claimant 90
4.5.2 A special relationship between defendant and third party 95
4.5.3 Creating a source of danger 96
4.5.4 A failure to abate a known danger 97
4.6 Summary of when a duty of care may be found for the actions of third parties 99
4.7 Conclusion 100
End-of-chapter questions 100
Further reading 101

5 Special duty problems: psychiatric harm 102
5.1 Introduction 103
5.2 What is psychiatric harm? 103
5.3 The general exclusionary rule 105
5.4 'Primary' and 'secondary' victims 107
5.5 Primary victims 108

5.6 Secondary victims 112
5.6.1 Relationship with the immediate victim 116
5.6.2 Proximity in time and space 118
5.6.3 The means by which the 'shock' is caused 119
5.7 Beyond primary and secondary victims 127
5.7.1 Rescuers 127
5.7.2 Involuntary participants 131
5.7.3 Communication of shocking news 132
5.7.4 Self-harm by the defendant 133
5.7.5 The 'assumption of responsibility' cases 134
5.8 Conclusion 136
End-of-chapter questions 136
Further reading 137

6 Special duty problems: public bodies 138
6.1 Introduction 139
6.2 The general exclusionary rule 140
6.2.1 Why is the judiciary reluctant to allow recovery? 140
6.3 When will public bodies owe a duty of care? 142
6.3.1 An alternative claim? 146
6.4 The impact of European jurisprudence 148
6.4.1 The *Osman* case 148
6.4.2 The *Z* and *TP and KM* cases 152
6.4.3 The implications for domestic law 154
6.5 The emergency services and armed forces 155
6.5.1 The fire service 155
6.5.2 The ambulance service 158
6.5.3 The police 160
6.5.4 The armed forces 171
6.5.5 The coastguard 173
6.5.6 Duty: the emergency services and armed forces—at a glance 174
6.6 Other types of public body 174
6.6.1 Justiciability 175
6.7 The recognition of new types of claim—'messed up lives'? 179
6.7.1 Education-based claims 180
6.7.2 Social claims 182
6.8 Conclusion 184
End-of-chapter questions 185
Further reading 186

7 Special duty problems: economic loss 188

7.1 Introduction 188
7.2 What is 'pure' economic loss? 190
7.3 Exceptions to the exclusionary rule: *Hedley Byrne* v *Heller* 195
7.4 Claims for pure economic loss in negligence before *Murphy* 197
7.5 Extending *Hedley Byrne* 201
7.5.1 A special relationship 201
7.5.2 Voluntary assumption of risk 203
7.5.3 Reasonable reliance 206
7.6 Beyond *Hedley Byrne*: the 'will cases' and a more flexible approach 210
7.7 Conclusion 215
End-of-chapter questions 215
Further reading 216

8 Breach of duty: the standard of care 217

8.1 Introduction 217
8.2 A test of reasonableness 219
8.3 An objective standard 221
8.3.1 Children 225
8.3.2 Common practice and special skills 226
8.3.2.1 The *Bolam* test 226
8.4 Setting the standard of care 236
8.4.1 Probability that the injury will occur 237
8.4.2 Seriousness of the injury 239
8.4.3 Cost of taking precautions 240
8.4.4 Social value of the activity 241
8.5 A balancing act 243
8.5.1 The Compensation Act 2006 and the Social Action, Responsibility and Heroism Act 2015 245
8.6 Establishing breach 247
8.7 Conclusion 248
End-of-chapter questions 249
Further reading 250

9 Causation and remoteness of damage 251

9.1 Introduction 251
9.2 Factual causation—the 'but for' test 254
9.2.1 Explaining the test 254
9.2.2 Problems with the test 256
9.2.2.1 Multiple potential causes 256

9.2.2.2 'Unjust' results 1: the mesothelioma exception 261
9.2.2.3 'Unjust' results 2: failure to inform 270
9.2.2.4 Indeterminate causes 271
9.2.2.5 Loss of chance 273
9.2.2.6 Uncertain actions 277
9.2.3 Multiple sufficient causes 277
9.3 Legal causation 279
9.3.1 Remoteness of damage 280
9.3.1.1 The 'egg shell skull' rule 282
9.3.2 Intervening acts 283
9.3.2.1 Later negligent acts 283
9.3.2.2 Acts of the claimant 285
9.4 Conclusion 287
End-of-chapter questions 287
Further reading 288

10 Defences to negligence 290
10.1 Introduction 290
10.2 Voluntarily assuming the risk (*volenti*) 291
10.2.1 Establishing the defence 293
10.3 Illegality 297
10.4 Contributory negligence 304
10.4.1 Did the claimant fail to exercise reasonable care for their own safety? 305
10.4.2 Did this failure contribute to the claimant's damage? 306
10.4.3 By what extent should the claimant's damages be reduced? 307
10.5 Conclusion 312
End-of-chapter questions 313
Further reading 314

PART II Special liability regimes 315

11 Occupiers' liability 319
11.1 Introduction 319
11.2 The Occupiers' Liability Act 1957 321
11.2.1 When is a duty owed? 322
11.2.1.1 Occupiers: 'control of premises' 323
11.2.1.2 Visitors: by invitation or permission only 325
11.2.1.3 Premises: including 'any fixed or moveable structure' 327
11.2.2 The standard of care 327
11.2.2.1 Children 329

11.2.2.2 'Persons in the exercise of a calling' 331
11.2.2.3 Warnings 331
11.2.2.4 Notices excluding liability 333
11.2.2.5 Faulty execution of work 334
11.2.2.6 Defences 335
11.3 The Occupiers' Liability Act 1957—annotated 337
11.4 The Occupiers' Liability Act 1984 339
11.4.1 Establishing a duty 340
11.4.1.1 Awareness of (or reasonable grounds to believe in the existence of) danger 344
11.4.1.2 Knowledge of (or reasonable grounds to believe in) the presence of a non-visitor in the vicinity of danger 345
11.4.1.3 Reasonable expectation of protection against the risk 345
11.4.2 The standard of care 346
11.4.2.1 Warnings 346
11.4.2.2 Risks willingly accepted by the non-visitor 346
11.5 The Occupiers' Liability Act 1984—annotated 347
11.6 The Occupiers' Liability Acts 1957and 1984—at a glance 349
11.7 Conclusion 351
End-of-chapter questions 351
Further reading 352

12 Product liability 353
12.1 Introduction 353
12.2 Defective products—claims in negligence 355
12.2.1 The scope of liability under *Donoghue* 356
12.2.1.1 Duty of care 356
12.2.1.2 Breach and causation 358
12.2.2 The limits of negligence liability 360
12.3 Defective products—claims under Part 1 of the Consumer Protection Act 1987 362
12.3.1 Bringing a claim 363
12.3.2 What is a 'defect'? 364
12.3.3 Causation and limitations 374
12.3.4 Defences 375
12.3.5 Overall effect of the Consumer Protection Act 1987 377
12.4 Part 1 of the Consumer Protection Act 1987—annotated 379
12.5 Claiming under Part 1 of the Consumer Protection Act 1987—at a glance 383
12.6 Conclusion 383
End-of-chapter questions 384
Further reading 385

13 Employers' liability 386
13.1 Introduction 386
13.2 An employer's personal non-delegable duty of care 388
13.2.1 Competent workforce 390
13.2.2 Adequate material and equipment 391
13.2.3 A proper system of working (including effective supervision) 392
13.2.4 A safe workplace 395
13.3 Conclusion 395
End-of-chapter questions 396
Further reading 396

14 Breach of statutory duty 397
14.1 Introduction 397
14.2 Does the statute give rise to a claim in tort law? 398
14.3 Is a duty owed to the claimant? 403
14.4 Has the duty been breached and does the harm fall within the scope of the duty? 404
14.5 Conclusion 405
End-of-chapter questions 405
Further reading 406

PART III The personal torts 407

15 Intentional interferences with the person 410
15.1 Introduction 410
15.2 Battery 414
15.2.1 Intentional application . . . 414
15.2.2 . . . of unlawful touching 415
15.2.3 Direct and immediate force 417
15.2.4 Lawful justification or excuse 417
15.3 Assault 418
15.3.1 Intention 418
15.3.2 Reasonable apprehension . . . 418
15.3.3 . . . of immediate and direct application of unlawful force 419
15.3.4 Lawful justification or excuse 421
15.4 False imprisonment 421
15.4.1 Intention 422
15.4.2 A complete restriction of the claimant's freedom of movement . . . 423
15.4.3 . . . without legal authorisation 428

15.5 Defences: lawful justification or excuse 431
15.5.1 Consent 431
15.5.2 Necessity 434
15.5.3 Self-defence 435
15.6 Intentional infliction of physical harm or distress 436
15.6.1 The tort in *Wilkinson* v *Downton* 436
15.6.2 The Protection from Harassment Act 1997 440
15.7 Conclusion 446
End-of-chapter questions 447
Further reading 447

16 Invasion of privacy 449
16.1 Introduction 449
16.2 A tort of invasion of privacy? 451
16.3 How has privacy been protected? 454
16.4 Breach of confidence 459
16.4.1 A new tort: 'misuse of private information' 463
16.4.1.1 What is a 'reasonable expectation of privacy'? 465
16.5 Towards the modern approach 469
16.5.1 The Human Rights Act 1998 and European case law 469
16.5.2 Balancing privacy and freedom of expression 471
16.6 Privacy claims today 473
16.6.1 Children and privacy 475
16.6.2 Iniquity 477
16.6.3 Limits to the current protection 480
16.7 Conclusion 482
End-of-chapter questions 483
Further reading 484

17 Defamation 485
17.1 Introduction 485
17.2 Establishing a claim in defamation 488
17.2.1 Who can sue? 488
17.3 Is the statement defamatory? 490
17.3.1 Innuendo 498
17.4 Does the statement refer to the claimant? 501
17.4.1 References to a group or class 503
17.5 Has the statement been 'published'? 504
17.5.1 Republication 505

17.6 Defences 506
17.6.1 Truth 506
17.6.2 Privilege 509
17.6.2.1 Absolute privilege 510
17.6.2.2 Qualified privilege 510
17.6.3 Publication in a matter of public interest 512
17.6.4 Honest opinion 518
17.6.4.1 An opinion not fact . . . 518
17.6.4.2 . . . that indicates the basis of the opinion 520
17.6.4.3 . . . and could be—and is—honestly held 521
17.7 Distributors, including operators of websites 522
17.8 Offer of amends 523
17.9 Remedies: damages and injunctions 524
17.10 The Defamation Act 2013—annotated 526
17.11 Conclusion 531
End-of-chapter questions 532
Further reading 533

PART IV The land torts 535

18 Trespass to land and nuisance 537
18.1 Introduction 538
18.2 Trespass to land 539
18.2.1 Intention 540
18.2.2 Defences 542
18.2.3 Trespass *ab initio* 544
18.2.4 Remedies 545
18.3 Private nuisance 545
18.3.1 What is private nuisance? 547
18.3.2 Who can sue? 550
18.3.3 The concept of the 'reasonable user' 553
18.3.3.1 Factors that are always considered 555
18.3.3.2 A factor that is sometimes considered, dependent on the type of claim 555
18.3.3.3 Other factors that are sometimes considered, if relevant on the facts 559
18.3.4 Defences to nuisance 564
18.3.4.1 Statutory authority 565
18.3.4.2 Twenty years' prescription and coming to nuisance 566
18.4 Remedies and the human rights dimension 570

18.4.1 Injunctions 570
18.4.2 Abatement and damages 571
18.4.3 Under the Human Rights Act 1998 574
18.5 Public nuisance 578
18.6 Conclusion 580
End-of-chapter questions 581
Further reading 582

19 Actions under the rule of *Rylands* v *Fletcher* 583
19.1 Introduction 583
19.2 The rule in *Rylands* v *Fletcher* 584
19.2.1 'The defendant brings on his land for his own purposes something likely to do mischief . . . ' 586
19.2.2 ' . . . if it escapes . . . ' 588
19.2.3 ' . . . which represents a non-natural use of land . . . ' 589
19.3 *Cambridge Water* v *Eastern Counties Leather plc* 590
19.3.1 ' . . . and which causes foreseeable damage of the relevant type' 591
19.4 *Transco* v *Stockport MBC* 594
19.5 Standing and defences 596
19.5.1 Who can sue? 596
19.5.2 Defences 597
19.6 The nuisance/*Rylands* v *Fletcher*/negligence overlap 599
19.6.1 The 'measured duty of care' 600
19.7 Where does *Rylands* v *Fletcher* fit today? 601
19.8 Conclusion 603
End-of-chapter questions 603
Further reading 604

PART V Liability, damages and limitations 605

20 Vicarious liability 607
20.1 Introduction 608
20.2 Stage 1: a relationship of, or akin to, employment 612
20.3 Stage 2: a tortious act . . . 618
20.4 . . . committed 'in the course of employment' 619
20.5 Conclusion 623
End-of-chapter questions 623
Further reading 624

21 Damages for death and personal injuries 625
21.1 Introduction 626
21.2 What are damages for? 629
21.3 Calculating damages 633
21.3.1 Forms of damages payments 633
21.3.2 Special and general damages 637
21.3.3 Death and damages 638
21.4 Independent, joint and several concurrent liabilities 640
21.5 Time limitations on claims 642
21.6 The problem with damages 646
21.6.1 Alternative sources of compensation 652
21.6.1.1 'No-fault' liability and simple compensation schemes 654
21.6.1.2 First-party insurance 657
21.7 Debunking the compensation myth 659
21.8 Conclusion 661
End-of-chapter questions 662
Further reading 663

APPENDIX: ANNOTATED PROBLEM QUESTIONS 665
INDEX 683

Table of cases

Case names in **bold** indicate that the case features in a 'case box' (which can be found on the page numbers given in **bold**).

United Kingdom

8 Representative Claimants & others v MGN Ltd [2016] EWHC 855 (Ch) . . . 464

A v B plc [2002] EWCA Civ 337; [2003] QB 195 . . . 467, 475, 478

A v East Kent Hospitals University NHS Foundation Trust [2015] EWHC 1038 (QB) . . . 235

A v Essex County Council [2003] EWCA Civ 1848; [2004] 1 FLR 749 . . . 183

A v Essex County Council [2010] UKSC 33; [2011] 1 AC 280 . . . 181, 646

A v Hoare; C v Middlesbrough Council; H v Suffolk County Council; X v Wandsworth LBC; Young v Catholic Care (Diocese of Leeds) [2008] UKHL 6; [2008] 1 AC 844 . . . 12, 40, **643–4**, 645, 646

A & B v Persons Unknown [2016] EWHC 3295 (Ch) . . . 459

A and others v National Blood Authority [2001] 3 All ER 289 (QBD) . . . 364, **372**, 373, 374, 377, 379, 380, 385, 674

A (Children) (Conjoined Twins: Medical Treatment) (No 1), Re [2001] Fam 147 (CA) . . . 434

A & S (Children) v Lancashire County Council [2012] EWHC 1689 (Fam) . . . 144

A-G *see* Attorney General

AA, Re [2012] EWHC 4378 (COP) . . . 434

AAA v Associated Newspapers Ltd [2013] EWCA Civ 554 . . . 467, 476, 477, 478, 677

AAA and others v Rakoff and others [2019] EWHC 2525 (QB) . . . 478

AB v Leeds Teaching Hospital NHS Trust [2004] EWHC 644 (QB); [2005] QB 506 . . . 134

AB v Nugent Care Society [2009] EWCA Civ 827; [2010] 1 WLR 516 . . . 646

ABB & others v Milton Keynes Council [2011] EWHC 2745 (QB) . . . 144

Abbey v Gilligan & others [2012] EWHC 3217 (QB) . . . 471

ABC (A Mother) v The Chief Constable of West Yorkshire Police [2017] EWHC 1650 (QB) . . . 511

ABC & others v Telegraph Media Group Ltd [2018] EWCA Civ 2329 . . . 461, 462

ABK v KDT & FGH [2013] EWHC 1192 (QB) . . . 442, 468

Abouzaid v Mothercare (UK) Ltd [2000] EWCA Civ 348 . . . 365, **371**, 372

Adam v Ward [1917] AC 309 (HL) . . . 510

Adams v Ursell [1913] 1 Ch 269 (Ch D) . . . 569

Addie & Sons (Collieries) v Dumbreck [1929] ACC 358 (HL) . . . 339

Airedale NHS Trust v Bland [1993] AC 789 (HL) . . . 434

AJ Allan (Blairnyle) Ltd & another v Strathclyde Fire Board [2016] CSIH 3 . . . 88, 156

AJS v News Group Newspapers Ltd [2017] (as yet unreported) . . . 468

Al Sadik v Sadik [2019] EWHC 2717 (QB) . . . 493

Alcock v Chief Constable of South Yorkshire Police [1992] 1 AC 310 (HL) . . . 20, 66, 72, 105, 107, 108, 111, 113, 114, **115–16**, 117, 120, 123, 126, 127, 128, 129, 130, 131, 132, 133, 137, 667

Alexandrou v Oxford [1993] 4 All ER 328; (1991) 3 Admin LR 675 (CA) . . . 155, 161

Ali & another v Channel 5 Broadcast Ltd [2018] EWHC 298 (Ch) . . . 467, 468, 473, 477

Ali & another v Channel 5 Broadcasting Ltd [2019] EWCA Civ 677 . . . 473

Allen v British Rail Engineering Ltd [2001] EWCA Civ 242; [2001] ICR 942 . . . 258

Allen v Gulf Oil Refining Ltd [1981] AC 1001 (HL) . . . 565

Allied Maples Group v Simmons and Simmons [1995] 1 WLR 1602 (CA) . . . 274

Allin v City & Hackney Health Authority [1996] 7 Med LR 167 (MCLC) . . . 133

AM v News Group Newspapers Ltd [2012] EWHC 308 (QB) . . . 441

AMC & another v News Group Newspapers Ltd [2015] EWHC 2361 (QB) . . . 467

Anchor Brewhouse Developments Ltd v Berkley House (Docklands Developments) Ltd (1987) 38 BLR 82 . . . 541

Anderton v Clwyd County Council [2002] EWCA Civ 933; [2002] 1 WLR 3175 . . . 180

Andreae v Selfridge & Co Ltd [1938] Ch 1 (CA) . . . 573

Andrews v Hopkinson [1957] 1 QB 229 (Leeds Assizes) . . . 360

Anns v Merton London Borough Council [1978] AC 728 (HL) . . . 36, 50, 63, 64, 65, 66, 67, 69, 70, 74, 76, 113, **198**, 199, 200, 201, 210

Anslow & others v Norton Aluminium Ltd [2012] EWHC 2610 (QB) . . . 554, 555, 570

ARB v IVF Hammersmith [2018] EWCA Civ 2803 . . . 203

Arcadia Group Ltd and others v Telegraph Media Group Ltd [2019] EWHC 223 (QB) . . . 462

Archbishop Bowen & another v JL [2017] EWCA Civ 82 . . . 646

Armes v Nottinghamshire County Council [2017] UKSC 60 . . . 614, 617, 644

Armsden v Kent Police [2009] EWCA Civ 631 . . . 306

Arthur JS Hall & Co v Simons [2002] 1 AC 615 (HL) . . . 152, 227

Ashley v Chief Constable of West Sussex Police [2008] UKHL 25; [2008] 1 AC 962 . . . 412, 435

Aswan Engineering Establishment Co v Lupdine Ltd [1987] 1 WLR 1 . . . 357

Atkinson v Newcastle & Gateshead Waterworks Co (1876–77) LR 2 Ex D 441 (CA) . . . 398

Attia v British Gas [1988] QB 304 . . . 105

Attorney General v Guardian Newspapers Ltd (No 2) [1990] 1 AC 109 (HL) . . . 459, 460

Attorney General v PYA Quarries Ltd [1957] 2 QB 169 (CA) . . . 579

Attorney General's Reference (No 6 of 1980) [1981] QB 715 . . . 432

Austin and other v Commissioner of Police of the Metropolis [2007] EWCA Civ 989 . . . 434

Austin and other v Commissioner of Police of the Metropolis [2009] UKHL 5; [2009] 1 AC 564 . . . 428, 429

Author of a Blog v Times Newspapers Ltd [2009] EWHC 1358 (QB); [2009] EMLR 22 . . . 465

AVB v TDD [2014] EWHC 1442 (QB) . . . 478, 480, 482

AXB v BXA [2018] EWHC 588 (QB) . . . 442

Axon v Ministry of Defence [2016] EWHC 787 (QB) . . . 473

Ayres v Odedra [2013] EWHC 40 (QB) . . . 306

Badger v Ministry of Defence [2005] EWHC 2941 (QB); [2006] 2 All ER 173 . . . 308

BAI (Run Off) Ltd & others v Durham & others [2012] UKSC 14 . . . 262, 267, 268

Bailey v Ministry of Defence [2008] EWCA Civ 883; (2008) 103 BMLR 134 . . . 257, 258, 259, 261, 262

Bailey & another v HSS Alarms Ltd (2000) *The Times*, 20 June (CA) . . . 80, 90

Baker v Quantum Clothing Group [2011] UKSC 17 . . . 389

Baker v TE Hopkins & Sons Ltd [1959] 1 WLR 966 (CA) . . . 128

Baker v Willoughby [1970] AC 467 (HL) . . . **277–8**, 279, 298, 310, 671

Ballard v Tomlinson (1885) LR 29 Ch D 115 (CA) . . . 590

Balls v Reeve & Anor [2021] EWHC 751 (QB) . . . 642

Banca Nazionale del Lavoro SPA v Playboy Club London Limited [2018] UKSC 43 . . . 206

Bank of Montreal v Dominion Gresham Guarantee and Casualty Co [1930] AC 659 (PC) . . . 227

Barber v Somerset County Council [2004] UKHL 13; [2004] 1 WLR 1089 . . . 135, 136

Barclays Bank v Various Claimants [2020] UKSC 13 . . . 612, 617

Barker v Corus UK Ltd [2006] UKHL 20; [2006] 2 AC 572 . . . 261, **263–4**, 265, 266, 267, 268, 269, 642

Barnes v Hampshire County Council [1969] 1 WLR 1563 (CA) . . . 81

Barnett v Chelsea and Kensington Hospital Management Committee [1969] 1 QB 428 (QBD) . . . **255**, 256, 273, 671

Barr & others v Biffa Waste Services Ltd [2012] EWCA Civ 312 . . . 553, 565, 569, 571

Barrett v Enfield LBC [2001] 2 AC 550 (HL) . . . 67, 72, 152, **182**

Barrett v Ministry of Defence [1995] 1 WLR 1217 (CA) . . . **87**, 88, 89, 171, 666

Barron v Vines [2016] EWHC 1226 (QB) . . . 516

Barry Congregation of Jehovah's Witnesses v BXB [2021] EWCA Civ 356 . . . 644

Batchellor v Tunbridge Wells Gas Co (1901) 65 JP 680 . . . 587

Baxter v Camden LBC (No 2) [2001] QB 1 (CA) . . . 557

Bayley v George Eliot Hospital [2017] EWHC 3398 (QB) . . . 236

BBC v Harper Collins Publishers Ltd & others [2010] EWHC 2424 (Ch) . . . 467

Beckett v Newalls Insulation Co Ltd [1953] 1 WLR 8 (CA) . . . 239

Bellefield Computer Services Ltd v E Turner and Sons Ltd [2000] BLR 97 . . . 200

Benarr v Kettering HA (1988) 138 NLH Rep 179 (QBD) . . . 36

Berisha v Stone Superstore Ltd [2014], Manchester County Court, 2 December . . . 119

Berkoff v Burchill [1996] 4 All ER 1008 (CA) . . . 498

Bici v Ministry of Defence [2004] EWHC 786 (QB) . . . 171

Bilta (UK) Ltd v Nazir (No 2) [2016] AC 1 . . . 300

Birch v Paulson [2012] EWCA Civ 487 . . . 223

Bird v Jones (1845) 7 QB 742 . . . 422, **424**

Blake v Galloway [2004] EWCA Civ 814; [2004] 1 WLR 2844 . . . 242, 243

Blamire v South Cumbria HA [1993] PIQR Q1 . . . 634

Bland v Moseley (1587) 9 Co Rep 58a . . . 549

Bloodworth v Gray (1844) 7 Man & G 334 . . . 490

Blyth v Birmingham Waterworks (1856) 11 Ex Ch 781 . . . 220

Bogle v McDonald's Restaurants Ltd [2002] EWHC 490 (QB) . . . 367, 368, 369, 380

Bolam v Friern Hospital Management Committee [1957] 1 WLR 582 (QBD) . . . 53, 181, 226, **227**, 228, 229, 230, 231, 233, 235, 236, 249, 277, 376, 670, 671

Bolitho v City and Hackney Health Authority [1998] AC 232 (HL) . . . 229, 230, 249, 277, 288, 670, 671

Bolton v Stone [1951] AC 850; [1951] 1 All ER 1078 (HL) . . . **46**, **237**, 249

Bone v Seale [1975] 1 WLR 797 (CA) . . . 572

Bonnington Castings Ltd v Wardlaw [1956] 2 WLR 707 (HL) . . . 257, 258, 259, 260, 261, 269

Borealis AB v Geogas Trading SA [2010] EWHC 2789 (Comm) . . . 285

Bottomley v Bannister [1932] 1 KB 458 . . . 325

Bottomley v Todmorden Cricket Club [2003] EWCA Civ 1575; [2004] PIQR P18 . . . 322, 323

Boumedien v Delta Displays Ltd [2008] EWCA Civ 368 . . . 110

Bourhill v Young [1943] AC 92 (HL) . . . 107, **112**, 113

Bourne Leisure Ltd (t/a British Holidays) v Marsden [2009] EWCA Civ 671; [2009] 29 EG 99 . . . 329

Bowen v National Trust [2011] EWHC 1992 (QB) . . . **328**, 350

Box v Jubb (1878–79) LR 4 Ex D 76 (Ex Div) . . . 597

BPE Solicitors & another v Hughes-Holland (in substitution for Gabriel) [2017] UKSC 21 . . . 196

Bradford Corporation v Pickles [1895] AC 587 (HL) . . . 563, 564

Bradford-Smart v West Sussex County Council [2002] EWCA Civ 7; [2002] 1 FCR 425 . . . 81

Brady v Southend University Hospital NHS Foundation Trust [2020] EWHC 158 . . . 236

Brett Wilson LLP v Persons Unknown [2015] EWHC 2628 (QB) . . . 488

Brevan Howard Asset Management LLP v Reuters Ltd & another [2017] EWCA Civ 950 . . . 459

Brice v Brown [1984] 1 All ER 997 (QBD) . . . 112

Bridlington Relay v Yorkshire Electricity Board [1965] Ch 436 (Ch D) . . . 560

Brink's Global Services Inc v Igrox Ltd [2009] EWHC 1817 (Comm) . . . 618

British American Tobacco UK Ltd & others, R (on the application of) v Secretary of State for Health [2016] EWHC 1169 (Admin) . . . 365

British Broadcasting Corporation & Eight Other Media Organisations, R (on the application of) v F & D [2016] EWCA Crim 12 . . . 459

British Celanese Ltd v AH Hunt (Capacitors) Ltd [1969] 1 WLR 959 (QBD) . . . 590

British Chiropractic Association v Singh [2010] EWCA Civ 350; [2011] 1 WLR 133 . . . 512, 518, **519**, 528

British Railways Board v Herrington [1972] AC 877 (HL) . . . 320, 339, 340, 347, 348, 349

Brock v Northampton General Hospital NHS Trust [2014] EWHC 4244 (QB) . . . 104, 121

Brooks v Commissioner of Police for the Metropolis [2005] UKHL 24; [2005] 1 WLR 1495 . . . 20, 154, 161, 163, 164, 166, 167, 170, 431

Brown v Paterson [2010] EWCA Civ 185 . . . 247

Buck v Norfolk and Waveney Health NHS Foundation Trust [2012] Med LR 266 . . . 92

Bull v Desporte [2019] EWHC 1650 (QB) . . . 467, 477

Bunt v Tilley [2006] EWHC 407 (QB) . . . 505

Burgon v News Group Newspapers [2019] EWHC 195 (QB) . . . 489

Burrell v Clifford [2016] EWHC 578 (Ch) . . . 474

Busby v Berkshire Bed Company Ltd [2018] EWHC 2976 (QB) . . . 363, 365, 374

Bussey Law Firm PC v Page [2015] EWHC 563 (QB) . . . 505

Butchart v Home Office [2006] EWCA Civ 239; [2006] 1 WLR 1155 . . . 134

BVG v LAR [2020] EWHC 931 (QB) . . . 478

Bybrook Barn Centre Ltd v Kent County Council [2001] BLR 55 (CA) . . . 601

C (A Person under a disability) v The Chief Constable of the Police Force of Northern Ireland [2014] NIQB 63 . . . 167

Cadet's Car Rentals v Pinder [2019] UKPC 4 . . . 634

Cairns v Modi [2012] EWHC 756 (QB) . . . 504, 523, 524, 525

Caldwell v Maguire [2002] EWCA Civ 1054; [2002] PIQR P6 . . . 242

Calvert v William Hill Credit Ltd [2008] EWCA Civ 888 . . . 134, 308

Cambridge Water Co Ltd v Eastern Counties Leather plc [1994] 2 AC 264 (HL) . . . 32, 536, 562, 584, 585, 586, 590–4, **591**, 596, 599, 601, 602, 603, 604, 680

Campbell v Mirror Group Newspapers Ltd [2004] UKHL 22; [2004] 2 AC 457 . . . 2, 21, 408, 453, **463**, 464, 465, 470, 471, 472, 477, 480, 482, 483, 484, 627, 677

Candler v Crane Christmas & Co [1951] 2 KB 164 (CA) . . . 195

Caparo Industries v Dickman [1990] 2 AC 605 (HL) . . . 28, 37, 49, 50, 52, 61, 65–74, 76, 77, 178, 196, 197, 205, **206**, **207**, 208, 209, 210, 212, 215, 356, 395, 669

Capital & Counties plc v Hampshire County Council [1997] QB 1004 (CA) . . . 88, 89, **155–6**, 157, 158, 159

Capps v Miller [1989] 1 WLR 839 (CA) . . . 309

Carder v The University of Exeter [2016] EWCA Civ 790 . . . 258, 259

Carlgarth, The [1927] P 93 (CA) . . . 325, 542

Carmarthenshire County Council v Lewis [1955] AC 549 (HL) . . . 81, 84

Carr-Glynn v Frearsons [1999] Ch 326 (CA) . . . 212

Cartledge v E Jopling & Sons Ltd [1963] . . . 31, 32

Carty v Croydon LBC [2005] EWCA Civ 19; [2005] 1 WLR 2312 . . . 181

Castle v St Augustine's Links (1922) 38 TTLR 615 . . . 580

Cattle v Stockton Waterworks Co (1874–75) LR 10 QB 453; [1874–80] All ER Rep 492 (QBD) . . . 194, 197

Cavalier v Pope [1906] AC 428 (HL) . . . 325

CDE v MGN Ltd [2010] EWHC 3308 (QB); [2011] Fam Law 360 . . . 479

CG v Facebook Ireland Ltd and Joseph McCloskey [2015] NIQB 11 . . . 445, 458

Chadwick v British Railways Board [1967] 1 WLR 912 (QBD) . . . 128, 130, 131

Charleston v News Group Newspapers Ltd [1995] 2 AC 65 . . . 496, 678

Chase v News Group Newspapers Ltd [2002] EWCA Civ 1772 . . . 507

Chatterton v Gerson [1981] QB 432 (QBD) . . . 432

Chaudry v Prabhaker [1989] 1 WLR 29 (CA) . . . 202

Chester v Afshar [2002] EWCA Civ 724 . . . 271

Chester v Afshar [2004] UKHL 41; [2005] 1 AC 134 . . . 230, 249, **270**, 271

Chic Fashions (West Wales) Ltd v Jones [1968] 2 QB 299 (CA) . . . 545

Chief Constable of Thames Valley Police v Earl Gideon Foster Hepburn [2002] EWCA Civ 184 . . . 431

Christian Brothers case *see* **Various Claimants v Catholic Child Welfare Society**

Christie v Davey [1983] 1 Ch 316 (Ch D) . . . **562–3**, 564

Chubb Fire Ltd v Vicar of Spalding [2010] EWCA Civ 981 . . . 255

Church v MGN Ltd [2012] EWHC 693 (QB) . . . 495

Church of Jesus Christ of Latter-Day Saints (Great Britain) v West Yorkshire Fire and Civil Defence Authority [1997] QB 1004 (CA) . . . 155

Cinnamond v British Airports Authority [1980] 1 WLR 582 (CA) . . . 545

Clark v Farley [2018] EWHC 1007 (QB) . . . 294

Clark v Molyneux (1877) 3 QBD 247 . . . 511

Clark Fixing Ltd v Dudley Metropolitan Borough Council [2001] EWCA Civ 1898 . . . 98, 99

Clarke v Bruce Lance & Co [1988] 1 WLR 881 (CA) . . . 211

Clough v First Choice Holidays & Flights Ltd [2006] EWCA Civ 15; [2006] PIQR P22 . . . 267

Clunis v Camden & Islington Health Authority [1998] QB 978 (CA) . . . 303

Co-operative Group (CWS) v Pritchard [2011] EWCA Civ 329 . . . 304, 431

Cockbill v Riley [2013] EWHC 656 (QB) . . . 238

Cockcroft v Smith (1705) 11 Mod Rep 43; 2 Salk 642; Holt KB 699 B . . . 435

Coco v AN Clark (Engineers) Ltd [1968] FSR 415 (Ch D) . . . 459, 461

Coker v Nwkanma [2021] EWHC 1011 (QB) . . . 494

Cole v Davies-Gilbert [2007] EWCA Civ 396; (2007) 151 SJLB 335 . . . 219

Cole v Turner (1704) 90 ER 958 (KB) . . . 416

Collett v Smith [2009] EWCA Civ 583 . . . 633

Collins v Secretary of State for Business, Innovation and Skills & another [2014] EWCA Civ 717 . . . 642

Collins v Wilcock [1984] 1 WLR 1172 (DC) . . . 411, 414, 416, 418, 421

Colour Quest v Total Downstream UK plc [2010] EWCA Civ 180; [2011] QB 86 . . . 598

Coltman v Bibby Tankers Ltd (The Derbyshire) [1988] AC 276 (HL) . . . 392

Commissioner of Police of the Metropolis v DSD and another [2018] UKSC 11 . . . 146, 148, 154, 163, 167, 171

Commissioner of Police of the Metropolis v DSD and NBV & others [2015] EWCA Civ 646 . . . 148

Conarken Group Ltd v Network Rail Infrastructure Ltd [2011] EWCA Civ 644 . . . 281

Condon v Basi [1985] 1 WLR 866 (CA) . . . 242, 297

Contostavlos v Mendahun [2012] EWHC 850 (QB) . . . 475, 477

Cook v Square D Ltd [1992] ICR 262 (CA) . . . 394

Cooke & Midland Heart Ltd v MGN Ltd & Trinity Mirror Midlands Ltd [2014] EWHC 2831 (QB) . . . 492

Cookson v Harewood [1932] 2 KB 478n (CA) . . . 506

Cookson v Knowles [1978] UKHL 3 . . . 639

Corby Group Litigation Claimants v Corby Borough Council [2008] EWCA Civ 463; [2009] QB 335 . . . 578, 588

Corby Group Litigation v Corby District Council [2009] EWHC 1944 (TCC) . . . 579

Cornish Glennroy Blair-Ford v CRS Adventures Ltd [2012] EWHC 2360 (QB) . . . 218

Corr v IBC Vehicles Ltd [2008] UKHL 13; [2008] 1 AC 884 . . . 103, 279, 286, 394

Correia v University Hospital of North Staffordshire NHS Trust [2017] EWCA Civ 356 . . . 271

Costello v Chief Constable of Northumbria Police [1999] 1 All ER 550 (CA) . . . **87**, 89, 91, 169

Coventry & others v Lawrence & another [2014] UKSC 13 . . . **554**, 556, 558, 564, 567, 570, 577, 578, 582, 679

Coventry & others v Lawrence & another [2015] UKSC 50 . . . 627

Cox (Sara) v MGN Ltd [2006] EWHC 1235 (QB) . . . 455

Cox v Ministry of Justice [2016] UKSC 10 . . . 609, 616, 618, 621

Cramaso LLP v Ogilvie-Grant, Earl of Seafield & others (Scotland) [2014] UKSC 9 . . . 205, 669

Craven v Davies [2018] EWHC 1240 (QB) . . . 296, 306, 307

Cross v Kirkby (2000) *The Times*, April 5 (CA) . . . 435

Crown River Cruises Ltd v Kimbolton Fireworks Ltd [1996] 2 Lloyd's Rep 533 (QBD) . . . 555, 589

Cruddas v Adams [2013] EWHC 145 (QB) . . . 504

Cruise (and Kidman) v Express Newspapers plc [1999] QB 931 (CA) . . . 508

CTB v NGN Ltd [2011] EWHC 1232 (QB) . . . 478

Cunningham v Reading Football Club Ltd [1992] PIQR P141 (QBD) . . . 323

Customs and Excise Commissioners v Barclays Bank plc [2006] UKHL 28; [2007] 1 AC 181 . . . 74, 204, **205**, 215

Cutler v Wandsworth Stadium [1949] AC 398 (HL) . . . 402

D v East Berkshire Community NHS Trust & another; MAK & another v Dewsbury Healthcare NHS Trust & another; RK & another v Oldham NHS Trust & another [2005] UKHL 23; [2005] 2 AC 373 . . . 31, 52, 142, **143**, 144, 145, 146, 148, 154, 177, 184, 400

D & F Estates Ltd v Church Commissioners for England [1989] AC 177 (HL) . . . 199, 201

D Pride & Partners v Institute for Animal Health [2009] EWHC 1617 (QB) . . . 191, 596

Daiichi UK Ltd v Stop Huntingdon Animal Cruelty [2003] EWHC 2337 (QB); [2004] 1 WLR 1503 . . . 445

Dann v Hamilton [1939] 1 KB 509 (KBD) . . . **293–4**, 295, 672

Darby v National Trust [2001] EWCA Civ 189; (2001) 3 LGLR 29 . . . 327, 332, **333**, 350

Darnley v Croydon Health Services NHS Trust [2018] UKSC 50 . . . 73, 74

Davie v New Merton Board Mills Ltd [1959] AC 604 (HL) . . . 391

Davies v Swan Motor Co [1949] 2 KB 291 . . . 308

Davis Contractors v Fareham Urban District Council [1956] AC 696 (HL) . . . 220

De Souza v Vinco Construction (UK) Ltd [2017] EWCA Civ 879 . . . 443

Delaney v Pickett [2011] EWCA Civ 1532 . . . 299

Delaware Mansions Ltd v Westminster City Council [2001] UKHL 55; [2002] 1 AC 321 . . . 572, 601

Dennis v Ministry of Defence [2003] EWHC 793 (QB); [2003] Env LR 34 . . . 569, 574, **577**, 578

Depp II v News Group Newspapers Ltd [2020] EWHC 2911 . . . 494, **508**, 509, 526

Depp II v News Group Newspapers Ltd [2021] EWCA Civ 423 . . . 508

Derbyshire County Council v Times Newspapers [1993] AC 534 (HL) . . . **489**

Desmond v Chief Constable of Nottinghamshire Police [2011] EWCA Civ 3 . . . 167

Dewey v White (1827) M & M 56 . . . 543

Deyong v Shenburn [1946] KB 227 (CA) . . . 394

DFT v TFD [2010] EWHC 2335 (QB) . . . 480

Diamond v Royal Devon & Exeter NHS Foundation Trust [2019] EWCA Civ 585 . . . 236, 271

Dickins v O2 plc [2008] EWCA Civ 1144; [2009] IRLR 58 . . . 258, 641

Dixon v Clement Jones Solicitors [2004] EWCA Civ 1005; [2005] PNLR 6 . . . 274

Dobson v Thames Water Utilities Ltd [2009] EWCA Civ 28; [2009] 3 All ER 319 . . . 575, 576, 578

Dobson v Thames Water Utilities Ltd (No 2) [2011] EWHC 3253 (TCC) . . . 576

Doe d Bishop of Rochester v Bridges [1824–34] 4 Dow & Ry KB 315 . . . 399

Donoghue v Folkestone Properties Ltd [2003] EWCA Civ 231; [2003] QB 1008 . . . 345, 346

Donoghue v Stevenson [1932] AC 562 (HL) . . . 28, 29, 32, **33–4**, 35, 36, 38, 42, 43, 56, 61, 63, 65, 66, 70, 72, 73, 74, 76, 79, 141, 142, 219, 354, 355, 356, 360, 384, 546, 674

Dooley v Cammell Laird & Co Ltd [1951] 1 Lloyd's Rep 271 (Liverpool Assizes) . . . 131, **132**, 667

Doughty v Turner Manufacturing Co [1964] 1 QB 518 (CA) . . . 281, 282

Douglas & others v Hello! Ltd & others [2007] UKHL 21 . . . 464

Douglas, Zeta-Jones and Northern & Shell plc v Hello! Ltd [2005] EWCA Civ 595 . . . **460–1**, 463, 474, 482, 483, 677

Doyle v Smith [2018] EWHC 2935 (QB) . . . 517

DPP v K (A Minor) [1990] 1 WLR 1067 (QBD) . . . 417

Dryden & others v Johnson Matthey plc [2018] UKSC 18 . . . 4, 6, 31, 32, 482, 550

DSD v The Commissioner of Police for the Metropolis [2014] EWHC 436 (QB) . . . 96, 147, 494

Dubai Aluminium Co Ltd v Salaam [2002] UKHL 48; [2003] 2 AC 366 . . . 612, 622

Duce v Worcestershire Acute Hospitals NHS Trust [2018] EWCA Civ 1307 . . . 234–5, 236, 271

Duke of Brunswick v Harmer (1849) 14 QB 185; 117 ER 75 (QB) . . . 505, 529

Dulieu v White & Sons [1901] 2 KB 669 (KBD) . . . 104, 108, 112

Dunnage v Randell [2015] EWCA Civ 673 . . . 225

Durham v BAI (EL Trigger Litigation) [2008] EWHC 2692 (QB); [2009] 2 All ER 26 . . . 262

Durham County Council v Dunn [2012] EWCA Civ 1654 . . . 646

Dutton v Bognor Regis Building Co Ltd [1972] 1 QB 373 (CA) . . . 198, 199

East Dorset District Council v Eaglebeam Ltd [2006] EWHC 2378 (QB); [2007] Env LR D9 . . . 580

East Suffolk Rivers Catchment Board v Kent [1941] AC 74 (HL) . . . 141, **142**, 156

Economou v De Freitas [2018] EWCA Civ 2591 . . . 494, 514, **516**, 517, 527

Edwards v London Borough of Sutton [2016] EWCA Civ 1005 . . . 328, 336

Edwards v Railway Executive [1952] AC 737 (HL) . . . 320

EL v The Children's Society [2012] EWHC 365 (QB) . . . 646

Elguzouli-Daf v Commissioner of Police for the Metropolis [1995] QB 335 (CA) . . . 167

Elias v Pasmore [1934] 2 KB 164 . . . 544, 545

Elizabeth Jagger v John Darling *see* Jagger v Darling

Ellis v Environment Agency [2008] EWCA Civ 1117; [2009] PIQR P5 . . . 258

Elton John v Associated Newspapers Ltd [2006] EWHC 1611 (QB) . . . 473

Emeh v Chelsea and Kensington AHA [1985] QB 1012 . . . 203

Enderby Town Football Club Ltd v The Football Association Ltd [1971] Ch 591 (CA) . . . 8

English Heritage v Taylor [2016] EWCA Civ 448 . . . 332

Equitas Insurance Ltd v Municipal Mutual Insurance Ltd [2019] EWCA Civ 718 . . . 264, 265

ERY v Associated Newspapers Ltd [2016] EWHC 2760 (QB) . . . 467

Esegbona v King's College Hospital Foundation NHS Trust [2019] EWHC 77 (QB) . . . 423

Essex Police v Transport Arendonk BVBA [2020] EWHC 212 (QB) . . . 168

Esso Petroleum v Southport Corporation [1956] AC 218 (HL) . . . 543

Esso Petroleum Co Ltd v Mardon [1976] QB 801 (CA) . . . 202, 206

Esterhuizen v Allied Dunbar Assurance plc [1998] 2 FLR 668 (QBD) . . . 213

ETK v Newsgroup Newspapers [2011] EWCA Civ 439 . . . 476, 477

Evans v Triplex Safety Glass Co Ltd [1936] 1 All ER 283 (KBD) . . . 359

Everett v Comojo (UK) Ltd (t/a The Metropolitan) [2011] EWCA Civ 13; [2011] PIQR P8 . . . 97, 99, 323

F v West Berkshire Health Authority [1990] 2 AC 1 (HL) *see* F (Mental Patient: Sterilization), Re

F (Mental Patient: Sterilization), Re [1990] 2 AC 1 (HL) . . . 416, 434

Fagan v Metropolitan Police Commissioner [1969] 1 QB 439 (DC) . . . 415

Fairchild v Glenhaven Funeral Services [2002] UKHL 22; [2003] 1 AC 32 . . . 261–2, 263, 264, 265, 266, 267, 268, 269, 272, 276, 322, 389, 641

Farrell v Avon Health Authority [2001] Lloyd's Rep Med 458 (QBD) . . . 133

FB (Suing by her Mother and Litigation Friend, WAC) v Princess Alexandra Hospital NHS Trust [2017] EWCA Civ 334 . . . 228

Fearn & others v The Board of Trustees of the Tate Gallery [2019] EWHC 246 (Ch) . . . 549, 559, 561, 679

Fearn & others v The Board of Trustees of the Tate Gallery [2020] EWCA Civ 104 . . . 549, 552, 559

Fenty & others v Arcadia Group Brands Ltd & others [2015] EWCA Civ 3 . . . 452

Ferdinand v MGN Ltd (Rev 2) [2011] EWHC 2454 (QB) . . . 478

Ferguson v British Gas Trading Ltd [2009] EWCA Civ 46; [2010] 1 WLR 785 . . . 445

Ferguson v Dawson [1976] 1 WLR 1213 (CA) . . . 614

Ferguson v Welsh [1987] 1 WLR 1553 (HL) . . . 322

Finesse Group Ltd v Bryson Products (A Firm) [2013] EWHC 3273 (TCC) . . . 357

Fitzgerald v Lane [1989] AC 328 (HL) . . . 42, 272, 642, 682

Flanagan & another v Greenbanks Ltd (t/a Lazenby Insulation) & Cross [2013] EWCA Civ 1702 . . . 285

Fletcher v Rylands (1865–66) LR 1 Ex 265 . . . 585

Flood v Times Newspapers [2012] UKSC 11 . . . 514, 515, 527

Flood v Times Newspapers [2014] EWCA Civ 1574 . . . 464

Flymenow Ltd v Quick Air Jet Charter GmbH [2016] EWHC 3197 (QB) . . . 525

Fowler v Lanning [1959] 1 QB 426 . . . 413

Frederick v Positive Solutions (Financial Services) Ltd [2018] EWCA Civ 431 . . . 617

French v Chief Constable of Sussex Police [2006] EWCA Civ 312; [2006] Po LR 19 . . . 108

Froom v Butcher [1976] QB 286 (CA) . . . 308, 309, 672

Frost v Chief Constable of South Yorkshire [1997] IRLR 173 . . . 107, 108
see also **White v Chief Constable of South Yorkshire Police**

Fullam v Newcastle Chronicle & Journal Ltd [1977] 1 WLR 651 (CA) . . . 499

Fytche v Wincanton Logistics plc [2004] UKHL 31; [2004] 4 All ER 221 . . . 404–5

G (A Child) v Bromley LBC (2000) 2 LGLR 237 (CA) . . . 180

Gallardo v Imperial College Healthcare Trust [2017] EWHC 3147 (QB) . . . 236

Galli-Atkinson v Seghal [2003] EWCA Civ 697; [2003] Lloyd's Rep Med 285 . . . 119, 667

Ganz v Childs & others [2011] EWHC 13 (QB) . . . 277

Garner v Salford County Council [2013] EWHC 1573 (QB) . . . 258

Geary v Wetherspoons plc [2011] EWHC 1506 (QB) . . . 335, 336, 339, 350

Geddis v Proprietors of the Bann Reservoir (1877–78) LR 3 App Cas 430 (HL) . . . 141

Gee & Others v DePuy International Limited [2018] EWHC 1208 (QB) . . . 370, 371, 372, 373, 374, 377, 674

General Cleaning Contractors v Christmas [1953] AC 180 (HL) . . . 331, 393

Gibbon v Pepper (1695) 1 Ld Raym 38 . . . 415

Giggs (formerly known as CTB) v NGN Ltd [2012] EWHC 431 (QB) . . . 478

Gilbert v Stone (1647) Style 72; 82 ER 59 . . . 540

Giles v Walker (1890) 24 QBD 656 (QBD) . . . 589

Gillingham Borough Council v Medway (Chatham) Dock Co Ltd [1993] QB 343 (QBD) . . . 557, 558

Glaister v Appleby-in-Westmoreland Town Council [2009] EWCA Civ 1325; [2010] PIQR P6 . . . 335, 673

Glasgow Corporation v Muir [1943] AC 448 (HL) . . . 221

Glasgow Corporation v Taylor [1922] 1 AC 44 (HL) . . . 329

Godfrey v Demon Internet Ltd (Application to Strike Out) [2001] QB 201 (QBD) . . . 504

Goldman v Hargrave [1967] 1 AC 645 (PC) . . . 88, 89, 97, 340, 600

Goldscheider v Royal Opera House Covent Garden Foundation [2019] EWCA Civ 711 . . . 240, 281

Goldsmith v Bhoyrul [1998] QB 459; [1997] 4 All ER 268 . . . 489

Goodwill v British Pregnancy Advisory Service [1996] 1 WLR 1397 (CA) . . . 203

Goodwin v NGN Ltd [2011] EWHC 1437 (QB) . . . 473, 478

Google Inc v Vidal-Hall & others [2015] EWCA Civ 311 . . . 21, 464, 482

Gorham v British Telecommunications plc [2000] 1 WLR 2129 (CA) . . . 204, 213

Gorringe v Calderdale Metropolitan Borough Council [2004] UKHL 15; [2004] 1 WLR 1057 . . . 50, 51, 176, 177

Gorris v Scott (1874) 9 LR Ex 125 (Ex Ct) . . . 404

Gough v Thorne [1966] 1 WLR 1387 (CA) . . . 225, 306

Gould v McAuliffe [1941] 2 All ER 527 (CA) . . . 325, 326

Gouldsmith v Mid-Staffordshire General Hospitals Trust [2007] EWCA Civ 397; [2007] LS Law Medical 363 . . . 277

GR v Wirral Metropolitan Borough Council [2009] EWCA Civ 827; [2010] 1 WLR 516 . . . 646

Graham v Dodds [1983] 1 WLR 808 . . . 639

Graiseley Properties Ltd & others v Barclays Bank plc & others [2013] EWHC 67 (Comm) . . . 479

Grant v Australian Knitting Mills Ltd [1936] AC 85 (PC) . . . 358–9, 361, 378

Gray v Thames Trains [2009] UKHL 33; [2009] 1 AC 1339 . . . 278, 279, 286, **297–8**, 299, 303, 313, 672

Greater Nottingham Co-Operative Society v Cementation Piling Ltd [1989] QB 71 . . . 199

Greatorex v Greatorex [2000] 1 WLR 1970 (QBD) . . . 134

Greenock Corporation v Caledonian Railway [1917] AC 556 (HL) . . . 598

Greenway v Johnson Matthey plc [2016] EWCA Civ 408 . . . 31

Gregg v Scott [2005] UKHL 2; [2005] 2 AC 176 . . . 274, 275, 276

Gregory v Piper (1829) 9 B & C 591 . . . 548

Griffiths & others v Suffolk Police & another [2018] EWHC 2538 (QB) . . . 95, 166, 171

Grimstone v Epsom and St Helier University Hospitals NHS Trust [2015] EWHC 3756 (QB) . . . 236

Grobbelaar v News Group Newspapers Ltd [2002] UKHL 40; [2002] 1 WLR 3024 . . . 629

Groves v Lord Wimborne [1898] 2 QB 402 (CA) . . . 400, 401, 402, 404

Guardian News & Media Ltd, Re [2010] UKSC 1; [2010] 2 AC 697 . . . 479

Gul v McDonagh [2021] EWHC 97 (QB) . . . 306, 312

Gulati & others v MGN [2016] EWHC 1482 (Ch) . . . 474

Gwilliam v West Hertfordshire Hospital NHS Trust [2002] EWCA Civ 1041; [2003] QB 443 . . . 327, **334**, 335, 338, 673

GYH v Persons Unknown [2017] EWHC 3360 (QB) . . . 445

Hale v Jennings [1938] 1 All ER 579 . . . 587, 596

Hale v London Underground Ltd [1993] PIQR Q30 (QBD) . . . 130

Haley v London Electricity Board [1965] AC 778 (HL) . . . 61

Hall v Brooklands Auto-Racing Club [1933] 1 KB 205 (CA) . . . 220

Halsey v Esso Petroleum Co Ltd [1961] 1 WLR 683 (QBD) . . . 573

Hambrook v Stokes Bros [1925] 1 KB 141 (CA) . . . 112

Harooni v Rustins [2011] EWHC 1632 (TCC) . . . 590

Harris v Birkenhead Corporation [1976] 1 All ER 279 . . . 324, 349

Haseldine v CA Daw & Sons Ltd [1941] 2 KB 343 (CA) . . . 334

Hassell v Hillingdon Hospitals NHS Foundation Trust [2018] EWHC 164 (QB) . . . 271

Hastings v Finsbury Orthopaedics Ltd and Stryker UK Ltd [2019] CSOH 96 (Scotland) . . . 371

Hatton v Sutherland [2002] EWCA Civ 76 . . . 112, 135, 136, 258, 446

Hayes v Willoughby [2013] UKSC 17 . . . 445

Hayes v Willoughby [2019] EW Misc 5 (CC) . . . 445

Haynes v Harwood [1935] 1 KB 146 (CA) . . . 30, 96, 97, 99

Hazell v British Transport Commission [1958] 1 WLR 169 (QBD) . . . 220

Heath v Mayor of Brighton (1908) 98 LT 718 . . . 559

Heaven v Pender (1883) 11 QBD 503 (CA) . . . 33, 35

Hedley Byrne v Heller & Partners [1963] UKHL 4; [1964] AC 465 . . . 49, **195–6**, 197, 198, 201, 202, 203, 206, 209, 210, 211, 212, 213, 214, 215, 216, 669

Henderson v Dorset Healthcare University NHS Trust Foundation [2020] UKSC 43 . . . 302, 303

Henderson v Merrett Syndicates Ltd [1995] 2 AC 145 (HL) . . . 204, 215

Heneghan v Manchester Dry Docks Ltd & others [2016] EWCA Civ 86 . . . 268, 269

Henry v Chief Constable of Thames Valley [2010] EWCA Civ 5; [2010] RTR 14 . . . 160

Herd v Weardale Steel, Coke and Coal Co [1915] AC 67 (HL) . . . 425, 427

Hicks v Chief Constable of South Yorkshire Police [1992] 2 All ER 65 (HL) . . . 104, 105, 107

Hicks v Young [2015] EWHC 1144 (QB) . . . 281, 282, 306, 424

Hill v Chief Constable of West Yorkshire Police [1989] AC 53 (HL) . . . 91, 92, **148**, 149, 150, 151, 152, 160, 161, 162, 163, 164, 166, 167, 168, 169, 170, 186, 668

Hirose Electrical v Peak Ingredients Ltd [2011] EWCA Civ 987 . . . 555

Hodge v Anglo-American Oil Co (1922) 12 Ll L Rep 183 . . . 355

Holbeck Hall Hotel Ltd v Scarborough Borough Council [2000] QB 836 (CA) . . . 601

Hollywood Silver Fox Farm Ltd v Emmett [1936] 2 KB 468 (KBD) . . . 564

Holtby v Brigham & Cowan (Hull) Ltd [2000] 3 All ER 421 (CA) . . . 258, 266, 269

Home Office v Dorset Yacht Co Ltd [1970] AC 1004 (HL) . . . 36, 64, 89, 90, 92, **95**, 96, 99, 141, 284, 666

Home Office v Wainwright & another [2001] EWCA Civ 2081 . . . 414

Hopps v Mott MacDonald Ltd [2009] EWHC 1881 (QBD) . . . 246

Horne-Roberts v SmithKline Beecham plc [2001] EWCA Civ 2006; [2002] 1 WLR 1662 . . . 374

Horrocks v Lowe [1975] AC 135 (HL) . . . 511

Hotson v East Berkshire Health Authority [1987] AC 750 (HL) . . . 255, **273**, 274, 276, 671

Hounga v Allen [2014] UKSC 47 . . . 299, 300, 301

Howmet Ltd v Economy Devices Ltd & others [2016] EWCA Civ 847 . . . 359

HRH Prince of Wales v Associated Newspapers Ltd [2008] Ch 57 . . . 465

HRH The Duchess of Sussex v Associated Newspapers Ltd [2021] EWHC 273 (Ch) . . . 472

HRH The Duchess of Sussex v Associated Newspapers Ltd [2021] EWHC 669 (Ch) . . . 472

Hudson v Ridge Manufacturing Co [1957] 2 QB 348 (Manchester Assizes) . . . 391

Hufford v Samsung Electronics (UK) Ltd [2014] EWHC 2956 (TCC) . . . 370

Hughes v Lord Advocate [1963] AC 837 (HL) . . . 50, 63, 281

Hulton & Co v Jones [1910] AC 20 (HL) . . . 501, **502**, 503, 504

Hunt v Severs [1994] 2 AC 350 (HL) . . . 637, 682

Hunter v Canary Wharf Ltd [1996] 1 All ER 482 (CA) . . . 551

Hunter v Canary Wharf Ltd [1997] AC 655 (HL) . . . 450, 549, 550, **551**, 552, 553, 560, 572, 576, 578, 581, 582, 596, 602, 603, 679, 680

Hurley v Dyke [1979] RTR 265 (HL) . . . 360

Hussain & another v Lancaster City Council [1999] 2 WLR 1142 . . . 93, 551

Hutcheson (formerly known as 'KGM') v News Group Newspapers Ltd [2011] EWCA Civ 808 . . . 473, 478

Huth v Huth [1915] 3 KB 32 (CA) . . . 505

Ide v ATB Sales Ltd & another [2008] EWCA Civ 424; [2009] RTR 8 . . . 370, 378

Imperial Chemical Industries Ltd v Shatwell [1965] AC 656 (HL) . . . 609

Indermaur v Dames (1867) LR 2 CP 311 (Ex Ch) . . . 351

Informer, An v Chief Constable [2012] EWCA Civ 197 . . . 168

International Energy Group Ltd v Zurich Insurance plc [2013] EWCA Civ 39 . . . 267

Iqbal v Dean Manson Solicitors [2011] EWHC 3185 (QB) . . . 442

Iqbal v Prison Officers Association [2009] EWCA Civ 1312; [2010] QB 732 . . . 413, 414, 422, 423, **426**, 427

Island Records, *ex p* [1978] Ch 122 . . . 398

J v North Lincolnshire County Council [2000] BLGR 269 (CA) . . . 248

J20 v Facebook Ireland [2016] NIQB 98 . . . 458

Jackson v Murray [2015] UKSC 5 . . . 305, **310**, 311

Jagger v Darling [2005] EWHC 683 (Ch D) . . . 467, 468, 477

Jain & Another v Trent Strategic Health Authority [2007] EWCA Civ 1186 . . . 178

Jain v Trent Strategic Health Authority [2009] UKHL 4; [2009] 1 AC 853 . . . 143, 183

Jalla v Shell International Trading and Shipping Company [2021] EWCA Civ 63 . . . 556, 584, 593

Jameel v Dow Jones & Co Inc [2005] EWCA Civ 75 . . . 492, 493

Jameel v Wall Street Journal Europe [2006] UKHL 44; [2007] 1 AC 359 . . . 488, 514, 515

James v DPP [2009] EWHC 2925 (Admin); [2010] Crim LR 580 . . . 442

James-Bowen & others v Commissioner of Police for the Metropolis [2016] EWCA Civ 1217 . . . 205, 394

James-Bowen & others v Commissioner of Police for the Metropolis [2018] UKSC 40 . . . 169

Janvier v Sweeney [1919] 2 KB 316 (CA) . . . 436

Jarvis v Hampshire County Council [2000] 2 FCR 310 (CA) . . . 180

JD v Mather [2012] EWHC 3063 (QB) . . . 274

JD & others v East Berkshire NHS Trust & others [2003] Lloyd's Law Reports 552 . . . 52, 53

Jebson v Ministry of Defence [2000] 1 WLR 2055 (CA) . . . 171, 393

Jeynes v News Magazines Ltd [2008] EWCA Civ 130 . . . 500

JGE v The Trustees of the Portsmouth Roman Catholic Diocesan Trust [2012] EWCA Civ 938 . . . 614, 615, 616, 644, 681

JIH v News Group Newspapers Ltd [2011] EWCA Civ 42 . . . 478, 479

Jobling v Associated Dairies Ltd [1982] AC 794 (HL) . . . **278**, 279, 283, 288, 298, 671

John v Central Manchester and Manchester Children's University Hospitals NHS Foundation Trust [2016] EWHC 407 (QB) . . . 259

John v MGN Ltd [1997] QB 586 (CA) . . . 525

John Munroe (Acrylics) Ltd v London Fire and Civil Defence Authority [1997] QB 983 (QBD) . . . 155

Johnson v Steele [2014] EWHC B24 (QB) . . . 504, 629

Jolley v Sutton London Borough Council [2000] 1 WLR 1082 (HL) . . . 50, 282, 327, **330**, 338, 350

Jones v Kaney [2011] UKSC 13 . . . 76, 196

Jones v Livox Quarries Ltd [1952] 2 QB 608 (CA) . . . **305–6**, 307

Jones & others v Secretary of State for Energy and Climate Change & another [2012] EWHC 2936 (QB) . . . 262, 263

Joseph v Spiller [2010] UKSC 53; [2010] 3 WLR 1791 . . . 518, 519, **520–1**, 526

Junior Books Ltd v Veitchi Co Ltd [1983] 1 AC 520 (HL) . . . 64, 197, **198**, 199, 201

JXJ v The Province of Great Britain of the Institute of Brothers of the Christian Schools [2020] [2020] EWHC 1914 (QB) . . . 644

K v Secretary of State for the Home Department [2002] EWCA Civ 775; [2001] Po LR 161 . . . 92, 96, 98, 99

Kambadzi v Secretary of State for the Home Department [2012] UKSC 23 . . . 429, 431

Karagozlu v Commissioner of Police for the Metropolis [2006] EWCA Civ 1691; [2007] 1 WLR 1881 . . . 429

Kaye v Robertson and Sport Newspapers Ltd [1991] FSR 62 (CA) . . . 452–3, 458, 461, 466, 481, 482

Kearn-Price v Kent County Council [2003] EWCA Civ 153; [2003] ELR 17 . . . 152

Kelsen v Imperial Tobacco Co [1957] 2 All ER 334 (QBD) . . . 540, 541

Kennaway v Thompson [1981] QB 88 (CA) . . . 555, **571**

Kennedy v London Ambulance Service NHS Trust [2016] EWHC 3145 (QB) . . . 257, 634

Kent v Griffiths [2001] QB 36 (CA) . . . 158, **159**, 161, 186, 668

Keown v Coventry Healthcare NHS Trust [2006] EWCA Civ 39; [2006] 1 WLR 953 . . . 340

Kerry Ingredients (UK) Ltd v Bakkavor Group Ltd & others [2016] EWHC 2448 (Ch) . . . 459

Khan v Meadows [2019] EWCA Civ 152 . . . 271

Khashoggi v IPC Magazines Ltd [1986] 1 WLR 1412 . . . 508

Khorasandjian v Bush [1993] 3 WLR 476 (CA) . . . 450, 551, 552

Khuja (formerly known as PNM) v Times Newspapers [2017] UKSC 49 . . . 479

Kiapasha (t/a Takeaway Supreme) v Laverton [2002] EWCA Civ 1656; [2002] All ER (D) 261 . . . 329

King v Liverpool City Council [1986] 1 WLR 890 (CA) . . . 97

Kirkham v Chief Constable of Greater Manchester [1990] 2 QB 283 (CA) . . . 85, 168, 286

Knauer v Ministry of Justice [2016] UKSC 9 . . . 638

Knight v Home Office [1990] 3 All ER 237 (QBD) . . . 241

Knightley v Johns [1982] 1 WLR 349 (CA) . . . 160, **284**, 285

Knowles v Liverpool City Council [1993] 1 WLR 1428 (HL) . . . 392

Knuppfer v London Express Newspapers Ltd [1944] AC 116 (HL) . . . 503, **504**

Kolasa v Ealing Hospital NHS Trust [2015] EWHC 289 (QB) . . . 325

Koutsogiannis v The Random House Group Limited [2019] EWHC 48 (QB) . . . 495

KR v Bryn Alyn Community (Holdings) Ltd [2003] EWCA Civ 85; [2003] QB 1441 . . . 645

Lachaux v Independent Print Ltd [2017] EWCA Civ 1334 . . . 526

Lachaux v Independent Print Ltd [2019] UKSC 27 . . . 492–3, 494

Lagden v O'Connor [2003] UKHL 64; [2004] 1 AC 1067 . . . 283

Laiqat v Majid [2005] EWHC 1305 (QB); [2005] 26 EG 130 (CS) . . . 540, 541

Lamb v Camden LBC [1981] QB 625 (CA) . . . 63, 90, 91, 97

Lambert & others v Barratt Homes Ltd & another [2010] EWCA Civ 681; [2010] BLR 527 . . . 601

Lane v Holloway [1968] 1 QB 379 (CA) . . . 435

Langridge v Levy (1837) 2 M & W 519; (1838) 4 M & W 337 . . . 33

Larner v Solihull Metropolitan Borough Council [2001] RTC 32 (CA) . . . 176

Latimer v AEC Ltd [1953] AC 643 (HL) . . . 240, 328, **395**, 675

Lau v DPP [2000] EWHC 182 (QB) . . . 442

Laugher v Pointer (1826) 5 B & C 547 . . . 615

Law Society v Kordowski [2011] EWHC 3185 (QB) . . . 442

Law Society v KPMG Peat Marwick [2000] 1 WLR 1921 (CA) . . . 208

Lawrence v Pembrokeshire County Council [2007] EWCA Civ 446; [2007] 1 WLR 2991 . . . 53, 144

Lawson v Glaves-Smith (Dawes Executor) [2006] EWHC 2865 (QB) . . . 412

Le Lievre v Gould [1893] 1 QB 491 (CA) . . . 36

League Against Cruel Sports v Scott [1986] QB 240 (QBD) . . . 20, 540

Leakey v National Trust for Places of Historic Interest or Natural Beauty [1980] QB 485 (CA) . . . 97, 600, 601

Leigh v London Ambulance Service [2014] EWHC 286 (QB) . . . 257

Leigh & Sillivan Ltd v Aliakmon Shipping Co Ltd (The Aliakmon) [1986] AC 785 (HL) . . . 191, 192

Lennon v Commissioner of Police of the Metropolis [2004] EWCA Civ 130; [2004] 1 WLR 2594 . . . 204

Les Laboratoires Servier v Apotex Inc [2014] UKSC 55 . . . 300, 301

Les Laboratoires Servier v Apotex Inc [2015] AC 430 . . . 303

Less & Carter v Hussain [2012] EWHC 3513 (QB) . . . 277

Letang v Cooper [1965] 1 QB 232 (CA) . . . 413

Levi v Bates [2015] EWCA Civ 206 . . . 441

Lewis v Daily Telegraph Ltd (No 2) [1964] 2 QB 601 (HL) . . . 491, 498, 499, 500, 507

Lewis v Six Continents plc (formerly Bass plc) [2005] EWCA Civ 1805 . . . 328

Lewis v Wandsworth London Borough Council [2020] EWHC 3205 (QB) . . . 237

Lim Poh Choo v Camden & Islington Area Health Authority [1980] AC 174 . . . 633, 637

Linklaters LLP & another v Mellish [2019] EWHC 177 (QB) . . . 463, 488

Lippiatt v South Gloucestershire Council [2000] QB 51 (CA) . . . 601

Lister v Hesley Hall Ltd [2001] UKHL 22; [2002] 1 AC 215 . . . 608, 618, 619, **620**, 621, 622, 623, 644, 681

Liverpool Women's Hospital NHS Foundation Trust v Ronayne [2015] EWCA Civ 588 . . . 119, **121–2**, 123

Livingstone v Ministry of Defence [1984] NILR 356 (Northern Ireland) . . . 415

Livingstone v Raywards Coal Co (1880) 5 App Cas 25 . . . 631

LJY v Persons Unknown [2017] EWHC 3230 (QB) . . . 477

LMS International Ltd & others v Styrene Packaging and Insulation Ltd & others [2005] EWHC 2065 (TCC) . . . 588

London Borough of Hackney v Persons Unknown In London Fields, Hackney (The 'prescribed Area') [2020] EWHC 1900 (QB) . . . 579

London Passenger Transport Board v Upson [1949] AC 155 . . . 398

Lonrho Ltd v Shell Petroleum Co Ltd (No 2) [1982] AC 173 (HL) . . . 398, **399**

Lord Bernstein of Leigh v Skyviews & General Ltd [1978] QB 479 (QBD) . . . 541

Lord Browne of Madingley v Associated Newspapers Ltd [2007] EWCA Civ 295 . . . 474

Loreena McKennitt v Niema Ash *see* McKennitt v Ash

Losinjska Plovidba v Transco Overseas Ltd (The Orjula) [1995] 2 Lloyd's Rep 395 (QBD) . . . 199

Loutchansky v Times Newspapers Ltd (No 2) [2001] EWCA Civ 1805; [2002] QB 783 . . . 506, 513

M v Newham [1995] 2 AC 633 . . . 152, 153, 177

McAlpine v Bercow [2013] EWHC 1342 (QB) . . . 489, **500**, 504, 532

McClaren v News Group Newspapers Ltd [2012] EWHC 2466 (QB) . . . 478

McCluskey v Wallace 1998 SC 711 . . . 311

McDermid v Nash Dredging & Reclamation Co Ltd [1987] AC 906 (HL) . . . 393

Macdonald v Aberdeenshire Council [2013] CSIH 83 . . . 176

McDonald (Deceased) v National Grid Electricity Transmission plc [2014] UKSC 53 . . . 404

McFarlane v EE Caledonia Ltd [1994] 2 All ER 1 (CA) . . . 117

McFarlane v Tayside Health Board [1999] UKHL 50 . . . 203, 220, 367

McGhee v National Coal Board [1973] 1 WLR 1 (HL) . . . 260, 261, 262, 263, 268, 269, 272

McGill v The Sports and Entertainment Media Group & others [2016] EWCA Civ 1063 . . . 274

McGlone v Greater Glasgow Health Board [2012] CSOH 190 . . . 271

McGuinn v Lewisham and Greenwich NHS Trust [2017] EWHC 88 (QB) . . . 229

McHugh v Okai-Koi [2017] EWHC 710 (QB) . . . 302, 306

McKenna v British Aluminium Ltd [2002] Env LR 30 (Ch D) . . . **553**

McKennitt v Ash [2006] EWCA Civ 1714; [2008] QB 73 . . . 465, **466**, 472

McKew v Holland & Hanmen & Cubitts (Scotland) Ltd [1969] 3 All ER 1621 (HL) . . . 285, 286

MacLeod v The Commissioner of the Police for the Metropolis [2015] EWCA Civ 688 . . . 241

McLoughlin v O'Brian [1982] 1 AC 410 (HL) . . . 36, 64, 105, **113**, 116, 119, 120, 667

McPherson v Daniels (1829) 10 B & C 263 . . . 507

McWilliam v Sir William Arrol & Co Ltd [1962] 1 WLR 295 (HL) . . . **392**

Maga v Birmingham Roman Catholic Archdiocese Trustees [2010] EWCA Civ 256; [2010] 1 WLR 1441 . . . 608

Majrowski v Guy's and St Thomas' NHS Trust [2006] UKHL 34; [2007] 1 AC 224 . . . 390, 442, 445, 609, **618**, 619

M'Alister (or Donoghue) (Pauper) v Stevenson *see* **Donoghue v Stevenson**

Malone v Commissioner of Police of the Metropolis (No 2) [1979] Ch 344 (Ch D) . . . 453, 470

Malone v Laskey [1907] 2 KB 141 (CA) . . . 550, 551

Manchester Building Society v Grant Thornton UK LLP [2019] EWCA Civ 40 . . . 189

Manchester Corporation v Farnworth [1930] AC 171 (HL) . . . 565

Manchester Ship Canal Developments v Persons Unknown [2014] EWHC 645 (Ch) . . . 545

Mansfield v Weetabix Ltd [1998] 1 WLR 1263 (CA) . . . 224, 225

Marc Rich & Co v Bishop Rock Marine Co Ltd (The Nicholas H) [1996] 1 AC 211 (HL) . . . 70, 72, 207

Marcic v Thames Water Utilities plc [2003] UKHL 66; [2004] 2 AC 42 . . . 574–5, 576, 577, 578

Mattis v Pollock (t/a Flamingos Nightclub) [2003] EWCA Civ 887; [2003] 1 WLR 2158 . . . 387, 618

Mayor of London v Hall [2010] EWCA Civ 817; [2011] 1 WLR 504 . . . 545

MB (Caesarean Section), Re [1997] 2 FLR 426 (CA) . . . 433, 434

Mbasogo v Logo Ltd (No 1) [2006] EWCA Civ 1370; [2007] QB 846 . . . 419, 438

Meering v Grahame-White Aviation Co (1919) 122 LT 44 (CA) . . . 427, 428

Megan Tanner (a child by her father and litigation friend) v Sarkar (2017) LTL 4 April . . . 118

Meiklejohn v St George's Healthcare NHS Trust & another [2014] EWCA Civ 120 . . . 270

Merlin Entertainments LPC, Chessington World of Adventures Operations v Cave [2014] EWHC 3036 (QB) . . . 443, 445

Mersey Docks and Harbour Board v Gibbs (1866) LR 1 (HL) . . . 141

Merthyr Tydfil County Borough Council v C [2010] EWHC 62 (QB); [2010] 1 FLR 1640 . . . 144

Michael v Chief Constable of South Wales Police [2015] UKSC 2 . . . 37, 50, 67, 68, 91, 93, 94, 99, 145, **147**, 154, 163, 164, 165, 166, 167, 170, 186, 668

Middleton and anothor v Person or Persons Unknown [2016] EWHC 2354 (QB) . . . 467

Midland Bank Trust Co Ltd & another v Hett Stubbs & Kemp (a firm) [1979] 1 Ch 384 (Ch D) . . . 49

Miller v Associated Newspapers [2016] EWHC 397 (QB) . . . 464

Miller v Jackson [1977] QB 966 (CA) . . . 546, 567, 568, 570, 571, 577

Ministry of Defence v AB & others [2010] EWCA Civ 1317; (2011) 117 BMLR 101 . . . 263

Ministry of Defence v AB & others [2012] UKSC 9 . . . 263, 269, 646

Ministry of Justice v Carter [2010] EWCA Civ 694 . . . 230

Mitchell v Glasgow City Council [2009] UKHL 11; [2009] 1 AC 874 . . . 51, 93, 99, 145, 146, 175, 177, 184

Mitton v Benefield [2011] EWHC 2098 (QB) . . . 442, 443

MM (An Adult), Re [2007] EWHC 2689 (Fam); [2009] 1 FLR 487 . . . 433

Mohamud v WM Morrison Supermarkets plc [2016] UKSC 11 . . . 621

Mohmed v Barnes and EUI Ltd [2019] EWHC 87 (QB) . . . 236

Monir v Wood [2018] EWHC 3525 . . . 501

Monk v PC Harrington Ltd [2008] EWHC 1879 (QB); [2009] PIQR P3 . . . 132

Monroe v Hopkins [2017] EWHC 433 (QB) . . . 492, 501, 504, 524

Monsanto plc v Tilly [2000] Env LR 313 (CA) . . . 543

Monson v Tussauds Ltd [1894] QB 671 (CA) . . . 490, **499**

Montgomery v Lanarkshire Health Board [2015] UKSC 11 . . . 230, **231–2**, 233, 234, 235, 236, 249, 271, 432, 670, 671

Morgan v Odhams Press Ltd [1971] 1 WLR 1239 (HL) . . . 501

Morris v CW Martin & Sons Ltd [1966] 1 QB 716 (CA) . . . 618

Morris v Murray [1991] 2 QB 6 (CA) . . . 292, 293, **294**, 295, 296, 672

Morrison Sports Ltd v Scottish Power [2010] UKSC 37 . . . 400

Mosley v Google [2015] EWHC 59 (QB) . . . 475, 627

Mosley v News Group Newspapers Ltd [2008] EWHC 1777 (QB); [2008] EMLR 20 . . . 467, 474, 477, 478, 483, 627, 677

Motto v Trafigura [2011] EWCA Civ 1150 . . . 627

Moy v Pettman Smith [2005] UKHL 7; [2005] 1 WLR 581 . . . 227

Muirhead v Industrial Tanks Specialties [1985] EWCA Civ 16 . . . 199

Mulcahy v Ministry of Defence [1996] QB 732 (CA) . . . 171

Mullaney v Chief Constable of West Midlands Police [2001] EWCA Civ 700 . . . 87, 169, 393

Mullen v Barr & Co [1929] SC 461 (IH) . . . 35, 356

Muller v King's College Hospital [2017] EWHC 128 (QB) . . . 229

Mullin v Richards [1998] 1 WLR 1304 (CA) . . . 226

Murphy v Brentwood District Council [1991] 1 AC 398 (HL) . . . 36, 64, 196–7, 197, **199–200**, 201, 210, 357

Murphy v Culhane [1977] QB 94 (CA) . . . 304, 431

Murray v Express Newspapers plc [2008] EWCA Civ 446; [2009] Ch 481 . . . 475, 476, 482, 483, 677

Murray v Ministry of Defence [1988] 1 WLR 692 (HL) . . . 427

Murrell v Healy [2001] EWCA Civ 486; [2001] 4 All ER 345 . . . 279

Muuse v Secretary of State for the Home Department [2010] EWCA Civ 453; (2010) 107(19) LSG 24 . . . 629

N v Chief Constable of Merseyside Police [2006] EWHC 3041 (QB); [2006] Po LR 160 . . . 621

National Coal Board v England [1954] AC 493 . . . 299

National Telephone Co v Baker [1893] 2 Ch 186 (Ch D) . . . 587

Naylor v Payling [2004] EWCA Civ 560; [2004] PIQR P36 . . . 335, 673

Nettleship v Weston [1971] 2 QB 691 (CA) . . . 44, 221, **222**, 223, 224, 226, 239, 242, 247, 249, 294, 295, 304, 631, 650, 657

Network Rail Infrastructure Ltd v Morris (t/a Soundstar Studio) [2004] EWCA Civ 172 . . . 561, 562, 581, 585, 679

Network Rail Infrastructure Ltd v Williams & another [2018] EWCA Civ 1514 . . . 549

Newstead v London Express Newspapers Ltd [1940] 1 KB 377 (CA) . . . 502, 503, 507

Nicholas H, The *see* Marc Rich & Co v Bishop Rock Marine Co Ltd

Nicholls v Ladbrokes Betting and Gambling Ltd [2013] EWCA Civ 1963 . . . 395

Nichols v Marsland (1876–77) LR 2 Ex D 1 (CA) . . . 598

NNN v D1 & another [2014] EWHC B14 (QB) . . . 477

North Glamorgan NHS Trust v Walters [2002] EWCA Civ 1792; [2003] PIQR P16 . . . 120, 121, 122, 123

Northumbrian Water Ltd v McAlpine Ltd [2014] EWCA Civ 685 . . . 590, 591, 595, 680

Northwestern Utilities Ltd v London Guarantee & Accident Co [1936] AC 108 (PC) . . . 597

Novartis Grimsby Ltd v Cookson [2007] EWCA Civ 1261 . . . 266, 267

NPV v QEL & another [2018] EWHC 703 (QB) . . . 477

NT1 & NT2 v Google LLC [2018] EWHC 799 (QB) . . . 468

Ntuli v Donald [2010] EWCA Civ 1276 . . . 478, 480

Nyang v G4S Care & Justice Services Ltd & others [2013] EWHC 3946 (QB) . . . 86, 255

O'Byrne v Aventis Pasteur SA Ltd [2008] UKHL 34; [2008] 4 All ER 881 . . . 375

O'Byrne v Aventis Pasteur SA [2010] UKSC 23 . . . 375

O'Byrne v Sanofi Pasteur MSD Ltd [2006] 1 WLR 1606 . . . 375

Officer L, Re [2007] UKHL 36; [2007] 1 WLR 2135 . . . 146

Ogwo v Taylor [1988] AC 431 (HL) . . . 128

O'Hare v Coutts & Co [2016] EWHC 2224 (QB) . . . 236

OLL Ltd v Secretary of State for Transport [1997] 3 All ER 897 (QBD) . . . 173

OPO v MLA [2014] EWCA Civ 1277 . . . 436, 439, 464

Orange v Chief Constable of West Yorkshire Police [2001] EWCA Civ 611; [2002] QB 347 . . . 85, 86, 169

Orchard v Lee [2009] EWCA Civ 295; [2009] ELR 178 . . . 225

O'Rourke v Camden London Borough Council [1998] AC 188 (HL) . . . 54, 399, 403

Osborn v Thomas Boulter & Son [1930] 2 KB 226 (CA) . . . 505

O'Shea v MGN Ltd [2001] EMLR 40 (QBD) . . . 502, 503, 678

Osman v Ferguson [1993] 4 All ER 344 (CA) . . . 91, 93, 148, **149**, 150, 151, 153, 161, 167

Overseas Tankship (UK) Ltd v Miller Steamship Co Pty Ltd (The Wagon Mound) (No 2) [1967] 1 AC 617 . . . 244, 280, 281, 562

Overseas Tankship (UK) Ltd v Morts Dock and Engineering Co (The Wagon Mound) (No 1) [1961] AC 388 (PC) . . . 62, 244, **280**, 281, 282, 572, 592, 671

P v Cheshire West and Chester Council; P and Q v Surrey County Council [2014] UKSC 19 . . . 428

P Perl (Exporters) Ltd v Camden LBC [1984] QB 342 (CA) . . . 91, 97, 99

Page v Smith [1996] AC 155 (HL) . . . 4, 63, 72, 104, 107, **108–9**, 110, 111, 112, 118, 127, 128, 129, 130, 282, 667

Palmer v Portsmouth Hospitals NHS Trust [2017] EWHC 2460 (QB) . . . 277

Palmer v Tees Health Authority (2000) 2 LGLR 69; [1999] Lloyd's Rep Med 351 (CA) . . . 91–2, 96, 98, 99, 152

Pape v Cumbria County Council [1992] 3 All ER 211 (QBD) . . . 392, 393

Paris v Stepney Borough Council [1951] AC 367 (HL) . . . 239–40

Parker v Chief Constable of Essex Police [2018] EWCA Civ 2788 . . . 431

Parkinson v St James & Seacroft University Hospital NHS Trust [2001] EWCA Civ 530; [2002] QB 266 . . . 203–4

Patchett v Swimming Pool & Allied Trades Association Ltd [2009] EWCA Civ 717; [2010] 2 All ER (Comm) 138 . . . 209

Patel v Mirza [2016] UKSC 42 . . . 297, 300, **301**, 302, 303, 313

Paul v Royal Wolverhampton NHS Trust [2020] EWHC 1415 (QB) . . . 124, **125**

Pearce v United Bristol Healthcare NHS Trust [1999] PIQR P 53 . . . 230

Peires v Bickerton's Aerodromes Ltd [2016] EWHC 560 (Ch) . . . 554, 578

Performance Cars v Abraham [1962] 1 QB 33 (CA) . . . 279

Perrett v Collins [1998] 2 Lloyd's Rep 255 (CA) . . . 49

Perry v Harris [2008] EWCA Civ 907; [2009] 1 WLR 19 . . . 219, 226, 238

Perry v Kendrick's Transport Ltd [1956] 1 WLR 85 (CA) . . . 596, 597

Perry v Raleys Solicitors [2019] UKSC 5 . . . 274

Phelps v Hillingdon London Borough Council [2001] 2 AC 619 (HL) . . . 37, 81, 152, **180**, 181, 399

Phillips v William Whiteley [1938] 1 All ER 566 . . . 226

Phipps v Rochester Corporation [1955] 1 QB 450 . . . 330

Pierce v Doncaster MBC [2007] EWHC 2968 (QB); [2008] 1 FLR 922 . . . 52, 179, 646

Pile v Chief Constable of Merseyside Police [2020] EWHC 2472 (QB) . . . 431

Pimlico Plumbers Ltd v Smith [2018] UKSC 29 . . . 612

Pinchbeck v Craggy Island Ltd [2012] All ER (D) 121 . . . 306

Pippin v Sheppard (1822) 147 ER 517 . . . 43

Pitts v Hunt [1991] 1 QB 24 (CA) . . . 308, 672

PJS v News Group Newspapers Ltd [2016] UKSC 26 . . . 464, 467, 468, 469, 473, 477

Playboy Club London Ltd v Banca Nazionale Del Lavoro Spa [2018] EWCA Civ 2025 . . . 206

PNM v Times Newspapers Ltd & others [2014] EWCA Civ 1132 . . . 477, 479

Polemis and Furness Withy & Co Ltd, Re [1921] 3 KB 560 . . . 280

Pollard v Tesco Stores Ltd [2006] EWCA Civ 393 . . . 365, 369, 372

Pollock v Cahill [2015] EWHC 2260 (QB) . . . 327

Polmear & another v Royal Cornwall Hospitals NHS Trust [2021] EWHC 196 (QB) . . . 125

Pomphrey v Secretary of State for Health and Anor [2019] 4 WLUK 483 . . . 271

Ponting v Noakes [1894] 2 QB 281 (QBD) . . . 597

Poole Borough Council v GN [2019] UKSC 25 . . . 37, 50, 68, 71, 93, 142, 143, **145–6**, 154, 175, 177, 178, 184, 205

Poppleton v Trustees of the Portsmouth Youth Activities Committee [2008] EWCA Civ 646; [2009] PIQR P1 . . . 295

Pratley v Surrey County Council [2002] EWHC 1608 (Admin) . . . 136

Priestly v Fowler (1837) 1 M&W 1 Ex Ch . . . 387, 401

Probert (A Child) v Moore [2012] EWHC 2324 (QB) . . . 305

Pusey v Somerset County Council [2012] EWCA Civ 988 . . . 560

R v Bournewood Mental Health Trust, *ex p* L [1998] UKHL 24; [1999] AC 458 . . . 427, 428, 434

R v Brown [1994] 1 AC 212 (HL) . . . 432

R v Central Independent Television plc [1994] Fam 192; [1994] 3 WLR 20 (CA) . . . 472

R v Chief Constable of Devon and Cornwall, *ex p* Central Electricity Generating Board [1982] 1 QB 458 (CA) . . . 414

R v Deputy Governor of Parkhurst Prison, *ex p* Hague [1992] 1 AC 58 (HL) . . . 399, 402, 426, 429, 430

R v Governor of Brockhill Prison, *ex p* Evans (No 2) [2001] 2 AC 19 (HL) . . . 423

R v Ireland [1998] AC 147 (HL) . . . 420, 421

R v Lincoln [1990] 12 Cr App R 250 . . . 432

R v Meade and Belt (1823) 1 Lew CC 184 . . . 420

R v Rimmington; R v Goldstein [2005] UKHL 63; [2006] 1 AC 459 . . . 579, 580

R v St George (1840) 173 ER 821 . . . 418

R v Venna [1976] QB 421 (CA) . . . 414

R v Williams (Owen Richard) [1923] 1 KB 340 (CCA) . . . 432

R (Greenfield) v Secretary of State for the Home Department [2005] UKHL 14; [2005] 1 WLR 673 . . . 21

R (on the application of Jalloh (formerly Jollah)) v Secretary of State for the Home Department [2020] UKSC 4 . . . **422**, 428

R (on the application of Lumba) v Secretary of State for the Home Department [2011] UKSC 12 . . . 429, **430**, 629

R (Mohamed) v Foreign Secretary (No 2) [2010] EWCA Civ 158 . . . 479

R (Smith) v Secretary of State for Defence [2010] UKSC 29 . . . 172

Rabone v Pennine Care NHS Trust [2010] EWCA Civ 698; [2010] PIQR Q4 . . . 86

Rabone & another v Pennine Care NHS Trust [2012] UKSC 2 . . . 86

Raggett v Society of Jesus Trust 1929 for Roman Catholic Purposes [2010] EWCA Civ 1002; [2010] CP Rep 45 . . . 646

Rahman v Arearose Ltd [2001] QB 351 (CA) . . . 258, 641

Ratcliff v McConnell [1999] 1 WLR 670 (CA) . . . 346, 350

Rathband v Northumbria Constabulary [2016] EWHC 181 (QB) . . . 169

Ravenscroft v Rederiaktiebolaget Transatlantic [1991] 3 All ER 73 (QBD) . . . 64

Raymond v Young [2015] EWCA Civ 456 . . . 572

RE (A minor by her mother and Litigation Friend LE) and others v Calderdale & Huddersfield NHS Foundation Trust [2017] EWHC 824 . . . 111, 119, 123, 124

Read v Lyons Co Ltd [1947] AC 156 (HL) . . . 236, 588, 590, 596, 680

Reaney v University Hospital of North Staffordshire NHS Trust [2014] EWHC 3016 (QB) . . . 283

Reaney v University Hospital of North Staffordshire NHS Trust & another [2015] EWCA Civ 1119 . . . 279, 283

Reaney v University Hospital of North Staffordshire NHS Trust & another (No 2) [2016] EWHC 1676 (QB) . . . 283

Reeman v Department of Transport [1997] 2 Lloyd's Rep 648 (CA) . . . 207

Rees v Darlington Memorial Hospital NHS Trust [2002] EWCA Civ 88; [2003] QB 20 . . . 550

Rees v Darlington Memorial Hospital NHS Trust [2003] UKHL 52; [2004] 1 AC 309 . . . 204, 367, 629

Reeves v Commissioner of Police for the Metropolis [2000] 1 AC 360 (HL) . . . **85**, 86, 89, 168–9, 286, 294, 304, 308, 431

Regan v Paul Properties Ltd [2006] EWCA Civ 1319; [2007] Ch 135 . . . 570

Rehill v Rider Holdings Ltd [2012] EWCA Civ 628 . . . 306

Reid v Price [2020] EWHC 594 (QB) . . . 467

Reilly v Merseyside RHA [1995] 6 Med LR 246 (CA) . . . 104

Revill v Newbery [1996] QB 567 (CA) . . . 347

Reynolds v Clarke (1725) 93 ER 747 . . . 417

Reynolds v Strutt and Parker LLP [2011] EWHC 2263 (QB) . . . 309

Reynolds v Times Newspapers [2001] 2 AC 127 (HL) . . . 510, **512–13**, 514, 515, 516, 517, 527, 528

Rhind v Astbury Water Park Ltd [2004] EWCA Civ 756 . . . **344**

Rhodes v OPO (by his litigation friend BHM) & another [2015] UKSC 32 . . . 436, **438–9**, 451, 464

Richard v The British Broadcasting Corporation (BBC) & another [2018] EWHC 1837 (Ch) . . . 467, 473, 474, 483, 629

Richards v London Borough of Bromley [2012] EWCA Civ 1476 . . . 219, 237

Richardson v LRC Products Ltd (2000) 59 BMLR 185 . . . 364, 367, 373, 380

Richardson v Mellish (1824) 2 Bing 229 . . . 8

Richardson v Pitt-Stanley [1995] QB 123 (CA) . . . 403

Rickards v Lothian [1913] AC 263 (PC) . . . 589, 597

Rigby v Chief Constable of Northamptonshire [1985] 1 WLR 1242 (QBD) . . . 160, 161, 589

Rihan v Ernst & Young Global Ltd and others [2020] EWHC 901 (QB) . . . 214

Rihanna v Topshop *see* Fenty & others v Arcadia Group Brands Ltd & others

Riley v Murray [2020] EWHC 977 (QB) . . . 495

RJW & SJW v The Guardian Newspaper & Person or Persons Unknown [2009] EWHC 2540 (QB) . . . 480

Roberts v Gamble [2007] EWCA Civ 721 . . . 515

Roberts v Ramsbottom [1980] 1 WLR 823 (QBD) . . . 223, 224

Robertson v Forth Road Bridge Joint Board (No 2) 1995 SC 364; [1996] SLT 263 (IH) . . . 117

Robinson v Balmain New Ferry Co Ltd [1910] AC 295 (PC) . . . 422, 424

Robinson v Chief Constable of West Yorkshire [2018] UKSC 4 . . . 37, 49, 50, 68, 70, **71–2**, 81, 140, 142, 145, 154, 160, 168, 175, 178, 205, 668

Robinson v Kilvert (1889) LR 41 Ch D 88 (CA) . . . 559, 560

Robinson v PE Jones (Contractors) Ltd [2011] EWCA Civ 9; [2011] CILL 2972 . . . 199, 204

Robinson v Post Office [1974] WLR 1176 (CA) . . . 285

Rocknroll v News Group Newspapers Ltd [2013] EWHC 24 (Ch) . . . 467, 476, 477

Roe v Ministry of Health [1954] 2 QB 66 (CA) . . . 12, **238**, 239

Roles v Nathan [1963] 1 WLR 1117 (CA) . . . 331, 332, 338, 350

Rookes v Barnard [1964] AC 1129 (HL) . . . 629

Rose v Plenty [1976] 1 WLR 141 (CA) . . . 622

Ross v Caunters [1980] Ch 297 (Ch D) . . . 210, 213

Rothwell v Chemical & Insulating Co Ltd & another; Topping v Benchtown Ltd (formerly Jones Bros Preston Ltd); Johnston v NEI International Combustion Ltd; Grieves v FT Everard & Sons Ltd & another [2007] UKHL 39; [2008] 1 AC 281 . . . 31, 32, 104, **110**, 111, 113, 276, 482, 550

Rouse v Squires [1973] 1 QB 889 (CA) . . . 284, 285

Rubenstein v HSBC Bank plc [2012] EWCA Civ 1184 . . . 281

Rylands v Fletcher (1868) LR 3 HL 330 (HL) . . . 2, 5, 32, 322, 454, 536, 538, 553, 570, 572, 584–90, **585**, 591, 592, 593, 594, 595, 596, 597, 598, 599, 600, 601, 602, 603, 604, 680

S, Re [2004] UKHL 47; [2005] 1 AC 593 . . . 469, 472

S v Gloucestershire County Council [2000] Fam 313; [2000] 3 All ER 346 (CA) . . . 183

S v W (Child Abuse: Damages) [1995] 1 FLR 862 (CA) . . . 645

Sabir v Osei-Kwabena [2015] EWCA Civ 1213 . . . 310

St George v Home Office [2008] EWCA Civ 1068; [2009] 1 WLR 1670 . . . 304, 307, 308

St George's Healthcare NHS Trust v S [1999] Fam 26 . . . 233

St Helens Smelting Co v Tipping (1865) 11 HLC 642; 11 ER 1483 (HL) . . . **548**, 549, 555, 556, 679

Sanderson v Hull [2008] EWCA Civ 1211; [2009] CP Rep 12 . . . 267

Sandhu Menswear Co Ltd v Woolworths plc [2006] EWHC 1299 (TCC); [2006] 24 EG 176 (CS) (QBD) . . . 98, 99

Sarjantson v Humberside Police [2013] EWCA Civ 1252 . . . 147

Saunders v Edwards [1987] 1 WLR 1116 (CA) . . . 298

Saunderson & others v Sonae Industria (UK) Ltd [2016] EWCA Civ 1177 . . . 579

Savage v South Essex Partnership NHS Trust [2008] UKHL 74; [2009] 1 AC 681 . . . 85

Savage v South Essex Partnership NHS Trust [2010] EWHC 865 (QB) . . . 86

Schembri v Marshall [2020] EWCA Civ 358 . . . 256

Scott v London and St Katherine Docks Co [1865] All ER Rep 248; (1865) 159 ER 665; 3 H & C 596 (Ex Ct) . . . 248

Scott v Shepherd (1773) 2 Wm Bl 892 . . . 417

Scout Association v Barnes [2010] EWCA Civ 1476 . . . 242, 243, 246, 342

Scullion v Bank of Scotland plc (trading as Colleys) [2011] EWCA Civ 693 . . . 209

Sebry v Companies House [2015] EWHC 115 (QB) . . . 205

Sedleigh-Denfield v O'Callaghan [1940] AC 880 (HL) . . . 97, 340, **599**, 600

Selwood v Durham County Council [2012] EWCA Civ 979 . . . 93, 99

Serafin v Malkiewicz and others [2017] EWHC 2992 (QB) . . . 473, 491

Serafin v Malkiewicz and others [2019] EWCA Civ 852 . . . 491

Serafin v Malkiewicz and others [2020] UKSC 23 . . . 491, 514

Shakil-Ur-Rahman v ARY Network Ltd [2016] EWHC 3110 (QB) . . . 525

Shelfer v City of London Electric Lighting Co [1895] 1 Ch 287 (CA) . . . 570, 571, 577, 578

Shell UK Ltd v Total UK Ltd [2010] EWCA Civ 180; [2011] QB 86 . . . 192, 193

Sherratt v Chief Constable of Greater Manchester Police [2018] EWHC 1746 (QB) . . . 166

Shiffman v Order of St John [1936] 1 All ER 557 . . . 587

Shorter v Surrey & Sussex Healthcare NHS Trust [2015] EWHC 614 (QB) . . . 121

Sidaway v Board of Governors of the Bethlem Royal Hospital [1985] AC 871 (HL) . . . 230, 231, 234, 270, 271

Siddiqui v University of Oxford [2016] EWHC 3150 (QB) . . . 180

Siddiqui v University of Oxford [2018] EWHC 184 (QB) . . . 60

Sienkiewicz v Greif (UK) Ltd [2009] EWCA Civ 1159 . . . 267

Sienkiewicz v Greif (UK) Ltd [2011] UKSC 10; [2011] 2 WLR 523 . . . 262, 263, **267–8**, 269

Sim v Stretch [1936] 2 All ER 1237 (HL) . . . 490

Simkiss v Rhondda Borough Council (1982) 81 LGR 460 (CA) . . . 330, 331

Simmons v British Steel plc [2004] UKHL 20; 2004 SC (HL) 94 . . . 258, 282

Simmons v Castle [2012] EWCA Civ 1288 . . . 628, 634

Simonds v Isle of Wight Council [2003] EWHC 2303 (QB); [2004] ELR 59 . . . 346, 652

Sion v Hampstead Health Authority [1994] 5 Med LR 170 (CA) . . . 105, 120

Six Carpenters Case (1610) 8 Co Rep 146; 77 ER 695; 1 Smith's Ld Cas 217 (QB) . . . 544

Slater v Clay Cross Ltd [1956] 2 QB 264 (CA) . . . 296

Slipper v BBC [1991] 1 QB 283 (CA) . . . 506

Smith v Charles Baker & Sons [1891] AC 325 (HL) . . . 291, 296, 401

Smith v Chief Constable of Sussex Police [2008] UKHL 50 . . . 93, 154, **162–3**, 164, 165, 166, 167, 170, 668

Smith v Eric S Bush [1990] AC 831 (HL) . . . **208–9**

Smith v Finch [2009] EWHC 53 (QB) . . . 309

Smith v Lancashire Teaching Hospitals NHS Foundation Trust & others [2017] EWCA Civ 1916 . . . 638

Smith v Lancashire Teaching Hospitals NHS Trust & another [2016] EWHC 2208 (QB) . . . 638

Smith v Leech Brain & Co Ltd [1962] 2 QB 405 (QBD) . . . 282, 283

Smith v Littlewoods Organisation Ltd [1987] 1 AC 241 (HL) . . . 50, 53, 64, 80, 89, 90, 97, 98, 99, 100, 600

Smith v Stone (1647) Sty 65 . . . 540

Smith v Youth Justice Board for England and Wales [2010] EWCA Civ 99 . . . 286

Smith & others v The Ministry of Defence [2013] UKSC 41 . . . 146, **171–2**, 173, 174, 175, 185

Snook v Mannion [1982] RTR 321; [1982] Crim LR 601 (DC) . . . 327

Sobrinho v Impresa Publishing SA [2016] EWHC 66 (QB) . . . 492

South Hetton Coal Co v North-Eastern News Association Ltd [1894] 1 QB 133 (CA) . . . 488

Southport Corporation v Esso Petroleum Co Ltd [1954] 2 QB 182 (CA) . . . 545

Southwark Borough Council v Mills [2001] AC 1 (HL) . . . 555

Southwark London Borough Council v William [1971] Ch 734 (CA) . . . 543

Spartan Steel & Alloys Ltd v Martin & Co (Contractors) Ltd [1973] 1 QB 27 (CA) . . . 45, **190–1**, 192, 193, 194, 195, 215

Spearman v Royal United Bath Hospitals NHS Foundation Trust [2017] EWHC 3027 (QB) . . . 305, **325–6**

Spelman v Express Newspapers (No 2) [2012] EWHC 355 (QB) . . . 476

Spencer v Wincanton Holdings Ltd [2009] EWCA Civ 1404; [2010] PIQR P8 . . . 286

Spicer v Commissioner of Police of the Metropolis [2019] EWHC 1439 (QB) . . . 496

Spring v Guardian Assurance plc [1995] 2 AC 296 (HL) . . . 167, 213, **214**, 394, 511

ST v Maidstone and Tunbridge Wells NHS Trust [2015] EWHC 51 (QB) . . . 261, 282

Standard Chartered Bank v Pakistan National Shipping Corp (No 2) [2002] UKHL 43; [2003] 1 AC 959 . . . 304, 431

Stannard (t/a Wyvern Tyres) v Gore [2012] EWCA Civ 1248 . . . 588, 590, 591, 595, 680

Stansbie v Troman [1948] 2 KB 48 (CA) . . . 80, 90, 97, 99

Stanton v Collinson [2010] EWCA Civ 81; [2010] CP Rep 27 . . . 308

Staples v West Dorset District Council [1995] 93 LGR 536 . . . 332

Stapley v Gypsum Mines Ltd [1953] AC 663 . . . 308

Star Energy Weald Basin Ltd v Bocardo SA [2010] UKSC 35; [2011] 1 AC 380 . . . **541–2**

Starr v Ward [2015] EWHC 1987 (QB) . . . 494

Steel and another v NRAM Limited (formerly NRAM Plc) (Scotland) [2018] UKSC 13 . . . 206, 208

Stennett v Hancock & Peters [1939] 2 All ER 578 (KBD) . . . 356

Stephen Anslow & others v Norton Aluminium Ltd *see* Anslow & others v Norton Aluminium Ltd

Stephens v Myers (1830) 4 C&P 350; (1830) 172 ER 734 (Assizes) . . . **419**, 676

Stephenson Jordan & Harrison Ltd v McDonall & Evans [1952] 1 TLR 101 (CA) . . . 614

Stinton v Stinton [1995] RTR 167 . . . 309

Stocker v Stocker [2018] EWCA Civ 170 . . . 504

Stocker v Stocker [2019] UKSC 17 . . . 494, **496–7**

Stokes v Guest, Keene and Nettlefold (Bolts and Nuts) Ltd [1968] 1 WLR 1776 . . . 389

Stovin v Wise [1996] AC 923 (HL) . . . 66, 69, 81, 82, 89, 101, 175, **176**, 178, 666

Stubbings v Webb [1993] AC 498 . . . 642

Sturges v Bridgman (1879) LR 11 Ch D 852 (CA) . . . 546, 556, **567**

Sube v News Group Newspapers Limited [2020] EWHC 1125 . . . 444

Sumner v Colborne Denbighshire CC and The Welsh Ministers [2018] EWCA Civ 1006 . . . 177

Surtees v Kingston upon Thames Borough Council [1992] PIQR P101 . . . 84

Sutradhar v National Environmental Research Council [2006] UKHL 33; [2006] 4 All ER 490 . . . 82, 89

Swain v Puri [1996] PIQR P442 (CA) . . . 345

Swinney v Chief Constable of Northumbria Police [1997] QB 464 (CA) . . . 91, 99, 134, 168

T (Adult: Refusal of Treatment), Re [1993] Fam 95; [1992] 3 WLR 782 (CA) . . . 432

Tamiz v Google Inc [2013] EWCA Civ 68 . . . 505

Tate & Lyle Industries Ltd v GLC [1983] 2 AC 509 (HL) . . . 580

Taylor v A Novo (UK) Ltd [2013] EWCA Civ 194; [2014] QB 150 . . . 108, 118, 125, 130

Taylor v Chief Constable of Hampshire Police [2013] EWCA Civ 496 . . . 281

Taylorson v Shieldness Produce Ltd [1994] PIQR 329 . . . 121

TCD v Harrow [2008] EWHC 3048 (QB); [2009] 1 FLR 719 . . . 646

Terry (John) v Persons Unknown [2010] EWHC 119 (QB); [2010] EMLR 16 . . . 478

Thake v Maurice [1986] QB 644 . . . 203

Thakrar v Secretary of State for Justice [2015] EW Misc B44 . . . 629

Theaker v Richardson [1962] 1 WLR 151 (CA) . . . 504, **505**

Theakston v MGN Ltd [2002] EWHC 137 (QB); [2002] EMLR 22 . . . 467, 475, 478

Theedom v Nourish Training Ltd [2015] EWHC 3769 (QB) . . . 492

Thefaut v Johnston [2017] EWHC 497 (QB) . . . 235, 271

Thomas v National Union of Mineworkers (South Wales Area) [1986] Ch 20 (Ch D) . . . **419–20**

Thomas v News Group Newspapers Ltd [2001] EWCA Civ 1233; [2002] EMLR 78 . . . 444, 445

Thompson-Schwab v Costaki [1956] 1 WLR 335 (CA) . . . 546

Thompstone v Thameside & Glossop Acute Services NHS Trust [2008] *The Times*, January 30 . . . 636

Thomson v Christie Manson & Woods Ltd [2005] EWCA Civ 555 . . . 202

Thornton v Telegraph Media Group [2010] . . . 492, 493

Times Newspapers Ltd & others v Flood & others [2017] UKSC 33 . . . 464

Tindall & another v Thames Valley Police & another [2020] EWHC 837 (QB) . . . 168

Tomlinson v Congleton Borough Council [2003] UKHL 47; [2004] 1 AC 46 . . . 15, 243, 321, 322, 327, 336, **341–2**, 343, 345, 351, **646–7**, 651, 652, 658, 659, 660, 673

Topp v London Country Bus (South West) Ltd [1993] 1 WLR 976 (CA) . . . 96, 97, 99, 284, 666

Trafigura super-injunction *see* RJW & SJW v The Guardian Newspaper & Person or Persons Unknown

Transco plc v Stockport MBC [2003] UKHL 61; [2004] 2 AC 1 . . . 536, 572, 578, 584, 585, **587**, 588, 590, 592, 594–5, 596, 599, 601, 602, 603, 604, 657, 680

Tremain v Pike [1969] 1 WLR 1556 (Exeter Assizes) . . . 63, 282

'Trigger Litigation' *see* BAI (Run Off) Ltd v Durham

Trimingham v Associated Newspapers Ltd [2012] EWHC 1296 (QB) . . . 444, 445, 467, 471, 478

Trotman v North Yorkshire County Council [1999] LGR 584 (CA) . . . 619

Tse Wei Chun v Cheng [2001] EMLR 777 . . . 521

Tuberville v Savage (1669) 1 Mod Rep 3; 2 Keb 545; 86 EnG Rep 684 . . . 420

Undre & Down to Earth (London) Ltd v London Borough of Harrow [2016] EWHC 2761 (QB) . . . 488

Uren v Corporate Leisure (UK) Ltd [2011] EWCA Civ 66 . . . 219, 246

Vacwell Engineering Co Ltd v BDH Chemicals Ltd [1971] 1 QB 111 (CA) . . . 282

Van Colle & another v Hertfordshire Police [2007] EWCA Civ 325 . . . 163

Van Colle v Chief Constable of Hertfordshire Constabulary [2008] UKHL 50; [2008] 3 WLR 593 . . . 146, 163, 668

Various Claimants v Catholic Child Welfare Society & others [2012] UKSC 56 . . . 609, 612, **614–16**, 617, 618, 620, 623, 624, 644, 681

Veakins v Kier Islington Ltd [2009] EWCA Civ 1288; [2010] IRLR 132 . . . 445, 446, 619

Vellino v Chief Constable of the Greater Manchester Police [2001] EWCA Civ 1249; [2002] 1 WLR 218 . . . 313

Venables v News Group Newspapers Ltd [2001] 2 WLR 1038 (Fam Div) . . . 21, 450, 459, 482

Venables & another v News Group Papers Ltd & others [2019] EWHC 494 (Fam) . . . 460

Vernon Knight Associates v Cornwall Council [2013] EWCA Civ 950 . . . 601

Viasystems (Tyneside) Ltd v Thermal Transfer (Northern) Ltd [2005] EWCA Civ 1151; [2006] QB 510 . . . 681

Victorian Railway Commissioners v Coultas (1888) LR 13 App Cas 222 (PC) . . . 108, 436

Vidal-Hall & others v Google Inc [2014] EWHC 13 (QB) . . . 2, 21, 450, 464

Vision Golf Ltd v Weightmans [2005] EWHC 1675 (Ch); [2005] 32 EG 66 (CS) . . . 642

Vowles v Evans [2003] EWCA Civ 318; [2003] 1 WLR 1607 . . . 95, 242

W v Essex County Council [2001] 2 AC 592; [2000] 2 WLR 601 (HL) . . . 37, 110, 127, 152, 183

Wade & Perry v British Sky Broadcasting Ltd [2016] EWCA Civ 1214 . . . 459

Wagon Mound (No 1), *see* **The Overseas Tankship (UK) Ltd v Morts Dock and Engineering Co (The Wagon Mound) (No 1)**

Wagon Mound (No 2), *see* **The Overseas Tankship (UK) Ltd v Miller Steamship Co Pty Ltd (The Wagon Mound) (No 2)**

Wainwright v Home Office [2003] UKHL 53; [2004] 2 AC 406 . . . 133, 411, 436, **437**, 438, 447, 450, 453, 470, 472, 480, 481

Walker v Northumberland County Council [1995] 1 All ER 737 (QBD) . . . 105, 134, **135**

Walker v The Commissioner of the Police of the Metropolis [2014] EWCA Civ 897 . . . 424, 629

Wallbank v Wallbank Fox Designs [2012] EWCA Civ 25 . . . 622, 681

Walter v Selfe (1851) 4 De G & S 315; 64 ER 849 (QB) . . . 549

Wan-Bissaka & Anor v Bentley [2020] EWHC 3640 (QB) . . . 467

Ward v Allies & Morrison Architects [2012] EWCA Civ 1287 . . . 634

Ward v Tesco Stores Ltd [1976] 1 WLR 810 (CA) . . . 248, 329

Waters v Commissioner of Police for the Metropolis [2000] UKHL 50; [2000] ICR 1064 . . . 134, 169, 170, 390, 394

Watson v British Boxing Board of Control Ltd [2001] QB 1134 (CA) . . . 95, 242

Watson v Buckley, Osborne, Garrett & Co Ltd [1940] 1 All ER 174 (Manchester Assizes) . . . 356

Watson v Croft Promosport Ltd [2009] EWCA Civ 15; [2009] 3 All ER 249 . . . 558, 571, 577

Watt v Hertfordshire County Council [1954] 1 WLR 835 (CA) . . . 241

Watt v Longsdon [1930] 1 KB 130; 69 ALR 1005 (CA) . . . 511

Webb v Beavan (1883) 11 QBD 609 . . . 490

Webster (A Child) v Burton Hospitals NHS Foundation Trust [2017] EWCA Civ 62 . . . 236, 271

Weir v Chief Constable of Merseyside Police [2003] EWCA Civ 111; [2003] ICR 708 . . . 620

Weld-Blundell v Stephens [1920] AC 956 (HL) . . . 284

Weller & Co v Foot and Mouth Disease Research Institute [1966] 1 QB 569 (QBD) . . . 197

Weller & others v Associated Newspapers Ltd [2015] EWCA Civ 1176 . . . 476, 477, 483, 677

Wellesley Partners LLP v Withers LLP [2015] EWCA Civ 1146 . . . 274

Wells v Cooper [1958] 2 QB 265 (CA) . . . 226

Wells v Wells [1999] 1 AC 345 (HL) . . . 634

Wells & Smith v University Hospital Southampton NHS Foundation Trust [2015] EWHC 2376 (QB) . . . 111, 230

Welton v North Cornwall District Council [1997] 1 WLR 570 . . . 202

Wendall v Barchester Healthcare Ltd [2012] EWCA Civ 25 . . . 622, 681

Wennhak v Morgan (1888) LR 20 QBD 635 (QBD) . . . 504

West v Bristol Tramways Co [1908] 2 KB 14 (CA) . . . 587

West Bromwich Albion Football Club Ltd v Al-Safty [2006] EWCA Civ 1299; [2006] All ER (D) 123 (Oct) . . . 205

Wheat v Lacon & Co Ltd [1966] AC 552 (HL) . . . **324**, 337, 338, 349

Wheeler v JJ Saunders Ltd [1996] Ch 19 (CA) . . . 558

Whiston v London SHA (successor body in law for the Queen Charlotte's Maternity Hospital) [2010] EWCA Civ 195; [2010] 1 WLR 1582 . . . 646

White v Blackmore [1972] 2 QB 651 (CA) . . . 292

White v Chief Constable of South Yorkshire Police [1999] 2 AC 455; [1998] 3 WLR 1509

(HL) . . . 104, 105, 106, 107, 108, 109, 110, 115, 126, **128–9**, 130, 131, 132, 135, 136, 667

White v Jones [1995] 2 AC 207 (HL) . . . **210**, 211, 212, 213, 214, 216, 669

White Lion Hotel v James [2021] EWCA Civ 31 . . . 292, **336**, 350

Wieland v Cyril Lord Carpets [1969] 2 All ER 1006 (QBD) . . . 285

Wild v Southend Hospital NHS Trust [2014] EWHC 4053 (QB) . . . 111, 120, 121

Wilkes v DePuy International Ltd [2016] EWHC 3096 (QB) . . . 364, 370, 371, 373, 374, 377

Wilkin-Shaw v Fuller & Kingsley School Bideford Enterprises Ltd [2012] EWHC 1777 (QB) . . . 219

Wilkin-Shaw v Fuller [2013] EWCA Civ 410 . . . 284

Wilkinson v Downton [1897] 2 QB 57 (QBD) . . . 2, 5, 104, 133, 408, 411, 421, 436–40, 442, 446, 454, 676

Williams v Humphrey (1975) *The Times*, February 20 . . . 415, 676

Williams v The Bermuda Hospitals Board (Bermuda) [2016] UKPC 4 . . . **259**, 260

Williams v University of Birmingham [2011] EWCA Civ 1242 . . . 238, 267

Williams & Reid v Natural Life Health Foods Ltd and Mistlin [1998] 2 All ER 577 (HL) . . . 205, 206

Willmore v Knowsley Metropolitan Borough Council [2009] EWCA Civ 1211; [2010] ELR 227 . . . 267

Willmore v Knowsley Metropolitan Borough Council [2011] UKSC 10 . . . 262, 268

Wilsher v Essex Area Health Authority [1987] 1 QB 730 (CA) . . . 227

Wilsher v Essex Area Health Authority [1988] 1 AC 1074 (HL) . . . 228, **256–7**, 261, 262, 263, 269, 272, 276, 360, 374

Wilson v Pringle [1987] QB 237 (CA) . . . 416

Wilson v Tyneside Window Cleaning Co [1958] 2 QB 110 (CA) . . . 390, 394

Wilsons & Clyde Coal Co Ltd v English [1938] AC 57 (HL) . . . 388, **389–90**, 394

Winterbottom v Wright (1842) 11 LJ Ex 415; 10 M&W 109; 152 ER 402 . . . 33, 34

WM Morrison Supermarkets plc v Various Claimants [2018] EWCA Civ 2239 . . . 618

WM Morrison Supermarkets plc v Various Claimants [2020] UKSC 12 . . . 622

Wood v Chief of Police for the Metropolis [2009] EWCA Civ 414; [2010] 1 WLR 123 . . . 477

Woodland v Essex County Council [2013] UKSC 66 . . . 387, 613

Woodland v Maxwell and Essex County Council [2015] EWHC 273 (QB) . . . 613

Woodland v Maxwell and Essex County Council (No 2) [2015] EWHC 1162 (QB) . . . 614

Woodroffe-Hedley v Cuthbertson [1997] (unreported), 20 June (QBD) . . . 2, 8–20, **9**

Woodward v Mayor of Hastings [1945] 1 KB 174 (CA) . . . 334

Wooldridge v George (QBD) (Judge Walden-Smith) 23rd January 2017 (unreported) . . . 223

Wooldridge v Sumner [1963] 2 QB 43 (CA) . . . 236, 292, 297

Wootton v J Docter Ltd [2008] EWCA Civ 1361; [2009] LS Law M 63 . . . 267

Worsley v Tambrands Ltd [2000] PIQR P95 (QBD) . . . 366, 380

Wright v Lewis Silkin LLP [2016] EWCA Civ 1308 . . . 274

Wright v Lodge [1993] 4 All ER 299 (CA) . . . 285

Wright v Troy Lucas (a firm) and George Rusz [2019] EWHC 1098 (HC) . . . 226

Wright v Ver [2020] EWCA Civ 672 . . . 489

Wright (A Child) v Cambridge Medical Group [2011] EWCA Civ 669 . . . 258, 276, 285

X (a woman formerly known as Mary Bell) v SO [2003] EWHC 1101 (QB); [2003] EMLR 37 . . . 450, 459, 460, 482

X and others (Minors) v Bedfordshire County Council [1995] 2 AC 663 (HL) . . . 7, 76, 140, 143, 145, 152, 153, 177, 178, 180, 182, 183, 399, 402

X & Y v London Borough of Hounslow [2009] EWCA Civ 286; [2009] 2 FLR 262 . . . 47, 48, 50, 51, 52, 53, 55, 93, 179, 181, 183, 184

X & Y (Protected parties represented by their litigation friend the Official Solicitor) v London Borough of Hounslow [2008] EWHC 1168 (QB); [2008] All ER 337 . . . 28, **47–55**, 56

XKF v BBC [2018] EWHC 1560 (QB) . . . 468

XLD v KZL [2020] EWHC 1558 (QB) . . . 478

XYZ v Schering Health Care Ltd [2002] EWHC 1420 (QB); (2003) 70 BMLR 88 . . . 374

YAH v Medway NHS Trust [2018] EWHC 2964 . . . 111

Yavuz v Tesco Stores Ltd & another [2019] EWHC 1971 (QB) . . . 493

Yearworth v North Bristol NHD Trust [2009] EWCA Civ 37; [2010] QB 1 . . . 108

Yetkin v Newham LBC [2010] EWCA Civ 776; [2010] RTR 39 . . . 177

Young v Downey [2020] EWHC 3457 (QB) . . . 629

Young v Kent County Council [2005] EWHC 1342 (QB) . . . 308, 673

Youssoupoff v Metro-Goldwyn-Mayer Pictures Ltd (1934) 50 TLR 581 (CA) . . . 492

Yuen Kun-Yeu v Attorney General of Hong Kong [1988] AC 175 (PC) . . . 64, 82

Zurich Insurance plc UK Branch v International Energy Group Ltd [2015] UKSC 33 . . . 267, 268, 269

ZXC v Bloomberg LP [2020] EWCA Civ 611 . . . 468, 484

ZYT & another v Associated Newspapers Ltd [2015] EWHC 1162 (QB) . . . 467

International cases

Australia

Amaca Pty Ltd v Booth [2011] HCA 53 . . . 266

Amaca Pty Ltd v Ellis; State of South Australia v Ellis; Millennium Inorganic Chemicals Ltd v Ellis [2010] HCA 5 . . . 266

Australian Broadcasting Commission v Lenah Game Meats [2001] 208 CLR 199 (HC (Aus)) . . . 465

Burnie Port Authority v General Jones Pty Ltd [1994] 179 CLR 520; 120 ALR 42 (HC (Aus)) . . . 599

Cook v Cook [1986] 162 CLR 376 (HC (Aus)) . . . 223

Gill v Ethicon Sàrl (No 5) [2019] FCA 1905 (Australia) . . . 370

Lowns v Woods (1996) 36 NSWLR 344 . . . 82

McHale v Watson (1966) 115 CLR 199 (HC (Aus)) . . . 226

Myerson v Smith's Weekly (1923) 24 SR (NSW) 20 . . . 518

Sutherland Shire Council v Heyman [1955–1995] PNLR 238; 157 CLR 424; (1985) 60 ALR 1; (1985) 59 ALJR 564 (HC (Aus)) . . . 52, 69, 199

Wallace v Kam [2013] HCA 19 . . . 271

Western Suburbs Hospital v Currie (1987) 9 NSWLR 511 (SC (NSW)) . . . 244

Canada

Canadian National Railway Co v Norsk Pacific Steamship Co Ltd (The Jervis Crown) [1992] lSCR 1021 (SC (Can)) . . . 194

Cook v Lewis [1951] SCR 830; [1952] 1 DLR 1 (SC (Can)) . . . 272

Doe v Metropolitan Toronto (Municipality) Commissioners of Police [1998] 160 DLR (4th) 289 (SC (Ont)) . . . 96, 167, 170

Doe 464533 v ND (2016) ONSC 541 . . . 453

Hill v Hamilton-Wentworth Regional Police (2007) 285 DLR (4th) 620; 2007 SCC 41 . . . 167

Horsley v MacLaren (The Ogopogo) *see* Ogopogo, The

Jones v Tsige [2012] ONCA 32 . . . 453

McKinnon Industries Ltd v Walker [1951] 3 DLR 577 . . . 560

Nor-Video Service v Ontario Hydro (1978) 84 DLR (3d) 221; 4 CCLT 244 (HC (Ont)) . . . 560

Ogopogo, The [1970] 1 Lloyd's Rep 257 (CA (Ont)) . . . 80

Queen, The v Saskatchewan Wheat Pool [1983] 1 SCR 205 . . . 406

Court of Justice of the European Union

Aventis Pasteur SA v O'Byrne (Case C-358/08) ECLI:EU:C:2009:744 . . . 375

Commission of the European Communities v United Kingdom (Case C-300/95) ECLI:EU:C:1997:35, Opinion of AG Tesauro . . . 376

Commission of the European Communities v United Kingdom (Case C-300/95) ECLI:EU:C:1997:255 . . . 376, 381, 385, 674

European Court of Human Rights

Austin and other v UK (App No 39692/09) (2012) 55 EHRR 14; [2012] ECHR 459 . . . 429

Earl Spencer v UK (App No 28851/95) (1998) 25 EHRR CD105 . . . 472

Hatton v UK (App No 36022/97) (2003) 37 EHRR 28 . . . 566, 571, 574, 575

HL v UK (App No 45508/99) (2005) 40 EHRR 32 . . . 428

Keenan v UK (App No 27229/95) (2001) 33 EHRR 38 . . . 85

Khatun v UK (App No 38387/97) (1998) 26 EHRR CD212 . . . 552, 553, 574, 578

Lillo-Stenberg and Sœther v Norway (App No 13258/09) [2014] ECHR 59, Chamber Judgment . . . 471

López Ostra v Spain (App No 16798/90) (1995) 20 EHRR 277 . . . 574

McKevitt and Campbell v UK (App Nos 61474/12 & 62780/12) [2016] . . . 19

MAK & RK v UK (App No 45901/05) [2010] ECHR 363 . . . 143

MGN Ltd v UK (App No 39401/04) [2011] EHCR 66 . . . 464, 627

Mosley v UK (App No 48009/08) (2011) 53 EHRR 30 . . . 475

Niemietz v Germany (App No 13710/88) (1993) 16 EHRR 355 . . . 472

Osman v UK (App No 23452/94) (2000) 29 EHRR 245 . . . 146, 148–52, **149–50**, 153, 154, 178, 179, 182

Peck v UK (App No 44647/98) (2003) 36 EHRR 41 . . . 451, 480, **481**, 482

Powell and Raynor v UK (App No 9310/81) (1990) 12 EHRR 355 . . . 566, 574

Renolde v France (App No 5608/05) (2009) 48 EHRR 42 . . . 85

S v France (App No 13728/88) (1990) 65 D & R 250 . . . 574

Stubbings v UK (App No 22083/93) (1997) 23 EHRR 213 . . . 643, 644, 645, 646

Times Newspapers (Nos 1 and 2) v UK (App Nos 3002/03 and 23676/03) [2009] EMLR 14 . . . 506

TP and KM v UK (App No 28945/95) (2002) 34 EHRR 2 . . . **152–3**, 154, 184, 400

Van Colle v UK (App No 7678/09) [2012] ECHR 1928 . . . 147

Von Hannover v Germany (App No 59320/00) [2004] EMLR 21 . . . 470, **471**, 476, 483

Von Hannover v Germany (No 2) (App No 40660/08) [2012] ECHR 228 . . . 471

Von Hannover v Germany (No 3) (App No 8772/10) [2013] ECHR 264 . . . 471

Wainwright v UK (App No 12350/04) (2006) ECHR 807 . . . 154, 437, 481

X, Y & Z v UK (App No 32666/10) [2011] ECHR 1199 . . . 154, 184

Z & others v UK (App No 29392/95) (2002) 34 EHRR 3; [2001] 10 BHRC 384 . . . **152–3**, 154, 184, 400

New Zealand

C v Holland [2012] NZHC 2155 . . . 453

Hosking v Runting [2004] 1 NZLR 1 (CA (NZ)) . . . 453

Invercargill City Council v Hamlin [1994] 3 NZLR 513 . . . 199

North Shore City Council v Body Corporate (2010) 188529 NZSC 158 . . . 199

United States

Grimshaw v Ford Motor Co, 119 Cal App 3d 757 (1981) . . . 245, 358

Larson v St Francis Hotel, 83 Cal App 2d 210; 188 P2d 513 (1948) . . . 248

Liebeck v McDonald's Restaurants, Dis T CT New Mexico (1994) . . . 368, 369

Osterlind v Hill, 160 NE 301 (1928) . . . 80

Palsgraf v Long Island Railroad Co, 162 NE 99 (NY 1928) . . . 61

Sindell v Abbott Laboratories, 26 Cal 3d 588; 607 P 2d 924; 163 Cal Rptr 132 (SC (US)) (1980) . . . 272

Summers v Tice, 33 Cal 2 d 280; 199 P 2d 1 (1948) . . . 272

Tarasoff v Regents of the University of California, 17 Cal. 3d 425, 551 P.2d 334, 131 Cal. Rptr. 14 (Cal. 1976) . . . 92

Ultramares Corp v Touche, Niven & Co, 255 NY 170; 174 NE 441 (1931) . . . 59

United States v Carroll Towing Co, 159 F2d 169 (1947) . . . 244

Wagner v International Railway Co, 232 NY 176; 133 NE 437 (1921) . . . 128

Table of legislation

Legislation in **bold** indicates that the statute or part thereof is reproduced in the text at the page location indicated in **bold** type.

United Kingdom

Statutes

Access to Medical Treatments (Innovation) Act 2016 . . . 228

Administration of Justice Act 1982
s 6 . . . 636

Betting and Lotteries Act 1934 . . . 402

Bill of Rights 1688
Art 9 . . . 510

Broadcasting Act 1990
s 166 . . . 490

Children Act 1989 . . . 403

Civil Aviation Act 1982 . . . 541
s 76 . . . 566
s 76(1) . . . 541

Civil Evidence Act 1968
s 11 . . . 247

Civil Liability Act 2018 . . . 16, 106, 654
s 3 . . . 654
s 3(2) . . . 654

Civil Liability (Contribution) Act 1978 . . . 42, 284, 285, 304, 606, 640, 641, 642
s 1(1) . . . 262
s 2 . . . 641

Communications Act 2003 . . . 457

Companies Act 1985 . . . 207

Compensation Act 2006 . . . 19, 245, 246, 650
Explanatory Notes . . . 652
s 1 . . . 178, **246**, 652
s 2 . . . 20, 650
s 3 . . . 265, 266, 267, 268
s 3(1)(a)–(c) . . . 268
s 3(1)(a)–(d) . . . 266
s 3(1)(d) . . . 268
s 3(3)(b) . . . 266
Pt 2 (ss 4–15) . . . 245, 653

Consumer Protection Act 1987 (CPA) . . . 254, 317, 318, 353, 354, 362, 363, 364, 365, 366, 367, 368, 370, 371, 372, 373, 374, 375, 377–8, 384, 391, 397, 550, 674
Pt 1 (ss 1–9) . . . 247, 317, 362–78, **379–82**, 383, 384, 642
s 1 . . . **379**, 384
s 1(1) . . . **362**, **379**
s 1(2) . . . 363, 364, **379**, 383
s 1(2)(a) . . . **379**
s 1(2)(b) . . . **379**
s 1(2)(c) . . . **379**
s 1(3) . . . **379**
s 2 . . . **379–80**
s 2(1) . . . 363, **379**, 383
s 2(2) . . . **379**
s 2(2)(a) . . . **379**
s 2(2)(a)–(c) . . . 363
s 2(2)(b) . . . **380**
s 2(2)(c) . . . 363, **380**
s 2(3) . . . 363, **380**
s 2(3)(a) . . . **380**
s 2(3)(b) . . . **380**
s 2(3)(c) . . . **380**
s 2(5) . . . 363, **380**
s 2(6) . . . **380**
s 3 . . . 364, 368, 369, 370, 373, **380**, 385, 674
s 3(1) . . . **380**, 383
s 3(2) . . . 372, **380**
s 3(2)(a) . . . **380**
s 3(2)(a)–(c) . . . 366, 383
s 3(2)(b) . . . **380**
s 3(2)(c) . . . **380**
s 4 . . . 375, **381**
s 4(1) . . . **381**
s 4(1)(a) . . . **381**
s 4(1)(a)–(f) . . . 383
s 4(1)(b) . . . **381**
s 4(1)(c) . . . **381**
s 4(1)(d) . . . **381**
s 4(1)(e) . . . 375, **376**, **381**, 385
s 4(1)(f) . . . **381**
s 5 . . . 363, **381–2**, 384
s 5(1) . . . 363, **381**, 383
s 5(2) . . . 363, **381**, 383
s 5(3) . . . **381**
s 5(3)(a) . . . **381**
s 5(3)(b) . . . **382**
s 5(4) . . . 363, **382**, 383
s 5(5) . . . **382**
s 5(6) . . . **382**
s 5(7) . . . **382**
s 5(7)(a) . . . **382**
s 5(7)(b) . . . **382**
s 5(8) . . . **382**
s 45 . . . 364, 379, 383

Consumer Rights Act 2015 . . . 209

Contracts (Rights of Third Parties) Act 1999 . . . 210
Countryside and Rights of Way Act 2000
Pt I (ss 1–46) . . . 348
s 2(1) . . . 338, 348, 349
s 13 . . . 339
County Courts Act 1984
s 66(3) . . . 530
Courts Act 2003 . . . 636
Crime and Courts Act 2013
s 34 . . . 629
s 40 . . . 458
Criminal Justice and Public Order Act 1994 . . . 539

Damages Act 1996
s 2 . . . 636
Damages (Scotland) Act 1976 . . . 379
Data Protection Act 1998 . . . 450, 475
s 4(4) . . . 622
Defamation Act 1952
s 2 . . . 490
s 5 . . . 497, 526
s 6 . . . 527
Defamation Act 1996 . . . 522, 529
s 1 . . . 522, 530
s 1(1)(b) . . . 522
s 1(3)(a) . . . 522
s 1(3)(d) . . . 522
s 1(3)(e) . . . 522
s 2 . . . 523
s 14 . . . 527
s 15 . . . 527
Defamation Act 2013 . . . 408, 487, 488, 489, 490, 515, 526–31, 532
Explanatory Notes . . . 492, 515
s 1 . . . 486, 488, 493, **526**, 678
s 1(1) . . . 490, 492, 493, **526**, 532
s 1(2) . . . 488, **526**
s 2 . . . 507, 509, **526**, 678
s 2(1) . . . **507**, **526**
s 2(2) . . . **507**, **526**
s 2(3) . . . 497, **507**, **526**
s 2(4) . . . **526**
s 3 . . . 518, **526–7**, 678
s 3(1) . . . **526**
s 3(2) . . . **526**
s 3(3) . . . **526**
s 3(4) . . . **526–7**
s 3(4)(a) . . . 521, **526**
s 3(4)(b) . . . 521, **527**
s 3(5) . . . **527**
s 3(6) . . . **527**
s 3(7) . . . **527**
s 3(8) . . . 526, **527**
s 4 . . . 510, 512, 514, 516, 517, 524, **527–8**
s 4(1) . . . 512, **527**
s 4(1)(b) . . . 514, 517
s 4(2) . . . 515, **527**
s 4(3) . . . 506, 515, **527**
s 4(4) . . . 515, **527**
s 4(5) . . . **528**
s 4(6) . . . 512, **528**
s 5 . . . 505, 522, 523, 528
s 5(1) . . . **528**
s 5(2) . . . 522, **528**
s 5(3) . . . 522, **528**
s 5(3)(a) . . . **528**
s 5(3)(b) . . . **528**
s 5(3)(c) . . . **528**
s 5(4) . . . **528**
s 5(11) . . . 523
s 5(12) . . . **528**
s 6 . . . 512, 528–9
s 6(1) . . . **528**
s 6(2) . . . 512, **528**
s 6(3) . . . 512, **528**
s 6(3)(a) . . . **528**
s 6(3)(b) . . . **529**
s 6(4) . . . **528–9**
s 6(4)(a) . . . **528**
s 6(4)(b) . . . **529**
s 6(5) . . . 512, **529**
s 6(6) . . . 512, **529**
s 7 . . . 509, 529
s 8 . . . 505, **529**
s 8(1) . . . **529**
s 8(1)(a) . . . **529**
s 8(1)(b) . . . **529**
s 8(2) . . . **529**
s 8(3) . . . **529**
s 8(4) . . . **529**
s 8(5) . . . **529**
s 8(5)(a) . . . **529**
s 8(5)(b) . . . **529**
s 8(6) . . . **529**
s 8(6)(a) . . . **529**
s 8(6)(b) . . . **529**
s 9 . . . 489, 529–30
s 9(1) . . . **529–30**
s 9(1)(a) . . . **530**
s 9(1)(b) . . . **530**
s 9(1)(c) . . . **530**
s 9(2) . . . 489, **530**
s 10 . . . 528, **530**
s 10(1) . . . **522**, **530**
s 10(2) . . . **530**
s 11 . . . 525, 530
s 11(1) . . . **530**
s 11(2) . . . **530**
s 14 . . . 490, **530**
s 14(1) . . . **530**
s 14(2) . . . **530**
s 15 . . . 530–1
Defective Premises Act 1972 . . . 200, 323, 324–5
s 1 . . . 200
s 4 . . . 325
s 4(1) . . . 325

Employers' Liability (Compulsory Insurance) Act 1969 . . . 388, 403, 648
s 5 . . . 403

Employer's Liability (Defective Equipment) Act 1969 . . . 387, 391, 392, 396, 675
s 1(1) . . . 391
s 1(3) . . . 392

Enterprise and Regulatory Reform Act 2013 . . . 16, 39, 391, 401, 402, 659
s 69 . . . 318, 387, 388, 392, 397, 401, 404, 405
s 69(3) . . . 401

Environmental Protection Act 1990 . . . 538

Factory and Workshop Act 1878 . . . 400
s 5 . . . 400

Fatal Accidents Act 1976 . . . 379, 638, 639, 646
s 1 . . . 638
s 1(1) . . . 638
s 1(3) . . . 638
s 1(3)(b) . . . 638
s 1A . . . 638
s 1A(2)(aa) . . . 638

Gulf Oil Refinement Act 1965 . . . 565

Health and Safety at Work Act 1974 . . . 387
s 47(2) . . . 401

Highways Act 1980
s 1(8) . . . 348

Housing Act 1985 . . . 403
s 63(1) . . . 54

Human Rights Act 1998 . . . 20–1, 22, 49, 53, 55, 86, 139, 142, 143, 146, 147, 154, 165, 181, 184, 185, 271, 408, 428, 429, 450, 451, 461, 464, 469, 470, 481, 482, 486, 552, 565, 570, 571, 574–8, 646, 653, 668
s 3(1) . . . 21, 565
s 6 . . . 21, 48, 55, 143, 470
ss 6–8 . . . 163
s 6(1) . . . 21, 470
s 6(3) . . . 21, 470
s 6(3)(a) . . . 143
s 7 . . . 20, 48, 55, 86, 470
s 7(5)(a) . . . 646
s 7(5)(b) . . . 646
s 8(3) . . . 576
s 12 . . . 469, 470
s 12(1) . . . 469
s 12(4) . . . **469**, 482
Appendix . . . 143

Law Reform (Contributory Negligence) Act 1945 . . . 40, 285, 304, 307, 308, 387
s 1(1) . . . 304, 307
s 4 . . . 304

Law Reform (Limitation of Actions, etc) Act 1954
s 2(1) . . . 413

Law Reform (Miscellaneous Provisions) Act 1934
s 1 . . . 638
s 1(1) . . . 488
s 1(4) . . . 638

Law Reform (Personal Injuries) Act 1948 . . . 39
s 1 . . . 388

Legal Aid, Sentencing and Punishment of Offenders Act 2012 (LASPO) . . . 15, 16, 628, 634
Pt 1 (ss 1–43) . . . 628
Pt 2 (ss 44–62) . . . 628
s 144 . . . 543

Limitation Act 1623 . . . 644

Limitation Act 1975 . . . 644

Limitation Act 1980 . . . 643, 646
s 2 . . . 642, 644
s 4A . . . 529
s 11 . . . 643, 644, 645
ss 11–14 . . . 642, 644
s 11(1) . . . 644
s 11A(3) . . . 374
s 14 . . . 642, 644, 645
s 32A . . . 529
s 32A(1)(a) . . . 529
s 33 . . . 644, 645

Mental Capacity Act 2005 . . . 423, 428, 433, 434
s 1 . . . 433
s 1(2) . . . **433**
s 1(3) . . . **433**
s 1(4) . . . **433**
s 1(5) . . . **433**
s 1(6) . . . **433**
s 2 . . . 433
s 3 . . . 433
s 3(1) . . . 433
s 3(1)(a) . . . 433
s 3(1)(b) . . . 433
s 3(1)(c) . . . 433
s 3(1)(d) . . . 433
s 4 . . . 433, 435
s 5 . . . 433, 435

Mental Health Act 1983 . . . 297, 428, 481

Mesothelioma Act 2014 . . . 268

Misrepresentation Act 1967 . . . 195

National Parks and Access to the Countryside Act 1949 . . . 338

NHS Redress Act 2006 . . . 655
s 3 . . . 655

Occupiers' Liability Acts . . . 97

Occupiers' Liability Act 1957 . . . 80, 317, 318, 319, 320, 321–39, 340, 341, 343, 344, 346, 347, 349–50, 351, 397, 542, 673

s 1 . . . **337–8**
s 1(1) . . . 321, 322, **337**
s 1(2) . . . 321, 322, 323, 325, **337**, 349, 542
s 1(3) . . . 327, **337**, 347, 349, 673
s 1(3)(a) . . . **337**
s 1(3)(b) . . . 325, **337**, 348
s 1(4) . . . **338**, 347
s 1(4)(a) . . . **338**, 346
s 1(4)(b) . . . **338**
s 2 . . . 332, 333, 336, **338–9**, 347
s 2(1) . . . 292, 321, 333, 337, **338**, 347, 349, 350
s 2(2) . . . 322, 327, 328, **338**, 342, 349
s 2(3) . . . 327, 328, 329, 331, **338**, 349, 350
s 2(3)(a) . . . 329, **338**, 350
s 2(3)(b) . . . 331, **338**, 350
s 2(4) . . . 331, **338**
s 2(4)(a) . . . 331, 332, **338**, 350
s 2(4)(b) . . . 334, **338**, 350
s 2(5) . . . 331, 335, 336, **339**, 350
s 2(6) . . . 331, **339**
s 4(a) . . . 348
s 5 . . . 321, 337, 349

Occupiers' Liability Act 1984 . . . 317, 318, 319, 320, 321, 322, 324, 325, 326, 330, 339–50, 351, 397, 673
s 1 . . . **347–8**
s 1(1) . . . 339, **347**
s 1(1)(a) . . . 321, **347**, 349
s 1(1)(b) . . . **347**
s 1(2) . . . 340, **347**, 349
s 1(2)(a) . . . **347**, 349
s 1(2)(b) . . . **347**
s 1(3) . . . 339, 340, 342, **347**, 349
s 1(3)(a) . . . 344, **347**
s 1(3)(b) . . . 345, **347**
s 1(3)(c) . . . 342, 345, **347**
s 1(4) . . . 346, **347**, 349
s 1(5) . . . 346, **348**, 350
s 1(6) . . . 338, 346, **348**, 350
s 1(6A) . . . 339, **348**
s 1(6A)(a) . . . **348**
s 1(6A)(b) . . . **348**
s 1(6B) . . . **348**
s 1(6C) . . . **348**
s 1(6C)(a) . . . **348**
s 1(6C)(b) . . . **348**
s 1(7) . . . **348**, 349
s 1(8) . . . 341, **348**, 349
s 1(9) . . . **348**
s 1A . . . 349
s 2(1) . . . 350

Offences Against the Person Act 1861 . . . 411

Police and Criminal Evidence Act 1984 . . . 542

Protection of Freedoms Act 2012 . . . 440

Protection from Harassment Act 1997 . . . 5, 136, 397, 408, 411, 420, 421, 436, 437, 440–6, 447, 450, 551, 608, 618, 676
s 1 . . . 441, 442
s 1(1) . . . 441
s 1(2) . . . 444
s 1(3) . . . 444
s 1(3)(a) . . . 444, 445
s 1(3)(c) . . . 443, 444, 445
s 1A . . . 441
s 1A(a) . . . 441
s 1A(c) . . . 441
s 2 . . . 441, 442
s 2A . . . 440
s 2A(3) . . . 440
s 3 . . . 398, 441
s 3(1) . . . 442
s 4A . . . 440
s 7(2) . . . 441
s 7(3) . . . 442
s 7(3)(b) . . . 441

Rehabilitation of Offenders Act 1974
s 8 . . . 507
s 8(5) . . . 507

Reservoirs Act 1975 . . . 602

Road Traffic Act 1930 . . . 648

Road Traffic Act 1988 . . . 672
s 14 . . . 309
s 15 . . . 309
s 149 . . . 294

Senior Courts Act 1981 (formerly Supreme Court Act 1981)
s 32A . . . 636
s 50 . . . 570
s 69(1) . . . 530
s 90 . . . 48

Serious Organised Crime and Police Act 2005 . . . 441

Slander of Women Act 1891 . . . 530
s 1 . . . 490

Social Action, Responsibility and Heroism Act 2015 . . . 17, 83, 245, 246
s 2 . . . 83
s 4 . . . 83

Stalking Protection Act 2019 . . . 440

Supreme Court Act 1981 *see* Senior Courts Act 1981

Theatres Act 1968
s 4 . . . 490

Third Parties (Rights Against Insurers) Act 1930 . . . 22

Unfair Contract Terms Act 1977 . . . 209, 292
s 1(1)(c) . . . 333
s 2 . . . 203, 350
s 2(1) . . . 292, 333, 338
s 2(2) . . . 333, 338

Vaccine Damage Payments Act 1979 . . . 375

Water Industry Act 1991 . . . 575, 576
s 18 . . . 576
s 94 . . . 576
Workmen's Compensation Act 1897 . . . 40, 401

Statutory Instruments

Asbestos Industry Regulations 1931, SI 1931/1140 . . . 404
Civil Procedure Rules 1998, SI 1998/3132 . . . 22
Control of Noise at Work Regulations 2005, SI 2005/1634 . . . 240
reg 6(1) . . . 240
Damages for Bereavement (Variation of Sum) (England and Wales) Order 2020, SI 2020/316 . . . 639
Damages (Variation of Periodical Payments) Order 2005, SI 2005/841 . . . 636
Damages-Based Agreements Regulations 2013, SI 2013/609 . . . 628
Defamation (Operators of Websites) Regulations 2013, SI 2013/3028 . . . 522
Electricity Supply Regulations 1988, SI 1988/1057 . . . 400
reg 17 . . . 400
Fatal Accidents Act 1976 (Remedial) Order 2020, SI 2020/1023 . . . 638
Noise at Work Regulations 1989, SI 1989/1790 . . . 389
Personal Protective Equipment at Work Regulations 1992, SI 1992/2966
reg 4 . . . 405
reg 7(1) . . . 405
Prison Rules 1964, SI 1964/388 . . . 402, 429, 437
Product Safety and Metrology etc. (Amendment etc.) (EU Exit) Regulations 2019, SI 2019/696 . . . 362, 363, 379, 380, 381
Urban Waste Water Treatment (England and Wales) Regulations 1994, SI 1994/2841 . . . 576

International Legislation

France

Code Penal
Art 223–6 . . . 82

Germany

Constitution . . . 452

United States

Restatement (Second) of Torts (2010) . . . 465
§ 652B . . . 452

European Secondary Legislation

Directive 80/778/EEC Relating to the Quality of Water intended for Human Consumption . . . 592
Directive 85/374/EEC Product Liability Directive . . . 317, 362, 364, 373, 376, 377, 379, 381
Art 6 . . . 373
Art 7 . . . 376
Art 7(e) . . . 376
Directive 1999/34/EC Amending Product Liability Directive . . . 364

International Instruments

European Convention on Human Rights (ECHR) . . . 20, 21, 49, 53, 143, 153, 172, 181, 453, 469, 470, 482, 486, 565, 566, 574, 576, 578
Art 2 . . . 20, 85, 86, 146, 147, 149, 151, 163, 166, 171, 172, 173, 460, 543
Art 3 . . . 20, 47, 55, 148, 153, 163, 184, 460
Art 5 . . . 20, 428, 429
Art 6 . . . 20, 47, 55, 149, 150, 151, 153, 154, 182, 184, 464, 627
Art 8 . . . 20, 21, 47, 55, 143, 149, 151, 153, 184, 408, 437, 450, 460, 464, 469, 470, 471, 472, 473, 474, 476, 477, 481, 482, 483, 536, 545, 574, 575, 576, 638, 677
Art 8(1) . . . 470, 471, 552, 553, 565, 566, 574, 577, 581
Art 8(2) . . . 471, 552, 566, 574
Art 10 . . . 20, 450, 460, 464, 469, 471, 472, 483, 502, 503, 545, 677
Art 10(1) . . . 471
Art 10(2) . . . 471, 486
Art 13 . . . 47, 55, 149, 150, 151, 153, 184, 437, 481, 566
Art 14 . . . 552, 578, 638
Protocol 1
Art 1 . . . 574, 575
Art 2 . . . 181
Lugano Convention . . . 489, 530

List of abbreviations of commonly cited works

Atiyah	Atiyah, Patrick *The Damages Lottery* (Hart, 1997)
Cane	Cane, Peter *Atiyah's Accidents, Compensation and the Law* (7th edn, CUP, 2006)
Conaghan & Mansell	Conaghan, Joanne and Wade Mansell *The Wrongs of Tort* (2nd edn, Pluto Press, 1999)
Harlow	Harlow, Carol Understanding Tort Law (Sweet & Maxwell, 2005)
Ibbetson	Ibbetson, David A Historical Introduction to the Law of Obligations (OUP, 1999)
Lunney, Nolan & Oliphant	Lunney, Mark, Donal Nolan and Ken Oliphant Tort Law: Text and Materials (6th edn, OUP, 2017)
Markesinis & Deakin	Deakin, Simon, Angus Johnston and Basil Markesinis Markesinis and Deakin's Tort Law (7th edn, OUP, 2012)
Peel & Goudkamp	Peel, WE and James Goudkamp Winfield and Jolowicz on Tort (19th edn, Sweet & Maxwell, 2014)
Steele	Steele, Jenny Tort Law: Text, Cases, and Materials (4th edn, OUP, 2017)
Weir	Weir, Tony An Introduction to Tort *Law* (2nd edn, OUP, 2006)

1 Introduction

1.1 Introduction

Consider the following examples:

→ *A pedestrian is knocked down and killed by a speeding motorist.*

→ *An office worker suffers psychiatric injury after being subjected to a campaign of transphobic bullying by her supervisor.*

→ *A runner trips over a loose paving slab on her morning run, breaking her ankle.*

→ *A school fails to diagnose a student's dyslexia, believing the student's poor performance is simply down to laziness. The student fails their GCSEs.*

→ *A house burns down as a result of an explosion at a nearby oil refinery.*

→ *A prisoner is kept in their cell for over 24 hours after prison guards walk out on an unofficial strike.*

→ *A group of ramblers take a shortcut over a field without the farmer's permission.*

→ *A student collapses unconscious after an evening of heavy drinking. His housemates lock him in the bathroom overnight while he sobers up.*

→ *A first-time buyer buys a house on the basis of an inaccurate survey. As a result, the property is worth significantly less than they paid for it.*

→ *A professional footballer wants to prevent a national newspaper publishing allegations about his private life.*

→ *The lead singer of a Smiths tribute band is branded a 'meat-eating wannabe who can't hold a note' on their former management's website.*

In each of these examples there is a potential tort claim. In fact, most of these scenarios (as with many of those that begin the following chapters) are drawn from cases you will study during your tort law course. Such tales—often tragic and bizarre in equal measure—go to the heart of tort law. There are few, if any, other subjects where you will encounter wayward cricket balls, learner drivers driving into lampposts and electroconvulsive therapy within the space of a few pages. And yet, despite its varied case law, many students find tort law a difficult subject to grasp—at least initially. (Something we acknowledge here in a spirit of supportive openness (we hope!) rather than with smug condescension.) Indeed, even before you begin your adventures into a subject where general principles at times appear to point one way and common sense the other, the title of the book might present a more immediate obstacle: what is 'tort law'?[1]

1.2 What is tort law?

A 'tort' is a civil (as opposed to criminal) wrong for which the law provides a remedy. The origins of the word 'tort' come indirectly from the Latin *tortus* (meaning crooked or twisted), although the more usual translation is that from modern French where it corresponds with 'wrong'. Thus, at its simplest, the law of tort is the law of non-criminal wrongs.[2] The plural 'wrongs' here is deliberate. Tort law is the name given to a diverse collection of legal wrongs. Some of these will, no doubt, be familiar—the torts of negligence, trespass to land, assault, battery, libel, for example often feature in the news. Others may be less familiar—such as the tort of nuisance, which protects an individual's use and enjoyment of their land, or those named after the cases from which they stem, such as the tort in *Wilkinson* v *Downton* [1897] which provides a remedy for indirect physical harm caused by an intentional act. Beyond this, however, there is no general agreement on what defines, and distinguishes, a 'tort'. Moreover, no one really knows quite how many torts there are.The boundaries between torts are fluid and the popularity of individual torts can change—'old' torts die out (the rule in ***Rylands* v *Fletcher* [1868]** may be a case in point here) while new ones emerge (e.g. the tort of misuse of private information (*Vidal-Hall* v *Google Inc* [2014])). So, it is clear that tort law covers a lot of ground. What is less clear is the extent to which the various individual torts—and so the law of torts as a whole—share common features, principles and justifications. The best view may be *Weir*'s, who has observed that '[t]ort is what is in the tort books, and the only thing holding it together is the binding' (p ix).

It is certainly true that in comparison to, say, contract law (traditionally, tort law's 'other half' in the law of obligations)[3] which is said to be grounded, among other things,

1. This chapter draws on and develops the ideas, insights and structure of Alan Thomson's introduction to tort law lectures given at the University of Kent. We both worked with Alan, who retired in 2010, and are grateful for his collegiate support. In particular, we thank him for his permission to use his case example of ***Woodroffe-Hedley* v *Cuthbertson* [1997]**.

2. There are, of course, other civil wrongs which fall outside the remit of tort—including breach of contract and equitable obligations. The principal distinction between torts and breaches of contract is that contracts are voluntarily undertaken obligations, whereas the wrongs which make up the law of torts are breaches of imposed obligations—in other words, obligations which we have not chosen to be subjected to. E.g. my obligation not to hit you is an obligation I am subjected to whether I like it or not. By contrast, if I contract to sell my car to you, my obligation to hand over the car is an obligation I have chosen to be subjected to. The distinction between torts and breaches of equitable obligations is less straightforward, essentially turning on an outdated jurisdictional division between the types of court which first recognised these obligations. These days it is increasingly common to see some equitable wrongs, such as breach of confidence, treated as a tort (***Campbell* v *Mirror Group Newspapers Ltd* [2004]**).

3. Though we should also acknowledge that it is now common to identify 'unjust enrichment' or 'restitution' as a third branch of the law of obligations.

in the morality of promise-keeping, tort law appears to lack any such common theme or ambition, and resembles little more than a miscellaneous collection of relatively self-contained wrongs. As we shall see, in recent years one particular tort—the tort of negligence—has gained prominence, and started to gain ground from other, older torts. If this development continues it may be possible that we will end up with a law of tort sharing a similar unity and coherence as is found in contract law. However, this move has not been universally welcomed and, in any case, we are not there yet.

In any event, definitions in the abstract may not be particularly helpful. The description of tort law as 'a collection of civil wrongs for which the law provides a remedy' or, Peter Cane's suggestion, that it is a way of protecting people's interests through 'a system of precepts about how people may, ought and ought not to behave in their dealings with others' (Cane 1997, p 13) simply prompts another question: what wrongs or interests are we talking about?

1.2.1 **What interests does tort law protect?**

To return to the earlier examples of situations where an action in tort law might arise, in each case someone has suffered an unwanted harm. Some involve *physical injury* (e.g. the damage caused to the runner tripping over the loose paving slab) or even *death* (in the case of the pedestrian killed by the speeding motorist). In others the harm is *psychiatric injury* (e.g. that suffered by the office worker). However, clearly not all cases involve physical or mental injury to the potential claimant; other types of harm include *damage to property* (e.g. that caused by the explosion at the oil refinery) and *financial loss* (e.g. in the case of the buyer whose house is not worth as much as they thought or, more controversially, the student who has not been recognised as dyslexic).

In some of these examples, there appears to be no damage or harm at all. However, even assuming for the sake of argument that the ramblers walk over the farmer's land without causing damage (they do not, e.g., tear up the ground or pick flowers) and that the housemates unlock the bathroom door before the drunk student wakes up the next morning (so he is unaware of having been locked in), we can still say that in these cases there is an interference with the individual's *rights*. One has a right to determine who has access to or makes use of their land—in other words, the law says that you get to control the use, if any, that others may make of your property. Similarly, each of us has a right to bodily freedom and autonomy. Others are not entitled to touch us or confine our movements (subject to certain exceptions) without our consent. Therefore, even though the farmer or the drunk student may not have been *harmed*, in the sense of being left worse off, as a result of these actions, we can say that they have been *wronged*.

As such, tort law is not just, or indeed primarily, concerned with harm as much as it is with rights. So what rights do we have? We have mentioned already rights to *bodily freedom and autonomy*, which we can also regard as embracing physical and psychological integrity. We have also noted rights to or *interests in property*, such as land. Others include rights to *reputation*—as in the example of the lead singer of the tribute band—and *privacy*—as with the professional footballer. This list is not, and should not be regarded as, closed. Indeed, one of the main roles of tort law is to mark out what rights or interests the law will recognise and protect.

There are three further points to make in relation to an understanding of tort law as a system of rules protecting our rights or interests.

First, while an understanding of tort law enables us to present it in a neat, linear form, it also involves something of a mis-description of the way the distinct torts are arranged and how they interrelate. What we mean by this is that while some torts exist and are defined only to protect a single interest (e.g. defamation protects a person's reputation, nuisance protects an individual's interest in enjoying their land), the tort of negligence—the biggest and most important of the torts—offers protection to *all* our legally recognised rights and interests.[4] What this means is that often, for any single harm or injury, there will be more than one tort upon which a claim may be founded. So, if you hit me (as well as any criminal claim) I may have a claim for battery (one of the torts specifically protecting my right to bodily integrity) or a claim in negligence—depending on the circumstances of the case.

Moreover, it is possible to define the rights and interests the law recognises and protects in broader or narrower terms. We could say that we have a single interest in our physical integrity, embracing both bodily and mental wellbeing. Alternatively, we could separate these into two. As we shall see, the law is somewhat ambivalent here; for some purposes it draws just such a distinction, yet for others it does not (see, for instance, ***Page* v *Smith*** [1996]). The same goes for our interest in our assets or property.

The position is muddied further when we note that even where a tort is designed to protect a single interest (e.g. defamation and nuisance), successful claimants can also recover for other harms suffered as a consequence of their interest having been infringed. For example, if you defame me, the basis of my claim is that you have harmed my reputation. However, if my claim is successful I can also recover for any financial losses I suffer as a result of my reputation having been tarnished (for instance, if it led to me losing my job and hence a loss of income). As such, we may say that even 'single interest' torts end up protecting a variety of interests and remedying a variety of harms (see **Table 1.1**).

Secondly, tort law does not recognise *all* interferences with an individual's interests as actionable harms. Tortious liability may be limited when it is thought to be undesirable for policy reasons. For example, we all have an interest in our mental wellbeing, but the courts have placed significant limitations on claims in respect of such harm.[5] At other times, the harm suffered may not be recoverable at all.[6]

Of course, the absence of tort liability does not mean that a defendant can act without fear of legal consequences. In particular, there may still be a criminal sanction. The speeding motorist who does *not* hit the pedestrian does not commit a tort (assuming they cause no other harm), however they may still be guilty of a criminal offence in relation to their dangerous driving.[7]

4. As a result, any attempt to study tort according to protected interest (see e.g. Cane 1997 and more recently Robert Stevens's suggestion for a tort textbook structured according to 'rights' (*Torts and Rights* (OUP, 2007), p 303)) would inevitably involve breaking up the tort of negligence, since this protects and so cuts across all such interests.

5. **Chapter 5**.

6. See further *Dryden and others* v *Johnson Matthey plc* [2018] and discussion in **section 2.1**.

7. Examples of torts which overlap with/are crimes include the torts of assault and battery and public nuisance (**Chapters 15** and **18** respectively). There are many torts where there is either no corresponding crime or where a criminal prosecution is very rare—e.g. medical negligence. The key difference between tort law and criminal law is that while actions in criminal law are brought by the state to punish the defendant, in tort law actions are brought by an individual (usually the injured party) to provide a remedy (i.e. compensation) for loss or harm.

TABLE 1.1 Interests protected by the torts discussed in this book

Interest	Tort
Personal (both physical and mental) integrity including the right to self-determination	Negligence (including occupiers' liability, employers' liability) Product liability Trespass to the person (assault, battery, false imprisonment) Breach of statutory duty The tort in *Wilkinson* v *Downton* Claims under the Protection from Harassment Act 1997 Nuisance (public)
Damage to property	Negligence (including occupiers' liability, employers' liability) Product liability Trespass to land Nuisance (public and private) The rule in ***Rylands*** v ***Fletcher***
'Pure' financial loss (i.e. loss *not* consequent on other injuries)	Negligence
'Consequential' financial loss	Negligence Product liability Defamation (libel and slander) Nuisance (public and private) Trespass to land
Possession, use and enjoyment of land	Trespass to land Nuisance (public and private) The rule in ***Rylands*** v ***Fletcher*** Negligence Claims under the Protection from Harassment Act 1997
Reputation	Defamation (libel and slander) Breach of confidence
Privacy	Negligence Trespass to land Nuisance (public and private) Breach of confidence Claims under the Protection from Harassment Act 1997 Misuse of personal information

We may also note that tort law does not protect the interests that it does recognise *equally*. Sexual harassment and (until recently) a person's interest in their private life, for example, have traditionally been only weakly protected in comparison with, say, physical injury or damage to an individual's reputation.[8]

Finally, and following on from the previous point, to say that the law of tort protects an individual's rights or interests does *not* mean that a claimant will succeed simply by showing that the defendant harmed them or infringed their rights. Tort law lays down a set of rules stating when exactly a harm or infringement of one's interest will give rise to legal liability.[9] Moreover, these rules—the hurdles a claimant must get over for their claim to succeed—vary from tort to tort. As such, we can speak only in very loose terms about there being general principles in the law of tort. So, although we can say that all claims in tort share the common feature that they concern infringements with a claimant's rights or interests, in reality you will gain a better understanding of how tort law actually operates in practice by recognising the individual torts as largely distinct.

Policy

At a number of points in your study of tort law you will come across references to 'policy'. For instance, judges or commentators sometimes explain decisions on the basis that they give effect to particular 'policy' considerations. As such, policy tends to be used to describe a certain type of factor or consideration which courts do or may take into account when deciding cases and framing legal rules. But what types of factor fall under the heading 'policy'?

The difficulty here is that the language of 'policy' appears to be used by different people at different times to mean different things. Even worse, those who make reference to 'policy' often fail to explain exactly what they mean by this.

Sometimes, the language of 'policy' is used to describe *all* factors that may have a bearing on how a case should be decided and how the law should develop. On this approach, every argument you might make about the law—what rules we should have, who should win a given case—is an argument of policy.[10] Policy here covers arguments of morality or justice, economic considerations, questions of resource allocation—in short, *everything*. The question here is not what role policy should play in the law—all law is necessarily driven by policy of some sort. Rather, it is simply what particular policies the law should advance or embody.

More commonly, however, 'policy' tends to be used to describe a particular subset of factors or arguments that the courts may employ when deciding cases. Here, policy is simply one thing the courts may turn to when determining the shape of the law, and is to be contrasted with other sorts of factors or considerations. This was most famously articulated by the legal

→

8. See generally Conaghan 2003.

9. These are both substantive and procedural. This book concentrates on the substantive rules, however it is important to remember that behind these lies a significant body of procedural rules, e.g. relating to jurisdiction, limitation periods and so on, that are crucial to the operation of tort law in practice. See further Stuart Sime *A Practical Approach to Civil Procedure* (23rd edn, OUP, 2020).

10. Lord Browne-Wilkinson in *X (Minors)* v *Bedfordshire County Council* [1995] seemed to be using 'policy' in this sense when he said that 'the public policy consideration which has first claim on the loyalty of the law is that wrongs should be remedied' (at 749).

→

philosopher Ronald Dworkin, who distinguished 'policy' from 'principle'.[11] His distinction was essentially that between moral standards and other sorts of arguments—principles are based on notions of individual fairness and justice, while policy by contrast covers so-called collective goals such as wealth maximisation or the encouragement of particular activities or trades. As such, policy is essentially defined by reference to what it is not. Policy is anything other than arguments of justice and morality.

The same point has been made by *Conaghan & Mansell*, who describe policy as a '"catch-all" phrase, used by judges and commentators alike, to describe judicial considerations which are "non-legal", that is not based on a recognised legal principle or an established precedent' (p 204). Typically then, policy arguments look beyond the particular facts of the case at hand and the relationship and dealings between the particular claimant and defendant, to consider the wider social, economic and political impact of imposing liability. In other words, the question is not simply 'is it fair to make the defendant liable to the claimant?' but rather 'what would be the consequences for society at large for imposing liability in situations such as this?' Unsurprisingly, perhaps, such arguments tend in practice to be used more commonly to deny rather than to allow claims.

Whether the courts *should* take policy considerations into account when deciding cases (and, if so, to what extent) is both controversial and disputed. Some lawyers argue that courts should *never* base their decisions on policy factors. This was Dworkin's argument and has, more recently, been repeated by Robert Stevens:

> We should not ask our judges to resolve questions of policy and, if asked, they should decline to provide answers that they have neither the ability nor legitimacy to give. Judges should adjudicate on rights and leave issues of policy to be discussed by academics and resolved by the legislature.[12]

What this assumes is that certain types of argument and consideration fall within the (democratic and/or intellectual) competence of judges and others do not, and that judges should therefore base their decisions only on the factors they are competent to evaluate. But how do we draw this line? And is it tenable in practice?

In many ways, the distinction between policy and principle draws a questionable dichotomy. Everyone is agreed that sometimes the courts modify or develop the law. In other words, sometimes courts do more than simply follow the decisions reached and rules set down in previous decisions and statute. As such, they have a 'creative' (quasi-)legislative function. This means that courts will sometimes have to look beyond the established precedent and statute law—to 'extra-legal' considerations of fairness or justice, economic efficiency and the like—to determine how a case should be decided.[13] Why then should we consider, as the likes of Dworkin and Stevens argue, that some 'extra-legal' considerations are acceptable for courts to take into account, while others must be excluded?

→

11. *Taking Rights Seriously* (Duckworth, 1977).

12. Stevens (**n 4**) p 311. See also Peter Cane's discussion of this in his review of Stevens's *Torts and Rights* ((2008) 71 MLR 641, 644–6).

13. Although cf Allan Beever *Rediscovering the Law of Negligence* (Hart, 2007).

→

The democratic argument—that it is the business of Parliament and not the courts to decide what the law should be—is an argument against *all* judicial creativity. It does not matter whether the courts employ moral arguments or other sorts of considerations. In each case the law is open to the challenge that key decisions about our rights and liabilities are not being taken by a democratically elected body. And, in each case, the answer is that this may not be democratically ideal but this is the way the law has always been and always will be.

Similarly, the argument that judges are not 'experts' on policy matters, and so should consider only 'moral' rights or questions of fairness and justice when deciding new points of law, makes little sense unless we can say that judges *are* experts on such moral questions. Otherwise, judges' lack of expertise should prevent them from making arguments of policy *or* of moral principle. And yet it seems that there is no reason to view our judges as having any particular understanding or competence in relation to questions of morality and justice or that, by contrast, their understanding of policy matters is noticeably weaker. As such, it is far from apparent why certain types of argument—of morality, fairness, etc—can be entrusted to judges while others—such as policy considerations—cannot.

Therefore, in the end the argument that courts should not take policy considerations into account when deciding cases appears rather dogmatic. Moreover, irrespective of whether courts really *should* take policy into account, it is clear that, at least on occasion, they *do*. However, here too we see a number of conflicting views as to what the correct role of policy should be in judicial decision-making. Compare the following:

> Public policy is 'a very unruly horse, and once you get astride of it you never know where it will carry you'. (Burrough J, *Richardson* v *Mellish* (1824) at 252)

> With a good man [or presumably woman] in the saddle, the unruly horse can be kept in control. It can jump over obstacles. (Lord Denning MR, *Enderby Town Football Club Ltd* v *The Football Association Ltd* [1971] at 606)

1.3 The disparate aims of tort law: a case study on *Woodroffe-Hedley* v *Cuthbertson*

Tort law has both backward- and forward-looking elements. It looks backwards at what happened—the 'wrong'—and addresses the harm done, while also looking to the future and at ways of regulating behaviour and developing responses to the risk of harm. It seeks to protect an individual's interests both *prospectively* (i.e. to prevent or deter future harm) and *retrospectively* (through the provision of compensation for past harms and the distribution of losses). Thus, tort law has a number of disparate functions or purposes—typically identified under the broad headings of (corrective) justice, compensation, deterrence, and, less often, vindication, that is inquiry and/or publicity.[14] It is to these

14. For a recent consideration of the purposes of tort law—focusing on the tort of negligence—see Steve Hedley 'Making Sense of Negligence' (2016) 36 LS 491 and, more generally James Goudkamp and John Murphy 'The Failure of Universal Theories of Tort Law' (2015) 21 Legal Theory 47.

functions that we now turn our attention, through an analysis of the little-known, and unreported, case of ***Woodroffe-Hedley* v *Cuthbertson*** [1997].[15]

Woodroffe-Hedley is of no great legal significance (although Dyson J's, later Lord Dyson, Justice of the UK Supreme Court, clear exposition of the elements of a claim in the tort of negligence deserves careful reading)[16] and is unlikely to appear on your reading lists. It is, nevertheless, indicative and revealing about the diverse purposes and functions of tort law. Our reason for introducing it here is to use it as an illustration of what tort law is about and how the courts balance its—at times competing—objectives.

see online resources

Woodroffe-Hedley v *Cuthbertson* (20 June 1997) QBD

This case involved a negligence claim following a climbing accident on the North Face of the Tour Ronde (one of the peaks of the Mont Blanc Massif, a mountain range in Europe). Gerry Hedley was an experienced rock climber. He hired David Cuthbertson, the defendant, an experienced alpine climber, to guide him to the summit of the Tour Ronde—a steep ice climb of about 350 metres. At the time of the accident, Cuthbertson was leading (i.e. going first). Concerned about the heat of the sun on the snow and the danger of rock fall, he decided to protect Hedley on a single ice screw belay in order to save time. Cuthbertson had no recollection of the accident; however, another climber on the mountain described how a large sheet of ice broke away from under his feet, dragging him down with it. The shock of the fall wrenched out the single ice screw and Hedley was also dragged down the mountain. The rope caught on a rocky outcrop and Hedley was killed instantly. Cuthbertson survived with a fractured knee.

The question for the court was whether Cuthbertson had negligently caused Hedley's death. The evidence was that had two ice screws and a running belay been used (as was good practice), Hedley would not have died. In response, Cuthbertson argued that given pressures of time it was reasonable to use a single screw. Dyson J disagreed. Cuthbertson, in deciding to dispense with a second screw and not to use a running belay, had fallen below the standard of care expected of a reasonably competent and careful alpine guide.[17]

The claimant (Hedley's young son) was awarded £150,000 in damages.

1.3.1 Doing (corrective) justice

The facts of the case paint a fairly bleak picture:

> Mr Cuthbertson made a serious mistake with tragic consequences which will live in his memory for the rest of his life. I am sure that he had Mr Hedley's best interests in mind when he made that fateful decision to move across the rocks, without taking the elementary and fundamental precaution of making the belay safe for Mr Hedley by driving in a

15. In so doing, we are mindful of *Weir*'s warning that before 'discussing the purpose of "tort", it is surely desirable to become familiar with what the ragbag actually contains: otherwise we shall be like adolescents spending all night discussing the meaning of life before, perhaps instead of, experiencing it' (p ix).

16. See further Lord Dyson on ***Woodroffe-Hedley*** and the criticism his judgment garnered in the press in his 2013 Holdsworth Club Lecture at para 33.

17. See **Chapter 8**.

> second screw. Objectively viewed, this was not a situation of emergency. Mr Cuthbertson had time to reflect. He reached a decision which, even without the benefit of hindsight, could not reasonably be justified. (Dyson J)

In short, the accident was Cuthbertson's fault; he was to blame for causing the accident and therefore, the argument goes, he should pay.[18]

The argument here is one of justice, specifically corrective justice.[19] Justice requires that we do not unreasonably interfere with others—their person and their property—when we go about our daily lives. So if we were to ask why we should not go around punching each other or destroying one another's property, the (or, at least, an) answer is that this is simply morally wrong. It is a requirement of justice that we do not treat each other in this way. Similarly, if I *do* punch you or destroy your property, justice requires me to do something about this—to correct or make good your loss.

This latter demand of justice is what is understood by corrective justice, and (as typically formulated) is built on two key elements—*fault* and *causation*. A defendant is liable to make good a claimant's losses because they (a) factually caused the claimant to suffer those losses and (b) were to blame (at fault) in so acting. By contrast, where either the defendant did not cause the claimant's losses or was not at fault in causing them, as a matter of justice we have no particular reason to require the defendant to make reparation. In the first case, the defendant can say 'it was nothing to do with me!'; in the second their defence is 'I couldn't help it!'

As such, corrective justice seems to provide a fairly good account of the typical tort claim. For the most part, defendants are liable in the law of tort only where they caused the claimant's loss and (though there are more exceptions here) where they were at fault in so doing. This, then, is what looks to be happening in ***Woodroffe-Hedley***. However, even on the comparatively simple facts of this case, the application of corrective justice may not be quite so clear.

Corrective justice rests on a notion of individual responsibility: if I am responsible for harming you, then justice requires me to put things right. However, in ***Woodroffe-Hedley***, it was not only Cuthbertson who was in some way responsible for what happened. Hedley also played a role. After all, as Dyson J acknowledged, 'mountain climbing is extremely dangerous. That is one of the reasons why so many risk their lives every year on mountains.' Hedley, as an experienced climber, knew this and willingly took the risk.

So even if we treat the role of a tort claim as being to determine who, if anyone, was (morally) responsible for the claimant's injuries, there may be no clear or single answer. To put the point another way, a case like ***Woodroffe-Hedley*** seems to present the court with a choice between the justice of righting a wrong (assuming this can be established) and avoiding the (possible) injustice of making someone else pay for another's self-chosen risk.[20]

18. In contrast, the professional standards committee of the British Mountain Guides found that David Cuthbertson was 'not at fault'. The climbing community has never accepted the *legal* decision in this case (Stephen Goodwin 'Climbers "acquit" colleague' *The Independent* 2 October 1997).

19. See Ernest Weinrib *The Idea of Private Law* (Harvard University Press, 1995) which is generally seen as setting out the 'purest' account of corrective justice.

20. As we shall see, the law has various mechanisms for splitting losses in cases where the claimant shares culpability (contributory negligence) or even preventing recovery completely (voluntarily assuming the risk/consent) (discussed in **Chapter 10**).

The court, in this case, through the mechanisms of negligence, allocated the loss to Cuthbertson. However, had the court found the situation to be an emergency, it would have been open to it to find his actions reasonable and the loss would have lain where it fell (i.e. with the claimant).

1.3.2 Compensation

In ***Woodroffe-Hedley***, as in the majority of tort cases, corrective justice is achieved by requiring the defendant to compensate (pay damages to) the claimant for the losses they have caused them. This may make it appear that corrective justice and compensation are effectively synonymous—to say that tort law is concerned with corrective justice is to say that it is about compensating harms. But this is not quite right.

While corrective justice often requires the payment of compensation, as we have seen, it does so only where the defendant is morally and legally responsible for the claimant's losses. This (typically) requires both causation and fault. As such, corrective justice requires the payment of compensation only where the defendant culpably caused the claimant's losses. Moreover, corrective justice is actually done only where it is *the defendant* who pays that compensation—otherwise it will not be *the defendant* who is making good the loss they have wrongfully caused—and that this money goes to *the claimant*—since otherwise it will not be *the claimant* who is then 'made good'.[21] This seems to impose significant limits on the role of tort law as a means for compensating losses. If tort law is simply about 'doing' corrective justice, then it can do nothing to remedy accidents and to make good losses which are no one's fault or where the party who is at fault cannot themselves pay compensation.

Look again at ***Woodroffe-Hedley***. The claimant was not the climber's estate but his young son, who was not even born at the time of the accident. It is not impossible to say that, by not using a second ice screw or a running belay, Cuthbertson was wronging Hedley's unborn son (as well as wronging Hedley himself), but nor is this self-evident. Even here, whether the claim can really be said to have given effect to corrective justice is far from clear.

Moreover, the extent to which tort law is really concerned with corrective justice can be challenged when we look at the motives of those who bring tort claims. In newspaper interviews at the time of the case, Hedley's widow was quoted as saying she felt deeply sorry for Cuthbertson.[22] It was clear that she was looking to allocate blame only insofar as was necessary to gain compensation for her son. Moreover, any compensation that Cuthbertson would be required to pay would be covered by his liability insurance. As such, it would not be Cuthbertson who was paying, but his insurance company. Thus, while on the surface tort law works to make the blameworthy pay, its corrective justice purposes are in truth undercut by the reality of insurance.

21. Indeed, Patrick Atiyah has argued that tort law no longer operates as a system of personal responsibility or corrective justice as the actual tortfeasor never pays ('Personal Injuries in the 21st Century: Thinking the Unthinkable' in Peter Birks (ed) *Wrongs and Remedies in the 21st Century* (OUP, 1996)).

22. Gary Younge 'Go tell it on the mountain' *The Guardian* 21 June 1997.

Indeed, claiming in tort is often, in practice, *conditional* on the defendant having insurance. After all, there is little point suing someone who will not in the end be able to pay:

> . . . it is seldom worth suing an uninsured negligent defendant.[23] Because of the operation of insurance, the plaintiff's loss is distributed, not to the careless defendant but, through insurance premiums, to all those who were not careless but who had insured against the possibility of being so. By the back door, the presence of insurance goes some way to the destruction of the central fault principle itself. (*Conaghan & Mansell* p 12)

Lord Sumption made a similar point in a speech to the Personal Injuries Bar Association in 2017.

> A system which makes compensation dependent on fault makes little sense if the damages are being paid not by the persons at fault, but by society as a whole. One is entitled to ask: why should the private law distribution of rights and liabilities between individuals or their employers determine the incidence of what is in reality a social cost? . . . [I]f the cost of compensating people for personal injury falls on society at large, there is no rational reason to distinguish between personal injury which has been caused by someone's fault, and personal injury which has occurred without fault.[24]

In such circumstances, the principles of corrective justice give way to the practicality of distributing losses. And, more fundamentally, the loss-*shifting* credentials and justifications of tort law (moving losses onto those who have culpably caused others to suffer them) are undermined. Losses, rather than being moved from one individual to another, are instead *spread* over a larger number of people. Tort law, while retaining its rhetoric of individual responsibility, effectively forces people to contract into the collective responsibility strategies of the welfare state (*Conaghan & Mansell* p 12).[25]

Tort law and the individual

Tort law, like all law, is political. By this we do not mean political in the party politics sense (although they may be relevant), but rather as 'being characterised by policy'.[26] Put simply, tort law embodies a philosophical perspective which prioritises individual over social or collective responsibility. Consider, for example, the decision in *Roe v Ministry of Health* [1954][27] or the fact that there exists no general legal duty to rescue.[28] The difficulty is that the politics of this understanding of tort law are rarely made explicit—they are, instead, presented as the way things are, as 'common sense'.

→

23. Though the case of the so-called 'lottery rapist' (***A* v *Hoare* [2008]**) may be an exception (David Batty 'Victim wins right to sue Lotto rapist' *The Guardian* 30 January 2008).

24. Sumption 2017.

25. Most notably in relation to workplace and road traffic accidents where statutory requirements that employers and motorists have liability insurance have been described by Jonathan Morgan as a '*partial* move towards a state-sanctioned compensation scheme' ('Tort, Insurance and Incoherence' (2004) 67 MLR 384, 400).

26. Wade Mansell, Belinda Meteyard and Alan Thomson *A Critical Introduction to Law* (Cavendish, 2004), p 2.

27. Discussed in **section 8.4.1**.

28. Discussed in **section 4.2**.

→

This understanding of tort law is not unproblematic: Joanne Conaghan and Wade Mansell argue that:

> if the basic subject matter of tort is concerned with how the law responds, or fails to respond, to the misfortunes which afflict individuals in our society, it can be strongly argued that the tort system represents a political solution which is undesirable both because of the arbitrariness of its results and because of the underlying callousness of its ideology. (1992, p 84)

This critique is, of course, itself political. It reflects a view that emphasises the importance of social or collective responsibility for an individual's misfortune and which questions the effectiveness of the tort law system—and in particular the centrality of the fault principle—as a mechanism for compensation and/or loss distribution (*Conaghan & Mansell* pp 3–4).

Our purpose here, however, is not to argue for one understanding of tort law over another. Rather, it is simply to make clear from the outset that more goes on beneath the surface of tort law than might at first be apparent and, in so doing, to encourage you to approach your study of it with a critical eye.

There is, however, as Lord Sumption noted in the earlier extract, another difficulty with tort law as a mechanism for compensation. As we have seen, the idea of corrective justice which underlies tort law's general requirements of causation and fault calls only for losses to be made good where they are the responsibility of someone else. However, while it might seem 'fair' that Hedley's young son is in some way compensated for the loss of his father, what about the many other children who lose a parent but have no one to blame for their death and, therefore, no one to sue in tort? Are they any less deserving of compensation? Similarly, would Hedley's son have been any *less* in need of compensation if the court had found the guide *not* to be negligent—if they had found one ice screw, in the circumstances of the case, to be sufficient?

The point here is not to question the requirements of corrective justice, but to ask whether the law of tort should put all its eggs in this one basket. Corrective justice provides *one* good reason for providing a claimant with compensation, but it does not follow that there are no other, equally good, reasons for compensating accident victims. Why should the law generally, and through the law of tort in particular, prioritise corrective justice? Should it not also provide compensation for those who suffer losses but who cannot find a defendant on which to pin them? Moreover, even where losses *are* caused by another's culpable conduct—and hence where corrective justice would seem to apply—as we have seen, the loss will often be borne either by an insurer or will not be made good at all (because the defendant does not have the resources to pay).[29] In the end, corrective justice actually seems to cover very little ground, protecting only a small minority of those whom we might feel should be compensated for their injuries.

29. Losses are also often borne by employers (or more accurately the employer's insurance company) through the mechanism of vicarious liability, discussed in **Chapter 20**.

Pause for reflection

Consider the following situations.

1. Leslie, an affluent 80-year-old, crashes his car while drunk and loses a leg.
2. Joan, an 18-year-old single parent, loses a leg when, while working as a traffic warden, she is struck by an unidentified hit-and-run driver.
3. Mary as a result of a congenital defect, is born with only one leg. She is now 5.
4. Dillon loses a leg as a result of contracting a serious disease.
5. John, a 'career burglar', loses a leg after being shot by a householder during a break-in.

Which of these people should receive compensation? Who or where should the compensation come from?

There is no 'right' answer to this exercise. Its purpose is simply to get you thinking about the variety of harms you will encounter in your study of tort law. Think about why you believe a person who loses a leg as the result of someone else's fault is more or less deserving of compensation than someone who, say, loses a leg after contracting a serious disease—what assumptions about the comparative severity of these harms and, importantly, the purpose of tort law, underpin your decision? Keep these questions (and your responses to them) in mind as you continue reading this and the following chapters so that you can reassess your position as you learn more about tort law.

As such *Atiyah* argues that the operation of tort law is largely arbitrary or—to use his words—a lottery. Tort law's effectiveness as a mechanism for compensation is limited by its allegiance to fault over need. In the absence of fault, tort victims are thrown back onto alternative sources of compensation and support: social security, insurance policies and other compensation schemes such as the Criminal Injuries Compensation Scheme.

see online resources

The compensation culture myth

There is much debate about the existence (and calls for eradication) of a so-called 'compensation culture', a culture that encourages us to 'blame and claim'.[30] Certainly, a cursory glance at the news media provides any number of examples of its (supposed) effects.[31]

→

30. See e.g. Sedley 2021; Saggerson 2018; Sumption 2017; Dyson 2015; Lewis 2014; Hand 2010; Kevin Williams 'State of Fear: Britain's "Compensation Culture" Reviewed' (2005) 25 LS 500.

31. See e.g. Anne Widdecombe 'We must get a grip on the compensation culture menace' *Daily Express* 3 March 2021; John O'Connell and Chris Keates 'Has the compensation culture gone mad?' *Daily Express* 30 March 2018; Hugh Morris, 'Compensation culture is ruining Britain's reputation abroad, tour operators warn' *Daily Telegraph* 21 June 2017; Emma Munbodh 'Attitudes to claiming: the "compensation culture"' *Mirror* 10 February 2015; Claire Carter 'Judge refuses whiplash damages as he criticises Britain's "compensation culture"' *The Telegraph* 26 March 2014; Jaya Navin 'Ridiculous compensation culture claims and pay-outs burden on tourist attractions' *Daily Mail* 26 April 2010; Sandra Laville and Sally James Gregory 'How a puppy, a paving slab and a passing cyclist made a bad break worth thousands: no-win no-fee firms blamed for compensation culture that costs £10bn a year' *The Guardian* 23 October 2004.

→

Moreover, this is something that courts have, for some time now, been conscious of and which they have sought to distance themselves from when imposing liability. For instance, Dyson J in ***Woodroffe-Hedley*** was careful to stress the following:

> Many accidents occur on guided climbs where no one is to blame. This decision should not be seen as opening the floodgate of claims against mountain guides whenever such accidents happen . . . Anyone who climbs with a guide is, as a matter of law, treated as consenting to the ordinary dangers of mountain climbing.[32]

But why should we be concerned about a compensation culture? After all, 'If the law entitles the victim of an accident to compensation, it ill becomes us to criticise him for knowing it and claiming.'[33] Surely the more accident victims are compensated for their losses, the better. Similarly, insofar as tort law is concerned with effecting corrective justice, more tort claims simply means more justice. What is undesirable about that?

At root, concerns about the existence and effects of 'an unrestrained culture of blame and compensation' (***Tomlinson*** v ***Congleton Borough Council*** [2003] at [81]), at least in part, seem to be a discomfort with the apparent unwillingness of individuals to take personal responsibility for their actions.[34] This may seem a strange argument to make. After all, as we have seen, tort law appears to be built on notions of individual responsibility, by holding people responsible for their actions and the harm they have caused. If so, how can an increase in the availability of tort claims be understood to *discourage* individual responsibility? The answer is that there is a danger that if we provide tort claims and compensation *too* readily—that is, if we make it too easy for people to demand that others make good the losses they suffer—it may discourage people from taking responsibility *for themselves*.

That would, of course, be a bad thing. But is there any evidence that this is really happening? Well, it depends who you ask. While the conclusion of the Labour Government's Better Regulation Task Force inquiry in 2004 was that the 'compensation culture is a myth, but the cost of this belief is very real',[35] six years later the (then) Prime Minister, David Cameron, took a different view:

> A damaging compensation culture has arisen, as if people can absolve themselves from any personal responsibility for their own actions, with the spectre of lawyers only too willing to pounce with a claim for damages on the slightest pretext. We simply cannot go on like this.[36]

Perhaps sensing a 'win', powerful insurance companies have continued to lobby the government,[37] keeping the issue on the political agenda. In 2013, the (then) Justice Secretary Chris Grayling, referring to a range of measures introduced in the Legal Aid, Sentencing and Punishment of Offenders Act 2012, stated:

→

32. Lord Dyson reiterated this point in his 2013 Holdsworth Club lecture: 'although I found for the widow in that case, I do not believe that it can be said that my decision made a contribution to compensation culture' (at [33]).

33. Sumption 2017. 34. Morgan (**n 25**) p 384.

35. Better Regulation Task Force *Better Routes to Redress* (2004), p 3.

36. Lord Young, *Common Sense, Common Safety* (Cabinet Office, 2010) p 5.

37. See e.g. Labour MP, Jo Stevens's, comment that the Civil Liability Bill reads like one that has been written by the insurance industry for the insurance industry (Civil Liability Bill [Lords], 4 September 2018, vol 646, col 94).

→

> We [the Government] are turning the tide on the compensation culture. It's pushing up the cost of insurance, and making it more expensive to drive a car or organise an event. It's time the whole system was rebalanced.[38]

In 2016, the (then) Justice Secretary, Liz Truss intervened pledging to cut down on 'whiplash claims' stating that '[f]or too long some have exploited a rampant compensation culture and seen whiplash claims an easy payday, driving up costs for millions of law-abiding motorists'[39] This was taken up by her successor, David Gauke who, notwithstanding government figures suggesting that personal injury claims were in 'freefall',[40] oversaw the passing of the Civil Liability Act 2018 which seeks to curb the number of whiplash claims, which he deemed were 'symptomatic of a wider compensation culture'.[41] More recently, personal injury lawyers have begun to 'fight back'. The Association of Personal Injury Lawyers' #RebuildingShatteredLives campaign launched in November 2020 which seeks to 'to tip the balance back towards empathy for injured people and put them at the heart of policy-making':

> The myths and misconceptions enshrouding personal injury have made people feel that if they try to seek redress they are fraudsters, or that they are part of the problem which has led to the so-called 'compensation culture'. In fact, multiple studies have found that the 'compensation culture' does not exist. But the belief that personal injury claims are a problem to be tackled is still strong among policymakers. The Overseas Operations (Service Personnel and Veterans) Bill, which now awaits scrutiny from the House of Lords, puts a six-year longstop on claims by injured armed forces personnel. . . . The Legal Aid, Sentencing and Punishment of Offenders (LASPO) Act 2012 was unjust and based on the deeply offensive notion that injured people should have 'skin in the game'. The Enterprise and Regulatory Reform Act 2013 was based on the misconception that businesses are sued unfairly by injured employees. . . . Rebuilding Shattered Lives is a push-back against this unfair situation.[42]

In fact, both views—as to the existence or otherwise of a compensation culture—share the same concern. Whether there really is an unhealthy expectation that all losses or injury ought to be compensated, or whether the real danger lies in the *perception* that such a culture exists, a consequence of *both* views is that people become over-cautious, abandoning activities which, though risky, also bring societal benefits. In other words, the *fear* of liability leads people to simply refuse to engage in generally beneficial activities—school trips are cancelled, horse

→

38. Ministry of Justice news release 'Government acts on compensation culture' 1 May 2013.

39. Brian Milligan, 'Whiplash plans to "cut car insurance premiums by £40"' BBC News, 17 November 2016.

40. Dropping to their lowest in a decade (John Hyde, 'Compensation culture? Stats reveal claims numbers in freefall' *Law Society Gazette* 24 April 2018). This fall has continued (John Hyde 'Personal injury claims fall again to eight-year low' *Law Society Gazette* 9 March 2020).

41. In January 2021, the government announced further delays to the implementation of the 'whiplash reform programme'. It is now due to go 'live' in May 2021. John Hyde 'Whiplash reforms delayed another month' *Law Society Gazette* 11 January 2021.

42. Mike Benner 'Trust in PI Lawyers' *Law Society Gazette* 18 November 2020. See further **https://rebuilding-shattered-lives.org.uk/about-us/**.

→

chestnut trees are stripped of their conkers and competitors are banned from running in pancake races for fear of being sued if things go wrong.[43]

This is the problem of *over*-deterrence. As James Hand notes:

> The compensation culture cliché may not be a reality, but if it discourages people from pursuing truly legitimate claims—or undertaking valuable activities—then it is, nevertheless, a very real cause for concern. (p 591)

Thus at the same time as fanning the flames of the 'compensation culture' myth (or reality), the government has also legislated to 'slay the health and safety culture' and protect the 'everyday heroes' deterred from participating in socially useful activities due to worries about risk and/or liability.[44] The Social Action, Responsibility and Heroism Act 2015 (SARAH) had a rough ride through the parliamentary process earning itself the epithet of 'the most unnecessary, indeed pointless piece of legislation to be considered by Parliament for a very long time'.[45]

The 'compensation culture' debate—like the search for the Loch Ness monster—looks set to continue for a while yet.

Pause for reflection

. . . the law of tort is an extraordinarily clumsy and inefficient way of dealing with serious cases of personal injury. It often misses the target, or hits the wrong target. It makes us no safer, while producing undesirable side effects. What is more, it does all of these things at disproportionate cost and with altogether excessive delay.[46]

43. See Frank Furedi and Jennie Bristow *The Social Cost of Litigation* (Centre for Policy Studies, September 2012).

44. Anon, 'Chris Grayling vows to "slay health and safety culture"' *The Telegraph* 19 June 2014. See and compare arguments in favour and against the Bill in the written evidence to the Public Bills Committee (PBC (Bill 009) 2014–2015).

45. Lord Pannick 'UK negligence law is already fit for heroes' *The Times* 13 November 2014. Lord Pannick continued his assault on the Bill in the House of Lords: 'Mr Grayling, the Lord Chancellor, has told us . . . that men and women up and down the land are standing ready to volunteer for social action. They are preparing themselves for acts of heroism, waiting only to receive the message that Parliament has approved this Bill to remove the concerns that they otherwise have about litigation. Then off to the youth clubs and old-age homes they will go to volunteer and into the lakes they will dive to rescue those in danger, and in those circumstances it would be irresponsible of me to delay the Bill any longer . . . This always was and it remains the most ridiculous piece of legislation approved by Parliament in a very long time. However, I pay genuine tribute—I emphasise "genuine tribute"—to the Minister [Lord Faulks], who has applied his formidable skills of reason and eloquence, and has done so with consummate courtesy, to a text that would barely muster a pass mark in GCSE legal studies, if there is such a thing' (HL Deb, 6 January 2015, vol 758(79), cols 261–2). See also Rachael Mulheron 'Legislating Dangerously: Bad Samaritans, Good Society, and the Heroism Act 2015' (2017) 81 MLR 88 and discussion in **section 8.5.1**.

46. However Sumption (2017) concludes that 'he has no doubt that' the current system 'will survive'. And will do so for three reasons: (a) the only alternative—a no-fault compensation scheme—would be enormously costly to introduce; (b) the benefits of tort law are visible to the public, while the costs are more subtle and indirect; and (c) public notions of personal responsibility and the proper function of law.

→

If tort law does such a bad job of compensating those whom we feel should be compensated, what are the alternatives?

One is simply to extend state provision for those who suffer misfortunes. In other words, the state should compensate those who suffer losses and should not limit such compensation to those injured as a result of another's fault. However, the costs of this might be considered prohibitive.[47] So, while the state does make some provision for the disadvantaged, including the operation of *some* so-called 'no-fault' compensation schemes, there is no prospect of it taking over responsibility for protecting us from all our losses.[48]

An even more radical solution was proposed by Patrick Atiyah in *The Damages Lottery*. He argued that in a system where people have a strong financial incentive to blame others for injury and where welfare support is increasingly provided through insurance and personal support systems, the solution to the inadequacy of the tort system to compensate for accidental harm lies in *personal*—that is first-party—*insurance*. The idea is that those engaged in risky activities would take out insurance to cover themselves should they be involved in an accident. People could insure themselves against *any* risks—from being run over to insuring against congenital disabilities that may affect their children (*Atiyah* p 191).

Do you think this is a good idea? Think about the other purposes and functions tort law serves.[49] Has Atiyah, as Joanne Conaghan and Wade Mansell argue, 'simply substituted one system of arbitrary and fortuitous distribution for another'?[50] What would happen, for example, to those who could not—or would not—buy insurance?

1.3.3 **Deterrence**

Tort law also plays a role in deterring future tortious activity. The imposition of liability in relation to a particular activity enables others to regulate their behaviour accordingly. Thus, it is argued, following ***Woodroffe-Hedley***, that mountain guides are more likely to use two ice screws rather than risk liability by relying on one. Moreover, one might think that anything that encourages safe practices is, in itself, a good thing.

However, as noted earlier, the problem is that sometimes the effect of the imposition of tortious liability in such circumstances is not to deter potentially negligent conduct but to stop the activity altogether 'just in case'. The deterrent effect of tort law is also weakened by the presence of insurance as it, once again, subverts that which it is said to reinforce. After all, the incentive to be careful is somewhat less strong when the result will merely be a rise in insurance premiums rather than having to bear a hefty compensation payout oneself. The financial impact on careless drivers of losing

47. See discussion of 'no-fault' compensation schemes in **section 21.6.1.1**.

48. Though see Sumption 2017.

49. As Jonathan Morgan (2018) notes in his reply to Sumption (2017): 'Tort law is, considered solely as a compensation scheme, outstandingly badly designed (in theory) and staggeringly inefficient to operate (in practice). But compensation is not tort's only legitimate role. Once this is acknowledged, the case for abolition is uncertain. Tort's other social functions could rationally justify its survival—although dubious moral sentiments (in my view) cannot' (at 23).

50. Joanne Conaghan and Wade Mansell 'From the Permissive to the Dismissive Society: Patrick Atiyah's Accidents, Compensation and the Market' (1998) 25 J L & Soc 284, 291.

their 'no claims bonus' coupled with higher premiums for those who fall into certain 'risky' categories does not always appear to have a significant deterrent effect. Though there may be more of such effect where insurance companies, as perhaps in relation to employers' or occupiers' liability, themselves put pressure on defendants to comply with safety regulations and meet other standards before agreeing to provide insurance.

1.3.4 **Vindication**

Finally, sometimes tort actions are brought to find out 'what really happened'. What happened in the operating theatre? Or on the streets of Omagh?

The Omagh bombing

Twenty-nine people—including a woman who was pregnant with twins—were killed and over 300 people were injured by a 500lb bomb in Omagh, a town in County Tyrone, Northern Ireland in August 1998. Although the bomb was 'claimed' by the Real IRA, no one has been convicted in a criminal court in relation to the bombing which has been described as 'the single worst atrocity in the course of the years of violence which occurred in Northern Ireland from the late 1960s onwards'.[51]

see online resources

Relatives of those killed initiated a landmark civil action against the five people they believed to be responsible. After a number of trials and retrials, four men were found civilly liable and ordered to pay the victims' families £1.6 million in compensation.[52] Responding to the decision at the successful retrial of two of the four men, Michael Gallagher, whose son Aidan was killed in the bombing, commented:

> We will be doing our best to try and recover the damages but at the moment, we're just happy that we've got a judgement [sic] that we, the families, the victims, have held someone to account for what happened at Omagh.[53]

Indeed, another reason Hedley's widow sued in ***Woodroffe-Hedley*** was because she wanted to know what had happened on the mountain (the French police had refused to give her the accident report).

Counterpoint

The tort system does little to encourage cooperation between the parties. It is, after all, dangerous—and, more importantly, costly—to apologise or admit responsibility (however limited) for an accident when litigation is likely (*Harlow* p 38). However, the Compensation Act 2006 →

51. *McKevitt and Campbell* v *UK* [2016], [5].
52. BBC News 'Real IRA chief to blame for Omagh' 8 June 2009. The European Court of Human Rights rejected an attempt by two of those found civilly liable to establish that their trial was 'unfair' in September 2016 (BBC News 'Omagh bombing: European court dismisses Real IRA men's claim' 29 September 2016).
53. BBC News 'Omagh bomb: Colm Murphy and Seamus Daly found liable at retrial' 20 March 2013.

→

attempts to go some way to remedying this by explicitly separating any admission of culpability from simply 'saying sorry': 'An apology, an offer of treatment or other redress, shall not in itself amount to an admission of negligence' (s 2).

This function of tort is often coupled with a wish to gain publicity about what has happened—to 'stop it from ever happening again'. This is often the line taken by relatives of those killed and injured by another's negligence, including Gerry Hedley's wife, Lydia.[54] Consider also the claims of the friends and family of those killed in the Hillsborough Stadium disaster (***Alcock* v *Chief Constable of South Yorkshire Police* [1992]**) or that of Dwayne Brooks against the Metropolitan Police following the murder of his friend, Stephen Lawrence (*Brooks* v *Commissioner of Police for the Metropolis* [2005]).[55]

A variant on this theme can be seen in *League Against Cruel Sports* v *Scott* [1986] a case about stag hunting on Exmoor. While formally this is a case about trespass to land, in reality it has very little to do with protecting land interests. Rather, it was a mixture of publicity and activism, of mobilising and using the law to further collectively held ends, in this case the desire of those opposed to stag hunting to put a stop to it on Exmoor by strategically buying up parcels of land so that the hunt, in passing over them, could be sued in trespass.

1.4 Tort law and the Human Rights Act 1998

The Human Rights Act (HRA) 1998 incorporates the majority of the European Convention on Human Rights (ECHR) into UK law.[56] What is the significance of this for tort law?

In the first instance, it imposes a duty on the state to respect and act consistently with the human rights set down in the Convention. These rights include: the right to life (Art 2), the right not to be subjected to inhuman or degrading treatment (Art 3), the right to liberty and security (Art 5), the right to a fair trial (Art 6), the right to respect for private and family life (Art 8) and the right to freedom of expression (Art 10). Accordingly, where the state does not do so, the HRA enables an individual to make a claim against the state (s 7). This is what is known as 'vertical effect'.[57]

54. See Younge (**n 22**).

55. Both of which, it should be noted, sparked government inquiries: The Right Reverend James Jones, Bishop of Liverpool, *The Report of the Hillsborough Independent Panel* (12 September 2012); Sir William Macpherson of Cluny, *Report on the Stephen Lawrence Inquiry* (Cm 4262-I, 1999). In April 2016, in what has been described as the victims' families' 'day of vindication', a new inquest found that the 96 people who died at the Hillsborough Stadium disaster had been unlawfully killed (David Conn 'Hillsborough inquests jury rules 96 victims were unlawfully killed' *The Guardian* 26 April 2016).

56. On the relationship between tort law and the HRA, see generally Jane Wright *Tort Law and Human Rights* (Hart, 2001).

57. It is important to note that this is not a claim in tort. It is a public, not a private, law claim; i.e. it creates a remedy in *public* law to enforce a Convention right.

More significantly, for our purposes, the HRA may have an influence on tort law claims between private individuals. This stems from section 6 of the HRA which makes it 'unlawful for a public authority to act in a way which is incompatible with a Convention right' (s 6(1)). What this appears to suggest is that courts (as 'public authorities' by virtue of s 6(3)) when deciding cases or framing legal rules are under a duty to respect the litigants' human rights (just as they are under an *express* obligation to read and give effect to legislation in a way that is HRA-compliant (s 3(1)). This is significant for the purposes of tort law because it would seem to mean that when determining the existence and scope of liability in tort, the courts must ensure that their decisions are HRA compatible. That in turn would seem to suggest that the content of the law of tort, and hence the rights and duties which exist between private individuals, must include adequate protection of the rights provided for in the Act (this is what is meant by the HRA having 'horizontal' effect).

To see how this might work, take the following example. One Convention right in respect of which English tort law has historically failed to offer much protection is the right to privacy (Art 8). As such, before the HRA, a claimant who went to court complaining that the defendant had interfered with their privacy would more than likely see their claim dismissed on the basis that it disclosed no cause of action. How has the HRA changed this? The HRA allowed a claimant, in bringing such a claim, to say that if the court does not recognise their claim it will be failing in its duty as a public body to protect their right to privacy. In other words, effective protection of the defendant's right to privacy has required the courts to recognise that an invasion of the claimant's privacy is an actionable wrong. Note that this does *not* mean that the HRA itself imposes duties on private individuals to respect each other's human rights. The House of Lords has stated that the HRA does not, itself, provide a remedy in tort (*R (Greenfield)* v *Secretary of State for the Home Department* [2005]), it simply imposes duties on public bodies—yet as developments in the law of privacy, as well as other areas, are beginning to show 'horizontal effect' has proven beneficial for tort (and other) litigants.

Early on, it was clear that while the courts were not willing to recognise any *new* torts, they were willing to modify existing torts to ensure that they are HRA compatible:

> [The] obligation on the court does not seem to me to encompass the creation of a free-standing cause of action based directly upon the articles of the convention . . . The duty of the court, in my view, is to act compatibly with the Convention rights in adjudicating upon existing causes of action, and that includes a positive as well as a negative obligation. (Butler-Sloss P, *Venables* v *News Group Newspapers Ltd* [2001] at 918)

This view was confirmed in ***Campbell* v *Mirror Group Newspapers* [2004]** where the House of Lords refused to recognise a new cause of action on the basis of the HRA but amended an existing action to protect the claimant's privacy. More recently, however, it seems the courts may be willing to go this extra step—see, for example, Tugendhat's development of the misuse of personal information as a distinct tort in *Vidal-Hall* v *Google Inc* [2014] (at [49]–[70]).[58]

58. Confirmed by the Court of Appeal in 2015. Discussed further in **section 16.4.1**.

1.5 A note on terminology

Since 1999 the victim or wronged party has been known in England and Wales as the *claimant*.[59] They were previously called the 'plaintiff' (and still are in some common law jurisdictions). You will therefore encounter both terms in your reading. In this book, we use 'claimant' whenever we are discussing the victim (even in relation to pre-1999 cases), reserving the term 'plaintiff' for when we quote directly from texts which predate the change.

On the other side is the *defendant*, who is also usually (but need not be) the alleged wrongdoer or *tortfeasor* (i.e. the person said to have committed the tort). This distinction is important and usually arises where an action is brought on the basis of *vicarious liability*, that is against an employer (or someone who is akin to an employer) (the defendant) who, it is argued, should be held vicariously liable for the torts of their employee or someone who is in a relationship akin to employment (the tortfeasor).[60] However, it may also arise where the case is brought against an insurer under the Third Parties (Rights Against Insurers) Act 1930, which allows the victim to sue an insolvent defendant's liability insurer directly.

1.6 Conclusion

In this introductory chapter we have considered the obvious, but essential, question: what is tort law? The answer has taken us from its origins in the simple mispronunciation of the French word for 'wrong'—tort—imported into England with the Norman Conquest to the recent and ongoing concerns about the so-called 'compensation culture'. Tort law is, then, the name given to a diverse collection of legal wrongs for which the law provides a remedy. These wrongs—or torts—protect an individual's interest in, among other things, their personal integrity, their property, their use and enjoyment of their land or their reputation. Many, but not all, of these interests are protected in different ways by a number of torts and, similarly, while some torts—for example, negligence—protect a wide variety of interests, others—for example, libel or slander—protect a single interest, in this case reputation.

Before considering the effects of the HRA on tort law, we explored the many—and at times conflicting—purposes and functions of tort law and the extent to which it is able to achieve them. Tort law tends to be about righting wrongs. It can be seen to operate as a mechanism of loss-shifting, ensuring that the victim of the tort is returned to the position they would have been in had the tort not occurred (usually through an award of damages). However, as we have seen, the corrective justice aspect of tort law is somewhat undercut by the presence of insurance liability which ensures the loss is spread amongst policy holders. Tort law is also forward-looking. It can have a deterrent effect, shaping potential wrongdoers' behaviour as they seek to avoid liability, as well as providing an avenue for publicity and inquiry.

59. Civil Procedure Rules 1998 (which implemented the so-called Woolf reforms designed to speed up and simplify civil litigation).

60. **Chapter 20**.

End-of-chapter questions

After reading the chapter carefully, try answering the questions which follow.

1 What is tort law and how does it differ from contract or criminal law?

2 What is the purpose of compensating for injury?

3 What is meant by the term 'compensation culture' and what does the use of the term imply?

4 Are the disparate aims of tort law conflicting or complementary? Give reasons for your answer.

If you would like to know what we think visit the **online resources**. www.oup.com/he/horsey7e

Further reading

The best place to start your reading is with Tony Weir's excellent introductory chapter in his *Introduction to Tort Law*.

Cane, Peter *The Anatomy of Tort Law* (Hart, 1997)

Conaghan, Joanne 'Tort Law and Feminist Critique' (2003) 56 CLP 175

Conaghan, Joanne and Wade Mansell 'Tort Law' in Ian Grigg-Spall and Paddy Ireland *The Critical Lawyer's Handbook* (Pluto Press, 1992), pp 83–90 (available online via the 'Critical Lawyers' Group website)

Dyson, Lord 'Compensation Culture: Fact of Fantasy?' Holdsworth Club Lecture, 15 March 2013

Dyson, Lord 'Magna Carta and the Compensation Culture' The High Sheriffs Law Lecture, Oxford, 13 October 2015

Hand, James 'The Compensation Culture: Cliché or Cause for Concern?' (2010) 37 J L & Soc 569

Harlow, Carol *Understanding Tort Law* (Sweet & Maxwell, 2005), Ch 2

Hershovitz, Scott 'Harry Potter and the Trouble with Tort Law' (2011) 63 Stan L Rev 67

Hutchinson, Allan and Derek Morgan 'The Canengusian Connection: A Kaleidoscope of Tort Theory' (1984) 22 Osgoode Hall LJ 69

Lewis, Richard 'Compensation Culture Reviewed: Incentives to Claim and Damages Levels' [2014] JPIL 209

Lewis, Richard and Ann Morris 'Tort Law Culture: Image and Reality' (2012) 39 J L & Soc 577

Morgan, Jonathan 'Abolishing Personal Injuries Law? A Response to Lord Sumption' [2018] Prof Neg 122

Saggerson, Alan 'Something Must Be Done: Recent Legislative Contributions to the Common Law' Lecture at Lincoln's Inn, 30 October 2018

Sedley, Stephen 'Mischief Wrought' London Review of Books, 4 March 2021

Sumption, Lord 'Abolishing Personal Injuries Law—A Project' Personal Injuries Bar Association Annual Lecture, London, 16 November 2017

Weir, Tony *An Introduction to Tort Law* (OUP, 2006), Ch 1

Williams, Glanville 'The Aims of the Law of Tort' (1951) 4 CLP 137

The tort of negligence

PART I

2 Introduction to the tort of negligence

2.1 Introduction

2.2 Mapping the historical development of the tort of negligence

2.3 Explaining the historical development of the tort of negligence

2.4 The role of the modern law of negligence

2.5 The elements of the tort of negligence

2.6 Case example: *X & Y* v *London Borough of Hounslow*

2.7 Conclusion

End-of-chapter questions

Further reading

3 Duty of care: basic principles

3.1 Introduction

3.2 From *Donoghue* to *Caparo*—a brief history of the duty of care

3.3 Establishing a duty of care: *Caparo Industries* v *Dickman*

3.4 Where does this leave us?

3.5 Conclusion

End-of-chapter questions

Further reading

4 Special duty problems: omissions and acts of third parties

4.1 Introduction

4.2 Acts and omissions

4.3 Summary of when a duty of care may be found in respect of omissions

4.4 Liability for acts of third parties: the general rule

4.5 When is there liability for the acts of third parties?

4.6 Summary of when a duty of care may be found for the actions of third parties

4.7 Conclusion

End-of-chapter questions

Further reading

5 **Special duty problems: psychiatric harm**
5.1 Introduction
5.2 What is psychiatric harm?
5.3 The general exclusionary rule
5.4 'Primary' and 'secondary' victims
5.5 Primary victims
5.6 Secondary victims
5.7 Beyond primary and secondary victims
5.8 Conclusion
End-of-chapter questions
Further reading

6 **Special duty problems: public bodies**
6.1 Introduction
6.2 The general exclusionary rule
6.3 When will public bodies owe a duty of care?
6.4 The impact of European jurisprudence
6.5 The emergency services and armed forces
6.6 Other types of public body
6.7 The recognition of new types of claim—'messed up lives'?
6.8 Conclusion
End-of-chapter questions
Further reading

7 **Special duty problems: economic loss**
7.1 Introduction
7.2 What is 'pure' economic loss?
7.3 Exceptions to the exclusionary rule: *Hedley Byrne* v *Heller*
7.4 Claims for pure economic loss in negligence before *Murphy*
7.5 Extending *Hedley Byrne*
7.6 Beyond *Hedley Byrne*: the 'will cases' and a more flexible approach
7.7 Conclusion
End-of-chapter questions
Further reading

8 **Breach of duty: the standard of care**
8.1 Introduction
8.2 A test of reasonableness
8.3 An objective standard
8.4 Setting the standard of care
8.5 A balancing act

8.6 Establishing breach
8.7 Conclusion
End-of-chapter questions
Further reading

9 Causation and remoteness of damage
9.1 Introduction
9.2 Factual causation—the 'but for' test
9.3 Legal causation
9.4 Conclusion
End-of-chapter questions
Further reading

10 Defences to negligence
10.1 Introduction
10.2 Voluntarily assuming the risk (*volenti*)
10.3 Illegality
10.4 Contributory negligence
10.5 Conclusion
End-of-chapter questions
Further reading

Introduction to Part I

1. The tort of negligence provides a remedy where injury or loss is caused to the injured party by the wrongdoer's failure to keep to a legal duty to take reasonable care (*Donoghue* v *Stevenson* [1932]). It plays a central role in the law of tort: more tort law claims are brought in the tort of negligence than in any other tort and it has influenced the interpretation of other torts.

2. Part I begins with two introductory chapters—**Introduction to the tort of negligence** and **Duty of care: basic principles**. The first of these chapters introduces the origins of the modern law of negligence and some of the key themes underpinning the tort. It outlines the essential ingredients of a claim in negligence—a duty of care, a breach of that duty and damage caused by that breach—before going on to explore these in practice through a close examination of the first instance judgment in *X & Y* v *London Borough of Hounslow* [2008]. The second introductory chapter tracks the development of the *duty of care*. It considers the various general tests developed and used by the courts in order to establish when a duty of care is owed. In novel cases where there is no existing precedent, since the decision of the House of Lords in *Caparo Industries* v *Dickman* [1990], the defendant will owe the claimant a duty of care only where there are positive reasons for them to do so (either because the circumstances of the case are very similar to another where a duty is already owed or because there is sufficient proximity and foreseeability between the parties and the harm suffered to make it fair, just and reasonable to impose a duty).

3. **Chapters 4** to **7** consider the circumstances in which the courts have developed specific rules as to when a duty of care is owed. These fall into three broad groups: liability in relation to particular harms—*pure psychiatric harm* and *economic loss; claims against public bodies*, for example local authorities, the police and other emergency services; and, finally, those relating to the way in which the harm was caused—either indirectly, such as through a failure to act (*an omission*), or where the immediate cause of the harm was the act of *a third party* (someone other than the claimant or defendant). As we shall see, duty of care is often used as a control mechanism in these cases to *deny* liability on the basis that the defendant was not, or ought not to be, held responsible for the claimant's injury.

4. **Chapter 8** focuses exclusively on the second of the requirements necessary to establish a claim in the tort of negligence—*breach of duty*. A breach occurs where a defendant has fallen below the particular *standard of care* demanded by the law. This is largely an objective test and is determined by comparing the actions of the defendant to those imagined to be done in the same circumstances by the so-called 'reasonable man'.

5. The final 'hurdle' for the claimant to overcome in the tort of negligence is *causation*. This is considered in **Chapter 9**. The claimant must prove that their injuries were caused by the defendant's actions in both *fact* and *law*. This is not always as straightforward as might be expected, especially in circumstances where there are multiple defendants and/or possible causes of the claimant's injury.

6. Finally, even if all the elements of a claim in negligence have been met, the defendant may still be able to avoid liability by raising a *defence*. In **Chapter 10**, we consider three key defences in the tort of negligence: *voluntarily assuming the risk* (*volenti non fit injuria* or consent), *contributory negligence* and *illegality*. It is important to note that although these defences are discussed in the context of the tort of negligence they are (with the exception of contributory negligence) applicable throughout tort law.

Introduction to the tort of negligence

2

2.1 Introduction

Consider the following examples:

→ ***A cyclist is knocked down and killed by a speeding car.***

→ ***A junior doctor mistakenly injects their patient with the wrong antibiotic causing permanent paralysis.***

→ ***An elderly woman breaks her hip tripping over a raised paving slab outside her local shop.***

→ ***A young child falls down a manhole left uncovered by Post Office employees earlier in the day and seriously injures his leg.***

In each of these examples the accident or injury suffered appears to be the fault (at least in part) of someone other than the injured party. The speeding motorist, the junior doctor, the local authority and the Post Office employees have all been, in some way, negligent, in the sense of having acted carelessly or neglectfully. They may therefore be liable for damages in the *tort of* negligence. It is important to distinguish at the outset between negligence in the former everyday or colloquial sense—whereby it is synonymous with carelessness or neglect—and negligence in the legal sense—that is, the type of liability which the law attaches to people who fall below a particular (legal) standard of care. Not all actions which are negligent in the first sense will be negligent in the second. It is only sometimes that the law *requires* us to act carefully and, therefore, it is important always to bear in mind that a person is not *automatically* liable for all, or indeed any, of the consequences of their negligent (in the sense of careless) actions. Moreover, as we shall see, a person may be liable in the tort of negligence even when their actions cannot realistically be described as careless.

'Negligence' in tort law therefore refers to a tort which, since the landmark case of ***Donoghue*** v ***Stevenson*** [1932], provides a remedy (usually in the form of damages) where injury or loss is caused to the injured party by the wrongdoer's failure to keep to a legal duty to take reasonable care.

Negligence liability may arise in relation to a range of diverse types of harm or injury—personal injury (physical and psychiatric), property damage, financial loss etc—and covers a wide range of activities—driving a car, giving financial advice, running a hospital operating theatre, playing football and so on. However, some harms or injuries are better protected by the tort of negligence than others. The courts have limited the operation of the tort in relation to some types of harm which they appear to view with suspicion—particularly psychiatric injuries and pure economic loss—and in claims against certain defendants—most notably public bodies, for example local authorities, the police and other emergency services. As such, though there is a single tort of negligence covering, potentially, all possible harms in all possible contexts, the courts have developed different approaches to deal with different sorts of harm in different contexts. We shall see examples of this in **Chapters 4** to **7**.

However, this should not obscure the general focus of the tort of negligence: to make people pay for the damage they cause when their conduct falls below an acceptable standard or level. It is this feature that makes the tort of negligence so important. Other torts we shall be looking at in this book are all identified by the type of interest or right they protect—for example, the tort of defamation protects the interest you have in your reputation, the trespass to the person torts protect rights to bodily freedom and safety. The tort of negligence is different. It is not defined by, and so is not limited to the protection of, any single type of right or interest. Instead, the focus of the tort of negligence is the 'quality' of the defendant's conduct—what must be shown is that the defendant acted unreasonably.

Of course, this is not to suggest that the actual harm caused by the wrongdoer is unimportant—far from it. It is crucial. Unlike, for example, the trespass torts which are actionable per se—meaning that the claimant need not show that they have suffered any loss for their claim to succeed—liability in negligence can only be established where the defendant's breach has resulted in harm: 'Negligence in the air will not do; negligence, in order to give a cause of action, must be the neglect of some duty owed to the person who makes the claim' (Greer LJ, *Haynes* v *Harwood* [1935] at 152).

It is, therefore, misleading to talk about 'liability for negligence' in the abstract—the wrongdoer will not be liable *in the tort of negligence* if no injury results from their careless action—the elderly man who *doesn't* trip over the broken paving slap as he does his weekly shop has no claim in negligence.

Pause for reflection

Consider again the examples at the start of the chapter. What if the speeding driver had at the last moment avoided hitting the cyclist or the doctor's mistake had caused the patient no ill effects? In such cases, although the wrongdoer's actions are just as careless or negligent, in law the driver and doctor would not be liable. Whether or not harm results from an individual's negligent conduct is more often than not a matter of luck rather than judgement. Why does it, therefore, make such a difference to the defendant's liability? You may find it helpful to refer again to the purposes of tort law (discussed in **Chapter 1**) and the tort of negligence in particular when thinking about your answer.

Even where the claimant has suffered harm, it doesn't mean that they will necessarily have a claim—the harm must be one that is *legally recognised*. The law does not provide compensation for *every* loss; harms which do not fall within the scope of negligence law, no matter how great and notwithstanding a defendant's clear breach of duty, will ground no liability in negligence.[1] As Lord Rodger notes in ***D* v *East Berkshire Community NHS Trust* [2005]**: 'the world is full of harm for which the law furnishes no remedy' (at [100]). Thus, to use Lord Rodger's examples, there is nothing *legally* preventing the owner of the local shop from injuring his rivals by destroying their businesses. Similarly,

> a young man whose fiancée deserts him for his best friend may become clinically depressed as a result, but in the circumstances the fiancée owes him no duty of care to avoid causing this suffering. So he too will have no right to damages for his illness. The same goes for a middle-aged woman whose husband runs off with a younger woman . . . However badly one of them may have treated the other, the law does not get involved in awarding damages. (Lord Rodger at [100])

Pause for reflection

It is not always clear whether a claimant has been harmed. Consider the differing approaches of the UK Supreme Court and Court of Appeal in *Dryden* v *Johnson Matthey plc* [2018]. The claimants were negligently exposed to high levels of platinum salts at work and, as a result, they had ended up developing sensitisation to platinum salts. The sensitisation itself carried no symptoms. It did, however, mean that there was a risk that the claimants would develop an allergy to platinum salts if they continued to be exposed to them, and this allergy would be manifested in adverse physical symptoms. In order to avoid further exposure, and hence to prevent any such allergic reaction, the claimants had their employment terminated or were reassigned to less well-paid jobs. They sued for their loss of earnings. To recover for these losses, they needed to establish that this financial loss was consequent on their suffering some form of personal injury. The claimants lost at trial and in the Court of Appeal.

> On the medical evidence, platinum sensitisation is not harmful in itself in any relevant sense. It is a physiological change analogous to the development of pleural plaques in the lungs in the *Rothwell* case [*Rothwell* v *Chemical & Insulating Co Ltd* [2007]], and hence does not constitute actionable damage or injury. Unlike the lung scarring from pneumoconiosis in the *Cartledge* case [*Cartledge* v *E Jopling & Sons Ltd* [1963]], platinum sensitisation is not a 'hidden impairment' which has the potential by itself to give rise to detrimental physical effects in the course of ordinary life. (Sales LJ, *Greenway* v *Johnson Matthey plc* [2016] at [30])

However in the Supreme Court, Lady Black, with whom the other Justices agreed, took a different view:

> The physiological changes to the claimants' bodies may not be as obviously harmful as, say, the loss of a limb, or asthma or dermatitis, but harmful they undoubtedly

→

1. On the categorisation of recoverable harm in negligence, see further Priaulx 2012.

→

are. *Cartledge* establishes that the absence of symptoms does not prevent a condition amounting to actionable personal injury, and an acceptance of that is also implicit in the sun sensitivity example, in which the symptoms would only be felt upon exposure to sunshine, just as the symptoms here would only be felt upon exposure to platinum salts. What has happened to the claimants is that their bodily capacity for work has been impaired and they are therefore significantly worse off. They have, in my view, suffered actionable bodily damage, or personal injury, which, given its impact on their lives, is certainly more than negligible. (at [40])[2]

The tort of negligence plays a central role in the law of tort. This is for two reasons:

(1) It is by far the most important tort in practice. More tort law claims are brought in the tort of negligence than in any other tort.

(2) The ideas and principles of negligence have influenced the interpretation of *other* torts—such as the infusion of the notion of foreseeability into private nuisance and the previously strict liability imposed by the rule in ***Rylands* v *Fletcher*** [1868] and in ***Cambridge Water Co Ltd* v *Eastern Counties Leather plc*** [1994].

The tort of negligence therefore usually forms a substantial part of tort law modules and textbooks. This book is no exception. The law relating to the tort of negligence occupies the whole of Part I (**Chapters 2** to **10**) and much of Part II on 'special liability regimes'. The purpose of this chapter is to explore the origins of the modern law of negligence and to introduce you to some of the key themes underpinning the tort before outlining the essential ingredients of a claim in negligence.

2.2 Mapping the historical development of the tort of negligence

The tort of negligence is a relatively modern tort. Unlike trespass, which by the 1270s had begun to develop a 'more sharply focused legal meaning' (*Ibbetson* p 39), the general principle of negligence as liability for conduct falling below a particular standard of care was only fully articulated in the early twentieth century in the House of Lords' ground-breaking decision in ***Donoghue*** in the 1930s.

So-called 'internal histories' of the development of the tort of negligence expounded by academics and legal historians such as Percy Winfield, Bob Hepple and, more recently, *Ibbetson*, typically adhere to the following form.[3] Originally, negligence was understood *as a way of* committing and understanding other torts rather than as a distinctive tort in itself.[4] The tort of negligence was 'thoroughly fragmented' (*Ibbetson* p 188). A duty of

2. For more on ***Rothwell*** mentioned in the extract from Sales LJ's judgment and a useful counterpoint to *Dryden*, see **section 5.5**.

3. Percy H Winfield 'The History of Negligence in the Law of Torts' (1926a) 42 LQR 184; Bob Hepple 'Negligence: The Search for Coherence' (1997) 50 CLP 69.

4. Winfield (**n 3**).

care was recognised only in very limited circumstances—for example, if someone had control of some dangerous thing, say a gun, they had a duty of care to prevent it from causing harm (*Langridge* v *Levy* [1837])—and/or in the context of particular relationships, such as between innkeeper and guest. Thus, though throughout the nineteenth century there were isolated pockets of negligence liability, there was no general principle of negligence (*Winterbottom* v *Wright* [1842]).

As the century progressed these 'pockets' began to join up and by the end of the century the judges were beginning to move towards the articulation of a general principle of a duty of care. This can be seen in Brett MR's judgment in *Heaven* v *Pender* [1883]:

> Whenever one person is by circumstances placed in such a position with regard to another that every one of ordinary sense who did think would at once recognise that if he did not use ordinary care and skill in his own conduct with regard to those circumstances he would cause danger of injury to the person or property of the other, a duty arises to use ordinary care and skill to avoid such danger. (at 509)

However, by the time ***Donoghue*** reached the House of Lords in 1932, there was still no *general* principle of negligence in tort law. Private law thinking continued to be dominated by contractual understandings of responsibilities and obligations between parties. This meant that, outside the limited pockets of liability mentioned earlier, an individual owed a duty of care to another only in situations where *they had specifically agreed to do so*—usually through a contract. As a result many people who were injured through another's carelessness had no claim. Take, for example, the situation where a consumer is injured by a defective and dangerous product. A contract would exist between the manufacturer and whoever had bought the article from them, say a shop owner. There would also be a contract between the shop owner and the person to whom they had sold the article. This then enabled the shop owner to sue the manufacturer and the buyer to sue the shop owner. But the lack of any general tort of negligence, combined with the doctrine of privity of contract—which, broadly speaking, means that only the parties to a contract could sue or be sued under it—meant that the consumer would have no claim against the manufacturer, whose carelessness was the cause of their injuries but with whom they had no contract. Moreover, if the injury was suffered by someone other than the person who had bought the article, that person would have no claim against *anyone*, since they had no contractual relationship on which to ground it. This was the stumbling block facing the claimant in ***Donoghue***.[5]

Donoghue v *Stevenson* [1932] HL

Mrs Donoghue and a friend were enjoying a drink in a café in Paisley, near Glasgow. Mrs Donoghue had already consumed some of her ginger beer (bought by her friend) when said friend poured the remainder of the beer, from its dark opaque glass bottle, into a glass tumbler

→

5. The full title of this case in the Law Reports reads '*M'Alister (or Donoghue) (Pauper)* v *Stevenson*' reflecting the Scottish practice of referring to a married woman in legal documents by both her married and maiden surnames. The correct citation is that which states her married surname: Donoghue.

→

together with what appeared to be the remains of a decomposed snail. The shock of what she saw, together with the thought of what she had already drunk, led Mrs Donoghue to suffer shock and serious gastro-enteritis. She sought compensation for the shock and her illness from Stevenson, the manufacturer of the ginger beer, claiming that they were negligent in their production of the bottle of ginger beer. (She could not sue the café owner as, having not bought the drink, she had no contract with him on which to sue.) The difficulty was that Mrs Donoghue also appeared to have no legal relationship with the manufacturer either. This was not, Stevenson argued, a pocket of 'exceptional circumstances'—such as where a product was inherently dangerous—where a duty of care was recognised outside a contractual relationship.

Eventually the case made its way to the House of Lords where the law lords heard preliminary arguments on whether the alleged facts could give rise to a legal claim.[6] Three of the five law lords thought they did and allowed Mrs Donoghue's claim, sending the case back down to the lower courts to be decided on its facts. Ultimately, however, the case was settled out of court—one result of which is that in the absence of any findings of fact, which would only have happened at trial, it was never established whether there was *in fact* a snail in Mrs Donoghue's bottle of ginger beer.

Without doubt ***Donoghue*** was a landmark decision. But why does it remain so important? An answer lies in the combination of three separate aspects of the majority's decision (*Ibbetson* pp 190–1).

First, at its most narrow, ***Donoghue*** overruled *Winterbottom* v *Wright* [1842] and recognised the existence of a new 'pocket' of liability, that is a further, isolated, situation where a duty of care was owed outside a contractual relationship:

> [A] manufacturer of products, which he sells in such a form as to show that he intends them to reach the ultimate consumer in the form in which they left him with no reasonable possibility of immediate examination, and with the knowledge that the absence of reasonable care in the preparation or putting up of the product will result in injury to the consumer's life or property, owes a duty to the consumer to take that reasonable care. (Lord Atkin at 599)

This understanding of the case, consistent with the reasoning of Lords Thankerton and Macmillan (who were in the majority with Lord Atkin), was the one preferred at the time ***Donoghue*** was decided.

Secondly, and following on closely from this, the decision demonstrates that the 'categories of negligence are never closed' (Lord Macmillan at 619). In other words, the courts were prepared to recognise that new duty situations may arise, even if they are not necessarily closely analogous to previously recognised duties.

Finally, and most broadly, ***Donoghue*** can be seen to establish a single, universal requirement to take reasonable care articulated in Lord Atkin's 'neighbour principle'

6. This means they were not deciding whether Mrs Donoghue's claim succeeded but rather whether *in law* she had an arguable case.

(discussed later in the chapter). It is *this* aspect that ensured ***Donoghue***'s centrality in the tort of negligence.

The significance, and innovative reasoning, of the majority opinions in ***Donoghue*** can best be seen in contrast with the dissenting opinion of Lord Buckmaster, the most senior law lord present on a bench otherwise entirely comprised of law lords who had been appointed within the preceding five years. Rejecting any possibility of Mrs Donoghue's claim succeeding, he sought to restrict such claims to those who entered into a contractual relationship in line with (then) current practice. He went on to quote with approval from the judgment of Lord Anderson in *Mullen* v *Barr & Co* [1929]:

> where the goods of the defenders are widely distributed throughout Scotland, it would seem little short of outrageous to make [manufacturers] responsible to members of the public for the condition of the content of every bottle which issues from their works. (at 578)

The result of the majority's reasoning was that ***Donoghue*** in fact established for the first time—and at a time of huge expansion of the market in consumer goods—that a manufacturer could be held liable to the ultimate consumer of their goods.[7] Indeed, this expansion of liability beyond the contractual relationship and rejection of the so-called privity fallacy (which prevented tort claims where *any* contract existed between *any* of the parties) laid the crucial foundations for the subsequent developments in consumer protection.[8]

However, more fundamentally, Lord Atkin's opinion represented a watershed in the tort of negligence. Despite a preface to the contrary in which he said that '[t]o seek a complete logical definition of the general principle is probably to go beyond the function of the judge, for the more general the definition the more likely it is to omit essentials or to introduce non-essentials' (at 580), Lord Atkin's leading majority opinion provided the foundations of a general principle of negligence liability. Noting that the courts had previously been 'engaged upon an elaborate classification of duties' as they existed in various factual scenarios (at 579), he argued that 'the duty which is common to all the cases where liability is established must logically be based upon some element common to the cases where it is found to exist' (at 580).

Lord Atkin's neighbour principle

> It is hard to discuss the significance which judges and authors since 1932 have attached to the neighbour principle without writing the whole history of the tort of negligence. (Heuston 1957, p 14)

Lord Atkin was not the first judge to attempt to formulate a general principle of negligence liability in tort law. Almost 50 years earlier, Brett MR (latterly Lord Esher), in *Heaven* v *Pender* [1883] had articulated a broad test grounded in the concept of foreseeability and again, somewhat

→

7. Most notably in the opinion of Lord Macmillan (at 609–11).
8. See **section 12.2**.

→

more narrowly, in *Le Lievre* v *Gould* [1893] in which he said: 'If one man is near to another, or is near to the property of another, a duty lies upon him not to do that which may cause a personal injury to that other, or may injure his property' (at 509). It was this latter formulation which met with more judicial and academic support, and ultimately formed the basis of Lord Atkin's neighbour principle:

> The rule that you must love your neighbour becomes in law: You must not injure your neighbour, and the lawyer's question: Who is my neighbour? receives a restricted reply. You must take reasonable care to avoid acts or omissions which you can reasonably foresee would be likely to injure your neighbour. Who then in law is my neighbour? The answer seems to be—persons who are so closely and directly affected by my act that I ought reasonably to have them in contemplation as being so affected, when I am directing my mind to the acts or omissions which are called in question. (Lord Atkin, *Donoghue* at 580–1)

In short, an individual must take reasonable care to avoid injuring those they can (or should) reasonably foresee will be injured if they do not take such care. Though note, however, that Lord Atkin makes no reference to the specific type of damage in relation to which a duty of care may arise or to the way that damage may be caused.

Initially, despite the rhetorical flair of Lord Atkin's speech, it was Lord Macmillan's more measured approach (that limited the *ratio* of ***Donoghue*** to claims between manufacturers and consumers) that won the day. However, gradually thinking began to change and, by the 1970s, the tort of negligence had come to be seen as 'an ocean of liability for carelessly causing foreseeable harm, dotted with islands of non-liability, rather than as a crowded archipelago of individual duty situations' (*Ibbetson* pp 192–3). That is, rather than a gradual widening of specific duties, the courts appeared to be operating from a (perhaps excessively) broad principle of (almost) default liability wherever harm was caused by a defendant's careless conduct. See, for example, ***McLoughlin* v *O'Brian* [1982]** (in which a mother recovered for the pure psychiatric harm caused by witnessing the aftermath of a negligently caused accident involving her family); ***Anns* v *Merton London Borough Council* [1978]** (where the local authority was liable for negligently failing to supervise the construction of a building) (overruled by ***Murphy* v *Brentwood District Council* [1991]**); *Benarr* v *Kettering HA* [1988] (where the claimants were awarded damages for the costs of bringing up a child, including the private school fees, where a child was born after a negligently performed sterilisation procedure); and ***Home Office* v *Dorset Yacht Co Ltd* [1970]** (in which liability was imposed on the Home Office for damage inflicted by escaping young offenders).

Foreshadowing the 'compensation culture' claims of the late 1990s, it was increasingly being argued that far too many people were being made liable in too many situations. Thus throughout the 1980s and 1990s there was a general retrenchment of the tort of negligence, primarily by cutting back the situations in which a duty of care was held to arise (discussed in **section 3.2**). There was a move by the judiciary to keep the tort of negligence in check by exercising greater caution and imposing liability only where there were clear precedents to do so or by relatively small incremental steps (***Caparo Industries plc* v *Dickman*** [1990]). As such, negligence law appeared to have gone almost full circle. Rejecting a single general principle, the judges once more adopted a more restrictive approach to claims, working from established pockets of liability.

In the late 1990s, however, there was a small, but significant, shift of mood. The judicial retrenchment of the 1980s and early 1990s was gradually relaxed allowing for the expansion of negligence liability into a number of new situations—for example, in relation to the 'messed up lives' claims (e.g. ***Phelps* v *Hillingdon London Borough Council*** [2001] (negligent failure to diagnose dyslexia); *W* v *Essex County Council* [2000] (abusive foster child)). However more recently, the Supreme Court has once more reasserted the importance of the law developing incrementally (see ***Michael* v *Chief Constable of South Wales Police*** [2015]; ***Robinson* v *Chief Constable of West Yorkshire*** [2018]; ***Poole Borough Council* v *GN*** [2019]) which could yet be the first signs of a new period of retrenchment.

Pause for reflection

The tort of negligence, like all legal rules and principles, is not 'timeless' or 'ageless'. It is important to keep this in mind as you begin to read the cases and learn more about the law. No law exists or develops in a vacuum. The law of tort—including negligence—has been shaped by the political, social and economic context of the time in which various cases were decided. Just as a case cannot be considered in isolation from other cases, nor should it be considered in isolation from the political backdrop against which it was decided. Consider, for example, the deliberate reining in of tortious liability during the rampant individualism of the Thatcher years (1979–90), particularly in response to financial losses, or the impact of the unfortunate spate of significant public disasters—the sinking of the *Herald of Free Enterprise* in Zeebrugge harbour, the fire in the underground station at King's Cross, the destruction of the Piper Alpha oil rig, the Hillsborough Stadium disaster—on the development of recovery for negligently caused psychiatric injuries or of the environmental movement on the torts of nuisance or trespass to land.

see online resources

2.3 Explaining the historical development of the tort of negligence

The historical map described earlier provides an important backdrop to the development of the tort of negligence and a starting point from which to begin to understand and contextualise contemporary debates and difficulties within it. It also suggests, contrary to some accounts, that the development of the tort of negligence was not seamless, nor can it be regarded as inevitable or logically necessary. As *Conaghan & Mansell* point out, there is a tendency to paint a picture of this process of development by which:

> Negligence emerges from the chaos of the discredited writ system to form a new order based on the apparent self-evident soundness of the principle of reasonable

> care . . . Nineteenth-century judges are presented as moving 'subconsciously' towards the negligence principle while scarcely aware of it, directed inexorably and unerringly by the demands of logic and reason. (*Conaghan & Mansell* p 88)

So, just as interesting and certainly as, if not more, important as *what* happened is *why* it happened—why did negligence triumph as a principle of liability? What was its intended (as opposed to actual) function? What effect, if any, did the values and influences of the society from which this 'new' tort emerged have on its form and structure? Why did this fledgling tort prioritise 'fault' over the more historically commonplace strict liability?

A number of arguments have been made in the academic literature. We will, following *Conaghan & Mansell*, look briefly at three:

(1) The influence of social and political thinking in an age of principles.

(2) A positive response to victims of workplace injuries.

(3) Strategic economic subsidisation of infant industries.[9]

2.3.1 The influence of social and political thinking in an age of principles

G Edward White, in his book *Tort Law in America—An Intellectual Tradition*, points to the importance of nineteenth-century intellectual trends and changing jurisprudential thought in reshaping the tort of negligence.[10] In the nineteenth century increased classification, conceptualisation and individualism were the order of the day—after all if, *Conaghan and Mansell* suggest, Charles Darwin had uncovered the hidden order of the natural and social worlds (*On the Origin of Species* was published in 1859) why, the 'lawyer-intellectuals' argued, should the same not be true for the legal world? Theorists in the United States took the lead,[11] until 1887—some 45 years *before* ***Donoghue***—when Sir Frederick Pollock attempted to articulate a general theory of English tort law in his textbook *The Law of Torts*.

In a similar vein, Patrick Atiyah has drawn attention to the overlap between the fault principle and the individualistic principles of Victorian society and liberal individualism.[12] The prioritisation of individual responsibility and minimal state interference meant that the fault principle was far more attractive than the strict imposition of liability for all injuries caused by one's actions. The fault principle, Atiyah argues, is liberal individualism made into law. No one is responsible for the fate of others unless there is a positive reason for making them so. One such reason is the responsibilities arising out of a contract, another is where the individual is at fault (the fact that they could have chosen to act in another way, and thereby avoided creating a risk of harm, is sufficient to establish liability).

9. For a more detailed exploration of the arguments outlined here, the best place to start is *Conaghan & Mansell*'s excellent discussion and critique of 'Historical Perspectives on Negligence', pp 81–104.

10. G Edward White *Tort Law in America—An Intellectual Tradition* (OUP, 2003, originally published in 1980), p 3.

11. Francis Hilliard *The Law of Torts* (2 vols, 1859); and Oliver Wendell Holmes 'Theory of Torts' (1873) 7 Am L Rev 652.

12. Patrick Atiyah *The Rise and Fall of Freedom of Contract* (Clarendon Press, 1979).

2.3.2 **A positive response to victims of workplace injuries**

Other commentators stress the importance of increased industrialisation in the development of the tort of negligence: 'the explosion of torts law and negligence in particular must be entirely attributed to the age of engines and machines.'[13] However, opinions differ on the precise nature of this causal connection.

On one view the development of the tort of negligence was a positive response to the victims of industrialisation and a way of shifting the loss from one party to another at a time when there was little or no state support or system of insurance. The development of railways, roads, factories, mines, quarries and such like had not only led to a vast rise in the numbers of accidents, but also to changes in the nature of the relationship between the claimant and the defendant. Accidental injuries between strangers—in both the everyday and legal sense—were increasingly becoming the norm. Increasing mass production made it less likely that individuals would have a direct, contractual relationship with the manufacturer or producer of the goods they used. Whereas requiring them to establish a special relationship with those who injured them would have significantly restricted their ability to recover, the recognition of these claims within the scope of the new general duty of care facilitated the expansion of liability.

2.3.3 **Supporting infant industries**

The opposing view is that liability was *restricted* by the courts during the industrial period, and the fault principle prioritised, in order to protect and nurture fledging industries.[14] The essential basis of liability of tort in the eighteenth century had been strict liability.[15] This meant that though liability only arose in limited circumstances, where it did wrongdoers were liable for all injuries their actions caused even if they were not at fault. In other words, the development of the tort of negligence, and particularly the primacy of fault, was instrumental: had the new industries been held to the earlier strict standard, Morton Horwitz argues, the ensuing liability would have seriously impaired their growth and development. Thus, far from being a humane response to personal injuries, the development of the fault principle within the tort of negligence was, *Conaghan & Mansell* conclude, an attempt by the courts to protect new industries from the crippling liability that would have followed had strict liability been imposed (p 91). Instead, they had to pay[16] only when the victim established 'fault' on the part of the defendant, which was not easy to do.

This view gains some support from the doctrine of common employment, which, until its abolition by the Law Reform (Personal Injuries) Act 1948, prevented claims by employees against their employers for injuries sustained at work where their injury was

13. Lawrence Friedmann *A History of American Law* (Simon & Schuster, 1972), p 261.

14. Morton Horwitz *The Transformation of American Law, 1780–1860* (Harvard University Press, 1977).

15. Although cf Winfield's criticism of this (Percy H Winfield 'The Myth of Absolute Liability' (1926) 41 LQR 437).

16. For a contemporary version of this debate see discussion of the Enterprise and Regulatory Reform Act 2013 in **section 14.2**.

caused by other employees.[17] Similarly, the defence of contributory negligence, until the Law Reform (Contributory Negligence) Act 1945, acted as an absolute bar to recovery in cases where the defendant was able to show that the claimant had (however slightly) contributed to their own injury.

Counterpoint

It is, of course, possible to respond to Horwitz's arguments with the more balanced suggestion that while insofar as liability is fault-based (as opposed to strict), then this does represent a lowering of the protection offered to an individual, a broad principle of negligence makes this (albeit) lower standard available to a greater number of people. If the courts were really concerned with insulating industry from legal liability, then it would have had no reason for expanding tort law in general, and the tort of negligence in particular, *at all*.

2.4 **The role of the modern law of negligence**

Today, despite greater state support for accident victims through social security payments and the NHS, the tort of negligence retains its place as the primary legal mechanism of accident compensation for personal injuries in the UK.[18] Moreover, alongside its role in determining compensation for accident victims, negligence—often treated as synonymous with 'accident law'—plays an important role in the *prevention* of accidents. The threat of a hefty compensation payout can have significant deterrent effects.[19] Unlike social security or other accident compensation schemes, awards of damages following a successful tort claim are (at least notionally) paid by the defendant responsible for inflicting the relevant harm.[20]

Despite its loss-shifting credentials, the tort of negligence operates more frequently as a loss-*spreading* device. Although the loss is shifted from the accident victim, the increasing availability of liability insurance means that it rarely falls on the individual defendant directly (indeed it is rarely worth suing an uninsured defendant, although the National Lottery-winning defendant in ***A* v *Hoare* [2008]** may be an exception). Rather, it is shifted once again to the defendant's insurance company and, from there, spread across all those who have, and shall take out, policies with the company:

> Thus from the very outset negligence proves paradoxical. The goal to which it claims to aspire (loss shifting on the grounds of fault), it rarely attains and the idea against which it stands in opposition (loss spreading among those who are not at fault), is its most commonplace effect. (*Conaghan & Mansell* pp 12–13)

17. Though the effects of this doctrine were somewhat reduced by the introduction of the Workmen's Compensation Act 1897.

18. See **section 21.6** and generally *Cane*.

19. On the deterrence aspect of tort law, see further *Harlow* pp 37–41 and **section 1.3.3**.

20. Though, it should be noted that there are exceptions to this—see, in particular, the discussion of vicarious liability in **Chapter 20**.

We may consider that this move away from the fault principle is no bad thing. Presumably, an increased use of insurance will mean that claims are met by those in the best position to pay with the result that more claims are likely to be met and more claimants are able to recover.

Pause for reflection

The fact that in many instances it is not the 'wrongdoer' who ends up compensating the claimant seems to clash significantly with the tort of negligence's intellectual and moral underpinnings (*Ibbetson* pp 196–9). But where does the responsibility for this lie? Could it perhaps—as suggested by Lord Sumption—lie with the centrality of traditional notions of fault?

> Personally, I would question whether there really is a moral case for imposing liability in damages on the ground of negligence. One might perhaps make an exception for professional failures where the defendant has undertaken to exercise an appropriate measure of care and the relationship with the victim, although not actually contractual, is equivalent to contract. Except in that situation, negligence is not morally culpable. It is a normal feature of human behaviour. . . . I can imagine a moral case for imposing an absolute liability on those who cause physical damage to others, simply on the ground that they are the agents of some invasion of the victim's physical integrity. That was the basis of the more limited and now largely redundant tort of trespass to the person.[21] I can also imagine a moral case for imposing liability on those who intentionally or recklessly cause physical damage to others. But liability for negligence does not depend on a person's mere infliction of damage, nor on his state of mind. It depends on his falling below some objective standard of conduct to which he has not usually assented, but which the law imposes upon him. It seems to me that the only possible justification for the law doing that is its social utility. Yet the arbitrary results and incomplete coverage of a fault-based system, combined with its prodigious cost and unwelcome side-effects, seriously undermine the social utility of the law of tort as a way of dealing with personal injury.[22]

Do you agree? Think again about the purposes of tort law discussed in **Chapter 1**.

2.5 The elements of the tort of negligence

The tort of negligence is, according to Percy H Winfield's enduring definition, 'the breach of a legal duty to take care by an inadvertent act or omission that injures another'.[23] His threefold presentation remains the mainstay of most tort textbooks and neatly

21. See **Chapter 15**. 22. Sumption 2017.

23. Winfield (**n 3**) 184. You should note now, however, that the tort of negligence is not limited to acts of inadvertence. Deliberate infliction of harms can also give rise to liability in the tort of negligence.

encapsulates the three essential elements of the tort. Thus, in order to establish a successful claim in the tort of negligence there needs to be:

(1) a legal *duty* owed by the defendant to the claimant to take care;

(2) a *breach* of this duty by the defendant; and

(3) damage to the claimant, *caused* by the breach, which is not considered by the courts to be too remote.

A number of preliminary points need to be made here before looking at each of these elements in more detail.

First, the defendant may be able to raise a *defence* which may either defeat the claim entirely or reduce the amount of damages paid.[24] Secondly, each element of a negligence claim is necessary, but not sufficient, in order to establish liability. Without a recognised legal duty of care between the defendant and claimant, for example, no liability will attach to even the most extreme acts of neglect; similarly, if no damage is caused by the defendant's breach of their duty of care—or if the damage caused is too remote—the defendant will not be liable.

Finally, in any given claim there may be more than one defendant, as well as multiple claimants. Where two or more parties act together in pursuit of a common design or plan and cause the same damage, each will be *jointly and severally liable*. This means that the claimant may choose to sue each party separately for the entirety of the damage or sue both jointly in the same action.[25] *Several concurrent* liability arises where the negligent actions of two or more parties acting independently cause the same damage—for example, where the claimant's car is hit by two cars both causing the claimant to suffer whiplash.[26] In this case, as with joint defendants, each party is liable separately for the entirety of the damage (although the claimant can only recover once). The distinction between the two types of defendant is largely historical; there is, in fact, very little substantive or practical difference between joint and several defendants. At other times, the defendant may be someone relatively distant from the facts of the case, but nonetheless—by virtue of their relationship to the tortfeasor—is vicariously liable for their actions.[27]

2.5.1 **Duty**

A defendant will only be liable for their carelessness if they owe the claimant a legal duty to take care. Carelessness alone (however great) is not enough:

> The law takes no cognizance of carelessness in the abstract. It concerns itself with carelessness only where there is a duty to take care and where failure in that duty has caused damage. (Lord Macmillan, ***Donoghue*** at 618)

The existence (or otherwise) of a duty of care is sometimes described as a control mechanism, by which the courts are able to restrict or extend the reach of negligence liability. That does not mean, however, that the courts exercise this control in every

24. See **Chapter 10**.

25. The Civil Liability (Contribution) Act 1978 allows the court to apportion damages between the parties responsible (or leave them to do this for themselves). See further **section 21.4**.

26. See e.g. *Fitzgerald* v *Lane* [1987].

27. See **Chapter 20**.

case. In the vast majority of cases, establishing a duty will be straightforward, with the law already making clear, unequivocal provision for duties of care in such situation. It is, for example, well established that a car driver owes a duty of care to other road users and that a doctor owes a duty of care to patients in their care (*Pippin* v *Sheppard* [1822]). Claims arising in these sorts of familiar contexts may yet raise difficult questions of fact and law—Has the duty been breached? Was the loss a result of the breach? Is there an available defence?—but the existence of the duty will not be one of them.

However, occasionally—but significantly—a court will have to consider whether a duty of care is, or should be, owed on the facts. Despite the broad statement of Lord Atkin in ***Donoghue***, the courts have latterly placed significant limitations on the situations in which a duty to take care will arise.[28] This is particularly apparent in what might be called 'problematic' duty areas—for example, where the injury suffered by the claimant is purely psychiatric or economic, where the defendant is a public body, where the harm is caused by someone for whom the defendant was responsible (acts of third parties) or where injury is suffered as a result of the defendant's failure to act (an omission) rather than a 'positive' action. In these areas, the courts in an effort to contain liability have typically held either that there is no duty on the part of the defendants or have severely restricted its scope (often citing 'public policy' reasons or justifications). In this way, the courts employ the concept of the duty of care as a means to *deny* liability (often in the context of significant carelessness) where they consider that it would be inappropriate to hold the defendant liable.

2.5.2 **Breach**

To say that the defendant owes a duty of care is also to say that their conduct must meet a certain standard—the standard of 'reasonable care'. Accordingly, a defendant will breach their duty of care where their conduct falls below the standard the law has set. The requirement that a defendant will be liable in the tort of negligence only where they have failed to exercise reasonable care suggests that negligence liability is both premised and dependent upon *fault*. It is not enough to show that the defendant has harmed the claimant—liability depends on the defendant having harmed the claimant *as a result of failing to show reasonable care*.

> The fault principle lies at the heart of the tort of negligence. It works in two ways: first . . . a person who causes loss or damage to another by fault should be required to compensate that other; and, secondly, . . . a person who causes loss or damage to another without fault should *not* be required to compensate that other. (*Cane* p 35)

However, though most would agree that liability should follow where fault is present, the converse is more problematic. The principle of 'no liability without fault' works well for defendants. It is, however, less attractive for claimants who, in the absence of fault, may be left to bear the entirety of their losses.

Finally, we may note that, since negligence in law is a failure to meet a standard of care, 'negligence' here does not describe a particular state of mind but rather the 'quality' of their conduct. A defendant who deliberately runs over a claimant with their car is just as negligent—in the sense of having failed to show reasonable care for the claimant—as one who inadvertently runs down the claimant because they are distracted by choosing a new track on their iPod.

28. See **Chapter 3**.

Pause for reflection

Though it is useful to talk about negligence law being fault-based, the concept of fault employed in the tort of negligence is a *legal*, and not necessarily a *moral*, standard. Only certain moral 'wrongs' give rise to liability in tort. Hence, it is possible to deliberately walk past an unknown child drowning in a puddle without (usually) fearing any *legal* consequences (see **section 4.2**). At other times, liability will attach in the tort of negligence to people whom most would consider in no way morally culpable (see e.g. ***Nettleship*** **v *Weston*** [1971]). Moreover, even where those liable in negligence are morally blameworthy, the consequences of liability can appear entirely disproportionate to their moral blame. A single, momentary lapse of concentration may lead to extraordinary legal culpability (*Cane* p 175).

2.5.3 **Causation and remoteness**

The final element of a claim in the tort of negligence is causation—the damage suffered by the claimant must have been *caused* by the defendant's breach of their duty. The claimant must prove not only that the defendant was at fault (that they breached their duty of care) and that they suffered a recognisable harm, but also that this was *as a result* of the defendant's actions—that is, that there is a causal link between the defendant's fault and the damage caused, which means both that the defendant factually *caused* the claimant's loss (factual causation) and that the loss caused is not too *remote* (sometimes called legal causation). This is not as straightforward as one might think. What constitutes a causal link in the tort of negligence is often a difficult question to answer.

2.5.4 **Putting it all together**

Establishing liability in the tort of negligence breaks down into three questions:

(1) Does the defendant owe the claimant a *duty of care*?

(2) Has the defendant *breached this duty* by falling below the required standard of care in the circumstances of the case? (Or, more roughly, is the defendant at fault?)

(3) Is the defendant's breach of their duty both the factual and legal *cause* of the claimant's injury?

To this can be added a fourth question:

(4) Is the defendant able to raise any partial or full *defences* to the claimant's action?

The elements of the tort of negligence

Duty + Breach + (Causation – Remoteness) – Defences = The tort of negligence

We will look at each of these questions in turn in Part I of this book; however, it is important to recognise from the outset that the elements of the tort of negligence are not as self-contained as Winfield's checklist suggests.

Counterpoint

The presentation of the tort in this way is theoretically problematic—it suggests the elements to the tort of negligence have clearer boundaries than they actually have. In fact, as we shall see, certain ideas and concepts—notably foreseeability—crop up at a number of different stages, and cut across these supposedly distinct elements. Moreover, this linear presentation of the elements of a negligence claim suggests a logic and consistency of approach which, some argue, fails to represent what the courts actually do, and the reasoning they really employ when deciding cases. Indeed, at times the judges have admitted as much:

> The more I think about these cases, the more difficult I find it to put each into its proper pigeon-hole. Sometimes I say: 'There was no duty.' In others I say: 'The damage was too remote.' So much so that I think the time has come to discard those tests which have proved so elusive. (Lord Denning MR, *Spartan Steel* v *Martin & Co* [1973] at 37)

It may be that Lord Denning is overstating things somewhat. These basic elements of duty, breach and causation are not simply interchangeable and they all tell us something, and indeed something different. Moreover, even if Lord Denning is right to say that there are times in which the same result can be presented in different ways, it is highly doubtful that *all* cases in which a claim is denied can be repackaged in the way he suggests. Nonetheless, it does help to bring out that those looking for a clear equation which determines when liability in negligence arises are likely to be left empty-handed. The tests and elements developed by the courts to analyse and decide such claims are not empty, but nor are they (at least in practice) concrete, clear and distinct.

Finally, it is worth stressing that insofar as we can meaningfully distinguish the various elements of a negligence claim, though each—duty, breach, causation—is essential for a claim to succeed, they are not always *all* at issue. For instance, as we have mentioned, often duty is straightforward (e.g. in relation to road traffic accidents), but at other times it is more problematic (e.g. in relation to claims for psychiatric injury). Similarly, while it is clear that the speeding driver (absent exceptional circumstances, such as transporting an accident victim) will usually be in breach of their duty of care, it may be more difficult to establish, for example, the appropriate standard of care required of a doctor in any given case and a causal link between the doctor's actions and the harm suffered by the claimant. Put another way, the legal 'hurdles' of duty, breach and causation may be easier or harder for the claimant to scale depending on the facts of the case. An example may help here:

FIGURE 2.1 Case example: ***Bolton* v *Stone* [1951]**

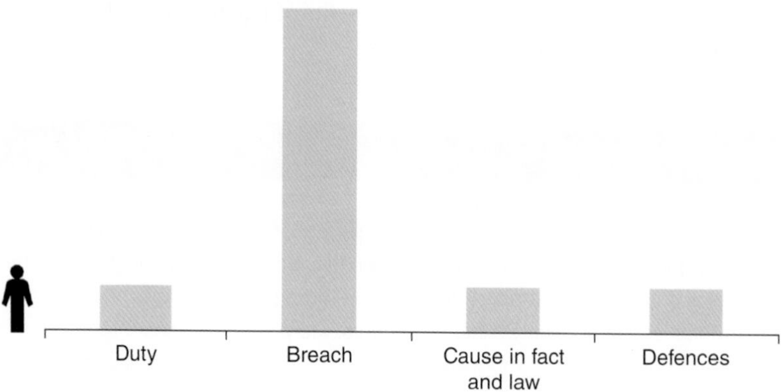

Bolton v *Stone* [1951] HL

In *Bolton* v *Stone* the claimant was hit on the head outside her house by a cricket ball hit by a player from an adjacent cricket pitch. It was clear that the defendant cricket club owed her a duty of care not to cause her physical injury. Moreover, there was no doubt that it was because of their activities—allowing cricket to be played at the ground—that the claimant suffered her injury. The key question for the court was one of breach—had the defendant fallen below the appropriate standard of care? Was, for example, the fence high enough? How often did cricket balls come over it? What damage was likely to be caused if they did? What were the costs of reducing the chances of this happening? The focus of the case was on the breach stage, with the duty and causation questions being more straightforward (see **Figure 2.1**).

Pause for reflection

The purpose of this very simple diagram is simply to illustrate the varying importance of, or difficulty in establishing, each element of the tort of negligence.[29] Of course, this diagram cannot convey the details of the case and it is not intended to be in any way mathematical. Its aim is purely to give the reader a general impression of the relative importance of each 'hurdle'. Though in *every* case each element of the tort must be present for the claim to succeed, typically only one or two are likely to be at issue. The uncontroversial aspects of the case will be glossed over relatively quickly.[30] You may find it helpful as you begin thinking about the tort of negligence to consider where the 'hurdle' or 'hurdles' arise in the cases you are reading and what a similarly constructed diagram of these cases would look like.

29. We have included further diagrams in the additional content that appears on the **online resources**—*Introduction to the tort of negligence: putting it together.*

30. The same is often true of problem question scenarios, which will typically (for pragmatic reasons such as word or time constraints) focus on a particular 'hurdle' or 'hurdles'. However, in our view, a complete answer will address each element, albeit with varying levels of detail.

2.6 Case example: *X & Y* v *London Borough of Hounslow*

In order for there to be a successful claim in the tort of negligence duty, breach and causation must be established. This is clearly demonstrated in ***X & Y* v *London Borough of Hounslow*** [2008]. Though the decision of Maddison J was not the end of the story for the claimants in this case,[31] his judgment remains an excellent example of how the ingredients of a negligence claim fit together. For this reason we have annotated in **Figure 2.2** *the first instance judgment*, making reference to the Court of Appeal judgment and the final outcome (see comments in bold).[32]

Pause for reflection

In his comment on *X and Y* Richard Mullender notes:

> The body of negligence doctrine applied by Maddison J and the Court of Appeal in *X and Y* is fraught with tension. Judges are sensitive to the demands of corrective justice . . . But judges are also aware that they may, by imposing liability on public bodies, deflect them from the pursuit of the public interest . . . [Both] were at work in *X and Y*. The Court of Appeal's response was to read the relevant doctrine narrowly and to emphasise the Council's many responsibilities to the public . . . [The alternative was to conclude] that the close relationship between the couple and the Council made them neighbours in Lord Atkin's sense. (p 509)

X & Y is then also an excellent example of the differing priorities of judges and the way in which legal rules can be interpreted to reach very different conclusions depending on their understanding of the issues at stake. Mullender suggests the Court of Appeal's decision ought to be understood in a context in which the growth of the welfare state is such that 'neighbourliness is a luxury that society cannot afford' (p 509). Do you think Maddison J would agree with Mullender's view?

31. Though the claimants were successful at first instance, this decision was overturned by the Court of Appeal. The legal issues raised by this case, and the Court of Appeal judgment (*X & Y* v *London Borough of Hounslow* [2009]), are discussed further in **section 6.7.2**. Permission to appeal to the House of Lords was refused. However, the claimants (and 'Z', X's mother) took their case to the European Court of Human Rights (ECtHR) alleging violations of Arts 3, 6, 8 and 13. But no ruling ever came. In 2011, the parties settled upon an agreement waiving any further claims against the UK. In light of this, it seems likely that the ECtHR was disposed to find that the local authority's actions had violated the human rights of their tenants, rendering the Court of Appeal's decision all the more unsatisfactory.

32. For a concise summary and discussion of the different approaches adopted by the trial judge and Court of Appeal see Richard Mullender 'Negligence, Neighbourliness, and the Welfare State' [2009] CLJ 507.

FIGURE 2.2 Annotated first instance judgment

X & Y (Protected parties represented by their litigation friend the Official Solicitor) v London Borough of Hounslow

An officer of the Supreme Court who acts for people with disabilities (see Senior Courts Act 1981, s 90).

High Court of Justice Queen's Bench Division [2008] EWHC 1168 (QB)

The claimants, X and Y, are claiming damages against the defendants, the London Borough of Hounslow, in the tort of negligence and under sections 6 and 7 of the Human Rights Act 1998. The claims arose out of an 'ordeal' which the claimants suffered in their council flat at the hands of local youths in November 2000 where, over the course of a weekend, the claimants (both of whom had learning difficulties) were imprisoned in their flat and repeatedly assaulted and (sexually) abused (often in front of their two children). This account of the facts is taken from Maddison J's judgment:

These claims were not revived in the Court of Appeal (at [36]). This is surprising given the decision to appeal to the ECtHR and, ultimately, to settle (which suggests that the ECtHR was expected to have found a violation of the claimants' human rights).

Note the date of the incident—compared with the date of trial—2007—and with the final resolution of the case in 2011.

[5]...X said that at one stage the youths confined him and Y to their bedroom, and made them perform sexual acts. They threw many of X's and Y's possessions over the balcony. They forced pepper and fluid into X's eyes. They locked him in the bathroom for a time, in the dark. They made him drink urine, eat dog biscuits, dog faeces and the faeces of one of the youths, threatening him that he would be stabbed if he did not. They made him put a vibrator up his bottom, and then lick it. They sprayed kitchen cleaner in his mouth, face and hair. They slashed him repeatedly all over his body with a knife or knives. Y's statement was to similar effect, adding that she too was made to put the vibrator in her mouth. The children too were abused, assaulted and locked in their bedroom from time to time. Even the family dog was abused. It is unnecessary to go into further detail, or into the physical and psychological injuries suffered by the claimants as a result.

The claimants argued that, amongst other things, the defendant should have foreseen that they were in imminent physical danger at their flat and should have arranged for them to be accommodated elsewhere. The claimants and their family were known to the defendants. Although they lived as a unit in the community, the family was seen as vulnerable and two sections of the defendant's Social Services Department had been engaged with the family prior to the relevant weekend. These were the Community Team for People with Learning Disabilities ('CTPLD') and the Children and Families section ('C & F').

The defendant strongly contested liability. They denied they owed the claimants a duty of care, pointing out that in no previous case had a local authority been held to be under a duty of care to protect vulnerable adults

→

from abuse by third parties and that any failings in this regard are only justiciable, if at all, within the forum of public law, and not by way of actions for damages of the kind brought here. Still less, argued the defendant, did it breach any such duty of care: what happened during the relevant weekend was caused by third parties, and was not reasonably foreseeable.

Essentially what the defendants are arguing is that the court is not in a position to judge or adjudicate on the case—that it falls outside its remit. See further on justiciability **section 6.6.1**.

This is true. The 'public bodies' chapter **(Chapter 6)** is one of the longest, and most complicated, chapters in this book.

After setting out the background to the case in detail, Mr Justice Maddison turned to the law:

The Law

[84] The liability of local authorities in negligence and under the Human Rights Act 1998 and the European Convention on Human Rights is a complex and developing area of the law. It is perhaps for this reason that I have been referred by Counsel to well over 40 authorities. I have found some helpful, but by no means all. In one of them, *Midland Bank Trust Co Ltd and Another* v *Hett Stubbs & Kemp (a firm)* [1979] 1 Ch 384 at 405B Oliver J said

> I have been led by counsel through a bewildering complex of authorities many of which are not easily reconciled with the principles established in subsequent cases in superior courts or, in some cases, with one another. The task of a judge of the first instance faced with this situation is not an easy one.

That observation, with which I sympathise, has provided some relief and comfort during my trawl of the authorities cited to me. Otherwise, I have not found the *Midland Bank* case helpful.

This is the leading case on establishing a duty of care in *novel* areas of the tort of negligence, that is where existing precedent doesn't settle whether a duty is owed.

Establishing a duty of care is the first element of any claim in the tort of negligence.

The Test to be Applied

[85] I first consider the test that should be applied to determine whether or not the Defendant owed the Claimants a duty of care. I have been taken to authorities in which it has been observed that the courts may be prepared to find that a duty of care exists more readily in cases involving injury or damage to person or property than in those involving only economic loss. (See e.g. ***Caparo Industries Ltd* v *Dickman*** [1990] 2 AC 605 at page 618, per Lord Bridge.) I have also been referred to authorities illustrating that important if not determinative factors in deciding whether or not a duty of care exists may be the assumption by the defendant concerned of responsibility toward the claimant concerned (see e.g. ***Hedley Byrne* v *Heller & Partners*** [1964] AC 465) or the degree of proximity between the parties (see e.g. *Perrett* v *Collins* [1998] 2 Lloyd's Rep 255 at page 261 per Hobhouse LJ). In the event, I do not need to consider such authorities in any detail because, at the conclusion of the oral argument, counsel appeared to accept that the proper test to apply in this case was the familiar tri-partite test deriving from the ***Caparo*** case referred to above. I agree with this approach. Given that I am dealing, as stated above,

'per' here means that the principle or dictum is quoted on 'the authority of' (that is, can be found in) Lord Bridge's opinion.

It is worth noting here that Sir Anthony Clarke MR in the Court of Appeal did not approach the case in this way. Rather, he adopted the incremental approach (as endorsed by *Robinson* v *Chief Constable of West Yorkshire* [2018]) and sought to develop existing case law that focused on whether the defendants had 'assumed responsibility' for the claimants noting that this claim falls outside cases where the courts have previously imposed negligence liability at ([60]). (see further section 3.3.3)

In fact, as the Supreme Court in ***Robinson*** confirms, the court in ***Caparo* [1990]** did not seek to set out the general three-stage 'test' described here. See further **section 3.3**.

→

This is good example of the 'confusion' as to the effect of ***Caparo*** referred to by Lord Reed in ***Poole Borough Council*** v ***GN*** [2019]:

'Confusion also persisted concerning the effect of ***Caparo*** until clarification was provided in ***Michael*** [2015] and ***Robinson***. The long shadow cast by ***Anns*** [1978] and the misunderstanding of ***Caparo*** have to be borne in mind when considering the reasoning of decisions concerned with the liabilities of public authorities in negligence which date from the intervening period. Although the decisions themselves are generally consistent with the principles explained in *Gorringe* [2004] and later cases and can be rationalised on that basis, their reasoning has in some cases, and to varying degrees, been superseded by those later developments.' (at [34]).

with a difficult and developing area of the law, and given that no previous case has established that a local authority owes a duty of care to adults in circumstances such as those arising in this case, I think it right that I should find that a duty of care existed only if I am satisfied that the injury and loss suffered by the Claimants was reasonably foreseeable; that their relationship with the Defendant was sufficiently proximate to warrant the imposition of the duty of care; and that it would be just, fair and reasonable to impose such a duty.

[Maddison J then established that the defendant could be treated as a single entity.]

This aspect of Maddison J's judgment was rejected by the Court of Appeal (at [67]).

Was the Injury and Loss Reasonably Foreseeable?

[93] I therefore turn to consider whether the Defendant should reasonably have foreseen the injury and loss which the Claimants suffered. The authorities cited to me establish that the Claimants must show that it was reasonably foreseeable that they would suffer an assault by local youths at their home of the general kind that actually happened; but need not show that the Defendant should have envisaged 'the precise concatenation of circumstances' which led up to the incident (see *Hughes* v *Lord Advocate* [1963] AC 837 at p 853 per Lord Morris) or the precise form the assault would take (see by way of analogy ***Jolley* v *London Borough of Sutton*** [2000] 1 WLR 1082). The fact that the injury and loss resulted from the acts of third parties would not by itself prevent that injury and loss from being foreseeable but it would be reasonable to expect someone to foresee such third party intervention only if it was highly likely or probable (see e.g. *Smith* v *Littlewoods Organisation Ltd* ([1987] 1 AC 241 at p 261 E to G per Lord Mackay of Clashfern).

In order for the injury to be reasonably foreseeable it must be of the same general kind. This is clarified in relation to the acts of third parties in the next sentence. We discuss issues relating to the establishment of a duty of care for the acts of third parties in more detail in **Chapter 4**.

[94] The chronology of events . . . seems to me to paint a picture of gradually mounting concern about the welfare and safety of the Claimants and their family. It is true that in some respects the Claimants could lead normal lives. It is also true that they were anxious to preserve their independence, to the extent that they sometimes resented and resisted the efforts of the Defendant's Social Services Department to help them. However, the repeated concerns, expressed by Z and the Defendant's own Social Services Department about the Claimants' vulnerability, their ability to keep themselves and their children safe, the unsuitability of their home and the condition in which they kept it, the way in which the children were being looked after, and the suspicion that the children had been sexually abused by others, tell their own story. In addition, there was information from Z that X had been attacked from time to time both in Wandsworth and Hounslow; and although there may have been times when the Defendant regarded Z as a thorn in its side, I see no reason why the information she provided should have been seen as unreliable.

'Z' is X's mother—now in her 80s.

[95] In my judgment, these mounting concerns made it reasonably foreseeable from an early stage that the Claimants and/or the children might in some manner come to some sort of harm. However, despite the number and variety of different concerns and the frequency with which they were expressed, they would not in my judgment be sufficient to satisfy the first of the three ***Caparo*** conditions as explained . . . above. What needs to be asked is whether, and if so when, events gathered pace to the extent that the harm that was reasonably foreseeable changed from harm of a general ill-defined

This seems to suggest foreseeability.

→

→

nature to harm resulting from an attack of the kind that happened during the relevant weekend. In my judgment, this development did indeed take place, and the events that made critical difference began early in September 2000. They took the form of the infiltration and ultimately the taking-over of the Claimants' flat by local youths; the development of a state of disorder and then of chaos or near-chaos at the flat; the assault on X at McDonalds; the making of threats to the Claimants; the obtaining of keys to the flat by youths who did not live there; and the reluctance of the Claimants through fear to complain about what was happening to them. That is not to say that the events occurring before September 2000 are irrelevant. Though insufficient by themselves in my view to establish the required degree of foreseeability, they did provide the background against which the events occurring in and after September 2000 could and should have been considered and assessed. [. . .]

However, in order for the claimant's injury to be 'reasonably foreseeable' it must be established that the defendants had (or should have had) *more* than a general awareness that the family might come to some sort of harm. That is, the defendants must have been aware of the possibility of the claimants suffering a serious physical assault.

[The judge then went on to detail the incidents of violence and intimidation against the claimants (known to the defendants) between September and November 2000.]

[106] . . . it was in my judgment reasonably, indeed clearly foreseeable that either or both of the Claimants would suffer a serious physical attack from local youths in their flat. In my judgment the danger of this happening should have been foreseen at the very latest by 7th November when, to the Defendant's knowledge, the prior assaults, threats, infiltration of the Claimants' home, dumping of stolen goods and arrests had been followed by the variety of complaints from neighbours referred to above. However, in my judgment it could and should reasonably have been foreseen by 20th October when Tajinder Hayre's letter of 18th October was received by the Defendant's Housing Department, given what was already known to the Defendant by then.

One of the claimants' social workers.

Was there a Relationship of Sufficient Proximity?

[107] The Claimants having thus cleared the first hurdle, as it were, I consider whether they and the Defendant were in a relationship sufficiently proximate to warrant the imposition of the duty of care. In my judgment they were, for reasons that can be explained comparatively briefly. The Defendant was the Claimants' landlord. More importantly, the Defendant, aware of the Claimants' disabilities, provided social services for them and indeed for their children. [. . .]

Note the Court of Appeal disagreed with this aspect of Maddison J's judgment.

Just, Fair and Reasonable

This aspect was considered by the Court of Appeal (at [91]–[93]) which held that: 'Given our view that there was here no relevant assumption of responsibility or other considerations such as those discussed in the *Gorringe* [relating to statutory duties] and *Mitchell* [2009] cases we have reached a different conclusion on the question whether it would be fair, just and reasonable to impose a duty of care of the kind suggested on the council. We do not think that it would' (at [93]).

[108] I therefore turn to consider whether it would be just fair and reasonable to impose a duty of care on the Defendant. It is convenient to begin by considering the scope of the duty contended for. The more widely based this is, the more difficult it might be to argue that it would be just, fair and reasonable to impose it.

This essentially allows the court to consider matters of policy etc that might weigh against (or for) there being a duty of care.

This is a point not often acknowledged—the narrower the scope of the duty is (if found), the less likely it is that allowing it will 'open the floodgates' to future claims.

[109] Vulnerable though they were, the Claimants do not suggest that the Defendant was under a general duty to protect them from harm. They were living independent lives in the community, and life is not free from risk

→

→

and danger. The Defendant did not purport to provide policing or security services. It would plainly not be fair, just and reasonable to impose such a broadly-based duty on the Defendant.

This is the potential scope of the defendant's duty—it is not a general duty to take care but rather a specific duty to move the claimants to alternative accommodation.

[110] However the Claimants do contend in essence that the Defendant became under a duty to protect them in a particular way, namely by moving them out of their flat and into some form of alternative accommodation at some stage before the relevant weekend. All parties accept that in practical terms there was nothing else the Defendant could have done to prevent the Claimants from being assaulted and abused as they were during the relevant weekend.

[The judge considers arguments as to when the defendants should have moved the claimants out of their flat.]

Compare the view of the Court of Appeal (at [91]–[93]).

[116] . . . if it was not the Defendant's duty to move the Claimants out of the flat long before the relevant weekend, it certainly became their duty to protect them by doing so in response to the developing crisis towards the end of 2000. I accept that submission. I return to my earlier findings that by about 20th October 2000 an attack of the kind that the Claimants suffered during the relevant weekend was reasonably foreseeable, and that the Defendant had the power and the procedures in place to move the Claimants on an emergency basis. Subject to the further discussion below, in those circumstances I would regard it as fair, just and reasonable to impose upon the Defendant a narrowly-defined duty to move the Claimants out of the flat in response to the unusual but dangerous situation which had developed.

Having established that the defendants might owe the claimants a narrowly framed duty to move them out of their flat once the dangerous situation had become apparent, Maddison J then goes on to consider arguments to the contrary.

This refers to the 'incremental approach' to establishing a duty of care discussed further in **section 3.3.3**.

[117] I now consider whether there are any other features of the case which would suggest that it would or would not be fair, just and reasonable to impose a duty of care. I have borne in mind the absence of any previous decided case establishing liability in similar circumstances. That is not of course determinative of the present case. However, regard must be had to the following dictum of Brennan J. in *Sutherland Shire Council* v *Heyman* (1985) ALR 1, at p 44:

> It is preferable, in my view, that the law should develop novel categories of negligence incrementally and by analogy with established categories, rather than by a massive extension of a prima facie duty of care restrained only by indefinable considerations which ought to negative or to reduce or to limit the scope of the duty or the class of persons to whom it is owed.

[118] This dictum has often been cited with approval in the courts of England and Wales, for example by Lord Bridge in the ***Caparo*** case at p 618.

This was one of the appeals in ***D* v *East Berkshire Community NHS Trust*** [2005].

[119] It is well-established that local authorities may, in certain circumstances, owe a duty of care to children, for example in relation to the investigation of suspected child abuse and the initiation and pursuit of care proceedings (*see JD and others* v *East Berkshire NHS Trust and Others* [2003] Lloyd's Law Reports 552) and in relation to the return of children previously placed in foster care to their natural parents (see *Pierce* v *Doncaster MBC* [2007] EWHC 2968). In the present case the Claimants, though adults, both functioned in many ways like children. No adult of normal intellect and

→

→

understanding was living in their household. The Defendant knew this, and had allocated a social worker to both their cases. In my judgment, the extension of a duty of care to the Claimants would involve a small step rather than a giant leap forward, and would not offend the 'incremental' principle enunciated by Brennan J. This is so particularly since, for the reasons explained above, the duty to be imposed, if any, would be of a very narrow and case-specific nature, and as such would not open the gates to a flood of future claims that would not otherwise have been brought.

[120] I have not overlooked the fact that in the *JD* case it was held by the Court of Appeal (and indeed by the House of Lords on a further appeal) that no separate duty of care was owed to the adult parents of the children concerned; and that a similar conclusion was reached by the Court of Appeal in *Lawrence* v *Pembrokeshire County Council* [2007] 1 WLR 2991. However, the position of the Claimants is in my judgment much closer akin to that of the children concerned in those cases than to that of their parents; and this case does not involve any conflict of interest between parent and child that prompted the refusal of the parents' claims in the cases just cited.

Here Maddison J is distinguishing the facts of *JD* v *Mather* [2012] and *Lawrence* [2007] from those in this case.

Often, as we shall see, it is hard to establish a duty of care when the harm was caused by the actions of third parties (such as the youths in this case)—see **Chapter 4**.

[121] Does the fact that the direct cause of the Claimants' injury and loss was the actions of third parties over whom the Defendant had no control mean that it would be unjust, unfair or unreasonable to impose a duty of care? In my view, it does not. It is clear from the *Littlewoods* case referred to in paragraph 93 above that the actions of such third parties are capable of founding an action in the tort of negligence. The Defendant is protected by the principle that a high degree of foresight is required in such cases.

[122] A further factor which it seems to me can properly be taken into account, though by itself it is not determinative of the issue, is the advent of the Human Rights Act 1998 and its incorporation of the European Convention on Human Rights into domestic law. The authorities appear to show a greater willingness to find the existence of duties of care subsequent to the passing of the Act.

[The judge then looks at two cases by way of example and dismisses the relevance of the defendant's apology to the claimants.]

[126] Accordingly, I find that it would be just, fair and reasonable to impose on the Defendant a duty of care of the kind contended for.

The considerations above only established a *duty*. The second hurdle in every claim in negligence is whether the defendant was 'at fault'. There are two questions that need to be addressed: (1) What is the standard of care required of the defendant? (2) Have they fallen below it?

Breach of Duty

Again the Court of Appeal came to a different conclusion in relation to this: 'If anyone assumed responsibility towards the claimants it was [the social worker] and, in our judgment, if anyone was at fault it was her. In our judgment, it follows from the fact that no such suggestion has been made that it is accepted that [the social worker's] approach was one which a reasonable social worker could reasonably take. It further follows that it is accepted that she could not be in breach of duty because of the principles in *Bolam v Friern Hospital Management Committee* [1957]' (at [98]).

[127] The next question to be considered is whether or not the Defendant was in breach of its duty of care to the Claimants. In the context of this case, the question becomes whether or not the Defendant could and should have moved the Claimants out of their flat before the relevant weekend.

[First the judge considered whether the defendants could have moved the claimants and their procedures for doing so.]

[132] . . . Given my earlier conclusion (which some might see as generous to the Defendant) that an assault of the kind that occurred during the relevant weekend first became reasonably foreseeable on or about 20th October 2000, in my judgment this emergency system was the only one available to the Defendant which could have been deployed to move the Claimants out of their flat before the relevant weekend.

So, the defendants could have moved the claimants out of their flat, which leads to a second question—should they have done so?

→

→

[133] I therefore turn to consider whether the Defendant *should* have invoked the emergency transfer system to move the Claimants from their flat. [...]

[137] ... I find that the Defendant should have invoked its emergency procedure to remove the Claimants from their flat on or very shortly after 20th October, 2000 but at the very latest on or very shortly after 7th November. The fact that this did not happen in my judgment pointed to and resulted from a lack of proper cooperation and communication between the Social Services and Housing Departments; a failure within those Departments sufficiently to appreciate the gravity and urgency of the situation which the Claimants faced (to which both Z and Tajinder Hayre were doing their best to draw attention); and a failure to give the Claimants' case the priority it deserved.

[138] Accordingly, I find that the Defendant was in breach of its duty of care to the Claimants.

> The defendants could and should have moved the claimants out of their flat and so by failing to do so the defendants fell below the standard of care expected of them, that is they breached their duty to the claimants to move them out of their flat once it became reasonably foreseeable that they were likely to suffer a serious physical assault.

Causation

[139] Finally, in the context of the tort of negligence I have to consider whether the Defendant's breach of its duty of care caused the injury and loss in respect of which this claim is brought. I can come clearly to the conclusion that it did. Self-evidently, had the Claimants left their flat before the relevant weekend, the assault of which they complain would not have happened. However, the Defendant has advanced two arguments in this regard.

> This is the final element that needs to be addressed. It can sometimes be tricky to establish that the defendant's actions *in fact* caused the claimant's loss or injury. Alternatively, it may be clear that the defendant caused the claimant's injury in fact, but not *in law*—that is, their injury or loss is considered to be too remote. However, here Maddison J deals with causation quickly, rejecting arguments made by the defendants in relation to whether the claimants would have agreed to move or have maintained contact with their eventual abusers. The defendant was unable to establish on the balance of probabilities that the claimants would have been assaulted even had they moved before the relevant weekend (at [141]).

Do the Claimants have a Right of Action at All?

[142] I have thus far assumed that the Claimants do in fact have a right of action for damages based on the tort of negligence. The Defendant submits, however that the Claimants do not. Though it may appear strange to leave this matter until this stage of the judgment, I have done so because it needs to be considered against the background of the matters already dealt with.

[143] Ultimately, it is said on behalf of the Defendant, the Claimants are complaining about the failure of the Defendant to re-house them; and decisions taken by local authorities in relation to the provision of social housing can be challenged only by way of an application for judicial review. In this connection, reliance is placed on the case of *O'Rourke* v *Camden London Borough Council* [1998] AC 188, in which the House of Lords held that the Plaintiff's claim for damages, arising out of the Council's failure to accommodate him as a homeless person pursuant to section 63(1) of the Housing Act 1985, should be struck out. Section 63(1) was part of a scheme involving the provision of social housing for the benefit of society in general, and created no private law duty sounding in damages, but was enforceable solely by way of judicial review.

> Put simply, the defendants are arguing that the claimants ought not be allowed to claim in the tort of negligence (private law) about something which is essentially a public law matter and which has a public law remedy (judicial review). *O'Rourke* [1997] is considered in the context of the tort of breach of statutory duty in **section 14.2**.

[...]

[148] ... The present case is distinguishable [from *O'Rourke*]. The Claimants were well-established tenants of the Defendant. The Defendant had already exercised its powers as to social housing in relation to the Claimants. Their claim is that they should have been moved *from* that accommodation, and not necessarily into further Council accommodation. Their claim is not based on narrow considerations of housing policy. There is, for example, no →

> And therefore already had a relationship that the law might recognise.

→

complaint that, being literally homeless, the Claimants were wrongly denied housing; or, being already housed by the Defendant, were wrongly placed in a transfer list below competing candidates. Their claim involves both the Housing and Social Services Departments; the interaction between them; and the manner in which these departments together reacted (or failed to react) to information they received about the Claimants' predicament.

[149] Finally, the evidence in and the reality of this case is that, by virtue of whatever statutory provisions, the Defendant actually had in place an emergency transfer procedure which it could have used before the relevant weekend, and which it did in fact use though only after that weekend.

Essentially, the defendant was able to do more than they did.

[150] I therefore regard the Claimants as having a valid cause of action.

This was overturned by the Court of Appeal in 2009. See section 6.7.2.

The Claim under the Human Rights Act 1998

[151] In addition to their claim based on the tort of negligence, the Claimants claim damages under the Human Rights Act, 1998 sections 6 and 7. This is on the basis that, in the circumstances already discussed, the Defendant failed to protect them from inhuman and degrading treatment, and to maintain the integrity of their private and family life, thus breaching Articles 3 and 8 respectively of the European Convention on Human Rights.

Claims under s 7 of the HRA are *not* claims in tort law. They are public law claims against the state for not ensuring that rights under the HRA are protected. Courts (as public bodies) are obliged under s 6 of the HRA to ensure that all their decisions are HRA compatible. Both claims are considered in more detail in the introduction to the book **(section 1.4)** and in the course of discussion of public body liability (see **Chapter 6**).

[…]

[153] However, I do not think that it is necessary for me to determine the claim, for several reasons. The first is that I have already found the Defendant liable in the tort of negligence. In doing so, incidentally, I have taken into account the impact of the Human Rights Act, albeit amongst many other factors when deciding that the Defendants owed a duty of care to the Claimants. The second reason is that in the course of argument the parties agreed (as do I) that in the circumstances of this case it is difficult to see how the claim under the Human Rights Act might succeed if that based on the tort of negligence failed. If the negligence claim failed, so would the Human Rights Act claim fail. Not having heard full argument on the point, however, it occurs to me that the converse may not necessarily apply. I have in mind that the 1998 Act came into force on the 2nd October, 2000 so that, on my earlier findings, the Claimants could rely on it only in relation to the period beginning on that date and ending on or about 20th October or, at the latest 7th November, 2000. Since I have found that the significant deterioration in the Claimants' situation began in September, 2000 and that developments after that month should have been assessed against the background of what had gone before, the claim in relation to the Human Rights Act is not without its complications. However, for the reasons I have given, I do not think it is necessary to extend any further what is already a lengthy judgment by detailed consideration of this claim.

The claimants (and 'Z', X's mother) took their case to the ECtHR alleging violations of Arts 3, 6, 8 and 13. Though there is no judgment from the ECtHR (the case having been settled), the fact that the case was settled suggests that the ECtHR was likely to have found the UK to have breached the claimants' rights. And if so this, in our view, makes the Court of Appeal's judgment even more unpalatable.

The claimants win.

Conclusion

[154] I therefore give judgment for the Claimants on the question of liability. Damages have been almost entirely agreed, any remaining issues can be resolved when the court convenes for the handing down of this judgment.

Compensation in the form of money—the primary remedy available in tort law. See further **Chapter 21**.

These were agreed at £97,000 at first instance. At settlement, X and Y each received €25,000, Z received €7,000 and €12,500 were awarded to cover all parties' costs.

2.7 **Conclusion**

The tort of negligence has a central role in the law of tort. This is for two reasons: more claims are brought under the tort of negligence than any other tort and its influence extends beyond the tort itself as in recent years it has gained prominence, and started to steal ground from other, older torts. The purpose of this chapter has been to explore the origins of the modern law of negligence, to highlight some of the key themes underpinning the tort and to outline the essential ingredients of a claim in negligence. The chapter began by mapping and explaining the historical development of the tort of negligence. It located the development of the tort within its political, social and economic context and against a backdrop of increasing industrialisation. It then went on to explore the origins of the modern tort of negligence in the landmark decision of the House of Lords in ***Donoghue*** and Lord Atkin's neighbour principle. Finally, the chapter outlined the three components which need to be established in order to succeed in a claim in the tort of negligence: duty, breach and causation (including remoteness) (as well as the absence of any relevant defences). Although in reality cases—and hence most judgments—will tend to focus on one or two of these elements, with the uncontroversial aspects of the case being glossed over very quickly, in every case every element of the tort must be present for the claim to succeed. A 'real life' application of these elements was considered in the case of ***X & Y***.

End-of-chapter questions

After reading the chapter carefully, try answering the questions which follow.

1. How do negligence in the everyday or general sense and the tort of negligence differ?
2. What must be established in order for there to be a successful claim in the tort of negligence?
3. Why would the courts ever want to deny a claim when someone is injured through another's carelessness?
4. What is the *ratio* of *Donoghue*?

If you would like to know what we think visit the **online resources**. www.oup.com/he/horsey7e

Further reading

The readings which follow provide a general introduction to development and purposes of the tort of negligence and the leading case of ***Donoghue***. The best place to start is with the chapters in Cane or Conaghan and Mansell.

Cane, Peter *Atiyah's Accidents, Compensation and the Law* (7th edn, CUP, 2006), Chs 2 and 3

Conaghan, Joanne and Wade Mansell *The Wrongs of Tort* (2nd edn, Pluto Press, 1999), Chs 4 and 5

Harlow, Carol *Understanding Tort Law* (3rd edn, Sweet & Maxwell, 2005), Ch 3

Hedley, Steve 'Making Sense of Negligence' (2016) 36 LS 491

Heuston, Robert '*Donoghue* v *Stevenson* in Retrospect' (1957) 20 MLR 1

Ibbetson, David *A Historical Introduction to the Law of Obligations* (OUP, 1999), Ch 10

Kleefeld, John C 'The Donoghue Diaries: Lord Atkin's Research Notes in *Donoghue v Stevenson*' (2013) 3 Jur Rev 375

Nolan, Donal 'Damage in the English Law of Negligence' (2013) 3 JETL 259

Priaulx, Nicky 'Endgame: On Negligence and Reparation for Harm' in Janice Richardson and Erika Rackley (eds) *Feminist Perspectives on Tort Law* (Routledge, 2012), pp 36–54

Robertson, Andrew 'On the Function of the Law of Negligence' (2013) 33 OJLS 31

Sumption, Lord 'Abolishing Personal Injuries Law—A Project' Personal Injuries Bar Association Annual Lecture, London, 16 November 2017

Weir, Tony 'The Staggering March of Negligence' in Peter Cane and Jane Stapleton (eds) *The Law of Obligations: Essays in Honour of John Flemming* (OUP, 1988), p 97

3 Duty of care: basic principles

3.1 Introduction

Consider the following examples:

→ ***A lorry driver crashes into a queue of traffic while talking on his mobile phone, killing the occupants of the car in front.***

→ ***A nurse misreads a doctor's handwriting and, as a result, gives a patient the wrong drug, causing them to suffer a serious allergic reaction.***

→ ***A university law lecturer fails to check departmental files properly before writing a reference to accompany a student's application to join an Inn of Court—unfortunately this means that a strong candidate ends up with a weak reference and their application is refused.***

→ ***A school caretaker injures their back falling off a stepladder while putting up decorations for the end of term play—the stepladder had not been properly maintained by his employer.***

In each of these cases the defendant owes the claimant a duty of care. The concept of the duty of care is central to the tort of negligence. It is one of three elements in the tort of negligence—the first 'hurdle' if you like—that must be established in order for a claim to be successful. Carelessness alone does not give rise to liability. The defendant must not only be careless but also be in a relationship to the claimant where their carelessness carries legal consequences. If the defendant does not owe a duty of care to the claimant, then the defendant will not be liable regardless of how carelessly they acted and how much loss they caused to the claimant, and there is no need to address the other elements of a negligence claim—that is breach, causation and remoteness. Moreover, the duty of care must be owed *in respect of the particular type of harm (or injury) suffered*—a defendant may owe the claimant a duty of care in respect of one type of loss (e.g. bodily injury) but not in respect of another (e.g. economic loss).

It is usually clear when a duty of care is owed. We know, for example, that an employer owes its employees a duty of care not to cause them foreseeable physical and psychiatric injury at work; that a driver owes a similar duty to other road users, and others in their vicinity; and that a doctor owes a duty to his patients (in both treating and, increasingly, advising them). In these, and many other cases, a duty of care is established by clear precedent: the courts have long recognised duties of care in these situations. Accordingly, in a road traffic accident case the key issue is not likely to be whether the defendant owed the claimant a duty of care, but rather whether they have breached this duty by falling below the standard of care expected in all the circumstances of the case.[1]

On occasion, however, cases arise where the question of whether a duty of care exists is not answered by precedent. In these 'novel' cases, the question for the court is whether the law *should* recognise a duty of care on such facts. To answer this question, the courts have made numerous attempts to identify a general test which can be used to identify when duties of care will arise. However, as we shall see, none of these attempts have been altogether successful.

Nonetheless, to repeat, this uncertainty about what general test or approach courts should take when faced with novel cases does not mean that there is significant uncertainty about when duties of care arise. Most cases are not novel but are covered by precedent. Accordingly, when considering whether a duty of care is owed, the starting point is *always* to look to existing precedent. If the cases give a clear answer one way or the other—that is, if they indicate that a duty is or is not owed—then that is the end of the matter. It is only in those rare, but nonetheless significant, cases where the precedents give no clear answer that the courts need to resort to a more general test or approach.

One thing which follows from what we have said already is that there is no universal duty to take care not to harm or injure each other. The law does not *always* require us to show reasonable care for those who may be harmed—however foreseeably—by our conduct. Indeed, the duty of care concept is seen by many as a sort of control device, which the courts employ to *limit* the scope of negligence liability. '[W]hereas Lord Atkin seems to have put forward the neighbour principle as a way of *expanding* the scope of liability for negligence, the duty of care concept is most commonly used in modern cases as a means of justifying *refusal* to impose liability' (*Cane* p 69, emphasis added). Notably, there are a number of situations where the law either denies a duty of care outright or makes establishing such a duty more onerous for claimants.[2] These relate to particular types of harm (e.g. where the defendant's actions cause psychiatric injury or economic loss), how the harm is suffered (e.g. where the claimant's loss or injury has been caused by the acts of a third party or through an omission rather than a positive act) and who the defendant is (e.g. where the defendant is a public body—such as a local authority, the police or other emergency services). This, of course, prompts a further question as to why the courts might wish to deny a duty of care in such cases.

There are a number of reasons why the courts might be reluctant to impose a duty of care. These include a wish to avoid imposing so-called 'crushing' liability on a particular individual or class of defendants—that is, 'liability in an indeterminate amount for an indeterminate time to an indeterminate class' (*Ultramares Corporation* v *Touche, Niven & Co* [1931]). A related wish may also be to prevent a 'flood' of claims—either in relation to one specific event or, more generally, in relation to a particular type of injury—which

1. See **Chapter 8**.
2. See further Nicky Priaulx, 'Endgame: On Negligence and Reparation for Harm' in Janice Richardson and Erika Rackley (eds) *Feminist Perspectives on Tort Law* (Routledge, 2012), pp 36–54.

may in turn clog up or slow down the tort system as a mechanism for compensation. The courts may also wish to seek to avoid the more negative aspects of deterrence—that is, the danger of 'overkill'—whereby beneficial yet 'risky' activities are restricted due to the over-self-regulation of would-be defendants. Finally, the courts may recognise that in some circumstances there is nothing wrong with the sort of harm the defendant has caused—that is, that it is sometimes entirely reasonable to act in ways that leave others worse off.[3] For example, failing a student's exam paper will inevitably leave them worse off both in terms of their future employment prospects as well as their current mental state. However, the examiner (assuming the paper is not of a sufficient standard to pass) is under no duty to prevent this from happening by not failing the student.[4]

Pause for reflection

Cane argues that the main function of the duty of care element in the tort of negligence is to:

> define the boundaries of liability for damage caused by negligent conduct by reference to what are commonly called 'policy considerations' . . . To say that a person owes a duty of care means (and means only) that the person will be liable for causing damage by negligence in that situation. (p 69)

Nicholas McBride disagrees. He argues that tort law's regulatory function—that is, the extent to which tort law tells people how they *ought* to behave—is *at least as* important. So viewed, it is wrong to say the imposition of a duty of care 'means only' that the defendant will be liable for carelessly harming the claimant. Rather we should take the notion of a duty of care seriously—it requires and directs a defendant to act with reasonable care (2004, pp 418–19).

This distinction, described by McBride as that between those who adopt a 'cynical' as opposed to 'idealist' view of the tort of negligence, is an important one. On one view tort law is about attributing or shifting losses, and hence the key question is: Do we want to impose liability in these circumstances, on this defendant, for this injury? On this basis the purpose of the duty of care inquiry is simply to weigh up the pros and cons of requiring the defendant to bear the claimant's losses. By contrast, the idealist view suggests that tort law is concerned primarily with telling people how they may and may not act. So, to impose a duty of care on a defendant is not simply to say that they will be liable if they carelessly injure someone, but that they must actually 'take care'.

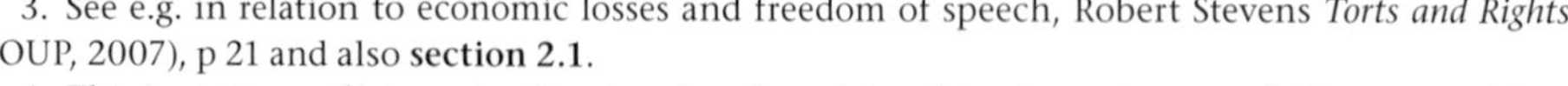

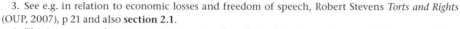

3. See e.g. in relation to economic losses and freedom of speech, Robert Stevens *Torts and Rights* (OUP, 2007), p 21 and also **section 2.1**.

4. This is not to say that an examiner is not under a duty of care to mark papers *fairly* or *accurately*—i.e. to give better papers better marks (it is also probably the case that teachers owe a duty of care to teach students adequately so as to enable them to pass the exam in the first place—see *Siddiqui* v *University of Oxford* [2018]). The point is rather that when an examiner gives a bad paper a bad mark, they are, consciously, leaving that student worse off than if they had awarded a higher mark. Nonetheless, as long as the mark is fair, no liability will attach since there is no duty to avoid causing such harm.

→

Keep this distinction in mind as you read more about the tort of negligence and, particularly, when reading **Chapters 4** to **7**, which deal with the types of claim in which the courts have struggled with whether and when to find a duty of care. To what extent, if any, can the distinction between the 'cynical' and 'idealist' views on negligence provide an explanation for some of the courts' more controversial decisions in relation to establishing a duty of care?

All this means is that it is important to know how, and in what circumstances, the courts will determine that a duty of care is established and it is to this that we shall now turn.

3.2 From *Donoghue* to *Caparo*—a brief history of the duty of care

Unsurprisingly the starting point in any consideration of the concept of a duty of care is ***Donoghue* v *Stevenson* [1932]**. As discussed in **Chapter 2**, the House of Lords set down a single, general test which could be applied in all cases to answer the question as to whether a duty was owed—Lord Atkin's 'neighbour principle':

> You must take reasonable care to avoid acts or omissions which you can reasonably foresee would be likely to injure your neighbour. Who then, in law, is my neighbour? The answer seems to be persons who are so closely and directly affected by my act that I ought reasonably to have them in contemplation as being so affected when I am directing my mind to the acts or omissions which are called in question. (at 580)

The basic test here is that, for a duty of care to arise, the claimant must fall within a class of individuals put at *foreseeable risk* by the defendant's action. It follows that duties of care are claimant-specific: the defendant does not owe a duty of care to the world at large. An example of this point is *Haley* v *London Electricity Board* [1965]. In this case, the claimant, who was blind, tripped over a hammer which had been placed on the pavement by the defendant to prevent pedestrians from walking along the pavement as they carried out their work. As a result of the fall the claimant became almost totally deaf. The House of Lords, finding for the claimant, held that the question of whether harm was reasonably foreseeable needed to factor in the characteristics of all those who might reasonably be expected to walk along the pavement—including blind pedestrians:

> In deciding what is reasonably foreseeable one must have regard to common knowledge . . . No doubt there are many places open to the public where for one reason or another one would be surprised to see a blind person walking alone, but a city pavement is not one of them. (Lord Reid at 791)[5]

5. See also the famous US case *Palsgraf* v *Long Island Railroad Co* [1928].

For some, Lord Atkin's neighbourhood principle is 'extraordinarily empty' (*Conaghan & Mansell* p 13). It simply prompts the question: what is, or ought to be, reasonably foreseeable? This is something which may ultimately depend on the imagination of the individual judge; what one judge may believe to be reasonably foreseeable, another may consider unusual and so on. Yet this requirement that harm be reasonably foreseeable before a duty of care is recognised has been the one constant in a period where much of the law of negligence has been in flux. And, while determining what harms are *reasonably* foreseeable is a question on which different people will sometimes come to different conclusions, the law cannot sensibly expect us to take care in respect of risks we could not reasonably have anticipated.

Pause for reflection

One constant in the quest for a general test for establishing duties of care is the requirement of foreseeability—that is, the claimant must be said to fall into a particular class of people in relation to whom it is reasonably foreseeable that the defendant's failure to take care could cause them damage. However, as we shall see, foreseeability also crops up as a requirement or relevant factor in other elements of the tort of negligence.

To recap, establishing a claim in negligence requires the claimant to prove not just that the defendant owed them a duty of care, but also that the defendant breached that duty, that the breach caused the claimant a loss and that this loss is not too remote. When we come to look at breach, in Chapter 8, we shall see that one of the key factors in determining whether the defendant did indeed act reasonably is the likelihood and gravity of the harm that could reasonably have been foreseen—so, for instance, the greater the likelihood of harm, the more care we expect the defendant to take to prevent it. Moreover, when determining whether the loss suffered by the claimant is too remote, we again turn to reasonable foreseeability—a loss is too remote if it was not reasonably foreseeable that a loss of that kind might follow from the defendant's breach (***Overseas Tankship (UK) Ltd*** v ***Morts Dock and Engineering Co The Wagon Mound (No 1)*** [1961]).[6]

This all appears rather confusing. If the claimant's loss was not reasonably foreseeable, then no duty of care can arise and their claim will fail before we get to questions of breach, causation and remoteness. By contrast, if a court has held that harm was reasonably foreseeable when looking at whether a duty arose, then it seems unnecessary to re-inquire into foreseeability when looking at breach and remoteness since that issue has already been addressed at the duty stage. To put much the same point another way, if it is held that the claimant's loss was *not* a reasonably foreseeable consequence of the defendant's carelessness, then it seems we can deny their claim on a variety of grounds: we could say that no duty was owed, that the defendant was not in breach or that the claimant's loss was too remote.

So, not only does it seem as though we are asking the same question two or three times but this also appears to muddy the relationship between the supposedly distinct elements of

→

6. See further Howarth 2006, pp 457–63.

→

a negligence claim. The same point has on occasion been made by the courts. For instance in *Lamb v Camden London Borough Council* [1981] Lord Denning MR had this to say:

> The truth is that all these three, duty, remoteness and causation, are all devices by which the courts limit the range of liability for negligence . . . As I have said . . . 'it is not every consequence of a wrongful act which is the subject of compensation'. The law has to draw a line somewhere. Sometimes it is done by limiting the range of persons to whom a duty is owed. Sometimes it is done by saying that there is a break in the chain of causation. At other times it is done by saying that the consequence is too remote to be a head of damage. All these devices are useful in their way. But ultimately it is a question of policy for the judges to decide. (at 636)

The best way to make sense of this all is to understand that at each stage—duty, breach, remoteness—we are, or should be, asking a slightly different question in relation to foreseeability. So, at the duty stage, we are asking whether harm of some broad variety—personal injury, psychiatric harm, property damage, pure economic loss, etc—was a reasonably foreseeable consequence of the defendant's carelessness. If a duty is established, we move on to breach. This involves asking whether the foreseeable harm was sufficiently grave or likely that the defendant should have done more than they did to avoid it happening. As such, the inquiry into foreseeability here is a little more detailed or focused—we are asking not only 'Was harm foreseeable?' but 'How likely was it that harm might be caused?' and 'How serious was the harm that the defendant could reasonably have foreseen?' Finally, when addressing remoteness, we are looking at the foreseeability of the specific harms that the claimant did in fact suffer. So, while at the duty stage we ask whether, for instance, physical harm, as broadly defined, was foreseeable, when turning to remoteness we look at the precise injury suffered by the claimant (and sometimes, too, the way in which they were injured), and we ask whether this was the *type of* physical harm that could reasonably have been foreseen (see e.g. *Tremain* v *Pike* [1969] and *Hughes* v *Lord Advocate* [1963], although compare *Page* v *Smith* [1996]).

Lord Atkin's neighbourhood principle from ***Donoghue*** was subsequently restated and refined in the dictum of Lord Wilberforce in ***Anns* v *Merton London Borough Council*** [1978]:

> . . . the question has to be approached in two stages. First one has to ask whether, as between the alleged wrongdoer and the person who has suffered damage there is a sufficient relationship of proximity or neighbourhood such that, in the reasonable contemplation of the former, carelessness on his part may be likely to cause damage to the latter, in which case a prima facie duty of care arises. Secondly, if the first question is answered affirmatively, it is necessary to consider whether there are any considerations which ought to negative, or to reduce or limit the scope of the duty or the class of person to whom it is owed or the damages to which a breach of it may give rise. (at 751–2)

So, on this reformulation of the test, the defendant owes the claimant a duty to take reasonable care (provided that it was ***reasonably foreseeable*** that a failure to take reasonable care by the defendant would cause damage to the claimant) ***unless*** there is some policy reason why, nonetheless, no duty should be held to be owed. This prompted Lord Goff in ***Smith* v *Littlewoods*** [1987] to acknowledge 'the broad general principle of liability for foreseeable damage is so widely applicable that the function of the duty of care is not so much to identify cases where liability is imposed as to identify those where it is not' (at 280).

Under the ***Anns*** test, the only positive reason needed to support the recognition of a duty of care was that harm to the claimant was indeed reasonably foreseeable. This first stage was pretty easy to satisfy—almost everything is foreseeable if you think about it long enough. Now, the second stage meant that courts were not compelled to find duties of care simply on account of the harm being reasonably foreseeable. However, the way the test was formulated created a sort of presumption that, *if* harm was reasonably foreseeable, then a duty of care was owed. As such, a defendant seeking to argue that he owed no duty faced an uphill battle, since they had to convince the court why they, exceptionally, should be permitted to cause careless harm.

The end result was an unprecedented, and increasingly unpopular, expansion of the tort of negligence in the late 1970s and early 1980s during which the courts seemed reluctant to refuse claims of any vaguely sympathetic claimant who came before them (see e.g. Roskill's leading opinion in ***Junior Books* v *Veitchi*** **[1983]**). Accordingly Lord Wilberforce's two-stage test soon fell into disfavour. It was rejected in *Yuen Kun-yeu* v *Attorney General of Hong Kong* [1987] and ***Anns*** itself was subsequently overruled by ***Murphy* v *Brentwood District Council*** **[1991]**.[7]

Counterpoint

Though many modern accounts of negligence fail to acknowledge this, the decision in *Anns* was not universally derided. Indeed, in *Ravenscroft* v *Rederiaktiebolaget Transatlantic* [1991] (decided after *Anns* was overruled in *Murphy*) Ward J had this to say:

> As I have tried to navigate my fragile craft to judgment, I have become aware that it is a tidal sea which flows as causes of action are extended and then ebbs as limitations are placed upon them. I can only console myself that if I am cast up among the flotsam and jetsam at the high water mark on the beach, I shall lie, I hope unnoticed but among such battered treasures as *Anns* v *Merton London Borough Council*. (at 76)

Moreover, it is far from clear that the test in *Anns necessitated* any expansion of liability. It may be that it was a victim of association—a casualty of the backlash against an increasing number of decisions (e.g. *McLoughlin* v *O'Brian* [1982]; *Home Office* v *Dorset Yacht Co* [1970]; even the decision in *Anns* itself) which appeared to threaten the principles of individual freedom and responsibility at a time when these were high on the political and governmental agenda (*Conaghan & Mansell* pp 17, 20).[8]

→

7. See **section 7.4**.
8. See also *Atiyah* in **Chapter 8**.

→

What do you think led the courts to the conclusion that the potential for liability had become too widespread? Think, in particular, about the so-called 'problematic' duty situations in relation to omissions, pure economic loss, public authorities, psychiatric harm and so on.

3.3 Establishing a duty of care: *Caparo Industries v Dickman*

The leading case on the duty of care in tort is now ***Caparo Industries plc* v *Dickman*** **[1990]**.[9] What test or approach ***Caparo*** stands for has, however, been a matter of some controversy. One thing which is clear is that the House of Lords sought to move away from the position of ***Donoghue*** and ***Anns*** whereby foreseeability of damage was enough to raise a prima facie duty of care, which would be negated only if there were public policy considerations which militated against such a duty. But, more than that, the court cast doubt on the broader idea which motivated Lord Atkin's judgment in ***Donoghue***: that there must be some general test which can determine when duties of care are owed.

3.3.1 The myth of the *Caparo* three-stage test

The more difficult question was, once the tests in ***Donoghue*** and ***Anns*** were rejected, what was to be put in their place. In setting these approaches aside, Lord Bridge suggested:

> . . . in addition to the foreseeability of damage, necessary ingredients in any situation giving rise to a duty of care are that there should exist between the party owing the duty and the party to whom it is owed a relationship characterised by the law as one of 'proximity' or 'neighbourhood' and that the situation should be one in which the court considers it fair, just and reasonable that the law should impose a duty of a given scope on the one party for the benefit of the other. (at 617)

Later courts came to treat this passage as setting down a new 'three-stage test' which must be applied to determine whether a duty of care arises. On this understanding, to know whether the defendant owes the claimant a duty of care we need to answer three questions:

(1) Was it reasonably foreseeable that the defendant's failure to take care could cause damage to the claimant?

(2) Was there a relationship of proximity between the claimant and the defendant?

(3) Is it fair, just and reasonable that the law should recognise a duty on the defendant to take reasonable care not to cause that damage to the claimant?

9. The facts of ***Caparo***, which concerned economic loss following reliance on information provided by auditors, are discussed in detail in **Chapter 7**. They are not relevant here.

Only if the answer to all three questions is 'yes' would a duty of care be found.

The first stage here is the familiar question of whether the claimant fell within a class of individuals put at *foreseeable risk* by the defendant's action. The second and third stages, however, marked a departure from the ***Anns*** test. Though the language of 'proximity' was used in ***Anns*** and indeed in ***Donoghue***, it appears that Lord Wilberforce, and (less clearly) Lord Atkin, did not intend the term to add anything to the notion of reasonable foreseeability. In other words, to say that there was 'proximity' between the claimant and defendant was to say no more than that it was reasonably foreseeable that the defendant's carelessness could cause the claimant harm. As such, 'proximity' did not describe a hurdle or requirement additional to the requirement of reasonable foreseeability. ***Caparo*** changed this. By employing 'proximity' as a second, additional, element to the test for establishing the existence of a duty of care, the House of Lords must have meant something more than simple reasonable foreseeability of harm. The difficulty was in identifying what this alternative understanding of proximity was and hence how to determine when it was present.

Clearly proximity does not describe simple physical closeness—a defendant can owe a duty of care to a claimant who is many miles away (indeed in ***Donoghue*** itself the claimant and defendant were not close in space and time). Rather proximity is perhaps better understood, to use Alistair Mullis and Ken Oliphant's expression, as a 'legal term of art';[10] a generic name for the more specific tests through which the existence of a duty of care is established in particular cases.[11] The fact that 'proximity' identified no single, definable idea or test was indeed admitted by the court in ***Caparo***. As Lord Oliver noted, 'proximity' is a 'convenient expression so long as it is realised that it is no more than a label which embraces not a definable concept but merely a description of circumstances from which, pragmatically, the courts conclude that a duty of care exists' (at 632). Similarly, in ***Stovin*** v ***Wise*** **[1996]** Lord Nicholls stated:

> [The ***Caparo***] formulation tends to suggest that proximity is a separate ingredient, distinct from fairness and reasonableness, and capable of being identified by some other criteria. This is not so. Proximity is a slippery word. Proximity is not legal shorthand for a concept with its own, objectively identifiable characteristics. Proximity is convenient shorthand for a relationship between two parties which makes it fair and reasonable one should owe the other a duty of care. This is only another way of saying that when assessing the requirements of fairness and reasonableness regard must be had to the relationship of the parties. (at 932)

As such, the proximity requirement tells us that, before a duty of care can arise, a certain type of relationship or connection must exist between the parties. However, importantly, and as Lord Oliver's quote reveals, ***Caparo*** itself tells us very little about what precise relationship or connection amounts to a relationship of proximity on any given set of facts. ***Donoghue*** and ***Anns*** both suggested that the only connection or relationship that needed to exist between the parties was that it was reasonably foreseeable that

10. *Tort* (4th edn, Palgrave Macmillan, 2011), p 22.

11. See e.g. the so-called ***Alcock*** control mechanisms which limit duty of care in relation to psychiatric injuries suffered by 'secondary victims' discussed in **section 5.6**.

the claimant might be harmed by the defendant's carelessness. ***Caparo*** tells us that this is not true (since otherwise this second stage of the ***Caparo*** 'test' would add nothing to the first) and that something more is needed. However, it does not say what this 'something more' is.

The final stage of the ***Caparo*** 'test'—that is, whether it is *fair, just and reasonable* to find that the defendant owed the claimant a duty to take reasonable care not to cause them damage—returns, once again, to notions of policy. In so doing, it has been argued that it leaves the courts with an inevitable 'residual discretion as to whether or not a duty of care should be recognised'.[12] Traditionally, judges have sought to play down this aspect of their role (especially during the period of retreat following ***Anns***). However, more recently, they have been more willing to engage in frank discussion of the various policy factors which weigh for and against the imposition of a duty of care. Indeed in ***Michael* v *Chief Constable of South Wales Police* [2015]** Lord Kerr (in dissent) appeared to suggest not only that a decision whether or not to impose a duty of care was necessarily informed by 'preponderant policy considerations' but that these might change over time:

> As to what is 'fair, just and reasonable', Lord Browne-Wilkinson in ***Barrett* v *Enfield London Borough Council* [2001]** 2 AC 550, 559 explained:
>
> > In English law the decision as to whether it is fair, just and reasonable to impose a liability in negligence on a particular class of would-be defendants depends on weighing in the balance the total detriment to the public interest in all cases from holding such class liable in negligence as against the total loss to all would-be plaintiffs if they are not to have a cause of action in respect of the loss they have individually suffered.

This passage clearly contemplates that, in deciding what is 'fair, just and reasonable', courts are called on to make judgments that are informed by what they consider to be preponderant policy considerations. Some assessment has to be made of what a judge considers the public interest to be; what detriment would be caused to that interest if liability were held to exist; and what harm would be done to claimants if they are denied a remedy for the loss that they have suffered. These calculations are not conducted according to fixed principle. They will frequently, if not indeed usually, be made without empirical evidence. For the most part, they will be instinctual reactions to any given set of circumstances. . . . It is, I believe, important to be alive to the true nature of these decisions, especially when one comes to consider the precedent value of earlier cases in which such judgments have been made. A decision based on what is considered to be correct legal principle cannot be lightly set aside in subsequent cases where the same legal principle is in play. By contrast, a decision which is not the product of, in the words of Lord Oliver, 'any logical process of analogical deduction' holds less sway, particularly if it does not accord with what the subsequent decision-maker considers to be the correct instinctive reaction to contemporaneous standards and conditions. Put bluntly, what one group of judges felt was the correct policy answer in 2009 should not bind another group of judges, even as little as five years later. (at [159]–[161])

12. Witting 2005, p 62.

3.3.2 Debunking the three-stage 'test'

The three-stage test, which ***Caparo*** was commonly read as setting down, posed a number of challenges. Its principal flaw or limitation was that it told us remarkably little about when a duty of care will arise or even how courts should go about determining when such duties arise. Yet this is the very thing a general test for establishing duties of care should do. However, what is striking when one reads the judgments in ***Caparo*** is that the House of Lords made clear that it was *not* intending to set down a test that could be used by courts in future cases to provide concrete answers to whether a duty of care arose on a given set of facts. On the contrary, the House of Lords in ***Caparo*** clearly took the view that it was impossible to find *any* single test which, in practice, could be used to identify those situations in which a duty of care will be owed. Lord Oliver put it thus:

> I think that it has to be recognised that to search for any single formula which will serve as a general test of liability is to pursue a will-o'-the wisp. The fact is that once one discards, as it is now clear one must, the concept of foreseeability of harm as the single exclusive test, even a *prima facie* test, of the existence of the duty of care, the attempt to state some general principle which will determine liability in an infinite variety of circumstances serves not to clarify the law but merely to bedevil its development in a way which corresponds with practicality and common sense. (at 632)

Moreover, not only did the House of Lords reject the possibility of formulating any single, practicable test, they also went on to deny the utility of the very concepts of 'proximity' and 'fairness, justice and reasonableness' that are employed in the so-called three-stage test:

> [T]he concepts of proximity and fairness embodied in these additional ingredients are not susceptible of any such precise definition as would be necessary to give them utility as practical tests, but amount in effect to little more than convenient labels to attach to the features of different specific situations in which, on a detailed examination of all the circumstances, the law recognises pragmatically as giving rise to a duty of a given scope. (Lord Bridge at 618)

Accordingly, while many lawyers came to view ***Caparo*** as setting down a new test which they must apply when working out when duties of care arise, this was not just a misreading of the judgments in ***Caparo*** but indeed the very opposite of what the court had intended. The Supreme Court has, in recent years, sought to resurrect and restate the true message of ***Caparo***. The point was emphasised by Lord Reed in ***Robinson*** v ***Chief Constable of West Yorkshire*** [2018].[13]

> The proposition that there is a ***Caparo*** test which applies to all claims in the modern law of negligence, and that in consequence the court will only impose a duty of care where it considers it fair, just and reasonable to do so on the particular facts, is mistaken. As Lord Toulson JSC pointed out in his landmark judgment in ***Michael*** v ***Chief Constable of Wales*** [2015] . . . that understanding of the case mistakes the whole point of the ***Caparo*** case, which was to repudiate the idea that there is a single test which can be applied in all cases in order to determine whether a duty of care exists, and instead to adopt an approach based, in the manner characteristic of the common law, on precedent, and on the development of the law incrementally and by analogy with established authorities. (at [21])

13. See too ***Poole Borough Council*** v ***GN*** [2019] at [30], [64], discussed in **section 6.3**.

This makes clear that we should not think of ***Caparo*** as setting down a test for establishing duties of care. But what does ***Caparo*** have to say to courts faced with novel cases, when the existing precedents do not give an answer to the question of whether a duty of care is owed?

One thing ***Caparo*** does is to change the starting point from which decisions on whether the defendant owes the claimant a duty to take reasonable care not to cause them injury are made. For Lord Wilberforce in ***Anns***, showing that it was reasonably foreseeable that the defendant's carelessness would harm the claimant was enough to establish a 'prima facie' duty of care. As we have seen, this effectively adopted a presumption that where harm was reasonably foreseeable, a duty of care would be owed. Of course, this presumption could be rebutted. Accordingly, the second stage of the ***Anns*** test asked whether there were policy considerations which nonetheless required the court to deny a duty of care. But this way of structuring the inquiry was significant. The test suggested that, all else being equal, a duty of care would be owed wherever it was reasonably foreseeable that the defendant's carelessness could harm the claimant and it was only in those (apparently) exceptional cases where policy considerations pointing *against* the imposition of a duty were sufficiently weighty, that a duty of care would nonetheless be denied. ***Caparo*** rejects this view. Instead the court must weigh up all the applicable reasons and arguments for and against recognising a duty of care. A duty of care will be found only if the court considers that, on balance, the combined reasons in favour of a duty of care are stronger than the combined reasons against, with no presumption that a duty will be owed when harm is foreseeable.

Pause for reflection

> The trend of authorities has been to discourage the assumption that anyone who suffers loss is *prima facie* entitled to compensation from a person (preferably insured or a public authority) whose act or omission can be said to have caused it. The default position is that he is not. (Lord Hoffmann, ***Stovin*** v ***Wise*** [1996] at 949)

Think again about McBride's understanding of the purpose of a duty of care. Even if we agree that there should be no assumption that anyone who suffers loss is prima facie entitled to compensation from whomever caused that loss, what is wrong with the assumption that we should all take care not to cause each other such losses?

3.3.3 **The incremental approach**

The principal steer ***Caparo*** gives to the courts came in its approval of a dictum of Brennan J in the Australian case of *Sutherland Shire Council* v *Heyman* [1985]: 'It is preferable, in my view, that the law should develop novel categories of negligence incrementally and by analogy with established categories' (at 481). This describes what has become known as the incremental approach. According to this approach, the courts should identify duties of care not by seeking a high-level, universal test of the kind the

House of Lords attempted to formulate in ***Donoghue*** and ***Anns***. Instead, their focus should be on the existing case law and the factual circumstances in which duties of care have already been found, and to work outwards from them. As Lord Bridge noted, this heralds a return to the pre-***Donoghue*** approach and 'the more traditional categorisation of distinct and recognisable situations as guides to the existence, the scope and the limits of the varied duties of care which the law imposes' (***Caparo*** at 618).

The suggestion that we should recognise duties of care in situations identical or analogous to those where the courts have recognised a duty of care previously (and that we should reject duties of care in situations where the courts have previously denied their existence) is clearly sensible and is hardly revolutionary. This is, one might say, just ordinary common law reasoning. The problem with this approach is what might be thought to be its implication: that, where no analogy can be found—that is, where there is no previously decided case analogous to the case at hand—a duty of care will be denied since the recognition of a duty of care cannot be understood as an incremental development of the law from existing, analogous authorities. In other words, if the law is to develop incrementally, we can *only* recognise duties of care in situations analogous to those where a duty of care has *already* been recognised.

But, if this is true, it then means that the outcome of cases depends not upon legal principle and the substantive merits of the case but upon the accidents of legal history—that is, on whether you are fortunate enough that an analogous case has already been decided by the courts. If we take the incremental approach seriously, where a party is unfortunate enough to suffer an injury in a truly novel way, so that no case similar to theirs has been brought to court before, then their claim will fail not because it is unmeritorious but for the simple (and highly unsatisfactory) reason that they are the first person to bring such a claim. Indeed, it is just this type of arbitrary and unfair result that the majority of the House of Lords in ***Donoghue*** rejected. The incremental approach appears to invite us to say that the minority in that case were right after all.[14]

Perhaps unsurprisingly, the courts have shown little enthusiasm for this approach, or at least the implication that *really* novel cases will lose out by reason of their novelty alone. For instance, in *Marc Rich & Co* v *Bishop Rock Marine Co Ltd* [1996] (also known as *The Nicholas H*) the House of Lords, faced with a novel type of negligence claim, effectively sidelined the incremental by analogy approach on the basis that, if there had been no analogous cases previously decided, then the past cases could offer no guidance either way as to whether a duty should be held to exist. Instead, the court decided the case pragmatically by analysing the reasons for and against the recognition of a duty and deciding whether on balance a duty ought to be recognised (albeit while using the language of fairness, justice and reasonableness).

Recent cases have seen the Supreme Court endorsing what might be considered a refined version of the incremental approach. We saw already in the earlier extract from ***Robinson* v *Chief Constable of West Yorkshire Police*** that Lord Reed held that it was the incremental approach, not the supposed three-stage test, which ***Caparo*** should be understood to stand for and it is this approach which courts should employ when dealing with novel claims (at [25]). But, in so doing, he did not endorse what we described as

14. See **section 2.2**.

the apparent implication of this approach: that truly novel claims fail simply by reason of their novelty. As he continued:

> Properly understood, the ***Caparo*** case . . . achieves a balance between legal certainty and justice. In the ordinary run of cases, courts consider what has been decided previously and follow the precedents (unless it is necessary to consider whether the precedents should be departed from). In cases where the question whether a duty of care arises has not previously been decided, the courts will consider the closest analogies in the existing law, with a view to maintaining the coherence of the law and the avoidance of inappropriate distinctions. They will also weigh up the reasons for and against imposing liability, in order to decide whether the existence of a duty of care would be just and reasonable. (at [29])

The clear suggestion here, then, is that even truly novel cases are to be decided on their merits, and the incremental approach is not a direction to courts to treat novelty alone as a basis for denying duties of care. On the contrary, courts faced with novel claims still have, in the end, to make a judgement of justness and reasonableness. But this judgement is to be made not by straight appeal to high principle but via a consideration of whatever analogous cases we can find (remembering that analogy is a matter of degree) and the more fact-specific considerations these cases identify.

In this way, ***Robinson*** seeks to reassert the true message of ***Caparo***.[15] But it also emphasises ***Caparo***'s limited role. As Lord Reed makes clear, if there *is* a previous decision which does cover the case at hand, then the court can say whether or not there is a duty of care by direct appeal to the precedent and so without any need to have recourse to ***Caparo***. Indeed, one of the important messages of ***Robinson*** is that courts not only do not *need* to resort to ***Caparo*** when a case falls within an established duty situation; *they should not do so*. This was true in ***Robinson*** itself.

Robinson v Chief Constable of West Yorkshire [2018] SC

The claimant, an elderly woman, was knocked to the ground and injured when two police officers attempted to arrest a suspected drug dealer. Her claim was dismissed at trial on the basis that the police had an immunity against claims in negligence. The Court of Appeal rejected her appeal on the grounds that the police generally owe no duty of care to members of the public and that, on the facts, there was no proximity between the parties and it would not be fair, just and reasonable to impose such a duty. The Supreme Court allowed the claimant's appeal, holding that the defendants both owed and breached a duty of care to the claimant. Lord Reed gave the lead judgment:

> Applying the approach adopted in the *Caparo* case, there are many situations in which it has been clearly established that a duty of care is or is not owed: for example, by motorists to other road users, by manufacturers to consumers, by employers

→

15. See ***Poole***: '***Robinson*** did not lay down any new principle of law' (at [64]).

→

to their employees, and by doctors to their patients. As Lord Browne-Wilkinson explained in ***Barrett* v *Enfield London Borough Council*** [2001] 2 AC 550, 559–60:

> Once the decision is taken that, say, company auditors though liable to shareholders for negligent auditing are not liable to those proposing to invest in the company . . . that decision will apply to all future cases of the same kind.

Where the existence or non-existence of a duty of care has been established, a consideration of justice and reasonableness forms part of the basis on which the law has arrived at the relevant principles. It is therefore unnecessary and inappropriate to reconsider whether the existence of the duty is fair, just and reasonable (subject to the possibility that this court may be invited to depart from an established line of authority). Nor, a fortiori, can justice and reasonableness constitute a basis for discarding established principles and deciding each case according to what the court may regard as its broader merits. Such an approach would be a recipe for inconsistency and uncertainty.

One of the principles of negligence law, clearly established through the case law, is that, we all owe each other duties of care not to cause one another foreseeable physical harm through our positive acts. This was the position that the defendant police officers found themselves in: it was reasonably foreseeable that, if they did not take reasonable care, in conducting their arrest, others in the vicinity might end up being physically harmed. Accordingly, it was, the court concluded, clear as a matter of precedent that they owed a duty of care and it was wrong for the Court of Appeal to ask whether it would be fair, just and reasonable to impose such a duty.

In summary, when determining if a duty of care is owed, the first place to look is to the decided cases. If they establish that a duty of care is, or is not, owed, then we have our answer, and the question of whether recognising such a duty would be fair, just and reasonable does not need to be asked and answered again. Even where the precedents provide no conclusive answer as to whether a duty of care is owed, they may nonetheless provide more concrete guidance than we get from ***Caparo***. So, for example, if the claimant suffers pure psychiatric injury, the courts will look to cases such as ***Alcock* v *Chief Constable of South Yorkshire Police*** [1992] and ***Page* v *Smith*** [1996], rather than ***Caparo***, to answer the duty of care question. Similarly, in cases concerning pure economic loss, the courts have developed more concrete principles to help establish when duties of care are owed. Furthermore, as ***Robinson*** shows, where personal injuries, and possibly property damage, are concerned, it will generally be the case that foreseeability of such injury will suffice to establish a duty; in other words, the test set down in ***Donoghue*** will be used (although there are exceptions to this—see e.g. *Marc Rich & Co* v *Bishop Rock Marine Co Ltd* [1996]). Only where and to the extent that the precedents do not provide an answer does the court need to consider the fairness and reasonableness of recognising a duty of care. In doing this—and this is the key idea of the incremental approach endorsed in ***Robinson***—the court must still focus on the decided cases to ensure that the law develops coherently and consistently.

However, it is not always easy to determine whether a case falls within an established duty situation or is, by contrast, novel. Take, for example, *Darnley* v *Croydon Health Services NHS Trust* [2018]. The claimant who went to hospital with a serious head injury and who was incorrectly told by a receptionist that he would have to wait four to five hours for treatment. The claimant went home rather than wait, where his condition deteriorated. By the time he returned to hospital, it was too late to save him from permanent brain damage. In the Court of Appeal, the case was seen as raising a novel duty question: do hospital receptionists owe a duty of care to patients concerning waiting times. The court concluded, by majority, that it would not be fair, just and reasonable to do so. On appeal, however, the Supreme Court considered that this was not a novel duty case at all. In Lord Lloyd-Jones's view:

> To my mind, . . . the present case falls squarely within an established category of duty of care. It has long been established that such a duty is owed by those who provide and run a casualty department to persons presenting themselves complaining of illness or injury and before they are treated or received into care in the hospital's wards. The duty is one to take reasonable care not to cause physical injury to the patient . . . In the present case, as soon as the claimant had attended at the defendant's A & E department seeking medical attention for the injury he had sustained, had provided the information requested by the receptionist and had been 'booked in', he was accepted into the system and entered into a relationship with the defendant of patient and health care provider. The damage complained of is physical injury and not economic loss. This is a distinct and recognisable situation in which the law imposes a duty of care. Moreover, the scope of the duty to take reasonable care not to act in such a way as foreseeably to cause such a patient to sustain physical injury clearly extends to a duty to take reasonable care not to provide misleading information which may foreseeably cause physical injury. While it is correct that no authority has been cited in these proceedings which deals specifically with misleading information provided by a receptionist in an A & E department causing physical injury, it is not necessary to address, in every instance where the precise factual situation has not previously been the subject of a reported judicial decision, whether it would be fair, just and reasonable to impose a duty of care. It is sufficient that the case falls within an established category in which the law imposes a duty of care. (at [16])[16]

Pause for reflection

Let's return to ***Donoghue*** v ***Stevenson***. What is the duty situation that case established? The case itself concerned a manufacturer of ginger beer in the Scottish city of Paisley. However, no one would say that the duty category it supports applies only to bottles of ginger beer or is limited only to those producing drinks in Paisley. The same rule would apply if the court was then faced with a claim by someone who had found a slug in a bottle of lemonade in Glasgow. But how do we know this? One way is by looking at the judgments given in the case. That it was ginger beer—rather than, say, lemonade—and that the bottle was produced in Paisley—rather

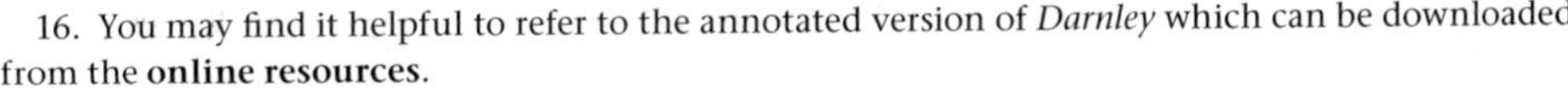

16. You may find it helpful to refer to the annotated version of *Darnley* which can be downloaded from the **online resources**.

see online resources

→

than, say, Glasgow—were not considerations which had any bearing on the decision and find no expression in the reasoning of the court. These, however, are easy examples. Does the ***Donoghue*** category extend beyond ginger beer and other drinks to food? Almost certainly. What about other potentially dangerous items? What about activities other than the provision of dangerous products? Does it extend, say, to dangerous *advice* (e.g. I tell you that it is safe to go into the nuclear reactor without protection). While none of these questions was addressed directly in ***Donoghue***, we might nonetheless say that they were by implication. Indeed, this was the key thrust of the neighbourhood principle: whenever you are doing something which poses a reasonably foreseeable risk of harm, *whatever that activity is*, you must take reasonable care.

Of course, this is precisely why the courts have rowed back on the neighbourhood principle: it goes too far. Nonetheless something like this process of generalisation—from the facts and decision in any given case to the broader rule or principle it stands for—is required every time we have to work out what range of cases is covered by a particular precedent or line of precedents. This then shows that, while the courts may say that they have 'abandoned the search for a general principle capable of providing a practical test applicable in every situation to determine whether a duty of care is owed' (*Darnley* at [15]), even the incremental approach depends on drawing generalisations from individual cases, indeed the sort of generalisation which ***Donoghue*** endorsed. Moreover, it also suggests why lower courts—told that there is no general principle to be found but also to look out for 'established' (and general) duty categories—might find their task rather difficult.

3.4 **Where does this leave us?**

It is important to remember that ultimately it is only a small minority of cases—where the courts are asked to determine whether new categories of claim should be recognised or existing precedents should be revised or extended—which call for the application of a general test or approach such as those propounded in ***Donoghue, Anns*** and ***Caparo***. As such, the practical need for some such test is not great and the number of cases in which the courts must struggle through without the guidance of such a test are few. Moreover, we have now at least some clarity. The approach put forward in ***Caparo*** does not itself determine when duties of care are owed in novel cases. This is something the judges faced with such cases must decide for themselves. What ***Caparo*** does is to provide a general steer when judges are making these decisions; a steer broadly as outlined in **Figure 3.1**.

Nonetheless, while the incremental approach affirms that courts are to look first to analogous cases, what cases are truly analogous and whether a duty of care should then be recognised on the basis of such an analogy are questions of what is just and reasonable; and neither ***Caparo*** nor indeed any conceivable test can offer real guidance as to how courts should answer *these* questions. As Lord Walker said, in ***Customs and Excise Commissioners*** v ***Barclays Bank plc*** [2006], there is an 'increasingly clear recognition

FIGURE 3.1 Establishing a duty of care in new cases

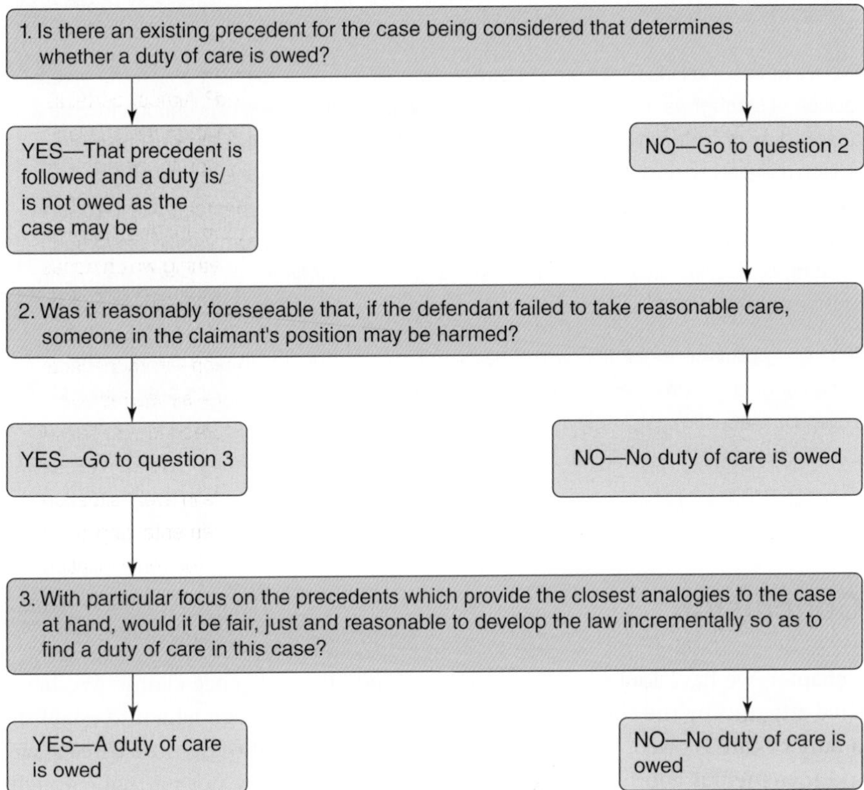

that the three-fold test . . . does not provide an easy answer to all our problems, but only a set of fairly blunt tools' (at [25]).[17] How these tools should be deployed is a question which is to be judged by reference to the particular facts of the case and is, in large measure, a matter for the judgement of the individual judge.

Important questions remain. Is this really the best we can do? What should we be looking for in a test, or broader approach, for establishing duties of care? Why, it might be asked, do we need the duty of care at all? Is the criticism of some of these cases directed to the content of the actual decisions or simply to the language that the courts have been using to explain their decisions? These are some of the questions you should be thinking about as you read the chapters that follow (which discuss situations where the law either denies a duty of care outright or makes establishing such a duty more onerous) and as you begin to learn more about duty and the tort of negligence as a whole.

17. Similar comments were made by Lord Hoffmann (at [14]) and Lord Bingham (at [7]).

Pause for reflection

As we have noted, the House of Lords in ***Caparo*** was determined to effect a shift away from the position of ***Donoghue*** and ***Anns*** whereby foreseeability of damage was enough to raise a prima facie duty of care, which would be negated only if there were public policy considerations which militated against such a duty. Do you think this shift has gone too far? Think about *Caparo* and the cases that have followed it (discussed in the following chapters). Are the courts now paying too little attention to the principle that carelessly caused harm should be compensated? After all, as Lord Browne-Wilkinson reminded us, in *X (Minors)* v *Bedfordshire County Council*, we should not lose sight of the compensatory purposes of the tort of negligence:

> the public policy consideration which has first claim on the loyalty of the law is that wrongs should be remedied and that very potent counter-considerations are required to override that policy. (at 749)[18]

3.5 **Conclusion**

In this chapter, we have looked at the concept of *duty* in negligence claims. We have considered attempts by the courts to establish general 'tests' through which to establish when a duty of care is owed, focusing on the most important of these—the three-stage 'test' and incremental approach from ***Caparo***. We concluded by noting that, though we should not downplay the significance of these general tests, they are used in a small minority of cases where the judges are being asked to develop a new area of the law. Thus, over the course of the next four chapters we shall consider the circumstances in which the courts have developed specific rules in order to establish when a duty of care is owed.

End-of-chapter questions

After reading the chapter carefully, try answering the questions which follow.

1 What purpose does the concept of duty of care serve? Why shouldn't everyone who falls below the standard of care of the reasonable person be liable if they injure someone?

2 In what situations is the issue of whether or not there is a duty of care unproblematic and when is it problematic? Why is this?

18. See also Lord Dyson in *Jones* v *Kaney* [2011]: 'The general rule that where there is a wrong there should be a remedy is a cornerstone of any system of justice. To deny a remedy to the victim of a wrong should always be regarded as exceptional. As has been frequently stated, any justification must be necessary and requires strict and cogent justification . . . If the position were otherwise, the law would be irrational and unfair and public confidence in it would be undermined' (at [113]).

3 In each of the following situations consider both whether there is a legal duty of care and whether there should be:

(i) Iris, a 2-year-old child, falls into two feet of water. Ben, an adult, walks by and offers no assistance. Iris drowns. What if Ben is Iris's father?

(ii) Doreen, an elderly woman, lives alone in an isolated farmhouse. Recently there have been a number of burglaries in the neighbourhood so she decides to protect herself by digging a hole beneath her front window, which she then covers with leaves. Unfortunately, Charlie, a postman, falls down this hole while looking through her window to see if Doreen is in to collect a parcel.

(iii) Dr Smith is a well-known magician. One night while performing his signature trick, which involves 'cutting' his assistant, Pip, in half, he accidently slices into her side causing her to bleed heavily. On seeing this, Pip's new boyfriend, Dan, who is in the audience, faints and falls and hits his head—he suffers severe concussion.

(iv) While out shopping, Kate's 7-year-old daughter slips out of her hand and runs into the road causing a serious accident.

(v) Helen negligently leaves the door of her fireworks factory unlocked one night. Some boys enter the factory and steal a large quantity of fireworks, which they light in the nearby park. This causes an explosion that seriously injures Ben who is walking his dog in the park.

4 '[T]he postulate of a simple duty to avoid any harm, that is, with hindsight, reasonably capable of being foreseen becomes untenable without the imposition of some intelligible limits to keep the law of negligence within the bounds of common sense and practicability' (Lord Oliver, *Caparo* at 633). How have the courts sought to place limits upon the duty of care owed in negligence and to what extent do you consider that such limits are 'intelligible'?

If you would like to know what we think visit the **online resources**. www.oup.com/he/horsey7e

Further reading

Much of the writing in this area focuses on the role of duty as an ingredient in the tort of negligence and asks the 'big questions' such as: 'Do duties of care exist?' 'If so, how many are there?' 'Do we need the concept of a duty of care?' and so on. The best place to start is with Nicholas McBride's discussion of the 'idealist' and 'cynical' views of negligence.

Cane, Peter *Atiyah's Accidents, Compensation and the Law* (7th edn, CUP, 2006), Ch 3

Hepple, Bob 'Negligence: The Search for Coherence' (1997) 50 CLP 69

Howarth, David 'Many Duties of Care—Or A Duty of Care? Notes from the Underground' (2006) 26 OJLS 449

McBride, Nicholas 'Duties of Care—Do They Really Exist?' (2004) 24 OJLS 417

Morgan, Jonathan 'The Outer Limits of "Personal Injury"' [2018] CLJ 461 (on *Dryden*)

Steele, Jenny 'Duty of Care and Ethic of Care: Irreconcilable Difference?' in Janice Richardson and Erika Rackley (eds) *Feminist Perspectives on Tort Law* (Routledge, 2012), pp 14–35

Tofaris, Stelios, 'Duty of Care in Negligence: A Return to Orthodoxy?' [2018] CLJ 454 (on ***Robinson***)

Witting, Christian 'Duty of Care: An Analytical Approach' (2005) 25 OJLS 33

4 Special duty problems: omissions and acts of third parties

Problem question

Read this problem question carefully, and keep it in mind while you are working through the chapter that follows. At the end of the chapter, you will be able to apply what you have learnt to the problem question and advise the relevant parties.

Margaret, who is 75, is in the supermarket on a busy Saturday afternoon when she feels pains in her chest. It transpires she is having a heart attack and she collapses to the floor. Although the supermarket is crowded, no one comes to help her.

Brian, the store manager, puts a call out over the PA system asking if there is a doctor present, but otherwise offers no assistance. Hearing the announcement, Karen, a nurse, comes forward and tries to help Margaret, but fails to put her in the recovery position. Margaret later dies.

Meanwhile, some youths see Margaret's car, which was left unlocked and with the key still in the ignition in the supermarket car park as she did not want to spend time looking for a parking space. The youths drive off in the car, failing to stop at a pedestrian crossing, hitting Jill and her daughter Heather who were crossing the road. Both are injured, Heather seriously. One of the youths, Luke, who was not wearing a seat belt, suffers a serious head injury.

Advise the parties.

4.1 Introduction

Consider the following situations:

- → ***A small child falls into a pond and is struggling to get out. A passing adult offers no assistance.***
- → ***A couple hire a motor boat at the seaside and are clearly in difficulties when the boat begins to sink. The hire shop owner sits on the beach and does nothing to help them.***

→ ***A doctor is driving along a road on which there has been a bad accident, but does not stop to help the victims.***

→ ***A man sees another man about to walk off the edge of a cliff, but does nothing to try and stop him.***

→ ***The door to a pub is left open one night by the cleaner. Some teenagers enter, consume a large amount of alcohol and cause lots of damage.***

→ ***The same teenagers, upon leaving the pub, vandalise a car belonging to a neighbour of the pub.***

In each scenario above the harm suffered by the various individuals is attributable to a 'third party' or occurred because the potential defendant did *not* do anything (as opposed to doing something that causes harm). It might seem logical that the defendant should incur no liability in any of these situations. As in all negligence claims liability here depends, first, on whether a duty of care was owed in respect of what happened or who it happened to. For example, we ask 'Does an adult walking past a drowning child owe that child a duty of care?' Whether a duty is owed by one party to another to whom they cause harm often depends on the *manner* in which that harm was inflicted. Generally, there is little problem establishing a duty to avoid the direct infliction of physical harm. However, when harm is inflicted indirectly, such as through a failure to act (what the law calls an omission, or non-feasance), or where the immediate cause of the harm was the act of a third party (someone other than the claimant or defendant), it becomes far harder to establish that a duty would—or should—be owed.

This chapter looks at two problematic duty areas. The first section considers when and why the courts have established that a duty of care should be owed by defendants when the harm was the result of their *omission*, while the second explores the situations when a defendant may owe a duty in relation to the *action(s) of a third party*. It might be thought strange that someone would ever compensate someone else for a harm that was not the result of their own actions. This is the stance the courts have generally taken: ordinarily you can be liable only for things that you do, not things you do not do. However, when someone *does not* do something that they *ought* to have done—perhaps because of the relationship between the parties concerned—a duty might be found. Similarly, while it appears odd that someone may be liable for harms that someone else caused, the courts have nonetheless found that in limited circumstances people who have responsibility for, or control over, others may incur a duty in respect of the harms caused by these 'third parties'.

4.2 **Acts and omissions**

Although Lord Atkin in ***Donoghue*** v ***Stevenson*** [1932] spoke of a duty of care arising in respect of 'acts or omissions',[1] later interpretations suggest that he only meant omissions in situations where a *pre*-tort relationship gives rise to a positive obligation to act (and,

1. ***Donoghue*** is outlined in **section 2.2**—see in particular the discussion of Lord Atkin's 'neighbour principle'.

therefore, where inaction would be a breach of that duty). This, broadly, is reflected in the law's position today. A relationship between the parties—for example, between parent and child, or school teacher and pupil, and also contractual relationships or those created by statute—may create a positive duty to act.[2] Outside specific pre-tort relationships, positive duties are not generally present in the tort of negligence and the courts seem unwilling to create them—most likely because negligence law developed against a social and political landscape that favoured individualism over collective responsibility.

In short, the exclusionary rule operates to prevent a duty being owed in respect of omissions. Lord Goff stated clearly in *Smith* v *Littlewoods* [1987] that 'the common law does not impose liability for what are called pure omissions' (at 271). If there is no duty, there can be no liability, so no compensation for harm(s) caused by the failure of someone to do something. Generally speaking, then, the duties of care that arise in negligence are duties not to cause harm to others by our actions. These do not extend to active or positive duties to act to help others (or even to try), even when to do so would be easy. An example commonly cited in this respect (including in our chapter-opening scenarios) is that of a child lying face down in a puddle of water and potentially drowning. A passing stranger has no duty to take any steps whatsoever to save that child, even if all it would take would be for them to grab the child's arm and pull them out of the water to safety. The principle is starkly illustrated by the US case *Osterlind* v *Hill* [1928]. In that case, the claimant rented a canoe from the defendant and took it out into the water. The canoe overturned and the defendant, who was a strong swimmer, did nothing: he sat on the shore and watched the claimant drown. When sued in negligence it was found that he owed no duty of care, despite the fact he had rented out the canoe.[3]

Pause for reflection

see online resources

Many people are shocked that the adult in the scenario described earlier would have no duty of care towards the child. Should this be the case, in your opinion? Do you think that the way the law operates might actually discourage people from going to the assistance of others? Allen Linden, a Canadian scholar, points out that this rule is 'particularly incomprehensible in an age when everyone carries a cell phone and can call for help without any risk whatsoever to him- or herself'.[4] Do you agree?

It is the 'pure' notion of omissions that concerns us here; that is, not those omissions which happen in the context of a relationship in which an obligation to act arises. In some circumstances there *would* be a duty to go to the rescue of the child in a puddle—if there was a pre-tort relationship that meant a duty to take positive action existed, such

2. e.g. the Occupiers' Liability Act 1957 fixes a positive duty on occupiers to ensure their premises are safe for lawful visitors (see **section 11.2.1**) and there are various statutory health and safety provisions that impose positive duties on employers.

3. So, in our example scenario, no duty of care would be owed by the owner of the hire shop to do anything to assist the person in trouble. However, in light of later cases (e.g. the Canadian case *The Ogopogo* [1970]), a *contractual* relationship might now be enough to create a positive duty to act. See also *Stansbie* v *Troman* [1948] and *Bailey and another* v *HSS Alarms* [2000].

4. Linden 2016, at 843. See also Carr 2019.

as if the parent or carer of the child was the person walking by,[5] or if the defendant had in some way 'assumed responsibility' for the claimant.[6] This general exclusion of liability for 'pure' omissions has been restated time and time again in case law—most notably by Lord Hoffmann in ***Stovin* v *Wise*** [1996]:

> There are sound reasons why omissions require different treatment from positive conduct. It is one thing for the law to say that a person who undertakes some activity shall take reasonable care not to cause damage to others. It is another thing for the law to require that a person who is doing nothing in particular shall take steps to prevent another from suffering harm from the acts of third parties . . . or from natural causes. (at 943)

He goes on to identify political, moral and economic reasons why no duty should be owed in such circumstances:

> In political terms it is less of an invasion of an individual's freedom for the law to require him to consider the safety of others in his actions than to impose upon him a duty to rescue or protect. A moral version of this point may be called the 'Why pick on me?' argument. A duty to prevent harm to others or to render assistance to a person in danger or distress may apply to a large and indeterminate class of people who happen to be able to do something. Why should one be held liable rather than another? In economic terms, the efficient allocation of resources usually requires an activity should bear its own costs. If it benefits from being able to impose some of its costs on other people (what economists call 'externalities'), the market is distorted because the activity appears cheaper than it really is. So liability to pay compensation for loss caused by negligent conduct acts as a deterrent against increasing the cost of the activity to the community and reduces externalities. But there is no similar justification for requiring a person who is not doing anything to spend money on behalf of someone else. Except in special cases (such as marine salvage) English law does not reward someone who voluntarily confers a benefit on another. So there must be some special reason why he should have to put his hand in his pocket. (at 943–4)

Lord Hoffmann suggests that the rule against liability in the context of pure omissions is an application of the 'Why pick on me?' aspect of modern life. After all, the argument goes, why should the burden to go to the assistance of anyone else be placed on one particular person purely because they were in that particular place at that particular time?

Pause for reflection

If a number of people are in a situation where they *could* prevent someone else from coming to harm, but no one actually does anything, should all of them be potentially liable for failing to help? Or does the fact that so many people *could* have done something indicate that we should not impose a positive obligation on any one of them?

→

5. See e.g. *Carmarthenshire County Council* v *Lewis* [1955], where the duty of parents was confirmed in the context of a claim against a school. From *Carmarthenshire* it can be seen that a similar duty arises in respect of schools when children are in their care: see also *Barnes* v *Hampshire County Council* [1969] and ***Phelps* v *Hillingdon London Borough Council*** [2001]. This positive obligation now also extends to ensuring children's educational and psychological needs and interests are met (*Bradford-Smart* v *West Sussex County Council* [2002]).

6. Most recently confirmed at the highest level in ***Robinson* v *Chief Constable of West Yorkshire*** [2018].

→

In *Stovin* v *Wise*, Lord Nicholls refers to these people (who do not help) as 'callous bystander[s]' (at 931). However, he goes on to say that 'something more is required than being a bystander. There must be an additional reason why it is fair and reasonable that one person should be regarded as his brother's keeper[7] and have legal obligations in that regard'—do you agree?

While there may be arguments made against a general exclusionary principle in respect of pure omissions, the rule was vigorously reiterated by the House of Lords in *Sutradhar* v *National Environmental Research Council* [2006]. The claimant was poisoned by arsenic after drinking water from an irrigation well, which had been tested for toxins (but not arsenic) on behalf of the British Government by the British Geological Survey (BGS). The claimant asserted that BGS had a positive duty to test for arsenic (particularly as arsenic-contaminated water was a major environmental problem, affecting 35–77 million of Bangladesh's inhabitants). The law lords held that no duty was owed in respect of BGS's failure to test for arsenic. Indeed, Lord Hoffmann found that 'BGS owed no positive duties to the government or people of Bangladesh to do anything. They can only be liable for the things they did . . . not for what they did not do' (at [27]).

Wrongly not doing something that you should have done (an omission or non-feasance), is to be contrasted with wrongly doing something (an act or misfeasance). Whether a case is one or the other depends either on the nature of the relationship between the parties (claimant and defendant) or the activity being undertaken and is closely linked to the notion of proximity (or closeness of relationship) that threads through all aspects of the duty question and in particular the so-called 'problematic' duty areas.

The duties imposed by law are those not to cause injury by your actions; they are not duties actively to help or become involved with others. The courts have found that there is no duty even to go to the rescue of another who is about to injure themself accidentally, or even to shout to warn them: as Lord Keith said in *Yuen Kun Yeu* v *Attorney General of Hong Kong* [1988], there will be no liability 'on the part of one who sees another about to walk over a cliff with his head in the air and forbears to shout a warning' (at 192).[8] This

7. The reference to being one's brother's keeper is biblical: God, after Cain had killed Abel, asked Cain where his brother was and Cain replied 'Am I my brother's keeper?' (Genesis 4:9). The answer to Cain's question differs according to one's political and ethical standpoint. While some might answer 'Yes, you are. WE are'—that is, we are all (and should be) responsible, at least to some extent, for the welfare of our fellow humans—others will respond differently, relying on conceptions of individual rather than collective responsibility to support the view that one should not have to expend time, energy or money on those who are not directly related (or proximate) to us in some way.

8. We can therefore infer that there would be no obligation in our example scenario for a bystander to take any measures to stop the man walking off the edge of the cliff, unless a special or pre-tort relationship existed between the parties. Nor would a doctor or nurse have to stop at the scene of an accident to help a stranger who might be injured or even dying (though see the Australian case *Lowns* v *Woods* [1996]). If they *did* stop and intervene, however, they may owe a duty not to make the situation worse. *Markesenis & Deakin* call this a 'rather extreme position', highlighting that the law fails to take into account either the magnitude of the harm that could be caused or the ease of preventing it (p 180).

stands in direct contrast to most civil law jurisdictions, in which such a duty *is* workably imposed upon citizens, even in relation to strangers.[9] Article 223-6 of the French *Code Penal*, for example, makes it a *criminal* offence not to try and assist someone in danger (as long as to do so would not mean taking undue risks to your own safety), which also translates into a civil obligation (and therefore potentially liability) when this does not occur.[10] In the UK, only when someone does act (i.e. they begin to attempt a rescue) does a duty become attached to them—they become obliged not to make the (claimant's) situation worse than it already was, though they are not obliged to make it better.[11]

Pause for reflection

Consider how a duty to rescue *could* work in practice in relation to the example of the drowning child. What would such a duty actually *consist* of? Would it be a duty to *save* the child or a duty to *try* to save the child by taking reasonable (but not dangerous) steps? Do you think there is a good reason why we should not owe this kind of duty? In any case, could we protect people from liability if they did try to help—by statute, for example? A number of US, Canadian and Australian states and territories have passed what are called 'Good Samaritan' statutes which provide those who try to help with an 'immunity from suit' (i.e. they cannot be sued for any consequences of trying to help).[12] Do you think the same should happen here?

The UK's Social Action, Responsibility and Heroism Act 2015 perhaps goes a little way towards this. While it does not create a *duty* to go to another's assistance where no duty previously existed, it impels the court, when considering whether any person who does so was in *breach* (i.e. fell below the expected standard of care), to consider that person's 'social action' (s 2) and/or 'heroism' (s 4). Though not providing 'immunity from suit', the Act may protect some of those who offer assistance. Whether what the Act contains is any different from existing common law principles that courts have always taken into account, is another question (see further **section 8.5.1**).

The rule that says that you are *not* obliged to go to someone's aid, even when it would be easy to do so, surprises a great many law students. It lies behind what we may term 'rescuer anxiety'. Many people faced with a situation in which they *could* intervene to help someone are often scared to, fearing that *if* they help, they may end up becoming liable for not being able to protect/save the person. In fact, this fear reflects an inaccurate understanding of the law. One can actually only be liable, once stepping in to help, for positive actions

9. See Basil Markesinis 'Negligence, Nuisance and Affirmative Duties of Action' (1989) 105 LQR 104.

10. The penalties apply to anyone who wilfully fails to offer assistance to a person in danger which he could himself provide without risk to himself or to third parties, or by initiating rescue operations. An example of this law in practice is where some press photographers at the scene of Princess Diana's fatal car accident in Paris were investigated for deliberately avoiding providing assistance to endangered persons.

11. This is also the position that applies to the duty of care that the fire service or coastguard owe to individuals. See **section 6.5.1** and **section 6.5.5** respectively.

12. See Linden (**n 4**).

that make the situation worse than it was before the intervention. So, in the example of the drowning child, exerting too much pressure while trying to resuscitate the child and breaking a rib while doing so may be 'making the situation worse'. *Liability*, however, is different from owing a duty of care. Liability simply means having legal responsibility for one's actions and only attaches once all the elements of a tort are made out by the claimant. So, for example, while someone who intervenes may owe a *duty* not to make the situation worse, their actions would still be judged against those of a 'reasonable person' in the circumstances (and so if a reasonable person would have tried to resuscitate the child in the same way, there will be no *breach* of duty and therefore no *liability* to pay compensation).

Pause for reflection

see online resources

If there was a duty to try and help, what would someone have to do in order to breach that duty? Failing to do anything at all might be a breach but this will depend on the circumstances. For example, say you walk down the high street late at night and happen to witness a mugging. If a general duty to rescue existed, your duty would be to try and do something to help, *if you can*—the least you could do is try to call the police or alert other people to what's happening—you would *not* have to take steps to stop the mugging yourself, as this may put you in danger. Why shouldn't this kind of duty be imposed on people? What does it say about our society and its values that such a duty is not imposed?

All this said, there are—as ever—some limited exceptions to the general exclusionary rule. These fall under three general headings:

(1) control;

(2) assumption of responsibility;

(3) creation (or adoption) of risks.

In one way or another, these exceptions increase the degree of proximity between the claimant and defendant, creating a relationship between them in which the foreseeability of harm becomes greater, therefore justifying the defendant's potential liability to that specific claimant for *not doing something* that they could or should have done.

4.2.1 **Control**

When we speak of control in this sense, we mean those situations where it is arguable that the defendant *should* owe a duty to the claimant *because* they exercise a high degree of control over them, or have express responsibility for them. A parent or carer of a small child, for example, has a sufficient degree of control over/responsibility for their child such that they *ought* to step in to try and help them if they were drowning in a pool of water.[13] However, this exception also extends to situations where it can be said that the

13. *Carmarthenshire County Council* v *Lewis* [1955], though note that this appears not to stretch beyond situations where an express or implied undertaking to care for the child exists and is not based merely on e.g. blood relationships. See also *Surtees* v *Kingston upon Thames Borough Council* [1992].

defendants, because they exercise control over the person harmed, owe them a positive duty to take steps to ensure they are not harmed by themselves or by anyone else. In so doing, it clearly overlaps in part with the 'assumption of responsibility' category, discussed in the next section.

An example of this can be seen in ***Reeves* v *Commissioner of Police for the Metropolis*** [2000].[14]

Reeves v *Commissioner of Police for the Metropolis* [2000] HL

A man called Martin Lynch committed suicide while being held in police custody. His partner claimed that the police had owed him a duty to prevent this from happening. Previous case law (see *Kirkham* v *Chief Constable of Greater Manchester* [1990]) had established that a duty of care was owed in respect of suicide attempts of prisoners known to be mentally ill, but a doctor had found Mr Lynch to be of sound mind. The police, who clearly owed him a duty of care not to physically harm him by their actions, argued that they owed him no duty of care in respect of his suicide because he was not mentally ill, and had deliberately taken his own life, even though the opportunity for him to do so had only arisen from their own carelessness.

A majority of the House of Lords disagreed, holding that the police's duty to prisoners in custody *did* extend to a positive duty to take reasonable steps to assess the suicide risk of all prisoners. This was justified by the degree of *control* exercised over prisoners in custody and the known (high) risk of suicide, even among those without a known mental illness. However, the court also took account of the deliberate nature of the prisoner's actions by finding him partially responsible for his own death. The damages awarded were consequently reduced by 50 per cent.[15]

In a later case also involving a suicide in police custody, however, it was held that the duty found in ***Reeves*** did not mean that the police have a duty of care requiring them to treat *all* prisoners as a suicide risk. In *Orange* v *Chief Constable of West Yorkshire Police* [2001], a man committed suicide by hanging himself with his belt from a grille on the door in a police cell after being arrested and detained for being drunk and disorderly. His widow claimed that the police had owed a duty to take away any means of suicide from him, such as his belt, and that they should have watched him more carefully. The Court of Appeal held that the duty from ***Reeves*** was only to take reasonable steps to *assess* whether a prisoner posed a suicide risk, and to act accordingly. As the police had no real reason to think that this particular prisoner would attempt suicide, the duty did not arise in this case. This distinction was later approved by the European Court of Human Rights in *Keenan* v *UK* [2001].[16] In *Savage* v *South Essex Partnership NHS Trust* [2008], the House of Lords found that a similar positive duty, based on Article 2 ECHR,

14. Notably, this case is also an exception to the general absence of duty owed by the police as a public body, discussed in **section 6.5.3**.

15. For an explanation of the principles of contributory negligence, see **section 10.4**.

16. The duty of state authorities to protect prisoners with mental health problems was more recently confirmed in *Renolde* v *France* [2009].

was owed to a patient detained in a mental hospital who had negligently been allowed to abscond, later committing suicide.[17]

Pause for reflection

Despite their differing outcomes, the facts of ***Reeves*** and *Orange* are very similar. In light of what we have said about the concept of duty being used as a 'control device', could it be argued that the Court of Appeal in *Orange* was seeking to 'put the brakes on' what could potentially be an expanding category of liability? Is it realistic to expect the police to owe a duty to all prisoners in their custody (and therefore under their control) to prevent them from attempting suicide? If not, why not? What positive obligations would this impose on the police, and are they unreasonable?[18]

Arguably, because the risk of suicide in custody is known to be high, the police should monitor all prisoners, even those without a history of mental illness (especially when they are first admitted), should design cells to minimise the risk of suicide and should remove items from prisoners (e.g. belts) that they could use to harm themselves. However, this must be balanced against the resources and time available to the police and a respect for the judgements they make in relation to who is at risk and who is not. Imposing an undue burden on the police constantly to monitor every prisoner might detract from their other functions. Again, however, it is important to note that imposing a duty of care is not enough to establish *liability* in the tort of negligence. Similarly, we might again ask what such a duty would *consist* of—would it be a duty to prevent all suicides in custody or merely a duty to take reasonable steps to try and ensure that prisoners do not commit suicide? Consider *Nyang* v *G4S Care & Justice Services Ltd and others* [2013], where, despite there being a duty in respect of the many omissions in relation to the care and assessment of the detainee claimant, his case failed because those omissions were deemed not to have *caused* his suicide.

4.2.2 **Assumption of responsibility**

As already stated, this category has obvious links with 'control'. When the defendant can be said to have 'assumed responsibility' for the claimant's wellbeing or safety, it seems obvious that positive obligations (in the form of a duty of care) should arise. The most common types of assumed responsibility (as opposed to more naturally arising relationships of responsibility, such as parent/child, which are better thought of as falling into the 'control' category) are those that arise out of a contract or from employment relationships.

17. The daughter of the woman who killed herself was later awarded £10,000 from the NHS in a Human Rights Act claim: *Anna Savage* v *South Essex Partnership NHS Trust* [2010]. In *Rabone* v *Pennine Care NHS Trust* [2010] the Court of Appeal ruled out such a claim where the patient was *voluntarily* receiving inpatient treatment for her mental health but, due to the hospital's negligence, was allowed on home leave, where she committed suicide. However, the Supreme Court overturned this, finding that the state has a positive obligation under Art 2 to prevent the suicide of voluntary mental patients and, though in *Rabone* the health trust admitted negligence and settled with the appellants (the patient's parents), this did not prevent them being recognised as 'victims' for the purposes of s 7 of the Human Rights Act 1998 (*Rabone and another* v *Pennine Care NHS Trust* [2012]).

18. Consider, e.g., the findings of the Office for National Statistics that male prisoners in England and Wales are 3.7 times more likely to die from suicide than the general population ('Drug related deaths and suicides in prison custody in England and Wales: 2008 to 2016', 25 July 2019). See also the Home Office report by Giles Lindon and Stephen Roe 'Deaths in police custody: A review of the international evidence', October 2017.

Costello v *Chief Constable of Northumbria Police* [1999] CA

A female police constable was attacked by a prisoner in a cell. Despite her calls for help, a police inspector in the vicinity did not come to her aid. Costello alleged that the police inspector owed a duty to assist a fellow officer when in trouble.

The Court of Appeal agreed. Police officers assume a responsibility to one another to 'watch each other's back'. Where a police officer's omission might lead to avoidable harm being suffered by a fellow officer, a positive duty to act would be imposed. Thus, in failing to act, the police inspector had breached that duty and the Chief Constable was vicariously liable.[19]

Another way that someone can assume responsibility for the wellbeing of someone else is by their actions. Put another way, *what* someone does in relation to someone else can indicate, by conduct, an assumption of responsibility. A clear example of this is seen in ***Barrett* v *Ministry of Defence*** [1995].

Barrett v *Ministry of Defence* [1995] CA

A naval pilot stationed on a remote Norwegian base where extreme drunkenness had become commonplace had been celebrating his 30th birthday and a promotion, when he became so drunk that he collapsed. The officer on duty ordered that he be taken to his bed—however, no one stayed to watch over him and he later choked to death on his own vomit.

At first instance, it was ruled that the senior officers had breached their duty to prevent irresponsible drinking on the base, but the damages to be awarded would be reduced by 25 per cent to account for Barrett's own contributory negligence.

The Court of Appeal agreed. However, to them, the senior officers' duty (and, through the doctrine of vicarious liability, that of the Ministry of Defence) was not owed in relation to the failure to prevent or discourage excessive drinking, as the court believed that adults should take responsibility for themselves in this respect. Rather, the duty was owed in relation to the duty officer's failure to have someone stationed to watch Barrett while he slept (a different omission) because, by that point, responsibility for his safety had been assumed by the officer concerned:

> [i]n the present case I would reverse the judge's finding that the defendant was under a duty to take reasonable care to prevent the deceased from abusing alcohol to the extent he did. Until he collapsed, I would hold that the deceased was in law alone responsible for his condition. Thereafter, when the defendant assumed responsibility for him, it accepts that the measures taken fell short of the standard reasonably to be expected. It did not summon medical assistance and its supervision of him was inadequate. (Beldam LJ at 1225)

The Court of Appeal also considered that more responsibility for his death lay with the deceased than with the officers, and reduced his damages by two-thirds.

19. See also *Mullaney* v *Chief Constable of West Midlands* [2001]. These cases are examples of an exception to the general rule that the police owe no duty of care, as discussed in **Chapter 6**. See further on vicarious liability **Chapter 20**.

Counterpoint

On closer inspection, the *ratio* of **Barrett** suggests that had no one found the naval officer when he was drunk or—more specifically, as this is what the case turns on—taken him back to his room, no one would have assumed responsibility and therefore no duty of care would or could have arisen. Can this be right? What this means is that if he had fallen unconscious outside (on the Norwegian naval base) and been left to freeze to death, either because he had not been found or because whoever did see him chose to ignore his plight and walk past (a 'pure' omission), no duty of care would have been owed. Would it be better to say that this was a situation in which the superior officers had 'control', and therefore *should* have done what they could to prevent excessive drinking? Or is it right that individual responsibility is taken into account *only until the point when someone else intervenes*?

4.2.3 **Creating or adopting risks**

The final exception to the general exclusionary rule in relation to omissions is based on the creation or adoption of a risk. If it can be said that the defendant—even accidentally—creates a dangerous situation, a positive duty to try and deal with that danger may be imposed. In ***Capital & Counties plc* v *Hampshire County Council*** [1997], it was found that a fire service, as a public body, will only owe a duty to a property owner when it either creates the danger in the first place or where its positive actions upon responding to an emergency make the situation worse. In this case, the county council was vicariously liable for the fire chief's decision to turn off a sprinkler system on the claimant's property, thereby allowing the fire to spread more rapidly than it would have had the sprinkler system still been operational. This general point flows through the law on omissions.[20]

In terms of 'adopting' risks, *Goldman* v *Hargrave* [1967][21] illustrates a similar idea. Here, a tree caught fire after being struck by lightning. The landowner ensured that the tree was cut down, but decided to let it burn itself out and took no further precautions to prevent the fire spreading. Therefore, although he did not cause the fire, in deciding to take no further steps to completely extinguish it he adopted the risk of it spreading (in a similar way to assuming responsibility for someone else he had, in a sense, assumed responsibility for the risk). Extensive damage was caused to a neighbouring property after the fire was revived by the wind. The Privy Council found that a duty of care was owed in relation to adopted dangers on one's land when that danger could spread to a neighbour's land.

20. See further **section 6.5.1**. A good summary of the rule from ***Capital & Counties plc*** was given by Lady Paton in a Scottish appeal case on liability of the fire service: *AJ Allan (Blairnyle) Ltd and another* v *Strathclyde Fire Board* [2016].

21. Discussed in more detail in the section on land torts, see **section 19.6**.

4.3 Summary of when a duty of care may be found in respect of omissions

This is summarised in **Table 4.1**.

TABLE 4.1 When a duty of care may be found in respect of omissions

Duty of care	
General rule: no duty of care	Exceptions:
Smith v *Littlewoods* [1987] *Stovin* v *Wise* [1996] *Sutradhar* v *National Environmental Research Council* [2006]	Control exercised over claimant by defendant *Reeves* v *Commissioner of Police for the Metropolis* [2000]
	Assumption of responsibility for claimant's welfare by defendant *Costello* v *Chief Constable of Northumbria Police* [1999] *Barrett* v *Ministry of Defence* [1995]
	Creation or adoption of a risk *Capital & Counties plc* v *Hampshire County Council* [1997] *Goldman* v *Hargrave* [1967]

4.4 Liability for acts of third parties: the general rule

There is no general duty to prevent other people causing damage. After all, why should someone owe a duty of care in respect of harm inflicted on another by a third party? Again, however, there are exceptions to this general rule, many of which relate to and overlap with those already discussed in the context of omissions, and stem from either a special or pre-tort relationship. For example, it is often because someone has not done something (an omission) that allows a third party the chance or opportunity to do something that they otherwise might not have done, this being what leads to the harm suffered.[22] The question for the courts is similar—in what circumstances should we depart from the general rule that people should not be liable for the actions of third parties?

4.5 When is there liability for the acts of third parties?

The law imposes liability for the acts of third parties in exceptional circumstances. In such circumstances, one of the logistical problems that might have been encountered—in relation to when or whether a defendant should be liable for the actions of a third party—is broadly met by the *content* of the duty being a 'duty to control the third party'

22. See e.g. ***Home Office* v *Dorset Yacht Co Ltd*** [1970].

or a 'duty to safeguard a dangerous thing'. However, this does not prevent there being causation problems—as we will see, a later act of a third party may actually operate to break the chain of causation back to the defendant (or may affect what damages can be paid if thought to be a supervening, rather than intervening event).[23] There is a very fine line between the consideration of a third party's actions as a duty issue or a causation issue and often the questions we ask are part and parcel of the same thing.[24] Some guidance on this point can be gleaned from the speech of Lord Reid in ***Home Office*** **v** ***Dorset Yacht Co Ltd*** **[1970]** where he said that an act of a third party:

> must have been something very likely to happen if it is not to be regarded as a *novus actus interveniens* breaking the chain of causation. I do not think that a mere foreseeable possibility is or should be sufficient, for then the intervening human action can more properly be regarded as a new cause than as a consequence of the original wrongdoing. (at 1030)[25]

There are some exceptional situations in which a duty has been imposed on a defendant in respect of the actions of a third party. Lord Goff (in *Smith* v *Littlewoods* [1987]) suggested that such a duty can arise in four circumstances:

(1) where there is a special relationship between the defendant and the claimant;

(2) where there is a special relationship between the defendant and the third party, such as a relationship of control or supervision;

(3) where someone creates a 'source of danger' that may be 'sparked' by a third party;

(4) where there is a failure to take steps to abate a known danger created by a third party.

We will look at examples from each of these categories in turn.[26]

4.5.1 A special relationship between defendant and claimant

Where the defendant and the claimant have a special (pre-tort) relationship, that is a relationship in which a sufficient degree of proximity can be found to justify the imposition of a duty of care from one to the other, a duty may arise in relation to the activities of a third party. Such a relationship may be defined by a contract between the two parties. For example, in *Stansbie* v *Troman* [1948], the claimant employed the defendant to decorate her premises. When she went out, she specifically requested that the decorator lock up after himself when he left. He failed to do this and she was subsequently burgled. The court found that the contractual relationship between them was enough to create the necessary proximity for the imposition of a duty on the defendant. Put simply, because of the relationship between them, he had a duty to lock the premises when he left, in order to prevent a burglary by a third party.[27]

23. **Section 9.2.3.**

24. See *Smith* v *Littlewoods* [1987], as one example of a case that clearly highlights the difficulty courts have in categorising third party actions as either a duty or causation issue.

25. Note there has been some criticism of Lord Reid's formulation—see e.g. Denning, Oliver and Watkins LJJ in *Lamb* v *Camden London Borough Council* [1981].

26. It should be clear from these categories where there is overlap between what is discussed here and in the earlier section on omissions. The first category, here, clearly has parallels with the idea of 'assumption of responsibility' in relation to omissions—and the others are even more obvious—so much so that you may find that other texts have some of the cases used to illustrate these ideas in the omissions section rather than in relation to third party liability and vice versa.

27. The principle was more recently confirmed in *Bailey and another* v *HSS Alarms* [2000].

Compare, however, *P Perl (Exporters) Ltd* v *Camden London Borough Council* [1984]. Here, two adjoining buildings were owned by Camden Council, one of which was leased by the claimant—the other was empty and unlockable. Thieves entered the unlocked premises, made a hole in the wall separating the two buildings and burgled the claimant's property. The Court of Appeal found that the council owed no duty in respect of the third parties' (the burglars') actions. Despite it being foreseeable that some harm might be caused by leaving their property unlocked, this was not enough to establish the necessary proximity between the defendant and the claimant.

Notably, however, this case falls into a clear group of cases in which property owners were not found—for various reasons—liable for the actions of third parties. This suggests that there may be underlying policy reasons for such decisions, not least the fact that property-owning claimants might be expected to have insurance.[28] However, presumably, *all* property owners might be expected to be insured, meaning that there are equally valid competing policy reasons in these cases.

The requisite proximity may also stem from an express or implied undertaking made by the defendant to the claimant. In such circumstances—for example, where the defendant promised not to do something that may endanger the claimant in some way—it seems right that a duty should arise. In *Swinney* v *Chief Constable of Northumbria Police* [1997] the Court of Appeal found that the police owed a duty of care not to leak confidential information about the claimant, a police informant, because she may be harmed by those about whom she had given information. Such undertakings can also be implied, as in ***Costello*** where it was found that one police officer has a duty to assist another if they come under attack from a third party in police custody.

However, it is also evident that there has to be a *direct* undertaking by the defendant in order for a duty to arise in these circumstances. In a string of police cases including ***Hill* v *Chief Constable of West Yorkshire*** [1989], ***Osman* v *Ferguson*** [1993] and ***Michael* v *Chief Constable of South Wales Police*** [2015], for example, no duty was owed by police to claimants who were victims of crimes committed by third parties. In these cases there was a general duty to the public at large, but no specific duty existed to protect specific claimants, as no promise—express or implied—had been made to this effect.[29]

The idea that there must indeed be a specific undertaking can be clearly seen in ***Palmer* v *Tees Health Authority*** [1999].

Palmer v *Tees Health Authority* [1999] CA

Mrs Palmer alleged that the defendant health authority had been negligent in its assessment of a mentally ill patient—Armstrong—who kidnapped, sexually assaulted, killed and mutilated her 4-year-old daughter Rosie upon his release from a secure unit. While under treatment for

→

28. Indeed, this point was explicitly acknowledged by Lord Denning MR in *Lamb* v *Camden London Borough Council* [1981], a case with similar facts to *P Perl (Exporters) Ltd*.

29. It should be noted here that there was a far higher degree of proximity in ***Osman*** and ***Michael*** than in ***Hill***, though still not enough for the court to consider imposing a duty on the police (see further **section 6.5.3**).

→

his illness, Armstrong stated that he had sexual feelings towards children and threatened to abduct and murder a child. Post-release, he failed to attend an outpatient's appointment.

The Court of Appeal, relying on *Hill*, found that the health authority owed neither Mrs Palmer nor Rosie a duty of care, as the necessary proximity between the parties did not exist. The child was not identifiable as a potential victim (like in *Hill*), meaning the health authority could have done nothing to prevent her murder, other than keep the patient detained. There was no special relationship that could give rise to a duty of care.

In his judgment in ***Palmer***, Stuart-Smith LJ said that 'once rules are established, it is not open to the courts to extend the accepted principles of proximity simply because the facts of a given case are particularly horrifying or heart-rending' (at 7). Nevertheless, it appears strange to us that the requisite proximity could not be found—or was not even argued on appeal—from the fact that Rosie lived in the same street as Armstrong.[30]

Following ***Palmer***, it was argued in *K* v *Secretary of State for the Home Department* [2002] that in situations where 'exceptionally serious' risks are posed by a known third party, sufficient proximity could exist between an injured claimant and a defendant whose negligence fails to prevent the harm occurring. Here a Kenyan man, who had been imprisoned for a number of violent crimes and was due to be deported, was released early by the Secretary of State. The claimant, who was subsequently raped by the man, sued the Secretary of State alleging that the decision to release him early was negligent, as he posed a known risk of committing a violent crime. The Court of Appeal found that because the victim was unidentifiable to the defendant, there was no relationship of proximity between them, following ***Hill*** and ***Palmer***, and this was not changed by the seriousness of the risk, even where it was clearly known by the defendant that such a risk existed.

Pause for reflection

Do you think it is right that the claimants in cases like *Palmer* and *K* have no cause of action? Where a psychiatric patient makes known his wish to harm a child, *should* he be released? *Why* was the criminal in *K* released before deportation? Surely both men did 'the very thing that was likely to happen' upon their release? As we have seen from Lord Reid in *Dorset Yacht*, this is, in different circumstances, enough to create a duty.[31] We would argue that simply because there was no undertaking between the defendant and the claimant, this should not mean that the claimants in cases like *Palmer* and *K* must fail. The crimes committed were just as severe, and the defendant's negligence just as intense, as they would have been if the criminal had told the

→

30. Contrast *Buck* v *Norfolk and Waveney Mental Health NHS Foundation Trust* [2012].

31. Also see Lord Morris in ***Dorset Yacht***, who said: 'If a person who in lawful custody has made a threat, accepted as seriously intended that, if he can escape, he will injure X . . . a duty [will be owed] to X to take reasonable care to prevent escape' (at 1039). Can parallels be drawn with those detained on mental health grounds? Compare the US case *Tarasoff* v *Regents of the University of California* [1976].

→

defendant who he was intending to attack. Arguably, also, preventative measures would have been easy to take in each of the cases.

In any case, as we see from cases like ***Osman* v *Ferguson***,[32] even where the victim is clearly identifiable (thus creating the requisite proximity), a positive duty to act may not arise for policy reasons. What policy reasons exist in relation to these cases?

The principle that a duty of care will not exist even where a potential victim is known to the defendant unless a specific undertaking has been given was underlined by the House of Lords in *Mitchell* v *Glasgow City Council* [2009]. Mitchell, a 72-year-old man, was beaten and killed with a stick or iron bar by his 60-year-old neighbour, Drummond. Both were tenants of the defendant, which had long been aware of Drummond's anti-social and hostile behaviour, including death threats made to Mitchell. Having issued many previous warnings, a further serious incident made the defendants summon Drummond to a meeting, where he was threatened with eviction if his anti-social behaviour continued. Leaving the meeting angry, Drummond returned home and attacked Mitchell. Acting on his behalf, Mitchell's widow contended that the council owed him a duty to inform him the meeting had taken place and warn both him and the police of the potential danger. The law lords found that the council owed Mitchell no duty of care:

> [a] duty to warn another person that he is at risk of loss, injury or damage as the result of the criminal act of a third party will only arise where the person who is said to be under that duty has by his words or conduct assumed responsibility for the safety of the person who is at risk. (Lord Hope at [29])

Given the high degree of foreseeability of harm, coupled with the council's proximate relationship (to both the claimant *and* the third party), as well as what *looks like* assumption of responsibility, it is not apparent to us that this is a clear-cut case where no duty should be owed.[33] More recently, in ***Poole Borough Council* v *GN* [2019]**,[34] the Supreme Court found that, despite knowledge of serious anti-social behaviour and violence from a neighbouring family towards the (child) claimants in council-arranged housing, this did not amount to an assumption of responsibility. Therefore, the council had no duty to protect the claimants from foreseeable harm. In contrast is the Court of Appeal decision in *Selwood* v *Durham County Council and others* [2012]. Here, a psychiatric patient threatened to kill the claimant social worker if he came into contact with her, though she was not informed of this threat. When she attended a case conference dealing with one of the patient's children, he stabbed her repeatedly. At first her claim was struck out, the decision relying in part on *Mitchell*. However, the Court of Appeal unanimously allowed her appeal, finding that assumption of responsibility need not be express or implied from conduct, it could also be inferred from the circumstances, and that the

32. Also see ***Smith* v *Chief Constable of Sussex Police* [2008]** and ***Michael* v *Chief Constable of South Wales Police* [2015]**.

33. Also see *Hussain and another* v *Lancaster City Council* [1999] and *X & Y* v *London Borough of Hounslow* [2009]. The latter case is discussed in **section 2.6** and **section 6.7.2**. The Court of Appeal decision relied heavily on the findings in *Mitchell*.

34. Discussed in **section 6.3**.

judge failed to consider whether the defendants' policy document[35] and/or working arrangements inferred such an assumption.

***Michael* v *Chief Constable of South Wales Police* [2015]** (discussed in detail at **section 6.3.1**) demonstrates the clear overlap between the problematic notions of imposing liability for omissions and for the action of third parties. Counsel for the claimant had raised an exception to the general rule on omissions as one ground of appeal, arguing that the police could be said to have assumed responsibility for Ms Michael's safety after the first 999 call, thus owing her a duty of care. Lord Toulson, giving the leading judgment, retreats into the long line of established authorities in this area and notes the exceptions of 'control' and 'assumption of responsibility' (at [98]–[100]), eventually finding that an assumption of responsibility could not (and should not) be established because the omission led to the harm being caused by a third party:

> It does not follow from the setting up of a protective system from public resources that if it fails to achieve its purpose, through organisational defects or fault on the part of an individual, the public at large should bear the additional burden of compensating a victim for harm caused by the actions of a third party for whose behaviour the state is not responsible. To impose such a burden would be contrary to the ordinary principles of the common law. (at [114])

Counterpoint

Arguably, collapsing the two areas of law into each other in that way led Lord Toulson to forget that additional exceptions, such as those discussed here, exist in relation to the actions of third parties. It is at least arguable that, as in the cases outlined earlier, a 'special relationship' existed between the defendant and claimant due to the nature of her call and the fact she would obviously rely on the police providing assistance to her,[36] even if that was not quite enough to amount to a 'true' assumption of responsibility. Being asked by a call handler (having dialled 999 while fearing an imminent violent attack) if she was able to lock the doors, and being told that the call would be passed on to the correct police force is, to us, clear indication that it was *reasonable* for Joanne Michael to rely on the police. Thus, they should have owed her a duty, despite the fact the harm was eventually caused by a third party. Had her call been handled properly, it is unlikely that she would have been killed.[37]

→

35. Which specifically stated that there might be circumstances in which confidential information might need to be disclosed without a patient's consent if the health or safety of a professional was at risk.

36. See Joanne Conaghan, 'Civil liability: addressing failures in the context of rape, domestic and sexual abuse' Inaugural Lecture given at the University of Bristol on 19 February 2015. The full lecture can be viewed at **www.youtube.com/watch?v=y1bawCpPr30&app=desktop**.

37. Also see Martin Evans, 'Woman was murdered by stalker ex-boyfriend after police blunders, report finds' *The Telegraph* 12 September 2018. There, the Independent Office for Police Conduct (IOPC) found multiple failures in the police response to the victim's reporting of worrying stalking behaviour by her ex-boyfriend. Contrast the response of Warwickshire police to the death of Julia Mendes, also following a miscategorised 999 call, where it could be argued that no such assumption of responsibility occurred, yet the victim's family were paid £21,687. See Diane Taylor 'Police apologise to dead woman's kin after failure to respond to 999 call' *The Guardian* 5 January 2017.

→

Lord Kerr (dissenting) said that the logic of the idea—that unless there was an explicit promise by the police coupled with express reliance by Joanne Michael, assumed responsibility cannot arise—must be questioned:

> Should someone in a vulnerable state, fearing imminent attack, who *believes that the assurance of timeous assistance has been made* when, through negligence on the part of the police, that impression has been wrongly created, be treated differently from another who has in fact received an explicit assurance of immediate help, if both have relied on what they believed to be a clear promise that police would attend and avert the apprehended danger? (at [165], emphasis added)

It would truly be an invidious distinction if—had the call handler said 'help is on its way, don't worry'—a duty of care could be found.[38]

4.5.2 A special relationship between defendant and third party

Again, when we speak of a 'special relationship' in this respect, we are talking about proximity. The more proximate (or close) the relationship between the defendant and the third party who caused the damage or harm, the more likely it is that a duty will be imposed on the defendant in respect of the third party's actions. As with liability for omissions, proximate relationships in this context include those where there is a degree of control exercised over the third party by the defendant, or where it can be said that the defendant has 'assumed responsibility' for the third party's actions. ***Dorset Yacht*** illustrates this principle well.[39]

Home Office v *Dorset Yacht Co Ltd* [1970] HL

In this case the court had to consider whether the acts of third parties (young offenders detained on Brownsea Island just off the Dorset coast) broke the chain of causation between the defendants' carelessness and the damage suffered by the claimants. The defendants, the boys' supervisors (for whom the Home Office would be vicariously liable), negligently allowed a group of boys to escape and damage the claimants' yachts moored in the harbour. The supervisory nature of the relationship created the requisite degree of proximity between the defendants and the third parties. Moreover, the damage suffered by the claimants was the direct consequence of this relationship 'failing': upon their escape, the boys did the exact thing that might be expected of them—they attempted to steal a boat to get off the island. The chain of causation was therefore intact and, correspondingly, a duty of care was owed in respect of the boys' actions. The duty arose because the actions of the boys following their negligent supervision were the thing 'very likely to happen' (Lord Reid at 1030).

38. See also *Griffiths and others* v *Suffolk Police and another* [2018].
39. Also see *Vowles* v *Evans and another* [2003] and *Watson* v *British Boxing Board of Control Ltd* [2001] in the context of sports officials.

Counterpoint

In the previous section we considered the cases of ***Palmer*** and *K*, where no duty was found on the basis that the defendant–claimant relationship lacked proximity. In our view, however, it is equally arguable that those cases fit into the category of a special relationship (based on control or assumption of responsibility) existing between the defendant *and the third party.*

Did the claimants fail to establish a duty only because the cases were looked at the wrong way? We can see no real differences between these cases; if anything, the case in ***Palmer*** is stronger than that in ***Dorset Yacht***. In the former, not only was the psychiatric patient still under the care of the health authority as an outpatient but he had expressed a *specific* wish to harm a child.

In ***Palmer***, no proximity was found between the defendant and the claimant as there had been no assumption of responsibility towards the victim, who was merely one member of a class of people who might be at risk. Was this the right question to ask, given Lord Goff's four exceptions to the general exclusionary rule for third party liability? Is it better to ask whether the defendant assumed responsibility for the conduct of (or the danger posed by) *the third party*?

Consider the Canadian case *Doe* v *Metropolitan Toronto (Municipality) Commissioners of Police* [1998], where the court found that a woman *was* owed a duty of care by the police in respect of her rape. She was one of many women in the potential target group of a serial rapist, who operated in a particular area of the city and was known as the 'Balcony Rapist' because he preferred to break into women's flats via balconies. Potential victims were neither warned nor adequately protected owing to a number of significant failings on the part of the police. Was this case decided differently from ***Palmer*** and *K* because the woman was in a smaller and more readily identifiable group of potential victims? If so, how few potential victims need there be before it can be said a duty would be owed to each of them? In ***Palmer***, it should be remembered, the victim lived on the same street as the man who killed her. How difficult would it have been to warn parents of children in the area? Or, if this is not the appropriate response, what else could the health authority have done? In our opinion, the fact that the claimant in ***Palmer*** could have been classified in a smaller group of potential victims should, like in *Doe*, have weighed more heavily with the court, as it is this feature that marks this case out from a law where the police would owe a duty in respect of all crimes committed by released prisoners and health authorities for psychiatric patients.[40]

4.5.3 **Creating a source of danger**

If a third party's actions exacerbate a dangerous situation originally created by the defendant, subsequently causing the claimant harm, the defendant may owe the claimant a duty of care. For example, in *Haynes* v *Harwood* [1935], the defendant left his horses untethered on a busy street; they bolted when some children threw stones at them. A police officer was injured trying to control the horses; it was found that the defendant owed him a duty of care, as he had created a source of danger that was 'sparked' by the third parties.

For a duty to arise in these circumstances, a special risk must be created. In *Topp* v *London Country Bus* [1993], the defendant's employee left an unlocked minibus unattended outside a pub, with keys in the ignition. When the pub closed, a patron entered

40. Consider also the High Court's decision (later upheld by the Supreme Court) in *DSD* v *The Commissioner of Police for the Metropolis* [2014], discussed at **section 6.3.1** as well as in the lecture by Joanne Conaghan, referred to in **n 36**.

the minibus and drove it away carelessly, killing a pedestrian. However, the Court of Appeal found that the minibus was no more a source of danger than any other vehicle parked on the road at that time, therefore leaving the minibus did not create the type of risk that would create a duty of care as in *Haynes*.[41]

Pause for reflection

Is an unlocked bus with the keys in the ignition, left outside a pub at closing time, really less dangerous than an untethered horse? Is the outcome of this case surprising, particularly as the driver/owners of the bus would be insured?

4.5.4 **A failure to abate a known danger**

In a sense, this is the reverse of the situation outlined earlier. There, we looked at instances where the defendant created a danger that could be 'sparked' by a third party. Here, we consider the situation where the danger is in fact created by a third party, but the defendant does nothing to abate it. However, the key word here is 'known'; unknown (or unknowable) dangers do not fall into this category. It can be explained as follows: if a defendant knows—or ought to have known—that a third party has created a danger that he *should* do something about (e.g. because it is on his property), then they will owe a duty of care to anyone injured as a result of that danger.[42] Put simply, the defendant has a duty to do something about the danger in order to prevent injury (to person or property) to others.

In *Smith* v *Littlewoods* [1987], the claimant's property was damaged by fire spreading from a derelict cinema owned by Littlewoods after vandals entered it at night and started a fire. The law lords—in particular Lord Goff—found that only where the danger was known, or foreseeable, would a duty be owed in respect of it.[43] On the facts, no such duty was owed as Littlewoods had no reason to suspect the vandals' entry and the only thing they could have done to prevent it would be to hire round-the-clock security, which would be disproportionate to the level of risk. As they had some security and had taken some precautions against trespassers, they had done all they reasonably should be expected to do.[44] In this sense *Smith* v *Littlewoods* went a long way towards clarifying the law in this area in which liability had previously been judicially controlled using various other aspects of the law of negligence.[45]

41. Would the same be true where a cleaner left the door to a pub open one night (as in the scenario at the beginning of the chapter)? The legal question is whether she should be held responsible for the damage to the pub and, also, for the damage to the car parked on the same street. By analogy with *Stansbie* it might be fairly easy to establish the duty in relation to the stolen alcohol and damaged pub—but might *Topp* stand in the way of the car owner claiming successfully?

42. See, in the context of land torts, ***Sedleigh Denfield* v *O'Callaghan* [1940]**, *Goldman* v *Hargrave* [1967] and *Leakey* v *National Trust* [1980], **section 19.6.1**. Also compare the position of occupiers of premises under the Occupiers' Liability statutes (**Chapter 11**).

43. Notably, although *Smith* v *Littlewoods* was a unanimous decision, each of the law lords reached their decision by different means.

44. Compare also Smith LJ's judgment in the context of a knife attack in a nightclub in the more recent case *Everett* v *Comojo (UK) Ltd (t/a The Metropolitan)* [2011], particularly [31]–[33].

45. Compare e.g. *Lamb* v *Camden London Borough Council* [1981] (third party's acts too remote a consequence of the defendant's breach (causation in law)), *P Perl (Exporters) Ltd* (no duty because the defendant could not be expected to control the actions of third parties) and *King* v *Liverpool City Council* [1986] (duty found but defendant not in breach as there was nothing they could reasonably have done to prevent the third parties' actions).

In *Clark Fixing Ltd* v *Dudley Metropolitan Borough Council* [2001], the reasoning from *Smith* v *Littlewoods* was used to find a duty in exactly the extended circumstances envisaged by Lord Goff. In *Clark*, Dudley Council owned property which shared a roof with an adjoining property owned by the claimant. As in *Smith*, trespassers entered the council's property and started a fire, which spread to the claimant's property, causing substantial damage. The council, unlike the cinema owners in *Smith*, was aware that trespassers had entered the premises—and had started fires—on a number of previous occasions, and in fact had received complaints about this from the claimants. The Court of Appeal therefore found that a duty was owed by the council, despite the actual harm being caused by third parties. Similarly, but without actual knowledge of the risk, a duty of care was found in *Sandhu Menswear Co Ltd* v *Woolworths plc* [2006], where the defendants had left piles of flammable material by storage units on an industrial estate, which when set alight had caused damage to the claimant's property. Even though in *Sandhu*, unlike *Clark*, there was no evidence that fires had previously been lit by third parties, the court held that it was foreseeable that fires *could* be lit by people trespassing in the area and therefore a duty could be found.

Pause for reflection

As outlined in **Chapter 2**, a claimant not only has to prove that a duty was owed to them, but that this was breached and that the breach *caused* the harm suffered by them. How is it possible, however, when the harm is the result of a third party's actions, to establish that the *defendant* was the *cause* of the claimant's harm?

Generally, this causation difficulty is overcome by the *content* of the duty—for example, it will be a 'duty to control a third party' or a 'duty to safeguard a dangerous thing'. When looked at this way, failure to control a third party or a dangerous thing (the breach) *is* what causes the claimant's harm. Do you agree with this statement? And if so, how do we explain cases like ***Palmer*** or *K*?

Counterpoint

Claire McIvor calls 'third party liability' a 'novel category of tortious liability' that 'evolved from a collection of disparate and isolated judicial decisions setting out *ad hoc* exceptions to the entrenched common law rules against liability for omissions and liability for the acts of others' (p 1). We agree, adding that the law defining if and when defendants owe a duty of care in respect of either an omission or for the actions of another seems to be based on judicial perceptions rooted wholeheartedly in the concept of individualism. While it may be admirable to suggest that people should only take responsibility for their own actions, this approach does not adequately encompass the fact that in many of the cases we have seen it may be more *morally* justifiable to adopt a broader conception of duty and allow breach to be used as a control on liability. Put simply, we would prefer the approach in these situations to be based on the level of fault or moral blameworthiness that could be attached to the defendant. McIvor is right to contend that due to 'the improvised nature of its development, the current law on third party liability is unstructured, unprincipled and incoherent' (p 1).

4.6 Summary of when a duty of care may be found for the actions of third parties

This is summarised in **Table 4.2**.

TABLE 4.2 When a duty of care may be found for the actions of third parties

General rule: no duty of care]	Exceptions (see *Smith* v *Littlewoods* [1987])	
	Proximity between defendant and claimant	
	Duty found in *Stansbie* v *Troman* [1948] *Swinney* v *Chief Constable of Northumbria Police* [1997] *Selwood* v *Durham County Council and others* [2012]	But not in *P Perl (Exporters)* v *Camden London Borough Council* [1984] *Palmer* v *Tees Health Authority* [1999] *K* v *Secretary of State for the Home Department* [2002] *Mitchell* v *Glasgow City Council* [2009] *Michael* v *Chief Constable of South Wales Police* [2015]
	Proximity between defendant and third party	
	Duty found in *Home Office* v *Dorset Yacht* [1970]	But not in *Palmer* v *Tees Health Authority* [1999] *K* v *Secretary of State for the Home Department* [2002] *Mitchell* v *Glasgow City Council* [2009]
	Creation of a source of danger	
	Duty found in *Haynes* v *Harwood* [1935]	But not in *Topp* v *London Country Bus* [1993]
	Failure to abate a known danger	
	Duty found in *Clark Fixing Ltd* v *Dudley Metropolitan Borough Council* [2001] *Sandhu Menswear Co Ltd* v *Woolworths plc* [2006] *Everett* v *Comojo (UK) Ltd (t/a The Metropolitan)* [2011]	But not in *Smith* v *Littlewoods* [1987]

4.7 Conclusion

In this chapter we have looked at the separate—but closely linked—concepts of liability for *omissions* and for the *actions of third parties*. A general exclusionary rule operates in respect of both. However, as usual, there are exceptions to these rules.

In relation to omissions, a duty of care can be established where the defendant and claimant have a relationship making it appropriate to depart from the general rule. As we saw, such relationships include those where a degree of control is exercised over the claimant by the defendant, that is, where the responsibility for them is explicit, such as parent–child relationships or with people held in custody and who constitute a known suicide risk. They may also be defined by the assumption of responsibility. If the defendant actively assumes responsibility for the claimant's wellbeing, this will usually be enough to establish a positive duty to act. Finally, we saw that positive obligations may arise in respect of omissions where a risk is created or adopted by a defendant.

Third party liability is controlled by similar concepts. Relationships between claimants and defendants are also important—the courts require a high degree of proximity before a duty will be imposed. This works in two ways: either there is sufficient proximity between the defendant and the claimant (e.g. as in many contractual relationships) that makes it appropriate for the defendant to be liable when a third party causes harm to the claimant, or there is sufficient proximity between the defendant and the third party. As with omissions, this may come from there being a relationship of control and/or responsibility between the defendant and the third party. Again, in a similar way to liability for omissions, a defendant may be liable for the actions of a third party when they have either created a danger that a third party's actions might cause harm or have failed to abate a known danger created by a third party.

End-of-chapter questions

After reading the chapter carefully, try answering the questions which follow.

1 Should a 'Good Samaritan' statute be passed in this country? What are the benefits of *not* having one?

2 Do the concepts of liberal individualism and personal autonomy carry more weight than collective or social responsibility? Should they?

3 In *Smith* v *Littlewoods* [1987], Lord Goff indicated that the legal treatment of omissions may one day need to be reconsidered. Was he correct?

If you would like to know what we think visit the **online resources**. www.oup.com/he/horsey7e

Answering the problem question

Consider again the problem question at the start of this chapter. Now having read about the topic, **what would be your advice to the various parties?**

Here are some pointers to get you started:

→ There are various claimants in this problem and various defendants. You should start by outlining who would claim against whom, and why.

→ M (her estate) will claim against B (and the supermarket vicariously, see **Chapter 20**). Though there is no general duty to assist someone in trouble, had B 'assumed responsibility' towards M?

→ M will also claim against K. The issues are similar to those against B, initially.

→ J and H will claim against M. However, the harm they suffered was the result of a third party's actions so it may be difficult to establish a duty.

→ L will also claim against M. Even if a duty can be established here there may be tricky causation points (see **Chapter 9**) and a potential defence to the claim (see **Chapter 10**).

If you need some more guidance

→ An **annotated version of the problem with issues and cases to consider** can be found in the Appendix.

→ A **suggested outline answer** to check your ideas against can be found in the online resources that accompany the book.

see online resources

Further reading

Literature on this area of law tends to focus on reform, highlighting inconsistencies and inadequacies in the existing law. Claire McIvor's book is a great starting point from which to critique the law on third party liability, while Jeroen Kortmann provides excellent analysis of the principles of altruism and rescue in the context of English law. Chapter 3 of the book contains a particularly good and persuasive critique of Lord Hoffmann's reasoning/justifications in ***Stovin* v *Wise***.

Carr, Nanci 'Am I My Brother's Keeper? How Technology Necessitates Reform of the Lack of Duty to Rescue or Duty to Report Laws in the United States' (2019) 2 Boston Uni Public Interest LJ 117

Conaghan, Joanne 'Challenging and Redressing Police Failures in the Context of Rape Investigations: The Civil Liability Route' (2015) 5(1) *feminists@law*

Kortmann, Jeroen *Altruism in Private Law: Liability for Nonfeasance and Negotiorum Gestio* (OUP, 2005)

Linden, Allen 'Toward Tort Liability for Bad Samaritans' (2016) 53 Alberta L Rev 837

McIvor, Claire *Third Party Liability in Tort* (Hart, 2006)

Randell, Melanie 'Sex Discrimination, Accountability of Public Authorities and the Public/Private Divide in Tort Law: An Analysis of *Doe* v *Metropolitan Toronto (Municipality) Commissioners of Police*' (2000–01) 26 Queen's LJ 451

Reid, Elspeth '*Smith v Littlewoods Organisation Ltd* (1985)' in Charles Mitchell and Paul Mitchell (eds) *Landmark Cases in the Law of Tort* (Hart, 2010)

5 Special duty problems: psychiatric harm

Problem question

Read this problem question carefully, and keep it in mind while you are working through the chapter that follows. At the end of the chapter, you will be able to apply what you have learnt to the problem question and advise the relevant parties.

Following months of speculation the legendary indie guitar band—*Blinking Idiot*—are about to embark on a reunion tour of the UK. They are performing a warm-up gig at a small intimate venue when a spotlight falls onto the stage causing a massive explosion killing the band members: Madeleine, Amish and Dave. Unfortunately, the lighting rig (onto which the spotlight was fitted) had been negligently maintained by Rack & Horse Lighting. The sight is particularly gruesome.

Hannah, Amish's wife, is watching the gig from the VIP area of the venue. She is physically unharmed, but later suffers nightmares and depression. This is particularly traumatic for her as she had previously suffered from depression but had sought help and recovered.

Pete, Madeleine's brother, is listening to the live radio broadcast of the gig from his hotel room in Paris. He hears the explosion and thinks he can hear Madeleine screaming. He rushes to the airport, managing to catch a flight that is just leaving, and arrives at the hospital three hours after the accident. Unfortunately, Madeleine's body has not yet been moved to the morgue and is still covered in blood and grime from the explosion. He develops post-traumatic shock disorder.

Lucy has attended every *Blinking Idiot* gig in the UK and has travelled to a number of their overseas concerts. She is a founder member of their fan club and regularly contributes to their fan magazine. She always tries to stand as close as possible to the stage. Miraculously she was not hurt by the explosion but has since been overcome with grief.

Tim was one of the first on the scene. He is a trainee paramedic and this was his first major incident. He rushes to the stage but quickly sees that there is little he can do. He spends the next two hours comforting distraught fans. He later suffers from recurring nightmares and panic attacks.

Stuart, one of the roadies, is overcome with feelings of guilt and depression. It was his job to fix the lighting and he feels the explosion was his fault. A subsequent investigation completely exonerates him.

Advise the parties.

5.1 Introduction

Consider the following examples:

→ ***A grandfather watches as his grandchild is hit and killed by a car driven by a drunk driver. He later develops severe depression.***

→ ***A woman is diagnosed with cancer and told she only has weeks to live. She settles her affairs, plans her funeral and waits to die. Six months later further medical tests reveal that there has been a misdiagnosis—her X-rays became mixed up with another patient's—and she is not sick after all. She is deeply embarrassed about seeing the people she told she was dying and becomes severely agoraphobic.***

→ ***A teenage boy is involved in a car accident. Though he escapes physical injury, he suffers a reoccurrence of chronic fatigue syndrome.***

→ ***An elderly woman is trapped in a poorly serviced lift for 12 hours. During the experience she is very frightened and afterwards suffers from claustrophobia and insomnia.***

→ ***The organisers of a gig negligently let too many people into the venue. The gig is being broadcast live and a young teenager sees his boyfriend caught in the crush at the front of the stage. Six hours later his mother tells him that his boyfriend has died. Subsequently, the teenager becomes increasingly withdrawn and is unable to sleep.***

In all these cases, the nature of the harm suffered is not physical but mental or psychological. The distinction between physical and (purely) psychiatric injuries is an important one. The courts have been far more cautious in recognising claims in respect of psychiatric harms than they have in relation to physical injuries, developing a restrictive body of rules severely limiting the circumstances in which victims may recover compensation for their mental injuries.[1] Whether this distinction can be justified as a matter of principle or policy—and indeed whether there is in fact any clear and coherent distinction between physical and psychiatric harms—is far from certain.

5.2 What is psychiatric harm?

Psychiatric harm is a form of personal injury. When the courts first started considering claims in respect of psychiatric injuries, they focused on the distinct ways in which such harm tends to be caused: that is, by an 'assault' on an individual's mind or senses rather

1. The focus of this chapter is on claims for negligently caused 'pure' psychiatric injuries, where the *only* injury suffered by the claimant is psychiatric. Where the claimant suffers psychiatric harm as a result of physical injuries negligently inflicted by the defendant, recovery is straightforward (*Corr v IBC Vehicles Ltd* [2008]).

than physical impact on the claimant's body. This explains archaic references to this area of law as relating to liability for 'nervous shock'. So construed, this grouped psychiatric harms together with certain physical harms also caused by what one has witnessed (for instance, a number of the early cases concerned miscarriages suffered by women after traumatic experiences). However, the distinct policy issues raised by psychiatric injuries have seen the focus shift away from the *way* the harm is caused to the *type* of harm suffered. As *Ibbetson* notes:

> Before the middle of the twentieth century the courts took a restrictive attitude towards liability for 'nervous shock'; the focus here was not on the type of injury but on the way in which it had been caused. Gradually this twisted round until 'nervous shock' was identified with 'post-traumatic stress disorder'—a type of harm rather than a mode of causation of harm—from which it shifted yet further into 'psychiatric injury'. (p 195)

Nowadays the courts maintain a clear distinction between physical and (pure) psychiatric harm with different rules applying to each. This is notwithstanding developing medical knowledge and increased awareness of the serious and incapacitating nature of mental illnesses and the difficulties in categorising injuries as either physical or psychiatric. Despite some judges acknowledging that this distinction is largely unreal and unsustainable,[2] there remains a general reluctance to let go of the common-sense perception that mental harm is not just different from but also 'less significant than physical harm, [that] inability to cope through neurosis is less serious than inability to walk by reason of amputation' (*Weir* p 49).

Though initially psychiatric harm was recoverable only if accompanied by physical injury, it is now clear that claimants can recover for pure psychiatric harm so long as it is a recognised psychiatric illness. It is not, therefore, possible to recover in the tort of negligence for mere grief, anxiety or distress (*Hicks* v *Chief Constable of South Yorkshire Police* [1992]; *Brock* v *Northampton General Hospital NHS Trust* [2014]).[3] As Lord Steyn noted in ***White* v *Chief Constable of South Yorkshire Police* [1998]** 'the law cannot compensate for all emotional suffering even if it is acute and truly debilitating' (at 491).[4] However, while some conditions such as depression, schizophrenia, post-traumatic stress disorder (PTSD) and anxiety neurosis are clearly recognisable as psychiatric illnesses, in other cases it is difficult to distinguish ordinary feelings of anxiety or distress from an actionable harm. It may be that the question is one of degree, rather than type, of harm.[5]

2. See e.g. Kennedy J in *Dulieu* v *White & Sons* [1901] at 677 and the comment of Lord Lloyd in ***Page* v *Smith* [1996]**: 'In an age when medical knowledge is expanding fast, and psychiatric knowledge with it, it would not be sensible to commit the law to a distinction between physical and psychiatric injury, which may already seem somewhat artificial, and may soon be altogether outmoded' (at 188).

3. Though a claimant may have a claim under one of the intentional torts, e.g. assault or libel or under the tort in *Wilkinson* v *Downton* [1897].

4. This was confirmed by the House of Lords in ***Rothwell* v *Chemical and Insulating Co Ltd and Johnston* v *NEI International Combustion Ltd*** [2007] discussed further in **section 5.5**.

5. It is crucial then that the elderly woman trapped in a lift (referred to in the examples at the start of this chapter) is able to show that her insomnia and claustrophobia are (or are symptoms of) a recognised psychiatric illness (cf *Reilly* v *Merseyside RHA* [1995] where the claimants (an elderly couple) were unable to claim for the fear and claustrophobia suffered whilst trapped in a hospital lift for an hour and 20 minutes).

Pause for reflection

Consider for a moment the facts of *Hicks*. The teenage claimants, Sarah and Victoria Hicks, were crushed and suffocated to death in the Hillsborough Stadium disaster (discussed in **section 5.6**). The House of Lords rejected a claim for psychiatric harm brought on their behalf (by their father, Trevor Hicks) holding that the police's negligence had only caused the Hicks sisters to suffer 'distress', which was not recoverable. The evidence suggested that they had become unconscious within seconds and died within five minutes. Do you agree with the House of Lords' decision? At what point, if any, should negligently inflicted 'distress' ground a claim for psychiatric injury? Why do you think Trevor Hicks brought this claim? Think again about the purposes of tort law discussed in **Chapter 1**.

5.3 The general exclusionary rule

In the early 1990s, the courts developed a number of control mechanisms in order to restrict recovery for negligently inflicted psychiatric harm. Opinions differ as to the extent to which these mechanisms are problematic. While some see them as necessary in order to protect defendants from crushing liability, others suggest that they represent a combination of invidious distinctions and convoluted, often contradictory rules grounded in shallow and inadequate theoretical foundations (*Conaghan & Mansell* p 36). Why is it, for example, that a house owner was able to recover in respect of psychiatric harm caused by witnessing a fire which extensively damaged her home (*Attia* v *British Gas* [1988]) while a brother who saw his sibling being crushed to death was unable to claim (***Alcock* v *Chief Constable of South Yorkshire Police* [1992]**)? Similarly, why was a mother who saw her family in hospital a few hours after a tragic road accident (***McLoughlin* v *O'Brian* [1982]**) able to recover when a father who watched his son slowly die over 14 days as a result of medical negligence was not (*Sion* v *Hampstead Health Authority* [1994])? And why allow recovery to a social worker whose traumatic caseload caused them to have a nervous breakdown (***Walker* v *Northumberland County Council* [1995]**) but not to the traumatised police officers involved in the Hillsborough Stadium disaster (***White***)?

It may be, *Conaghan & Mansell* suggest, that 'all of these outcomes can be explained in terms of the web of rules which have been spun round cases of psychiatric harm but that does not make them any more defensible when placed side by side and considered in terms of justice and basic common sense' (p 36). More recently, the application and the development of these control mechanisms has been somewhat haphazard; the courts have largely acted without clear policy goals with the result that their reasoning and, on occasions, decisions have been motivated both towards and away from allowing recovery according to the—typically tragic—circumstances of particular cases.

Arguments for restricting compensation for pure psychiatric harm

The key arguments for restricting compensation in relation to negligently inflicted psychiatric harm were summarised by Lord Steyn in ***White***.

(1) The difficulties of drawing a line between acute grief and psychiatric illness and the greater diagnostic uncertainty in relation to psychiatric claims (based on a fear of sham claims and doubts as to causation).
(2) The effect the increased availability of compensation might have on potential claimants, particularly as a disincentive to rehabilitation.
(3) The significant increase in the class of claimants who could recover and the alleged danger of an over-proliferation of claims (the 'floodgates' argument).
(4) The potential unfairness to the defendant of imposing damages out of all proportion to the negligent conduct (including the increased burden on insurers and, ultimately, all insurance policy holders) (at 493–4).

Counterpoint

As long ago as 1998, the Law Commission considered arguments for limiting liability for negligently inflicted psychiatric harm in its *Report on Liability for Psychiatric Illness*. It concluded that most of the arguments for restricting liability do not stand up to close scrutiny. Moreover, it suggested that many apply equally well to claims for physical injury. Consider, for example, the momentarily careless car driver—the absence of proportionality between culpability and consequences in this situation is as prominent and problematic whether a claim following an accident is for physical or psychiatric injury (although, of course, it is important to note that, unlike psychiatric harm, physical injuries are likely to be limited to those in physical proximity to the accident). Moreover, despite a general distrust in relation to psychiatric illnesses, fraudulent or exaggerated claims are just as likely in relation to physical harm: although medically it can be determined that an injury has occurred it often cannot establish to any degree of certainty the extent or duration of the pain and suffering it has caused. A classic example is a neck injury (whiplash) usually following a car accident. There is no way of 'proving' the pain the claimant is in—the courts have to go on their word. However, the existence of many specialist whiplash claims companies suggests that this is big business, with claims for severe whiplash reaching up to £44,630.[6]

6. Figure cited on claim helpline website (www.national-accident-helpline.co.uk/personal-injury-claims/whiplash-claims.html). Indeed, such is the number and impact of whiplash claims on, e.g., car insurance costs that the government has legislated to limit such claims. The Civil Liability Act 2018, which should have come into force in 2020 (see John Hyde, 'MOJ confirms whiplash delay to 2020' *Law Society Gazette* 17 July 2018), was further delayed by the Covid-19 pandemic. At the time of writing, implementation was expected to begin May 2021 (see Neil Rose 'Whiplash reforms delayed until April 2021' *Legal Futures* 21 April 2020).

5.4 'Primary' and 'secondary' victims

Typically, when discussing claims in respect of psychiatric harm a distinction is drawn between 'primary' and 'secondary' victims with different rules applying to each. The distinction reflects different ways that psychiatric injuries may be suffered. Very broadly, a claimant may suffer such injuries because of something that has happened to *them* (for instance, being involved in a car accident) or, alternatively, by seeing or hearing about something that has happened to *someone else* (e.g. witnessing a car crash involving other people). Though the language of 'primary' and 'secondary' victim is usually traced to Lord Oliver's opinion in ***Alcock***, the factual distinction between those who suffer psychiatric injury as a result of being involved in an accident and those who suffer psychiatric injury through witnessing an accident involving others can be found in the earlier case of ***Bourhill*** **v** ***Young*** **[1943]**, discussed in **section 5.6**.

Alcock was one of a number of cases arising out of the Hillsborough Stadium disaster.[7] Faced with a tragedy involving multiple victims and a huge number of potential claimants, Lord Oliver drew a distinction between cases in which the claimant is 'involved, either mediately or immediately [that is, indirectly or directly], as a participant' (primary victims), and those in which the claimant was 'no more than the passive and unwilling witness of injury caused to others' (at 407). In relation to the latter group of claimants—secondary victims—the House of Lords went on to articulate a number of limits on the availability of claims (detailing what constitutes a relationship of sufficient proximity between the claimant and defendant—described by Henry LJ in the Court of Appeal as the 'nearness, hearness and dearness' requirements (*Frost* v *Chief Constable of South Yorkshire Police* [1997] at 278[8])).

Since ***Alcock*** this distinction, particularly in relation to primary victims, has been applied in differing ways. In contrast to Lord Oliver who clearly envisaged a fairly wide class of claimants falling within the primary victim category, including rescuers and unwitting agents, Lord Lloyd in ***Page*** **v** ***Smith*** **[1996]** appeared to restrict it to those within the range of foreseeable physical danger. Significantly, Lord Lloyd's restrictive interpretation of the primary victim category was utilised to strategic effect by the majority of the House of Lords in another Hillsborough-related case—***White***.

Nonetheless, and in contrast to the restrictive approach adopted by the House of Lords in ***Page***, more recent case law has shown some willingness to widen the class of claimants who can recover for psychiatric harms.

Counterpoint

The lack of precision as to the definition of a primary—or (less often) a secondary—victim is problematic.[9] Though we may consider any such distinction unsatisfactory, if we are to continue to distinguish between primary and secondary victims, it is important that we define these →

7. See also, in **section 5.2**, *Hicks* v *Chief Constable of South Yorkshire Police* [1992] and ***White***.
8. As ***White*** was known in the Court of Appeal. These requirements are set out in full in **section 5.6**.
9. See e.g. Mulheron 2008 and Case 2010.

→

terms with a measure of certainty. We should be wary of extending them (and their accompanying rules) to cases they don't fit:

> The distinction is well established in our law and the relevant principles were stated by the House of Lords in *Alcock* and Frost [*White*] . . . the courts should not seek to make any substantial development of these principles. That should be left to Parliament, although the case law shows that some modest development by the courts may be possible. (Lord Dyson MR, *Taylor* v *A Novo (UK) Ltd* [2013] at [24])

In light of this, while it is important to understand the various uses of the 'primary' and 'secondary' victim classifications as different rules apply to them, the terms are, at best, a means to the end of determining what the claimant needs to establish in order to succeed in their claim. As Lord Phillips CJ noted in *French* v *Chief Constable of Sussex Police* [2006] 'there is no magic in this terminology' (at [31]). As such, it is more important to be familiar with the substance of these rules rather than to become too sidetracked by questions of classification.[10]

5.5 **Primary victims**

It has long been established that a claimant is able to recover damages for psychiatric injury stemming from actual physical injury or from a reasonable fear or apprehension of danger to their physical safety (*Dulieu* v *White* [1901]).[11] This was expanded in ***Page* v *Smith***.

Page v *Smith* [1996] HL

The claimant's car was involved in a minor road traffic accident caused by the defendant's negligence. Although the claimant suffered no physical injury, the accident triggered the recurrence of his myalgic encephalomyelitis (ME), a condition which causes severe fatigue, which had been in remission at the time of the accident.[12] The claimant argued that this had become chronic and permanent as a result of the accident.

Although initially successful, the claimant lost in the Court of Appeal on the ground that his injury was not reasonably foreseeable in a person of ordinary courage and fortitude.

→

10. Indeed, in *Yearworth* v *North Bristol NHS Trust* [2009] the Court of Appeal assumed that the claimants who had banked sperm with the hospital prior to embarking on treatment for cancer could recover for psychiatric harm suffered as a result of the defendant's negligent destruction of their samples without considering whether they were primary or secondary victims.

11. In this case, the court refused to follow the earlier case of *Victorian Railways Commissioners* v *Coultas* [1888] in which the Privy Council denied the claimant's claim for psychiatric injury on the basis that her injuries were too remote.

12. The claimant's condition was variously described as myalgic encephalomyelitis (ME), or chronic fatigue syndrome (CFS) or post viral fatigue syndrome (PVFS), which had manifested itself from time to time with different degrees of severity.

→

Nevertheless, a bare majority of the House of Lords allowed his appeal. In his leading opinion, Lord Lloyd held that, where it is reasonably foreseeable that the defendant's negligence may cause *physical* harm to the claimant, they can also recover for the *psychiatric* harm they suffer, even where no physical injury actually occurred:

> Suppose, in the present case, the plaintiff had been accompanied by his wife, just recovering from a depressive illness, and that she had suffered a cracked rib, followed by an onset of psychiatric illness. Clearly, she would have recovered damages, including damages for her illness, since it is conceded that the defendant owed the occupants of the car a duty not to cause physical harm. Why should it be necessary to ask a different question, or apply a different test, in the case of the plaintiff? Why should it make any difference that the physical illness that the plaintiff undoubtedly suffered as a result of the accident operated through the medium of the mind, or of the nervous system, without physical injury? If he had suffered a heart attack, it cannot be doubted that he would have recovered damages for pain and suffering, even though he suffered no broken bones. It would have been no answer that he had a weak heart. (Lord Lloyd at 187)

Thus, as the claimant was in the zone of physical danger, he was able to recover for the psychiatric harm he suffered notwithstanding that (a) no physical harm was in fact suffered and (b) the psychiatric injury itself was not reasonably foreseeable. On this basis, as long as some form of physical injury was foreseeable, it does not matter whether it was foreseeable that the claimant's particular *psychiatric* illness would have occurred in a person of ordinary moral courage and fortitude.[13] In cases where *physical* harm is reasonably foreseeable, physical and psychiatric harms are to be treated as equivalent, so that if the former is foreseeable, the claimant can recover in respect of both physical *and* psychiatric harms, even in cases where the latter is *not* foreseeable.

The decision in ***Page*** has been the subject of much criticism.[14] Academic criticism has tended to focus on Lord Lloyd's restrictive definition of a primary victim as a party who is *necessarily* within the zone of physical danger.[15] Opinions differ over whether Lord Lloyd intended to limit the primary victim category to those claimants who were in physical danger, and it remains unclear as to when a claimant *who is not in peril* will be

13. This extension of the 'thin' or 'egg shell' skull rule (discussed in more detail in **section 9.3.1.1**), whereby, so long as the relevant kind of harm is foreseeable, it does not matter that its precise form or extent is not, puts the primary victim at a considerable advantage over secondary victims. Unlike secondary victims, primary victims can 'recover damages for negligently inflicted pure psychiatric illness, even if it was sustained because he lacked the fortitude or "natural phlegm" of an ordinary person' (Mulheron 2008, p 106 arguing for the reintroduction of a rule of normal fortitude in all cases of psychiatric harm).

14. See e.g. Bailey and Nolan's conclusion to their detailed exploration of ***Page*** in which they remark '[f]ortunately, the long-term prospects for *Page*'s survival look slim' and accompanying references (2010, pp 527–8), Lord Goff's dissenting opinion in ***White*** (at 468–81) and Peter Handford 'A New Chapter in the Foresight Saga' (1996) 4 Tort L Rev 5.

15. Though insofar as it removes the requirement that the psychiatric harm be foreseeable, the treatment of primary victims in ***Page*** is extremely generous.

recognised as a primary victim.[16] This was considered by the House of Lords in ***Rothwell* v *Chemical and Insulating Co Ltd*** [2007].

Rothwell v Chemical & Insulating Co Ltd and another; Topping v Benchtown Ltd (formerly Jones Bros Preston Ltd); Johnston v NEI International Combustion Ltd; Grieves v FT Everard & Sons Ltd and another [2007] HL

The claimant had been exposed to asbestos in the course of his employment and had developed pleural plaques. He was physically healthy and the pleural plaques themselves would not have caused any illness.[17] They were, however, evidence that asbestos had entered his body and showed that the claimant, therefore, might in the future develop a more serious asbestos-related disease. As a result, the claimant became *so* worried about the risk that he was clinically depressed (a recognisable psychiatric illness). He argued that since it was reasonably foreseeable that the defendant's negligence put him at risk of physical injury (of contracting asbestosis or mesothelioma) he was a primary victim and hence should be owed a duty of care in respect of his psychiatric illness on the basis of ***Page***.

His claim failed. Neither the pleural plaques themselves nor the claimant's anxiety that he might become seriously ill was enough to ground his claim. In addition, his reaction was unforeseeable. While it was to be expected that the developing pleural plaques would cause anxiety to the person of reasonable fortitude, there was no evidence that it would lead them to have such a serious reaction that they would become mentally ill. Moreover, 'the category of primary victim should be confined to persons who suffer psychiatric injury caused by fear or distress resulting from involvement in an accident caused by the defendant's negligence or its immediate aftermath' (Lord Hope at [54]). The claimant's psychiatric injury, which resulted from a fear as to something that might happen in the future, therefore fell within 'an entirely different category' (at [54]). Similarly, Lord Hoffmann confined ***Page*** to psychiatric injury caused by events (accidents) that had actually occurred, arguing that 'it would be an unwarranted extension of the principle in ***Page*** to apply it to psychiatric illness caused by apprehension of the possibility of an unfavourable event which had not actually happened' (at [33]).[18]

Pause for reflection

Quite why it was necessary to refine ***Page*** in this way is unclear, although Lord Hope's reference to Lord Steyn's opinion in ***White*** in which he cautions against judicial expansion in relation to recovery for negligently inflicted psychiatric harm and, his own view that 'the

→

16. See further Mulheron on the changing definitions of a primary victim in ***Page*** [1996], ***White*** [1998], *W* v *Essex County Council* [2001], ***Rothwell*** [2007] (2008, pp 84–6) and discussion in **section 5.7.2** and **section 5.7.5**.

17. If they had, he would have been able to recover.

18. Compare Smith LJ's view in *Boumedien* v *Delta Displays Ltd* [2008] in which she stated that the claimant was a primary victim if 'the defendant can reasonably foresee that his conduct will expose the plaintiff to risk of personal injury, whether physical or psychiatric' (at [7]).

→

labels . . . identified in ***Page* v *Smith*** should not be extended beyond what was in contemplation in that case' (at [54]) may provide an explanation. It is likely Lord Hope was mindful of the extent of liability should the claimant succeed.[19]

Consider the following example. A potentially deadly virus is negligently allowed to escape from a research laboratory. Following ***Rothwell*** will the employees of the laboratory be owed a duty of care in respect of psychiatric illness caused by anxiety for their future health? What about local residents who face a similar risk of contracting a serious illness—should they be able to claim for any subsequent psychiatric harm caused by their fears? If not, why not?

One context in which the courts have been willing to allow claims which do not involve an accident is in a clinical setting, specifically where a mother sustains psychiatric injury due to negligence during the management of labour and before the child is born (see e.g. *Wild* v *Southend University Hospital NHS Foundation Trust* [2014]; *Wells and Smith* v *University Hospital Southampton NHS Foundation Trust* [2015]; *RE (A minor by her mother and Litigation Friend LE) and others* v *Calderdale & Huddersfield NHS Foundation Trust* [2017]). This was recently confirmed in *YAH* v *Medway NHS Trust* [2018] in which the claimant was awarded damages in relation to psychiatric harm suffered following the traumatic delivery of her daughter who, as a result, suffered cerebral palsy.

> . . . it is settled law that a baby is part of its mother until birth; there is, up to that point, a single legal person. Each of the three cases to which I was referred (*Wild, Wells* and *RE*) illustrate this principle. There is, of course, a much larger body of case law and commentary which establishes the principle . . . It flows from that principle that the mother is a primary victim in so far as she suffers personal injury consequent on negligence which occurs before the baby is born. I believe this also to be settled law. Certainly, it is endorsed in the three cases to which I was referred. (Wipple J at [21]–[22])

Nor was it necessary for a primary victim to demonstrate that their injury was caused by 'shock' (whether in the ***Alcock*** or some other sense).

> . . . on any view the Claimant had endured a longer and more stressful birth than she should have done, by virtue of the Defendant's negligence. She therefore had a claim for physical injury (in the form of additional pain and suffering), if she had wished to bring it. If she had included a claim for physical injury of that sort, and whether or not she succeeded on that aspect of her claim, . . . she would not have to demonstrate that shock was the trigger for the psychiatric element of her claim. . . . ***Page v Smith*** establishes the approach in personal injury claims, whether the injuries consist of physical or psychiatric injuries or both. There is no requirement for a primary victim who brings a claim for 'pure' psychiatric injury to show that the injury was caused by shock. To return to Lord Ackner's axiom [in ***Alcock***],

19. In February 2010, following a consultation process (Pleural plaques, CP 14/08), the government introduced an extra-statutory scheme, which will make payments of £5,000 to individuals *who had started but not resolved* a claim for compensation before the decision in ***Rothwell***. The payment broadly reflects the level of compensation likely to have been received if pleural plaques had continued to be compensatable (Pleural plaques: Jack Straw statement, Ministry of Justice, 25 February 2010).

old-fashioned though it is, a primary victim *can* in principle claim for psychiatric injury which has been caused not by shock, but by 'the accumulation over a period of time of more gradual assaults on the nervous system', which have given rise to a recognised psychiatric condition. (at [33]–[34])

5.6 Secondary victims

A secondary victim suffers psychiatric injury as a result of witnessing someone else being harmed or endangered.[20] Recovery in such cases is limited by a number of policy-orientated control mechanisms. The first of these is that the psychiatric injury suffered must be reasonably foreseeable in a person of 'ordinary fortitude' in the same circumstances.[21] The notion of ordinary phlegm or fortitude, derived from ***Bourhill* v *Young* [1943]**, is invoked as a means of assessing the 'validity' of a claimant's emotional reactions in the face of trauma.

> ***Bourhill* v *Young* [1943] HL**
>
> The claimant, who was eight months pregnant, witnessed a serious motorbike accident. Though she did not see the accident itself, she heard it, and saw the motorcyclist's blood on the pavement. She later suffered serious psychiatric harm and her child was stillborn about a month after the accident. The House of Lords rejected her claim on the grounds that her injuries were not foreseeable—she was never in physical danger *and* that, as a pregnant woman, she was particularly susceptible to shock.

If, therefore, a secondary victim suffers psychiatric harm in circumstances where the ordinarily courageous person would not, the defendant will not be liable even if a severe psychological reaction results. However, once some psychiatric harm is foreseeable, the defendant will—on the basis of the 'egg shell' or 'thin' skull rule—be liable in full, even if a particular vulnerability or susceptibility means that the claimant suffers much greater psychiatric harm than might have been anticipated (*Brice* v *Brown* [1984]).

> **Pause for reflection**
>
> It has been argued that the notion of 'ordinary phlegm or fortitude' not only allows for the incorporation of evaluative judgements (and possible gender bias) in the consideration of what is a 'normal' reaction to any given event, but also perpetuates the false assumption that there is (or →

20. The first 'secondary victim' case was *Hambrook* v *Stokes Bros* [1925] in which the Court of Appeal refused to follow the bar against recovery in such cases set down by the Divisional Court in *Dulieu* v *White*.

21. As noted earlier, typically a primary victim does not need to show that their reaction corresponds with that of a person of ordinary fortitude (***Page***) though following *Hatton* v *Sutherland* [2002] it seems that this exception does not apply to employees who suffer psychiatric harm due to stress at

→

can be) a reasonable response to a tragic event. Do you agree? Consider, again, the facts of *Bourhill*. To what extent are the characteristics of the claimant significant here? What degree of fortitude is to be expected of an 'ordinary pregnant woman'? Or is a pregnant woman, by definition, not 'ordinary'?

The foundations for the modern approach to secondary victims were laid down in ***McLoughlin***.

McLoughlin v *O'Brian* [1982] HL

The claimant suffered psychiatric harm after witnessing the 'immediate aftermath' of a serious car accident, which killed her daughter and injured her husband and three other children. Arriving at the hospital some two hours after the accident, she encountered circumstances that were 'distressing in the extreme and . . . capable of producing an effect going well beyond that of grief and sorrow' (at 417); her husband and children, visibly upset and bruised, were still covered in grime and dirt from the accident.

The House of Lords allowed her claim on the basis that she had come upon 'the immediate aftermath' of the accident. However, their lordships were not in full agreement as to *why* she should be able to recover. In particular, there was tension as to whether the issue of recovery should be determined, as Lord Bridge suggested, on the ordinary principles of *reasonable foreseeability* or, as Lord Wilberforce argued, by reference to independent *policy-based* factors (including the *closeness of the relationship* between the claimant and the accident victim, the *proximity* of the claimant to the accident itself and whether the shock was induced by what the claimant *saw or experienced* as opposed to what she was *told* after the event).[22]

Even at the time, ***McLoughlin*** was viewed as a borderline case—on 'the margin of what the process of logical progression would allow' (Lord Wilberforce at 419). Nevertheless, it encapsulated the judicial understanding of the time; a time when judges were more generous to claimants in negligence than they are today. However, darker clouds were building on the horizon, as the mood within tort law generally shifted towards a more restrictive approach to the duty of care (the so-called 'retreat from ***Anns***').[23] Then

work (unless the employer knows of a particular problem or vulnerability on the part of the claimant) or (following ***Rothwell***) to those who suffer an 'unforeseeable' reaction caused by the apprehension of an illness. See further Mulheron 2008, pp 106–9.

22. It may be that there is greater overlap between the two approaches than this suggests. Lord Bridge made it clear that the three factors set down by Lord Wilberforce would be taken into account when determining whether on the facts the shock was reasonably foreseeable (Nolan 2010, p 282). However, as Paula Case notes, the differing approaches of Lords Bridge and Wilberforce are 'broadly representative of an "assimilation approach" which uses ordinary negligence principles to determine duty of care (articulated by Lord Bridge) . . . [and an] "isolation approach" [(articulated by Lord Wilberforce)] which views psychiatric damage as distinct from other harms and needing to be insulated from ordinary negligence principles'. She continues: 'Though the latter approach won the day in ***Alcock***, more recently case law suggests a movement toward a gradual assimilation of psychiatric harm into mainstream negligence principles in order to determine whether a duty care exists' (Case 2010, pp 34–5).

23. See further **section 3.2** and **section 7.4**.

the unthinkable happened, a tragedy with multiple victims and a vast number of potential claimants and this mood was cemented—the Hillsborough Stadium disaster.[24]

The Hillsborough Stadium disaster

see online resources

'The tragedy that claimed the lives of 96 Liverpool football fans shattered a community and shook the world of football took a matter of minutes to unfold. In its simplest terms, Hillsborough was a case of overcrowding in the central standing area allocated to Liverpool fans at the FA Cup semi-final match against Nottingham Forest . . . The disaster began to unfold at approximately 2.30pm. With half an hour before kick-off, most of the Nottingham Forest supporters were in their seats. Meanwhile the area reserved for the Liverpool supporters—the Leppings Lane end of the stadium—was half empty. But outside, it was a different story, with more than 2,000 Liverpool supporters building up against the turnstiles to the Leppings Lane entrance. Some had arrived late from their journey across the Pennines. Others had stayed outside to make the most of the sunshine. There were also those who had come without tickets to the all-ticket match, hoping to buy them at the ground. But whatever the reason for the late rush, anxiety among both fans and police was mounting as the minutes to kick-off ticked by.

By 2.45pm the crowd had swelled to over 5,000, making entry to turnstiles virtually impossible. Those who did get through were short of breath and sweating profusely from the crush. As the minutes passed, it became increasing clear that, despite police efforts, the mass of people would never get through by 3pm. There was also a more serious risk of some being dangerously hurt. Something had to be done.

Suddenly at 2.52pm, the large blue, concertina steel door—Gate C—in the perimeter wall was slid open by a police officer. Those at its entrance tumbled through. Those at the back pushed harder still. The logjam was unstuck. But things quickly got out of control. Where fans had been entering in ones and twos through the turnstiles, there was now a wave of about 2,000 racing to see the start of the game. The majority took the most obvious route: straight ahead through the tunnel of gangway 2. They piled into the back of pens 3 and 4, which were already uncomfortably full, crushing those at the front.

At 2.54pm the teams came onto the pitch. Fans at the back of the pens pushed forward for a better view, unaware that people were dying in the front. As the excitement of the game grew, there were more surges, each causing a squeeze more perilous than the last. Finally, with fans spilling through a narrow escape onto the pitch or being lifted to the seating areas above, a policeman realised what was happening. At 3.06pm, six minutes into the game, he ordered the

→

24. In fact, as Donal Nolan notes, the Hillsborough Stadium disaster was one of a number of man-made disasters during the UK's 'disaster era' (1985–89), which included the Bradford football stadium fire in 1985 (40 fatalities), the sinking of the *Herald of Free Enterprise* car ferry (187) and the King's Cross underground station fire in 1987 (31), the Piper Alpha oil rig fire in 1988 (167) and, in 1989, the East Midlands Kegworth plane crash (47) and the sinking of the *Marchioness* pleasure boat (51). The fact that there were so many man-made disasters in the years preceding ***Alcock***, Nolan argues (he lists ten events, totalling 979 fatalities), each giving rise to litigation (including for psychiatric injury), combined with the 'topicality of trauma-induced psychiatric injury . . . can only have reinforced long-standing judicial concerns about the opening of floodgates in nervous shock litigation' (2010, p 292).

→

referee to stop the game. Only then did the scale of the disaster become clear. Bodies were lifted forward and laid out on the pitch—many teenagers and children. People screamed for their loved ones as ambulance staff fought to save lives. Advertising hoardings were torn down as makeshift stretchers in a desperate attempt to bring faster relief.

By 4.50pm, the scheduled end of the game, the ground was empty. Abandoned clothing and programmes littered the scene of the disaster. While nearby the bodies of the dead lay in the stadium's gymnasium.'

(BBC News 'Timetable to a tragedy' 14 April 1999 referring to Taylor LJ's vivid account in *Interim Report on the Hillsborough Stadium Disaster* (Cm 765, 1989))

Ninety-six people were crushed to death and over 400 people were injured at Hillsborough Stadium. At the time, it was 'one of the most televised, monitored and photographed disasters in the UK'.[25] Many thousands of people watched the tragedy unfold on live TV or listened to it on the radio, even more saw later news reports and press coverage. The number of potential claims for psychiatric harm was immense. The court's response was to abandon its aspiration to 'provide a comprehensive system of corrective justice . . . in favour of cautious pragmatism' (Lord Hoffmann, ***White*** at 502).

Alcock v *Chief Constable of South Yorkshire Police* [1992] HL

Alcock was a test case involving representatives of the friends and families of the victims of the disaster at Hillsborough Stadium. The claimants included grandparents, friends, spouses, siblings and fiancés of the victims who had either been at the ground when the incident occurred, or who had arrived at the ground later or seen or heard about it on the TV or radio. As they had not been *directly* involved in the disaster (in the sense of having been in physical danger), the claimants were not able to recover as primary victims. Rather, they argued that their psychiatric injuries were caused by what they saw happen to and/or feared had happened to their loved one and that, as such, they were secondary victims.

The defendant, the Chief Constable of South Yorkshire Police, admitted negligence in respect of those who had been killed or injured at Hillsborough but argued that he did not owe

→

25. Phil Scraton 'Justice: Hillsborough's Final Victim' (1992) April *Legal Action* 7. In April 2016, after almost 27 years of campaigning by friends and family members of those who died at Hillsborough, an inquest ruled that they were unlawfully killed and a catalogue of failings by police and the ambulance services contributed to their deaths (David Conn 'Hillsborough inquests jury rules 96 victims were unlawfully killed' *The Guardian* 26 April 2016). In November 2016, 465 people were granted a group litigation order to seek damages for the 'anguish' and psychiatric harm they suffered as a result of the disaster and the 'prolonged cover-up'. In January 2018 it was reported that South Yorkshire Police had set aside £11.6 million in connection with estimated payouts (Chris Burn, 'Hillsborough disaster and Rotherham scandal compensation costs leave South Yorkshire police facing "very serious situation"' *The Yorkshire Post* 2 January 2018). See the **online resources** for updates.

see online resources

→

a duty of care to those who had suffered psychiatric damage as a result of seeing or hearing the news of what had happened.[26]

Despite limited success at first instance, both the Court of Appeal and House of Lords rejected the claims. The lack of *proximity* between the claimants and the police meant that no duty of care arose such as was necessary to ground a claim in the tort of negligence: they were not 'in contemplation of law, in a relationship of sufficient proximity to or directness with the tortfeasor as to give rise to a duty of care' (at 410). Drawing on and developing the more restrictive approach of Lord Wilberforce in ***McLoughlin***, Lord Oliver set out guidelines—subsequently known as the *Alcock* control mechanisms—as to when proximity will be established. These relate to the following issues:

(1) the *class of persons* whose claim should be recognised (defined by their relationship to the victim);
(2) the *closeness* of the claimant—both physically and temporally—to the accident;
(3) the necessity of, and the means by which, the *shock* is caused.

It is worth spending some time looking at the ***Alcock*** control mechanisms in a little more detail—noting again that in all instances it is necessary for the claimant to establish first that they are suffering from a medically recognised psychiatric illness.

5.6.1 **Relationship with the immediate victim**

There must be what is described as 'a close tie of love and affection' between the claimant and the accident victim. Despite subsequent interpretations of this requirement, it is clear that the law lords did *not* want to establish a rigid list of categories of relationship within which claimants would succeed (at 415). Rather,

> [w]hether the degree of love and affection in any given relationship, be it that of relative or friend, is such that the defendant . . . should reasonably have foreseen the shock-induced psychiatric illness, has to be decided on a case by case basis. (Lord Ackner at 404)

The court held that this will be presumed in the case of spouses, parents and children—although, of course, this can be rebutted if the defendant can show that such closeness did not exist. This does not mean that siblings and other relatives can never claim; however, they must bring evidence to prove such ties existed.[27] Thus, Brian Harrison, who

26. It was accepted, for the purposes of argument, that the claimants were suffering from a recognised psychiatric illness and that the Chief Constable had breached his duty of care. The question of breach, in light of the Hillsborough Inquest's findings that the failure of David Duckenfield, the Hillsborough police match commander, to close a tunnel 'was the direct cause of the deaths of 96 people' now seems unarguable (BBC News 'Hillsborough inquests: David Duckenfield admits causing 96 deaths' 17 March 2015).

27. A grandfather (e.g. the one in the example at the start of the chapter) would as a secondary victim need to establish, alongside the other ***Alcock*** control mechanisms, that he had a close tie of love and affection with his grandchild—this would not be presumed by their familial relationship.

watched the scenes at Hillsborough unfold from the West Stand knowing that both his brothers were in pens three and four behind the goal was unable to recover. He did not have—or did not show that he had—a close enough relationship with his late brother, perhaps because he did not know he had to.

Counterpoint

The 'love and affection' requirement has been subject to widespread and severe criticism. In Jane Stapleton's words:

> That, at present, claims can turn on the requirement of 'close ties and affection' is guaranteed to produce outrage. Is it not a disreputable sight to see brothers of Hillsborough victims turned away because they had *no more* than brotherly love towards the victim? In future cases will it not be a grotesque sight to see relatives scrabbling to prove their especial love for the deceased in order to win money damages and for the defendant to have to attack that argument? ('In Restraint of Tort' in Peter Birks (ed) *The Frontiers of Liability: Volume 2* (OUP, 1994), p 95)

Do you agree?

Pause for reflection

The familial relationships of the claimants in ***Alcock*** are not the only ones which may exhibit close ties of love and affection. Other relationships, including that of work colleagues, teacher and student and close friends, can also—so long as a close tie of love and affection can be established on the facts of each case—fall within this category.

However, this is not always straightforward. Consider the Scottish case of *Robertson* v *Forth Road Bridge Joint Board* [1996]. The claimant suffered psychiatric harm after his colleague died while trying to remove a sheet of metal from the Forth Road Bridge in windy conditions. His claim was denied despite evidence showing that they had spent the greater part of their employment working together, and that they had often walked to and from work together and had gone out socially during the week. Though clearly their relationship went beyond that of work colleagues, the court held that it was not enough to demonstrate the necessary close tie of love and affection.

Although usually the claimant will have to establish a close tie of love and affection with the immediate victim, the House of Lords in ***Alcock*** did not rule out the possibility of a mere bystander being able to recover if the circumstances were 'particularly horrific' (at 397). Quite what would be more horrific than the events of the Hillsborough Stadium disaster is difficult to imagine, although Lord Ackner imaginatively suggested that witnessing an out-of-control petrol tanker crash into a school may be such an event (at 403). In *McFarlane* v *EE Caledonia Ltd* [1994] the claimant developed PTSD after witnessing the Piper Alpha oil rig disaster from a boat which was engaged in trying to fight the fire which had engulfed the rig. He argued that, as the fire was especially horrific, the oil-rig owners (who had admitted responsibility for the disaster) owed him a duty of care, despite the fact he was a mere bystander (he did not have a close relationship with the people injured or killed in the explosion). This was rejected by the Court of Appeal. Not only was it impossible to establish a hierarchy of horrific events, but to do so would wrongly reduce establishing a duty in such cases to a question of foreseeability: the more horrific the accident, the more likely psychiatric harm would occur.[28]

5.6.2 **Proximity in time and space**

In relation to the second requirement of 'proximity'—closeness to the accident in time and space—Lord Oliver summed up the general position thus:

> The necessary element of proximity between plaintiff and defendant is furnished, at least in part, by both physical and temporal propinquity and also by the sudden and direct visual impression on the plaintiff's mind of actually witnessing the event or its immediate aftermath. (at 416)

This was confirmed in *Taylor* v *A Novo (UK) Ltd* [2013]. The claimant's mother died suddenly three weeks after being negligently injured at work. The claimant developed PTSD, as a result of witnessing her mother's death (she was not present at the original accident or its immediate aftermath). In bringing her claim against her mother's employers, the claimant sought to establish proximity by arguing that there were, in fact, two 'events'—the accident and her mother's collapse and death—and that, as the cause of her injuries, the latter was 'operative' or a relevant event in determining proximity. This was rejected by the Court of Appeal:

> In reality there was a single accident or event . . . which had two consequences. The first was the injuries to [the mother's] head and arm; and the second (three weeks later) was her death . . . if [the claimant] had been in physical proximity to her mother at the time of the accident and had suffered shock and psychiatric illness as a result of seeing the accident and the injuries sustained by her mother, she would have qualified as a secondary victim on established principles. But in my view, to allow [her] to recover as a secondary victim on the facts of the present case would be to go too far . . . if . . . right, [she] would have been able to recover damages for psychiatric illness even if her mother's death had occurred months, and possibly years, after the accident (subject, of course, to proving causation). This suggests that the concept of proximity to a secondary victim cannot reasonably be stretched this far. (Lord Dyson MR at [29]–[30])[29]

But what about the immediate aftermath—how far does this extend? While Mrs McLoughlin arriving at the hospital two hours after the accident was sufficient, Robert

28. His claim as a primary victim also failed. Though the boat he was on had come within 80 metres of the oil rig, his fear for his own life was not reasonable. This aspect of the case should now be read in light of ***Page***.

29. See also *Megan Tanner (a child by her father and litigation friend)* v *Sarkar* [2017]—the first reported secondary victim claim involving a child. The defendant had admitted liability in relation to H (M's 2-year-old brother) who had died of sepsis after his GP had failed to refer him for urgent treatment. M, who was 5, was unable to claim for the psychiatric harm she suffered as a result of the witnessing her brother's decline over three days, travelling in the ambulance with him and seeing his body in the hospital mortuary and at the funeral home as these did not form the 'immediate aftermath' of

Alcock's search at the ground and arrival at the temporary mortuary in the stadium's gymnasium around midnight (about eight hours after the match was abandoned) where he identified his brother-in-law's body which was blue with bruising, his chest red, was not—the blood on his brother-in-law's body has been memorably described as 'too dry' to allow recovery.[30] In *Galli-Atkinson* v *Seghal* [2003], the 'immediate aftermath' relatively generously allowed a mother's claim for psychiatric harm following the death of her daughter in a road traffic accident. It was suggested that the immediate aftermath of an accident could be viewed as being made up of different component parts, in particular the mother's visit to the scene of the accident and the hospital morgue. However, in *Berisha* v *Stone Superstore Ltd* [2014], the court adopted a more restrictive approach.[31] In this case, the claimant arrived at the hospital five hours after her partner had been seriously injured at work. By the time she arrived he was on a life-support machine. The claimant stayed with him for 36 hours until—with her permission—life-support was removed. Striking out her claim, District Judge Hassell commented:

> There is nothing unusual following a catastrophic or fatal accident for a next of kin to be met by the police and summoned to hospital. In the modern world there is nothing unusual in the next of kin then being involved in difficult but inevitable decisions concerning maintenance of life support. The essential facts of going to hospital, seeing an unconscious loved one and taking the decision to withdraw life support have never been found, individually or collectively, to confer secondary victim status on the claimant in an accident case . . . Although few of us have to cope with tragedy, there is nothing inherently unusual, amongst tragedies, of the circumstances of the accident that befell [the claimant's partner] or what happened thereafter. [The claimant] neither witnessed the accident, nor attended the scene, not witnessed a continuation of the scene, nor the immediate aftermath of the accident, nor did she participate in a seamless tale beginning with the accident. Given that, her claim clearly falls on the wrong side of the existing control mechanisms. (at [62], [72])

The Court of Appeal in ***Liverpool Women's Hospital NHS Foundation Trust*** **v** ***Ronayne*** **[2015]** confirmed a strict approach to the control mechanisms for secondary victims, particularly in cases of clinical negligence.[32] Tomlinson LJ observed that while ***McLoughlin*** is understood as an 'aftermath' case, 'it could properly be said that Mrs McLoughlin came upon the accident, albeit transposed into the setting of the hospital' (at [16]).

5.6.3 The means by which the 'shock' is caused

It is clear that the psychiatric harm must be sustained as a result of a sudden 'shock' rather than as the result of a continuous process of dealing with or responding to such events. Lord Ackner described this as a 'sudden appreciation by sight or sound of a

the doctor's failure to refer H as they occurred 12 hours after the family had returned home from the doctor. Nor had she established that she had suffered a recognisable psychiatric illness.

30. Stapleton 1994, p 84. Further, unlike in ***McLoughlin***, it was argued that the purpose of his visit was for identification rather than aid or comfort.

31. Indeed, counsel in *Berisha* suggested that ***McLoughlin*** and *Galli-Atkinson* are the only examples of a claimant who attends hospital after an unexpected accident has befallen a loved one successfully recovering damages for psychiatric harm (at [35]).

32. Though see *RE (A minor by her mother and Litigation Friend LE) and others* v *Calderdale & Huddersfield NHS Foundation Trust* [2017] discussed in **section 5.6.3**.

horrifying event, which violently agitates the mind' (at 401). In *Sion* v *Hampstead Health Authority* [1994], for example, a father was unable to recover for psychiatric harm sustained as a result of watching his son die over a period of 14 days while becoming increasingly aware that the hospital was negligent in its treatment of him.

This requirement was criticised by the Law Commission in its *Report on Liability for Psychiatric Illness* (1998) and judges have on occasion tried to eschew its more restrictive effects. In *North Glamorgan NHS Trust* v *Walters* [2002] a mother was able to recover as a secondary victim for psychiatric harm she suffered as a result of the negligent treatment leading to the death of her baby son. The court held that such a shocking event was not confined to a single moment in time and, taking a realistic approach to the facts, the 36-hour period prior to her son's death could be classed as a single horrifying event. Referring to Lord Wilberforce's opinion in ***McLoughlin***, Ward LJ continued: 'One looks to the totality of the circumstances which bring the claimant into proximity in both time and space to the accident. It seems to me, therefore, to be implicit in [Lord Wilberforce's] judgment read as a whole that when he said . . . "the shock must come through the sight or hearing of the 'event' or its 'immediate aftermath'" he was not intending to confine "the event" to a frozen moment in time' (at [27]).

However, *Walters* was distinguished in *Wild* v *Southend Hospital NHS Trust* [2014]. In this case, the claimant was the father of a foetus who died in utero as a result of the defendant's negligence and was later delivered stillborn. He suffered psychiatric harm as a result of being present when the death of the foetus was discovered and during the birth. Dismissing his claim, the judge, Michael Kent QC, held that the claimant's witnessing of the consequences of the defendant's negligence did not equate to witnessing a horrific 'event':

> [The claimant] was experiencing a growing and acute anxiety which started when the second midwife failed to find a heartbeat. This developed to the point at which, simply because of the behaviour (and no doubt body language) of the clinical staff and the words of the doctor '*I concur*', he had a correct realisation that the baby had died. But none of that, in my judgment, equates to actually witnessing horrific events leading to a death or serious injury. That what [the claimant] experienced was capable of and did generate sufficient shock to have foreseeably caused psychiatric illness is not in dispute. But the authorities show that the control mechanisms often have the effect of excluding such cases . . . In my judgment this case is materially different from the facts in *Walters* being based on an 'event' which starts with the realisation that Matthew [the foetus] has already died. (at [47], [53])

Pause for reflection

There is little to distinguish the facts of *Walters* and *Wild*. As the judge in *Wild* commented:

> It has also been objected that the effect of the [*Alcock*] control mechanisms . . . is to give rise to and perpetuate a distinction between different classes of claimant which will create an understandable sense of grievance even beyond the effects of the arbitrary

→

→

> distinction between those who experience an event and those who are merely told about the consequences of an event (who are already excluded). Miss Whipple [counsel for the claimant and now Whipple J] points out that, for example, [the claimant] would not then be able to recover in circumstances where his wife has recovered damages for distress arising out virtually the same set of circumstances. That imports a gender bias as fathers would never be able to recover in still-birth cases whatever the facts may show. She suggests that it also draws an arbitrary distinction between accident cases (meaning cases such as road accidents where the negligence and consequences are all played out at the same time in front of the secondary victim) and clinical negligence or disease cases where the effects of acts or omissions may become manifest (and only be capable of becoming manifest) some time (perhaps many years) later. (at [49])

However, the judge in *Wild* was not convinced:

> . . . given the acceptance that there is an arbitrary line drawn between classes of claimant in these cases, it does not seem to me that the fact that cases similar to the one before me might never be able to succeed can be a ground for extending or modifying the control mechanisms in nervous shock cases, particularly when the subject has been so comprehensively travelled over by the higher courts. (at [50])

Do you agree?

In fact, as noted in ***Ronayne***, *Walters* was (until recently) the only reported case involving the consequences of observing in a hospital setting the effects of clinical negligence in which the claimant was successful (at [17]).[33]

Liverpool Women's Hospital NHS Foundation Trust v Ronayne [2015] CA

The claimant's wife suffered a series of complications after undergoing a hysterectomy at the defendant's hospital (it was common ground that this was as a result of the defendant's negligence). The claimant suffered psychiatric injury as a result of the 'shock' of his wife's rapid deterioration over the course of 36 hours and in particular seeing her connected to various machines, including drips, monitors and her appearance which he later described as resembling the 'Michelin Man'.[34]

→

33. See e.g. *Taylorson* v *Shieldness Produce Ltd* [1994]; *Brock* v *Northampton General Hospital NHS Trust* [2014]; *Shorter* v *Surrey & Sussex Healthcare NHS Trust* [2015].

34. As Burrows and Burrows note, the claimant easily met the close tie of love and affection to the primary victim (his wife), proximity in time and space and had seen the condition of his wife deteriorate through his own unaided senses. What was at issue was whether his illness had been caused by a shocking (or horrifying) event (Andrew S Burrows and John H Burrows 'A Shocking Requirement in the Law of Negligence Liability for Psychiatric Illness: *Liverpool Women's Hospital NHS Foundation Trust* v *Ronayne* [2015] EWCA Civ 588' (2016) 24 Med L Rev 278, 282).

→

Rejecting his claim, the Court of Appeal held there was no 'shock' but rather 'a series of events which gave rise to an accumulation during that period of gradual assaults on the claimant's mind . . . [which] at each stage . . . the claimant was conditioned for what he was about to perceive' (at [40]):

> [I]t as wholly artificial to describe the sight of his wife in her post-operative condition as the end of a distinct event. It was all part of a continuum. Thankfully it was very different in nature from the death which occurred in *Walters*. The claimant knew that the next 24 hours were critical, and that the story was far from over. As it turned out, the story had many weeks and months to run (at [38]).[35]

Nor was what the claimant saw objectively 'horrifying'. On both occasions the appearance of the claimant's wife was as would ordinarily be expected of a person in hospital in the circumstances in which she found herself. Tomlinson LJ continued:

> What is required in order to found liability is something which is exceptional in nature . . . There is I think a danger of the 'Michelin Man' epithet acquiring a significance greater than it deserves . . . I can readily accept that the appearance of Mrs Ronayne on this occasion must have been both alarming and distressing to the claimant, but it was not in context exceptional and it was not I think horrifying in the sense in which that word has been used in the authorities. Certainly however it did not lead to a sudden violent agitation of the mind, because the claimant was prepared to witness a person in a desperate condition and was moreover already extremely angry (at [41]).

Pause for reflection

It has been suggested that the decision in ***Ronayne*** was 'a welcome result for the NHS'.

To have allowed recovery in this case would be to allow recovery for almost any person who developed a psychiatric disorder after witnessing their loved ones in a hospital setting following treatment for clinical negligence. Such a wide ambit for recovery would significantly increase the NHS's liability for clinical negligence claims.[36]

This may be true; however, as Burrows and Burrows argue 'it is hard to resist the conclusion that the need for a sudden shocking event is an unnecessary and arbitrary restriction'—not least because many psychiatric illnesses are *not* caused by a sudden shock.

→

35. Happily, after nine weeks in intensive care during which time she developed an MRSA infection and had to deal with other extremely unpleasant complications, the claimant's wife made a full recovery.

36. Joanne Hughes 'Husband not entitled to damages as a secondary victim as sight of his wife in hospital was not sufficiently "horrifying"' *Lexology* 18 June 2015 (Hughes was part of litigation team which represented the defendants in ***Ronayne***).

→

Admittedly, the Court of Appeal was bound by precedent to apply the sudden shocking event requirement so that any development of the law would appear to require a decision of the Supreme Court. But that there is flexibility in applying the sudden shocking event requirement is shown by the enlightened decision in *North Glamorgan NHS Trust* v *Walters* [and] one would expect that, if given the opportunity, the Supreme Court would act to remove this requirement.[37]

Following ***Ronayne***, is it particularly difficult for secondary victims to recover in clinical contexts. A recent exception to this is *RE (A minor by her mother and Litigation Friend LE) and others* v *Calderdale & Huddersfield NHS Foundation Trust* [2017]. In this case, a grandmother was able to recover as a secondary victim for psychiatric harm suffered as a result of being present during her daughter's chaotic and distressing labour and delivery of RE.[38] The midwife had negligently failed to diagnose shoulder dystocia and summon emergency assistance. Had she done so, RE would have been born 11 minutes earlier and would have avoided all harm. It was accepted that the relationship between the grandmother and her daughter was one of 'close love and affection' and that, in being present at the birth, she was sufficiently proximate in time and space. The question for the court was then whether the event was sufficiently shocking to ground a claim. Goss J held that it was:

> She was present throughout the birth and witnessed the aftermath. She, too, was convinced that RE was dead. There is agreement between the Consultant Psychiatrists that she has suffered PTSD as a result of observing the events of RE's birth. I am satisfied that her first-hand observation of the first 15 minutes of life, that is the period immediately following her birth, was the triggering event for PTSD. . . . I find that the event was sufficiently sudden, shocking and objectively horrifying to reach the conclusion that . . . [her] claim for damages for nervous shock is established. (at [48])

Pause for reflection

RE is the first case in a number of years where the claim of a secondary victim has succeeded. Given criticisms of the decision in ***Ronayne***, we might expect that the apparent loosening of the ***Alcock*** criteria at least in the context of cases such as *RE*, and the subsequent possible

→

37. Burrows and Burrows (**n 34**) p 284.

38. The mother was either a primary victim (on the basis that the negligence had occurred when RE was still in utero and so the damage occurred when the mother and foetus were still considered to be one person) (at [40]) or a secondary victim on the basis that she had the necessary close tie of love and affection with RE, she had witnessed the scene directly, and that judged objectively it was 'exceptional in nature and horrifying' and was not an event of the kind to be expected as 'part and parcel' of the demands and experience of childbirth (at [47]).

→

expansion in claims, would be widely welcomed. However, as Jaime Lindsey points out, while the judge in finding that the mother was a primary victim rightly 'hold[s] a firm line in protecting a pregnant woman's bodily autonomy and confirming this in the clearest possible terms', the aspects of the decision relating to the claims of secondary victims are more concerning.[39] In particular, Lindsey suggests that the judge's characterisation of the birth as a 'shocking event' may make it harder for pregnant women generally to exercise their autonomy when it comes to decisions about childbirth:

> One difficulty with this case arises in relation to the finding that the birth was a shocking event. Of course, childbirth is in many ways shocking: it often occurs over an extended period of time, sometimes a matter of days, it is usually extremely painful and it can involve the risk of death or serious bodily injury for both the woman and child. . . . However, despite the obvious dangers of childbirth, it is a still normal life experience which the human species relies upon for its very existence. Turning what is a normal and necessary life experience into a medically and legally recognised cause of psychiatric harm has potentially dangerous consequences in the way that we view childbirth, both from a legal and social perspective . . . [W]hen law frames childbirth as a sudden, shocking and horrifying event of such a nature that it can create psychiatric injury in others, it characterises childbirth as dangerous and abnormal.[40]

Moreover, what about the impact of the decision on the well-publicised scarce resources of the NHS? In 2017/18 the NHS paid out more than £1.63 billion in damages to claimants.[41] Without doubt, there are difficult choices to be made as to the allocation of such resources. However, in cases such as *RE*, life-changing decisions are made under extreme pressure and often in a matter of minutes. Reasonable people may well disagree as to whether placing a system and staff that are already under strain under yet more pressure by allowing the claims for psychiatric injury of friends and family, who happen to be present with the patient, is a helpful or reasonable thing to do. What do you think?

More recently, there are further signs of movement towards a less restrictive interpretation of what a sudden shocking event can be. The decision of Chamberlain J in ***Paul* v *Royal Wolverhampton NHS Trust*** [2020] is one example.

39. Jaime Lindsey, 'Psychiatric Injury Claims and Pregnancy: *Re (a Minor) and Others v Calderdale & Huddersfield NHS Foundation Trust* [2017] EWHC 824' (2018) 26(1) Med L Rev 117 at 117.

40. At 221–2. Of course, some births may be more 'shocking' than others. In her witness statement, the mother described RE's birth as follows: 'I couldn't believe what was happening. I felt that I was living in a nightmare. The doctor clamped RE's cord and as I looked down at her I could see that her body was completely white and lifeless, her head was purple and swollen, she did not make sound. I remember thinking to myself "my baby is dead my baby is dead". . . . I had stuck in my mind the picture of her lying between my legs, her head was completely purple and bruised and swollen, her body was white and lifeless' (at [42]). It took a further 12 minutes for RE to take her first breath.

41. NHS Resolution Annual Report 2017–2018 (HC 1251), p 19.

Paul v *Royal Wolverhampton NHS Trust* [2020] EWHC 1415 (QB)

Mr Paul collapsed and died while on a shopping trip with his two daughters, who suffered psychiatric harm as a result. Negligent medical care received by their father 14 months previously when he had been admitted to hospital with chest pain was the cause of his later death. It was the claimants' case that Mr Paul's collapse and death was the first manifestation of the defendant's breach of duty.

In determining whether the death was capable of being the 'relevant event', Master Cook found that as the death occurred so long after the initial negligence, it could not be the 'relevant event' to establish sufficient proximity. On appeal, Chamberlain J concluded that the Master had been wrong to strike out the claims and that they should proceed to trial:

> When the negligence and the damage are separated, and assuming there is no requirement for the negligence and the damage to be synchronous, the 'scene of the tort' can only mean 'the scene where damage first occurred'. In the context of the tort of negligence, this is the point when the tort becomes actionable or complete. (at [65])

On this basis, he concluded that 'there was . . . only one event: Mr Paul's collapse from a heart attack' (at [75]):

> . . . it was a sudden event, external to the secondary victims, and it led immediately or very rapidly to Mr Paul's death. The event would have been horrifying to any close family member who witnessed it, and especially so to children of 12 and 9. The fact that the event occurred 14½ months after the negligent omission which caused it does not . . . preclude liability. Nor does the fact that it was not an accident in the ordinary sense of the word, but rather an event internal to the primary victim. In a case where such an event is the first occasion on which the damage is caused, and therefore the first occasion on which it can be said that the cause of action is complete, *Taylor* v *A. Novo* does not preclude liability. (at [75])

Crucially, this does not indicate that witnessing *any* death many months after a negligent act will enable a successful claim as a secondary victim. The issue is when the consequences of the negligence first become apparent.

Chamberlain J dismissed arguments that this decision would open the floodgates to future claims, maintaining that stringent limits remain in relation to claims by secondary victims. ***Paul***, alongside another case in which the claimants witnessed their young daughter's collapse and death some months after a negligently missed diagnosis (*Polmear* v *Royal Cornwall Hospitals NHS Trust* [2021]), are due to be heard by the Court of Appeal in late 2021. It remains to be seen whether these cases, alongside *RE*, mark the beginnings of a move towards the expansion of liability.[42]

42. Like ***Paul***, *Polmear* was initially heard by Master Cook who, by then, was bound by the later decision in ***Paul***, thus he had to refuse the defendant's application to strike out the claim. He also gave permission for the case to 'leapfrog' to the Court of Appeal, being clear that there was an important point of principle to be decided (at [54]). It might therefore be that both cases are heard together in the Court of Appeal. The outcome of those appeals will be interesting, as it appears there are a number of similar other cases stayed in advance of the decisions.

The House of Lords in ***Alcock*** made it clear that there would be no liability to a secondary victim who is merely told about the shocking event by a third party (including newspaper coverage and television broadcasts):

> Although the television pictures certainly gave rise to feelings of the deepest anxiety and distress, in the circumstances of this case the simultaneous television broadcasts of what occurred cannot be equated with the 'sight or hearing of the event or its immediate aftermath.' Accordingly shocks sustained by reason of these broadcasts cannot found a claim. (Lord Ackner at 405)[43]

Nevertheless, Lord Ackner left open the possibility that watching a live broadcast could exceptionally ground a claim if it is clear that the victims had died—for example if, to use Nolan LJ's example in the Court of Appeal, a hot-air balloon carrying a number of children were to explode live on television (at 405).

Pause for reflection

see online resources

Without doubt, despite developments relating to primary victims, ***Alcock*** remains the 'single most important English authority on liability for nervous shock' (Nolan 2010, p 273). It is, in Lord Steyn's words, the 'controlling decision' on secondary victims (***White*** at 496).

Nevertheless, it has been the subject of trenchant criticism. See, for example, Lord Hoffmann in ***White***, commenting that in ***Alcock*** 'the search for principle was called off' (at 511); the Law Commission's recognition that the restrictions 'have been almost universally criticized as arbitrary and unfair' (*Report on Liability for Psychiatric Illness* (1998) [6.3]); and Jane Stapleton's description of this area of law as one where 'silliest rules prevail' (1994, p 36). The ***Alcock*** control mechanisms have come to be seen, by many, as arbitrary and unfair rules designed to restrict recovery and avoid a 'flood' of liability.[44]

However, Donal Nolan suggests the ***Alcock*** control mechanisms have been used in a way that was unintended by the House of Lords (2010, pp 307–8). He argues that the law lords did not seek to lay down rigid rules precisely because, in Lord Jauncey's words, 'to draw such a line would necessarily be arbitrary and lacking in logic' (***Alcock*** at 422). Thus, as well as being a landmark case in tort, ***Alcock*** is, in his view, also a 'misunderstood decision':

> A case that is often painted as retrograde and reactionary was in fact rather conservative, and even in some respects mildly progressive, not least when one takes into account the circumstances in which it was decided. (Nolan 2010, p 308)

What do you think? Is it time judges stopped 'blaming' ***Alcock*** and took responsibility for the limitations of their own decisions?

The traditional distinction between primary and secondary victims can be summarised in **Table 5.1**.

43. In ***Alcock***, none of the live television coverage, in line with broadcasting policy, showed pictures of suffering by recognisable individuals. Had it done so, it was accepted that this would break the chain of causation between the defendant's alleged breach of duty and the psychiatric illness (at 410).

44. See e.g. Deborah Evans 'A Miscarriage of Justice' APIL blog, 5 March 2014.

TABLE 5.1 The traditional distinction between primary and secondary victims

Primary victims	Secondary victims
Physical injury must be foreseeable; however psychiatric injury itself need not be foreseeable. No need for the claimant to be of 'ordinary fortitude' (*Page*)	Psychiatric harm must be foreseeable in a person of 'ordinary fortitude' in the same circumstances as the claimant
Application of *Page*—is the claimant in the 'zone of danger'?	Application of *Alcock* control mechanisms: close tie of love and affection; proximity to the accident and means by which the shock is caused
No policy considerations to limit the number of claimants	Policy used to limit the number of claimants

5.7 Beyond primary and secondary victims

The examples of psychiatric harm claims we have discussed up until now have all arisen in the context of accidents caused by the defendant's careless acts or omissions. It is in this context that the distinction between primary and secondary victims was first drawn and makes best sense: primary victims are those involved in, and endangered by, the accident; secondary victims are those who were not involved but witnessed, or later learned of, what happened to the primary victims. Clearly, however, psychiatric harms can be suffered in other ways. Though the courts have, on occasion, sought to fit all psychiatric injury claims within the framework of primary and secondary victims,[45] the safer approach is to acknowledge that there are some claimants—as we have seen—who suffer (pure) psychiatric harm *other than* through being involved in or witnessing an accident. At times, these claimants fall outside the classification of primary and secondary victims. In what other circumstances does the law recognise victims of psychiatric harms as having a claim in negligence?

5.7.1 Rescuers

One area where the primary–secondary victim distinction has proved problematic is in relation to rescuers. Those who seek to assist and save those injured in an accident will not always be exposed to the risk of personal harm, but nor are they mere bystanders.

45. See e.g. Lord Slynn in *W* v *Essex County Council* [2001] who found the parents of children seriously abused by a child they were fostering to be primary victims: 'Is it clear beyond reasonable doubt that the parents cannot satisfy the necessary criteria as "primary" or "secondary" victims? As to being primary victims it is beyond doubt that they were not physically injured by the abuse and on the present allegations it does not seem reasonably foreseeable that there was risk of sexual abuse of the parents. But the categorisation of those claiming to be included as primary or secondary victims is not as I read the cases finally closed. It is a concept still to be developed in different factual situations . . . I do not consider that any of the cases to which your Lordships have been referred conclusively shows that, if the psychiatric injury suffered by the parents flows from a feeling that they brought the abuser and the abused together or that they have a feeling of responsibility that they did not detect earlier what was happening, prevents them from being primary victims' (at 601).

In this sense they are not simply witnesses but participants. For this reason, when the primary–secondary victim distinction was first set down, rescuers who suffered psychiatric injury as a result of their participation were often thought to fall within the class of primary victim. For instance, Lord Oliver, in ***Alcock***, clearly envisaged primary victims as encompassing a broad range of claimants including rescuers and unwitting agents (discussed in **section 5.7.2**). However, more recently, the courts have favoured the narrower conception of primary victim set out by Lord Lloyd in ***Page*** so that rescuers can only recover if they were also at foreseeable risk of physical injury.

Traditionally, the courts treated rescuers favourably: 'Danger invites rescue. The cry of distress is the summons of relief . . . the act, whether impulsive or deliberate, is the child of the occasion' (*Wagner* v *International Railway Co* [1921]). So, where a defendant endangered someone by their carelessness, the courts typically held that it is reasonably foreseeable that others may put themselves at risk by trying to save the victim. As such, defendants have been held to owe a duty of care not just to those they initially endanger by their actions, but also to those who intervene to rescue them (see e.g. *Ogwo* v *Taylor* [1988] and *Baker* v *TE Hopkins* [1959]).[46]

Moreover, this expansive approach appeared to extend beyond cases where the rescuer was *physically* harmed in their attempted rescue to those where the rescuer suffered *psychiatric* harm. In *Chadwick* v *British Railways Board* [1967] the widow of a window cleaner was able to recover for the psychiatric harm suffered by her husband as a result of his particularly harrowing and gruesome experience giving help and relief to victims of a severe rail crash over the course of 12 hours. And as recently as ***Alcock***, Lord Oliver recognised the 'well-established' principle that a defendant owes a duty of care to those 'induced to go to the rescue' of those in peril as a result of their negligence (at 408).

However, this simple proposition no longer stands in light of another case arising out of the Hillsborough Stadium disaster—***White*** **v** ***Chief Constable of South Yorkshire Police***—involving claims by police officers who had suffered psychiatric harm as a result of their work during the disaster.

White v *Chief Constable of South Yorkshire Police* [1998] HL

The claimants were police officers who had been on duty the day of the Hillsborough Stadium disaster. Three were on duty at the ground itself, one had attempted to free spectators, two had attended the makeshift morgue in the gymnasium and another two were among those drafted in later that afternoon and who, with the others, witnessed the chaotic and gruesome scenes. A final officer had worked as a liaison officer at a nearby hospital. All had suffered psychiatric illness as a result of their participation in the events of that day.

The claimants could not satisfy the conditions set out in *Alcock* (so they could not be considered secondary victims), nor could they establish that they were in danger of physical harm,

→

46. In the same vein, rescuers' actions will usually not be treated as *novus actus interveniens*, nor will they be held to be contributorily negligent in respect of any harms they suffer in attempting their rescue.

→

such as to ground liability as primary victims following ***Page***. Instead, the claimants argued that they were entitled to recover on the basis that they were either rescuers or employees and, as such, fell outside the remit of the previous cases.

A bare majority of the House of Lords held that neither a rescuer nor an employee was placed in any special position in relation to recovery for psychiatric harm.

Accepting the narrow definition of primary victim given by Lord Lloyd in ***Page***, Lord Steyn in the majority held that a rescuer could only be considered a primary victim if he 'objectively exposed himself to danger or reasonably believed he was doing so' (at 499). The police officers were never in (nor did they reasonably believe themselves to be in) actual physical danger. To extend the category of primary victims to include rescuers would be, in Lord Steyn's view, 'unwarranted' (at 500).

Nor could the claimants recover on the basis that the defendant owed them a duty of care because they were his employees. Though employers clearly owe a duty of care to their employees in respect of physical injuries, the majority held that it did not follow that there was *also* a duty in respect of psychiatric harms suffered in the course of their employment.[47] Moreover, to allow the claimants to recover on the basis of their employment with the defendants would lead to 'striking anomalies': the police officers would be given rights denied to others, including doctors and ambulance workers, who had assisted the injured at Hillsborough out of a sense of moral, as opposed to legal, obligation (Lord Hoffmann at 506).

Accordingly, the claimants' status as rescuers and as employees made no difference to the legal principles determining recovery for psychiatric injury. Since the claimants were not exposed to any risk of physical harm (to allow for recovery under ***Page***) and could not satisfy the ***Alcock*** criteria (the claimants had no close ties of love and affection to the victims, nor did they all meet the requirements of proximity in space and time) their claims failed.

In dissent, Lord Goff, found it 'inconsistent' to make foreseeability of physical injury not merely a sufficient but also a *necessary* condition of liability for psychiatric harm (at 479). To do so, he argued, was not only inappropriately restrictive, but also in opposition to Lord Lloyd's expansive strategy in ***Page*** and Lord Oliver's categorisation of rescuers as primary victims in ***Alcock***. Similarly, Lord Griffiths (who would have allowed the appeal on the basis of the police officers' position as employees) also rejected the distinction between physical and psychiatric injury; '[i]f it is foreseeable that the rescuer may suffer personal injury in the form of psychiatric injury rather than physical injury, why should he not recover for that injury?' (at 464).

Counterpoint

Controversially, in the Court of Appeal, the claims of all but one of the police officers had been successful on the basis that they were rescuers and/or employees. Unsurprisingly, this decision was highly criticised. Many believed it was unfair to allow the police (who in another

→

47. Claims for psychiatric injury by employees against their employers are discussed further in **section 5.7.5**.

→

capacity were the defendants in ***Alcock*** and ***White***) to recover when the claims of friends and family had been dismissed in ***Alcock***.[48] As Lord Steyn notes 'The claim of the police officers on our sympathy, and the justice of the case, is great but not as great as that of others to whom the law denies redress' (***White*** at 498).[49]

By the time the police officers' case reached the House of Lords it was clear that the law in this area was in a 'genuine doctrinal muddle' (*Conaghan & Mansell* p 40). It was, in the words of Lord Steyn, so far beyond judicial repair that 'the only sensible general strategy for the courts is to say thus far and no further . . . to treat the pragmatic categories as reflected in the authoritative decisions such as the ***Alcock*** case . . . and ***Page*** v ***Smith*** as settled for the time being' (***White*** at 500). Any further development was the responsibility of Parliament.[50]

In short, the law lords' acknowledged aim in ***White*** was one of damage limitation—with the result, we would argue, that the police officers were abandoned within a tangled web of largely arbitrary and illogical distinctions between physical and psychiatric harm, primary and secondary victims.

In ***White***, therefore, the courts' usual inclination to protect rescuers was trumped by their lordships' inclination to limit recovery for pure psychiatric harm. Lord Hoffmann puts it thus:

> There does not seem to me to be any logical reason why the normal treatment of rescuers on the issues of foreseeability and causation should lead to the conclusion that, for the purpose of liability for psychiatric injury, they should be given special treatment as primary victims when they were not within the range of foreseeable physical injury . . . such an extension would be unacceptable to the ordinary person . . . He would think it wrong that policemen, even as part of a general class of persons who rendered assistance, should have the right to compensation for psychiatric injury out of public funds while the bereaved relatives are sent away with nothing. (at 510)

In light of this the majority considered that the decision in *Chadwick* could be supported only on the basis that the rescuer was in fact in physical danger (even if he did not realise this himself and this was not part of the original court's reasoning) when he sought to extract the victims from the wreckage of the train.

Pause for reflection

see online resources

Lord Hoffmann frames the decision in ***White*** as a choice between distributive and corrective justice. We are forced to choose between the two alternatives: either the police officers are able to recover (as dictated by the principles of corrective justice) or their claims are denied

→

48. See e.g. the reaction of Trevor Hicks, who was at the stadium during the disaster with his daughters (both of whom died). (*Daily Mirror* 'Families' fury at cash bid by Hillsbro cops' 1 November 1996)

49. By way of contrast, in *Hale* v *London Underground* [1992] a fireman involved in rescuing the victims of the King's Cross underground station fire was able to recover for his psychiatric injury, despite the fact that he was a professional rescuer and, presumably, hardened to horrifying scenes.

50. Echoed by the Master of the Rolls in *Taylor* v *A Novo Ltd* [2013] at [31].

→

(in accordance with both the principle of distributive justice and, in line with, the decision in *Alcock*). His (and our) decision is presented as an either/or choice between the police officers and the families and friends in *Alcock*. This dichotomy underpins his refusal to extend liability to rescuers not in physical danger. Corrective justice is abandoned in favour of 'cautious pragmatism' (at 502) as the burden of distributive justice falls on the police officers.[51]

What do you think of this either/or alternative? To what extent, if any, do you believe the House of Lords should have responded to the earlier decision in *Alcock*?

Counterpoint

Lord Goff, in his dissenting opinion in ***White***, highlights the constrained and doctrinally flawed character of the majority opinions. In particular, he criticises the introduction of further 'control mechanisms' (akin to the highly criticised ***Alcock*** restrictions) through the creation of 'unacceptable' and 'unjust' distinctions, which distinguish claimants according to their physical location (at 487). The imposition of a requirement of fear of physical injury in such cases is, he argues, both capricious and misplaced. Drawing on *Chadwick*, and responding to the majority's attempt to distinguish it, he poses the following analogy:

> Suppose that there was a terrible train crash and that there were two Chadwick brothers living nearby, both of them small and agile window cleaners distinguished by their courage and humanity. Mr A Chadwick worked on the front half of the train, and Mr B Chadwick on the rear half. It so happened that, although there was some physical danger present in the front half of the train, there was none in the rear. Both worked for 12 hours or so bringing aid and comfort to the victims. Both suffered PTSD in consequence of the general horror of the situation. On the new control mechanism now proposed, Mr A would recover but Mr B would not. To make things worse, the same conclusion must follow even if Mr A was unaware of the existence of the physical danger present in his half of the train. This is surely unacceptable. (at 487–8)[52]

5.7.2 **Involuntary participants**

Another category of claimants who fall outside the primary–secondary victim distinction are those known as involuntary participants or 'unwitting agents'. This stems from ***Dooley* v *Cammell Laird & Co Ltd*** [1951].

51. Although see Richard Mullender and Alistair Spier's defence of the decision in ***White*** on the principles of distributive justice ('Negligence, Psychiatric Injury, and the Altruism Principle' (2000) 20 OJLS 645).

52. An alternative way to distinguish *Chadwick* and ***White*** would have been to introduce the so-called 'fireman's rule', whereby the police officers in ***White*** as professional rescuers are considered to be persons 'of extraordinary phlegm' and recovery is restricted accordingly. This solution was rejected by the majority of the Court of Appeal and by Lord Hoffmann in ***White***.

Dooley v *Cammell Laird & Co Ltd* [1951] Liverpool Assizes

The claimant was operating a crane at the docks where he worked when, as a result of his employer's negligence, the sling connecting the load to the crane-hooks snapped causing the load to fall into the hold of a ship where men were working.

He successfully recovered from the psychiatric illness he suffered as a result of his fear that the falling load would injure or kill some of his fellow workmen.

Though Lord Oliver held that ***Dooley*** had been correctly decided in ***Alcock***, there was some doubt as to whether it survived the 'thus far and no further' sentiment of Lord Steyn in ***White***. Nevertheless, a number of more recent cases factually analogous to ***Dooley*** have sidestepped the requirement of physical imperilment, preferring the view of Lord Oliver in ***Alcock***—where his status as a 'primary victim' arose out of his role as a 'participant' in the accident—he 'had been put into the position of being or believing that he is, has been, or is about to be the involuntary cause of another's death or injury' (at 408)—rather than as a result of being in physical danger. In *Monk* v *PC Harrington Ltd* [2008], for example, the claimant was a foreman working on a construction site at Wembley Stadium. A temporary working platform became dislodged (as a result of the defendant's negligence) and fell 60 feet and hit two workmen below, killing one and injuring the other. The foreman heard of the accident on a portable radio and went to help the injured workmen. He subsequently developed significant psychiatric injury which prevented him from working. He claimed either as a rescuer, who reasonably feared for his own safety, or as an 'unwilling participant' in the accident—he believed his actions had caused the accident as he had supervised the installation of the platform that fell. Denying his claim on both grounds, the court held that though the primary victim category extended to 'unwilling participants', and that this extended to those who reasonably felt that they had put another in danger, on the facts there was no reasonable basis for the claimant's belief that he was responsible for his co-worker's death.[53]

5.7.3 Communication of shocking news

In ***Alcock***, the House of Lords made it clear that there would be no liability to a secondary victim who does not witness the accident or its immediate aftermath and is merely told about an accident involving a loved one by a third party. However, could the claimant sue the *communicator* of the news if it was the *manner* of communication that caused the psychiatric injury? Suppose the live TV broadcasts coming from the Hillsborough Stadium during the disaster had included (in breach of the broadcasters' code of practice) close-up pictures of individuals caught in the crush and close to death—could the relatives claim that the TV company was at fault in showing the pictures and so should be liable for the psychiatric injury they suffered as a consequence of seeing them?

53. His claim as a rescuer was denied on the basis that he was not physically endangered or reasonably in fear of his own safety.

Pause for reflection

It is far from obvious that the courts would recognise a duty of care in such cases—the public interest in the dissemination of information might well be taken to preclude liability for the negligent communication of distressing news. However, while we may well feel that there should be media freedom to convey important information to the public, even if some find it shocking and that we should not allow people to recover simply on the basis that they have been upset by what they have seen or heard, we may not think that this should entitle broadcasters to sensationalise or misrepresent such information particularly where this in itself shocks viewers. So, while we value freedom of expression, this need not preclude claims where there has been some sort of abuse of this freedom. Where would you draw the line?

Where false, but distressing, news is communicated *with the intention to shock or harm the claimant*, the teller of the falsehood is liable for any physical and psychiatric damage caused.[54] The same is likely to be true where false, but distressing, news is *negligently* communicated. In *Farrell* v *Avon Health Authority* [2001] the court held that a duty of care was owed in respect of the psychiatric injury suffered by a father who was told on arriving at the hospital where his former girlfriend had just given birth that his son had died. He sat for 20 minutes holding the baby he thought was his, before being told that there had been a mistake and that his son was in fact alive.[55] This position might seem somewhat anomalous in light of ***Alcock***. After all, as Michael Jones notes, 'which event is worse—being told (correctly) that someone has negligently killed your child or negligently being told (incorrectly) that your child has died?'[56]

5.7.4 Self-harm by the defendant

What about where a claimant suffers psychiatric harm as a result of witnessing the defendant negligently placing *themselves* in danger? Would, for example, a mother be able to bring a claim against her son for psychiatric harm caused by witnessing his imperilment when he negligently walked in front of an oncoming car (Lord Oliver, ***Alcock*** at 418)? The reasons for denying such a claim, Lord Oliver continued, can only be grounded in policy 'for it is difficult to visualise a greater proximity or a greater degree of forseeability' (at 418). The key policy issue here is that of self-determination: a person ought to be free to choose to incur personal risks, without exposing themselves to liability to others.

54. *Wilkinson* v *Downton* [1897]; confirmed in the House of Lords in ***Wainwright* v *Home Office* [2003]** discussed further in **section 15.6.1**.

55. See also *Allin* v *City & Hackney Health Authority* [1996] where the claimant recovered damages for psychiatric injury suffered as a result of being told after a difficult birth that her baby had died; she found out six hours later that the baby had in fact survived.

56. Michael Jones 'Negligently Inflicted Psychiatric Harm: Is the Word Mightier than the Deed?' (1997) 13 PN 111, 113. Consider again the woman misdiagnosed with cancer (in the examples at the beginning of the chapter). The decisions in *Farrell* and *Allin* suggest that she will be owed a duty of care in these circumstances (assuming her agoraphobia amounts to a recognised psychiatric illness). The issue is then one of breach—i.e. whether the defendant had been negligent in mixing up her test results.

In *Greatorex* v *Greatorex* [2000] the court refused to hold the defendant liable for the claimant's psychiatric injuries suffered as a result of witnessing the aftermath of his negligent driving. John Greatorex, the defendant, was involved in a car accident (he had been drinking and crashed the car while driving on the wrong side of the road). When the fire service arrived he was trapped in the car, injured and unconscious. Coincidently, the lead fire officer was his father, Christopher Greatorex, who later suffered psychiatric harm as a result of what he had seen. He brought a claim against his son (which would have been met by the Motor Insurers' Bureau as his son was uninsured). The father's claim was denied on the grounds that as the defendant's injuries were self-inflicted it was against public policy to hold him liable.[57]

5.7.5 The 'assumption of responsibility' cases

Finally, a claimant will be able to establish that the defendant owes a duty of care not to cause them psychiatric harm where the defendant has 'assumed responsibility' to ensure that the claimant avoids reasonably foreseeable psychiatric injury.[58] Examples of relationships in which such an assumption of responsibility has been found include employer and employee (*Waters* v *Commissioner of Police for the Metropolis* [2000][59]); bookmaker and gambler (*Calvert* v *William Hill Credit Ltd* [2008]); doctor and patient (*AB* v *Leeds Teaching Hospital NHS Trust* [2005]); police and police informant (*Swinney* v *Chief Constable of Northumbria Police* [1997][60]); and prison officer and prisoners (*Butchart* v *Home Office* [2006]). In the latter case, the claimant (who the prison authorities knew to be in a depressed and suicidal state) was housed with another suicidal prisoner, who subsequently went on to commit suicide. The claimant woke up to find his cell mate had hanged himself. He suffered severe shock. He was later told that his cell mate's suicide was his fault. The Court of Appeal held that prison authorities owed the claimant a duty of care to ensure the health and safety of prisoners and that this could extend to preventing or minimising the risk of a vulnerable prisoner claimant suffering psychiatric harm as a result of being placed in a cell with a suicidal prisoner.

This category also includes occupational stress claims.[61] As with the other assumption of responsibility cases, these do not usually involve the apprehension of physical impact (or danger), rather their psychiatric injury typically stems from unreasonable direct pressure or stress they feel as employees. An employer was first found liable for their employee's work-related stress in ***Walker* v *Northumberland County Council*** [1995].

57. The Law Commission recommended that such claims be allowed ([5.34]–[5.43]); however, as with the rest of their recommendations, this has not been adopted.

58. The case law here is explored in detail by Mulheron 2008, pp 99–106.

59. Discussed in **section 6.5.3**.

60. Discussed in **section 6.5.3**.

61. See generally Jesse Elvin 'The Legal Response to Occupational Stress Claims' (2008) 16 Tort L Rev 23.

Walker v *Northumberland County Council* [1995] QBD

The claimant was a social services manager with a heavy and emotionally demanding caseload of child abuse cases who suffered a second nervous breakdown as a result of pressure at work (after his earlier breakdown he had been promised additional support, which had not materialised).

Colman J held that there was no logical reason for excluding the risk of psychiatric injury from an employer's duty to provide a safe system of work:[62]

> Whereas the law on the extent of this duty has developed almost exclusively in cases involving physical injury to the employee as distinct from injury to his mental health, there is no logical reason why risk of psychiatric damage should be excluded from the scope of an employer's duty of care. (at 710)

Though there was no breach on the part of the employer at the time of the first breakdown (as this was unforeseeable on the part of the employer), in light of this, the claimant's second breakdown *was* reasonably foreseeable if his workload was not reduced. The employer was in breach of duty in respect of the claimant's second breakdown.

Counterpoint

The approach in ***Walker*** seems somewhat at odds with the decision in ***White***. Lord Hoffmann distinguished ***Walker*** in ***White*** on the basis that in ***Walker*** the claimant's psychiatric harm 'was caused by the strain of doing the work which his employer had required him to do' (at 506), whereas in ***White*** the police officers' injuries stemmed from their *witnessing* of the death and injury of others.

Paula Case argues that the House of Lords in ***White*** drew an 'absurd' distinction between employees' claims for psychiatric injury caused by 'occupational stress' and those arising out of a single traumatic incident (2010, p 38). While in the former the employer–employee relationship is sufficient to ground a claim, in the latter the claimant/employee is thrown back on the ordinary principles of negligence for recovery for psychiatric harm—that is, the primary/secondary victim distinction. Unsurprisingly, 'the legacies of ***White*** [including its "exclusive" definition of primary victims] have been routinely ignored, distinguished, qualified or undermined' in the more recent 'stress at work' case law (*Cane* p 34).

Walker was confirmed by the Court of Appeal in *Hatton* v *Sutherland* [2002] in which the court accepted that a duty was owed in respect of psychiatric injury caused by stress at work. Though only one of the claimants was successful in the House of Lords (where the case was reported as *Barber* v *Somerset County Council* [2004]), the law lords approved the guidance setting out when an employer would be in breach offered by Hale LJ in the Court of Appeal. In line with the ordinary principles of employer's liability, the

62. See further **section 13.2.4**.

'threshold question' was whether the kind of harm to the particular employee was (or ought to have been) reasonably foreseeable. So viewed, foreseeability depends on the interrelationship between the individual characteristics of the relevant employee and the requirements made of them by their employer, including (but not limited to) the nature and extent of the work being undertaken, signs of stress shown by the employee themselves, the size and scope of the business and the availability of resources. Once the threshold is crossed, it is immaterial whether a person of ordinary fortitude would have suffered the same harm.

Pause for reflection

It has been suggested that the foreseeability hurdles in *Hatton* (as approved by the House of Lords in *Barber*) appear to be set at a level which effectively insulates the employer from liability in the quite typical case where the employee will not admit to experiencing stress for fear of appearing unable to cope (*Pratley* v *Surrey County Council* [2002])—do you agree?[63]

5.8 Conclusion

In this chapter we have considered the law in relation to recovery for negligently inflicted psychiatric injury in the *absence* of physical injury. The law in this area has been shaped by prejudice and tragedy. Assumptions that suffering psychiatric harm is less than suffering physical injury and fears of exaggerated and/or fraudulent claims as well as a number of high-profile, negligently caused, disasters have led to the introduction of 'control mechanisms' limiting recovery. Central to this is the distinction between claimants deemed 'primary' victims, 'secondary' victims and, more recently, those who fit neither category. So understood, Lord Steyn's conclusion in ***White*** that 'the law on the recovery of compensation for pure psychiatric harm is a patchwork quilt of distinctions which are difficult to justify' (at 500) remains apposite.

End-of-chapter questions

After reading the chapter carefully, try answering the questions which follow.

1 Why does the law distinguish psychiatric from physical injury? To what extent, if at all, is this distinction justifiable?

2 What is the distinction between primary and secondary victims and does it produce defensible consequences?

3 Does the law relating to psychiatric damage apply coherent principles?

If you would like to know what we think visit the **online resources**. www.oup.com/he/horsey7e

63. See also discussion relating to the use of the Protection from Harassment Act 1997 by claimants in order to avoid the restrictions of the guidelines set down in *Hatton* (**section 15.6.2**).

Answering the problem question

Consider again the problem question at the start of this chapter. Now having read about the topic, **what would be your advice to the various parties?**

Here are some pointers to get you started

→ Don't jump straight to the most obvious classification. Though Hannah is most likely to be a secondary victim, could she be a primary victim? You should explore what she'd need to establish for this to be the case.

→ Will Pete be able to satisfy the proximity in time and space element of ***Alcock***? Has he arrived during the 'immediate aftermath' of the explosion?

→ It is clear that Stuart is an 'involuntary participant', but could he also be a primary victim? What would he need to establish for this to be the case?

If you need some more guidance

→ An **annotated version of the problem with issues and cases to consider** can be found in the Appendix.

→ A **suggested outline answer** to check your ideas against can be found in the online resources that accompany the book.

see online resources

Further reading

Numerous articles and case notes have been written on the issues surrounding psychiatric damage. The best place to start is Donal Nolan's excellent chapter on *Alcock*.

Bailey, Stephen and Donal Nolan 'The *Page* v *Smith* Saga: A Tale of Inauspicious Origins and Unintended Consequences' [2010] CLJ 495

Case, Paula 'Now You See It, Now You Don't: Black Letter Reflections on the Legacies of *White* v *Chief Constable of South Yorkshire Police*' (2010) 18 Tort L Rev 33

Chamallas, Martha and Linda Kerber 'Women, Mothers, and the Law of Fright: A History' (1990) 88 Mich L Rev 814

Mulheron, Rachael 'The "Primary Victim" in Psychiatric Illness Claims: Reworking the "Patchwork Quilt"' (2008) 19 Kings LJ 81

Nolan, Donal '*Alcock* v *Chief Constable of South Yorkshire Police* (1991)' in Charles Mitchell and Paul Mitchell (eds) *Landmark Cases in the Law of Tort* (Hart, 2010), p 273

Teff, Harvey *Causing Psychiatric and Emotional Harm Reshaping the Boundaries of Legal Liability* (Hart, 2008)

6 Special duty problems: public bodies

Problem question

Read this problem question carefully, and keep it in mind while you are working through the chapter that follows. At the end of the chapter, you will be able to apply what you have learnt to the problem question and advise the relevant parties.

PC Plod and PC Bill both work for the Countyshire Constabulary. They are involved in investigating a high-profile criminal case involving a bank robbery.

One night, PCs Plod and Bill are on motorway patrol, when a car passes them at a fairly high speed. PC Plod, who is driving the patrol car, recognises the car as belonging to one of his neighbours, Mr Smith, with whom he has had a long-standing feud since Mr Smith had an affair with his wife. Determined to get his own back on Mr Smith, PC Plod, despite PC Bill's objection, decides to give chase. As the cars approach 110 mph, PC Plod loses control and the two cars collide. Mr Smith's car turns over several times before eventually coming to a stop. PC Bill is injured.

PC Plod calls an ambulance from the Countyshire Ambulance Service. This takes 30 minutes to arrive and, even then, because of staff shortages, the paramedic on board is an unqualified trainee. He examines Mr Smith and concludes that he is dead, so devotes his attention to a fairly minor leg wound suffered by PC Bill. Half an hour later a doctor arrives at the scene. When he examines Mr Smith he realises he is actually alive, but deeply unconscious. Despite the doctor's best efforts, Mr Smith dies on the way to hospital.

Meanwhile, the criminal gang under investigation take part in another bank robbery in a nearby town, during which a hostage is killed. Witnesses seeing the hostages being dragged into the bank at gunpoint had called the police and been assured that they were on their way. In fact, the call had gone to PC Plod, who had ignored it because he was more interested in chasing Mr Smith. Bruce, the husband of the hostage who died, believes the police could have done more to prevent her death. The owner of the bank believes the police were negligent in failing to prevent the robbery.

Advise the families of Mr Smith and the hostage as to any potential claims in negligence.

6.1 Introduction

Consider the following examples:

- ***An educational psychologist employed by the local authority fails to diagnose a teenager's special learning needs, with the result that she does not get the support necessary to do well enough in her exams to go to university.***
- ***The police fail to act on multiple reports of harassment of a woman by a man who has become obsessed with her. The man later assaults and kills her.***
- ***A fire service turns up late to a scene of a raging fire and is unable to put it out because the fire officers did not bring the right tools to connect the hose to the nearby hydrant.***
- ***Children suffering from abuse at the hands of their parents are not removed from their home and placed in the care of the local authority, despite calls from teachers and neighbours that suggest the abuse is escalating.***
- ***A highways authority resurfaces a road then fails to re-paint the road markings exactly as they were before. When wrongly exiting a junction where she should in fact have given way (but the road was not marked as such), a driver is hit and killed by a lorry which simply could not stop in time.***

This chapter considers the limited circumstances when public bodies will owe private law duties of care to individuals who claim they were negligent. A public body is a state-funded (i.e. through taxes) organisation, including local councils, educational authorities, the emergency services and even the armed forces. The volume of public body negligence cases has increased greatly in recent years. This may be due to the introduction of the Human Rights Act (HRA) in 1998, which brought into sharper focus the harms that public bodies can cause and made people generally more rights-aware. However, it is not easy to establish liability on the part of a public body. As usual, liability (or otherwise) is established through the mechanism of duty of care—that is, the existence of a duty or, more likely, its non-existence, is the tool by which the courts shape whether liability can be found. In other contentious areas of negligence controlled via the concept of duty of care, judges take into account the nature or *type of harm* (e.g. psychiatric rather than physical, see **Chapter 5**), or *how* it is caused (for instance, by an omission rather than a positive act, see **Chapter 4**); this serves to justify limiting the extent of liability that a defendant might owe. Public body liability, however, is the only area where the *type of defendant* is taken into account in terms of whether recovery is appropriate or should be limited.

This seems counter-intuitive—if tort is (at least partly) about compensating harms suffered due to the wrong of another, why should it matter who that other is? With public body defendants, a general exclusionary rule operates, preventing a duty of care from arising in the majority of cases. This is because there are 'public policy' reasons which justify public bodies being generally exempt from negligence liability—denying that a duty of care exists in the first place is the most effective way to ensure this.

6.2 **The general exclusionary rule**

As case examples show, the term 'public bodies' is wide-ranging and encompasses many agencies which have great potential to cause harm, in terms of both volume and severity. One problem is that, as a public *body,* there is no single entity as such—it becomes harder to pin down exactly what the negligent act was when we are considering a sequence of events (or omissions), all of which add up to negligence. It is also difficult to pinpoint exactly who among an organisation staffed by many was actually to blame for what happened in any given situation.[1]

Counterpoint

Is incompetence—including gross incompetence—the same as negligence? Often not, as the case law proves, even when this amounts to serious harm including loss of life, sexual abuse or the destruction of property. If negligence is about accidents—or 'preventable' accidents—then we believe that accidents that can result in this extent of harm are exactly what the law should protect us against, particularly given the fact that public bodies have the capacity to harm in more diverse and severe ways than individual defendants.

A further problem is that the negligence of public bodies or, more so, the liability for it, is often clouded by the *manner* in which it is caused. Omission and neglect are already difficult to attach liability to, as are harms 'really' caused by the actions of a third party (who the public body may be responsible for). Should, for example, the police be held liable for harm caused by a criminal they *negligently* failed to apprehend? Additionally, the *types* of harm that may be caused often seem unrecognisable at law—if someone suffers emotional distress as a result of a health authority's carelessness, should this be compensated?

6.2.1 **Why is the judiciary reluctant to allow recovery?**

Much judicial reluctance in this area has to do with the public law notions of parliamentary sovereignty and the separation of powers, resulting in an unwillingness to interfere with statutory provisions. However, there is little or no reluctance to allow claimants to recover in respect of those twin paragons of harm: personal injury and property damage. If either is negligently caused by the direct actions (and often inactions) of a public body or its agent—say a van negligently driven by a council employee caused property damage or personal injury—then compensation will be available, without difficulty.[2]

The general exclusionary rule operates where the actions of the public body are *not* direct, do not cause these 'easily recognised' harms or do not make a situation worse. Despite the

1. See e.g. *X (Minors)* v *Bedfordshire County Council* [1995].

2. This is explained well in the Law Commission's 2008 consultation document on public body liability (at [3.104]) and also explains the perceived 'ease' of suing in e.g. 'slip and trip' cases. The principle that public bodies will be liable *in the same way as private individuals* for harms caused by direct, positive acts has been definitively confirmed by the Supreme Court in ***Robinson* v *Chief Constable of West Yorkshire Police*** [2018].

fact that a number of (often very high) hurdles must be overcome by claimants—duty being only the first of these—the courts have tasked themselves with weighing up the 'social contract', asking how far and in what circumstances it is appropriate to provide private law remedies where the state has not conferred a benefit on an individual and where there may be other (arguably less effective, less attractive) public law remedies already available. The courts have often stressed the difference between public and private and asserted on a number of occasions that political, moral and economic reasons justify the non-imposition of a private law duty on public bodies to confer benefits on individuals (as opposed to the lesser duty merely to refrain from causing direct harm).

It might be thought that because public bodies are paid for by the public, avoidable harms caused by their carelessness (or worse) ought to attract compensation. However, it is often precisely this that makes courts shy away from finding a duty of care—the fact that taxpayers' money pays for public bodies and taxpayers are thought unlikely to want to 'fund' their negligence through compensation payouts. Put like this, it is unattractive, but phrased in terms of redressing wrongs committed (with the dual benefit that lessons will be learnt so that—with luck—similar negligent acts will not happen in the future) and alongside the loss-spreading effects and principles of distributive justice, liability in such circumstances may seem more appealing.

The counter-argument is that making public bodies pay compensation strains the public purse and diverts resources away from public services—this argument holds particular force in times of financial austerity and cuts to public spending. It is also suggested, often by judges, without empirical or other evidence to support such assertions, that allowing claims would lead inexorably to increased unmeritorious and vexatious claims and to dangerous (but undefined) 'defensive' practices being adopted.[3] Negligent actions/inactions of public bodies can potentially harm vast numbers of people, so it is suggested by the courts, when denying that a duty should be owed, that actions against them are or could become common—that claims will be made precisely *because* the body concerned is viewed as having deep pockets and is able to bear the loss.

Historically, organs of the state could not be liable at all in negligence: the Crown had immunity from suit. This changed with *Mersey Docks and Harbour Board Trustees* v *Gibbs* [1866], later confirmed in *Geddis* v *Proprietors of the Bann Reservoir* [1878], where Lord Blackburn said that while no action could be taken for harms caused by an agent of the Crown in doing what it was authorised to do by an Act of Parliament if it was done without negligence, but if the harm was the result of negligence then an action would lie (at 455). Later, ***East Suffolk Rivers Catchment Board* v *Kent* [1941]** considered, for the first time, whether public bodies owe a common law duty of care to individuals harmed by their negligent actions where they have a public law *power* to act, but not a public law *duty* to do so. This distinction (between powers and duties) still leads to many of the problems with finding public bodies liable today.

3. Note that not all judges have been swayed by the notion of liability resulting in 'defensive practices'. In ***Home Office* v *Dorset Yacht Co Ltd* [1970]**, Lord Reid rejected it, saying that 'Her Majesty's servants are made of sterner stuff' (at 1033). In this case—a good example of the complex nature of public body cases, as it also involved both an omission and the actions of third parties—the House of Lords *did* impose liability on the Home Office for damage caused by escaping young offenders. Carol Harlow described this as 'setting the scene for a liability revolution as great as, if not greater than, that usually attributed to *Donoghue* v *Stevenson*' (*State Liability: Tort Law and Beyond* (OUP, 2004), p 17).

East Suffolk Rivers Catchment Board v Kent [1941] HL

At high tide, flood waters breached a sea wall maintained by the catchment board. It took a long time to fix the wall, during which the claimant's land continued to be flooded with sea water. He sued for the losses this caused him, unsuccessfully in the High Court, but recovering in the Court of Appeal.

On the catchment board's appeal to the House of Lords, the question was whether this was a breach of a public law *duty* or whether the catchment board was simply exercising *powers* given to it under statute. The Lords held it was the latter: there was no existing duty that said that the board *should* repair the wall—or even to complete the work once started—it merely had the power to do so. So, the issue became whether the exercise of this power could attract a common law duty of care, owed to individuals who suffered harm as a result of the negligent exercise of the power. The law lords thought not, stating (with one notable dissent from Lord Atkin, referring back to principles he had expounded in ***Donoghue*** v ***Stevenson*** [1932]) that public bodies would be liable only for the negligent exercise of a statutory power where doing so had made matters worse.

In ***East Suffolk***, the House of Lords determined that no duty would be owed to a claimant in respect of the negligent exercise of a power, unless that action made the claimant worse off than they were before. This general exclusionary rule is still in operation, albeit with exceptions, and the particular issue raised in ***East Suffolk***—'justiciability'—is something the courts have returned to many times, as we will later see.

The rest of this chapter is divided into sections dealing first with the current status of the general law on public body liability, then a closer look at the emergency services (as a particular type of public body, responsible by their very nature for the wellbeing of citizens) and armed forces. This is followed by a section on other types of public bodies, including educational and highway authorities and child protection services. The final section considers the impact of human rights jurisprudence and the passage of the HRA on this contentious area of tort law, particularly in relation to new 'types' of claim.

6.3 When will public bodies owe a duty of care?

Public bodies will be liable where the negligent exercise of their powers makes a situation worse than it already was or causes direct physical harm to person or property.[4] However, where this is not the case, it is more difficult to establish a duty, particularly when harm is caused via an omission and/or by the actions of third parties.[5]

Two cases help to illustrate the current position: ***D*** **v** ***East Berkshire Community NHS Trust and another*** [2005] (and its conjoined cases *MAK and another* v *Dewsbury Healthcare NHS Trust and another* and *RK and another* v *Oldham NHS Trust and another*) and ***Poole Borough Council*** **v** ***GN and another*** [2019].

4. ***Robinson***, discussed in **section 3.3.3**. 5. See **Chapter 4**.

D v *East Berkshire Community NHS Trust* and other cases [2005] HL

D v *East Berkshire* concerned a mother who was wrongly suspected of harming her daughter. In *MAK*, a man and his daughter claimed that the daughter had been wrongly and unjustifiably taken into care because of suspicions (wrongly held) that the father was abusing her. *RK and another* concerned a couple who had been wrongly accused of abuse; their daughter had been taken into care on the basis of these false allegations.

In each case, the local authority contended that it owed no duty to the claimants, relying on the authority of *X (Minors)* v *Bedfordshire County Council* [1995]. In *X*, the House of Lords ruled that no duty was owed by local authorities in respect of decisions about whether to take children into care. The law lords felt that to find such a duty would cut across the statutory framework in which such decisions were made and potentially lead to staff working less effectively as they would always keep one eye on the avoidance of liability (commonly referred to as 'defensive practices'). However, in *D* v *East Berkshire* and its conjoined cases, the Court of Appeal had ruled that the duty question in this type of claim must be considered in light of the HRA (Lord Phillips MR at [79]–[83]). This brought into domestic focus rights contained in the European Convention on Human Rights,[6] giving citizens the right to sue public bodies in a domestic court for violations of these rights.[7] In addition, the Act named the *courts* as a public body,[8] meaning that domestic courts may not make any decision that impinges on a citizen's human rights guaranteed under the Convention.

The Court of Appeal ruled that the HRA's effect meant that the policy argument that workers would adopt defensive practices for fear of being sued in negligence no longer held weight in cases where human rights issues were at stake (in these cases Art 8 (at least)—the right to private and family life—was almost certainly engaged). In other words, as individuals could sue the state *directly* under the HRA, this kind of risk avoidance was not unique to the tort of negligence and a duty should not be denied on this basis. Consequently, there could be no other interpretation than that it *was* 'fair, just and reasonable' to impose a duty on authorities charged with making decisions about whether to take children into care. However, the court said that this duty was owed only to the *child* and not to its parents (at [86]–[87]). To allow both could amount to a conflict of interest where abuse by a parent was being alleged and/or investigated.[9]

The claimants appealed to the House of Lords on the issue of whether a duty should be owed to the parents as well, arguing that no such conflict of interest arose: it was in *all* parties' interests that the authorities acted with care in making decisions about whether to remove children from their parents. However, their appeal was unsuccessful: the majority ruled that although a more general duty was owed to the whole family, where there was a suspicion or allegation of abuse there had to be a duty to the child only to ensure that this was properly and sensitively investigated, which inevitably might not be in the interests of the parents, meaning that the conflict of interest still existed (Lord Bingham dissented on this point).[10]

6. Not all of the Convention rights are directly actionable under the HRA, only those listed in the Appendix to the Act.

7. Section 6. 8. Section 6(3)(a).

9. Also, in a different context, see *Jain* v *Trent Strategic Health Authority* [2009]. Note also that the decision in ***Poole*** suggests that while it is possible to find a duty owed to children by public bodies, this will not arise *because of* policy or human rights reasons, but because it can be argued that an 'assumption of responsibility' exists.

10. See also *MAK* v *UK* [2010], in which the girl in the second case listed under ***D* v *East Berkshire*—*and her father***—successfully argued that their Art 8 rights had been violated.

Pause for reflection

see online resources

Is this issue really one of semantics? In other words, in distinguishing between a duty of care owed to children, parents or a family as a whole, do you think that the House of Lords was playing with words deliberately in order to limit the category of people to whom a duty of care can be owed—and is it right that they should do so? Could it be said that authorities charged with investigating abuse should owe a duty to *all* parties involved to investigate any allegations *carefully*, in which case there would be no conflict of interest, as it would be in both the parents' and the children's interest that decisions are based on a careful investigation? If you only relate a duty to whether the investigations should be *sensitively* conducted, it becomes easier to see where a conflict of interest might arise.

Pause for reflection

There have been various high-profile instances of mishandled abuse cases by public authorities in recent years, either where the authorities had been notified that abuse was occurring but failed to properly investigate, or where agents of an authority simply did not recognise signs that ought to have been clear.[11] Does the fact that such failures are seemingly commonplace support the idea that public bodies charged with this kind of protective role ought to owe duties of care to those individuals harmed by their actions or inactions?

D v ***East Berkshire*** and its conjoined cases are so significant because a duty was found to be owed to *someone* by the public bodies concerned in respect of the alleged negligence. Prior cases, as already indicated, had more commonly shown there to be no duty, so this represented a marked change of direction.[12] Lord Bingham (dissenting) in *D* v ***East Berkshire*** suggested that more reliance could be placed on using breach as a 'control device' to limit recovery and there was thus no reason to distinguish which of the parties the duty was owed to. Even where a duty was recognised and 'breach rather than duty were to be the touchstone of recovery, no breach could be proved without showing a very clear departure from ordinary standards of skill and care' (at [49]). Do you agree?

The Supreme Court has recently handed down an important decision clarifying the position in this area.

see online resources

11. See, among other examples: BBC News 'Rochdale abuse: social services "missed opportunities"' 27 September 2012 (in relation to the Rochdale abuse scandal); BBC News 'Jimmy Savile scandal: report reveals decades of abuse' 11 January 2013; BBC News 'South Yorkshire authorities attacked by MPs over grooming' 10 June 2013; Helen Pidd 'Rotherham abuse scandal: IPCC to investigate conduct of 10 police officers' *The Guardian* 19 November 2014. More on these stories and others can be found on the **online resources**. A case showing the kind of negligence that can occur and the harms that can be caused is *A & S (Children)* v *Lancashire County Council* [2012]).

12. Consider the implications of ***D* v *East Berkshire*** in relation to the abused children in the scenario outlined at the start of this chapter. On the basis of this case, which parties would be owed a duty of care and which would not? See also *ABB and others* v *Milton Keynes Council* [2011]. The 'no duty to parents' rule withstood subsequent challenge in *Lawrence* v *Pembrokeshire County Council* [2007], but was later refined, with the court saying no absolute rule about parents (or otherwise) was ever laid down by ***D* v *East Berkshire***. Instead, the rule is that no duty will be owed to those *suspected of abuse*, parents or otherwise (*Merthyr Tydfil County Borough Council* v *C* [2010]).

Poole Borough Council v *GN and another* [2019] UKSC

Brothers CN (then aged 9) and GN (aged 7) were housed by the council on an estate in Poole with their mother in May 2006. CN has severe mental and physical disabilities. The council failed to take appropriate and necessary steps under anti-social behaviour legislation to safeguard the boys from prolonged abuse, harassment and violent assaults from members of a 'delinquent' family who lived on the estate, which caused foreseeable physical and psychological harm, including suicide attempts by CN. The High Court found that a duty of care was owed by the council to protect vulnerable children. However, this was unanimously rejected by the Court of Appeal which suggested that the principle from *D* v *East Berkshire* had been implicitly overruled by later cases dealing with harms caused by the actions of third parties (e.g. see *Michael* (section 6.3.1); *Mitchell* (section 4.5.1)). Thus, the council should not be liable for the wrongdoing of a third party (the abusive neighbours), even where that wrongdoing is foreseeable. Irwin LJ also resurrected the idea from *X* v *Bedfordshire* that invoking a duty would cut across the many decision-making processes in a difficult area, and result in defensive practice (at [94]).

The case was appealed to the Supreme Court, which agreed that no duty of care existed, but for slightly different reasons.[13] Lord Reed found that *X* v *Bedfordshire* is no longer good law in that it relied on public policy reasons for denying the existence of a duty of care owed by local authorities to children in the context of exercising their statutory functions, or for whom they assume responsibility (at [74]). He also cautioned against courts relying on public policy as a basis for deciding whether duties of care exist, saying:

> public authorities are prima facie subject to the same general principles of the common law of negligence as private individuals and organisations, and may therefore be liable for negligently causing individuals to suffer actionable harm but not, in the absence of some particular reason justifying such liability, for negligently failing to protect individuals from harm caused by others. Rather than justifying decisions that public authorities owe no duty of care by relying on public policy, it has been held that even if a duty of care would ordinarily arise on the application of common law principles, it may nevertheless be excluded or restricted by statute where it would be inconsistent with the scheme of the legislation under which the public authority is operating. In that way, the courts can continue to take into account, for example, the difficult choices which may be involved in the exercise of discretionary powers. (at [75])

Therefore, the rule that there is no liability for the wrongdoing of third parties, or in the context of 'failing to confer a benefit', can be displaced if there is an assumption of responsibility. The fact that a local authority is only exercising its statutory powers does not preclude a duty of care from arising, and each case would be concluded on its facts. In *Poole*, however, Lord

→

13. It is notable that ***Robinson*** had been handed down by the Supreme Court in the time between the Court of Appeal and Supreme Court decisions in ***Poole***.

→

Reed found that there had been no assumption of responsibility, which meant that no duty arose on the facts:

> the council's investigating and monitoring the claimants' position did not involve the provision of a service to them on which they or their mother could be expected to rely … Nor could it be said that the claimants and their mother had entrusted their safety to the council, or that the council had accepted that responsibility. Nor had the council taken the claimants into its care, and thereby assumed responsibility for their welfare. (at [81])

6.3.1 **An alternative claim?**

Given the steer from ***D* v *East Berkshire***, some claimants have attempted to pursue human rights claims rather than claiming in negligence.[14] A good example is *Van Colle* v *Chief Constable of Hertfordshire Constabulary* [2008]. Here, the claimants were the parents of Giles van Colle, a man shot dead days before he was due to give evidence for the prosecution in a criminal trial. In the period before the trial, the accused, Daniel Brougham, was alleged to have intimidated witnesses and evidence was provided to show that the police knew (or should have known) this. Despite this, van Colle was offered no protection. Brougham was convicted of his murder. The van Colles argued that the police had put Giles at risk—they could and should have offered him further protection from Brougham and it was likely that his death could have been prevented had this been given. They argued that this meant that the police had violated Article 2 of the Convention (which guarantees the right to life), bringing their claim under the HRA, instead of in negligence.

As we will see, a negligence claim against the police would have been likely to fail (the court noted that a negligence claim would have been 'fraught with difficulty'). The defendants based their defence to the Article 2 claim in terms of existing (negligence) precedents and the policy arguments within them—but the Court of Appeal said that it was exactly these arguments which led to the obligation of the police to provide protection for the life of witnesses: the claimants succeeded. However, the House of Lords found that there was, in fact, no violation of Article 2 as there had been no 'direct and immediate threat' to Giles's life. The threshold test for this was high.[15] The van Colles further appealed to the ECtHR. The ECtHR reaffirmed the ***Osman* v *UK*** test, later finding that though the police should have realised that there was an escalating situation of

14. Some high-profile examples include ***Smith and others* v *Ministry of Defence* [2013]**, discussed in **section 6.5.4** and *Commissioner of Police of the Metropolis* v *DSD and another* [2018], discussed later in this section.

15. The threshold was set in ***Osman* v *UK* [1999]** (see **section 6.4.1**). That the threshold is high has been confirmed in *Re Officer L* [2007] (considered in *Van Colle*) and *Mitchell* v *Glasgow City Council* [2009] (see **section 4.5.1**). Note that police forces may now issue 'Osman warnings' whereby someone under threat of serious harm is warned by the police—potentially a litigation-avoidance strategy. See BBC News 'Police letters warn 1,900 people of "threat to life"' 28 October 2015.

intimidation of a number of witnesses, including Giles, there was no decisive stage in the events leading up to the murder when the police knew or ought to have known of a 'real and immediate risk' to his life.[16] The same issue arose in ***Michael*** v ***Chief Constable of South Wales Police*** [2015].

Michael v *Chief Constable of South Wales Police* [2015] SC

Joanna Michael dialled 999 from her mobile phone at 2.29 am. She told the call handler at Gwent Police that her ex-boyfriend was at her house, was aggressive, had bitten her ear and had dragged her current boyfriend into his car, threatening to be back 'any minute' and saying 'I'm going to drop him home and ... [fucking kill you]' (in evidence, the call handler later said she thought she heard 'hit' rather than 'kill'). Gwent Police graded the call as requiring immediate response and called South Wales Police (who covered the area where Joanna Michael lived). In summarising the call, Gwent Police's call handler made no mention of the threat to kill. South Wales Police graded the call as one in which officers should respond within 60 minutes.

Joanna Michael called 999 again at 2.43 am. The operator heard screaming, then the line went silent. South Wales Police were immediately informed and arrived at her house at 2.51 am. She was dead, having been stabbed multiple times.

Joanna Michael's parents and children claimed against both police forces in negligence and under the HRA, for failure in their Article 2 duty to protect her right to life. At first instance, both claims were allowed to proceed. The Court of Appeal, while ruling out a duty of care in negligence (on proximity grounds), thought the case should go to trial on the Article 2 claim. Both parts of the decision were appealed to a seven-member Supreme Court. It unanimously upheld the finding on Article 2, but was split 5:2 on the negligence claim (Lord Kerr and Lady Hale dissenting). Lord Toulson, giving the lead judgment, found that in respect of the Article 2 claim, whether the call handler should have heard the threat was to 'kill' rather than 'hit'—and whether, if she had, this should have alerted her to a 'real and immediate' threat to life—were matters of fact to be determined at trial (at [139]).

Thus, though it appears that it will be difficult to succeed in this type of claim, it may not be impossible.[17]

Similar issues arose in *DSD* v *The Commissioner of Police for the Metropolis* [2014], a test case seeking to establish the potential liability of the police to victims of the notorious 'Black Cab Rapist', John Worboys. Green J found a human rights 'duty imposed upon the police to conduct investigations into particularly severe violent acts perpetrated by private parties in a timely and efficient manner' (at [14]). The systemic failings by the police in investigating

16. *Van Colle* v *UK* [2012].

17. Encouraging in this respect may be the Court of Appeal decision in *Sarjantson* v *Humberside Police* [2013], also in relation to the police's obligations under Art 2, this time in the context of an ongoing physical attack. Interestingly, leave to appeal to the Supreme Court was refused, the review panel stating that the Court of Appeal's decision was correct, for the reasons given. The ***Michael*** decision may also increasingly result in future similar cases being settled—see e.g. Diane Taylor 'Police apologise to dead woman's kin after failure to respond to 999 call' *The Guardian* 5 January 2017.

the large number of rapes and sexual assaults (over 100) perpetrated by Worboys amounted to a breach of the victims' rights under Article 3 ECHR (right to be free from inhumane and degrading treatment). The decision was upheld by the Court of Appeal which ruled that the police have a positive duty under Article 3 to conduct investigations into alleged ill-treatment by private individuals, and the margin of appreciation afforded to the state in relation to its failings would operate on a 'sliding scale' basis (becoming wider at the lower end of the scale).[18] The Supreme Court later rejected an appeal by the Metropolitan Police.[19] This decision is important, as it means that allegations of ill-treatment of the gravity stipulated by Article 3 give rise to a duty to properly conduct an official investigation. Moreover, this duty can also arise where crimes are committed by private individuals.[20]

6.4 The impact of European jurisprudence

6.4.1 The *Osman* case

The first European case to impact on domestic law interpretations (leading to the decision in ***D* v *East Berkshire***) was ***Osman* v *UK* [1999]**, which stemmed from decisions in two earlier domestic cases (***Hill* v *Chief Constable of West Yorkshire* [1989]** and ***Osman* v *Ferguson* [1993]**).

Hill v *Chief Constable of West Yorkshire* [1989] HL

A woman sued on behalf of her daughter, the final murder victim of serial killer Peter Sutcliffe ('the Yorkshire Ripper'). She alleged that the police had been negligent in failing to catch him earlier than they had.

The courts held that although it was foreseeable that if the police failed to apprehend the killer, he would go on to kill another young woman in the area, no proximity existed between the police and the victim as the police could have no idea exactly who or where any victim was likely to be—all females within the large area in which the murders were being committed were equally at risk. Therefore, no duty of care could be owed to the victim and the claim could not proceed. Though it was not necessary to do so, the House of Lords then considered policy reasons upon which a finding of no duty should rest. Confirming the Court of Appeal's decision, their lordships held (*obiter*) that poor investigative decisions should attract no duty as this might have an 'inhibiting effect' on the judgement of police officers. Furthermore, though many such claims against the police would be likely to fail, even preparing a defence would waste police resources in terms of time, manpower and financial expenditure.

18. *Commissioner of Police of the Metropolis* v *DSD and NBV and others* [2015].

19. *Commissioner of Police of the Metropolis* v *DSD and another* [2018].

20. This also opens avenues of possibility in relation to third parties' actions—see **section 4.5**. For more on the significance of this decision, see Joanne Conaghan, 'Investigating Rape: Human Rights and Police Accountability' (2016) 37 LS 54. For a different potential interpretation of the opportunities this decision might bring, see *The Guardian* 'Rotherham child sexual abuse victims to take police to court' 25 February 2016. For further discussion of tort's potential in the context of domestic violence, see Kirsty Horsey and Erika Rackley 'Tort Law' in Rosemary Auchmuty (ed) *Great Debates on Law and Gender* (Palgrave, 2018).

Osman v *Ferguson* [1993] CA

Mrs Osman and her son Ahmet alleged that the police were negligent in failing to prevent an attack on the family in which the boy was badly injured and his father was killed. The Osmans had been targeted by Paget-Lewis (a teacher at Ahmet's school, who had become obsessed by the teenage boy) who had, inter alia, crashed his car into the family's car, damaged their home, smeared dog excrement on the door, assaulted one of Ahmet's friends and verbally abused Ahmet in public. Despite numerous reports to the police, and assurances that they were 'aware that Paget-Lewis was the perpetrator of those acts and that [the deceased] should not worry for his own safety or that of his family' (at 347), records of the family's complaints were neither kept nor linked to previous complaints. Paget-Lewis was never cautioned, despite being interviewed by the police more than once (including at his own instigation) and even though he declared his own criminal insanity and claimed that he might 'do a Hungerford' (in reference to a series of killings in the town of that name in the 1980s). Paget-Lewis went on to steal a gun and shoot Ahmet Osman and kill his father.

The Court of Appeal struck out the Osmans' claims, relying on the policy arguments from *Hill*. Leave to appeal to the House of Lords was refused.

In ***Osman*** v ***Ferguson***, McCowan LJ considered the case 'doomed' to fail because of the policy reasons from ***Hill***, which provided immunity for the police from negligence claims of this type (at 354). Having exhausted any possibility of a domestic remedy, the Osmans took their case to the ECtHR.

Osman v *UK* [1999] ECtHR

The Osmans claimed that multiple human rights violations occurred when the UK's domestic courts refused to consider their negligence claim against the police. They claimed that the striking-out procedure meant they were denied a fair hearing, and asked the ECtHR to rule on violations of Article 2 (the right to life, in relation to the father), Article 6 (the right to a fair trial), Article 8 (the right to private, home and family life) and Article 13 (the right to an effective remedy).

The ECtHR ruled that there was no violation of Article 2 because there was never a 'real and immediate risk to the life of an identified individual or individuals from the criminal acts of a third party' (at [116]). Had there been, the question would have been whether the police had taken appropriate 'measures within the scope of their powers which, judged reasonably, might have been expected to avoid that risk'. Similarly, the ECtHR found no violation of Article 8, on the basis that the police did not themselves interfere with the Osmans' private and family life.

However, on Article 6, where it was alleged that *Hill* effectively meant that the police had 'blanket immunity' against negligence claims—meaning that the courts would never look at the individual merits of claims relating to police negligence and the prevention of crimes—a

→

→

violation was found. The ECtHR found that the way ***Hill*** was used in ***Osman*** v ***Ferguson*** did in effect confer immunity from suit upon the police in this type of claim, amounting to a disproportionate restriction of the Osmans' ability to access a fair hearing. The UK courts had neither looked at the merits of the Osmans' case nor at whether the facts of their case differed sufficiently from those in ***Hill*** so as to distinguish their case. The ECtHR thought that proper consideration should have been given to opposing policy arguments, which should have been more carefully balanced against those from ***Hill*** before reaching a decision. In their view, the Court of Appeal had simply struck out the case on the grounds that the exclusionary rule from ***Hill*** was directly applicable, even though the Osmans clearly had a far greater degree of proximity to the police than ***Hill*** did and despite the fact that the police had arguably assumed some responsibility for their safety.

Article 6 gives what is known as a qualified right—some exceptions can apply which may justify its violation in some cases. However, in ***Osman*** v ***UK***, the ECtHR found that no exception applied. It acknowledged that the policy arguments from ***Hill*** were legitimate, but considered that the *way* those arguments had been used in ***Osman*** v ***Ferguson*** violated the Osmans' Article 6 rights. In particular, potentially competing policy arguments had not been able to be brought forward, such as the fact that the case involved the protection of a minor, that a life had been lost and that the errors on the part of the police amounted to very serious negligence, rather than mere 'incompetence' as in ***Hill***. These factors, the ECtHR said, should have been examined, and the police's 'immunity' should have at least been challenged. As it was, these factors were automatically excluded from consideration, and this was what in their view violated the Osmans' right to a fair hearing.

The UK Government claimed that the ***Hill*** rule did not amount to blanket immunity for the police—that negligence suits against the police in relation to criminal investigations and the suppression of crime would not inevitably fail. It also argued that alternative mechanisms—outside the tort of negligence—existed whereby the Osmans could have claimed compensation.[21] The ECtHR dismissed these arguments, finding that the Osmans had good reason to sue the police. Their purpose in doing so was not only compensation, but also to draw attention to the police's negligence and have them account for it.

The finding of a violation of Article 6 also meant that Article 13 (the right to a remedy) was engaged and the Osmans were ultimately awarded around £30,000 compensation by the British Government in recognition of the violation of their Article 13 right (see **Table 6.1**).

21. e.g. they could have taken a civil action against Paget-Lewis directly, or his psychiatrist (who had concluded that he was not mentally ill before he went on to attack the Osmans), or they could have claimed from the Criminal Injuries Compensation Board.

TABLE 6.1 Summary of the human rights issues in *Osman* v *UK*

Claim/Article	Reason for claim	ECtHR finding	Result
Article 2—right to life	Claim on behalf of the father who was shot and killed	Article 2 not engaged as there was no 'real and immediate risk' to life; therefore there could be no violation	No violation—threshold test not met
Article 6—right to a fair trial	Claim that the striking-out process in the domestic courts did not enable a fair hearing taking into account all the facts of the case	Striking out the case merely on the basis of the 'immunity' established in *Hill* constituted a disproportionate restriction of the right to a court hearing	Violation of this right, therefore 'just satisfaction' should be given, engaging Article 13 (see the following section)
Article 8—right to private, home and family life	Claim that the actions of the police in failing to do anything about Paget-Lewis amounted to disruption of the family's home and family life	Article 8 not engaged as it was not the police themselves who had interfered with the Osmans' enjoyment of home and family life	No violation
Article 13—right to a remedy	Claimed in respect of breaches of the other three rights; if a right had been violated then a remedy must be awarded (there must be 'just satisfaction')	Was engaged because a right had been violated (Art 6) yet no remedy had been provided for this	Approx £30,000 compensation awarded (from the UK Government)

Pause for reflection

Thinking back to the aims of the tort system, and what the interests of claimants might be, do you think that *Osman* v *Ferguson* made sense? Is there another way to control liability in this area (in respect of the police and crime) rather than saying it simply cannot come under court scrutiny, even where the negligence is as stark as in *Osman*? What aim of the tort system, if any, do you think the ECtHR decision in *Osman* v *UK* achieved?

The implications of ***Osman* v *UK*** for domestic law were great. Effectively, the ECtHR said that where serious negligence was alleged in respect of a public body's acts or omissions, coupled with serious harm being attributable to that negligence, a case against a public body should not necessarily be struck out on policy grounds, as there may be countervailing policy arguments pushing the opposite way: in *favour* of a duty of care. In practical terms, this would mean that domestic courts should consider the merits of every case where public body negligence was alleged and only strike out those cases where they were *absolutely certain* there was good reason to do so. Consequently, the courts became more cautious about striking out, as seen in numerous claims that were *not* struck out in the years immediately following ***Osman*** **v** ***UK*** that, we suggest, *would have been* had it not been for that decision.[22]

6.4.2 The *Z* and *TP and KM* cases

The next ECtHR cases to impact on the domestic law of negligence, and in particular the role of the duty of care control device, were ***Z and others*** **v** ***UK*** [2001] and ***TP and KM*** **v** ***UK*** [2001].

Z and others v *UK* [2001] and *TP and KM* v *UK* [2001] ECtHR

These cases related back to domestic cases decided by the House of Lords conjoined under the name of *X* v *Bedfordshire* [1995]. Two of the cases within *X* had concerned victims of child abuse. In *X* itself, it was alleged that the child protection services of the local council were negligent in failing to remove a group of siblings from their parents, where they were suffering horrendous cruelty and neglect. The children's teachers, as well as neighbours and the police, had at various times been in contact with social services over a period of years, expressing concern about the children. Five years after the first concerns were expressed, the children were finally taken away from their parents and placed in care—and only then at the instigation of the children's mother—but by this time three of the children had suffered psychiatric harm as a result of the way they had been treated. The Official Solicitor claimed on their behalf against the council in respect of the harms they had suffered, the impact on their health and the impairment of their proper development. The House of Lords struck out the claims, holding that no duty of care arose between social services and the children.

In the second case, *M* v *Newham*, it was alleged that social services incorrectly removed a child from her mother and placed her into care. The girl, who was being sexually abused, had told a social worker and psychiatrist interviewing her on behalf of the authority that her abuser was called 'John'. They wrongly assumed that this was the mother's cohabiting boyfriend of the same name, without adequate further investigation. It turned out that John was a cousin who had previously lived with the family. When the mistake was discovered, the girl was allowed to return home. Both mother and daughter sought compensation from the council (as vicariously liable for the social worker and psychiatrist's negligence) for the psychiatric harm they suffered as a result of the traumatic experience and imposed separation. These claims were also struck out.

→

22. e.g. *W* v *Essex County Council* [2001]; ***Barrett*** **v** ***Enfield London Borough Council*** [2001]; ***Phelps*** **v** ***Hillingdon London Borough Council*** [2001]; *Hall* v *Simons* [2002]; *Kearn-Price* v *Kent County Council* [2003]. However, in ***Palmer*** **v** ***Tees Health Authority*** [1999] (discussed in **section 4.5.1**) the opposite decision was reached (though this may be because of the surface similarity with the facts of ***Hill***, even though there are clearly a number of distinguishing features that would point towards a duty being at least arguable on the facts).

→

On appeal to the ECtHR, *X* v *Bedfordshire* became ***Z and others* v *UK***. It was claimed that the children's rights under Article 3 (the right to be free from inhumane and degrading treatment) and Articles 6, 8 and 13 had been violated. In *M* v *Newham*, now ***TP and KM* v *UK***, violations of Articles 6, 8 and 13 were alleged.

In both cases, the ECtHR retreated from its previous position on Article 6, saying that the striking-out procedure used by the UK courts was not, in fact, a Convention violation. Whilst Article 6 was concerned with *procedural* blocks to a fair trial (for example, if particular categories of people were arbitrarily prevented from making claims in the first place, or in respect of particular types of harm), it should not be concerned with *substantive* legal barriers. The court recognised that viewing the striking-out procedure as conferring 'immunity' on public bodies (like the police or social services) against negligence claims was incorrect. Instead, it understood that the decision whether to strike out a claim was part of the substantive law of negligence and as such was a legal barrier to a claim, but did not prevent a claim being made. The fact that a domestic court may not impose a duty of care in respect of a public body's actions was not a procedural barrier and was in fact *the result* of a claim being decided by a court. Although such hearings (striking-out applications) did not *examine* the facts of the case, they were adversarial, proceeded on the basis that the facts alleged were true and, having assumed this, asked whether there was a case to answer. That is, did a duty arise, given the circumstances and the negligence alleged? If no duty could be found, then the defendants had no case to answer: this was not to say that they were immune from liability, only that no liability could arise in that instance for them to be immune from.

Crucially, however, the ECtHR found, on the established facts, violations of Article 3 in *Z* and Article 8 in *TP and KM*.

Despite both cases having been struck out without detailed investigation of the claims, as in ***Osman* v *Ferguson***, in a retreat from its position in ***Osman* v *UK***, the ECtHR admitted, perhaps capitulating to various judicial and academic criticisms, that it had misinterpreted English law on negligence—essentially admitting that its decision in ***Osman* v *UK*** had been wrong. In ***Z*** and ***TP and KM*** the ECtHR found instead that the striking-out action was a *result* of competing policy arguments (in favour of and against there being a duty of care) being carefully considered and was not about conferring immunity but about whether to extend existing categories of case where a duty could be found. According to the ECtHR, this was sufficiently fair access to a court for the purposes of Article 6.

However, in ***Z***, Article 3 was violated due to the local authority's failure to remove the children from a situation in which they suffered 'inhumane and degrading treatment'. In ***TP and KM***, Article 8 was violated because the child was wrongly separated from her mother. In both cases, the right to an effective remedy had also been denied, so Article 13 was also violated. These findings, while not as explosive as the Article 6 finding in ***Osman* v *UK***, still mean that public bodies must be extremely careful in the way they handle certain situations, particularly post-HRA, and may lead indirectly to a finding that a duty should be owed in respect of certain claims.[23]

Pause for reflection

In 'striking-out' procedures, the court assumes the alleged facts are all true—that is, that the defendant *was* negligent—and then decides whether the defendant has a case to answer. What purpose do you think this procedure serves? Why not hear every case and then decide on the facts whether there was liability?

6.4.3 The implications for domestic law

After ***Z*** and ***TP and KM***, domestic courts were again 'free' to strike out cases. This did not mean, however, that they went back to striking out as many claims as they had prior to ***Osman* v *UK***. Although the Article 6 ruling in ***Osman* v *UK*** was effectively, though not explicitly, overturned by ***Z*** and ***TP and KM***, some points about what courts actually must do when striking out were absorbed by the judiciary. Furthermore, the ***Z*** and ***TP and KM*** decisions were not unanimous; five dissenting judges (of 17) believed, even after the legal position had been explained, that ***Osman* v *UK*** was still correct. However, the question for the courts, where there is existing precedent, is now: 'Can this case be distinguished?' Are there, for example, competing policy reasons which should outweigh those previously taken into account? Unless the court thinks there are, the claimant's case will be struck out.[24]

Where no analogous precedent exists, the courts remain 'careful' about which claims they strike out. As a direct result, as well as the findings that there *were* human rights violations in ***Z*** and ***TP and KM***, some claims against public bodies for previously unrecognised 'types' of harm have—luckily in our opinion—been able to proceed.

The ECtHR may pronounce again on issues regarding the existence of duties of care in future cases. In ***Z***, it stated that it would continue to scrutinise legal rules which have the effect of meaning that defendants cannot be liable domestically. If it decides that such a rule *is* a procedural rather than a substantive barrier to a claim, Article 6 will apply and the policy arguments flowing each way will have to be considered to see whether the barrier amounts to a disproportionate impediment to the claimant's ability to have their case heard. In essence, we are talking about whether there is *immunity*, or *blanket immunity*, from suit. It seems that some immunity, for example that in relation to a particular aspect of a public body's activities (e.g. the police's discretion to investigate

23. ***D* v *East Berkshire*** rests quite considerably on the findings in ***Z*** and ***TP and KM*** (though now see ***Poole***); so subsequently does *Commissioner of Police of the Metropolis* v *DSD and another* [2018]. Also see *Wainwright* v *UK* [2006] (**Chapter 16**) and *X, Y & Z* v *UK* [2011] ECHR 1199, discussed in **section 6.7.2**.

24. See e.g. *Brooks* and ***Smith*** (**section 6.5.3**) and ***Michael*** (**section 6.3.1**). See also comments on the procedure to be followed after ***Robinson*** in particular in relation to the 'incremental approach' (discussed in **section 3.3.3**) and ***Poole***.

crimes as they see fit and according to their current resources and priorities), will be considered proportionate, as long as this does not close every avenue of claim against that particular public body.

6.5 The emergency services and armed forces

Some particular categories of public body have, in a sense, their own rules- or at least well-established precedents. As indicated in the previous section, where clear precedents exist, they will be relied upon, rather than courts seeking features that might distinguish a new claim. This is particularly apparent in claims brought against the emergency services and armed forces. We look here at these particular types of public body individually, as different rules regarding whether a duty can be found have been created for the different services.

6.5.1 The fire service

Whether a duty of care can be owed by the fire service to individuals to whom it responds was considered in the conjoined cases of ***Capital & Counties plc* v *Hampshire County Council*** [1997]; *John Munroe (Acrylics) Ltd* v *London Fire and Civil Defence Authority* [1997]; *Church of Jesus Christ of Latter-Day Saints (Great Britain)* v *West Yorkshire Fire and Civil Defence Authority* [1997]. The facts differed in each case, but the question for the court was the same: did the fire service owe a duty of care to the claimants in relation to its negligent acts or omissions? In each case, the claimant's property had been severely damaged by fire and each was claiming that, at least in part, this was the fault of the defendant fire service.

***Capital & Counties plc* v *Hampshire County Council* and other cases [1997] CA**

In *Capital & Counties*, the fire service responded to an emergency call to a building on fire. Upon arrival, the officer in charge instructed that the building's sprinkler system, which was operational, be turned off. This allowed the fire to worsen and cause more damage than it would otherwise have done. In *John Munroe*, smouldering debris from a fire in an adjacent property set light to the claimant's building. The alleged negligence on behalf of the fire service was in relation to the inspection of the first property and their satisfaction that all the fires were out: had they visited the claimant's building, they would have found and dealt with the smouldering debris. In the third case, the fire service was unable to fight a fire in a church because the nearest fire hydrants were poorly maintained (the responsibility of the fire service under statute), resulting in an inadequate supply of water.

The Court of Appeal considered first whether the fire service had a duty even to respond to emergency calls. Relying on *Alexandrou* v *Oxford* [1993], where it was found that the police owed no duty to a member of the public to respond to an activated burglar alarm, the court

→

found similarly that the fire service had no duty to respond to an emergency call or to turn up and attempt to fight a fire.

Though the emergency services do have a duty (once they have responded) not to *positively* make the situation worse, there is usually no duty in relation to mere omissions—that is, if the situation worsens because they *fail* to do something.

Pause for reflection

The Court of Appeal said that the fire service (like the police before it) owes no private duty of care to individuals calling in an emergency, meaning that those individuals have no right to sue the fire service if it negligently fails to respond. This is not the same as saying that fire fighters can ignore fires if they want to—there is a duty in public law and evidently a social or moral obligation for them to do so, as well as duties under fire officers' individual employment contracts. But does this make it sound any better?

Next, the court considered whether, if a fire service *did* respond to an emergency call, it would owe a duty of care in respect of *how* the fire was fought. In ***Capital & Counties***, the decision to turn off the sprinkler system was a positive act that had the effect of making the fire worse than it would have been had this decision not been taken. Following ***East Suffolk***, it was found that this action had made the claimants worse off than they were before; therefore a duty was owed. However, in the other two cases, no direct positive action had made the situation worse than it was before the fire service's arrival.[25] The claimants argued that by responding, the fire service had 'assumed responsibility' for the situation and that the claimants relied on this, creating the necessary proximity between the defendant and the claimants; as a result the fire service had created an obligation to take care.

The Court of Appeal refused to find a duty in these two cases.[26] It said that the duty of the fire service was to the public at large and that if a duty was owed to individual property owners, the two duties could come into conflict, which, for policy and pragmatic reasons, would be undesirable. They also questioned who in fact would be owed such a duty. Would it be only the owner of the building on fire about which the emergency call had been made? If so, they said, this would leave neighbouring property owners outside the sphere of the duty unless they too (or someone on their behalf) lodged an emergency call. This, the court held, would be untenable, as other property owners would be unprotected, and the fire service may act to protect those buildings whose owners were owed a duty of care but not the surrounding properties—and this may be contrary to the way the fire service itself would choose to fight fires.

25. So, would the fire officers' failure to bring the correct equipment to connect their hose be an instance of them making the situation worse (in which case a duty could be established) or merely an example of them failing to make it better (with the result that no duty would exist)?

26. See also *AJ Allan (Blairnyle) Ltd and another* v *Strathclyde Fire Board* [2016].

As professionals, fire fighters would know how best to proceed, and this should not be dictated by whether a duty is owed to a potential claimant. If other building owners were to be included within the duty, this too would cause problems, as anyone in the locality and potentially at risk would be owed a duty, and the fire service could not protect everyone all the time.

Counterpoint

The claimants' argument in these cases seems perfectly sensible, particularly when we consider why the fire service exists in the first place (or at least what the public's perception of this would be). Furthermore, the Court of Appeal's decision seems very conservative given that the question is not actually whether the fire service should owe a duty to protect properties on fire when they are called out in an emergency, but to whom they might end up being liable if they are negligent when doing so. Why would the *standard* of care concept not sufficiently control liability? That is, could the court have said that the fire service owes a *duty* to all of the building owners as outlined earlier, but that this duty would be *breached* only if the fire service actually performed negligently according to the usual practices of the profession or in comparison with the actions a competent fire service might have taken in the same situation? As we will see, this is what happens when the liability (or otherwise) of doctors and other professionals is considered, where there is usually no question of whether a duty is owed,[27] and it is also the case that the standard of care can be relaxed in emergency situations.[28]

The third reason the Court of Appeal gave for not finding that the fire service owe individuals a duty of care was that it would be irrational to impose a duty about how a fire was fought when it had already been decided that there was no duty to turn up and fight the fire in the first place.

Counterpoint

Where was this principle decided? It might be argued here that the court was talking in circles to convince itself. It could equally have held that the fire service both owed a duty to respond *as best it could* to emergency calls and that, once there, would have to take care about *how* the fire was fought. Again, with public expectations in mind, wouldn't this seem more logical? As the situation stands following ***Capital & Counties***, there is no obligation to respond *and* no obligation to take care having done so, *unless* there is a negligent positive act on the part of the fire service which makes the situation worse than it would have been if the fire service failed to respond at all.

27. See **section 8.3.2.1**. 28. See **section 8.4.4**.

Pause for reflection

If a fire service negligently fails to turn up at a building with a fire that could easily be contained (but the owners of the building have done nothing, in reliance on the fire service which has answered their call), have they made the situation worse than it would have been? The difficulty here is the distinction between acts and omissions.[29] Not turning up would be an omission, about which the law struggles to find situations in which a duty should be owed, as opposed to positive acts, where a finding of duty is more likely. Does this seem a logical distinction to you in these circumstances?

The public policy ground in ***Capital & Counties*** is that the fire service owes a more general duty to all property owners and so owing a duty to individuals would cut across this. As a result, a duty is owed to individuals only where the situation is worsened, as this establishes the necessary proximity between the parties. However, even where a fire service had not made the harm worse than it would have been with no intervention, the court easily—and unusually—rejected the usual public policy argument that is put forward in relation to public bodies: the fact that imposing a duty might lead to a flood of unmeritorious claims or that damages paid out would be funded by taxes and would divert money away from funding other useful activities. These points applied equally to other public and emergency services, such as the ambulance service, yet were not enough to lead to a finding of no duty in those cases.

Pause for reflection

Although this wider public policy angle did not have to be considered by the Court of Appeal, it was still mentioned. But does what the court said make sense? Why do those arguments apply to the ambulance service and fire service (in theory at least) but *not* always to the police? What role does—or should—insurance play here? Most buildings are insured, so the question comes down to whether we think the owners of property should pay the price (of fire service incompetence) through increased premiums (which are, in the long run, spread across all policy holders) or whether this is better distributed among taxpayers (as it would be if the fire service paid compensation).

6.5.2 The ambulance service

The ambulance service owes a duty of care to individuals in certain circumstances. In fact, the ambulance service, unlike the fire service, has a duty to respond to an emergency call. Both points come from ***Kent* v *Griffiths*** [2001].

29. See **Chapter 4**.

Kent v *Griffiths* [2001] CA

An emergency call was made by a GP who had been called to the home of a pregnant woman having an asthma attack. He was told that an ambulance was on its way. When it failed to arrive promptly, the GP called twice more. In the end the ambulance took 38 minutes to arrive. In that time, the woman temporarily stopped breathing. This caused her to lose her baby and subsequently suffer psychiatric harm including personality changes and memory loss. In her claim against the London Ambulance Service, the defendants—who admitted they had no good reason for the failure to arrive promptly—claimed that the case should be struck out because they owed her no duty of care, based on ***Capital & Counties***, so had no case to answer in respect of their admitted negligence.

The Court of Appeal rejected the strike-out application, holding that the ambulance and fire services were distinguishable due to the nature of the service provided. Thus, the ambulance service did owe a duty to respond to the call.

The Court of Appeal found that the ambulance service is distinguishable from the fire service because it can be seen as an extension of the National Health Service, which is understood to owe a duty of care towards its patients. It said that the service provided by fire fighters and the police is for the benefit of the public as a whole and could not, except in certain situations, extend to a duty owed to an individual member of the public, for the reasons outlined in ***Capital & Counties***. In contrast, once the ambulance service accepts a call in relation to a named individual, it must be seen as providing a service to that individual. Crucially, that individual is the only one who could be harmed as a result of the ambulance service's negligence when responding. In short, the ambulance service owes a duty of care to individuals, once it has accepted the emergency call in relation to them, both to respond and to respond without carelessness.

Although the issue did not arise in ***Kent***, the court went on to draw a distinction between operational or procedural matters and those involving policy or the exercise of discretion. In essence, if a delay was caused by a lack of resources or a decision to deploy resources in a particular way rather than as a result of operational or procedural negligence, it is far less likely—as in other types of case against public bodies where policy/operational distinctions are used—that a duty would arise.

Counterpoint

It might at first glance seem sensible that the ambulance service owes a duty of care because an ambulance is sent out to deal with one individual, whereas the fire service responds to fires and is a service to the public at large. It may also seem sensible to

→

→

maintain the policy/operational decision in relation to these services. But consider the following two scenarios:

(1) An emergency call is made and the ambulance service is asked to respond to a multi-car motorway accident in which over a dozen people are hurt. It sends five ambulances. It does not send any more as it has decided that staff overtime cutbacks are needed, despite it being the beginning of the busy holiday season on the roads. All the ambulances are delayed, resulting in many deaths and more serious injuries than would have been suffered if there were more ambulances and they had arrived promptly.
(2) A man in an isolated Grade II-listed cottage calls the fire service when his cottage is hit by lightning and catches fire. The fire service has a free engine, but does not send it for half an hour. When it does, the cottage is beyond saving and the man has lost everything.

Which of the affected parties, if any, can make a claim?[30]

6.5.3 The police

Similar policy/operational distinctions arise in claims against the police. As ever, a duty is owed when the police, by direct and positive negligent action, cause property damage or personal injury. This has been recently confirmed at the highest level in ***Robinson* v *Chief Constable of West Yorkshire Police*** **[2018]**. However, distinctions are drawn between operational negligence (that which happens in regard to the way in which they do their job), for which the police *can* be held liable, and policy matters (decisions about resource allocation, prioritisation of cases or investigations and so on), for which they generally *cannot*. This distinction is clearly illustrated by *Rigby* v *Chief Constable of Northampton* [1985], where the police were sued for causing damage to the claimant's shop when they used inflammable CS gas to try and drive out a burglar hiding there. While it was a policy decision to arm themselves with CS gas in the first place (as opposed to a non-flammable alternative), the *action* of using the gas without having the necessary equipment to fight any resulting fire, which was clearly foreseeable, was an operational matter, so a duty could arise. A duty was also found in *Knightly* v *Johns* [1982] in relation to an operational decision by a police inspector who instructed a constable to drive against the flow of traffic in a tunnel in which the police were dealing with an accident, resulting in injury to the constable (see also *Henry* v *Thames Valley Police* [2010]).

Most recently, in ***Robinson***,[31] overturning the decision of the Court of Appeal (which had relied on ***Hill***), the Supreme Court found that police officers owed a duty to a 76-year-old woman who was knocked to the ground and injured during the negligent arrest of a drug dealer on a city street. Lord Reed found that the case concerned an

30. In the first scenario, part of the reason for the ambulances being late is operational and part of it is due to policy. Would any of the potential claimants be able to show that they were affected by one and not the other? Clearly, in the second scenario the man would have no claim at all—the fire service eventually responded, but did not 'make things worse'.

31. See **section 3.3.3**.

application of established principles of the law of negligence and so the existence of a duty did not depend on whether it would be 'fair, just and reasonable' for the police to owe Mrs Robinson a duty of care (at [30]). Like other public authorities, in accordance with the general law of tort the police are subject to liability for causing personal injury (at [45]–[48]). Lord Mance stated that the 'direct physical interface between the police and the public, in the course of an arrest placing an innocent passer-by at risk', should now be recognised as 'an established area of general police liability for positive negligent conduct which foreseeably and directly inflicts physical injury' (at [97]).

Pause for reflection

As *Rigby* illustrates, policy and operational matters are not always easy to differentiate. It seems that the difference in that case was in the police deciding to arm themselves with the gas versus the actual usage of the gas during the incident. Does this seem a logical distinction, particularly because if the police had chosen to use a non-flammable gas in the first place, no claim could have arisen?

Although the distinction is often difficult to see, some types of case have been long identified as falling within the sphere of police policy: the way the police conduct and prioritise their investigations of crimes. An additional layer of the exclusionary rule in this area stems from ***Hill***. Given that the investigation and suppression of crime is a primary function of the police (which could directly affect a great number of people), it is strange how highly unlikely it is that liability can ever arise in this area. Like the fire service, the police owe a general duty to society; cases show that a private law duty is *not* owed to individuals; seemingly no matter how closely connected they are to the police's negligence (proximity) and how likely it is that they may be affected by it (foreseeability).

The policy justifications raised in ***Hill*** have been relied on consistently in subsequent cases including *Alexandrou* v *Oxford* [1993] and ***Osman*** **v** ***Ferguson*** to prevent a duty arising.[32] Similar reasoning resurfaced in *Brooks* v *Commissioner of Police for the Metropolis* [2005]. Duwayne Brooks was attacked alongside his friend Stephen Lawrence, who was murdered in a racially motivated attack in 1993.[33] Brooks suffered post-traumatic stress disorder, initially as a result of witnessing the murder. He also claimed that his treatment at the hands of the police worsened the condition and that they owed him a duty of care on three grounds: to take reasonable steps to ascertain whether he was a victim of the attack and, if so, to treat him accordingly; to take reasonable steps to give him adequate and appropriate support as a witness to a serious crime; and to treat his statements with reasonable care and attention. The police investigation into Stephen Lawrence's murder was later found by an official inquiry to have been grossly mishandled, and the same inquiry highlighted 'institutional racism' in the Metropolitan Police.[34]

32. Though the Court of Appeal in ***Kent*** **v** ***Griffiths*** **[2001]** later held that *Alexandrou* should be confined to its own facts in order for it to be able to find a duty in respect of the ambulance service (at [21]).

33. Described by Lord Bingham in the House of Lords as 'the most notorious racist killing which our country has ever known' (at [1]).

34. Sir William Macpherson of Cluny, *Report on the Stephen Lawrence Inquiry* (Cm 4262-I, 1999).

One of the findings was that the police had begun mishandling the case whilst at the scene of the attack.[35] When officers found Duwayne Brooks at the scene he was in a state of high anxiety, agitated and, according to the police officers, 'aggressive'. They therefore assumed that the two men had been fighting, rather than that both had been attacked, and treated Duwayne more like a suspect than a witness or victim of violent hate crime. They did not consider that he would understandably be anxious and agitated after being racially attacked and seeing his friend murdered. The inquiry report found that this mistake was made because of racist stereotyping by officers at the scene and meant that the police, having failed to take his evidence seriously, lost any advantage they might have had in being able to track down the attackers.

While the actions of the police in this case were clearly extremely negligent—far more so than in ***Hill***, for example—the law lords ruled unanimously that Duwayne Brooks was owed no duty of care, relying almost entirely on the policy arguments from ***Hill***. They reiterated that the police's primary duty (to the public) is to investigate and suppress crime and that finding they owed a private law duty in the way that Brooks was claiming they did, and having to treat all potential victims or witnesses of crime in the way he was arguing they should, would eat up valuable police time, diverting resources away from their primary functions. While acknowledging the *desirability* of victims and witnesses of crime being treated seriously and with respect, the law lords found that this was not the same as saying that there was a duty to do so. To impose such a duty was to them a step too far and would be 'bound to lead to an unduly defensive approach in combating crime' (Lord Steyn at 1509). ***Smith*** **v** ***Chief Constable of Sussex Police*** [2008] upheld these entrenched assumptions.

Smith v *Chief Constable of Sussex Police* [2008] HL

Stephen Smith sued the police in negligence for serious injuries (including three skull fractures and associated brain damage, as well as continuing physical and psychological injury) that he sustained when attacked with a claw hammer by his former boyfriend, Gareth Jeffrey. Smith had informed the police of a series of 'violent, abusive and threatening telephone, text and internet messages, including death threats' (at [23]) that he had received from Jeffrey prior to the attack. According to the facts as laid out by Lord Bingham in the House of Lords:

> There were sometimes ten to 15 text messages in a single day. During February 2003 alone there were some 130 text messages. Some of these messages were very explicit: 'U are dead'; 'look out for yourself psycho is coming'; 'I am looking to kill you and no

→

35. This was later confirmed by another inquiry headed by Mark Ellison QC, which looked into a 'cover-up' by the Metropolitan Police of corruption in its ranks in relation to the case: 'The Stephen Lawrence Independent Review: possible corruption and the role of undercover policing in the Stephen Lawrence case' House of Commons, 6 March 2014. See also Tom Harper 'Employees at Scotland Yard ordered to carry out "mass shredding" of Stephen Lawrence evidence, claims damning review of the Met' *The Independent* 18 March 2014. The Ellison report suggests that Brooks' civil case against the police may also have been tainted by their actions outside the courtroom (at 5.2).

→

> compromises'; 'I was in the Bulldog last night with a carving knife. It's a shame I missed you'. (at [23])

Notwithstanding the severity of the threats, officers assigned to the case treated it as a domestic matter and took no steps to arrest Jeffrey or otherwise protect Mr Smith: 'The officers declined to look at the messages (which Mr Smith had offered to show them), made no entry in their notebooks, took no statement from Mr Smith and completed no crime form' (at [24]). Later, 'Mr Smith told an inspector that he thought his life was in danger ... He offered to show the inspector the threatening messages he had received, but the inspector declined to look at them and made no note of the meeting. He told Mr Smith the investigation was progressing well, and he should call 999 if he was concerned about his safety' (at [25]).

Smith's claim was struck out in the county court on the basis of previous case law (*Hill*; *Brooks*). However, the Court of Appeal ruled [2008] that it was at least arguable that the police owed him a duty of care as a known potential victim of violent crime—a duty to take reasonable steps to prevent a foreseeable attack by an identified person. Sedley LJ said that where:

> someone's life or safety has been so firmly placed in the hands of the police as to make it incumbent on them to at least take elementary steps to protect it, unexcused neglect to do so can sound in damages if harm of the material kind results. (at [27])

The Court of Appeal was particularly influenced by a comparable rights-based duty owed by the police as a result of Article 2 ECHR,[36] which they considered should influence the content of the common law duty of care in negligence (see e.g. Rimer LJ at [45] and Pill LJ at [55]).

The House of Lords overturned the Court of Appeal's decision. Lords Hope, Phillips, Carswell and Brown found that some of the policy reasons outlined in *Hill* and restated in *Brooks* applied equally to Smith's case. They relied on two in particular. First, the danger that a duty of care would detrimentally affect the working practices of the police, causing them to 'act defensively' in order to avoid legal proceedings against them. Secondly, the fact that time and resources would both have to be diverted towards the handling of such claims and away from the ordinary functions of the police in serving the public. These policy considerations, they felt, were enough to deny the possibility that a duty could be found, even though some of their lordships expressed regret, concern or difficulty in reaching this opinion (Lord Phillips at [36]; Lord Carswell at [107]; Lord Brown at [127]).

36. Which the Court of Appeal had recently found in *Van Colle* [2007] (later overturned by the House of Lords, which heard *Van Colle* alongside ***Smith***). On the Court of Appeal's findings in *Van Colle*, see JR Spencer 'Tort Law Bows to the Human Rights Act' [2008] CLJ 15, where the HRA, ss 6–8 are compared to Heineken, the beer that it is claimed 'refreshes the parts that other beers cannot reach'. Now see ***Michael*** on the potential for using Art 2 (discussed in **section 6.3.1**) (and also consider the potential for using Art 3 in police claims, since *Commissioner of Police of the Metropolis* v *DSD and another* [2018], discussed in Joanne Conaghan 'Investigating Rape: Human Rights and Police Accountability' (2017) 37 LS 54).

After *Brooks*, the principle was that only an 'outrageous' case would be enough to show that a duty of care should exist to a private individual. The ineptitude of the police in ***Smith*** *could* have been seen this way—and indeed was by four out of eight of the country's most senior judges across the Court of Appeal and House of Lords. Lord Bingham, dissenting in the House of Lords, agreed with the Court of Appeal that a duty of care was arguable. In fact, he went further, saying that:

> if the pleaded facts are established, the Chief Constable *did* owe Mr Smith a duty of care ... I would hold that if a member of the public (A) furnishes a police officer (B) with apparently credible evidence that a third party whose identity and whereabouts are known presents a specific and imminent threat to his life or physical safety, B owes A a duty to take reasonable steps to assess such threat and, if appropriate, take reasonable steps to prevent it being executed. I shall for convenience of reference call this 'the liability principle'. (at [44], emphasis added)

Lord Bingham did not consider this 'liability principle' to be inconsistent with ***Hill*** and *Brooks*, which he agreed were correctly decided. In his view, the three decisions stood independently of each other. He then set out reasons why the policy arguments from ***Hill*** were not appropriate in the context of ***Smith*** and why they would not affect the operation of the 'liability principle' (at [48]–[53]). He did not see that adopting the principle would 'induce a detrimentally defensive frame of mind', for example, as the only thing the police would need to do would be to make a 'reasonable assessment of the threat posed to an identified potential victim by an identified person' (at [49])—this would essentially test the police on *standard* of care (breach). Nor did he believe that accepting the principle would detract from the police's primary function of investigating and suppressing crime, a factor which had clearly weighed particularly heavily in *Brooks*. Unfortunately, Lord Bingham's 'liability principle' was not accepted by the four other law lords.[37] Lord Hope, for one, plainly believed that the policy reasons in favour of denying the existence of a duty were still as strong in ***Smith*** as they had been in *Brooks* and this fact, to him, made the 'liability principle' unworkable. This is evident from the fact that he viewed the case as a 'domestic' issue:

> So-called domestic cases that are brought to the attention of the police all too frequently are a product of [the breakdown of relationships]. One party tells the police that he or she is being threatened. The other party may say, when challenged, that his or her actions have been wrongly reported or misinterpreted. The police have a public function to perform on receiving such information. A robust approach is needed ... Not every complaint of this kind is genuine ... Police work elsewhere may be impeded if the police were required to treat every report from a member of the public that he or she is being threatened with violence as giving rise to a duty of care ... (at [76])

This dismissive attitude towards domestic violence is part of the problem and is not helped by senior judges making such comments. In ***Michael***, Lady Hale agreed with Lord Kerr (dissenting) that a duty of care should arise on the facts.[38] Moreover, she

37. Three of whom (Lords Hope, Carswell and Brown) disagreed specifically with it in their speeches (at [77], [109] and [129] respectively).

38. See **section 6.3.1**.

explicitly recognised the countervailing policy arguments that apply in cases where domestic violence is at issue:

> [I]n developing the law it is wise to proceed on a case by case basis, and the formulation offered by Lord Kerr would be sufficient to enable this claim to go to trial at common law as well as under the Human Rights Act 1998. It is difficult indeed to see how recognising the possibility of such claims could make the task of policing any more difficult than it already is. It might conceivably, however, lead to some much-needed improvements in their response to threats of serious domestic abuse. This continues to be a source of concern to Her Majesty's Inspectorate of Constabulary: see *Everyone's Business: Improving the Police Response to Domestic Abuse* (2014). I very much regret to say that some of the attitudes which have led to the inadequacies revealed in that report may also have crept into the policy considerations discussed in *Smith* (by Lord Carswell at para 107 and Lord Hope at para 76). If the imposition of liability in negligence can help to counter such attitudes, so much the better. (at [198])

Though she went on to say that even without such strong counter-policy arguments the principles suggested by Lord Kerr should apply to 'all specific threats of imminent injury to individuals which the police are in a position to prevent, whatever their source', it is this aspect of her judgment that potentially leaves the door open for future claimants.

Counterpoint

Lady Hale is right. If the starting point is taken to be that events in cases like *Smith* or *Michael* arose from 'domestic' issues then the policy arguments will always be able to be used to justify a finding of no duty. Worse, policy arguments pointing in the other direction can be ignored.[39] 'Domestic' implies that people should sort things out for themselves (although we—like Lady Hale—would have hoped that changes in emphasis for both the police and the courts in relation to 'domestic' violence would bring some recognition that 'domestic' does not mean that these issues are easily resolved and that many such problems arise from imbalances of power within relationships).[40]

Lord Bingham also recognised the seriousness of the facts in *Smith* and, it seems, found it hard to believe that no duty could arise when the threats made were so numerous, plainly violent and escalating in severity. His 'liability principle' only outlined a duty mirroring what most of us would *expect* from the police in a situation of that type: where the evidence is 'credible' (as opposed to where it is not) and the threat is 'specific and imminent', 'reasonable steps' must be taken to assess the threat and, if necessary, do something about it.

→

39. Similarly, Joanne Conaghan contends that the threat of liability is exactly what may be needed if we seriously want the police force to do better for victims of domestic violence. Without advocating a 'liability free-for-all', opening the door to potential liability might allow true reform to take place ('Civil liability: Addressing failures in the context of rape, domestic and sexual abuse' Inaugural Lecture given at the University of Bristol, 19 February 2015). The full lecture can be viewed at **www.youtube.com/watch?v=y1bawCpPr30&app=desktop**. See also Conaghan (**n 36**).

40. See Horsey and Rackley (**n 20**).

→

Positing the rejection of the 'liability principle' in ***Smith*** as perhaps its failure to engage directly with the proximity question (at [156]), Lord Kerr in ***Michael*** attempted a different formulation, foregrounding proximity as a marker of foreseeable harm, which would be established on the facts:

> It appears to me incontestable that a proximity of relationship can be created by interaction between parties such as potential victim and police. The nature of that interaction, when it has taken place, is crucial to the question whether the necessary degree of proximity exists. (at [163])

To Lord Kerr, a proximate relationship would 'transcend the ordinary contact that a member of the public has with the police force', though need not go as far as an assumed responsibility (at [167]). He considered that when the police are provided with sufficient information that would enable them to prevent imminent harm to an individual, the 'duty is personalised to that individual' (at [169]).

Despite the clear potential to have distinguished the existing precedents in ***Smith*** and ***Michael***, coupled with the countervailing policy arguments that would seem to make imposing a duty of care less problematic than in ***Hill***, it seems that the police *do* in fact have a blanket protection in respect of the way they conduct investigations (including whether they choose to investigate in the first place). Four senior judges thought that a duty could (Court of Appeal) or should (Lord Bingham) have arisen in ***Smith***. Two Supreme Court Justices would have found a duty in ***Michael***. We are hopeful that this means there are cracks beginning to show in the reasoning used to uphold this immunity.[41]

In *Brooks*, the House of Lords said that the judgment rested solely on the facts of the case and that the 'blanket immunity' that it might be thought arose from ***Hill*** did not exist. To illustrate, Lord Keith said that there *could* be some 'cases of outrageous negligence by the police' that would fall beyond the general principle and in which a duty could be found. If the facts of *Brooks*, ***Smith*** and now ***Michael*** are not outrageous enough, however, it is hard to picture exactly the degree of negligence Lord Keith was imagining.[42] If it must happen, we would at least prefer to see a less disingenuous 'cloak and dagger' approach to the protection of the police by the courts. Reliance on assumptions of responsibility leave us with similar problems: is it not likely that the police simply *will not* assume responsibility, for risk of liability? Thus we are left in a situation as in ***Smith***—the police can and will simply do nothing.

41. An encouraging case in this respect may be *Sherratt* v *Chief Constable of Greater Manchester Police* [2018], where a duty of care *was* established, on the basis of assumed responsibility and reliance, towards a woman who had committed suicide about which a 999 call had been placed. Cf *Griffiths and others* v *Suffolk Police and another* [2018].

42. So, in fact, it seems unlikely that the police would owe the woman assaulted by her harasser a duty of care, despite the high degree of proximity in that scenario, in contrast to the position we might have thought she would be in earlier in the chapter. She may, however, depending on the immediacy of the threat, have an alternative human rights claim based on Art 2 (see **section 6.3.1**).

Pause for reflection

Compare ***Hill***, ***Osman*** v ***Ferguson***, *Brooks*, **Smith** and ***Michael*** to a Canadian case: *Doe* v *Metropolitan Toronto (Municipality) Commissioners of Police* [1998]. In this case, the police negligently mishandled the investigation of a series of rapes in an area of Toronto. One reason for this was the police force's overall reliance on 'rape myths': stereotypical assumptions about women who allege rape, women who are raped and how women would respond if warned about a serial rapist operating in their vicinity. The claimant was a victim of the serial rapist. She argued that the police were negligent in failing to catch him sooner and, in the alternative, that they should have warned women in the area so that they could take steps to protect themselves. In *Doe*, the judge vehemently refused to follow ***Hill***, pointing out that clear policy arguments militated in the other direction, meaning that the police *should* owe a duty of care to any woman who was then raped, as a result in part or whole of their failings.[43]

What about the policy arguments operating in the other direction in **Smith** or ***Michael***? Do you think this is the type of 'outrageous negligence' that Lord Keith had in mind in *Brooks*? Why do you think *Doe* was not mentioned in either *Brooks*, **Smith** or ***Michael***?[44]

The ***Hill*** 'immunity' has extended to cases on the very edge of negligent police activities. In *Elguzouli-Daf* v *Commissioner of Police for the Metropolis and another* [1995], the claimants sued the police and the Crown Prosecution Service (CPS) on the basis that their prosecutions were negligently delayed, resulting in them being kept in custody for longer than they should have been. However, no duty of care was found: the Court of Appeal held that to find such would be dealing with 'individualised justice' as opposed to general principles of justice serving the entire community (Steyn LJ at 349) and would risk defensive practices and a diversion of resources from the CPS. In *Desmond* v *Chief Constable of Nottinghamshire Police* [2011], the Court of Appeal found that no duty could be owed by the police in respect of information disclosed (wrongly) on an Enhanced Criminal Record Certificate in relation to the claimant securing a job as a teacher. Part of the reason for this was the conflict of interest between the claimant's right to gain employment and the public interest in protecting children. Further, the police had not assumed responsibility to the claimant in respect of the economic loss he suffered (at [49]).[45]

There have, however, been some cases where a duty of care has been found to be owed by the police to an individual, even where the matter was not 'operational', arguably

43. In Canada, then, the family of the assaulted woman (in the scenarios at the beginning of the chapter) may well have a claim. See also *Hill* v *Hamilton-Wentworth Regional Police* [2007] (case failed on breach).

44. Human rights claims may, however, prove fruitful in respect of future negligently investigated rapes, see *Commissioner of Police of the Metropolis* v *DSD and another* [2018] (discussed in **section 6.3.1**), as well as the Northern Irish case *C (A Person under a disability)* v *The Chief Constable of the Police Force of Northern Ireland* [2014], even merely in terms of inducing a settlement payment and admissions of failure.

45. Contrast similar cases relating to pure economic loss. See e.g. ***Spring*** **v** ***Guardian Assurance*** **[1995]**, discussed in **section 7.6**.

proving that ***Hill*** does not grant immunity. However, all can probably be explained by the concept of 'assumption of responsibility'. In *Swinney* v *Chief Constable of Northumbria Police* [1997] the claimant, a pub landlady and police informant, was owed a duty of care in respect of the police's negligence in not keeping her identity safe. She had provided information about a violent criminal and had made it known that she would be likely to face repercussions if she was identified as the source. Despite this, police documents containing details of the case, including her name, were left in an unlocked police car and were, inevitably perhaps, stolen—eventually reaching the criminal against whom the evidence was given. Swinney was then subjected to a vicious campaign of harassment from which she suffered psychiatric harm and the loss of her pub. At first, the police argued that there was no proximity between them and her as a victim and that the ***Hill*** policy reasons served equally in her case. The Court of Appeal disagreed with both grounds. Swinney's case was distinguishable from ***Hill*** as it was clearly known by the Northumbria Police who might potentially be harmed as a result of their negligence (in fact that was exactly what they were charged with preventing), as opposed to ***Hill*** where no particular potential victim was identifiable. The court found that the police had *assumed responsibility* for the claimant's protection against the criminal she gave evidence about.

In dealing with the policy arguments, the Court of Appeal found that although many of the arguments put forward in ***Hill*** were *relevant*, they could not be viewed in isolation, and counterbalancing policy arguments must also be considered. In essence, the court performed a balancing act, weighing up policy reasons both for and against there being a duty owed, ultimately finding that the policy arguments *for* there being a duty of care outweighed those against.[46] Informants perform a public duty and deserve the protection of the police. Without such protection in place, the number of people prepared to inform would drop, making the prevention and detection of crime more difficult. Informers were more than ordinary members of the public and the police assumed a responsibility towards them when relying on them for information. Unfortunately, on the facts of *Swinney*, the police were later found not to be in *breach* of the duty that they owed. The Court of Appeal has given further guidance as to the extent of the duty of care owed to informers, finding that though the duty extends to their safety and wellbeing, no duty exists in respect of economic loss (*An Informer* v *Chief Constable* [2012]).[47]

Other exceptions to the ***Hill*** 'immunity' have come in different types of case, though not always easily. In *Kirkham* v *Chief Constable of Greater Manchester* [1990], the police were found to owe a duty to a remand prisoner in respect of whose suicidal tendencies they had failed to tell the prison authorities. He later hanged himself in custody. A similar duty was found to be owed to a prisoner held overnight in police cells in ***Reeves***

46. Recently confirmed in ***Robinson*** to be the correct approach (see **section 3.3.3**). See also *Essex Police* v *Transport Arendonk BVBA* [2020] and *Tindall and another* v *Thames Valley Police and another* [2020].

47. See Janet O'Sullivan 'Is it a Fair Cop? Police Informers, Financial Loss and Negligence' [2012] CLJ 267, who argues that in fact the case may be viewed as one where the judges elided duty and breach, with it possibly being able to be read as a 'duty but no breach' outcome. She contends that 'English law's fascination with employing the duty concept frequently hides the fact that a nuanced approach to the standard of care ... can solve many difficult problems traditionally left to the duty of care, ensuring the flexibility to give a remedy in a truly egregious case of wrongdoing without a problem of blanket immunity'.

v ***Commissioner of Police for the Metropolis*** [2000]. Similarly, the Court of Appeal held in ***Costello* v *Chief Constable of Northumbria Police*** [1999] that a police officer was owed a duty of care by her employers in relation to her safety while at work. Costello was attacked by a prisoner in a cell. Despite hearing her scream, the inspector on duty (and who was specifically charged with her protection) had negligently failed to help her—it was found that he did owe her a duty (for which the commissioner would be vicariously liable) to act where his failure to do so would result in a colleague being unnecessarily exposed to an increased risk of injury. However, all of these cases can be easily classified into the category of 'assumption of responsibility'.[48] In other words, why shouldn't the police owe a duty to those actually in their care at the time the negligence is alleged, if a risk of harm is foreseeable? It is this known potential harm that seems to exist as a common thread in these cases—reinforced by the fact that the courts have also found that it would be unreasonable to hold that the police had assumed responsibility for every person in police custody in relation to suicide. Only when a known risk of this happening exists will the positive duty be owed (*Orange* v *Chief Constable of West Yorkshire Police* [2001]).

A more difficult case to pigeonhole is *Waters* v *Commissioner of Police for the Metropolis* [2000]. Eileen Waters, a young female police officer, claimed in negligence (as well as discrimination where her claim was dismissed) against her employers for negligently failing to prevent a campaign of harassment mounted against her by fellow officers after she had alleged that she had been raped by one of them in police quarters. Following her allegation, she was snubbed and victimised by her colleagues and bullied and harassed on more than 80 separate occasions. She claimed that her employers had not dealt seriously with either her complaint or the harassment she suffered following it. Relying on ***Hill***, the defence argued (and the lower courts agreed) that allowing her action to proceed would divert officers and resources from the police's primary function; the prevention and detection of crimes. However, the House of Lords considered that all relevant circumstances of her case had to be taken into account. Only in the House of Lords, for example, did any judge (Lord Hutton) allude to the actual harms suffered by Eileen Waters, which could only have been exacerbated by the length of time it took for her claim to get that far (ten years). Their lordships eventually found that the policy arguments *for* there being a duty of care owed to Miss Waters by her employer outweighed those against. If, as happens in a striking-out action, the court must proceed assuming the facts alleged were true, then public interest *demanded* that a duty should be owed and that the serious problem the police had in dealing with complaints of this nature by one of their own officers should be made public. Showing that the police owed a duty of care would in theory force something to be done to change the way such claims were handled in the future; the knock-on effect also had to be considered. How could the

48. The cases are discussed in **section 4.2.1** and **section 4.2.2**. For a case in which the assumption of responsibility (to police officers by the police force in the context of protecting their interests during civil litigation against them) argument failed, see *James-Bowen and others* v *Commissioner of Police of the Metropolis* [2018]. Cases where a duty was owed to police officers harmed as a result of negligent colleagues/superiors include *Mullaney* v *Chief Constable of West Midlands Police* [2001]. More recently, however, no duty was found in relation to failure to warn officers on duty of threats to kill police officers made by known murderer Raoul Moat (*Rathband* v *Northumbria Constabulary* [2016]), following ***Hill***.

public have any confidence in the way the police would handle rape allegations made by an ordinary citizen if it was known that circumstances such as those faced by Eileen Waters were allowed to continue?

Pause for reflection

see online resources

Compare what happened in *Waters* to the Canadian case of *Doe*. What do the two cases tell you about the way the tort system typically deals with harms suffered primarily by women?[49] Do you think Eileen Waters should have had to fight so hard merely for the right for her case to proceed to trial?

Counterpoint

Overall, it seems that any case taken against the police about non-operational matters will be, at best, a fight. ***Hill*** (in our view, unreasonably) stands the test of time. There are, it seems to us, clear policy reasons operating counter to those expounded by Lord Keith in ***Hill***, notwithstanding their lordships' admission in both *Brooks* and ***Smith*** (confirmed in ***Michael***) that *some* of these can no longer necessarily be relied upon. It is at least arguable that policy issues like those apparent in *Doe* and *Waters* (e.g. keeping public faith in the efficacy of the police force) are apparent in *all* these cases (as the Macpherson Report would seem to suggest of *Brooks*). Even exceptions to the rule, which appear to be based on the idea of the defendant police force having 'assumed responsibility' for the wellbeing of the claimant, do not seem consistent. If it is arguable, for example, that an informant should be owed a duty of care so as not to discourage future informants from coming forward, or that a serving police officer should be owed a duty of care in respect of her treatment after making an allegation of rape against another officer, so that the public have more confidence in the way the police generally handle rape cases and—more importantly—rape victims, why do they not owe a duty to a likely victim of a serious racist attack, particularly when he was also the witness to a murder? Even before ***Smith*** was decided by the House of Lords, *Markesinis & Deakin* commented that 'the pattern of the decided cases suggests that of all the decisions in the area of duty of care, ***Hill*** comes closest to providing a "safe haven" for public bodies in the exercise of certain functions'.[50] Hopefully, for the sake of public confidence in the police as well as the ability of the courts to deal with police negligence, this safe haven will not last forever. However, in light of the most recent authorities on the police in negligence claims, it seems that a case even more 'outrageous' on its facts will be needed to

→

49. You could also consider the fact that ***Smith*** concerned two gay men and both ***Smith*** and ***Michael*** concerned domestic violence. For further discussion of tort's potential in the context of domestic violence, see Kirsty Horsey and Erika Rackley 'Tort Law' in Rosemary Auchmuty (ed) *Great Debates on Law and Gender* (Palgrave, 2018).

50. *Markesinis & Deakin* (6th edn, 2008, OUP), p 213.

→

persuade the majority of their lordships to depart from ***Hill***. That said, where the high threshold is met for a human rights claim to succeed, another avenue is now possible, as *Commissioner of Police of the Metropolis* v *DSD and another* [2018] illustrates.[51]

6.5.4 The armed forces

In respect of the armed forces, cases suggest that a private law duty of care will only be owed to individuals where a highly proximate relationship arising out of an 'assumption of responsibility' exists. In ***Barrett* v *Ministry of Defence* [1995]**, for example, a drunken naval officer was found to have been owed no duty of care until the point where a superior officer stepped in to order that he was helped back to his room, thus assuming responsibility for his safety.[52] In *Jebson* v *Ministry of Defence* [2000], a drunken soldier suffered injuries after climbing onto—then falling off—the roof of an army truck. The Court of Appeal found that the defendants owed a duty to provide suitable transport and provisions for soldiers after a night out. The assumption of responsibility idea seemingly extends only to civilian circumstances: in *Mulcahy* v *Ministry of Defence* [1996], it was found that 'common sense' and policy reasons (including the 'defensive practices' argument) meant that the army should not owe a duty to soldiers in battle conditions, even though the claimant was injured by friendly fire from his own sergeant.[53]

Recent military negligence cases have been controversial, decided very much in the public eye, and have brought in human rights claims alongside negligence.[54]

Smith and others v *Ministry of Defence* [2013] SC

Family members of six soldiers killed or injured in Iraq sued in relation to the provision of inadequate equipment/training and/or inadequate protection from 'friendly fire'. There were three sets of claims:

(1) The ' Challenger claims': it was alleged that the MOD was negligent in failing to properly equip tanks and give soldiers adequate training to prevent 'friendly fire' incidents.
(2) The 'Snatch Land Rover claims': allegations that the MOD failed to take adequate preventative measures to protect the 'real and immediate risk to life' (thereby engaging Art 2 ECHR) of soldiers travelling in those vehicles, who were killed by roadside bombs.
(3) The 'Ellis negligence claim': one of the claimants in (2) also alleged various failures on the part of the MOD.

→

51. Though see *Griffiths and others* v *Suffolk Police and another* [2018], a case in which the threshold was not reached.

52. See **section 4.2.2**.

53. In *Bici* v *Ministry of Defence* [2004] it was established that this 'combat immunity' applies only where soldiers are actively 'under threat'.

54. See **section 3.3.1**.

→

The MOD argued that the Article 2 claims should be struck out on the basis that the soldiers were outside the jurisdiction of the Convention at the time of the soldiers' deaths and that even if that was not the case, Article 2 imposed no positive obligation to protect life during operations against the enemy. It also argued that the negligence claims should all be struck out on the basis of combat immunity or, alternatively, because it would not be fair, just or reasonable to impose a duty of care on the MOD. The Court of Appeal, following an earlier Supreme Court decision, struck out the Article 2 claims,[55] but ruled that the negligence claims could proceed. Both parts of that judgment were appealed.

A seven-member Supreme Court unanimously held that the soldiers *had* been within the UK's jurisdiction for the purposes of the Convention. A 4:3 majority held that the 'Snatch Land Rover claims' should not be struck out. The majority found that high-level military policy decisions and battlefield operations would fall outside the scope of Article 2, but whether 'claims which are between these two categories' might engage Article 2 would be a matter of judgement on a case-by-case basis.[56]

On the negligence claims, the Supreme Court found that the combat immunity principle should be narrowly construed and thus not extended beyond 'active combat' to planning and preparation for active operations. It viewed the 'Challenger claims' as clearly falling outside the combat immunity principle, though was less sure that the same was true of the 'Ellis negligence claim'. Nonetheless, the majority found that neither claim should be struck out.

Pause for reflection

Lord Mance (with whom Lord Wilson agreed) would have struck out all of the claims, viewing them as non-justiciable.[57] He thought the majority decision would 'make extensive litigation almost inevitable after, as well as quite possibly during and even before, any active service operations undertaken by the British army. It is likely to lead to the judicialisation of war' (at [150]). Why would this be a problem?

Policy Exchange, a think tank, subsequently issued a report showing that 5,827 claims were brought against the MOD in 2012/13 with an average of £70,000 compensation being paid to the 205 claimants who were successful.[58] It warned that the armed forces risked being 'paralysed' by sustained legal assault and 'judicial mission creep', with 'catastrophic consequences' for national safety. It proposed various options, including that Parliament should legislate to define 'combat immunity' (at 56); that the principle of Crown immunity be revived in wartime situations (at 57); or that the UK should derogate from the ECHR during military operations (at 58–9). In 2016, then Prime Minister Theresa May vowed to end such

→

55. *R (on the application of Smith)* v *Secretary of State for Defence and another* [2010] had upheld this claim.

56. Though it was thought that given the wide margin of appreciation given to states, that 'it is far from clear that the claimants will be able to demonstrate ... a breach' (at [78]–[81]).

→

claims against soldiers (including commanding officers).[59] Further, in December 2016 the MOD launched a public consultation on plans to prevent courts adjudicating on allegations that injuries or deaths in combat were the result of negligence, proposing an internal compensation scheme instead, alongside legislation dealing with combat immunity (MOD, *Better Combat Compensation*, 1 December 2016). The plan was critiqued by many for sidestepping the principles of justice.[60] The consultation closed on 23 February 2017 but at the time of writing no response from government had appeared, with the explanation being that the policy is 'under further consideration following breadth of consultation responses and change over of Secretary of State'.

Duncan Fairgrieve described the Policy Exchange report as largely 'premised on anecdote and assumption'. He asked: 'Might it not be just as convincingly argued that the possibility of liability will reinforce rather than undermine standards?'[61] Which do you think is the right response to the decision in *Smith* v *MOD*? Do you think that independent judicial oversight offers protection to serving personnel and creates accountability for those who make negligent operational decisions?

It should be noted that the majority Justices in ***Smith* v *MOD*** did not view it as certain that the claimants would succeed. All they did was find that the claims in negligence and arising under Article 2 ECHR should be allowed to be determined at full trial. The claimants must still prove that there was a breach (and policy decisions about wartime conditions will come into play here) which caused their loss.

6.5.5 **The coastguard**

Similar restrictions to those that attach to the fire service operate in relation to the coastguard. In *OLL Ltd* v *Secretary of State for Transport* [1997], the court held that, like the fire service, the coastguard owes no duty to respond to calls from people in trouble at sea, only a duty not to make the situation worse when they do. In this case children and teachers on a school canoeing trip got into severe difficulties at sea, with some canoes capsizing and the party becoming separated in the water. The coastguard's response was both slow and inefficient and, the claimants argued, made the situation worse. However, the court disagreed; the claims were struck out as disclosing no cause of action.

57. See at [125]–[137], [146] and [151]–[152]. Lord Carnwath would have struck out the 'Challenger claims' for the same reason (at [156]). 'Justiciability' is discussed in **section 6.6.1**.

58. Thomas Tugendhat and Laura Croft 'The Fog of Law: An introduction to the legal erosion of British fighting power' *Policy Exchange* 18 October 2013.

59. *The Times* 'British Troops to be Exempted from Human Rights Law' 4 October 2016.

60. See Owen Boycott and Damien Gayle 'Combat immunity plan will deny soldiers justice, says Law Society' *The Guardian* 14 February 2017.

61. Fairgrieve 2014.

Pause for reflection

Interestingly, according to Lord Bingham in ***Smith***, this was another case where a duty should have been obvious on the facts, following his 'liability principle'. After discussing the facts and outcome of the case, he said: 'My Lords, I feel bound to say that a law of delict [as tort is known in Scotland] which denies a remedy on facts such as these, in the absence of any statutory inhibition, fails to perform the basic function for which such a law exists' (at [57]). Think back to what the functions of tort law are. Do you agree? Do you think the fact that the coastguard (and the lifeboat service) is funded through charitable donations and relies heavily on volunteers swayed the court in *OLL*?

6.5.6 **Duty: the emergency services and armed forces—at a glance**

The position is summarised in **Table 6.2**.

TABLE 6.2 Duty: the emergency services and armed forces—at a glance

Which service/body	When is a duty of care owed?
Fire service	• No duty to respond to emergency call • Once responded, the duty is not to, by any positive act, make the situation worse
Ambulance service	• Must respond to an emergency call to a named individual
Police	• No duty to respond to emergency call • Duty can be owed when the negligent conduct in question is 'operational' • In non-operational matters, such as investigations, duty only exists when there is an 'assumption of responsibility' for the wellbeing of the claimant
Armed forces	• No duty in battle conditions while 'under threat' • Duty owed where the defendant can be said to have 'assumed responsibility' towards the claimant
Coastguard	• No duty to respond to emergency call • Once responded, duty is not to, by any positive act, make the situation worse

6.6 **Other types of public body**

Other public bodies include local and district councils and authorities (e.g. health or highways authorities) and the various agencies within these. Such organisations have posed problems when determining whether a duty should arise in relation to harm suffered by individuals as a result of negligence. Even where there is a high degree of foreseeability that negligent action (or inaction) would cause harm or where, because of the claimant's relationship with the public body concerned, there exists a high degree of 'proximity', the courts have tended to fall back on the idea that it would not be 'fair, just or reasonable' to impose a duty.[62] Of course, this must all now be understood in light of the Supreme Court decisions in ***Robinson*** and ***Poole***.

One reason commonly cited for this reluctance is the fact that compensation would ultimately be paid by taxpayers. The courts are disinclined to spend public money in this way, particularly when that might mean diverting it from other sources and/or eventually leading to increased taxes. Also, there is a concern that—in a similar vein to the arguments in relation to the police—making public authorities and agencies pay compensation would divert the focus of the employees of such organisations to litigation-avoidance and thereby instil defensive working practices. However, as with the police, it is at least arguable that changed working practices (e.g. to avoid negligence or, put another way, to ensure that *more care* is taken) are not necessarily as bad as the picture is painted judicially.

6.6.1 **Justiciability**

When it comes to litigation against public bodies, a further layer of complexity causes the courts a problem: 'justiciability'. This has been described as 'the constitutional concept which recognises [that] the capabilities of the courts are limited'[63] and operates only in the context of cases taken against public bodies, in both public and private law. It is an extremely effective control device by which the courts limit claims, 'because it requires the court to strike out a claim without even proceeding to ask whether a duty of care should be owed'.[64] In other words, because public bodies were created by statute, the courts often wonder whether they are actually *able* to question the actions of these authorities or whether there is a more suitable forum in which to do so. In many cases, according to the justiciability argument, the proper actions and decisions taken by these bodies need to be examined by reference to factors that adversarial court proceedings are not suited to.

What this comes down to, in a very general sense, is again the distinction between statutory powers and duties. Under statutes, public bodies are authorised to take decisions on particular matters (i.e. they have the *power* to do so), but *how* and *when* and *whether* they exercise these powers is a matter for their discretion, and may come down to a number of different factors such as resource-allocation, prioritisation of resources or services and so on. We have already considered this type of distinction when discussing whether operational or policy matters are capable of giving rise to a duty of care. A good example of the justiciability issue can be seen in ***Stovin* v *Wise* [1996]**.[65]

62. See e.g. *Mitchell* v *Glasgow City Council* [2009].

63. Bruce Harris 'Judicial Review, Justiciability and the Prerogative of Mercy' [2003] CLJ 631, cited in the Law Commission's consultation paper *Administrative Redress: Public Bodies and the Citizen* (2008), [3.121].

64. Law Commission (**n 63**) [3.121].

65. Also see Lord Mance in ***Smith* v *MOD***, as discussed in **section 6.5.4**.

Stovin v *Wise* [1996] HL

The claimant motorcyclist was injured in a collision with the defendant's car at a junction. The defendant alleged that the collision was partly caused by negligence of the highways division of the local authority, which he therefore joined to the action as a co-defendant. The defendant claimed that his view of the claimant exiting the junction was obstructed by a bank of earth which the local authority had not moved. Although not the landowners, the authority had the power under statute to do this and, in fact, had previously asked the landowners to remove the earth, in response to previous accidents at the same junction, but had failed to follow this up when no action was taken. The claimant alleged that the existence of the statutory power was enough to create the requisite relationship of proximity between road users and the authority. The question was whether the local authority's failure to follow up was an action (or omission) that the court had the right to question. There were worse accident 'black spots' in the area under the authority's control *and* there were other things than accident black spots that needed to be dealt with under the same limited budget.

So, asked the court, what authority would it have to question how these resources were allocated and which aspects of the many tasks undertaken by the authority within its statutory remit and limited budget were examinable in a court? Their lordships were, they said, not equipped with—and nor should they be—the power to decide whether the authority should have put more resources and manpower into ensuring that the obstruction was moved. Striking out the claim, the majority (Lords Nicholls and Slynn dissenting) said that the situation regarding the exercise of a statutory power was similar to that regarding a statutory duty.[66] Therefore, in order to determine whether this could give rise to the right of an individual to sue in negligence—that is, whether a common law duty of care could be owed—it was necessary to examine the statute itself and identify whether Parliament had *intended* to give individuals the right to claim compensation if the power was not exercised or was exercised incorrectly.

This inevitably proved to be a circular argument. The very fact that Parliament had decided to confer a power on a public body to do something, rather than make it a duty to do so, could be taken to indicate that no right for individuals to be able to make claims was intended.[67] Lord Hoffmann admitted as much: 'the fact that Parliament has conferred a discretion must be some indication that the policy of the Act conferring the power was not to create a right to compensation. The need to have regard to the policy of the statute therefore means that exceptions will be rare' (at 953).

In ***Stovin***, while it was held that the presence of a statutory power was not enough, in itself, to create a positive duty to act, the law lords stopped short of saying that individuals harmed by the negligent exercise of (or failure to exercise) that power would *never* have a right to compensation. In order for this to be the case, they said, two strict requirements must be met. First, the non-exercise or negligent exercise of the power must have

66. **Chapter 14**.

67. So this principle would therefore seem to preclude any claims in respect of the lines not being repainted on the road in the scenarios at the beginning of the chapter. See *Larner* v *Solihull Metropolitan Borough Council* [2001], *Gorringe* v *Calderdale Metropolitan Borough Council* [2004] and *Macdonald* v *Aberdeenshire Council* [2012].

been irrational (in the public law sense)[68] in all the circumstances and, secondly, there must be what Lord Hoffmann called 'exceptional grounds' for creating the obligation to compensate (at 953). He envisaged that these might include situations in which there is 'general reliance' on the correct exercise of power under consideration, so much so that 'the general pattern of social and economic behaviour' is affected (an example might be the setting of insurance premiums) (at 954). These exceptions, he continued, should reflect general expectations of the wider community, not merely those of the defendant, and general reliance could exist only where the benefit to be provided by the exercise of the power would be 'uniform and routine' in nature (at 954), so that it would be indisputable what the defendant had been expected to do. A claimant could not establish reliance purely by the fact that he relied upon it himself; this reliance must be shared more widely among the general public.[69] Lord Hoffmann highlighted the imperfection of the road network and that it is the primary duty of drivers to take care, taking the road as they find it, including hazardous bends, intersections and junctions.[70]

Similar issues regarding justiciability had been raised in *X*, in 1995. The authorities concerned applied to have all five claims struck out, because they argued they did not owe the individual claimants a common law duty of care.[71] As we have already seen, the first two claims (*X*, and *M* v *Newham* [1995]) concerned allegations that the social services arm of the local authority had acted negligently in exercising its powers to prevent and deal with child abuse. The three other claims were made in relation to the authority's power to make provisions for the education of children with special needs.

In *X*, the House of Lords found that it would not be 'fair, just and reasonable' to impose a duty of care on the local authority in respect of the way it exercised its power with relation to child abuse (Lord Browne-Wilkinson at 749). There were a number of reasons for this: in exercising this power the authority had a degree of discretion, and people might well have different opinions on the best way of acting and on the wisdom or otherwise of decisions taken. If a duty of care was attached to the authority towards the children and families it used its discretion in relation to, employees would always worry about whether they might be sued for reaching particular conclusions or taking particular decisions. This would make their practices less efficient and consequently divert resources from child protection services. Moreover, said the law lords, citizens have alternative ways of challenging public bodies, including statutory appeals procedures and ombudsmen, and it would cut across this statutory framework if a duty of care were to be imposed.[72]

However, in relation to the claims about special needs education in *X*, their lordships stated that it was at least arguable that a duty of care might arise, as there was not the same risk of defensive practices and because information was provided to individual parents/families from a position of responsibility with the assumption that it would be relied upon.

68. Though Lord Hoffmann later retreated from this in *Gorringe* v *Calderdale Metropolitan Borough Council* [2004] as it would be too difficult to apply irrationality principles to pure omissions (at [32]). For an exception to the rule, in the context of foliage planted *on* rather than adjacent to the highway, see *Yetkin* v *Newham London Borough Council* [2010].

69. This principle was affirmed in *Mitchell* v *Glasgow City Council* [2009], again in the context of a public body's omission (at [7]).

70. See also *Sumner* v *Colborne Denbighshire County Council and The Welsh Ministers* [2018].

71. Note that since ***Poole***, *X* is no longer regarded as good law, as discussed earlier.

72. If a case arose now with similar facts, this would not be the case—a duty to the children *could* be found (following ***D* v *East Berkshire***), though now see ***Poole*** for the correct approach in such cases.

Pause for reflection

Is it not at least arguable that there is always a high degree of reliance from the children involved with the child protection services of a local authority? Why wasn't the reliance argument made in this respect?

Some later cases appear to pull back from such strict restrictions on liability towards individuals. But this should not be seen as a change in direction by the courts in favour of a less strict approach to the duty of care issue with regard to public bodies. In fact, we would argue, it has more to do with events subsequent to *X* and ***Stovin*** which were outside the control of the courts and which bring into stark relief the real issues created by denying that public bodies owe no duty of care in negligence. We have already encountered these events and cases earlier when looking at the background to the current focus of the law in relation to public body liability; they stem from the appeal to the ECtHR in ***Osman* v *UK***.

Counterpoint

Stephen Bailey has argued that the justiciability issue is a 'blind alley' and only serves to further complicate the law of negligence relating to public bodies. He says that the 'justiciability proposition' should simply be removed, as it is 'difficult to see any proper basis' for it (2006, p 169) and indicates a preference for breach-based considerations. In a 2008 consultation paper published to assess the efficacy of 'mechanisms through which claimants can obtain redress from public bodies for substandard administrative action' (*Administrative Redress: Public Bodies and the Citizen*, later abandoned), the Law Commission described the position regarding justiciability. It stated that the '[c]ourts have struggled to articulate workable criteria for determining what should and should not be justiciable. The most that can be said under the current state of law is that certain matters are deemed "unsuitable for judicial determination" and that these are revealed on a rather unpredictable, case-by-case basis' (at [3.127]). Further, in *Jain* v *Trent Strategic Health Authority* [2008], Arden LJ in the Court of Appeal indicated that considerations of justiciability when determining duty are less 'likely in the future to be as important or have the same weight' as the 'fair, just and reasonable' consideration from *Caparo* (at [62])—now as restated in ***Robinson*** and ***Poole***. We would agree that the justiciability point makes matters less clear than they need to be, particularly in an area of law which is already confused and confusing. As Bailey suggests, it would be better to allow all claims to be judicially determined and then 'the more complex the decision and the more sensitive the relevant considerations, the more difficult it will be for the claimant … to establish breach of duty' (p 170). Breach would seem to us to be a sufficient control device for public body liability, particularly given that section 1 of the Compensation Act 2006 allows courts to adjust the standard of care to take account of the fact that the defendant was undertaking a socially 'desirable activity'.

→

→

In its consultation the Law Commission stated that:

> in private law, we consider that the current situation is unsustainable. The uncertain and unprincipled nature of negligence in relation to public bodies, coupled with the unpredictable expansion of liability over recent years, has led to a situation that serves neither claimants nor public bodies. (at [2.7])[73]

We would agree that the law in relation to the liability of public bodies in negligence is both 'uncertain and unprincipled' and would welcome proper reform. At the core of the Law Commission recommendations for claims in private law lay a requirement to show 'serious fault' on the part of the public body concerned (at [4.145]–[4.147], [4.152]). This looked very much like a move towards a breach-based test and, from our perspective, this move would have been welcome (at [2.9]).[74] However, the Commission also proposed that certain activities—those regarded as 'truly public' in nature (defined at [4.110]–[4.131])—would be placed in a specialised scheme, whereby claimants would have to first meet public law requirements in order to establish liability (at [4.99]). Only cases not considered 'truly public' would be considered under the ordinary rules of negligence (at [2.11]–[2.12], [4.5], [4.10]). This seems a little like the justiciability test and would serve to limit redress against public bodies—although if it had been clearly defined it may have been less problematic—despite the Commission's supposed commitment to a principle of 'modified' corrective justice (at [4.2], [4.9]). The proposals encountered a great deal of opposition and critique, mainly from academic quarters.[75] For this reason the Commission announced in May 2010 that it would not continue to pursue reform.[76]

6.7 The recognition of new types of claim—'messed up lives'?

Despite the justiciability issue and what seems to be a general desire of the courts to protect public bodies from negligence claims, the aftermath of ***Osman* v *UK*** seemed to lay the foundation for some new types of claim to succeed against public bodies. These claims fall outside the more traditional claims relating to more easily recognised harms and refer to lives being negatively affected or 'messed up' in some way by a public body's negligence. We have broken these down further in the following two sections: to

73. The Commission made similar comments in relation to breach of statutory duty.

74. Though it should be noted that using the standard of care as the threshold test for liability in the context of public bodies is also likely to present difficulties for claimants (*Pierce* v *Doncaster* [2007]; *X & Y* v *London Borough of Hounslow* [2009]).

75. See, in particular, Tom Cornford 'Administrative Redress: The Law Commission's Consultation Paper' [2009] PL 70; Richard Mullender 'Negligence, Public Bodies, and Ruthlessness' (2009) 72 MLR 961. A full summary of the responses to the consultation is available online.

76. The Law Commission *Administrative Redress: Public Bodies and the Citizen* (Law Com No 322, 2010). One proposal that did survive—and may eventually prove very useful—is for costs of compensation paid by public bodies to be collated and published by government.

'educational' claims where the claimants essentially allege that negligence has caused them to be less well educated than they ought to be,[77] and 'social' claims which relate to the disturbance of lives in a more general sense.

6.7.1 Education-based claims

In ***Phelps*** v ***Hillingdon London Borough Council*** [2001], four cases were jointly considered by the House of Lords. ***Phelps*** itself was the only one at full trial; the others were striking-out actions.

Phelps v *Hillingdon London Borough Council* and other cases [2001] HL

In *Phelps*, the claimant, by then an adult, had learning difficulties as a child. At the time, an educational psychologist had been employed by the local authority to make an assessment of her educational needs. The resulting report said that the child's difficulties stemmed from emotional and behavioural problems, whereas in fact she was later properly diagnosed with dyslexia. She claimed that the negligent assessment of her needs led to a failure to provide the right kind of schooling, affecting her educational development and subsequently her employment prospects as an adult.

The second case (*Jarvis* v *Hampshire County Council*) also concerned a dyslexic claimant, who alleged not a failure to diagnose the condition, but that the local authority had given the wrong advice about schooling once the diagnosis had been made. In the third case, *G (a child)* v *Bromley London Borough Council*, the local authority failed to provide the right equipment to the claimant who had a muscle-wasting disease and needed special equipment to be able to communicate. He alleged that this failure caused his education to suffer and that this resulted in psychological damage. The final case (*Anderton* v *Clwyd County Council*) concerned a woman who was seeking access to her educational records, claiming that inadequate education had damaged her.

The Court of Appeal dismissed Miss Phelps's claim on policy grounds. Primarily it was thought that not to dismiss it would open the door to all manner of vexatious and inconsequential claims being made against schools and education authorities. A seven-member House of Lords, however, refused to dismiss any of the four claims raised in the ***Phelps*** group, referring back to its own decision in *X* (this aspect of *X* survives), in which it had ruled that there may be duties owed by local education authorities to children in respect of educational services, on the basis of assumed responsibility. It said that an authority owes a duty of care in respect of the provision of an education appropriate to a child's needs and that where this fails to materialise due to the negligence of a teacher or other employee of the authority, such as an educational psychologist, the authority could be liable according to the principles of vicarious liability.

77. Such claims do not only arise against public bodies, as a recent case shows: *Siddiqui* v *University of Oxford* [2016].

This novel approach served to justify the House of Lords' decision as well as paving the way for future cases to be taken on a vicarious liability basis.[78] However, because their lordships decided ***Phelps*** in this way it became—unfortunately in our view—unnecessary to consider whether the authority could owe a *personal* duty to such children. Their lordships stressed that whether there was liability in such a situation would depend not on whether a child had or had not done badly at school, or if they had not realised their potential, but on whether this was a direct result of a failure of the employee to live up to the standard of care expected of them, which would be governed according to the standard of others in a similar profession (***Bolam* v *Friern Hospital Management Committee*** [1957]).[79] This, they said, would be enough to prevent floods of claims to every local education authority, alleging poor educational standards and decreased employment potential.

Counterpoint

This House of Lords' opinion suggests that *breach* could be used as a sufficient control device in *all* educational claims against public bodies (although it is not hard to see the concept being workable in other types of claim, as we have already indicated). Could we say that public bodies should, in general, owe a duty of care to individuals to deal carefully with their business, in order to avoid harming those whose day-to-day lives could be affected by their actions—but then say that this is a professional (high) standard, as with doctors, thereby using the standard of care to control liability? Again, it seems that imposing a high *standard* of care might serve both to prevent liability in the majority of cases (if this is what is deemed to be desirable) *as well as* improving the quality of the service provided and increasing public confidence.

The breach-based test appears to have been adopted in educational cases. In *Carty* v *Croydon London Borough Council* [2005], it was confirmed by the Court of Appeal (who it must be remembered were squarely resistant to educational claims in ***Phelps***) that the approach now to be taken from ***Phelps*** applied not only to educational authority employees such as psychologists or teachers, but also to the authority's administrative staff responsible for decisions about education. If such a matter was justiciable, it could be found that the employee concerned had assumed a responsibility to the child to provide services according to their needs. However, only where the decisions made in this respect are obviously wrong (i.e. they have fallen clearly below the standard of care expected) will a claim succeed.

Future claims may alternatively be made under the HRA in respect of negligent educational provision, as the right to education is guaranteed under the European Convention.[80] In *A* v *Essex County Council* [2010], however, such a claim failed in the Supreme Court, in

78. See **Chapter 20**. Though cf *X & Y* v *London Borough of Hounslow* [2009] discussed in **section 2.6**.
79. Thus it should be fairly easy to establish that a duty of care was owed by the educational psychologist in the scenario at the beginning of the chapter, with the result that the local education authority would be (vicariously) liable for any negligence on her part: breach then becomes the 'control device' used to establish liability.
80. Protocol 1, Art 2 begins 'No person shall be denied the right to education'.

relation to a child who had special educational needs and was left without formal educational provision for 18 months. The majority concluded that there was no absolute right to education meeting the claimant's particular special needs, only a right to have access to the education that was actually available. An alternative claim based on him being given *some* education during the 18-month period was thought possible—but was time-barred.

6.7.2 Social claims

Barrett v *Enfield London Borough Council* [2001] HL

The claimant was a 17-year-old boy who had been in local authority care since he was 10 months old. He had been moved frequently and, as a consequence, had a difficult and unpleasant childhood in which he formed no lasting bonds and which had negatively affected him when older: he ended up suffering various psychiatric illnesses. He argued that the local authority owed him a duty of care and had breached this by failing to find him suitable adoptive parents, locate suitable foster parents or initiate and supervise a meeting with his biological mother, as it was meant to do.

At trial and in the Court of Appeal, his case was struck out on the authority of the 'abuse' cases (rather than the 'education' cases) in *X*, the courts ruling that there were good policy reasons why it would not be 'fair, just and reasonable' to impose a duty of care in this situation, despite the high degree of proximity and foreseeability of the harm occurring. On appeal to the House of Lords, however, the local council's strike-out application was refused. The law lords held that without a proper hearing of the facts it was impossible to say whether the actions of the council in respect of the boy's upbringing were policy decisions (conferred via a statutory power) and therefore not justiciable, or operational decisions which would be justiciable and could therefore give rise to a duty of care.

Barrett is an interesting case study in judicial attitude and political comment, as well as forming the basis for future decisions along similar lines. There seem to be several different reasons for the case succeeding. In the House of Lords, the decision was given with a degree of judicial reluctance. Chronologically, it followed ***Osman* v *UK*** and is illustrative of a period where the courts were reluctant to strike cases out in case this was viewed as a violation of the claimant's Article 6 right to a fair hearing. This is particularly apparent in Lord Browne-Wilkinson's speech (made all the more striking as he also gave the leading opinion in *X*, see in particular the passage at 560). The Court of Appeal had followed *X*, striking out Barrett's claim, finding it not fair, just or reasonable to impose a duty on the local authority concerned and, in any case, that the matter was not justiciable. The House of Lords, however, given the impact of ***Osman* v *UK***, distinguished ***Barrett*** from *X* (and other subsequent cases), arguing that while *X* had been concerned with decisions about *whether* to take a child into care, ***Barrett*** concerned what happened once a child *was* in care, when the authority had clearly assumed responsibility for his wellbeing. Politically, it seems that the law lords knew this was something that they must do—though the (tenuous) distinction, if one has to be made at all, is in our view correct.

In *W* v *Essex County Council* [2000], the House of Lords found a duty was owed by a local authority to the claimants, who were council foster parents suing on behalf of their own children. Before accepting a foster child into their home, the claimants had specifically told the council that they could not take a child who was a known or suspected abuser. Negligently, and without informing the claimants, the council placed with the couple a 15-year-old boy who they knew had sexually assaulted his sister. While placed with the family, he sexually assaulted the claimants' children. Here, however, the Court of Appeal did not strike out the claim. While it could point to policy reasons why a duty should not be owed that were similar to those stemming from *X*, it also acknowledged that some strong opposing arguments existed—the most pressing being that the council had broken its own express promise to the claimants. The House of Lords upheld this decision on appeal.

Similarly, in *S* v *Gloucestershire County Council* [2000], the Court of Appeal confirmed that no blanket immunity should be thought to exist regarding claims made against local authorities in relation to child abuse. Making a connection to the education cases, they held that only in the clearest of cases, once the whole context of the case had been carefully considered, should any claim of this type be struck out. Later, in *A* v *Essex County Council* [2003], a claim was made by a married couple who had been on the council's adoption register. They had specified to the council that they would take children with relatively mild emotional or behavioural difficulties but could not cope with anything more severe. The council had—(similarly to *W* v *Essex*)—agreed to this, but later placed a brother and sister with the couple where it was known that the boy had considerable behavioural problems. In the course of his stay, inter alia, the boy physically attacked the couple and tried to harm himself by electrocution. The couple sued alleging that the council had not provided them with correct information about the boy's behavioural problems and as a result their lives had suffered unreasonable disruption. The Court of Appeal upheld their claim saying that although a council did not have a general duty to provide information about children being placed with adoptive parents, once a decision had been made in relation to the type and amount of information that was to be provided to prospective adopters, reasonable care should be taken to ensure that this informational target was met. However, it should be noted that this then becomes an operational matter rather than a policy decision.

Later, however, the courts retreated to a stricter approach on duty.[81] A harrowing example is found in a case involving vulnerable adults with learning difficulties living in local authority housing (*X & Y* v *London Borough of Hounslow* [2009]). Here, a claim was made in respect of the authority's failure to re-home the claimants and their two young children after the family was subjected to bullying and harassment by local youths who were known to be, inter alia, entering the premises and preying on the claimants' vulnerability.[82] Representatives acting for the claimants contended that because the authority (or the social worker for whom it would be vicariously liable) had not taken this emergency action when the harassment escalated, the claimants were subjected to a particularly horrendous incident of prolonged serious physical and sexual abuse in their

81. See e.g. *Jain* v *Trent Strategic Health Authority* [2009].

82. Thus the harm was highly foreseeable. The facts of the case are discussed in full in **section 2.6**, where the *first instance* judgment is annotated as a good example of the rules of negligence in action.

home by the youths. Though their claim succeeded at first instance, this was overturned by the Court of Appeal, which found that the defendant authority owed the claimants no duty. Partly this was due to the nature of the claim involving both an omission and the actions of third parties.[83] The House of Lords had at that time recently confirmed in *Mitchell* v *Glasgow City Council* [2009] that there was no general duty for a defendant to take care to prevent a third party from deliberately causing damage to a claimant, absent any assumption of responsibility. In any case, the Court of Appeal said that it could not be established in *X & Y* that there *had* been any lack of care. Having been refused leave to appeal to the House of Lords, the claimants took their case to the ECtHR alleging violations of Articles 3, 6, 8 and 13.[84] However, no ruling ever came, as the parties in 2011 settled upon an agreement 'under which the applicants agreed to waive any further claims against the United Kingdom'[85] in return for X and Y each being paid €25,000 (Z received €7,000), as well as a sum of €12,500 to cover all parties' costs. In a short comment, the ECtHR stated that it was satisfied that this was because the settlement was based on the UK Government's 'respect for human rights'. To us, this indicates that, like ***Z*** and ***TP and KM*** (discussed earlier), the ECtHR would have been prepared to find that the local authority's actions had violated the human rights of their tenants, rendering the finding of no duty of care all the more distasteful.

6.8 Conclusion

In this chapter we considered when *public bodies* will owe an individual a *private law* duty of care. Often, it seems that this will depend on the nature of the public body itself as the scope of the liability of some has been more affected by European jurisprudence and the impact of the HRA than others.

Of the *emergency services and armed forces* it can be said that a duty is easily established only in relation to the ambulance service which, by analogy to the NHS and medical profession, owes a duty of care towards any individual to whom it agrees to respond. By contrast, the fire service, coastguard and armed forces owe a duty only when it can be shown that their positive actions (rather than 'mere' failures to act) made a situation worse than it was or where responsibility for the safety or wellbeing of the claimant was assumed. Similarly, the notion of assumption of responsibility can be used to establish a duty on the part of the police, but rarely (and controversially) does this extend into non-operational matters such as the investigation of crimes, even where the negligence alleged is gross and the injuries suffered due to police incompetence are highly foreseeable and severe.

Greater in-roads have been made in respect of other types of public body, such as child welfare and protection services or the educational services of *local authorities*. Here, it seems, the impact of decisions from the ECtHR have been absorbed most strongly, with potential breaches of human rights being considered alongside (explicitly or implicitly)

83. See **Chapter 4** to explore the difficulties inherent in claims involving either (or both) of these elements. See also ***Poole***, which has notable similarities.

84. *X, Y & Z* v *UK* Application no 32666/10, 8 June 2010 ('Z' is X's mother, by then in her 80s).

85. *X, Y & Z* v *UK* [2011] ECHR 1199.

claims in negligence. To an extent, it seems that there is movement towards the use of breach as a control device for liability in these areas (particularly in the educational context).

End-of-chapter questions

After reading the chapter carefully, try answering the questions which follow.

1 Why are the courts reluctant to make a finding that a public body owes a duty of care to individuals harmed by its negligence? Would breach be a better tool to control liability?

2 Should the liability of public bodies be treated any differently from that of private bodies/individuals?

3 Is there any valid reason to treat the emergency services differently from each other when dealing with whether a duty of care is owed?

4 Why should the police be afforded what seems like a greater degree of protection from negligence claims taken against them, as compared with other emergency services?

5 What impact have decisions of the European Court of Human Rights and the passage of the Human Rights Act 1998 had on negligence litigation against public bodies?

6 Was the Supreme Court's decision in *Smith* v *MOD* correct?

If you would like to know what we think visit the **online resources**. www.oup.com/he/horsey7e

Answering the problem question

Consider again the problem question at the start of this chapter. Now having read about the topic, what would be your advice to the various parties?

Here are some pointers to get you started

→ Mr Smith's family/estate will sue PC Plod because of the car chase which led to his death, as well as the paramedic for the inadequate assessment of Mr Smith at the scene (as well as the chief constable and the Ambulance Service through vicarious liability (see Chapter 20)). It will need to be established whether *each* of the potential tortfeasors owed Mr Smith a duty of care, using the relevant case law. The Ambulance Service may also be sued *directly* for turning up late.

→ In respect of PC Plod's duty, you should remember that driving a police car is an operational matter so it is likely that the same duty was owed as any other road user might have. In emergency situations, the standard of care might be relaxed (see Chapter 8), but was this an emergency?

→

- The Ambulance Service will owe a duty to respond (*Kent* v *Griffiths*) (but again there would be a question about breach).
- Although this is a problem about duty of care, you should also be aware that there might be causation issues, particularly due to the interaction between the two defendants' potential breaches of duty.
- The hostage's family/estate will also need to establish that the hostage was owed a duty of care by the police. This is a different kind of claim from the one above, as it relates to the police's role in the 'investigation and suppression of crime' and so the authorities stemming from ***Hill*** will be relevant. Consider whether, unlike in ***Michael***, the police here can be said to have assumed responsibility.

If you need some more guidance

- An **annotated version of the problem with issues and cases to consider** can be found in the **Appendix**.
- A **suggested outline answer** to check your ideas against can be found in the online resources that accompany the book.

Further reading

Numerous books, articles and case notes have been written on the liability of public bodies. For a relatively up-to-date critique of the inconsistency of the law in this area, Stephen Bailey's article is good, in particular as it questions whether civil claims in negligence are the best place to deal with many of these issues, though care should be taken not to get too bogged down in public law issues. Many of the others are useful for the historical context and analysis they provide, or comment on specific cases.

Bailey, Stephen 'Public Authority Liability in Negligence: The Continued Search for Coherence' (2006) 26 LS 155

Conaghan, Joanne 'Law, Harm and Redress: A Feminist Perspective' (2002) 22 LS 319

Cornford, Tom 'The Negligence Liability of Public Authorities for Omissions' [2019] CLJ 545

du Bois, Francois 'Human Rights and the Tort Liability of Public Bodies' (2011) 127 LQR 589

Fairgrieve, Duncan 'Pushing Back the Boundaries of Public Authority Liability: Tort Law Enters the Classroom' [2002] PL 288

Fairgrieve, Duncan 'Suing the Military: The Justiciability of Damages Claims Against the Armed Forces' [2014] CLJ 18

Gearty, Conor '*Osman* Unravels' (2002) 65 MLR 87

Giliker, Paula '*Osman* and Police Immunity in the English Law of Torts' (2000) 20 LS 372

Hartshorne, John, Nicolas Smith and Rosemaire Everton '"*Caparo* under Fire": A Study into the Effects Upon the Fire Service of Liability in Negligence' (2000) 63 MLR 502

Horsey, Kirsty 'Trust in the Police? Police Negligence, Invisible Immunity and Disadvantaged Claimants' in Janice Richardson and Erika Rackley (eds) *Feminist Perspectives on Tort Law* (Routledge, 2012)

Horsey, Kirsty and Erika Rackley 'Tort Law' in Rosemary Auchmuty (ed) *Great Debates on Law and Gender* (Palgrave, 2018)

Law Commission *Administrative Redress: Public Bodies and the Citizen* (Law Com No 322, 2010)

McBride, Nicholas '*Michael* and the Future of Tort Law' (2016) 32 PN 14

McIvor, Claire 'The Positive Duty of the Police to Protect Life' (2008) 24 PN 27

McIvor, Claire 'Getting Defensive About Police Negligence: The *Hill* Principle, the Human Rights Act 1998 and the House of Lords' [2010] CLJ 133

Palmer, Phil (2011) 'Can the Police ever be Liable for Negligent Investigation or a Failure to Protect?' (2011) 1 IJPLAP 100

Steele, Iain 'Negligence Liability for Failing to Prevent Crime: The Human Rights Dimension' [2008] CLJ 239

Steele, Jenny '(Dis)owning the Convention in the Law of Torts' in James Lee (ed) *From House of Lords to Supreme Court* (Hart, 2010)

Tofaris, Stelios, 'Duty of Care in Negligence: A Return to Orthodoxy?' [2016] CLJ 454

Tofaris, Stelios and Sandy Steel, 'Negligence Liability for Omissions and the Police' [2016] CLJ 128

Wright, Jane '"Immunity" No More: Child Abuse Cases and Public Authority Liability in Negligence after *D v East Berkshire Community Health NHS Trust*' (2004) 20 PN 58

7 Special duty problems: economic loss

Problem question

Read this problem question carefully, and keep it in mind while you are working through the chapter that follows. At the end of the chapter, you will be able to apply what you have learnt to the problem question and advise the relevant parties.

Rachael and Chris invested £600,000 in Read-Sing-Sign, a children's charity bookshop, after speaking to Amanda, a personal friend who is also an auditor. Amanda had prepared a financial report for the trustees of the shop, but showed it to Rachael and Chris 'off the record'. This showed that the bookshop was doing well and made good annual profits. It later transpired that the audit was inaccurate as Amanda failed to include some unpaid debts in the figures. The shop was in fact worthless.

Meanwhile, Rachael, who was relying on a £200,000 inheritance from her grandfather in order to be able to pay for her share of the shop, was told by the solicitors dealing with her grandfather's will that it is invalid and the terms of his previous will, which left everything to a local cats' home, would have to be followed. This is because he failed to sign both copies of the latest version of the will. The solicitor's copy was filed without checking the signature was present.

Advise Rachael and Chris as to the likelihood of success of any claims in negligence that they may take.

7.1 Introduction

Consider the following situations:

→ ***A driver negligently crashes his car in the Dartford Tunnel, blocking both lanes. As a result, a ten-mile tailback develops. Caught in this tailback are:***

(a) ***Guy, a businessman, hurrying to close a lucrative contract for his company;***

(b) ***Vicki, trying to get to the sales early to buy a cheap 4K TV, one of only 25 available;***

(c) ***Benny, who needs to get to work on time or his wages will be docked.***

→ ***In the same accident, another driver is seriously injured and is unable to work for a year.***

→ ***A council workman negligently cuts a power cable supplying a factory. The factory has to shut for two days, losing profit as a result.***

→ ***A financial advisor negligently advises a client to invest in a company, which later goes bankrupt, causing the client to lose his investment.***

→ ***A builder negligently constructs the foundations of a house. When new owners move in the walls start cracking, causing the house's value to decrease.***

→ ***A man buys a washing machine and, after only a week, it malfunctions, flooding his kitchen and ruining the flooring. It cannot be fixed.***

Many of the losses we encounter when looking at negligence (and tort law more generally) are 'economic'. Even some non-economic losses may *appear* financial in nature because the way tort law 'fixes' many of the harms caused by negligence is to pay compensation. Because money is usually the answer, there is a tendency to view all harms economically, asking 'how much is that worth?'[1]

In this chapter, we are concerned with losses that are truly *only* economic in nature—so-called 'pure' economic losses. These differ from 'consequential' economic losses, where financial loss is suffered as a secondary consequence of another harm, such as personal injury or property damage. The tort of negligence distinguishes between these, using duty of care as a device to control whether and when claimants will be able to recover their pure economic losses. It is difficult, as we shall see, to establish a duty in respect of pure economic loss, even if that loss is indisputably caused by the defendant's negligence. Like psychiatric harm, pure economic loss is a harm that negligence does not easily recognise. One reason for this is that liability for such losses is often regarded as better dealt with elsewhere, such as in contract law or the 'economic torts'.[2]

This chapter considers when and how the courts have found that a duty of care should be owed by defendants when the harm caused by them is purely economic. As we will see, this depends on the *type* of negligence that the harm originates from; this distinction stems from the complicated history of liability in this area. Pure economic loss is, generally speaking, recoverable if it stems from carelessly made statements or advice in the context of certain relationships in which there is an 'assumption of responsibility', but not when it results from what has been termed a careless 'activity'.[3]

1. See e.g. **Figure 21.1** in **section 21.3.1**.
2. These torts rely on a defendant's intention, rather than carelessness, and are not covered in this book.
3. There is also a difference between advice and 'information', as recently confirmed by the Court of Appeal in *Manchester Building Society* v *Grant Thornton UK LLP* [2019].

7.2 What is 'pure' economic loss?

The starting point is to decide whether a financial loss is 'pure' economic loss. Financial losses caused by negligence can generally be split, initially, into two categories: pecuniary (related to money) and non-pecuniary (i.e. loss not susceptible to precise arithmetical calculation, including pain, suffering, mental distress and so on). A further distinction can be made between pecuniary losses that are consequent on another type of harm having occurred (e.g. lost earnings after being injured in an accident or the cost of repairing a car after someone has crashed into it) and those financial losses that are 'pure'—that is, *not* consequent on any other type of harm. The categorisation of some losses as 'purely' economic is best understood as a judicial construction designed to distinguish between different types of economic loss in order to prevent (or limit) recovery (see **Figure 7.1**).

FIGURE 7.1 Types of loss in negligence

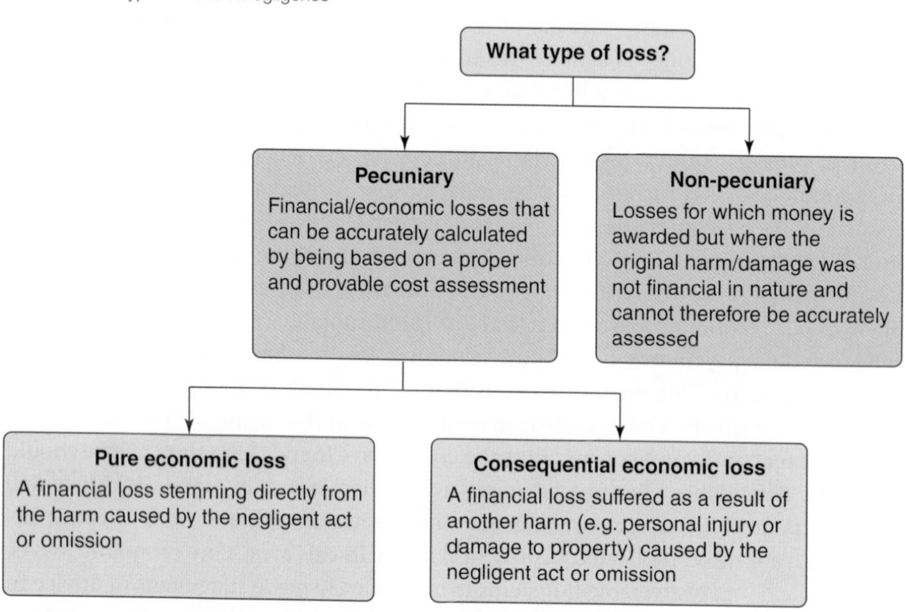

The difference between pure and other types of economic loss is illustrated well by ***Spartan Steel & Alloys Ltd* v *Martin & Co (Contractors) Ltd*** [1973].

Spartan Steel & Alloys Ltd v *Martin & Co (Contractors) Ltd* [1973] CA

While digging up a road the defendant contractors negligently cut an electricity cable supplying power to the claimant's factory, leaving it without power for 14 hours. In this time the factory owners could not operate their steel furnace. There was a possibility that the molten steel

→

→

inside the furnace (the 'melt') would solidify and cause damage; the 'melt' had to be poured away and the factory closed. The factory owners claimed damages under three heads:

(1) the damage to the steel in the furnace at the time of the power cut, which had to be thrown away;
(2) the loss of profit that could have been made by selling the steel in the furnace; and
(3) the anticipated lost profit on other steel that would have been processed during the period the factory was closed.

A majority of the Court of Appeal allowed recovery for the first two heads of damage but found that the third, the *anticipated* profit, was not recoverable.

The first loss was straightforward physical damage to property, which poses few problems to recovery in tort. The second was consequential economic loss (the lost profit was directly consequent on the damaged property). The third, however, was regarded as a pure economic loss (although a result of the negligence it was not consequent on any damage to property) in respect of which no duty of care arose.

Spartan Steel shows that a duty of care is owed only in respect of financial losses relating to damage directly caused by the defendant's negligence. This includes any additional financial losses (e.g. lost profit) that are incurred as a *direct* result of the damage. However, lost profits which are not a direct result of the defendant's negligence are deemed to be 'purely economic', attracting no duty.[4] On this view, the losses incurred by Guy, Vicki and Benny in the scenarios at the start of the chapter are pure economic losses, whereas the loss of earnings suffered by the driver injured in the accident in the tunnel would be consequential upon his injuries and, therefore, recoverable.

Pause for reflection

Would the outcome of *Spartan Steel* have been any different if the cable supplying the electricity had been owned *by the factory*?

It appears so. Had the factory owned the cable then damage caused by the contractors would be recoverable property damage, making all the other losses 'consequential', including the lost profit on the steel that could not be processed while the factory was closed.

Do you think that such a relatively small factual difference (the ownership of the cable) should have such a significant effect on the amount of damages recoverable?

The ownership idea seems to be supported by *Leigh and Sillavan Ltd* v *Aliakmon Ltd (The Aliakmon)* [1986]. The claimants were purchasers of steel coils negligently damaged in transit

→

4. See also *D Pride & Partners (A Firm)* v *Institute for Animal Health* [2009] where it was found that no duty of care was owed to livestock farmers who sustained pure economic losses as a result of a negligently caused outbreak of foot and mouth disease which resulted in the establishment of control zones and a ban on exports designed to prevent the spread of the disease.

→

while being shipped on *The Aliakmon*. They had neither legal nor possessory title until after the goods had been paid for so were deemed unable to recover for the economic loss suffered. Explaining the extent of the exclusionary rule, Lord Brandon said:

> in order to enable a person to claim in negligence for loss caused to him by reason of loss of or damage to property, he must have had either the legal ownership of or a possessory title to the property concerned at the time when the loss or damage occurred. (at 809)

In *The Aliakmon*, the claimants argued that they had *equitable* ownership of the goods despite not having legal title and that equitable ownership should be enough to enable them to bring an action for damage to the cargo. Lord Brandon rejected that submission because the legal owner had not been joined as party to the action.

In *Shell UK Ltd and others* v *Total UK Ltd and others* [2010] (part of the litigation following the explosions at the Buncefield oil storage depot in 2005), Shell claimed damages for economic losses it suffered because two oil pipelines it used—but did not own—were damaged. This caused it to lose money on aviation fuel it normally delivered to major airports, as well as fuel it usually sent out in tankers. The Court of Appeal distinguished *The Aliakmon* because Shell had a *beneficial* interest in the damaged property, so could claim for economic losses provided they joined the legal owners as parties to the action:

> [A] duty of care is owed to a beneficial owner of property (just as much as to a legal owner of property) by a defendant, such as Total, who can reasonably foresee that his negligent actions will damage that property. If, therefore, such property is, in breach of duty, damaged by the defendant, that defendant will be liable not merely for the physical loss of that property but also for the foreseeable consequences of that loss, such as the extra expenditure to which the beneficial owner is put or the loss of profit which he incurs. Provided that the beneficial owner can join the legal owner in the proceedings, it does not matter that the beneficial owner is not himself in possession of the property. (at 142)[5]

In ***Spartan Steel,*** Lord Denning MR articulated various policy considerations that precluded recovery of damages for the anticipated lost profits, not least the fact that power failures were a fact of life:

> This is a hazard which we all run. It may be due to a short circuit, to a flash of lightning, to a tree falling on the wires, to an accidental cutting of the cable, or even to the negligence of someone or other. And when it does happen, it affects a multitude of persons: not as a rule by way of physical damage to them or their property, but by putting them to inconvenience, and sometimes to economic loss. The supply is usually restored in a few hours, so the economic loss is not very large. Such a hazard is regarded by most people as a thing they must put up with—without seeking compensation from anyone. Some there are who install a stand-by system. Others seek refuge by taking out an insurance policy against breakdown in

5. An appeal to the Supreme Court was scheduled for 2011 but the parties settled out of court instead.

> the supply. But most people are content to take the risk on themselves. When the supply is cut off, they do not go running round to their solicitor. They do not try to find out whether it was anyone's fault. They just put up with it. They try to make up the economic loss by doing more work next day. This is a healthy attitude which the law should encourage. (at 38)

He went on to say that if such claims were allowed, inflated claims might be made for lost profits that were simply not provable and for which the level of mitigation attempted could not be established. He was also conscious of the burden of 'crushing liability':

> [T]he risk of economic loss should be suffered by the whole community who suffer the losses ... rather than on the one pair of shoulders, that is, on the contractor on whom the total of them, all added together, might be very heavy. (at 39)

It seems then, that policy considerations lie behind the courts' continued reliance on an exclusionary rule in relation to pure economic loss, including the fear that allowing such claims would lead to a flood of further claims of that nature. This, in turn, could lead to what is known as 'crushing liability', where one defendant, from one careless act, ends up being substantially liable to numerous claimants.[6]

Consider again the first scenario outlined at the start of the chapter. While the negligent driver of the car would clearly owe a duty of care to other drivers not to cause them physical harm or property damage (and would also be liable for any financial losses consequent on those harms, such as loss of earnings or the cost of repairs), if he was found to owe a duty in respect of pure economic losses, he would have to compensate anyone in the tailback behind him who suffered an economic loss of any kind. Thus, if Guy failed to make his meeting and secure his lucrative contract, the driver would be liable for the sum that he expected to make. Similarly, if Vicki failed to make it to the shop before closing time, she would have to be compensated for the difference in price between the sale TV and the usual price.

This argument—often referred to as a 'floodgates' argument—is grounded in the assumption that it is better to prevent *all* claims by denying a duty than to allow a 'flood' of claims. Moreover, it is generally accepted that a role of the law in a market economy is to shape and develop the framework in which the market should operate with maximum efficiency and one way this is achieved is by preventing claims for pure economic losses.[7]

Counterpoint

Edmund Davies LJ, dissenting in ***Spartan Steel***, saw the central question differently:

> Where a defendant who owes a duty of care to the plaintiff breaches that duty and, as both a *direct* and a *reasonably foreseeable* result of that injury, the plaintiff suffers only economic loss, is he entitled to recover damages for that loss? (at 39, emphasis added)

→

6. Though this does not always preclude recovery. In relation to the Buncefield oil depot explosions referred to earlier (*Shell UK Ltd and others* v *Total UK Ltd and others* [2010]), it was estimated that Total would be liable for compensation running to over £600 million (see Chris Green 'Final Cost of Buncefield Fire could hit £1bn' *The Independent* 12 December 2008).

7. See e.g. Stapleton 1991.

→

He sought guidance from a similar earlier case: *Cattle* v *Stockton Waterworks Co* [1875]. In *Cattle*, the defendant's pipes had leaked, causing delay to the construction of the claimant's tunnel, which in turn delayed and caused the claimant a loss of profit on his construction contract. Blackburn J refused to allow the claimant's recovery, but his judgment was interpreted by Edmund Davies LJ as turning on the specific facts of the case and not ruling out recovery for direct and foreseeable economic losses in the future. The facts of ***Spartan Steel***, he suggested, were different. It was clearly foreseeable that if the power supply is negligently disrupted, surrounding factories would be *directly* affected and would suffer foreseeable loss. Put simply, it is inevitable that cutting an electricity supply to a factory will cause the owners to lose money. As such, it is not clear to us, as it was not to Edmund Davies LJ, why this foreseeable loss should, as a matter of course, be unrecoverable.

This formulation would arguably put enough restriction on the ability to recover economic loss. Not all losses will be foreseeable to a party at the time of the negligent act.[8] Thus, rather than saying outright that there is no duty owed in relation to pure economic loss, issues related to crushing liability could be dealt with by saying that the loss suffered was unforeseeable (as acknowledged by Lord Denning MR at 36). Again, consider the Dartford Tunnel scenario at the start of the chapter. While it is clearly foreseeable that people caught in the traffic jam would suffer delays and even that their cars may then overheat and break down (causing foreseeable economic loss if they have to have the cars towed away and repaired), Guy's particular loss is not foreseeable—it would not be foreseeable that a particular person in the ensuing tailback would fail to make a lucrative business contract.

In ***Spartan Steel*** Lord Denning MR's public policy considerations seem to have won the day. For him, at the heart of the case lay the failure of the factory owners to insure against loss. However, it is not at all obvious which of the two companies in ***Spartan Steel***—the factory or the construction company which, presumably, could be held to foresee the consequences of its (admitted) negligence[9]—was in a better position to insure against such losses.

Pause for reflection

In *Canadian National Railway Co v Norsk Pacific Steamship Co (The Norsk)* [1992], a claim was allowed for 'relational' economic loss when a ship was negligently steered into and damaged a railway bridge owned by a third party. The claimant rail company, which had a contractual licence to use the bridge, lost profits as a result. The claim was allowed on the basis that operations of the claimant and the bridge owner were 'closely allied' (i.e. they both wanted to use the bridge for the same thing (to make profits) and each needed the other to do so).

This case is distinguishable from ***Spartan Steel*** on the ground that there was no close alliance between the interests of the factory owners and the defendant. Do you agree? Couldn't the same be said of the factory and the electricity company? Moreover, even if this distinction can be sustained—should it make a difference to the outcome of the case?

8. Which is when foreseeability is assessed, see **section 9.3.1**.
9. The alternative policy argument that imposing a duty to compensate for foreseeable economic loss might act as a deterrent and encourage workers to take more care at work was rejected.

Another reason for the courts' reluctance to extend a duty of care to pure financial losses is that these are more traditionally and readily dealt with by contract law. Accordingly, if people want to protect their economic interests, they should use contracts to do so.[10] In ***Spartan Steel*** the factory owners were prevented from being able to claim damages from the electricity company for its failure to supply power by an exclusion clause in the contract. Had they been able to recover in tort, this contractual limitation would have been circumvented and, in so doing, the benefits and extent of the contract would have been called into question—something the court was extremely reluctant to encourage.

7.3 Exceptions to the exclusionary rule: *Hedley Byrne v Heller*

Although there is a *general* rule against recovery of pure economic losses, as we have already seen with the exclusionary rules operating in relation to other aspects of the duty of care in negligence, such a rule does not prevent *all* recovery: there are some limited exceptions, which stem primarily from ***Hedley Byrne* v *Heller* [1963]**. This is an important case in both contract and tort law. It introduced the tort of 'negligent misstatement' into law and set out guidelines as to when and how it would operate.[11]

Hedley Byrne & Co Ltd v *Heller and Partners* [1963] HL

Hedley Byrne, an advertising agency, was asked to buy some advertising space for a company called Easipower Ltd. To ensure that Easipower could pay for this service, Hedley Byrne decided to credit check the company. Hedley Byrne's bank twice contacted Easipower's bank, Heller, to ask if the company was creditworthy, and both times was told that it was. The second check asked specifically whether Easipower was 'trustworthy, in the way of business, to the extent of £100,000 per annum'. On the basis of Heller's positive responses, Hedley Byrne contracted with Easipower and bought advertising space for them for £17,000. Easipower

→

10. In the washing machine example at the start of the chapter, although the cost of replacing the washing machine itself would be considered pure economic loss in tort, it would in fact be recoverable under contract if it was the *machine* that was faulty—a distinction we encounter when looking at product liability in **Chapter 12**.

11. ***Hedley Byrne*** was decided at a time when only 'fraudulent' and 'innocent' misrepresentations were legally recognised—in the context of making a statement that induced someone to enter into a contract. Because fraud required proof on the part of the claimant, few cases were successful. But, at the same time, often there was something more than wholesome innocence on the part of the statement-maker. In ***Hedley Byrne***, Lord Denning referred back to his dissenting judgment in the Court of Appeal case of *Candler* v *Crane Christmas & Co* [1951], where he had found that a duty of care could be owed by accountants preparing accounts knowing that the figures they provided would be *relied* upon by potential investors. In ***Hedley Byrne***, he used this to 'create' a new tort of negligent misstatement, increasing the categories of potential claim for misrepresentation in contractual situations by including negligence for the first time. (This was followed shortly afterwards by a statutory form of negligent misrepresentation in the Misrepresentation Act 1967.) It also enabled claims to be made in three-party situations, where a misstatement is made by A to B, which induces B to enter a contract with C (rather than with A).

→

later collapsed, and Hedley Byrne sought to claim back the £17,000 from Heller on the basis that they had been negligent when preparing the statement about the creditworthiness of Easipower.

However, when issuing its statements, Heller had included a disclaimer saying that each was prepared 'without responsibility on the part of this Bank or its officials'; a clause excluding their liability, should it arise. The House of Lords held that in view of this disclaimer, no liability could arise on the facts of this particular case.

However, the law lords also considered what the position would be had there been no disclaimer. On this, their lordships found (*obiter*) that a duty of care could arise in some situations where advice was given, even where the only harm caused was what would otherwise be regarded as 'pure' economic loss. But, they said, this was limited to situations where the following four conditions were met:

(1) a special (or 'fiduciary') relationship of trust and confidence exists between the parties; and
(2) the party preparing the advice/information has voluntarily assumed the risk (express or implied); and
(3) there has been reliance on the advice/information by the other party; and
(4) such reliance was reasonable in the circumstances.

On the facts of ***Hedley Byrne***, had there not been a disclaimer attached to the information given, Heller would have owed a duty of care and would have been liable for Hedley Byrne's losses.[12]

The ***Hedley Byrne*** principles continue to form the basis of any duty of care that can be owed in relation to pure economic loss when such loss is based on reliance on a *statement* of some kind.[13] Put another way, it is only where these principles can be applied that an exception to the general exclusionary rule will be made.

But what about economic losses caused by what someone has done—that is, by the 'activity' of the defendant? After ***Hedley Byrne*** and until ***Caparo Industries plc* v *Dickman* [1990]**, there was a period of significant expansion of liability for pure economic loss. During this period recovery extended beyond losses caused by misstatements (i.e. poor advice) to include 'activity'-related losses (e.g. loss of value caused when the walls of a house crack due to the negligent construction (an activity) of the foundations). This particular expansion was curtailed by the House of Lords in ***Murphy* v**

12. Thus, it seems that the financial advisor in the scenarios outlined at the beginning of this chapter would be liable, as long as the four ***Hedley Byrne*** conditions are met, and there was no disclaimer in his contract of service.

13. And since the Supreme Court decision in *Jones* v *Kaney* [2011], this principle has been extended to expert witnesses in court paid for by a client to give evidence on their behalf—in this case it was a medical expert—who were until this point immune from suit. Note, however, that there is a distinction between 'advice' and mere 'information' provided by the defendant, as illustrated by *BPE Solicitors and another* v *Hughes-Holland (in substitution for Gabriel) (Rev 1)* [2017]. In that case, Lord Sumption defined 'information' cases as those in which 'a professional adviser contributes a limited part of the material on which his client will rely in deciding whether to enter into a prospective transaction' (at [41]).

Brentwood District Council [1991], which closed the door on claims for pure economic loss relating to defective products or buildings.

We can now generalise about when and on what basis recovery will be possible for pure economic loss: there is a difference between statement-based losses and activity-based losses. Recovery is allowed for the first, subject to the ***Hedley Byrne*** criteria, but not the second. Put another way, the criteria *only* apply where the claimant's pure economic loss has been caused by what the defendant has *said* (rather than what they have done), and only then within the context of a fiduciary relationship, an assumption of responsibility and reliance. However, as we shall see, the distinction between what is 'said' and what is 'done'—between statements and activities—is not always an easy one to draw and is an even harder one to maintain.

Pause for reflection

Does it make sense to draw a distinction about *how* an economic loss was caused? Why prioritise economic losses that are caused by what someone else *said*, but not what they *did*?

7.4 Claims for pure economic loss in negligence before *Murphy*

Broadly speaking, until ***Murphy*** there were three 'phases' of judicial development of the duty of care for pure economic loss, which can be roughly summarised, as in **Table 7.1**.

TABLE 7.1 Claims for pure economic loss before ***Murphy***

Phase 1	Pre-1963 (*Hedley Byrne*)	No recovery of pure economic loss in negligence[14]
Phase 2	*Hedley Byrne–Junior Books* v *Veitchi* 1963–83	Period of expansion of the type of situation for which pure economic loss was recoverable, following expansion of duty in negligence more generally and of the *Hedley Byrne* principles
Phase 3	Post-*Junior Books* 1983–90	Closing down of the exceptions: a retreat from a more generous position regarding pure economic loss, culminating in *Caparo* and *Murphy*

Indirectly, ***Hedley Byrne*** opened the door to recovery for other types of pure economic loss claim (i.e. those not based on statements).[15] This coincided with a more general relaxation of the duty of care concept in the tort of negligence as a whole.[16] In particular, the courts

14. See e.g. *Cattle* v *Stockton Waterworks* [1875].

15. See e.g. *Weller & Co* v *Foot and Mouth Disease Research Institute* [1966], a case concerned with lost profit after negligence caused the closure of local cattle markets. Undoubtedly this case—though ultimately unsuccessful—was brought in the wake of ***Hedley Byrne*** to test the extent of the relaxation.

16. See **section 2.2**.

began to allow claims for what could be described as economic losses based on defective products (which for these purposes included buildings, each being based on the activity of production). In *Dutton* v *Bognor Regis Building Co Ltd* [1972], for example, the purchaser of a house successfully sued a local authority for carelessly approving the foundations, which turned out to be insecure, rendering his house physically defective with badly cracked walls.[17] Pre-***Hedley Byrne***, entering the contract to buy the house would have been seen merely as a 'bad bargain' (the house was simply worth less than was paid for it) and the purchaser would have had no remedy for the economic loss suffered as a result: the cost of repairing the walls. Post-***Hedley Byrne***, in a changed climate, it may have been in the court's mind that the local authority had assumed the risk of its building approvals (which were made pursuant to statutory powers) and that the buyer had been entitled to rely on this. Whatever the reason, *Dutton* seemed to call into question whether any distinction could continue to be drawn between defects in property and pure economic losses.

Anns v *Merton London Borough Council* [1978] HL

The claimant alleged that the local authority had negligently failed to supervise the construction of a building, with the result that cracks appeared in the walls, caused by sinking foundations.

In the House of Lords, Lord Wilberforce classified this as 'material physical damage' (as opposed to pure economic loss) meaning that damages for the cost of repairs were recoverable.

Following ***Anns***, the distinction between material physical damage and pure economic loss seemed to have been lost entirely. This became even more apparent in ***Junior Books Ltd* v *Veitchi Co Ltd*** [1983].

Junior Books Ltd v *Veitchi Co Ltd* [1983] HL

A claim was made by the owners of land in relation to a factory under construction. The building company contracted to build the factory was instructed by the claimant to subcontract the defendant, a specialist flooring company, to lay a floor designed to support heavy machinery. The floor was laid negligently and had to be rebuilt. While this was done the factory had to be closed and the claimants lost profits. As the landowners had no contract with the subcontractors (they only had one with the building company), they sued them in negligence.

The House of Lords allowed the claim in negligence for the pure economic loss (cost of relaying the floor and lost profits),[18] categorising the claim as one where the supply of a defective product (the floor) caused economic loss. They found, drawing on *Hedley Byrne*, that Veitchi, which had special skill, had 'assumed responsibility' for the condition of the floor and the claimants had relied upon this.[19]

17. Arguably, granting of approval falls somewhere between statements/advice and activity.

18. Their lordships based their decision on Lord Wilberforce's two-stage duty test from ***Anns***, see **section 3.2**.

19. Although note the dissent of Lord Brandon, who argued that the type of liability being found in this case was one that should only be recoverable in contract.

Not only did confusion ensue from these decisions but, by the late 1980s, the social and economic climate had once again changed and, in simplistic terms, the courts were looking for a way to 'rein in' the situations in which a duty of care in negligence could be owed—in all contentious areas, not only in relation to pure economic loss.[20]

The first indication of this change of approach came in *D & F Estates Ltd* v *Church Commissioners for England and others* [1989]. The claimants sought damages for the cost of repairing defective plastering on the walls of a flat they had purchased 15 years previously, which was part of a building owned by the defendants. The plastering had been done negligently by a plasterer subcontracted by the co-defendant building firm. At first instance, following *Dutton* and ***Anns***, the claimants won. Reversing the decision, the Court of Appeal held that the builders owed a duty only to employ competent subcontractors and on the facts this duty had not been breached. The House of Lords agreed, finding also that, in any case, the cost of repairing the defective plaster was not a recoverable loss in negligence. It was distinguishable from defective foundations in that it was simply a defect in the product (the flat) itself and could cause no further direct harm. The first seeds of doubt about the correctness of ***Anns*** were sown,[21] paving the way for the decision in ***Murphy***.

Murphy v *Brentwood District Council* [1991] HL

Mr Murphy purchased a semi-detached house in Brentwood, which had been built by a company called ABC Homes. Over ten years later, serious cracks started appearing in the walls. These were found to be caused by a defect in the foundations, the design of which had been approved by the district council. The defect made the house structurally unsound and worth £35,000 less than Mr Murphy had paid. At first instance the judge found that the council had owed and breached a duty of care in relation to its buildings approvals.

The House of Lords decided otherwise, also taking the opportunity to reflect on the correctness of *Anns*. They held that the damage in *Anns* (and therefore in *Murphy*) should properly be considered pure economic loss and *not* a form of material physical damage. They found that faulty foundations cause no loss or damage, other than a financial loss, unless they are

→

20. It seems now that the ***Junior Books*** decision is confined to its own facts and will therefore not be resurrected or followed in future cases (see e.g. *Muirhead* v *Industrial Tanks Specialties* [1985]; *Greater Nottingham Co-operative Society* v *Cementation Piling Ltd* [1989]; *Losinjska Plovidba* v *Transco Overseas Ltd (The Orjula)* [1995]). In fact, Burnton LJ said that 'the decision of the House of Lords in ***Anns*** v ***Merton LBC***, like its ... decision in ***Junior Books Ltd*** v ***Veitchi Co Ltd* [1983]**, must now be regarded as aberrant, indeed as heretical' (*Robinson* v *PE Jones (Contractors) Ltd* [2011] at [92]).

21. Interestingly, the High Court of Australia had by this time already declined to follow ***Anns*** in *Sutherland Shire Council* v *Heyman* [1985]. New Zealand still allows claims from home owners for defective inspections, etc that cause economic loss (*Invercargill City Council* v *Hamlin* [1994], confirmed by the New Zealand Supreme Court in *North Shore City Council* v *Body Corporate* [2010]). The ***Junior Books*** decision was also called into question in *D & F Estates*, particularly by Lord Bridge, who preferred the dissenting opinion of Lord Brandon, and who stated there was such a 'unique scope of the duty of care owed by the defender to the pursuer arising from that relationship that the decision cannot be regarded as laying down any principle of general application in the law of tort' (at 19).

→

dangerous or cause further physical damage to the 'fabric of the house' by subsidence or collapsing walls—it is merely the cost of repairing the foundations that is at issue. This, in their view, was pure economic loss for which no duty should be owed. Thus, in ***Murphy*** the House of Lords overturned ***Anns*** on this point.[22]

Counterpoint

Much of the reasoning in ***Murphy*** focused on whether a house could be considered a 'complex structure'. Complex structures are those where each part of a whole can be treated as individual pieces of property. This means that if one part is defective (which would be classified as pure economic loss) but *causes damage to another part* (damage to property), the cost of rectification will be recoverable. This is particularly helpful in the context of product liability. If a faulty component causes damage to another component or to the product itself, recovery is possible for the damaged component but not for the cost of replacing the original faulty component (see **Chapter 12**).

The application of the 'complex structure' theory was rejected in ***Murphy***:[23]

> to apply the complex structure theory to a house so that each part of the entire structure is treated as a separate piece of property is unrealistic. A builder who builds a house from foundations upwards is creating a single integrated unit of which the individual components are interdependent. To treat the foundations as a piece of property separate from the walls or the floors is a wholly artificial exercise. If the foundations are inadequate the whole house is affected. (Lord Jauncey at 497)

Lunney, Nolan & Oliphant suggest that this argument in itself poses difficulties when translated to other products. They ask whether:

> purchaser[s] of a bottle of wine whose contents were ruined by a defective cork suffer property damage (because one item of property, the cork, had damaged another, the wine) or pure economic loss (because one single composite item of property, the bottle of wine, had damaged itself)?[24]

→

22. One reason for this, in addition to the general closing down of the scope of liability in negligence, was the passage of the Defective Premises Act 1972, which had not been considered in ***Anns***. Section 1 imposes obligations on builders of domestic premises in respect of the quality and fitness of their work, which exist for a period of six years after construction is complete. In ***Murphy***, Lord Bridge argued that '[i]t would be remarkable to find that similar obligations … applicable to buildings of every kind and subject to no such exclusions or limitations as are imposed by the Act of 1972, could be derived from the builder's common law duty of care' (at 480–1).

23. This rejection has been confirmed in cases since, including *Bellefield Computer Services Ltd* v *E Turner and Sons Ltd* [2000].

24. At p 404.

→

Realistically, of course, even if it was the wine manufacturer who was negligent, one could take a bottle of wine back to the retailer, who would be obliged, having sold a product not of 'satisfactory quality', to provide either a refund or a replacement. This is not true of houses. It may be that, given the extent of the potential loss, houses *should* be viewed as complex structures. Perhaps the real problem here is that many of the claims we have seen in relation to houses and other properties were against public authorities—meaning that courts would be less likely to want to find liability.[25]

The period from ***Hedley Byrne*** to ***Murphy*** was clearly a turbulent time in relation to pure economic loss, with a number of important House of Lords' decisions relating to the scope and content of the duty of care. This reached a 'high point' with ***Anns*** and ***Junior Books***, which was later retreated from in *D & F Estates* and ***Murphy***.

7.5 Extending *Hedley Byrne*

Post-***Murphy***, the only way to claim in negligence for pure economic loss is to rely on the four principles established in ***Hedley Byrne***.[26] However, these principles have themselves been applied in ways which seem to be *extensions* of the way they were first formulated. This is particularly notable given the policy reasons elucidated for not recognising claims for pure economic loss in the first place, and the 'closing down' of liability for economic loss described in the previous section. We turn next to where these principles have (and have not) been applied.

7.5.1 A special relationship

In ***Hedley Byrne*** Lord Reid envisaged that a special (or fiduciary) relationship—a relationship of trust and confidence—would arise where it was clear that:

> the party seeking information or advice was trusting the other to exercise such a degree of care as the circumstances required, where it was reasonable for him to do that, and where the other gave the information or advice when he knew that the inquirer was relying on him. (at 486)

From this definition it is apparent that the four ***Hedley Byrne*** principles in fact overlap, as the reliance and assumption of risk elements are clearly both *part* of what makes a special relationship in the first place. The question of whether it 'was reasonable for him to do that' seems to mean that this type of relationship ought only to arise in a business/

25. See further **Chapter 6**. 26. See **section 7.3**.

commercial context.[27] Therefore, if we were to advise you here to invest your money in a certain company's shares, no such special relationship could arise in which we would owe you a duty of care in respect of pure economic loss suffered by you even in reliance on our advice.

Pause for reflection

see online resources

The limitation of the 'special relationship' to business contexts seems appropriate given the closeness of economic loss claims in negligence to contractual claims. Where people are seeking to promote their business interests (and it is someone's job to assist in this, when asked) is there any good reason why that person should not be liable for any negligent advice they give, when they are being asked to give it for that very reason?

Why, in *Hedley Byrne*, did the claimants not sue for breach of contract?

An example of the type of special relationship required to be able to sue for economic loss can be seen in ***Esso Petroleum Co Ltd* v *Mardon*** [1976].

Esso Petroleum Co Ltd v *Mardon* [1976] CA

An employee of Esso, whose job it was to assess the potential output of petrol stations, advised Mr Mardon, who was thinking of leasing a petrol station, that the station in question would sell at least 200,000 gallons of petrol per year. Mr Mardon entered the lease in reliance on this advice, but sold only 78,000 gallons in the first 15 months of trading. The advice of the Esso employee (for whom Esso would be vicariously liable) was found to be negligent. The question was whether a duty of care could be owed to Mr Mardon in respect of the loss he had suffered, which was purely economic.

The Court of Appeal held that the required special relationship had been created because, in making the statement, Esso's employee had assumed a responsibility to Mr Mardon based on his expertise in assessing the market for petrol sales, and Mr Mardon had reasonably relied on this. Therefore, a duty of care was owed.

The principle has also been extended to cover an auctioneer's advice to potential bidders (*Thomson* v *Christie Manson & Woods Ltd* [2005]) and an environmental health officer's assessment of premises (*Welton* v *North Cornwall District Council* [1997]).

27. Though cf *Chaudry* v *Prabhaker* [1989] where the claimant relied on the advice of a friend who 'had a lot to do with motor cars' to find her a used car. He negligently found and recommended her to buy a car that had been in an accident, rendering it worthless. By a majority, the Court of Appeal agreed that he owed the claimant a duty of care in respect of her economic loss. Presumably this was because she had asked him to act as her agent, bringing this closer to a business arrangement and away from a purely domestic one.

7.5.2 Voluntary assumption of risk

It is a reasonable extension of the special relationship idea that where such a relationship exists, any party giving advice, without a disclaimer, can be said to have assumed the risk that the statement they make is reliable. If they did not want to assume the risk, they could, as in ***Hedley Byrne*** itself, attempt to exclude their liability.[28]

In *Goodwill* v *British Pregnancy Advisory Service* [1996], the defendants negligently advised the claimant's partner that his vasectomy had been successful. The claimant relied on this information and stopped using other methods of contraception, subsequently falling pregnant and giving birth to a child. The claim was for the costs associated with bringing up the child. While agreeing that the relationship in which the advice was given could be regarded as one of 'trust and confidence', the Court of Appeal was unwilling to find that the risks of making the statement negligently had been assumed (and particularly not to the man's partner, who only entered a relationship with him after he had already had the vasectomy). Because of this, the court found, the claimant was not entitled to have relied on the advice given and no duty of care was owed.

Counterpoint

In recent years the courts have more generally, in a range of different circumstances, found against claimants who claim for the costs associated with bringing up an unwanted child (both in negligence and in relation to defective contraceptive products).[29] In the tort of negligence, one way this has been achieved is by constructing the parents' claim as a pure economic loss.

Do you think that such costs—such as feeding and clothing the child—are *purely* economic? Could the cost of raising a child which was born because of someone else's negligent advice or action be classified as *consequential* economic loss? Consider *McFarlane* v *Tayside Health Board* [1999] which had similar facts to *Goodwill* except that the claimants were a married couple who already had four children and were trying to avoid having another precisely *because* they could not afford the costs of bringing up a fifth child. The McFarlanes were also denied recovery. Alongside categorising their loss as purely economic, the parents' harm (having a healthy—albeit unwanted—child) was said to be unrecognised in law:

> The law must take the birth of a normal, healthy baby to be a blessing, not a detriment ... It would be repugnant to [society's] own sense of value to do otherwise. It would be morally offensive to regard a normal, healthy baby as more trouble and expense than it is worth. (Lord Millett at 1347)

The decision in *McFarlane* has been subjected to significant academic and judicial criticism.[30] It should now be read in light of the later House of Lords' decisions in *Parkinson* v *St James &*

→

28. This would be, in the context of professional negligence, subject to the Unfair Contract Terms Act 1977, s 2, thus any disclaimer could be struck out of the contract if its terms were deemed unreasonable by a court or if the negligence resulted in personal injury or death.

29. Previous cases of this nature had been successful, e.g. *Emeh* v *Chelsea and Kensington AHA* [1985] and *Thake* v *Maurice* [1986].

30. Though its core policy was recently confirmed in *ARB* v *IVF Hammersmith* [2018].

Seacroft University Hospital NHS Trust [2001] (in which damages were awarded only for the *additional* costs of bringing up an unwanted child who was disabled) and *Rees* v *Darlington Memorial Hospital NHS Trust* [2003]. In *Rees*, while not allowing recovery of the costs of raising an unplanned yet healthy child (born to a disabled mother), the law lords (by a slim 4:3 majority) controversially reconceptualised the harm suffered by the mother as damage to her autonomy for which there should be a 'conventional award', despite this idea having been raised and rejected in *McFarlane*. The award was set at £15,000.

see online resources

The modern test for determining assumption of responsibility was outlined by the House of Lords in *Henderson* v *Merrett Syndicates Ltd* [1995], a case involving a number of claims by investors (known as 'Names') who, in syndicates, had underwritten insurance policies for Lloyds. They suffered substantial losses when numerous insurance claims were made against Lloyds in the early 1990s, and alleged that the agents who had set out the syndication of the Names had been negligent in doing so. Their lordships found that the agents had assumed responsibility for the financial affairs of the Names, despite there being no statement or advice that this was based on:[31]

> [T]here is no problem in cases of this kind about liability for pure economic loss; for if a person assumes responsibility to another in the respect of certain services, there is no reason why he should not be liable in damages in respect of economic loss which flows from the negligent performance of those services. (Lord Goff at 238)

An interesting example of the principle in action is found in *Lennon* v *Commissioner of Police of the Metropolis* [2004]. In this case a police officer was negligently advised by a personnel officer about the impact on the terms of his employment contract of transferring from one police force to another, resulting in him permanently losing his housing entitlement. The Court of Appeal found that it was well established that liability for pure economic loss could arise where there was an express voluntary assumption of responsibility on which the claimant had relied. In this case, the personnel officer had expressly assumed responsibility for the claimant's transfer and for giving advice in relation to the housing allowance and had led him to believe that he could rely on her to handle the arrangements; a duty therefore arose in respect of the economic loss he suffered.[32]

The assumption of responsibility principle was revisited by the House of Lords in ***Customs & Excise Commissioners* v *Barclays Bank*** [2006].

31. The House of Lords also confirmed in this case that when there are concurrent obligations in contract and tort, the claimant can choose which one to sue in (though not if the contract expressly provides that liability may be contractual only: see *Robinson* v *PE Jones (Contractors) Ltd* [2011]).

32. Similar points were made in respect of a claim about a pension fund in *Gorham* v *British Telecommunications plc* [2000].

Customs & Excise Commissioners v *Barclays Bank* [2006] HL

Customs officers obtained 'freezing orders' on the bank accounts of two companies which were in debt with regards their tax payments. This meant that the bank (Barclays) was legally obliged not to let any payments leave the companies' bank accounts. However, Barclays negligently allowed some withdrawals to be made. Customs & Excise sought to recover this money by suing Barclays in negligence, alleging that this was recoverable economic loss. They contended that, once a freezing order had been received, a bank assumed responsibility for the loss that would be suffered if money was allowed to leave the frozen accounts.

The House of Lords ruled that there had been *no* assumption of responsibility in the required sense, because it could not truly be said that the responsibility assumed was *voluntary* where the bank was obliged by law to accept the freezing order, therefore the claim failed.

In ***Barclays Bank***, the reasoning of the law lords suggested that the 'assumption of responsibility' concept is an imprecise tool with which to determine liability for pure economic loss.[33] Rather than being a blunt concept that is either present or not in any given case, it will need to be interpreted flexibly and in accordance with the precise facts and policy considerations in each case:[34] 'although it may be decisive in many situations, the presence or absence of a voluntary assumption of responsibility does not necessarily provide the answer in all cases' (Lord Rodger at [20]).

Thus it would have seemed that the concept, though retained by the House of Lords, would be able to be more loosely relied upon in the future, or sidestepped where policy considerations are deemed to override it.[35] In *Sebry* v *Companies House* [2015], a slightly novel twist arose. Here, an employee at Companies House erroneously altered the status of a company to show that it had gone into liquidation. As a result, many of its creditors

33. Though Lord Hoffmann continued to believe the existence of a voluntary assumption of risk is 'critical' when establishing a duty of care in respect of economic loss (at [14]) and Lord Mance defined it as 'a core area of liability' (at [28]). Compare Lord Bingham, who thought it was a 'sufficient but not necessary condition' (at [4]). *Lunney, Nolan & Oliphant* suggest that 'the role of assumption of responsibility seems to be a means of satisfying the three-stage test [***Caparo***], but not the only means' (p 452). In *Sebry* v *Companies House* [2015], Edis J said that the assumption of responsibility and three-stage tests overlap, and followed the approach of Lord Bingham in ***Barclays Bank*** (at [107]), though noting later that the tests could give different answers. All this should now be read in light of comments in ***Robinson* v *Chief Constable of West Yorkshire* [2018]** and ***Poole Borough Council* v *GN* [2019]**, which suggest that no general test was laid down in ***Caparo*** (see **section 3.3.2**).

34. Similar points were made about the three-stage duty test from ***Caparo*** (by Lord Walker at [25], Lord Hoffmann at [14] and Lord Bingham at [7]). As we shall see, both the wider impact of ***Caparo*** (used to incrementally extend the disputed categories of duty) and its narrower *ratio* have been taken into account in economic loss claims. See also *Cramaso LLP* v *Ogilvie-Grant, Earl of Seafield and others (Scotland)* [2014].

35. Compare *Williams and Reid* v *Natural Life Health Foods Ltd and Mistlin* [1998] and *West Bromwich Albion Football Club Ltd* v *Al-Safty* [2006]. Seemingly it matters who makes the statement, in what context and which party is deemed best able to bear the loss. Also see *James-Bowen and others* v *Commissioner of Police for the Metropolis (Rev 1)* [2016], where a claim for economic loss based on assumption of responsibility was rejected, but the overall claim was not struck out as it was deemed potentially arguable on normal common law duty of care principles (at [50]–[52]).

withdrew, and it ended up in administration, suffering a loss of £9 million. Edis J found that Companies House had assumed responsibility towards—and therefore owed a duty to—the company (to maintain accurate records), though this duty did not extend to anyone else, for example creditors or potential investors.

Similarly, in *Banca Nazionale del Lavoro SPA* v *Playboy Club London Ltd* [2018], Playboy asked a company, Burlington, to obtain a credit reference from his bank for a man gambling at the club who required more funds. Burlington asked the bank about the man's finances, without mention of Playboy. The bank confirmed that the man held an account there and was trustworthy for up to £1.6 million per week. Relying on the bank's reference, Playboy granted the man a cheque-cashing facility of £1.25 million. After accumulating net winnings of £427,400 the man returned home to Lebanon. His (fraudulent) cheques were returned unpaid; it transpired that the bank had opened his account two days after providing the reference. The account was closed shortly afterwards, having never held any funds. The Supreme Court found that Playboy had not been entitled to rely on the reference; the duty of care owed by the bank was only owed to the addressee (Burlington) and there was no assumption of responsibility to Playboy, of whom it was unaware.[36]

The importance of an assumption of responsibility should not therefore be understated. In *Steel and another* v *NRAM Ltd (formerly NRAM plc) (Scotland)* [2018], a solicitor negligently prepared a statement in respect of the sale of a commercial property, which was sent by email to the opposite party, who later suffered substantial financial loss. One issue was whether she had assumed responsibility for the truth of her statement. Lord Wilson cited with approval the finding of Lord Steyn in *Williams* v *Natural Life Health Foods Ltd* [1998] 'there [is] no better rationalisation for liability in tort for negligent misrepresentation than the concept of an assumption of responsibility' (at 837), adding that '[i]t has therefore become clear that, although it may require cautious incremental development in order to fit cases to which it does not readily apply, this concept remains the foundation of the liability' (at [24]). The Supreme Court found that it was not generally the case that a solicitor would assume such a responsibility towards the other side, 'unless it was reasonable for the latter to have relied on what the solicitor said and unless the solicitor should reasonably have foreseen that he would do so' (at [32]).

7.5.3 Reasonable reliance

Whether the claimant can be said to have relied on a statement or advice is also important in providing an exception to the general exclusionary rule. As already indicated, the idea of reliance overlaps with the other ***Hedley Byrne*** principles. For example, it is often precisely *because* a 'special relationship' exists that one party will rely on the other's advice, particularly when this is given in a professional context (as in ***Esso* v *Mardon***).

The nature of the reliance, coupled with the fourth principle from ***Hedley Byrne***—that the reliance must be reasonable in the circumstances—is important. In ***Caparo*** (a case perhaps better known for statements on whether a duty of care exists at all in contentious cases),[37] for example, it was held that the reliance was not reasonable, given the context in which the statement had been made.

36. Interestingly, though the Playboy Club failed with its negligence claim, it was later allowed to reframe the claim in the tort of deceit in the light of new evidence: see *Playboy Club London Ltd* v *Banca Nazionale Del Lavoro Spa* [2018].

37. See **section 3.3**.

Caparo Industries plc v _Dickman_ [1990] HL

Caparo was considering a takeover bid of another company, Fidelity. In pursuance of this, Caparo looked at information prepared by Fidelity's auditors, which it received because it already held a number of shares in Fidelity. This information showed that Fidelity was doing well and, in reliance on this audit, Caparo launched its takeover bid only to find later that Fidelity was almost completely worthless. Caparo sued, alleging negligence in the preparation of the audit.

The House of Lords found that no duty of care was owed in respect of the economic loss caused by Caparo's reliance on the information provided. This was because it was not reasonable for Caparo to have relied on this information when preparing its takeover bid of Fidelity. Company audits were an annual requirement for businesses under the Companies Act 1985, and the information within them was provided for shareholders; not for potential investors as this would include a class of persons of an indeterminate size.[38] Thus, in Caparo's capacity as a shareholder of Fidelity, the information could be relied upon, but in its capacity as a potential investor, it could not be.

In ***Caparo***, because the reliance on the information was not *reasonable*, no special relationship could arise between the two companies. Lord Bridge clarified this position further, saying that there would be a difference where:

> the defendant giving advice or information was fully aware of the nature of the transaction which the plaintiff had in contemplation, knew that the advice or information would be communicated to him directly or indirectly and knew that it was very likely that the plaintiff would rely on that advice or information in deciding whether or not to engage in the transaction in contemplation. (at 620–1)

He explained that because audit information under the Companies Act 1985 is put into 'more or less general circulation', it could foreseeably be relied on by anyone for any purpose and those preparing the audit should not owe a duty to anyone and everyone who relied on it. Put another way, the provision of information for one particular purpose should not (or cannot) *reasonably* be relied on for any other purpose, not least because there is no assumption of risk in respect of any alternative purpose for which the information is used. A similar idea was used to deny the existence of a duty of care to a fisherman in *Reeman* v *Department of Transport* [1997], when the certificate of seaworthiness that had been issued for his boat turned out to have been negligently written. The boat in fact was almost worthless. The Court of Appeal, following ***Caparo***, held that such certificates were issued to enhance maritime safety, not to establish the commercial value of boats, so should not have been relied on in this way.[39]

38. Therefore, finding the accountants liable would set a precedent potentially exposing accountants and auditors to vast sums in damages. The decision is clearly policy-based, designed to avoid opening the 'floodgates' of liability, perceived knock-on consequences of which would be inflated prices of accountancy services more generally and therefore a deleterious effect on all business transactions in society.

39. Also see *Marc Rich & Co* v *Bishop Rock Marine Co Ltd* [1995].

In *Steel and another* v *NRAM Ltd (formerly NRAM plc) (Scotland)* [2018], the claim ultimately failed because it was not reasonable for the defendant to have relied on the solicitor's statement. In a situation where a statement is provided by a solicitor for the other party, and could be easily checked, 'it is not reasonable for the representee to rely on the representation without checking its accuracy and ... it is, by contrast, reasonable for the representor not to foresee that he would do so' (at [38]).

Pause for reflection

Do you think the distinction drawn in ***Caparo*** is valid? If, as an existing shareholder in Fidelity, Caparo would have been entitled to rely on the information provided in relation to the investment they already had, why should they not also be able to rely on it in relation to any further investment they might be considering making? If the idea was to curtail the situations in which a duty of care might arise—and this certainly was one of the aims of the House of Lords, given the climate of the time—then to say that the duty would arise only in the context of existing shareholders—but not *prospective* shareholders—would still have this effect, with the exception that Caparo itself would have been owed a duty of care.

In contrast to ***Caparo***, in *Law Society* v *KPMG Peat Marwick* [2000], the claimants sued when the defendants—the accountants for a firm of solicitors—failed to discover that a senior partner was siphoning off money and defrauding many of the firm's clients. When the fraud was discovered, more than 300 of the firm's clients claimed compensation from the Law Society, via a no-fault compensation fund established for this very purpose. Trying to recover its economic loss, the Law Society sued the accountants, saying they had been negligent in preparing the firm's annual accounts. Relying on ***Caparo***, the accountants contended that their duty was only to the solicitors' firm and not to anyone else who relied on the accounts prepared for them for any other purpose. However, the Law Society argued that the duty extended as far as them, as law firms had to have their accounts prepared annually for the benefit of the Law Society, and it was known by the accountants involved that the society would rely on the information provided. The Court of Appeal agreed, holding that because the accountants knew the purpose for which such accounts were prepared, and because it was foreseeable that failure to correctly prepare accounts would lead to claims being made against the fund, it was appropriate to impose a duty.

A decision was reached on similar grounds in ***Smith* v *Eric S Bush*** [1990].

***Smith* v *Eric S Bush* [1990] HL**

The claimant purchased a house, relying on a survey of the property prepared by the defendants. The survey had been carried out negligently and the house was in fact worth much less than was paid for it. The survey, as is normal practice, had been commissioned by the building

→

→

society with which the claimants had taken out their mortgage—the principal purpose of such a survey is to satisfy the building society that the value of the house being purchased is at least that of the amount of money being lent.

The House of Lords held that although a contract exists only between the mortgage lender and surveyor, surveyors would owe a duty of care to the buyer, as they would be aware that the buyer would rely on the information provided by them, and it would be reasonable for buyers to do so.

Part of the reasoning in ***Smith*** is that it is commonly understood that surveys provided primarily for mortgage lenders are often relied on by homebuyers as well. While it is possible for buyers to commission their own detailed structural survey, this is more expensive, so many purchasers simply rely on the survey carried out by the mortgage lender, especially as it is actually the buyer who has to pay for this survey to be conducted. In ***Smith*** this fact was particularly important—the court recognised that Mrs Smith was making one of the most important purchases of her life and, as she was not wealthy, was fully entitled to rely on the valuation provided for the mortgage lender.[40] In ***Smith***, the surveyors had used a disclaimer which, as in ***Hedley Byrne***, would ordinarily prevent a duty of care from arising. However, the disclaimer used in ***Smith*** was rendered ineffective by the Unfair Contract Terms Act 1977.[41] In contrast, in *Scullion* v *Bank of Scotland plc (trading as Colleys)* [2011], the Court of Appeal considered whether a duty of care was owed by a valuer to the purchaser of buy-to-let property, rather than to a homebuyer. Lord Neuberger MR distinguished ***Smith*** on exactly that basis: that in *Scullion* the property was an investment.

Counterpoint

It is interesting to consider how the notion of *assumption of responsibility* works in *Smith*. It does not seem to us that it can be said that the surveyors assumed responsibility for the accuracy of the information they were providing *to Mrs Smith*. Furthermore, the disclaimer that was included, though falling foul of contract legislation, surely at least points to the fact that no responsibility had *actually* been assumed (as in *Hedley Byrne*).[42]

40. It was probably helpful that her case is distinct from ***Caparo*** on another ground: that it was only she who would be relying on the information, meaning there was no wider class of people about which to be concerned.

41. In a consumer context such as this, the relevant legislation would now be the Consumer Rights Act 2015.

42. It was this that precluded liability for a statement on a website in *Patchett* v *Swimming Pool & Allied Trades Association Ltd* [2009]. While the Court of Appeal found that online representations could in theory give rise to a duty of care, it also found that the website in question made clear that its information should not be solely relied upon.

7.6 Beyond *Hedley Byrne*: the 'will cases' and a more flexible approach

Despite the idea behind ***Caparo***, and the cases that followed, being to limit the situations in which a duty of care arises in relation to pure economic loss, some later decisions appeared to have expanded this area of liability once again, into areas which could be defined as relating to the provision of services rather than the making of a statement or the giving of advice. This expansion started with what have become colloquially known as the 'will cases' but, as we shall see, the principle has been further extended to other services.

The first of the so-called will cases was *Ross* v *Caunters* [1980]. A solicitor negligently drew up a will for his client, so much so that the will ran contrary to the law on probate and the intended beneficiary (the claimant) was unable to inherit. The claimant's loss, however, was purely economic—in fact it may be better described as a failure to make an anticipated gain, more commonly encountered in contract law.[43] Furthermore, rather than this being a case where 'advice' was given in the form of a *statement*, this was a negligent *action* or *service*. Notwithstanding this difference, the claimant won and was able to recover the sum she had lost (or not gained) from the negligent solicitor.

Ross v *Caunters* was not considered particularly significant at the time of its judgment. In 1980, as indicated earlier, negligence liability was in a period of expansion, with the courts willing to find duties of care in new situations following the formula laid out in ***Anns***. *Ross* becomes more significant because it was later followed in cases that came *after* this period of expansion had been closed down (following ***Murphy*** and ***Caparo***), when any successful claim for pure economic loss had to, in theory, be based on the four ***Hedley Byrne*** principles (and so therefore relate to statements, advice or similar). The first case to do this was ***White* v *Jones*** [1995].

White v *Jones* [1995] HL

Two sisters were cut out of their father's will following an argument. Later, the rift in the relationship between the sisters and their father was mended and the father instructed his solicitor to redraft the will, including an inheritance of £9,000 for each daughter. When, after a month, he discovered that this had not yet been done, he reissued his instruction. After his death, it was found that the will had not been changed and the daughters sued the solicitor.

The House of Lords found in the claimants' favour, awarding them the economic loss they had suffered as a result of the solicitor's negligence.

43. The claimant had no contract with the solicitor and due to the restrictive laws on privity of contract in operation at the time would have been entirely unable to sue in contract. The principle of privity of contract is that only the parties to a contract have any rights or obligations under it, thus only they can sue or be sued. After 1999, a claimant in a similar position to the woman in *Ross* v *Caunters* may be able to circumvent the privity rule, as the Contracts (Rights of Third Parties) Act 1999 allows parties outside a contract to sue if they were an intended beneficiary of the contract and were identified as such in the terms of the contract itself.

Considering that the principles from ***Hedley Byrne*** supposedly formed the only basis for recovery of economic losses at the time ***White*** was decided, it is difficult to see how this case fits. In ***White***, a *service* was provided and the loss caused to the claimants came as a result of negligent provision of that service rather than as a statement made in the context of a special relationship where the risk of its accuracy was assumed and relied upon. Moreover, though solicitors in the provision of will-drafting services clearly have a special relationship (of trust and confidence) with *their clients*, it would seem to raise the risk of a conflict of interest if this relationship also extended to the intended beneficiaries of wills. The decision truly marks a more flexible approach to the ***Hedley Byrne*** principles.[44] Similar claims have, however, been denied where it appears that the interests of the testator and beneficiaries differ (i.e. where there is an *actual* conflict of interest). It is only where these interests are identical that the ***White*** exception comes into play (see e.g. *Clarke* v *Bruce Lance & Co* [1988]).

Pause for reflection

Do you think the House of Lords was swayed by the need to do 'justice' in *White*? Failures in the context of service provision are certainly more familiar territory in contract law. The problem was that the only party in the contract with the solicitor (the father, or more accurately his estate) had suffered no loss as a result of the breach of contract/negligence. The claimants, who *had* suffered loss, were not parties to the contract. Outside a contractual relationship, to be able to sue in negligence the defendant must owe the claimant a duty of care and the 'rules' on pure economic loss in negligence at this time would not have allowed such a duty to arise. In reality the House of Lords in *White*, by extending the *Hedley Byrne* principles, created such a duty. Do you think they did the right thing?

The situation is analogous to *Hedley Byrne* itself. Why shouldn't a solicitor be liable for negligently failing to do what they ought to have done (e.g. by not acting on an instruction)? Furthermore, arguably the solicitor's firm is more likely to be able to absorb the losses than those affected by the negligence, who might be people of 'modest means'. Lord Goff referred to this when he spoke of the unfairness that he felt would come from not providing the claimants a remedy:

> The injustice of denying such a remedy is reinforced if one considers the importance of legacies in a society which recognises ... the right of citizens to leave their assets to whom they please, and in which, as a result, legacies can be of great importance to individual citizens, providing very often the only opportunity for a citizen to acquire a significant capital sum; or to inherit a house, so providing a secure roof over the heads of himself and his family; or to make special provision for his or her old age. (at 260)

In other cases, courts have been keen to stress the importance of insurance. Here, a solicitors' firm could clearly insure against losses of this nature, whereas those who benefit from a will would not be able to do so, often because they will not know that they were supposed to benefit until it is too late.

44. Indeed, in his dissenting judgment, Lord Mustill says that the extended duty found by the majority went 'far beyond anything so far contemplated by the law of negligence' (at 291).

Counterpoint

White is a case where the law lords seemed to have decided the outcome they wanted to achieve before embarking on their judgment. In order to do so, and to address what Lord Goff referred to as a 'lacuna in the law which needs to be filled' (at 260), they extended the ***Hedley Byrne*** principles. Unfortunately, the result is not a perfect fit. The hardest to reconcile are the principles of 'assumption of risk' and 'reliance': it can clearly be said that solicitors preparing wills assume some kind of responsibility to their clients (to do the job properly), but not to the intended beneficiaries (some of whom might not even know they were due to inherit and so cannot be said to rely on the fiduciary nature of the relationship). Acknowledging this, Lord Goff stated:

> [T]here is great difficulty in holding, on ordinary principles, that the solicitor has assumed any responsibility towards an intended beneficiary under a will which he has undertaken to prepare on behalf of his client but which, through his negligence, has failed to take effect in accordance with his client's instructions. The relevant work is plainly performed by the solicitor for his client; but, in the absence of special circumstances, it cannot be said to have been undertaken for the intended beneficiary. Certainly, again in the absence of special circumstances, there will have been no reliance by the intended beneficiary on the exercise by the solicitor of due care and skill; indeed, the intended beneficiary may not even have been aware that the solicitor was engaged on such a task, or that his position might be affected. (at 262)

Lord Browne-Wilkinson circumvented this problem by stating that when a solicitor takes on the drafting of a will, they accept responsibility (and therefore all the risks attached) for doing this properly. The *scope* of the responsibility was for the law to decide and that was what the House of Lords had done in extending the duty to the intended beneficiaries, according to the principles of ***Caparo***, which he said demanded that:

> the law will develop novel categories of negligence 'incrementally and by analogy with established categories.' In my judgment, this is a case where such development should take place since there is a close analogy with existing categories of special relationship giving rise to a duty of care to prevent economic loss. (at 275)

Seen in this sense, ***White*** is not an extension of principle but remains firmly based on the existing principles established in ***Hedley Byrne***. Lord Goff, on the other hand, held that responsibility was factually assumed only to the father but that the law should extend this duty implicitly to the claimants (at 268). Either way, as we have indicated, this seems to be the result of a desire to do practical justice for the claimants, who would otherwise have no means of recovery. It also prevents solicitors 'getting away with negligence', in the sense that they can now be sued by those parties who would actually suffer the loss as a result.

The principle from ***White*** was further extended in ***Carr-Glynn* v *Frearsons* [1999]**. In this case, a woman instructed her solicitors to prepare a will in which the claimant was bequeathed a share in some property. The solicitors advised the woman that her will might be ineffective, as the way the property was owned meant that her share of it might automatically pass to the co-owners when she died. However, they also advised her how this situation could be avoided, but she died before this could be done. As a result, the claimant lost out on the property share that was meant to pass under the will and, in contrast to *Ross* and ***White***, the woman's estate *also* suffered a loss, as the property share was lost. The Court of Appeal held that although the estate had suffered a loss and a claim would therefore be able to be made in this respect, if this happened, the estate would receive the damages. This would *then* amount to a situation similar to that which arose in ***White***—where the intended beneficiary lost out and had no way of seeking a remedy, but in the long term the estate would suffer no loss. On that basis, a duty was found to be owed to the claimant by the solicitor, who should have done what was necessary to make sure the will would operate as required.

Pause for reflection

While it might seem like a logical extension to find a duty of care to the beneficiary even where the estate could already claim compensation (as this seems merely an intermediate point in the fact of assessing that the estate would end up suffering no loss, but those who were intended to benefit from a will would do so), do you think the solicitor was *actually* negligent in this case? By framing the duty as 'a duty to make sure the will would work as the testator intended it to', there would clearly be a breach, as this is not what eventually occurred. But given that the solicitor advised the woman what she needed to do, is it simply *bad luck* on the claimant's part that she died before it could be done? Should bad luck be compensated in this way?

In *Esterhuizen* v *Allied Dunbar Assurance plc* [1998], the principle of the will-drafting cases was extended beyond solicitors to other companies offering will-making services. This seems a natural extension of the principle guided by market expansion. It would seem odd that one could sue a solicitor for negligently drafting a will that you expected to benefit under, but not a commercial company that does essentially the same job. Similarly, in *Gorham* v *British Telecommunications plc* [2000], the Court of Appeal held that the widow of a man who had been advised to switch pension schemes could sue for the economic loss she suffered when the benefits of the pension could not be transferred to her on the death of her husband. He had opted out of his employer's pension scheme on the negligent advice of an insurance company. Had he not done so, insurance benefits would have been paid to his family upon his death. Instead, these were lost when he transferred the pension to the new provider. In awarding his widow damages for the economic loss suffered, the Court of Appeal drew analogies with wills, finding that the pension advisor had assumed the risk of his advice, which would be relied on, to the family as well as his client.

Beyond wills, the ***Hedley Byrne*** principles were extended in ***Spring* v *Guardian Assurance* [1995]** to cover the writing of references (perhaps more obviously a statement—albeit of a different type). In this case, Lord Goff clearly outlined the House of Lords' position on pure economic loss, finding that recovery should not be confined to cases based on statements or advice but could include the provision of a service, where there had been the appropriate assumption of responsibility and reliance (at 318).

Spring v *Guardian Assurance* [1995] HL

Spring had worked for the defendant company but had been made redundant. He sought a reference when he was trying to find new employment with a different company. The reference provided stated that he was dishonest and incompetent and, as a result, Spring was not employed. He sued the defendants in negligence for the economic losses caused to him by not getting the new job.

At trial it was found that although the employer genuinely believed in the truth of the reference it had prepared, it had reached these conclusions wrongly and was therefore negligent. A duty of care to take care in providing accurate references was owed. The House of Lords agreed that this duty had been owed and that it had been breached.

Notably, unlike in ***Hedley Byrne*** and ***White***, the claimant was not the person the statement (in the reference) was made to or prepared for—he was the person the statement was *about*.[45] This seems to indicate that the ***Hedley Byrne*** principles can operate in a slightly different direction. The other components of 'assumption of responsibility' and 'reasonable reliance' are apparent in this type of situation; only the relationship is different. Arguably, however, a comparable relationship of trust and confidence exists when a past employer is asked to provide a reference.

Counterpoint

It was argued in *Spring* that the claim was essentially one about damage to the claimant's reputation and would therefore be better suited to defamation (**Chapter 17**). The defendants argued that to allow a claim in negligence (as well as or instead of a claim in defamation) would undermine the rules and limits of the law on defamation. However, it seems to us that where there *is* negligence that causes harm—as happened in *Spring*—there should be no reason that a claim should not be viable as long as there is no potential for double recovery. That is, if a successful claim for damages is made in one area, then a separate claim in the other should be precluded. It seems that in this case the House of Lords merely sought—again—to achieve Lord Goff's 'practical justice'. They perhaps recognised (here and in *White*) that the radical early 1990s 'closing down' of the areas in which a duty of care for economic loss could arise had been too sweeping in its nature.

45. See also the recent case of *Rihan* v *Ernst & Young Global Ltd and others* [2020], which seems to extend the situations in which an employer may be under a duty to protect an employee from pure economic loss.

7.7 Conclusion

The starting point in relation to pure economic losses—those financial losses that are not consequential on another type of loss—was that no recovery can be made for pure economic loss if it was caused by negligence (***Spartan Steel***). Much of the justification for this was based on policy considerations: a fear of indeterminate or 'crushing' liability and that allowing recovery would interfere too much with contract law and the role of insurance. As we have seen, however, the law on pure economic loss came to be defined more by *how* the loss was caused—by a negligent statement or a negligent activity or defective product. Economic loss stemming from activities (e.g. building houses) or defective products (including houses) is not recoverable in the tort of negligence, whereas economic loss arising from negligent statements or services can be, providing certain conditions are met.

In ***Barclays Bank***, the House of Lords suggested that three categories of case now exist in which a claimant may succeed in a claim for pure economic loss. The first exception to the general exclusionary rule can occur where there is a clear analogy to an existing situation that has already been recognised by the courts, as in other types of negligence claim. Secondly, where this is not possible, a claimant following ***Caparo*** may fulfil the test for the incremental expansion of tortious liability into a new area (showing 'proximity', 'foreseeability' and that it would be 'fair, just and reasonable' to impose liability in that situation).

Lastly, there are situations where the claimant can establish that their claim satisfies the four ***Hedley Byrne*** principles. These are based on the special (fiduciary) nature of a relationship in which there is an assumption of responsibility coupled with reasonable reliance. The principles have, however, in more recent years been applied beyond statements to encompass negligent provision of certain services, reflecting a more flexible approach and a willingness on the part of the courts to do practical justice. In adopting this more flexible approach, the courts have relied heavily on the reformulation of the 'assumption of responsibility' test outlined by Lord Goff in *Henderson* v *Merrett*, as adapted by ***Barclays Bank***.

End-of-chapter questions

After reading the chapter carefully, try answering the questions which follow.

1 Is it possible to give a coherent account of the development of the law on pure economic loss in negligence?

2 Jane Stapleton describes the principles on which pure economic loss in negligence can be found to attract a duty of care as 'soft concepts'. Do you agree?

If you would like to know what we think visit the **online resources**. www.oup.com/he/horsey7e

Answering the problem question

Consider again the problem question at the start of this chapter. Now having read about the topic, what would be your advice to the claimants?

Here are some pointers to get you started

- → There is generally no duty of care in cases where the damage is 'pure' economic loss. To establish a duty, you would need to look at the exceptions to this rule, which stem from *Hedley Byrne*.
- → R & C would sue A for their loss caused by her financial audit if their claim falls within the *Hedley Byrne* principles, including a relationship of trust and confidence, assumed responsibility and whether their reliance on the report was reasonable.
- → R would also sue the solicitors. Though there is a negligent act, the question would be whether any duty of care was owed by the solicitors *to R*. *White* v *Jones* may help R here.

If you need some more guidance

see online resources

- → An **annotated version of the problem with issues and cases to consider** can be found in the **Appendix**.
- → A **suggested outline answer** to check your ideas against can be found in the online resources that accompany the book.

Further reading

A good place to start further reading is Paula Giliker's article. Although it discusses Canadian law, it provides useful commentary on the issues outlined in this chapter as well as suggestions for reform.

Barker, Kit 'Wielding Occam's Razor: Pruning Strategies for Economic Loss' (2006) 26 OJLS 289

Giliker, Paula 'Revisiting Pure Economic Loss: Lessons to be Learnt from the Supreme Court of Canada' (2005) 25 LS 49

Hughes, Andrew and Nicolas J McBride '*Hedley Byrne* in the House of Lords: An Interpretation' (1995) 15 LS 376

Quill, Eoin 'Consumer Protection in Respect of Defective Buildings' (2006) 14 Tort L Rev 105

Stapleton, Jane 'Duty of Care and Economic Loss: A Wider Agenda' (1991) 107 LQR 249

8 Breach of duty: the standard of care

Problem question

Read this problem question carefully, and keep it in mind while you are working through the chapter that follows. At the end of the chapter, you will be able to apply what you have learnt to the problem question and advise the relevant parties.

Kate and Iris have spent the afternoon looking at wedding dresses. Before heading home they go to a new champagne bar to celebrate finding 'the one'. Iris offers Kate a lift home in her car, assuring Kate that she's alright to drive as she's 'probably only just over the drink-drive limit'. On the journey home Iris loses control of the car and crashes into a lamp post. Kate suffers minor cuts and bruises and is taken to hospital for a check-up. At the hospital Kate contracts an infection in a cut to her right arm. The doctor on duty decides not to treat the infection with antibiotics immediately as he has recently read a report in a little-known medical journal which suggested that it is better to allow the body 'time to heal' following a trauma. Kate's right arm is partially paralysed.

Advise Kate.

8.1 Introduction

Consider the following examples:

→ *A cricketer hits a ball for six. It flies over the boundary fence hitting a passer-by on the head, causing serious injury.*

→ *A learner driver mistakes the accelerator for the brake and hits a tree, injuring her instructor.*

→ *A stressed junior doctor misreads the instructions on the back of a packet of drugs and injects a patient with 250 ml, rather than 25 ml as stated, paralysing the patient from the neck down.*

There are three vital ingredients of the tort of negligence: duty of care, breach of duty and damage caused by the breach (factual and legal causation). This chapter focuses on the second of these requirements—breach of duty. In each of the previous examples the defendant may have breached their duty of care not to cause the claimant physical injury. In practical terms, breach is an important factor. Many everyday negligence cases turn on issues of breach—was the defendant driving too fast given the particular road conditions? Did the doctor follow the correct procedure or administer the correct drug? Was appropriate safety equipment provided by the employer, and so on?

Breach occurs where the defendant falls below the particular standard of care demanded by the law. Establishing this involves making a value judgement on the defendant's behaviour: 'It cannot be *proved* that a person was negligent; one can merely *argue* that a person was negligent and hope to persuade the judge' (*Cane* p 37). The key issue to be addressed is how and where the courts set the acceptable standard or level of care owed towards one's neighbours. There are two questions to be considered.

(1) How the defendant *ought* to have behaved in the circumstances—what was the required standard of care in these circumstances? This is often described as a matter of law.

(2) How the defendant *did* behave—did they (as a matter of fact) fall below the standard of care required?

As the majority of cases turn largely on the facts at hand—the speed of the car and whether it was appropriate for the time of day, location and so on—it is difficult (although not impossible) to make generalisations about how the defendant *ought* to have behaved, that is where the standard of care will be set. As such, despite its practical importance, arguably there is relatively little to say about breach of duty in negligence—the actual *law* here is relatively limited. The most we can do is identify a few broad and rather open-ended propositions. Indeed, *Weir* argues that 'decisions on breach are not citable as *authorities*; they are merely *illustrations* of the application of the indubitable rule that if one is under a duty at common law such care must be taken as is called for in all the circumstances' (p 57).

However, this only goes so far. While clearly the determination of whether a breach has occurred depends on the particular facts of the case, it is nevertheless possible to identify some broad principles that the courts use when seeking to define the appropriate standard of care, which give some indication as to what the law requires us to do in order to avoid causing harm to others.

Pause for reflection

Some of the most familiar negligence cases—that is the ones most often reported in the media—involve 'freak accidents' during entertainment events or school trips.[1] These have often been followed by calls for a public inquiry (to investigate the cause of the tragedy and

→

1. See e.g. Press Association 'Paralysed teacher loses £5m "welly-wanging" damages claim' *The Guardian* 13 August 2012 (discussing *Cornish Glennroy Blair-Ford* v *CRS Adventures Ltd* [2012]), BBC

→

make recommendations to prevent similar accidents from happening in the future) or a review of health and safety guidelines,[2] as well as claims for compensation.[3] In deciding these claims, the courts seek to strike a balance between ensuring safety and curtailing legitimate activities and/or commercial interests (*Cane* p 40). The balance can be a tricky one:

> Accidents happen, and sometimes they are what can be described as pure accidents in the sense that the victim cannot recover damages for the resulting injury because fault cannot be established. If the law were to set a higher standard of care than that which is reasonable . . . the consequences would quickly become inhibited. There would be no fêtes, no maypole dancing and none of the activities that have come to be associated with the English village green for fear of what might conceivably go wrong. (Scott-Baker LJ, *Cole* v *Davies-Gilbert* at [36])

As you are reading the cases in this and other chapters, consider where you think the line should be drawn.

8.2 A test of reasonableness

The first thing to note about the standard of care in negligence is that it is *not* a standard of perfection. The standard allows for *some* errors and mistakes. As Lord Atkin held in ***Donoghue* v *Stevenson* [1932]**: 'You must take *reasonable care* to avoid acts or omissions which you can *reasonably foresee* would be likely to injure your neighbour' (at 580, emphasis added). The key requirement is that the defendant behaves reasonably. Of course, this simply prompts the question: what is reasonable behaviour? Or, put another way, what standard of care did the circumstances require?

The courts answer this question by comparing what the defendant has done to the imagined actions of the so-called 'reasonable man' and asking what a reasonable man in the position of the defendant would have done in the circumstances, If the defendant has done something that the reasonable man *would not* have done (or has omitted to do

News 'Charlotte Shaw mother loses death claim' 28 June 2012 (discussing *Wilkin-Shaw* v *Fuller & Kingsley School Bideford Enterprises Ltd* [2012]) and BBC News 'Former RAF man wins right to sue MoD over game injury' 2 February 2011 (discussing *Uren* v *Corporate Leisure (UK) Ltd* [2011]); Alexandra Topping 'Parents win appeal over head injury on bouncy castle' *The Guardian* 1 August 2008 (discussing *Perry* v *Harris* [2008]).

2. See e.g. Ragnar E Löfstedt 'Reclaiming Health and Safety for all: a review of progress one year on' January 2013; Ragnar E Löfstedt 'Reclaiming Health and Safety for all: an independent review of health and safety legislation' November 2011; Health and Safety Executive 'School trips and outdoor learning activities: tackling the health and safety myths' 6 June 2011.

3. While one may have a certain amount of sympathy with Tomlinson LJ's observation in *Richards* v *London Borough of Bromley* [2012] that '[i]t needs to be understood that not every misfortune occurring on school premises attracts compensation' (at [15]), school compensation claims are increasingly 'big business'—see e.g. Matthew Davis 'Schools pay £1.5m in compensation cases including £7,500 for a child who had a splinter' *Daily Mirror* 22 August 2015.

something that the reasonable man *would* have done) then they will be in breach of their duty (*Hazell* v *British Transport Commission* [1958] at 171). In short,

> [n]egligence is the omission to do something which the reasonable man, guided upon those considerations which ordinarily regulate the conduct of human affairs, would do, or doing something which a prudent and reasonable man would not do. (Alderson B, *Blyth* v *Birmingham Waterworks* (1856) at 784)

So who is this apparent paragon of virtue against whom all others are to be judged? Over the years various descriptions have been attempted, often involving some mode of transport: the reasonable man is 'the man on the Clapham omnibus' (Greer LJ, *Hall* v *Brooklands Auto-Racing Club* [1933] at 224) or, more recently, a 'traveller on the London underground' (Lord Steyn, *McFarlane* v *Tayside Health Board* [1999] at 82). Rather more grandly, he is 'the anthropomorphic conception of justice' (Lord Radcliffe, *Davis Contractors* v *Fareham Urban District Council* [1956] at 728).

Yet, while it is agreed that the reasonable man is neither all-seeing nor all-knowing and that, on occasions, he makes *reasonable* mistakes, there is less agreement (particularly among feminist legal scholars) about whether these qualities should be tied to the physical characteristics of a *man*. Moreover, it is clear that even if we adopt the more politically correct (if not less contentious) 'reasonable *person*' terminology, questions remain: what is her or his ethnicity, religion, class, sexual orientation, age, education, and so on?

> Is the reasonable person . . . [m]ale or female? Young, middle-aged or old? Christian, Muslim or of some other, or no, religion? Rich, poor or averagely affluent? Perhaps none of these differences between people is relevant, for instance, to questions about how a reasonable person would drive a car, but some or all of them may be thought relevant in some contexts. (*Cane* p 37)

Feminist critiques of the reasonable man

Feminist and other legal scholars have argued that despite claims to gender-neutrality, the standard of the reasonable man in fact embodies a male point of view and as such holds women to a standard devised without them in mind. This criticism goes beyond a dislike of the way the standard is expressed: 'his gender-specificity is not just a linguistic convention, whereby both sexes are denoted by reference to the masculine: the reasonable man is, in fact, male' (Conaghan 1996, p 52).

What does this mean? There are a number of aspects to this critique. One focuses on the fact that the notion of the 'reasonable man' is not based on statistical evidence of what most people actually do think and do. Rather, it is a conception conjured up by the judges themselves embodying a standard set and considered appropriate *by them*. Given the continuing under-representation of women, ethnic minorities and other non-traditional groups within the judiciary, it is likely that the 'reasonable man' reflects the particular perspectives, assumptions and (possibly) prejudices of a subset of society—that is, those (white, middle-class men) who make up the judiciary.

More controversially, it is argued that the standard of reasonableness not only assumes but *prioritises* the ability to adopt a position of detached objectivity from which to weigh up

→

→

the costs and benefits of a particular course of action—an ability traditionally (and, perhaps, essentially) associated with men. Assuming this is true, then the very idea of applying 'a standard of reasonable care' seems to embody a peculiarly *male* way of thinking and to exclude differences in the way women think and act. As such, the problem is not with the language of the reasonable 'man', but with the very notion of 'reasonableness'. On this view, it may well be 'dangerously misleading' to adopt the rebranding of the reasonable person—since it attributes a 'false universality to what is in fact a partial and loaded standard' (Conaghan 1996, p 58).[4]

The truth of the matter is, of course, that there is no such individual as the reasonable man (or indeed person). The reasonable man is a judicial construct—or shorthand—through which the judges seek to determine what was reasonable conduct in the circumstances of the particular case: the reasonable man is the personification of the judicial view of reasonableness. This does not mean, however, that the reasonable man is simply the personification *of the judges themselves*, or a decoy behind which they can and do pursue their own preferences and prejudices.[5] Not least because there is a whole series of rules, developed through the case law, setting out the qualities and conduct—the 'standard of care'—expected of the defendant. It is to these that we now turn.

8.3 **An objective standard**

The first thing to note is that the test of 'what the reasonable man would do in the circumstances of the case' is objective. This means that the standard of care expected of the defendant is not dependent on, or skewed in favour of, certain characteristics and/or capabilities of the defendant; the personal idiosyncrasies of the defendant are largely (although, as we shall see, not completely) irrelevant (*Glasgow Corporation* v *Muir* [1943] at 457). Put simply (except for in a very few, limited, circumstances) the appropriate question is not 'what could *this particular* defendant have done?' but rather 'what level of care and skill did the activity the defendant was undertaking require?' Thus, even though certain individuals may, due to certain inherent characteristics (e.g. experience and so on), be more or less able to take care, the law imposes the same standard of care on everyone.[6] The defendant cannot (usually) argue against, or raise as a defence in response to, the imposition of liability on the grounds that they 'did their best' according to their education, experience, health and so on where their best falls below the standard of care expected of the reasonable man. This is clearly seen in the case of ***Nettleship* v *Weston*** **[1971]**.

4. See also Mayo Moran *Rethinking the Reasonable Person* (OUP, 2003).
5. Although cf *Cane* (p 39) who argues that the reasonable person is invoked in order to obscure the role of the judge as a policy-maker.
6. However, as we will see later, the courts have developed a number of modifications to the general standard, e.g. in relation to children and people professing to have a particular skill.

Nettleship v *Weston* [1971] CA

The claimant had agreed to give the defendant driving lessons. The defendant (the learner driver) was holding the steering wheel and controlling the pedals, while the claimant moved the gear lever and handbrake. Unfortunately, after turning a corner, the defendant failed to straighten the steering wheel and panicked. Despite her best efforts, and the fact that the car was only travelling at walking pace, the car mounted the pavement and hit a lamp post breaking the claimant's knee cap. The defendant was convicted of driving without due care and attention.[7] The claimant sued in negligence.

The majority of the Court of Appeal held that all drivers, *including those learning to drive*, are held to the same standard: 'The standard of care . . . is measured objectively by the care to be expected of an experienced, skilled and careful driver' (at 702). The standard of care in negligence is not dependent on the particular defendant's characteristics and/or capacities. The fact that, as a learner, she was by definition incapable of meeting this standard was irrelevant: 'The learner driver may be doing his best, but his incompetent best is not good enough. He must drive in as good a manner as a driver of skill, experience and care' (at 699). Nevertheless, the claimant's damages were reduced by 50 per cent for contributory negligence as he was jointly controlling the car at the time of the accident.

The decision of the Court of Appeal in ***Nettleship*** is perhaps a little harsh. As a learner driver Mrs Weston was unable to reach the standard of care to which she was ultimately held. Moreover, the claimant was well aware of the defendant's limited driving capabilities—he was in the car *because* he had agreed to give her driving lessons. As Salmon LJ, in dissent, noted, a learner driver cannot owe an instructor a duty to drive with a degree of skill they both know is not possessed (at 705). In taking the opposite view and holding the defendant to an objective standard, the majority sought to avoid the 'endless confusion and injustice' that would follow should the standard of care be varied according to someone's knowledge of another's skill (at 700). By applying the same standard to all drivers, the decision in ***Nettleship*** ensures that victims of road accidents do not lose out simply because they were unlucky enough to be injured by someone who is learning to drive. The alternative is that the innocent victim of a learner driver who had driven as well as could be expected (albeit to a standard somewhat lower than that expected of an experienced driver) would be denied compensation.

Counterpoint

The 'objective standard of care can be understood as the law's attempt to strike a fair balance between the competing interests in freedom of action and personal security that we all share' (*Cane* p 49). But does the decision in ***Nettleship*** strike a 'fair balance' between the parties? Is it fair?

→

7. On the relevance of a criminal conviction on a civil claim see **section 8.6**.

→

The reason we make liability in negligence conditional upon the defendant having failed to exercise reasonable care (rather than, for instance, making liability strict) is the belief that it is only where the defendant is at *fault* (and that fault causes the claimant's injuries) that the law should require the defendant to pay compensation. Corrective justice does not require that we compensate all the harms we cause, only those that we cause through our fault or neglect. The problem with the decision in ***Nettleship*** is that it imposes liability without genuine fault.[8]

The decision in ***Nettleship*** is perhaps better understood as resting on a more pragmatic motivating factor—compulsory motor insurance. The majority judges 'see to it' that the defendant is liable so that the claimant can be compensated out of the insurance fund (at 700). In so doing, the Court of Appeal elevates the function of tort as a mechanism of compensation over that of achieving corrective justice, something that Lord Denning MR clearly recognises:

> Thus we are, in this branch of the law, moving away from the concept: 'No liability without fault'. We are beginning to apply the test: 'On whom should the risk fall?' Morally the learner driver is not at fault; but legally she is liable to be because she is insured and the risk should fall on her. (at 700)

Ultimately, of course, the financial loss falls neither on the claimant nor the defendant but on the defendant's insurance company (and in turn other insurance policy holders). It is more accurate therefore to suggest that in ***Nettleship*** the fault principle is subordinated not only to ensure the claimant is compensated, but also to the loss-shifting goals of distributive justice.

Nevertheless, it is clear that the objective standard of care is not a standard of perfection. In *Birch* v *Paulson* [2012], for example, the defendant was not liable for the serious injuries suffered by a drunk pedestrian who stepped out in front of her car. The Court of Appeal held that:

> [while] it would have been very easy indeed for the defendant, as she approached this man on the kerb, either to have taken her foot off the accelerator or to have steered towards the centre of the road or both . . . the legal test is not a question . . . of perfection using hindsight. Of course it is not, and drivers are not required to give absolute guarantees of safety towards pedestrians. The yardstick is by reference to reasonable care . . . there was nothing here to require the defendant as a reasonably careful driver to act in any way other than a way in which she did act given the situation in which she found herself at the time. (at [32])[9]

The objective standard of care, independent of the characteristics and capacities of the defendant, was taken to an extreme in *Roberts* v *Ramsbottom* [1980]. In this case, the defendant had (unknowingly) suffered a stroke before starting to drive into town. Though he realised his consciousness was impaired, he was unaware that he was unfit

8. The Australian High Court, in a case on very similar facts, refused to follow ***Nettleship*** and described it as 'contrary to common sense and the concept of what is reasonable in the circumstances' (*Cook* v *Cook* [1986]) (though in this case the defendant had fallen below the (lower) standard of care required of a learner driver).

9. See also *Wooldridge* v *George* [2017].

to drive. As he was driving along, he suddenly began to feel much worse. He subsequently collided with a stationary van, narrowly avoided two men working in the road, knocked a cyclist onto the pavement, before ploughing into the claimant's car, seriously injuring the claimant and damaging the car. The defendant argued that from the moment of his stroke he was unable, through no fault of his own, to control his car properly or appreciate that he was unfit to drive. Neill J disagreed. Though the defendant was in no way to blame morally, he was nonetheless liable in the tort of negligence. He had fallen below the objective standard of the reasonable driver in relation to both in his collision with the claimant and also in continuing to drive despite feeling increasingly unwell and following his earlier collision with the parked van, even though he was, at the time, unable to appreciate their significance. It was acknowledged that if he had suffered a complete loss of consciousness he might have had a defence of 'automatism'.

In ***Nettleship*** and *Roberts* v *Ramsbottom* liability in negligence was imposed even though the defendant was not (or may not have been) genuinely at fault. However, the relevance of fault was reasserted in another dangerous driving case a few years later, *Mansfield* v *Weetabix Ltd* [1998], where the Court of Appeal held that the defendant was not liable for the damage caused to a shop (and shop owner's home) when the lorry he was driving crashed into it. Unknown to the defendant, he had a medical condition (malignant insulinoma), which starved his brain of glucose so that it was unable to function properly. The final accident, which formed the basis of the claim, was the culmination of a gradual lowering of his blood sugar level. However, crucially, the court held that at no time had the defendant been aware of his condition, despite the fact that over the course of 40 miles he had been involved in three distinct incidents, one of which involved the police. Of course, if the defendant had been aware of his condition, he would, following *Roberts* v *Ramsbottom*, have been liable. The defendant had not, therefore, fallen below (or breached) the standard of care applied by the court, which was of 'a reasonably competent driver unaware that he is, or may be, suffering from a condition that impairs his ability to drive' (at 1268).

Pause for reflection

Of course, the practical result of *Mansfield* v *Weetabix* is that the claimants whose shop and home had been destroyed were left uncompensated and the pot of insurance money (at least on the side of the defendant) remained untouched. Though they were aware of the harshness of the decision to the claimants, the Court of Appeal judges in *Mansfield*, unlike those in *Nettleship*, were unwilling to find the innocent lorry driver liable simply in order to compensate the claimants—who, after all, had (or should have had) their own *household* insurance. Responsibility for any change in the law, they argued, lay at the feet of Parliament (at 1268). Which approach do you prefer? Why? Think again about the arguments made earlier in relation to *Nettleship*.

As seen in *Mansfield* v *Weetabix*, the courts do, on occasion, modify or vary the objective standard to take into account *certain* characteristics of *some* defendants.[10] Illness is one example; other examples include where the defendant is a child or professes to have a special skill or competence.

8.3.1 Children

In relation to children, the courts acknowledge that the capacity of children to recognise the dangers of a particular activity, take care to avoid them and not hurt others varies according to the age of the child (unlike in criminal law there is no minimum age for liability in tort). The standard of care is still objective, it is simply scaled according to age to that which can be 'objectively expected of a child of that age' (***Orchard* v *Lee* [2009]** at [9]). The question for the court is, in the words of Salmon LJ, 'whether any ordinary child of 13½ [for example] can be expected to have done any more than this child did. I say "any ordinary child". I do not mean a paragon of prudence; nor do I mean a scatter-brained child; but the ordinary girl of 13½' (*Gough* v *Thorne* [1966] at 1387).

Orchard v *Lee* [2009] CA

Two 13-year-old boys were playing a game of tag in a courtyard and walkway designated for their year group during their school lunch break. During the course of the game the defendant was running backwards, taunting the other boy. Unfortunately he ran into the claimant, who was working as a lunchtime assistant supervisor at the school. The back of his head hit her cheek and, though the injury initially seemed insignificant, it later became quite serious. The trial judge dismissed the supervisor's claim finding that 'it was a simple accident caused by "horseplay between two 13-year-old boys in and around an outside court yard . . . boys doing what boys do"' (at [2]).

The Court of Appeal agreed. A child will only be held liable in negligence if their conduct is careless to a very high degree or falls significantly outside the norm for a child of their age. In assessing whether this is the case 'the question is whether a reasonable 13-year-old boy, in the situation that [the defendant] was in, would have anticipated that some significant personal injury would result from his actions' (Aikens LJ at [24]). As there was nothing to suggest that the defendant was playing tag 'in a manner in which a 13-year-old boy would reasonably foresee there was likely to be injury beyond that normally occurring while a game of tag was in progress', the defendant had not fallen below the standard of care required of him (Waller LJ at [12]).

10. However, see *Dunnage* v *Randell* [2015]. The claimant, an undiagnosed paranoid schizophrenic, set himself on fire injuring his nephew (who was attempting to prevent the accident). He was found to have fallen below the standard of care of a reasonable man. Rejecting the application of *Mansfield* v *Weetabix*, the Court of Appeal held that 'unless a defendant can establish that his condition entirely eliminates responsibility . . . he remains vulnerable to liability if he does not meet the objective standard of care. It is the entirety of the elimination which drives this conclusion, and once that entirety is eroded or diminished, he is fixed with the standard. The evidence was that [the claimant's] responsibility came very close to complete elimination, but the experts stopped short of finding that it was complete' (Rafferty LJ at [114]). See further Goudkamp and Ihuoma at pp 138–44 and Maria Orchard 'Liability in Negligence of the Mentally Ill: A Comment on *Dunnage v Randell*' (2016) 45 CLWR 366.

Pause for reflection

As noted in the Australian case of *McHale* v *Watson* (1966), 'Children, like everyone else, must accept as they go about in society the risks from which ordinary care on the part of others will not suffice to save them. One such risk is that boys of 12 may behave as boys of 12' (at 216). Or, indeed, that 15-year-old schoolgirls will 'play as somewhat irresponsible girls of 15' (*Mullin* v *Richards* [1998] at 1312).

The 'reasonable child' standard invoked by the court effectively prevents a child-defendant's action being measured against a standard of care that they are unable to reach. How—if at all—can this be reconciled with the Court of Appeal's decision in ***Nettleship***?

8.3.2 **Common practice and special skills**

Where a person professes to have a special skill or competence, the law requires that when dealing with people in the context of a calling or profession they do so with an appropriate level of competence.

> Nobody expects the passenger on the Clapham omnibus to have any skill as a surgeon, a lawyer, a pilot, or a plumber, unless he is one; but if he professes to be one, then the law requires him to show such a skill as any ordinary member of the profession or calling to which he belongs, or claims to belong, would display.[11]

Thus, in *Phillips* v *William Whiteley* [1938] the court denied a claim for damages in respect of an infection the claimant developed after having her ears pierced in a jewellery store. Ear-piercing is not something which requires a surgical level of skill and so the claimant could expect only that her ears were pierced to the standard of a reasonably competent jeweller, which they had been in this case.[12] In 2019, in *Wright* v *Troy Lucas (a firm) and George Rusz* [2019], Eady J held an unqualified legal advisor to the standards of a professional lawyer: 'I have no hesitation in finding that the defendants should be held to the duty and standard of care that they had chosen to assume when holding themselves out as competent to carry out legal services for the claimant in his clinical negligence litigation' (at [82]). Though the defendant had never described himself as a solicitor, he had held himself out as having 'extensive experience' of these types of claims and as being 'as good as, if not better, than any solicitor or barrister' (at [18]). He was ordered to pay over £260,000 in damages to compensate the claimant for what they were likely to have received had their original claim against the NHS been properly handled (on the advice of Rusz, the claimant had previously settled for £20,000 and incurred £73,000 in legal costs).

8.3.2.1 The *Bolam* test

Typically, a defendant cannot escape liability in negligence simply by arguing that they followed common practice: 'Neglect of duty does not cease by repetition to be neglect

11. *Peel & Goudkamp* p 277.

12. See also e.g. *Wells* v *Cooper* [1958], where a do-it-yourself (DIY) carpenter was not liable for injuries caused by his failure to use adequate screws to fix a door handle. He had not fallen below the standard of care expected of a reasonably competent non-professional carpenter (which was lower than that required of a professional carpenter). See also *Perry* v *Harris* [2008] (discussed in **section 8.4.1**).

of duty' (*Bank of Montreal* v *Dominion Gresham Guarantee and Casualty Company* [1930] at 666). However, there is one important exception to this rule. The courts give wide latitude to professionals, acting in their professional capacity, to determine the standards by which they are to be judged. In cases where the defendant has a special skill or competence (i.e. a skill that the reasonable man ordinarily does not have) and the circumstances are such that they are required to exercise that skill or competence, the courts have developed a different approach. In such cases, the actions of the defendant are judged against those of the ordinary skilled man *professing to exercise that skill*—the so-called ***Bolam*** test.

Bolam v *Friern Hospital Management Committee* [1957] QBD

The claimant was a patient who had been given electro-convulsive therapy without being given a relaxant drug and without the appropriate physical restraints. In the course of the treatment he fractured his hip, a possible consequence of the treatment about which he had not been warned. At the time, the medical profession held conflicting views on whether it was necessary to administer relaxant drugs before the procedure as a way of reducing the likelihood of injury and whether it was necessary to warn the patient of the risk of injury. In assessing the standard of care, the court held:

> a man need not possess the highest expert skill . . . it is sufficient if he exercises the ordinary skill of an ordinary competent man exercising that particular art . . . [and acts] in accordance with a practice accepted as proper by a responsible body of medical men skilled in that particular art. (McNair J at 586)

As such, the defendant was not in breach of his duty, as other responsible doctors would have acted in the same way.

It is clear that ***Bolam*** applies to *all* professionals exercising a special skill or competence. In *Moy* v *Pettman Smith* [2005], a case involving a claim in negligence against a barrister, Baroness Hale approved Lord Hobhouse's view in *Arthur JS Hall & Co* v *Simons* [2002] that:

> the standard of care to be applied in negligence actions against an advocate is the same as that applicable to any other skilled professional who has to work in an environment where decisions and exercises of judgment have to be made in often difficult and time-constrained circumstances. It requires a [claimant] to show that the error was one which no reasonably competent member of the relevant profession would have made. (at [25])

However, a distinction is drawn between the defendant's own 'rank or status' and the 'post' they are occupying at the time of the alleged breach (*Wilsher* v *Essex Area Health Authority* [1987] (CA) at 751). The defendant's conduct is assessed according to the standard reasonably expected of a reasonably competent person occupying such a post. The law makes no allowances for inexperience or for the fact that everyone must, to a certain extent, gain practical experience 'on the job'. Thus in *Wilsher* a junior doctor was held to the standards of the more senior post they were occupying at the time, notwithstanding the fact that this was effectively part of their training: 'the standard is not just that of the averagely competent and well-informed junior houseman (or whatever the position of the doctor) but of such a person who fills a post in a unit offering a highly specialised service' (Mustill LJ at 751).[13]

What this means in practice is that the courts generally defer to the standards of a particular profession as to what is considered appropriate behaviour. This is important: 'judges are not qualified to make professional judgements on the practices of other learned professions . . . A professional should not be penalised, and held to be incompetent, just because a judge fancies "playing" at being architect, solicitor or doctor' (Brazier and Miola 2000, p 87).

Counterpoint

A balance needs to be struck between respect for expert opinions and showing them undue deference.[14] It is argued that the courts have been reluctant to impose liability on members of the medical profession. Traditional justifications for this include: the importance of the doctor's reputation as a member of a respectable and responsible profession, a reluctance to interfere in a specialised branch of knowledge, the view that doctors are motivated by altruistic reasons and that it would therefore be unfair to penalise them for every error and, finally, a fear of increased claims and defensive medical practices (Sheldon 1998, pp 20–1).

In her exploration of the gendered dimensions of the ***Bolam*** principle and its conflation of *accepted* with *acceptable* practice (p 19), Sally Sheldon suggests a number of justifications which point in the opposite direction. These include the need to compensate the victims of medical misadventures, the potential of negligence claims to discourage bad practice and reinforce the accountability of doctors (especially given their high status and remuneration), the current failure to recognise the vulnerability of the patient in the doctor/patient relationship and, crucially, the existence of liability insurance.[15]

Which of these two positions do you find more persuasive?

13. Note: the decision in *Wilsher* was appealed to the House of Lords on the issue of causation where the standard of care issue was not discussed. For a recent application of *Wilsher*, see *FB (Suing by her Mother and Litigation Friend, WAC)* v *Princess Alexandra Hospital NHS Trust* [2017] in which a Senior House Officer (SHO), Dr Rushd, was found to have fallen below the standard of care required by a reasonably competent SHO in her treatment of a young child: 'Dr Rushd in the present case must be judged by the standard of a reasonably competent SHO in an accident and emergency department. The fact that Dr Rushd was aged 25 and "relatively inexperienced" . . . does not diminish the required standard of skill and care. On the other hand, the fact that she had spent six months in a paediatric department does not elevate the required standard. Other SHOs in A&E departments will have different backgrounds and experience, but they are all judged by the same standard . . . Thus in professional negligence, as in the general law of negligence, the standard of care which the law requires is an imperfect compromise. It achieves a balance between the interests of society and fairness to the individual practitioner' (at [63], [60]).

14. The issue as to the extent to which 'doctors know best' was alive and kicking in the heated debates surrounding the (failed) Medical Innovation Bill 2014–15 (the so-called 'Saatchi Bill') and its later reincarnation as the Access to Medical Treatments (Innovation) Act 2016. They both attracted significant—and well-judged—criticism from legal and medical professionals alike. See e.g. José Miola 'Bye-Bye *Bolitho*? The Curious Case of the Medical Innovation Bill' (2015) 15 Med L Int 124.

15. For an insightful 'update' of Sheldon's critique of the standard of care, see Miola 2012.

Bolam established that a doctor will not have fallen below the standard of care expected of a reasonable doctor, if they have acted in accordance with a respectable body of the medical profession (even if it is a minority viewpoint). However, this is qualified by a 'gloss' applied by the House of Lords in *Bolitho* v *City and Hackney Health Authority* [1998]. In this case a young boy suffered brain damage and later died of a cardiac arrest following respiratory failure while in hospital. Two serious incidents of respiratory difficulties had preceded his death, during which nurses had called for the doctor, who never arrived. As a result, the young boy had not been intubated (which the claimant argued would have prevented his death). The doctor argued that, even if she had attended, she would not have intubated the young boy and that, as a result, her failure to attend had not caused his death. Ultimately, though the majority of witnesses agreed that the boy should have been intubated, the House of Lords was persuaded that—as a reasonable body of opinion would have acted as the defendant did—she had not fallen below the standard of care required of her. However, the court went on to stress that the common practices of a profession should not go completely unchecked:

> In the vast majority of cases the fact that distinguished experts in the field are of a particular opinion will demonstrate the reasonableness of that opinion . . . But if, in a rare case, it can be demonstrated that the professional opinion is not capable of withstanding logical analysis, the judge is entitled to hold that the body of opinion is not reasonable or responsible. (Lord Browne-Wilkinson at 243)

The upshot of *Bolitho* is that 'doctor knows best' *only* 'if he [sic] acts reasonably and logically and gets his facts right'.[16] If a particular practice, even if widely accepted within a profession, is logically insupportable, a defendant cannot escape liability simply by showing that others would have acted as they did.[17] What this means is that the ***Bolam*** test is now better understood, to use Rachael Mulheron's formulation, as a two-stage test:

(1) Has the doctor acted in accordance with a practice accepted as proper by a respectable body of medical opinion?

(2) If yes, is the practice itself 'reasonable' and 'logical' (Mulheron 2010, p 613).

16. Lord Woolf 'Are the Courts Excessively Deferential to the Medical Profession?' (2001) 9 Med L Rev 1–16 at 1.

17. See further *McGuinn* v *Lewisham and Greenwich NHS Trust* [2017] applying *Bolitho* to find the doctor in breach of their duty of care (in failing to appreciate that the foetus the claimant was carrying was at risk of suffering from microcephaly) because their actions 'lacked a sufficiently logical and rational basis' (at [175]) and *Muller* v *King's College Hospital* (2017) in which Kerr J sought to distinguish between cases of 'pure treatment' (i.e. 'where the nature of the patient's condition is known, and the alleged negligence consists in a decision to treat (or advice treatment of) a condition in a particular manner' (at [50]) which may be viewed through the lens of ***Bolam*** and *Bolitho*) and cases of 'pure diagnosis' (i.e. 'where the patient's condition is unknown, and what is alleged to be negligent is a doctor's diagnosis of the condition, in the form of a report, with no decision made or advice given about treatment or further diagnostic procedures. The diagnosis is either right or wrong and, if wrong, either negligently so or not') (at [49]) where recourse to ***Bolam*** is 'ill-fitting' (at [68]). However, he concluded, 'I am bound by the law as it currently stands, to approach that issue by reference to a possible invocation of the *Bolitho* exception. I must not, therefore, reject [the defendant's view] unless I am persuaded that it does not hold water, in the senses discussed in Lord Browne-Wilkinson's speech in *Bolitho* and developed in other cases; that is to say, if it is untenable in logic or otherwise flawed in some manner rendering its conclusion indefensible and impermissible (at [79]).

However, crucially, Mulheron notes, the courts have not added a third stage in which they choose between two reasonable and logical schools of thought:

> [I]t is *not* for the court to venture into a consideration of two contrary bodies of opinion and to decide the case on the basis of which, of the patient's and the doctor's expert medical opinion, it prefers . . . Once ***Bolam*** applies, the fact of differences in expert opinion cannot lead to a rejection of ***Bolam*** evidence. (p 614)[18]

The assumption that 'doctors know best' (albeit qualified by the *Bolitho* gloss) has been especially controversial in relation to warning patients of the risks of treatment and the treatment of medically incapacitated adults and mature minors (Brazier and Miola 2000). The former now appears to have been resolved following the recent case of ***Montgomery* v *Lanarkshire Health Board* [2015]** in which the Supreme Court rejected the application of the ***Bolam*** test in cases involving the disclosure of risks in a medical context.

Until ***Montgomery***, the leading case on the duty of doctors to inform their patients of the risks of their treatment was the 30-year-old decision in *Sidaway* v *Bethlem Royal Hospital* [1985]. In *Sidaway*, the claimant had been paralysed while undergoing an operation on her back. There was no evidence that the operation had been performed negligently. However, the claimant argued that she should have been told of the known (albeit very small) risk of paralysis accompanying the procedure and that, had she been told, she would not have had the operation. The majority of the House of Lords, applying ***Bolam***, held that the doctor had not breached his duty of care in failing to inform her of the risks associated with her treatment as other reasonable doctors would have acted in the same way. There was one caveat, however. In cases involving a failure to warn of 'a substantial risk of grave adverse consequences' 'a judge might . . . come to the conclusion that disclosure of a particular risk was so obviously necessary to an informed choice on the part of the patient that no reasonably prudent medical man would fail to make it' (Lord Bridge, *Sidaway* at 24).

Nevertheless, as Lords Reed and Kerr noted, it is 'wrong to regard *Sidaway* as an unqualified endorsement of the application of the ***Bolam*** test to the giving of advice about treatment' (***Montgomery*** at [57]). The majority view has been the subject of extensive and scathing criticism, much of which has focused on Lord Scarman's dissenting opinion, in which he argued that the courts 'cannot stand idly by if the profession, by an excess of paternalism, denies its patients real choice. In a word, the law will not allow the medical profession to play God' (at 1028). Over the years, the unsatisfactory nature of the majority's analysis in *Sidaway* has meant that the courts in England and Wales have tacitly departed from it (in favour of Lord Woolf MR's test in *Pearce* v *United Bristol Healthcare NHS Trust* [1999]): a position that 'was effectively endorsed, particularly by Lord Steyn, in the causation case ***Chester* v *Afshar* [2005]**'[19] and was unequivocally confirmed in ***Montgomery***.

18. Indeed, in *Ministry of Justice* v *Carter* [2010] the Court of Appeal overturned the decision of a trial judge who did this. For a clear example of the judicial process of determining whether a defendant has breached their duty of care, see *Wells and Smith* v *University Hospital Southampton NHS Foundation Trust* [2015].

19. Lords Reed and Kerr, ***Montgomery*** at [86]. In ***Chester*** the majority of the House of Lords eschewed *Sidaway* (stepping around *Sidaway* rather than deviating from it) to hold that a doctor who had not informed the patient of a very small risk, which accompanied the course of treatment he was suggesting, had not only breached his duty of care but also that the patient's ability to make an informed choice about her treatment was so important that they were willing to extend the rules on causation in order to allow her claim: 'Her right of autonomy and dignity can and ought to be vindicated by a narrow and modest departure from traditional causation principles' (Lord Steyn at [24]). On the causation aspects of ***Chester***, see further **section 9.2.2.3**.

Montgomery v *Lanarkshire Health Board* [2015] SC

In 1999, the claimant gave birth to a baby boy. As a result of complications during the birth, during which the baby was starved of oxygen, the baby was born with significant disabilities. The claimant sued in negligence (on behalf of her son). The claimant was a relatively small woman and diabetic. Women with diabetes are more likely to have large babies and there is a 9–10 per cent risk of shoulder dystocia during vaginal delivery (the baby's shoulders being too wide to pass through the mother's pelvis). The claimant was told that she was having a larger than usual baby, however she was not told about the risks of her experiencing mechanical problems during labour. Her doctor accepted that there was a high risk of shoulder dystocia, but despite this, she said that her practice was not to spend a lot of time, or indeed any time at all, on it 'because, in her estimation, the risk of a grave problem for the baby resulting from shoulder dystocia was very small . . . and that if the condition was mentioned, "most women will actually say, 'I'd rather have a caesarean section' . . . and it's not in the maternal interests for women to have caesarean sections"' (at [13]).

The primary question for the court was whether, in failing to warn the claimant of the risk, the doctor was in breach of her duty of care towards the claimant. (The lower courts had found the doctor's actions to accord with a responsible body of medical opinion (as required by ***Bolam***) and—surprisingly—not to fall within the small group of cases involving 'a substantial risk of grave adverse consequences' where the court may substitute its own view.)

The Supreme Court unanimously found in favour of the claimant. It held that patients have a right to make their own decisions and to be given sufficient information to do so. Doctors, therefore, have a corresponding duty to take reasonable care to ensure that a patient is aware of material risks inherent in treatment, and of any alternatives:

> Since *Sidaway*, however, it has become increasingly clear that the paradigm of the doctor–patient relationship implicit in the speeches in that case has ceased to reflect the reality and complexity of the way in which healthcare services are provided, or the way in which the providers and recipients of such services view their relationship . . . patients are now widely regarded as persons holding rights, rather than as the passive recipients of the care of the medical profession . . . In the law of negligence, this approach entails a duty on the part of doctors to take reasonable care to ensure that a patient is aware of material risks of injury that are inherent in treatment . . .
>
> An adult person of sound mind is entitled to decide which, if any, of the available forms of treatment to undergo, and her consent must be obtained before treatment interfering with her bodily integrity is undertaken. The doctor is therefore under a duty to take reasonable care to ensure that the patient is aware of any material risks involved in any recommended treatment, and of any reasonable alternative or variant treatments. The test of materiality is whether, in the circumstances of the particular case, a reasonable person in the patient's position would be likely to attach significance to the risk, or the doctor is or should reasonably be aware that the particular patient would be likely to attach significance to it. (Lords Reed and Kerr at [75], [82], [87])

→

→

The Justices made clear that significance of a risk is fact-sensitive and cannot be reduced to percentages, and that (in line with guidance issued by the General Medical Council) in order to advise, the doctor must engage in dialogue with her patient (at [89]).

There is one important caveat (as well as the expected exceptions related to emergency treatment) to the doctor's duty to inform in the form of a 'therapeutic exception'. This allows a doctor to withhold information where 'he reasonably considers that its disclosure would be seriously detrimental to the patient's health' (at [88]). The court anticipates that use of this caveat will be limited: 'it is not intended to subvert that principle by enabling the doctor to prevent the patient from making an informed choice where she is liable to make a choice which the doctor considers to be contrary to her best interests' (at [91]).

A secondary question for the court related to causation. The lower courts held that the claimant had not established on the facts that she would have elected to have a caesarean section, had she been properly informed. Given the evidence of the doctor herself that 'if you were to mention shoulder dystocia to every [diabetic] patient, if you were to mention to any mother who faces labour that there is a very small risk of the baby dying in labour, then everyone would ask for a caesarean section', and the claimant's own statements, it is unsurprising that the Supreme Court concluded that the claimant would have chosen a caesarean section had it been offered to her.[20]

Pause for reflection

Montgomery is also—particularly in Lady Hale's 'footnote' to the main judgment—a timely and important recognition of patient—and in particular women's—autonomy. It offers a 'robust' defence of women's choice in the context of pregnancy and childbirth.[21]

> . . . it is not possible to consider a particular medical procedure in isolation from its alternatives. Most decisions about medical care are not simple yes/no answers. There are choices to be made, arguments for and against each of the options to be considered, and sufficient information must be given so that this can be done . . . Pregnancy is a particularly powerful illustration [of this] . . . That is not necessarily to say that the doctors have to volunteer the pros and cons of each option in every case, but they clearly should do so in any case where either the mother or the child is at heightened risk from a

→

20. It took 16 years for ***Montgomery*** to make its way through the courts. At its heart, is the care of a—now—16-year-old boy. It has since been reported that Ms Montgomery has been awarded between £5–5.25 million in damages which will allow her, in her words 'to ensure Sam receives the best possible care for the rest of his life' (BBC News 'Nadine Montgomery wins £5m from NHS Lanarkshire over brain damage to son' 11 March 2015).

21. See Kirsty Keywood 'The Death of *Sidaway*: Values, Judgments and Informed Consent' Journal of Medical Ethics blog, 15 March 2015.

→

vaginal delivery. In this day and age, we are not only concerned about risks to the baby. We are equally, if not more, concerned about risks to the mother. And those include the risks associated with giving birth, as well as any after-effects. One of the problems in this case was that for too long the focus was on the risks to the baby, without also taking into account what the mother might face in the process of giving birth. (at [109]–[111])

Lady Hale continued,

We do not have a full transcript of the evidence, but in the extracts we do have Dr McLellan [the defendant doctor] referred to explaining to a mother who requested a caesarean section 'why it may not be in the mother's best interest' and later expressed the view that 'it's not in the maternal interests for women to have caesarean sections'. Whatever Dr McLellan may have had in mind, this does not look like a purely medical judgment. It looks like a judgment that vaginal delivery is in some way morally preferable to a caesarean section: so much so that it justifies depriving the pregnant woman of the information needed for her to make a free choice in the matter. Giving birth vaginally is indeed a unique and wonderful experience, but it has not been suggested that it inevitably leads to a closer and better relationship between mother and child than does a caesarean section.

In any event, once the argument departs from purely medical considerations and involves value judgments of this sort, it becomes clear . . . that the ***Bolam*** test, of conduct supported by a responsible body of medical opinion, becomes quite inapposite. A patient is entitled to take into account her own values, her own assessment of the comparative merits of giving birth in the 'natural' and traditional way and of giving birth by caesarean section, whatever medical opinion may say, alongside the medical evaluation of the risks to herself and her baby. She may place great value on giving birth in the natural way and be prepared to take the risks to herself and her baby which this entails. The medical profession must respect her choice, unless she lacks the legal capacity to decide (*St George's Healthcare NHS Trust v S* [1999]). There is no good reason why the same should not apply in reverse, if she is prepared to forgo the joys of natural childbirth in order to avoid some not insignificant risks to herself or her baby. She cannot force her doctor to offer treatment which he or she considers futile or inappropriate. But she is at least entitled to the information which will enable her to take a proper part in that decision . . . Gone are the days when it was thought that, on becoming pregnant, a woman lost, not only her capacity, but also her right to act as a genuinely autonomous human being. (at [114]–[116])[22]

Lady Hale retired from the Supreme Court in January 2020. However, her comments in ***Montgomery*** are indicative of what we came to expect—and welcome—from the first woman Justice on the Supreme Court during her time on the court.[23] Why do you think she decided to add a 'footnote' in this case? Do you think it is important that she did so?

22. See discussion of the so-called forced caesarean section cases in **section 15.5.1**.

23. See further Erika Rackley *Women Judging and the Judiciary: From Difference to Diversity* (Routledge, 2013), Chs 5 and 6.

Counterpoint

And yet, while ***Montgomery*** calls for the opening up of lines of communication between medical professionals and patients, as Kirsty Keywood notes, the effectiveness of the case in promoting and protecting patient choice is—at least in part—dependent on resources being available to support their choices.[24] Could the decision in ***Montgomery*** itself work against this?

After all, one consequence of the decision in ***Montgomery*** is that a substantial sum of the Lanarkshire NHS Board's budget has been taken out of the collective pot. Maternity claims already represent the highest value, and the second highest number, of all NHS claims (though these represent just 0.1 per cent of all births).[25] However, while Lords Reed and Kerr acknowledged that the decision *could* lead to an increase in defensive practices, as well as in claims from women claiming that they had not been adequately advised, they did not expect this to be the case:

> [A]n approach to the law which, instead of treating patients as placing themselves in the hands of their doctors (and then being prone to sue their doctors in the event of a disappointing outcome), treats them so far as possible as adults who are capable of understanding that medical treatment is uncertain of success and may involve risks, accepting responsibility for the taking of risks affecting their own lives, and living with the consequences of their choices . . . in so far as the law contributes to the incidence of litigation, an approach which results in patients being aware that the outcome of treatment is uncertain and potentially dangerous, and in their taking responsibility for the ultimate choice to undergo that treatment, may be less likely to encourage recriminations and litigation, in the event of an adverse outcome, than an approach which requires patients to rely on their doctors to determine whether a risk inherent in a particular form of treatment should be incurred. (at [81], [93])

Do you agree?[26]

Without doubt ***Montgomery*** is a landmark decision. And without doubt *Sidaway* is dead[27] and '"Informed consent" has arrived' and is now 'firmly part of English law' (Lady Hale at [107]).[28] Doctors have 'a duty to take reasonable care to ensure that the patient is aware of any material risks involved in any recommended treatment, and of any reasonable alternative or variant treatments' (at [87]). In *Duce* v *Worcestershire Acute*

24. Keywood (**n 21**).

25. NHS Litigation Authority 'Ten Years of Maternity Claims: An Analysis of NHS Litigation Authority Data' 2012.

26. See here the Royal College of Surgeons guidance on ***Montgomery*** discussed in David Hart 'Informed consent: Surgeons respond to *Montgomery*' UK Human Rights blog, 30 October 2016.

27. See David Hart 'Supreme Court reverses informed consent ruling: *Sidaway* is dead' UK Human Rights blog, 13 March 2015.

28. Andrew Hockton '"Informed consent" has arrived' *The Times* 19 March 2015.

Hospitals NHS Trust [2018], Hamblen LJ suggested this involved a two-stage test (paragraph numbers refer to ***Montgomery***):

(1) What risks associated with an operation were or should have been known to the medical professional in question. That is a matter falling within the expertise of medical professionals [83].

(2) Whether the patient should have been told about such risks by reference to whether they were material. That is a matter for the Court to determine [83]. This issue is not therefore the subject of the ***Bolam*** test and not something that can be determined by reference to expert evidence alone [84]–[85]. (at [33])

But when is a risk 'material'? And, more importantly, how does a doctor determine what is material to a specific patient? The test of materiality, as set out in ***Montgomery***, is 'whether, in the circumstances of the particular case, a reasonable person in the patient's position would be likely to attach significance to the risk, or the doctor is or should reasonably be aware that the particular patient would be likely to attach significance to it' (at [87]). The test is both subjective and objective. However, what is less clear is the extent to which subjective factors relating to the patient are relevant:

> [T]he greater degree of subjectivity inserted into the assessment the further one departs from the standard of the reasonable patient. Some characteristics of a patient are obvious: In particular that person's actual medical condition which would include its severity. Other personal factors may be less self-evident: such as the patient's tolerance for or stoicism towards pain, or the ability to manage pain. Other factors might be quite remote from the medical or physiological condition of the patient, such as the patient's need to return to work, or the fact that the patient has suffered a recent event in his/her life (such as a bereavement or a divorce) which renders that person unusually fragile and (say) unwilling to take chances at that particular time. (Green J, *Thefaut* v *Johnston* [2017] at [55])

The test was applied by the High Court in *A* v *East Kent Hospitals University NHS Foundation Trust* [2015] (which was heard just five days after the judgment in ***Montgomery***). The claimant argued that the defendant had negligently failed to warn her that the foetus she was carrying might be suffering from a chromosomal abnormality. It was common ground that were the risk of such an abnormality found to be 'material' then it ought to have been raised with the claimant. Finding for the defendant, the judge held that while a risk 'somewhere in the region of 1–3 per cent' would, in this context, be considered 'material' (and, as such, should be raised with the claimant), 'the decision in ***Montgomery*** . . . is not authority for the proposition that medical practitioners need to warn about risks which are theoretical' or 'background', as was the case here (Dingeman J at [90], [101]).[29]

Inevitably, perhaps, many legal arguments have been made, and much judicial and academic ink[30] has been spilt, since ***Montgomery*** as doctors, lawyers and their clients

29. See further, Nigel Poole 'After *Montgomery*—Part Two: Recommended Treatment, Risk and Dialogue' *Learned Friend* 12 September 2018.

30. See e.g. Cave and Milo 2020; Gemma Turton 'Informed Consent to Medical Treatment Post-*Montgomery*: Causation and Coincidence' (2018) Med L Rev; George G Buttigieg 'Re-visiting *Bolam* and *Bolitho* in the light of *Montgomery v Lanarkshire Health Board*' (2018) 86 Medico-Legal J 42; Louise V Austin '*Grimstone v Epsom and St Helier University Hospitals NHS Trust*: (It's Not) Hip to Be Square' (2018) 26 Med L Rev 665; Nigel Poole 'After *Montgomery*—Part Two: *Bolam* Returns' *Learned Friend* 12 September 2018; Sarah W Chan et al '*Montgomery* and Informed Consent: Where Are We Now?' (2017) 357 BMJ 2224.

attempt to work out its impact on clinical practice. What is clear is that ***Bolam*** is far from dead. It continues to inform both stages of the ***Montgomery*** test (see e.g. *Grimstone* v *Epsom and St Helier University Hospitals NHS Trust* [2015]; *Bayley* v *George Eliot Hospital* [2017]; *Duce* v *Worcestershire Acute Hospitals NHS Trust* [2018]); *Diamond* v *Royal Devon and Exeter NHS Foundation Trust* [2019] EWCA Civ 585; *Brady* v *Southend University Hospital NHS Foundation Trust* [2020]). Nor has ***Montgomery*** been confined to consent cases (as was originally thought). Its principles have been applied in cases where treatment in general is in question (see e.g. *Webster* v *Burton Hospitals NHS Foundation Trust* [2017]), to the duty to inform a patient of the need for follow-up treatment (*Gallardo* v *Imperial College Healthcare Trust* [2017]) and outside a medical context in *O'Hare* v *Coutts & Co* [2016] in which the defendant, a private bank, was found to owe a duty to take reasonable care to warn its customers of risks relating to suggested investments (although, on the facts, it had not breached that duty).

8.4 Setting the standard of care

Having determined that the courts generally apply a common standard, we now need to consider how the courts go about *setting* that standard. While the courts do not (usually) take into account the characteristics of the individual defendant, they do take into account the circumstances of the situation in which the accident or injury occurred. The standard of care does not exist in the abstract: 'The law in all cases exacts a degree of care commensurate with the risk' (Lord Macmillan, *Read* v *Lyons Co Ltd* [1947] at 173).

When seeking to define the standard of care required of the defendant—that is, what the defendant *ought* to have done or what is *reasonable* in the circumstances of the case—the courts take a number of factors into account: probability or risk of the injury; the seriousness of the injury; the cost of taking precautions; and the social value of the activity. So, if we ask what is a reasonable speed to drive, the answer will vary—the reasonable car driver will drive at different speeds at different times and according to different circumstances.[31]

Some examples may help here. All things being equal, it is reasonable to drive at 70 mph on a clear motorway but not on residential streets. It will be reasonable to drive faster in clear weather conditions than when it is pouring with rain or foggy. Why is this? The answer is straightforward. The risks posed by driving at 70 mph in a residential street are higher than those on a clear motorway. Similarly, accidents are more likely to occur in adverse weather conditions. The reasonable driver may be expected to take more care when driving near a school, where potential injuries may not only be more likely (e.g. a child running out from behind a parked car) but more severe (a child is more likely to be more seriously injured than an adult if hit by a car) than if, say, they have an injured friend in the back of their car who they are rushing to hospital (where the social utility of their act may outweigh the risks it creates).

Thus, in *Wooldridge* v *Sumner* [1963], for example, a photographer who was injured while working at the National Horse Show was unable to recover for the serious injuries

31. For a recent application of this principle see *Mohmed* v *Barnes and EUI Ltd* [2019].

he suffered when one of the riders he was photographing had come round the corner of the arena at excessive speed causing the horse to become temporarily out of control. Rejecting his claim, the Court of Appeal held that '[t]he law of negligence has always recognised that the standard of care which a reasonable man will exercise depends upon the conditions under which the decision to avoid the act or omission relied upon as negligence has to be taken' (Diplock LJ at 67). In the absence of recklessness or an intention to harm the claimant, the horse rider was free to concentrate on winning the competition.

8.4.1 Probability that the injury will occur

One of the first factors the courts will take into account is likelihood of the injury occurring. The general rule is the more likely—or foreseeable—the outcome, the greater the possibility that the courts will find the defendants liable for failing to take steps to avoid it.

Bolton v *Stone* [1951] HL

The claimant was hit on the head outside her house by a cricket ball hit by a player from an adjacent cricket pitch. The hit was substantial, although possibly not exceptional. The ball had travelled some 100 yards (approx 91 m) and over a seven-foot fence (which, due to the slope of the pitch, was in effect 17 feet high). The claimant sued in negligence and nuisance.

The House of Lords, rejecting both claims,[32] held that although there was evidence that over a period of years balls had been hit out of the ground, this was, in fact, very rare. It had happened six times in 30 years. Thus, although the possibility of a ball being hit out of the ground was foreseeable, this was not sufficient to establish negligence since the chances of the ball hitting someone were so low that a reasonable person would not have taken precautions to stop it happening.

> The standard of care in the law of negligence is the standard of an ordinarily careful man, but in my opinion an ordinarily careful man does not take precautions against every foreseeable risk . . . He takes precautions against risks which are reasonably likely to happen . . . there are many footpaths and highways adjacent to cricket grounds and golf courses on to which cricket and golf balls are occasionally driven, but such risks are habitually treated both by the owners and committees of such cricket and golf courses and by the pedestrians who use the adjacent footpaths and highways as negligible and it is not, in my opinion, actionable negligence not to take precautions to avoid such risks. (Lord Oaksey at 863)[33]

Thus, in *Richards* v *London Borough of Bromley* [2012], the Court of Appeal held that an injury suffered by a school pupil (who had injured her heel when leaving the school through a pair of swing doors) was not reasonably foreseeable. Though there had been one incident four months earlier, this was only superficially similar to the accident in

32. It was agreed that nuisance could not be established in the absence of negligence (at 860).
33. See also *Lewis* v *Wandsworth London Borough Council* [2020].

question and '[i]n any event the trivial nature of the earlier incident and the risk which it brought to light, seen in the context of thirty years' safe use of the doors by thousands of children and staff, rendered reasonable both the nature of the remedial action which the school authorities proposed to take and the timescale within which they proposed to do it' (at [14]).

In *Perry* v *Harris* [2008], a case involving the liability of a parent for the severe and permanent injuries sustained by a child using a bouncy castle hired for her children's birthday party, the Court of Appeal, finding for the defendant, held that in setting the standard of care what mattered was not merely whether *some* harm was foreseeable but also the *severity* of the foreseeable harm:

> A reasonable parent could foresee that if children indulged in boisterous behaviour on a bouncy castle, there would be a risk that, sooner or later, one child might collide with another and cause that child some physical injury of a type that can be an incident of some contact sports. We do not consider that it was reasonably foreseeable that such injury would be likely to be serious, let alone as severe as the injury sustained by the claimant. (Lord Phillips CJ at [38])[34]

It is also clear from the cases that the conduct of the defendant is assessed at the time of the alleged breach; it is a test of foresight, not hindsight (***Roe* v *Ministry of Health* [1954]**). If something seems to be acceptable at the time—that is, if the risk of injury is low—then it is unlikely to be considered negligent.

Roe v *Ministry of Health* [1954] CA

The claimants were paralysed after being injected with contaminated nupercaine (a spinal anaesthetic) during a routine, minor operation. The nupercaine had been contained in sealed glass ampoules and stored in a solution of phenol prior to use. Unknown to the hospital, the phenol had percolated into the ampoules through invisible cracks or molecular flaws, causing the claimants' paralysis.

Rejecting the claims, the Court of Appeal held that, though it was clear in hindsight that the hospital was at fault, *at the time of the operation* neither the anaesthetist nor any of the hospital staff knew of the dangers of storing glass ampoules in the phenol solution. The test applied was the standard of medical knowledge when the accident occurred in 1947: 'We must not look at the 1947 accident with 1954 spectacles' (Denning LJ at 84).

The approach in ***Roe*** was affirmed in *Williams* v *University of Birmingham* [2011]. The widow of a former physics undergraduate, who had conducted experiments in an asbestos-lagged service tunnel under the science department at the University of Birmingham

34. See also *Cockbill* v *Riley* [2013] in which the claimant fractured his spine resulting in incomplete tetraplegia after entering a paddling pool (it was not clear how he had done so) while at a party to celebrate the end of his GCSEs. The court held that it was *not* reasonably foreseeable that someone would attempt to carry out a dive or a belly-flop (which can very easily turn into a dive) and thus suffer grave injury and so the defendant was not in breach of his duty of care to the claimant.

and who had since died of malignant mesothelioma in his left lung, brought a claim against the university in negligence. The university admitted that the claimant's husband would have been exposed to asbestos as a student, but argued that the exposure was too small to ground a claim. Rejecting the claim, Atkins LJ (giving the leading judgment), adapting Denning LJ's 'graphic phrase', argued that 'we must not look at what happened in the tunnel in 1974 through 2009 or 2011 spectacles' (at [38]). The state of the lagging was not such as should have alerted the university to a reasonably foreseeable risk that people using the tunnel might be exposed to an unacceptable risk of an asbestos-related injury (at [60]–[61]).

Pause for reflection

A leading medical textbook published in 1951 (after the accident which formed the basis of the claim in ***Roe***) warns medical practitioners to 'never place ampoules of local anaesthetic solution in alcohol or spirit. This common practice is probably responsible for some cases of permanent paralysis reported after spinal analgesia' (***Roe*** at 86). However, despite this significant societal *benefit*—it was the injuries suffered by the claimants in ***Roe*** which first alerted the medical profession to this particular danger—the effect of the Court of Appeal's decision was that the full *cost* or burden of this medical advance was borne solely by the unfortunate men. This apparent injustice was justified by Denning LJ thus:

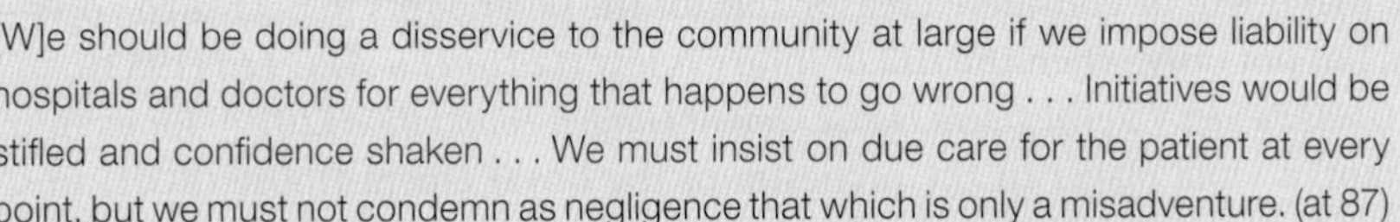

> [W]e should be doing a disservice to the community at large if we impose liability on hospitals and doctors for everything that happens to go wrong . . . Initiatives would be stifled and confidence shaken . . . We must insist on due care for the patient at every point, but we must not condemn as negligence that which is only a misadventure. (at 87)

Do you agree? Compare Denning LJ's reasoning here with that in ***Nettleship***—why do you think he adopted such a markedly different approach in this case?

8.4.2 **Seriousness of the injury**

The second factor the courts take into account is the seriousness of the injury should it occur. Generally, the more serious the potential injury, the more likely the defendant will be found to have fallen below the required standard of care should it materialise: 'the law expects of a man a great deal more care in carrying a pound of dynamite than a pound of butter' (Singleton LJ, quoting Percy H Winfield, in *Beckett* v *Newalls Insulation Co Ltd* [1953] at 15). One illustration from the case law will suffice here.

***Paris* v *Stepney Borough Council* [1951] HL**

The claimant, a garage hand, suffered serious injury when a metal chip flew into one of his eyes while he was working. Unfortunately, he was already (as his employers knew) blind in his other eye. The injury, therefore, left him effectively blind. He sued his employers, claiming they were

→

→

negligent in failing to provide safety goggles and to require their use as part of a safe system of work.[35]

The majority of the House of Lords agreed. Though the chance of injury was low, the seriousness of the consequences should an accident occur must also be taken into account when assessing the precautions a reasonable employer should take to ensure the safety of their workforce. The provision of safety goggles was 'obviously necessary when a one-eyed man was put to [this] kind of work' (at 383).

8.4.3 **Cost of taking precautions**

The courts also consider the cost to the defendant of taking precautions against the risk. The lower the cost—whether in terms of time or money—the more reasonable it is that someone should take precautions. Thus, it is likely (all things being equal) that the courts would consider a driver who fails to slow down while driving near a school at the end of the school day to have fallen below the standard of care required of a reasonable driver; the cost to the driver of driving more slowly is unlikely to be seen as unreasonably high. If, on the other hand, the cost of taking precautions is very onerous, it is less likely that it will be considered reasonable for the defendants to bear such costs—especially, but not only, when the risk of injury is low (***Latimer* v *AEC Ltd* [1953]**).

In *Goldscheider* v *Royal Opera House Covent Garden Foundation* [2019], for example, the claimant, a viola player in the orchestra of the Royal Opera House (ROH) in Covent Garden, London, was able to recover for the damage caused to his hearing as a result by being placed too close to the trumpet section in the orchestra 'pit' in breach of the Control of Noise at Work Regulations 2005. Regulation 6(1) states '(1) The employer shall ensure that risk from the exposure of his employees to noise is either eliminated at source or, where this is not reasonably practicable, reduced to as low a level as is reasonably practicable'. McCombe and Bean LJJ in the Court of Appeal, rejecting the ROH's appeal, held that despite undertaking a risk assessment and providing performers with ear plugs and training, it had failed to take 'all reasonably practical steps' to protect the claimant's hearing. They continued:

> [O]ne might have expected evidence on the following lines. Firstly, it might have been shown that [high noise] level . . . is regularly reached in public performances of Wagner operas at the ROH whatever the configuration of the pit, whatever the number of brass instruments used and whoever is conducting. Secondly, evidence might have been led to show that to keep within the upper [noise limits] . . . EAV [exposure action value] would mean that Wagner could not be performed at all at the ROH, or that his works could be performed only in a way which would compromise artistic standards to an unacceptable extent. Thirdly, the defendant might have attempted to prove that the only way in which the rehearsals could have been scheduled is on the basis of six hours rehearsal per day on consecutive days, with no consideration being given to whether it was essential for the loudest passages to be played again and again throughout the day at full volume. It is in our judgment particularly significant

35. See further **section 13.2.3**.

> that the pit was [later] reconfigured . . . with the brass instruments being split up. There is no evidence that this caused an unacceptable reduction (or indeed any reduction at all) in the artistic standards of . . . [the Wagner opera the claimant was performing] when it came to be performed in public. Alterations made by defendants after a workplace accident do not necessarily demonstrate liability retrospectively, but they do make it very difficult for the defendant to prove that all reasonably practicable steps had already been taken. (at [41]–[42])

The courts are also reluctant to interfere with the budgetary decisions made in relation to limited resources by public authorities. In *Knight* v *Home Office* [1990], a mentally ill prisoner committed suicide. As a known suicide risk, he had been observed every 15 minutes. The court recognised that while lack of funds could never be a complete defence to insufficient safety precautions, the facilities of a prison hospital were necessarily different to a specialist psychiatric hospital and so, on the facts, there was no breach of the prison officers' duty of care.

8.4.4 **Social value of the activity**

While an assessment of the 'cost of taking precautions' goes to the *private* costs of adhering to a particular standard of care imposed on the individual, this final factor relates to the *social* costs of the activity. The greater the social value of the activity, the more likely the courts will find it reasonable to have dispensed with safety precautions.

While there is no special exemption for any of the emergency services from the law of negligence (the question remains whether the defendant has behaved as a reasonable man), the court will take into account the emergency in which the defendant is acting. The standard of care will usually therefore be lower where the defendant is acting in the 'heat of the moment' or in an emergency or rescue situation.

***Watt* v *Hertfordshire County Council* [1954] CA**

A fireman was seriously injured by heavy lifting-gear while travelling in the back of a lorry on the way to an accident where a woman was trapped under a vehicle. The lorry had not been specially fitted to carry the gear in an emergency.

The Court of Appeal, rejecting the fireman's claim, held that the public benefit justified taking the risks associated with failing to adequately secure the lifting-gear in the back of the lorry:

> It is well settled that in measuring due care you must balance the risk against the measures necessary to eliminate the risk. To that proposition there ought to be added this: you must balance the risk against the end to be achieved . . . The saving of life or limb justifies taking considerable risk. (Denning LJ at 838)

If, therefore, the same accident had occurred in pursuit of a commercial end then the claimant would have recovered: 'the commercial end to make a profit is very different from the human end to save life or limb' (at 838).[36]

36. See more recently *MacLeod* v *The Commissioner of the Police for the Metropolis* [2015] discussed in Karen O'Sullivan 'Sound the Alarm' (2015) 165 NLJ 10.

In sporting events the standard of care is usually lower as the participants are understood to be acting 'in the heat of the moment', concentrating on winning and so are likely to pay less attention to what is going on around them. This adjusted standard was extended to cases involving other forms of consensual activity, such as 'horseplay' in *Blake* v *Galloway* [2004] in which a teenager was injured while playing a 'game' which involved throwing bark and twigs at each other. Finding for the defendant, the Court of Appeal held that there had been no breach of duty:

> If the defendant in the present case had departed from the tacit understandings or conventions of the play and, for example, had thrown a stone at the claimant, or deliberately aimed the piece of bark at the claimant's head, then there might have been a breach of the duty of care. But what happened here was, at its highest, 'an error of judgment or lapse of skill' (to quote from Diplock LJ), and that is not sufficient to amount to a failure to take reasonable care in the circumstances of horseplay such as that in which these youths were engaged . . . This was a most unfortunate accident, but it was just that. Young persons will always want to play vigorous games and indulge in horseplay, and from time to time accidents will occur and injuries will be caused. But, broadly speaking, the victims of such accidents will usually not be able to recover damages unless they can show that the injury has been caused by a failure to take care which amounts to recklessness or a very high degree of carelessness, or that it was caused deliberately (i.e. with intent to cause harm). (Dyson LJ at [15], [25])

However, while the standard of care owed between participants in a sporting event is lower, it is never eliminated entirely (*Caldwell* v *Maguire* [2002]).[37] Thus while a footballer may have to put up with the odd foul or high tackle, where these fall below what could be reasonably expected in anyone playing the game, liability will arise. The objective standard of care in competitive sports varies according to the level at which it is played. The standard of care expected of a footballer in a premiership match will be higher than that of a Sunday league player (*Condon* v *Basi* [1985]).[38]

It is also clear from *Scout Association* v *Barnes* [2010] that the social value of an activity *as a whole* does not mean that *all* examples of that activity are acceptable, whatever the risk:

> Of course, the law of tort must not interfere with activities just because they carry some risk. Of course, the law of tort must not stamp out socially desirable activities. But whether the social benefit of an activity is such that the degree of risk it entails is acceptable is a question of fact, degree and judgment, which must be decided on an individual basis and not by a broad brush approach. (Smith LJ at [49])

In *Barnes*, the claimant was injured while playing a game called 'Objects in the Dark' which involved running around a pile of wooden blocks in a scout hall and attempting to grab a block once the lights were switched off (with only minimal lighting provided by emergency exit lights). The majority of the Court of Appeal upheld the trial judge's

37. See, in relation to the standard of care expected of referees and organisers of sporting events, *Vowles* v *Evans* [2003] and *Watson* v *British Boxing Board of Control Ltd* [2001].

38. In this way *Condon* v *Basi* appears to depart from ***Nettleship*** (which was not considered by the court). Of course, even if negligence is established, the defendant may still raise a defence (usually *volenti* or contributory negligence) against the claim (see **Chapter 10**).

decision that the defendant had breached its duty—the value of playing the game in the dark as a way of adding 'spice' to increase the boys' enjoyment of the game did not justify the additional risk:

> [T]he particular justification for playing this game in the dark was only that it added excitement. The darkness did not add any other social or educative value but it did significantly increase the risk of injury . . . the added excitement of playing the game in the dark, which might well encourage boys to attend scouts—a desirable objective—did not justify the increased foreseeable risk. (Smith LJ at 46)

Pause for reflection

Though it is clear from the majority judgments in *Barnes* that the trial judge had appropriately weighed the costs and benefits of the competing factors at issue in the case, there is considerable force in Ward LJ's dissenting opening paragraph:

> I have to confess that I have found it uncommonly difficult to reach a confident judgment in this case. Here was a big strong thirteen year old lad, well-used to rough and tumble, playing rugby with distinction for his county, ever ready to take the bumps and the bruises, ever willingly to put his body on the line for the thrill of his sport. For him, you get hurt, you get up, and you get on with it. He brought the same enthusiasm and competitive instincts to his participation in his local Scout troop. He was the least likely boy to need wrapping in cotton wool. So, is awarding him damages for an injury suffered playing the game, 'Objects in the Dark', not an example of an overprotective nanny state robbing youth of fun simply because there was some risk involved in the exercise? Is this a decision which emasculates those responsible for caring for our children and in so doing, enfeebles the children themselves? Where do you draw the line? I have found that hard to answer. (at [50])

Do you think that the majority drew the line correctly in this case? To what extent, if at all, can it be reconciled with the decision in *Blake* v *Galloway*?

8.5 **A balancing act**

When determining the standard of care required by the defendant, the courts are engaged in a balancing act. As Lord Hoffmann noted in ***Tomlinson* v *Congleton Borough Council*** [2003]:

> the question of what amounts to 'such care as is in all the circumstances of the case is reasonable' depends upon assessing . . . not only the likelihood that someone may be injured and the seriousness of the injury which may occur, but also the social value of the activity which gives rise to the risk and the cost of preventative measure. These factors have to be balanced against each other. (at [34])

No factor is viewed in isolation from the others. In each case the courts weigh up the likelihood of injury and the seriousness of harm against the cost of taking precautions and the social value of the activity before coming to a decision as to what was reasonable in all the circumstances of the case—what the reasonable man would have done. An example may help here.

Overseas Tankship (UK) Ltd v *Miller Steamship Co Pty Ltd (The Wagon Mound) (No 2)* [1967] PC

The defendants carelessly transferred furnace oil from a nearby wharf onto a vessel, the *Wagon Mound,* which was moored in Sydney Harbour, causing a large quantity of the oil to spill into the harbour where it accumulated around the wharf and the claimants' vessels. The owners of the wharf were carrying out repairs on the claimants' ships which caused pieces of hot metal to fly off and into the wharf. On one such occasion it is thought that the metal fell onto an object supporting a piece of inflammable material in the oil-covered water, which subsequently ignited. This caused the oil to catch alight and the ensuing fire quickly destroyed the wharf and the claimants' vessels.

The Privy Council held that although the chance of the oil catching fire was very low it was nevertheless a real one and, given the very grave consequences should the risk materialise, there was no justification for the defendant's failure to take steps to eliminate it given how easy it was for them to prevent the spillage (had they taken reasonable care in the first place when filling up the vessel). On this basis, the defendants had fallen below the standard of care required—the reasonable man would have taken precautions.

> If a real risk is one which would occur to the mind of a reasonable man in the position of the defendant's servant and which he would not brush aside as far-fetched . . . then surely he would not neglect such a risk if action to eliminate it presented no difficulty, involved no disadvantage, and required no expense. (at 643–4)[39]

Pause for reflection

This process through which the courts distinguish between acceptable and unacceptable carelessness—that is, the balancing of the probability (P) and likely seriousness of injury (L) against the private and social costs[40] (B) of the necessary precautions—was reduced to a quasi-mathematical formula by a US judge named Learned Hand J (in *United States* v *Carroll Towing Co* [1947]).

→

39. Note this is the second of the ***Wagon Mound*** cases. The first, ***Overseas Tankship (UK) Ltd*** v ***Morts Dock and Engineering Co (The Wagon Mound) No 1*** [1961], brought by the owners of the wharf, is discussed in the context of remoteness in **Chapter 9**.

40. 'Social costs' include not only financial but also 'immeasurable "soft" values such as community concepts of justice, health, life and freedom of conduct' (*Western Suburbs Hospital* v *Currie* [1987]). The assessment of community values can be problematic. How are we to compare, to use *Cane's* example, the social value of playing cricket with the safety of passers-by so as to decide whether it is negligent to play cricket without a fence (p 42)?

→

$B < LP$ = a reasonable person would take precautions = defendant liable if they do not take precautions

$B > LP$ = a reasonable person would not take precautions = defendant not liable if they do not take precautions

The 'Learned Hand test' holds that where the private and social costs of taking precautions (B) is less than the probability (P) multiplied by the likelihood of injury (L), the defendant will be held to have fallen below the standard of care of the reasonable man if they fail to take such precautions. Conversely, where the costs of taking precautions (B) are greater than the probability (P) multiplied by the seriousness of the injury (L) occurring, it would be unreasonable to expect the defendant to take such precautions.

Of course, the formula only tells us so much. Nevertheless, it remains a helpful *illustration* of the sort of balancing exercises the courts are undertaking when setting the appropriate standard of care in all the circumstances of the case.

Counterpoint

The Learned Hand test is essentially an economic one: 'If it can be shown that expenditure of £X on avoiding or minimising the risk of an accident will prevent accident costs of £X + Y, then it is clearly desirable that £X should be spent. On the other hand, it is said, there is no point in spending £X to prevent accident costs which are less than £X' (*Cane* p 41). This reduction of value of life and limb to a mathematical formula is described by *Conaghan & Mansell* as 'ideologically objectionable in its shallow and impoverished view of human activity' (p 62). Do you agree? Consider the US case of *Grimshaw* v *Ford Motor Company* [1981], discussed in **Chapter 12**.

8.5.1 The Compensation Act 2006 and the Social Action, Responsibility and Heroism Act 2015

The Compensation Act 2006 was enacted to address the *perception* of a growing compensation culture in the UK.[41] Speaking in 2005, the then Prime Minister, Tony Blair, suggested its purpose was to:

> clarify the existing common law on negligence to make clear that there is no liability in negligence for untoward incidents that could not be avoided by taking reasonable care or exercising reasonable skill . . . This will send a strong signal and it will also reduce risk-averse behaviour by providing reassurance to those who may be concerned about possible litigation, such as volunteers, teachers and local authorities.[42]

41. Part 2 of the Act addresses the aggressive marketing of the claims management industry, which the government stressed was responsible, alongside irresponsible media reporting, for fostering the *perception* of a compensation culture (see generally **Chapter 1** and Herbert 2006). The Compensation Act is discussed in more detail in **Chapter 21**.

42. Tony Blair 'Common Sense Culture not Compensation Culture' speech delivered at Institute of Public Policy Research, 26 May 2005.

To this end, section 1 requires the courts to 'have regard to' the wider impact of their assessment of the appropriate standard of care in a particular case.

Compensation Act 2006

1. Deterrent effect of potential liability

A court considering a claim in negligence or breach of statutory duty may, in determining whether the defendant should have taken particular steps to meet a standard of care (whether by taking precautions against a risk or otherwise), have regard to whether a requirement to take those steps might—

(a) prevent a desirable activity from being undertaken at all, to a particular extent or in a particular way, or

(b) discourage persons from undertaking functions in connection with a desirable activity.

In fact, section 1 adds little to our understanding of the tort of negligence. As Jackson LJ in *Barnes* notes, it simply restates what we already know: that 'the function of the law of tort [is] to deter negligent conduct and to compensate those who are the victims of such conduct. It is not the function of the law of tort to eliminate every iota of risk or to stamp out socially desirable activities' (at [34]).[43]

But what 'desirable' activities does this include? The Act's remit clearly extends to injuries caused while scouting, on school trips, as well as the playing of sports and games and the provision of public amenities more generally. But does it apply to injuries sustained while in a military zone? *Hopps* v *Mott MacDonald Ltd* [2009] suggests that it does. The claimant, a civilian electrical engineer, lost his shoulder when he was hit by an improvised explosive device (IED) while travelling on a road known as 'bomb alley' in a civilian vehicle while working on rebuilding projects in Iraq following the invasion in 2003 (at [93]).[44] He sued his employers and the Ministry of Defence who were responsible for his security. The judge, while acknowledging the claimant's contribution 'at much personal cost . . . to improving the lot of the Iraqi people' (at [133]) rejected his claim. Referring to section 1 of the Compensation Act, the judge held that given the small risk of injury and desirability of the rebuilding work, it was not unreasonable for the claimant to have been carried around in an unarmoured (civilian) vehicle.

The Social Action, Responsibility and Heroism Act 2015 was intended to work alongside the Compensation Act 2006 to buttress the law of negligence. Just 176 words long, it lists the matters—social action, responsibility and heroism—to which a court must have regard in determining a claim in negligence or breach of statutory duty. Enacted as part of the Coalition Government's 'wider programme to encourage participation in civil society and . . . a specific commitment to "take a range of measures to encourage volunteering and involvement in social action"' (Bill's Explanatory Notes at [6]), it is yet to be cited in a reported case.

43. See also comment of Smith LJ in *Uren* v *Corporate Leisure (UK) Ltd* [2011] that 'it was common ground that [the Act] . . . did not add anything to the common law position' (at [13]).

44. The case also established that s 1 of the Compensation Act 2006 had retrospective effect (at [92]).

8.6 Establishing breach

You will remember that in order to establish whether the defendant has breached their duty of care two questions need to be considered:

(1) How the defendant *ought* to have behaved in the circumstances—what was the required standard of care in these circumstances?

(2) How the defendant *did* behave—did they fall below the standard of care required?

So far, this chapter has concentrated solely on the first of these questions. The second question—that is, proof of negligence—is largely a question of fact to be determined by the court on the evidence before them. The burden is on the claimant to establish, on the balance of probabilities—that is, that it is more likely than not—that the defendant's actions fell below the required standard of care.[45]

At times this can be extremely difficult. In many cases the claimant will have to rely on the defendant releasing certain information to them (which they are unlikely, understandably, to be willing to do) or the information may be highly technical or simply very dense. The latter is particularly so in relation to litigation arising out of a defective drug where it can be very time-consuming and expensive to sift through the scientific and medical evidence.[46] Things are slightly more straightforward in relation to road traffic accidents. Section 11 of the Civil Evidence Act 1968 shifts the burden of proof onto the defendant to show that he was *not* negligent and that his conduct (although criminal) does not amount to civil negligence. Similarly, while criminal conviction (or breach of the Highway Code (*Brown* v *Paterson* [2010])) does not automatically establish negligence, it is admissible in civil proceedings as prima facie evidence of negligence. It is highly likely, therefore, that a driver who, for example, is convicted of injuring another by their careless driving, will also be found to be negligent.[47]

The courts may also infer negligence from the circumstances in which the accident or injury took place. This process is usually described by the phrase *res ipsa loquitur* meaning 'the thing speaks for itself'. Academics disagree on the precise status of the 'doctrine'.[48] Some argue that it simply reflects the common-sense view that sometimes the likelihood that the accident was caused by the defendant's negligence is such that it is not necessary to explain it, while others suggest that it is a more formal doctrine which, in certain circumstances, shifts the burden of proof from the claimant to the defendant (meaning that they will be liable if they are unable to prove, on the balance of probabilities, the *absence* of fault on their part). Most agree that this latter view goes too far. *Steele* describes *res ipsa loquitur* as not so much a doctrine 'so much as a complex name for a common-sense inference from the facts' (p 137). *Res ipsa loquitur* does *not* shift or reverse the burden of proof onto the defendant. It simply means that sometimes the

45. The claimant must provide evidence of carelessness if an action in negligence is to disclose a good cause of action. If the claimant is unable to do this, the defendant may apply for summary judgment (which means the claim will fail without further argument).

46. This difficulty was addressed by Parliament in Part 1 of the Consumer Protection Act 1987, see **Chapter 12**.

47. See Lord Denning MR's discussion of the claimant's liability in ***Nettleship*** at 698–9.

48. Patrick Atiyah '*Res Ipsa Loquitur* in England and Australia' (1972) 35 MLR 337.

circumstances of the negligence can be evidence of carelessness. As such it is a welcome and effective means of redressing the balance of power between claimant and defendant where evidential difficulties make it hard for the claimant to establish negligence.

The 'doctrine' stems from the judgment of Erle CJ in *Scott* v *London and St Katherine Docks Co* [1895] where, in response to the claimant's failure to explain how his injury occurred, he stated:

> There must be reasonable evidence of negligence, but, where the thing is shown to be under the management of the defendant, or his servants, and the accident is such as, in the ordinary course of things, does not happen if those who have the management of the machinery use proper care, it affords reasonable evidence, in the absence of explanation of the defendant, that the accident arose from want of care. (at 601)

Two things need to be met in order for the rule to come into play (although these often run together). First, the thing which caused the accident needs to be 'under the management of the defendant, or his servants', that is, the defendant needs to have control of the thing that caused the injury. A defendant will not be liable if, for example, someone steals their car and causes an accident or for a hotel guest throwing furniture out of a hotel window (*Larson* v *St Francis Hotel* [1948]). Secondly, the accident must be such as 'in the ordinary course of things, does not happen if those who have the management of the [things] use proper care'. This will, largely, depend on the circumstances of the case—it will be easier to prove negligence if you slip on a wet floor near a swimming pool or gym (where the occupiers may be expected to know that the floor might be wet and take appropriate precautions) than in a shopping centre (*Ward* v *Tesco Stores Ltd* [1976]). The question for the court is whether the evidence taken as a whole points in the direction of the defendant's negligence. Thus, where the defendant is unable to explain how the accident occurred but is able to show that they exercised all reasonable care in the circumstances, they will not be found liable (*J* v *North Lincolnshire County Council* [2000]).

8.7 **Conclusion**

In this chapter, we have considered the second part of a claim in the tort of negligence—*breach of duty of care*. This occurs where a defendant has fallen below the standard of care demanded by the law. In setting the standard of care, the courts seek to balance issues relating to the public benefit against individual freedom and responsibility. This takes the form of two questions: (1) what was the required standard of care in these circumstances? (2) And did the defendant fall below this standard? When setting the standard of care the courts compare the actions of the defendant to those of the 'reasonable man'. This is an objective test (although the courts, on occasions, may incorporate the defendant's age and skills into their assessment). When setting the standard of care required of the defendant—that is, what the defendant *ought* to have done or what is *reasonable* in the circumstances of the case—the courts take a number of factors into account: probability or risk of the injury; the seriousness of the injury; the cost of taking precautions; and sometimes the social value of the activity.

The second question—that is, proof of negligence—is largely a question of fact to be determined by the court on the evidence before them. The claimant is sometimes helped when seeking to establish on the balance of probabilities that the defendant breached their duty of care by the 'doctrine' of *res ipsa loquitur*.

End-of-chapter questions

After reading the chapter carefully, try answering the questions which follow.

1 In *Bolton* v *Stone* the cricket club was not held liable. What was the role of reasonable foreseeability? Do you agree with the outcome of the case?

2 What was the reasoning behind ***Nettleship***? Is it a fair decision? Fair (or unfair) to whom?

3 'It is better to control liability by adjusting the standard of care than by restricting the circumstances in which a duty of care arises.' Discuss.

If you would like to know what we think visit the **online resources**. www.oup.com/he/horsey7e

Answering the problem question

Consider again the problem question at the start of this chapter. Now having read about the topic, **what would be your advice to the various parties?**

Here are some pointers to get you started

→ Kate has two potential claims in this problem question. The claim against Iris is relatively straightforward (it is unlikely that Iris will be considered to be acting as a reasonable driver if she's 'probably just over the drink-drive limit'). But could Kate be contributorily negligent?

→ Her claim against the doctor is more complicated. You will need to consider both whether she has breached her duty of care *and*, if so, whether this has caused her injury. Key here is whether Kate has been given the opportunity to give her 'informed consent'—see ***Bolam***, *Bolitho*, ***Chester*** and ***Montgomery***.

→ Also remember the question asks you to 'advise Kate' so although this is a 'breach' question you should consider all the elements to a claim in negligence.

If you need some more guidance

see online resources

→ An **annotated version of the problem with issues and cases to consider** can be found in the Appendix.

→ A **suggested outline answer** to check your ideas against can be found in the online resources that accompany the book.

Further reading

Much of the academic writing in this area focuses on medical negligence and, in particular, the effect of ***Bolam*** and more recently ***Montgomery***. For a general discussion of the role and purpose of fault as a basis of negligence liability, see Chapter 2 of *Cane*.

Beever, Allan 'Negligence and Utility' (2017) 17 Ox Uni Commonwealth LJ 85

Brazier, Margaret and José Miola 'Bye-Bye *Bolam*: A Medical Litigation Revolution?' (2000) 8 Med L Rev 85

Cave, Emma and Caterina Milo 'Informing Patient: The *Bolam* Legacy' (2020) 20 Med L International 103

Conaghan, Joanne 'Tort Law and the Feminist Critique of Reason' in Anne Bottomley (ed) *Feminist Perspectives on the Foundational Subjects of Law* (Cavendish, 1996), p 47

Gardiner, Bruce 'Liability for Sporting Injuries' [2008] JPIL 16

Goudkamp, James and Melody Ihuoma 'A Tour of the Tort of Negligence' [2016] Professional Negligence 137

Herbert, Rebecca 'The Compensation Act 2006' [2006] JPIL 337

Heywood, Robert and José Miola 'The Changing Face of Pre-operative Medical Disclosure: Placing the Patient at the Heart of the Matter' (2017) 133 LQR 296

Miola, José 'The Standard of Care in Medical Negligence—Still Reasonably Troublesome?' in Janice Richardson and Erika Rackley (eds) *Feminist Perspectives on Tort Law* (Routledge, 2012), p 163

Mulheron, Rachael 'Trumping *Bolam*: A Critical Legal Analysis of *Bolitho*'s "Gloss"' [2010] CLJ 609

Nolan, Donal 'Varying the Standard of Care in Negligence' [2013] CLJ 651

Sheldon, Sally 'A Responsible Body of Medical Men Skilled in that Particular Art: Rethinking the *Bolam* Test' in Sally Sheldon and Michael Thomson (eds) *Feminist Perspectives on Health Care Law* (Cavendish, 1998)

Causation and remoteness of damage

9

Problem question

Read this problem question carefully, and keep it in mind while you are working through the chapter that follows. At the end of the chapter, you will be able to apply what you have learnt to the problem question and advise the relevant parties.

Stefaan and Gavin spend the evening drinking in the pub. Stefaan offers Gavin a lift home in his car, assuring Gavin that this will be fine as he is 'probably only just over the limit'. Driving home, Stefaan swerves to avoid a fox and crashes the car. The paramedics who arrive at the scene find that Gavin has broken his arm but otherwise only has minor cuts and bruises. Gavin is taken to hospital to be checked by a doctor.

At the hospital Gavin is seen by Cheryl, the doctor on duty. Cheryl disagrees with the paramedics' opinion and, deciding Gavin's arm is not broken but only sprained, puts it in a sling, without setting it in a cast. As she was so busy that evening, she decided not to bother sending him for an X-ray first. Gavin returns to hospital the following month with pain in his arm. It transpires that his arm *was* in fact broken and, because it was not set in the proper cast, the bones have fused together wrongly, resulting in a permanent disability. An expert witness says that there was a chance this might have happened anyway, even if Cheryl had not been negligent. Gavin has to have an operation to try and re-set the bones, but this will not improve his arm to the condition it was in before the accident.

A week later Gavin is knocked down by a speeding motorist who fails to stop and cannot be traced. His right arm is so badly injured that it has to be amputated.

Advise Gavin in relation to the claims in negligence he may bring.

9.1 Introduction

Consider the following examples:

→ ***Peter goes to hospital complaining of stomach pains after eating some badly prepared fish. A doctor negligently examines him and sends him home. Later, he dies from severe food poisoning. Medical evidence showed that there was nothing the doctor could have done to save him.***

→ ***David negligently causes a collision on a motorway. Pauline, who was driving one of the other vehicles, was dazed by the collision and went to sit on the hard shoulder. A police car, rushing to the scene of the accident, hit and seriously injured Pauline.***

→ ***Judy had pains in her chest and went to hospital. A doctor gave her a cursory examination and told her to stay in the waiting room, where she later had a heart attack and died. Medical evidence suggested that even if the doctor had treated her properly, she would still have had only a 30 per cent chance of living.***

→ ***Bern contracts lung cancer as a result of exposure to asbestos. Medical evidence has proved that the type of cancer he has is caused by a single asbestos fibre entering the lung. Two of Bern's previous employers negligently exposed him to asbestos.***

Once a duty of care and breach are established, claimants must also show that the defendant's breach *caused* their harm. Causation is central to any negligence claim, as it links the defendant's breach to the claimant's harm. The purpose of establishing causation is to allocate responsibility for (the costs of) harm and, to some extent, risks. Causation has two aspects: 'factual' and 'legal'. The first of these is analysed almost mathematically, using a balance of probabilities test (though some exceptions exist, as we will see later) to establish whether the defendant *in fact* caused the harm. The 'legal' aspect of causation (including a test of 'remoteness') simply asks whether any of the factual causes should be excluded from being seen as a cause in law. If either causation test 'fails', the defendant escapes liability.

Although we use causal language in everyday speech, our meaning is not always clear. The answer to a question about the cause of something often depends on who we ask, or why we ask the question in the first place—different people see causes in different ways, particularly when cause is associated with *responsibility*. Any given event has numerous (often infinite) causes—that is, factors without which it could not have happened. Put another way, any number of things may have caused it. The same is true of a tort or harm. The problem of multiple potential causes runs through causation, leaving the courts having to pin down or 'find' the 'real' cause from one of a number of factors. In so doing, two questions must be addressed (see **Table 9.1**).

TABLE 9.1 Considering factual and legal causation in negligence

	'Cause in fact'	**'Cause in law'**
The questions being asked	• What happened factually in the situation as it occurred? • On the balance of probabilities, did the breach cause the harm alleged ('but for' the negligence, would the harm have been suffered)? • If not, have the courts created an exception to the usual rule?	• Even if the breach was the cause in fact of the harm suffered, what is the legal interpretation of the facts—was the harm too remote? • Are there any policy or other reasons to justify denying liability? • Was there a break in the chain of causation?

(1) What are the prerequisite conditions for the harm (factual causation)?

(2) What is the 'relevant' or 'real' cause of it (legal causation)?

In law as in life, it is not always possible to pinpoint the single *factual* cause of a harm. A road accident, for example, may have many 'real' causes—both drivers may have been going too fast on a winding country lane in the fog, in which case there are at least three factors—the speed of each driver and the weather conditions—that might have caused the harm.

Pause for reflection

A stolen and abandoned car is set on fire. Consider this list of potential causes:

- Adam, who stole the car, didn't tell his parents where he was going.
- Adam's parents did not check where he was going when he left the house earlier that evening.
- The area lacks recreational facilities for teenagers.
- The police have failed to catch car thieves in the area.
- Adam and the police were involved in a chase; Adam abandoned the car so that he could get away.
- The police failed to notify the Highway Authority that the car was abandoned.
- No one removed the car from the side of the road.
- Ben, who set the car on fire, is only 12, but was out unsupervised at night.
- Ben's parents don't know that Ben has left the house.
- Ben is sold cigarettes and matches at a local newsagent.
- Ben thinks it will be fun to throw lit matches in the abandoned car.

Which of these is/are *the* cause/causes of the harm?

Don't worry if you don't know the 'legal' answer at this stage. The purpose of this exercise is for you to think quickly about which of these facts, if any, you would consider the cause of the harm (and which you would not). Thinking through the issues in this way will help you prepare for the material to follow.

As this example helps to illustrate, the process of determining *factual* causation comes down to one of elimination rather than inclusion. How do we go about reducing the list of possible causes? Put another way, are some causes more likely to be legally relevant than others? The answer, it seems, is yes. Hart and Honoré suggest that we are more likely to find a cause in something out of the ordinary or unusual and that where both natural factors and human actions are involved, we will tend to focus on the human actions.[1] Similarly, positive actions, rather than omissions, are more likely to be considered causative and, when deciding between human actions, we are more likely to focus on voluntary rather than involuntary actions and those that we deem unreasonable rather than reasonable.

1. HLA Hart and AH Honoré *Causation in the Law* (2nd edn, OUP, 1985).

In tort law, the question is more sharply focused than simply asking 'what caused the injury or harm?' After all, if this were the question, then any or all of the potential reasons given in the list in the previous box could be said to be a 'cause' of the car burning: the car would not have burnt without—or 'but for'—each of the listed facts. Rather, when seeking to establish a claim in negligence, the question is: 'Did the defendant's *negligence* (i.e. their breach of duty) cause this harm?' Or, more precisely, 'Can we say that the act or omission that we have identified as negligent is a "real" cause (it may be one of many) of the harm?' The law approaches this wider question in two stages as just identified:

(1) was the defendant's action/inaction a necessary pre-condition for the harm to occur and, if so;

(2) is it therefore *the* cause of the harm?

These two stages are known as factual causation (or 'cause in fact') and legal causation (or 'cause in law') respectively and, as each contains different principles and tests, will be dealt with separately in this chapter.

9.2 Factual causation—the 'but for' test

In determining liability for a breach of duty we must first decide whether the defendant's wrong *in fact* caused the claimant's harm. At first glance, this may seem to be a question of common sense. If we ask whether the harm was *a consequence* of the defendant's breach then we can reach a yes or no answer quite easily. However, in law, the question of causation is actually more difficult, in part due to the fact that there are various *legal* meanings of the word 'cause' which differ from its ordinary meanings.

9.2.1 Explaining the test

Sometimes, liability is established simply by showing that the defendant's actions caused the harm. This is how strict liability systems work. In fault-based systems like negligence, however, this is not enough. We have to establish that the defendant's *breach of duty*, as opposed to simply his *actions*, caused the harm. In other words, the harm suffered by the claimant must be caused by the fact that the defendant's actions fell below the appropriate standard of care for liability to arise.[2]

The cause in fact question is whether the defendant's negligent action or omission was a necessary condition for the harm to occur.[3] Put differently, if the harm would have occurred *without* the defendant's carelessness, there is no cause in fact. This is often expressed in the form of a 'but for' test: we ask the question 'But for the defendant's

2. The same rule applies in every tort where proof of harm or damage is required, so what is said in this chapter about causation as it relates to negligence should also be remembered in the context of other fault-based torts, as well as some strict liability ones (e.g. claims under the Consumer Protection Act 1987).

3. Questions of cause in relation to a defendant's *failure* to do something only arise if there was a duty to act—see **Chapter 4**.

carelessness (breach), would the claimant have escaped harm?' If the answer is 'yes', the cause in fact is identified: no harm would have come to the claimant without the added element of the defendant's carelessness.

Almost all answers to the factual causation question, however, retain an element of uncertainty. It is probably fair to say that we can never be entirely sure how events would have turned out—for example, whether a particular loss would have been suffered—if the circumstances had been different—for instance, if the defendant *had* exercised reasonable care. Confusingly, we are asking what would have happened in an alternative situation, and yet how can we know, since, by definition, this is not what *did* happen? We deal with this through the 'burden of proof'. Unlike criminal law, where the burden of proof must be established beyond reasonable doubt, in tort law the claimant must only establish that something was, on the balance of probabilities, a necessary condition for the harm occurring. This is a lower standard. To succeed, the claimant need only show that it was more likely than not that the defendant's breach caused their harm. If they cannot establish that the defendant's negligence made the likely difference between something happening and not happening, then it cannot be a cause of their injuries.[4] Put another way, it is more likely than not that the defendant's breach did *not* contribute to the harm suffered by the claimant and so was essentially coincidental and unconnected.

The classic example of the 'but for' test is found in ***Barnett* v *Chelsea and Kensington Hospital Management Committee*** [1969].

Barnett v *Chelsea and Kensington Hospital Management Committee* [1969] QBD

A doctor failed to properly examine a man who presented himself at the hospital's emergency department. It transpired that the man was suffering from arsenic poisoning from which he subsequently died. The doctor admitted negligence, but said that he had not caused the man's death. *Even if he had have acted properly, the man would have died anyway* as it was too late to do anything to save him. It could not be said that 'but for' the doctor's negligence the man would not have died.

The court held that as the doctor's negligence was not a necessary condition for the man's death, he could not be held liable for it.[5]

In *Nyang* v *G4S Care & Justice Services Ltd and others* [2013], a similar issue arose. Mr Nyang, detained at an immigration removal centre pending deportation to Gambia, tried to kill himself by running head first into a concrete wall at speed. He broke his

4. In this respect the cause in fact test is purely a negative test as it can be said that it merely excludes things that might have been a cause.

5. Thus we would arrive at the same outcome in respect of Peter and his food poisoning in the chapter-opening scenario. Also, although the facts seem different on first glance, the same would apply to Judy (see ***Hotson***). For similar reasoning in a different context (property damage) see *Chubb Fire Ltd* v *Vicar of Spalding* [2010].

spine and rendered himself tetraplegic. Some of the actions (and inactions) of the detention and medical staff at the centre, particularly in respect of failures to determine his psychological condition, were found to be breaches of duty. However, Lewis J determined that 'but for' the breaches the claimant would have suffered the same harm.

9.2.2 **Problems with the test**

Establishing or disproving cause in fact is not always as easy as in ***Barnett***.[6] We cannot always imagine what would have happened if the defendant had not been negligent. Two situations in particular make dealing with factual causation complicated. Here, various policy reasons have led, on some occasions, to judicially devised ways around—exceptions to—the usual 'but for' test.

The first problem is situations where there are multiple potential causes of the harm and a lack of, for example, scientific or forensic knowledge means that it would be too difficult (or even impossible) to establish what would have happened in the absence of negligence. There are some fairly obvious examples of situations where this might lead to an unclear outcome, such as in complex medical situations or accidents involving multiple vehicles. The second problem, perhaps more contentiously, covers situations where we *could* work out the factual cause, but the result appears unjust and we therefore want to reject it.

This, of course, prompts questions as to when such exceptions to the 'but for' test of factual causation are to be recognised, their extent and rationale. Answers can be found in careful analysis of the difficult and often seemingly contradictory case law and it is to this that we now turn.

9.2.2.1 Multiple potential causes

Where there is more than one potential cause of harm, it becomes factually hard to establish, in the absence of clear evidence or proof, that any of the potential causes is more likely than any other to be *the* cause. For example, where there are two competing potential causes, each seeming equally plausible, each will only be 50 per cent likely to be the cause of the harm suffered, thus neither would satisfy the 'but for' test. Where there are three competing potential causes, each of these will only be 33.3 per cent likely to be the cause, and so on. A good example of this is found in ***Wilsher* v *Essex Area Health Authority*** [1988].

> ***Wilsher* v *Essex Area Health Authority* [1988] HL**
>
> Martin Wilsher was cared for in the special care baby unit of a hospital, after being born prematurely. A doctor was negligent in monitoring his blood. Consequently, he was, on two separate occasions, given too much oxygen. Wilsher developed retrolental fibroplasia (RLF)—an incurable retinal condition—which eventually left him blind in one eye and with seriously impaired
>
> →

6. See e.g. *Schembri* v *Marshall* [2020], in particular at [51]–[56].

→

vision in the other. Too much oxygen in the blood is a known possible cause of RLF. The defence contended that there were a number of other 'innocent' potential causes, including his premature birth (RLF is a known risk to premature babies). In total there were five competing causes, each equally probable, thus 20 per cent likely to be the true cause of the harm.

Wilsher's claim against the negligent doctor succeeded in the lower court and by a majority in the Court of Appeal. However, the House of Lords was not persuaded that, on the balance of probabilities, the doctor's negligence and not any other factor had caused the harm.

From ***Wilsher***, even where there is a negligent act that common sense tells us might potentially be the cause of someone's harm, if there are other, alternative possible causes of that harm, especially 'natural' ones, we cannot establish that 'but for' the negligent act, the claimant would not have suffered harm. As a result, the defendant will escape liability.[7] The practical problem in multiple potential cause cases is always whether enough evidence can be gathered to prove that the defendant's negligence caused the harm. Variants of the 'alternatives' issue arise all the time, but this does not always mean that the claimant will be unsuccessful, as the courts have sometimes deviated from the 'but for' test in such situations.

Material contribution to harm

In *Bonnington Castings Ltd* v *Wardlaw* [1956] (predating ***Wilsher***), a factory employee contracted pneumoconiosis, a lung condition, from the inhalation of silica dust. He sued his employer in negligence. Some dust inhalation was an inevitable consequence of the work being done (this dust was therefore deemed to be 'innocent' dust). However, the House of Lords found that there was a higher level of dust in the air than there should have been (they deemed this extra quantity 'guilty' dust), due to the employer's negligence in not adequately ventilating the factory. The question was, then, whether the 'guilty' dust made any difference to the claimant's chances of contracting the disease.

Crucially, medical evidence established that the disease was progressive, or *cumulative*—it was caused by the *build-up* of silica dust in the lungs. It could not be established exactly at what point the disease occurred. As the question was not how much dust was in the lungs or how long it had been there, it could not be established, on the balance of probabilities, whether the 'guilty' dust was the cause. That is, it could not be said that 'but for' the defendant's negligence in allowing the 'guilty' dust into the air, the defendant would not have suffered the harm.[8] However, the House of Lords

7. Though see the Court of Appeal decision in *Bailey* v *Ministry of Defence* [2008]. Here, there were two potential causes of the claimant's cardiac arrest and brain damage—one negligent and one 'natural' and it could not be established which was the 'but for' cause. Following ***Wilsher***, there should have been no liability. However, the Court of Appeal, treating the case as one of *cumulative* cause (see later), found that the hospital's negligence made a 'material contribution' to the harm. See also *Leigh* v *London Ambulance Service* [2014] and *Kennedy* v *London Ambulance Service NHS Trust* [2016].

8. In fact the medical evidence said that it made a *difference*; but because the case was argued as 'all or nothing', what it could not say was whether the entire disease would have been avoided in the absence of the guilty dust. This case makes much more sense if the language of 'divisible harm' is used (which was not the language used in the 1950s).

found that *in this case*, because *cumulatively* the 'innocent' and 'guilty' dust were *more likely* to cause harm, it was enough to show that the defendant's negligence made a *material* ('more than negligible'[9]) *contribution* to the condition. The law lords effectively bypassed the 'but for' test (perhaps for policy reasons related to the employer–employee relationship and the existence of employers' liability insurance). Crucially, when the 'but for' test produced—according to the House of Lords—unsatisfactory results, they manufactured a way around it.[10]

The extent of the effect of this diversion from the 'but for' test was somewhat more diluted by *Holtby* v *Brigham & Cowan (Hull) Ltd* [2000].[11] Following *Bonnington*, where a disease is contracted as a result of *cumulative* exposure to toxins, it need only be proved that the negligent part of that exposure would materially contribute to the condition, and not that the negligent exposure was *the* likely cause of the condition. In such cases, the claimant could receive full compensation. However, in *Holtby*, the Court of Appeal ruled that claimants in such situations may only recover damages proportionate to the defendant's negligence. The claimant in *Holtby* was negligently exposed to asbestos by a number of employers over a period of years, contracting asbestosis (a cumulative condition) as a result. The Court of Appeal awarded damages proportionately by defendant, based on the extent of exposure (time plus intensity) under each negligent employer.[12] The decision can be viewed as significant because the injury (asbestosis) was treated as 'divisible'. However, it is not a divisible injury in the sense that one defendant caused the claimant harm and another defendant caused a different type of harm entirely.

Pause for reflection

Why do you think the Court of Appeal treated asbestosis as a divisible injury in *Holtby*? What would have been the position, with regard to damages, had they not done so? Was the court looking for the 'fairest' outcome for both the claimant (who would receive full compensation) *and* the defendants (so all of them became liable to pay at least something, but none would be liable for the full amount)? If so, do you think this is an appropriate role for the court? See the judgment of Stuart-Smith LJ for an indication of how he viewed the court's role: 'in my view the

→

9. *Bailey* v *Ministry of Defence* [2008] (at [46]). Confirmed in *Garner* v *Salford County Council* [2013] where the claim failed for lack of evidence that the defendant's negligence exposed the claimant to more than minimal levels of asbestos. The opposite conclusion was reached, in relation to a small proportion of total exposure, in *Carder* v *The University of Exeter* [2016].

10. See also **section 9.2.2.2**.

11. See also *Ellis* v *Environment Agency* [2008]. Cf *Simmons* v *British Steel* [2004] in which the *Bonnington* test was used to hold the defendant fully liable for the (psychiatric) injury suffered by the claimant.

12. See also *Allen* v *British Rail Engineering* [2001], a case relating to 'vibration white finger', *Wright (a child)* v *Cambridge Medical Group* [2011] (baby with severe chicken pox symptoms negligently not referred to hospital by doctor, then negligently treated when eventually admitted to hospital, resulting in permanent hip damage); *Rahman* v *Arearose Ltd* [2001] (claimant beaten then later receiving negligent medical treatment, both cumulatively found to have caused him psychiatric harm); and *Hatton* v *Sutherland* [2002] (a stress-at-work case) (*obiter*). This approach to apportionment in relation to *psychiatric* harm was later doubted: see *Dickins* v *O2 plc* [2008].

→

court must do the best it can to achieve justice, not only to the claimant but the defendant, and among defendants' (at [20]).

On the other hand, consider the position of the claimant in this kind of 'divisible' claim who cannot locate one of his previous employers, or who finds out that one of them has long ago gone bankrupt? Does the decision to award proportionate damages seem as fair then, particularly when compared with the position of the claimant in *Bonnington*, or those where the harm is 'indivisible'? See *Carder* v *The University of Exeter* [2016], a case illustrating not only the potential perils of apportionment but also the 'justice' that may or may not be done. Recognising the award eventually received by the claimant (just over £1,500) was small, especially when compared to his litigation costs, Lord Dyson MR recommended that future claims should be settled early (at [43]).

Williams v _The Bermuda Hospitals Board (Bermuda)_ [2016] PC

Mr Williams went to a hospital emergency department with severe abdominal pain. The doctor who examined him ordered a CT scan to determine whether he had appendicitis or another condition. There was a 4–5-hour delay in performing the scan. Williams's appendix ruptured and he developed sepsis, leading to myocardial ischemia (reduced blood flow to the heart) and his needing life support. He could not prove that 'but for' the hospital's failure to provide adequate diagnosis and treatment, his condition would have been avoided and his claim failed for this reason at first instance. On appeal, the court found that the negligent diagnosis and subsequent treatment delay had materially contributed to the injury. Bermuda Hospitals Board appealed to the Privy Council.

Lord Toulson applied *Bonnington*, finding the 'parallel with the present case . . . obvious' (at [35]), that there had been both 'innocent' (already beginning to occur before the scan) and 'guilty' (attributable to the negligence) sepsis. Crucially, he found that the myocardial ischemia resulted from the effect of both. Therefore, the hospital's negligence had materially contributed to the ischemia.

In ***Williams***, the hospital board (with the NHS Litigation Authority intervening) pursued the appeal 'because of its concern about the Court of Appeal's judgment as a precedent'. It wanted to see 'orthodox legal principles' restored in medical cases (see [3]). However, though non-binding on the domestic courts, the Privy Council's judgment suggests that despite some 'distaste' for the idea after *Bailey*, material contribution to harm *can* be applied to medical cases where the final claim relates to an indivisible injury, and the usual 'but for' test can be dispensed with.[13]

13. It has since been applied in the High Court in *John* v *Central Manchester and Manchester Children's University Hospitals NHS Foundation Trust* [2016], in the context of a brain injury suffered in part as a result of a fall, compounded by a double delay in diagnosis and treatment at hospital.

Pause for reflection

SH Bailey contends that 'the significance of the decision in ***Williams*** should be taken at face value as involving an inference of fact that but-for causation was established', that the (flawed) reasoning in the case obscures this, and that 'to award full damages in cases where but-for causation cannot be established needs proper justification'.[14] Given the difficulties in reasoning, and the various interpretations and criticisms of the decision that Bailey discusses, he argues that 'the question whether there is a "material contribution" exception to proving but-for causation is crying out for review afresh by the Supreme Court. The accumulated dicta to date are unclear, inconsistent and unhelpful and proceed largely by assertion. Clarity is needed on the exact parameters of such an exception and on what are the reasons of legal policy that justify it.'

Do you agree? Can it be argued that ***Williams*** is in fact a straightforward application of the 'but for' test?

Material increase in risk

The 'material contribution' route around the problem caused by the rigidity of the 'but for' test was revisited in *McGhee* v *National Coal Board* [1973]. This case was similar in its facts to *Bonnington* but with an important difference. Again, scientific evidence was unable to determine whether 'innocent' or 'guilty' causes were the factual cause of the claimant's condition, a kind of dermatitis caused by exposure to brick dust. The claimant encountered the 'innocent' dust while he was at work, but this same dust became 'guilty' *after* work (it stayed on the claimant longer than it should have done, as the employers negligently failed to provide adequate washing facilities for employees' use at the end of their shift). The question was whether the extra time the dust was on the claimant's skin caused his skin condition to develop. Unlike *Bonnington*, it was recognised that dermatitis was *not* a cumulative condition—it could be triggered by a single exposure to the dust—it may, therefore, have occurred from working with 'innocent' dust. Thus, the 'guilty' dust did not materially contribute to the harm itself, but rather only to the *risk* of harm occurring.

The question became whether the claimant's condition was caused by his innocent exposure to dust *or* by the 'guilty' dust that remained on his body while he cycled home. Only if it could be shown to be the latter would the employer's negligence be the factual ('but for') cause of the claimant's condition. As in *Bonnington*, the evidence was not strong enough to prove it either way. However, what could be shown was that the longer the dust lay on someone's skin, the greater risk that person had of contracting dermatitis. The House of Lords held that this was enough—the fact that the *risk* of the claimant developing the condition was increased was enough to establish causation.

In *McGhee, material increase of risk* was treated as equivalent to *material contribution*. In so doing, on another view, the House of Lords in fact reversed the burden of proof—shifting it onto the *defendant* who then had to show that there was another, more likely,

14. SH Bailey, '"Material Contribution" after *Williams v The Bermuda Hospitals Board*' (2018) 38 LS 411 at 425.

cause than their negligence.[15] Where this cannot be done (as in *McGhee*), the defendant remains liable. It should be noted, however, that there is still a 'but for' calculation involved. To succeed, a claimant has to show, *on the balance of probabilities*, that the alleged negligence materially increased the risk of the harm being suffered.

Pause for reflection

The decisions in *Bonnington* and *McGhee* may seem like logical developments to a fairly rigid rule that can, because of its reliance on probability, produce some harsh results. However, look again at the dates of the two cases, and then at ***Wilsher***.

Both cases predate (and, importantly, survive) ***Wilsher***. In fact, the *McGhee* argument was rejected by the House of Lords in ***Wilsher***, which did not think that *McGhee* had established a new test for causation.[16] They said that although there *was* a materially increased risk of blindness caused by the doctor's negligence, this was not enough to establish factual causation. There were four other possible 'innocent' causes, any of which may have led to the condition, and the doctor's carelessness was not the most likely cause. Why was there a difference in this case? Does the fact that there was *more than one* other potential cause make the difference? Or is the decision in ***Wilsher*** based purely in policy, this time (as is often the case in relation to establishing breach—see **Chapter 8**) showing undue deference to the medical profession? If so, is the Court of Appeal's decision in *Bailey* v *Ministry of Defence* [2008] consistent?[17] For a visual outline of the judicially created exceptions to the normal causation rules, see **Figure** 9.1 later.

A key development in this area came with the House of Lords' decision in ***Fairchild* v *Glenhaven Funeral Services*** [2002]. However, despite the clear overlap with issues relating to 'material increase in risk', discussed previously, this case fits better into another category: that where the court feels the result of using the 'but for' test is an unjust one.

9.2.2.2 'Unjust' results 1: the mesothelioma exception

Fairchild v *Glenhaven Funeral Services* [2002] HL

A group of claims were made against multiple defendants by three employees who developed mesothelioma (an inevitably fatal type of lung cancer), caused by exposure to asbestos dust. Two of the claims failed at first instance, as the claimants could not satisfactorily show where the asbestos that caused their mesothelioma had come from.

In relation to the claim in ***Fairchild***, however, there was no problem in establishing that the employer had been negligent in allowing the claimant to be exposed to asbestos—the problem was that the employee had been exposed *by a series* of negligent employers, not just one. As

→

15. This approach was resoundingly rejected in later cases; see e.g. ***Barker* v *Corus UK Ltd*** [2006].
16. See e.g. Lord Bridge at 1090.
17. Also see Swift J in *ST* v *Maidstone and Tunbridge Wells NHS Trust* [2015] at [195]–[198].

→

in *McGhee*, the experts agreed that mesothelioma could be caused in a single moment—for example, even by a single asbestos fibre entering the lung—and was not necessarily caused by prolonged exposure.[18] The difficulty was that the claimants could not show *when* that causative exposure occurred, so they could not show, on the balance of probabilities, which of the employers was the factual cause. On that basis, strictly following the 'but for' test, the Court of Appeal dismissed the claim, and the claimant appealed to the House of Lords.

The law lords held that the 'but for' test produced an unjust result and the idea that no defendant would be liable for the harm suffered by the claimant, when there was no doubt that the cause had been negligence, clearly sat uncomfortably with them. Accordingly, they resurrected *McGhee*, approving the 'material increase of risk' interpretation and stating that in this *exceptional* type of case (perhaps defined as employment/industry)[19] this would be enough to establish factual causation; the defendants were therefore liable.[20]

In finding in ***Fairchild*** that each defendant had materially increased the risk of the claimant contracting mesothelioma, the House of Lords did not overrule ***Wilsher***, which seemed to potentially stand in the way of this interpretation. Instead, they distinguished it, holding that ***Wilsher*** had been correctly decided on its facts.[21] The law lords stressed that ***Fairchild*** was an *exception* to normal causation principles. The final outcome of ***Fairchild*** was that each of the negligent employers was jointly and severally liable. It would therefore be up to the employers who had been brought before the court to seek contributions from others who had not (under s 1(1) of the Civil Liability (Contribution) Act 1978).

Pause for reflection

Does the fact that *Wilsher* and *Fairchild* are both good law have any impact on the type of case the 'material increase of risk' test can be applied to in the future? We do not find the explanation that *Wilsher* should be confined to its facts very convincing, and would rather have seen a more carefully stated exposition of the policy and other distinguishing arguments behind the decision to depart from what seemed to be binding authority. Was it, for example, the difference between finding employers (who were likely to be insured) liable and the NHS? Did the shorter

→

18. Note, however, that the 'single fibre' theory has since been discredited by experts (***Sienkiewicz* v *Grief (UK) Ltd*** [2011]; *Durham* v *BAI (EL Trigger Litigation)* [2008], later *BAI (Run Off) Ltd and others* v *Durham and others* [2012]). It is enough that the harm is 'indivisible' and that the state of scientific knowledge renders proof of causation impossible.

19. Though now cf *Willmore* v *Knowsley Metropolitan Borough Council* [2011].

20. This may mean that Bern, in the scenario at the start of this chapter, would have a successful claim.

21. Perhaps it is the small difference in the facts—that there were only two potential causes, rather than five—that led to the Court of Appeal's finding (distinguishing ***Wilsher***) that there *could* be liability based on 'material contribution' in *Bailey* v *Ministry of Defence* [2008]. Though cf *Jones and others* v *Secretary of State for Energy and Climate Change and another* [2012].

→

timescale in *Wilsher* indicate a different outcome—the claimants in *Fairchild* had worked and were exposed to asbestos over a long period of time, followed by the slow onset of their disease and the inevitable nature of their death?

A clearer explanation might be found in *Ministry of Defence* v *AB and others* [2012], a test case involving claims relating to around 1,000 people harmed (including various cancers) by nuclear testing in the Pacific in the 1950s. Evidence showed there were a number of potential causes of the cancers other than radiation. While the judge at first instance thought that the higher courts might be happy to extend the ***Fairchild*** exception to this kind of case 'as a matter of policy', the Court of Appeal found 'no foreseeable possibility that the Supreme Court would be willing to extend the ***Fairchild*** exception' in cases where multiple potential causes exist, some of which were impossible to identify.[22] And they were correct: in the Supreme Court Lord Phillips observed that, in light of the observations made in ***Sienkiewicz*** v ***Greif (UK) Ltd*** [2011], the Court of Appeal's conclusion that the ***Fairchild*** exception would not be extended was correct (at [157]). There is clearly 'no appetite in the appellate courts for extending the ***Fairchild*** exception to cases involving diseases other than mesothelioma'.[23]

In ***Barker*** v ***Corus UK Ltd*** [2006], the House of Lords revisited similar issues, though with the added complication of a period of self-exposure and a new question regarding apportionment of damages.

Barker v *Corus UK Ltd* [2006] HL

A number of claims were made on behalf of people who had died from mesothelioma contracted as a result of exposure to asbestos dust at work. Some of the exposure was negligent on the part of the employers concerned and the claims were brought against them (those that had not gone bankrupt since the injury occurred). In one of the claims, the exposure to asbestos could be clearly broken down to three distinct periods of time: a period when the claimant was working for a now insolvent employer (who therefore could not be sued); a period when working for the defendant; and a period of self-employment. At both first instance and in the Court of Appeal, the defendants were held, following ***Fairchild***, jointly and severally liable.

The difference was that, to reflect the claimant's own negligence during the period of self-employment, contributory negligence (a partial defence, see **Chapter 10**) was found, with the claimant's damages reduced by 20 per cent to take this into account. The defendants in all of the cases appealed the finding of joint and several liability to the House of Lords, arguing that liability should be proportionately divided to reflect the actual risk that was caused by their negligence (e.g. based on the proportion of time that the claimant was negligently exposed to asbestos dust by the employer).

→

22. *Ministry of Defence* v *AB and others* [2010] at [154].

23. *Jones and others* v *Secretary of State for Energy and Climate Change and another* [2012] (at [6.18]). As *Peel & Goudkamp* point out, however, 'one obstacle is the decision in *McGhee*, which was not a mesothelioma case' (at 7-021).

→

A majority of the House of Lords agreed that the damages ought to be apportioned among the defendants according to their contributions to the increased risk.[24] They agreed that the most 'practical' method of apportionment would be based on the amount of time the claimant was negligently exposed to the asbestos dust by each employer, Lord Hoffmann noting that 'allowance may have to be made for the intensity of the exposure and the type of asbestos' (at [48]).

In ***Barker***, the House of Lords departed from the idea that the employers, all of whom had contributed by their negligence to an increased risk of the claimant contracting a fatal lung cancer, should be jointly and severally liable. Instead they preferred the idea that compensation payments should be based on the period of time (and intensity of exposure, etc) that the claimant worked for the employer and was negligently exposed to asbestos.[25] This issue was never raised in ***Fairchild***. In practice this means that, for example, in a situation where an employee was negligently exposed to asbestos by a series of four employers and one of these employers had subsequently gone bankrupt, compensation—but not full compensation—would be divided between the remaining three solvent employers on the basis of the period of time the claimant was employed by them. This means that the claimant cannot fully recover the damages that have been calculated according to their (or their dependants') need. This principle is illustrated in **Table 9.2**.

TABLE 9.2 Division of damages between a series of employers (following *Barker*)

	Risk increased by negligent defendant	Period of time employed by defendant	Defendant solvent or bankrupt	Proportion of damages paid
Harm suffered by claimant (e.g. mesothelioma)	A	10 years	Solvent	20%
	B	20 years	Bankrupt	None
	C	15 years	Solvent	30%
	D	5 years	Solvent	10%
Total proportion of (full) damages recoverable by claimant				60%

24. The point is that although mesothelioma is indivisible, if the harm is construed as 'risk of damage', that is divisible.
25. A principle recently confirmed in *Equitas Insurance Ltd* v *Municipal Mutual Insurance Ltd* [2019].

Pause for reflection

In *Fairchild*, the Court of Appeal found none of the defendants liable, as it could not be established, on the balance of probabilities, that any one of them had caused the harm suffered by the claimants. They said that the required 'leap over the evidential gap' would not only defy logic but would be 'susceptible of unjust results':

> If we were to accede to the claimants' arguments, we would be distorting the law to accommodate the exigencies of a very hard case. We would be yielding to a contention that all those who have suffered injury after being exposed to a risk of that injury from which someone else should have protected them should be able to recover compensation even when they are quite unable to prove who was the culprit. (Brooke LJ at [103])

The House of Lords disagreed. Lord Bingham, dealing with this exact point, explained:

> There is a strong policy argument in favour of compensating those who have suffered grave harm, at the expense of their employers who owed them a duty to protect them against that very harm and failed to do so, when the harm can only have been caused by breach of that duty and when science does not permit the victim accurately to attribute, as between several employers, the precise responsibility for the harm he has suffered. I am of the opinion that such injustice as may be involved in imposing liability on a duty-breaking employer in these circumstances is heavily outweighed by the injustice of denying redress to a victim. (at [33])

Which of the opinions do you agree with most? How does your opinion fit with the result of *Barker*?[26]

Dissenting in ***Barker***, Lord Rodger said that redefining the harm to justify apportioning damages between defendants would unfairly shift the risk that defendants had gone bankrupt, or were otherwise untraceable, onto the claimants, who had been negligently injured by the defendants in the first place. ***Barker***, unsurprisingly, caused great concern among workers who had been negligently exposed to asbestos dust during their employment.[27] These concerns were recognised by Parliament which, at the time, was debating the (then unrelated) Compensation Bill. As a result of the hostility to ***Barker***, the Bill was amended to legislatively reverse ***Barker***'s effect. Section 3 of the Compensation Act 2006 provides that, where the conditions for applying ***Fairchild*** are met (i.e. where negligent exposure to asbestos by a series of employers causes mesothelioma, but it cannot be shown which of the employers actually, or most likely, caused the disease), any or all

26. See also *Peel & Goudkamp* at 7-022, who say 'given the uncertainty surrounding the *Fairchild* exception and the quixotic process it unleashed, it may be that the law should have been left unaltered while the state of scientific knowledge was left to develop, notwithstanding the policy based impulse for alteration'. A similar view was expressed by the Court of Appeal in *Equitas Insurance Ltd v Municipal Mutual Insurance Ltd* [2019]. Males LJ said that 'once the courts can be confident that the objective of ensuring victim protection has been achieved, it is desirable that the anomalies should be corrected and that the law should return to the fundamental principles of the common law. Put shortly, once unorthodoxy has served its purpose, we should revert to orthodoxy' (at [91]).

27. Or, more importantly perhaps, to claimant lawyers and unions.

employers will be liable for the whole sum of damages.[28] This applies even where other sources of exposure existed, including self-employment or other (non-negligent) sources (though damages may still be reduced for the claimant's own contributory negligence under section 3(3)(b)). It is, of course, open to the liable defendant to seek contributions from others under the principles governing joint and several liability.[29]

Counterpoint

Had section 3 of the Compensation Act 2006 not been enacted, we would, in our opinion, have been left in an undesirable and contradictory position regarding House of Lords' decisions on asbestos-related claims. In ***Fairchild***, the position was that claimants should be allowed to recover *full* damages for the harm (and it must be remembered that this is a fatal lung cancer), even though they could not possibly have established which of the defendants was the likely cause. In this sense, the ***Fairchild*** decision is claimant-centred and is based on the fact that the claimant would receive nothing if the 'material increase of risk' exception to the 'but for' rule was not used.

In contrast, *Holtby*, while a good result for the actual claimant in that case, means that in future claimants suffering from asbestosis (as opposed to mesothelioma) may not recover in full if one or more of their previous employers has become insolvent.[30] This is less claimant-friendly. The same can be seen in the House of Lords' decision in ***Barker*** on the same point in relation to mesothelioma.

In ***Barker***, Lord Rodger pointed out that while it may seem harsh that a single defendant becomes liable for the total sum of a claimant's damages, purely because his negligence made a material contribution to the risk that the claimant would suffer mesothelioma, this result was also settled law. He went on to say that this principle 'is a form of rough justice which the law has not hitherto sought to smooth, preferring instead, as a matter of policy, to place the risk of insolvency of a wrongdoer or his insurer on the other wrongdoers or their insurers' (at [90]). ***Barker***, he claimed, meant that this risk has to be 'shouldered entirely by the innocent claimant' (at [90]). This does not appear consistent with the policy-orientated decision made by the House of Lords that sometimes wrongdoers should pay even where it cannot be proved that it was *their* wrong that caused the harm. As Lord Rodger found in ***Barker***, 'the desirability of the courts, rather than Parliament, throwing this lifeline to wrongdoers and their insurers at the expense of claimants is not obvious' (at [90]). This is particularly true given the fact that a claimant who contracted mesothelioma and was only ever employed by one negligent employer over the course of their working life would be able to recover full damages based on the 'but for' principle. Claimants should not be hindered by the fact that they have worked for *more* than one negligent employer.

Clearly Parliament agreed and section 3 of the Compensation Act 2006 removes this risk from claimants who have contracted or died from mesothelioma.[31] What section 3 does not legislate is what happens when ***Fairchild*** is applied *outside* a claim for mesothelioma. There, ***Barker*** will still apply (proportionate liability).[32]

28. Section 3(1)(a)–(d). Thus, in the scenarios at the beginning of this chapter, Bern's claim will not be unduly affected by ***Barker***.

29. See **Chapter 21**.

30. Though they may have recourse to some damages via the Financial Services Compensation Scheme.

31. Compare two decisions of the High Court of Australia, however: *Amaca Pty Ltd* v *Ellis* [2010] (where the claimant was also a smoker), distinguished in *Amaca Pty Ltd* v *Booth* [2011].

32. Though see the comments (*obiter*) of Smith LJ in *Novartis Grimsby Ltd* v *Cookson* [2007], a bladder cancer case, in which she indicates that she would have applied the ***Fairchild*** principle in the

Because the effect of the interaction of the decisions in ***Fairchild*** and ***Barker*** was not immediately clear, a flurry of causation cases based on the idea of material increase in risk was encouraged. Few succeeded.[33] More recently, the Supreme Court has indicated that the idea that there is a separate claim for material increase in risk *outside* of mesothelioma is wrong.[34]

Though ***Fairchild*** will apply in mesothelioma cases where there have been multiple potential negligent exposures to asbestos, there remained a question about what happens when there has only been a single (negligent) exposure coupled with 'ordinary' environmental exposure. The impact of section 3 of the Compensation Act 2006 was called into question in this respect in ***Sienkiewicz***.

Sienkiewicz v Greif (UK) Ltd [2011] SC

An action was brought on behalf of Mrs Costello, who died from mesothelioma in 2006. Mrs Costello had worked in offices at the defendant's factory in Ellesmere Port in Cheshire for nearly 20 years until 1984. Her job required her to enter areas of the factory that were contaminated with asbestos. At first instance, this exposure was found to be negligent. However, the judge also found that the claimant had been exposed to low levels of asbestos in the general atmosphere around Ellesmere Port, which might also have been significant enough to have caused mesothelioma.

The defendants argued that where there was only one employer, the correct test was the 'but for' test, not the *Fairchild* exception. They contended that the claimant had to prove on the balance of probabilities that the negligent exposure caused the disease and that to do this she would need to establish that the negligent exposure more than doubled the risk.[35] The judge accepted this argument, finding also that the doubling of risk could not be established on the facts—the negligent exposure had only increased the risk by 18 per cent. The claimant appealed, arguing that the correct test was whether the (negligent) occupational exposure had *materially* increased the risk: the increase did not have to be twofold, only more than minimal. The Court of Appeal agreed.[36] On the issue of apportionment, Smith LJ first acknowledged that the *Fairchild* judges *might* not have thought the exception appropriate where there was only one negligent employer and the other asbestos source was environmental. However, whether this was the case or not,

→

absence of an (almost straightforward) application of the 'but for' test, as the two potentially causative agents 'act on the body in the same way' (at [72]).

33. See e.g. *Clough* v *First Choice Holidays* [2006]; *Sanderson* v *Hull* [2008]; *Wootton* v *J Docter Ltd* [2008]. Note that it has been confirmed that the ***Fairchild*** test does not change how the duty is formulated and, to get to the stage of applying it, the duty and breach elements of a claim must be established in the ordinary way: *Williams* v *University of Birmingham* [2011].

34. In *Employers' Liability Insurance 'Trigger' Litigation: BAI (Run Off) Ltd and others* v *Durham and others* [2012] (*'Trigger Litigation'*). In *International Energy Group Ltd* v *Zurich Insurance plc* [2013], the claimants contended that ***Barker*** should continue to be applied to a claim arising in Guernsey (where s 3 of the Compensation Act 2006 does not apply). The Court of Appeal ruled that the approach of the Supreme Court in *BAI (Run Off)* (based on Lord Rodger's approach in ***Barker***) was to be preferred. Following an appeal heard in July 2014, with further submissions in January 2015, a seven-member Supreme Court confirmed that this is the position (*Zurich Insurance plc UK Branch* v *International Energy Group Ltd* [2015]).

35. This principle was used in *Novartis Grimsby Ltd* v *Cookson* [2007]—but this was not a mesothelioma case.

36. *Sienkiewicz* v *Grief (UK) Ltd* [2009]. Also see *Willmore* v *Knowsley Metropolitan Borough Council* [2009].

→

she found that section 3 of the Compensation Act 2006 rendered this irrelevant, as it covered the situation in this case.[37] Lord Clarke thought the case was clearly the type of case considered in *Fairchild*, as interpreted in **Barker** (as the non-occupational exposure could be viewed in a similar way to the period of self-employment in **Barker**). Unanimously, the appeal was allowed.

The defendants appealed to the Supreme Court. The seven-member court considered the '*Fairchild* exception', the effect of section 3 of the Compensation Act 2006, how 'material' a material increase in risk has to be (rejecting the so-called 'doubling of risk' idea), as well as the importance of epidemiological evidence, eventually dismissing the appeal unanimously.[38] Lord Phillips (at [98]–[106]) explained that a continuing justification for maintaining the exception is that the gaps in our knowledge as to how mesothelioma is triggered 'justifies the adoption of the special rule of causation that the House of Lords applied in *Fairchild* and **Barker**' (at [103]).[39]

This decision tells us that the '***Fairchild*** exception' also applies in mesothelioma cases where only *one* defendant is proved to have negligently exposed the victim to asbestos, even though there was a risk of developing the disease from a non-negligent exposure.[40] The Supreme Court found that proof that the injury would not have happened 'but for' the defendant's negligence is unnecessary. It also confirmed that section 3 only applies when the defendant has committed a tort.[41] As confirmed in *Zurich* [2015], and taking us back to the question of what exactly 'cause' means, we now know that under ***Fairchild***, as confirmed in '*Trigger Litigation*', mesothelioma is 'caused' in any period in which exposure occurs which materially increased the risk of contracting it.[42] The Court of Appeal has more recently determined that ***Fairchild*** also applies to lung cancer caused by exposure to asbestos.[43]

37. Section 3(1)(d) was the point of contention, as the conditions in s 3(1)(a)–(c) were clearly made out.

38. Alongside the defendant's appeal in *Willmore* v *Knowsley Metropolitan Borough Council* [2011], which was heard at the same time.

39. The implication appears to be that if the evidential uncertainties disappear by future findings that fill the scientific gaps in our knowledge, the mesothelioma exception would also disappear.

40. This fits more closely with *McGhee* v *National Coal Board* [1973], upon which ***Fairchild*** was originally based (see **section 9.2.2.1**).

41. Reflecting further an attempt to do justice for those who contract mesothelioma due to negligent employers, the Mesothelioma Act 2014 established the Diffuse Mesothelioma Payment Scheme, which allows parties who contracted the disease after 25 July 2012, but who have no one to sue (as the employer(s) who negligently exposed them, or their insurers, have become insolvent), to claim from a compensation fund paid for by levies from the insurance industry (though only for 80 per cent of the amount of the average damages obtainable via legal action).

42. See the opinion of Lord Mance, especially at [45]–[49].

43. *Heneghan* v *Manchester Dry Docks Ltd and others* [2016]. Part of the reasoning was based on the fact that in *Zurich*, Lords Neuberger and Reed said that the *Fairchild* exception was 'applicable to any disease which has the unusual features of mesothelioma' (at [191]). Note, however, that the ***Barker*** rule on apportionment would apply.

FIGURE 9.1 Problems and solutions to multiple potential cause claims

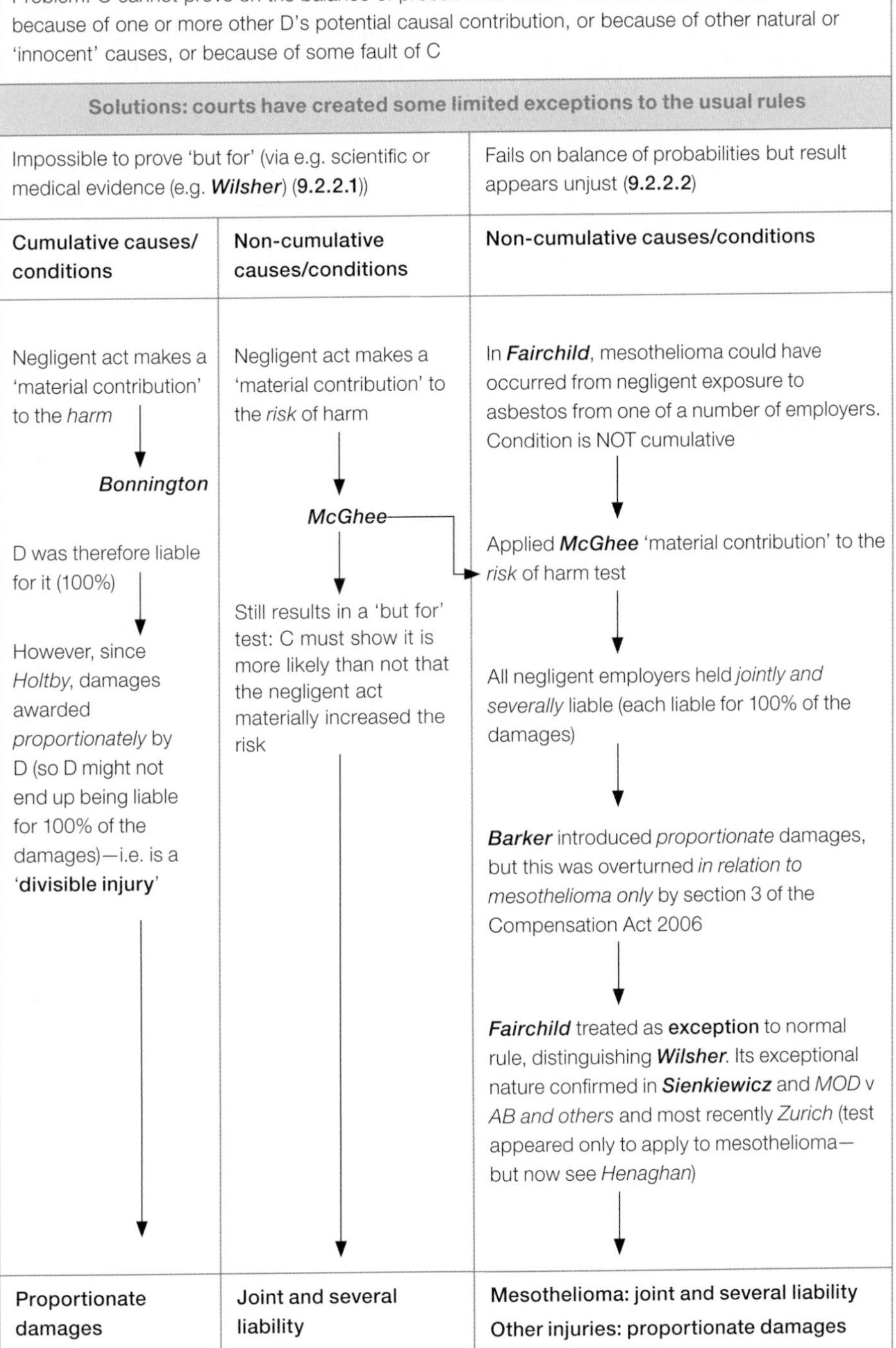

Multiple potential causes in fact		
Problem: C cannot prove on the balance of probabilities that D was the cause in fact, either because of one or more other D's potential causal contribution, or because of other natural or 'innocent' causes, or because of some fault of C		
Solutions: courts have created some limited exceptions to the usual rules		
Impossible to prove 'but for' (via e.g. scientific or medical evidence (e.g. ***Wilsher***) (**9.2.2.1**))		Fails on balance of probabilities but result appears unjust (**9.2.2.2**)
Cumulative causes/ conditions	**Non-cumulative causes/conditions**	**Non-cumulative causes/conditions**
Negligent act makes a 'material contribution' to the *harm* → ***Bonnington*** → D was therefore liable for it (100%) → However, since *Holtby*, damages awarded *proportionately* by D (so D might not end up being liable for 100% of the damages)—i.e. is a **'divisible injury'** →	Negligent act makes a 'material contribution' to the *risk* of harm → ***McGhee*** → Still results in a 'but for' test: C must show it is more likely than not that the negligent act materially increased the risk →	In ***Fairchild***, mesothelioma could have occurred from negligent exposure to asbestos from one of a number of employers. Condition is NOT cumulative → Applied ***McGhee*** 'material contribution' to the *risk* of harm test → All negligent employers held *jointly and severally* liable (each liable for 100% of the damages) → ***Barker*** introduced *proportionate* damages, but this was overturned *in relation to mesothelioma only* by section 3 of the Compensation Act 2006 → ***Fairchild*** treated as **exception** to normal rule, distinguishing ***Wilsher***. Its exceptional nature confirmed in ***Sienkiewicz*** and *MOD* v *AB and others* and most recently *Zurich* (test appeared only to apply to mesothelioma—but now see *Henaghan*) →
Proportionate damages	**Joint and several liability**	**Mesothelioma: joint and several liability** **Other injuries: proportionate damages**

9.2.2.3 'Unjust' results 2: failure to inform

Outside asbestos-related litigation, the courts have departed from ordinary 'but for' causation in order to secure just results in medical negligence cases involving 'informed consent'. In *Sidaway* v *Board of Governors of the Bethlem Royal Hospital* [1985], a surgeon failed to disclose a 1–2 per cent risk of spinal damage to a patient undergoing a spinal operation, which later materialised. In all probability, the House of Lords agreed, he had failed to disclose the risks. However, other experts said they would not have disclosed the risks in the same situation either, so counsel for Sidaway tried to invoke the transatlantic informed consent doctrine. The law lords refused to entertain this (Lord Scarman dissenting), declaring the doctrine impractical and stating that the time was not right to substantially change the rules on informing of risks. However, Lord Templeman noted that if Sidaway had *asked* about the specific risks, she should have been informed of them.

Chester v _Afshar_ [2005] HL

The claimant developed a serious spinal condition (cauda equina syndrome) following an operation on her spine, which she had been advised to undergo by the defendant. The claimant had reluctantly agreed to the operation. The defendant had not warned her of the small risk that she might develop the condition, even if the operation was performed without negligence. When this risk materialised, the claimant sued in negligence arguing that had she been aware of the risk she would have sought advice on alternatives to surgery and the operation would not have taken place when it did (although it may well have taken place at a later date). The trial judge found that the possibility that the claimant might have consented to surgery in the future was not sufficient to break the causal link between the defendant's failure to warn and the damage sustained by the claimant. The Court of Appeal agreed.

So did the majority of the House of Lords. They found that the claimant had not been able to establish sufficient causation on conventional principles. Because she may well have had the operation later, the defendant's failure to warn neither affected the risk nor was the effective cause of the injury she sustained.[44] However, the law lords went on to modify these principles. The defendant doctor owed her a duty to advise her of the disadvantages of the treatment he proposed and this was closely connected with her ability to give consent and make an informed choice as to whether to have treatment. Since the injury she sustained was within the scope of the defendant's duty to warn and was the result of the risk of which she was entitled to be warned, the defendant's failure to warn the claimant was a breach of this duty *and* the cause of the claimant's injury: 'Her right of autonomy and dignity can and ought to be vindicated by a narrow and modest departure from traditional causation principles' (Lord Steyn at [24]).

44. Compare *Meiklejohn* v *St George's Healthcare NHS Trust and another* [2014].

Counterpoint

Note that *Sidaway* was decided at a time when medical paternalism was rife, whereas ***Chester*** came at a time when patient rights were more carefully considered (following the implementation of the Human Rights Act 1998) and, despite not being argued this way, Carole Chester's human rights certainly seem to have been championed (also see *McGlone* v *Greater Glasgow Health Board* [2011], a Scottish case). That said, ***Chester*** did not get rid of the *breach* question in relation to informed consent, merely sidestepped it. There remained a question about what risks it was legitimate for a doctor to tell or not tell, without falling below the standard of care expected of them. On this, see ***Montgomery* v *Lanarkshire Health Board*** [2015], discussed in **section 8.3.2.1** and subsequent cases in this area.

Though the law lords viewed ***Chester*** as a departure from ordinary 'but for' principles, another interpretation is that it represents merely a (less than) straightforward application of the 'but for' test. But for the defendant's negligent advice, Ms Chester would have avoided injury (on the balance of probabilities) as she would either not have had the operation at all or, even if she had had the operation on another day, there would only have been a 1–2 per cent chance of the risk materialising. That is, it was 98–99 per cent unlikely that she would have suffered the injury. Indeed, this had been the view of the Court of Appeal,[45] and has latterly been interpreted as the correct view by the High Court of Australia.[46]

In *Correia* v *University Hospital of North Staffordshire NHS Trust* [2017] the Court of Appeal emphasised that if the ***Chester*** principle is to be relied upon it remains necessary for the claimant to prove that, if correctly warned of the risk, they would have declined or deferred the operation. This was confirmed in *Duce* v *Worcestershire Acute Hospitals NHS Trust* [2018] and in *Diamond* v *Royal Devon & Exeter NHS Foundation Trust* [2019]. In *Duce* it was found that the claimant could not establish that she would not have gone ahead with the operation, which had left her with nerve damage, had she been warned of the risks. In *Diamond* it was established that the claimant would have proceeded with abdominal mesh surgery even if she had been informed of the risks in relation to potential future pregnancies. An example of a case where it *was* established that, had the claimant been warned of the risks of her surgery, she would *not* have undergone the operation (which left her paralysed) is *Hassell* v *Hillingdon Hospitals NHS Foundation Trust* [2018].[47] In *Khan* v *Meadows* [2019] it was confirmed that only the risk that it was the duty to be warned against was actionable, not the risk of any additional harms that might materialise.[48]

9.2.2.4 Indeterminate causes

What is the situation when there is more than one negligent defendant, but *neither* can be proved to be the cause of the harm suffered? This is what is known as an 'indeterminate cause'. If it is accepted that mesothelioma, for example, is caused by a single fibre

45. See *Chester* v *Afshar* [2002] (CA) (at [40]).
46. *Wallace* v *Kam* [2013].
47. See also *Thefaut* v *Johnston* [2017]; *Webster (A Child)* v *Burton Hospitals NHS Foundation Trust* [2017].
48. See also *Pomphrey* v *Secretary of State for Health and another* [2019].

of asbestos entering the lung, then ***Fairchild*** becomes a case of indeterminate causes, because each negligent employer was equally likely to have exposed the claimants to the asbestos that caused the disease. Neither satisfies the 'but for' test. By contrast, *McGhee*, on which the decision in ***Fairchild*** rests, is not a case of indeterminate cause, as the dust all came from the same place, albeit some 'innocent' and some 'guilty'.

In cases from other jurisdictions raising the issue of the inability to prove which of two negligent defendants actually caused the harm, courts found another novel way to circumvent the 'but for' test. In the US case of *Summers* v *Tice* [1948] and the similar Canadian case of *Cook* v *Lewis* [1951], the court shifted the burden of proof to the defendants. In both cases the issue was which of two negligent hunters fired the shot that hit the claimant (and hence who should be liable). Both had fired their guns at approximately the same moment. Evidence could show only that the shot fired came from one of their two guns—applying the 'but for' test the claimant could never win, as neither defendant would be more than 50 per cent likely to have fired the offending shot. Shifting the burden of proof meant that the court asked the defendant to prove that he was *not* responsible—if neither could do this then they should be jointly and severally liable. In ***Fairchild***, the House of Lords, discussing the 'two hunters' scenario, explicitly rejected the idea of reversing the burden of proof, deeming it artificial: proof was the problem in the first place (Lord Hutton at [110]).

Similar to the 'two hunters' problem is *Fitzgerald* v *Lane* [1987], where a pedestrian crossing a road was hit first by one negligent driver and then almost immediately by another, rendering him tetraplegic. It was impossible to establish which impact actually caused the tetraplegia (and it may well have been a combination of both) and applying the 'but for' test would therefore have rendered each of the negligent drivers equally (50:50) responsible but, crucially, neither liable for the harm. The Court of Appeal, using the *McGhee* 'material increase in risk' principle, found each defendant liable.[49]

Pause for reflection

In another US case, *Sindell* v *Abbot Laboratories* [1980], the problem of indeterminate causes was resolved differently. Five pharmaceutical companies were all held liable for supplying a drug that caused vaginal cancer in women even though, because the cancer developed a long time after the drugs had been taken, it could not be established by any of the claimants which company had supplied the particular drug that caused their harm. Any of the five companies could have been responsible, as the problem was in the design of the drug itself, rather than a manufacturing error. Had the 'but for' test been applied, none of the companies would have been liable. The court surmounted this problem by adapting the rule from *Summers* v *Tice* and apportioning liability on the basis of each defendant's market share. Therefore, *all* the companies were liable (and so all had to pay), but the court also decided that the *amount* each should pay should be based on that company's share of the market.

Do you think this is a justifiable decision? Is apportioning the damages to be paid in this way more appropriate when the harm is caused by a product (rather than employers), particularly when all companies posed an equal *risk* of causing vaginal cancer?

49. Notably, this case was decided before ***Wilsher*** reached the House of Lords, as recognised by Lord Bingham in ***Fairchild*** at [28].

9.2.2.5 Loss of chance

There has been an interesting and different response to the idea that while we know and can identify an increase in the *risk* of something happening, we cannot always say the same for the actual cause. These are sometimes referred to as 'loss of chance' cases.

> ***Hotson* v *East Berkshire Health Authority* [1987] HL**
>
> A boy fell from a tree, injuring his hip. In hospital, he was negligently diagnosed: the doctors who saw him failed to notice that vascular necrosis (a condition where blood vessels die) had developed and he was sent home without adequate treatment. Five days later he returned to hospital and his condition was correctly diagnosed, though by this time nothing could be done about it and paralysis was inevitable. Expert medical evidence indicated that had the diagnosis been made correctly at the time the boy first came to hospital, there would have been a 25 per cent chance that the condition could have been prevented. However, five days later, that chance had gone.
>
> The House of Lords found that it could not be shown on the balance of probabilities that the boy would have avoided the condition had the doctors not been negligent: there was a 75 per cent chance that he would have developed the condition even with proper diagnosis. Therefore, his claim failed.

Hotson, like ***Barnett***, perfectly illustrates exactly what a claimant needs to pass the 'but for' test: it being more likely than not that the defendant's negligent actions caused the damage. Though the final outcome of ***Hotson*** is a straightforward application of the 'but for' test, the case raises further interesting issues. Both lower courts accepted an alternative argument (or an alternative definition of the *harm*) that the claimant *could* have established that he had *'lost a chance'*—the 25 per cent chance of not having the condition—and that this harm was definitely caused (on the balance of probabilities) by the negligence in question.[50] Because of this, they had awarded him 25 per cent of the total damages he would have received had he been successful in his initial claim. This 'lost chance' idea was rejected by the House of Lords.[51]

While a 'lost chance' claim was a novel approach, it was not without basis in law (damages for lost chance are, in some circumstances, available in economic loss claims and also in contract law). However, the idea clearly did not attract the House of Lords. The question, they said, was whether Hotson had been 'doomed' when he came to the hospital in the first place, in a similar way to ***Barnett***. It was 75 per cent likely that he was, so the negligent treatment therefore made no difference. Translating percentages into legal certainties, he had *no chance* of recovery.[52]

50. So, in this sense, lost chance is the reverse corollary of 'material increase in risk'.

51. Applying ***Hotson***, Judy's claim in the scenarios outlined at the beginning of the chapter would also fail.

52. The difference is that in ***Barnett*** the claimant was 100 per cent certain to die from the original arsenic poisoning: he literally had 'no chance'.

Pause for reflection

Is it right that if a claimant can show a 51 per cent likelihood that negligence caused their harm it will be treated as a legal certainty that it did (and 100 per cent of the damages will be recoverable), whereas if you can show only a 49 per cent likelihood that the negligence caused the harm it will be treated as a legal certainty that it did not (and no damages will be recoverable)? This is known as the 'all or nothing' rule. It might seem fairer if we were talking about certainties, rather than probabilities.

It is not, however, clear whether in ***Hotson*** the law lords meant to rule out permanently the possibility of 'lost chance' claims in medical/personal injury cases. Interestingly, a number of cases post-***Hotson*** have recognised the idea of a 'lost chance' when the claim has been one for economic loss,[53] so clearly the *type* of loss is recognised within the law of negligence. In relation to medical negligence, the issue was revisited in ***Gregg*** **v** ***Scott*** **[2005]**.

Gregg v *Scott* [2005] HL

The claimant consulted a doctor complaining about a lump under his arm, which the doctor failed to accurately diagnose as cancerous. As a result, the cancer treatment that the claimant eventually received was delayed by nine months, and his chance of survival decreased.

Evidence showed that 17 in every 100 people who developed the same kind of cancer could be cured by prompt treatment (defined as within one year of the tumour appearing) and a further 25 in every 100 people would be cured even with a delay of one year. The other 58 would be incurable, no matter when the cancer was diagnosed or treated. Using these figures, the claimant contended that he initially had a 42 per cent chance of being cured, had his treatment not been delayed, which had decreased to 25 per cent because of the delay that occurred.

A 3:2 split House of Lords rejected his claim, the majority stating that the claimant needed to show that the doctor's negligence made it more likely than not that he could not be cured. Since, at the outset, he was 58 per cent likely to die anyway, he could not do so. Therefore, it could not be shown that 'but for' the doctor's negligence he could not be cured.

In the alternative, the claimant argued that he had lost a 17 per cent chance of survival (the difference between 42 per cent and 25 per cent). This claim was also rejected, the majority holding that loss of chance could not form the basis of a medical negligence claim.

The 'lost chance' argument in ***Gregg*** differs from that in ***Hotson*** in an important way—in ***Hotson*** there was an either/or situation: when he reached hospital the first time it was either too late to do something about his hip, or it was not (see also *JD* v *Mather* [2012]).

53. See e.g. *Allied Maples Group* v *Simmons and Simmons* [1995], *Dixon* v *Clement Jones Solicitors* [2004], *Wellesley Partners LLP* v *Withers LLP* [2015] (in relation to concurrent liability in contract and tort), *McGill* v *The Sports and Entertainment Media Group and others* [2016]; *Wright* v *Lewis Silkin LLP* [2016] and *Perry* v *Raleys Solicitors* [2019].

In *Gregg*, the situation was different: even when the claimant first went to the doctor the chances of survival were against him and, on balance, he was 58 per cent likely to die from the cancer rather than survive. What the delay in diagnosis did was to *reduce* his *chance of survival*, not eradicate it, thus raising what is, arguably, the straightforward issue of whether someone can recover for a calculable lost chance.[54]

Counterpoint

see online resources

Lord Nicholls, in the opening paragraph of his powerful dissent in Gregg, described the issue as follows:

> This appeal raises a question which has divided courts and commentators throughout the common law world. The division derives essentially from different perceptions of what constitutes injustice in a common type of medical negligence case. Some believe a remedy is essential and that a principled ground for providing an appropriate remedy can be found. Others are not persuaded. I am in the former camp. (at [1])

Arguably, this passage sums up most of the law on factual causation—or at least those cases where an unorthodox approach has been taken or departure from the 'but for' test has been suggested. Lord Nicholls goes on to describe the idea that a patient can only recover damages if his original chance of recovery had been more than 50 per cent as not only 'irrational and indefensible' (at [3]) but makes the duty of care a doctor owes their patients to take reasonable care 'hollow' (at [4]). We would agree.

Baroness Hale (who was in the majority in *Gregg*), commented on the loss of chance argument, pointing out that if it could be concluded that a doctor's negligence had affected a claimant's chances to some calculable extent, then we would have 'a "heads you lose everything, tails I win something" situation', operating in favour of the claimant (at [224]). We suggest this is better than a 'heads I win something, tails I win nothing' situation, operating wholly in favour of defendants, particularly when they are clearly negligent.[55] The policy arguments supporting a →

54. On an alternative view, the 'loss' that the claimant identified in *Gregg* is essentially fictional. On this view it is inaccurate to say that the claimant lost a chance—either the claimant was one of the 42 people out of 100 who would have survived with immediate treatment, or he was one of the 58 who would not. As one of the former group, the claimant had a 100 per cent chance of survival, if in the latter they had no chance. The difficulty is that we cannot know which group the claimant fell into so we are thrown back onto the statistical probability (58:42) that he fell within the latter class. Importantly, just because 42 out of 100 people survive in such a situation, it does not mean that *each one of those people* had a 42 per cent chance of survival; rather 42 of them had a 100 per cent chance of survival and 58 had no chance.

55. However, an alternative view should again be noted, which suggests that recognising loss of chance claims would potentially change the outcome of almost every negligence claim. As discussed earlier, as things stand, if a claimant can establish on the balance of probabilities that the defendant's negligence caused their loss, they recover all of their losses. Where claimants cannot prove this, they recover nothing. However, very rarely are we 100 per cent sure that the claimant would have been harmed even without the breach, so almost every claimant could argue that they lost some chance of escaping unharmed. Moreover, where negligence claims succeed, we are rarely 100 per cent certain that the harm would not have been suffered but for the breach, because the question is necessarily

→

claimant-favouring system stem from the underlying aims of the tort system itself, not least the desire to compensate those who have suffered harm due to the wrongs of another, but also in the more 'practical' aspects such as making people (in this example, doctors) act more *carefully* than they might otherwise do, reducing the number of *future* potential claimants. However, when the defendant has *not* harmed the claimant, as may be the case, it would be unjust to make them pay. Crudely, as the law stands, it could be argued that the 'chance' of the claimant making a financial gain (or avoiding an economic loss) is valued more highly than the chance of the claimant not suffering a physical harm or even death.

Furthermore, the type of calculation that the court is asked to make in a loss of chance claim is not one that is wholly unknown to them (not only because lost chance is recognised in other types of claim, outside medical negligence or other personal injury). When damages for an 'ordinary' personal injury are calculated, reductions and increases in the amount to be awarded can be based on the 'chance' of something happening in the future.[56] Arguably, it would not be difficult to extend the principle.

see online resources

After ***Gregg*** it seems that it will be extremely difficult for claims to be based on lost chance in personal injury/medical negligence. Opinions differ as to whether the decision in ***Gregg*** rules out this type of claim in its entirety or merely restricts it to as yet undefined situations (Lord Phillips and, possibly, Baroness Hale refused to rule out lost chance claims in other contexts).[57] Perhaps such a situation might fall factually somewhere between ***Hotson*** and ***Gregg*** or be an extension of the facts in ***Gregg*** where the lost chance claimed has *literally* been lost.

Pause for reflection

Do you think that the fact that Gregg was still alive at the time the House of Lords issued its decision in the case counted against him? If he had actually lost the chance of survival (by dying), might the decision have gone the other way? Consider the speech of Lord Phillips, who was in the majority, but seems to indicate that he might have ruled the other way (thus making the outcome 3:2 in favour of the claimant), had Gregg in fact died (at [188]).

hypothetical. Would acceptance of the loss of a chance argument entail reductions in claimants' damages to reflect the fact that there was a chance that the harm would have been suffered anyway? The loss of a chance approach involves a shift away from the all or nothing approach we currently have. If so, cases like ***Hotson***, ***Wilsher*** and even ***Fairchild*** (where 100 per cent of the loss was recoverable despite the uncertainties) would have to be overruled, unless we could say that, *in some situations*, the all or nothing approach applies, *whereas in others*, the lost chance approach does. This is something, it is suggested, which would be difficult to do without arbitrariness and inconsistency, though Lord Nicholls in his dissent sought to do just this.

56. This is simply a question of apportionment. See e.g. *Rothwell* v *Chemical and Insulating Co Ltd* [2007].

57. See Lord Neuberger MR in *Wright (A Child)* v *Cambridge Medical Group* [2011] at [82]–[84].

9.2.2.6 Uncertain actions

So far we have looked at cases where it has been difficult to show what has actually happened, thus making the application of the 'but for' test problematic. A different problematic situation arises in circumstances when either the claim being made relates to something that has not been done, but should have been (an omission), or—more precisely—when we cannot be quite *sure* what would or should have been done in a given situation.

In *Bolitho* v *City and Hackney Health Authority* [1998], it was alleged that a hospital consultant was negligent in failing to respond promptly to her pager, as a result of which the 2-year-old claimant died. In seeking to establish a causal link the House of Lords had to consider what the consultant *would* have done had she responded. The consultant argued that even if she had attended the child, she would not in fact have intubated him. Medical evidence showed that this was the only course of action that could have saved him at that time. So viewed, on the balance of probabilities, the child would have died whether the consultant had responded or not. However, the law lords approached the case differently, finding that it must first be established whether the doctor's failure to intubate would also have been negligent (applying the test from ***Bolam* v *Friern Hospital Management Committee* [1957]**). If it was, legal causation was *also* established because it could be said that what the doctor *should* have done, but negligently did not do, was the likely cause of the child's death.[58]

9.2.3 Multiple sufficient causes

We have already considered problems encountered where a claim involves multiple defendants who each *could have* caused the harm complained of, but cannot be proven to have done so, according to the 'but for' test. A similar but different problem arises where there is more than one defendant, each of whom *does* pass the 'but for' test, but where one of their actions comes later than that of the other. Or, the later action may be non-tortious, but still capable of giving rise to the harm. Here, instead of indeterminate or multiple *potential* causes, we have what are known as multiple *sufficient* causes; the question is whether the action of the second party (negligent or otherwise) absolves the original tortfeasor from blame. Put another way, should the original defendant, who is clearly liable for *some* harm, *remain* liable after the unrelated actions of another party?

> ***Baker* v *Willoughby* [1970] HL**
>
> The claimant suffered injury to his leg as a result of a car accident negligently caused by the defendant. Resulting pain and stiffness meant that he had to find alternative employment. Later, while working in a scrap-metal yard, but before the first case went to trial, he was shot in the same leg by armed robbers. His leg was later amputated. The question for the House
>
> →

58. See also *Gouldsmith* v *Mid-Staffordshire General Hospitals Trust* [2007], *Ganz* v *Childs and others* [2011], *Less & Carter* v *Hussain* [2012] and *Palmer* v *Portsmouth Hospitals NHS Trust* [2017].

→

of Lords was whether the negligent driver should pay compensation for the effect of his negligence (the pain and stiffness) for the rest of the claimant's life, or whether his liability ended when the claimant was shot. The defendant argued that the act of the robbers in shooting the man in the leg 'obliterated' the effect of the injury caused by him. This argument had been accepted by the Court of Appeal, who awarded damages for the leg injury up until the time the later injury occurred. It was not in dispute that the criminals who shot the claimant would have been liable for the additional extent of the injury they caused to the leg, but these men had never been found, so could not be sued.

The House of Lords felt that this might lead to a gap in damages. If the original defendant was liable for the original injury only to the point in time that a later, more serious, injury caused by another party occurred and that other party (if able to be sued) was only liable for the *additional* harm caused, then there would be no compensation awarded for the continuing effects of the first injury. On this basis, they said that the original defendant's negligence continued to operate even after the additional harm caused by the gunshot.[59]

By way of contrast, what is the position when the later event is either non-tortious or even naturally occurring? In such a situation, no one would have any liability for the additional harm caused by the later event.

Jobling v *Associated Dairies Ltd* [1982] HL

The claimant injured his back at work, subsequently reducing his earning capacity. Before the trial against his employer, he contracted an unrelated back disease which rendered him completely incapable of any work. As in ***Baker***, the question for the House of Lords was whether the defendant should continue to be liable for the original injury and the loss of earnings associated with it past the point where the later (and greater) harm was suffered.

The House of Lords refused this claim. They relied on the fact that when assessing damages, account could be taken of the ordinary 'vicissitudes of life' (hardships) that a person might be expected to encounter, and that damages were usually reduced accordingly to take account of these. This meant that Jobling could only be compensated up until the point that he contracted the disease, as it could be said that this would have happened anyway.

Jobling is a case where the later 'sufficient cause' of the harm complained of overtakes or *supersedes* or 'obliterates' the original cause. When this happens, the defendant will be liable only for the damages relating to the extent of the injury they caused, up until the

59. One tenuous way of putting this is that the decision could be justified on the ground that the claimant would not have been working in the scrap-metal yard (and so would not have been shot) had it not been for the negligence of the first defendant. For a more concrete exposition of this idea (though rejected), see ***Gray* v *Thames Trains*** [2009], where ***Baker*** was doubted.

time of the superseding event. The point is that the superseding event, such as the disease in ***Jobling***, would have happened anyway, whether the claimant was previously injured or not and, as in this case, damages after that point in time are rendered irrelevant.

While ***Jobling*** did not explicitly overrule ***Baker***, it is probable that ***Baker*** is now 'confined to its facts'. It is therefore possible that if a similar situation arose today, the later event, even if tortious or criminal, would supersede the first (though see Lord Brown, ***Gray* v *Thames Trains* [2009]** at [96]–[97]).[60] The question whether or not ***Baker*** 'survives' ***Jobling*** may in part be answered by *Murrell* v *Healy* [2001]. The claimant was injured in a car accident, for which he received £58,500 compensation from the other driver in an out-of-court settlement. Later the same year, he was involved in another accident—the court was asked whether the defendant should pay a reduced sum of damages to make allowance for the fact that the claimant had already been compensated for *some* injury. The Court of Appeal held that the defendant should compensate Murrell only for additional damage caused by the accident (the reverse of ***Baker***, where the second tortfeasors were unable to be sued) and that if the first defendant's liability was unaffected by the second tort, the second defendant cannot be liable for any of the original losses. Murrell also developed joint problems in his legs which were unattributable to either of the accidents—following ***Jobling*** and the 'vicissitudes of life' idea, the damages he had been awarded were then reduced.[61]

Pause for reflection

Note that the question whether something is a supervening cause is very similar to the question whether the actions of a later tortfeasor (or otherwise) break the chain of causation back to the original defendant (thereby absolving them entirely from liability). Where the line is drawn between these two points is very hard to define, and people have different opinions—where do you think it is? Is *Murrell* a case where the chain of causation would have broken, but the claimant was lucky enough to have already settled out of court with the first defendant?

9.3 Legal causation

When one or more factors, including the defendant's negligence, *are* found to be necessary conditions of the claimant's harm (factual causation), the 'real' or 'operative' cause in law (legal causation) must still be determined. This involves two distinct tests, the first asking whether the harm was too remote a consequence of the defendant's negligence, and the second asking whether any subsequent event could be said to have broken the chain of causation stemming from the defendant's negligent act. Each test represents a value judgement about how far we think defendants' liabilities should extend—that

60. Cf *Corr* v *IBC Vehicles Ltd* [2008].

61. In *Performance Cars* v *Abraham* [1962] the same idea is used in a case concerning property damage. See now also *Reaney* v *University Hospital of North Staffordshire NHS Trust and another* [2015], discussed in **section 9.3.1.1**.

is, regarding the final question about to whom responsibility for harm is appropriately allocated.

9.3.1 Remoteness of damage

When a court asks whether a harm was too 'remote' a consequence of the defendant's negligence, it is essentially asking whether the consequences of the negligent action were so far removed from it as to have been *unforeseeable* by the defendant (judged by the standard of the 'reasonable person') at the time the action occurred. Put another way, the defendant may argue that the consequences of their action were *not* foreseeable—that is, that they were too remote. If so, cause *in law* is not established and the claimant's case fails. Whether something is too remote is judged in light of what was known at the time the breach occurred; that is, with foresight, not hindsight.

Overseas Tankship (UK) Ltd v Morts Dock and Engineering Co (The Wagon Mound) No 1 [1961] PC

The defendants were responsible for a ship that had been loading in Sydney Harbour, Australia. Due to the negligence of a crew member, some oil leaked into the water and formed a thin film over its surface, spreading to a neighbouring wharf owned by the claimants, where welders were working repairing another ship. Some days later, sparks from the welding managed to ignite the oil—the resulting fire caused serious damage to the wharf and other nearby ships.

At first instance, the damage caused by the oil itself (e.g. to the slipway of the wharf) was deemed reasonably foreseeable but, because evidence showed that oil spread thinly on water is difficult to ignite, damage to the claimant's property caused *by fire* would *not* have been foreseeable to a reasonable person (at the time the oil was spilt). The Privy Council agreed, finding that a reasonable person could not have foreseen fire damage as a possible consequence of the negligent act.[62]

Before ***The Wagon Mound (No 1)***, a defendant was liable for *all* direct physical consequences of their negligent act (*Re Polemis and Furness, Withy & Co Ltd* [1921]). This meant that defendants would be liable for any consequences of their breach of duty, as long as they were directly the result of the breach, whether or not these could have been foreseen, even if the consequences may have been substantially different from those a reasonable person might expect, and even if the consequences ended up being far more serious than could have been anticipated. ***The Wagon Mound (No 1)*** substantially narrowed the *Re Polemis* test (indeed, the Privy Council stated that *Re Polemis* was no longer

62. By the time of ***The Wagon Mound (No 2)***, evidence showed that though *unlikely*, it was quite *possible* for oil spread thinly on the surface of water to be ignited if a certain temperature was reached, such as if a welder's spark fell onto something floating in the oily water and smouldered for a while (as had, in fact, happened in this situation). Therefore, the issue in that case was not about foreseeability but whether, given that the damage *could* now be considered foreseeable, a reasonable person would have taken steps to prevent it—a breach issue (**section 8.5**).

good law), establishing a far more defendant-friendly test. Following ***The Wagon Mound (No 1)***, the question asked in order to establish whether the claimant's harm is too remote is: 'Was the *kind* of damage suffered by the claimant reasonably foreseeable at the time the breach occurred?' This remains the primary test for remoteness of damage in negligence—and indeed extends further into other torts.[63] ***The Wagon Mound (No 2)* [1967]** did not change the nature of this test—it is simply that on the new evidence presented to the court by this time, the Privy Council could conclude that even a thin film of oil on water would ignite—although the risk of damage by fire was small, it still existed.

The way the remoteness test is formulated means that only the *type* of damage must have been foreseeable, not the *extent*. So, for example, as long as *some* physical damage was a foreseeable consequence of the breach, the *amount* of physical damage suffered need not be.[64] Take a simple example of driving a car. It is clear to any reasonable person that if a car is driven negligently, physical injury to other road users (including other drivers, passengers, cyclists, pedestrians and so on) is foreseeable, as would be property damage to any other vehicle. So, it does not matter in law that, even with a small amount of carelessness (e.g. a momentary lapse of concentration), a pedestrian is seriously injured or even killed. The equation is:

NEGLIGENT DRIVING = FORESEEABLE RISK OF PHYSICAL INJURY = LIABLE FOR ALL PHYSICAL CONSEQUENCES

Similarly, if a negligent driver hits another person's vehicle, it is evident that damage to the vehicle itself would be foreseeable, as would be damage to the vehicle's contents. It would not matter what the contents of the vehicle are—so if a truck was transporting cheap beans or expensive designer clothing, the negligent driver would be liable for the full costs of whatever was damaged.

While this distinction (type versus extent of damage) appears relatively straightforward, it has not always proved to be so. In *Doughty* v *Turner Manufacturing Co* [1964] a factory worker suffered serious burns when an asbestos lid was knocked into a vat of hot liquid, causing a chemical reaction that made the liquid boil up over the edge. The specific chemical reaction was not foreseeable to the reasonable person—but the claimant contended that as it would be foreseeable that the lid falling in would cause some liquid to splash out, and that the likely result of this would be that the claimant would be burnt, the *type of injury* he had suffered *was* foreseeable. However, the court disagreed with this interpretation, finding that an eruption of boiling liquid was different from being splashed by liquid.

Another case, however, appears to tell a different story. In *Hughes* v *Lord Advocate* [1963], an 8-year-old boy fell down a manhole in the street which had been left open by Post Office employees earlier that day. Upon finishing work, the men had covered the hole with a canvas tent and surrounded this with paraffin lamps to alert to the danger. The boy picked up a lamp and took it into the tent. While playing, he knocked the lamp over into the manhole, which caused an explosion of paraffin vapour and the boy fell into the

63. See e.g. **section 19.3.1**. *Steele*, however, says that it is perhaps 'time to update' ***The Wagon Mound (No 1)*** test (p 209).

64. Confirmed in *Conarken Group Ltd* v *Network Rail Infrastructure Ltd* [2011], *Taylor* v *Chief Constable of Hampshire Police* [2013], *Hicks* v *Young* [2015] and most recently by the Court of Appeal in *Goldscheider* v *Royal Opera House Covent Garden Foundation* [2019]. In the context of financial losses, see *Rubenstein* v *HSBC Bank plc* [2012].

hole and was badly burnt. The defendants claimed that they could not have foreseen that the boy would enter the tent with the lamp and be burnt by a subsequent explosion. The House of Lords disagreed. Finding the defendants liable, they held that it was reasonably foreseeable that the *type* of damage would be burns, therefore the exact means by which the burns occurred did not matter (see also *Jolley* v *Sutton London Borough Council* [2000]; *ST* v *Maidstone and Tunbridge Wells NHS Trust* [2015]; *Hicks* v *Young* [2015]).

Pause for reflection

How can the difference between the two previous cases be explained? Do you think the fact that both of the cases were decided in the two years immediately after *The Wagon Mound (No 1)*, which created a 'new' test, could have anything to do with it? Perhaps the judges were simply struggling to implement the new test. Or perhaps the court was simply more sympathetic towards a child?

In the years following the reformulation of the remoteness test in ***The Wagon Mound (No 1)***, there were numerous inconsistencies in attempts to convince a court that physical damage suffered was too remote to be attributed to the defendant. For example, in *Tremain* v *Pike* [1969], a defendant negligently allowed his farm to become infested with rats. The claimant farm worker contracted Weil's disease as a result of exposure to rats' urine. Although clearly arguable that physical injury from rats is foreseeable, the claimant lost because the court held that while injury from rat bites would be foreseeable, Weil's disease was not. However, in *Vacwell Engineering Co Ltd* v *BDH Chemicals Ltd* [1971], it was held that because a small chemical explosion might be foreseeable, all damage caused by a large explosion that occurred when ampoules of chemicals were being washed in water was foreseeable even though no one could have predicted this happening.

Pause for reflection

It seems unlikely that a court today would follow the 'version' of the foreseeability test seen in *Doughty*. *Lunney, Nolan & Oliphant* suggest that the 'modern trend', at least in relation to personal injuries, seems to be to interpret the *type* of injury in a broad sense (see e.g. *Smith* v *Leech Brain* [1962], discussed later), so the extent of the harm or the exact way in which it was caused poses no problems to claimants (p 280). This may also explain the decision to include psychiatric harm with physical injury under the more generous heading of 'personal injury' in ***Page* v *Smith* [1996]** and *Simmons* v *British Steel plc* [2004].[65]

9.3.1.1 The 'egg shell skull' rule

We have seen that the remoteness test is used to determine whether the type of damage suffered is foreseeable, not the extent. Once the type of harm is judged foreseeable, the defendant incurs liability for all the damage caused, even where its extent was not

65. See **section 5.5**.

foreseeable. Because of this, a rule has been developed to protect even those claimants who suffer what may be called 'extreme' damage because they already have some kind of susceptibility or 'weakness'.

The 'egg shell skull' rule, as it has become known, is simply a principle that states that a defendant will be liable for the full extent of the harm they caused, even if the person harmed suffered more harm than might be expected, due to existing weaknesses or frailty. The maxim is expressed as 'the defendant must take the victim as they find them'. The classic example comes from *Smith* v *Leech Brain & Co Ltd* [1962] where, because of the defendant's negligence, the claimant was burnt on the lip. The claimant had a pre-cancerous skin condition, which became cancerous as a result of the burn, and he eventually died. The defendant was held liable for the full consequences of his negligence (i.e. all the physical damage (*type*), so this included the cancer (*extent*)). The court held that as long as physical injury had been foreseeable, it did not matter what the extent of this was, or that the claimant was already more susceptible to a greater level of harm. This approach was followed in *Reaney* v *University Hospital of North Staffordshire NHS Trust* [2014], but on appeal the Court of Appeal described the correct approach as objectively determining whether the claimant's needs before and after the negligently caused injury were 'quantitatively' or 'qualitatively' different (see [19]). If quantitatively different (i.e. more of the same), then a defendant is only liable for any additional needs flowing from their negligent act. If qualitatively different (i.e. different in kind), then a claimant may recover in full.[66]

In *Lagden* v *O'Connor* [2003] it was confirmed that the 'egg shell skull' principle also applies to economic harms. Thus, if a claimant suffers heightened economic loss as a result of an already weak economic circumstance, a defendant will be liable for the full extent of the loss.

9.3.2 **Intervening acts**

Even if the defendant 'causes' an accident by starting a sequence or chain of events, a later event might be held to be the 'real' cause of the eventuating harm. In such circumstances, the 'chain of causation' (which began with the defendant's negligence) is said to be 'broken', leaving the defendant not liable for the claimant's harm. The later event is known as a *novus actus interveniens* (literally, a new intervening act, already familiar to those who have studied criminal law).

This is the second aspect to establishing cause in law (the first being to assess whether the harm was not too remote). However, there is a very fine line between 'supervening' events (as seen in ***Jobling*** and which go to questions of cause in *fact*) and later 'intervening' acts (which involve questions relating to cause in *law*).

9.3.2.1 Later negligent acts

One question is what *kind* of later act is required in order for the chain of causation to be broken. It is clear that subsequent *deliberately* wrongful acts (e.g. crimes) will be

66. *Reaney* v *University Hospital of North Staffordshire NHS Trust and another* [2015]. The matter was reverted to a further trial applying that test: see *Reaney* v *University Hospital of North Staffordshire NHS Trust and another (No 2)* [2016].

sufficient (*Weld-Blundell* v *Stephens* [1920]).[67] Beyond this, the question remains whether a later act has itself to be *negligent* in order to break the chain of causation. Whether what happens subsequently is foreseeable is also relevant—if it is something that is clearly likely to happen as a result of the defendant's negligence then it is unlikely to break the chain. This was plainly expressed by Lord Reid in ***Home Office* v *Dorset Yacht Co Ltd* [1970]**, who said that a subsequent negligent act of a third party must 'have been something very likely to happen if it is not to be regarded as a *novus actus interveniens* breaking the chain of causation. I do not think a mere foreseeable possibility is or should be sufficient' (at 1030).[68]

In *Rouse* v *Squires* [1973] a lorry driver negligently caused his lorry to jack-knife and block part of a motorway. A car subsequently drove into the rear of the lorry. A second lorry driver stopped to assist, pulling over some distance in front of the accident. A third lorry driver stopped before the accident scene, leaving his headlights on for illumination. The driver of a fourth lorry was less careful and did not see the accident until he was almost upon it. He skidded into the back of the third lorry, killing its driver. The question for the court was which negligent lorry driver caused the death. At first instance, the trial judge held the fourth lorry driver wholly responsible as his negligent driving had broken the chain of causation in relation to the original negligent lorry driver. However, the Court of Appeal found that the chain of causation had not been broken. *Both* drivers were responsible and damages were apportioned between them.

Knightley v *Johns* [1982] CA

A serious traffic accident in a one-way tunnel was caused by the defendant's negligent driving and police were called to the scene. Having forgotten to stop traffic entering the tunnel, the police inspector in charge sent two officers on motorcycles, one of whom was the claimant, against the direction of the oncoming traffic to go back and close the tunnel. Both the instruction and driving against the flow of traffic were expressly contrary to police standing orders, but nevertheless the two officers complied with the instruction. Near the entrance to the tunnel, the claimant suffered injury when he was hit by a car.

At first instance, the judge found that neither the officer's instruction nor the claimant had been negligent and that their actions did not break the chain of causation back to the original defendant (the driver), who would therefore be liable for the claimant's injuries in full. However, the Court of Appeal found that the inspector's instruction *had* been negligent and that his negligence was sufficient to break the chain of causation between the defendant car driver's original negligence and the claimant's injuries. As a result, no claim could succeed against the defendant.

Where more than one party can be said to be responsible for causing harm, it is unusual for the courts to find only one of them legally responsible. The Civil Liability (Contribution) Act 1978 means that the court can apportion damages between the parties responsible (or leave them to do this for themselves). Because of this, it is not

67. This obviously has links to the situations in which a *duty* in respect of the acts of a third party can arise (see **Chapter 4**, but contrast *Topp* v *London Country Bus (South West) Ltd* [1993], **section 4.5.3**).

68. Contrast *Wilkin-Shaw* v *Fuller* [2013], where the actions of the intervening third party with regard to a party of schoolchildren in difficulty on a moor were at the very least well-meaning.

common for a court to find that a later negligent act breaks the chain of causation back to the original defendant.[69]

Thus, in *Wright* v *Lodge* [1993],[70] the first defendant's Mini broke down on a dual carriageway and she negligently failed to move it to the hard shoulder. While she was trying to restart the car, it was hit by a lorry being driven negligently over the speed limit, injuring a passenger in the car as a result. The lorry skidded across the central reservation, tipped on its side and collided with oncoming vehicles on the other side of the carriageway, injuring two drivers, one fatally. The injured parties sued the driver of the lorry, who joined (using the Civil Liability (Contribution) Act 1978) the driver of the Mini as a co-defendant. For her negligence, she was ordered to pay 10 per cent of her passenger's damages (the lorry driver paid the remainder). However, with respect to the injuries to the other claimants, the lorry driver was found to have broken the chain of causation from her negligence and, as a result, was wholly liable.[71]

9.3.2.2 Acts of the claimant

Can the claimant's *own* negligence break the chain of causation? It is rare for this to be the case, because generally if a claimant negligently contributes to their own injuries, this can be dealt with via the defence of contributory negligence.[72] Since 1945 this has been only a 'partial' defence, meaning that the claimant's contribution to their own harm can be assessed and their damages reduced accordingly.[73] However, there may still be occasions where the claimant's own actions after the original negligence of the defendant are considered *so* careless that they should remove any share of the responsibility from the original defendant—but we know that 'mere unreasonable conduct on a claimant's part' will not necessarily break the chain.[74] In *McKew* v *Holland and Hannen and Cubitts (Scotland) Ltd* [1969], the claimant suffered a leg injury at work due to his employer's negligence, which resulted in stiffness and impaired mobility. Subsequently, he went to inspect a flat in the course of his work, which could only be accessed by descending a steep staircase without a handrail. As he was about to descend the stairs, his leg buckled and to avoid falling down the stairs and landing on his head, he threw himself forwards, breaking his ankle. McKew claimed that the defendant should be liable for this damage, as it was an extension of the original injury. However, the House of Lords rejected his claim. The claimant had negligently thrown himself down the stairs and had broken the chain of causation. The defendant was not, therefore, liable for his broken ankle.

McKew can be contrasted with *Wieland* v *Cyril Lord Carpets* [1969] where, as a result of the defendant's negligence, the claimant had to wear a neck brace. This restricted her

69. Unless it is *considerably* negligent or 'egregious': see Lord Neuberger MR's discussion of this in *Wright (A Child)* v *Cambridge Medical Group* [2011] at [37].

70. Contrast to *Rouse* v *Squires* [1973].

71. Consider this in relation to Pauline's claim against David. Did the police break the chain of causation? Compare ***Knightley* v *Johns* [1982]**, *Rouse* v *Squires* [1973] and *Wright* v *Lodge* [1993]. Also see *Robinson* v *Post Office* [1974].

72. See **section 10.4**.

73. Law Reform (Contributory Negligence) Act 1945.

74. *Borealis AB* v *Geogas Trading SA* [2010], applied in *Flanagan and another* v *Greenbanks Ltd (t/a Lazenby Insulation) and Cross* [2013].

ability to use her bifocal glasses properly with the result that she fell down some stairs and injured her ankle. The court found that she had been as careful as she could have been and therefore her actions could not break the chain of causation and her ankle injury was also caused by the defendant's negligence.

Pause for reflection

Do you think the difference between the two cases just described can be attributed to the amount of care the claimants took for themselves after they had sustained their original injury? Was it not reasonable for McKew to choose to fall in the way he did rather than risk suffering a different type of injury? What do you think the situation would have been if McKew's injured leg had buckled completely while actually on his way down the stairs? See *Spencer* v *Wincanton Holdings Ltd* [2009], where the claimant, who had failed to secure his prosthetic leg when he stopped to refuel his car, fell over, exacerbating an existing serious injury. The Court of Appeal found the case was not like *McKew* in that Spencer had not acted so unreasonably that he had broken the chain of causation; contributory negligence was appropriate to deal with the sharing of responsibility.[75]

A claimant's own actions in committing suicide while imprisoned (*Kirkham* v *Chief Constable of Greater Manchester Police* [1990]) or while being held in police custody (***Reeves* v *Commissioner of Police for the Metropolis* [2000]**) have been found not to break the chain of causation back to the defendant. While this might seem surprising, as suicide is a deliberate act, the reasoning of the courts was that because the police had a duty of care to protect the specific claimant from suicide (in *Kirkham* by passing on the information that the prisoner was depressed and may become a suicide risk), the claimant doing exactly what may be expected of them should not negate that duty. In ***Reeves***, however, the damages awarded were reduced for the contributory negligence of the claimant.

In *Corr* v *IBC Vehicles Ltd* [2008], a similar question arose. A man was seriously injured and almost killed in an accident at work. The accident and injuries led to him suffering clinical depression, and he later committed suicide. Here, his employers (the defendants) did not, as in ***Reeves*** and *Kirkham*, owe him a specific duty of care to prevent suicide. Instead, the question was whether the suicide had been caused by the original breach of duty (to keep employees reasonably safe) or whether the claimant's deliberate action had broken the chain of causation. The House of Lords found that the chain of causation was not broken, Lord Bingham in particular being swayed by the idea that the suicide was not a free and voluntary choice *because* of the effect of the accident on the mind of the claimant (at [16]). In contrast, the House of Lords found in ***Gray* v *Thames Trains* [2009]**, that a later *criminal* act committed by the claimant, who had sustained

75. See also *Smith* v *Youth Justice Board for England and Wales and another* [2010] where the claimant's own contribution to the post-traumatic stress disorder she suffered after the death of a 15-year-old boy in custody who she was involved in forcibly restraining in effect broke the chain of causation (on grounds of 'fairness'): see Sedley LJ at [29]–[37].

both physical and psychiatric injuries in a train crash negligently caused by the defendants, did break the chain.

9.4 **Conclusion**

After a claimant establishes breach of a duty of care owed to them by the defendant, the next 'hurdle' is establishing *causation*. This has two parts: *cause 'in fact'* and *cause 'in law'*.

To establish cause in fact, the claimant must show, on the balance of probabilities, that the defendant's *breach* caused their harm. This is often expressed as a 'but for' test: can the claimant establish that 'but for' the defendant's negligent act, they would not have suffered harm? There are many flaws with this test. In particular, its inflexibility can cause unjust outcomes, especially when there are multiple potential causes of the harm. The courts have therefore devised exceptions to the test, used in specific types of exceptional case, usually where the outcome that would be generated by the 'but for' test is deemed to be unsatisfactory in some way. However, it should be remembered that the principal exceptions to the 'but for' test created here do not and cannot apply in all cases. To a very large extent they are limited to the type of case in which the decision was first made (e.g. the material contribution test originated from industrial cases, and is only now beginning to apply in some medical negligence cases; and the 'lost chance' idea seems limited to claims for economic loss, having been ruled out—for the moment at least—in medical claims).

The second part of causation is cause in law, which has two parts (though it may be that only one of them is relevant/arguable in a particular case scenario). They encompass a *remoteness* test (which involves establishing whether the damage that occurred was foreseeable to the defendant at the time of the negligence) where it is the *type* of harm (e.g. personal injury) that must be foreseeable, not its *extent*. The second test is to ask whether any *intervening acts* (acts that occurred after the defendant's breach) broke the chain of causation. If so, the defendant will not be liable.

End-of-chapter questions

After reading the chapter carefully, try answering the questions which follow.

1 Is there a coherent way of explaining the difference between supervening and intervening acts?

2 Does the remoteness test lose some of its impact or validity with the incorporation of the 'egg shell skull' rule?

3 What policy reasons can you identify that have affected the courts' decisions in asbestos-related injury cases? Are they consistent?

4 To what extent do the rules on factual and legal causation help to achieve the general aims of tort law?

If you would like to know what we think visit the **online resources**. www.oup.com/he/horsey7e

Answering the problem question

Consider again the problem question at the start of this chapter. Now having read about the topic, **what would be your advice to Gavin?**

Here are some pointers to get you started

- → It seems obvious that S will owe G a duty of care and has breached this. The question is whether G's broken arm is a 'but for' cause (cause in fact) of S's negligence.
- → G will also sue C. If a breach could be established (see **Chapter 8**), this claim raises causation points similar to those seen in *Bolitho*. There is also a 'but for' issue raised by the evidence of the expert witness.
- → If the 'but for' test can be satisfied in the previous claims, the issue of foreseeability of harm will arise (cause in law), as will potential intervening acts. Did, for example, C's treatment of G break the chain of causation back to S?
- → Another question is how the later injury caused by the speeding motorist affects any claim. Is this a supervening event which obliterates any earlier causes (see *Jobling*)?

If you need some more guidance

see online resources

- → An **annotated version of the problem with issues and cases to consider** can be found in the Appendix.
- → A **suggested outline answer** to check your ideas against can be found in the online resources that accompany the book

Further reading

Reading on causation is often quite difficult, and many articles focus solely on one or two cases. Reading these—and case notes—is good to gain a detailed understanding of some of the more difficult or controversial cases. Many of the articles and case notes listed below focus on a particular case or cases.

Bailey, Stephen 'Causation in Negligence: What is a Material Contribution?' (2010) 30 LS 167

Hoffmann, Lord '*Fairchild* and After' in Andrew Burrows, David Johnston and Reinhard Zimmermann (eds) *Judge and Jurist: Essays in Memory of Lord Rodger of Earlsferry* (OUP, 2013)

Laleng, Per 'Causal Responsibility for Uncertainty and Risk in Toxic Torts' (2010) 18 Tort L Rev 102

Laleng, Per '*Sienkiewicz* v *Greif (UK) Ltd* and *Willmore* v *Knowsley Metropolitan Borough Council*: A Material Contribution to Uncertainty?' (2011) 74 MLR 777

Laleng, Per 'Is *Fairchild* a Leading Case of the Common Law?' (2014) The Honourable Society of the Inner Temple Lecture Series

Lee, James 'Causation in Negligence: Another Fine Mess' (2008) 24 PN 194

Miller, Chris 'Causation in Personal Injury After (and Before) *Sienkiewicz*' (2012) 32 LS 396

Morgan, Jonathan, 'Reinterpreting the Reinterpretation of the Reinterpretation of *Fairchild*' [2015] CLJ 395

Stapleton, Jane 'The *Fairchild* Doctrine: Arguments on Breach and Materiality' [2012] CLJ 32

Stapleton, Jane 'An "Extended But-For" Test for the Causal Relation in the Law of Obligations' (2015) 35 OJLS 697

Steel, Sandy 'Justifying Exceptions to Proof of Causation in Tort Law' (2015) 78 MLR 729

Steele, Jenny 'Breach of Duty Causing Harm? Recent Encounters Between Negligence and Risk' (2007) 60 CLP 296

Voyiakis, Emmanuel 'Causation and Opportunity in Tort' (2018) 38 OJLS 26

Wellington, Kate 'Beyond Single Causative Agents: The Scope of the *Fairchild* Exception Post-*Sienkiewicz*' (2013) 20 Torts LJ 208

10 Defences to negligence

Problem question

Read this problem question carefully, and keep it in mind while you are working through the chapter that follows. At the end of the chapter, you will be able to apply what you have learnt to the problem question and advise the relevant parties.

Ben, Graeme and Andy are old school friends. Every year they go camping together in Snowdonia National Park. After they arrive on the Friday night, they decide to go to the pub where Ben and Graeme spend several hours reminiscing and by the time they leave they are both over the legal driving limit. Andy has not been drinking. On their way back to the campsite they pass a farm and notice a tractor with its keys in the ignition. Graeme gets in and starts the engine. Ben and Andy quickly jump in beside him. None of them wears a seat belt. At first, Graeme drives slowly around the farmyard but when Ben says 'Is that the best you can do?' he decides to go 'off-road' and drives it into a field. Unfortunately, on the rough ground Graeme loses control of the tractor and it overturns. Ben and Andy are thrown out onto the field. Ben is seriously injured. Though Andy escapes with only minor physical injuries, he later develops post-traumatic stress disorder (PTSD) as a result of the incident. One day while walking home from work Andy 'snaps' lashing out at an innocent passer-by and causing them serious injury. Though it is recognised that his actions were as a result of his PTSD, he is jailed for six months and loses his job.

Advise the parties (you should assume that, in the absence of applicable defences, Ben and Andy would have a good claim in negligence).

10.1 Introduction

Consider the following examples:

- ***A cycle-courier is knocked down and seriously injured as she swerves to avoid a pedestrian crossing the road. She is not wearing a cycle helmet.***
- ***A footballer is seriously injured by a late, high tackle in the closing minutes of a crucial cup tie.***

→ ***A driving instructor suffers a serious knee injury when the student, to whom she is giving driving lessons, crashes into a lamp post.***

In all these scenarios, even if all the other elements of a claim in negligence—that is, duty, breach and causation—have been met, the defendant may be able to raise a defence. In so doing, what the defendant is effectively saying is 'though I did carelessly injure the claimant, there is nonetheless a good reason why the law should not hold me responsible'. The defendant might, for example, argue that the claimant was (at least in part) to blame for their injuries or that they had accepted the risk of them occurring. Alternatively, they may suggest that an award of damages would be inappropriate on the basis that the claimant was injured while they were engaged in an illegal, or inherently risky, activity. Where a defendant is able to successfully raise a defence, it may work to defeat the claim entirely or merely reduce the amount of damages payable.

This chapter considers three key defences in the tort of negligence: *voluntarily assuming the risk (volenti non fit injuria)*,[1] *contributory negligence* and *illegality*. While contributory *negligence* (as the name suggests) is confined to claims in negligence,[2] *volenti* and illegality are general defences and, as such, are applicable throughout tort law.[3]

10.2 Voluntarily assuming the risk (*volenti*)

The defence of *volenti* is based on the common-sense notion that 'one who has invited or assented to an act being done towards him cannot, when he suffers it, complain of it as a wrong' (Lord Herschell, *Smith* v *Baker* [1891] at 360).[4] This idea is encapsulated in, and often referred to using, the Latin maxim *volenti non fit injuria* (literally: 'no wrong will be done to the willing'), sometimes abbreviated to *volenti*. It is a complete defence. This means that where it is made out it will defeat the claim and no damages will be payable.

The defence of *volenti* can arise in two different ways. First, the defence applies where the claimant consents to the specific harm caused by the defendant and (sometimes) where they have consented to the risk of that harm. For instance, if I agree to you hurting me or damaging my property—say I invite you to punch me in the stomach or to tear up my textbook—you will have a defence to any tort claim I may bring against you. Similarly, if I willingly put myself into a dangerous situation—for instance, I agree to be taken for a ride on a pedalo with a 'driver' who is clearly drunk—my claim for any injuries I then suffer may well be defeated on the basis that I voluntarily undertook the

1. A note on terminology: typically the case law refers to 'consent' in the context of intentional torts and '*volenti*' or voluntary assumption of risk in relation to negligence.

2. This includes the statutory negligence regimes considered in **Chapters 11** to **14**.

3. Consent is also discussed in **section 15.5.1**. There are other defences that are peculiar to specific torts—most obviously in relation to defamation and nuisance. These are discussed in the appropriate chapters.

4. In this case the House of Lords rejected the application of *volenti* in relation to injuries suffered by an employee at work as a result of his employers not warning him of the moment of a reoccurring danger (even though he was aware of the general risk of the danger occurring). See further **Chapter 13**.

risk of such injuries. In the context of negligence claims this involves consenting to not simply the risk of harm but the risk of being harmed by the defendant's negligence.[5]

Secondly, the defence will apply where the claimant consents (or, at least, is *to be treated as* consenting) to the defendant excluding their liability for any injuries they may cause (though here the defence may be restricted by the provisions of the Unfair Contract Terms Act 1977). This version of the defence is best exemplified in cases of occupiers' liability. As we shall see, occupiers owe a duty of care to those they allow onto their premises. However, an occupier who is keen to avoid liability may put up a notice saying that visitors 'enter at their own risk' or, more straightforwardly, that they 'exclude liability for any injuries visitors may suffer on the premises'. If a visitor sees such a notice and enters the premises nonetheless—or indeed even if they do not see it but the occupier is held to have taken 'reasonable steps' to bring it to the visitor's attention—their claim for any injuries they then suffer will be defeated (see Occupiers' Liability Act 1957, s 2(1)).[6]

Although both forms of the defence are based on the consent of the claimant, the difference between them is that in each case the claimant is consenting to something different. In the first case, the claimant is consenting to the specific factual harms which they suffer and/or the risks to which they are exposed—for example, a punch in the stomach or a pedalo capsizing. By contrast, in the second case, the claimant's consent is not to any particular factual harm or danger but rather to the defendant's exclusion or waiver of liability. Here the claimant is saying not 'I accept that what I am doing is dangerous' but rather 'I accept that I cannot sue you if I end up injured'.

This difference between the two versions of the defence is reflected in how the defence is proved. You can only (meaningfully) consent to something if you know about it (though, as we shall see, the defence of *volenti* requires something more than just knowledge). However, because the two versions of the defence involve consent to different things, each requires a different type of knowledge. With the first version (where the claimant consents to the specific factual harm caused or the risk run) the defendant must show that the claimant did indeed consent to the harm which in turn requires that they were aware of the risk of that injury. By contrast, the second version of the defence can be made out even where the claimant has no idea that they are in a dangerous situation and has not given any thought at all to the possibility of their being injured. Rather, since the defence is based on their consent to the defendant excluding liability, the question is whether they knew (or should have known) that the defendant was indeed intending to exclude liability for injuries the claimant may suffer.

Because of this, although the two versions of the defences were described by Buckley LJ in *White* v *Blackmore* [1972] as 'somewhat analogous' (at 668), they do not always run together. In this case, the claimant's husband was fatally injured while watching a motor race. At the time of his injury, he was standing with his family behind the spectators'

5. This doesn't happen very often. It is not the same as 'consenting' to the risk of being injured, e.g. by a kick in a football match or sustaining injury in any other 'risky' activity. See further Lord Diplock in *Wooldridge* v *Sumner* [1963] at 69–70. ***Morris* v *Murray* [1991]** (discussed in this chapter) is a very good example of just how far someone has to go for the courts to consider that the claimant consented to the risk of being harmed by another's negligence.

6. Unless the premises are business premises, in which case the occupier cannot exclude liability for negligently caused personal injury or death (Unfair Contract Terms Act 1977, s 2(1)). See further **section 11.2.2.4**. For a discussion of the operation of *volenti* in the context of an occupier's liability claim see ***White Lion Hotel* v *James* [2021]**.

ropes some way from the track. A car's wheel became tangled up in the safety rope which set in motion a chain of events which culminated in the claimant being thrown into the air. The Court of Appeal held that, because the victim did not have full knowledge of the factual risks he was running, the first version of the defence could not succeed:

> It might not have been at all obvious to the deceased that he was standing in a particularly dangerous place when the accident occurred. Accepting this I do not think it can be said . . . that the deceased had full knowledge of the risk he was running. (at 668)

However, the court held that the second version of the defence *was* available, since the defendants had taken reasonable steps to inform the victim that they were seeking to exclude liability. The various warnings were 'sufficient to exclude any duty of care on the part of the organisers . . . towards the deceased, the defendants were not guilty of negligence and consequently they do not need the shield of the doctrine of *volenti*' (at 668).

We shall look at the second version of the defence in greater detail in **Chapter 11**, when we deal with occupiers' liability. For now we shall focus on the first version of the defence.

10.2.1 **Establishing the defence**

In order for the defence to be established the defendant must show that the claimant either agreed to, or voluntarily took the risk of, the harm that materialised. While cases where the claimant has consented to the harm or tortious action—for example, a battery by agreeing to surgery or to give blood—are (usually) relatively straightforward,[7] those where the agreement is to the *risk* of such harm are more tricky. In such cases it is necessary to show that the claimant at the material time:

(1) knew the nature and extent of the risk of harm; and

(2) voluntarily agreed to it (***Morris* v *Murray*** **[1991]** at 18).

The test is a subjective one; it is not enough that a reasonable person might have been aware of the risk—the particular claimant must know and, importantly, agree to it. It is well established that awareness or knowledge of the risk is not enough: 'A complete knowledge of the danger is in any event necessary, but such knowledge does not necessarily import consent' (***Dann* v *Hamilton*** **[1939]** at 515).

Dann* v *Hamilton **[1939] KBD**

The claimant was injured in a car accident. It was clear that the accident was the result of the negligent driving of the defendant, Hamilton, who had been drinking. Dann brought a claim for damages against Hamilton's estate (he had been killed outright at the scene). The question for the court was whether the claimant had voluntarily assumed the risk *of the defendant's negligence*.

→

7. Discussed further in **section 15.5.1**.

→

The court found that the following exchange had taken place when another passenger was leaving the car the claimant was travelling in: 'You two [referring to the claimant and her mother, who was also in the car] have more pluck than I have', to which the claimant answered 'You should be like me. If anything is going to happen, it will happen' (at 514). Nevertheless Asquith J held that, though the claimant was aware that the defendant had been drinking and that this would materially reduce his ability to drive safely, she had not consented to, or absolved him from liability for, any negligence on his part that might cause her harm. Simply knowing the risk is not enough; the claimant must accept it.

IMPORTANT NOTE: the application of *volenti* in relation to passengers in road traffic accidents is now excluded by section 149 of the Road Traffic Act 1988.[8]

While it is clear that the claimant must be shown to have consented to (rather than simply having been aware of) the risk of injury, what is less clear is what exactly this requires. Lord Denning MR in ***Nettleship* v *Weston*** [1971] took a very formalistic approach: 'knowledge of the risk of injury is not enough. Nor is a willingness to take the risk of injury. Nothing will suffice short of an agreement to waive a claim for negligence' (at 701). This view was approved by the House of Lords in ***Reeves* v *Commissioner of Police for the Metropolis*** [2000]. However, other cases appear to be less demanding.

Morris v *Murray* [1991] CA

After spending an afternoon drinking, during which the defendant had consumed the equivalent of over half a bottle of whisky, he and the claimant decided to take the defendant's light airplane for a spin. The claimant drove to the airfield and helped to prepare the plane for take-off. Shortly after take-off the plane crashed, killing the defendant and seriously injuring the claimant. The defendant's estate met the claimant's claim for compensation with the defence that he had either voluntarily assumed the risk of injury or was contributorily negligent.

The Court of Appeal held that Morris had voluntarily assumed the risk of injury. He was not so drunk as to be unable to appreciate the extent and the nature of the risks involved and had willingly embarked upon the flight knowing that Murray was so drunk that he was very likely to be negligent.[9]

8. As a result, defendants in similar cases today seek to rely on illegality and/or contributory negligence in order to prevent or reduce their liability. See further *Clark* v *Farley* [2018].

9. The latter requirement may mean that a claimant who is completely drunk is better protected than someone who is sober or only slightly tipsy. However, providing the claimant is still able to be aware of risk, it makes no difference if the alcohol makes them more likely to take the risk or, indeed, to give the risk no thought at all.

Pause for reflection

In *Morris* Fox LJ described the facts of the case as 'a drunken escapade, heavily fraught with danger' (at 12) and that 'the wild irresponsibility of the venture is such that the law should not intervene to award damages and should leave the loss where it falls' (at 17). In a similar vein, more recently, May LJ noted that '[a]dults who chose to engage in physical activities which obviously give rise to a degree of unavoidable risk may find that they have no means of recompense if the risk materialises so that they are injured' (*Poppleton* v *Trustees of the Portsmouth Youth Activities Committee* [2008] at [1]).[10]

This reflects what *Cane* describes as an increasing emphasis on self-reliance and 'personal responsibility' by the courts (p 81). Even if we accept that the courts are right to stress that individuals must take responsibility for their own actions, and that the law of torts should limit the protection it offers to those who have little regard for their own safety, should the law leave those who are injured when acting irresponsibly without *any* legal claim? A better response in some of these cases would be to use the *partial* defence of contributory negligence, discussed later, since it is designed to deal with just this problem and allows the court to reduce a claimant's damages in line with their own fault while not depriving them of all compensation.

Morris shares a number of parallels with ***Dann***. In both cases, the claimant agreed to take a ride in a vehicle being driven by a defendant who had been drinking heavily, with full knowledge of the risks this involved. In both cases, the vehicle crashed, the driver was killed and the claimant badly injured. Yet in ***Dann*** the claim succeeded, while in ***Morris*** the defence of *volenti* was made out. Though the Court of Appeal in ***Morris*** sought to distinguish ***Dann*** on the basis that there the claimant was a reluctant passenger who felt unable to extricate herself from the drunken drive, this does not seem to have been the basis for the court's rejection of the defence in that case.

More fundamentally, ***Morris*** brings out the difficulty in identifying what is meant by consent. It is clear that the claimant knew that he was taking a great risk but, as cases such as ***Dann*** and ***Nettleship*** stress, knowledge of—or willingness to take—a risk is not the same as consent. But if something more is needed, what is it? Certainly the claimant in ***Morris*** did not *want* to be injured, though he did willingly engage in a course of conduct which might lead to that result. It is hard to resist the conclusion that, sometimes—where the risk run is particularly great or the activities of the claimant particularly irresponsible—the courts do treat knowledge as tantamount to consent.

10. Although this case was decided on the grounds of duty of care rather than *volenti*, the issues it raises are on point. The claimant was badly injured after falling awkwardly from a climbing wall. Allowing the appeal, the Court of Appeal held that in light of the inherent and obvious risks in the activity which the claimant had voluntarily undertaken, the climbing centre was not under a duty to prevent the claimant from undertaking said risks, or to train and/or supervise him while he did so.

Counterpoint

In order to establish a defence based on the claimant's voluntary assumption of the risk, the claimant needs to have done more than simply put themselves in a dangerous situation. As Lord Halsbury LC pointed out in *Smith* v *Baker & Sons* [1891], anyone crossing a London street knows that a substantial percentage of drivers are negligent. If a man crosses deliberately, with that knowledge, and is negligently run down, he is certainly not consenting to the risk of injury, and so without a remedy (at 337).[11] Similarly, it might be argued that a young man walking home alone late at night knows that they run a greater risk of being attacked than if they take a taxi.[12] However, no one would argue that they have voluntarily assumed the risk of any injury they may suffer.

This seems straightforward enough. But things become less clear if we compare these examples with ***Morris***. As we have seen, there the claimant knowingly and willingly engaged in an inherently dangerous activity. When he was then injured, the court held that he had voluntarily assumed that risk. Yet the same appears also to be true in the earlier examples. The man who crosses the road knows there is the risk of being run over but crosses the road anyway. The man knows there is a danger of being attacked but walks home late at night nonetheless. Of course, neither *wants* to be injured, but nor did the claimant in ***Morris***.

One possible distinction between these cases lies in the likelihood of the risk eventuating. So, the chances of the plane crashing in ***Morris*** were greater than the likelihood of being run over crossing the road or of being attacked late at night. But should this be enough? It is unlikely that the man's claim would be defeated by his voluntary decision to walk home however great the likelihood of him being attacked. And rightly so. Perhaps what distinguishes them is an element of culpability. The claimant in ***Morris*** was factually and morally responsible for his injury. Whereas few would argue that a man crossing a road or walking home alone late at night is (wholly) responsible for his injuries.

A claimant may consent to some harms or risks and not others. The claimant must have consented to the risk of the injury caused in the way it occurred, which in the context of negligence includes the defendant causing that injury by failing to take reasonable care. So, while Morris may have consented to the risk of injury that was likely to follow from embarking on a flight with a drunken (and therefore likely to be negligent) pilot, if the defendant had instead been harbouring a long-term grudge against the claimant and decided to take the opportunity to teach him a lesson, it seems clear that Morris's consent to the negligent consequences of the drunken adventure would not have provided a defence (*Slater* v *Clay Cross Ltd* [1956]).

Volenti, then, only goes so far. Similar issues arise in relation to consent in the context of sporting events. Here, though the potential claimant is not courting injury—in fact they wish to avoid it—they know it might happen. The courts have held that, by willingly engaging in such activities, the claimant voluntarily assumes the risks inherent in

11. See also *Craven* v *Davies* [2018].

12. Let us assume that, like the claimant in ***Morris***, they could easily have avoided the risk by returning home earlier or taking a taxi.

the relevant sport (dependent on the level at which the sport is being played). That said, it is unlikely that their consent would be seen as extending to injuries or risks which are not part and parcel of the game. So, while a footballer would be regarded as consenting to being tackled, even fouled, and any injuries so caused, their consent would not extend to serious foul play, such as a dangerously high and/or late tackle (*Condon* v *Basi* [1985]).[13]

10.3 **Illegality**

The defence of illegality denies recovery to certain claimants injured while committing unlawful activities. Like *volenti*, it is a complete defence. It is typically seen to invoke a special rule of public policy. Lord Hoffmann in ***Gray* v *Thames Trains*** [2009] identified two formulations of the illegality defence. At its most narrow, the defence ensures that a claimant cannot recover in civil law for the consequences of a criminal sanction imposed as a result of one's own unlawful act (at [29]). If the law imposes a harm or loss (e.g. imprisonment or a fine) on someone as punishment for their wrongdoing, they cannot seek compensation for that loss by bringing an action in tort against a defendant they claim caused them to commit the wrong. Its wider formulation holds that a claimant ought not to be able to recover damages for losses they suffer while engaged in criminal activity: *ex turpi causa non oritur actio* (literally: no action may be founded on an illegal act). While the former is justified on the grounds of consistency, the latter is typically thought to rest on the broader idea that 'it is offensive to public notions of the fair distribution of resources that a claimant should be compensated (usually out of public funds) for the consequences of his own criminal conduct' (at [51]).[14] However, as we shall see, the public notions of fairness can be a tricky thing to predict—especially when it comes to 'compensating criminals'.

Gray v *Thames Trains* [2009] HL

The claimant developed PTSD after being involved in the Ladbroke Grove rail crash, which killed 31 people and injured over 500 others. The crash was caused by the defendants' negligence. Two years later, under the effects of this condition, Gray stabbed and killed a pedestrian in a 'road-rage' incident and was convicted of manslaughter on the grounds of diminished responsibility and sentenced to be indefinitely detained in hospital under the Mental Health Act 1983. Gray sued the defendants for, amongst other things, loss of earnings both before and during his detention as well as general damages for his detention, conviction and feelings of guilt and remorse and for the damage to his reputation. He also sought an indemnity against any claims that might be brought by the relatives of the pedestrian.

→

13. The same applies to spectators (*Wooldridge* v *Sumner* [1963]) though in such cases it is more likely that the claim will fail on the grounds that the conduct was not, in the circumstances of the case, negligent; discussed further in **section 8.4**.

14. For further discussion of the rationales of the illegality defence, see ***Patel* v *Mirza*** [2016].

→

The House of Lords rejected his claim. An award of damages would set the civil law against the criminal law. Lord Rodger cited with approval the Law Commission's view in 2001 that 'it would be quite inconsistent to imprison or detain someone on the grounds that he was responsible for a serious offence and then to compensate him for the detention' (at [66]).[15] Gray's counter-argument that his earning potential had already been diminished by the defendants' negligence before his criminal act and that they remained responsible for this continuing partial loss also fell foul of the consistency principle, as well as being rejected by analogy with ***Jobling*** v *Associated Diaries Ltd* [1982].[16]

Counterpoint

As Lord Brown notes, the facts of ***Gray*** and ***Jobling*** are not directly analogous. While the harm suffered by the claimant in the latter was superseded by a wholly unconnected disabling illness (the so-called 'vicissitudes principle'), there was no doubt in ***Gray*** that the manslaughter and detention were factually caused by the defendant's negligence: 'But for [their] negligence there would have been no manslaughter and no detention. That here is a given' (at [96]). Though *Baker* v *Willoughby* [1970] allows for some modification of the 'vicissitudes principle' in order to occasion justice, despite his sympathy for the 'tragedy' suffered by the claimant (at [89]) Lord Brown ultimately rejects this argument:

> Whilst recognising that . . . the tortfeasor benefits from criminality which in one sense he himself has contributed to bringing about, the opposite conclusion would result in the claimant being able to ignore a vicissitude for which he for his part has been held responsible (if only for a diminished extent). (at [101])

Do you agree? ***Gray*** leaves open what the position would be if the claimant had been found to be legally irresponsible by reason of insanity but is still indefinitely detained. It is not clear whether *ex turpi causa* would apply in such circumstances (see Lord Phillips at [15] and Lord Rodger at [83]). What do you think a court would—and should—decide?

The existence of the defence of illegality does not, however, mean that one can *never* recover in tort for injuries suffered against a backdrop of criminality. As Bingham LJ noted in *Saunders* v *Edwards* [1987], it is not for the court to 'draw up its skirts and refuse all assistance to the [claimant], no matter how serious his loss' (at 1134). If the illegal act of the claimant is trivial or simply forms the background to the defendant's tort, then it will not bar the claim. So, for example, if someone negligently damages your car while it is parked on double yellow lines, a court will not hold that your claim for damages is defeated on the basis that you were parked illegally. Your illegality is both trifling and

15. In *The Illegality Defence in Tort* (2001), [4.100].
16. ***Jobling*** is discussed in **section 9.2.3**.

in no meaningful way contributes to the damage you suffered.[17] Nor are participants in criminal activity *necessarily* prevented from recovering from each other. To use Lord Asquith's example in *National Coal Board* v *England* [1954]:

> A and B are proceeding to the premises which they intend burglariously to enter, and before they enter them, B picks A's pocket and steals his watch, I cannot prevail on myself to believe that A could not sue in tort . . . The theft is totally unconnected with the burglary. (at 429)

How, then, do the courts determine when a claimant's unlawful conduct is sufficient to bar his claim in tort? One approach can be seen in the Court of Appeal's decision in *Delaney* v *Pickett* [2011]. The claimant and defendant were transporting a large quantity of cannabis (one package was about the size of a small football) when the defendant negligently lost control of the car he was driving. The claimant was very seriously injured. The trial judge rejected his negligence claim against the driver on the basis that the parties were engaged in an unlawful enterprise. The Court of Appeal, applying the wider interpretation of Lord Hoffmann's reasoning in ***Gray***, allowed his appeal:

> [T]he crucial question is whether . . . the criminal activity merely gave occasion for the tortious act of the defendant to be committed or whether, even though the accident would never have happened had they not made the journey which at some point involved their obtaining and/or transporting drugs with the intention to supply, . . . the immediate cause of the claimant's damage was the negligent driving. The answer to that question is in my judgment quite clear. Viewed as a matter of causation, the damage suffered by the claimant was not caused by his or their criminal activity. It was caused by the tortious act of the defendant in the negligent way in which he drove his motor car. In those circumstances the illegal acts are incidental and the claimant is entitled to recover his loss. (Ward LJ at [37])

Another approach to determining when a claimant's illegality will provide a defence can be seen in the Supreme Court's decision in *Hounga* v *Allen* [2014]. The claimant had entered the UK illegally to work as a 'sort of *au pair*' (at [12]) for Mrs Allen, the defendant. During this time she was regularly subjected to serious physical abuse, culminating in an incident in which the defendant evicted her, causing her to sleep outside in wet clothes. The claimant was taken to social services and later brought a number of claims in contract and tort, including for harassment and discrimination. The Supreme Court unanimously held that the illegality defence did not defeat her claim in relation to the statutory tort of discrimination (the court was divided on the position in relation to the contract claim) as there was not a 'sufficiently close connection between the illegality and the tort to bar the claim' (Lord Hughes at [59]). The illegality 'was no more than the context in which Mrs Allen then perpetrated the acts of physical, verbal and emotional abuse' (Lord Wilson at [40]). Lord Wilson continued:

> to uphold Mrs Allen's defence of illegality to her complaint runs strikingly counter to the prominent strain of current public policy against trafficking and in favour of the protection of its victims. The public policy in support of the application of that defence, to the extent that it exists at all, should give way to the public policy to which its application is an affront. (at [52])

17. Though, depending on the facts, it is possible that your actions may be contributorily negligent.

The approach adopted here involves weighing up all the relevant policy arguments and, in light of these, to determine whether allowing the claim would run counter to public policy. So, the illegality defence is supported by a policy to avoid inconsistency in the law and to ensure that wrongdoers aren't unfairly rewarded for their wrongdoing. But these policies are stronger or apply more strongly in some cases than others. Moreover, there will often be policies which count against applying the illegality defence. For example, in *Hounga*, though the claimant acted unlawfully, since she knew she had entered the country illegally, laws against people trafficking are designed to protect people like the claimant and denying her claim would run counter to the important policy behind such laws. How these policy considerations weigh out will, of course, vary from case to case.

Pause for reflection

The benefit of the 'range of factors' approach adopted in *Hounga*, whereby the courts weigh up the various policy arguments for and against applying the defence, is that it enables the court to address these arguments directly and explicitly, such that the illegality defence will be made out only in those cases where the court considers that it really would be against public policy for the claim to succeed. The downside of this approach, however, is that it makes the application of the defence significantly uncertain. It will typically be unclear how a court will, or indeed how it should, weigh up the competing policies, and different judges are likely to differ on how these policies balance out. However, is this uncertainty a problem? Certainty is something the law rightly strives for. We cannot obey the law unless and until we know what the law expects of us. Nonetheless, certainty is not the only—or even an overriding—value for the law to promote and there are times when the law can do justice only at the cost of some uncertainty. Moreover, the people who are primarily affected by uncertainty in the application of the illegality defence are those engaged in illegal conduct. One way to avoid the uncertainty of the illegality defence is therefore not to break the law in the first place. Is this a good response to concerns about the uncertainty of the defence? What about, for example, other parties, who are not themselves engaged in unlawful conduct, who might need to know where the defence operates?[18]

For some judges, the uncertainty entailed by the sort of range of factors approach adopted in *Hounga* is simply too great. Their preference is for a less flexible and hence more predictable rule that the illegality defence will operate to defeat claims where, but only where, the claimant has to rely on their unlawful conduct to make out their claim. This division of opinion has been laid bare over recent years in the Supreme Court: while *Hounga* supported the range of factors approach, a majority favoured the narrower reliance rule only a year later in *Les Laboratoires Servier* v *Apotex Inc* [2014]. When the court considered the illegality defence once more in *Bilta (UK) Ltd* v *Nazir (No 2)* [2015] this split was evident once again, prompting Lord Neuberger to say that the court needed to settle the correct approach to the illegality defence 'as soon as appropriately possible' (at [15]). It got the chance in ***Patel* v *Mirza***.

18. See ***Patel* v *Mirza* [2016]** at [158].

Patel v *Mirza* [2016] SC

The claimant and defendant entered into a contract under which the claimant was to pay money to the defendant, which the defendant would then use to bet on the price of shares on the basis of inside information. Investing on the back of such information is criminal and the contract was accordingly unlawful too. In the end, the defendant did not obtain the information he needed to put the plan into action and the claimant sought the return of the money he had paid him. The question was whether the defendant could raise the claimant's illegality as a defence to this claim.

A panel of nine Supreme Court Justices was convened to hear the appeal. All nine agreed that the illegality defence should not defeat the claim. The importance of the case, however, comes not in the result but in what the court had to say about the approach to be adopted in such cases. Once more the court was split but, by a 6:3 majority, it rejected the narrow reliance rule and endorsed a variant of the range of factors approach employed in *Hounga* v *Allen*. Lord Toulson, giving the lead judgment, stated:

> The essential rationale of the illegality doctrine is that it would be contrary to the public interest to enforce a claim if to do so would be harmful to the integrity of the legal system. . . . In assessing whether the public interest would be harmed in that way, it is necessary (a) to consider the underlying purpose of the prohibition which has been transgressed and whether that purpose will be enhanced by denial of the claim, (b) to consider any other relevant public policy on which the denial of the claim may have an impact and (c) to consider whether the denial of the claim would be proportionate response to the illegality, bearing in mind that punishment is a matter for the criminal courts. (at [120])

Lord Toulson acknowledged the concerns that this sort of approach could create uncertainty, but made the point that the need for the law to be certain is less pressing when it comes to those contemplating unlawful activity and that the alternative rule-based approach, adopted in cases like *Les Laboratoires Servier* v *Apotex Inc* and favoured by the minority, did not in fact provide significantly greater certainty, as the courts have tended to bend, or to create exceptions to, these rules in a bid to reach satisfactory results:

> The public interest is best served by a principled and transparent assessment of the considerations identified, rather than by the application of a formal approach capable of producing results which may appear arbitrary, unjust or disproportionate. (at [120])

Pause for reflection

As you will have spotted, *Patel* was not itself a tort case. The claimant's allegation was not that the defendant had wronged him; rather, he simply claimed that the defendant should not be entitled to retain the money that the claimant had paid him, since the contract under which that money was paid was void and the purpose of the payment (to bet on share price movements) had failed. As such, the claim did not fall within the domain of tort law but instead belongs to the

→

→

law of unjust enrichment. Nonetheless, the court made clear that the approach courts should take to the illegality defence should be, in broad terms, the same whether the claimant is looking to enforce a contract, recover compensation for a tort, claim an item of property or seeking restitution of an unjust enrichment.[19]

The approach set out by Lord Toulson may well end up operating rather differently in various types of case: there is, for instance, less danger of a claimant being seen to gain from his unlawful conduct where he is seeking compensation for an injury than where he is looking to have a contract enforced. Nonetheless, in the first instance decision in *McHugh* v *Okai-Koi* [2017] it appeared to be common ground that ***Patel*** should apply in a personal injury tort claim. The judge, working through Lord Toulson's criteria, considered that 'the grounds of public interest' would not be 'enhanced' by denying the claim of the family of a woman killed following a particularly nasty incident of 'road rage'. (The defendant had been convicted of causing death by careless driving after the deceased, who had climbed onto the car's bonnet in order to prevent the defendant from driving away, slipped hitting her head on a Belisha beacon.[20])

As we have noted, a minority in the Supreme Court dissented from the majority's 'range of factors' approach, preferring instead a narrower and (so they considered) more certain rule-based approach. Nonetheless, we might expect ***Patel*** to mark a decisive commitment to the range of factors approach, putting an end to the back and forth the courts have been engaged in over the correct approach to adopt in these cases. The very point of convening the nine-judge panel was, after all, to settle this question, at least for the time being.

Though ***Patel*** marks, in this way, a clean break from the disagreements which have plagued the illegality defence in recent years, the majority did not, with very few exceptions, think that the courts had been coming to the wrong decisions in illegality cases. The point of clarifying the approach the courts should adopt in relation to the illegality defence was to see that courts could come to the right decisions more directly and transparently and that the same approach should be adopted whatever the nature of the claim.[21] As such, much of the older case law remains a useful guide as to the sorts of situation in which the defence will be made out, even if some of the reasoning in these cases would now be rejected.[22]

In 2020, the illegality defence was considered yet again by the Supreme Court in *Henderson* v *Dorset Healthcare University NHS Trust Foundation* [2020]. The claimant, who

19. This was confirmed in *Henderson* v *Dorset Healthcare University NHS Trust Foundation* [2020] in which Lord Hamblen noted 'there can be little doubt that it was intended to provide guidance as to the proper approach to the common law illegality defence across civil law more generally' (at [76]).

20. The judge did, however, consider that the deceased's share of the responsibility was 'considerably greater' than that of the defendant and that a 'just and equitable division of responsibility' was 75/25 in favour of the defendant.

21. See further Sarah Green and Alan Bogg (eds) *Illegality after Patel v Mirza* (Hart, 2018).

22. As Lord Hamblen explicitly notes: '***Patel v Mirza*** does not represent "year zero" and that in all future illegality cases it is ***Patel*** and only ***Patel*** that is to be considered and applied. That would be to disregard the value of precedent built up in various areas of the law to address particular factual situations giving rise to the illegality defence. Those decisions remain of precedential value unless it can be shown that they are not compatible with the approach set out in ***Patel*** in the sense that they cannot stand with the reasoning in ***Patel*** or were wrongly decided in the light of that reasoning. Lord Toulson made it clear in ***Patel*** that the principles he identified were to be found in the existing case law' (*Henderson* v *Dorset Healthcare University NHS Trust Foundation* [2020] at [77]).

was under the care of the defendant's community mental health team, had killed her mother while experiencing a serious psychotic episode. She was later convicted of manslaughter by reason of diminished responsibility. The NHS Trust admitted it had negligently failed to return the claimant to hospital following a deterioration of her condition and that, had it done so, the tragic events would not have taken place. However, they argued that the claimant's claim for damages for the losses she had suffered as a result of her actions was barred on the basis of illegality because the damages she claimed resulted from: (a) the sentence imposed on her by the criminal court; and/or (b) her own criminal act of manslaughter. A key question for the court was whether, following ***Patel***, they were still bound by the House of Lords' opinion in ***Gray***.[23] Rejecting the claimant's claim, the court unanimously agreed that ***Gray*** remained good law and compatible with the approach set out in ***Patel***. The application of the illegality defence was justified on two public policy considerations: consistency between the criminal law and tort law and the need to maintain public confidence in the legal system: 'For one branch of the law to enable a person to profit from behaviour which another branch of the law treats as being criminal or otherwise unlawful would tend to produce inconsistency and disharmony in the law, and so cause damage to the integrity of the legal system . . . the decision in ***Gray*** should be affirmed as being "***Patel*** compliant"—it is how ***Patel*** "plays out in that particular type of case". The clearly stated public policy based rules set out in ***Gray*** should be applied and followed in comparable cases' (Lord Hamblen at [119], [145]).

Pause for reflection

Lord Hamblen in ***Henderson*** left open the possibility, raised by Lords Phillips and Roger in ***Gray*** and more recently by Lord Sumption, that there may be some exceptional cases in a criminal act where the illegality defence will not succeed:

> In *Les Laboratoires Servier v Apotex Inc* [2015] Lord Sumption stated at para 23 that: 'The paradigm case of an illegal act engaging the defence is a criminal offence.' . . . [T]here may be some exceptional cases where a criminal act will not constitute turpitude. The reservation made in ***Gray*** in relation to trivial offences may be an example of such a case, as may be strict liability offences where the claimant is not privy to the facts making his act unlawful. (at [112])

While Lord Hamblen was clear that 'the serious criminal offence of manslaughter by reason of diminished responsibility does not come close to falling within such an exception and clearly engages the defence' (at [112]), the *possibility* of the existence of such a category means the limits of the illegality are likely to be tested again at some point in the not too distant future.

What offence do you think might—or should—fall outside its remit?

23. The Supreme Court also declined to overrule *Clunis* v *Camden & Islington Health Authority* [1998] in which the claimant had killed a man at Finsbury Park Underground station, for which he was later convicted of manslaughter on the grounds of diminished responsibility. The claimant had a long history of mental illness and seriously violent behaviour but had been discharged from hospital to be cared for within the community. He argued that the health authority had been negligent in their assessment of his condition and that, as a result, he had not been prevented from committing the attack. His claim was rejected by the Court of Appeal on the ground of illegality—his claim arose directly out of a criminal offence he himself had committed.

10.4 Contributory negligence

Contributory negligence is a defence that operates not to defeat the claimant's claim entirely but rather to reduce the amount of damages the defendant must pay. It is a partial defence. It will be raised by a defendant where the claimant has failed to take reasonable steps for their own safety *and* this failure has contributed to the injury the claimant has then suffered.[24]

> In a typical accident case, where there are faults on the part of the victim (C) and the defendant (D) both of which then and there directly contribute to the accident, [where] there is no difficulty in finding that C suffers damage partly as a result of his own fault and partly as a result of the fault of D. Such cases are the regular diet of judges in the courts day in and day out. (Dyson LJ, *St George* v *Home Office* [2008] at [54])

Section 1(1) of the Law Reform (Contributory Negligence) Act 1945 states that a court can reduce the claimant's damages by whatever amount seems just according to their share in responsibility for the damage.[25]

Law Reform (Contributory Negligence) Act 1945

Where any person suffers damage as the result partly of his own fault and partly of the fault of any other person or persons, a claim in respect of that damage shall not be defeated by reasons of the fault of the person suffering the damage, but the damages recoverable in respect thereof shall be reduced to such an extent as the court thinks it is just and equitable having regard to the claimant's share in the responsibility for the damage (s 1(1)).

'Fault' is defined in section 4 of the Act as 'negligence, breach of statutory duty or other act or omission which gives rise to a liability in tort'.[26] The same section also establishes that damage includes loss of life, personal injury, economic loss and property damage.

In order for the defence to be raised, three questions need to be addressed:

(1) Did the claimant fail to exercise reasonable care for their own safety?

(2) Did this failure contribute to the claimant's damage? and

(3) By what extent should the claimant's damages be reduced?

24. e.g. the driving instructor in the scenarios at the start of this chapter is likely to be contributorily negligent if they fail adequately to supervise the learner driver (see further ***Nettleship* v *Weston* [1971]** discussed at length in **section 8.3**).

25. Where the defence is raised successfully it will mean that both the claimant and the defendant are responsible, at least in part, for the claimant's losses and accordingly those losses are split between them. This is similar to, but should not be confused with, the situation where more than one *defendant* is liable for the claimant's losses (as joint tortfeasors) where the law also splits losses between those responsible for causing them under the Civil Liability (Contribution) Act 1978 (see further **section 21.4**).

26. Despite suggestions that the defence of contributory *negligence* might apply in cases involving intentional harm (see e.g. *Murphy* v *Culhane* [1977]; Lord Hope in ***Reeves* v *Commissioner of Police for the Metropolis* [2000]**), this was rejected by Lord Rodger in *Standard Chartered Bank* v *Pakistan National Shipping Corp (No 2)* [2002] (at [43]–[45]) and more recently by Atkins LJ in *Co-operative Group (CWS)* v *Pritchard* [2011] (at [62]).

10.4.1 Did the claimant fail to exercise reasonable care for their own safety?

When determining whether the claimant has taken reasonable care for their own safety an objective standard is applied. In other words, the question is 'what would a reasonable person in the claimant's position have done to avoid being hurt?'[27] This standard will vary according to the circumstances though it is clear that 'the law certainly does not require the claimant to proceed on his way like a timorous fugitive constantly looking over his shoulder for threats from others' (*Peel & Goudkamp* p 703).

***Jones* v *Livox Quarries Ltd* [1952] CA**

The claimant was riding on the back of a slow-moving tracked vehicle at work, contrary to company regulations, when a dumper truck crashed into the back of it seriously injuring the claimant. He sued his employer, claiming that the driver of the dumper truck was negligent in failing to keep a proper look-out. In response, the defendants argued that the claimant had caused or contributed to his own injuries by his own carelessness in riding on the back of the truck.

The Court of Appeal agreed: 'A person is guilty of contributory negligence if he ought reasonably to have foreseen that, if he did not act as a reasonable prudent man, he might be hurt himself; and in his reckonings he must take into account the possibility of others being careless' (Denning LJ at 615). The claimant's award of damages was reduced by 20 per cent.

Pause for reflection

While at first sight contributory negligence appears to be a useful mirror image of negligence, which allows for the reduction of damages where the claimant is also 'at fault', the practical effects of a finding of contributory negligence are, *Cane* argues, somewhat less satisfying:

> To find a defendant guilty of negligence shifts the loss away from the claimant and typically spreads it by means of insurance . . . A finding of contributory negligence usually →

27. Though as with setting the standard of care for the defendant, the law does allow for some modification of this objective standard, e.g. in relation to children. See *Probert (A Child)* v *Moore* [2012] in which a schoolgirl was not found contributorily negligent after being hit by a speeding motorist despite the fact that she was walking along a dark country road in the same direction as the traffic, while wearing dark clothing and (probably) listening to her iPod. (Though this case must now be read in light of the Supreme Court decision in ***Jackson* v *Murray*** [2015].) Similarly, in ***Spearman* v *Royal United Bath Hospitals NHS Foundation Trust*** [2017], the judge rejected an argument that a claimant, who was being treated in a hospital's emergency department, was contributorily negligent in relation to the serious injures he had sustained after climbing onto, and subsequently falling from, a flat roof on the hospital's premises: 'Whether as a result of the ongoing effects of the hypoglycaemic attack or the effects of the pre-existing brain injury [caused by an accident some 30 years early] or a combination of the two, the claimant did not appreciate the danger he was in, in climbing the fence . . . Just as a young child is not guilty of contributory negligence in running out into a road where the child is so young as not to appreciate the danger of so doing, so too where a person's state of mind is such that, whether temporarily or permanently, they do not appreciate that they are putting themselves in danger and it cannot be said that they should have so appreciated. Otherwise, that would be to penalise a person for being ill or of unsound mind, and the law does not do that' (at [74]).

→

> has precisely the opposite effect, which is to leave part or all of the loss on the claimant, who will typically be without insurance. Thus, reduction of damages for contributory negligence falls much more heavily on the claimant than liability for negligence bears on the defendant. (p 56)

This may be behind the courts' willingness (within the objective standard) to make allowances for the personal characteristics and qualities of the claimant—for example, their age—when making findings of contributory negligence. As Lord Denning noted in *Gough* v *Thorne* [1966]:

> A very young child cannot be guilty of contributory negligence.[28] An older child maybe. But it depends on the circumstances. A judge should only find a child guilty of contributory negligence if he or she is of such an age to be expected to take precautions for his or her safety: and then he or she is only to be found guilty if blame should be attached to him or her. A child has not the road sense or experience of his or her elders. He or she is not to be found guilty unless he or she is blameworthy. (at p 1390)

This is particularly important given that children and the elderly are disproportionately represented among pedestrians seriously injured or killed in road traffic accidents (*Cane* p 56).

Other examples of situations in which the claimant has been found to have failed to exercise reasonable care for their own safety include pulling out from a side road in front of a police car travelling at speed and with its blue light flashing (*Armsden* v *Kent Police* [2009]), attempting to cross the road when the red man at a pedestrian crossing was against the pedestrian (*Rehill* v *Rider Holdings Ltd* [2012]),[29] jumping off (rather than climbing down) an indoor climbing wall (*Pinchbeck* v *Craggy Island Ltd* [2012]), jumping from a moving taxi (*Hicks* v *Young* [2015]), standing in the middle of the road in order to 'moon' at passing cars while in an intoxicated state (*Ayres* v *Odedra* [2012]) and climbing onto the bonnet of a car to prevent it from moving (*McHugh* v *Okai-Koi* [2017]).

10.4.2 **Did this failure contribute to the claimant's damage?**

The claimant's own carelessness will only provide a defence to the defendant's negligence when it makes some contribution *to the injuries they suffered*. Though usually this

28. In *Gul* v *McDonagh* [2021] counsel noted that no reported case had been found in which a finding had been made against a child under the age of 8 (at [11]).

29. This is not to suggest that failure to use a designated crossing (or to do so safely) will *always* be negligent. See *Craven* v *Davies* [2018] in which a man hit by a car doing 86 mph in a 40 mph limit late at night was not found to be contributorily negligent for failing to use a nearby crossing: 'Much will depend upon the construction of the carriageway, the volume of traffic, the time of day, lighting and visibility. Given that this accident occurred at about 1 am, it is virtually certain that the volume of traffic would have been light. It is clear from the report from Mr Sorton that the road was well illuminated by street lighting during the hours of darkness. The unobstructed field of view from the nearside kerb where the deceased crossed was approximately 300 metres. In these circumstances, in my judgment, it would not be reasonable to conclude that the deceased failed to take reasonable care for his own safety by not using the Puffin crossing' (at [10]).

will mean that the claimant contributed in some way to the accident which caused their injury, it also includes cases such as where the claimant's failure to wear a seat belt has contributed to their injury. It is important to note that in all successful cases of contributory negligence there will be more than one cause of the claimant's injuries—that is, both the claimant and defendant will have contributed to the accident (if the defendant's breach of duty was not a 'but for' cause of the injury then any claim would fail even before we get to the question of defences).[30] Equally, if the claimant is careless but that carelessness did not have any bearing *on their injury* then there will be no defence (their negligence is not contributory).[31]

Even where the claimant's carelessness was a 'but for' cause of their own injuries the defence will not be available if the injuries they suffered arose from some risk or danger of which they were not aware and against which they could not have been expected to take precautions. For example, in ***Jones* v *Livox Quarries Ltd***, Denning LJ considered what the position of the claimant would have been had he been negligently shot while riding on the back of the truck. In this case, he suggested, the claimant would not be contributorily negligent *even though* he was partly to blame—after all, had he not been acting unreasonably by riding on the back of the truck he would have been elsewhere when the shot was fired. In this example, we might say that the claimant's actions merely provide the setting or the circumstances in which the injuries were suffered, rather than being a cause of them; his loss—being shot—would have had nothing to do with why it was unreasonable to travel on the back of the truck (at 616).

Thus in *St George* v *Home Office* [2008] the claimant, a prisoner who suffered severe brain damage after falling from a top bunk as a result of an epileptic seizure brought on by drug and alcohol withdrawal, was not found to be contributorily negligent. Though 'but for' his addiction he would not have fallen from the bunk, his addiction was too remote in time and place to allow his injury to be properly regarded as a potent cause of the injury as required by the Act: 'The fault is not sufficiently closely connected with the defendant's negligence. Rather, the fault is part of the claimant's history which has led to his being a man who is suffering from a particular medical condition' (Dyson LJ at [58]). As such this can be distinguished, Dyson LJ suggested, from a situation where the claimant is intoxicated and walks into the path of a negligently driven car:

> [t]he fault of such a person (negligently walking into the path of a car) is a potent cause of the injury which he sustains in the accident. The fault (walking in the road in a drug-induced state of intoxication) is closely connected in time and place with the accident which is caused then and there by a combination of the negligence of the claimant and the defendant. (at [57])

10.4.3 By what extent should the claimant's damages be reduced?

Section 1(1) of the 1945 Act offers no guidance as to how the award of damages is to be reduced, or responsibility is to be apportioned, save for requiring that the damages be

30. See **section 9.2**.

31. e.g. the mere fact that a claimant is intoxicated does not necessarily mean that he is culpable, so long as his actions—judged by reference to those of a sober person—remain reasonable (*Craven* v *Davies* [2018] at [11]).

reduced to such extent as the court thinks 'just and equitable having regard to the claimant's share in the responsibility for the damage' (as opposed to responsibility for the accident). When deciding by how much to reduce the award of damages to the claimant, the courts look to the *comparative blameworthiness* of the parties and to the 'relative importance of [the claimant's] acts in causing the damage' (*Stapley* v *Gypsum Mines Ltd* [1953] at 682; *Davies* v *Swan Motor Co* [1949]).

If the parties are equally to blame the damages will be reduced by 50 per cent; if the defendant is twice as blameworthy as the claimant they will be reduced by 33 per cent, and so on.[32] In *Young* v *Kent County Council* [2005], for example, a 12-year-old boy who was seriously injured after falling through a roof while attempting to retrieve his football was considered by the court to be 'as much to blame as the defendants' (at [34]). His damages were reduced by 50 per cent to reflect this. In *Badger* v *Ministry of Defence* [2005], the claimant's damages were reduced by 20 per cent to reflect the extent to which his failure to give up smoking had made a material contribution to his lung cancer (which was also caused by the defendants negligently exposing him to asbestos).[33]

Froom v *Butcher* [1976] CA

The claimant suffered head and chest injuries and a broken finger when his car was negligently hit by the defendant. The claimant was not wearing a seat belt. At the time there was no statute requiring people to wear seat belts and the claimant preferred not to wear one because he had at one time seen an accident where the driver would have been trapped if he had been wearing one.

The Court of Appeal held that the claimant was contributorily negligent *in respect of the injuries he would have avoided if he had worn a seat belt.* His damages were reduced by 20 per cent (as had been previously agreed by the parties).

The Court of Appeal went on to lay down guidelines in relation to the appropriate reduction in damages for failing to wear a seat belt (see **Table 10.1**). In *Stanton* v *Collinson* [2010], the Court of Appeal found that a teenager who suffered serious head injuries in a car accident in which he was not wearing a seat belt was *not* contributorily negligent on the grounds that it had not been shown that a belt, if worn, would sufficiently have reduced the injuries suffered. Hughes LJ continued:

> [The Law Reform (Contributory Negligence) Act 1945] . . . permits an approach such as adopted in ***Froom* v *Butcher*** . . . and the general proposition that, absent something exceptional, there should be no reduction in a case where the injury would not have been reduced

32. The wording of the Act may be thought to suggest that the claimant can never be 100 per cent contributorily negligent. This was certainly the view of the Court of Appeal in *Pitts* (although cf Lord Hoffmann in ***Reeves***).

33. The fact that a claimant smokes (or has made similar lifestyle choices) will not amount to contributory negligence where, e.g., the defendant's negligence relates to a failure to treat, or take into account, their condition or where these choices were made long before the defendant's negligence (*St George* v *Home Office* [2008] at [58]; *Calvert* v *William Hill Credit Ltd* [2008]).

> 'to a considerable extent' by the seat belt . . . Both parties in this appeal urged upon us, in different contexts, the undesirability of a prolonged or intensive enquiry in these cases. They were right to do so; there is a powerful public interest in there being no such enquiry into fine degrees of contributory negligence, so that the vast majority of cases can be settled according to a well-understood formula and those few which entail trial do not mushroom out of control. ***Froom* v *Butcher*** so states, and is binding. (at [26])

The ***Froom* v *Butcher*** guidelines have subsequently been applied in relation to a claimant's failure to wear a motorbike helmet in *Capps* v *Miller* [1989] and in relation to cycle helmets in *Smith* v *Finch* [2009] and *Reynolds* v *Strutt and Parker* [2011].

TABLE 10.1 Reduction in damages payable for failure to wear a seat belt or appropriate crash helmet on a motorbike

Level of injury	Reduction
Prevented completely	25%
Less severe	15%
No difference	0%

Damages will be reduced by up to one-third in cases of injury to a passenger where the driver is drunk, unless the passenger engages in conduct that affects the driver's performance, for example by encouraging them to speed (*Stinton* v *Stinton* [1995]).

Pause for reflection

It is clear from the judgment in *Froom* v *Butcher* that the claimant was reluctant to wear a seat belt and dubious of the safety benefits in so doing. At the time, wearing seat belts was not compulsory and, in the face of considerable parliamentary opposition, the government had to fall back on its Highway Code to 'strongly advise' motorists to fit and wear seat belts. This meant that although wearing seat belts remained, in principle, optional, the failure to wear one could be brought as evidence in civil proceedings. By finding the claimant in *Froom* v *Butcher* contributorily negligent, the Court of Appeal relied on the deterrent effects of tort law to fill this 'legislative gap'.[34] Motorists who may be willing to risk more serious injury by not wearing a seat belt were not, it seemed, as willing to risk a proportion of their award of compensation should the worst happen and began to buckle up (*Harlow* p 38). It remains to be seen whether the High Court's decision in *Smith* v *Finch* will have a similar effect in relation to cycle helmets.[35]

34. It is now compulsory to wear a seat belt (Road Traffic Act 1988, ss 14 and 15).

35. The Cyclists' Defence Fund suggests that deductions for contributory negligence for not wearing a helmet in head injury claims are now commonplace in out-of-court settlements (see further: **www.cyclistsdefencefund.org.uk**).

Jackson v Murray [2015] SC

The claimant, a 13-year-old child, suffered severe, life-changing injuries after being hit by a car when she ran into the road after alighting from her school bus. The driver of the car was liable in negligence. However, the Lord Ordinary (the trial judge) found the 'principal cause' of the accident was the 'reckless folly' of the claimant: either she did not look before crossing the road or, having looked, she failed to identify and react sensibly to the presence of the car in close proximity. In light of this, she was contributorily negligent and her damages were reduced by 90 per cent, reduced to 70 per cent on appeal.

Allowing her appeal, by majority, the Supreme Court found the parties to be 'at least equally as blameworthy' (at [43]), increasing the claimant's award to 50 per cent of the agreed damages (amounting to a reported £1.1 million). While there is no demonstrably correct apportionment—different judges will take different views on what is 'just and equitable'—meaning that the decision is 'inevitably a somewhat rough and ready exercise . . . [and] it follows that those differing views should be respected, within the limits of reasonable disagreement' (Lord Reed at [28]), in this case, the views of both the Lord Ordinary and Extra Division judges fell beyond these limits, hence the majority's increase of the claimant's award.

There were two central questions in ***Jackson***. How should responsibility be apportioned? And what principles should govern the review of an apportionment by an appellate court? There was agreement among the Justices that the former should be answered in light of the respective causative potency of the parties' acts and their respective blameworthiness and that an appellate court should only alter the assessment of the court below where the court 'has manifestly and to a substantial degree gone wrong' (at [46]). However, as the split decision demonstrates, these principles allow for considerable differences of opinion.

Pause for reflection

But what of the claimant's age—after all, she was only 13 at the time of the accident, 11 years earlier? And what of the defendant's negligence—it was agreed by the parties that 'if he had been driving at a reasonable speed, and had been keeping a proper look-out, he would not have hit her' (at [1]).

The courts have consistently imposed a high burden on car drivers, to reflect the potentially dangerous nature of driving:

> A pedestrian has to look to both sides as well as forwards. He is going at perhaps three miles an hour and at that speed he is rarely a danger to anyone else. The motorist has not got to look sideways though he may have to observe over a wide angle ahead: and if he is going at a considerable speed he must not relax his observation, for the consequences may be disastrous . . . In my opinion it is quite possible that the motorist may be very much more to blame than the pedestrian. (Lord Reid, *Baker* v *Willoughby* [1970] at 490)[36]

→

36. See e.g. discussion in *Sabir* v *Osei-Kwabena* [2015] at [13]–[18].

→

This was applied in the Scottish case of *McCluskey* v *Wallace* [1998] where a 10-year-old child was found to be 20 per cent responsible for her injuries when she failed to take reasonable care when crossing a road and was hit by a car. The driver was travelling at an appropriate speed but had failed to notice her, and could have avoided her if he'd been paying proper attention. The trial judge's decision to find the claimant in Jackson 90 per cent responsible for her injuries seems particularly harsh—especially given it was clear that the motorist had failed to drive with reasonable care:

> It was then about 40 minutes after sunset, and the light was fading. Vehicles had their lights on. The bus stopped, with its headlights on, and signs to the front and rear indicating that it was a school bus. The driver put on the bus's hazard lights. A number of vehicles following the bus stopped behind it. The defender was driving home in the opposite direction. His lights were switched on. As he approached the scene, he saw the stationary bus on the other carriageway. He had a view of the stationary bus for at least 200 metres. He had seen the school bus on this road before. He was travelling at about 50 mph. He did not slow down. His position in evidence was that he could not remember whether he had thought at the time that the bus might have stopped to drop children off. He regarded the risk of children running out unexpectedly as irrelevant: such a risk was 'not his fault', as he put it . . . The defender was unaware of her presence until the moment of impact. Since she must have been within his line of vision for approximately 1.5 seconds between emerging from behind the bus and the moment of impact, the Lord Ordinary inferred that he was not keeping a look-out for the possibility of such an event occurring. If he had had in mind the possibility that someone might emerge, he would have seen her earlier than he did. (Lord Reed at [7], [9])

Clearly, the claimant had also failed to take reasonable care for her own safety. As the Lord Ordinary noted:

> either she did not look to her left within a reasonable time before stepping out, or she failed to make a reasonable judgment as to the risk posed by the defender's car. On the other hand, . . . regard has to be had to the circumstances of the [claimant]. . . . [S]he was only 13 at the time, and a 13 year old will not necessarily have the same level of judgment and self-control as an adult. . . . [S]he had to take account of the defender's car approaching at speed, in very poor light conditions, with its headlights on. . . . [T]he assessment of speed in those circumstances is far from easy, even for an adult, and even more so for a 13 year old. It is also necessary to bear in mind that the situation of a pedestrian attempting to cross a relatively major road with a 60 mph speed limit, after dusk and without street lighting, is not straightforward, even for an adult. (cited at [41])

But was her failure to take reasonable care significantly worse than that of the claimants in *McCluskey*? ***Jackson*** is a good example of the difficulty courts have in relation to how to apportion responsibility between two negligent parties. The claimant was variously found to be between 90 and 50 per cent responsible for her injuries. Do you think the Supreme Court reached the right decision in this case?

More recently the High Court in *Gul* v *McDonagh* [2021] found that the claimant's failure to recognise that the car was being driven much faster than usual and adjust his actions accordingly amounted to contributory negligence. The claimant—a 13-year-old boy—suffered 'catastrophic injuries' when he was hit by a car which was being driven at over twice the 20 mph speed limit (the defendant was later convicted for dangerous driving):

> In my judgment that should have been apparent to a reasonable adult who had made an appropriate assessment of the dangers he faced in crossing the road. I then have to consider whether a reasonable 13 year old with the claimant's experience should be expected to have made the same judgment. I accept that many children cannot judge how fast vehicles are going or how far away they are. However, at 13, I consider it likely that the claimant would have experience of crossing roads on his own, even roads where traffic might be going at 40mph. It would be wholly wrong to expect the claimant to have been able to estimate the precise speed of the Focus. However, . . . a reasonable 13 year old making a careful assessment would have realised that the Focus was being driven much faster than usual. Further, although the claimant did not have far to go, I consider that a reasonable 13 year old would have considered that the Focus represented a source of potential danger and would have waited for the Focus to pass. Further, even if a reasonable 13 year old had set off, I consider that they would have kept the Ford Focus under observation so that, if necessary, they could hurry across the very short distance . . . In determining what reduction it is just and equitable to make on account of the claimant's contributory negligence, it is necessary to evaluate the relative degree of blameworthiness and causative effect of the acts and omissions which constitute negligence on the part of the claimant and the first defendant respectively. It is generally expected that a court will impose a high burden on drivers of cars to reflect the fact that a car is potentially a dangerous weapon. The first defendant's driving in this case was particularly egregious. His speed excessive, the risk of injury obvious and his motivation the desire to avoid arrest. Insofar as the claimant could see the defendant so too the defendant could see the claimant and could and should have slowed down. It would not have taken much adjustment on the part of the defendant to allow the claimant to complete that final 30cm across the road. The causative potency of all these factors is extremely high and must weigh heavily against the first defendant. . . . Whilst deeply sympathetic to the claimant, I do not think his culpable misjudgment can be wholly ignored. However, when balanced against the conduct of the first defendant it falls very much at the lowest end of the scale . . . I consider that the just and equitable reduction in all the circumstances of this case is 10%. (at [89], [97]–[98], [100])

10.5 **Conclusion**

Even if all the other elements of a claim in negligence have been met, the defendant may still be able to limit their liability in whole or in part by raising a defence. This chapter has considered the application of three defences—*voluntary assumption of risk, illegality* and *contributory negligence*. Although the latter is confined to negligence, the others apply generally throughout tort. In order to establish *voluntary assumption of risk* the defendant must show that the claimant consented to (rather than was simply aware of) the full extent and nature of the risk. As such it works to encourage the claimant to take personal responsibility for their actions, particularly when they are involved in inherently risky activities while *illegality* operates to defeat a claim where the action arises out of an illegal activity. While ***Patel*** appears to have gone some way to quelling debates as to the application of illegality, at least for the time being, it, remains—to paraphrase Sedley LJ—a somewhat 'blunt instrument' with which to do justice (*Vellino* at [55]). Finally, we looked at *contributory negligence*. This is the most common and successful defence in negligence. Unlike the other defences considered in this chapter, which exonerate the defendant from having to pay anything, contributory negligence *reduces* the damages of a claimant whose failure to exercise reasonable care for their own safety has contributed to their injury.

End-of-chapter questions

After reading the chapter carefully, try answering the questions which follow.

1 Outline each of the three defences discussed in this chapter. What do you think are their strengths and weaknesses?

2 The defence of illegality 'expresses not so much a principle as a policy. Furthermore, that policy is not based upon a single justification but on a group of reasons, which vary in different situations' (Lord Hoffmann, *Gray* v *Thames Trains* [2009] at [30]). Discuss with reference to recent case law.

If you would like to know what we think visit the **online resources**. www.oup.com/he/horsey7e

Answering the problem question

Consider again the problem question at the start of this chapter. Now having read about defences, what would be your advice to Ben and Andy? Do you think they are likely to recover compensation in respect of their injuries from Graeme? (You should assume that, in the absence of applicable defences, they would have a good claim in negligence.)

Here are some pointers to get you started

→ Will Andy's claim against Graeme be defeated by the defence of illegality?

→ Has Ben been contributorily negligent—both in relation to jumping in beside Graeme and failing to wear a seat belt?

If you need more guidance

see online resources

→ An **annotated version of the problem with issues and cases to consider** can be found in the Appendix.

→ A **suggested outline answer** to check your ideas against can be found in the online resources that accompany the book.

Further reading

The references below are a good place to start your further reading; however, you should bear in mind that—particularly, but not only, in relation to illegality—there has been a lot of recent case law and so some of the discussions of the law may be a little out of date.

Field, Ian D 'Contributory Negligence and the Rule of Avoidable Losses' *(2018) 38 OJLS* 475

Goudkamp, James 'Rethinking Contributory Negligence' in Erika Chamberlain, Jason Neyers and Stephen Pitel (eds) *Challenging Orthodoxy in Tort Law* (Hart, 2013)

Goudkamp, James *Tort Law Defences* (Hart, 2013)

Goudkamp, James and Donal Nolan 'Contributory Negligence in the Court of Appeal: An Empirical Study' (2017) 37 LS 437

Green, Sarah and Alan Bogg (eds) *Illegality after Patel v Mirza* (Hart, 2018)

Jaffey, AJE '*Volenti Non Fit Injuria*' [1985] CLJ 87

Law Commission *The Illegality Defence* (Law Com No 320, 2010)

Lord Mance '*Ex Turpi Causa*: When Latin Avoids Liability' (2014) 18 Edin L Rev 175

Lord Sumption 'Reflections on the Law of Illegality' (2012) 20 Restitution L Rev 1

Lunney, Mark 'Personal Responsibility and the "New" *Volenti*' (2005) 13 Tort L Rev 76

Webb, Charlie 'Illegality' in William Day and Sarah Worthington (eds) *Challenging Private Law: Lord Sumption on the Supreme Court* (Hart, 2020)

Special liability regimes

PART II

11 Occupiers' liability
11.1 Introduction
11.2 The Occupiers' Liability Act 1957
11.3 The Occupiers' Liability Act 1957—annotated
11.4 The Occupiers' Liability Act 1984
11.5 The Occupiers' Liability Act 1984—annotated
11.6 The Occupiers' Liability Acts 1957 and 1984—at a glance
11.7 Conclusion
End-of-chapter questions
Further reading

12 Product liability
12.1 Introduction
12.2 Defective products—claims in negligence
12.3 Defective products—claims under Part 1 of the Consumer Protection Act 1987
12.4 Part 1 of the Consumer Protection Act 1987—annotated
12.5 Claiming under Part 1 of the Consumer Protection Act 1987—at a glance
12.6 Conclusion
End-of-chapter questions
Further reading

13 Employers' liability
13.1 Introduction
13.2 An employer's personal non-delegable duty of care
13.3 Conclusion
End-of-chapter questions
Further reading

14 Breach of statutory duty
14.1 Introduction
14.2 Does the statute give rise to a claim in tort law?

14.3 Is a duty owed to the claimant?
14.4 Has the duty been breached and does the harm fall within the scope of the duty?
14.5 Conclusion
End-of-chapter questions
Further reading

Introduction to Part II

1. In this Part we consider three 'special liability' regimes relating to occupiers and defective products and the tort of breach of statutory duty. Though much of tort law is based on general principles of common law, there are a number of situations where the legislature has intervened to introduce statutory rules. Typically, their purpose is to mitigate the harshness and inadequacies of the common law, though other factors have also played a part—in the case of product liability, for example, statutory intervention was necessary in order to implement a European Community Directive. In this Part we look at three 'special liability' regimes relating to occupiers, employers and defective products.[1]

2. We begin, in **Chapter 11**, with *occupiers' liability*. An occupier may be liable where a person who comes onto their land is injured in or by unsafe premises if the occupier has not taken reasonable care to ensure that they, and those entering on them, are safe.

3. In such cases the common law has been superseded by the Occupiers' Liability Acts (OLAs) of 1957 and 1984. Before this, a complex system of common law rules governed this area of law, whereby the scope of the duty owed by the occupier depended on the circumstances in which the claimant came onto the premises. It continues to be important to define at the outset the category of visitor who has been injured: the Occupiers' Liability Act 1957 covers the safety of lawful visitors, whereas the Occupiers' Liability Act 1984 covers unlawful visitors (typically trespassers).

4. Although the OLAs define the circumstances in which a duty of care will be owed (and tell us something as to its extent, as well as matters relating to its discharge and limitation), questions of breach and causation still need to be established by reference to the ordinary principles of negligence.

5. In **Chapter 12**, we turn to the special liability regime related to those injured by defective products. As with occupiers' liability, *product liability* is primarily governed by statute (Part 1 of the Consumer Protection Act 1987). However, whilst in the context of occupiers' liability Parliament intervened in order to remedy the perceived failings of the common law, here they did so in response to a European Community Directive which *required* near-uniform product liability legislation across EU member states.

6. Unlike the OLAs, the Consumer Protection Act (CPA) 1987 has not replaced the common law. A claimant may still claim in the tort of negligence in relation to defective products. Though such claims will generally be more difficult to establish than under the CPA (which creates a form of *strict liability*), they remain necessary given problematic statutory limitations in relation to certain types of claim.

7. We then turn in **Chapter 13** to *employers' liability*. An employer owes a *non-delegable duty of care* to their employees to ensure that they are reasonably safe when at work. This works to ensure that an employer remains responsible for key tasks even when their obligations have been delegated to another.

1. The grouping mirrors that of Mark Lunney, Donal Nolan and Ken Oliphant in *Tort Law: Text and Materials* (6th edn, OUP, 2017).

8. Finally, in **Chapter 14**, we consider the tort of *breach of statutory duty*. Unlike the statutory duties contained in, for example, the OLAs or the CPA where liability arises directly according to the provisions of the statute itself, in a civil action in the tort of breach of statutory duty, liability arises *indirectly* where a statute imposes a duty (typically relating to criminal liability) but does not identify a civil remedy in the event of its breach. The tort is a combination of statute and the tort of negligence; the duty is defined by statute, while the action lies in the common law. While historically the tort played an important role in the employment context, its application in this context has been significantly curtailed by section 69 of the Enterprise and Regulatory Reform Act 2013.

Occupiers' liability

11

Problem question

Read this problem question carefully, and keep it in mind while you are working through the chapter that follows. At the end of the chapter, you will be able to apply what you have learnt to the problem question and advise the relevant parties.

'Camden Cool', an after-school youth club run by the local authority, is holding an open day to raise funds for the club. One of the main attractions is a large bouncy castle supplied, erected and supervised by Elsinore Castles, a small local company. Joseph and Harry are the first to try it out. They both suffer minor cuts and bruises when the castle breaks free from its moorings and lifts into the air. It later turns out that it had not been appropriately tethered to the ground. Unfortunately, despite assuring Jake, the club's youth worker, when he phoned to book the castle, that they had the necessary documentation, Elsinore's public liability insurance had expired two months before the accident.

In the chaos that follows, Iris (Joseph's sister) wanders off alone. She is too young to be a member of the club and so doesn't know her way around the buildings. She is seriously injured when she falls down a flight of stairs after going through a door marked 'Private: No Unauthorised Entry'.

Meanwhile Frank and Bill (who are members of the club) have sneaked off to play football. After a particularly poor shot at goal their ball lands on a flat roof. Although they know the roof is 'out of bounds', as everyone is busy at the open day, they decide to climb onto the roof to retrieve it. As they do so one of the skylights breaks. Bill falls through the roof hitting his head hard, causing him to lose his hearing.

Advise the parties of any claims they may have under the Occupiers' Liability Acts 1957 and 1984.

11.1 Introduction

Consider the following examples:

→ ***While on a picnic with some friends, a student dives into a lake to cool off. Unfortunately, he misjudges his dive into the shallow water and, as a result, hits his head on the lake bed and breaks his neck.***

→ ***A shopper slips on some spilt milk in the dairy aisle of his local supermarket injuring his back and ruining his new suede jacket. The warning sign had been moved by another shopper to get to the food on the shelves.***

→ ***A dinner guest trips over a child's toy left at the top of a flight of stairs and tumbles to the bottom, twisting her ankle.***

→ ***On his way home from a night out, a student trips over an uneven paving stone on the driveway leading to his halls of residence.***

Occupiers' liability deals with the risks posed, and harms caused, by dangerous places and buildings. In such cases, similar to those described above, the occupier of the premises—broadly understood to include not only buildings but also driveways, fire escapes and so on—may be liable if they have not taken reasonable care to ensure that those entering their premises are safe. What makes these claims distinctive is that the general principles of negligence (whereby if a breach of duty has caused injury, liability will usually follow) have been incorporated into, and modified by, statute in the form of the Occupiers' Liability Acts 1957 and 1984.[1]

This statutory intervention was a response to the harshness and complexity of the common law, whereby the scope of the duty owed by the occupier varied according to the circumstances in which the claimant came on to the premises. Those who were on the premises by virtue of a contract (e.g. a plumber coming to fix a leaking tap) were owed a higher standard of care than so-called 'invitees' (e.g. a shopper), or a friend the occupier had invited round for dinner, who was merely a 'licensee'. Although they all fared better than 'uninvited' persons or trespassers who, until *British Railways Board* v *Herrington* [1972], were owed no positive duty of care at all; occupiers were simply under an obligation not to deliberately or recklessly cause trespassers harm (*Edwards* v *Railway Executive* [1952]).

Pause for reflection

Despite the enactment of the 1957 Act and, more particularly, its companion—the 1984 Act—Richard Buckley argues that the imposition of liability on occupiers remains 'an aspiration rather than an accurate statement of contemporary law' (2006, p 215). More recently, this traditional reluctance to impose liability—usually relating to a desire to leave landowners alone to enjoy their land as they wish—has been given a contemporary twist. The imposition of liability has been framed as an attack on the liberties of both individuals who choose to engage in dangerous pastimes at their own risk *and* those who wish to simply enjoy the countryside and other public spaces. Consider, for example, the following extract from the speech of Lord Hobhouse

→

1. In this chapter we will use the abbreviation OLAs when referring to both of the Occupiers' Liability Acts and OLA 1957 or OLA 1984 when referring to a specific Act.

→

in *Tomlinson* v *Congleton Borough Council* [2003] in which he mirrors the concerns of many about the effects of 'an unrestrained culture of blame and compensation':

> [I]t is not, and should never be, the policy of the law to require the protection of the foolhardy or reckless few to deprive, or interfere with, the enjoyment by the remainder of society of the liberties and amenities to which they are rightly entitled. Does the law require that all trees be cut down because some youths may climb them and fall? Does the law require the coastline and other beauty spots to be lined with warning notices? Does the law require that attractive waterside picnic spots be destroyed because of a few foolhardy individuals who choose to ignore warning notices and indulge in activities dangerous only to themselves? The answer to all these questions is, of course, no. (at [81])

Do you agree with Lord Hobhouse? Think again about the purposes of tort law, contrasting the idea of corrective justice and its focus on individual responsibility and fault with the concerns of providing compensation and distributing losses across the community.[2]

Though there are now just two categories of visitor—lawful and unlawful—it remains important to identify from the outset which category the person who has been injured falls into as this will determine which of the OLAs applies.

- The 1957 Act—covers lawful visitors (including invitees and licensees at common law and contractual visitors) (ss 1(2), 5).
- The 1984 Act—covers unlawful visitors (typically trespassers) (s 1(1)(a)).

There is one further point to note here. Although the Acts define the circumstances in which a duty of care will be owed and tell us something as to its extent, as well as matters relating to its discharge and limitation, when determining whether the duty has been breached and whether this breach caused the claimant loss we revert back to the ordinary principles of negligence.

11.2 **The Occupiers' Liability Act 1957**

The 1957 Act provides that an occupier owes a duty of care to visitors in respect of dangers posed by the state of the premises or by things done or omitted to be done on them (s 1(1)). In line with its objective to simplify the common law, the 1957 Act abolishes the various categories of visitor (and hence the varying duties owed to contractors, licensees and (implied) invitees) and provides that all lawful entrants should be owed the same common duty of care in respect of personal injury and property damage suffered on the premises (s 2(1)). The Act applies only to injuries suffered on the occupier's premises; if the injury is suffered outside their premises then there can be no claim on the basis of

2. See further Jane Stapleton 'Tort, Insurance and Ideology' (1995) 58 MLR 820 and Morgan 2004.

occupiers' liability, though, of course, a claim may lie under the ordinary principles of negligence, in the tort of nuisance (if there is an unreasonable interference with land) or under the rule in ***Rylands* v *Fletcher*** **[1868]** (if the damage is caused by the escape of a dangerous thing).[3]

11.2.1 **When is a duty owed?**

Under the 1957 Act an *occupier* owes a common duty of care to all *lawful visitors* who suffer injury on their *premises* (s 1(1)). It also states that occupiers and visitors are to be defined in the same way as at common law (s 1(2)).

Pause for reflection

There is some ambiguity as to the scope of the 1957 Act. The reference in section 1(1) to 'dangers due to the state of the premises *or to things done, or omitted to be done on them*' and in section 2(2) to 'a duty to take such care as in all the circumstances of the case is reasonable to see that the visitor will be reasonably safe *in using the premises* for the purposes for which he is invite or permitted by the occupier to be there' (emphasis added) has led to debate as to whether the Act extends the occupier's duty to include injuries caused by activities which are taking place on their premises (an 'activity' duty) or whether it is limited to injuries caused by the static condition of the premises themselves (an 'occupancy' duty).[4] It seems, however, that section 1(1) of the 1957 Act *only* applies to dangers posed, and harms caused, by the condition of the premises (though these may be rendered dangerous by virtue of some activity that has previously taken place on them).[5] The Act has no application where a claimant is injured by an activity that is happening on the defendant's premises. In *Bottomley* v *Todmorden Cricket Club* [2003], for example, the claimant was injured when helping to set up a firework display. As his injuries arose from activities conducted on the defendant's land rather than due to the state of the land itself, his claim under the Act failed.[6] This, Buckley argues, is the better view of the scope of the 1957 Act: 'All activities which take place do so *somewhere*, and the law relating to occupiers' liability would be extraordinarily wide if it were expanded to include all the activities

3. Discussed in **Chapters 2–10**, **18** and **19** respectively.

4. This distinction between so-called 'occupancy' and 'activity' duties predates the OLAs. It was developed by the courts as a way of avoiding the harshness of the common law. While liability in relation to the former depended on the status of the visitor, the ordinary rules of negligence applied to the latter.

5. Though the case law is not consistent on this. Compare Lord Goff in *Ferguson* v *Welsh* [1987] (approved in *Fairchild* v *Glenhaven Funeral Services* [2002] (CA) at [122]–[133]) with Lords Hoffmann and Hobhouse in ***Tomlinson*** at [26]–[29] and [69]–[70] respectively: 'There are two alternatives. The first is . . . [the] state of the premises is the physical features of the premises as they exist at the relevant time. It can include foot paths covered in ice and open mine shafts . . . The second alternative is dangers due to things done or omitted to be done on the premises. Thus if shooting is taking place on the premises, a danger to visitors may arise from that fact. If speed boats are allowed to go into an area where swimmers are, the safety of the swimmers may be endangered' (at [69]).

6. His claim relying on the ordinary tort of negligence was successful.

→

which a defendant happens to carry out on his land' (2006, p 208). And, in any case, as Brooke LJ noted in *Bottomley*, there is likely to be little difference, if any, between the duty owed under the 1957 Act and that under the ordinary principles of negligence (at [42]).

That said, an occupier may, in certain circumstances, be liable to a visitor for the harm caused by another visitor. In *Cunningham* v *Reading Football Club Ltd* [1992] a policeman was able to recover under the 1957 Act for his injuries suffered as a result of being hit by a concrete missile thrown by football hooligans. Although the actions of the hooligans (described by one witness as 'the worst they had seen at any football ground in Britain' (at 144)) might seem more akin to an activity (and, as such, to fall outside the scope of the 1957 Act), the court held that the defendants had breached their duty as occupiers under the 1957 Act. The premises were in a particularly dilapidated state and this allowed the hooligans to break off bits of concrete with their feet to use as missiles. Therefore the claimant's injuries could be attributed to the state of the premises and hence the defendant's breach of their occupancy duty. However, this should now be read in light of *Everett* v *Comojo (UK) Ltd (t/a The Metropolitan)* [2011] in which Smith LJ suggested that the duty of care imposed by the 1957 Act might be relevant when seeking to establish whether it is fair, just and reasonable to impose a common law duty of care on the occupier in situations where the potential liability does not relate to the condition of the premises: 'It would be surprising if management could be liable to a guest who tripped over a worn carpet and yet escape liability for injuries inflicted by a fellow guest who was a foreseeable danger—for example in that he had previously been excluded on account of his violent behaviour and who on this occasion had been allowed in carrying an offensive weapon' (at [33]).

In order to establish when a duty of care is owed it is necessary to look to both the 1957 Act and the case law for answers to the following questions.

- Who is an occupier?
- Who is a lawful visitor?
- What are premises?

11.2.1.1 Occupiers: 'control of premises'

The duty imposed by the 1957 Act is owed by those in occupation of premises. Occupation is different from ownership; an occupier need not be the owner of the premises and nor is the owner necessarily the occupier. Neither is occupation simply a matter of who is physically present on the premises. Rather, the occupier is the person who has, or is able to exercise, a sufficient degree of *control* over the premises (s 1(2)).[7] Importantly, there may be more than one occupier at any given time. For example, a landlord and tenant may, depending on the circumstances, both be considered occupiers for the purpose of the 1957 Act.

7. This explains why landlords are not (usually) liable under the 1957 Act (although they may be liable under the Defective Premises Act 1972).

Wheat v *Lacon & Co Ltd* [1966] HL

The defendants, Lacon & Co brewery, had let their public house to Mr Richardson to manage under a service agreement. They had also given Richardson and his wife permission (on an informal basis) to live on the first floor of the public house and to rent the other rooms to paying guests. The claimant's husband, Mr Wheat, was fatally injured after falling down a flight of poorly lit stairs while staying at the pub. The light bulb at the top of the stairs had been removed, which meant that he was unable to know when he reached the last step and was unable to see that the handrail finished three steps short of the end of the staircase. The question for the court was whether the brewery (who owned the public house) was an occupier for the purposes of a claim under the 1957 Act (a claim in negligence against Mr and Mrs Richardson had failed).

The House of Lords held that *both* the brewery and Mr and Mrs Richardson were occupiers for the purposes of the 1957 Act and, as such, owed a common duty of care to the claimant (and other lawful visitors). The brewery, by simply granting a concession to allow Mr and Mrs Richardson to occupy the first floor, had not relinquished complete control of the premises: 'In order to be an "occupier" it is not necessary for a person to have entire control over the premises. He need not have exclusive occupation. Suffice that he has some degree of control. He may share the control with others' (Lord Denning at 578).

However, on the facts, neither party had fallen below the standard of care required of them. The fact that the stairs had a short handrail did not, in itself, make the stairs unreasonably hazardous and nor were they responsible for the actions of the stranger who had plunged the stairs into darkness by removing the light bulb, shortly before Mr Wheat attempted to walk down them.

Wheat* v *Lacon shows that an occupier need not have actual physical possession of the premises. Indeed one may be an 'occupier' for the purposes of the 1957 (and 1984) Act despite never having resided in or physically occupied the premises. For instance, in *Harris* v *Birkenhead Corporation* [1975], as part of a slum clearance programme, a tenant was served with a compulsory purchase order, which stated that the corporation would enter and take possession of the property a fortnight after the notice was served. The tenant moved out. Three months later the corporation had still not secured the property despite knowing that vacant properties in the area were often vandalised. As a result, vandals had broken down the front door and caused considerable damage inside the property, including removing the glass from a second-floor window. The claimant (a 4-year-old girl), who had entered the property through the damaged door, fell out of the window suffering severe brain damage. The Court of Appeal held that even though the corporation had never been to the premises, they nevertheless were the occupiers as soon as the previous tenant had left. They had control over the property and, though they did not exercise it, the ability *and duty* to secure it.

Liability under the Defective Premises Act 1972

Typically, a landlord who has leased out premises will not have retained sufficient control to be treated as an occupier for the purposes of the OLAs. In such situations, a tenant who suffers an injury as a result of a defect in the premises they are renting will have no claim under the

→

→

1957 Act; there is no 'occupier' (other than themselves) to sue. Nor does the common law offer much protection in such circumstances (*Cavalier* v *Pope* [1906]; *Bottomley* v *Bannister* [1932]).

This gap is addressed by section 4 of the Defective Premises Act 1972.[8] Where a lease imposes on the landlord an obligation in respect of the maintenance and repair of the property, the landlord will be held to owe a duty of care to all those who might reasonably be expected to be affected by any defects in the state of the premises, so long as (a) the landlord knows or ought to have known of the relevant defect and (b) the defect is one which the landlord should have remedied by virtue of the obligation to repair imposed by the lease. The important point to note here is that the duty is owed not only to the tenant, but also to others who may foreseeably be affected by defects, such as partners and other family members (s 4(1)).

11.2.1.2 Visitors: by invitation or permission only

An occupier only owes a duty under the 1957 Act to those they have invited or have (or are treated as having) given permission to enter or use the premises (s 1(2)).[9] The key question is then: did the claimant have express, or implied, permission to be on the premises?

Such permission is rarely unlimited. As Scrutton LJ notes: 'When you invite a person into your house to use the staircase, you do not invite him to slide down the banisters' (*The Carlgarth* [1927] at 110).[10] By limiting the extent of the permission they give to a visitor, an occupier can restrict the duty they owe to them. For example, they might place restrictions on the time a visitor can spend on their premises (e.g. opening hours), the purposes for which they can use it, or limit their permission to particular parts of the property. If a visitor goes beyond what they have been invited or given permission to do at that point, and to that extent, they will cease to be treated as a visitor and will fall outside the provisions of the 1957 Act—although in these circumstances the 1984 Act will apply.

Spearman v _Royal United Bath Hospitals NHS Foundation Trust_ [2017] QBD

The claimant, James Spearman, had been taken to hospital by ambulance after suffering from a hypoglycaemic attack. The claimant had a phobia of hospitals. Within 15 minutes, he had left the emergency department of the hospital, climbed five flights of stairs to a flat roof, climbed over a protective barrier and either fallen or jumped into a courtyard below where he suffered a severe traumatic brain injury and multiple fractures including fractures

→

8. The Defective Premises Act 1972 is also discussed in relation to negligence liability for economic loss in **section 7.4**. See also JR Spencer 'The Defective Premises Act 1972—Defective Law and Defective Law Reform' [1975] CLJ 48.

9. This duty also extends to the lawful visitor's property (s 1(3)(b)).

10. This is largely a matter of common sense. Consider again the dinner guest who fell down the stairs. They will remain a lawful visitor (and the occupier will be liable) so long as their presence on the stairs was reasonable. See further *Gould* v *McAuliffe* [1941] and *Kolasa* v *Ealing Hospital NHS Trust* [2015].

→

to his lower limbs, sternum, ribs, lumbar spine and left wrist leaving him dependent on others for care and assistance with all activities of daily living.

But was Spearman a 'visitor' (and so owed a duty under the 1957 Act) or a 'trespasser' (and so falling within the more limited remit of the OLA 1984) at the time of the accident? Interestingly, the judge held that—despite his actions in leaving the emergency department and making his way up two flights of stairs and onto the roof—he remained a visitor:

> in my judgment whether a person is or is not a trespasser is not solely determined by whether the place where they are is or is not an 'authorised' place. A person's state of mind and intention is an important additional factor. If a patient, who is a lawful visitor to a hospital (whether the Emergency Department or any other department) has finished his or her treatment and is leaving, he or she does not cease to be a visitor in general until they leave the hospital premises. The position may be different if they deliberately enter an area marked 'no entry', or 'private' or know that they are entering a part of the hospital where they have no right to be. But if the patient simply makes a mistake and goes the wrong way, it could not possibly be suggested that such a person was now a trespasser. So here, intending to leave the Emergency Department, Mr Spearman, in his confused state of mind, thought (wrongly but honestly) that he needed to go upstairs to get out and, indeed, go over the barrier to get out. His belief meant that he remained a lawful visitor and, in my judgment, he did not become a trespasser at any time material to this case. Just as, for Goddard LJ in *Gould's* [v *McAuliffe* [1941]] case, it was determinative that 'there was nothing to show that an invitee to this garden ought not to go through the gate in question', so here, the lack of any notice over door 1 and the lack of any lock on door 1 had the same effect. . . . [T]he suggestion that the mere act of climbing over the wall, not being an act covered by the general permission to be on the site as a patient nor being part of the permission given by the defendant to patients leaving the site after treatment, was enough to convert the claimant in that case from being an invitee or visitor to being a trespasser is too simplistic as it fails to take account of the state of mind of the claimant . . . [T]he claimant was mentally disturbed and did what he did as a result of a genuine and honest mistake, made in his state of confusion, it being wholly foreseeable that confused and mentally unstable patients would be part of [the] cohort of visitors to the department. (at [56])

Finding the hospital liable (both in breach of their duty under the 1957 Act and a 'superimposed duty at common law' (at [75])), the judge concluded: the hospital 'had failed to take reasonable steps to ensure that the premises were reasonably safe for him as a vulnerable patient who was confused and mentally unstable at the time that he was in the emergency department of the hospital' (at [75]).[11]

11. The judge also refused to find the claimant contributorily negligent, see further **section 10.4.1**.

A person may be a visitor for some purposes and not for others depending on the scope of the permission granted by the occupier (compare e.g. ***Darby*** v ***National Trust*** [2001] and ***Tomlinson***).

The occupier may change the terms of their permission and even revoke it entirely while the visitor is on the premises, changing the status of the 'visitor'. However, to be effective, this must be done in a way that is obvious to the visitor. A rather extreme example of this is provided by *Snook* v *Mannion* [1982] where a motorist told the policeman who had followed him up his driveway in order to breathalyse him to 'f**k off'. The court held that these words—which were taken to refer to the policeman's presence as well as his attempts to breathalyse the motorist—were not sufficient to revoke the licence usually implied to allow people to use a driveway to approach the house on legitimate business. In the same way, notices merely stating 'keep out' or 'private' may also not be sufficient.

11.2.1.3 Premises: including 'any fixed or moveable structure'

Under the 1957 Act the definition of premises extends to 'any fixed or movable structure, including any vessel, vehicle or aircraft' (s 1(3)). Clearly this broad interpretation of premises not only includes buildings, driveways, fire escapes and other real property but also encompasses less permanent structures such as scaffolding, a derelict boat left on a council estate (see e.g. ***Jolley*** v ***Sutton London Borough Council*** [2000]; ***Gwilliam*** v ***West Hertfordshire Hospitals NHS Trust*** [2002]).

11.2.2 The standard of care

Under the 1957 Act, an occupier owes a positive duty to act to take 'such care as in all the circumstances of the case is reasonable to see that the visitor will be reasonably safe in using the premises for the purposes for which he is invited' (s 2(2)). The first thing to note is that it is the *visitor*, not the premises, that must be reasonably safe. Thus, where the occupier is aware of a particular vulnerability of the visitor, and can reasonably be expected to take steps to guard against it, their duty of care will be higher. This was illustrated in *Pollock* v *Cahill* [2015] in which the claimant, who was blind, suffered serious brain and spinal injuries after falling out of an open second-floor window while staying at his friends' house: 'the reference to "such a visitor" [in s 2(3) of the OLA 1957] requires the occupier to have regard to any known vulnerability . . . If [the claimant] had been a sighted person, the open window would not have rendered the premises unsafe. It was the fact that he was blind that made them so. [The defendant] was fully aware of his position . . . [and] failed to discharge the common duty of care they owed as occupiers. The open window was a real risk to [the claimant]. [The defendants] created that risk. They ought to have appreciated the risk and taken steps to prevent it by keeping the window closed or by warning [the claimant] about it with particular reference as to the extent of the drop from the window (Davis J at [51], [53]).[12]

see online resources

12. The defendants' appeal was unsuccessful. The claimant—a Commonwealth Games medal winner and the first blind man to reach the South Pole—expressly limited his claim to £2 million, the limit of the defendants' insurance. Without this, the value of his claim would have been 'significantly greater' (at [1]).

Secondly, the occupier's duty only applies for the purposes for which the visitor was invited onto the premises and finally that the occupier is not under 'an obligation to ensure the safety of visitors, merely to take reasonable care to provide reasonable safety' (Mackay J, ***Bowen* v *National Trust*** [2011] at [6]).

Bowen v *National Trust* [2011] QBD

The claimant was killed when a 21-metre tree branch fell entirely without warning on a group of school children sheltering under the tree while on a school trip to Felbrigg Hall in Suffolk (owned by the National Trust). Three other children were seriously injured. The claimants argued that the defendant's tree inspectors, for whom the National Trust was vicariously liable, failed to exercise reasonable care in failing to spot the defect in the tree and 'tagging' it as requiring remedial action. Rejecting their claim, Mackay J suggested it was 'the cruellest coincidence' that the branch fell just as the children were standing underneath it (at [43]). Nevertheless, he continued,

> I accept these inspectors used all the care to be expected of reasonably competent persons doing their job, and the defendant had given them adequate training and instruction in how to approach their task. To require more would serve the desirable end of compensating these claimants for their grievous loss and injuries. But it would also be requiring the defendant to do more than was reasonable to see that the children enjoying the use of this wood were reasonably safe to do so. I regretfully conclude that I cannot find that the defendant was negligent or in breach of its duty in respect of this tragedy. (Mackay J at [43])

In short, in the words of McCombe LJ in *Edwards* v *London Borough of Sutton* [2016], 'not every accident (even if it has serious consequences) has to have been the fault of another; and an occupier is not an insurer against injuries sustained on his premises' (at [61]).

Whether the occupier has breached their duty of care is determined by the same basic principles as in the common law of negligence (as reflected by the fact that some of the leading cases on breach are cases of occupiers' liability).[13] So, for instance, in determining what amounts to reasonable care, we take into account the likelihood and gravity of harm resulting from the state of the premises and the costs involved in rectifying any potential dangers. In particular, the 1957 Act requires courts to consider what is reasonable 'in all the circumstances of the case' (s 2(2)), including the degree of care expected from the visitor/claimant (s 2(3)). We looked at breach in detail in **Chapter 8**, and the cases discussed there are relevant here too. Here we shall draw attention only to a handful of issues which are either specific to occupiers' liability or are mentioned in the 1957 Act.

It is clear that the courts will take into account the resources of the occupier when considering what steps they might reasonably be expected to take to ensure the visitor is reasonably safe.[14] The common duty of care is not owed 'in the abstract' but by particular defendants to particular claimants (*Lewis* v *Six Continents* [2005] at [24]).

13. See e.g. ***Latimer* v *AEC Ltd*** [1953].

14. Thus, in relation to the examples posed at the beginning of the chapter, while an occupier might be reasonably expected to ensure that children's toys are tidied away before hosting a dinner party (this being fairly easily achieved), more information is needed (in relation to the resources of

Kiapasha (t/a Takeaway Supreme) v *Laverton* [2002] CA

The claimant broke her ankle after slipping over in the defendant's busy takeaway after a night out. It had been raining earlier in the evening and the shop floor was wet and slippery. The shopkeeper had taken a number of precautions to prevent accidents: the shop floor had been re-laid using slip-resistant tiles; there was a doormat to limit the amount of water brought in on the feet of the customers (although this may have been kicked out of the way at the time of the accident); and there was a system for mopping up excess water, which usually took place six or seven times on a busy night.

The majority of the Court of Appeal held that the shopkeeper had done all that could reasonably be expected of him in his attempts to keep his shop floor dry:

> In some large businesses it may be reasonable to expect stringent precautions at the shop door, including mats large enough to absorb moisture from large numbers of customers who do not wipe their feet and/or a member of staff stationed near the door to mop up as required . . . The question is what was reasonable to expect of the defendant in the particular circumstances of the case and whether anything else would have made a difference. In my view, it would not . . . [I]n that particular shop, at that particular time, it was not reasonable to expect the shopkeeper to ensure that the mat was in place and to mop the floor often enough and efficiently enough to prevent its being wet, even significantly or considerably so. (Hale LJ at [19]–[23])[15]

Similarly, and again as with breach more generally, the occupier's duty to ensure that the visitor will be reasonably safe while on their premises does not mean that the visitor cannot be expected to take reasonable care for their own safety (s 2(3)). The 1957 Act makes particular reference to children and professionals.

11.2.2.1 Children

Children invited onto premises are owed a common duty of care like all other visitors. However, where the visitor is a child more may be required of the occupier to ensure that they are kept *reasonably* safe. Though the courts recognise that it may be impossible to make the premises *completely* safe for children—especially when they are not under the supervision of their parents (*Bourne Leisure Ltd* v *Marsden* [2009]). In particular, the occupier must take into account that children will be less careful than adults (s 2(3)(a)). As such, occupiers will generally owe a higher standard of care to children than to older visitors (*Glasgow Corporation* v *Taylor* [1922]).

the occupier, extent of the unevenness, cost of repair and so on) before the same can be said in relation to the uneven paving stone at the students' halls of residence.

15. Consider again the spilt milk in a supermarket aisle in the examples at the beginning of the chapter—what additional information would the court need in order to decide whether the occupier was in breach of their duty? See further *Ward* v *Tesco Stores Ltd* [1976].

Jolley v *Sutton London Borough Council* [2000] HL

A boat had been abandoned for at least two years on land owned by the defendant. Although it appeared to be in relatively good condition, it was in fact rotten. The claimant, a 14-year-old boy, was crushed when the boat fell on him (he and a friend had decided to repair it) suffering serious spinal injuries which left him paralysed. He brought an action against the council for damages under the 1957 Act.

Holding the council liable, the House of Lords noted that the boat was likely to be a particular attraction—or an 'allurement'—to children. Though the boat was not likely to pose a danger to adults, who were more likely to steer clear of it, it was reasonably foreseeable that children might approach the boat and be tempted to climb onto it. As Lord Hoffmann noted: children's 'ingenuity in finding unexpected ways of doing mischief to themselves and others should never be underestimated' (at 1093). The claimant was found to be contributorily negligent, and his damages were reduced by 25 per cent.

It is worth stressing that the 'allurement' of the boat in ***Jolley*** was relevant to establishing the foreseeability of the children climbing onto the boat, and hence whether it was reasonable to have expected the council to have taken steps to ensure the boat was safe or to remove it. In other words, its relevance was to determining whether the defendant breached its duty to the claimant. Clearly, this question only arises once we have established that the child claimant is indeed a visitor, that is, has the occupier's permission to enter or use the premises, and so is owed a duty under the 1957 Act.

At one point, it seemed that the courts were willing to stretch the notion of permission in relation to children to ensure that they were always treated as visitors, most likely because, as already noted, trespassers were afforded little protection at common law. However, now the 1984 Act has extended the protection accorded to those injured when on another's premises without permission, there is far less need for the courts to stretch the notion of visitors when dealing with children. As such, the better view is that in determining both whether the claimant has permission to enter the defendant's premises and how far that permission extends—that is, determining whether a child is a visitor for the purposes of the 1957 Act—the same rules apply to adults and children alike.

Nevertheless, it is usually argued that, in deciding whether the common duty of care has been breached, an occupier is entitled to assume that parents will take reasonable care of young children:

> [T]he responsibility for the safety of little children must rest primarily on the parents; it is their duty to see that such children are not allowed to wander about by themselves, or at least to satisfy themselves that the places to which they do allow their children to go unaccompanied are safe for them to go to. It would not be socially desirable if parents were, as a matter of course, able to shift the burden of looking after their children from their own shoulders to those who happen to have accessible bits of land. (*Phipps* v *Rochester Corporation* [1955] at 472)

In *Simkiss* v *Rhondda Borough Council* [1983], a child was seriously injured whilst playing with a friend on a steep bank. In the course of argument it became clear that the child's father did not believe the bank to be dangerous. The Court of Appeal held that it was not reasonable to hold the council to a higher standard of care than a reasonably prudent parent—if the child's father did not consider the bank to be dangerous, then why should the council? Moreover, even if the father *had* considered the bank to be dangerous, the council was entitled to assume that the father would warn his child of familiar and obvious dangers. The fact that he had not either meant that he thought the bank was safe or was evidence of negligence on *his* part.

Counterpoint

The decision in *Simkiss* appears somewhat harsh. Do you think it would have been decided differently if the father had given a different answer to the question of whether he considered the bank dangerous? Why should the fact that the claimant's parents fail to give sufficient regard to their child's safety entitle occupiers to escape liability for their own neglect? It is one thing to say that occupiers should not be expected to make up for parents' shortcomings, quite another to hold them to a lower standard simply because the child's parents would have done no better.

11.2.2.2 'Persons in the exercise of a calling'

While greater care must be taken in relation to children invited onto one's premises, less is required of occupiers in respect of visitors who are considered able to look after themselves. In particular, skilled visitors are expected to guard against special risks associated with their profession (s 2(3)(b)).

In *Roles* v *Nathan* [1963] two chimney sweeps died whilst trying to mend the chimney of a coke-fired boiler. Though they had been warned repeatedly that the boiler room was dangerous and were told to leave, they had carried on working. The majority of the Court of Appeal dismissed a claim under the 1957 Act by the chimney sweeps' widows on two grounds: first, a householder can reasonably expect a specialist to appreciate and guard against dangers associated with their trade (s 2(3)); and, secondly, the warning had been sufficient to ensure that the sweeps were, in all the circumstances, 'reasonably safe' within the meaning of section 2(4). Accordingly, though Lord Denning MR was of the view that no duty of care was owed to the sweeps, in any event 'the duty was discharged . . . in regard to the dangers that caused their deaths. If it had been a different danger, as for instance if the stairs leading to the cellar gave way, the occupier might no doubt be responsible, but not for these dangers which were special risks ordinarily incidental to their calling' (at 1123–4).[16]

11.2.2.3 Warnings

An occupier may discharge their duty by giving a warning of the potential danger (s 2(4)(a)) (or alternatively it may raise the defence of *volenti* (s 2(5)) or contributory negligence (s 2(6))). Warnings may be verbal, but can also be visual or written—for example, a notice

16. A similar claim against an occupier also failed in *General Cleaning Contractors* v *Christmas* [1953] (discussed in **section 13.2.3**).

on the edge of a cliff, a barrier around a building site or a large yellow 'warning' sign on a shop floor. However, whatever its form, a warning will only be sufficient to discharge an occupier's duty to a particular visitor if, in all the circumstances, it is enough to enable that visitor to be reasonably safe.[17] Lord Denning MR in *Roles* v *Nathan* uses this example:

> Supposing, for instance, that there was only one way of getting into and out of premises, and it was by a footbridge over a stream which was rotten and dangerous . . . [previously] the occupier could escape all liability to any visitor by putting up a notice: 'This bridge is dangerous', even though there was no other way by which the visitor could get in or out, and he had no option but to go over the bridge. In such a case, s 2(4)(a) [of the 1957 Act] makes it clear that the occupier would nowadays be liable. But if there were two footbridges, one of which was rotten, and the other safe a hundred yards away, the occupier could still escape liability, even today, by putting up a notice: 'Do not use this footbridge. It is dangerous. There is a safe one further upstream'. Such a warning is sufficient because it does enable the visitor to be reasonably safe. (at 1124)

In *English Heritage* v *Taylor* [2016], the claimant was able to recover for the serious head injury he sustained after falling over a sheer drop while on a day out with his grandchildren at Carisbrooke Castle. The defendant had failed to provide a sign warning of the drop, which was not obvious. The claimant was found to be 50 per cent contributorily negligent.

> [A]s with many public organisations which have large areas of land and premises open to the public, [English Heritage] has acted (as an occupier) in a way consistent with the principle that adult visitors do not require warnings of obvious risks except in cases where they do not have a genuine and informed choice . . . I accept that questions of whether a danger is obvious may not always be easy to resolve . . . But there are many areas of life in which difficult borderline judgments have to be made. This is well understood by the courts and is taken into account in deciding whether negligence or a breach of section 2 of the Act has been established. In this context, it is highly relevant that the common duty of care is to take such care 'as in all the circumstances is reasonable' to see that the visitor is 'reasonably' safe in using the premises for the purpose for which he is invited or permitted by the occupier to be there. The court is, therefore, required to consider all the circumstances. These will include how obvious the danger is and, in an appropriate case, aesthetic matters. If an occupier is in doubt as to whether a danger is obvious, it may be well advised to take reasonable measures to reduce or eliminate the danger. But the steps need be no more than reasonable steps. That is why the decision in this case should not be interpreted as requiring occupiers like English Heritage to place unsightly warning signs in prominent positions all over sensitive historic sites. (Etherton MR at [28]–[30])[18]

see online resources

Where the danger is obvious, however, there is usually no need to give a warning. Thus, in *Staples* v *West Dorset District Council* [1995] the occupiers were under no duty to warn of the inherent dangers of a famous sea wall in Lyme Regis known as 'the Cobb', which is covered in seaweed and algae and obviously very slippery. Nor will the failure to warn about one type of danger help the claimant if they subsequently suffer personal injury as a result of an unrelated danger (***Darby***).

17. A warning that might suffice to alert adults to dangers on the premises may be not be sufficient to warn children. Similarly, simply placing a warning sign in the supermarket aisle (in the example at the beginning of the chapter) may not be enough, in itself, to absolve the occupiers of liability.

18. Inevitably, perhaps, this latter point was lost on certain parts of the British press. See e.g. Nicola Harley 'Historic sites could be littered with "irritating" warning signs after pensioner fell in moat' *The Telegraph* 12 May 2016.

Darby v National Trust [2001] CA

The claimant's husband drowned while swimming in a pond at Hardwick Hall in Derbyshire owned by the National Trust. He was a competent swimmer, but the pond was murky and very deep in places. Visitors often swam or paddled in the pond and the National Trust did little to discourage this. There was a legible but inconspicuous notice near the car park, which—among other things—forbade bathing and boating and wardens occasionally patrolled the ponds, discouraging people from swimming in them by warning of the dangers of catching Weil's disease from the water. The claimant argued that the National Trust's failure to place 'No Swimming' notices around the pond (or to similarly warn of the risk of catching Weil's disease) amounted to a breach of their common duty of care under section 2 of the 1957 Act.

The Court of Appeal held that such notices would have told Mr Darby 'no more than he already knew' about the risks relating to swimming in open water and that the National Trust's failure to warn about one type of danger (Weil's disease) could not help the claimant if they subsequently suffered personal injury as a result of an unrelated danger (drowning) (at [25]–[26]). There were no special or hidden dangers in relation to this particular pond and no duty on the part of the National Trust to warn him of obvious dangers. The National Trust had done all that was reasonable in the circumstances of the case to see that the claimant's husband was reasonably safe while using its premises:

> It cannot be the duty of the owner of every stretch of coastline to have notices warning of the dangers of swimming in the sea. If it were so, the coast would have to be littered with notices in places other than those where there are known to be special dangers which are not obvious. The same would apply to all inland lakes and reservoirs. (May LJ at [27])

11.2.2.4 Notices excluding liability

The presence of an effective warning notice will defeat a claim under the 1957 Act because it means that, in the circumstances, the defendant has taken reasonable care to ensure that visitors are safe on their premises. By issuing a warning the defendant has told visitors what they must do and not do to avoid being harmed, and has, in so doing, discharged their duty to the visitors. This should be distinguished from the situation under section 2(1) where, by a written notice or otherwise (e.g. through an express term of a contract), an occupier seeks to restrict, exclude or otherwise modify their duty to a visitor. Unlike warning notices that seek to ensure that visitors are reasonably safe, thus satisfying the duty imposed on the occupier under the 1957 Act, such exclusions operate to prevent a duty from arising in the first place (or at least to limit its scope by setting out the conditions on which the claimant enters the premises).

Where the premises are occupied for business purposes, an occupier's ability to limit their liability is restricted by sections 2(1) and 2(2) of the Unfair Contract Terms Act 1977.[19] Such an occupier is unable to restrict liability for death or personal injury resulting from

19. Section 1(1)(c) of the Unfair Contract Terms Act 1977 specifically refers to notices excluding or limiting liability under the 1957 Act.

negligence, however they are able to restrict their duty in relation to other damage where it is reasonable to do so. If the premises are in private use, the occupier is free to extend, restrict or otherwise modify their liability as much (or as little) as they choose.

11.2.2.5 Faulty execution of work

Where an accident is the result of a subcontractor's work on the premises, the occupier will not be liable if, in all the circumstances, they have acted reasonably in entrusting the work to an independent contractor and have taken reasonable steps (if appropriate) to check that the contractor is competent and that the work has been properly done (s 2(4)(b)). Usually, the more technical the work, the more reasonable it will be to entrust it to an independent contractor (compare *Woodward* v *Mayor of Hastings* [1945] and *Haseldine* v *CA Daw & Sons Ltd* [1941]).

Of course, a claimant who is injured as a result of a subcontractor's faulty work may have a claim against that subcontractor under the ordinary principles of negligence. This raises an interesting related question as to when an occupier is under a duty to ensure that subcontractors who they entrust to do work on their premises are insured or otherwise have sufficient resources to meet any claims that may arise from their negligence.

Gwilliam v *West Hertfordshire Hospitals NHS Trust* [2002] CA

The 63-year-old claimant was injured while using a 'splat wall' (a Velcro wall which people attempt to stick themselves to by jumping off a trampoline) run by an independent contractor at a charity fun day organised by the defendant occupier, the NHS Trust. Her injuries were caused by the independent contractor's negligence. Unfortunately, the contractor's insurance policy had lapsed and so it was unable to meet her claim in full. The claimant sued the NHS Trust for failing to ensure that the contractor was adequately insured.

The Court of Appeal denied her claim for the outstanding amount of damages. The majority of the court held that though the NHS Trust owed the claimant a duty to check that the contractor had adequate insurance (on the basis that this went to the competence of the contractor and so was relevant to the reasonableness of the occupier in choosing the particular contractor), on the facts the NHS Trust had done enough (under s 2(4)(b) of the 1957 Act) to discharge their duty and so there was no breach. It would, the majority suggested, be unreasonable to require the occupier to go any further by, for example, checking the specific terms of the policy.

> Sedley LJ strongly dissented on the existence of a duty (though all members of the court concurred in dismissing the appeal).[20] There was, he suggested, a big difference between a duty to protect visitors from physical injury and a duty to protect them from an inability to recover damages (at [56]).

20. Sedley LJ also disagreed with Lord Woolf CJ and Waller LJ on the issue of breach. If the Trust had owed a duty of care, he argued, given the ease with which the insurance certificate could have been checked (e.g. by being faxed or sent to the hospital), the Trust would have, on the facts of the case, breached their duty.

The upshot of the decision in ***Gwilliam*** is that a defendant occupier may be liable to the victims of a third party's wrong, if they fail to ensure that the third party is in a position to meet any such liabilities. It is difficult to see why the simple fact that the third party's negligence happened on the defendant's premises is sufficient reason for holding the occupier liable. As Jonathan Morgan suggests, ***Gwilliam*** appears to be grounded in a particular view of the functions of tort law:

> All three judges seem to agree that the overriding purpose of liability in tort law is to compensate loss by spreading it through an insurance pool, and therefore that a failure to bring this about by failing to carry insurance is itself, in principle at least, a wrongful act. (2004, p 389)

It is worth noting that in *Naylor* v *Payling* [2004] the Court of Appeal held that the owner of a nightclub had taken reasonable care to see that visitors to the club were safe and that, save in special circumstances, there was no general duty to take reasonable steps to ensure that an independent contractor was insured. In *Glaister* v *Appleby-in-Westmoreland Town Council* [2009], the Court of Appeal affirmed Neuberger LJ's view in *Naylor* of ***Gwilliam*** as 'a difficult case' stating a preference for the approach of Sedley LJ (at [54]). Rather than focusing on the loss-spreading benefits of insurance, the Court of Appeal in *Glaister* focused on the deterrent effect of such claims:

> I would reject the idea that those bodies, public or private, which try to encourage attendance at such events or undertake some responsibility in relation to them thereby expose themselves to legal liability for the negligence of other bodies participating in the event. I do not see the justice of it and I am concerned that the fear of it is likely to act as a deterrent to those . . . who freely give their time and energies to the encouragement of such events. If that were to happen, the result would be an impoverishment of our community life. (Toulson LJ at [48])

Pause for reflection

While the judges in *Glaister* were keen to praise the claimant's 'selfless and public spirited' act (at [64])—he was seriously injured after being kicked in the head attempting to catch a horse that had broken loose from his tethering at the Appleby Horse Fair—the upshot of their decision is that the claimant was left uncompensated for his injuries. Do you think this is the right outcome? What extent do you think concerns about the so-called 'compensation culture' played in the court's decision?

11.2.2.6 Defences

An occupier will not be liable where a visitor's injuries arise from 'risks willingly accepted as his by the visitor' (s 2(5)).[21] In *Geary* v *Wetherspoons plc* [2011], for example, the claimant fractured her spine and was paralysed after falling four metres onto a marble floor while

21. The statutory defence found in s 2(5) of the 1957 Act is indistinguishable from the common law defence of *volenti*, discussed further in **Chapter 10**.

attempting to slide down a banister: 'The claimant freely chose to do something which she knew to be dangerous . . . She knew that sliding down the banisters was not permitted, but she chose to do it anyway. She was therefore the author of her own misfortune. The defendant owed no duty to protect her from such an obvious and inherent risk. She made a genuine and informed choice and the risk that she chose to run materialised with tragic consequences' (Coulson J at [46]).

White Lion Hotel **v** ***James*** **[2021] CA**

Christopher James died after falling from a second-floor window while staying at the White Lion Hotel. At first instance, the judge found that the hotel owners had failed to take reasonable care for the safety of the deceased in using the room (as required by s 2 of the 1957 Act), but made a finding of 60 per cent contributory negligence. There was no appeal against these findings. Rather the appeal was on a point of law: that the judge had failed to apply the principle derived from ***Tomlinson***, *Edwards* v *London Borough of Sutton* and *Geary* v *Wetherspoons plc*, that 'a person of full age and capacity who chooses to run an obvious risk cannot found an action against a defendant on the basis that the latter has either permitted him to do so, or not prevented him from so doing' (at [5]).

The Court of Appeal disagreed: 'There is no absolute principle that a visitor of full age and capacity who chooses to run an obvious risk cannot found an action against an occupier on the basis that the latter has either permitted him so to do, or not prevented him from so doing' (at [88]).

> What a claimant knew, and should reasonably have appreciated, about any risk he was running is relevant to that analysis and, in cases such as *Edwards* and ***Tomlinson***, may be decisive. In other cases, a conscious decision by a claimant to run an obvious risk may, nevertheless, not outweigh other factors: the lack of social utility of the particular state of the premises from which the risk arises (the ability to open the lower sash window); the low cost of remedial measures to eliminate the risk (£7 or £8 per window); and the real, even if relatively low, risk of an accident recognised by the guilty plea. This was a risk which was not only foreseeable, it was likely to materialise as part of the normal activity of a visitor staying in the bedroom. (Davies LJ at [83])

Davies LJ continued, that James had consciously chosen to sit on the window sill and accepted the risk of falling if he leant too far out was not sufficient to amount to *volenti* under section 2(5) of the Act.

> The defence of *volenti non fit injuria* was always a defence available to the occupier of the property and section 2(5) expressly preserves it. . . . There is no finding that [James] was aware of, and expressly or impliedly accepted, that the risk had been created by the appellant's breach of duty and by his actions he was deliberately absolving or forgiving the appellant for creating the risk ... In my judgment these are findings which provide a basis for the determination of contributory negligence. They do not go sufficiently far to meet the requirements of section 2(5). (at [89], [97])

11.3 The Occupiers' Liability Act 1957—annotated

In **Figure 11.1** we have annotated extracts from the OLA 1957 highlighting the key issues discussed in this chapter.

FIGURE 11.1 The Occupiers' Liability Act 1957

Occupiers' Liability Act 1957

Preliminary

1.— (1) The rules enacted by the two next following sections shall have effect, in place of the rules of the common law, to regulate the duty which an occupier of premises owes to his visitors in respect of dangers due to the state of the premises or to things done or omitted to be done on them.

(2) The rules so enacted shall regulate the nature of the duty imposed by law in consequence of a person's occupation or control of premises and of any invitation or permission he gives (or is to be treated as giving) to another to enter or use the premises, but they shall not alter the rules of the common law as to the persons on whom a duty is so imposed or to whom it is owed; and accordingly for the purpose of the rules so enacted the persons who are to be treated as an occupier and as his visitors are the same (subject to subsection (4) of this section) as the persons who would at common law be treated as an occupier and as his invitees or licensees.

(3) The rules so enacted in relation to an occupier of premises and his visitors shall also apply, in like manner and to the like extent as the principles applicable at common law to an occupier of premises and his invitees or licensees would apply, to regulate—

(a) the obligations of a person occupying or having control over any fixed or moveable structure, including any vessel, vehicle or aircraft; and

(b) the obligations of a person occupying or having control over any premises or structure in respect of damage to property, including the property of persons who are not themselves his visitors.

→

Puts the common law to one side; see s 1(2) in relation to definitions of who is an occupier and visitor.

See discussion in **section 11.2.1** relating to the distinction between so-called 'activity' duties and 'occupancy' duties.

Definition of an occupier as someone who has control of the premises; see ***Wheat v Lacon*** [1966].

Definition of a visitor as someone invited onto, or given permission to be on, premises. Remember this permission can be revoked and/or restricted under s 2(1).

The common law is incorporated into the Act—'licensees' and 'invitees' are combined into a single category 'lawful visitor'. Contractors are incorporated by s 5.

Very broad definition of premises.

e.g. the shopper's suede jacket in the examples at the beginning of the chapter—even if it belonged to someone else.

(4) A person entering any premises in exercise of rights conferred by virtue of—

(a) section 2(1) of the Countryside and Rights of Way Act 2000, or

(b) an access agreement or order under the National Parks and Access to the Countryside Act 1949, is not, for the purposes of this Act, a visitor of the occupier of the premises.

Extent of occupier's ordinary duty

2. —(1) An occupier of premises owes the same duty, the "common duty of care", to all his visitors, except in so far as he is free to and does extend, restrict, modify or exclude his duty to any visitor or visitors by agreement or otherwise.

(2) The common duty of care is a duty to take such care as in all the circumstances of the case is reasonable to see that the visitor will be reasonably safe, in using the premises for the purposes for which he is invited or permitted by the occupier to be there.

(3) The circumstances relevant for the present purpose include the degree of care, and of want of care, which would ordinarily be looked for in such a visitor, so that (for example) in proper cases—

(a) an occupier must be prepared for children to be less careful than adults; and

(b) an occupier may expect that a person, in the exercise of his calling, will appreciate and guard against any special risks ordinarily incident to it, so far as the occupier leaves him free to do so.

(4) In determining whether the occupier of premises has discharged the common duty of care to a visitor, regard is to be had to all the circumstances, so that (for example)—

(a) where damage is caused to a visitor by a danger of which he had been warned by the occupier, the warning is not to be treated without more as absolving the occupier from liability, unless in all the circumstances it was enough to enable the visitor to be reasonably safe; and

(b) where damage is caused to a visitor by a danger due to the faulty execution of any work of construction, maintenance or repair by an independent contractor employed by the occupier, the occupier is not to be treated without more as answerable for the danger if in all the circumstances he had acted reasonably in entrusting the work to an independent contractor and had taken such steps (if any) as he reasonably ought in order to satisfy himself that the contractor was competent and that the work had been properly done.

Section 1 establishes when a duty is owed, this section establishes the standard of care.

e.g. the rules and regulations made and published under statutory authority—such as certain conditions in relation to rail travel—which are not 'agreed to' by the visitor.

Takes into account the fact that visitors ought to be responsible for their own safety, to an extent, and allows for the defence of contributory negligence.

See e.g. ***Jolley* v *Sutton*** [2000].

i.e. the standard of care necessary in order to discharge (or not breach) the duty.

This section is somewhat vague—it is likely that the courts will extend this beyond its strict reading and was applied 'by analogy' by the majority of the Court of Appeal in ***Gwilliam*** [2002].

i.e. met the standard of care expected of them.

See s 1(6) of the OLA 1984.

Note restrictions under s 2(1) and (2) of the Unfair Contract Terms Act 1977 (UCTA) in relation to business premises.

It is the *visitor* rather than the premises, which must be reasonably safe.

Definition of the common duty of care—effectively the common law duty in tort of negligence—see further Lord Denning's description of it in ***Wheat* v *Lacon***, as 'a particular instance of the general duty of care which each man owes to his "neighbour"' (at 578).

i.e. a professional, or skilled, visitor. See e.g. *Roles* v *Nathan* [1963].

A warning does not automatically absolve an occupier from liability. It must enable the visitor to be reasonably safe in order to discharge the occupier's duty of care. Note also here the difference between a warning notice and a notice seeking to exclude or limit liability (s 2(1))—the former seeks to discharge an occupier's duty while the latter seeks to prevent it from arising in the first place.

→

(5) The common duty of care does not impose on an occupier any obligation to a visitor in respect of risks willingly accepted as his by the visitor (the question whether a risk was so accepted to be decided on the same principles as in other cases in which one person owes a duty of care to another).

(6) For the purposes of this section, persons who enter premises for any purpose in the exercise of a right conferred by law are to be treated as permitted by the occupier to be there for that purpose, whether they in fact have his permission or not.

e.g. the police entering with a warrant or employees of public utilities (gas and electricity) entering to read the meter enter the premises 'as of right' and as such are 'lawful visitors' even if the occupier may object to their presence.

This statutory defence is effectively the same as the common law defence of *volenti* (see *Geary* v *Wetherspoons plc* [2011]).

11.4 **The Occupiers' Liability Act 1984**

Under the 1984 Act,[22] an occupier owes a duty (provided certain conditions are met (s 1(3)) to take reasonable care in all the circumstances to see that persons 'other than his visitors'—typically trespassers—do not suffer injury as a result of 'danger due to the state of the premises or to things done or omitted to be done on them' (s 1(1)).[23]

Pause for reflection

Imagine for a moment a 'trespasser'. Who do you have in mind? A burglar? A squatter? Someone sneaking a shortcut home across a neighbour's garden? A group of teenagers up to mischief on a building site? An elderly person who's entered the wrong property by mistake? A child fetching their football from a neighbour's roof? A person swimming in a lake in a country park?

Traditionally the law relating to trespassers has been very strict. Trespassers went onto premises at their own risk and occupiers were simply under an obligation not to deliberately or recklessly cause them harm (*Addie & Sons (Collieries) Ltd* v *Dumbreck* [1929]). This was seen to be particularly harsh, especially in relation to young children. The turning point came in *British Railways Board* v *Herrington* [1972] where the courts introduced a 'duty to act humanely'. In this case, a child suffered severe burns while playing on an electrified railway track. Although the defendant knew that a gap in their fence was regularly used as a

→

22. You may find it helpful to refer to the **annotated version of the 1984 Act (section 11.5)** or the **OLAs 'at a glance' (section 11.6)**. These can also be downloaded from the **online resources**.

see online resources

23. However, the term also applies to people exercising a private right of way and ramblers *lawfully* exercising a public right of way by using a footpath across private land (subject to some exclusions) (s 1(6A) as inserted the Countryside and Rights of Way Act 2000, s 13).

→

shortcut and had seen children on the line they took no action. The House of Lords held that the claimant was able to recover. The defendant knew of the risk of children playing near the railway tracks and in failing to take the necessary steps to repair the gap in the fence was in breach of its duty.[24] However, while the duty imposed on occupiers in *Herrington* clearly went beyond a duty not to intentionally or recklessly cause harm, it was still lower than the duty set 15 years earlier in the 1957 Act. And, it wasn't until almost 30 years after its predecessor that the 1984 Act finally extended the same 'common duty of care' to trespassers—albeit in more limited circumstances.

Why do you think it took Parliament so long to pass the 1984 Act? Think about the policy reasons behind the harshness of the common law—the reluctance of the courts to interfere with a landowner's freedom to use and enjoy their property coupled with the understanding of a trespasser as a 'wrongdoer' deserving of their fate. Can the latter argument be justified given that the term 'trespasser' covers a wide variety of cases like those listed at the start of this box?

Section 1(2) of the 1984 Act defines an occupier and premises in the same way as the 1957 Act. Similarly, as with the 1957 Act, the duty imposed on occupiers under the 1984 Act extends only to harm caused by the state of the premises rather than by the activities of those on the premises. In *Keown* v *Coventry National Health NHS Trust* [2006], for example, the Court of Appeal held that the claimant's injuries were caused by his activity (in climbing up the underside of a fire escape) rather than the state of the premises (that is, the fire escape itself).

11.4.1 **Establishing a duty**

A crucial difference between the 1957 Act and the 1984 Act is that while an occupier will *always* owe a duty of care to a visitor, this is not the case in relation to a non-visitor. In order for a duty to be owed under the 1984 Act the following conditions, set out in section 1(3), must be met:

(1) that the occupier is *aware* of the danger or has reasonable grounds to believe that it exists; and

(2) the occupier *knows*, or has reasonable grounds to believe that someone is, or may come, in the vicinity of the danger (whether or not they have lawful authority to do so); and

24. There is an interesting parallel here with land negligence cases such as ***Sedleigh-Denfield* v *O'Callaghan* [1940]**; *Goldman* v *Hargrave* [1967] and so on, discussed in **Chapter 19**, where an awareness of a danger on one's land has resulted in liability if the landowner fails to do something about it.

(3) the risk is one against which, in all the circumstances of the case, the occupier may *reasonably be expected* to offer some protection.

If these three conditions are satisfied the occupier will owe a duty of care in respect of any *personal* injury suffered by a non-visitor. Unlike the 1957 Act, the 1984 Act does not extend to property damage (s 1(8)).

Tomlinson v Congleton Borough Council [2003] HL

The claimant hit his head on the bottom of a lake (in a public park managed by the defendants) while attempting a shallow dive. He broke his neck and, apart from some small movement in his hands and arms, was paralysed from the neck down. Although boating and fishing were allowed, swimming was forbidden at the lake; prominent notices read: 'Dangerous water: no swimming'. However, visitors frequently ignored these, as well as the verbal warnings from council-employed park rangers, and several accidents had already occurred. The council knew this and had planned, for a number of years, to plant vegetation on the 'beach' areas to prevent people from entering the water. They had not yet done this for financial reasons. The claimant sued the council on the grounds that the council had breached their duty of care under the 1984 Act. The claimant's status as a lawful visitor to the park was limited to the time *before* he entered the lake. As he did not have the occupier's permission to enter the water (he had ignored the warning signs) he became a trespasser as soon as he did so.

The House of Lords rejected his claim, overturning a majority Court of Appeal decision. There was no risk to the claimant due to 'the state of the premises or anything done or omitted upon the premises', and so no risk of a kind which gave rise to a duty under either of the OLAs:

> There was nothing about the mere at Brereton Heath which made it any more dangerous than any other ordinary stretch of open water in England . . . [Tomlinson] was a person of full capacity who voluntarily and without any pressure or inducement engaged in an activity which had inherent risk. The risk was that he might not execute his dive properly and so sustain injury. Likewise, a person who goes mountaineering incurs the risk that he might stumble or misjudge where to put his weight. In neither case can the risk be attributed to the state of the premises. (Lord Hoffmann at [26]–[27])

Nor did it make a difference that the council themselves had intended to take steps to reduce the danger by making it harder for people to gain access to the lake. Though the defendants were aware of the danger and had reasonable grounds to believe that people were in the vicinity of it, the risk was not one against which they could be reasonably expected to offer protection. Lord Hoffmann continued:

> It will be extremely rare for an occupier of land to be under a duty to prevent people from taking risks which are inherent in the activities they freely choose to undertake

→

→

> upon the land. If people want to climb mountains, go hang-gliding or swim or dive in ponds or lakes, that is their affair. Of course the landowner may for his own reasons wish to prohibit such activities. He may think that they are a danger or inconvenience to himself or others. Or he may take a paternalist view and prefer people not to undertake risky activities on his land. He is entitled to impose such conditions, as the Council did by prohibiting swimming. But the law does not require him to do so . . . [Moreover,] even if swimming had not been prohibited and the Council had owed a duty under section 2(2) of the 1957 Act, that duty would not have required them to take any steps to prevent Mr Tomlinson from diving or warning him against dangers which were perfectly obvious. If that is the case, then plainly there can have been no duty under the 1984 Act. The risk was not one against which he was entitled under section 1(3)(c) to protection. (at [45], [50])[25]

Thus, the requirements for establishing a duty of care under section 1(3) of the 1984 Act had not been met.

Counterpoint

In ***Tomlinson*** the House of Lords affirmed the 'principle of individual responsibility' (Morgan 2004, p 401) and an understanding of tort law as a set of rules and principles of 'personal responsibility (and freedom) which concern how people may, ought or ought not behave in their dealings with others' (*Cane* p 24).

> The law does not provide such compensation simply on the basis that the injury was so disproportionately severe in relation to one's fault or even not one's own fault at all. Perhaps it should, but society might not be able to afford to compensate everyone on that principle, certainly at the level at which such compensation is now paid. The law provides compensation only when the injury is someone else's fault. (Lord Hoffmann at [4])

Of course, one significant consequence of the claimant's inability to establish fault was that he bore the entirety of the costs of his injury. His condition was no one's *fault*, but his own.

Lord Hoffmann also considered the 'social cost' of finding the council liable. The principles of distributive justice are used to limit, rather than (as is more usual) to enable recovery:

> There is an important question of freedom at stake. It is unjust that the harmless recreation of responsible parents and children with buckets and spades on the beaches

→

25. Compare Lord Hoffmann's opinion in ***Tomlinson*** with the majority of the Court of Appeal in *Scout Association* v *Barnes* [2010] discussed in **section 8.4.4**.

→

should be prohibited in order to comply with what is thought to be a legal duty to safeguard irresponsible visitors against dangers which are perfectly obvious. The fact that such people take no notice of warnings cannot create a duty to take other steps to protect them. (Lord Hoffmann at [46])

Whichever view one prefers, the conclusion was, perhaps, inevitable.[26]

Tomlinson provides an excellent example of the operation of the 1984 Act, and the difference between this Act and its 1957 counterpart. Under the 1957 Act, all the claimant needs to establish is that they were a lawful visitor to the defendant's premises. Once this is proved, the occupier will automatically owe the claimant a duty of care and attention shifts to the other stages of a claim: Was the duty breached? Did it cause the claimant loss? Are there any defences? Under the 1984 Act, however, establishing a duty is less straightforward, and more claims will be defeated at this stage.[27]

Pause for reflection

In *Tomlinson* the claim was rejected on the basis that no duty was owed to the claimant. This is because a duty will not arise under the 1984 Act unless the risk is one against which the occupier may reasonably be expected to offer some protection. In the circumstances, the House of Lords held that the council should not be expected to take steps to protect people from the obvious risks of diving into shallow water. As Lord Hoffmann noted, however, the same result would in substance have been reached had the claimant been classed as a lawful visitor and his case had been dealt with under the 1957 Act. The only difference would have been that the

26. It is worth noting, however, that the Court of Appeal in ***Tomlinson*** came to the opposite conclusion. It held that the council not only owed the claimant a duty of care but also that they were in breach of this duty—though it reduced the claimant's damages by two-thirds to reflect the extent to which he was contributorily negligent. Ward LJ noted: 'Congleton Beach, as the place was also known, was as alluring to "macho" young men as other dangerous places were to young children. In my judgment the gravity of the risk of injury, the frequency with which those using the park came to be exposed to the risk, the failure of warning signs to curtail the extent to which the risk was being run, indeed the very fact that the attractiveness of the beach and the lake acted as a magnet to draw so many into the cooling waters, all that leads me to the conclusion that the occupiers were reasonably to be expected to offer some protection against the risks of entering the water. It follows that in my judgment the defendants were under a duty to the [claimant] . . . The authorities were inviting public use of this amenity knowing that the water was a siren call strong enough to turn stout men's minds. In my judgment the posting of notices, shown to be ineffective, was not enough to discharge the duty' (at [29], [31]).

27. Consider again the student injured when diving into a lake in the examples at the beginning of the chapter. What additional information would you need in order to determine which Act to apply and advise them as to the potential outcome of their claim?

→

claim would have failed not at the duty stage (since the 1957 Act automatically imposes a duty to all visitors) but at the breach stage (since, as the House of Lords held, it was not reasonable to expect the council to take any steps to make the premises safer).

As such, although the two Acts will often lead to the same results, they will often do so for slightly different reasons. Cases that fail on the basis that there was no breach under the 1957 Act will often be dismissed under the 1984 Act on the ground that no duty arises in the first place. This reflects an important but subtle difference in emphasis between the two Acts: 'Parliament has made it clear that in the case of a lawful visitor, one starts from the assumption that there is a duty whereas in the case of a trespasser one starts from the assumption that there is none' (Lord Hoffmann at [38]).

If, as Lord Hoffmann suggests, the end result is (or at least can be) the same, why then do you think Parliament has created this difference in the operation of the two Acts? Think again about the distinction between visitors and non-visitors and the policy reasons for limiting liability in respect of trespassers.

11.4.1.1 Awareness of (or reasonable grounds to believe in the existence of) danger

In order for an occupier to owe a non-visitor a duty of care, they must be aware of the danger, or have reasonable grounds to believe that it exists (s 1(3)(a)). While the first part of this ground is subjective—it requires the occupier to *know* about the danger—the second part is (at least partly) objective—it asks whether the occupier *reasonably ought* to know about it.

***Rhind v Astbury Water Park Ltd* [2004] CA**

The claimant suffered serious injuries after he hit his head on a fibreglass container diving into Astbury Mere in Cheshire to retrieve his football. The container was not visible from the surface; it was lying on the bed of the Mere, covered in silt. As there were clear notices near the Mere saying: 'Private Property: Strictly No Swimming Allowed' the claimant was a trespasser and so the question for the Court of Appeal was whether the defendants owed a duty of care under the 1984 Act.

Denying the claimant's claim, the court held that the defendants had no knowledge, nor were there reasonable grounds for them to believe, that the container was hidden beneath the surface of the Mere and that, as a result, no duty was owed.

11.4.1.2 Knowledge of (or reasonable grounds to believe in) the presence of a non-visitor in the vicinity of danger

The occupier must also be aware, or have reasonable grounds to believe, that a non-visitor is in the vicinity of the danger (s 1(3)(b)). When we say that a person has reasonable grounds to believe that something is true, this means that, from the knowledge they do in fact have, they should have worked out or discovered something else. So, for instance, you may have reasonable grounds to believe that a problem question on occupiers' liability will appear on this year's exam paper if such a question has been included in every paper in the past ten years. From your knowledge of fact A—the contents of the past exam papers—you have reason to infer fact B—that such a question will appear in this year's paper. Accordingly, before we can say that an occupier had reasonable grounds to believe that a non-visitor is, or may arrive, in the vicinity of the danger on his premises, he must have actual knowledge of such 'background' or 'primary' facts as would support such an inference (*Swain* v *Puri* [1996]).

So, for example, if I know that people are playing football next to my field and that, in the past, people have come onto my field to fetch their ball, I have reasonable grounds to believe (i.e. I should have figured out) that they may do so again. However, if I had no knowledge that people had ever played football there or had gone onto the field to fetch their balls, *even if I should have known this*, I cannot be said to have reasonable grounds to believe they may do this in the future. To this extent, those who know less are less likely to be held liable, even though complete ignorance may be no less (and, indeed, may be more) culpable than partial ignorance.

The other point to note is that the defendant must know, or have reasonable grounds to believe, that the claimant (or someone like them) is in the vicinity of the danger *at the time the claimant was injured*. So it is not in itself enough to show that the defendant knew that the claimant had been on the premises previously, or even that they were likely to do so again. This *may* provide grounds for a reasonable belief that the claimant was in the vicinity of the danger at the time of the accident but whether it does will depend on the circumstances. For example, in *Donoghue* v *Folkestone Properties Ltd* [2003], the claimant's claim in respect of injuries he suffered while diving into the defendant's harbour was denied because, although the defendant was aware that people swam in the harbour during summer, they were not, and could not reasonably have been expected to be, aware that this would happen during a midwinter night, when the claimant was injured.

11.4.1.3 Reasonable expectation of protection against the risk

Finally, the risk must be such that in all the circumstances of the case the defendant may be reasonably expected to offer some protection from it (s 1(3)(c)). As we have seen, this is where the claim failed in ***Tomlinson***. In determining whether it is reasonable to expect the occupier to offer protection, the courts must engage in a balancing exercise similar to that which they embark upon when determining whether a duty of care has been breached. This would include taking into account the costs of requiring the occupier to take steps to make the premises safer. For example, in *Simonds* v *Isle of Wight Council* [2004] a 5-year-old boy fell off a swing breaking his arm. The swing was near to a playing field being used for a school sports day. It was argued that the school was under a responsibility to discourage the pupils from using the swings, for example by placing a cordon around them. This was rejected. One of the reasons the courts gave for this was that a likely consequence of finding the school liable was: 'that sports days and other simple pleasurable sporting events would not be held . . . Such events would become uninsurable or only insurable at prohibitive cost' (at [30]).

11.4.2 **The standard of care**

The occupier's duty, once it is established, is to 'take such care as is reasonable in all the circumstances of the case to see that the [non-visitor] does not suffer injury on the premises' (s 1(4)). We may think that an occupier should not be expected to go as far to secure the safety of those they have *not* invited onto their land as they would in respect of those they have invited. As such, it is likely that in determining what will amount to reasonable care the courts will take into account that the claimant will not have been invited (expressly or by implication) onto the premises and that the occupier's duty under the 1984 Act is not as exacting as the duty under the 1957 Act (*Donoghue* v *Folkestone Properties Ltd* (at [31])). Beyond this, and as with the 1957 Act, in assessing what amounts to reasonable care the courts will weigh up the same sorts of factors as in ordinary common law negligence claims including, for example, the resources of the defendant and the cost of taking precautions (*Ratcliff* v *McConnell* [1999]).

11.4.2.1 Warnings

It is possible for an occupier to discharge their duty under the 1984 Act by giving a warning or by discouraging people from entering the premises (e.g. a locked gate) (s 1(5)). However, unlike under the 1957 Act where the warning must be such as to enable the visitor in all the circumstances to be reasonably safe (s 1(4)(a)), under the 1984 Act all the occupier needs to do is to take reasonable steps to bring the danger to the claimant's attention.

11.4.2.2 Risks willingly accepted by the non-visitor

As under the 1957 Act, no duty will be owed by the occupier in respect of risks willingly accepted by the non-visitor (s 1(6)). Thus in *Ratcliff* the Court of Appeal held that no duty was owed to a claimant who accepted the risk of serious injury from diving into water of an unknown depth when he climbed over a fence surrounding his college open-air swimming pool on his way home after a night out.

11.5 The Occupiers' Liability Act 1984—annotated

In **Figure 11.2** we have annotated extracts from the OLA 1984 highlighting the key issues discussed in this chapter.

FIGURE 11.2 The Occupiers' Liability Act 1984

Occupiers' Liability Act 1984

Duty of occupier to persons other than his visitors.

1. —(1) The rules enacted by this section shall have effect, in place of the rules of the common law, to determine—

(a) whether any duty is owed by a person as occupier of premises to persons other than his visitors in respect of any risk of their suffering injury on the premises by reason of any danger due to the state of the premises or to things done or omitted to be done on them; and

(b) if so, what that duty is.

(2) For the purposes of this section, the persons who are to be treated respectively as an occupier of any premises (which, for those purposes, include any fixed or movable structure) and as his visitors are—

(a) any person who owes in relation to the premises the duty referred to in section 2 of the Occupiers' Liability Act 1957 (the common duty of care), and

(b) those who are his visitors for the purposes of that duty.

(3) An occupier of premises owes a duty to another (not being his visitor) in respect of any such risk as is referred to in subsection (1) above if—

(a) he is aware of the danger or has reasonable grounds to believe that it exists;

(b) he knows or has reasonable grounds to believe that the other is in the vicinity of the danger concerned or that he may come into the vicinity of the danger (in either case, whether the other has lawful authority for being in that vicinity or not); and

(c) the risk is one against which, in all the circumstances of the case, he may reasonably be expected to offer the other some protection.

(4) Where, by virtue of this section, an occupier of premises owes a duty to another in respect of such a risk, the duty is to take such care as is reasonable in all the circumstances of the case to see that he does not suffer injury on the premises by reason of the danger concerned.

→

This section establishes the scope of the Act.

An occupier's duty under the 1984 Act has to be established (s 1(3)) (cf OLA 1957, s 2(1)).

The 'content' of the duty.

Same wide definition of 'premises' as the OLA 1957 (s 1(3)).

Definition of an occupier.

The requirements of this section must be met to establish the existence of a duty.

This section establishes the content of the duty.

As in *British Railways Board v Herrington* [1972].

Most obviously trespassers, but also includes ramblers by virtue of s 1(4) of the OLA 1957. Defined negatively—'non-visitors'.

As with the 1957 Act, the risk of injury must be due to the state of the premises rather than as a result of an activity on them (*Revill v Newberry* [1996]).

→

(5) Any duty owed by virtue of this section in respect of a risk may, in an appropriate case, be discharged by taking such steps as are reasonable in all the circumstances of the case to give warning of the danger concerned or to discourage persons from incurring the risk.

Warnings: simply has to be given (cf OLA 1957, s4(a)).

Application of defence of consent or voluntarily assuming the risk (see **section 10.2**).

(6) No duty is owed by virtue of this section to any person in respect of risks willingly accepted as his by that person (the question whether a risk was so accepted to be decided on the same principles as in other cases in which one person owes a duty of care to another).

(6A) At any time when the right conferred by section 2(1) of the Countryside and Rights of Way Act 2000 is exercisable in relation to land which is access land for the purposes of Part I of that Act, an occupier of the land owes (subject to subsection (6C) below) no duty by virtue of this section to any person in respect of—

This section details certain circumstances where an occupier's duty is restricted in relation to ramblers.

(a) a risk resulting from the existence of any natural feature of the landscape, or any river, stream, ditch or pond whether or not a natural feature, or

(b) a risk of that person suffering injury when passing over, under or through any wall, fence or gate, except by proper use of the gate or of a stile.

(6B) For the purposes of subsection (6A) above, any plant, shrub or tree, of whatever origin, is to be regarded as a natural feature of the landscape.

(6C) Subsection (6A) does not prevent an occupier from owing a duty by virtue of this section in respect of any risk where the danger concerned is due to anything done by the occupier—

Incorporation of common law principle of 'common humanity' (*British Railways Board v Herrington*).

(a) with the intention of creating that risk, or

(b) being reckless as to whether that risk is created.

An occupier does not owe a duty to people using the highway (Highways Act 1980, s 1(8)).

(7) No duty is owed by virtue of this section to persons using the highway, and this section does not affect any duty owed to such persons.

(8) Where a person owes a duty by virtue of this section, he does not, by reason of any breach of the duty, incur any liability in respect of any loss of or damage to property.

An occupier does not owe a duty in relation to property damage (cf OLA 1957, s 1(3)(b)).

(9) In this section—

"highway" means any part of a highway other than a ferry or waterway;

"injury" means anything resulting in death or personal injury, including any disease and any impairment of physical or mental condition; and

"movable structure" includes any vessel, vehicle or aircraft.

11.6 The Occupiers' Liability Acts 1957 and 1984—at a glance

See **Table 11.1**.

TABLE 11.1 Summary of the Occupiers' Liability Acts 1957 and 1984

	1957	1984
Type of damage (to claimant)	*Property damage and personal injury* (as old common law).	*Personal injury only* (ss 1(1)(a) and 1(4)). Property damage excluded (s 1(8)) but may be covered by common law (*Herrington* v *British Railways Board* [1972]).
'Premises'	Wide definition: 'any fixed or moveable structure' including vehicles (s 1(3)).	As 1957 Act (s 1(2)).
'Occupier'	Person who would have been at common law (s 1(2); ***Wheat*** v ***Lacon***; *Harris* v *Birkenhead Corporation*).	As 1957 Act (s 1(2)(a)).
'Visitor'	All *lawful visitors* (s 1(2)) including invitees, licensees at common law and contractual visitors (s 5).	All *non-visitors* (usually trespassers) (s 1(1)(a)). Also, subject to certain restrictions, includes ramblers (exercising a right under s 2(1) of the Countryside and Rights of Way Act 2000). However, it does not cover people using the highway (s 1(7)) or people using other public rights of way (s 1A).
Duty	Occupier owes 'a *common duty of care*' to all visitors simply by virtue of the fact that they are visitors (s 2(1)).	Occupier *only* owes a duty (defined in s 1(4)) if: (1) aware of danger (or has reasonable grounds to believe it exists); and (2) knows (or has reasonable grounds to believe) a non-visitor is (or may be) in vicinity of danger; and (3) the risk is one in all circumstances the occupier may be reasonably expected to protect against (s 1(3)).
Extent of the duty (or standard of care)	A duty to take *such care that the visitor is reasonably safe* while using the premises for the purposes for which they are invited (s 2(2)). It is the visitor, not premises, who must be reasonably safe; different standards of care apply for different visitors (s 2(3)).	A duty to '*take such care as is reasonable in all the circumstances of the case to see that the [non-visitor] does not suffer injury on the premises*' (s 1(4)).

TABLE 11.1 *Continued*

	1957	1984
Discharging duty (or breach)	As *ordinary principles of breach* (see **Chapter 8**). The occupier's duty to ensure that the visitor will be reasonably safe while on their premises, not obligation to ensure safety of visitors (***Bowen*** v ***National Trust***). However, this does not mean that the visitor cannot be expected to take reasonable care for their own safety (s 2(3)). Standard of care may vary depending on the identity and expertise of the visitor, in particular: (1) the standard of care expected will be higher in relation to *children*, who are 'less careful than adults' ((s 2(3)(a)); ***Jolley***); (2) professional visitors can be expected to 'appreciate and guard against special risks' (s 2(3)(b); *Roles v Nathan* [1963]). May be discharged by taking reasonable steps to give *warnings* must enable visitor to be 'reasonably safe' (s 2(4)(a); ***Darby***). Generally there will be no liability for harms caused where *independent contractors have done faulty work on the premises as long as occupier has acted reasonably in entrusting the work to them* (s 2(4)(b)).	As *ordinary principles of breach* (see **Chapter 8**). May be discharged by taking reasonable steps to give: a warning of the danger concerned (s 1(5)) (no requirement of reasonable safety); discouragement to persons from incurring the risk (s 1(5)).
Limitations and defences	Occupier can *extend, restrict, modify or exclude their duty* (so far as they are free to do so) ***via a notice*** or contract (s 2(1) (subject to UCTA, s 2)). Generally no duty in relation to *risks* 'willingly accepted as his' by the visitor (s 2(5)) (*Geary* v *Wetherspoons plc* cf ***White Lion Hotel*** v ***James***). *Contributory negligence* (implied by s 2(3) although not mentioned in the statute used by courts).	No express provision—but probably as 1957 Act (s 2(1)). Generally no duty in relation to risks 'willingly accepted as his' by the visitor (s 1(6); *Ratcliff* v *McConnell*). Contributory negligence (not mentioned in the statute, but used by courts).

11.7 **Conclusion**

All injuries that do not happen at the claimant's home or on the road must happen on someone else's property. In this chapter we have considered the circumstances in which an occupier may be liable for injuries sustained on their premises. Despite *Weir*'s suggestion (p 20) that accidents on private property have been marked out for special attention since 1866 when an employee of the gas company fell into an unfenced vat in a sugar factory (in *Indermaur* v *Dames* [1867]), traditionally there has been a reluctance to allow such claims—usually relating to a desire to leave landowners alone to enjoy their land as they wish. This has been given a contemporary twist. The imposition of liability has been framed as an attack on the liberties of both the individual who chooses to engage in dangerous (but otherwise harmless) pastimes at his own risk *and* citizens as a whole to enjoy the countryside. This is particularly apparent in ***Tomlinson*** where the House of Lords reasserted the importance of individual responsibility, fault and interpersonal justice as the foundations of tortious liability.

Nevertheless, an occupier will be liable if they have not taken reasonable care to ensure that those they have invited, and sometimes not invited, onto their premises are reasonably safe. Determining the scope and nature of occupiers' duty is a heady mix of common law and statute. However, while the OLAs define the circumstances in which a duty of care will be owed (and tell us something as to its extent, as well as matters relating to its discharge and limitation), it is important to remember that questions of breach and causation still need to be established by reference to the ordinary principles of negligence.

End-of-chapter questions

After reading the chapter carefully, try answering the questions which follow.

1 What are the main similarities and differences between the Occupiers' Liability Act 1957 and the Occupiers' Liability Act 1984?

2 Do you think the House of Lords would have come to the same decision in *Tomlinson* if the claimant had been a 4-year-old child? Also, given the evidence before the House of Lords about 'macho male diving syndrome' what if the claimant had been an 18-year-old woman?

If you would like to know what we think visit the **online resources**. www.oup.com/he/horsey7e

Answering the problem question

Consider again the problem question at the start of this chapter. Now having read about the topic, **what would be your advice to the various parties?**

Here are some pointers to get you started

- Are Iris, Frank and Bill visitor or non-visitors? You need to consider this in relation to each of them as this will determine which Act applies.
- Breach and causation are straightforward here, but could Bill be found contributorily negligent?

If you need more guidance

- An **annotated version of the problem with issues and cases to consider** can be found in the Appendix.
- A **suggested outline answer** to check your ideas against can be found in the online resources that accompany the book.

see online resources

Further reading

Much of the academic writing in this area concentrates on one or other of the two Acts. The best place to start your reading is with Buckley's 2006 article which looks at both Acts and will give you an overview of the law with a comparative twist.

Buckley, Richard 'The Occupiers' Liability Act 1984—Has *Herrington* Survived?' [1984] Conv 413

Buckley, Richard 'Occupiers' Liability in England and Canada' (2006) 35 CLWR 197

Jones, Michael 'The Occupiers' Liability Act' (1984) 47 MLR 713

Morgan, Jonathan 'Tort, Insurance and Incoherence' (2004) 67 MLR 384

Payne, Douglas 'The Occupiers' Liability Act' (1958) 21 MLR 359

Product liability

12

Problem question

Read this problem question carefully, and keep it in mind while you are working through the chapter that follows. At the end of the chapter, you will be able to apply what you have learnt to the problem question and advise the relevant parties.

After many years of research, Rack and Horse Pharmaceuticals (RHP) developed a drug to treat breast cancer. After only 18 months of clinical trials, it received a licence and went on the market in the UK in March 2016. Although the drug itself is completely pure, it is now known that in less than 0.5 per cent of patients (those who carry a particular gene) it can produce an undesirable side effect known as Tort Syndrome. This side effect is not widely publicised as both RHP and the government are keen to encourage widespread uptake of the drug in relevant groups of women.

In 2021, 20 claimants who were given the drug between 2016 and 2018 and who contracted Tort Syndrome begin an action against RHP alleging both negligence and liability under the Consumer Protection Act 1987. RHP argues against liability because up until 2019, there was no genetic test that could determine which individuals carried the gene in question.

The claimants bring evidence to show there was an article in an Outer Mongolian scientific journal, published both in hard copy and on the internet in 2017, which suggested a test to determine whether individual women carried the specific gene for the reaction to the drug that causes Tort Syndrome. Had RHP conducted clinical trials for longer, the company would have been able to identify the characteristics of the women likely to react badly to the drug and to issue appropriate warnings and advice.

Advise the parties.

12.1 **Introduction**

Consider the following examples:

→ ***Stuart buys Bluetooth headphones from an electrical store. He later finds out that they do not work because a small but crucial component is missing.***

→ ***Chris buys Bluetooth headphones from an electrical store. He later tries to charge them but the internal wiring is faulty; he receives a small electric shock.***

→ ***Theresa receives Bluetooth headphones for her birthday. She later finds out that they do not work because a small but crucial component is missing.***

→ ***Alison buys a car for Marion. Two weeks later, one of the tyres explodes while Marion is driving, causing the car to swerve into her garden wall, which will cost £500 to rebuild. The car costs £1,000 to repair.***

→ ***Rosie buys a car for Molly. After a year, the two front tyres need replacing. Two weeks later, one of the replaced tyres explodes while Molly is driving, causing the car to swerve into her garden wall, which will cost £500 to rebuild. The car costs £1,000 to repair.***

→ ***Josh takes a drug to stop his head aching, but later finds out that he has a stomach ulcer caused by an unusual reaction to the drug.***

At first sight, it might seem odd that we are considering product liability in a book on tort law, when most of us are more accustomed on a day-to-day basis to dealing with 'products' and the consequences of their defects via contract law. However, ***Donoghue* v *Stevenson*** **[1932]**, the foundational case for all modern claims in negligence, *is* itself a case about a defective product (contaminated ginger beer) that harmed the end-user (gastroenteritis).

Liability for defective products is, therefore, also possible in negligence, though the picture is, as we shall see, more complicated than might be expected. Much depends on what type of defect is being claimed for. It is more appropriate to sue in contract for some harms caused by defects in products and in negligence for others. In basic terms, this depends on whether the claimant takes their case against the retailer (contract) or the manufacturer (negligence) of the item. Often, a claim in contract might be preferable where possible, as 'strict liability' (i.e. liability without the need to establish fault) is imposed by statute on retailers in respect of the quality of the goods that they sell, and the remedies are set out. When claiming in negligence against a manufacturer, the usual hurdles of duty, breach and—in particular—causation must be overcome.

see online resources

Because an understanding of liability for defective products in contract law is an important part of the overall picture regarding defective products in law, we have included a basic summary of the liabilities that may arise in contract on our **online resources**.

It is worth either refreshing your memory about these liabilities, or gaining a brief overview of them, if you have yet to study contract law, before reading on.

This chapter looks at *tortious* liabilities for defective products, beginning with manufacturers' liability in negligence and the problems claimants may encounter. This leads us to a later development relating to product liability—the Consumer Protection Act (CPA) 1987—enacted to ensure better protection of consumers from defective goods by making *producers* strictly liable for harms caused by the products they market.

12.2 Defective products—claims in negligence

As already mentioned, at its narrowest interpretation, ***Donoghue*** is a landmark product liability case. The case not only lays the foundations of the entire tort of negligence but also specifically allows for claims in negligence to be taken directly against the manufacturers of defective products.[1]

Before ***Donoghue***, a person injured (either personally or through damage to their property) by defective goods had limited grounds for recovery. If they had a contract with the retailer of the goods then they may have had a claim for breach of contract and (subject to the various rules governing this type of claim) compensation could be awarded for both the cost of replacing the product itself *and* of putting right any damage to person or property caused by the product. Contract law, however, is limited in the protection it can offer (see the content on this on the **online resources**)— not least only (usually) to those who are party to the contract, which Mrs Donoghue was not. Further, in the tort of negligence, though someone in Mrs Donoghue's position could be compensated for their illness and distress, the cost of the *product itself* would have been regarded as a pure economic loss and, as such, unrecoverable.[2] The claimant could only have received compensation (in contract rather than tort law) covering the cost of the ginger beer itself if she had paid for it. If, as was the case in ***Donoghue***, she had no contract with the seller, she would be limited to a claim in negligence against the manufacturer.

see online resources

Prior to 1932, manufacturers could only be liable in relation to products if the product itself was classed as 'dangerous' or was manufactured to be dangerous, in which case a warning had to be given. However, the distinction between 'dangerous' and 'not-dangerous' was not always helpful.[3] In ***Donoghue***, the House of Lords overturned the distinction and also discarded what it termed the 'privity of contract fallacy', holding that there should be no reason why the same facts should not give one person a right in contract and another person a simultaneous right to sue in negligence. It drew no distinction between the type or nature of the product (though it seems logical that this would be a relevant factor when assessing the *standard* of care to which the manufacturer should be held and whether that has been breached). That is, it seems common sense to say that manufacturers of inherently dangerous products ought to be even more careful.

Pause for reflection

The law lords in *Donoghue* were split 3:2 in favour of the claimant. Two dissented, mainly because of concerns about opening the 'floodgates' to claims (similar reasoning is often seen in negligence cases today, where a court is asked to expand the types of situation or

→

1. The facts of ***Donoghue*** are set out in **section 2.2**.
2. See **Chapter 7**.
3. See e.g. Scrutton LJ in *Hodge* v *Anglo-American Oil Co* [1922], who described goods rendered 'dangerous' by negligent construction as 'a wolf in sheep's clothing' (at 187).

→

relationship in which a negligence claim might succeed). Within the majority opinions, Lord Macmillan took a more pragmatic approach to the finding of liability than Lord Atkin's broad 'neighbour' principle—favouring a more cautious case-by-case approach (similar to that used in novel types of claim following ***Caparo Industries plc*** v ***Dickman*** [1990]).

Interestingly, three years prior to ***Donoghue*** a case with very similar facts had been dismissed. In *Mullen* v *AG Barr* [1929] it was alleged that a bottle of ginger beer contained a decomposing mouse but, as there was no precedent for the type of claim being made (ginger beer not being 'dangerous' in and of itself), the case failed. The same lawyers represented Mrs Donoghue—and were clearly very persistent—so it is them we need to thank for the law as it stands today!

Generally, the wide scope of the tort of negligence (and negligence in relation to product liability) is these days taken for granted and the impact and importance of the ***Donoghue*** decision is not really seen amongst all the later developments, limitations and rules. Consider how negligence might look if the claimant in ***Donoghue*** had failed or if Lord Macmillan's approach had been favoured over Lord Atkin's.

12.2.1 The scope of liability under *Donoghue*

As ***Donoghue*** is a negligence case, liability in relation to harm caused by products must be assessed by considering the various factors—duty, breach and causation—that a claimant must establish when making any claim in the tort of negligence. As these have all been discussed in far greater detail in **Chapters 2** to **10** of this book, we concentrate here on the more pertinent issues regarding product liability.

12.2.1.1 Duty of care

The duty owed is the ordinary common law duty of care—based on the presumed intention to supply the goods to the ultimate consumer in the same state they left the production line. The duty extends beyond the manufacturer/consumer relationship to include, for example, packers, machine operators and distributors. Similarly, the 'ultimate consumer' not only covers the 'end-purchaser' of the product concerned, but includes also the ultimate user (as in ***Donoghue***) and any person coming into contact with the product. In *Stennett* v *Hancock & Peters* [1939], for example, the manufacturer's duty of care extended to a pedestrian who was hit by a wheel of a lorry when it fell off.

The duty may also extend *beyond* the product itself to include, for example, containers, packaging or instructions (*Watson* v *Buckley, Osborne, Garrett & Co Ltd* [1940]). In ***Donoghue***, Lord Atkin defined the type of products that the duty covers as 'articles of common household use, where everyone, including the manufacturer, knows the articles will be used by persons other than the ultimate purchaser' (at 46). Clearly, however, given the example of *Stennett*, mentioned earlier, the definition of 'products' must extend beyond 'household items' and could, logically, include *any* product where the definition of 'consumer' is taken in its broadest sense.

Despite the range of relationships covered and a broad understanding of what a product is, it should be noted that the principles *preventing* a duty of care from arising in the wider law of negligence also apply here. Damage to (or a defect in) the product itself, for which the only claim is the cost of replacement, is regarded as pure economic loss, for which no duty can arise (***Murphy* v *Brentwood District Council*** [1991]).[4] A claimant can therefore recover damages for anything the defective product causes injury *to*, but not for any injury to the product itself. The remedy in tort would seem, in this respect, to be less useful than that in contract.

Pause for reflection

Is there a good reason for regarding the cost of replacing the item itself as pure economic loss, thereby preventing a remedy in tort? Does it seem fair that if you bought the item for yourself, you would be able to claim this cost against the retailer (in contract), but if you were given the product as a gift, you could not obtain a replacement? While it might be thought that the person who bought the present could always bring a claim on your behalf (e.g. the position of Alison in the examples at the beginning of this chapter), in reality they cannot as they will have suffered no harm.

Before we leave 'duty' some mention should be made of what is known as the 'complex structure' theory.[5] Under this theory, component parts of a product are (sometimes) seen as a separate product entirely.[6] Therefore, if the component part is the defective 'product', and it causes damage to the rest of the product or another part of it, this can be classed as consequential damage and not pure economic loss (though the cost of the defective component itself would be pure economic loss).[7] Consider how this relates to the Alison/Marion and Rosie/Molly situations outlined at the beginning of the chapter. If the tyre exploded soon after the car was purchased, then it is likely that the courts would view this as a defective *car* and Marion would have no claim (she did not buy the car herself so cannot claim against the retailer) for the cost of fixing the car, although she would be able to claim for the cost of rebuilding her wall. However, if Molly's *replacement* tyre exploded, this could be considered to be one component of a 'complex structure' (the car) and subsequently any damage to the car, as well as the wall, would be consequential loss.[8] All that Molly would be unable to claim would be the cost of replacing the tyre.

4. See **Chapter 7**.
5. This theory is also discussed in **Chapter 7** in relation to ***Murphy*** (see Counterpoint box in **section 7.4**).
6. Although this has now been ruled out for buildings in the sense that foundations cannot be regarded as a separate component of a building.
7. The idea was considered in *Finesse Group Ltd* v *Bryson Products* [2013], see in particular [28]–[29].
8. See also the (*obiter*) comments of Lloyd LJ in *Aswan Engineering* v *Lupdine Ltd* [1987].

Pause for reflection

Should a manufacturer's duty extend to taking steps to recall any defective products that have already gone into circulation?

In the US case *Grimshaw* v *Ford Motor Co* [1981], Ford was alleged to have discovered a defect in the Ford Pinto which sometimes caused the cars to explode if they were hit by another car from behind. However, the company calculated that it would be cheaper to pay compensation to anyone injured or killed in such an explosion than it would be to recall all the cars in circulation and repair the defects. If there had been a duty to recall the cars once the defect was known then Ford would have been in breach for not doing so. At trial, Ford was ordered to pay punitive damages in excess of $125 million, though this was reduced to $3.5 million on appeal (plus compensatory damages of just under $3 million).[9] This case illustrates many of the problems associated with using private law remedies in relation to product liability. The fact that producers can be sued is meant to have a deterrent effect, thus changing their behaviour. Yet, it seems, sometimes producers (particularly large-scale producers) will weigh the risks and benefits to their profits and shareholders when considering whether to recall and rectify defects in their products (even where these are dangerous enough to pose a risk to life, as in the *Ford* case). In this sense, it seems that stronger *public law* regulation might be a better deterrent.[10]

12.2.1.2 Breach and causation

Breach of duty of care was considered in **Chapter 8**. The question here is: did the defendant manufacturer exercise reasonable care when making the product? This is, as ever, to be assessed on a case-by-case basis.

Breach is not normally problematic as it may often be inferred from the presence of the defect. That is, it is often assumed that any defect can only exist because there was negligence during the manufacturing process—how else could a snail come to be in a sealed bottle of ginger beer, for example? The manufacturer must rebut the presumption of carelessness with evidence. This principle can clearly be seen in operation in ***Grant* v *Australian Knitting Mills Ltd*** [1936].

Grant v _Australian Knitting Mills Ltd_ [1936] PC

Mr Grant purchased some woollen underpants and, after wearing them, suffered from a painful skin condition. This was caused by a reaction to sulphites present in the wool, left over

→

9. For explanation of these different types of damages, see **section 21.2**.

10. Recent examples of producers recalling products with dangerous defects include Samsung recalling its Galaxy phone (see Cristina Criddle 'Why is the Samsung Galaxy Note 7 catching fire?' *The Telegraph* 11 October 2016) and Whirlpool's tumble dryers (BBC News 'Whirlpool told to recall dryers in "unprecedented" government move' 12 June 2019).

→

from the manufacturing process. The claimant could not prove negligence on the part of the manufacturer and the manufacturer claimed that there had been no carelessness during the manufacturing process, and that reasonable care had been taken to ensure that chemicals used did not remain in the wool.

The court found that there could be no other explanation for the sulphites in the wool than that one of the employees had, at some point during the manufacture of the underpants, been careless. The manufacturers were therefore held liable.

Defects in products that are present when the product reaches the end-user can be inferred to have been caused by the manufacturer's carelessness, unless the manufacturer did not intend the product to reach the end-user in the same condition it left the factory. Following ***Grant***, it is relatively easy to establish a breach of duty, as courts are willing to infer carelessness unless there is evidence to the contrary. This inference is not always made, however. In *Evans* v *Triplex Glass Co Ltd* [1936], for example, a claim against the manufacturer of windscreen safety glass did not succeed as the court found that the fault was more likely to lie with the fitters of the glass than its manufacturer.

Once breach is established, it must be decided whether the breach actually caused the harm complained of. The tests for causation in fact and in law are the same in product liability as for any other area of negligence.[11] In a sense, however, the duty requirement that the item must not have been subject to intermediate examination between leaving the manufacturer and reaching the end-user can also be viewed as a breach/causation question. To find the defendant liable, a court must satisfy itself that they were responsible for the defect and that it was not due to the fault of someone else further down the chain of supply. If someone else—for example, a distribution company who inspected the goods before they were supplied to retailers—could be said to be responsible for the defect, this will 'break the chain' of causation back to the manufacturer. In addition, an end-user of a product will be unsuccessful in a claim if it can be shown that they had knowledge (actual or constructive) of the defects.[12]

In ***Grant***, the defendants argued that the goods may have been tampered with after leaving the factory and the fact that this might have happened (there was no real way of proving whether it had) should enable the manufacturer to escape liability. They argued that because the garments had been wrapped in paper packets and could be sold separately, there was a possibility that they had been interfered with. The court dismissed this argument, finding that interference was a question of fact (i.e. evidence must be shown to prove that there was actually interference, otherwise the presumption will be that there was none). However, *Evans* (decided in the same year) tells us that if there is a 'reasonable possibility' or a probability of interference with the product, this will be enough to exonerate the manufacturer from liability.

11. See **Chapter 9**.
12. *Howmet Ltd* v *Economy Devices Ltd and others* [2016].

The question of inspection may be a difficult one, especially if a party in the supply chain had the *opportunity* to inspect the goods but did not take it. There is no obligation on intermediate parties (or, indeed, the end consumer) to exhaustively examine goods that pass through their control, so a manufacturer will remain liable unless they have a genuine or specific reason to believe that the goods will be inspected by another party before they leave the supply chain. This, of course, prompts another question: when *can* a manufacturer reasonably expect another party to examine the goods? While in *Andrews* v *Hopkinson* [1957] a second-hand car salesman had the opportunity to check cars and was held liable for failing to do so for any obvious faults (although a full and exhaustive inspection was not required), in *Hurley* v *Dyke* [1979] a seller of a defective second-hand car avoided liability as he had informed the buyer that it was 'as seen and with all its faults' (the warning moved the duty onto the buyer to inspect the car for himself).

12.2.2 The limits of negligence liability

So far we have considered the position under ***Donoghue*** in relation to manufacturing defects. However, products can be also defective because of the way they are *designed* and in these circumstances we begin to see the limits of a claim in negligence. This is problematic. Design defects by their very nature are likely to affect greater numbers of end-users—possibly even every consumer of a product—and are also likely to be difficult to discover by examination of the product either before it leaves the supply chain or by the ultimate consumer. In short, design defects are more serious and increase the possibility of harm to the product's end-users.

Unfortunately, it is also more difficult for someone to succeed in a negligence claim in relation to design defects. While duty is easy to establish, it is difficult to show that there was carelessness in designing a product, that is, that the designers fell below—or breached—the standard of care expected of them. In relation to causation, the claimant must show two things: first, that the design defect *can* cause harm and, secondly, that the design defect *was* the actual or material cause of the specific harm being claimed for. This is a high threshold. For example, a claimant may be able to show that a particular drug, because of a design flaw, can cause cancer. However, it will be very difficult for them to prove, on the balance of probabilities, that taking the drug caused *their particular cancer*, particularly as other factors such as environment, genetics and lifestyle may also all be relevant (as in ***Wilsher* v *Essex Area Health Authority* [1988]**).[13]

The particular difficulties associated with design defects became very apparent in the 1960s with the Thalidomide tragedy.

The Thalidomide tragedy

Thalidomide is a drug that was initially sold from the mid-1950s to 1961 in many countries worldwide and under many different product names. It was primarily prescribed to pregnant

→

13. So Josh, in the earlier scenarios, may have difficulties establishing that the drug was the cause of his stomach ulcer.

→ women, to help combat morning sickness and in order to help them sleep. However, it later transpired that Thalidomide is a potent teratogen, which means that it can cause severe birth defects if taken during pregnancy. The drug had been inadequately tested before being put on the market and approximately 10,000 children were born with birth defects after their mothers took it while pregnant. These defects included phocomelia, characterised by the shortness of the long bones in the arms or legs and therefore often severely shortened limbs, as well as problems with the heart or kidneys, or with digestion. Life expectancy was also shortened and many affected children died in infancy.[14]

In 1962, in reaction to the tragedy, the US Congress enacted laws requiring tests for safety during pregnancy before any drug can receive approval for sale in the United States and numerous other countries enacted similar legislation. Thalidomide was not prescribed or sold for decades. However, perhaps surprisingly, it was never withdrawn completely from the medical marketplace and is used today to treat a number of conditions, including leprosy and several types of cancer.

see online resources

The Thalidomide tragedy is a perfect example of harm caused by a design defect. Nothing in the *manufacturing* process had gone wrong, causing a particular batch of the drug to produce negative side effects in those for whom it had been prescribed. Instead, part of the *design* process had been faulty. The parents of some of the children affected by Thalidomide claimed in negligence against the producers of the drug. The legal outcomes of their claims are forever unknown as they were settled before reaching court, however it is clear that although the manufacturers owed those affected a duty of care as the ultimate consumers, because the consequences of the drug were not foreseeable by a reasonable manufacturer at the time it was circulated, it would have been very difficult for them to show that the manufacturer had breached this duty by failing to take reasonable care in the design process. It would have also been difficult to establish causation—the birth defects could have been caused by a number of different things.[15]

What the Thalidomide tragedy did highlight was the need for change. While the common law was in a fairly satisfactory position in relation to manufacturing defects, as courts were willing to infer negligence (***Grant***) and generally had a fairly 'flexible' approach to liability, the Thalidomide cases showed what problems claimants might face if trying to claim for harms caused by *design* defects. This led to demands for legal reform and, in particular (perhaps because it was 'fashionable' at the time), a call for strict liability to be placed on manufacturers of defective products.

Strict liability is liability without fault. What it would mean for manufacturers to be strictly liable for defective products is that even if they did nothing wrong in the manufacturing

14. This does not mean that similar scandals cannot happen again. Recently, campaigners have highlighted the use of sodium valproate (used to treat epilepsy, bipolar disorder and other conditions) by pregnant women, despite being known by the medical profession to be teratogenic. See Sarah Boseley 'Birth defect risks of sodium valproate "known 40 years ago"' *The Guardian* 26 September 2017.

15. In fact scientists only discovered *how* the drug caused the side effects it did in 2009, though this still would not prove that the drug *did* do this in any individual case, as other (genetic) factors could also cause the same symptoms. For a discussion of the difficulties posed by multiple potential causes, see **section 9.2.2.1**. Thalidomide manufacturers have never admitted negligence, though they have issued apologies—see BBC News 'Thalidomide apology insulting, campaigners say' 1 September 2012.

or design process (i.e. there was nothing that could technically be called a 'breach'), they would have to compensate someone who suffered harm caused by a defect in their product. The main reasons suggested for the introduction of strict liability were threefold:

- manufacturers create products and therefore create the hazard or harm. Since this is done in the pursuit of profit, it is reasonable for them to accept the risk of liability for any harms actually caused by the product;
- manufacturers are in the best position to insure against the risks of any such hazards or harms (and the price of such insurance can be reflected in the product price and therefore distributed amongst all end-users of a product);
- imposing strict liability on manufacturers provides an incentive for them to take all possible safety precautions during the design and manufacturing processes.

In light of increasing pressure worldwide in favour of strict liability, the European Community issued a Directive in 1985[16] requiring member states to change and harmonise their laws on product liability.[17] In the UK, this took the form of Part 1 of the CPA.[18]

12.3 **Defective products—claims under Part 1 of the Consumer Protection Act 1987**

Section 1(1) of the CPA stipulates that:

> This Part shall have effect for the purpose of making such provision as is necessary in order to comply with the product liability Directive and shall be construed accordingly.[19]

Thus, it may be that it is the terms of the Directive itself that should be followed, rather than the terms of the Act, as the CPA must be construed in line with the original meaning intended by the Directive—a point to which we shall later return.

The CPA makes the manufacturer of a product (and others along the supply chain) liable *without proof of fault* (strictly liable) for personal injury and some property damage caused

16. Directive 85/374/EEC.

17. This is kept under almost constant review. In 2017, the European Commission evaluated the application and performance of the Directive, including how it meets its objectives and whether it continues to meet consumers' and others' needs—and, interestingly, whether it is fit for purpose in an increasingly technological age, with specific reference to the 'Internet of Things' (European Commission 'Public Consultation on the rules on liability of the producer for damage caused by a defective product' 10 January 2017)—it received responses from 657 stakeholders. The fifth report on the Product Liability Directive (covering 2011–15) was published in 2018. It concluded that the evaluation showed that despite products having increased in complexity since the Directive was issued, and although some legal terms (including 'defect' and 'product') may need better definition (especially in light of emerging technologies), it continues to be an adequate tool. In addition, the Commission established an expert group on liability and new technologies to keep these areas under review and to 'issue guidance on the Product Liability Directive and a report on the broader implications for, potential gaps in and orientations for, the liability and safety frameworks for artificial intelligence, the Internet of Things and robotics'. Its report was published in February 2020.

18. Brought into force 1 March 1988.

19. Post-Brexit, Regulations have been passed which will change the tense of s 1(1) so that it reads 'This part was enacted for the purpose . . . ' and ' . . . as was necessary . . . ' (Product Safety and Metrology etc. (Amendment etc.) (EU Exit) Regulations 2019, SI 2019/696).

wholly or in part by a defect in the product concerned. This looks to be a step forward from, and a contrast to, the tort of negligence, where fault must be proved. As formulated, strict liability as (supposedly) provided by the CPA should provide an easier route to redress.

Manufacturers are, however, granted a number of specific defences under the CPA. These are problematic. The imposition of strict liability is considerably less strict if the defendant is able to defend claims against them. One of the defences in particular has caused considerable controversy, as we shall see later in this section.

Essentially, establishing liability under the CPA requires a series of questions to be asked. The Act defines concepts such as 'product' and 'defect' and it is within these confines that claims must proceed.

12.3.1 **Bringing a claim**

Unfortunately, the CPA does not clearly set out who can sue and who can be sued.[20] Reading between the lines, it appears that anyone who suffers damage covered by the Act as a result of a defective product can bring a claim (ss 2(1) and 5(1)). The definitions in section 1(2) and a further outlining of who potential defendants might be in section 2(2)(a)–(c) suggest that manufacturers and producers of goods can be sued, as well as 'own-branders' (companies who put their name to a product made for them by someone else)[21] and importers.[22] Similarly, *suppliers* of goods can be sued if the conditions in section 2(3) are met. The purpose of the Act is to increase the protection of consumers (in the spirit intended by those advocating strict liability for defective products) by ensuring that *someone* can be found liable in relation to defective products. This is underlined by section 2(5) which states that if more than one potential defendant can be liable for the same damage they will be jointly and severally liable.

To claim, the right 'kind' of damage is needed. This is defined in section 5 as death or personal injury, or property damage with a value of more than £275 (s 5(4)). Thus, small monetary claims for property damage are excluded (perhaps to limit the number and ensure the 'seriousness' of claims). There is no upper limit to the total amount of damages that may be claimed (despite an option to limit this when implementing the Directive). Pure economic loss is also specifically excluded by section 5(2), which means that, as in the tort of negligence, the cost of *replacing* a defective product is not recoverable.

Pause for reflection

Does a figure of £275 as the minimum claimable limit for property damage seem (a) quite arbitrary and (b) relatively low? Consider what you can buy for £275 these days and what could have been bought for that sum when the CPA came into force. Should this figure be increased?

20. You may find it helpful to read this section alongside the **annotated version of the CPA (section 12.4)** or the **CPA 'at a glance' table** in **section 12.5**. These can also be downloaded from the **online resources**.

21. See e.g. *Busby* v *Berkshire Bed Co Ltd* [2018] at [21].

22. Post-Brexit, s 2(2)(c) is to be amended to remove reference to imports into 'member states', replacing it with '. . . imported the product into the United Kingdom' (Product Safety and Metrology etc. (Amendment etc.) (EU Exit) Regulations 2019).

'Products' are defined in section 1(2) and include 'any goods or electricity and . . . a product which is comprised in another product, whether by virtue of being a component part or raw material or otherwise'. 'Goods' are further defined (s 45) to include 'substances, growing crops and things comprised in land by virtue of being attached to it, and any ship, aircraft or vehicle'. This definition is quite broad and possibly encompasses things that, as a consumer, one might not ordinarily have considered.[23]

The key aspect of the CPA is its coverage of 'defective' products—so the definition of defect is one that needs detailed analysis. It is here that most of the case law under the CPA can be found: the courts have found themselves tasked, on occasion, with ruling on whether or not a certain product is 'defective' for the purposes of the Act.

12.3.2 **What is a 'defect'?**

Defects in products for the purposes of the CPA are defined in section 3. As a defendant is strictly liable for any damage (of the right kind) caused wholly or in part by a 'defective product', this definition is a key part of the Act. Section 3 defines a defect as follows:

> [T]here is a defect in a product for the purposes of this Part if the safety of the product is not such as persons generally are entitled to expect . . .

The burden of proof is on the claimant to show that a defect exists, and that this caused them harm. In addition, defects are about safety, not quality. However, it seems that the standard (regarding what is and what is not defective) is set by 'persons generally'—not, for example, by manufacturers, consumers or any other specific group or individual (see *Richardson* v *LRC Products Ltd* [2000]). But the way the definition is phrased does mean that, objectively, the perspectives of those groups or individuals have to be taken into account when considering what 'persons generally' might think. This is a rather weak and circular definition. Indeed, in *Wilkes* v *DePuy International Ltd* [2016], Hickinbottom J pointed out that as an objective, rather than a subjective, *consumer* expectation test, it is rather an 'empty vessel' (at [68]).

Counterpoint

If the CPA really is about consumer protection, it seems odd that the expectations of manufacturers and others with vested interests should be taken into account when deciding whether a product is 'defective'. Manufacturers base their considerations on a cost/benefit analysis—for example, to them, a product will be 'defective' only if the magnitude of the danger it poses and the cost of preventing any harm occurring outweigh the product's utility—this risk/utility

→

23. e.g. blood products provided for transfusion purposes: ***A* v *National Blood Authority*** [2001]. The original definition did not include agricultural produce or game, unless this had been subjected to an industrial process (e.g. in a meat-packing factory). EU member states were free to include or exclude this produce under the 1985 Directive. However, a further EU Directive made inclusion compulsory after the BSE ('mad cow disease') crisis—agricultural produce has therefore been included within the definition of 'product' under the CPA since 2000.

→

analysis is more familiar to us from the tort of negligence and in particular an assessment of the standard of care and whether a defendant has fallen below it. This, therefore, implies *fault*—and the CPA is meant to bring no-fault (strict) liability.

On the other hand, it is questionable whether strict liability is desirable in this area at all. Manufacturers have to absorb the costs and risks of development in other ways and, unless clearly negligent in the way they make a path to market (e.g. if a pharmaceutical company did not undertake any testing to determine whether a drug it was producing had any harmful side effects), it can seem unreasonable that they also have to pay for harms suffered by people using their products. Consumers generally welcome choice, innovation and competition (more products on the market, prices are kept down by competition, etc), so is imposing strict liability on producers allowing consumers the best of both worlds? Perhaps it is arguable that consumers should take more responsibility for themselves when it comes to injuries suffered in this context (see ***Abouzaid* v *Mothercare (UK) Ltd*** [2000] and *Pollard* v *Tesco Stores Ltd* [2006] as just two examples of cases where it might well be argued that had more care been taken by the consumer, the risk would not have materialised).[24]

Evidently, the CPA's definition of 'defect' allows products into the market that are potentially dangerous—but not defective. As the concept of a defect is linked to 'safety' and about what may be reasonably expected, this means that certain items that are inherently dangerous cannot be classed as defective. For example, a cut-throat razor or a serrated bread knife will not be 'defective' products, as people are 'generally entitled to expect' that razors and knives will be sharp.

Pause for reflection

Where does this leave products such as cigarettes and alcohol? Are these as safe as 'persons generally are entitled to expect'? If so, what makes them this 'safe'? It could be argued that the damaging effects of cigarettes and alcohol are well publicised. For example, the potential consequences of smoking are already clearly pointed out on packaging,[25] and government campaigns have highlighted that people who consume alcohol should take into account how many 'units' they consume, with products now labelled to allow consumers to find this information

→

24. See also *Busby* v *Berkshire Bed Co Ltd* [2018], where the claimant fell off her new bed during sex, resulting in paralysis. Despite a finding of fact that the bed was not 'of satisfactory quality' (for contract law purposes), it was not found to be defective under the CPA, and her injury had been merely an accident which 'required a most unfortunate and unusual combination of positioning on the bed and movement which I do not believe would have been foreseeable by any reasonable person prior to the incident' (HHJ Cotter QC, at [142]).

25. New rules on cigarette packaging came into force in May 2016 after tobacco firms lost a legal challenge (*British American Tobacco UK Ltd and others, R (on the application of)* v *Secretary of State for Health* [2016]). Packets of ten cigarettes are no longer available and for larger packs standardised green packaging is used. Pictures depicting the harmful effects of smoking must now cover 65 per cent of the front and back of every packet of cigarettes, with additional warnings on the top of the pack.

→

easily. It is very unlikely that policy-makers would think it wise or practical to take tobacco and alcohol out of circulation (consider the 'Prohibition' experiment in the United States during the 1920s and 30s, which drove the supply of alcohol underground and created a criminal sub-culture). There are cultural issues with regulating an existing product which has been found to be dangerous long after release, as opposed to regulating the safety of a new product coming onto the market. So, while it might be said that tobacco and alcohol are not as 'safe' as other products, public expectations in relation to these substances clearly differ greatly from those in relation to others.

The question when deciding whether a product is defective for the purposes of the CPA is: what *are* 'persons generally entitled to expect'? As this is an objective standard it can be difficult to assess, although section 3(2)(a)–(c) sets out guidelines as to what factors may be taken into account when considering the safety/defectiveness of a particular product, including:

- the manner in which, and purposes for which, the product has been marketed;
- the 'get-up' (packaging);
- use of marks (e.g. the British Standards Institution 'Kitemark');
- instructions or warnings accompanying the product when sold;
- what might reasonably be expected to be done with the product; and
- the time at which the product was supplied.

Counterpoint

The issue of defectiveness or non-defectiveness is perhaps a common-sense interpretation of the safety of a product, according to how and why it is marketed, how it is packaged, what people (consumers) are meant to do with it (and what they are not) and, importantly, any warnings accompanying the product. It can be assumed that an adequate warning would be enough to make an otherwise defective (i.e. unsafe) product non-defective. This, too, does not sound like strict liability in any real sense. Either a product is unsafe or it is not—should giving a warning be enough to remove liability? Put another way, if there is a product which would be deemed unsafe if no warning came with it, are we saying the manufacturer is *at fault* for not supplying an adequate warning, and should therefore be liable? Conversely, if a warning is included, is there no fault and therefore no liability? Is this really a form of negligence?

When considering 'defectiveness', the question of whether adequate warnings were given (thus rendering a product 'safe') has arisen in case law generated by the CPA (of which there is surprisingly little). For example, in *Worsley* v *Tambrands Ltd* [2000], a woman complained that a tampon she had used was defective when she suffered toxic shock syndrome after using it. She claimed that while it was known that the risk of this syndrome appearing was greater with misuse of the product, she had used it according to the instructions. As the evidence showed that she had read the comprehensive instructions, including the warnings given about the product, the court held that the tampon had not been defective as 'people generally' (in this case, women using the product) should know, as it was stated in the instructions and warnings, that a small risk of toxic shock syndrome was present even with ordinary use. Similarly, in *Richardson* v *LRC Products Ltd* [2001], the question for the court was whether a condom, from which the whole tip had sheared off during use (i.e. it had more than just split or punctured during sex), was defective. The claimants were claiming for the costs associated with pregnancy and birth of an unwanted child. Again, because it was considered well known that condoms are not 100 per cent effective, due to the warnings to this effect that always accompany them (including on the outer packaging), the condom was not found to be defective.

Counterpoint

Richardson may be viewed outside the ambit of product liability as a case where a claim for 'wrongful birth' was being made. In other cases of this type (e.g. when a sterilisation operation has been performed negligently), the House of Lords was adamant in its view that this is not a compensable harm.[26] While the courts are prepared to award damages for the pain and suffering associated with the 'physical harm' of pregnancy and birth caused by negligence, damages for 'wrongful birth' are generally unavailable. This is largely due to policy reasons: either the harm suffered is not viewed as a legal harm, or the harm (the cost of raising an unwanted child) has been deliberately classified as 'pure economic loss' (see *McFarlane* v *Tayside Health Board* [1999]—discussed in **section 7.5.2**). Given the date of *Richardson*, it may well be assumed that this decision also had the weight of the public policy arguments from the wrongful birth negligence cases behind it, even though the same harm was caused in a different way.

see online resources

In *Bogle and others* v *McDonald's Restaurants Ltd* [2002], customers of McDonald's fast-food restaurants sued the company (in negligence as well as under the CPA) for scalding caused by hot coffee. The product—that is, the coffee—was 'defective' in two ways: first, the temperature at which it was served was too high and, secondly, the lids on the cups in which it was served came off too easily. The High Court dismissed the claims, holding that 'persons generally' would know that hot coffee could cause scalding if spilt and that care should be taken with hot drinks to avoid spillages. Because people want hot coffee, they have to suffer the 'inevitable' risk that comes with it. Field J said that:

> if McDonald's were going to avoid the risk of injury by a deep thickness burn they would have had to have served tea and coffee at between 55C and 60C. But tea ought to be brewed with boiling water if it is to give its best flavour and coffee ought to be brewed at between 85C and 95C. Further, people generally like to allow a hot drink to cool to the temperature

26. Controversially, since *Rees* v *Darlington Area Health Authority* [2002] a 'conventional' award of £15,000 for loss of autonomy may now be awarded in such cases, though this in no way compensates for the financial losses caused by the negligence.

> they prefer. Accordingly, I have no doubt that tea and coffee served at between 55C and 60C would not have been acceptable to McDonald's customers. Indeed, on the evidence, I find that the public want to be able to buy tea and coffee served hot, that is to say at a temperature of at least 65C, even though they know (as I think they must be taken to do . . .) that there is a risk of a scalding injury if the drink is spilled. (at [33])

Put another way, the decision says that coffee-buying customers (who were usually adults and teenagers) should generally expect coffee to be hot and should guard against spillages themselves. On the second issue, the court found that the lids needed to come off easily to allow customers to put sugar and milk in their drinks; the fact they came off easily if the cups were knocked over did not make them defective. The test used here seems to be one of 'legitimate consumer expectation' and can probably be linked back to the use of the words '*entitled* to expect' in section 3 of the CPA—that what persons generally are 'entitled' to expect may well be different from what an individual claimant or claimants did in fact expect (i.e. some people may have higher standards, but they may not be 'entitled' to these standards under the CPA).

Pause for reflection

Bogle may be compared to the infamous US case of *Liebeck v McDonald's Restaurants* [1994], which is often used as an example of the US 'compensation culture'. The case became a flashpoint in the US debate over tort reform after a jury awarded nearly $3 million to a woman who burned herself with hot coffee bought from McDonald's.[27] Stella Liebeck, a 79-year-old woman, bought a cup of coffee from the drive-through window of her local McDonald's restaurant. She was sitting in the passenger seat of her grandson's car, which he had parked to allow Mrs Liebeck to add cream and sugar to her coffee. She placed the coffee cup between her knees and pulled the lid towards her to remove it, spilling the entire cup of coffee on her lap and burning herself in the process. Her award was reduced to $640,000 by the trial judge,

→

27. It should be noted here that one of the major differences—and possibly a contributing factor to the commonly held perception that in the United States you can sue for anything—between the US and UK tort systems is the presence of a jury on tort cases. Typically, jurors tend to feel more sympathy to claimants (and antipathy to defendants) and this may be particularly true where cases are taken against large corporations. Jurors also 'decide' damages awards, and in the United States there is far more scope for non-compensatory damages (e.g. punitive or aggravated damages) than in the UK (see **Chapter 21**). In a 1998 case against Philip Morris tobacco (one of the world's largest producers of cigarettes), a jury awarded $81 million to the widow and children of a man who had smoked the company's Marlboro cigarettes for 40 years (since before the time tobacco companies acknowledged the dangers of smoking). The family had sued for $100 million but the award was reduced as the court found the man 50 per cent responsible for the harm he suffered. Less than two months later, in another claim against Philip Morris, another jury awarded $51.5 million to a cigarette smoker with terminal lung cancer (though this was later appealed). More recently, in 2018, Monsanto (now owned by Bayer) was found liable for gardener DeWayne Johnson's terminal cancer caused by 'Roundup', one of the company's weedkiller products. The jury awarded him $289 million damages. There have also been subsequent successful cases, with substantial damages awards. See also Patricia Cohen 'Roundup maker to pay $10 billion to settle cancer suits' *The New York Times* 24 June 2020—reportedly one of the biggest settlements in US litigation history.

→

though the case was later settled out of court for an unknown amount (thought to be less than $600,000) before an appeal was decided.

Do you think *Bogle* is evidence of a 'compensation culture' in the UK? Or do you think the claims were legitimate? Some often unreported information (or facts that are conveniently forgotten by those arguing that a compensation culture exists) about the *Liebeck* case is that the coffee, which had been absorbed by Mrs Liebeck's clothing, was then held against her skin as she sat in the puddle of hot liquid for over 90 seconds, scalding her thighs, buttocks and groin. She was taken to hospital, where doctors determined that she had suffered third-degree burns on 6 per cent of her skin and lesser burns over 16 per cent. She remained in the hospital for eight days while she underwent skin grafting, which was then followed by two years of further treatment. During the trial, the court heard that that McDonald's required its franchises to serve coffee at 180–190°F (82–88°C). At that temperature, it was said that the coffee could cause a third-degree burn in between two and seven seconds. Other evidence showed that from 1982 to 1992 the company had received more than 700 reports of people burned by its coffee, to varying degrees of severity, and had previously settled claims arising from scalding injuries for more than $500,000.

Mrs Liebeck had not intended this outcome: initially, she sought to settle with McDonald's for $20,000 to cover her medical costs, which were $11,000, but the company offered only $800. When McDonald's refused to raise its offer, she claimed against them, alleging 'gross negligence' for selling 'unreasonably dangerous' and 'defectively manufactured' coffee. McDonald's then refused her lawyer's offer to settle for $90,000. Just before the trial, a mediator suggested a settlement of $225,000, but McDonald's again refused. In part, it can be said that all the refusals on the part of McDonald's were part of the reason for the high award of damages from the court. Another often-ignored fact is that the trial judge found Mrs Liebeck to be 20 per cent contributorily negligent.[28]

'Consumer expectation' was also relevant in *Pollard* v *Tesco Stores Ltd* [2006]. There, the Court of Appeal found that the child-resistant top of a bottle of dishwasher detergent was not defective, despite the fact that in this case it had been opened by a child. The bottle top did not conform to the relevant British Design Standard, but even so, the claim was dismissed on the grounds that consumers would not generally know what the relevant design standard was; all they would expect would be that a 'child-proof' cap was harder for a child to remove than a normal cap. As this was still the case, the product was not defective.

Pause for reflection

Does the outcome of the *Tesco* case seem like 'strict liability' to you? Would you think a bottle of chemicals from which a child could remove the supposedly child-proof cap fits the definition of a 'defective' product under section 3 of the CPA? This certainly does not seem like strict liability. Furthermore, it seems as though the expectation of the manufacturers (who would or

see online resources

28. See **Chapter 10**. Further information on this case is available on the **online resources**.

→

ought to know the relevant design standard), rather than of the public, was the driving factor in this case. The CPA, it should be remembered, specifies that the relevant expectations should be those that 'persons generally' (including manufacturers) are 'entitled to expect' when determining whether or not a product is defective (s 3). Does the outcome of this case now mean that consumers are not entitled to expect that 'child-proof' caps on dangerous substances are, in fact, child-proof?

A question about whether claimants need to prove the exact way in which a defect manifests itself, or if it is enough to show that there is 'some defect' (a 'broad-brush' approach) was answered in *Hufford* v *Samsung Electronics (UK) Ltd* [2014]. The claimant sought to show that his fridge was defective, as it had unexpectedly and seemingly inexplicably caught fire—he could not point to the exact cause, but was only operating the fridge in conditions of 'normal use'. The defendant argued that as the claimant could not be reasonably specific about the nature of the defect, he should not succeed. Grant HHJ found:

> in relation to a claim under the 1987 Act, a claimant does not have to specify or identify with accuracy or precision the defect in the product he seeks to establish, and thus prove. It is enough for a claimant to prove the existence of a defect in broad or general terms, such as 'a defect in the electrics of the Lexus (motor car)'. (at [25])

Thus, it appears that the 'broad-brush' approach will be acceptable.[29] Unfortunately, in *Hufford*, the claim eventually failed, as the claimant was unable to discharge the burden of proof that a defect in the fridge had caused the fire, rather than any other cause.

A claimant must also prove that the item they allege to be defective would be defective with 'ordinary use'. In *Wilkes*, the claimant sought to render the defendant company, which had provided the artificial hip joint used in his hip-replacement operation, liable under the CPA. One part of the artificial hip was a steel femoral shaft called a 'C-Stem'. Three years after Wilkes' operation, the C-stem fractured inside his body, leaving metal debris around the joint. However, the court found that it was not the case that the hip implant had been subject to normal use and had failed earlier than expected. Instead, it was found that the implant failed because of the excessive and unpredictable load it had been subjected to. Hickinbottom J said that no medicinal product could be absolutely safe or risk-free, and 'persons generally' were therefore not entitled to expect that they will be (at [65]). Again, this seems like a move further away from strict liability.[30]

In *Gee and others* v *DePuy International Ltd* [2018], a case was brought by 312 individuals affected by 'adverse reaction to metal debris' following hip replacements, including damage to surrounding tissue and pain, swelling and numbness in the leg, resulting in the need for further corrective surgery. In a lengthy judgment (170 pages) Mrs Justice Andrews DBE found that the claimants had failed to establish that the safety of the product at the

29. See also *Ide* v *ATB Sales Ltd & Anor* [2008].

30. Contrast the decision in an Australian case brought on behalf of hundreds of women left with excruciating pain and other symptoms due to transvaginal mesh implants. In *Gill* v *Ethicon Sàrl (No 5)* [2019], Katzmann J found that lack of an adequate warning affected consumer expectations and that '[w]hat persons generally are entitled to expect of medical devices is also affected by what the manufacturer says or does not say about them' (at 3370). The producers, Johnson & Johnson, were subsequently unsuccessful in an appeal.

relevant time (2002) did not meet the standard that the public generally were entitled to expect. The test applied was whether the product had an abnormal tendency to result in damage or harm, compared with comparable products. Factors such as cost, avoidability of the harm and the benefit to society of the product were found to be relevant.[31]

> The Council considered that the economic risk of producing a defective product should fall on the person best equipped to take precautionary steps or to insure against it, namely, the producer. That is something the Court must not forget. Nevertheless, depending on the circumstances and the product, and particularly on the harm, it may be that in an appropriate case the Court could legitimately conclude that the public would not be entitled to expect the producer to achieve something in terms of safety that is scientifically impossible or prohibitively expensive or which it would be impossible to insure against. It all depends on the nature of the product and its intended use, and all the other relevant circumstances. (at 167)

Despite there being only a limited number of cases concerning the meaning of 'defect' for the purposes of applying liability under the CPA and, more to the point, that manufacturers (as can be seen in the cases discussed) seem quite easily to be able to avoid their products being classed as defective, there have been some successful claims.

Abouzaid v *Mothercare (UK) Ltd* [2000] CA

The claimant, a 12-year-old boy, was injured when trying to fasten a clasp on the strap used to affix a 'cosytoes' (a detachable cover that envelops a baby's torso and legs) to a pushchair. While the elastic on the strap was stretched, he let the strap go and it recoiled, hitting him in the eye, causing injury to the retina and leaving him with impaired sight.

The court found that the product (the cosytoes) was defective. In its view, the manufacturer could have done more to prevent accidents of this type occurring, such as by using a different method to fasten the product to a pushchair, or providing a warning. Because it was so easy to avoid the danger, and the manufacturer had not taken adequate steps to do so, the product was defective and Mothercare was liable for the harm it caused.[32] Put another way, the ease with which the risk of injury could have been avoided was taken into account when determining liability.

In ***Abouzaid*** the Court of Appeal found that the relevant test was that the product must be judged against the expectations of persons generally in all the circumstances of the case—that is, whether the product had the level of safety which the general public would expect of such a product at the time the injury occurred. As the public would not expect injury to be able to be caused by something as generally innocuous as a cosytoes, this particular product *could* be deemed unsafe, and therefore defective, because it had unexpectedly caused injury.

31. Note, however, that the product in question was removed from sale in 2013. It is also unlikely that this case marks the end of litigation about hip replacements—further group litigations are being planned, resting on different harms and differing factual scenarios. In *Hastings* v *Finsbury Orthopaedics Ltd and Stryker UK Ltd* [2019], for example, the Scottish court considered the impact of *Wilkes* and *Gee*, agreeing with the general approach but rejecting the specific aspect of *Gee* that rested on a comparison with other products, instead agreeing, as the claimant argued, that consumer expectation would be that a product would be at least as good as alternatives. The claimant later failed on causation.

32. This may partly have been because of the manufacturer's own reputation as a leader in the baby products market—see Pill LJ at [27].

Pause for reflection

Compare the decision (in particular the reasoning) in *Abouzaid* with *Tesco*. Are the two decisions consistent in the way they have determined what a defective product is (or is not)? Which do you think is the better decision and why? One difference between the two cases is that a cosytoes will obviously come into close proximity with children, due to its very nature, whereas it might be expected that a cleaning chemical would be kept in a safe place away from children by responsible parents as an additional safeguard, despite it supposedly being child-proof. However, overall the decision in *Abouzaid* does seem to be more logical and 'in tune' with what the expectations of 'persons generally' might be.

***A and others* v *National Blood Authority* [2001] QBD**

The claimants contracted Hepatitis C, a liver disease, after being supplied with contaminated blood during blood transfusions. The people who donated the blood had been infected with the Hepatitis C virus but, at the time they donated, there was no way of testing for its presence. At the time of the transfusions the medical profession was aware that Hepatitis C existed and that it could be transmitted by a blood transfusion, but there was still no way of testing the blood. Thus, it was known that some blood provided for transfusions *could* be contaminated with Hepatitis C, but no way of telling *which* blood this was. The public was not warned of this small risk.

The court had to decide whether the contaminated blood was defective for the purposes of establishing liability under the CPA. The defendants argued that the blood could not have been defective because the public was only 'entitled' to expect the product to be as safe as it could be if reasonable precautions had been taken when handling it and there was nothing more that the blood authority could have done to make the product safer. In short, they argued that the risk was unavoidable and this fact had to be considered when the court looked at 'all the circumstances' that must be taken into account (under the CPA, s 3(2)). However, the claimants argued that to take such things into account would let 'questions of fault back in by the back door' (at 316).

The defendant's argument was roundly rejected by Burton J, who found the blood to be defective. He held that the question of avoidability or otherwise should not be taken into account as section 3(2) could be interpreted to mean 'all *relevant* circumstances': what the producer could or could not have done, therefore, was not a *relevant* consideration when looking at strict liability (as opposed to negligence).[33] He defined the infected blood as a 'non-standard' product—one that does not perform as the producer of the product intends—adding that where there is a harmful characteristic in a non-standard product, a decision that the product is defective would be 'straightforward'. The primary question would be whether the public accepted the non-standard nature of the product—that is, whether it could be said that the risk of some blood being affected was one that had been accepted by the general public. On this point, he found that the public was entitled to expect blood that was 100 per cent safe. Therefore the blood authority was liable.

33. It should be noted that this determination may not have survived an appeal had this case gone further. It is also potentially in doubt after *Gee*.

Burton J paid close attention to the meaning of 'defect' under the CPA. Because the Act itself says that it must be interpreted in line with the EC Directive, he used the definitional terms of the Directive rather than the provisions of the Act. In so doing he provided a three-stage test when determining under Article 6 of the Directive (and therefore presumably s 3 of the CPA) whether a product is defective:

(1) What harmful characteristic in the product caused the injury?

(2) Was the product 'standard' or 'non-standard'?

(3) What are the consumer's legitimate expectations as to the product?

From the way the test is constructed, it becomes harder to establish that there is a defect in a 'standard' product than a 'non-standard' one. This would be similar to arguing that the problem came at the design stage rather than the manufacturing stage. However, even with non-standard products, the legitimate expectations of consumers must be considered, so being non-standard clearly does not equate to being 'defective' in and of itself (see *Richardson* v *LRC Products* [2000] and now *Gee and others* v *DePuy International Ltd* [2018]). What consumers are entitled to expect will depend on whether any risk associated with the product is public knowledge and, crucially, whether this risk can be objectively considered socially acceptable. Infected blood, according to Burton J, clearly was not socially acceptable in any sense (at [56]).

The ***A*** judgment was the leading authority on 'defectiveness' for nearly 20 years. According to ***A***, if a product is 'non-standard', and the public would not accept this 'non-standard' nature, the defendant will be liable. This is true irrespective of whether the 'non-standard' product could have been made standard (the only option being to withdraw the product from circulation) or whether the wholesale withdrawal of the product would have significant disadvantages to society. The decision in ***A*** proved controversial and many have argued that it was wrongly decided. In light of *Wilkes* [2016] and *Gee* [2018], which as we saw earlier did consider other factors in arriving at the decisions that the products were non-defective, at least part of the decision must now be in doubt. Which approach is now to be followed has yet to be resolved in a subsequent case or in a higher court.

If the point of the CPA was to achieve strict liability for 'defective' products that cause harm, then we might consider that ***A*** was in fact correct despite it not necessarily seeming to be fair that the blood authority was held liable, as there was literally nothing it could have done at the time to have made the blood safe. Strict liability is, however, not meant to be 'fair', it is meant to be strict, and the desirability of the outcome (compensation for the harm suffered by the claimants) supposedly justifies this. However, ***A*** seems somewhat inconsistent with most other claims taken under the Act and it might be questioned why this is—was Burton J, perhaps, swayed by the number of potential claimants or the very serious nature of the harm done to them, or by the nature of blood transfusions being a necessary life-saving measure?

In 2017, the High Court granted a group litigation order to a group of 500 people comprising some of the surviving victims and family members of those who died following the contaminated blood scandal of the 1970s and 1980s. Thousands of people are estimated to have died after receiving blood products imported from the United States which were infected with Hepatitis C and HIV. The claims against the government have been stayed pursuant to an ongoing public inquiry into the scandal, announced by the then Prime Minister Theresa May in July 2017.[34] It may therefore matter very much whether the *A* or *Wilkes/Gee* approach is followed in the future.

12.3.3 **Causation and limitations**

If a defect is found, a claimant must still show that the defect caused the damage. The ordinary principles of legal causation apply.[35] Therefore, at the point of determining causation, when the claim is against the manufacturer of a medical product (e.g. a drug) in particular, the claimant would seem to be no better off than under the common law, particularly where there are multiple potential causes of the harm, especially given that the idea of 'materially increasing the risk of harm' in this type of case appears to have been ruled out in ***Wilsher* v *Essex Area Health Authority* [1988]**.[36] This point was clearly illustrated in *XYZ* v *Schering Health Care Ltd* [2002], where Mackay J concluded that because the evidence suggesting a causal connection between the third-generation oral contraceptive pill and cardio-vascular problems was contradictory and insufficient, the case would be doomed to fail on causation, so there was no need to decide whether and how the CPA would apply.[37]

Furthermore, time limitations are placed on claims under the CPA. A claimant must bring the claim within three years of the harm being suffered (though in 'latent harm' situations where the claimant only discovers later that harm has been suffered, the three years run from this time, not from when the harm was literally caused). While this is quite generous, another limitation period exists, giving claimants only ten years to claim from the time the particular product was put into circulation.[38] This is to take into account consumer expectations—arguably if a product has (successfully) been on the market for ten years, it is not defective. What these limitations mean in practice, however, is that if a product has been on the market for nine years and 11 months, and then the claimant is harmed by a defect in the product, a claim must be taken almost immediately in order not to run out of time. If injury occurs a month later, no claim will be possible.

As long as an action is initiated within the ten-year period it can be decided. In *Horne-Roberts* v *SmithKline Beecham* [2001] the Court of Appeal ruled that this was the case even where proceedings had originally been mistakenly initiated against the *wrong* producer. The correct producer was later allowed to be substituted in the action even though the ten-year period had by then expired. In 2008, the House of Lords referred this issue to the European Court of Justice (ECJ), asking for clear guidance on the position where a

34. See BBC News Online 'Contaminated blood: Victims can launch court damages action' 26 September 2017; Jim Duffy 'Contaminated blood: statutory inquiry announced' UK Human Rights blog, 7 November 2017. The progress of the Inquiry can be found at **www.infectedbloodinquiry.org.uk/news**.

35. As outlined in **Chapter 9**.

36. For a full discussion of the development and treatment of the concept of 'material increase of risk', see **section 9.2.2.1**.

37. The reason for the failure of the claim in *Busby* v *Berkshire Bed Co Ltd* [2018] was that the injury had not been caused by the bed, but by the activity of the claimant (at [105]). Though this was the case, HHJ Cotter QC also considered whether there was a defect under the CPA and/or a breach of contract and/or negligence.

38. Limitation Act 1980, s 11A(3).

claimant mistakenly names the wrong producer in an action commenced within the limitation period.[39] The ECJ ruled that certain circumstances would permit substitution of a producer after the expiry of the time limit, despite the fact this limit was strict. These included those where the party sued is a wholly owned subsidiary of the producer, and 'the putting into circulation of the product' had in fact been determined by that producer.[40] Upon the case's return (then to the Supreme Court), it was unanimously found that domestic law did not allow a producer to be substituted as the defendant in place of a wholly owned subsidiary, unless the parent company had actually determined when the supplier put the product in circulation. On the facts, this had not happened and the appeal was unsuccessful—the claimant was out of time.[41]

12.3.4 **Defences**

The availability of defences in the CPA appears to allow manufacturers to say 'it was not my fault'. Strict liability, by definition, ought not to be fault-based.[42] While the presence of explicit defences in the CPA is controversial, it may be argued that liability under the Act should be strict, but not absolute.

However, of the six defences built into the CPA in section 4,[43] one in particular has proved especially contentious. Under section 4(1)(e) a manufacturer or other party who finds themselves liable under the Act can claim:

> [t]hat the state of scientific and technical knowledge at the relevant time was not such that a producer of products of the same description as the product in question might be expected to have discovered the defect if it had existed in his products while they were under his control.

This has become known as the 'development risks' or 'state of the art' defence. It covers circumstances where, some time after the product was produced, scientific or technical knowledge renders it 'defective'. Put another way, if a discovery is made after the product is put into circulation by the manufacturer, meaning that the product would now be regarded as defective, the manufacturer escapes liability (on that occasion only, as any time after the first time the defect would be known). Ironically, therefore, under the CPA the Thalidomide claimants are unlikely to have been better off, despite this tragedy and other pharmaceutical harms being key factors leading to the movement to strict liability.[44] As Ross Cranston has pointed out, the large pharmaceutical companies operating from the UK are the biggest beneficiaries of the inclusion of the (optional) defence

39. *O'Byrne* v *Aventis Pasteur SA* [2008]. The ECJ had already once provided guidance on the matter, in *O'Byrne* v *Sanofi Pasteur MSD Ltd* [2006], though evidently this was not clear.

40. *Aventis Pasteur* v *O'Byrne* [2009].

41. *O'Byrne* v *Aventis Pasteur SA* [2010].

42. Compare the Vaccine Damage Payments Act 1979, under which a tax-free statutory sum is awarded to people who become severely disabled as a result of vaccination against certain diseases, without proof of fault. The one-off lump sum payment increased from £100,000 to £120,000 in July 2007, having previously increased from £40,000 to £100,000 in 2000. In December 2020 the Department of Health and Social Care announced that the government was adding Covid-19 vaccines to the Vaccine Damage Payments Scheme.

43. Contributory negligence is also available though not listed in s 4.

44. Which is exactly why the Law Commission recommended that parties injured by defective products should be compensated no matter what care had been taken by the producer (*Liability for Defective Products* (Law Com No 82, Cmnd 6831, 1977)).

(Scott and Black 2000, p 194). In fact, the UK Government was one of the most vocal when it came to implementing the Directive and was very much in favour of not using the derogation provision that would have allowed the defence to be excluded.

Pause for reflection

Does the development risks defence sound, in essence, like a crude version of the ***Bolam*** test in negligence which applies to professionals when determining whether they have fallen below the expected standard of care? In that test, if the professional concerned can show that they acted in the same way as others from a respectable body of professional opinion would have done, they will not be in breach of their duty of care. This makes it harder to find professionals liable in negligence.[45] The development risks defence, as it is phrased in section 4(1)(e), appears to give manufacturers the ability to say that 'other manufacturers would not have been able to spot the defect, given the state of scientific and technical knowledge'. Do you think this is what it means? Is this a subjective or an objective test?

***Commission of the European Communities* v *UK* (*EC* v *UK*) [1997] ECJ**

The CPA was meant to implement the terms of the EC Directive. The European Commission was concerned that the terminology of section 4(1)(e) of the CPA (the 'development risks defence') deviated from the wording of the defence under Article 7 of the Directive, creating what could be called a subjective test, as it focused on the conduct and abilities of the 'reasonable manufacturer'. Article 7(e) had been differently worded and required an objective assessment of the state of scientific and technical knowledge at the time the product was put into circulation. It said that the defence would apply when:

> [t]he state of scientific and technical knowledge at the time when the producer put the product into circulation was not such as to enable the existence of the defect to be discovered.

In ***EC*** v ***UK***, the ECJ said that the relevant test was to ask whether the information (that would make the product defective) was 'accessible' to the producer of the product concerned at the relevant time.

Relying on 'accessibility' of knowledge means that even if someone in the world might know the product is unsafe (because this is shown by later scientific or technical discoveries), the *producer* might not necessarily be able to know this. This, however, appears to be a subjective rather than objective assessment. The ECJ suggested that this meant, for example, that if a scientific discovery was made in a remote part of Manchuria (a region of China), and written up only in an obscure Manchurian journal (or not at all), then this information will not be 'accessible' to all producers.[46] However, if a discovery is made

45. See **section 8.3.2**.
46. ***Commission*** **v** ***UK*** [1977], Opinion of AG Tesauro at [23].

in France, even if this was written up in French and published in a French journal, the information would be likely to be deemed to be accessible to the majority of manufacturers (particularly European manufacturers covered by the Directive). In short, accessible information means that risks become foreseeable, and therefore the defence cannot apply.

In *A*, the defendant blood authority also contested the claim on the basis that even if a defect in the product could be established, they could avail themselves of the development risks defence. Burton J, however, ruled that the defence was not applicable, as the general risk that the blood was contaminated with the virus was known (albeit unavoidable, as this knowledge did not extend to being able to find out whether a particular bag of blood was defective). This decision means that the defence could only be used the very first time a risk becomes known. The blood authority knew the risk existed, so the defence could no longer apply.

Pause for reflection

Do you think the National Blood Authority should have been found liable, especially given that it is obliged under statute to provide blood and could not at the time screen for the presence of the Hepatitis C virus in blood samples?

see online resources

12.3.5 Overall effect of the Consumer Protection Act 1987

There have been very few cases under the CPA. While this might be in part due to high litigation costs, it might be argued that the Act has had a more silent effect in that the notion that manufacturers can be found to be strictly liable for harm caused by their products, even without negligence, may encourage more out-of-court settlements or have encouraged manufacturers to actually make their products safer. It might have been thought that the decision in *A*, where strict liability appeared to be taken to its strictest point, would mean that more claims would be brought by consumers. However, this does not appear to have happened and more recent cases tend to suggest that there is little benefit to bringing a claim under the Act rather than a claim in negligence, as well as a move away from the consumer-friendliness of *A*. Considerations of 'fault' seem to have crept into the CPA, particularly in the sense of what a defect can be said to be, despite Burton J's attempts in *A* not to 'dilute' the intentions underlying the CPA. That said, as mentioned earlier, it is yet to be seen which approach to determining defectiveness—that in *A* or the *Wilkes/Gee* approach—will be relied on in future cases.

Counterpoint

It also appears that the development risks defence actually undermines the aims of the CPA. Arguably, what it does is switch the burden of proof onto producers to show that when they designed the product that has caused harm, they took the care expected of an

→

→

expert/manufacturer at that time. In this respect, although strict liability in general and the CPA in particular were meant to make things easier for claimants in terms of *design* defects (remember that at common law the duty is clear and the courts are often willing to infer that a manufacturer was in breach (***Grant***),[47] meaning that it is relatively easy to sue for defects caused by the *manufacturing* process), it does not seem to have improved much at all. Claimants in the Thalidomide cases, for example, would have been no better off than they were in taking their claims in negligence. This, combined with the small number of cases actually taken under the CPA (and the even smaller number of successful claims), seems to suggest that it has been largely ineffective in achieving its supposed aims.[48]

Manufacturers have argued throughout the history of the implementation of the CPA that strict liability would, for example, hinder innovation and the placement of new, better and more cost-effective products onto the market. Strict liability, in their eyes, leads to increased costs, which in turn must be passed on to consumers. In turn, this leads to the question of whether private law mechanisms are an appropriate response to defects in products at all, or whether increased public law regulation would better benefit society. In relation to strict liability for products the argument is whether we feel it is better that manufacturers/producers should bear the costs of unknown risks (through insurance?) or whether consumers, through product choice, would be better equipped to make decisions based on the level of risk they are prepared to accept. Forcing producers to compensate through a strict liability regime forces product prices up (as producers bear all, or most, of the risk). In any case, imposing new or additional burdens on producers in the current economic climate would seem very unlikely.

However, the inhibition of innovation and design does not seem to have occurred in the 30 plus years since the CPA came into force—perhaps again suggesting that the Act itself is not as 'strict' as it could have been in imposing liability on manufacturers and that the behaviour of producers is unlikely to have been significantly altered by the presence of the Act.

47. It seems that this is also a possibility under the CPA: see *Ide* v *ATB Sales* [2008].

48. Though of course it may have a 'hidden' effect in encouraging either out-of-court settlements or swift(er) recall of defective products by manufacturers. See e.g. David Sanderson 'Hundreds burnt by toxic sofas to share £20 million compensation' *The Times* 27 April 2010; BBC News 'Pushchair maker Maclaren agrees compensation' 6 May 2010; BBC News 'Robinsons Fruit Shoot children's drink in safety recall' 3 July 2012; BBC News 'Aston Martin recalls 17,000 cars over possible defective part' 5 February 2014; BBC News 'Aldi chocolate recalled in salmonella scare' 5 January 2015; Hilary Osborne 'Ikea recalls child safety gates following accidents' *The Guardian* 23 June 2016; Mared Gruffydd 'B&Q adds another heater to recall list amid electric shock and fire fears' *Daily Express* 20 March 2021 and other examples on our **online resources**.

see online resources

12.4 Part 1 of the Consumer Protection Act 1987—annotated

In **Figure 12.1** we have annotated Part 1 of the Consumer Protection Act 1987, highlighting the key issues discussed in this chapter.

FIGURE 12.1 The Consumer Protection Act 1987, Part 1

Post-Brexit, regulations have been passed which will change the tense of s 1(1), so that it will read 'This part was enacted for the purpose...' and '...as was necessary...' (Product Safety and Metrology etc. (Amendment etc.) (EU Exit) Regulations 2019, SI 2019/696).

It is this EC Directive (85/374/EEC) that the UK had to implement, and did so by passing Part 1 of the CPA 1987—see the definition in s 1(2).

The Consumer Protection Act 1987

Part 1

1.—(1) This Part shall have effect for the purpose of making such provision as is necessary in order to comply with the product liability Directive and shall be construed accordingly.

(2) In this Part, except in so far as the context otherwise requires—

["agricultural produce" means any produce of the soil, of stock-farming or of fisheries;]

"dependant" and "relative" have the same meaning as they have in, respectively, the Fatal Accidents Act 1976 and the Damages (Scotland) Act 1976;

Anything in square brackets means this is a section inserted by later legislation or regulations.

See **Chapter 21**.

"producer", in relation to a product, means—

(a) the **person who manufactured it**;

(b) in the case of a substance which has not been manufactured but has been won or abstracted, **the person who won or abstracted it**;

(c) in the case of a product which has not been manufactured, won or abstracted but essential characteristics of which are attributable to an industrial or **other process having been carried out** (for example, in relation to agricultural produce), **the person who carried out that process**;

'Producers' are those that can be held liable under the Act—as the rest of this section reveals (see emboldened text), the concept of who a producer is has been quite broadly defined.

"product" means any goods or electricity and (subject to subsection (3) below) includes a product which is comprised in another product, whether by virtue of being a component part or raw material or otherwise;

Definition of 'products' for the purposes of the Act—see also s 45. The case ***A v National Blood Authority*** [2001] says that blood received in transfusions is also a 'product' covered by the Act.

and

"the product liability Directive" means the Directive of the Council of the European Communities, dated 25th July 1985, (No. 85/374/EEC) on the approximation of the laws, regulations and administrative provisions of the member States concerning liability for defective products.

(3) For the purposes of this Part a person who supplies any product in which products are comprised, whether by virtue of being component parts or raw materials or otherwise, shall not be treated by reason only of his supply of that product as supplying any of the products so comprised.

This is what makes a defendant liable—if they produce a product that has a defect which causes ***harm***.

2.—(1) Subject to the following provisions of this Part, where any damage is caused wholly or partly by a defect in a product, every person to whom subsection (2) below applies shall be liable for the damage.

(2) This subsection applies to—

See definition of 'producer', above (s 1).

(a) the producer of the product;

→

→

(b) any person who, by putting his name on the product or using a trade mark or other distinguishing mark in relation to the product, has held himself out to be the producer of the product;

(c) any person who has imported the product into a member State from a Place outside the member States in order, in the course of any business of his, to supply it to another.

(3) Subject as aforesaid, where any damage is caused wholly or partly by a defect in a product, any person who supplied the product (whether to the person who suffered the damage, to the producer of any product in which the product in question is comprised or to any other person) shall be liable for the damage if—

(a) the person who suffered the damage requests the supplier to identify one or more of the persons (whether still in existence or not) to whom subsection (2) above applies in relation to the product;

(b) that request is made within a reasonable period after the damage occurs and at a time when it is not reasonably practicable for the person making the request to identify all those persons; and

(c) the supplier fails, within a reasonable period after receiving the request, either to comply with the request or to identify the person who supplied the product to him.

...

(5) Where two or more persons are liable by virtue of this Part for the same damage, their liability shall be joint and several.

(6) This section shall be without prejudice to any liability arising otherwise than by virtue of this Part.

3.—(1) Subject to the following provisions of this section, there is a defect in a product for the purposes of this Part if the safety of the product is not such as persons generally are entitled to expect; and for those purposes "safety", in relation to a product, shall include safety with respect to products comprised in that product and safety in the context of risks of damage to property, as well as in the context of risks of death or personal injury.

(2) In determining for the purposes of subsection (1) above what persons generally are entitled to expect in relation to a product all the circumstances shall be taken into account, including—

(a) the manner in which, and purposes for which, the product has been marketed, its get-up, the use of any mark in relation to the product and any instructions for, or warnings with respect to, doing or refraining from doing anything with or in relation to the product;

(b) what might reasonably be expected to be done with or in relation to the product; and

(c) the time when the product was supplied by its producer to another;

and nothing in this section shall require a defect to be inferred from the fact alone that the safety of a product which is supplied after that time is greater than the safety of the product in question.

→

This means that 'own-branders' can be construed as producers, even if they did not actually make the product but someone else made it for them—e.g. Co-op's own-brand cornflakes. However, the situation is less clear if the distinction 'made for X' or 'selected for X' is used on a product—does this imply that the own-brander does not 'hold himself out to be the producer'?

Importers can also be construed as producers, meaning that there will always be someone in the EU who can be sued.

Post-Brexit, s 2(2)(c) is to be amended to remove reference to imports into 'member States', replacing it with '...imported the product into the United Kingdom' (Product Safety and Metrology etc. (Amendment etc.) (EU Exit)Regulations 2019).

This section provides that even suppliers (retailers) can be liable in certain (limited) circumstances, e.g. where the retailer either cannot or does not identify the producer.

For an explanation of this term, see the chapter on damages, **Chapter 21**.

People are generally entitled to expect what is 'socially accepted' as a risk that comes with the product—see e.g. *Richardson* v *LRC Products* [2000]; *Bogle* v *McDonald's* [2002] and contrast ***A* v *National Blood Authority***.

Definition of 'defect'—the key part of the Act and what most of the case law pertains to.

Later (controversially) re-defined by Burton J in ***A* v *National Blood Authority*** as 'all the relevant circumstances', excluding consideration of whether reasonable care was taken by the manufacturer.

e.g. the packaging.

e.g. industry standard marks such as the 'Kite Mark'.

Instructions or warnings with a product can render it 'safe' and therefore not defective—see e.g. *Worsley* v *Tambrands* [2000].

→

4.—(1) In any civil proceedings by virtue of this Part against any person ("the person proceeded against") in respect of a defect in a product it shall be a defence for him to show—

> It is controversial that any defences are built into the Act—but the liability is 'strict', not 'absolute'.

(a) that the defect is attributable to compliance with any requirement imposed by or under any enactment or with any Community obligation; or

> Post-Brexit, s 4(1)(a) is to be amended to read 'any retained Community obligation' (Product Safety and Metrology etc. (Amendment etc.) (EU Exit) Regulations 2019).

(b) that the person proceeded against did not at any time supply the product to another; or

(c) that the following conditions are satisfied, that is to say—

(i) that the only supply of the product to another by the person proceeded against was otherwise than in the course of a business of that person's; and

(ii) that section 2(2) above does not apply to that person or applies to him by virtue only of things done otherwise than with a view to profit; or

(d) that the defect did not exist in the product at the relevant time; or

(e) that the state of scientific and technical knowledge at the relevant time was not such that a producer of products of the same description as the product in question might be expected to have discovered the defect if it had existed in his products while they were under his control; or

> The 'development risks' or 'state of the art' defence. This is the most controversial of all the defences and the wording used in the CPA was challenged by the European Commission in ***EC* v *UK* [1997]**. They alleged that the CPA definition allowed a subjective interpretation of what a 'reasonable producer' could have been expected to know at the time, when the standard set by the Directive was meant to be objective. In that case it was deemed that all 'accessible' information or knowledge had to be taken into account.

(f) that the defect—

(i) constituted a defect in a product ("the subsequent product") in which the product in question had been comprised; and

(ii) was wholly attributable to the design of the subsequent product or to compliance by the producer of the product in question with instructions given by the producer of the subsequent product.

...

5.—(1) Subject to the following provisions of this section, in this Part "damage" means death or personal injury or any loss of or damage to any property (including land).

> Definition of 'damage'—i.e. what harms can be claimed for under the CPA. It is surprising, perhaps, that this definition comes so late.

(2) A person shall not be liable under section 2 above in respect of any defect in a product for the loss of or any damage to the product itself or for the loss of or any damage to the whole or any part of any product which has been supplied with the product in question comprised in it.

> This would be pure economic loss in negligence and is also irretrievable under the Act.

(3) A person shall not be liable under section 2 above for any loss of or damage to any property which, at the time it is lost or damaged, is not—

(a) of a description of property ordinarily intended for private use, occupation or consumption; and

→

→

(b) intended by the person suffering the loss or damage mainly for his own private use, occupation or consumption.

(4) No damages shall be awarded to any person by virtue of this Part in respect of any loss of or damage to any property if the amount which would fall to be so awarded to that person, apart from this subsection and any liability for interest, does not exceed £275.

To take a claim for property damage, the loss must amount to more than £275. This means small claims are excluded under the Act.

(5) In determining for the purposes of this Part who has suffered any loss of or damage to property and when any such loss or damage occurred, the loss or damage shall be regarded as having occurred at the earliest time at which a person with an interest in the property had knowledge of the material facts about the loss or damage.

(6) For the purposes of subsection (5) above the material facts about any loss of or damage to any property are such facts about the loss or damage as would lead a reasonable person with an interest in the property to consider the loss or damage sufficiently serious to justify his instituting proceedings for damages against a defendant who did not dispute liability and was able to satisfy a judgment.

(7) For the purposes of subsection (5) above a person's knowledge includes knowledge which he might reasonably have been expected to acquire—

(a) from facts observable or ascertainable by him; or

(b) from facts ascertainable by him with the help of appropriate expert advice which it is reasonable for him to seek;

but a person shall not be taken by virtue of this subsection to have knowledge of a fact ascertainable by him only with the help of expert advice unless he has failed to take all reasonable steps to obtain (and, where appropriate, to act on) that advice.

(8) Subsections (5) to (7) above shall not extend to Scotland.

...

12.5 Claiming under Part 1 of the Consumer Protection Act 1987—at a glance

See **Table 12.1.**

TABLE 12.1 Summary of the Consumer Protection Act 1987, Part 1

Issue	Relevant sections	Explanation
Who can sue?	Sections 2(1) and 5(1)	A person who 'suffers damage as a result of a defective product' (see definitions of 'damage' and 'defect')
Who can be sued?	Sections 1(2) and 5(2)	Manufacturers, producers, 'own-branders' and importers into the EU.* Some suppliers can also be sued
What damage can be claimed for?	Section 5(1) See also ss 5(2) and 5(4)	Death, personal injury and property damage Pure economic loss excluded and property damage must exceed £275
What is a 'product'?	Section 1(2) See also s 45	Goods and electricity, component parts and raw materials 'Goods' includes substances, growing crops, things on land and any ship, aircraft or vehicle
What is a 'defect'?	Section 3(1) See also s 3(2)(a)–(c)	A defect exists when 'the safety of a product is not such that persons generally are entitled to expect'—this is the most analysed aspect of the legislation in case law Packaging, normal use, instructions and warnings may be taken into account
Are any defences appropriate?	Section 4(1)(a)–(f)	There are six defences available under the Act Contributory negligence is also applicable

* As discussed in **n 22** earlier, post-Brexit this is to be amended to say 'importers into the United Kingdom'.

12.6 Conclusion

In this chapter we have considered the ways in which liability for defective products is regulated in tort law. This should be understood against a background knowledge of the provisions of *contract law*, which provide the backdrop to the development of the law of negligence in this area. A basic outline of the generous protections consumers can expect from contract law is included on our **online resources**. However, despite this protection, as well as reform to the doctrine of privity of contract, many end-users of products remain unable to take contractual claims in relation to faulty or defective

see online resources

products. There are two main reasons for this. First, end-users who did not purchase the product (and thereby enter a contract with the retailer) usually cannot sue despite changes to the doctrine of privity. Secondly, under contract it is impossible to directly sue the manufacturer, which in many cases will be the preferred option. Thus the law of contract has limitations in terms of consumer protection.

This chapter outlined the way the tort of *negligence* has been used by claimants who suffer damage as a result of a defective product. As in all negligence claims, the hurdles of establishing duty, breach and causation must be overcome. While the first two are not generally difficult (as ***Donoghue*** gives the duty and a breach is often inferred on the facts), causation issues can often stand in the way of a successful claim. This is particularly true when considering design defects and it was recognition of these limitations in negligence that led in part to calls for strict liability in this area.

Strict liability (where the producer of a product is held liable without the need for the injured party to show fault) for defective products was meant to have been introduced by the enactment of Part 1 of the CPA. However, the Act's definition of defect is weak, being based on what 'persons generally are entitled to expect' and much of the little case law has been devoted to finding that products are *not* defective. Furthermore, the inclusion of defences in the Act, particularly the *'development risks defence'* seems to suggest that liability remains somewhat subjective and contains elements of fault, thus not rendering it totally strict.

End-of-chapter questions

After reading the chapter carefully, try answering the questions which follow.

1 What are the advantages and disadvantages of having a system of strict liability in relation to defective products? Does strict liability make more sense when the harm suffered is personal injury?

2 Who should bear the risks and costs associated with innovation and increased consumer choice?

3 Do the provisions of Part 1 of the Consumer Protection Act 1987 achieve their aims?

If you would like to know what we think visit the **online resources**. www.oup.com/he/horsey7e

Answering the problem question

Consider again the problem question at the start of this chapter. Now having read about the topic, **what would be your advice to the claimants?**

Here are some pointers to get you started

→ The claimants would need to sue the 'producer', RHP, under s 1 of Part 1 of the Consumer Protection Act 1987, if they have suffered harms that are recognised under the Act (s 5). They would also need to establish that the drug is a 'product' covered by the Act. If they

→

→

succeed in their claim, RHP will be strictly liable (i.e. without the need to prove fault), subject to any defences.

- The central question is whether the drug was 'defective' (s 3). The different approaches in *A* v *National Blood Authority* and *Wilkes/Gee* should be considered, as well as other cases looking at the meaning of 'defect'.
- If it is, does RHP have any defences? Of particular interest here would be the 'development risks defence' (s 4(1)(e)). One criterion is that any knowledge that was published should have been 'accessible' (*EC* v *UK*)—was it?

If you need some more guidance

- An **annotated version of the problem with issues and cases to consider** can be found in the Appendix.
- A **suggested outline answer** to check your ideas against can be found in the online resources that accompany the book.

Further reading

Further reading on this subject often centres on critiques of the Consumer Protection Act 1987 and in particular the development risks defence. More recent work includes Eisler and Nolan, who both provide critical commentary on the decision in ***Wilkes*** about how 'defects' should be determined (though note both are pre-***Gee***), while reaching somewhat different conclusions.

Department of Trade and Industry *Guide to the Consumer Protection Act 1987*

Eisler, Jacob 'One Step Forward and Two Steps Back in Product Liability: The Search for Clarity in the Identification of Defects' [2017] CLJ 233

Fairgrieve, Duncan and Geraint Howells 'General Product Safety—A Revolution Through Reform?' (2006) 69 MLR 59

Gerling, Andrea 'A Matter of Degree: How a Jury Decided That a Coffee Spill is Worth $2.9 Million' *Wall Street Journal* 1 September 1994

Giliker, Paula 'Strict Liability for Defective Goods: The Ongoing Debate' (2003) 24 Bus L Rev 87

Howells, Geraint and Mark Mildred 'Infected Blood: Defect and Discoverability: A First Exposition of the EC Product Liability Directive' (2002) 65 MLR 95

Newdick, Christopher 'The Development Risks Defence of the Consumer Protection Act 1987' (1988) CLJ 455

Nolan, Donal 'Strict Product Liability for Design Defects' (2018) 134 LQR 176

Wuyts, Daily 'The Product Liability Directive—More Than Two Decades of Defective Products in Europe' (2014) 5 JETL 1

13 Employers' liability

Problem question

Read this problem question carefully, and keep it in mind while you are working through the chapter that follows. At the end of the chapter, you will be able to apply what you have learnt to the problem question and advise the relevant parties.

Every Tuesday, Thursday and Friday evening there is a drop-in centre for young people between the ages of 11 and 16 at Kings Wharf, a local community centre. It is run by a team of youth workers employed by James.

Harry is youth counsellor at the centre. He is busy setting up the hall for the evening's activities when he slips on a puddle of greasy water from a leaking radiator and breaks his wrist. He had reported the leak to his supervisor, Dougie, over a week earlier and it had not been fixed. Tom, a youth worker at the centre and Harry's partner, sees him fall. Frustrated by Dougie's lack of action, Tom punches him on the nose.

Danny works in the centre kitchen, making snacks and drinks for the young people. He is using a food processor to make some cookies when a fragment of metal is thrown off by the machine and enters his eye. The food processor had been serviced two weeks earlier in accordance with the provisions of the Kitchens Safety Act 2003 [a fictitious statute] which states that 'all moving parts on food-mixers must be maintained'.

Advise the parties.

13.1 Introduction

Consider the following situations:

→ ***A factory worker is seriously injured when a piece of metal breaks off the machine he is using and hits him in the eye.***

→ ***A window cleaner falls from her ladder. Her supervisor had not told her about the safety harness provided by her employers.***

→ ***An employee working in a fast-food restaurant accidentally slips on a pool of grease, which has seeped from a poorly maintained deep-fat fryer, breaking his ankle.***

→ ***A customer at a local nightclub is seriously injured when the club's bouncer beats him up for (wrongly) suspecting that he was attempting to jump the queue.***

All these are cases in which tortious liability might arise in the workplace. The common law and the various statutory provisions governing liability in the workplace impose a heavy burden on employers not only to ensure the safety of their workforce, but also in relation to torts committed by their employees against others in the course of their employment. An employer will typically be liable in tort in one of three ways:

(1) An employer owes a non-delegable common law duty of care to their employees and therefore may be *personally* liable for harm caused to their employees.[1]

(2) An employer may also be *personally* liable for the breach of a specific statutory duty, such as that arising out of the Employer's Liability (Defective Equipment) Act 1969.[2]

(3) An employer may be liable *vicariously* for injuries caused by an employee's tort committed in the course of their employment.

This chapter focuses on an employer's personal liability. Vicarious liability is discussed in **Chapter 20**.[3]

Pause for reflection

Historically it was extremely difficult for employees to recover for injuries suffered at work. The 'unholy trinity'—comprising the doctrine of common employment, which prevented an employee from suing their employer for injury negligently inflicted by a fellow employee (*Priestly v Fowler* [1837]), the defences of contributory negligence (an absolute bar to recovery until the Law Reform (Contributory Negligence) Act 1945) and *volenti non fit injuria*—effectively insulated employers from liability. Responsibility for safety in the workplace rested primarily with

→

1. Non-delegable duties do not only arise in an employment context or between employers and employees. See e.g. *Woodland* v *Essex County Council* [2013] which established that a school owed a non-delegable duty of care towards its pupils, as do hospitals towards their patients (discussed in **section 20.2**).

2. Until recently an employer could also be liable in the tort of breach of statutory duty, which enables a claimant in certain circumstances to recover compensation for losses caused by the defendant's failure to comply with a statutory obligation. However, s 69 of the Enterprise and Regulatory Reform Act 2013 prevents claims from being brought against an employer unless specifically provided for by the statute or where it can be proven, on ordinarily common law principles, that the employer has been negligent (see further **section 13.2**). The Employer's Liability (Defective Equipment) Act 1969 is unaffected because it is not classified as 'health and safety legislation' under the Health and Safety at Work Act 1974.

3. The nightclub owner in the example at the start of the chapter may be both *personally* liable to the injured customer (e.g. if they were negligent in their selection and/or control of the bouncer) and *vicariously* liable (see *Mattis* v *Pollock (t/a Flamingos Nightclub)* [2003] discussed in **Chapter 20**).

→

those least able to ensure it—the employees. The situation began to change towards the end of the nineteenth century as a combination of the growth in the power of trade unions, greater awareness of hazardous working conditions (particularly on the railways) and the increasing availability of employers' liability insurance encouraged the judiciary and the legislature to mitigate the harshness of these rules. And, by the mid-twentieth century, all three obstacles had either been abolished or strictly confined.[4]

Until recently employees were in a stronger position than many other accident victims and, as a result, workplace litigation (which includes actions for vicarious liability against employers) has generated a large number of tort claims.[5] The threat of adverse publicity and a desire to maintain labour/public relations means that many employers are likely to settle out of court and the Employers' Liability (Compulsory Insurance) Act 1969, which makes it compulsory for employers to insure against workplace accidents, means that employers are likely to be able to meet any award of damages.

As a result, someone injured at work (or by an employee acting 'in the course of their employment') is more likely to be able to claim and, importantly, recover than someone who suffers the same injury outside the workplace. Do you think this is fair? What are the justifications for this? Consider the following arguments: (a) employees often have limited control over the situations they find themselves in at work, while employers are in a position to ensure that the conditions they provide are safe; (b) imposing liability on employers encourages them to improve working conditions (something they are uniquely able to do); and (c) employers are (or at least should be) better informed about the various hazards of the working environment (e.g. the machinery or chemicals they use), unlike an employee who may be inexperienced in the industry and may not be aware of the risks and, therefore, know how to take care.

13.2 An employer's personal non-delegable duty of care

An employer's personal duty of care, established in ***Wilsons & Clyde Coal Co Ltd* v *English*** **[1938]** requires an employer to see that reasonable care is taken for their employees' safety. That an employer owes their employees a personal duty to take reasonable care to ensure their health and safety at work, competent work colleagues and so on is perhaps unremarkable. What is more remarkable is the form this duty takes. Unusually, this duty is non-delegable in nature.[6] This means that it is not enough for the employer themselves to take reasonable care to see that their employees are safe. Rather, their duty

4. The doctrine of common employment was abolished by the Law Reform (Personal Injuries) Act 1948, s 1.

5. Compensation claims against employers comprised the third highest number of claims registered with the Department for Work and Pensions Compensation Recovery Unit in 2017–18, which amounted to just over 8 per cent of the overall claims (n = 69,230). This is down from 105,291 claims in 2013–14, which is likely to be, at least in part, a result of the Enterprise and Regulatory Reform Act 2013, s 69 (see further **section 13.2.2**).

6. Though see Robert Stevens 'Non-Delegable Duties and Vicarious Liability' in Jason Neyers, Erika Chamberlain and Stephen Pitel (eds) *Emerging Issues in Tort Law* (Hart, 2007).

is to ensure that reasonable care *is* taken. This may not sound like much of a difference. Its significance can be seen when we consider that in many businesses it is simply not feasible for the owner themselves to supervise all aspects of the day-to-day running of the business. In practice, all we can expect employers to do in such situations is to take reasonable care to ensure that the people they choose to delegate these jobs to are capable of doing so. However, the consequence of an employer's duty of care being non-delegable means that an employer will have breached their duty if those they have entrusted with responsibility fail to exercise reasonable care in respect of the employees' safety, *even if the employer has exercised reasonable care in the appointment of those they entrusted*. The employer cannot escape liability by showing that they themselves acted reasonably in delegating this task to the relevant person. In other words, if reasonable care is not taken to ensure that employees are reasonably safe when at work, the employer will be held to have breached their duty of care.[7] It makes no difference that it was not the employer but rather the person to whom they had delegated this responsibility who had acted carelessly. In short, while *factual* responsibility for employees' safety may (and often will have to) be delegated, *legal* responsibility cannot be.

Once an employer is found to be in breach of their non-delegable or statutory duty of care (i.e. to have fallen below the standard of a 'reasonable and prudent employer'),[8] it is necessary to establish a causal link between this breach and the claimant's harm. This can be easier stated than done (see e.g. ***Fairchild* v *Glenhaven Funeral Services Ltd* [2002]** and related litigation) and to consider any potential defences (usually contributory negligence).

Wilsons & Clyde Coal Co Ltd v *English* [1938] HL

A miner was crushed in a mining accident after haulage equipment was set in motion as he was travelling through the pit at the end of the day (contrary to recognised mining practice). He sued the mine owners on the basis that they had failed to provide a reasonably safe system of work. The defendants claimed they had discharged their duty by appointing (as required by statute) a competent and qualified manager to control the machinery.

The House of Lords unanimously rejected the employer's argument. Finding the employer personally liable, Lord Wright said:

> [T]he [employer's] obligation is fulfilled by the exercise of due care and skill. But it is not fulfilled by entrusting its fulfilment to employees, even though selected with due care

→

7. Conversely, if reasonable care is taken the employer will not be liable. An example of this is the Supreme Court's decision in *Baker* v *Quantum Clothing Group* [2011] in which the claimants had suffered hearing loss as a result of industrial noise before the Noise at Work Regulations were introduced in 1989. On the employer's common law duty in negligence, the majority held that until the regulations were introduced (and allowing a period for implementation) the harm suffered by the claimants was not foreseeable, and hence there was no liability in negligence.

8. See *Stokes* v *Guest, Keene and Nettlefold (Bolts and Nuts) Ltd* [1968] and discussion in **section 8.3.2** and **section 8.4**.

→

> and skill. The obligation is threefold, the provision of a competent staff of men, adequate material, and a proper system and effective supervision. (at 78)

The failure of the manager to ensure the health and safety of the claimant had put the employer, the defendant mine company, in breach of *its* duty of care.

Pause for reflection

It might be asked why the claimant did not sue the defendants on the ground that they were vicariously liable for the actions of the manager. The answer lies in the doctrine of 'common employment' which, until its abolition in 1948, prevented an employee from suing their fellow employees for injuries they had negligently caused—and hence an employer could not be vicariously liable. An employee was deemed to have assumed the risk of negligence by their fellow employees (provided they had been selected with reasonable care by their employer) as one of the terms of their employment contract. Thus, as the miner had no claim against his manager, there could be no vicarious claim against the mine owner.

Where similar facts to *Wilsons & Clyde Coal Co Ltd* arise today, employees would be able to argue that their employer is both personally *and* vicariously liable for the actions of their manager.

An employer's non-delegable duty is typically said to have four components (building on Lord Wright's statement in ***Wilsons & Clyde Coal Co Ltd***) comprising the provision of:

- a competent workforce;
- adequate material and equipment;
- a safe system of working (including effective supervision);
- a safe workplace.

Although often considered separately for the sake of convenience or argument, as is the discussion below, they are, in fact, best regarded as manifestations of a single duty on the part of an employer to take reasonable care to ensure the safety of their workforce (*Wilson* v *Tyneside Window Cleaning Co* [1958]).

13.2.1 Competent workforce

An employer owes their employees a duty to ensure that they employ competent colleagues, including effective supervision and training. This extends to the bullying, victimisation or harassment of an employee by another employee (*Waters* v *Commissioner of Police for the Metropolis* [2000]).[9] This aspect of an employer's personal non-delegable duty is of less

9. An employer may also find themselves vicariously liable in respect of such behaviour (see ***Majrowski*** v ***Guy's and St Thomas' NHS Trust*** [2006] discussed in **Chapter 20**).

importance following the abolition of the doctrine of common employment; however, it may still be useful in circumstances where an employer is not vicariously liable. In *Hudson v Ridge Manufacturing Co* [1957], for example, an employee was injured when a colleague, who had a reputation for being a practical joker, tripped him up. Though the joker had been officially reprimanded for his behaviour by his employer, the court nevertheless held that given the seriousness of his conduct the employer should have done more to deter it, and in failing to do so, was in breach of their duty of care to the injured employee.

13.2.2 **Adequate material and equipment**

An employer also has a duty to take reasonable care to provide all necessary equipment (including safety equipment), as well as instructions on how to use it and to maintain it in a reasonable condition.

Here the common law has been supplemented by the Employer's Liability (Defective Equipment) Act 1969. Section 1(1) establishes that if an employee is injured in the course of employment by a defect in equipment provided by their employer and the employee can prove that the defect was (wholly or partly) caused by the fault of a third party (usually the manufacturer) then the employer will be liable.[10] The purpose of the Act was to overcome the effects of *Davie* v *New Merton Board Mills Ltd* [1959]. In this case, an employee was blinded in one eye when a piece of metal chipped off the tool he was using. The tool had been negligently manufactured (causing it to become too hard for its purpose), although externally it appeared to be in good condition. Rejecting the claimant's claim for compensation from his employer, the House of Lords held that the employers had discharged their responsibility to provide proper tools by purchasing them from a reputable supplier. The practical effect of this decision was to leave the employee without compensation where the supplier or manufacturer could not be identified or was bankrupt.

Counterpoint

Despite its wide scope, the Employer's Liability (Defective Equipment) Act 1969 does not completely remedy the problems posed by *Davie* v *New Merton Board Mills Ltd*. As well as establishing causation—that is, that the defect in the equipment caused the accident—the employee needs to prove 'fault' against the third party—that is, that on the balance of probabilities the defect was due to the fault of some other person (usually during its manufacture). This is not always easy. Potential claimants may, however, be helped in this by the Consumer Protection Act 1987 as the definition of fault in the 1969 Act includes 'breach of statutory duty or other act or omission which gives rise to liability in tort'.

Despite its limitations, the Employer's Liability (Defective Equipment) Act 1969 is likely to have a new lease of life following the enactment of the Enterprise and Regulatory Reform Act 2013. Nigel Tomkins notes:

→

10 Thus, while the employee, in order to succeed against their employer, first has to succeed against a third party, if successful, the employer will usually have a claim for contribution/indemnity from the third party.

→

[quoting Lord Oliver in *Coltman* v *Bibby Tankers Ltd (The Derbyshire)* [1988]]: 'The purpose of the Act was manifestly to saddle the employer with liability for defective plant of every sort with which the employee is compelled to work in the course of his employment . . . ' I have no doubt that the 1969 Act is about to be dusted off and used again. This is just one of the inevitable consequences of [section 69]. (2013, p 211)

Equipment, defined by section 1(3) of the 1969 Act as 'any plant and machinery, vehicle, aircraft or clothing', has been construed relatively broadly, extending in *Coltman* v *Bibby Tankers Ltd (The Derbyshire)* to include a ship provided by the employer for the purposes of employment. In *Knowles* v *Liverpool City Council* [1993] the House of Lords held that 'equipment' also included any material used by the employee for the purposes of the business—in that case a paving stone which the claimant was laying and was injured by.

However, an employer may be able to avoid liability in relation to a failure to provide safety equipment if they can establish that, even if such equipment had been provided, the employee would not have used it. The argument here is one of causation: the employer is in clear breach of their duty, but as the claimant would have suffered the same injury in any case, their failure to provide safe equipment cannot be said to have been a cause of the employee's injuries.

McWilliam v _Sir William Arrol & Co Ltd_ [1962] HL

The claimant, a steel erector, fell to his death at work. He was not wearing a safety harness. His employers had failed (in breach of their statutory duty) to provide safety equipment. However, the House of Lords held that they were not liable for the claimant's death. The employers were able to provide strong evidence that the employee rarely, if ever, used a safety harness and so, even if one had been provided, it was reasonable to infer that he would not have worn it. As such, he would have suffered the same injury even if the employers had provided the necessary equipment.

13.2.3 A proper system of working (including effective supervision)

An employer has a duty to ensure a reasonably safe system of working and to give employees general safety instructions about their job. This includes the physical layout of the job, the sequence in which work is carried out and the provision, where appropriate, of warnings and notices. Thus, in *Pape* v *Cumbria County Council* [1992] a part-time cleaner who contracted dermatitis after working with various detergents and chemical cleaning products was able to recover as, although the defendants had provided rubber gloves, they did not warn her of the possibility of developing dermatitis, nor instruct her to wear them. It was not, it seems, enough to simply *provide* the rubber gloves, the employer should also have taken reasonable steps to ensure that the safety equipment was properly understood and used by the claimant.

Pause for reflection

It could be argued that *Pape* makes the employer liable for something which is really the employee's responsibility: after all, should employees really need to be told when to use the safety equipment provided? Why do you think the court came to this decision? It could be suggested that holding an employer liable in these circumstances will encourage safer working practices more generally. Do you agree?

The employer must not only ensure that there is a safe system of work, they must also take care to see that the system is implemented (*Mullaney* v *Chief Constable of West Midlands Police* [2001]). They are expected to be aware that employees are often careless about taking safety precautions and that dangerous working practices can develop. In *General Cleaning Contractors* v *Christmas* [1953] a window cleaner was standing on the sill outside a first-floor window when the window unexpectedly closed. The court held that the employer should have given the employee clearer instructions so as to ensure such accidents did not happen and in failing to do so they had not provided a safe system of work.

The nature and extent of an employer's supervision was extended further in *Jebson* v *Ministry of Defence* [2000]. A group of soldiers had gone for a night out. Anticipating that they would be worse for wear, the defendants—the soldiers' employer—sent a lorry to pick them up and bring them back to barracks. The claimant, who was very drunk, fell and injured himself as he attempted to climb onto the roof of the lorry on its way home. In allowing his claim for compensation, the Court of Appeal held that the defendants had failed to ensure an effective system of supervision. Knowing the soldiers' drunken state, the defendants ought to have had a supervisor in the back of the lorry to ensure that none of them injured themselves.

An employer remains under a duty to ensure a safe system of work for an employee even when the employee is temporarily posted elsewhere. In *McDermid* v *Nash Dredging & Reclamation Co Ltd* [1987] an 18-year-old deckhand was instructed by his employer, the defendant company, to work on a tug owned by the defendants' parent company. He suffered serious injuries to his leg as a result of the captain of the tug's negligence. The issue was whether the deckhand's employer was liable for the captain's failure to operate a safe system of work. The House of Lords held that the defendants were liable on the basis that they retained personal responsibility for the deckhand's safety notwithstanding that he was working outside their workplace:

> It matters not whether one says that there was no 'system' in operation at all, or whether one says that the system provided was unsafe, or whether one says that the system in fact provided was not in use at the crucial stage. In any event the defendants had delegated their duty to the plaintiff to Captain Sas [the captain of the tug], the duty had not been performed, and the defendants must pay for the breach of their 'non-delegable' obligation. (Lord Hailsham at 911)

However, an employer's duty to ensure a safe system of work only extends so far. As Pearce LJ noted in *Wilson* v *Tyneside Window Cleaning Co*:

> Now it is true that in ***Wilsons & Clyde Coal Co Ltd*** **v** ***English*** **[1938]** Lord Wright divided up the duty of a master into three main headings, for convenience of definition or argument; but all three are ultimately only manifestations of the same duty of the master to take reasonable care so to carry out his operations as not to subject those employed by him to unnecessary risk. Whether the servant is working on the premises of the master or those of a stranger, that duty is still, as it seems to me, the same; but as a matter of common sense its performance and discharge will probably be vastly different in the two cases. The master's own premises are under his control: if they are dangerously in need of repair he can and must rectify the fault at once if he is to escape the censure of negligence. But if a master sends his plumber to mend a leak in a respectable private house, no one could hold him negligent for not visiting the house himself to see if the carpet in the hall creates a trap. Between these extremes are countless possible examples in which the court may have to decide the question of fact: Did the master take reasonable care so to carry out his operations as not to subject those employed by him to unnecessary risk? Precautions dictated by reasonable care when the servant works on the master's premises may be wholly prevented or greatly circumscribed by the fact that the place of work is under the control of a stranger. Additional safeguards intended to reinforce the man's own knowledge and skill in surmounting difficulties or dangers may be reasonable in the former case but impracticable and unreasonable in the latter. So viewed, the question whether the master was in control of the premises ceases to be a matter of technicality and becomes merely one of the ingredients, albeit a very important one, in a consideration of the question of fact whether, in all the circumstances, the master took reasonable care. (at 266–7)

Thus, in *Cook* v *Square D Ltd* [1992], the Court of Appeal held that though the employer is under a duty to take reasonable steps to ensure the safety of their employee, they could not reasonably be expected to be responsible for daily events on a site in Saudi Arabia and so were not in breach of their duty when the employee was injured after slipping on a raised floor tile. Where an employer is on another's premises, their liability will depend on what is reasonable in the circumstances—including the place of work, the nature of the building, the experience of the employee, the nature of the work, the degree of control exercised by the employer and his knowledge of the premises.

In recent years, the courts have recognised that as well as ensuring an employee's physical safety, an employer's duty also encompasses (at least in some cases) that reasonable care is taken to prevent *psychiatric* injury, including workplace stress[11] and suicide (*Corr* v *IBC Vehicles Ltd* [2008]; *Waters* v *Commissioner of Police for the Metropolis* [2000]). It may also extend to some aspects of an employee's *economic* wellbeing—such as writing a reference (***Spring*** **v** ***Guardian Assurance*** **[1995]**)[12]—though this does not extend to protection of an employee's property (*Deyong* v *Shenburn* [1946]).

11. See further discussion in **section 5.7.5**.

12. See also *James-Bowen and others* v *Commissioner of Police for the Metropolis (Rev 1)* [2016], in which the Court of Appeal refused to strike out the claim of four police officers for economic and reputational harm suffered in the conduct of litigation (at [33]–[36]): 'Although the existence of a duty of care as between employer and employee is well established, no case has been drawn to our attention in which the court has been asked to consider whether it extends to the conduct of litigation and if so whether it extends to economic or reputational harm. Whether it does, or may do so, is likely to depend to a large extent on whether the court considers that the third requirement identified in

13.2.4 A safe workplace

An employer must take reasonable care to provide a safe place of work. However, this does not mean that the employer must ensure that the workplace is completely safe.[13]

> ***Latimer* v *AEC Ltd* [1953] HL**
>
> Heavy rainfall flooded the defendant's factory. The rainwater mixed with an oily liquid, which usually collected in channels in the floor. This meant that when the water drained away the floor became very slippery. The defendants put down sawdust to remedy this; however there was insufficient sawdust to cover the entire floor. Nevertheless, the majority of the floor was covered. The claimant slipped on part of the untreated floor and broke his ankle.
>
> The House of Lords held that the defendants were not liable. They had done everything that could reasonably be expected of them. The danger of injury to their employees was not such as to impose on the employer further costly and inconvenient measures, for example closing the factory until the floor had completely dried out.[14]

13.3 Conclusion

In this chapter we have considered ways in which an employer may be personally liable in tort for injury suffered by one of their employees. An employer owes a personal non-delegable duty of care to their employees to ensure a safe workplace for their employees. This sees that the employer remains responsible for key tasks even when the performance of them has been delegated to another. The duty arises from the direct nature of the relationship between the claimant and the defendant—the conduct of the delegated employee is used to establish breach. An employee may also recover compensation for losses caused by the employer's failure to comply with a statutory obligation.

Caparo* v *Dickman is satisfied, namely, that it would be fair, just and reasonable for a duty of care to be imposed on the employer in those circumstances. That is likely to involve a question of legal policy and I agree with the judge that the court should not strike out a claim on that ground at an early stage unless the position is very clear' (Moore-Bick LJ at [34]).

13. See also *Nicholls* v *Ladbrokes Betting and Gambling Ltd* [2013] in which the claimant suffered psychiatric harm as a result of being traumatised during an armed raid at the betting shop where she worked as a cashier. The employer was held not to be in breach of his duty of care in failing to instruct the employee to use the magnetic lock on the premises: 'In my view it cannot ordinarily be negligent to fail to ensure that a safety or security device is used if it would not have been negligent not to have installed the device in the first place' (Tomlinson LJ).

14. Are the facts of ***Latimer*** distinguishable from those of the example at the beginning of the chapter where the employee slips on a pool of grease in a fast-food restaurant? The answer depends on whether efforts have been made to make the floor safe. As you are told that the machine is poorly maintained it is likely that the manager would have had an opportunity to put this right (unlike the sudden effects of the heavy rainfall in ***Latimer***).

End-of-chapter questions

After reading the chapter carefully, try answering the question which follows.

1 Critically evaluate the development of the common law duty of care employers owe to their employees.

If you would like to know what we think visit the **online resources**. www.oup.com/he/horsey7e

Answering the problem question

Consider again the problem question at the start of this chapter. Now having read about the topic, **what would be your advice to the various parties?**

Here are some pointers to get you started

→ The potential claim between Harry and James raises an almost classic case of an employer's non-delegable duty of care.

→ Danny has two potential actions: one relying on the Employer's Liability (Defective Equipment) Act 1969 and one for breach of statutory duty (under the fictitious Kitchens Safety Act 2003).

→ James will be vicariously liable for Tom's actions—see further discussion in Chapter 20.

If you need more guidance

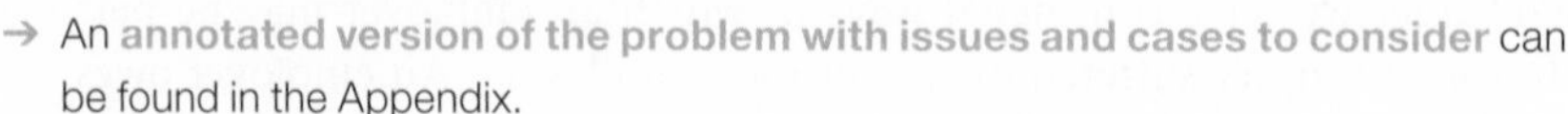

→ An **annotated version of the problem with issues and cases to consider** can be found in the Appendix.

see online resources

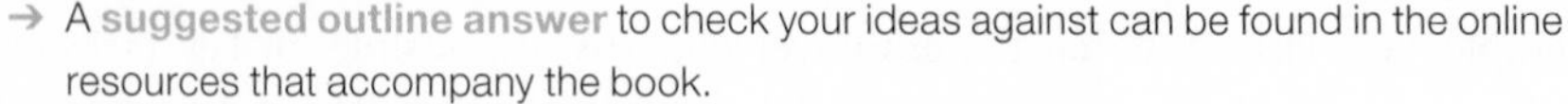

→ A **suggested outline answer** to check your ideas against can be found in the online resources that accompany the book.

Further reading

The best place to start your further reading is with Tomkins' 2010 article which explores the evolution of an employer's common law duty of care.

Collins, Hugh *Employment Law* (2nd edn, OUP, 2010)

Patten, Keith 'Personal Injury: Step Back in Time' (2013) 163 NLJ 62

Tomkins, Nigel 'First Principles in Employers' Liability' [2010] JPIL 131

Tomkins, Nigel 'Civil Health and Safety Law after the Enterprise and Regulatory Reform Act 2013' [2013] JPIL 203

Breach of statutory duty

14

14.1 Introduction

Consider the following situations:

→ ***A postal worker contracts mesothelioma caused by regular visits to a factory where he is exposed to asbestos dust.***

→ ***A farmer's sheep are swept overboard in rough seas. They had not been securely penned.***

→ ***A bus driver suffers frostbite as a result of a hole in his left boot (which had been supplied by his employer) after attempting to dig out his bus after it gets stuck in snow.***

Although the expression 'breach of statutory duty' can be used to describe *any* breach of a tortious duty created by statute, 'breach of statutory duty' is also a tort in its own right. As such it is separate to and conceptually distinct from the general common law principles of the tort of negligence. The tort of breach of statutory duty enables a claimant in certain circumstances to recover compensation for losses caused by a defendant's failure to comply with a statutory obligation. Historically, the tort has played an important role in ensuring safety in the workplace by providing employees with an avenue for compensation that avoided the harshness of the doctrine of common employment—though its role in this regard has been substantially restricted by section 69 of the Enterprise and Regulatory Reform Act 2013.

Unlike the statutory duties contained in the Occupiers' Liability Acts 1957 and 1984, the Protection from Harassment Act 1997 or the Consumer Protection Act 1987 where liability arises directly according to the provisions of the statute, a civil action for the tort of breach of statutory duty liability arises *indirectly* where a statute imposes a duty (typically relating to criminal liability) but does not identify a civil remedy in the event of its breach. The tort of breach of statutory duty is, therefore, a combination of common law and statute—the duty lies in the statute, the action in the common law:

> A claim for damages for breach of a statutory duty intended to protect a person in the position of the particular plaintiff is a specific common law right which is not to be confused in

> essence with a claim for negligence. The statutory right has its origin in the statute, but the particular remedy of an action for damages is given by the common law in order to make effective, for the benefit of the injured plaintiff, his right to performance by the defendant of the defendant's statutory duty . . . It is not a claim in negligence in the strict or ordinary sense . . . (Lord Wright, *London Passenger Transport Board* v *Upson* [1949] at 168–9)

The tort of breach of statutory duty exists alongside—and independently of—the tort of negligence. Such that a defendant may be liable for breach of statutory duty (e.g. where an Act imposes strict liability) but not so in negligence and, conversely, a defendant may be liable in negligence even where they have fulfilled their statutory duty.

Moreover, not every breach of a statutory duty gives rise to a claim in tort (***Lonrho Ltd* v *Shell Petroleum Co Ltd (No 2)*** [1982]). Civil liability does not arise automatically. In order to establish the tort of breach of statutory duty four questions (in addition to the usual requirements relating to causation and defences) need to be addressed:

(1) Does the statute give rise to a claim in tort law?

(2) Is a duty owed to the claimant?

(3) Has the defendant breached their duty?

(4) Does the claimant's loss or injury fall within the scope of the duty?

The first of these questions—that is, whether Parliament intended there to be a civil remedy—is often the most contentious.

14.2 Does the statute give rise to a claim in tort law?

Clearly there is no problem where a statute explicitly states whether a breach of its provisions gives rise to a remedy in tort as, for example, in section 3 of the Protection from Harassment Act 1997. Rather, difficulties arise when the statute imposes a duty but is silent as to whether it intended there to be a civil action for its breach. In such circumstances, the court must 'divine' the will or intention of Parliament. This is essentially a matter of statutory interpretation. It is clear that a breach of a public statutory duty does not always give rise to a claim, however nor does it follow that because Parliament has not included such a provision, that no remedy exists. Everything turns on the object and language of the particular statute (*Atkinson* v *Newcastle Waterworks Co* [1877]).

The process of establishing whether Parliament intended there to be a civil remedy in relation to a particular statute has been described by Glanville Williams as 'looking for what is not there' (1960, at 244). Lord Denning MR said something similar in *Ex p Island Records Ltd* [1978]:

> The truth is that in many cases the legislature has left the point open . . . the dividing line between the pro-cases and the contra-cases is so blurred that you may as well toss a coin to decide it. (at 135)

Pause for reflection

Why do you think this is? Why might Parliament be unwilling to specify whether a civil remedy is available should a defendant breach a statutorily imposed duty? Think about who the defendants in an action for breach of statutory duty are likely to be. Although traditionally actions for breach of statutory duty were more likely to have been brought against individuals, usually employers, the tort is not limited in this way. And more recently a number of largely unsuccessful claims have been brought against public authorities (see e.g. *R* v *Deputy Governor of Parkhurst, ex p Hague* [1992]; *X (Minors)* v *Bedfordshire County Council* [1995]; ***Phelps* v *Hillingdon London Borough Council*** [2001]; *O'Rourke* v *Camden London Borough Council* [1997]). Given the subject matter of these claims—the treatment of prisoners, child protection, education and the provision of social housing—it may well be politically astute to place responsibility for the absence of a civil law remedy following a public body's failure to perform its statutory duty at the feet of the judiciary rather than to explicitly state it in the statute itself.

***Lonrho Ltd* v *Shell Petroleum Co Ltd (No 2)* [1982] HL**

Lonrho Ltd brought an action for breach of statutory duty in respect of heavy financial losses it had sustained (in contrast to its competitors) as a result of complying with sanctions imposed on the supply of oil following the unilateral declaration of independence (UDI) by Southern Rhodesia (now the Republic of Zimbabwe) in 1965.

The House of Lords rejected the claim. In his leading opinion, Lord Diplock identified a number of factors that the courts should take into account when assessing whether breach of a statutory obligation gives rise to civil liability. Accepting the presumption in *Doe d Bishop of Rochester* v *Bridges* [1824–34], that '[w]here an Act creates an obligation and enforces the performance in a specified manner we take it as a general rule that performance cannot be enforced in any other manner' (Lord Tenterden at 859), Lord Diplock outlined two exceptions to this general rule: where the statutory duty is imposed for the protection of a limited class of people and where the statute creates a public right and a particular member of the public suffers 'special damage'[1] (at 185–6).

Neither exception was applicable in this case as the sanctions, in the words of Fox LJ in the Court of Appeal, were not 'concerned with conferring rights either on individuals or the public at large. Their purpose was the destruction, by economic pressure, of the UDI regime in Southern Rhodesia; they were instruments of state policy on an international matter' (at 86).

In *X (Minors)* v *Bedfordshire County Council,* Lord Browne-Wilkinson confirmed that though there is no general rule by which to determine whether a statute gives rise to civil liability, courts may refer to a number of 'indicators'. These include whether the duty was imposed for the protection of a limited class of the public; other remedies

1. e.g. where the defendant's breach amounts to a public nuisance (see **section 18.5**) or misfeasance in public office.

provided for by the statute;[2] the extent to which the statute's scope is limited and specific or general and administrative; as well as various, ubiquitous policy considerations (at 731–2).[3] An example may help here.

Groves v *Lord Wimborne* [1898] CA

The claimant, a young boy, seriously injured his arm in the cog-wheels of a steam winch while working in the defendant's iron works (his forearm was later amputated). The machinery had been left unfenced contrary to section 5 of the Factory and Workshop Act 1878, which imposed an absolute duty on the employer to ensure that certain dangerous machinery was fenced.

The Court of Appeal allowed Groves's claim against his employer. The question for the court was whether the existence of alternative sanctions for breaching this duty (in the form of fines or penalties) prevented a claim for breach of statutory duty on the part of the claimant. The Court of Appeal recognised the existence of alternative means of enforcing the duty as a *factor* to be taken into account, however, it was, Vaughan Williams LJ argued, 'by no means conclusive or the only matter to be taken into consideration' when determining whether an action will lie for non-performance of that duty (at 416). Other factors included whether the statute was passed for the benefit of the public at large or a particular class of people.

Pause for reflection

Consider the timing of the decision in ***Groves***. Since the early nineteenth century, the development of the railway system and increasing industrialisation had led to a huge rise in the numbers of accidents and injuries, particularly in the workplace. Working conditions in many factories and quarries were extremely hazardous—hence the need for Acts of Parliament such as the Factory and Workshop Act 1878. Nevertheless, the onus was very much on the *employee* to take responsibility for their own safety and, importantly, to bear the severe personal and

→

2. See e.g. *Morrison Sports Ltd* v *Scottish Power* [2010], in which the claimants sought to bring a civil action against Scottish Power UK on the basis that its breach of reg 17 of the Electricity Supply Regulations 1988 had caused a fire which had damaged their property. The court concluded that the overall legislative scheme suggested that Parliament had not intended that a breach of the relevant provisions of the 1988 Regulations should give rise to a private law statutory right of action: 'There is no basis whatever for thinking that the drafter of the provision intended to introduce a civil right of action but—somehow—botched that comparatively straightforward task and came up with the words in the subsection which are so singularly ill-suited to the supposed purpose' (Lord Rodger at [16]). Rather, the wording of the subsection was to allow for both the payment of a criminal fine and a civil remedy, if so provided for by the Secretary of State (at [27]).

3. As well as the claim for breach of statutory duty, the claimants also sued in negligence (see discussion of ***Z and others* v *UK*** **[2001]** and ***TP and KM* v *UK*** **[2001]** in **section 6.4.2**). It is possible given the considerable doubting of the negligence aspects of this decision in ***Z*** and ***D* v *East Berkshire Community NHS Trust*** **[2005]** that the court's reasoning in relation to breach of statutory duty may also be reconsidered in future cases.

→

financial consequences of any injuries suffered—a view encapsulated in the doctrine of common employment set down in *Priestly* v *Fowler* [1837].

However, towards the end of the century there were signs that societal attitudes were beginning to change. The Workmen's Compensation Act 1897 imposed, for the first time, liability on employers in relation to 'accidents arising out of and in the course of employment'. This change was also reflected in the courts. Just six years earlier, the House of Lords had sought to limit the scope of the defence of consent in a case involving an employee who was injured when a stone fell from an overhead crane. The court held that the employer could not escape liability by arguing that the employee had 'voluntarily accepted the risk' by virtue of the fact that the employee had continued to work there despite knowing of the danger of injury (*Smith* v *Charles Baker & Sons* [1891]).

The decision in ***Groves*** was another blow to the so-called 'unholy trinity'.[4] At the time there was no other way the claimant could have obtained a remedy in tort (a claim in negligence would have been defeated by the doctrine of common employment). The statutory duty, however, was absolute and, importantly, imposed directly on the employer. Its approach reflected the mood of the time and the case was hugely important in establishing an oasis of protection for employees.

More recently, it seems the mood has swung the other way. Buoyed by a general feeling of antagonism towards health and safety 'madness',[5] in 2013 the Coalition Government enacted the Enterprise and Regulatory Reform Act.[6] Section 69 amends section 47(2) of the Health and Safety at Work etc Act 1974 by reversing the original section—which provided that a 'breach of a duty imposed by health and safety regulations shall, so far as it causes damage, be actionable except in so far as the regulations provide otherwise'—with a presumption in the opposite direction: a 'breach of a duty imposed by a statutory instrument containing (whether alone or with other provision) health and safety regulations shall not be actionable except to the extent that regulations under this section so provide' (s 69(3)).[7]

→

4. The 'unholy trinity' comprising the doctrine of common employment, which prevented an employee from suing their employer for injury negligently inflicted by a fellow employee (*Priestly* v *Fowler* [1837]), contributory negligence (which until 1945 was an absolute bar to recover) and *volenti non fit injuria* effectively insulted employers from liability. Responsibility for safety in the workplace rested primarily on those who were least able to do something about it: the employees.

5. See e.g. the 'Map of Elf and Safety Madness' leaflet produced by the Department for Work and Pensions in November 2013: www.gov.uk/government/uploads/system/uploads/attachment_data/file/260847/elf-safety-map-251113.pdf, Lord Young's *Common Sense, Common Safety* (October 2010) and Professor Löfstedt's *Reclaiming health and safety for all: an independent review of health and safety legislation* (November 2013).

6. The Act also introduces a number of other reforms limiting employees' rights, including the introduction of up-front employment tribunal fees and a cap on the maximum compensation paid for unfair dismissal.

7. The Act applies only to health and safety breaches since October 2013 (allowing for further claims relating to illnesses with a long latency period, e.g. mesothelioma). Of course, it is still possible for the employee to bring a claim in negligence and as Lord Faulks noted during a parliamentary debate on the Bill, 'a breach of regulation will be regarded as strong prima facie evidence of negligence. Judges will need some persuasion that the departure from a specific and well-targeted regulation does not give rise to a claim in negligence' (HL Deb, 22 April 2013, vol 744, col 1328).

→

The government's intention was to limit an employee's remedy to cases where the employer can be said to have been negligent, with the aim of changing 'the perception of employers towards health and safety regulations' and reducing 'unnecessary costs and burdens'.[8] It is notable, however, that Professor Löfstedt, the author of one of the reports relied on by the government, commented when the Bill was before Parliament that:

> the approach being taken is more far-reaching than I anticipated in my recommendation [which related to the imposition of strict liability] and, if this amendment becomes law I hope that the Government will carefully monitor the impact to ensure that there are no unforeseen consequences. (*Reclaiming health and safety for all: a review of progress one year on* (January 2013) at [30])

What is clear is that the Act—in effectively overturning ***Groves*** and a right of action which has existed since the nineteenth century—represents a radical change of approach and attitude in this area of law.

In *Cutler* v *Wandsworth Stadium* [1949] the courts considered another factor indicative of whether a civil claim may arise: who the statute is intended to benefit. In this case, the House of Lords held that the primary intention of the Betting and Lotteries Act 1934 (under which the claimant sought to claim) was to regulate ringside betting operations and that, while changes made under its regulation may benefit some bookmakers, this was not the intended purpose of the Act. In *R* v *Deputy Governor of Parkhurst, ex p Hague* [1992], a group of lawfully detained prisoners claimed that their treatment in prison was in breach of the Prison Rules 1964. Rejecting the prisoners' claims, Lord Jauncey held that the Prison Rules were intended to ensure the management and smooth running of the prisons: '[t]he fact that a particular provision was intended to protect certain individuals [the approach in ***Groves***] is not of itself sufficient to confer private law rights of action upon them, something more is required to show that the legislature intended such conferment' (at 170–1).[9] This has had a significantly limiting effect on the scope of the tort of breach of statutory duty.

Pause for reflection

The prisoners in *Ex parte Hague* were not, perhaps, overly sympathetic claimants—but what about the children in *X* v *Bedfordshire*? In this case, Lord Browne-Wilkinson goes even further

→

8. Matthew Hancock MP (Parliamentary Under-Secretary of State for Skills), HC Deb, 16 October 2012, vol 551, col 151.

9. The claimants in this case also brought actions for false imprisonment. These were also unsuccessful (a change in prison conditions did not make the imprisonment unlawful) and are discussed further in **section 15.4.3**.

→

and suggests that the starting point is a presumption *against* a right of civil liability unless this is clearly what Parliament intended. Thus, while the duties imported into the Children Act 1989 were clearly intended to benefit children in the position of the claimants, they were 'no more than public duties' and, as such, not intended to be enforced at civil law (at 748): 'Although regulatory or welfare legislation affecting a particular area of activity does in fact provide protection to those individuals particularly affected by that activity, the legislation is not to be treated as being passed for the benefit of those individuals but for the benefit of society in general' (at 731–2). Similarly, in *O'Rourke* v *Camden London Borough Council* [1998] the duty to provide temporary housing under the Housing Act 1985 was held to be enforceable only through judicial review.

Think back to what you learnt about the difficulty of establishing a duty of care in the tort of negligence against a public body. Do you think who the defendant is also makes a difference to these claims for breach of statutory duty? If so, is this problematic?

In July 2008, the Law Commission consulted on how best to achieve a clear, simple and just system of redress for individuals who have suffered loss as a result of seriously substandard administrative action. One of its suggestions was to abolish or significantly limit the ambit of breach of statutory duty as it applies to public bodies as it 'neither meets the requirements of aggrieved citizens or properly addresses the legitimate concerns of public bodies faced with seemingly ever expanding liability' (Law Commission *Administrative Redress: Public Bodies and the Citizen*, [4.34], [4.106]). Do you agree? Is a private law remedy in these cases an effective or justifiable use of public funds? Can these cases be distinguished from, say, cases against the NHS? Think about who ultimately pays the compensation—does this fit the distributive justice aims of tort law?

14.3 **Is a duty owed to the claimant?**

As well as establishing that an Act gives rise to a statutory duty, it also needs to be established that the claimant is a member of the protected class. In *Richardson* v *Pitt-Stanley* [1995], for example, the claimant severely injured his right hand at work and successfully sued the company employing him in negligence and breach of statutory duty. Unfortunately, his employer company was uninsured (contrary to the Employers' Liability (Compulsory Insurance) Act 1969) and so was unable to meet his claim. In response, the claimant sued the directors of the company personally for breach of their statutory duty under section 5 of the Act. The majority of the Court of Appeal held that there was no cause of action. The statute was not, in their view, *solely* intended for the benefit of those injured at work but rather was also intended to protect the insured against the effects of multiple and/or large claims:

> Although these consequences may not be so catastrophic as they are for a seriously injured employee who cannot enforce his judgment, they are likely to be serious, more widespread and more frequent. (Stuart-Smith LJ at 131)

In 2014, the majority of the Supreme Court in *McDonald (Deceased)* v *National Grid Electricity Transmission plc* [2014], adopted a more expansive approach allowing the claim, relying on the Asbestos Industry Regulations 1931, of a lorry driver who came into contact with asbestos dust when he attended Battersea Power Station between 1954 and 1959 to collect pulverised fuel ash as part of his work. The duty imposed by the regulations to 'persons employed', was not limited to any particular employment (at 103).[10]

14.4 Has the duty been breached and does the harm fall within the scope of the duty?

Once it is established that a statute allows for an action for breach of statutory duty and that a duty is owed to the claimant, the claimant must establish that the duty has been breached and that the harm suffered falls within the scope of the duty. The first is usually straightforward. The scope and content of the duty will typically be defined by the statute. Liability may be strict (as in ***Groves***), or qualified, for instance by requiring 'reasonable care' to be taken or for the employer to do what is 'reasonably practicable' (akin to the standard of common law negligence) or, more onerously, to take certain steps 'so far as practicable' or 'as are necessary'. Either way, the standard of care is found in the statute, so once we know what the duty requires of the defendant, we shall know what constitutes a breach of that duty.

Additionally, the harm or damage suffered by the claimant must be of the type that the duty was intended to prevent. See, for example, *Gorris* v *Scott* [1874] which involved a cargo of sheep. The defendant shipowner was under a statutory duty to keep them securely penned when in transit in order to prevent the spread of disease. He did not do so—in breach of his duty—and as a result the sheep were swept overboard in bad weather. The claim for breach of statutory duty was unsuccessful. The duty was imposed in order to prevent disease, the damage in fact suffered was accordingly 'something totally apart from the object of the Act' (at 129–30).

Fytche v Wincanton Logistics plc [2004] HL

Mr Fytche was employed by the defendant company to drive a milk tanker to collect milk from farms at night. One morning, after a particularly heavy snow shower, the tanker became stuck on an icy country road. Contrary to the company's standard procedures, the claimant attempted to dig the tanker out. It took three hours in sub-zero temperatures. Unfortunately, as a result, the claimant suffered frostbite in his little toe as a result of a leak in his right boot,

→

see online resources

10. Though the application of this case on its facts is likely to be restricted in the future by s 69 of the Enterprise and Regulatory Reform Act 2013. Don't forget you can watch the UK Supreme Court Justices explaining their judgments via the Supreme Court's YouTube channel, (UKSupremeCourt):youtube.com/user/UKSupremeCourt.

→

provided under regulation 4 of the Personal Protective Equipment at Work Regulations (PPE) 1992. The majority of the House of Lords held that there was no claim for breach of statutory duty in respect of the small hole in his boot (despite an obligation under regulation 7(1) of the PPE 'to maintain equipment in good repair'). The boots had not been provided to protect his toes against frostbite (or similar weather risk), but rather to protect from impact injuries (e.g. from falling milk churns) and for which purpose they were still in good repair (at [15]). The employers were not, therefore, in breach of regulation 7(1).

However, Baroness Hale, in her dissenting opinion, saw things rather differently:

> A boot with a hole, however small, which lets in water is not in good repair. The issue in this case . . . is who should bear the risk that the boots supplied for a particular reason turn out to have an incidental defect which causes the employee injury at work. I have no difficulty with the conclusion that the employer rather than the employee should bear that risk . . . I venture to suggest that a non-lawyer would find it odd indeed that Mr Fytche would have recovered damages if his employer had also thought the boots should protect against a weather risk but does not do so because his employer had a different risk in mind. (at [69]–[70])

14.5 **Conclusion**

In this chapter, we have considered the tort of breach of a statutory duty. This enables a claimant in certain circumstances to recover compensation for losses caused by the defendant's failure to comply with a statutory obligation. However, not every breach of a statutory duty gives rise to a claim in tort. Parliament must have intended for liability to arise. Although its existence as a separate tort is largely the result of an attempt in the late nineteenth century to eschew the harshness of the common law in relation to employers' liability, it need not be confined to workplace-related injuries. Indeed, recent legislative changes have restricted the operation of the tort in this area.

End-of-chapter questions

After reading the chapter carefully, try answering the questions below.

1 What are the 'indicators' used by the courts to determine whether Parliament intended there to be a civil remedy?

2 To what extent, if at all, is section 69 of the Enterprise and Regulatory Reform Act 2013 a backward step in the regulation of health and safety in the workplace?

3 The pretence of seeking what has been called a 'will-o'-the-wisp', a non-existent intention of Parliament to create a civil cause of action, has been harshly criticised. It is capricious and

arbitrary, 'judicial legislation' at its very worst (Dickson J in *The Queen* v *Saskatchewan Wheat Pool* [1983] at 216). Discuss.

4 Consider the examples at the beginning of this chapter—what would the claimants need to show to establish a claim for breach of statutory duty? See also the problem question at the beginning of Chapter 13. What more information would you need in order to know whether Danny would be able to use the (fictitious) Kitchens Safety Act 2003 in order to establish a claim for breach of statutory duty?

If you would like to know what we think visit the **online resources**. www.oup.com/he/horsey7e

Further reading

Foster, Neil 'The Merits of the Civil Action for Breach of Statutory Duty' (2011) 33 Sydney LR 67

Lee, James 'Breach of Statutory Duty' in Ken Oliphant (ed) *The Law of Tort* (LexisNexis, 2015)

Matthews, M H 'Negligence and Breach of Statutory Duty' (1984) 4 OJLS 429

Patten, Keith 'Step Back in Time' (2013) 163 NLJ 62

Stanton, Keith *Breach of Statutory Duty in Tort* (2nd edn, Sweet & Maxwell, 1986)

Stanton, Keith 'New Forms of the Tort of Breach of Statutory Duty' (2004) 120 LQR 324

Tomkins, Nigel 'Civil Health and Safety Law after the Enterprise and Regulatory Reform Act 2013' [2013] JPIL 203

Williams, Glanville 'The Effect of Penal Legislation in the Law of Tort' (1960) 23 MLR 233

The personal torts

PART III

15 Intentional interferences with the person

15.1 Introduction
15.2 Battery
15.3 Assault
15.4 False imprisonment
15.5 Defences: lawful justification or excuse
15.6 Intentional infliction of physical harm or distress
15.7 Conclusion
End-of-chapter questions
Further reading

16 Invasion of privacy

16.1 Introduction
16.2 A tort of invasion of privacy?
16.3 How has privacy been protected?
16.4 Breach of confidence
16.5 Towards the modern approach
16.6 Privacy claims today
16.7 Conclusion
End-of-chapter questions
Further reading

17 Defamation

17.1 Introduction
17.2 Establishing a claim in defamation
17.3 Is the statement defamatory?
17.4 Does the statement refer to the claimant?
17.5 Has the statement been 'published'?
17.6 Defences
17.7 Distributors, including operators of websites
17.8 Offer of amends
17.9 Remedies: damages and injunctions
17.10 The Defamation Act 2013—annotated
17.11 Conclusion
End-of-chapter questions
Further reading

Introduction to Part III

1. In this Part we look at specific torts which protect an individual's interest in some aspect of their person—specifically their personal or bodily integrity, reputation and privacy.

2. We begin, in **Chapter 15**, by looking at the torts comprising trespass to the person—*battery, assault* and *false imprisonment*. Each seeks to protect an individual against an infringement of their personal or bodily integrity, that is against the infliction, or fearing the infliction, of unlawful force (battery and assault) and the unlawful restriction of a person's freedom of movement (false imprisonment).

3. The three trespass to the person torts have the same characteristics: the defendant must have intended both the *conduct* itself and (usually) *consequences* of their action (though they need not have intended to harm or hurt the claimant); the defendant's action must cause direct and immediate harm; and they are actionable per se, that is, without proof of loss. These characteristics distinguish these torts from the tort of negligence: while trespass to the person compensates the claimant in relation to direct and intentional harm (e.g. being deliberately hit), negligence compensates the claimant for that which is unintentional or indirect (i.e. accidental injury).

4. The chapter then goes on to consider the tort in *Wilkinson* v *Downton* [1897], which provides a remedy for physical harm caused by an intentional act (as opposed to physical impact or fear of such) and the *Protection from Harassment Act 1997*, which imposes both civil and criminal liability for harassing conduct. Though the 1997 Act was originally introduced as a response to stalking, it is of general and (potentially) wide application as seen in its use in cases of workplace harassment and the disclosure of private sexual images.

5. **Chapter 16** considers the tort of misuse of private information. This area of law is highly topical and somewhat contentious, particularly in the era of anonymity orders and 'super-injunctions'. As with *defamation*, an action to protect an individual's (often, but not always, someone in the public eye) *privacy* involves delicately balancing their right to a private and family life free from *unwanted* intrusion against media freedom against the public's 'right to know'.

6. Although a number of legal mechanisms have offered some protection of privacy interests (e.g. *trespass to the person*, private nuisance and breach of confidence), none of them protected privacy per se and all have quite substantial limitations. The Article 8 right to privacy is incorporated into UK law through the Human Rights Act 1998, but this does not create a free-standing action, except against public authorities. There is no general 'tort' of invasion of privacy (confirmed by the House of Lords in ***Campbell*** v *MGN* [2004]). It was recognised, however, that existing causes of action may require amending with the goal of protecting *privacy*. As a result, changes particularly in the action for breach of confidence (an action for unjustified publication of private information) alongside the use of Article 8 now indicate that such a tort exists as the tort of misuse of private information.

7. *Defamation*—libel and slander—discussed in **Chapter 17** is perhaps one of the most familiar torts and certainly one of the most glamorous (although increasingly it may have to share this honour with the new invasion of privacy torts). It is also one of the most controversial—the spectre of reform has hung over this area of law for a number of years. This finally arrived in the form of the Defamation Act 2013. This makes a number of changes to the common law, particularly in relation to defences.

The law of defamation enables an individual (or, more controversially, a company) to prevent the publication of, or recover damages for, public statements which make, or are likely to make, people think less of them. As such it is unsurprising that many of the cases involve people in the public eye—celebrities, TV personalities, politicians and so on—and/or multinational corporations who are not only more aware of, but certainly have a greater interest in, their reputations. However, none of this should detract from the central question at the heart of the law of defamation: when should an individual's interest in what people think of them trump or silence the freedom of others to be able to say what they know, or think they know, about them?

8. Only a false statement can be defamatory. However, a claimant need not be able to prove that it is false to bring (and win) a claim—it is up to the defendant to prove that the statement is true in order to avoid liability. Other defences include honest opinion, publication on a matter of public interest and privilege (where the statement is made in the performance of a duty). Remedies include an injunction to prevent publication, a permanent injunction to prevent further publication and damages (which, unusually, can include exemplary damages).

15

Intentional interferences with the person

Problem question

Read this problem question carefully, and keep it in mind while you are working through the chapter that follows. At the end of the chapter, you will be able to apply what you have learnt to the problem question and advise the relevant parties.

Henry, Mark, Mary and Anne are sitting in the students' union bar discussing their outfits for the forthcoming 'Law Society Spring Ball'.

Thomas, Mary's ex-boyfriend, walks by and says quietly to Henry, 'I'll get you! No one steals my girl and gets away with it'. Although Henry is not particularly upset by this, he decides to teach Thomas a lesson. When no one is looking, he deliberately trips Thomas up. Thomas falls over but is not hurt. He quickly jumps up and runs after Henry. Thomas hits Henry and pushes him away and Henry falls awkwardly and hits his head. As Mary rushes to get a doctor, Thomas corners her and whispers, 'I miss you, let's try again'. She pushes him away.

Meanwhile Mark and Anne have sneaked into the bar's storeroom for some time alone. On seeing this, Thomas locks the storeroom door. It remains locked until Rafe, the barman, comes on duty some time later and unlocks it.

Later that evening, Thomas calls Catherine, Henry's pregnant ex-girlfriend, who lives some distance away, and tells her Henry has been badly hurt. She takes the news very badly. Thomas then calls Mary's mobile; as she is still at the hospital with Henry she does not answer it. By the time she checks her phone she has 12 missed calls.

Advise the parties.

15.1 Introduction

Consider the following examples:

→ ***An infatuated student makes multiple phone calls to a classmate's mobile suggesting that they meet up.***

→ ***A man is shopping with his 3-year-old daughter in the toy department of a large department store. They are both locked in when the store closes for the evening.***

→ ***A woman enters a lift with a male colleague at work. He sidles up to her, standing very close (but not touching) and whispers 'sweet nothings' in her ear. They are alone in the lift.***

→ ***A jilted lover sends private sexual images of her ex-partner to his friends and family and threatens to put them online.***

→ ***A doctor delivers a healthy child after performing a caesarean section on the mother without her consent.***

All of these cases involve a possible infringement of an individual's personal or bodily integrity. As such the harm lies not in whether the defendant's actions have caused physical damage but rather in the violation of the claimant's right to be free from unjustifiable interference. Trespass to the person is made up of three torts: battery, assault and false imprisonment. These were defined by Goff LJ in *Collins* v *Wilcock* [1984] (at 1177) as laid out in **Table 15.1**.

TABLE 15.1 The trespass to the person torts

The trespass to the person torts		
Assault 'an act which causes another person to apprehend the infliction of immediate, unlawful force on his person'	Battery 'the actual infliction of unlawful force on another person'	False imprisonment 'the unlawful imposition of constraint on another's freedom of movement from a particular place'

In addition to these three torts, this chapter also considers the tort in *Wilkinson* v *Downton* [1897]. While assault and battery provide a remedy for those who fear, or who experience, the immediate infliction of unlawful physical force, the tort in *Wilkinson* v *Downton* provides a remedy for those who suffer physical or psychiatric injury as a result of another's intentional conduct. Though the House of Lords' decision in ***Wainwright* v *Home Office*** **[2003]** and the enactment of the Protection from Harassment Act 1997 have limited its role, it appears more recently to have had something of a revival and the rule continues to offer the possibility of recovery for harm suffered in circumstances not covered by the trespass torts, the 1997 Act or the tort of negligence.

Pause for reflection

The torts which comprise trespass to the person have close connections with the criminal law and, in particular, the offences found in the Offences Against the Person Act 1861. Sulphuric acid being placed into washroom hand dryers, threats of violence at a parish council meeting,

→

→

a car deliberately running over a policeman's foot or a spurned lover's harassment of a former partner all amount to criminal offences. So why then does the law also recognise a civil action in these, and other, cases? And, why would the victim wish to bring a claim?

Think again about the purposes of tort law outlined in the introduction to the book. Many of the cases highlight abuses of, and discrepancies in, power—for example, between men and women, police officer and suspect, doctor and patient, and prisoner and the state. A civil action may be used to highlight a refusal of the Director of Public Prosecutions (DPP) to bring a criminal prosecution in a particular case, or following an unsuccessful prosecution (see *Ashley* v *Chief Constable of Sussex Police* [2008]).[1] Consider, for example, rape and other forms of sexual assault. Given the very low number of criminal convictions in such cases, the civil law might be invoked here to strategic effect (see e.g. *Lawson* v *Glaves-Smith* [2006]).[2] Do you think this would be a good idea? Think about the purpose of civil, as opposed to criminal, law.

Conventionally, the trespass to the person torts are described as having the same characteristics:

- they must be committed intentionally;
- they must cause direct and immediate 'harm';[3] and
- they are actionable per se, that is, without proof of loss.

These characteristics distinguish the trespass to the person torts from the tort of negligence. Put simply, trespass compensates the claimant in relation to direct and intentional harm (e.g. being deliberately hit), while negligence compensates the claimant for unintentional or indirect harm (i.e. accidental injury).

It is worth noting at the outset that the term 'intention' is ambiguous. It can describe two different aspects of a person's conduct. First, we can speak of intentional *conduct*, that is, willed, voluntary action. The contrast here is with conduct which was out of the defendant's control—for example, a spasm or when they are physically manipulated by someone else. Secondly, and more commonly, the language of intention is used in connection with the *consequences* of one's willed actions—for example, to touch or hurt someone or to score a goal. In this sense, intention requires a particular state of mind or attitude in respect of the result of one's conduct. Typically, one intends a particular consequence when one's purpose is to bring about that consequence through one's actions. The contrast here is with recklessness or negligence which involves, at most, an awareness of the risk that one's conduct will bring a particular result without intending to cause such a result.

It is clear that the torts we are concerned with in this chapter require intention in the first sense. A defendant will not be liable if they were not in control of their actions

1. On this case and point, see further Nicholas McBride 'Trespass to the Person: The Effect of Mistakes and Alternative Remedies on Liability' [2008] CLJ 461.

2. See further Godden 2012; Horsey and Rackley 2018; Antonsdóttir 2020.

3. It may be that the reference to 'harm' here is misleading. The effect of the torts of trespass to the person being actionable per se is that the claimant need not show that they have suffered any loss for their claim to succeed. As such, the claimant need not have suffered any tangible (physical or psychiatric) harm. Rather, they simply need to show that they have been unlawfully touched (battery), apprehended an immediate unlawful touching (assault) or been physically restrained (false imprisonment).

at the relevant time. It is less clear if intention in the second sense is needed—that is, whether the defendant need intend the specific consequences of their actions (e.g. unlawful touching, or the claimant's fear of such touching, in the case of battery and assault respectively) or whether it is enough that the defendant was simply careless as to the possibility of the result occurring.

At one point it seemed that a trespass could be committed negligently (*Fowler* v *Lanning* [1959]). However, the Court of Appeal decision in *Letang* v *Cooper* [1965] marked a change in direction. In this case, the claimant (wishing to avoid restrictions imposed by the Law Reform (Limitation of Actions, etc) Act 1954, s 2(1)) sued in trespass for injury caused by the defendant negligently driving his car over her legs as she sunbathed in the hotel car park more than three years earlier.[4] In denying her claim, Lord Denning MR proposed that a clear line be drawn between trespass and negligence: trespass requires that the defendant intended to touch the claimant, whereas 'when the injury is not inflicted intentionally but negligently . . . the only cause of action is in negligence and not trespass' (at 240).[5]

This position was endorsed by the Court of Appeal in ***Iqbal* v *Prison Officers Association* [2009]**, which held that 'it is well established that all forms of trespass require an intentional act. An act of negligence will not suffice' (Smith LJ at [71]). However, Smith LJ then went on to hold that intention here also includes subjective recklessness, that is where the defendant *foresees* that their actions will have the relevant consequences (e.g. the application of force in the case of battery, the deprivation of the claimant's liberty in that of false imprisonment) and goes ahead with those actions nonetheless (at [73]). On this understanding, the person who throws a stone in a crowded area not intending (i.e. setting out) to hit anyone *but knowing it is likely that someone may be hit* will be liable in the tort of battery.

Pause for reflection

While Smith LJ in *Iqbal* does much to clarify the mental element needed for the trespass to the person torts, some difficulties remain. First, the use of the phrase 'intentional act' is unhelpful and potentially misleading. As we saw previously, intention can be used in two senses: to describe action which is voluntary (rather than involuntary) or to describe a person's attitude to certain consequences of their action (that their purpose was to bring about those consequences). So if A locks the door to a room, not knowing that B is inside, A's locking of the door is intentional (in the first sense) even though A has no intention (in the second sense) to lock B in.

Because of this, saying there must be an 'intentional act' is ambiguous. Now we know from *Iqbal* that A does not falsely imprison B *unless* he intends to lock B in (or is aware that by locking the door he may lock B in but does this anyway). But then we would be better off making clear that what needs to be intended is *the imprisonment*—that is, A needs to lock the door

→

4. The Act stated that personal injury actions for 'negligence, nuisance or breach of duty' must be brought within three years, while other tort actions were barred after six years.

5. It may be that disagreements as to whether a trespass can be committed negligently are somewhat academic. After all, if a claimant is unable to sue for negligently touching in trespass, so long as they have suffered some form of physical injury, a remedy will lie in the tort of negligence. And if they have not suffered such harm, then a claim in trespass would be largely useless since no more than nominal damages would be awarded.

→

with the objective of locking B in (or at least knowing that by locking the door this is likely to happen). Similarly, in battery what needs to be intended is not (simply) the defendant's physical conduct—such as throwing a stone—but *the application of force*—the stone hitting someone (or knowing it is likely to hit someone and doing it anyway).

This relates to the other difficulty with the judgment: the view that subjective recklessness is a sufficient mental element for the trespass to the person torts. This aligns the law of torts with the criminal law offences of assault and battery, where it has long been clear that subjective recklessness is sufficient mens rea (*R* v *Venna* [1976]). Again, however, the courts could have made this point more clearly. In ***Iqbal***, Smith LJ stated that 'in the criminal law a reckless disregard of the consequences is taken as sufficient to satisfy the requirement of intention', before holding that the same should go for the law of torts (at [73]). Not only does this misdescribe the criminal law, where the courts have repeatedly stressed the difference between intention and recklessness, but also it is clear that there is a difference between trying to hit someone and doing something which one knows may hit someone. As such, the clearer formulation would be to say that trespass requires intention *or* recklessness, rather than pretending that recklessness is a type of intention.

15.2 **Battery**

A battery is the intentional application of unlawful force to another person: typically A stabs B; X shoots Y; Henry punches Thomas. It is the 'physical interference with' or 'invasion of' the claimant's body or person (Buxton LJ in *Home Office* v *Wainwright and another* [2001] at [67]). As we shall see, there is no need to show that the defendant caused the claimant actual harm or injury by touching them, or indeed that they intended to cause (or were reckless as to causing) them harm or injury. As such any unwanted physical touching—from a pat on the back to a violent blow to the head—can amount to a battery. Nor does it matter *why* the touching occurred; the fact that the contact was the result of a practical joke or intended to convey affection is irrelevant: 'an unwanted kiss may be a battery although the defendant's intention may be most amiable' (*R* v *Chief Constable of Devon and Cornwall, ex p Central Electricity Generating Board* [1982] at 471).

Fortunately, this somewhat broad prohibition of unwanted conduct is qualified. In order to be unlawful, the force must exceed 'physical contact which is generally acceptable in the ordinary conduct of daily life' and must be applied to the claimant by immediate and direct means (*Collins* v *Wilcock* at 1177). An actionable battery therefore requires:

(1) the intentional application of unlawful force (the touching or contact);

(2) which is direct and immediate; and

(3) for which the defendant has no lawful justification or excuse (i.e. no defence).

15.2.1 **Intentional application . . .**

The trespass torts are typically said to require intention on the part of the defendant. However, as we have seen, the word 'intention' can be used in different ways. So, the voluntary throwing of a stone is an *intentional act*, whether or not the thrower *intends to hit* anyone. What is clear is that there needs to be more than an intentional throwing. There is no battery unless the stone-thrower intends to hit someone with the stone (or at least is aware that the stone might hit someone and throws it nonetheless). Nor is there a battery if the defendant acts involuntarily—for example, if Anne trips over and stumbles into Henry. Though, if Thomas pushes Anne into Henry, he has committed a battery against both Anne and Henry (*Gibbon* v *Pepper* [1695]). The mental element necessary for the tort of battery requires either:

(1) an *intention* (i.e. setting out) to apply force to another person; or

(2) *recklessness* as to (i.e. foreseeing the likelihood of) one's actions causing the application of force to another person.

There are two further points to make. First, if the defendant intends to make contact with A but instead touches B, the tort of battery will be committed against B. So, if Henry while trying to hit Thomas hits Catherine instead, she has a claim in battery against Henry by virtue of the rule of 'transferred intent' (*Livingstone* v *Ministry of Defence* [1984]). Secondly, the defendant will be liable to compensate the claimant for any harm suffered as a result of the unlawful touching even if he did not intend to cause the claimant harm, or the possibility of causing harm never crossed their mind. In *Williams* v *Humphrey* [1975], the defendant pushed the claimant into a swimming pool causing him to fall awkwardly and break his ankle. The defendant argued that he did not intend to hurt the claimant, but this did not matter. He had clearly intended to touch the claimant and there is no further requirement of intending any injury that follows. Similarly, a doctor who performs a medical operation without the patient's consent will commit a battery, even though their intention is to help rather than harm the patient.

A battery can also be committed, even if the original action by the defendant was involuntary, if the defendant has the opportunity to stop inflicting the unlawful force and fails to do so. In *Fagan* v *Metropolitan Police Commissioner* [1969], a police officer was directing the defendant as to where to park when the defendant accidentally drove his car on to the police officer's foot. Despite being aware of what he had done, the defendant deliberately left his car on the officer's foot for a period of time, causing injury to his toe. The defendant was found guilty of criminal assault. Though Fagan's initial—unintentional—action of stopping his car on the constable's foot did not amount to a (criminal) assault, his failure to move his car, once he had knowledge of his car's position and until the police officer had shouted 'Get off my foot' several times, did. Though this is a criminal case, the same reasoning would apply, by analogy, in the civil courts: the defendant's failure to move his car also fulfils the intention requirement of the tort of battery.

15.2.2 **. . . of unlawful touching**

Applied literally, battery covers all forms of contact—with the result that Anne would commit a battery simply by tapping Mary on her shoulder to get her attention. It would clearly be nonsense if there were an actionable battery in such circumstances. Nevertheless, whilst some limitation on the scope of battery is common sense, the courts have experienced difficulties in finding a theoretical basis as to where to draw the line between unlawful and acceptable ordinary everyday contact.

An early, somewhat narrow, attempt to distinguish lawful from unlawful touching was made by Lord Holt CJ in *Cole* v *Turner* [1704], who stated that 'the least touching of another in anger is a battery' (at 149). Thus, in *Wilson* v *Pringle* [1987], the Court of Appeal suggested that in order for the defendant's actions to be unlawful, and for there to be an actionable battery, there needed to be 'hostile intent'. The claimant, a 13-year-old boy, suffered serious injury to his hip when the defendant, a fellow pupil, pulled his school bag off his shoulder in an act of horseplay. The defendant's liability turned on whether his actions had, as a matter of fact, been 'hostile' rather than a schoolboy prank.

This is not particularly helpful. All it does is restate the question that needs to be answered: what is hostile intent? In *Wilson* v *Pringle*, the Court of Appeal equates 'hostility' with 'acting unlawfully' (at 253). On this view, hostile intent appears here to mean 'little more than that the defendant has interfered in a way to which the claimant might object' (*Peel & Goudkamp* p 60). But what is 'hostile' to one person may seem quite the opposite to another. When does an overenthusiastic slap on the back become hostile? And is, to use Lord Goff's example, a surgeon's mistaken, but non-hostile, amputation of a patient's leg not therefore a battery?

A better approach is that of Goff LJ in the earlier case *Collins* v *Wilcock* [1984], who stated that touching will only amount to a battery where it does not fall within the category of physical contacts 'generally acceptable in the ordinary conduct of daily life' (at 1177). What is considered generally acceptable will depend on the context. So, while you wouldn't expect to be pushed while in the queue at the Post Office, being jostled at the bar in a busy nightclub is the sort of thing about which people cannot reasonably complain and is likely to be considered generally acceptable. Though being 'goosed' (i.e. having your bottom pinched) while waiting at the bar may well cross the line.

Although this approach was criticised as 'not practical' by Croom-Johnson LJ in *Wilson* v *Pringle* (at 252), Lord Goff restated his views and won the day—rejecting the hostility requirement—once he had joined the House of Lords in the case of *Re F (Mental Patient: Sterilization)* [1990]:

> it has recently been said that the touching must be 'hostile' to have that effect . . . I respectfully doubt whether that is correct. A prank that gets out of hand; an over-friendly slap on the back; surgical treatment by a surgeon who mistakenly thinks that the patient consented to it—all these things may transcend the bounds of lawfulness, without being characterised as hostile. (at 73)

Pause for reflection

In fact, Lord Goff's notion of generally acceptable touching falls foul of the same definitional difficulties as Croom-Johnson LJ's in *Wilson* v *Pringle*. What constitutes contact 'generally acceptable in the ordinary conduct of human life' is just as difficult to define as hostile contact. Consider, for example, the over-familiar (female) work colleague who greets everyone—male and female—with a 'friendly' pat on their bottom—does this constitute acceptable or unacceptable behaviour? Would it make a difference if the colleague was male?

Conaghan & Mansell may well think so. They argue that Lord Goff's notion of 'generally acceptable conduct' is open to feminist charges of bias, as male perceptions of acceptable

→

→

conduct are hidden under a guise of neutrality, thereby precluding the recognition of women's experiences and their divergence from those of men: 'what men may see as a compliment, women often experience as an insult; what men offer as a gesture of intimacy and friendship, women may perceive as an invasion of privacy' (pp 164–5). A woman who pursues a battery claim in circumstances that involve 'minor' touching, a wolf-whistle or similar, *Conaghan & Mansell* suggest, is likely to be regarded as petty or vindictive: 'her sense of insult and embarrassment discounted as an "over-reaction", precisely because the original act is perceived as benign' (p 166). Do you agree?

15.2.3 Direct and immediate force

Finally, the unlawful touching must be the direct and immediate result of the defendant's actions. A common example used to illustrate this point is the distinction between the claim of a person who is hit by a log as it is deliberately thrown onto the road and the claim of someone who later trips over it. While the former lies in battery, the latter is said to be restricted to the tort of negligence (*Reynolds* v *Clarke* [1725]). In practice, however, it seems the courts have interpreted the 'directness' requirement extremely flexibly. In *Scott* v *Shepherd* [1773], the defendant who had thrown a lit squib (firework) into a market place was liable in battery, despite the fact that two stallholders had caught the squib and thrown it on to protect themselves and their wares before it had eventually exploded in the claimant's face injuring his eye. Similarly, the defendant in *DPP* v *K (A Minor)* [1990], a schoolboy aged 15, was found liable for the injuries caused to another pupil as a result of his pouring sulphuric acid into the upturned nozzle of an electronic hand-drying machine, and which had subsequently been blown onto the pupil's face, leaving a permanent scar.[6] In both these cases the unlawful force appears to be a consequential rather than direct result of the defendant's actions. Nevertheless, it appears that the shortness of time between the act and the contact is sufficient to satisfy the 'direct and immediate' requirement in battery. On this basis Alastair Mullis and Ken Oliphant argue that the directness requirement serves little purpose, and that it is likely that a person who trips over a log left in the road (assuming it happened relatively quickly after the log was thrown and the necessary intention could be established) would have a claim in trespass (as well as negligence).[7]

15.2.4 Lawful justification or excuse

Once it has been established that the defendant has intentionally touched the claimant and that the contact is both unlawful and direct and immediate, the defendant will have committed a battery unless she has a lawful justification or excuse for her actions. As these justifications and excuses are also applicable to the torts of assault and false imprisonment, they are discussed at **section 15.5**, after we have considered the elements of these torts.

6. The defendant was convicted of assault occasioning actual bodily harm. The case has since been held to have been wrongly decided on another ground.

7. Alastair Mullis and Ken Oliphant *Torts* (Palgrave Macmillan, 2012), p 219.

15.3 **Assault**

Consider again the example of the woman in the lift at the beginning of the chapter. Clearly, there is no battery—but could the man's actions constitute an assault (*Conaghan & Mansell* p 170)?

Defined by Goff LJ in *Collins* v *Wilcock* as 'an act which causes another person to apprehend the infliction of immediate, unlawful force on his person' (at 1177), assault protects the claimant who fears or apprehends a battery. Unlike battery, the wrong of assault lies not in the unwanted physical contact, but in the *anticipation* of such contact. The tort of assault is committed where the defendant's actions cause the claimant to reasonably apprehend the direct and immediate infliction of force upon their person. Assault and battery will usually, but not always, occur together: unless, for example, the assailant changes their mind, misses their target or a third party intervenes, the immediate anticipation of a battery (an assault) will almost always be followed by a battery (actually being hit). Thus, if Henry points a gun at Thomas he has committed an assault. It makes no difference whether the gun is loaded (assuming Thomas does not know this is the case) as he has reason to apprehend a battery (*R* v *St George* [1840]). But Henry will only commit a battery if he shoots the gun and hits Thomas. If Henry's aim is poor and he misses Thomas, there will be no battery—but there will be an actionable assault. Equally, not every threat of a battery will give rise to an assault. If Henry says to Thomas, 'I'm going to shoot you dead', but Thomas knows that Henry has no means of doing this it is unlikely that Henry's threat will satisfy the requirements of an assault. Similarly, if Henry shoots Thomas while he is asleep, his actions will constitute a battery, but not an assault. An actionable assault requires that:

(1) the defendant intends that the claimant apprehends the application of unlawful force;

(2) the claimant reasonably apprehends the immediate and direct application of unlawful force;

(3) for which the defendant has no lawful justification or excuse.

15.3.1 **Intention**

The same issues relating to the difficulties in establishing the meaning of 'intention' discussed earlier also apply here. However, it is clear that the defendant must have acted voluntarily, and have intended to cause the claimant to apprehend the application of immediate unlawful force, or be subjectively reckless as to the possibility that their actions will cause the claimant to apprehend the application of such force.

15.3.2 **Reasonable apprehension . . .**

For there to be an assault the claimant must reasonably anticipate or expect the application of unlawful force—that is, the infliction of a battery. Thus, if Rafe creeps up behind Henry and strikes him, Rafe has committed a battery, but not an assault. It would only be an assault if Henry knew Rafe was about to hit him. Conversely, if Henry sees Rafe coming and moves so that he successfully avoids Rafe's blow, Rafe will have committed an assault but no battery. The test of reasonable apprehension is an objective one. It does not matter whether the particular claimant was overly timid or if they could have defended themselves successfully.

Stephens v _Myers_ [1830] Assizes

The claimant was chairing a parish council meeting, sitting at the head of the table. The defendant was also at the table with about six or seven people between him and the claimant. The defendant was asked to leave the meeting (he had become disruptive during the course of the meeting's discussions), in response to which he threatened the claimant with violence, advancing towards the claimant with a clenched fist. Fortunately, his approach was stopped by the timely intervention of the churchwarden and he was never within striking distance of the claimant. The defendant was liable for assault (and so the claimant's apprehension of a battery was held to be reasonable), though the jury clearly thought the claimant was somewhat timid—their award of one shilling was trivial.

15.3.3 . . . of immediate and direct application of unlawful force

In order for there to be an assault the claimant must reasonably apprehend the infliction of immediate and direct unlawful force. If she knows that the defendant is not in a position to do this then there can be no assault: 'It is not every threat, when there is no actual violence, that constitutes an assault, there must, in all cases, be the means of carrying that threat into effect' (***Stephens*** **v** ***Myers***). This was confirmed in ***Thomas*** v ***National Union of Miners (South Wales Area)*** **[1986]**, and by the Court of Appeal in *Mbasogo* v *Logo Ltd* [2006].

Thomas v _National Union of Miners (South Wales Area)_ [1986] Ch D

see online resources

During the 1984–5 miners' strike, a group of working miners sought an interlocutory injunction against the National Union of Mineworkers to prevent its members (who were striking miners) from verbally abusing and harassing them as they went to work. Each day a crowd of some 50–70 picketers gathered at the colliery gates as the working miners entered the workplace in vehicles surrounded by a police guard.

Dismissing their claim, Scott J held that the actions of the striking miners did not meet the requirements of immediacy or directness necessary to establish an assault: 'the working miners are in vehicles and the pickets are held back from the vehicles, I do not understand how even the most violent of threats or gestures could be said to constitute an assault' (at 62).

However, this is not to say that there can never be an assault where the defendant lacks the immediate means to put it into effect. A bank robber who points a gun at the cashier and threatens to shoot unless his demands are met commits an assault—whether or not the gun is loaded—so long as the cashier reasonably believes that the gun is loaded and hence that the threat could be carried out.

Traditionally, the requirement of directness meant that threatening words needed to be accompanied by a physically intimidating gesture: 'No words or singing are equivalent to an assault' (*R* v *Meade and Belt* [1823]). Though a threatening gesture can be negated by words suggesting that an assault is *not* imminent. Thus in *Tuberville* v *Savage* [1669] there was no assault when the defendant placed his hand on his sword and stated, '[i]f it were not assize time [that is, the time when judges from the King's Bench were visiting] I would not take such language from you'. As it *was* assize time, he was, in fact, stating that he *did not intend* to strike the claimant. The key point remains whether the claimant reasonably apprehended the infliction of immediate and direct force. Circumstances in which the defendant's words negate their threatening gestures are distinguishable from conditional threats where the claimant is merely given an option by the defendant to avoid violence. This is clearly an assault. It is no excuse for the highwayman to claim that his victims had a viable alternative option when he said, 'Stand and deliver, your money or your life'.

Highwaymen aside, the reason for judicial emphasis on gestures rather than words, *Conaghan & Mansell* suggest, lies in a concern to 'distinguish a mere insult (for which there is generally no legal remedy) from a serious and immediate threat' (p 170); to balance the conflicting interests of freedom of speech and public order. It follows, they continue, 'that the harasser who makes obscene remarks, "amorous" proposals or embarrassing or intimate comments has traditionally not been significantly inhibited by the tort of assault from doing so. There is, after all, no harm in asking' (*Conaghan & Mansell* p 170)—though there may now be a claim under the Protection from Harassment Act 1997.

However, the House of Lords' decision in ***R* v *Ireland* [1998]**—another criminal law case with applicability to the law of tort—ended any doubt over whether mere words could amount to an assault.

R v *Ireland* [1998] HL

Three women had suffered psychiatric illness as a result of being subjected to a lengthy period of harassment by the defendant, including repeated silent telephone calls, often at night. Lord Steyn in the House of Lords rejected the proposition that an assault could never be committed by words alone: 'A thing said is also a thing done. There is no reason why something said should be incapable of causing apprehension of immediate personal violence, e.g. a man accosting a woman in a dark alley saying "come with me or I will stab you"' (at 162).

Liability, therefore, depends on whether the claimant in the circumstances reasonably believed that the oral threat could be carried out in the sufficiently near future to qualify as an immediate threat of personal violence. On the facts, the court was prepared to accept that silence would be capable of giving rise to such fears:

> Just as it is not true to say that every blow which is struck is an assault . . . so also it is not true to say that mere words or gestures can never constitute an assault. It all depends on the circumstances . . . The words and gestures must be seen in their whole context. (Lord Hope at 166)

Pause for reflection

Despite the saying 'sticks and stones may break my bones, but words will never hurt me', this seems to require an unduly high level of courage by the recipient of the verbal threats. As Lord Steyn notes at the beginning of his opinion:

> it is easy to understand the terrifying effect of a campaign of telephone calls at night by a silent caller to a woman living on her own. It would be natural for the victim to regard the calls as menacing. What may heighten her fear is that she will not know what the caller may do next. The spectre of the caller arriving at her doorstep bent on inflicting personal violence on her may come to dominate her thinking. After all, as a matter of common sense, what else would she be terrified about? (at 152)

Do you agree with Lord Steyn's reasoning here? Would it make a difference if the calls had been made to the claimants' mobile phones? Or by text? Or via Facebook or Twitter? The caller may not know the claimant's precise location, it is unlikely that this would have a significant (if any?) impact on their state of mind. Nor is the claimant likely to be significantly (any?) less distressed or worried. Nonetheless, in such a case it is likely that the claimant would find it harder to establish an assault—the caller's inability (subject to any evidence to the contrary) to pinpoint their exact location (which, of course, could still be in their own home) may well make their fear of *imminent* and direct force less reasonable.[8]

As we shall see, a claimant who is the victim of harassing conduct but which does not fulfil the requirements necessary to establish the tort of assault may nonetheless still be able to recover using the tort in *Wilkinson* v *Downton* or the Protection from Harassment Act 1997.

15.3.4 **Lawful justification or excuse**

Again, even if the other elements of the tort have been made out, there will be no actionable assault if the defendant has a lawful justification or excuse for her actions.[9]

15.4 **False imprisonment**

The tort of false imprisonment sits alongside battery and assault as the third in the family of torts comprising trespass to the person. Goff LJ in *Collins* v *Wilcock* [1984] defines false imprisonment as involving the 'unlawful imposition of constraint on another's freedom of movement from a particular place' (at 1177). As such, 'imprisonment' extends to any action that deprives the claimant of their freedom of movement—so long as there is a *complete* restriction of this freedom and the defendant has no lawful justification or

8. Consider again the phone calls made by the student in the examples at the beginning of the chapter—***R* v *Ireland*** suggests that, if sufficiently serious, they could amount to an assault. There may also be a claim under the Protection from Harassment Act—see **section 15.6.2**.
9. See **section 15.5**.

excuse the claimant will have been falsely imprisoned. There is no need to show force, though a claimant must not be taken to be consenting to the imprisonment simply because they do not resist.

R (on the application of Jalloh (formerly Jollah)) v Secretary of State for the Home Department [2020] SC

The claimant, a Liberian national named Ibrahima Jalloh, had been placed under an unlawful curfew after being released from an immigration detention centre on bail. These included a requirement to live at a specified address in Sunderland, to submit to electronic tagging and to stay at home each night between the hours of 11.00 pm and 7.00 am. This had lasted a total of 891 days. He sought damages for false imprisonment, arguing that he had been confined to his house without any legal basis for long periods of time. The Supreme Court, upholding the decision of the first instance judge and the Court of Appeal, agreed:

> The essence of imprisonment is being made to stay in a particular place by another person. The methods which might be used to keep a person there are many and various. They could be physical barriers, such as locks and bars. They could be physical people, such as guards who would physically prevent the person leaving if he tried to do so. They could also be threats, whether of force or of legal process . . . In this case there is no doubt that the defendant defined the place where the claimant was to stay between the hours of 11.00 pm and 7.00 am. There was no suggestion that he could go somewhere else during those hours without the defendant's permission. This is not a case like ***Bird v Jones*** where the claimant could cross the bridge by another route or *Robinson v Balmain New Ferry Co Ltd* where he had agreed to go onto the wharf on terms that he could only get out if he paid a penny. (Lady Hale at [24]–[25])

Nor would the fact that the claimant had at times ignored his curfew (for example, to attend family court proceedings) make a difference to his situation while he was obeying it.

> Like the prisoner who goes absent from his open prison, or the tunneller who gets out of the prison camp, he is not imprisoned while he is away. But he is imprisoned while he is where the defendant wants him to be. (Lady Hale at [26])

In order for there to be an actionable claim for false imprisonment:

(1) the defendant must intend to completely restrict the claimant's freedom of movement;

(2) without lawful justification or excuse.

15.4.1 **Intention**

As Smith LJ held in ***Iqbal***, false imprisonment, like the other trespass torts, requires an intentional act. However, as we have seen this requirement is a little misleading. To use Smith LJ's example:

> If a security guard in an office block locks the door to the claimant's room believing the claimant has gone home for the night and not realising that he is in fact still inside the room, he has committed a deliberate act. However, he did not intend to confine the claimant. He may well be guilty of negligence because he did not check whether the room was empty but he would not be guilty of the intentional tort of false imprisonment. (at [72])

In this example, the fact that the locking of the door was intentional is not enough. The defendant must intend thereby to confine the claimant to that room. However, it is also clear from ***Iqbal*** that subjective recklessness will also suffice, so that there will be liability even where the defendant doesn't set out to imprison the claimant but he is nonetheless aware that this is a likely consequence of his actions. So if, in the previous example, the defendant locked the door suspecting (and not caring) that the claimant may still be inside then, though he doesn't strictly *intend* to imprison him, he is nonetheless liable for false imprisonment.[10]

While the defendant needs to intend to restrict the claimant's freedom of movement, it is not necessary for the defendant to intend to do so *unlawfully*. In *R* v *Governor of Brockhill Prison, ex p Evans (No 2)* [2001], for example, the claimant was lawfully imprisoned for various criminal offences. However, the prison governor miscalculated her release date with the consequence that the claimant was held for longer than she should have been. Her claim for false imprisonment was successful, even though the prison governor clearly did not intend to hold the claimant for any longer than the lawful duration. Similarly, in *Esegbona* v *King's College Hospital Foundation NHS Trust* [2019], the NHS Trust was found to have falsely imprisoned a patient for almost five months. Mrs Esegbona had suffered heart failure. After almost three months of treatment in the hospital's Intensive Care Unit, she wished to return home. The doctors believed her to be confused and suffering from cognitive impairment and communication difficulties. A psychiatrist advised that there needed to be an assessment of her capacity. The hospital failed to carry this out and safeguards under the Mental Capacity Act 2005 had not been followed. The patient was ultimately transferred to a nursing home. The court awarded damages of £130 a day—almost £15,000 in total.[11]

15.4.2 A complete restriction of the claimant's freedom of movement . . .

As there must be a *complete* restriction of the claimant's freedom of movement the conditions for the tort are not satisfied if the claimant is able to move in another direction

10. This is different still to the situation where the defendant entirely innocently locks the claimant in a room (for which there will likely be no liability) and to where a defendant ought to have known that there was someone in the room (in which case there will be a claim in negligence). The law distinguishes between the situation where you lock the door knowing that someone *is* inside (false imprisonment), where you lock the door knowing that someone *might* be inside (which we tend to call (subjective) recklessness—but which will, it seems, still meet the intention requirements of false imprisonment)—and the situation where you lock the door not thinking that someone might be inside but when you *ought* to have known this (negligence).

11. Sadly, Mrs Esegbona died a week later after she (again) attempted to self-excubate herself. The NHS Trust was found negligent in failing to give the nursing home sufficient advice in relation to her treatment.

(***Bird* v *Jones*** [1845]; ***Hicks* v *Young*** [2015]) or if there is a reasonable means of escape (though if the claimant is reasonably unaware of the means of escape, their detention is likely to amount to false imprisonment). However, if the claimant's freedom of movement is completely restricted, it does not matter how long this restriction lasts. This means that acts which are most immediately recognisable as batteries may also amount to false imprisonment—so, for example, if A rapes B, B will have a claim in battery, false imprisonment and (possibly) assault. In *Walker* v *The Commissioner of the Police of the Metropolis* [2014] the Court of Appeal held that the claimant had been 'technically' falsely imprisoned in a narrow doorway by a police officer for a few seconds immediately prior to his lawful arrest (the police were attending a domestic dispute during which 'all hell broke loose' and there was a violent scuffle between the police officer and claimant):

> It is not acceptable for an ordinary citizen to interfere with a person's liberty by confining him or her in a doorway. Although the confinement was for only a few seconds, the principle in question is framed in terms of 'for however short a time' (***Bird* v *Jones***, *Halsbury's Laws*). It is understandable that where liberty is in question . . . there is no room for complaisance. (Rix LJ at [30])

However, it was clear that the court was uncomfortable with the decision, Tomlinson LJ continued:

> Mr Walker's [the claimant] conduct attracts no sympathy [the trial judge had rejected his version of events in which he claimed the police officers had assaulted him as a 'tissue of lies'] but that is of course often the way when a fundamental constitutional principle is at stake. The detention was indeed trivial, but that can and should be reflected in the measure of damages and does not render lawful that which was unlawful. The judge's assessment of £5.00 as the appropriate figure was I think generous to Mr Walker, but there is no appeal against that assessment. (at [46])[12]

Bird v *Jones* [1845] QBD

The defendant's employer had, without permission, installed seating to view a regatta on the River Thames across the public footway on Hammersmith Bridge in London. Although this prevented the claimant using the footway, the defendants were not liable for false imprisonment as his freedom of movement was not completely restrained; he was able to turn back the way he had come: 'imprisonment is . . . a total restraint of the liberty of the person . . . and not a partial obstruction of his will, whatever inconvenience it may bring on him' (at 742).

It also seems to be the case that where the defendant imposes reasonable conditions on the manner in which the visitor leaves his premises, these will be considered to amount to a reasonable means of escape and the restriction of the claimant's freedom will not be considered 'complete'. In *Robinson* v *Balmain New Ferry Co Ltd* [1910] the claimant had paid a penny to enter a wharf in order to catch a ferry but then changed his mind. He

12. Despite ultimately winning his case, the claimant had to pay all his costs for the original trial (at which his claim was unsuccessful), and recovered just 25 per cent of his costs for the appeal.

tried to leave the way he came, and claimed he was falsely imprisoned when he refused to pay the defendants a further penny to leave the wharf. His claim failed. It was reasonable for the defendants to have the payment barriers on one side of the wharf, and, in any case, the claimant had known about the charge to leave when he entered the wharf.[13]

Pause for reflection

Of course much turns here on what is considered 'reasonable'. Consider the following examples: a man has been deliberately locked in a room on the first floor of a building. The window is unlocked and there is a rope near it long enough for him to climb down safely—is this a reasonable means of escape to defeat a claim in the tort of false imprisonment? Would your answer change if there was no rope?

see online resources

This was taken further in *Herd* v *Weardale Steel, Coke and Coal Co Ltd* [1915]. A miner had descended into the pit at 9.30 am and was due to remain until the end of his shift at 4 pm. At 11 am, he refused to do certain work on the basis that it was dangerous, and demanded to be taken to the surface. His employer initially refused. He was brought to the surface at 1.30 pm although the lift had been available to carry men to the surface from 1.10 pm—which meant that he had been detained in the mine against his will for 20 minutes. The House of Lords held that the employer was not liable for false imprisonment. The miner had voluntarily entered the mine under a contract of employment and so was deemed to have (impliedly) consented that he would not be brought to the surface until the end of the shift:

> If a man gets into an express train and the doors are locked pending its arrival at its destination, he is not entitled, merely because the train has been stopped by signal, to call for the doors to be opened to let him out. He has entered the train on the terms that he is to be conveyed to a certain station without the opportunity of getting out before that, and he must abide by the terms on which he has entered the train. So when a man goes down a mine, from which access to the surface does not exist in the absence of special facilities given on the part of the owner of the mine, he is only entitled to the use of these facilities (subject possibly to the exceptional circumstances to which I have alluded) on the terms on which he has entered. (Viscount Haldane LC at 71)

Counterpoint

Paula Giliker and Silas Beckwith suggest that it is difficult to see *Herd* as anything other than a harsh ruling in favour of employers' rights over employees.[14] It is, they argue, scarcely legitimate to suggest that imprisonment is a reasonable response to the employee's breach of

13. See further Mark Lunney's interesting discussion of the historical and commercial context of this controversial case, including an explanation for the misprinting of the claimant's name—as Robinson rather than *Robertson*—in the authorised report of the Privy Council (2009).

14. *Tort* (Sweet & Maxwell, 2008), p 353.

→

contract. There is, however, another way of viewing the court's decision: as a case of omission. On this view, there could be no liability because the restriction on the claimant's movement was the result of an omission; the employers had not done anything to positively restrain the claimant, they had simply failed to provide him with a route out. As such, there could be no action for false imprisonment. Trespass is concerned with immediate and direct actions, not omissions—the employers had simply failed to do something they were not obliged to do in the first place.

The view that false imprisonment cannot be committed by an omission was affirmed by the Court of Appeal in ***Iqbal***.

Iqbal v *Prison Officers Association* [2009] CA

The Prison Officers Association (POA) called an unlawful strike which meant that very few prison officers turned up for work. In light of this, the prison governor decided that prisoners should remain in their cells for the entire day. The claimant, a prisoner who was normally allowed out of his cell for six hours a day for work and recreation, brought a claim against the POA for false imprisonment for the period that he would usually be allowed out of his cell, there being no claim against the prison governor (at [21]).[15]

The Court of Appeal rejected his claim. The majority saw the central question as whether the prison officers could be held liable for an omission: their failure to release the claimant from his cell (both sides agreed that if the prison officers were liable then so too was the POA). They held that an omission could ground liability only if the defendants were under a positive duty to act *in relation to the claimant*. Since, in their view, there was no such duty—the prison officers' duty to release the claimant from his cell was a contractual duty owed to the prison governor and not the claimant—there could be no claim.

> At least as a general principle, defendants are not to be held liable in tort for the results of their inaction, in the absence of a specific duty to act, a duty which would normally arise out of the particular relationship between the claimant and the defendant. Such a hard and fast distinction between action and inaction may seem arbitrary to some people, but it is not unprincipled, and, while it may lead to apparent injustice in particular cases, it does help to ensure a degree of clarity and certainty in the law. (Lord Neuberger MR at [21])

> Sullivan LJ dissented in *Iqbal* on the ground that the POA's action in calling the strike could not be sensibly considered a 'mere omission'. It was a positive act (at [94]). And, as such, the claimant's right not to be further restrained by the prison officers' unauthorised action was infringed.

15. Following *Ex p Hague* it is well established that a prisoner 'cannot maintain an action for false imprisonment against the [prison] governor even if he is deprived of any limited degree of freedom which he usually enjoys under the prison regime. His detention anywhere within the prison is lawful' (***Iqbal*** at [62]).

Pause for reflection

The extent to which, to use Lord Neuberger's phrase, the 'apparent injustice' in ***Iqbal*** (and *Herd*) is outweighed by the need to ensure clarity and certainty in the law will depend on one's views of the different interests of the parties. As Sullivan LJ notes, the prison governor's response to the strike was 'entirely predictable' (at [102]). In any industrial dispute resulting in strike action, third parties—here the prisoners—will often bear the brunt of the disruption. In the context of a prison this is likely to be felt through the loss of the measure of liberty afforded to the prisoners by the governor as part of the prison regime. However, he continued:

> in so far as there is a conflict between the prisoners' right not to be deprived of that liberty by persons, including prison officers, acting otherwise than in accordance with the prison governor's authority, and the right of prison officers (absent any statutory prohibition) to strike, the former right must take precedence over the latter. While the right to strike is important, the right not to be falsely imprisoned is of fundamental importance. (at [103])

Do you agree?

Though it is necessary to show a complete restriction of the claimant's freedom of movement, the claimant need not be aware of the restriction. Nor does the claimant need to have suffered any additional harm (beyond the restriction of their movements) from his false imprisonment:

> it appears to me that a person could be imprisoned without his knowing it. I think a person can be imprisoned while he is asleep, while he is in a state of drunkenness, while he is unconscious, and while he is a lunatic . . . Of course the damages might be diminished and would be affected by the question whether he was conscious of it or not. (Atkin LJ, *Meering* v *Grahame-White Aviation* [1920] at 53–4)

This was confirmed *obiter* by the House of Lords in *Murray* v *Ministry of Defence* [1988] (though in that case the claimant knew her freedom of movement was restricted): 'the law attaches supreme importance to the liberty of the individual and if he suffers a wrongful interference with that liberty it should remain actionable even without proof of special damage' (at 529). However, a person who is unaware of their imprisonment is likely to receive only nominal damages (see Smith LJ, ***Iqbal*** at [83]).[16]

But what if the claimant is not yet imprisoned, but the defendant has decided that if they attempt to leave they will be imprisoned? In *R* v *Bournewood Mental Health Trust (ex p L)* [1998], the *potential* deprivation of a claimant's liberty was not held to be sufficient to ground a claim. In this case a mentally ill patient was voluntarily held in an unlocked hospital ward—the staff at the hospital had agreed that should he try to leave he would

16. Thus if the father and daughter, in the example at the start of this chapter, were found by the security guard before they realised they were imprisoned, their damages for false imprisonment (assuming the other elements of the tort can be established) would be reduced accordingly.

be detained compulsorily under the Mental Health Act 1983. This is indeed what happened. A bare majority of the House of Lords overruled a unanimous Court of Appeal and dismissed the patient's claim for false imprisonment in relation to the period prior to his compulsory detention. There was, they concluded, no imprisonment until the claimant was sectioned; an agreement to imprison the claimant was not the same as actually imprisoning him.

This rationalisation is, to say the least, somewhat difficult to grasp. The decision is certainly at odds with that in *Meering*. In both cases the imprisonment consisted in the certainty that total restraint would have been enforced had either of the claimants tried to leave, even though neither had the knowledge that this would happen. As Lord Steyn noted in dissent, the idea that the claimant could go free seems something of a 'fairy tale' (at 475), nevertheless he, and Lord Nolan who also dissented, both agreed with the majority that the defendant's actions were justified by the necessity principle. Given the unanimous recognition of a violation and lack of adequate protection of the claimant's Article 5 right (right to liberty and security) by the European Court of Human Rights (ECtHR) in *HL* v *UK* [2004] at [91] and that the circumstances in which a mentally ill patient can be detained have been clarified by the Mental Capacity Act 2005, it is unlikely that the majority's decision in *Bournewood* will be followed, in this context, in future (*P* v *Cheshire West and Chester Council; P and Q* v *Surrey County Council* [2014]). Indeed, as Lady Hale notes in ***Jalloh***: 'So far as is known, *Bournewood* is the only example of a deprivation of liberty which did not amount to imprisonment at common law: generally speaking, one may well be imprisoned without being deprived of one's liberty, but the other way round is harder to envisage' (at [23]).

15.4.3 **. . . without legal authorisation**

The essence of false imprisonment is the restriction of an individual's freedom of movement without lawful justification or excuse. What amounts to a lawful justification or excuse is explored further in **section 15.5**, however unlike the torts of battery and assault the tort of false imprisonment has a strong constitutional element, which is worth exploring separately. In particular, where the defendant is a public authority (under the Human Rights Act (HRA) 1998), a claim for false imprisonment may coexist with one in respect of Article 5 of the European Convention on Human Rights (ECHR). An example of this is the case of *Austin and other* v *Commissioner of Police of the Metropolis* [2009]). This case was brought in response to a police cordon on Oxford Street, London on 1 May 2001, which restricted the movement of some 3,000 people. The police had imposed the cordon after a large number of demonstrators—so-called 'May Day' protesters—some of whom were violent, had converged at Oxford Circus. The claimant was caught within the cordon and was prevented from leaving for several hours. She brought claims for false imprisonment and a breach of her right to liberty under Article 5 ECHR. The House of Lords held that there had been no infringement of the claimant's Article 5 right. The police's actions in seeking to ensure crowd control had been resorted to in good faith, were proportionate and were not enforced any longer than was reasonably necessary (at [37]).[17] Despite heavy criticism of the House of Lords' decision in *Austin* by commentators and academics, the majority of the Grand Chamber of the ECtHR agreed that:

> in the circumstances the imposition of an absolute cordon was the least intrusive and most effective means to be applied . . . [but continued] that measures of crowd control should not be used by the national authorities directly or indirectly to stifle or discourage protest, given the fundamental importance of freedom of expression and assembly in all democratic societies. Had it not remained necessary for the police to impose and maintain the cordon in order to prevent serious injury or damage, the 'type' of the measure would have been different, and its coercive and restrictive nature might have been sufficient to bring it within Article 5. (*Austin and other* v *UK* [2012] at [66], [68])

In most cases of false imprisonment, the claimant would otherwise be free to go wherever they please. But what about a person who is lawfully imprisoned—can they be falsely imprisoned in relation to acts subsequent to their lawful imprisonment? In *R* v *Deputy Governor of Parkhurst Prison, ex p Hague* [1992] the House of Lords held that the claimant, a category A prisoner, was unable to establish a claim for false imprisonment in relation to his continued segregation following a prison transfer (in breach of the Prison Rules) as to do so would be to confuse the fact of confinement (the essence of a claim of false imprisonment) with the conditions of confinement (which fall outside the remit of the tort). This is surprising. One might expect that a breach of the Prison Rules would negate the prison governor's statutory authority, thereby rendering lawful imprisonment *unlawful*. It is likely that the court was mindful of a desire to limit claims from disgruntled prisoners for technical breaches of the Rules.[18] A similar issue was considered by the Supreme Court in ***R (on the application of Lumba)*** v ***Secretary of State for the Home Department*** [2011].[19]

17. The claim for false imprisonment was rejected by the Court of Appeal and was not considered by the House of Lords. The claimant accepted that if the House of Lords found that there was no infringement of her rights under Art 5 then her claim for false imprisonment must also fail, as her containment within the cordon would be justified by the lawful exercise of police powers (at [11]).

18. It may also be that there are other avenues to compensation in such a case: e.g. an action for breach of statutory duty, negligence, misfeasance in public office (*Karagozlu* v *Commissioner of Police for the Metropolis* [2006]) or using the HRA.

19. ***Lumba*** was followed just two months later by *Kambadzi* v *Secretary of State for the Home Department* [2012] on a similar issue. The appellant was a foreign national who had been detained pending the making of a deportation order. However, the Secretary of State had not complied with a policy on the frequency of review of the detention. A majority of the Supreme Court held that the appellant's detention was unlawful (and that the appellant had been falsely imprisoned) during the periods where there had been no review. Though the full facts of the case had yet to be argued, if it is found that the appellant would have been detained even if his case had been reviewed, the court held that it is likely that only nominal damages would be awarded. Lord Brown (with whom Lord Rodger agreed) dissented on the basis that ***Lumba*** did not compel the majority's decision as it concerned a substantive entitlement under a policy, not a procedural one, and because it held that not every breach of public law will result in the detention being unlawful.

R (on the application of Lumba) v Secretary of State for the Home Department [2011] SC

The claimant was a foreign national prisoner (FNP) serving a four-year prison sentence in the UK. In April 2006, the Home Secretary notified him that on the conclusion of his sentence, he would be deported and that he would be detained pending deportation. As a result, the claimant, who was due to be released from prison in June 2006, remained in custody until he left the UK voluntarily in February 2011. The claimant brought a claim for false imprisonment for the period of detention following the completion of his prison sentence on the basis that the Home Secretary had detained him without lawful authority to do so. During the relevant period, despite a published policy stating that there was a presumption in favour of a FNP's release, pending a final decision relating to their deportation, in fact decisions had been made on the basis of an *unpublished* policy which operated on the opposite presumption, that is in favour of detention. The key issues for the court to determine were (a) whether the unpublished policy was unlawful; (b) if so, whether the detention on the basis of this policy amounted to false imprisonment where a FNP would have been lawfully detained in any event (as was the case here); and (c) if it was unlawful, what was the appropriate measure and award of damages.

The Supreme Court unanimously held that it was unlawful for the Secretary of State to maintain an unpublished policy which was inconsistent with the published policy and which applied a near blanket on the release of a FNP prior to deportation. Secondly, the court held that though a breach of a public law duty was capable of rendering the detention unlawful, not all forms of public law unlawfulness will ground a claim. Nevertheless, in this case, the majority (6:3) found the Home Secretary liable in the tort of false imprisonment on the basis that the statutory power used to detain the claimant was exercised in breach of her public law duties:

> all that the claimant has to do is to prove that he was detained. The Secretary of State must prove that the detention was justified in law. She cannot do this by showing that, although the decision to detain was tainted by public law error . . . a decision to detain free from error could and would have been made. (Lord Dyson at [88])

However, the fact that the claimant would have been detained whichever policy was applied was, the majority held, relevant when determining the issue of damages. Here the Justices were split. While Lords Dyson, Kerr and Collins's view was that, since the claimant had suffered no loss, only nominal damages of £1 should be awarded, the other Justices, in favour of an award, thought that it should be either £1,000 or £500 in order to underline the serious and 'deplorable' abuse of power (Lord Hope at [176]): 'to recognise that the claimant's fundamental constitutional rights have been breached by the state and to encourage all concerned to avoid anything like it happening again' (Lady Hale at [218]). On the basis that the three dissenting judges (who would not have awarded anything), would go for the lowest award, this left the award of £1 in the majority (6:3).

Nevertheless, it is clear that if a prisoner is 'imprisoned' by another prisoner within the confines of the prison (or by a prison officer acting in bad faith) they will be able to bring an action for false imprisonment (*Ex p Hague* at 164). Things are slightly more complicated in relation to cases where a police officer 'detains' a suspect (without arresting them) on the basis of a 'reasonable suspicion', which might justify the detention.[20] While generally trespass to the person is concerned with unlawful and not unreasonable conduct, in such cases the burden of proof is on the claimant to show that the defendant's exercise of discretion was unreasonable (*Chief Constable of Thames Valley Police* v *Earl Gideon Foster Hepburn* [2002]; *Brooks* v *Commissioner of Police for the Metropolis* [2005]).

15.5 Defences: lawful justification or excuse

A common element of each of the trespass torts is that the defendant must not have a lawful justification or excuse for their actions. As seen in the earlier discussion of statutory authority, this usually operates as a defence to a claim, with the onus being on the defendant to establish that they can justify or excuse their actions. In this section we consider three further defences that typically arise in this context—consent, necessity and self-defence.[21]

15.5.1 Consent

As already noted, the tort of battery potentially covers all forms of contact, subject to the requirement that the contact exceeds that which is generally acceptable in everyday life. However, the scope of battery (as well as the torts of assault and false imprisonment) is also limited through the mechanism (or defence) of consent. There is no battery when the claimant consents to the direct and immediate application of force by the defendant. If, for example, Anne consents to being kissed by Mary, she cannot later sue her for a battery—her consent provides her with a lawful justification or excuse for this action. Similarly, there will be no false imprisonment or assault if you consent to being tied up and threatened, say as part of a role-play or acting class. In the colourful case of *Pile* v *Chief Constable of Merseyside Police* [2020] the claimant, who had been arrested for being drunk and disorderly, in the words of Turner J:

> had emptied the contents of her stomach all over herself and was too insensible with drink to have much idea of either where she was or what she was doing there. Rather than leave the vulnerable claimant to marinade overnight in her own bodily fluids, four female police officers removed her outer clothing and provided her with a clean dry outfit to wear. The claimant was so drunk that she later had no recollection of these events. (at [1])

20. See e.g. *Parker* v *Chief Constable of Essex Police* [2018] in which Leveson P held that though the actual arrest (in relation to the death of Mr Lubbock at his house in 2001) was unlawful, 'there were reasonable grounds both to suspect Mr Parker [otherwise known as Michael Barrymore] of committing an offence and that it was necessary to arrest him . . . . [And] that had things been done as they should have been done (to quote Lady Hale in *Kambadzi*), a lawful arrest would have been effected' (at [132]). As a result, Parker was only entitled to nominal damages, not the £2.4 million he was asking for.

21. There has been some uncertainty as to whether the defence of contributory *negligence* applies in cases involving intentional harm (see e.g. *Murphy* v *Culhane* [1977]; ***Reeves* v *Commissioner of Police for the Metropolis* [2000]**). However, in *Standard Chartered Bank* v *Pakistan National Shipping Corp (No 2)* [2002] Lord Rodger suggested that contributory negligence was not applicable in cases of intentional wrongdoing (at [43]–[45]) and more recently in *Co-operative Group (CWS)* v *Pritchard* [2011] Atkins LJ held that the defence of contributory negligence does not apply to the torts of assault and battery (at [62]).

Dismissing the claimant's appeal, the judge held:

> Where someone is so intoxicated that she is unable to make an informed choice then circumstances will arise in which a police officer can readily assume that consent to the removal of clothing can be implied. Normally, someone in custody who has vomited all over themselves, but lacks the ability to articulate their preference, may be safely taken to have given implied consent to the removal of their outer clothing and its replacement by clean clothing so long as all reasonable considerations of safety and the preservation of dignity have been taken into account. (at [37])

Issues relating to consent often arise in the context of medical treatment.[22] A doctor does not commit a battery when operating on or treating a patient if the patient has given valid consent to the treatment. Of course, this simply prompts a second question: when is a patient's consent valid? An answer to this is found in *Chatterton* v *Gerson* [1981], in which the court ruled that a patient's consent to an operation was valid, despite the fact that she had not been fully informed of the risks, because she broadly understood the nature of the operation:

> [O]nce the patient was informed in broad terms of the nature of the procedure which is intended, and gives her consent, that consent is real, and the cause of the action on which to base a claim for failure to go into risks and implications is negligence, not trespass. (at 443)[23]

This is not to suggest that trespass has no role to play in a medical context. Bristow J continued: 'if by some accident . . . a boy was admitted to hospital for a tonsillectomy and due to an administrative error was circumcised instead, trespass would be the appropriate cause of action against the doctor' (at 432).

But what about refusal of consent? If an individual is able to consent to what would otherwise be a battery, surely it follows that there is a corresponding ability to refuse consent to such actions? Consider again the example of a doctor who delivers a healthy child after performing a caesarean section on the mother without her consent. Does—or should—she have an action against the doctor in battery? The law is clear that an individual has an absolute right to the inviolability of their body:

> [A]n adult patient who . . . suffers from no mental incapacity has an absolute right to choose whether to consent to medical treatment, to refuse it, or to choose one rather than another of the treatments being offered. This right of choice is not limited to decisions which others might regard as sensible. (Lord Donaldson MR, *Re T (Adult: Refusal of Treatment)* [1993] at 102)

22. For examples of the role and validity of consent in other contexts see e.g. *R* v *Lincoln* [1990] concerning 'rough and tumble' on the football pitch—there is no battery when the claimant has voluntarily taken the risk of touching—and *R* v *Williams* [1923] in which a singing teacher was found guilty of raping a naïve claimant who had 'consented' to his actions on the basis of his false assertion that his conduct would improve her singing voice. Her consent was invalid on the basis that she had not really understood what was happening. Finally, consent will not be valid when it is to actions which are deemed contrary to public policy (see *AG's Reference (No 6 of 1980)* [1981] and *R* v *Brown* [1994]).

23. To repeat, this does not mean that the patient has no claim where they have not been fully informed of the risks of the medical procedure. Rather that the claim is more appropriately brought in negligence. The UK Supreme Court has recently confirmed the practice of a patient-friendly, 'informed consent', approach to a doctor's failure to warn of risks adopted by the General Medical Council (GMC)—see ***Montgomery* v *Lanarkshire NHS Trust*** **[2015]** discussed in **section 8.3.2.1**.

A competent adult may therefore withhold their consent to any treatment (including the provision of food if provided by an intravenous tube or similar) even if said treatment is in their best interests, is necessary to save their life or, somewhat more controversially, the life of their unborn child (*Re MB (Caesarean Section)* [1997] at 533). This common law position—and the test of capacity more broadly—has been enshrined in statute (for those over 16) in the Mental Capacity Act 2005.[24]

The Mental Capacity Act 2005, s 1

(2) A person must be assumed to have capacity unless it is established that he lacks capacity.

(3) A person is not to be treated as unable to make a decision unless all practicable steps to help him to do so have been taken without success.

(4) A person is not to be treated as unable to make a decision merely because he makes an unwise decision.

(5) An act done, or decision made, under this Act for or on behalf of a person who lacks capacity must be done, or made, in his best interests.

(6) Before the act is done, or the decision is made, regard must be had to whether the purpose for which it is needed can be as effectively achieved in a way that is less restrictive of the person's rights and freedom of action.

A doctor can only treat a patient in the absence of consent where a patient is unable to consent, that is, they *lack the capacity* to make such a decision themselves. To determine when a patient will lack capacity, it is useful here to adopt Shaun Pattinson's explanation of sections 2 and 3 of the 2005 Act as setting out a two-stage test.[25] A patient will only be considered to lack capacity if both stages of the test are met. First, the patient must be suffering from an 'impairment of, or a disturbance in the functioning of, the mind or brain', which means they are unable to make a decision for themselves (s 2). This may be temporary or long term, and caused by a number of factors including mental illness, brain injury or alcohol or drug abuse. Secondly, the patient will be considered unable to make a decision if the doctor reasonably believes, and takes reasonable steps to ensure (as required by s 5), that the patient is unable to meet any of the requirements of section 3(1): (a) to understand the information relevant to the decision; (b) to retain that information; (c) to use or weigh that information as part of the process of making the decision; or (d) to communicate his decision (whether by talking, using sign language or any other means). Where this test is satisfied, a doctor will not incur liability so long as they reasonably believe that the treatment or procedure is in the patient's 'best interests' (ss 4 and 5).

By contrast, it follows that where a patient *is able* to, for example, understand the information relevant to the decision, they have the capacity to make decisions about

24. In *Re MM (An Adult)* [2007] Munby J held that there is 'no relevant distinction between the test in s 3(1) of the Act and the pre-existing common law' (at [74]).

25. Shaun Pattinson *Medical Law and Ethics* (4th edn, Sweet & Maxwell, 2014), Ch 5.

how they are to be treated and to give—and withhold—their consent and the doctor who operates or treats them will commit a battery.

Counterpoint

The 2005 Act, like the common law, places considerable emphasis on the *doctor's* belief in the patient's capacity. Despite judicial rhetoric upholding an individual's right to self-determination, in cases where medical treatment is necessary to save the life of a woman and the foetus she is carrying, the case law suggests that the former's refusal to consent to medical intervention is less than likely to be considered valid.[26] *Re MB (Caesarean Section)* [1997] is a case in point. In this case, the claimant consented to a caesarean section but withheld consent in relation to an accompanying medical procedure, without which the caesarean section could not be performed. The court held that, in continuing with the procedures, the doctor had not committed a battery. The claimant's withholding of consent was held to be invalid, because she was found to be suffering from an impairment or disturbance of mental functioning (due to a fear of needles). Of course, the reality of the situation was that if the doctors had not intervened, the claimant *and the foetus* would have died. Nevertheless, an individual's right to make bad decisions is recognised in both common and statute law—how far do you think this should extend to decisions which would negatively impact on the life of the foetus?[27]

15.5.2 **Necessity**

Previously in medical situations where a claimant is unable to consent a defendant might rely on the limited common law defence of necessity.[28] This solved a practical problem experienced by emergency services and other medical professionals where an unconscious patient is incapable of consenting to necessary medical treatment. On this basis, where a patient is unconscious but otherwise competent, and not known to object to the treatment, doctors may intervene in the best interests of the patient (*Re F; F* v *West Berkshire Health Authority* [1990]). The defence was also used in cases of permanent incapacity, for example where the patient is in a coma or mentally ill (e.g. *Airedale NHS Trust* v *Bland* [1993]).

Again, the common law in relation to this has been codified by the Mental Capacity Act 2005. As noted earlier, a medical professional will not incur liability for treating a

26. Celia Wells 'On the Outside Looking In: Perspectives on Enforced Caesareans' in Sally Sheldon and Michael Thomson (eds) *Feminist Perspectives on Health Care Law* (Cavendish, 1998), p 237. See also Emma Cave, 'Protecting Patients from their Bad Decisions: Rebalancing Rights, Relationships, and Risk' (2017) 25 Med L Rev 527.

27. For a recent application of the principles in *Re MB* (and the first published judgment approving a caesarean section since the enactment of the Mental Capacity Act 2005), see *Re AA* [2012].

28 Though necessity is most often used where the claimant is temporarily unable to consent, it also applies in other situations (see e.g. the extended discussion in *Re A (Conjoined Twins)* [2001]) and in relation to false imprisonment (*Bournewood*; *Austin and other* v *Commissioner of Police of the Metropolis* [2007] (CA)—although note that the House of Lords did not discuss the application of necessity).

patient who is temporarily or permanently incapacitated, so long as before doing so they take reasonable steps to establish, and reasonably believe, that the patient lacks capacity and the treatment or procedure is in the patient's 'best interests' (s 5). Where the patient's lack of capacity is only temporary—due to shock or anger or as a result of an accident—the medical professional may treat the patient in accordance with their best interests, though they should also take into account when the person is likely to regain capacity in relation to the matter in question and, if possible, wait until the patient has regained capacity before continuing with further treatment (s 4).

15.5.3 **Self-defence**

The defendant may be able to argue that they acted in self-defence. However, unlike the defendant in criminal proceedings who simply needs an honest belief (even if that belief is unreasonable) that they were about to be attacked, the tort defendant's belief must be not only honest but also *reasonable* (*Ashley* v *Chief Constable of West Sussex Police* [2008]). Moreover, it has long been established that the defendant's actions must be proportionate to the force (about to be) exerted against them. Thus, in *Cockcroft* v *Smith* [1705], the claimant's act of running with his finger extended towards the defendant's eyes did not justify the defendant's action of biting off part of the offending finger. Similarly, in *Lane* v *Holloway* [1968] the defendant's severe blow to the claimant's eye was out of proportion to the claimant's punch to his shoulder. *Lane* is also authority for the proposition that provocation is not a valid defence in relation to cases of trespass to the person.

However, *Lane* can be contrasted with the decision in *Cross* v *Kirkby* [2000]. Here a farmer, who had been struck by a hunt saboteur with a baseball bat, wrestled the bat from him and struck a single blow to the head which caused the claimant serious injuries. In upholding the defendant's raising of self-defence the Court of Appeal took into account the anguish of the moment in assessing whether this was an excessive or disproportionate response to the threat posed and held that the law did not require the defendant to measure the violence to be deployed with mathematical precision.

Pause for reflection

Views will differ on what response is or is not reasonable in 'self-defence'. Consider again the woman alone in a lift with an amorous male colleague. Suppose she takes matters into her own hands and knees the man in the groin—could he have a successful claim for battery against her? Or is her conduct excusable on the grounds of self-defence? Much will turn on whether her actions are considered a reasonable exercise of force. After all, to whisper sweet nothings is not to threaten violence—in fact quite the opposite—nor are the words in themselves likely to be sufficient indication that they would be followed by any immediate unlawful force in, say, the form of a kiss or embrace—and, even if they were, surely the harm or injury of, for example, a stolen kiss isn't comparable with that of a knee in the groin? Is it?

15.6 **Intentional infliction of physical harm or distress**

So far this chapter has considered the three torts which comprise trespass to the person: battery, assault and false imprisonment. All these involve direct actual or potential physical infringements of the claimant's person: touching them, putting them in fear of such touching or restricting their movement. However, it is possible to cause another harm *indirectly*; that is, without physically interfering (or threatening to physically interfere) with them or their movements. In such cases, the trespass to the person torts offer no remedy. While the tort of negligence may offer some redress (though only if the claimant's distress amounts to a recognisable psychiatric illness),[29] where such harm is intentional a claimant in such cases will usually turn to the tort in *Wilkinson* v *Downton* and the Protection from Harassment Act 1997.

15.6.1 **The tort in *Wilkinson* v *Downton***

In *Wilkinson* v *Downton* [1897] the defendant falsely told the claimant that her husband had been involved in an accident in which he had been seriously injured. The defendant later claimed that he had intended it as a practical joke. Unfortunately for him it was misjudged. The claimant took the news very badly, causing her to suffer severe physical and psychological reactions. Finding for the claimant, Wright J held that a cause of action arises when:

> [t]he defendant . . . wilfully do an act calculated to cause physical harm to the . . . [claimant]—that is to say, infringe her right to personal safety, and thereby in fact caused physical harm to her. That proposition, without more appears to me to state a good cause of action, there being no justification alleged for the act. (at 57)[30]

However, over the years the status of the 'well-known but seldom used principle in *Wilkinson* v *Downton*' (Arden LJ, *OPO* v *MLA* [2014] at [30]) has been in some doubt—most notably following Lord Hoffmann's suggestion in ***Wainwright*** that it should have 'no leading role in the modern law of tort' and should instead be allowed to 'disappear beneath the surface of the law of negligence' (at [40]–[41]). This may be sensible in relation to *negligently* inflicted psychiatric injury—not least because (in Hoffmann's view) the tort in *Wilkinson* v *Downton* was only established in order to circumvent a now defunct decision (*Victorian Railways Commissioners* v *Coultas* [1888]) which *prevented* recovery in negligence for such injuries.[31] But what about an intentional act that causes physical injuries?

29. See **Chapter 5**.
30. *Wilkinson* v *Downton* was approved by the Court of Appeal in *Janvier* v *Sweeney* [1919].
31. Though see Lady Hale and Lord Toulson's rejection of this as an 'interesting reconstruction [that] shows the pitfalls of interpreting a decision more than a century earlier without a full understanding of jurisprudence and common legal terminology of the earlier period' (***OPO*** at [61]–[63]).

As with the trespass to the person torts, it is clear that the defendant must have had the actual intention to *act*; what is less clear, however, is whether the defendant need also to have intended the *consequences* of his act—what does it mean to say that the defendant's act was 'calculated to cause physical harm'?[32] This was addressed by the House of Lords in ***Wainwright***.

Wainwright v *Home Office* [2003] HL

The claimants, Mrs Wainwright and her son, Alan, were strip-searched by prison officers before visiting a family member in Leeds prison. The searches were a humiliating and distressing experience for both claimants. It was agreed that the search had been 'sloppily' carried out and not in accordance with the Prison Rules 1964. The claimants sought, in part, to rely on the tort in *Wilkinson* v *Downton* in order to ground a claim for the anxiety and distress they had suffered as a result of the prison officers' actions.[33]

Unanimously rejecting their claims, the court held that liability under the Rules required, at the very least, the defendants to have acted without caring whether they caused harm (recklessly). This was not established on the facts of the case: the 'deviations from the procedure laid down for strip-searches were . . . not intended to increase the humiliation necessarily involved but merely sloppiness' (Lord Hoffmann at [45]).

Pause for reflection

Lord Hoffmann continued that *even if the necessary intention had been established* in ***Wainwright*** not all intentionally caused distress should give rise to liability under the *Wilkinson* v *Downton* tort:

> Even on the basis of a genuine intention to cause distress, I would wish . . . to reserve my opinion on whether compensation should be recoverable. In institutions and workplaces all over the country, people constantly do and say things with the intention of causing distress and humiliation to others. This shows lack of consideration and appalling manners but I am not sure that the right way to deal with it is always by litigation . . . The requirement of a course of conduct [in the Protection from Harassment Act 1997] shows that Parliament was conscious that it might not be in the public interest to allow the law

→

32. See further Denise Réaume 'The Role of Intention in the Tort in *Wilkinson* v *Downton*' in Jason Neyers, Erika Chamberlain and Stephen Pitel (eds) *Emerging Issues in Tort Law* (Hart, 2007), p 533.

33. A battery claim in relation to the touching of Alan's penis was allowed by the Court of Appeal (and was not appealed by the Home Office). The claimants also argued there was a breach of their Art 8 rights (right to private and family life). This was rejected by the House of Lords, but upheld in the ECtHR which unanimously held that there had been a breach of both their Art 8 and 13 rights (*Wainwright* v *UK* [2006]). The privacy aspects of the case are discussed in **section 16.6.3**.

→

> to be set in motion for one boorish incident. It may be that any development of the common law should show similar caution. In my opinion, therefore, the claimants can build nothing on *Wilkinson* v *Downton*. It does not provide a remedy for distress which does not amount to recognised psychiatric injury and so far as there may be a tort of intention under which such damage is recoverable, the necessary intention was not established. (at [46]–[47])

Wainwright then prevents the application of the tort in *Wilkinson* v *Downton* in cases of intentionally caused anxiety or distress that falls short of a recognised psychiatric illness.[34] (Though this should now be read in light of Lord Neuberger's comments in *OPO* (at [119]).)

Jonathan Morgan has argued that the decision in ***Wainwright*** reflects a continuing judicial reluctance to recognise the significance of *distress* as an actionable harm:

> it is characterised respectively as a flowing from a failure of etiquette, or from the good natured fun of traditional rites of initiation . . . Such a dismissive attitude to mental distress is perhaps a little surprising, when the facts of ***Wainwright*** itself provide a glaring example of degrading behaviour, by a public authority at that. A rule that only 'serious' distress is actionable would better meet concerns of a flood of trivial claims, while allowing recovery in cases of truly humiliating conduct.[35]

What do you think? Think about the increasing prevalence of image-based sexual abuse, for example taking and/or publishing a private sexual image of someone without his or her consent. Should the fact that the victim's distress does not develop into a psychiatric illness restrict their ability to claim? What if the victim's primary emotion was anger rather than anxiety?[36]

It is clear, following the Supreme Court decision in ***Rhodes* v *OPO* [2015]**, that the defendant must have *intended* to cause physical harm or severe mental or emotional distress. Recklessness is not sufficient. Nor can intention be imputed as a matter of law, though it may be inferred as a matter of fact (Lady Hale and Lord Toulson at [81]–[87]).

Rhodes v *OPO (by his litigation friend BHM) and another* [2015] SC

The case involved the publication of a memoir by James Rhodes, a well-known performing artist, in which he detailed the sexual abuse he suffered while at school and his subsequent mental health issues. The case was brought on behalf of his son, OPO, who suffers from a combination of attention deficit hyperactivity disorder, Asperger's, Dysgraphia and Dyspraxia,

→

34. Confirmed in *Mbasogo* v *Logo Ltd* [2006].
35. Jonathan Morgan 'Privacy Torts: Out with the Old, Out with the New' (2004) 120 LQR 393, 395.
36. On the role of the civil law in addressing the harm of image-based sexual abuse, see further Clare McGlynn and Erika Rackley 'Image-based Sexual Abuse' (2017) 37 OJLS 534; Horsey and Rackley 2018.

→

and sought to prevent publication on the basis that in revealing such details of his father, its publication would be likely to cause him severe emotional distress. The Court of Appeal held—somewhat surprisingly—that the claimant had an arguable case under the tort in *Wilkinson* v *Downton* and granted an interim injunction until the case went to trial.

The Supreme Court allowed the defendant's appeal. Lady Hale and Lord Toulson gave the leading judgment. There are three elements in the *Wilkinson* v *Downton* tort: a conduct element, a mental element and a consequence element. The first (conduct) requires that 'words or conduct directed to the claimant for which there is no justification or reasonable excuse' ([74]). The burden of proof is on the claimant to demonstrate this and, in this case, the court held, this had not been met:

> The book is for a wide audience and the question of justification has to be considered accordingly, not in relation to the claimant in isolation . . . [the Court of Appeal's approach] excluded consideration of the wider question of justification based on the legitimate interest of the defendant telling his story to the world at large in the way he wishes to tell it, and the corresponding interest of the public in hearing his story. When those factors are taken into account . . . there is every justification for the publication (Lady Hale and Lord Toulson at [75]–[76]).

Nor was there any suggestion that the appellant actually intended to cause psychiatric harm, severe mental or emotional distress to the claimant—the second element of any claim (at [89]). The third element (consequence) did not arise in this case; however, it was common ground that the necessary consequence for liability was physical harm or a recognised psychiatric illness. The court left open the question as to whether intentionally causing severe distress might be actionable. Lord Neuberger, in a short concurrence, suggested that it should be:

> As I see it, therefore, there is plainly a powerful case for saying that, in relation to the instant tort, liability for distressing statements, where intent to cause distress is an essential ingredient, it should be enough for the claimant to establish that he suffered significant distress as a result of the defendant's statement. It is not entirely easy to see why, if an intention to cause the claimant significant distress is an ingredient of the tort and it enough to establish the tort in principle, the claimant should have to establish that he suffered something more serious than significant distress before he can recover compensation. (at 119)

see online resources

Pause for reflection

The Court of Appeal judgment in *Rhodes* v *OPO* (or *MLA* v *OPO* as the case was then known) was greeted with dismay and regret by many commentators.[37] At the heart of many of the objections was the view that, were it to stand, the judgment had potentially significant →

37. Liew 2015; Dan Tench 'Case Law: *OPO v MLA*, Shock and Disbelief at the Court of Appeal' Inforrm's blog, 13 October 2014.

→

ramifications for freedom of expression and was 'likely to lead to a "chilling effect" on free speech'.[38] Jo Glanville, the director of English PEN, a worldwide writers' association (who were intervenors in the case at the Supreme Court), commented:

> This sets a worrying precedent for injuncting memoirs or any non-fiction that may expose or investigate the past, whether personal or political. It would allow anyone to cite the distress of a relative or friend as grounds for censorship.[39]

The Supreme Court, in what has been described as a 'paean to freedom of expression'[40] accepted these arguments:

> A person who has suffered in the way that the appellant has suffered, and has struggled to cope with the consequences of his suffering in the way that he has struggle, has the right to tell the world about it . . . Freedom to report the truth is a basic right to which the law gives a very high level of protection . . . . It is difficult to envisage any circumstances in which speech which is not deceptive, threatening or possibly abusive, could give rise to liability in tort for wilful infringement of another's right to personal safety. The right to report the truth is justification in itself. That is not to say that the right of disclosure is absolute, for a person may owe a duty to treat information as private or confidential. But there is no general law prohibiting the publication of facts which will cause distress to another, even if that is the person's intention. (Lady Hale and Lord Toulson at [76]–[77])

15.6.2 **The Protection from Harassment Act 1997**

The Protection from Harassment Act (PfHA) was a response to increasing public concern about harassment and, in particular, stalking.[41] Its enactment attracted considerable media and celebrity attention, most notably from Princess Diana. The Act has since been used by celebrities such as Cheryl Cole, Russell Brand and Harry Styles to try and prevent or restrict press intrusion.

38. MLA 'Notice of appeal in the Supreme Court of the United Kingdom' 6 November 2014.

39. Ian Cobain and Matthew Taylor 'Ex-wife of well-known performer obtains injunction against book to protect son' *The Guardian* 11 October 2014.

40. Dan Tench 'Case Law: ***OPO v James Rhodes*** (formerly MLA): Pianist's book unbanned, no intention to cause distress' Inforrm's blog, 20 May 2015.

41. This aspect of the Act has been strengthened through the creation of two new offences of stalking inserted into the PfHA as ss 2A and 4A by virtue of the Protection of Freedoms Act 2012. Though the Act does not include a formal definition of stalking, s 2A(3) gives examples of behaviours typically associated with it, including following or spying on a person, monitoring their use of the internet or email, loitering and interfering with their property. The introduction of 'Stalking Protection Orders' introduced in the Stalking Protection Act 2019, allows courts to ban perpetrators from going to certain locations and from contacting victims and requires them to seek help.

The Act introduces a civil remedy for harassment (s 3) as well as a criminal offence of harassment (s 2).[42] In line with its principal purpose to prevent and protect rather than compensate, the Act provides for the imposition of an injunction, alongside damages and criminal sanctions for non-compliance (s 3).[43] The key provision, in section 1(1), states that 'a person must not pursue a course of conduct (a) which amounts to harassment of another, and (b) which he knows, or ought to know, amounts to harassment of the other'.[44] In *Levi* v *Bates* [2015] the Court of Appeal confirmed that an individual may be harassed by the defendant even if their actions are aimed at someone else. This is usually likely to be the intended victim's partner or spouse or close family member:

> It is right that, for the statutory tort of harassment to occur, there must be a course of conduct which is aimed (or targeted) at an individual since that is inherent in the term 'harassment'. But I see no reason why it should be only that individual who can sue, if the defendant knows or ought to know that his conduct will amount to harassment of another individual. The tort . . . of harassment does not require an intent to harass any one individual; section 1 of the Act is clear that the question whether conduct is harassing conduct is an objective question for the fact-finder. If therefore a defendant knows or ought to know that his conduct amounts to harassment, he should be liable to the person harassed, even if the conduct is aimed at another person . . .
>
> It may not be often that a person who is not the target of the harassing conduct will, in fact, be harassed. But a wife, or other close family member, may well suffer a feeling of harassment if a defendant publishes her and her husband's address with a view to encouraging members of the public to visit that address in an aggressive or hostile manner. The same applies to publication of a telephone number or a reminder to the public that what is her telephone number (as well as her husband's) can be found in the telephone book. If it is reasonable for one private individual to publish such information about another private individual, there will be no tort; but publication of such information in pursuance of a private grudge may well not be reasonable at all and was not reasonable in this case. (Longmore LJ at [55]–[56])

The Act leaves the definition of harassment deliberately wide. The Act states that harassment may include 'alarming the person or causing the person distress' (though conduct can still amount to harassment even where no distress or alarm is caused) (s 7(2)). Merely

42. The focus here is on civil claims. On the relationship between the criminal and civil aspects of the 1997 Act see Emily Finch 'Stalking the Perfect Stalking Law: An Evaluation of the Efficacy of the Protection from Harassment Act 1997' [2002] Crim LR 703.

43. See e.g. *AM* v *News Group Newspapers Ltd* [2012] in which interim injunctions were granted against journalists and photographers to prevent them from waiting outside—so-called 'door stepping'—the homes of people they wished to photograph or interview. On the impact of the Act on the activities of the media, see Nicole Moreham 'Harassment by Publication in the Media' Inforrm's blog, 26 January 2016.

44. Section 1A (added by Serious Organised Crime and Police Act 2005) extends the remit of the 1997 Act to include a course of conduct directed at *two or more people* which the harasser knows or ought to know amounts to harassment *and* by which 'he intends to persuade any person (whether or not one of those mentioned (in s 1A(a)) (i) not to do something that he is entitled or required to do, or (ii) to do something that he is not under any obligation to do (s 1A(c)). In such circumstances, a course of conduct is defined as 'conduct on at least one occasion in relation to each of those persons' (s 7(3)(b)).

annoying or aggravating matters of everyday life will not amount to harassment: 'the Protection from Harassment Act 1997 is not designed to interfere with the ordinary give and take of everyday life' (*Mitton v Benefield* [2011] at [10]). The behaviour must be of a level that is 'oppressive and unacceptable': Courts are well able to recognise the boundary between conduct which is unattractive, even unreasonable, and conduct which is oppressive and unacceptable. To cross the boundary from the regrettable to the unacceptable the gravity of the misconduct must be of an order which would sustain criminal liability under section 2 (Lord Nicholls, ***Majrowski*** at [30]).

The 1997 Act defines a 'course of conduct' as harassing conduct on 'at least two occasions' (s 7(3)).[45] The incidents must be similar in type and in context: 'the fewer incidents there are and the further in time they are apart, the less likely it will be that they can properly be treated as constituting a course of conduct' (Elias LJ, *James* v *DPP* [2009] at [11]).[46] Whether the defendant's actions amount to a 'course of conduct' will then depend on the facts of the case. It appears that a single publication of a harassing statement or image online will amount to a 'course of conduct' where the defendant does so 'in the knowledge that such publications will inevitably come to [the claimant's] attention on more than one occasion and on each occasion cause them alarm and distress constitutes harassment under the PHA' (Tugendhat J, *Law Society* v *Kordowski* [2011] at [61]). Tugendhat J continued:

> The publication is an ongoing one on a prominent website; accordingly the distress and alarm caused by the publication will also be continuous. It is reasonable to infer in every case that those posted would suffer such distress and alarm on at least two occasions. (at [64])

Pause for reflection

This understanding of a 'course of conduct' allows victims of image-based sexual abuse to utilise the provisions of the 1997 Act in circumstances where a single act (e.g. uploading a single picture) has been done in the knowledge that it would be viewed by a large number of people.[47] In fact, in light of the difficulties and inadequacies of the *criminal* law in this area,

→

45. The Act does not, therefore, cover one-off incidents, such as the practical joke in *Wilkinson* v *Downton*, however serious. Though a victim who fears that a single incident of harassing conduct *might* in the future *become* a course of conduct may be able to claim under s 3(1) which provides a remedy for the 'apprehension' of a breach of s 1. See further, David Ormerod, Case Comment: 'Harassment: Whether Two Incidents of Harassment Constitute a Course of Conduct' [2000] Crim LR 580 discussing *Lau* v *DPP* [2000].

46. The Act is concerned with courses of conduct rather than individual instances of harassment. However, as Rix LJ noted in *Iqbal* v *Dean Manson Solicitors* [2011] involving a series of letters from a firm of solicitors containing allegations against the personal and professional integrity of an assistant solicitor previously employed by them, it is not necessary for those two occasions to amount individually to harassment: 'Take the typical case of stalking, or of malicious phone calls. When a defendant, D, walks past a claimant C's door, or calls C's telephone but puts the phone down without speaking, the single act by itself is neutral, or may be. But if that act is repeated on a number of occasions, the course of conduct may well amount to harassment. That conclusion can only be arrived at by looking at the individual acts complained of as a whole . . . So it is with a course of communications such as letters. A first letter, by itself, may appear innocent and may even cause no alarm, or at most a slight unease. However, in the light of subsequent letters, that first letter may be seen as part of a campaign of harassment' (at [45]).

47. See e.g. *ABK* v *KDT & FGH* [2013]; *AXB* v *BXA* [2018] and generally Horsey and Rackley 2018.

→

victims are increasingly exploiting civil law avenues of redress (usually harassment and misuse of private information).

But what of the (alleged) perpetrators of sexual violence and/or harassment, can they too turn to the civil law? Do they too have a remedy in tort?

> '#MeToo': Five letters that have been tweeted millions of times in the past month, and demonstrate the enormous power of social media and how it can bring about change for the good. The feeling of solidarity is a cathartic experience for many who have been the victim of sexual abuse, harassment or other forms of coercive behaviour. But, what if a victim wants to go further and name someone they say has acted inappropriately towards them?[48]

The simple answer is yes. The laws of harassment, defamation, and misuse of private information apply to victims and perpetrators of on- and offline abuse alike. However, naming the person who has abused you in a public forum—even in a single tweet—is not without risk. While the threshold for harassment is high, it has been used in cases of online 'campaigns' or 'trolling' including where the campaign has involved the repeated tweeting of a derogatory or abusive statement.[49] As Brett Wilson, a media law specialist, explains:

> For a claimant there are a number of advantages in bringing a harassment claim:–
>
> 1. Truth is not a defence to a harassment claim.[50] The issue is whether the conduct is reasonable or not.[51] Standing outside someone's house with a megaphone every day of the week shouting 'John Smith sexually harasses women' is likely to be deemed unreasonable even if it is true that John Smith has sexually harassed women in the past. Whilst it would depend on the facts of the case, the same logic could be applied to an online campaign where these allegations are repeatedly tweeted or posted.
> 2. It is not necessary to prove serious harm or any harm to reputation [as in cases in defamation].[52] Whilst there is often an overlap with defamation, the tort is not concerned with injury to reputation. Damages are awarded for distress and injury to feelings.[53] An injunction can be imposed to prohibit repetition of the conduct.
> 3. It is not even necessary to show that anyone read the statements. The question is whether the conduct was harassing and whether the defendant knew or should have known this. Harassment may be established by unwanted communications to the claimant alone.
> 4. The legal process is often more straightforward, quicker and cheaper (in relative terms).[54]

48. Brett Wilson '#MeToo, naming and shaming: a risky business?' Inforrm's blog, 2 November 2017.

49. While the conduct must target an individual, this can be direct or indirect (*Mitton v Benefield* [2011]).

50. Unlike in defamation, see **section 17.6.1**. See *Merlin Entertainments LPC, Chessington World of Adventures Operations v Cave* [2014].

51. It may be that in cases of public figures, a general public interest in exposing the wrongdoer would be sufficient to make the conduct reasonable—see discussion of s 1(3)(c) of the 1997 Act below.

52. See **section 17.3**.

53. The amount of damages awarded in injury to feelings cases typically range from £800 to £42,000, with only the most 'exceptional cases' exceeding £42,000 (Presidential Guidance, 'Employment Tribunal awards for injury to feelings and psychiatric injury following *De Souza v Vinco Construction (UK) Ltd* [2017] EWCA Civ 879'.

54. Wilson (**n 48**): other avenues include defamation, privacy (misuse of private information/breach of confidence) and malicious falsehood.

The defendant need not have foreseen that their conduct would harass or cause the claimant anxiety. Liability is based on actual or constructive knowledge that their conduct amounts to harassment, that is whether the defendant *ought* to have known that their conduct amounts to harassment. The test is whether 'a reasonable person in the possession of the same information would think the course of conduct amounted to harassment of the other' (s 1(2)). The PfHA excludes certain conduct from the remit of harassment. These defences are listed in section 1(3) and include activity for the purpose of detecting or preventing crime (s 1(3)(a)) and that which is 'in the particular circumstances . . . reasonable' (s 1(3)(c)).

Pause for reflection

Joanne Conaghan argues that a key difficulty with the 1997 Act is that it 'assumes a degree of consensus [as to what constitutes harassing behaviour] which may not exist' (1999, pp 207–8). Despite the view of the Court of Appeal in *Thomas* v *News Group Newspapers Ltd* [2001] that 'harassment is . . . a word which has a meaning that is generally understood' (at [30]), this may not always be the case. Opinions may differ on when, for example, an ex-lover's attempts to win a partner back become threatening or a series of newspaper articles amount to harassment.[55]

Moreover, she continues, the 'adoption of the "reasonable harasser's" perspective' fails to directly engage with the effect of the harasser's conduct on the *claimant* and 'inevitably incorporates a gender dimension into the standard applied, certainly where the conduct in question has a sexual dimension' (pp 207–8). Do you agree? Think again about the infatuated student in the examples at the start of the chapter—at what point do you think their phone calls will constitute harassment?

55. See further Tugendhat J's application of Phillips LJ's view, in *Thomas* v *News Group Newspapers Ltd* [2001], that 'in general, press criticism, even if robust, does not constitute unreasonable conduct and does not fall within the natural meaning of harassment . . . a series of articles that have foreseeably caused distress to an individual . . . discloses no arguable case of harassment' (referred to in *Trimingham* v *Associated Newspapers Ltd* [2012] at [34] and discussed in Eleanor Steyn 'Associated Cost of Overstating Media Harassment Claim' (2012) 23 Ent L Rev 228). See also *Sube* v *News Group Newspapers Ltd* [2020], in which a married couple with nine children had been the subject of a series of newspaper articles detailing their dissatisfaction with their social housing offered by Luton Borough Council. Although the couple had originally approached the press (hoping to put pressure on the council), they were unhappy with the 'indignant tone' of the articles, published under headlines such as: 'Jobless dad whines about £15k-a-year council home—and turns down five bedroom house'. Rejecting their claim for harassment, Warby J held that:

> nothing short of a conscious or negligent abuse of media freedom will justify a finding of harassment: ' . . . the test [of reasonableness] requires the publisher to consider whether a proposed series of articles, which is likely to cause distress to an individual, will constitute an abuse of the freedom of press which the pressing social needs of a democratic society require should be curbed.' *Thomas* v *News Group* [50] (Lord Phillips MR). (at [68])

In *Hayes* v *Willoughby* [2013], the defendant, Willoughby, had embarked on a campaign against his former employer alleging fraud, embezzlement and tax evasion in relation to his management of his companies. A subsequent investigation found no basis in the allegations, however the defendant continued with his campaign. The majority of the Supreme Court held that the defendant had no section 1(3)(a) defence to his harassing behaviour. The test was neither wholly objective (as that would render the reasonableness defence in section 1(3)(c) otiose), nor subjective (a mere belief that he is preventing a crime, however absurd, cannot justify the defendant persisting in a course of conduct which the law recognises as harassment). Rather the defendant's actions must pass an 'undemanding' 'test of rationality':

> He must have thought rationally about the material suggesting the possibility of criminality and formed the view that the conduct said to constitute harassment was appropriate for the purpose of preventing or detecting it. If he has done these things, then he has the relevant purpose. The court will not test his conclusions by reference to the view which a hypothetical reasonable man in his position would have formed. (Lord Sumption at [15])

In contrast *Willoughby* was described by Lord Sumption as having a 'vendetta' against Hayes which 'was more than objectively unreasonable. It was irrational. His persistence was obsessive' (at [16]).[56]

Despite its initial focus on stalking, the PfHA has an extremely wide remit. It has been used in response to the publication of victimising newspaper articles (*Thomas* v *News Group Newspapers Ltd; Trimingham* v *Associated Newspapers Ltd* [2012]), sending mass emails and setting up websites (*Merlin Entertainments LPC, Chessington World of Adventures Operations* v *Cave* [2014]), a Facebook page revealing the identity and whereabouts of a convicted sex offender (*CG* v *Facebook Ireland Ltd and Joseph McCloskey* [2015]),[57] unjustified bills and threats of legal action (*Ferguson* v *British Gas* [2009]), posting of personal information or purported information online (*GYH* v *Persons Unknown* [2017), multiple, unjustified letters demanding payment (*Ferguson* v *British Gas*), paparazzi photographers,[58] bullying in the workplace (***Majrowski***; *Veakins* v *Kier Islington Ltd* [2009]) and intimidating public demonstrations (*Daiichi UK Ltd* v *Stop Huntington Animal Cruelty* [2004]).

However, even if there is found to be no harassment, other remedies may be available—see e.g. clause 4 of the Independent Press Standards Organisation's 'Editors' Code of Practice' which states that 'journalists must not engage in intimidation, harassment or persistent pursuit' and 'must not persist in questioning, telephoning, pursuing or photographing individuals once asked to desist; nor remain on their property when asked to leave and must not follow them' unless, of course, such behaviour is in 'the public interest' (see further **www.ipso.co.uk/IPSO/harassment.html**).

56. In 2019, Willoughby was given a six-month suspended sentence for five breaches of a harassment injunction, originally ordered in 2011 by the Court of Appeal (*Hayes* v *Willoughby* [2019]).

57. See also Iain Wilson 'Case Law: *Suttle v Walker*, Facebook "Keyboard warrior" order to pay £55,000 libel and harassment damages' Inforrm's blog, 30 January 2019.

58. 'News: Harry Styles harassment case, photographers consent to permanent injunctions' Inforrm's blog, 11 March 2014; Natalie Peck 'Harassment and injunctions: Cheryl Cole' Inforrm's blog, 7 July 2011.

Pause for reflection

Maurice Kay LJ in *Veakins* v *Kier Islington* drew attention to the increasing use of the PfHA in the context of workplace harassment in order, he suggested, to avoid the more restrictive requirements to succeed in a negligence action following *Hatton* v *Sutherland* [2002].[59] Though there is nothing in the language of the Act to prevent its application in this context, it was doubtful, he suggested, that this is what the legislature had in mind when enacting the provisions:

> It should not be thought from this unusually one-sided case that stress at work will often give rise to liability for harassment. I have found the conduct in this case to be 'oppressive and unacceptable' but I have done so in circumstances where I have also described it as 'extraordinary'. I do not expect that many workplace cases will give rise to this liability. It is far more likely that, in the great majority of cases, the remedy for high-handed or discriminatory misconduct by or on behalf of an employer will be more fittingly in the Employment Tribunal. (at [17])

Similarly, Conaghan suggests that 'the idea that persistent criticism at work should be viewed and treated in the same way as stalking threatens the credibility and legitimacy of the Act' (1999, p 210). Do you agree?

15.7 **Conclusion**

This chapter explores the torts which comprise trespass to the person—battery, assault and false imprisonment. These torts protect an individual against an infringement of their personal integrity through the infliction of unlawful force (battery), the fear of the infliction of said force (assault) and the unlawful restriction of their freedom of movement (false imprisonment). The three torts have the same characteristics: they must be committed intentionally; they must cause direct and immediate harm; and they are actionable without proof of loss. These characteristics distinguish the trespass to the person torts from the tort of negligence: while trespass compensates the claimant in relation to direct and intentional harm (e.g. being deliberately hit), negligence compensates the claimant for unintentional or indirect harm (i.e. accidental injury).

The chapter also considered the tort in *Wilkinson* v *Downton*, which provides a remedy for intentional acts causing *indirect* physical harm and the Protection from Harassment Act 1997 which imposes civil and criminal liability for harassment, that is a 'course of conduct' that is 'oppressive and unacceptable'.

59. Keith Patten notes that a claim under the PfHA has three advantages over a claim in negligence: (a) no foreseeability requirement; (b) an ability to sue for 'anxiety' in absence of recognised psychiatric illness; and (c) a longer limitation period (2010).

End-of-chapter questions

After reading the chapter carefully, try answering the questions which follow.

1 Outline the trespass to the person torts; how do they differ from the tort of negligence?

2 'Tort law has, in recent years, come a long way toward removing the barriers which previously stood in the way of complainants seeking redress in the context of harassing conduct.' Assess the accuracy of this statement.

If you would like to know what we think visit the **online resources**. www.oup.com/he/horsey7e

Answering the problem question

Consider again the problem question at the start of this chapter. Now having read about the topic, **what would be your advice to the various parties?**

Here are some pointers to get you started

→ There are a few potential assaults here: Thomas's threat to Henry, his whispered advances to Mary and (if he saw it coming) Henry's tripping up of Thomas.

→ Could Thomas's missed calls to Mary be considered harassing behaviour under the Protection from Harassment Act?

→ Don't forget defences—is Mary's battery of Thomas in self-defence?

If you need more guidance

→ An **annotated version of the problem with issues and cases to consider** can be found in the Appendix.

→ A **suggested outline answer** to check your ideas against can be found in the online resources that accompany the book.

Further reading

Though some of the academic writing in this area predates the decision in ***Wainwright***, it continues to offer an insightful and relevant critique of the law in this area.

Antonsdóttir, Hildur Fjóla 'Compensation as a Means to Justice? Sexual Violence Survivors' Views on the Tort Law Option in Iceland' (2020) 28 Fem LS 277

Chamallas, Martha 'Will Tort Law Have its #MeToo Moment?' 4 September 2018, Ohio State Public Law Working Paper No 456

Conaghan, Joanne 'Enhancing Civil Remedies for (Sexual) Harassment: s 3 of the Protection from Harassment Act 1997' (1999) 7 Fem LS 203

Godden, Nikki 'Tort Claims for Rape: More Trials, Fewer Tribulations?' in Janice Richardson and Erika Rackley (eds) *Feminist Perspectives on Tort Law* (Routledge, 2012), pp 163–78

Horsey, Kirsty and Erika Rackley 'Tort Law' in Rosemary Auchmuty (ed) *Great Debates on Law and Gender* (Palgrave, 2018)

Hunt, Chris DL '*Wilkinson v Downton* Revisited' [2015] CLJ 392

Liew, Ying Khai 'The Rule in *Wilkinson v Downton*: Conduct, Intention and Justifiability' (2015) 78 MLR 349

Lunney, Mark 'False Imprisonment, Fare Dodging and Federation—Mr Robertson's Evening Out' (2009) 31 Sydney L Rev 537

Patten, Keith 'Defining Harassment' (2010) 160 NLJ 331

Trindale, F A 'Intentional Torts: Some Thoughts on Assault and Battery' (1982) 2 OJLS 211

Invasion of privacy

16

Problem question

Read this problem question carefully, and keep it in mind while you are working through the chapter that follows. At the end of the chapter, you will be able to apply what you have learnt to the problem question and advise the relevant parties.

Elizabeth is the fiancée of a Premiership footballer, Alessandro Talentti. She has always been happy to be photographed with Alessandro at awards evenings, film premieres and charity events and also while out with her girlfriends shopping or lunching, or with other footballers' wives and girlfriends watching football matches.

Recently, as she has started to organise her wedding, which she wants to be intimate and private, Elizabeth has found the media attention intrusive and has had several arguments with photographers wanting to take her picture whilst out shopping or in small, quiet restaurants. One photographer, Chris, is particularly persistent and takes photographs when she is leaving a hospital after visiting her mother who is very ill. He also photographed her (using a long-range lens) going in to a small London bridal boutique when she was shopping for bridesmaids' dresses with her young sister and niece.

On the wedding day—the press having been successfully excluded from the venue—one of the caterers secretly takes some pictures of the ceremony and the reception, where there were many famous guests. He sells these pictures to *Peachy!*, a well-known celebrity glossy magazine; the pictures are published in the following week's issue and online as an 'exclusive'. Meanwhile, a journalist contacts Alessandro saying he has found out that he had a brief affair the previous year while away at a football tournament and that this information is going to be published the following day.

Advise Elizabeth and Alessandro as to any legal actions they might be able to pursue.

16.1 Introduction

Consider the following examples:

- → ***Karen, a famous pop singer, is photographed entering an eating disorders treatment centre and the pictures are published in a tabloid newspaper.***
- → ***Long-range photographs are taken of Molly, a television newsreader, with her children on holiday, sunbathing and swimming in the sea. These are published on the website of a tabloid newspaper.***

→ ***Nancy, a British actress, marries a Hollywood actor. They agreed to sell their wedding photos to Look and See! magazine but secret photos of the ceremony are published in Look Here! magazine.***

→ ***Eric, a teenager, is caught on CCTV vandalising a shop front. Images of him are published in a local newspaper and put on the local TV news.***

→ ***David, an Olympic gold-medallist, is discovered to be having an extramarital affair by a reporter who wants to publish this information 'in the public interest'.***

In each of these examples the parties' privacy has, in some way, been invaded. Privacy is consistently a 'hot topic', from the 2012 Leveson Report into media practices, to the recent treatment of Meghan Markle, Duchess of Sussex, by sections of the British media. In modern society, there are obviously many ways in which information about others can be collected and transmitted, meaning that the protection of our privacy is more relevant than ever.

That said, it took a long time for privacy to be protected by tort—and really this was driven by developments flowing from the Human Rights Act (HRA) 1998. Some limited protection of privacy was always possible: torts of trespass (to person and land), private nuisance, malicious falsehood and defamation all overlap to some extent with aspects of privacy. Further protection comes from property rights, equity and copyright laws, as well as, inter alia, the Protection from Harassment Act 1997 and the Data Protection Act 1998.[1] However, it was not until 2014 that we could say there was an actual privacy tort—this is when the court confirmed that there was a tort of misuse of private information.[2]

Article 8 of the European Convention on Human Rights (ECHR) gives everyone 'the right to respect for . . . private and family life . . . home and . . . correspondence'. This, brought into domestic focus by the HRA, helped the law develop in ways to bring about new protection of privacy in tort. However, there is a competing and equally important Convention right: the right to freedom of expression (Art 10). Most recent case law focuses on the interplay between these rights.

Many (but not all) claims regarding privacy violations are made by 'celebrities'—who (usually but not always) allege media intrusion into their private lives. 'Privacy' has therefore become somewhat contentious. When asking whether someone should have the right to remain private in a particular situation, regard is often had to their fame, notoriety or their own self-exposure via social media. Some believe that celebrities should accept the inevitable media and other interference fame brings. However, celebrity cases set precedents that apply for everyone and, while many of us will never be intruded upon by the media, others are (see e.g. *Venables* v *News Group Newspapers* [2001]; *X (a woman formerly known as Mary Bell)* v *SO* [2003]) and there are numerous other ways our privacy can be invaded (see e.g. ***Wainwright* v *Home Office* [2003]**;

1. However, none of these protects an individual's privacy per se and all are limited in the protection offered. E.g. despite protectionist in-roads made in *Khorasandjian* v *Bush* [1993], since ***Hunter* v *Canary Wharf*** [1997] individuals require a proprietary interest in land to claim in private nuisance (**section 18.3.2**). Similarly, for recovery under the 1997 Act, there must be a 'course of conduct' that amounts to harassment (**section 15.6.2**).

2. *Vidal-Hall and others* v *Google Inc* [2014].

Peck* v *UK [2003]; ***Rhodes* v *OPO*** [2015]). In light of findings from the Leveson Inquiry, including those on illegal phone hacking of teenage murder victim Milly Dowler and others' mobile telephones, as well as high-profile sports, music, television, political and business personalities and others seeking injunctions and super-injunctions to prevent information about them being published, media intrusion and the consequent invasions of privacy it causes are rarely not in the spotlight.

This chapter considers how tort protects against invasions of privacy, by looking at the development of breach of confidence, a legal concept straddling tort and equity, once concerned with 'secrets' and now judicially adapted to protect privacy, in the form of 'misuse of private information'. We then ask whether developments in the law protecting privacy—particularly in the wake of the HRA—threaten freedom of expression and therefore the public's 'right' to information, particularly about celebrities, including royalty and politicians.

16.2 **A tort of invasion of privacy?**

Successive Parliaments have been unwilling to create a privacy tort—despite numerous calls to do so—which has been a major obstacle in developing privacy protection. This legislative reluctance can be illustrated with a short review of Committee Reports and Bills presented to Parliament and parliamentary opinion thereafter.

In the 1960s three Bills were presented before Parliament directly relating to privacy; two of which expressly provided for an actionable right for citizens to claim that their privacy had been infringed. Each failed. Lord Mancroft's Bill (1961) was withdrawn due to lack of governmental support; Mr Alexander Lyon's Bill (1967) was rejected for being too limited; and Mr Brian Walden's Bill (1969) was rejected for encroaching too far into freedom of expression.[3]

Soon after, the Younger Committee presented its *Report on Privacy*.[4] This concluded by stating that there was 'no need to extend the law of privacy further'. The principal objection related to defining 'privacy', but it was also thought that sufficient remedies for intrusion of one's privacy already existed, and self-regulation of media outlets was preferred. Similar views were advocated by the McGregor Commission in 1977.[5] These reports were followed by two Bills presented within the 1988–9 parliamentary sessions—again, both failed.[6]

In 1990, the Calcutt Committee again rejected the creation of a tort of privacy in favour of press self-regulation through the Press Complaints Commission.[7] Even after reviewing the laws of France, Germany and the United States, the Committee could not find a satisfactory definition of privacy. A final statement of the Calcutt Committee expressing the government's view was presented in 1995. Once again self-regulation was

3. The complete text of each of the three Bills is available in the appendix of the Younger Report.

4. *Report of the Committee on Privacy*, Chairman: Kenneth Younger (Cmnd 5012, 1972).

5. *(Third) Royal Commission on the Press* (Cmnd 6810, July 1977).

6. Bill on Protection of Privacy and Right of Reply introduced by John Browne MP and Tony Worthington MP.

7. *Committee on Privacy and Related Matters Report of the Committee on Privacy and Related Matters*, Chairman: David Calcutt (Cm 1102, June 1990).

preferred and no intention to introduce a tort of privacy was expressed.[8] Although in 2004 the House of Commons Culture, Media and Sport Committee advocated a specific right of privacy,[9] it later acknowledged that:

> To draft a law defining a right to privacy which is both specific in its guidance but also flexible enough to apply fairly to each case which would be tested against it could be almost impossible. Many people would not want to seek redress through the law, for reasons of cost and risk. In any case, we are not persuaded that there is significant public support for a privacy law.[10]

As already noted, a key problem has been the lack of a coherent definition of what privacy is, despite a number of attempts having been made. One reason for this may be that 'privacy' is not the same for all people. It has variously been described as 'the right to be let alone',[11] to be free from an 'unwanted gaze' or 'unauthorised interference with a person's seclusion of himself'[12] or to have unfettered control of information about or images of oneself.[13]

Other nations have well-established privacy protection, suggesting that workable definitions are possible.[14] However, these protections vary in their intensity and, consequently, such variation may be one of the factors making finding a universal definition so difficult. In France, for example, invasion of privacy is a crime, supported by civil injunctions; therefore people, including 'celebrities', can keep their private lives very private indeed.[15] German law offers less protection but the Constitution written after the Second World War protects information about citizens' personal and private lives. The notion of what is considered private has been developed by the courts over time in a flexible way and many claimants satisfactorily resolve their claims.

As early as 1931, Percy H Winfield said that he hoped the House of Lords would develop a new tort specifically to protect privacy. However, 60 years later, the common law still had no defined privacy protection, as clearly illustrated by ***Kaye* v *Robertson and Sport Newspapers Ltd*** **[1991]**.

Kaye v *Robertson and Sport Newspapers Ltd* [1991] CA

Gordon Kaye (at the time a well-known TV personality) suffered extensive brain injuries when a billboard collapsed onto his car. While in hospital, an editor and a photographer from the *Sunday Sport* newspaper gained entry to his room. They photographed him lying semi-conscious in →

8. *Privacy and Media Intrusion* (Cm 2918, July 1995).

9. This was rejected by the government at the time (Privacy and Media Intrusion: Replies to the Committee's Fifth Report 2002–2003, First Special Report (HC 213, February 2004)).

10. Culture, Media and Sport Committee 'Self Regulation of the Press' Seventh Report of Session 2006–2007 (HC 375, July 2007), [53].

11. Thomas Cooley *Cooley on Torts* (2nd edn, 1888), p 29; SD Warren and LD Brandeis 'The Right to Privacy' (1890) 4 Harv L Rev 193, 205.

12. Percy H Winfield 'Privacy' (1931) 47 LQR 23.

13. William L Prosser 'Privacy' (1960) 48 Cal L Rev 383, 389. See *Fenty and others* v *Arcadia Group Brands Ltd and others* [2015]—otherwise known as *Rihanna* v *Topshop*—where the singer successfully sued the retail chain for unauthorised use of her image on a vest top.

14. See e.g. the US *Restatement (Second) of Torts* (2010), especially s 652B.

15. See Lisa O'Carroll and Caroline Davies 'William and Kate win French injunction over topless photos' *The Guardian* 18 September 2012.

→

bed and conducted an 'interview', later marketing these as a 'scoop'. His injuries meant Kaye had no memory of this occurring. Kaye's agent sought an injunction to prevent the pictures and story being published, alleging that these were an invasion of privacy. As there was no specific privacy tort, he resorted to other existing torts, including defamation, passing off, malicious falsehood and trespass to the person.

All but the malicious falsehood claim failed. This meant only that the newspaper had to remove any references that said Kaye had consented to being interviewed or photographed—the photos were still published. The Court of Appeal recognised that it was a clear invasion of privacy to be photographed in a hospital bed, particularly when one had no power to prevent this, but nothing more could be done. English tort law had created various 'boxes' of liability which, if a claim does not fit into them, leave no redress:

> If ever a person has a right to be let alone by strangers with no public interest to pursue, it must surely be when he lies in hospital recovering from brain surgery and in no more than partial command of his faculties. It is this invasion of his privacy which underlies the [claimant's] complaint. Yet it alone, however gross, does not entitle him to relief in English law. (Bingham LJ at 70)

In ***Kaye***, the Court of Appeal recognised the need for a tort of invasion of privacy but deferred responsibility for this to Parliament: 'The facts of the present case are a graphic illustration of the desirability of Parliament considering whether and in what circumstances statutory provision can be made to protect the privacy of individuals' (Glidewell LJ at 66).

Similarly, in *Malone* v *Metropolitan Police Commissioner (No 2)* [1979], a case concerning telephone tapping, Sir Robert Megarry V-C emphasised that the courts should not 'legislate' where no right has been created. He stated that 'where Parliament has abstained from legislating on a point that is plainly suitable for legislation, it is indeed difficult for the court to lay down new rules of common law or equity that will carry out the Crown's treaty obligations' (at 373, referring to the state's obligations under the ECHR). This desire to refrain from judicial intervention in favour of legislative action was also acknowledged in ***Wainwright***. Lord Hoffmann (with whom the other law lords all agreed) explicitly agreed with Sir Robert Megarry V-C, rejecting any 'broad brush approach' of the common law (at [33]). Lord Hoffmann stated that English law neither contained nor needed a specific privacy tort, and might even be *unable* to create one (at [18]). A year later, in ***Campbell* v *Mirror Group Newspapers* [2004]**, Lady Hale said: 'our law cannot, even if it wanted to, develop a general tort of invasion of privacy' (at [133]).[16]

Thus, both the judiciary and Parliament have long been averse to the idea of creating a tort to protect privacy. Various reasons for this have been proffered, including lack of precedent, lack of a suitable definition of privacy, concerns about frivolous claims, the appropriate remedy (and whether any remedy could be effective, especially after the event) and concern about placing restraints on freedom of expression.

16. Interestingly, the Ontario Court of Appeal has recognised a common law tort of invasion of privacy: *Jones* v *Tsige* [2012]. Other Canadian provinces have statutory torts protecting privacy. In *Doe 464533* v *ND* [2016] the Ontario Superior Court of Justice recognised a tort of 'publication of embarrassing private facts'. In New Zealand, the tort was recognised in *Hosking* v *Runting* [2004] (at 109) and a further tort of 'intrusion on seclusion' in *C* v *Holland* [2012].

Counterpoint

In our view, none of these reasons are convincing. Lack of precedent does not prevent Parliament enacting legislation nor, in other areas, has it stopped the courts 'creating law' (see e.g. the tort in *Wilkinson* v *Downton* [1897] or the action under ***Rylands* v *Fletcher*** [1868]). Definition may be problematic but it is not insurmountable. The 1972 Younger Committee report described privacy as 'privacy of information, that is the right to determine for oneself how and to what extent information about oneself is communicated to others'.[17] This subjective interpretation fits well with the majority of the cases we discuss shortly—perhaps indicating that defining privacy has never been as problematic as is assumed or that a definition is in fact relatively unimportant.

The concern about frivolous claims surfaces each time a potential new harm is identified in tort. Yet the 'floodgates' that the judiciary seem so concerned to avoid opening do not seem to have opened in other jurisdictions and, given the personal and financial cost of bringing any legal claim, particularly as legal aid would not be available, few would be able to bring so-called frivolous claims. If the courts are concerned that there will be *more* claims, this is a different issue—but an increased number of claims may simply reflect an increased number of invasions of privacy, which should be no barrier to making a claim and may also indicate that those who continuously infringe individuals' personal and private lives (e.g. the press) ought to be reined in by private law actions against them.

Remedies are more problematic. Most claimants seek to prevent information reaching, or to have information withdrawn from, the public sphere. Often it will be too late to do this (e.g. in the form of an injunction prohibiting publication). However, this difficulty is not used as a reason to *deny* remedies in other areas: for personal injuries caused by negligence there is no remedy that can give a claimant back a lost limb, yet the 'appropriateness' of the remedy, which has to be monetary, does not prevent actionable claims. In any case, damages can be awarded in lieu of an injunction in appropriate cases.

Concerns about infringements on the right to freedom of expression are more valid. It is right in a democratic society that people, including the media, are free to form and speak their opinions. However, again (and as the cases discussed later show) the problem is not insurmountable: a balancing exercise is undertaken and in fact the development of this balancing exercise may even have been what opened the door for the recent acknowledgement that a tort exists.

16.3 **How has privacy been protected?**

Despite the lack of common law protection, as indicated earlier the legislature has favoured non-intervention and self-regulation, not wanting to be seen to be curbing the important, and protected, right to freedom of expression. This view was supported by the Culture, Media and Sport Select Committee which, in its 2007 report *Self-Regulation of the Press*, concluded that significant progress had been made to ensure the correct

17. At p 10.

balance between protecting privacy and the right to publish—so much so that any statutory regulation would, in its view, 'represent a very dangerous interference with the freedom of the press. We continue to believe that statutory regulation of the press is a hallmark of authoritarianism and risks undermining democracy' (at [54]).

More authority was instead given to the Press Complaints Commission (PCC), an organisation that supposedly monitored British press adherence to ethical guidelines, which was closed down in September 2014.[18]

Pause for reflection

The PCC marketed itself as 'fast, free and fair'—its main advantage supposedly that it was quicker to achieve adjudication than through the court system. People who considered that their privacy had been violated by the print media could complain to the PCC, which—after considering the allegation alongside the 'justifications' for the intrusion—could obtain a retraction and an apology, but could provide no further remedies.

Sara Cox, the radio DJ and TV presenter, complained to the PCC after a tabloid newspaper published long-range photographs of her sunbathing topless on a private beach on her honeymoon. She complained that the photographs were taken when she was in a place where she had a reasonable expectation of privacy and were published in breach of her right to respect for her private life. Following adjudication by the PCC, the newspaper's editor published a prominent apology and wrote privately to Ms Cox, but she sued anyway,[19] later settling out of court.

Why did Sara Cox sue even after an apology was obtained? Once private photographs have been published, they cannot be retracted—is an apology enough? Do you think the fact that the newspaper settled out of court is an indication or an admission of wrongdoing?

As Sara Cox's case illustrates, the PCC lacked 'teeth'. Its board was comprised mainly of press representatives, including editors of national newspapers—so to an extent it had a vested interest in what was and was not published.

The Leveson Inquiry

The PCC's ineffectiveness was something that vexed Lord Justice Leveson in his inquiry into the culture, practices and ethics of the press in 2011–12.[20] While not specifically concerned with privacy (it was ordered by then Prime Minister David Cameron in the wake of public outrage surrounding the newspaper phone-hacking scandal), many of the recommendations from

→

18. The PCC operated an Editors' Code of Practice addressing invasions of privacy (clause 3), including, e.g., guidance restricting the use of long-range lenses and in relation to people grieving, children and people in hospital.

19. *Sara Cox* v *MGN Ltd* [2003].

20. Lord Justice Leveson, *Report into the Culture, Practices and Ethics of the Press* (2012). See especially from p 219 (and in the Executive Summary from p 12).

→

the 2,000-page report have affected the law in some way and are likely to continue to do so.[21] The recommendations included the following:

- Dissolution of the PCC and the creation of a new, wholly independent regulatory body comprised of people with media experience but no serving editor, government minister or politician.
- This body should create a Standards Code recognising the importance of freedom of speech and of publishing matters in the public interest, such as the exposure of serious impropriety or crime, particularly of public figures.
- The Code should address the way individuals are treated by the press, especially with regard to accuracy, avoiding misrepresentation of facts and maintaining appropriate respect for their privacy.
- The body should be empowered to grant appropriate remedial action for breach of its standards, to direct the nature and placement of apologies/corrections and to impose sanctions including financial penalties (Leveson envisaged fines of up to 1 per cent of annual turnover up to a maximum of £1 million for serious systemic violations).
- Legislation should 'underpin' the proposed system of self-regulation.

Welcoming the Leveson Report, David Cameron agreed that a new and independent regulator of the press, with a new code of standards, was required. However, he viewed using legislation to underpin this as 'crossing the Rubicon' and political opinion on the matter was very much divided.[22] The government nonetheless committed to implementing Leveson's key recommendation: the media should regulate itself but there should be some independent verification (or 'recognition') of those regulatory arrangements. The three major parties eventually reached agreement on establishing an independent regulator backed by Royal Charter.[23] This was granted by the Privy Council in October 2013, despite legal challenges.[24] In November 2014 the Press Recognition Panel (PRP) was established to independently verify the media's new self-regulatory body: the Independent Press Standards Organisation (IPSO).[25]

21. This was Part 1 of the Leveson Inquiry—Part 2, also requested by David Cameron, cannot begin until any criminal proceedings stemming from Part 1 have been concluded. From November 2016 to January 2017 the Department for Culture, Media & Sport and the Home Office opened a new consultation asking in part 'whether it is still appropriate, proportionate and in the public interest' to go ahead with Part 2. In March 2018 the government controversially confirmed that Part 2 of the Inquiry would not go ahead.

22. See e.g. Patrick Wintour and Dan Sabbagh 'Leveson Report: David Cameron refuses to "cross Rubicon" and write press law' *The Guardian* 29 November 2012; Lisa O'Carroll 'Leveson debate prompts criticism over "draconian" punitive damages plan' *The Guardian* 11 January 2013.

23. Department for Culture, Media and Sport 'Leveson Report: Final draft Royal Charter for proposed body to recognise press industry self-regulator' (Policy paper) 11 October 2013. See also Patrick Wintour 'Press regulation: a back-channel deal sealed with a 3am text message' *The Guardian* 18 March 2013; Patrick Wintour, Lisa O'Carroll and Nicholas Watt 'Press regulation: newspapers bridle at "historic" deal' *The Guardian* 19 March 2013.

24. See BBC News 'Press regulation: Privy Council grants royal charter' 30 October 2013.

25. Royal Charter, art 2.2.

IPSO was established 8 September 2014, replacing the discredited PCC. More independent of media interests than the PCC, under the terms of its Editors' Code of Practice, it can deal with inaccurate reporting, invasion of privacy, intrusion into grief or shock and harassment by the press.[26] It too has the power to obtain apologies and corrections, but may also issue fines in sufficiently serious cases.[27]

Clause 2 of IPSO's Editors' Code, the current version of which came into effect on 1 January 2021, is laid out as follows:

2 *Privacy

i) Everyone is entitled to respect for their private and family life, home, physical and mental health, and correspondence, including digital communications.
ii) Editors will be expected to justify intrusions into any individual's private life without consent. In considering an individual's reasonable expectation of privacy, account will be taken of the complainant's own public disclosures of information and the extent to which the material complained about is already in the public domain or will become so.
iii) It is unacceptable to photograph individuals, without their consent, in public or private places where there is a reasonable expectation of privacy.

The asterisk denotes a section of the Code from which IPSO allows derogation if it is in 'the public interest' to do so. This is defined at the end of the Code:

The Public Interest

1. The public interest includes, but is not confined to:
   - Detecting or exposing crime, or the threat of crime, or serious impropriety.
   - Protecting public health or safety.
   - Protecting the public from being misled by an action or statement of an individual or organisation.
   - Disclosing a person or organisation's failure or likely failure to comply with any obligation to which they are subject.
   - Disclosing a miscarriage of justice.

→

26. e.g. in September 2016 it upheld a breach of privacy complaint from the Duchess of Cambridge after she objected to online publications about herself and Prince George (Press Association 'Duchess of Cambridge has privacy breach complaints upheld' *The Guardian* 15 September 2016).

27. Ofcom, the independent regulator for the UK communications industries—with responsibilities across television, radio, telecommunications and wireless communications services—has similar powers in that it can issue fines and withdraw licences from repeat offenders. One principal duty, established under statute (Communications Act 2003), is maintaining 'adequate protection for audiences against unfairness or the infringement of privacy'.

→

- Raising or contributing to a matter of public debate, including serious cases of impropriety, unethical conduct or incompetence concerning the public.
- Disclosing concealment, or likely concealment, of any of the above.

2. There is a public interest in freedom of expression itself.
3. The regulator will consider the extent to which material is already in the public domain or will become so.
4. Editors invoking the public interest will need to demonstrate that they reasonably believed publication—or journalistic activity taken with a view to publication—would both serve, and be proportionate to, the public interest and explain how they reached that decision at the time.
5. An exceptional public interest would need to be demonstrated to over-ride the normally paramount interests of children under 16.

Pause for reflection

It is hard to establish how effective IPSO is, especially as some major news publishers have opted out of its system and it refuses to apply for recognition by the PRP. Further, in October 2016 another regulator—IMPRESS (the Independent Monitor for the Press)—was established in 'opposition' to IPSO, claiming to be 'the first truly independent press regulator in the UK'. It has its own Standards Code, with different (broader) definitions of privacy and public interest, and is said to be 'Leveson compliant'.[28] As you read further, consider whether any changes are likely to alter the way the press operates, especially given these internal disagreements, and as IPSO's Editors' Code mirrors exactly what was said in the PCC Code of Practice.[29]

Also consider the fact that Leveson paid little attention to the burgeoning sphere of social media, the development of which he viewed as 'largely irrelevant to his considerations' and not lending itself to regulation. What role do you think the expansion of social media plays in the privacy debate? Can the mainstream press be effectively regulated (and should it be) while others are free to post almost anything (subject to criminal law) online?[30]

Existing 'boxes' of liability (***Kaye***), as well as self-regulatory bodies, have so far proved to have limited effect when an individual claims infringement of their privacy. More recently, however, the courts developed another route which offers greater protection of privacy: actions for breach of confidence.

28. IMPRESS was recognised by the Press Recognition Panel in 2016.

29. Note that unless or until the government decides to implement s 40 of the Crime and Courts Act 2013, there is no sanction for publishers who do not sign up as members of a formally recognised regulator.

30. IMPRESS has more guidance on the use of social media by journalists than IPSO. An interesting take on this is the use of social media as a *source* of information, especially by regional publications. See e.g. Hold the Front Page 'Law Column: IPSO and the use of social media as a source' 31 January 2017. Two courts in Northern Ireland have given potentially significant judgments on the civil liability of social media companies for content posted by users: see *J20* v *Facebook Ireland* [2016] and *CG* v *Facebook Ireland & McCloskey* [2015].

16.4 Breach of confidence

Breach of confidence stems from equity and is designed to protect 'secrets' or confidential information. In *Coco* v *AN Clark (Engineers) Ltd* [1968], the duty was said to be breached when:

- information exists which has 'the necessary element of confidence about it';
- the defendant could be said to be obliged to keep the information confidential; and
- 'unauthorised use' of the information was made by the defendant.

Thus, it can be used only when a *duty* of confidentiality is established. As the action was primarily used to protect commercial secrets, it would initially appear to have little application to the type of privacy cases we are concerned with.[31] Conventionally, a pre-existing relationship was required to bring about the duty. So, there would only be limited application in the context of personal secrets, for example in a marital relationship or between a party and someone taken into their confidence.

However, in *Attorney General* v *Guardian Newspapers Ltd (No 2)* [1990], a case relating to the publication of the controversial *Spycatcher* book, Lord Goff declared that a duty of confidentiality exists when:

> confidential information comes to the knowledge of a person . . . in circumstances where he *has notice or is held to have agreed* that the information is confidential with the effect that it would be just in all the circumstances that he should be precluded from disclosing the information to others. (at 281, emphasis added)

Thus, a pre-existing relationship is not necessarily required. A duty will arise if a party gains information and knows (or ought to know) that they would be expected to keep it confidential, however it was obtained. This has far broader implications for the protection of privacy, particularly in relation to press intrusion into people's personal lives. This is clearly illustrated by *Venables* v *News Group Newspapers* [2001] and *X (A woman formerly known as Mary Bell)* v *SO* [2003].[32] In *Venables* an injunction was imposed *contra mundum* (against the whole world) to prevent disclosure of information that might reveal the identity or whereabouts of the killers (who had themselves been children at the time of the murder) of toddler Jamie Bulger. The justification for this was that another right was at issue—the right to life of the claimant—who might suffer at the

31. As was the case in *Kerry Ingredients (UK) Ltd* v *Bakkavor Group Ltd and others* [2016], concerning the recipes for flavour-infused cooking oils. Cf *Wade & Perry* v *British Sky Broadcasting Ltd* [2016] where the Court of Appeal found that Sky did not misuse confidential information in commissioning a music talent show with multiple similarities to one pitched to it previously by the claimants. See also *Brevan Howard Asset Management LLP* v *Reuters Ltd and another* [2017] where the Court of Appeal upheld the confidential nature of information provided to potential hedge fund investors.

32. See also *British Broadcasting Corporation & Eight Other Media Organisations, R (on the application of)* v *F & D* [2016], regarding anonymity of the teenage girls who murdered Angela Wrightson and a clampdown on social media reporting of the trial (by news agencies and members of the public). In December 2016, two brothers who tortured three other children in South Yorkshire (when they were aged only 10 and 11) were granted lifelong anonymity, also for their own protection (see BBC News 'Edlington boy torturers granted anonymity' 9 December 2016 and *A & B* v *Persons Unknown* [2016]).

hands of members of the public if his identity was revealed (at 1069).[33] Similarly, in *X*, an injunction was imposed to prevent the publication of information that might identify Mary Bell (who had also killed children when she was a child herself) and also her own, now adult, daughter.

Pause for reflection

Following these cases, do you think that what might make information confidential depends on how much *harm* would be caused to the parties concerned if the information was leaked? As you read through the chapter, think how a harm-based analysis fits with other cases decided in favour of the claimants. Do you think this is an appropriate test? Photographs of holidays, weddings or even of someone's sexual activities in public being published without consent can be viewed as causing little or no real harm when compared to a risk to the right to life. But, on the other hand, it depends what we consider 'harm' to be—if the harm is the invasion of privacy itself then are all of the claimants in these cases equally deserving?

The defence to a breach of confidence claim is to show that disclosure of the information, though confidential in nature, is justified in the public interest. That is, the public interest in disclosure must be weighed against the interest of the claimant in maintaining confidentiality (*Attorney General* v *Guardian Newspapers Ltd (No 2)*).[34]

In ***Douglas, Zeta-Jones and Northern & Shell plc* v *Hello! Ltd*** [2005] breach of confidence essentially became a privacy action in all but name.

***Douglas, Zeta-Jones and Northern & Shell plc* v *Hello! Ltd* [2005] CA**

The celebrity couple Michael Douglas and Catherine Zeta-Jones married in a New York hotel. They entered a £1 million contract with *OK!* magazine to publish exclusive photographs of the wedding and it was a term of the contract that the couple would have the final say regarding which photographs could be used. The wedding was otherwise private. Its location had not been made public, guests were asked not to bring cameras and it was an invitation-only event. However, despite the security provided by the couple, a freelance photographer managed to get into the wedding and take covert pictures, which he then sold to rival magazine *Hello!* The couple sought and failed to achieve an interim injunction to prevent *Hello!* publishing the

33. See, in respect of criminal penalties that can be applied for violation of the injunction, 'Two narrowly avoid jail after sharing "photos of James Bulger killer" online' *The Telegraph* 31 January 2019. In 2019, an application to vary the confidentiality order from 2001 (preventing Venables' identification) was refused by Sir Andrew MacFarlane, President of the Family Division, on the grounds that Venables' Arts 2 and 3 rights outweighed the applicant's Arts 8 and 10 rights: *Venables and another* v *News Group Papers Ltd and others* [2019].

34. See further discussion of the new 'responsible publication on a matter of public interest' in the context of defamation (**section 17.6.3**).

→

pictures, relying in part on breach of confidence and the new 'privacy' law (which they argued had been created by the HRA).

The court disagreed with the claimants' submission that the HRA had created a new action in law on the basis that existing law was enough to protect people's privacy interests. It found that there had been a breach of confidence, relying on the *Coco* definition. It said that *Hello!* should clearly have realised that 'an obligation of confidence' existed in relation to the photographs (otherwise the photographer would not have had to obtain them secretly) and that there was no authority for their use, especially as it had been widely publicised that the wedding was to be a private event. The couple was awarded £14,500 damages for interference with the remaining right of privacy they had after selling the photographic rights in the first place. (*OK!* magazine was also awarded more than £1 million for lost profit; this award was overturned by the Court of Appeal but later restored by the House of Lords in 2007.)

Pause for reflection

If hundreds of people were at the wedding anyway, and the photographs were to be sold to a publication that would be seen by millions, was this really a private affair? What made the unauthorised photographs an invasion of the claimants' privacy, when they had already contracted to share their wedding day with the world? Does this case fit with the 'harm' analysis mentioned earlier? The claimants would presumably feel saddened to know that covert photography had taken place on their wedding day by someone seeking to make a profit—but is this harmful?

Do you agree with the decision? If not, is this *because* the couple had entered a contract that was designed for them to have control over which information (photographs) stayed private and which was made public?

The court in ***Douglas*** found that it did not matter that there were so many people at the wedding as everyone there *knew* it was private. So understood, the photographs, because of the design of the contract with *OK!*, were confidential precisely *because* of their commercial value. In effect, the Court of Appeal was simply applying the normal rules on breach of confidence. As in ***Kaye***, the court made it clear that it was for Parliament to create a tort of invasion of privacy, not judges, who could only work with existing laws. However, because of the nature of the case—and who brought it—it was seen as establishing, even for people in the public eye, a (limited) right to privacy.

Breach of confidence resurfaced more recently in *ABC and others* v *Telegraph Media Group Ltd* [2018]. In this controversial case, the Court of Appeal granted an interim injunction to the claimant (one a prominent businessman) in relation to allegations made by five previous employees about his 'discreditable conduct'. A journalist had approached the claimants, informing them that details of the allegations were to be published, as well as the fact that the complainants had all signed non-disclosure agreements (NDAs), for which they had received substantial monetary payments. The claimants (two companies and the businessman concerned) immediately sought an injunction preventing them from being named, or information about the allegations or NDAs being published. The Court of Appeal (overturning an earlier judgment of the High Court) found that an interim injunction should be granted, as the information concerned carried the necessary degree of confidence. It recognised the importance of protecting duties of confidence and was not persuaded that the 'public interest in publication outweighs the confidentiality attaching to the information pending a speedy trial' (at [31]). The Court of Appeal essentially made it clear that this was not a test of whether the information was in the public interest, but whether it is in the public interest that the duty of confidence should be breached. The case was later discontinued by the claimants in February 2019, reportedly leaving them with a £3 million legal bill. This also meant that the Court of Appeal's injunction was discharged, and the *Daily Telegraph* immediately published its allegations that Sir Philip Green, the businessman concerned (owner of Topshop/Topman), had subjected five individuals to racial, physical and sexual abuse and other bullying behaviour.[35]

Pause for reflection

The *ABC* decision had meant that an *interim* injunction would be in place—up until the point of a full trial that would decide whether a permanent injunction should be granted. This meant that the information may still have come to light, after a proper trial of the facts, which the Court of Appeal had ordered to be expedited in recognition of the undesirability of delay in the publication of matters of potential public interest. However, the Court of Appeal's decision was overtaken by the actions of Lord Hain in the House of Lords who, exercising parliamentary privilege, named Sir Philip Green in October 2018, which undoubtedly led to the claimants' later discontinuation of the case.

Notwithstanding the rights and wrongs of naming the claimant at that stage in the proceedings, the case should make us think. Presumably, there is a public interest in the disclosure of multiple allegations of sexual harassment, bullying and racial abuse by a senior executive who then paid large sums to prevent victims telling their stories publicly. The use of NDAs in this respect should give us cause for concern.[36] Strong criticism was voiced against them by *The Telegraph* in response to the judgment. Though this was not unexpected, given that it was the defendant in this case (and had spent eight months researching the story), the criticism referred to concerns about NDAs being used to cover up potential wrongdoing, particularly by powerful individuals, saying it would 'reignite the #MeToo movement against the mistreatment of women, minorities and others by powerful employers'. Maria Miller MP, chair of the House of Commons' Women and Equality Committee, said it was 'shocking' that NDAs were still being used to gag victims and that they should not be used 'where there are accusations of sexual misconduct and wider bullying'.[37]

→

35. See Robert Mendick 'Sir Philip Green backs down: the inside story of the court case that never was' 8 February 2019; *Arcadia Group Ltd and others* v *Telegraph Media Group Ltd* [2019].

36. Similar issues arise in relation to defamation claims—see **section 17.3** and the pause for reflection box there.

37. Claire Newell 'The British #MeToo scandal which cannot be revealed' *The Telegraph* 25 October 2018.

→

In *Linklaters LLP and another* v *Mellish* [2019], the issue of how large 'Magic Circle' law firms deal with sexual harassment in the workplace arose. Mellish, who had left the firm after a short period of employment, emailed the senior partners announcing that he intended to share his 'impressions of the current culture at Linklaters', especially 'the ongoing struggle Linklaters has with women in the workplace'. Mellish highlighted three incidents in particular, and said he would go on record about how the company had handled them. Mr Justice Warby, granting an interim injunction, ruled that Linklaters had a 'legitimate interest' in maintaining confidentiality over such matters, and that this outweighed the public interest in the conduct of large firms. Commenting on the decision, Richard Moorhead says:

> He [Warby J] does not consider the possibility that stifling a discussion of firm culture is more likely to inhibit the coming forward of complainants. Judges need to think more carefully if protecting the reputation of men, whilst claiming to protect the interests of women.[38]

16.4.1 A new tort: 'misuse of private information'

Douglas opened the door for other privacy claims, most involving high-profile claimants. The major turning point for the law on privacy came when supermodel Naomi Campbell tried to suppress publication of details of her rehabilitation from drugs.

Campbell v *Mirror Group Newspapers* (MGN) [2004] HL

The *Daily Mirror* published stories referring to the fact that Naomi Campbell was seeking treatment for drug addiction. On one occasion it published a photograph showing the model leaving a Narcotics Anonymous meeting in London as well as details about what her treatment might entail. Having tried and failed to sue for invasion of privacy, Campbell framed her action as a claim for breach of confidence, on the grounds that any 'reasonable person' would realise that details of her actual treatment and where this was taking place were clearly confidential.

A bare majority of the House of Lords upheld her claim—in part. Because she had previously denied having a drugs problem, despite acknowledging that many models did take drugs, the law lords held that the story detailing the fact that she did in fact use illegal drugs, and was attending Narcotics Anonymous for help in overcoming this problem, could be published, as this was correcting an inaccurate image she had portrayed of herself. However, they went on to hold that the details of her treatment as well as the photograph of her leaving the meeting could not be published. Medical information is always a confidential matter, and publishing the photograph may allow people to discover where her treatment was taking place. Both things, if published, could have negative effects on the treatment itself.

38. Richard Moorhead, 'New York, London, Paris,* Munich,. [sic] Everyone's talking about . . . Linklaters' *LawyerWatch* 6 February 2019.

Campbell is significant.[39] In ***Campbell***, their lordships clarified the relationship between breach of confidence and privacy. Lord Nicholls (dissenting), while accepting that the nature of breach of confidence had changed once the pre-existing relationship requirement was removed, maintained that there was 'no over-arching, all-embracing cause of action for "invasion of privacy"' (at [11]). However, he acknowledged that developments in the law, particularly with regard to breach of confidence, had been prompted by the HRA and that because the duty of confidence now arose where 'a person receives information he knows or ought to know is fairly and reasonably to be regarded as confidential' this had in essence created a tort of 'misuse of private information' (at [14]). Furthermore, the HRA, plus jurisprudence from the European Court of Human Rights (ECtHR), prompted him to acknowledge that 'the values enshrined in Articles 8 and 10 are now part of the cause of action for breach of confidence' (at [17]). Thus, future cases—now understood as 'misuse of private information' claims—would need to concentrate more on confidential/private information and the balance of the claimant's right to private, home and family life (Art 8) and the defendant's right to freedom of expression (Art 10). This balance is explored more fully shortly.

That there is a *tort* of misuse of private information was confirmed by the High Court in *Vidal-Hall and others* v *Google Inc* [2014] in the context of Google's misuse of personal data obtained via the Safari browser. Tugendhat J cited Lord Nicholls in *Douglas and others* v *Hello! Ltd and others* [2007] as authority that 'breach of confidence, or misuse of confidential information, now covers two distinct causes of action, protecting two different interests: privacy, and secret ("confidential") information' (at [255]), leading him to conclude that a distinct 'tort of misuse of private information' exists (at [70]). This was upheld by the Court of Appeal in *Google Inc* v *Vidal-Hall and others* [2015]. Also in 2014—though this part of the claim was ultimately unsuccessful—it was considered a tort by the Court of Appeal in *OPO* v *MLA* [2014], a case where a child (by his litigation friend) sought to prevent publication of his father's (a successful musician and public figure) autobiography.[40] The Supreme Court confirmed the tort in *PJS* v *News Group Newspapers Ltd* [2016].

39. Though note that, ironically perhaps, the ECtHR ruled that the *Daily Mirror*'s right to freedom of expression was violated by having to pay the £1 million legal costs (partly lawyers' 'success fees') when it lost the original case (*MGN Ltd* v *UK* [2011]). Similar arguments have arisen in other cases considering Conditional Fee Agreements (CFAs) and After the Event (ATE) insurance (see **Chapter 21**). In *8 Representative Claimants and others* v *MGN Ltd* [2016] (*The Mirror* 'phone hacking' case), Mann J found that the regime permitting the recovery of the additional liabilities was compatible with Art 10 ECHR (see also *Miller* v *Associated Newspapers* [2016]). Both defendants were granted 'leapfrog' permission to appeal so that the issues could be considered by the Supreme Court alongside the appeal of *Flood* v *Times Newspapers* [2014] (considering whether having to pay the entire costs of the other side, including success fees and ATE premiums arising from a CFA (amounting to nearly £1.7 million, before interest), in a libel case in which it was partly successful, violated the defendant's Arts 6 and 10 rights). In April 2017 the Supreme Court unanimously dismissed all three appeals (*Times Newspapers Ltd and others* v *Flood and others* [2017]).

40. Arden LJ (at [12]). What defeated OPO's claim on this point was that the information to be published, though it would potentially affect him, was not *about* him (at [45]). A Supreme Court decision ultimately allowed full publication of the book (***Rhodes* v *OPO (by his litigation friend BHM) and another*** **[2015]**; see further **section 15.6.1**).

Since ***Campbell***, a new two-stage test has been used to determine whether/when a breach of confidence or 'misuse of private information' has occurred. The test is as follows.

(1) Did the claimant have a 'reasonable expectation of privacy' with regard to the information? If so,

(2) Does the claimant's interest in maintaining their right to privacy outweigh the defendant's interest in freedom of expression (i.e. the ability to publish the information)?

16.4.1.1 What is a 'reasonable expectation of privacy'?

In ***Campbell***, it was held that a reasonable expectation of privacy would arise when it was 'obvious' that the information being disclosed was private (see also e.g. ***Loreena McKennitt* v *Niema Ash*** [2006]; *HRH Prince of Wales* v *Associated Newspapers Ltd* [2008]).[41] Clearly, detail relating to treatment for drug addiction is private, even if the person being treated is well known. In relation to Naomi Campbell, while the majority of the law lords thought that information about treatment *was* obviously private, they did not think the same of the photograph, as this was taken on a public street.[42]

Pause for reflection

Lord Nicholls (dissenting) argued that treatment for an addiction at Narcotics Anonymous followed a well-known pattern and as such the disclosure of information about this was no more significant than 'saying a person who has fractured a limb has his limb in plaster or that a person suffering from cancer is undergoing a course of chemotherapy' (at [26]).

Do you agree? Or does the fact that drug addiction is connected with a person's mental well-being and is associated with judgements that can be made about their personality and private life, as well as their physical health, distinguish the two examples?

A secondary test was proposed for situations—like the photo—where it is not 'obvious' that information was private. Then, we must ask whether disclosure of the information would cause offence to a 'person of ordinary sensibilities' if it was about them.[43] This is a fairly bizarre subjective–objective test, particularly as the courts must put themselves into the minds of a 'person of ordinary sensibilities' in the same situation as

41. An interesting issue may arise in relation to this in the context of 'deadnaming'—see Izzy Lyons 'Transgender lawyer launches UK's first "deadnaming" case against Father Ted writer Graham Linehan' *The Telegraph* 7 October 2018.

42. Nor, it seems, is the identity of a secret blogger, particularly when the blog in question criticised the internal workings of the police force from an insider's perspective: see *Author of a Blog* v *Times Newspapers Ltd* [2009].

43. This is similar to, yet different from, the formulation in the US *Second Restatement of Torts* and the Australian case of *Australian Broadcasting Commission* v *Lenah Game Meats* [2001]: that disclosure must be 'highly offensive to the reasonable person' in order to ground an action (Gleeson CJ at [42]). In ***Campbell***, Lord Nicholls said that the phrase 'highly offensive' should not be relied on as it suggested a stricter test than 'reasonable expectation of privacy' and 'could be a recipe for confusion' (at [22]).

the claimant—often situations that are unlikely to happen to most 'ordinary people'. Because on this secondary test it could be harmful to Naomi Campbell's treatment of and recovery from addiction to publish a photograph from which the location of her treatment could be identified, publication was prevented. In other words, because to publish a photograph which could enable people to find out where an obviously private medical treatment was taking place might cause offence to 'a person of ordinary sensibilities', she could *also* establish a 'reasonable expectation of privacy' in relation to the photographs. As Baroness Hale noted, it would have been different if Campbell was merely 'going about her business in a private street' because:

> she makes a substantial part of her living out of being photographed looking stunning in designer clothing. Readers will obviously be interested to see how she looks if and when she pops out to the shops for a bottle of milk. (at [154])

Pause for reflection

Look again at *Kaye*. If the same events happened today, would the case be decided differently? The images of him in hospital would have a 'reasonable expectation of privacy' attached (as photographs of a person in hospital, unable to give their consent, can easily be considered 'obviously' private) and it would be unlikely that the photographs of him would be in the public interest, even if the public was interested in the fact that he had been injured. The question is about where the line should be drawn about what information the public should be given about the private lives of others.

In ***McKennitt***, the 'reasonable expectation of privacy' test was used in relation to personal information shared between friends.

Loreena McKennitt v _Niema Ash_ [2006] CA

Niema Ash, a former close friend of Canadian folk artist Loreena McKennitt, wrote a book detailing her time on tour with her. The book included information about McKennitt's sexual relationships and health, an ongoing legal dispute with Ash and her business partner over some property and McKennitt's emotional response to the death of her fiancé. McKennitt sued, alleging breach of confidence.

The Court of Appeal found that McKennitt had a reasonable expectation of privacy in relation to the personal information she had shared with Ash during their friendship. In fact, Ash herself acknowledged this, as her book was prefaced with a comment saying that it contained information that would be known only because of the close nature of the two women's friendship. An injunction against further publication was granted and £5,000 damages were awarded.[44]

44. The House of Lords refused leave to appeal, suggesting that they agreed fully with the Court of Appeal's reasoning.

A 'reasonable expectation' of privacy will, therefore, generally be quite 'obvious'.[45] Examples include *Elizabeth Jagger* v *John Darling* [2005], where Elizabeth Jagger (the daughter of Mick Jagger) obtained an injunction preventing the publication of pictures and CCTV footage of her and Calum Best (the son of footballer George Best) engaged in 'sexual activities' in the doorway of a nightclub. Mr Justice Bell found that she had a reasonable expectation of privacy as, although in a public space, she was unaware of being observed in any way, particularly by CCTV (at [13]). In *Mosley* v *NGN* [2008] it was confirmed that one's sexual activities are generally to be considered private. This was restated in *AMC and another* v *News Group Newspapers Ltd* [2015], a case about an affair conducted by a 'prominent and successful professional sportsman, who has, from time to time held positions of responsibility in his sport' (at [6]). In a non-celebrity context, private intimate relationships were held to attract a reasonable expectation of privacy in *ZYT and another* v *Associated Newspapers Ltd* [2015] and *Bull* v *Desporte* [2019].

In *ERY* v *Associated Newspapers Ltd* [2016], Nicol J found that a suspect in a police investigation had a reasonable expectation of privacy. This was reiterated in *Richard* v *BBC and another* [2018], even once the information (about investigations being conducted into historic child sex abuse allegations under Operation Yewtree) had come into the hands of the media. In *Middleton and another* v *Person or Persons Unknown* [2016], Pippa Middleton, the sister of the Duchess of Cambridge, and her then fiancé, were granted an urgent injunction preventing publication of some 3,000 photographs stolen from her iCloud account, on reasonable expectation of privacy grounds. In *Ali and another* v *Channel 5 Broadcast Ltd* [2018] the claimants were found to have a reasonable expectation of privacy in relation to the filming and broadcast of their eviction from their privately rented home on the TV programme *Can't Pay? We'll Take it Away.* In *Wan-Bissaka and another* v *Bentley* [2020] the Premiership footballer succeeded in a claim against his former partner to prevent her disclosing details of their relationship, including text conversations.

When there is already some public awareness of the so-called private information, the 'reasonable expectation' of privacy may be lost. In *Theakston* v *MGN Ltd* [2002], for example, an attempt by a television and radio presenter to prevent further publication of information about his visit to a brothel failed due to knowledge of the event already being in the public domain.[46] However, what is considered to be in the public domain is a fine line—for example, Ned Rocknroll (the husband of actress Kate Winslet and nephew of Sir Richard Branson) succeeded in preventing the publication of partially naked photographs of himself in a national newspaper, despite those photographs having been visible for a period of time on his friend's Facebook page.[47] In *PJS* [2016] a majority of the Supreme Court—somewhat controversially—upheld an injunction preventing publication of the names of a celebrity and his partner allegedly involved in an

45. Would this be the case for Karen, in the scenarios outlined at the beginning of this chapter? If so, would her right to privacy outweigh the newspaper's freedom of expression? Would this depend on anything she had said/done in relation to eating disorders before?

46. However, the publication of photographs depicting the event was prohibited. See also *A* v *B plc* [2002]; *BBC* v *HarperCollins Publishers Ltd and another* [2010]; *Trimingham* v *Associated Newspapers Ltd* [2012]; *AAA* v *Associated Newspapers Ltd* [2013].

47. *Rocknroll* v *News Group Newspapers Ltd* [2013]. See also *Reid* v *Price* [2020], where some of the information about the claimant's sexual conduct that he successfully sued the defendant—Katie Price—for disclosing was already publicly known.

extramarital threesome, despite widespread knowledge of who the celebrity might be following publication of the information outside the jurisdiction and on social media.[48]

Once reasonable expectation of privacy is established, the second part of the test asks whether the claimant's interest in maintaining their right to privacy outweighs the defendant's interest in freedom of expression (i.e. the ability to publish the information)? In *Jagger*, Bell J said there was 'no legitimate public interest in further dissemination of the images which could serve only to humiliate the claimant for the prurient interests of others' (at [14]).[49] Similarly, in *ABK* v *KDT and another* [2013], in the context of a 'revenge pornography' harassment claim, the female claimant was granted an order protecting her reasonable expectation of privacy in respect of personal photographs and information that was held (threatened to be disclosed to friends, family and employer) by the defendant, with whom she had had an extramarital affair. In *AJS* v *News Group Newspapers Ltd* [2017], Nicol J granted an injunction to prevent *The Sun* newspaper from naming a famous individual (AJS), a witness in a serious police investigation into allegations of a 'serious criminal offence' that took place at AJS's home in February 2017.[50] He found that there was no public interest in publishing AJS's private details and that he maintained a reasonable expectation of privacy. Likewise, in *XKF* v *BBC* [2018] the claimant, an ex-police officer who had been imprisoned for corruption, successfully prevented the BBC from showing an interview with him on their *Panorama* programme. Though there might not be a reasonable expectation of privacy in relation to his initial *conviction* (even though it was by then spent), there was in respect of his *rehabilitation* (including his change of identity).[51]

Similarly, in *ZXC* v *Bloomberg LP* [2020], the Court of Appeal upheld a decision that the publication of confidential information obtained from a law enforcement agency investigating a businessman is a misuse of private information. This confirms the approach that, as a matter of general principle, those under *investigation* by law enforcement agencies maintain a reasonable expectation of privacy. Such investigations may therefore only be reported where there is a proven public interest justification.[52] Giving judgment for the Court of Appeal, Simon LJ said:

> I would take the opportunity to make clear that those who have simply come under suspicion by an organ of the state have, in general, a reasonable and objectively founded expectation of privacy in relation to that fact and an expressed basis for that suspicion. The suspicion may ultimately be shown to be well-founded or ill-founded, but until that point the law should recognise the human characteristic to assume the worst (that there is no smoke without fire); and to overlook the fundamental legal principle that those who are accused of an offence are deemed to be innocent until they are proven guilty. (at [82])

In what may prove to be a defining case in this contentious area, an appeal by Bloomberg to the Supreme Court is scheduled to be heard in late 2021.

48. This wider knowledge had earlier persuaded the Court of Appeal to overturn the injunction (see [47]) and Lord Toulson in dissent. In *PJS* v *News Group Newspapers Ltd* [2016] the High Court approved an agreed final order in the action. See further Tommy Chen 'PJS and the Tort of Misuse of Private Information' (2016) 11 JIPLP 892.

49. See also *Ali and another* v *Channel 5 Broadcast Ltd* [2018] where Arnold J referred to the televised footage as 'voyeuristic' in nature (at [215]).

50. Reported in the *Sun on Sunday* on 12 March 2017 under the headline 'Judge gags press'. No public judgment has ever been handed down and the only details are those from the newspaper, which had been allowed to report on the anonymised proceedings.

51. See also *NT1 & NT2* v *Google LLC* [2018].

52. Not everyone agrees that this is the correct approach–see Nicole Moreham 'Why Police Investigations should not be regarded as private, Part 1' Inforrm's blog 18 February 2020.

Essentially this becomes a battle between privacy and freedom of expression: these concepts must be balanced to determine the outcome. The following section explores the way misuse of private information claims have developed, as affected by human rights considerations.

16.5 Towards the modern approach

16.5.1 The Human Rights Act 1998 and European case law

Lord Irvine (then the Lord Chancellor) said, during parliamentary debate on the Human Rights Bill, that:

> judges are pen-poised regardless of the incorporation of the Convention to develop a right of privacy to be protected by the common law . . . it will be a better law if the judges develop it after incorporation because they will have regards to Articles 8 and 10, giving Article 10 its due high value . . . I believe that the true view is that the courts will be able to adapt and develop the existing domestic principles in the laws of trespass, nuisance, copyright, confidence and the like to fashion a common law right to privacy.[53]

Human Rights Act 1998, s 12(4)

The court must have particular regard to the importance of the Convention right to freedom of expression and, where the proceedings relate to material which the respondent claims, or which appears to the court, to be journalistic, literary or artistic material (or to conduct connected with such material), to—

(a) the extent to which—
    (i) the material has, or is about to, become available to the public; or
    (ii) it is, or would be, in the public interest for the material to be published;
(b) any relevant privacy code.

Section 12(4) of the HRA requires the courts to undertake a balancing exercise when considering the competing rights from Articles 8 and 10. Section 12 is, however, headed 'freedom of expression' and applies when 'a court is considering whether to grant any relief which, if granted, might affect the exercise of the Convention right to freedom of expression' (s 12(1)). Clearly, granting someone a remedy for infringement of their privacy (e.g. by the press) may have an effect on freedom of expression. Section 12 in a way seems to prioritise this freedom above the right to privacy, by assigning it special status.[54] However, later cases indicate that the two rights (and the ability to derogate from them) are to be treated equally.[55]

53. HL Deb, 24 November 1997, vol 583, col 784.
54. It is notable, e.g., that freedom of expression and 'freedom of thought, conscience and religion' are the only Convention rights given this express treatment under the HRA—i.e. only these rights are singled out as deserving special attention by the courts.
55. Confirmed in *Re S* [2005] and most recently reiterated by the Supreme Court in *PJS* [2016] at [19]–[20], [51] and [65].

Section 6(1) of the HRA makes it 'unlawful for a public authority to act in a way which is incompatible with a Convention right'. Courts and tribunals are deemed 'public authorities' (s 6(3)), as is 'any person certain of whose functions are functions of a public nature', which may include organisations such as IPSO and Ofcom. Furthermore, section 7 of the HRA allows individuals to bring proceedings in domestic courts against any public authority that has acted in contravention of a Convention right. This means that a citizen may claim in a domestic court that their right to private and family life, granted by Article 8(1), has been infringed by a public authority or other who falls within the definition in section 6. However, if the proceedings taken relate to 'journalistic, literary or artistic material' (i.e. we are talking about information about someone's private life being published in some way, as most of the case law seems to deal with),[56] section 12 comes into play, and the court must weigh up whether giving relief for the invasion of privacy would unjustifiably impact on freedom of expression.

see online resources

Pause for reflection

In *Wainwright* Lord Hoffmann, referring to ECtHR jurisprudence, remained unconvinced that a general privacy principle was required. Instead, he said, domestic courts could provide an adequate remedy for invasions of privacy made contrary to Article 8. In this context, he described sections 6 and 7 of the HRA as 'substantial gap fillers' (at [34]), suggesting that in conjunction with Article 8(1) the job of protecting privacy could be done adequately, without the need to create a free-standing tort.

He concluded his speech saying that:

> a finding that there was a breach of Article 8 will only demonstrate that there was a gap in the English remedies for invasion of privacy which has since been filled by sections 6 and 7 of the 1998 Act. It does not require that the courts should provide an alternative remedy which distorts the principles of the common law. (at [52])

Lord Hoffmann seems to suggest that invasion of privacy is a harm that has always been recognised—but that the law has not always provided suitable remedies when the harm has occurred, and it is this remedial gap that is filled by the HRA. Do you agree? Consider cases decided since the coming into force of the Act—have the decisions become any easier for judges to make? Are they making the right decisions and providing the right remedies for the right claimants?

The most notable ECtHR decision in the context of evolving judicial attitudes to privacy came in ***Von Hannover* v *Germany*** **[2004]**. This judgment was handed down a short time after ***Campbell***, and remains influential in determining how judges should balance the two competing rights.

56. Exceptions include *Malone* v *Commissioner of Police for the Metropolis (No 2)* [1979], which concerned phone tapping by the police, and ***Wainwright***, concerning an intimate strip-search of visitors to a prison.

Von Hannover v *Germany* [2004] ECtHR

Princess Caroline of Monaco alleged that media intrusions into her daily routine were infringing her rights under Article 8. Princess Caroline has celebrity status in much of Europe—she is the eldest child of the late Prince Rainier III of Monaco and his wife, the late American film actress Grace Kelly and was the presumptive heir to the throne of Monaco. She claimed that numerous paparazzi photographs of her undertaking daily activities, including some which showed her children, were an invasion of her right to private, home and family life. She had previously taken her claim in the German courts, but had failed on the grounds that, as a public figure *par excellence*, she should expect members of the public to take an interest in her daily life.

The ECtHR upheld her claim, holding that the key issue when weighing up the rights under Articles 8 and 10 was to ask how far the information being published would be in the 'public interest', which the judges found was different from what the public might genuinely be interested in. They also distinguished between Princess Caroline's public functions and private life. Clearly, they said, when performing or attending a public function, there would be a legitimate public interest in pictures of her being published but, when going about her private life, she had a 'reasonable expectation' of privacy.[57]

16.5.2 Balancing privacy and freedom of expression

Like the Article 8(1) right to private and family life, home and correspondence, Article 10(1) ECHR gives the right to freedom of expression. Both are 'qualified' rights, meaning that while they must be protected by the state, certain things (listed in Arts 10(2) and 8(2) respectively) are considered legitimate infringements of a person's exercise of that right. Among other things, Article 10(2) states that the right to freedom of expression may be curtailed in the public interest (e.g. in the interests of national security) or where other, competing, individual rights are at stake (e.g. the right of people to protect their reputations or to prevent the disclosure of information given in confidence). So, at the outset, neither right is absolute. By definition, each right impinges on the other, particularly in the context of claims about media invasions of privacy. The media, as part of a democratic society, has a vital role to play in disseminating information. The question is how far the press can go—especially into someone's 'private' affairs—before they are deemed to have gone 'too far'.[58]

57. Compare the ECtHR decision in *von Hannover* v *Germany (No 2)* [2012], in which Princess Caroline attempted to prevent the continued use of the same pictures. This time, with a different understanding of the claimant as a 'public figure', rather than a 'private individual' the Court found no violation of Art 8 and that publication of the pictures alongside the article in question contributed to a debate of public interest. A similar conclusion was reached in *von Hannover* v *Germany (No 3)* [2013]. Also see *Lillo-Stenberg and Sæther* v *Norway* [2014].

58. This was essentially the question for the law lords in ***Campbell***. It has become even more apposite in light of press scandals and the increase in social media forums, blogging etc in recent years. An interesting example of where the press was deemed not to have gone 'too far' is in the privacy/harassment claim brought by Carina Trimingham (the lover of married former MP Chris Huhne), who was herself formerly in a civil partnership: *Trimingham* v *Associated Newspapers Ltd* [2012]. In February 2013, following the conviction of Huhne for perverting the course of justice, Trimingham withdrew her appeal against this decision. See also *Abbey* v *Gilligan and others* [2012].

Pause for reflection

What does the term 'private and family life' encompass? In *Niemietz* v *Germany* [1993] the ECtHR deemed it neither 'possible nor necessary to' attempt an exhaustive definition (at [29]). The Court added:

> However, it would be too restrictive to limit the notion to an 'inner circle' in which the individual may live his own personal life as he chooses and to exclude therefrom entirely the outside world not encompassed within that circle. Respect for private life must also comprise to a certain degree the right to establish and develop relationships with other human beings. (at [29])

Thus, it seems that one's 'inner circle', at least, may be protected, as well as—to a degree—one's relationships with others, but each case will be decided on its own facts.

How far do you think one's private and family life extends? Is this the same for ordinary citizens and for celebrities? Clearly there is no right or wrong answer to this—people have their own perceptions about how far celebrities open themselves up to invasions of privacy. It is likely that there is a 'spectrum' of private information: ranging from the very private (e.g. an evening spent at home with one's young children) to less private (e.g. being seen in public). But celebrity lifestyles make for difficult cases. For instance, where on the spectrum would a celebrity's wedding sit if the kind of measures Michael Douglas and Catherine Zeta-Jones took to try and keep it private were not used? What about Prince Harry and Meghan Markle's private lives, after the televised interview on *Oprah*?[59]

Lord Hoffmann once described freedom of expression as 'the trump card that always wins' (*R* v *Central Independent Television plc* [1994] at 203). It appears highly unlikely that the statement is true today—if it was then. This position is underscored by *Earl Spencer* v *UK* [1998] where, according to Lord Hoffmann, the UK satisfied the ECtHR that breach of confidence is capable of providing an adequate remedy where Article 8 has been violated.[60] In a fresh look at the balance of freedom of expression against privacy, in ***Campbell***, he said that there is 'no question of automatic priority. Nor is there a presumption in favour of one rather than the other' (at [55]). The House of Lords in *Re S* [2005] found the correct approach when both Article 8 and Article 10 rights are involved to be:

> [f]irst, neither Article as such has precedence over the other. Secondly, where the values under the two Articles are in conflict, an intense focus on the comparative importance of the specific rights being claimed in the individual case is necessary. Thirdly, the justifications for interfering with or restricting each right must be taken into account. Finally, the proportionality test—or 'ultimate balancing test'—must be applied to each. (Lord Steyn at [17])

By 2006, in ***McKennitt***, it was acknowledged by Buxton LJ, with whom Latham and Longmore LJJ agreed, that both Article 8 and Article 10 ECHR are 'now the very content

59. Note that in February 2021, just weeks before the interview was televised, the Duchess of Sussex succeeded in her claim for misuse of private information with respect to a series of newspaper articles reproducing parts of a private letter she wrote to her father in 2018: *HRH The Duchess of Sussex* v *Associated Newspapers Ltd* [2021].

60. Speaking in ***Wainwright*** at [32].

of the domestic tort that the English court must enforce' (at [11]). In *PJS* [2016], the Supreme Court restated that neither Article takes precedence—justifications for and the proportionality of interfering with each Article should be considered on the facts. In *Ali and another* v *Channel 5 Broadcast Ltd* [2018], for example, though the broadcast complained of was found to be highlighting a debate of general public interest,[61] this was considered to have been outweighed by the invasion of private life suffered by the claimants.[62] Similarly, in *Richard* v *BBC* [2018], Mann J found that:

> It does not follow that, because an investigation at a general level was a matter of public interest, the identity of the subject of the investigation also attracted that characterisation. I do not think that it did. Knowing that Sir Cliff was under investigation might be of interest to the gossip-mongers, but it does not contribute materially to the genuine public interest in the existence of police investigations in this area. (at [282])

The BBC's interest in freedom of expression was not found to have outweighed the claimant's right to privacy. This was in part because reporting on allegations against someone in Sir Cliff Richard's position would cause 'very serious' consequences for him, particularly bearing in mind 'the failure of the public to keep the presumption of innocence in mind at all times [which] means that there is inevitably going to be stigma attached to the revelation, which is magnified in this case by the nature of the allegations against him, which were allegations (especially in the then climate) of extreme seriousness' (at [316]).

16.6 **Privacy claims today**

Today, our right to privacy is protected by the tort of misuse of private information underpinned by the Article 8 right to privacy, but balanced against competing considerations of freedom of expression. Assessing whether a claimant's right to privacy has been infringed will now always entail a careful balancing of these interests.[63] Where public figures are concerned, this exercise will continue to be difficult. In *Elton John* v *Associated Newspapers* [2006], Sir Elton John complained that a picture taken of him walking away from his car with his driver was an invasion of his privacy. The court found that the picture contained no obviously private information and was merely a snapshot of him going about his ordinary life. In *Serafin* v *Malkiewicz and others* [2017] a

61. '[I]ncreasing levels of personal debt, and in particular rent arrears of tenants in privately-rented accommodation; the dependence of tenants on benefits, and in particular housing benefit; the effect of enforcement of writs of possession by HCEAs [High Court Enforcement Agents]; and the consequences for both landlords and tenants' (at [185]).

62. The programme was said to have had 9.65 million viewers, as well as clips of it being shared on Facebook and other social media. The claimants were each awarded £10,000. An appeal (to increase the award of damages) and cross-appeal (on the public interest) was heard in December 2018. Neither was successful (*Ali and another* v *Channel 5 Broadcasting Ltd* [2019]).

63. Though the first step to a *successful* claim is still to establish a 'reasonable expectation of privacy' so as to engage Art 8: see *Hutcheson (Formerly Known As 'KGM')* v *News Group Newspapers Ltd and others* [2011]; *Goodwin* v *NGN Ltd* [2011]. This was not established in *Axon* v *Ministry of Defence* [2016] in the context of leaks to a national newspaper about a former Royal Navy commanding officer who had been removed from command following allegations of bullying.

photograph of the claimant (who was engaged in a more detailed defamation claim and argued the photograph showed him in a negative light) gesticulating with two fingers was found to be 'no big deal' in the modern age (at [351]), and did not engage a reasonable expectation of privacy. However, in *Lord Browne of Madingley* v *Associated Newspapers Ltd* [2007], the law was extended to include confidential business information within the protection zone of Article 8. Soon after, in ***Douglas***, discussed earlier, damages were awarded, albeit minimal, for violation of Article 8 rights when information of a commercially sensitive nature was distributed by a third party without authorisation.

Pause for reflection

Although it seems that the courts will now protect someone's privacy if it would be more harmful not to do so, it might be argued that the harm is not what 'might happen' to the claimant if the photographs were printed, or the news story was run, but simply the very fact that this might happen. Hundreds of celebrities and well-known public figures are captured on camera every day, their photographs ending up in newspapers and glossy magazines or on websites. But not all of them take legal action—so is taking legal action *itself* the actual (first) indicator that harm has been suffered? In our view, it is hard to qualify harm objectively and therefore its subjective nature must be taken into account.

In *Mosley* v *News Group Newspapers Ltd* [2008], the late Max Mosley, then the head of the International Automobile Federation (FIA), won a privacy claim against the *News of the World* over the publication of an article about him taking part in a Nazi-style orgy.[64] Mosley, the son of 1930s British Fascist leader Sir Oswald Mosley, was covertly filmed by the paper with five prostitutes in a basement flat in London. The now defunct *News of the World* described a 'sick Nazi orgy' and a 'truly grotesque and depraved' event, posting the film on its website and alleging that Mosley had assumed the role of a concentration camp commandant, saying: 'In public he rejects his father's evil past but secretly he plays Nazi sex games'. The film was viewed by 3.5 million people. In court, Mosley admitted involvement in sadomasochistic extramarital sex, but denied the link to Nazism. Mr Justice Eady ruled that Mosley had a reasonable expectation of privacy in

64. *News of the World* 'F1 Boss has Sick Nazi Orgy with 5 Hookers' 30 March 2008. Mosley sued for both aggravated (punitive) and compensatory damages (see **section 21.2**) but was awarded only compensatory damages, plus costs. The award was £60,000, reported to be over three times higher than the previous highest privacy award (though note that the BBC reported that the same judge awarded Hugh Grant, Liz Hurley and Arun Nayar £58,000 in May 2008 in a case concerning long-range photographs of them on a private beach (BBC News 'Grant and Hurley Win Privacy Payout' 17 May 2008)). These awards—thought to mark the ceiling of what may be awarded in privacy claims—were overtaken in *Gulati and others* v *MGN* [2016] where significant payments ranging from £72,500 to £260,250 were ordered following the serious and repeated criminal invasions of privacy in the 'celebrity' phone-hacking cases. Now, the highest award seems to have been made to Sir Cliff Richard, who was awarded £210,000 general and aggravated damages, plus an amount for special damages (see **Chapter 21**) to be later determined (*Richard* v *BBC and another* [2018]). South Yorkshire Police, the second defendant in the case, had already settled the case for £400,000 plus costs in 2017. In contrast, an award of £5,000 (plus costs, despite the defendant arguing against these) was ordered in *Burrell* v *Clifford* [2016]. The case illustrates potential issues about access to justice and the fact that claimants with 'low value' claims would find it hard to take cases if normal costs rules were not followed.

relation to his sexual activities, though unconventional, if they took place between consenting adults on private property (at [232]). He said that the authorities tend to show that 'people's sex lives are to be regarded as essentially their own business—provided at least that the participants are genuinely consenting adults and there is no question of exploiting the young or vulnerable' (at [100]; see also *Contostavlos* v *Mendahun* [2012]). Given that the link to Nazism was not proved, Mr Justice Eady further concluded that there was:

> no public interest or other justification for the clandestine recording, for the publication of the resulting information and still photographs, or for the placing of the video extracts on the *News of the World* website—all of this on a massive scale. Of course, I accept that such behaviour is viewed by some people with distaste and moral disapproval, but in the light of modern rights-based jurisprudence that does not provide any justification for the intrusion on the personal privacy of the claimant. (at [233])

Notably, Eady J stressed that this was not a 'landmark' decision (at [234]), but one that applied 'recently developed but established principles' to an unusual set of facts.[65] In 2008 Mosley asked the ECtHR to uphold a right to prior notification—that is, for the government to pass a law obliging newspapers, etc to warn people in advance when intimate or sexual details were about to be published. His claim was rejected,[66] though he was unwilling to concede defeat. In *Mosley* v *Google* [2015] he defeated Google's arguments that his claim under the Data Protection Act should be struck out, meaning that Google must block images of the original photographs via its search engine. The case was later settled out of court.

16.6.1 Children and privacy

The Court of Appeal in ***Murray* v *Express Newspapers plc* [2008]** considered the approach to be taken in relation to children.

> #### *Murray* v *Express Newspapers plc* [2008] CA
>
> JK Rowling, the author of the Harry Potter books, claimed on behalf of her then 18-month-old son David, after a long-lens photograph of him in his pushchair was published in 2004. Rowling (whose married name is Murray), sought damages for the infringement of David's right to privacy as well as an injunction to prevent further publication of similar pictures. Her case failed in the High Court. Mr Justice Patten said that the law did not provide for a 'press-free zone' (at [66]) for celebrities and their children in respect of everything that they do, adding that 'an area of routine activity which, when conducted in a public place, carries no guarantee of privacy'.
>
> The Court of Appeal overturned the decision, finding that David had a legitimate expectation of privacy, even while on a public street.

65. Though the recognition of a 'reasonable expectation of privacy' in this case does *not* seem consistent with either *Theakston* v *MGN Ltd* [2002] (brothel visitation by single man) or *A* v *B plc* [2003] (extramarital affairs), particularly given that Max Mosley was married. Eady J may, however, have been referring to the 'recently developed' principle of the 'reasonable expectation of privacy'.

66. *Mosley* v *UK* [2011]. See, in particular, at [119].

Interestingly, Express Newspapers settled out of court when the claim was still at the High Court—the action survived only against the picture agency that took and supplied the photographs to the newspaper. Giving the judgment of the Court of Appeal, Sir Anthony Clarke said:

> As we see it, the question whether there is a reasonable expectation of privacy is a broad one, which takes account of all the circumstances of the case. They include the attributes of the claimant, the nature of the activity in which the claimant was engaged, the place at which it was happening, the nature and purpose of the intrusion, the absence of consent and whether it was known or could be inferred, the effect on the claimant and the circumstances in which and the purposes for which the information came into the hands of the publisher. (at [36])

This interpretation allowed the court to find that the High Court judge had not given enough consideration to the fact that the claimant was a child. Sir Anthony Clarke found that:

> if a child of parents who are not in the public eye could reasonably expect not to have photographs of him published in the media, so too should the child of a famous parent. In our opinion, it is at least arguable that a child of 'ordinary' parents could reasonably expect that the press would not target him and publish photographs of him. The same is true of David, especially since on the alleged facts here the photograph would not have been taken or published if he had not been the son of JK Rowling. (at [46])

Murray suggested that there will always be a legitimate expectation of privacy if you are the (young) child of a famous person, because you cannot be said to have sought celebrity status for yourself.[67] This argument was used in *AAA* v *Associated Newspapers Ltd* [2013], where pictures of the infant child claimant were published alongside claims that her father was a famous (even perhaps notorious) politician. The claim was ultimately unsuccessful, largely due to the mother's inconsistent approach to the level of privacy to be afforded the information; it also raised a matter of general public interest. While children's interests do not have automatic precedence over others, not only should their *best* interests be considered, but courts should also accord particular weight to the Article 8 rights of any children likely to be affected by a publication, a principle confirmed by the Court of Appeal in *ETK* v *Newsgroup Newspapers* [2011].[68] *Weller and others* v *Associated Newspapers Ltd* [2015] confirmed that children may have different expectations regarding their privacy when compared to adults and that these expectations could, in fact,

67. The IPSO Editors' Code should be remembered in this context—clause 6 applies to children specifically—part (v) states that 'editors must not use the fame, notoriety or position of a parent or guardian as sole justification for publishing details of a child's private life'. The 'public interest' section of the Code (discussed at **section 16.3**) may apply however, though para 5 of that states that in 'cases involving children under 16, editors must demonstrate an exceptional public interest to override the normally paramount interests of the child'.

68. See also *Rocknroll* v *News Group Newspapers Ltd* [2013]. However, the determinant factor, from ***von Hannover*** is always 'the contribution the published information will make to a debate of general interest' (Ward LJ at [23]). See also Tugendhat J in *Spelman* v *Express Newspapers* [2012] (from [55]).

be affected by the actions of the parents, as had been the case in *AAA*.[69] In *PJS* [2016], the Supreme Court found that the Court of Appeal had failed to adequately consider the impact that the publication of the information would have on PJS's children.[70] The principles are, however, not confined to the children of celebrities.[71]

Whether celebrity *parents* are equally deserving of protection from being photographed going about their ordinary lives is more debatable. Some people feel strongly about this, arguing that if you become famous, you should expect what comes with the territory. As Lady Hale reminded us in ***Campbell***, many people are interested in what celebrities look like when they pop to the shops for a pint of milk. With regard to adults, it has seemed that only when to publish photographs or news stories might cause tangible harm does the question of protecting privacy seem to arise.[72] This appears to include harm to the wider family unit, particularly where children are involved.[73] Ward LJ in *ETK* v *Newsgroup Newspapers* [2011] confirmed this in the context of a claim to protect information about an adulterous affair between two 'entertainment industry' personalities from being made public (at [22]).[74] He was prepared to protect their identities because children were involved and because:

> there is no political edge to the publication. The organisation of the economic, social and political life of the country, so crucial to democracy, is not enhanced by publication. The intellectual, artistic or personal development of members of society is not stunted by ignorance of the sexual frolics of figures known to the public . . . (at [21])

16.6.2 **Iniquity**

One question left unresolved relates to 'iniquity'. When the claimant has done something they shouldn't (e.g. something illegal) this may justify, in the name of freedom of expression, publication of information which may otherwise seem to be an invasion of privacy.[75] *Jagger, Contostavlos, Mosley* and *PJS* show that adult sexual activity—even

69. In March 2016, the defendants in *Weller* were refused leave to appeal the decision to the Supreme Court. What would be the issues and likely outcome of a claim by Molly, in the scenario described at the beginning of the chapter?

70. See especially Lord Mance at [35]–[37] and Lady Hale's judgment from [72]. See also *Ali and another* v *Channel 5 Broadcast Ltd* [2018] (at [152]).

71. See e.g. *Bull* v *Desporte* [2019].

72. Though see the successful claim in *Wood* v *Chief of Police for the Metropolis* [2009], where the Court of Appeal ruled that the retention of photographs taken of the claimant (an arms trade protestor) by the police was a violation of his Art 8 right.

73. cf *PNM* v *Times Newspapers Ltd and others* [2014] (note: a seven-member Supreme Court heard the claimant's appeal in this case in January 2017).

74. Also see *Rocknroll* v *News Group Newspapers Ltd* [2013]. Contrast *AAA* v *Associated Newspapers*.

75. Conversely, the iniquitous behaviour of the *defendant* in *NNN* v *D1 and another* [2014] (blackmail), may have been one of the reasons for granting an injunction and anonymity to the claimant. It certainly was in *LJY* v *Persons Unknown* [2017] (see Warby J at [2]), where a threat was made against a well-known person 'in the entertainment business' that information about an alleged historic offence would be disclosed to the authorities and the press, as well as in *NPV* v *QEL and another* [2018] in relation to 'a successful businessman'. In *LJY*, Warby J explained that 'The blackmail element strengthens the claim. Such conduct considerably reduces the weight attached [or] to be attached to any freedom of expression argument and correspondingly increases the weight of the arguments in favour of restraining publication' (at [26]).

extramarital—is generally considered private.[76] Cases involving anonymity orders and so-called 'super-injunctions'[77]—in particular in relation to the sexual activities of famous people—support the idea that the public's interest (as opposed to public interest) will not always be enough to warrant publication of such stories (or even the names of the individuals concerned): something more is required.[78] The idea of exposing iniquity may also have to be balanced against the risk of intrusion and harassment.[79]

In *John Terry* v *Persons Unknown* [2010], this 'something more' was the public interest in exposing the iniquity of the claimant in having an affair with his team-mate's girlfriend, particularly when he was seen as a 'role model'.[80] Terry's counsel had argued, relying on an interpretation of *Mosley*, that private conduct must have been unlawful before it was able to be publicly criticised, but this was rejected.[81] In *Hutcheson (Formerly Known As 'KGM')* v *News Group Newspapers Ltd and others* [2011], Gross LJ found that information about chef Gordon Ramsay's father-in-law and business colleague was publishable 'in the public interest' where both family and commercial matters were intertwined. Hutcheson had for years maintained a secret second family—one issue was whether he had inappropriately used Ramsay company money to fund the second family and that this, apparently, was one of the reasons his employment had been terminated.

In contrast, the Court of Appeal did grant anonymity to 'a well known sportsman' (at [7]), though not an injunction protecting the disclosure of certain facts about his infidelities (*JIH* v *NGN Ltd* [2011]).[82] Lord Neuberger, giving the judgment of the court, said:

76. Confirmed recently in *XLD* v *KZL* [2020] and *BVG* v *LAR* [2020]. Compare *A* v *B plc* [2003], a case relating to disclosure of information about Premiership footballer Garry Flitcroft's extramarital affairs. Allowing publication in 'the public interest', the Court of Appeal seemed keen to stress that the protection afforded to information about sexual behaviour in 'transient relationships' should not be as great as that afforded to that within marriage (see e.g. Lord Woolf CJ at [11] and [43]). How might this impact on David, in the scenarios at the beginning of the chapter? Also consider *Trimingham* v *Associated Newspapers Ltd* [2012] and *AAA* v *Associated Newspapers Ltd* [2013].

77. Injunctions granting not only anonymity but also prohibiting publication of information about the very existence of legal proceedings.

78. See e.g. *AVB* v *TDD* [2014]. Though note, however, that the fact that *details* of a sexual relationship are generally considered private does not necessarily mean that the 'bare fact' of the existence of a sexual relationship is: see e.g. *Ntuli* v *Donald* [2010], *Goodwin* v *NGN Ltd* [2011]; or vice versa (details can be published but anonymity granted): see e.g. *JIH* v *NGN Ltd* [2011]. Injunctions preventing the press from naming an individual may also be maintained even after that individual has been named elsewhere (in one case, in Parliament and many internet/social media sites): *CTB* v *NGN Ltd and another* [2011] (later *Giggs (formerly known as CTB)* v *NGN Ltd and another* [2012]). In *AAA* v *Rakoff* [2019] anonymity orders were refused to nine dancers at Spearmint Rhino's 'sexual entertainment venues' among comments that anonymity should not be seen by claimants as an inevitability.

79. *CTB* v *NGN Ltd and another* [2011].

80. This was perhaps compounded by the fact that he was the captain of the England football team and the exposure of his wrongdoing came in the run-up to the 2010 World Cup. Similarly, in finding nothing to substantiate Terry's application for a super-injunction, the court appeared influenced by the claimant's desire (or that of his agent) to protect his commercial interests. See Sam Jones 'John Terry case sparks government concern over super-injunctions' *The Guardian* 31 January 2010. See also *Ferdinand* v *MGN Ltd (Rev 2)* [2011] for similar issues raised regarding the player who succeeded John Terry to the England captaincy and *McClaren* v *News Group Newspapers Ltd* [2012] in relation to the former England manager.

81. Tugendhat J at [100].

82. The anonymity order was granted despite indications that some of the information about the claimant's affairs was already in the public domain. This seems contrary to some earlier cases, notably *Theakston* [2002].

> There is obvious force in the contention that the public interest would be better served by publication of the fact that the court has granted an injunction to an anonymous well known sportsman . . . than by being told it has granted an injunction to an identified person to restrain publication of unspecified information of an allegedly private nature. (at [33])

In *JIH* the Court of Appeal was apparently swayed that an injunction granting anonymity would better balance the claimant's and public's interests because information was already in the public domain relating to an earlier, similar story about the claimant. Lord Neuberger said that if his identity but not the information was disclosed, the public and the media would easily be able to work out what information the injunction was designed to protect, thus defeating its purpose—it would be a 'classic, if not very difficult, jigsaw exercise' (at [40]).

Pause for reflection

The Supreme Court has found that the right of freedom of expression in relation to legal proceedings means to be able to report them, providing that the reporting is fair and accurate. That right includes being able to *name* those involved rather than simply referring to anonymous people in a disembodied way (*Re Guardian News and Media Ltd* [2010]).[83] See also *R (Mohamed)* v *Foreign Secretary (No 2)* [2010], *Graiseley Properties Ltd and others* v *Barclays Bank plc and others* [2013], and *PNM* v *Times Newspapers Ltd and others* [2014]. Lord Rodger said: 'if newspapers can identify the people concerned they may be able to give a more vivid and compelling account which will stimulate discussion . . . Concealing identities simply casts a shadow over entire communities' (at [65]).

In *CDE* v *MGN Ltd* [2010] Eady J considered a case brought by a married man who 'often appears on television' (at [4]) and his wife, seeking to protect their family from the revelation of a 'virtual' (i.e. via text message, email, etc) affair he had briefly conducted with another woman (the second defendant in this case—who had been persuaded by a journalist to sell her story to the *Sunday Mirror*). The claimants had always, it was found, 'guarded their private lives closely' and 'never sought publicity' (at [4]). They were granted anonymity, though this was *also* extended to several individuals not actually party to the case, including the couple's teenage children, the child of the second defendant *and* one of the journalists on the defendant newspaper, the second defendant's solicitor and her 'publicity advisor'! Is this taking anonymity too far?

Concealing one or other feature of a case may, however, be more favourable in the interests of 'open justice' than the granting of 'super-injunctions'.[84] Surely allowing the press to publish *something* is preferable to restrictions on publishing *anything*?[85] This was addressed by

→

83. Note that this was in the context of preserving the anonymity or otherwise of three brothers subject to freezing orders in connection with terrorism allegations.

84. In a slightly different but related context, in January 2017, a seven-member Supreme Court heard an appeal against *PNM* v *Times Newspapers* [2014], an important case considering the basis of the open justice principle in the context of whether information that was mentioned in open court (concerning a person who was arrested but not charged) could be reported. A 5:2 majority dismissed the appeal from the refusal of Tugendhat J and the Court of Appeal to grant an injunction to prevent his name being disclosed. The man was named and the case became *Khuja (formerly known as PNM)* v *Times Newspapers* [2017].

85. e.g. in January 2017, *The Times* reported that it was subjected to a gagging order pursued by Ryan Giggs in relation to the terms and financial aspects of his divorce.

→

a committee chaired by Lord Neuberger MR which considered the use of super-injunctions (as well as interim injunctions and anonymity orders) in the wake of concerns expressed in Parliament, the media, the courts and by the public following the *Trafigura*[86] and John Terry super-injunctions.[87] It recommended that:

> exceptions to the principle of open justice will only be allowed when they are strictly necessary in the interests of justice, and that when allowed they will go no further than is strictly necessary. This should mean that super-injunctions will only be granted in very limited circumstances and, at least normally, for very short periods of time. (p ii)

Further, any derogations from the principles of open justice would have to be justified by the claimant and it was envisaged that this would be 'a heavy burden'.[88] That said, in February 2017, reports emerged of a new super-injunction, preventing publication of any information which might lead to the identity of the celebrity involved, including their gender and what they are famous for.[89] The *Sunday Times* reported that it had initiated legal proceedings. Nevertheless, the identity of the celebrity concerned was leaked by overseas media outlets.[90]

16.6.3 **Limits to the current protection**

Despite the development of the breach of confidence action and its reformulation in ***Campbell***, leading to a recognised tort of misuse of private information, the limits to the protection that can be offered remain clear. This is particularly evident in non-celebrity, non-publication cases, for example ***Wainwright*** and ***Peck***.

In ***Wainwright***, the claimants sued the Home Office for invasion of their privacy (as well as in trespass to the person),[91] following a 'sloppily' performed strip-search conducted when visiting a family member in prison. The House of Lords stated categorically that no tort of invasion of privacy exists,[92] reiterating the feeling of the time that it was an interest that could, and should, only be protected by using other existing

86. *RJW & SJW* v *The Guardian Newspaper & Person or Persons Unknown* [2009].

87. Lord Neuberger MR 'Report of the Committee on Super-Injunctions: Super-Injunctions, Anonymised Injunctions and Open Justice', May 2011. Interestingly, the report confirmed that from the beginning of 2010 until the date of publication, there had only been two super-injunctions, one lasting only for one week (*DFT* v *TFD* [2010]) and the other overturned on appeal (*Ntuli* v *Donald* [2010]). Now see *AVB* v *TDD* [2014].

88. As an indication of the number of cases we are talking about, there were 41 privacy claims in the Media and Communications list of the Queen's Bench Division in 2020 (11 per cent of the total list), according to Inforrm (Inforrm 'Media and Communications List: Analysis of Claims Issued in 2020' 2 January 2021).

89. *Mail on Sunday* 'The return of the "super injunction": Celebrity gags press from reporting story on their "personal and professional life"' 5 February 2017.

90. *The Guardian* 'Publication of hacked David Beckham emails renders injunction worthless' 6 February 2017.

91. The facts and other claims in ***Wainwright*** are discussed in **section 15.6.1**.

92. See, in particular, the speech of Lord Hoffmann at [31]–[35], with whom Lords Hope and Hutton agreed. Lord Hoffmann later reiterated the same point in ***Campbell*** at [43].

legal mechanisms (as in ***Kaye***). ***Wainwright*** failed because there was no question of there being any private information (or photographs) being disclosed: it did not fall into the same category of 'privacy' (or confidence) that had by then been recognised, even though what happened to Mrs Wainwright was a clear invasion of her privacy (in terms of personal autonomy) in the commonly understood sense. Note, however, that if prison visitors were treated the same way today, an action would lie directly against the Home Office under the HRA—this was later confirmed by the ECtHR in *Wainwright* v *UK* [2006], where violations of Articles 8 and 13 ECHR were found.

Peck v *UK* [2003] ECtHR

Peck was filmed on CCTV in a town centre trying to commit suicide with a knife. The police detained him under the Mental Health Act. He was later released. His claim arose after the CCTV footage of him was used by the local authority and passed to TV and newspapers to demonstrate the effectiveness of the CCTV system. Although his face was somewhat obscured when the images of him were published, people who knew him were able to recognise him, and he alleged this infringed his right to privacy. He complained to the predecessor of Ofcom and to the local authority but his claims were dismissed. He then took his case to the ECtHR alleging breaches of his Article 8 and 13 rights.[93] The government relied on the fact that the information had lost any characteristic of confidentiality as it was already in the public domain—that is, Mr Peck's actions were committed in public.

The ECtHR found that Article 8 had been violated as, although his actions took place in a public place, showing him on TV and in newspapers was not the same as him being seen by passers-by. The relevant moment was judged to have been 'viewed to an extent which far exceeded any exposure to a passer-by or security observation' (at [53]). Consequently, as no remedy had been provided in UK law, there was also a breach of Article 13.[94]

Thus, it appears that even where breach of confidence or misuse of private information is an inadequate means of providing a remedy for invasion of privacy, a human rights claim may still be fruitful.

Counterpoint

It is arguable that a gender issue exists in the developed domestic law relating to privacy. While it has become apparent that a perceived 'harm' will attract judicial protection under what can loosely be termed Article 8 principles—in that privacy appears to override freedom of →

93. Article 13 guarantees the right to an effective remedy.

94. Would the same be the case for Eric, the teenager in the scenarios at the beginning of the chapter, caught on CCTV committing an act of vandalism? It is not clear that it was merely the fact that publication of the pictures or also the fact that his actions were *inherently* of a private nature that was decisive in that case.

→

expression when to invade the private sphere would or could cause 'harm' in some way (e.g. a set-back in drug rehabilitation or health (***Campbell***), right to life issues (*Venables*; ***Peck***), breach of a contractual obligation (***Douglas***), concern for children (*Bell*; ***Murray***))—these are all harms that the law might find it fairly easy to recognise and, as such, deem 'deserving' of protection.

But when the claimant's harm becomes less tangible, such as the mere 'distress' suffered by Mrs Wainwright, the sympathetic application of Article 8 by the domestic courts seems to greatly diminish.[95] As with other areas of tort law, *who* is protected turns on what is understood as 'harm':[96] '[p]erceptions of harm are closely linked to law, and legal recognition—in the form of a right to redress—is a key signifier that harm has been incurred'.[97] Moreover, judicial reluctance to widen the scope of the nascent privacy laws—to include privacy-related harms such as those suffered by Mrs Wainwright—may well have gender implications, as restrictions are placed on recovery in relation to harms which (historically at least) tend to be associated with (although, of course, not exclusively suffered by) women (especially mothers).[98]

16.7 **Conclusion**

As we have seen in this chapter, there was a long-standing reluctance on the part of both Parliament and the judiciary to create a specific tort of invasion of privacy. Early cases had to be moulded into legal actions that did not necessarily fit and, it seems, could offer little protection even when they did (***Kaye***). Largely, the problems stemmed from difficulty in defining (or unwillingness to define) what the right to protect one's privacy would actually encapsulate.

However, in more recent years, via cases such as ***Campbell*** and ***Douglas***, the (equitable) principle of breach of confidence has been shaped into a tort of misuse of private information (as confirmed in *Google Inc* v *Vidal-Hall and others* [2015]). To establish the tort, a claimant must establish that they had a legitimate expectation of privacy and that disclosure of the information about them was not in the public interest.

This brings into sharp focus (and in fact the development of the law has been shaped by) human rights considerations. A right to private life is enshrined in the ECHR and by the HRA in domestic law. However, rights must be balanced against competing rights and here the right to freedom of expression becomes important (HRA, s 12(4)). That said, while this may once have 'trumped' any notion of a right to privacy, it is apparent from the most recent case law that neither right is paramount and each must be weighed against the other, according to the facts of each particular case.

95. Compare *AVB* v *TDD* [2014].

96. Compare the decision in ***Rothwell* v *Chemical and Insulating Co Ltd*** [2007] on the harm caused by the development of pleural plaques following negligent exposure to asbestos fibres (**section 5.5**) (see also *Dryden and others* v *Johnson Matthey plc* [2018]) or the birth of unwanted children after a doctor's negligent action or advice (**section 7.5.2**).

97. Joanne Conaghan 'Law, Harm and Redress: A Feminist Perspective' (2002) 22 LS 319, 322.

98. Joanne Conaghan 'Tort Law and Feminist Critique' (2003) 56 CLP 175, 186.

End-of-chapter questions

After reading the chapter carefully, try answering the questions which follow.

1 Why do you think the judiciary and various governments in the UK have been so reluctant to formulate a specific law relating to the invasion of privacy?

2 Look at the cases that revolve around invasions of privacy (e.g. *Von Hannover*, *Douglas*, *Campbell*, *Murray*, *Mosley*, *Richard*). How many of the claimants in these cases really had a 'reasonable expectation of privacy' in respect of the information they did not want to be in the press? Can you define 'a reasonable expectation of privacy' any more easily than 'privacy'?

3 What harm(s) does the law find should be recognised as invasion of privacy? Is there any common element among the successful cases?

If you would like to know what we think visit the **online resources**. www.oup.com/he/horsey7e

Answering the problem question

Consider again the problem question at the start of this chapter. Now having read about the topic, **what would be your advice to Elizabeth and Alessandro?**

Here are some pointers to get you started

→ E will want to claim against the photographer for the invasive photographs (perhaps also on behalf of her sister and niece). Following *Campbell*, the first issue is whether she (and the others) can be said to have had a reasonable expectation of privacy in that situation. There is much case law (including *Campbell* itself) that can be used in the analysis. It may be different for E and for the children (*Murray*; *Weller*). If there is a reasonable expectation of privacy then her interest in keeping the information private (derived from Art 8 ECHR) must be weighed against any potential public interest in publication (derived from Art 10 ECHR).

→ E and A will want to claim against *Peachy!* The situation is similar but not the same as that in *Douglas* v *Hello!* The question is still whether there was a reasonable expectation of privacy—this was demonstrated in *Douglas* v *Hello!* but would it be here?

→ A may want to seek an injunction to prevent publication of the story about his alleged affair. The purpose of injunctions must be considered against the implications for freedom of speech. Many cases are similar and relevant (particularly in the context of private sexual relationships) and should be analysed to come to a conclusion on whether or not an injunction would be justified.

If you need some more guidance

→ An **annotated version of the problem with issues and cases to consider** can be found in the Appendix.

→ A **suggested outline answer** to check your ideas against can be found in the online resources that accompany the book.

see online resources

Further reading

Much has been written on the subject of privacy in recent years, many articles focusing on a particular case or cases. A good place to start is with some of the general comment pieces, such as by Aplin or McLean, or with Bennett's theoretical explorations of 'horizontal privacy' post-***Campbell***. Hargreaves writes an interesting article focusing on relational harm in the privacy context. Moreham brings us right up to date analysing the controversial case of ***ZXC* v *Bloomberg***. Unfortunately, as the law in this area moves so fast, some of the writing, even the more recent articles, may need updating!

Aplin, Tanya 'The Development of the Action for Breach of Confidence in a Post-HRA Era' [2007] IPQ 19

Bennett, Thomas 'Corrective Justice and Horizontal Privacy: A Leaf out of Wright J's Book' (2010) 7 The Journal Jurisprudence 545

Bennett, Thomas 'Horizontality's New Horizons—Re-Examining Horizontal Effect: Privacy, Defamation and the Human Rights Act: Part 1' (2010) 21 Ent L Rev 96

Bennett, Thomas 'Horizontality's New Horizons—Re-Examining Horizontal Effect: Privacy, Defamation and the Human Rights Act: Part 2' (2010) 21 Ent L Rev 145

Eady, Mr Justice, Speech at University of Hertfordshire, 10 November 2009 (available from Judiciary of England and Wales website)

Hargreaves, Stuart '"Relational Privacy" and Tort' (2017) 23 William & Mary J Women and the Law 433

McLean, Angus and Claire Mackey 'Is there a Law of Privacy in the UK? A Consideration of Recent Legal Developments' (2007) 29 EIPR 389

Moreham, Nicole 'Privacy in Public Places' [2006] CLJ 606

Moreham, Nicole 'Unpacking the Reasonable Expectation of Privacy Test' (2018) 134 LQR 651

Moreham, Nicole 'Privacy and Police Investigations: *ZXC* v *Bloomberg*' [2021] CLJ 5

Morgan, Jonathan 'Privacy in the House of Lords, Again' (2004) 120 LQR 563

Neuberger, Lord PSC '"What's in a name?"—Privacy and anonymous speech on the Internet' Conference 5RB Keynote speech, 30 September 2014

Richardson, Janice 'If I Cannot Have Her Everybody Can: Sexual Disclosure and Privacy Law' in Janice Richardson and Erika Rackley (eds) *Feminist Perspectives on Tort Law* (Routledge, 2012), pp 145–62

Schreiber, Arye 'Confidence, Crisis, Privacy Phobia: Why Invasion of Privacy Should Be Independently Recognised in English Law' [2006] 2 IPQ 160

Defamation

17

Problem question

Read this problem question carefully, and keep it in mind while you are working through the chapter that follows. At the end of the chapter, you will be able to apply what you have learnt to the problem question and advise the relevant parties.

In the Hood is a weekly blog focusing on fashion and TV and is famous for its celebrity 'scoops'. This week's posts (written by members of the blog's 'community') include the following stories:

'TV CHEF IN JUNK FOOD SHAME!'—a story about a TV chef, who prides herself on her healthy recipes, and who has been spotted buying an unhealthy snack in her local supermarket. In fact, she was accompanied by a film crew and was buying it for the new series of her show. The post does not mention this.

'BOOZED-UP & KICKED OUT'—a photo spread (accompanied by brief captions) of 'celebrities' appearing worse for wear after a night out. Underneath the headline—but in much smaller print—there is an explanation that these are staged photos using celebrity look-a-likes.

'MarTWO'—an opinion piece naming the mystery woman at the centre of a recent #MarTWO investigation as 'a celebrity influencer closely associated with Marmite'. This post has been shared on Twitter over 1 million times, including from the *In the Hood* Twitter account.

Advise the authors of the posts and *In the Hood* about potential liability in the tort of defamation.

17.1 Introduction

Consider the following examples:

→ ***A national newspaper suggests that a well-known celebrity couple are 'bad parents' to their three children.***

→ ***A newly married TV presenter is revealed live on-air by her co-presenter as having had an affair with her dance partner while filming a TV show.***

→ ***A TV 'self-help' guru is accused of plagiarism.***

→ ***The CEO of a multinational company is 'exposed' as engaging in sadomasochistic sexual activities with allegedly fascist overtones.***

→ ***A presenter on BBC Radio 5's Test Match Special accuses an England cricketer of fixing matches in return for significant sums of money.***

In each of these examples there is a potential claim in the tort of defamation. In contrast with, say, the torts of trespass to the person and negligence, which protect an individual's bodily or physical integrity, defamation protects a person's reputation. The law of defamation enables an individual (or, more controversially, a company) to prevent the publication of, or recover damages for, public statements which make, or are likely to make, people think less of them. As such, unsurprisingly many of the cases involve people in the public eye—celebrities, politicians and so on—and/or multinational corporations who are inevitably not only more aware of, but certainly have a greater interest in, what other people think of them. However, defamation is not a tort exclusively for the rich and famous; we all have an interest in our reputation being maintained. The principles of defamation are applicable to everyone—though the high costs of bringing a claim, combined with the absence of legal aid to support such claims may mean that its universality is more theoretical than real.

In the tort of defamation an individual's reputation is said to be pitted against freedom of expression. At its heart lies the question as to when an individual's interest in what people think of them should trump or silence the freedom of others to be able to say what they know, or think they know, about them. Freedom of expression is considered so important that (in contrast with one's interest in one's reputation) it is protected under the European Convention on Human Rights (ECHR) and the Human Rights Act 1998. However, as both make clear, one's right to freedom of expression is not unlimited. Individuals do not have complete freedom to say whatever they like, whenever they like. Article 10(2) provides that an individual's ability to exercise this right can be restricted in the interests of a democratic society including 'for the protection of the rights and freedoms of others'. Accordingly, one of the fundamental questions that the tort of defamation has to resolve is where to strike the balance between the right to freedom of expression and an individual's desire to protect their reputation.

Inevitably there is disagreement as to whether and when the courts have struck the right balance. Certainly there are examples where defamation has been used by individuals and companies[1] to suppress criticism with disquieting effect—not least because until relatively recently the tort of defamation essentially allowed an individual to sue another who said *anything* that might make a third party think less of the claimant without having to show that what was said was untrue, that it caused them harm or that the speaker was unreasonable or at fault. This has now changed. Section 1 of the Defamation Act 2013 introduced a 'serious harm' requirement intended to ensure that only the most egregious cases are brought.[2]

1. See e.g. the so-called 'McLibel' trial (**www.mcspotlight.org**).

2. In 2020, there were 147 new defamation claims, compared to 265 in 2018 and 560 in 1995 ('Media and Communications List: Analysis of Claims Issued in 2020' Inforrm's blog, 2 January 2021; 'Defamation claims in 2018 up by 70%, the highest number for nine years, will ***Lachaux*** reverse the trend?' Inforrm's blog, 11 June 2019).

Pause for reflection

In fact, the tort of defamation provides an individual or company with relatively heavy-duty tools with which to protect their reputation against another's fundamental right to free speech and expression. However, does an individual's reputation really require this much protection? *Weir* continues:

> [T]he protection may be thought to be all the odder in that the only kinds of harm apt to result from being badmouthed are emotional upset and financial loss, neither of which is very readily redressed in the law even where the defendant's negligence has been demonstrated. (p 176)

Do you agree? Think again about the purposes of tort law (discussed in **section 1.3**).

The Defamation Act 2013, which came into force on 1 January 2014,[3] was the result of a long campaign arguing that the common law on defamation was not fit for purpose. The Act was touted as turning 'English libel laws from an international laughing stock to an international blueprint'.[4] Certainly the Act introduces wide-ranging reforms including the seriousness threshold, 'new' statutory defences of responsible publication on matters of public interest, truth (replacing the common law defence of justification) and honest opinion (replacing the common law defence of honest comment) as well as changes to the multiple publication rule and measures designed to inhibit so-called 'libel tourism'.

Crucially, the new Act has not *replaced* the common law (in the sense that the common law is now irrelevant). The Act not only develops many common law principles, but is intended (in places) to *mirror* the previous common law position. The Act, to adopt Matthew Collins's analogy, is:

> Frankenstein's monster: countless complications and piecemeal reforms riveted to the rusting hulk of a centuries' old cause of action . . . No-one [he concludes] starting from scratch, would devise defamation laws of the kind with which England and Wales, and the rest of the common law world, have been saddled.[5]

What this means for our purposes is that it is necessary to understand *both* the common law and new Act.[6]

3. As the limitation period for libel is 12 months, cases were still able to be brought under the old law until the end of 2014.

4. Patrick Wintor '"Laughing stock" libel laws to be reformed, says Nick Clegg' *The Guardian* 6 January 2011.

5. Collins 2014. For a helpful overview and assessment of the Act six years on see 'Defamation Act 2013: A summary and overview six years on, Part 1, Sections 1 to 3—Brett Wilson LLP' Inforrm's blog, 29 January 2020 and 'Defamation Act 2013: A summary and overview six years on, Part 2, Sections 4 to 14—Brett Wilson LLP' Inforrm's blog, 30 January 2020.

6. You may find it helpful to refer to the annotated version of the Defamation Act 2013 (**section 17.10**). You can also download this from the **online resources**.

see online resources

17.2 Establishing a claim in defamation

While the Defamation Act 2013 makes changes to the *substance* of the law, it has not changed the *structure* of defamation claims. In order to establish a claim in the tort of defamation four questions need to be addressed:

(1) Is the statement defamatory?

(2) Does the statement refer to the claimant?

(3) Has the statement been published or communicated to a third party?

(4) Are there any applicable defences?

We shall take each question in turn. However, before we do so there is one further point to address: who can bring a claim in defamation.

17.2.1 Who can sue?

A defamation claim can be brought by any living human being. Whatever other reasons there may be for adhering to the old adage not to speak ill of the dead, fear of a defamation claim is not one of them—an action does not survive the death of either party (Law Reform (Miscellaneous Provisions) Act 1934, s 1(1)). More controversially, companies are also able to bring a defamation claim (*South Hetton Coal Co* v *North-Eastern News Association Ltd* [1894]). After all, as Lord Bingham noted in *Jameel* v *Wall Street Journal Europe* [2007], they too have a reputation to protect:

> the good name of a company, as that of an individual, is a thing of value. A damaging libel may lower its standing in the eyes of the public and even its own staff and make people less ready to deal with it, less willing and less proud to work for it . . . I find nothing repugnant in the notion that this is a value which the law should protect. (at [26])[7]

This may be true. However, it is not immediately obvious why a company's reputation needs quite *as much* protection as that of an individual. This has been (partly) addressed in section 1 of the Defamation Act 2013. As with any other defamation claimant, a company (or any other 'body that trades for profit') needs to establish that the defamatory statement has caused, or is likely to cause, 'serious harm' to its reputation (discussed in **section 17.3**). In addition, section 1(2) requires that this harm is manifested as 'serious *financial* loss' (rather than, say, the company's goodwill or public image). Though, in truth, this is not a particularly high hurdle—not least because it extends to potential (as well as actual) losses.[8]

Others go even further and argue that companies should not be able to bring defamation claims *at all*. Allowing them to do so, it is suggested, ignores the power of big business and can have a 'chilling effect' upon potential critics and challengers.[9] Limiting

7. Though he went on to say that where the company has suffered no financial loss, damages should be kept within modest bounds (at [27]).

8. See further *Brett Wilson LLP* v *Persons Unknown* [2015] and *Undre & Down to Earth (London) Ltd* v *London Borough of Harrow* [2016].

9. For a recent example, see *Linklaters LLP* v *Frank Mellish* [2019] in which Warby J granted Magic Circle law firm, Linklaters, an injunction against a former employee preventing him from talking about the firm's 'ongoing struggle with women in the workplace'.

companies' ability to claim in defamation would, it is argued, be in line with the decision in ***Derbyshire County Council* v *Times Newspapers Ltd* [1993]** in which the House of Lords recognised that restricting an individual's ability to openly criticise national and local government would be contrary to the democratic process and would 'place an undesirable fetter on freedom of speech' (at 549).

Derbyshire County Council v *Times Newspapers Ltd* [1993] HL

Derbyshire County Council sued *The Times* newspaper over two articles which had questioned the propriety of its financial dealings. However, before the case could proceed, the court had first to decide whether the council was able to bring an action. The House of Lords unanimously held that the council was unable to sue in defamation:

> It is of the highest public importance that a democratically elected governmental body, or indeed any governmental body, should be open to uninhibited public criticism. The threat of a civil action for defamation must inevitably have an inhibiting effect on freedom of speech. (Lord Keith at 547)

The reasoning in ***Derbyshire*** was applied to political parties in *Goldsmith* v *Bhoyrul* [1997]. However, crucially, these decisions do not prevent politicians and parliamentarians from bringing defamation claims (see e.g. Lord McAlpine's defamation claims against a number of high-profile tweeters, including comedian Alan Davies and Sally Bercow for tweets linking him to child sex abuse).[10] An argument can be made that this ability to bring, or threaten to bring, defamation proceedings has the same 'chilling effect' on political debate and commentary and that, at least in relation to comments about their performance as MPs, this should similarly be restricted.[11]

A further restriction on who can sue was introduced by the 2013 Act. Purporting to address so-called 'libel tourism',[12] section 9 of the Defamation Act 2013 creates a 'threshold test' for acceptance of jurisdiction in defamation cases by courts in England and Wales in cases against non-domiciled persons (i.e. persons not living in the UK, EU or in a Lugano Convention state). In such cases, courts in England and Wales lack jurisdiction unless they are 'satisfied that, of all the places in the world in which the statement complained of has been published, England and Wales is clearly the most appropriate place in which to bring an action in respect of the statement' (s 9(2); *Wright* v *Ver* [2020]).

10. Ben Dowell 'McAlpine libel: 20 tweeters including Sally Bercow pursued for damages' *The Guardian* 23 November 2012; *McAlpine* v *Bercow* [2013].

11. See e.g. Owen Bowcott 'Complaints to solicitors' regulator over libel demands from Galloway's lawyers' *The Guardian* 4 March 2015. Although there are other times when an MP's ability to bring defamation claims is right and proper. See e.g. Richard Burgon MP's successful claim—amounting to £30,000—against *The Sun* newspaper suggesting he had joined a band which 'delights in Nazi symbols' (at [1]) (*Burgon* v *News Group Newspapers* [2019]).

12. Though cf Gavin Phillipson 'London: the capital of libel tourism?' *The Guardian* 29 March 2010.

The torts of defamation: libel and slander

The tort of defamation comes in two forms: libel and slander. A distinction is drawn at common law between libel (a defamatory statement in permanent form, typically writing, but also including, for example, 'a statue, a caricature, an effigy, chalk marks on a wall, signs, or pictures' (*Monson* v *Tussauds Ltd* [1894] at 692)) and slander (i.e. statements that are temporary or transitory, usually speech but also mimicry, gestures and sign language). The test is one of 'permanence' rather than form.[13] Thus, not all spoken insults or 'speech' are treated as slander—for example, defamatory song lyrics are libellous, despite the fact they are spoken. Ultimately, the question of classification is largely a matter of common sense. Clearly, there are borderline cases—for instance, an insult written in sand on a beach. However, such cases arise more often in the imagination of tort textbook writers than in the courtroom.

Although the distinction between the torts of libel and slander had long been criticised as an unnecessarily historical relic,[14] the 2013 Act did not abolish it. Section 1(1) makes clear that in *all* cases of defamation (i.e. both libel and slander) the claimant needs to demonstrate that the publication of the defamatory statement has 'caused or is likely to cause serious harm'—or injury—'to the reputation of the claimant'. On top of this, the Act mirrors the common law position by requiring in cases of slander that the claimant demonstrate some sort of material *loss* flowing from this; for example, by losing money as a result of being shunned by business clients—with the exception of cases of imputation of criminal conduct and incompetence in business dealings where, reflecting the previous common law position, there is no need to demonstrate special damage.[15]

17.3 Is the statement defamatory?

A statement will be considered defamatory if it is likely to make others think less of the person referred to: the words or statement must tend to 'lower the claimant in the estimation of right-thinking members of society in general' causing them to be shunned or avoided (*Sim* v *Stretch* [1936] at 1240). The meaning of the defamatory statement is not, then, that which people may actually have attached to it, but rather that derived from an objective assessment to be determined by 'right-thinking members of society'. But who are these right-thinking members of society? The answer, of course, is the

13. Though some non-permanent forms of publication are treated as libel by virtue of various statutory provisions—e.g. radio and television (Broadcasting Act 1990, s 166) and public theatre performances (Theatres Act 1968, s 4).

14. See e.g. Faulks Committee *Report of the Committee on Defamation* (Cmnd 5909, 1975), [91]; J M Kaye 'Libel or Slander: Two Torts or One' (1972) 91 LQR 524.

15. Until the 2013 Act there were four exceptions to the need to prove special damage in cases of slander: where the statement imputed (a) criminal conduct (*Webb* v *Beavan* (1883)); (b) that the claimant has a contagious disease (*Bloodworth* v *Gray* [1844]); (c) incompetence in business dealings (as clarified by the Defamation Act 1952, s 2); and (d) a lack of chastity in a *woman* (Slander of Women Act 1891, s 1). However, s 14 of the 2013 Act abolishes the dated and potentially discriminatory 'contagious diseases' and 'lack of chastity in a woman' exceptions.

ubiquitous reasonable person—here the reasonable reader, viewer or listener—described by Lord Reid in *Lewis* v *Daily Telegraph* [1964] as 'someone who is fair-minded, who is not avid for scandal, nor overly suspicious nor unduly naïve, nor bound to select one defamatory meaning when non-defamatory meanings are possible' (at 260).

This is a relatively low threshold. Where a statement, for example, suggests that the claimant has broken or ignored the beliefs or practices of a particular group to which they belong, it is the implication of hypocrisy or disloyalty which is actionable, even if the ordinary person is indifferent to the claims made in the original statement. For example, to suggest that someone places the occasional bet is not in itself defamatory, however to suggest this of a local vicar who has campaigned vociferously against a new bingo hall may be. The point here is not whether people generally think badly of occasional gamblers, but rather the implication of double standards which could have a significant negative impact on an individual's reputation.[16]

Counterpoint

Pursuing a libel claim can be a double-edged sword.[17] In 1992, Jason Donovan, an actor and singer, sued *The Face* magazine over claims that he was gay. The defamatory statement was not, Donovan argued, being called 'gay', but rather the implication of hypocrisy in the suggestion that he was lying to his fans about his sexuality. Unfortunately, despite the niceties of this distinction his actions were seen by many as homophobic. Despite winning his case, in trying to protect his reputation he succeeded in destroying it. A last-minute agreement to take less →

16. In the same way, the suggestion that an individual buys processed unhealthy food is not, in and of itself, defamatory (it is unlikely to detrimentally affect what people generally think of an individual). However, the implication of dishonesty which underpins the same statement in relation to a TV chef who has publicly campaigned for healthy eating, as in the example at the beginning of this chapter, will give rise to an action in defamation.

17. See also Jay J's comment in *Serafin* v *Malkiewicz and others* [2017]: 'The claimant observed somewhat wistfully towards the conclusion of the trial that had he anticipated what was entailed, he would not have brought this claim in the first place. Without prejudice to the terms of any order for costs that I will make after receiving written submissions, this litigation has proved to be enormously costly for him as well as for the defendants. It is, in a different way perhaps from the article itself, a modern morality tale: a cautionary warning that litigation of this sort, having regard to the nature of the issues at stake, should not be initiated out of almost unbounded self-confidence and lack of judgment, coupled with a misplaced belief that the court will surely succumb to the same charm and eloquence that has worked so effectively in the world outside' (at [354]). These comments must now be read in light of the Court of Appeal's comprehensive reversal of Jay J's decision: 'In our view, the Judge not only seriously transgressed the core principle that a judge remains neutral during the evidence, but he also acted in a manner which was, at times, manifestly unfair and hostile to the claimant . . . the nature, tenor and frequency of the Judge's interventions were such as to render this libel trial unfair' (*Serafin* v *Malkiewicz and others* [2019] at [119]). The case was ultimately considered by the Supreme Court, which found, 'with a degree of embarrassment in relation to respected colleagues' (at [78]), the Court of Appeal to have wrongly applied the law in relation to s 4 of the Act (see further **section 17.6.3**) and remitted the case for a full re-trial (rather than simply on the determination of costs as ordered by the Court of Appeal) (*Serafin* v *Malkiewicz and others* [2020]).

→

than the £200,000 he was awarded (in order to prevent the magazine from closing down) and an apology was not enough to prevent the loss of a huge proportion of his fan base.

In many ways, the tort of defamation itself treads a similarly thin line. There are certain things which in the eyes of most 'right-minded people' will not lower their estimation of an individual. Being gay, for example, or having been raped (compare *Youssoupoff* v *Metro-Goldwyn-Mayer Pictures Ltd* [1934]) or having a serious contagious illness or disease will (or should) not make people generally think badly of the person involved. The claimant—and then the law—is faced with a problem. While such allegations *should not* be considered damaging, and in the minds of properly *right-thinking* people *are not*, sadly they often are. Not all people are right-minded (however much we might wish otherwise). Given this, statements which should not negatively impact on people's views of the claimant will nonetheless do so, sometimes seriously. The dilemma here is that if we take the requirement that the statement must lower the claimant's standing in the eyes of right-minded people there will be situations where a claimant's reputation *is* unfairly damaged but for which the law provides no remedy. However, if the law is to recognise a claim in these circumstances then the law risks lending its support to the view that being gay, having been raped, suffering from a serious contagious illness and the like are negative attributes.

In *Jameel* v *Dow Jones & Co Inc* [2005] and *Thornton* v *Telegraph Media Group Ltd* [2010], the courts added a further 'seriousness' requirement to considerations as to whether a statement is defamatory. Section 1(1) of the Defamation Act 2013 was intended to 'raise the bar' further still so that 'only cases involving serious harm to the claimant are brought'.[18] Libel is no longer actionable per se. A defamatory statement is only actionable if it causes, or is likely to cause, serious harm to the claimant's reputation. However, as with any new statutory requirement, there has been a period of 'bedding in' as judges interpret and apply it.[19]

Lachaux v *Independent Print Ltd* [2019] SC

The case involved a series of articles published in *The Independent*, *i*, the *Evening Standard* and *Huffington Post*, about events that had taken place in the United Arab Emirates, including details of allegations that the claimant had kidnapped his and his ex-wife's son, as well as allegations of domestic violence made by the claimant's ex-wife. In the High Court, Warby J held that Lachaux had demonstrated, by evidence, that the harm caused by the defamatory

→

18. Explanatory Notes to the Defamation Act 2013 at [11] (hereinafter Explanatory Notes).

19. See e.g. *Cooke & Midland Heart Ltd* v *MGN Ltd & Trinity Mirror Midlands Ltd* [2014]; ***Lachaux* v *Independent Print Ltd*** [2019]; *Theedom* v *Nourish Training Ltd* [2015]; *Sobrinho* v *Impresa Publishing SA* [2016]; *Monroe* v *Hopkins* [2017]; and generally Tom Rudkin 'Defamation Act 2013: You cannot be serious' Inforrm's blog, 3 March 2016 and Oliver Lock and Tom Rudkin 'A time to reflect: the serious harm test' Inforrm's blog, 31 July 2016.

→

publications complained of was 'serious', within the meaning of section 1(1). The Court of Appeal, while agreeing with Warby J's conclusion on the substance of the case, thought that he had gone too far in his interpretation of 'serious harm'. The question for the Supreme Court was therefore how section 1(1) should be interpreted.

Unanimously dismissing the newspapers' appeal, the Supreme Court held that section 1:

> not only raises the threshold of seriousness above that envisaged in *Jameel (Yousef)* and *Thornton*, but requires its application to be determined by reference to the actual facts about its impact and not just to the meaning of the words. (at [12])

To find otherwise, Lord Sumption continued, would mean that section 1 did nothing to alter the common law, which was clearly contrary to Parliament's intention:

> [S]ection 1 necessarily means that a statement which would previously have been regarded as defamatory, because of its inherent tendency to cause some harm to reputation, is not to be so regarded unless it 'has caused or is likely to cause' harm which is 'serious'. The reference to a situation where the statement 'has caused' serious harm is to the consequences of the publication, and not the publication itself. It points to some historic harm, which is shown to have actually occurred. This is a proposition of fact which can be established only by reference to the impact which the statement is shown actually to have had. It depends on a combination of the inherent tendency of the words and their actual impact on those to whom they were communicated. (at [14])

On the facts, the court largely adopted Warby J's approach to determining whether the harm caused, or likely to be caused, was 'serious':

> [Warby J] based his finding of serious harm on (i) the scale of the publications; (ii) the fact that the statements complained of had come to the attention of at least one identifiable person in the United Kingdom who knew Mr Lachaux and (iii) that they were likely to have come to the attention of others who either knew him or would come to know him in future; and (iv) the gravity of the statements themselves, according to the meaning attributed to them by Sir David Eady. Mr Lachaux would have been entitled to produce evidence from those who had read the statements about its impact on them. But I do not accept, any more than the judge did, that his case must necessarily fail for want of such evidence. The judge's finding was based on a combination of the meaning of the words, the situation of Mr Lachaux, the circumstances of publication and the inherent probabilities. There is no reason why inferences of fact as to the seriousness of the harm done to Mr Lachaux's reputation should not be drawn from considerations of this kind.[20]

20. For an application of s 1(1) post-***Lachaux***, see and compare *Yavuz* v *Tesco Stores Ltd and another* **[2019]** and *Al Sadik* v *Sadik* [2019].

Pause for reflection

> [*Lachaux* is] another example of the worrying trend where wealthy men who are accused of abuse are able to buy victims' silence.[21] Libel proceedings are extremely costly and few can risk speaking out for fear of punitive costs awards against them despite the huge public interest in exposing serious wrongdoing. In libel, serious harm to reputation seems to be valued more highly than the serious harm of violence against women that may be exposed by victims speaking out. (Harriet Wistrich, Centre for Women's Justice)[22]

Do you agree? Southall Black Sisters, the Nia Project and the Centre for Women's Justice sought (and were denied) intervenor status in ***Lachaux*** when it was heard by the Supreme Court. Central to their argument was that its 'outcome may well serve to shape the future reporting of violence against women in the media' and, in particular, that a 'narrow and context-free approach to the meaning of "serious harm" could serve to deny women vital access to the media to highlight the injustices perpetrated against them'.[23]

In the age of #MeToo, the women's groups argued, the media has become an important way for women (and some men) to expose, challenge and seek acknowledgement for harms they have suffered. In a world where we continue to see high levels of sexism, misogyny and systemic institutional failings—not least within the legal system itself—the media play a vital role in validating the remarkably similar stories of routine violence and abuse perpetrated on women in the workplace, on the streets and in their homes. Not only can public reporting of all forms of violence against women and girls (VAWG) lead to investigation and redress for individuals, it can also encourage other victims to come forward, contributing to a much-needed overthrow of public stereotypes, myths and attitudes surrounding violence against women.[24]

Lined up against this is the full force of defamation laws, non-disclosure agreements and super-injunctions which remain usually, though not always, in the hands of rich men.[25]

Lachaux—and other cases like it—are then about far more than statutory interpretation. They are about (abuse of) power. They are about freedom of expression. They are about the role of the media in aiding—and hindering—the pursuit of justice. And while ***Stocker* v *Stocker*** [2019] and ***Depp II* v *News Group Newspapers Ltd*** [2020] may offer a chink in the armour, it remains to be seen how far the law is willing to go to protect (some) reputations.

21. See ***Stocker* v *Stocker*** [2019]; ***Lachaux* v *Independent Print Ltd*** [2019]; and ***Economou v de Freitas*** [2018].

22. Southall Black Sisters, 'Press Release: *Lachaux* v *Independent News Print Ltd and Another*' (no date): **www.southallblacksisters.org.uk/news/press-release-lachaux-v-independent-news-print-limited-and-another**.

23. See **n 22**. Though see *Coker v Nwkanma* [2021].

24. See e.g. in the cases of the so-called 'Black Cab Rapist' (*DSD* v *The Commissioner of Police for the Metropolis* [2014] discussed in **section 6.3.1**) and Jimmy Savile. Southall Black Sisters (**n 22**) and Julie Bindel 'Women who allege abuse mustn't be silenced by rich men's libel threats' *The Guardian* 23 January 2019.

25. See further Brett Wilson, '#MeToo, naming and shaming: a risky business?' Inforrm's blog, 2 November 2017. See also *Starr* v *Ward* [2015] in which a woman said she was groped by comedian Freddie Starr in 1974 behind the scenes of Jimmy Savile's *Clunk Click* TV show when she was 15. She successfully defended a defamation claim brought by Starr against her. It was reported that Starr faced a £1 million costs bill and lost £300,000 from shows being cancelled over the allegations ('Freddie Starr loses groping defamation case' BBC News, 10 July 2015).

In deciding whether the statement is defamatory, the courts will then look at the statements in context including the scale of the publications, actual and potential readership (and their relationship to the claimant) and the gravity of the statements themselves. Some examples may help here. In *Church* v *MGN Ltd* [2012], for example, Tugendhat J held that a fabricated newspaper article titled 'MARRYOKE' in which it was suggested that singer Charlotte Church had drunkenly proposed to her boyfriend at a pub karaoke night could be seen as defamatory. While a marriage proposal to a long-term partner is not in itself defamatory, 'whether or not words complained of are defamatory depends on the context in which they appear . . . [and so] to attribute such drunken behaviour to a star such as the claimant [was in the judge's opinion] clearly capable of defaming her' (at [16]).[26] Similarly in *Riley* v *Murray* [2020] a tweet by the defendant, a stakeholder manager in the office of Jeremy Corbyn, then the leader of the Labour Party which stated 'Today Jeremy Corbyn went to his local mosque for Visit My Mosque Day, and was attacked by a Brexiteer. Rachel Riley tweets that Corbyn deserves to be violently attacked because he is a Nazi. This woman is as dangerous as she is stupid. Nobody should engage with her. Ever' was defamatory. Nicklin J concluded:

> This is a straightforward case. My findings are these:
>
> *i)* The natural and ordinary meaning of the Tweet is:
>
> (1) Jeremy Corbyn had been attacked when he visited a mosque.
> (2) The claimant had publicly stated in a tweet that he deserved to be violently attacked.
> (3) By so doing, the claimant has shown herself to be a dangerous and stupid person who risked inciting unlawful violence. People should not engage with her.
>
> *ii)* Paragraphs (1) and (2) are statements of fact. Paragraph (3) is an expression of opinion.
>
> *iii)* Paragraphs (2) and (3) are defamatory at common law.
>
> An imputation that a person had publicly supported a violent attack on someone is plainly defamatory at common law; it is conduct which would substantially affect, in an adverse manner, the attitude of other people towards the claimant or have a tendency so to do. Had it stood alone, the description of the claimant as 'dangerous' and 'stupid' would also have been defamatory, but the gravity of the defamatory meaning is largely supplied by the allegation of fact rather than the expression of opinion based upon it. (at [25], [29])

Nor is it enough for the claimant to point to the headline or a particular sentence or paragraph in isolation from the piece as a whole in order to ground a claim. As Nicklin J noted in *Koutsogiannis* v *The Random House Group Ltd* [2019]:

> The publication must be read as a whole, and any 'bane and antidote' taken together. Sometimes, the context will clothe the words in a more serious defamatory meaning (for example the classic 'rogues' gallery' case). In other cases, the context will weaken (even extinguish altogether) the defamatory meaning that the words would bear if they were read in isolation (e.g. bane and antidote cases). (at [12])

26. As the case was one in which the defendant was seeking to have the claim 'struck out', the judge made no comment on whether the words were *in fact* defamatory. The case was later settled for an undisclosed sum.

Counterpoint

In *Charleston* v *News Group Newspapers Ltd* [1995] the House of Lords held that the defendants were not liable in defamation for an article featuring degrading, faked photographs of the claimants—two popular Australian TV soap actors in the early 1990s—as the accompanying text made it clear that the photographs were not real. The decision as to whether the material was capable of being defamatory must be determined according to the meaning an ordinary, reasonable, fair-minded reader would understand from it, rather than on its effect on a sub-group of limited readers who looked only at pictures and headlines. Similarly in *Spicer* v *Commissioner of Police of the Metropolis* [2019] the headline 'Two guilty of killing a woman while racing their cars' on the police's Met Website was not defamatory against the driver of one of the cars who had been acquitted of causing death and causing injury by dangerous driving:

> The headline is inconsistent with the text. It is not true that two men were 'guilty of killing a woman'. But ordinary reasonable readers would not allow the headline to distort the meaning they took from the article as a whole. Readers are familiar with discordance between headlines and articles. Here, the more detailed explanation of events was in the article itself. It clearly stated that one man had been convicted of killing and another acquitted. Reading the headline and article together a reasonable reader would conclude that the headline was wrong. Some readers might think this odd, or sloppy, and move on. Discordance between headline and text is hardly unknown. But whatever conclusion (if any) the reader drew about the reasons for it, I am confident the reader would not see the claimant as a convicted killer. (at [35])

Do you agree? Think about the last time you read a newspaper—did you read to the end of every article?

But what about where the meaning of the potentially defamatory statement is unclear? How should a judge go about determining the meaning of what has been said?

Stocker v *Stocker* [2019] SC

The defendant, Nicola Stocker, had posted a number of comments on the Facebook wall of her ex-husband's new partner in which she claimed her ex-husband, Ronald Stocker, had 'tried to strangle me'. She also made a number of allegations about threats, 'gun issues' and the breach of a non-molestation order, all of which contributed a 'picture of acute marital breakdown' (at [4]). Mr Stocker began proceedings against her for defamation. The question for the court was what the words 'He tried to strangle me' conveyed to the 'ordinary reasonable reader' of a Facebook post? (at [1]).

At trial (finding for Mr Stocker) the judge, Mitting J, relied (in error) on the Oxford English Dictionary in his determination of meaning: either Mr Stocker had tried to kill his wife, or

→

→
he had constricted her neck or throat painfully. On this view, the fact that Mrs Stocker said that her husband had tried to strangle her precluded the possibility of the latter meaning being attributed (as he had in fact done this): the only possible meaning of Mrs Stocker's posts was that Mr Stocker had tried to kill her, something which Mrs Stocker was unable to justify.

Despite his success in the lower courts, Mr Stocker lost in the Supreme Court. The trial judge, a unanimous Supreme Court held, had simply got it wrong in law:

> Mitting J fell into legal error by relying upon the dictionary definition of the verb 'to strangle' as dictating the meaning of Mrs Stocker's Facebook post, rather than as (as Sharp LJ [in the Court of Appeal] suggested) a check. In consequence, he failed to conduct a realistic exploration of how the ordinary reader of the post would have understood it. Readers of Facebook posts do not subject them to close analysis. They do not have someone by their side pointing out the possible meanings that might, theoretically, be given to the post. . . . Taking a broad, overarching view, and keeping in mind that only one meaning could be chosen, the choice to be made between the meaning of the words being that Mr Stocker grasped his wife by the neck or that he tried to kill her is, in my opinion, a clear one. If Mrs Stocker had meant to convey that her husband had attempted to kill her, why would she not say so explicitly? And, given that she made no such allegation, what would the ordinary reasonable reader, the casual viewer of this Facebook post, think that it meant? In my view, giving due consideration to the context in which the message was posted, the interpretation that Mr Stocker had grasped his wife by the neck is the obvious, indeed the inescapable, choice of meaning. (Lord Kerr at [47]–[48])

Lord Kerr went on to consider the defence of justification:

> In light of my conclusion as to the correct meaning to be given to the words, 'tried to strangle me', section 5 of the Defamation Act 1952[27] must occupy centre stage. It is beyond dispute that Mr Stocker grasped his wife by the throat so tightly as to leave red marks on her neck visible to police officers two hours after the attack on her took place. It is not disputed that he breached a non-molestation order. Nor has it been asserted that he did not utter threats to Mrs Stocker. Many would consider these to be sufficient to establish that he was a dangerous and disreputable man, which is the justification which Mrs Stocker sought to establish. . . . Even if all her allegations were considered not to have been established to the letter, there is more than enough to satisfy the provision in section 5 of the 1952 Act that her defence of justification should not fail by reason only that the truth of every charge is not proved, having regard to the truth of what has been proved. (at [61]–[62])

27. Which has since been replaced by s 2(3) of the Defamation Act 2013.

A statement may be defamatory even if the hearer does not believe it, it is no excuse for the defendant to say that they did not intend the words to be defamatory (although intention may be relevant to possible defences and may reduce the award of damages). The tort of defamation protects an individual's reputation, and a statement can damage an individual's reputation, even where it turns out that the defendant did not mean what they said.

However, a defendant may argue that the words were 'mere abuse', uttered in rage and not intended to be taken seriously. Mere abuse is not (usually) defamatory. The line between mere abuse and a defamatory statement is a fine one.

Berkoff v _Burchill_ [1996] CA

Steven Berkoff, an actor and film director, sued Julie Burchill, a well-known journalist, for libel over two comments made about him in her column in the *Sunday Times* in which she referred to him as 'hideously ugly' and, on the second occasion, a review of a production of Frankenstein compared him to Frankenstein's monster. The defendants argued that the essence of the tort of defamation was damage to reputation, not hurt feelings or annoyance, and that while the statement may have caused the latter, it had not caused the former.

This was rejected by the majority of the Court of Appeal. Holding that the word 'reputation' is to be interpreted 'in the broad sense as comprehending all aspects of a person's standing in the community' (at 151), Neill LJ went on to hold that the words 'hideously ugly' could be defamatory 'even though they neither impute disgraceful conduct to the [claimant] nor any lack of skill or efficiency in the conduct of his trade or business or professional activity, if they hold him up to contempt, scorn, or ridicule or tend to exclude him from society' (at 146). At the time it was for a jury to decide whether the statement was *in fact* defamatory.

Counterpoint

We would suggest the better view in this case is offered by Millett LJ's dissent, in which he pointed out that Burchill's words were an attack on Berkoff's *appearance* rather than reputation. Burchill had simply made a cheap joke at Berkoff's expense: 'it is [he argued] one thing to ridicule a man; it is another to expose him to ridicule . . . people must be able to poke fun at each other without fear of litigation' (at 153).

17.3.1 Innuendo

The tort of defamation is not confined to openly defamatory statements. This makes sense—were the law otherwise it would be possible to frame an attack on an individual's reputation indirectly, in the knowledge that they would be unable to do anything about it. The detrimental impact on a person's reputation is the same whether one says 'there was a miscarriage of justice when X was cleared of murder' or 'X is a murderer' (*Lewis* v *Daily Telegraph* [1964] at 258).

> ***Monson* v *Tussauds Ltd* [1894] CA**
>
> The claimant had been tried for murder in Scotland and released on a verdict of 'Not Proven', a form of acquittal. The defendants placed a waxwork of the claimant with a gun in a room adjoining the 'Chamber of Horrors'. The Court of Appeal held that the scene was capable of being defamatory.

These implied or veiled attacks on someone's reputation are called innuendo. Innuendo is a mechanism through which the courts are able to attribute to a statement its *legal* meaning. It typically arises in relation to statements that do not appear defamatory, but which, because of background knowledge or information, nevertheless make people think worse of the claimant. The test for determining whether the ascribed meaning is capable of being defamatory remains an objective one: what view would right-thinking people knowing the additional information make of the statement?

Traditionally there are said to be two types of innuendo, although the line between them may, at times, be difficult to draw:

- false or popular innuendo—where the reader needs to simply read between the lines to uncover the true meaning of the defamatory statement;
- true or legal innuendo—where the defamatory nature of the statement is not apparent on its face but depends on facts or circumstances known to those to whom the statement is published.

An example of false or popular innuendo is *Lewis* v *Daily Telegraph* [1964]. The *Daily Telegraph* reported that the company (of which Lewis was the chairman) was being investigated by the Fraud Squad. It included reference to the claimant's name. After the investigation the company was absolved of all wrongdoing. The claimant sued in defamation claiming that ordinary readers would 'read between the lines' and assume that the company's affairs had been conducted dishonestly. The defendants admitted the articles were defamatory, but argued that they didn't go so far as to include actual guilt of fraud and so could be defended on the grounds of truth. The majority of the House of Lords agreed:

> [w]hat the ordinary man, not avid for scandal, would read into the words complained of must be a matter of impression. I can only say that I do not think that he would infer guilt of fraud merely because an inquiry is on foot. (Lord Reid at 260)

Indeed, were it otherwise it would be impossible to report any criminal investigation.

Legal or true innuendo relies on some additional information known only to those to whom the statement is published. So, for example, the statement that the claimant 'is no Florence Nightingale' might imply to the ordinary reader that the claimant lacks compassion—as Florence Nightingale is well known for her compassion. Whereas to say that the claimant was seen having an intimate dinner with her dance partner is not in itself defamatory, it becomes so only in relation to people who know that she is recently married, to whom it might carry the implication that she is having an affair (see e.g. *Fullam* v *Newcastle Chronicle & Journal Ltd* [1977]).

A discussion of innuendo arose in the context of one of the most high-profile 'Twibel' (Twitter libel) cases involving a defamatory tweet sent by Sally Bercow about former Deputy Chairman and Treasurer of the Conservative Party, Lord McAlpine (***McAlpine* v *Bercow*** [2013]).

McAlpine v *Bercow* [2013] HC

In November 2012, the defendant sent a tweet: 'Why is Lord McAlpine trending? *Innocent face*'. At the time, Bercow had over 56,000 followers. It followed a BBC *Newsnight* report which included a serious allegation of child abuse and references to 'a leading Conservative politician from the Thatcher years' and 'a prominent Tory politician at the time'. Following the broadcast there was intense media speculation as to the politician's identity, as well as on Twitter which led to McAlpine's name 'trending'. Unfortunately, it was a case of mistaken identity: it was quickly accepted that Lord McAlpine was entirely innocent. In deciding the meaning of the tweet, Tugendhat J stated:

> In respect of an innuendo meaning, a claimant must, in addition to identifying the meaning complained of, prove the extrinsic facts relied upon and prove that these facts were known to readers . . . The claimant will have been defamed in the minds of those readers, but not in the minds of the readers who did not know the extrinsic facts. (at [50])

He continued:

> The legal principles to be applied when determining the question of meaning are in part derived from the [*Lewis* v *Daily Telegraph*] case. They were summarised by Sir Anthony Clarke MR in *Jeynes* v *News Magazines Ltd* [2008] at [14]–[15] (where 'he' means 'he or she'):
>
>> The legal principles relevant to meaning have been summarised many times and are not in dispute. . . . They may be summarised in this way: (1) The governing principle is reasonableness. (2) The hypothetical reasonable reader is not naïve but he is not unduly suspicious. He can read between the lines. He can read in an implication more readily than a lawyer and may indulge in a certain amount of loose thinking but he must be treated as being a man who is not avid for scandal and someone who does not, and should not, select one bad meaning where other non-defamatory meanings are available. (3) Over-elaborate analysis is best avoided. (4) The intention of the publisher is irrelevant. (5) The article must be read as a whole, and any 'bane and antidote' taken together. (6) The hypothetical reader is taken to be representative of those who would read the publication in question.
>
> It is important in this case to stress point (6). The tweet was not a publication to the world at large, such as a daily newspaper or broadcast. It was a publication on Twitter. The hypothetical reader must be taken to be a reasonable representative of users of Twitter who follow the Defendant. (at [57]–[58])

Tugendhat J rejected the defendant's claim that she was simply asking for information, and found that the tweet meant 'in its natural and ordinary defamatory meaning, that the claimant

→

→

was a paedophile who was guilty of sexually abusing boys living in care' (at [90]). However, he continued, 'If I were wrong about that, I would find that the Tweet bore an innuendo meaning to the same effect. But if it is an innuendo meaning it is one that was understood by that small number of readers who, before reading the Tweet on 4 November, either remembered, or had learnt, that the Claimant had been a prominent Conservative politician in the Thatcher years' (at [91]), that is to those people who had the *additional* knowledge to interpret the meaning of the tweet.[28]

The defendant later apologised for her 'irresponsible use of Twitter' and agreed to pay the claimant undisclosed damages.

17.4 **Does the statement refer to the claimant?**

The defamatory statement must refer to the claimant. The question to be asked is this: would a reasonable person understand the statement as referring to the claimant? Where the claimant is named—including by a nickname, initials or even job title (e.g. 'Home Secretary')—there is usually no difficulty. However, the more obscure the reference, the more need there is for a 'peg or pointer' in the statement itself or to be provided by the context in which the statement was made that identifies the claimant. In such cases, the test is whether the hypothetical reasonable reader, having knowledge of the circumstances, would believe that the article was referring to the claimant (*Morgan* v *Odhams Press Ltd* [1971]).

If the claimant is not clearly identified in the statement, and so where one would need to know certain additional background information to connect the claimant to the statement made by the defendant, the claimant must show that the statement was actually published to people who knew the additional information—that is, to people who could have made the connection between the statement and the claimant. Otherwise all there is a statement which *might* have defamed the claimant if addressed to the right people, but which, in the end, did not.

What about statements that unintentionally refer to the claimant? For instance, certain names are common, and so a statement referring to, say, Dave Smith, may refer to any potential number of individuals who share that name. Can the author be liable in defamation, even where they did not intend their statement to refer to the claimant, and indeed intended it to identify someone else? The short answer is yes. The tort of defamation is not concerned with whether the defendant *intended* to harm an individual's reputation, but rather whether their words are capable of causing this outcome. Thus, a defendant may be liable even when they intended their statement as a piece of fiction (***Hulton & Co* v *Jones* [1910]**).[29]

28. See also discussion in *Monroe* v *Hopkins* [2017] at [44]–[59].

29. Or indeed even if they had no knowledge of the defamatory statement at the time it was published (*Monir* v *Wood* [2018]).

Hulton & Co v Jones [1910] HL

The defendants (a newspaper company) published a fictional account of a motor festival in Dieppe featuring 'Artemus Jones', a church warden from Peckham. The claimant was a barrister also called Artemus Jones. He was unknown to the author of the story and his editor (although he had once worked for the newspaper). He was not a church warden. He did not live in Peckham, nor had he attended the motor festival in Dieppe. Nevertheless, he sued in libel, claiming that a number of his friends had read the story and believed it to refer to him. The House of Lords agreed. There was sufficient evidence to suggest that a jury could reasonably conclude that a reasonable person would believe that the story referred to the claimant.

Similarly, in *Newstead* v *London Express Newspaper Ltd* [1940], the defendant newspaper published an account of the trial for bigamy of 'Harold Newstead, a thirty year old Camberwell man'. Unfortunately for the newspaper, this description was true of more than one man. Another Harold Newstead, a non-bigamist who also lived in Camberwell and who was about the same age as the other Harold Newstead, successfully sued for libel. Although recognising the considerable burden their decision would place on newspapers, the Court of Appeal held that it was not unreasonable, given the significant consequences for the 'wrong' man, to expect the party who publishes such statements to make sure they identify the person so closely that little or no confusion arises.[30]

However, not every unintentional reference will ground a claim. In *O'Shea* v *MGN Ltd* [2001] the *Sunday Mirror* ran an advertisement for an adult internet service featuring a model who closely resembled the claimant. O'Shea sued in libel claiming that people who did not realise that the model in the advert was not in fact her would conclude that she had consented to appear on a highly pornographic website. Rejecting her claim, Morland J held that although the image was at common law defamatory, to hold the newspaper liable in defamation would be contrary to Article 10 ECHR. Distinguishing ***Hulton*** and *Newstead* as cases where the claimant could have more easily been identified, Morland J suggested it would impose an 'impossible burden on a publisher if he were required to check if the true picture of someone resembled someone else who because of the context of the picture was defamed' (at [43]).[31]

30. For a recent example, see Lena Durham's post on Buzzfeed in which she apologises to the man mistakenly identified as her rapist after matching the pseudonym she used in her book *Not that Kind of Girl* ('Why I choose to speak out' 9 December 2014).

31. But what if a man is wrongly identified in the local and national press as a rapist? In April 2014, it was reported that the police paid 'substantial damages' to a man who was wrongly identified as a rapist on the BBC News website and in the *Oxford Mail* newspaper. In this case, the police had supplied the press with the wrong photo, and so there was a straightforward claim against them (the case was settled). Following *O'Shea* what do you think are the chances of a successful claim against the BBC and *Oxford Mail* (Dominic Ponsford 'Police pay substantial damages to man wrongly identified in the press as a rapist' *PressGazette* 22 April 2014)?

Pause for reflection

O'Shea appears to create a distinction between unintentional defamation in photographs and unintentional defamation in writing, with only the latter being actionable. Is this distinction sustainable?

Morland J's point is that it would be virtually impossible for defendants to ensure that the individuals in photos they publish could not be wrongly identified—after all most, if not all, of us look more or less like someone else. By contrast, when writing, there is more scope for ensuring that the correct person is identified, simply by including more information. So while there may be any number of people named Dave Smith, there are likely to be fewer who live in, say, Oadby, Leicester, and even fewer aged 24 and so on. In the end, by providing enough information, it will be possible to ensure that no mis-identification can occur.

However, is this a realistic demand to make of publishers? Though we *could* demand that every time someone is named in a newspaper article, sufficient information is included to ensure that no one else will be wrongly identified, this would also appear to impose a significant burden on publishers, and one which jars with the demands of newspaper and television reporting. This is, of course, the point that was made and rejected in *Newstead*, where the court reasserted that liability in defamation was strict and that it was no defence that the defendant acted reasonably and never intended to identify the claimant.

But it seems to be precisely this argument that is accepted by the court in *O'Shea*. The fact that *O'Shea* concerned pictures and *Newstead* words, allowed Morland J to distinguish the decision and rule in *Newstead*. However, in substance both cases seem to raise the same basic question: should a publisher who acts entirely reasonably and innocently, not intending their statement or story to identify the claimant, be held liable in defamation? It may be that mis-identification is more likely to occur where pictures are used, but, as cases such as *Newstead* show, the same problems can arise with words.

As such, to treat *O'Shea* as an exception to the general rule of strict liability, which applies to visual images only, may not be a satisfactory solution. If so, which way should the law go? Should we view *O'Shea* as wrongly decided or, alternatively, should the reasoning be extended to cases such as *Hulton* and *Newstead*? Do you think the reasoning in *Hulton* and *Newstead* is likely to withstand an Article 10 challenge? Think again about the balance the courts need to strike between the right to freedom of expression and an individual's desire to protect their reputation.

17.4.1 **References to a group or class**

Where the defamatory statement refers to a class or group of people, there is no liability unless the class or group is so small that the claimant can establish that the statement must apply to every member of the class or, alternatively, that the statement refers to them directly: 'In order to be actionable the defamatory words must be understood to be published of and concerning the [claimant]' (Lord Atkin, ***Knupffer* v *London Express Newspaper Ltd* [1944]** at 121). So, for example, the statement that 'all MPs are liars' is not actionable; while a statement suggesting that 'all the candidates for London Mayor are corrupt'—where there were only ten people in the running—may be. While there is no clear guidance on just how small the group needs to be it is suggested that the best approach is to apply the ***Hulton*** test—that is, would a reasonable person believe that the statement referred to the claimant?

Knupffer v London Express Newspaper Ltd [1944] HL

During the Second World War the defendant newspaper referred to the 'quisling activities' (meaning they were colluding or sympathising with Hitler and the Nazi Party) of the Young Russian political party, Mlado Russ (or Young Russia). As there were only 24 British members of the party, the claimant, a Russian resident in London, argued that, as head of the British branch of the party, British readers would assume that the remarks referred to him.

This was rejected by the House of Lords. The article referred only to the party's activities in France and the United States. Since there were several thousand international members, there was no evidence that the claimant had been singled out: 'No doubt it is true to say that a class cannot be defamed as a class, nor can an individual be defamed by a general reference to the class to which he belongs' (Lord Porter at 124).

17.5 Has the statement been 'published'?

The third element of a claim in defamation is the requirement that the defamatory statement has been published. The term 'publication' can be misleading. The requirement is better understood as a need for 'communication'—the defamatory statement must be communicated to a third party. A private conversation or correspondence between the defendant and the claimant—however insulting or hurtful it may be to the claimant—cannot give rise to a claim in defamation.[32] The wrong remedied by the tort of defamation is the injury to an individual's reputation—that is, to what *others* think of them—so if no one but the claimant hears or understands what the defendant says there is no risk of this sort of harm. Though traditionally the statement need only be published to one person, this will now need to be considered in light of the 'serious harm' requirement.

It is clear that 'publication' extends beyond the print media to include websites (*Godfrey* v *Demon Internet* [2001]; *Johnson* v *Steele* [2014]), tweets, including retweets (*Cairns* v *Modi* [2012]; *McAlpine* v *Bercow* [2013]; *Monroe* v *Hopkins* [2017]), blogs (*Cruddas* v *Adams* [2013]) and posts on Facebook (***Stocker* v *Stocker* [2018]**).

But what about where the publication is unintentional? Where the defendant did not intend anyone to read/hear what they wrote/said? Here the test is one of reasonable foreseeability. If it was reasonably foreseeable that a third party would see/hear the statement the defendant will be liable (***Theaker* v *Richardson* [1962]**).

32. Similarly, statements exchanged between *married* couples are not regarded as being published. One's spouse is not a third party. Insofar as there is good sense in allowing partners to be able to communicate as they wish without fear of legal consequences, so as to avoid 'disastrous results to social life' (*Wennhak* v *Morgan* [1888] at 639) this should apply to *all* partners, married or otherwise.

Theaker v *Richardson* [1962] CA

The defendant wrote to the claimant accusing her of shoplifting, being 'a very dirty whore' and 'a lying low-down brothel-keeping whore and thief'. He put it in an envelope on which he typed the claimant's name and address and put it through her letter-box. Her husband opened it, thinking it was an election address. The claimant sued for libel. Allowing her claim and awarding her £500 damages, the jury found that it was reasonably foreseeable that someone other than the claimant might open the envelope.

The decision in ***Theaker* v *Richardson*** can be contrasted with that in *Huth* v *Huth* [1915], where a man sent his wife a letter which was defamatory of both his wife and their children. It was opened and read by the butler. The children sued (at the time, a wife was prohibited in law from suing her husband). The Court of Appeal held that it was not foreseeable that a butler would open his employer's mail: 'it is no part of a butler's duties to open letters . . . addressed to his master or mistress' (Lord Reading CJ at 38). Conversely, it is not possible to publish information you are unaware of and have no control over.[33] In *Bunt* v *Tilley* [2006], an Internet Service Provider (ISP) was held not to have 'published' allegedly defamatory postings made in internet chat rooms—though this now needs to be read in light of *Tamiz* v *Google Inc* [2013] in which it was suggested that Google was the 'second publisher' of the blog of a third party once it had been drawn to its attention (though the action was struck out on the facts on the basis that the damage to the claimant's reputation was not sufficiently serious), and the 'operators of website' defence in section 5 of the Defamation Act 2013.[34]

While publication can be avoided by marking the mail 'private and confidential', messages on the back of postcards sent through the post are always treated as published, as are documents (if read) left open, for example, on a desk (in both paper and electronic form) or dictated to a personal assistant or secretary (*Osborn* v *Thomas Boulter & Son* [1930]).

17.5.1 **Republication**

At common law, every time a defamatory statement is republished a new cause of action arises (*Duke of Brunswick* v *Harmer* [1849]). So a single statement may have a number of different 'publishers'. Section 8 of the Defamation Act 2013 introduces an exception. The single publication rule introduces a 12-month limitation period, from the date of the first publication of that material to the public or a section of the public, which prevents an action being brought in relation to publication of the *same material* (notwithstanding

33. Compare *Bussey Law Firm PC* v *Page* [2015] in which the defendant's 'unknown hacker' defence was rejected. The defendant, who was being sued by a US law firm in respect of defamatory posts on Google Maps (which had been traced to his account), had argued that his Google account had been 'hacked' and that the hacker had posted the words complained of. The defendant was ordered to pay £50,000 in damages and £50,000 costs.

34. As yet there are no reported cases on s 5.

any subsequent publication that was substantially the same) by the *same publisher.* Its aim is to reduce the number of so-called 'stale publications'.[35] The rule only applies once the material is published to the public, or section of the public and does not apply when the defamatory material is published in a different manner (e.g. if it is moved from an obscure part of a website to the front page) or by someone else.

One clear application of the rule is in relation to newspaper archives. Under the common law, each time a user accessed an archive a new course of action arose (*Loutchansky* v *Times Newspapers (No 2)* [2001]). There was a concern that this was having 'chilling effect' restricting the creation of such archives (though a claim that this amounted to a violation of the newspaper's Art 10 rights was rejected in *Times Newspapers (Nos 1 and 2)* v *UK* [2009] on the basis that the publisher could place a note warning of the veracity of the article).

But what about where your defamatory statement is repeated by someone else? Certainly the person repeating the statement will be liable, subject to the operation of section 10 (in relation to secondary publishers) or the neutral reporting without adoption public interest defence (s 4(3)). It is no defence that defendant was simply repeating what someone else said. Though, generally a defendant will not usually be liable for another person's voluntary republication of the original publication unless: (a) they have authorised the repetition or intended that the statement be repeated (e.g. by speaking at a press conference); or (b) the person who repeated the statement was under a legal or moral duty to do so; or (c) the republication is, on the facts, reasonably foreseeable (*Slipper* v *BBC* [1991]).

17.6 **Defences**

The tort of defamation is framed very broadly. A claimant may sue in respect of any statement which might cause right-thinking people to think less of them and that is likely to cause them serious harm, irrespective of fault on the part of the defendant, even if the statement was not intended to refer to the claimant, and—subject to a few exceptions—they can sue anyone who played a role in its publication. Liability is limited through the operation of a number of defences specific to defamation: truth, absolute and qualified privilege, honest opinion and responsible publication on a matter of public interest. In addition, there are also rules relating to the operators of websites and the defendant may, in certain circumstances, choose to apologise and make an offer of amends—rather than fight the action through the courts.[36] We shall look at each of these in turn.

17.6.1 **Truth**

Not all defamatory statements are untrue. Calling a thief a thief may damage his reputation but this is hardly something the thief can complain about. Unsurprisingly, therefore, it has long been the case that establishing the truth of a defamatory statement could defend a claim in defamation: 'the law will not permit a man to recover damages in respect of an injury to a character which he does not or ought not possess' (*McPherson*

35. Price and McMahon 2013, p 127.

36. Also where the claimant has consented (either expressly or impliedly) to the publication of the defamatory material, this will be a defence (*Cookson* v *Harewood* [1932]).

v *Daniels* [1829] at 272).[37] Section 2 of the Defamation Act 2013 has put this on a statutory footing (replacing the common law): 'It is a defence to an action for defamation for the defendant to show that the imputation conveyed by the statement complained of is substantially true' (s 2(1)). The defence applies to statements of fact, not opinion. The motive of the defendant is irrelevant, as is whether the statement is in the public interest, and pre-2013 case law while helpful is not binding.

In order to rely on the defence the defendant needs to show that the imputation of the statement is 'substantially true'. The burden of proof therefore rests on the defendant to demonstrate that it is more likely than not that the statement was substantially true in the meaning that it bore. It is not necessary, however, for the defendant to demonstrate that *everything* they said was true.

As stated in section 2 of the Defamation Act 2013:

> '*(1)* It is a defence to an action for defamation for the defendant to show that the imputation conveyed by the statement complained of is substantially true.
>
> *(2)* Subsection (3) applies in an action for defamation if the statement complained of conveys two or more distinct imputations.
>
> *(3)* If one or more of the imputations is not shown to be substantially true, the defence under this section does not fail if, having regard to the imputations which are shown to be substantially true, the imputations which are not shown to be substantially true do not seriously harm the claimant's reputation.'

This reflects the position at common law: 'the defendant does not have to prove that every word he/she published was true. He/she has to establish the "essential" or "substantial" truth of the sting of the libel' (Brooke LJ, *Chase* v *News Group Newspapers Ltd* [2002] at [34]).

However, identifying the 'sting' of the defamation—the imputation of the statement—can be tricky. It is clear that what matters is whether the defamation of the defendant can be shown to be true, not whether the statement can be shown to be true in some other sense or for some other purpose. For example, in *Newstead* the statement about Harold Newstead was true of the other Harold Newstead but not the claimant. Similarly, in *Lewis* v *Daily Telegraph* the paper accurately reported that the company was being investigated for fraud. While it was not enough to show that there was indeed such an investigation, nor was it necessary to show that the claimant had indeed been fraudulent. Rather, what needed to be shown to be true was that right-thinking people would assume that the claimant had conducted his affairs in such a way as to raise a suspicion of fraud.[38] But what about where various connected statements are made? Where a number of defamatory statements have been made the claimant may choose only to sue in relation to one. Here it seems likely that, as in the common law, the defendant will not be able to defend themselves by establishing the truth of the other claims: 'it is no defence to a charge that "you called me A" to say "Yes, but I also called you B on the same

37. The Rehabilitation of Offenders Act 1974, s 8 provides a statutory exception to this. When referring to a spent conviction, the defendant must show both that it is true and an absence of malice in publishing the information (s 8(5)).

38. Consider again the BBC Radio 5 presenter's comment in the examples at the beginning of the chapter. His statement is clearly defamatory. But could he rely on the defence of truth? This will depends on how the specific allegations are interpreted.

occasion, and that was true"' (Brooke LJ, *Cruise (and Kidman)* v *Express Newspapers* [1999] at 954). Though the defendant may seek to argue that together the various statements had a common 'sting' and that the 'sting' is true (*Khashoggi* v *IPC Magazines Ltd* [1986]).

Billed as the libel trial of the century, the much-discussed ***Depp II* v *News Group Newspapers Ltd*** [2020] adds little to the legal development of libel law, but is nonetheless a useful example of where the truth defence has been successfully used.

Depp II v *News Group Newspapers Ltd* [2020] HC

Johnny Depp, an American actor, sued the publisher and author of an article which made several allegations that Depp had been violent towards his ex-wife, actor Amber Heard, during their relationship. Though there was some disagreement as to meaning, it was common ground that the natural and ordinary meaning of the words complained of was that '(i) the claimant had committed physical violence against Ms Heard; (ii) this had caused her to suffer significant injury; and (iii) on occasion it caused Ms Heard to fear for her life' (at [80]–[81]). Without an effective defence, the articles were clearly defamatory (at [585]).

After a 14-day trial conducted during the coronavirus pandemic, in which both Depp and Heard gave evidence in person, Nicol J reviewed each incident before 'stepping back' to consider the evidence 'in a more global sense' (at [108]). He found that 12 of the 14 incidents of assault raised at trial were proven, with the result that the defendants had 'established the substantial truth of the words that they published in the meanings which I have held those words to bear' (at [575]).

In March 2021, the Court of Appeal refused Depp's request to present future evidence or appeal on the basis that neither had a real prospect of success (*Depp II* v *News Group Newspapers Ltd* [2021]. He was ordered to make an initial payment towards costs of £630,000.

Pause for reflection

Nicol J's judgment was welcomed by Refuge and other women's organisations as sending a 'powerful message':

> Every single survivor of domestic abuse should be listened to and should be heard. No survivor should ever have her voice silenced. A common tactic used by perpetrators of domestic abuse is to repeatedly tell victims that no one will believe them—and to use power and control to try and silence them. What we have seen today is that power, fame and financial resources cannot be used to silence women. That is a welcome message for survivors of domestic abuse around the world.[39]

→

39. Refuge responds to Johnny Depp losing his libel case, 2 November 2020.

However, beyond the Hollywood cast, extensive media coverage and eye-watering costs, at its heart *Depp* is yet another case involving a rich, powerful man seeking to harness the might of defamation law to silence a victim-survivor of domestic abuse. As others have noted:

> In this case, the defendants were able to rely Ms Heard's evidence of the abuse she endured in her marriage to Mr Depp. Without Ms Heard's participation, a [section] 2 truth defence was unlikely to succeed. Not all victims of domestic abuse will be so willing to have their private lives forensically examined in a courtroom by lawyers and available to be reported in the press and on social media.[40]

For some (many?) victim-survivors it is likely that this—understandably—will be too high a price to pay.

The claimant need only show that the statement was defamatory—she does not also have to show that the defamatory statement was untrue. However, pursuing an action in defamation for a true statement (on the assumption that the defendant will be unable to prove its truth) is often a dangerous ploy—as Oscar Wilde, Jonathan Aitken, Neil Hamilton, Jeffrey Archer and now Johnny Depp have learnt to their cost. Even if they are successful, and that is not always the case, it's unlikely that they will leave court completely vindicated. They may have been awarded substantial damages, but they will not have *proved* that the statement was false—simply that the defendant has been unable to produce sufficient evidence to prove the truth of the allegation. Given the additional damage a prolonged court case may do to their reputation, it's not always clear whether it is worth the risk.

17.6.2 **Privilege**

The defence of privilege allows people to speak and, crucially, publish without fear of defamation proceedings in circumstances where it is important that people are able to speak freely. In such situations—described as 'privileged'—freedom of expression takes priority over an individual's right to protect their reputation.

The defence of privilege comes in two forms: absolute and qualified. Absolute privilege covers situations where it is crucial that people are able to speak with complete freedom. In such circumstances, it is not possible to bring a claim in defamation, however outrageous or false the statement and however malicious the speaker. In contrast, qualified privilege only protects the maker of a defamatory statement who speaks honestly and without malice. Here it falls to the claimant to prove malice, once the privilege has been established. Section 7 of the Defamation Act 2013 extends the circumstances in which both forms of the defence can be used.

40. Tamsin Allen and Daniel Shaw 'Case Comment: *Depp* v *NGN*—an analysis of the judgment', Bindmans website, 14 December 2020.

17.6.2.1 Absolute privilege

Where the defence of absolute privilege operates it ensures that no action can be taken against a person who makes a defamatory statement. Key situations which are absolutely privileged include:

(1) parliamentary proceedings, including statements in Parliament and in reports published by Parliament;

(2) contemporaneous reports of judicial proceedings;

(3) court proceedings—including those before the UK and international domestic courts, the Court of Justice of the European Union, the ECtHR and UN international tribunals.

No statement in Parliament could ever lead to liability in court: 'the freedom of speech and debate or proceedings in Parliament ought not to be impeached or questioned in any court or place out of Parliament' (Art 9 of the Bill of Rights 1688). This meant that anything said in either House (statements made by parliamentarians outside the House are not privileged)—however ludicrous or false—was absolutely privileged and, as such, could not give rise to a claim in defamation.[41]

17.6.2.2 Qualified privilege

Qualified privilege is much wider in scope than absolute privilege. It offers a defence:

> on an occasion where the person who makes a communication has an interest or duty, legal, social or moral, to make it to the person to whom it is made, and the person to whom it is made has a corresponding interest or duty to receive it. The reciprocity is essential. (Lord Atkinson, *Adam* v *Ward* [1917] at 334)

Until the creation of the 'publication in a matter of public interest' defence in section 4 of the Defamation Act 2013, qualified privilege was often relied on by the media in the form of the so-called ***Reynolds*** defence. As we shall see in the following section, section 4 abolishes the common law ***Reynolds*** defence, however the defence of qualified privilege extends beyond the category of privilege recognised in ***Reynolds***.

As noted earlier, the defence protects the publisher of a defamatory statement where the defendant was under a duty to communicate the relevant information (if it were true) and the recipient has an interest in receiving it. A straightforward example is the provision of a reference concerning a prospective employee to his potential employer. Here the employer has a clear interest in hearing the honest views of the referee as to the qualities and failings of the prospective employee. Of course, what this means is that even if the reference turns out to be inaccurate, the subject of that reference will have no claim in defamation as long as the referee has acted without malice. This meant that traditionally claimants who lost out on jobs because of inaccurate and bad references

41. This has been used by MPs and members of the House of Lords to circumvent reporting restrictions imposed by the courts. In October 2018, Lord Hain relied on privilege in order to name Sir Philip Green as the businessman at the centre of an injunction linked to allegations known as the 'British #MeToo scandal'. (See further Jessica Elgot 'Sir Philip Green named as man at heart of "UK #MeToo scandal"' *The Guardian* 26 October 2018.)

could obtain no remedy in law, unless they could show that the referee had acted dishonestly. However, their position has been improved—and the protection afforded by the defence of qualified privilege undercut—by recent developments in the tort of negligence (***Spring* v *Guardian Assurance* [1995]**).

It is clear then that the defence only applies in situations where the statement is made without malice. A defendant acts maliciously, in this context, if they use 'the occasion . . . for an indirect or wrong motive' (*Clarke* v *Molyneux* [1877])—for instance, if the statement is made with the intention of damaging the claimant's reputation—or where the defendant does not believe that the statement is true, or makes the statement without caring whether it is true or not. However, where the defendant honestly believes in the truth of the statement they are entitled to the protection of qualified privilege however unreasonable or prejudiced the defendant was in coming to the conclusion that the statement was true:

> In ordinary life it is rare indeed for people to form their beliefs by a process of logical deduction from facts ascertained by a rigorous search for all available evidence and a judicious assessment of its probative value. In greater or in less degree according to their temperaments, their training, their intelligence, they are swayed by prejudice, rely on intuition instead of reasoning, leap to conclusions on inadequate evidence and fail to recognise the cogency of material which might cast doubt on the validity of the conclusions they reach. But despite the imperfection of the mental process by which the belief is arrived at it may still be 'honest', that is, a positive belief that the conclusions they have reached are true. The law demands no more. (Lord Diplock, *Horrocks* v *Lowe* [1975] at 150)

Similarly, while we might be interested in hearing all sorts of idle and frivolous gossip, the question is not whether the recipient would be 'interested' in receiving the information, it is whether the recipient has 'an interest' in receiving such information which is sufficiently strong that the law should protect the maker of the statement even if the information is wrong, as long as they do not act maliciously.

In *Watt* v *Longsdon* [1930], for example, the defendant, a company director, received information suggesting that the claimant, who was employed overseas, was acting immorally and dishonestly and, in particular, that he was misbehaving with women. Without waiting for the information to be verified, the defendant informed the chairman of the company and the employee's wife. The information was not true and the claimant sued. The Court of Appeal held that although the defendant's communication of the information to the chairman of the company was privileged (there being a common interest in the affairs of company), this privilege did not attach to his telling the employee's wife. While she may have been 'interested' in knowing what her husband was getting up to, the company director was under no duty to tell her—which is to say that the public interest in wives learning whether their husbands are misbehaving (at least not from their husbands' employers) is not sufficiently great as to merit the protection of qualified privilege.[42]

42. For a recent application of the defence of qualified privilege, see *ABC (A Mother)* v *The Chief Constable of West Yorkshire Police* [2017].

Section 6 of the Defamation Act 2013 introduces an entirely new category of qualified privilege, that of a 'peer reviewed statement in a scientific or academic journal etc'. This is aimed at facilitating academic debate and its introduction is likely due to a small number of cause célèbre cases which were influential in the campaigns surrounding the enactment of the new Act, most notably ***British Chiropractic Association* v *Singh*** **[2010]** in which the British Chiropractic Association sued Singh, a journalist, for critical statements made in a newspaper article. Though this action was ultimately unsuccessful (discussed in **section 17.6.4.1**), it was a stark example of the difficulties individuals may face in defending defamation claims. The defence only applies to statements relating to scientific or academic matter (s 6(2)), that have been independently peer-reviewed by the editor of the journal and one or more experts (s 6(3)).[43] Where such statements are privileged, 'the publication of a fair and accurate copy of, extract from or summary of the statement or assessment is also privileged' (s 6(5)). As with all forms of qualified privilege, the defence is defeated by malice (s 6(6)).

17.6.3 Publication in a matter of public interest

Section 4 of the Defamation Act 2013 introduces an entirely new defence of 'publication in a matter of public interest'. This applies where the defamatory statement—whether of fact or opinion—is (a) on a matter of public interest and (b) the defendant reasonably believed that publishing the statement was in the public interest (s 4(1)).

It is based on—though also abolishes (by virtue of s 4(6)—the so-called ***Reynolds*** defence, which itself was a development of qualified privilege in the case of ***Reynolds* v *Times Newspapers*** [2001].

Reynolds v *Times Newspapers* [2001] HL

Libel proceedings were brought against the *Sunday Times* for an article suggesting that Albert Reynolds, the former Prime Minister of the Republic of Ireland, had misled the Irish Parliament. The article made no attempt to put his side of the story. Reynolds sued in defamation and *The Times* argued that it was protected by qualified privilege.

In the House of Lords, the defendants argued that the common law should recognise a separate category of qualified privilege for 'political information' covering all reporting of such matters, except where motivated by malice. This was unanimously rejected by the court, with the majority holding that the existing protection provided by the defences of privilege and honest comment was adequate when dealing with matters of public interest and it would be wrong to single out political debate from other matters of public importance.

The appeal therefore failed. Though there was a public interest in the reasons for the claimant's resignation, it was not established that the public interest in the particular story published by the

→

43. Leaving open the question as to whether the defence would have been successful in ***Singh*** (cf Price and McMahon 2013, p 102).

→

defendants, given how it was presented, was such as to attract the protection of qualified privilege: '[t]he publisher must show that the publication was in the public interest and he does not do this by merely showing that the subject matter was of public interest' (Lord Hobhouse at 239).

However, though the defendant newspaper lost in ***Reynolds*** it nonetheless marked a significant shift in the law of defamation in favour of media freedom most notably through Lord Nicholls's 'responsible journalism' test in which he listed ten (non-exhaustive) factors to be taken into account when determining whether publication of the relevant information is in the public interest and hence whether the defence of qualified privilege will be available. He held that, when balancing the competing interests of an individual in protecting their reputation against freedom of expression, the court should take into account the following factors:

> 1.The seriousness of the allegation. The more serious the charge, the more the public is misinformed and the individual harmed, if the allegation is not true. 2. The nature of the information, and the extent to which the subject matter is a matter of public concern. 3. The source of the information. Some informants have no direct knowledge of the events. Some have their own axes to grind, or are being paid for their stories. 4. The steps taken to verify the information. 5. The status of the information. The allegation may have already been the subject of an investigation which commands respect. 6. The urgency of the matter. News is often a perishable commodity. 7. Whether comment was sought from the plaintiff. He may have information others do not possess or have not disclosed. An approach to the plaintiff will not always be necessary. 8. Whether the article contained the gist of the plaintiff's side of the story. 9. The tone of the article. A newspaper can raise queries or call for an investigation. It need not adopt allegations as statements of fact. 10. The circumstances of the publication, including the timing . . .
>
> The weight to be given to these and any other relevant factors will vary from case to case . . . In general, a newspaper's unwillingness to disclose the identity of its sources should not weigh against it. Further, it should always be remembered that journalists act without the benefit of the clear light of hindsight. Matters which are obvious in retrospect may have been far from clear in the heat of the moment. Above all, the court should have particular regard to the importance of freedom of expression. The press discharges vital functions as a bloodhound as well as a watchdog. The court should be slow to conclude that a publication was not in the public interest and, therefore, the public had no right to know, especially when the information is in the field of political discussion. Any lingering doubts should be resolved in favour of publication (at 205).

Pause for reflection

Though perhaps the most significant development of the law on privilege, as early as 2002 the Master of the Rolls, in *Loutchansky* v *Times Newspapers Ltd (No 2)* [2002], suggested that '***Reynolds*** privilege' is 'a different jurisprudential creature from the traditional form of privilege from which it sprang' (at 806). This was endorsed by Lord Hoffmann and Baroness

→

→

Hale in *Jameel* v *Wall Street Journal Europe* [2007], who went on to suggest that '[i]t might more appropriately be called the ***Reynolds*** public interest defence rather than privilege' (Lord Hoffmann at 46).

The traditional forms of privilege attach to the *occasion* on which the statement is made. These are occasions marked out by a reciprocity of duty (on the part of the maker of the statement) and interest (on the part of its recipient)—such as statements made in court, the provision of references and so on. The privilege then attaches to any statements made on such occasions, unless in turn that privilege was abused by demonstrating malice on the part of the defendant. As such, there is, as Lord Hoffmann described it, a 'two-stage process' (at [50]): first, we ask if the statement was made on a privileged occasion; and, secondly, if so, we ask whether that privilege is defeated by the defendant's malice.

By contrast, the defence outlined in ***Reynolds*** works differently. Here what is privileged is not the *occasion* on which the statement is made but the *material* that is communicated. And whether this material is privileged depends not simply on the occasion on which the statement is made, but also the contents of the statement and the conduct of the parties in publishing this material in that form. Accordingly, there is no need for a separate inquiry into the possibility of the privilege being removed on the basis of the defendant's malice since 'the propriety of the conduct of the defendant is built into the conditions under which the material is privileged' (at [46]).

In transplanting the new public interest defence as a separate defence away from its roots in qualified privilege, section 4 brings with it the possibility of some much needed conceptual clarity to both defences. Though the break might not be as clean as we might have hoped.[44]

Once again, Parliament's intention was to essentially 'codify' and 'reflect' the current common law defence as developed from ***Reynolds*** and affirmed by the Supreme Court in *Flood* v *Times Newspapers* [2012]. However, 'public interest' is used in different ways in each limb of the test. In the first it is directed to the subject matter of the statement—was it a matter of public interest? While in the second it goes to whether, in all the

44. See eg *Serafin* v *Malkiewicz* [2020] in which the Supreme Court approving the decision of the Court of Appeal in ***Economou* v *de Freitas*** emphasised the material difference between the ***Reynolds*** defence and that in s 4 and that they should not be equated, nor should the ***Reynolds*** factors be used as a checklist in the context of s 4:

> . . . the Bill, as introduced, *did* in effect make reference to the ***Reynolds*** factors but later they were deliberately omitted. Subject to what some may regard as only a quibble, the observations of Sharp LJ [in ***Economou* v *de Freitas***] are valid. The quibble, if such it be, relates to her use of the word 'checklist'. I suggest that a check list is a list of factors to which reference ought to be made, in particular in order to check whether a preliminary conclusion should be confirmed. . . . But, in removing the listed matters from the Bill and in proceeding to substitute a reference to all the circumstances, Parliament made clear its intention that the ***Reynolds*** factors, upon which the list had been based, were not to be used as a check list. Even if, at the time of the decision in the ***Reynolds*** case, it was appropriate to describe the factors identified by Lord Nicholls as a check list, it is clearly inappropriate so to regard them in the context of the statutory defence. But, as Sharp LJ proceeded to explain, that is not to deny that one or more of them may well be relevant to whether the defendant's belief was reasonable within the meaning of subsection (1)(b). (at [69])

circumstances, it was in the public interest for the defamatory statement to be published.[45] The test mirrors the common law, incorporating 'both a subjective element—what the defendant believed was in the public interest at the time of publication—and an objective element—whether the belief was a reasonable one for the defendant to hold in all the circumstances'.[46]

The Act does not define 'the public interest', though section 4(2) requires the court when determining whether the defence has been made out to 'have regard to all the circumstances of the case', subject to the conditions relating to 'reportage' and 'editorial discretion'. James Price and Felicity McMahon suggest that 'public interest' has been left deliberately wide in order to dissuade the courts from returning to a ***Reynolds***-style checklist. They continue:

> One of the complaints about ***Reynolds*** was that it was difficult in practice to advise defendants (or claimants) pre-publication whether it would be effective as a defence. However, the existence of the 'checklist' did at least enable some structure to be given to an analysis of what should be done to enable publication at as low a risk as possible. Without guidance from the courts on which circumstances might be relevant and what their relevant weight might be, advising pre-publication is likely to become less certain again.[47]

Section 4(3) makes it clear that when determining whether the defamatory statement is on a matter of public interest, the statement may be considered on its own or in the wider context of the article or document in which it was published, thereby incorporating the common law doctrine of 'reportage' (see e.g. *Roberts* v *Gamble* [2007]), which allows for the disregarding of a defendant's failure to verify the truth of the imputation behind the statement where it is presented as, or forms part of, 'an accurate and impartial account of a dispute to which the claimant was a party' (s 4(3)).

Section 4(4) states that 'when determining whether it was reasonable for the defendant to believe that publishing the statement complained of was in the public interest, the court must make such allowance for editorial judgment as it considers appropriate'. The category of exercising editorial judgement is not limited to newspaper editors. This section expressly recognises the importance of editorial judgement and discretion as affirmed in *Flood* (which was decided as the draft Defamation Bill was before Parliament), in which the Supreme Court affirmed Lord Hoffmann's observation in *Jameel* v *Wall Street Journal Europe* [2007] that the intention of ***Reynolds*** was to promote 'greater freedom for the press to publish stories of genuine public interest' (Lord Brown at [118]) and the role of editors in setting boundaries around this:

> The courts . . . give weight to the judgment of journalist and editors not merely as to the nature and degree of the steps to be taken before publishing the material, but also as to the content of the material to be published in the public interest. The courts must have the last word in setting the boundaries of what can properly be regarded as acceptable journalism, but within those boundaries the judgment of responsible journalists and editors merits respect. (Lord Mance, *Flood* at [137])

45. Price and McMahon 2013, p 75.
46. Explanatory Notes at [29].
47. Price and McMahon 2013, p 75.

The leading case on section 4 is ***Economou* v *de Freitas*** [2018].[48]

Economou v *de Freitas* [2018] CA

The claimant, Alexander Economou, was the ex-boyfriend of Eleanor de Freitas, the late daughter of the defendant. Ms de Freitas had accused Economou of raping her. Economou was arrested but not charged. Eight months later, he brought a private prosecution (which the CPS subsequently took over) against Ms de Freitas claiming she had sought to pervert the course of justice by falsely accusing him of rape. Four days before the trial started, Ms de Freitas, who suffered from bipolar affective disorder, committed suicide. Mr de Freitas wanted the inquest into his daughter's death expanded to include an examination of the role of the CPS. He was advised to raise the issues publicly, which he did, authoring—or authorising to be written—seven articles. It is these articles which formed the basis of Economou's claim.

At first instance, Warby J held that only two of the seven articles were actionable (the others failing to meet the 'serious harm' threshold) and that the public interest defence was made out in relation to all of them. The central issue was not simply whether the articles raised issues of public importance (which they did), but whether Mr de Freitas 'reasonably believed that the publication of the particular statement was in the public interest'. Referring extensively to *Reynolds*, Warby J concluded:

> I would consider a belief to be reasonable for the purposes of s 4 only if it is one arrived at after conducting such enquiries and checks as it is reasonable to expect of the particular defendant in all the circumstances of the case. Among the circumstances relevant to the question of what enquiries and checks are needed, the subject-matter needs consideration, as do the particular words used, the range of meanings the defendant ought reasonably to have considered they might convey, and the particular role of the defendant in question. (at [241])

In addition, Mr de Freitas's role was 'closer to that of a source or contributor than that of a journalist' (at [242]). As such, it would be 'wrong in principle' to require him to undertake inquiries expected of a journalist (at [246]).[49]

→

48. See also *Barron* v *Vines* [2016]. Two Labour MPs brought a defamation claim against a UKIP counsellor who alleged during a Sky News interview that they knew for years of the large scale sexual abuse of children in Rotherham, and that they were still failing to ensure the perpetrators were brought to justice. Finding for the claimants, Warby J offered 'tentative and provisional view' potential application of the defence (which had not been raised by the defendant—he had received inadequate legal advice) (at [64]) adjourning the claimants' summary judgment application, to enable him to take advice and, if so advised, raise the defence at a later hearing. The defendant chose not to do this. He was later ordered to pay £80,000 in damages and the claimant's costs.

49. This case is another example of the extent to which bringing a defamation claim can be a double-edged sword. As Oliver Lock notes: 'Being accused of a sexual crime is, of course, one of the most damaging accusations that can be made against an individual and, if that allegation is false, he or she will want to do all in their power to fight it. However, this case . . . should be a warning against taking such robust action when doing so may harm your reputation further. In pursuing a libel case against the Defendant, Mr Economou has found his name at the centre of a widely publicised libel

→

The Court of Appeal rejected the claimant's argument that Warby J had effectively conferred 'contributor immunity' on the defendant. Recognising that the case raised difficult and important issues of free speech on the one hand, and reputation on the other, Sharp LJ reaffirmed the importance of ***Reynolds*** when assessing the reasonableness of the defendant's belief.

> Section 4 requires the court to have regard to all the circumstances of the case when determining the all-important question arising under section 4(1)(b) . . . In my judgment, all the circumstances of the case must include the sort of factors carefully identified by the judge, including, importantly, the particular role of the defendant in question. The statute could have made reference to the ***Reynolds*** factors in this connection, but it did not do so. That is not to say however, that the matters identified in the non-exhaustive checklist may not be relevant to the outcome of a public interest defence, or that, on the facts of the individual case, the failure to comply with one or some of the factors, may not tell decisively against a defendant. However, even under the ***Reynolds*** regime, as Lord Nicholls made clear, the weight to be given to those factors, and any other relevant factors, would vary from case to case. As with ***Reynolds*** therefore, with its emphasis on practicality and flexibility, all will depend on the facts. (at [110])

Pause for reflection

What is clear from ***Economou* v *de Freitas*** is that 'mere contributors' (and by extension bloggers and others who have not practised traditional journalism) will not be held to the same standards as professional journalists in order to qualify for the public interest defence.

Do you think this strikes a fair balance between freedom of expression and the protection of an individual's reputation? Should it make a difference where the defamatory statement is published? After all, as Lord Hobhouse stated in ***Reynolds*** 'No public interest is served by publishing or communicating misinformation' (at 128). Indeed, as Sharp LJ noted in ***Economou* v *de Freitas***:

> The implications of the publication of false information are, if anything, more serious now than they were when ***Reynolds*** was decided. The fact that information is present on the Internet, gives it permanence and reach, which may have profound implications for the life and future prospects of the person defamed. A successful public interest defence leaves a claimant whose reputation is damaged without vindication, damages or the ability to obtain injunctive relief . . . It might also be said, that in an era of distrust and 'fake news', it is more important than ever that the public should, so far as possible, be put in the picture as to where the truth, or some approximation of it, lies. (at [109])[50]

judgment. The particular sensitivities of this case also called for thoughtfulness when Mr Economou was deciding how to deal with the allegations that had been made against him. Perhaps it would have been more prudent to take action against the publishers of the story, rather than a grieving father.' 'Case Law: *Economou v de Freitas*, Is it interesting? New judgment considers the scope of the "public interest" defence' Inforrm's blog, 28 September 2016.

50. See further and compare *Doyle* v *Smith* [2018] and discussion in Jacob Rowbottom 'Citizen journalists, standards of care, and the public interest defence in defamation' Inforrm's blog, 18 December 2018.

17.6.4 **Honest opinion**

Section 3 replaces the common law defence of honest or fair comment with the statutory defence of honest opinion. This provides a defence where three conditions are met:

(1) The defamatory statement is one of opinion.

(2) The statement indicates, whether in general or specific terms, the basis of the opinion.

(3) An honest person could have held that opinion on the basis of true facts or facts alleged to be true under privilege.

Unlike in the common law defence, there is no need for the statement to be on a matter of public opinion, nor does it depend on malice.

17.6.4.1 An opinion not fact . . .

There is a fine line between a comment *on* facts as opposed to a statement *of* fact and to suggest that comment is restricted to statements of opinion risks oversimplification. A basic rule of thumb is that facts are simply descriptive, whereas comments and opinions are evaluative. So to say, for example, that the fifth edition of this book has 21 chapters is a statement of fact; to say that it is the best yet is a statement of opinion. The veracity of statements of fact is not dependent on the perspectives and values of the person who makes the statement: there is in such cases *a fact of the matter*, and this is the case even if people disagree over what this is. By contrast, opinions are *necessarily* dependent on an individual's values and preferences.

Though sound in principle, drawing this distinction in practice can be difficult. Indeed, the courts have on occasion suggested that the same statement could be either a statement of fact or a statement of opinion depending on the context. A famous example of this was given by Ferguson J in the New South Wales case of *Myerson* v *Smith's Weekly* [1923]: 'To say that a man's conduct was dishonourable is not a comment, it is a statement of fact. To say that he did certain specific things and that his conduct was dishonourable is a statement of fact coupled with a comment.' As noted by the Supreme Court in ***Joseph* v *Spiller*** **[2010]**, this cannot be right. To say that a man's conduct was dishonourable is not a simple statement of fact. It is a comment coupled with an allegation of unspecified conduct upon which the comment is based. In fact (no pun intended), a defamatory comment about a person will almost always be based, either expressly or inferentially, on conduct on the part of that person (Lord Phillips at [5]). So, while comments that do not identify the conduct on which they are based have sometimes been treated as if they were statements of fact, the better view is that they remain statements of opinion.

What is clear, however, is that the defence of honest opinion (as with the common law defence) will not succeed in such cases. Instead, only the defence of truth would be open to the defendant, which requires that they prove the existence of facts that justify the comment. ***Singh*** highlights the difficulties of distinguishing fact and opinion.

British Chiropractic Association v *Singh* [2010] CA

The defendant published a newspaper article containing the following statement:

> The British Chiropractic Association claims that their members can treat children with colic, sleeping and feeding problems, frequent ear infections, asthma and prolonged crying, even though there is not a jot of evidence. This organisation is the respectable face of the chiropractic profession and yet it happily promotes bogus treatments.

The claimant sued for libel and the defendant sought to rely on the defence of fair comment. The question for the court was whether these were assertions of fact (in which case the defence would not be available) or statements of opinion. The trial judge, Eady J, held that they were statements of fact, but the Court of Appeal allowed the defendant's appeal.

Though the words 'not a jot of evidence' may be thought to involve a question of fact—either such evidence exists or it does not—the court said that the words should be read as meaning there is 'no worthwhile or reliable evidence'. And whether evidence not only exists but is *worthwhile* is a value judgement, and so a matter of opinion. The claim that the treatments were 'bogus' was to be understood in the same light.

Pause for reflection

Some of the cases have been prepared to treat *inferences of fact* as amounting to comment for the purposes of fair comment, as long as the facts from which the inference is drawn are identified and true. An inference of fact is a statement of fact which is drawn (inferred) from other factual material. So one might infer from the fact that a married TV presenter has a private dinner with her dance partner a further fact: that they are having an affair. ***Singh*** appears to endorse this view, at least insofar as we are concerned with scientific or medical matters where the question of what inferences (of fact) can be drawn from the available evidence is contested.

The Supreme Court in ***Joseph*** v ***Spiller*** noted that one possible reform of the *common law* defence of honest comment would be to extend it to inferences of fact. However, Lord Phillips was unconvinced by the merits of such a reform:

> Some decisions have gone further and treated allegations of verifiable fact as comment . . . It is questionable whether this is satisfactory. Prejudiced commentators can draw honest inferences of fact, such as that a man charged with fraud is guilty of fraud. Should the defence of fair comment apply to such inferences? Allegations of fact can be far more damaging, even if plainly based on inference, than comments on true facts. (at [114])

Do you agree? Is it correct to say that allegations of fact will typically be taken more seriously and hence will cause more damage than comments and statements of opinion? Can we maintain the line between statements (including inferences) of fact and statements of opinion without severely limiting individuals' freedom to challenge (potentially) bogus scientific claims?

17.6.4.2 . . . that indicates the basis of the opinion

The defence of honest opinion will be available only where the statement is one of opinion rather than fact *and* the facts on which that opinion is based are sufficiently identified, whether in general or specific terms. This reflects the test approached by the Supreme Court in ***Joseph* v *Spiller***.

Joseph v *Spiller* [2010] SC

The claimants were musicians who had entered into a contract with the defendant booking agency. The contract included a 're-engagement clause', which provided that if the claimants were to perform at a venue for a second time within a 12-month period, this second booking was to be arranged through the defendant. The defendant wrote to the claimants complaining that they had breached this clause by arranging a second booking directly with the venue. In their reply by email, the claimants wrote: 'your contract . . . holds no water in legal terms'. The defendant then posted a notice on their website stating that they would no longer accept bookings for the claimants as 'following a breach of contract' they had advised that 'the terms and conditions of "contracts hold no water in legal terms"'.

In response to the claimants' defamation claim, the defendant pleaded fair comment. The claimants applied to have this defence struck out on, among other things, the basis that the facts to which the comments were directed were not identified with sufficient particularity in the notice on their website, since the details of the alleged breach of contract were not specified. The application succeeded at first instance and in the Court of Appeal, but not before the Supreme Court.

Giving the leading judgment, Lord Phillips held that for the defence to be available:

> the comment [need not] identify the matters on which it is based with sufficient particularity to enable the reader to judge for himself whether it was well founded. The comment must, however, identify at least in general terms what it is that has led the commentator to make the comment, so that the reader can understand what the comment is about and the commentator can, if challenged, explain by giving particulars of the subject matter of his comment why he expressed the views that he did. A fair balance must be struck between allowing a critic the freedom to express himself as he will and requiring him to identify to his readers why it is that he is making the criticism. (at [104])

More generally, he noted the need for the defence of fair—or, as the Supreme Court preferred, honest—comment to develop to fit modern modes of communication.

> Today the internet has made it possible for the man in the street to make public comment about others in a manner that did not exist when the principles of the law of fair comment were developed, and millions take advantage of that opportunity. Where the comments that they make are derogatory it will often be impossible for other readers to evaluate them without detailed information about the facts that have

→

→

> given rise to the comments. Frequently these will not be set out. If [the defendant] were required to provide sufficient facts as to enable a reader to judge if the comments are well founded] the defence of fair comment will be robbed of much if its efficacy. (at [99])

Lord Walker echoed these sentiments:

> The creation of a common base of information shared by those who watch television and use the internet has had an effect which can hardly be overstated. Millions now talk, and thousands comment in electronically transmitted words, about recent events of which they have learned from television or the internet. Many of the events and the comments on them are no doubt trivial and ephemeral but from time to time (as the present appeal shows) libel law has to engage with them. The test for identifying the factual basis of honest comment must be flexible enough to allow for this type of case, in which a passing reference to the previous night's celebrity show would be regarded by most of the public, and may sometimes have to be regarded by the law, as a sufficient factual basis. (at [131])

17.6.4.3 . . . and could be—and is—honestly held

The defendant must prove that there is a true factual basis to form a sufficient basis for the comment such that an honest person could have held the opinion. The defendant need not prove that all the facts on which his opinion is based are true, just enough to make it possible to hold the opinion in question. This is an objective test and asks whether an honest person could have held the opinion either 'on the basis of any fact which existed at the time the statement complained of was published' (s 3(4)(a)), or 'on the basis of anything asserted to be a fact in a privileged statement published before the statement complained of' (s 3(4)(b)). The test then is not one of reasonableness, but rather whether the view is one that an honest person might hold. To use Lord Nicholls's formulation in *Tse Wei Chun* v *Cheng* [2001] it asks whether the comment was 'one which could have been made by an honest person, however prejudiced he might be, and however exaggerated or obstinate his views' (at [20]). Thus, while the defendant cannot rely on an honestly held opinion if that opinion was based on incorrect facts and there were no other facts which could have supported it, it may be possible for the defendant to rely on the defence where the opinion is based on a honest but distorted view of the underlying facts or event where an honest person shared their view by reference to facts of which the defendant was not aware at the time the defamatory statement was published (and so upon which the opinion was not based).

Like the common law defence, there will be no defence if the defamatory opinion offered by the defendant is not an opinion they in fact hold or, where the statement is said by someone other than the defendant, where the defendant knew or ought to have known that the author did not hold the opinion.

17.7 Distributors, including operators of websites

A distinction is drawn between those who publish and republish defamatory material—authors, editors, publishers and so on—and mechanical distributors—those who simply disseminate the material (usually booksellers, libraries, newsagents). Section 1 of the Defamation Act 1996 provides the latter with a defence of 'innocent defamation' if he is able to show:

(1) he was not the author, editor or publisher of the statement complained of;

(2) he took reasonable care in relation to its publication; and

(3) did not know, or had no reason to believe, that what he did caused and contributed to the publication of a defamatory statement.

The 1996 Act extends the defence to 'mechanical distributors' to include 'printers, producers, distributors and sellers of material containing the statement' (s 1(3)(a) as well as to broadcasters of live programmes where they have no effective control over the person making the statement (s 1(3)(d)). The latter claim is comparatively rare. Most potentially defamatory programmes are either pre-recorded or, in order to meet the requirement of reasonable care (s 1(1)(b)), shown 'as live' where transmission is slightly delayed. The Act also extends to 'operators of or providers of access to a communications system by means of which the statement is transmitted, or made available, by a person over whom he has no effective control' (s 1(3)(e)), that is, ISPs or Twitter where the quantity of material means that it may have limited awareness of what is being added to the system.

Section 10(1) of the 2013 Act adds a further layer of protection for 'secondary' publishers. It states that:

> A court does not have jurisdiction to hear and determine an action for defamation brought against a person who was not the author, editor, or publisher of the statement complained of unless the court is satisfied that it is not reasonably practicable for an action to be brought against the author, editor or publisher.

Section 5 of the 2013 Act extends the protection offered to website operators making it 'a defence for the operator to show that it was not the operator who posted the statement on the website' (s 5(2)). The defence is limited in section 5(3), which states that the defence does not apply if the claimant is able to show:

> (a) it was not possible for the claimant to identify the person who posted the statement,
>
> (b) the claimant gave the operator a notice of complaint in relation to the statement, and
>
> (c) the operator failed to respond to the notice of complaint in accordance with any provision contained in regulations.[51]

51. The Defamation (Operators of Websites) Regulations 2013 came into force in January 2014 and set out the procedures which operators must follow if they wish to rely on this defence. In essence, these require the operator to either hand over the details of the poster to the complainant (with the poster's consent) or to remove the offending publication within a stipulated time frame.

The defence is also defeated by malice on the part of the operator (s 5(11)). While the effect of this defence means that website operators will not be automatically liable in defamation (even if they moderate comments), they may become liable if they do not act in accordance with the regulations and where users use pseudonyms (thus preventing the claimant from identifying the poster directly). In light of this Iain Wilson and Max Campbell suggest that while section 5 appears to strike a balance between freedom of expression and regulation, in reality it allows internet operators to provide a forum for 'internet "trolls" many of whom', they suggest, are 'vexatious in nature and may even be happy to engage in tortious litigation with the subject of their defamatory comments' and, if the claimant is unable or unwilling to engage in this, the website operator is free to continue to provide a space for such action while also potentially gaining materially from them (e.g. through advertising revenue).[52]

17.8 **Offer of amends**

Where the defamatory statement is unintentional (or innocent)—for example, where the defendant knows that the statement refers to the claimant but honestly and reasonably believes that it is true or where (as in cases of mistaken identity described earlier) the defendant never intends to refer to the claimant—the defendant can choose to make an offer of amends (usually an apology and correction, and appropriate damages) under section 2 of the Defamation Act 1996. An offer of amends is not strictly a defence aimed at showing that the defamatory statement was justified or excusable, rather it provides an opportunity for defendants to acknowledge they were wrong and to prevent the claim from going any further.

Timing is crucial here. The offer must be made before the service of a defence to the claim; that is, the defendant must choose whether they are going to fight the defamation action or admit they were wrong. This is to ensure the effectiveness of the apology. As the Judge LCJ noted in *Cairns* v *Modi* [2012]:

> It is virtually self-evident that in most cases publication of a defamatory statement to one person will cause infinitely less damage than publication to the world at large, and that publication on a single occasion is likely to cause less damage than repeated publication and consequent publicity on social media. By the same token, rapid publication of the withdrawal of a defamatory statement, accompanied by an apology, together with an admission of its falsity given as wide publicity as the original libel diminishes its impact more effectively than an apology extracted after endless vacillation while the libel remains in the public domain, unregretted and insidiously achieving greater credibility. (at [24])

52. Iain Wilson and Max Campbell 'Defamation Act 2013: A Summary and Overview' Inforrm's blog, 21 January 2014.

If the defendant's offer is accepted, the action stops and damages are agreed by the parties.[53] If damages cannot be agreed, then damages will be assessed by the court. If the offer is not accepted, the defendant can use the fact that the offer was made in their defence (unless the claimant is able to show that the defendant *knew* that the comments referred to the claimant and were false and defamatory) (s 4).

There are many examples of an offer of amends in practice—see, for example, the *Daily Express* and *Daily Star*'s front-page apology to the parents of Madeleine McCann for suggestions that they had in some way contributed to her death,[54] *The People*'s apology to the father of Baby P, whom the paper had falsely accused of being a convicted rapist (*Cairns* v *Modi* [2012]), the Metropolitan Police's apology to a man who was wrongly pictured on 'wanted posters' following the London Riots in 2011[55] and the *Daily Telegraph*'s apology (and payment of 'substantial damages') to Melania Trump.[56]

A recent example where the defendant failed to take up the opportunity of an offer of amends is *Monroe* v *Hopkins* [2017]. Monroe tweeted Hopkins saying 'Dear @KTHopkins, public apology +£5k to migrant rescue & I won't sue. It'll be cheaper for you and v. satisfying for me' (at [17]). The offer was later repeated in a letter from Monroe's solicitor. However, it was not taken up. In his concluding comments Warby J, the trial judge, noted: 'The case could easily have been resolved at an early stage. There was an open offer to settle for £5,000. It was a reasonable offer' (at [83]). Instead, Monroe was awarded £24,000 in compensation and costs were reported to be £300,000.[57]

17.9 **Remedies: damages and injunctions**

An award of damages is the primary remedy in defamation. The amount of damages awarded in defamation cases often appears out of proportion with those awarded for personal injuries. This is partly because an action in defamation is one of the few times in tort law where a compensatory award may be supplemented by aggravated or exemplary damages. Thus, while the purpose of personal injury damages is primarily

53. See e.g. Archie Bland 'Julie Burchill agrees to pay Ash Sarkar "substantial damages" in libel case' *The Guardian*, 16 March 2021.

54. BBC News 'McCanns welcome papers' apology' 19 March 2008.

55. Press Association 'Riots Good Samaritan wins poster libel payout from Met police' *The Guardian* 3 May 2013.

56. 'Melania Trump—An Apology' *Daily Telegraph* 26 January 2019.

57. Harry Cockburn 'Katie Hopkins' legal bills to top £300,000 after losing High Court battle to Jack Monroe' *The Independent* 10 March 2017. In January 2018, Hopkins's application for appeal was refused.

compensatory, damages for defamation (as well as being compensatory in respect of hurt feelings and distress as well as material losses caused by the defamatory statement) incorporate the additional purposes of vindication (repairing and re-establishing the claimant's reputation), and—to a lesser extent—punishment and deterrence (*John* v *MGN Ltd* [1997] at 607). In addition, in *Cairns* v *Modi* the Court of Appeal recognised the potential of the so-called 'percolation phenomenon' to increase the amount of damages awarded where the defamatory statement has 'gone viral':

> we recognise that as a consequence of modern technology and communication systems any such stories will have the capacity to 'go viral' more widely and more quickly than ever before. Indeed it is obvious that today, with the ready availability of the world wide web and of social networking sites, the scale of this problem has been immeasurably enhanced, especially for libel claimants who are already, for whatever reason, in the public eye. In our judgment, in agreement with the judge, this percolation phenomenon is a legitimate factor to be taken into account in the assessment of damage. (Judge LCJ at [27])

Traditionally damages were assessed by the jury. This led to a wide variety in level of awards particularly when compared to those for personal injury as the jurors were, in Bingham MR's words, left 'in the position of sheep loosed on an unfenced common, with no shepherd' (*John* v *MGN* at 608). Since the Court of Appeal's decision in *John* v *MGN*, judges have been able to inform juries of the level of damages in personal injury cases as a way of trying to guide their decision and prevent disproportionate libel awards. And, of course, now that the presumption of a jury trial has been abolished (Defamation Act 2013, s 11), this is now a matter for the judge.[58]

An award of damages can be accompanied by a final injunction prohibiting further publication of the defamatory material. An injunction is an immediate court order preventing someone from taking certain steps, and a defendant who fails to comply can be imprisoned for contempt of court. An injunction can be obtained in a matter of days or, in extremely urgent cases, a matter of hours. The award of an injunction after a statement has been accepted by the courts as defamatory is relatively uncontroversial. More problematic are super-injunctions which seek to prevent publication until a full trial. Traditionally the courts have been reluctant to grant such orders—though these are increasingly being used by celebrities keen to protect their public image.[59]

58. See further and compare the award of 'top bracket' damages (£185,000) in *Shakil-Ur-Rahman* v *ARY Network Ltd* [2016] with the award of just £10 (reflecting the *claimant's* 'disgraceful' behaviour before and during the litigation) in *Flymenow Ltd* v *Quick Air Jet Charter GmbH* [2016].

59. See **section 16.6.2**.

17.10 The Defamation Act 2013—annotated

In **Figure 17.1** we have annotated extracts from the Defamation Act 2013, highlighting the key issues which have been discussed in this chapter.

FIGURE 17.1 The Defamation Act 2013

Defamation Act 2013

1. Serious harm

(1) A statement is not defamatory unless its publication has caused or is likely to cause serious harm to the reputation of the claimant.

(2) For the purposes of this section, harm to the reputation of a body that trades for profit is not 'serious harm' unless it has caused or is likely to cause the body serious financial loss.

2.Truth

(1) It is a defence to an action for defamation for the defendant to show that the imputation conveyed by the statement complained of is substantially true.

(2) Subsection (3) applies in an action for defamation if the statement complained of conveys two or more distinct imputations.

(3) If one or more of the imputations is not shown to be substantially true, the defence under this section does not fail if, having regard to the imputations which are shown to be substantially true, the imputations which are not shown to be substantially true do not seriously harm the claimant's reputation.

(4) The common law defence of justification is abolished and, accordingly, section 5 of the Defamation Act 1952 (justification) is repealed.

3. Honest opinion

(1) It is a defence to an action for defamation for the defendant to show that the following conditions are met.

(2) The first condition is that the statement complained of was a statement of opinion.

(3) The second condition is that the statement complained of indicated, whether in general or specific terms, the basis of the opinion.

(4) The third condition is that an honest person could have held the opinion on the basis of—

(a) any fact which existed at the time the statement complained of was published;

→

This section replaces the common law defence of justification (see s 2(4)). It is intended to broadly reflect—while clarifying certain elements of—the common law. See ***Depp II v News Group Newspapers Ltd*** [2020].

The defendant does not have to prove that every word was true—all that he needs to establish is the 'sting' of the claim.

As in the common law, the defence doesn't fail just because the defendant cannot establish the truth of every statement.

This section replaces the common law defence of fair comment (see s 3(8)).

However, unlike the common law defence there is no need for the statement to be on a matter of public opinion.

It must be clear, either generally or specifically, what formed the basis of the opinion (this is the test laid down by Lord Phillips in ***Joseph v Spiller***).

This is a new requirement aimed at ensuring that only the most serious cases are brought (see ***Lachaux v Independent Print Ltd*** [2017]). Note: it does not change who can sue.

This ensures that the harm to the reputation of a company (or similar) is not serious harm unless it has caused, or is likely to cause, serious financial loss.

What matters is whether the defamation of the defendant can be shown to be true, not whether the statement can be shown to be true in some other sense or for some other purpose.

The defence does not apply to statements of fact. See ***Joseph v Spiller*** [2010] for discussion of the difficulty sometimes of distinguishing between statements of fact and statements of opinion.

Honesty was a requirement of the common law defence. However, unlike the common law, there is no need to prove the absence of malice.

→

(b) anything asserted to be a fact in a privileged statement published before the statement complained of.

(5) The defence is defeated if the claimant shows that the defendant did not hold the opinion.

(6) Subsection (5) does not apply in a case where the statement complained of was published by the defendant but made by another person ("the author"); and in such a case the defence is defeated if the claimant shows that the defendant knew or ought to have known that the author did not hold the opinion.

This section allows the defence, in certain circumstances, to cover the statements of others.

(7) For the purposes of subsection (4)(b) a statement is a "privileged statement" if the person responsible for its publication would have one or more of the following defences if an action for defamation were brought in respect of it—

(a) a defence under section 4 (publication on matter of public interest);

(b) a defence under section 6 (peer-reviewed statement in scientific or academic journal);

(c) a defence under section 14 of the Defamation Act 1996 (reports of court proceedings protected by absolute privilege);

(d) a defence under section 15 of that Act (other reports protected by qualified privilege).

By abolishing the commonlaw defence, and repealing s 6 of the 1952 Act, the 2013 Act prevents defendants from arguing the common law defence alongside (or even instead of) the statutory defence.

(8) The common law defence of fair comment is abolished and, accordingly, section 6 of the Defamation Act 1952 (fair comment) is repealed.

Note the different ways 'public interest' is used in this section.

4. Publication on matter of public interest

This defence replaces the so-called ***Reynolds* [2001]** defence.

(1) It is a defence to an action for defamation for the defendant to show that—

(a) the statement complained of was, or formed part of, a statement on a matter of public interest; and

(b) the defendant reasonably believed that publishing the statement complained of was in the public interest.

(2) Subject to subsections (3) and (4), in determining whether the defendant has shown the matters mentioned in subsection (1), the court must have regard to all the circumstances of the case.

See ***Economou* v *de Freitas*** **[2018].**

(3) If the statement complained of was, or formed part of, an accurate and impartial account of a dispute to which the claimant was a party, the court must in determining whether it was reasonable for the defendant to believe that publishing the statement was in the public interest disregard any omission of the defendant to take steps to verify the truth of the imputation conveyed by it.

This section is intended to capture the common law doctrine of 'reportage'.

This directly reflects the Supreme Court decision in *Flood* v *Times Newspapers* [2012].

(4) In determining whether it was reasonable for the defendant to believe that publishing the statement complained of was in the public interest, the court must make such allowance for editorial judgement as it considers appropriate.

→

In cases where website operators do not 'edit' the content of the website they will also be protected under s 10 so long as they are not the 'author, editor or publisher' of the statement and it is 'reasonably practicable' for the claimant to pursue the author, editor or publisher of the statement.

→

(5) For the avoidance of doubt, the defence under this section may be relied upon irrespective of whether the statement complained of is a statement of fact or a statement of opinion.

(6) The common law defence known as the ***Reynolds*** defence is abolished.

5. Operators of websites

This section extends the protection offered to operators of websites.

(1) This section applies where an action for defamation is brought against the operator of a website in respect of a statement posted on the website.

(2) It is a defence for the operator to show that it was not the operator who posted the statement on the website.

(3) The defence is defeated if the claimant shows that—

(a) it was not possible for the claimant to identify the person who posted the statement,

(b) the claimant gave the operator a notice of complaint in relation to the statement, and

(c) the operator failed to respond to the notice of complaint in accordance with any provision contained in regulations.

This section may extend the scope of the defence in relation to websites that allow users to post comments using a pseudonym.

(4) For the purposes of subsection (3)(a), it is possible for a claimant to "identify" a person

...

This section offers protection to website moderators.

(12) The defence under this section is not defeated by reason only of the fact that the operator of the website moderates the statements posted on it by others.

6. Peer-reviewed statement in scientific or academic journal etc

This section is introduced as a direct result of the case of ***British Chiropractic Association v Singh*** [2010].

(1) The publication of a statement in a scientific or academic journal (whether published in electronic form or otherwise) is privileged if the following conditions are met.

(2) The first condition is that the statement relates to a scientific or academic matter.

(3) The second condition is that before the statement was published in the journal an independent review of the statement's scientific or academic merit was carried out by—

(a) the editor of the journal, and

(b) one or more persons with expertise in the scientific or academic matter concerned.

(4) Where the publication of a statement in a scientific or academic journal is privileged by virtue of subsection (1), the publication in the same journal of any assessment of the statement's scientific or academic merit is also privileged if—

(a) the assessment was written by one or more of the persons who carried out the independent review of the statement; and

→

(b) the assessment was written in the course of that review.

(5) Where the publication of a statement or assessment is privileged by virtue of this section, the publication of a fair and accurate copy of, extract from or summary of the statement or assessment is also privileged.

(6) A publication is not privileged by virtue of this section if it is shown to be made with malice.

...

7. Reports etc protected by privilege

This section amends some of the provisions in the Defamation Act 1996 relating to absolute and qualified privilege.

...

8. Single publication rule

This section introduces a single publication rule—reversing the common law rule established in *Duke of Brunswick v Harmer* [1849].

One clear application of the rule is in relation to newspaper archives.

(1) This section applies if a person—

(a) publishes a statement to the public ('the first publication'), and

(b) subsequently publishes (whether or not to the public) that statement or a statement which is substantially the same.

In order for this rule to apply, the statement must be published by the same person and in substantially the same way. It does not apply when the defamatory material published is substantially different to the original, or is published in a different manner (e.g. if it is moved from an obscure part of a website to the front page) or by someone else (see ss 8(4) and 8(5)).

(2) In subsection (1) "publication to the public" includes publication to a section of the public.

(3) For the purposes of section 4A of the Limitation Act 1980 (time limit for actions for defamation etc) any cause of action against the person for defamation in respect of the subsequent publication is to be treated as having accrued on the date of the first publication.

(4) This section does not apply in relation to the subsequent publication if the manner of that publication is materially different from the manner of the first publication.

(5) In determining whether the manner of a subsequent publication is materially different from the manner of the first publication, the matters to which the court may have regard include (amongst other matters)—

(a) the level of prominence that a statement is given;

(b) the extent of the subsequent publication.

(6) Where this section applies—

(a) it does not affect the court's discretion under section 32A of the Limitation Act 1980 (discretionary exclusion of time limit for actions for defamation etc), and

(b) the reference in subsection (1)(a) of that section to the operation of section 4A of that Act is a reference to the operation of section 4A together with this section.

9. Action against a person not domiciled in the UK or a Member State etc

This section was introduced in order to address the problem of so-called 'libel tourism'.

(1) This section applies to an action for defamation against a person who is not domiciled—

→

(a) in the United Kingdom;
(b) in another Member State; or
(c) in a state which is for the time being a contracting party to the Lugano Convention.

(2) A court does not have jurisdiction to hear and determine an action to which this section applies unless the court is satisfied that, of all the places in which the statement complained of has been published, England and Wales is clearly the most appropriate place in which to bring an action in respect of the statement.

…

This section offers additional protection to so-called 'secondary publishers'.

10. Action against a person who was not the author, editor etc

(1) A court does not have jurisdiction to hear and determine an action for defamation brought against a person who was not the author, editor or publisher of the statement complained of unless the court is satisfied that it is not reasonably practicable for an action to be brought against the author, editor or publisher.

(2) In this section "author", "editor" and "publisher" have the same meaning as in section 1 of the Defamation Act 1996.

This section abolishes the (unusual) presumption in favour of a jury trial in defamation cases. It leaves the courts with a residual discretion to order a jury trial, but gives no guidance on when it might be appropriate to so order.

11. Trial to be without a jury unless the court orders otherwise

(1) In section 69(1) of the Senior Courts Act 1981 (certain actions in the Queen's Bench Division to be tried with a jury unless the trial requires prolonged examination of documents etc) in paragraph (b) omit "libel, slander,".

(2) In section 66(3) of the County Courts Act 1984 (certain actions in the county court to be tried with a jury unless the trial requires prolonged examination of documents etc) in paragraph (b) omit "libel, slander,".

…

This section abolishes two dated and discriminatory provisions which set out exceptions to the need to prove special damage in cases of slander.

14. Special damage

(1) The Slander of Women Act 1891 is repealed.

(2) The publication of a statement that conveys the imputation that a person has a contagious or infectious disease does not give rise to a cause of action for slander unless the publication causes the person special damage.

15. Meaning of "publish" and "statement"

In this Act—

→

→

"publish" and "publication", in relation to a statement, have the meaning they have for the purposes of the law of defamation generally;

"statement" means words, pictures, visual images, gestures or any other method of signifying meaning.

...

17.11 Conclusion

Defamation protects an individual's or a company's reputation by allowing them to prevent the publication of, or recover damages for, public statements that have caused or are likely to cause serious harm to the reputation of the claimant. In so doing, the courts have to decide whether an individual's interest in what people think of them should trump the freedom of others to be able to say what they know, or think they know, about them.

In order to bring a claim, the statement must be defamatory (as opposed to simply insulting), it must refer to the claimant and must be published. The defendant can, however, defeat a claim in defamation by virtue of a number of defences, many of which have been put on a statutory footing in the Defamation Act 2013.

The law on defamation has recently undergone a significant period of change, the long-term effects of which are not yet clear. In fact, it may well turn out to be a bit of a damp squib! As Matthew Collins notes:

> While in a number of respects the reforms are radical, as a package, they cannot be so described. The 2013 Act does not redefine the elements of the cause of action or reduce the panoply of available defences. It does little to simplify the complexity of the law. As with reforms past, it mostly bolts new principles onto the existing structure although, to labour the metaphor [see **section 17.1**], some of the monster's organs have been transplanted or received grafts.[60]

60. Collins 2014.

End-of-chapter questions

After reading the chapter carefully, try answering the questions which follow.

1 Who can and who cannot sue in defamation? Explain the reasons for this.

2 Outline the key changes introduced by the Defamation Act 2013. What are the key differences between absolute privilege, qualified privilege and the new public interest defence?

3 When will defendants who disseminate or host a defamatory statement made by another escape liability?

4 The Defamation Act 2013 has done much to clarify and improve the balance between protecting an individual's reputation and the freedom of speech of others. Do you agree?

If you would like to know what we think visit the **online resources**. www.oup.com/he/horsey7e

Answering the problem question

Consider again the problem question at the start of this chapter. Now having read about the topic, **what would be your advice to the editor of *In the Hood*?**

Here are some pointers to get you started

→ Is the 'Junk Food Shame' article likely to have caused the TV chef 'serious harm' as required by s 1(1)? What if her show had been cancelled as a result?

→ Might the authors of *In the Hood* be able to rely on the defence of 'publication in a matter of public interest' in relation to one or more of the stories? Would it make a difference here that *In the Hood* is a blog, rather than a traditional magazine or newspaper?

→ Is the 'MarTWO' post defamatory? Could the innuendo case law help here? Think again about *McAlpine* v *Bercow*. If it is, what difference, if any, would the fact it has been retweeted so many times make?

If you need some more guidance

→ An **annotated version of the problem with issues and cases to consider** can be found in the Appendix.

see online resources

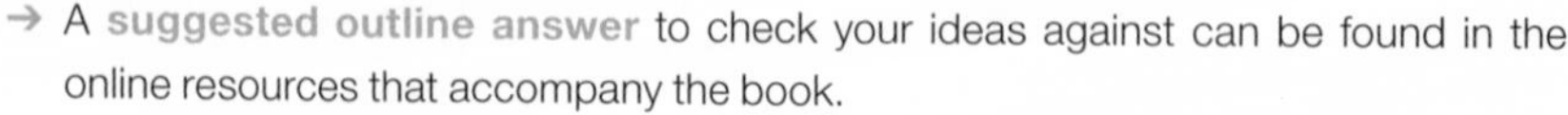

→ A **suggested outline answer** to check your ideas against can be found in the online resources that accompany the book.

Further reading

In addition to the academic articles listed, the Inforrm blog (**www.inforrm.wordpress.com**) has some interesting articles and links to recent cases. It is also worth taking a look at the various weblinks on the online resources.

Barendt, Eric 'Libel and Freedom of Speech in English Law' [1993] PL 449

Collins, Matthew 'Reflections on the Defamation Act 2013, one year after Royal Assent' Inforrm's blog, 25 April 2014

Erdos, David 'Serious Harm to Reputation Rights? Defamation in the Supreme Court [2019] CLJ 510

Gibbons, Thomas 'Defamation Reconsidered' (1996) 16 OJLS 587

Howarth, David 'Libel: Its Purpose and Reform' (2011) 74 MLR 845

McNamara, Lawrence *Reputation and Defamation* (OUP, 2007)

Mullis, Alastair and Andrew Scott 'Something Rotten in the State of English Libel Law? A Rejoinder to the Clamour for Reform of Defamation' (2009) 14 Communications Law 173

Mullis, Alastair and Andrew Scott 'Tilting at Windmills: The Defamation Act 2013' (2014) 77 MLR 87

O'Callaghan, Patrick 'The Law of Defamation—Part 1 and Part II' in *Butterworths Common Law Series: The Law of Tort* (Butterworths, 2014), Chs 25 and 26

Price, James and Felicity McMahon (eds) *Blackstone's Guide to the Defamation Act 2013* (OUP, 2013)

The land torts

PART IV

18 Trespass to land and nuisance

18.1 Introduction

18.2 Trespass to land

18.3 Private nuisance

18.4 Remedies and the human rights dimension

18.5 Public nuisance

18.6 Conclusion

End-of-chapter questions

Further reading

19 Actions under the rule of *Rylands* v *Fletcher*

19.1 Introduction

19.2 The rule in *Rylands* v *Fletcher*

19.3 *Cambridge Water* v *Eastern Counties Leather plc*

19.4 *Transco* v *Stockport MBC*

19.5 Standing and defences

19.6 The nuisance/*Rylands* v *Fletcher*/negligence overlap

19.7 Where does *Rylands* v *Fletcher* fit today?

19.8 Conclusion

End-of-chapter questions

Further reading

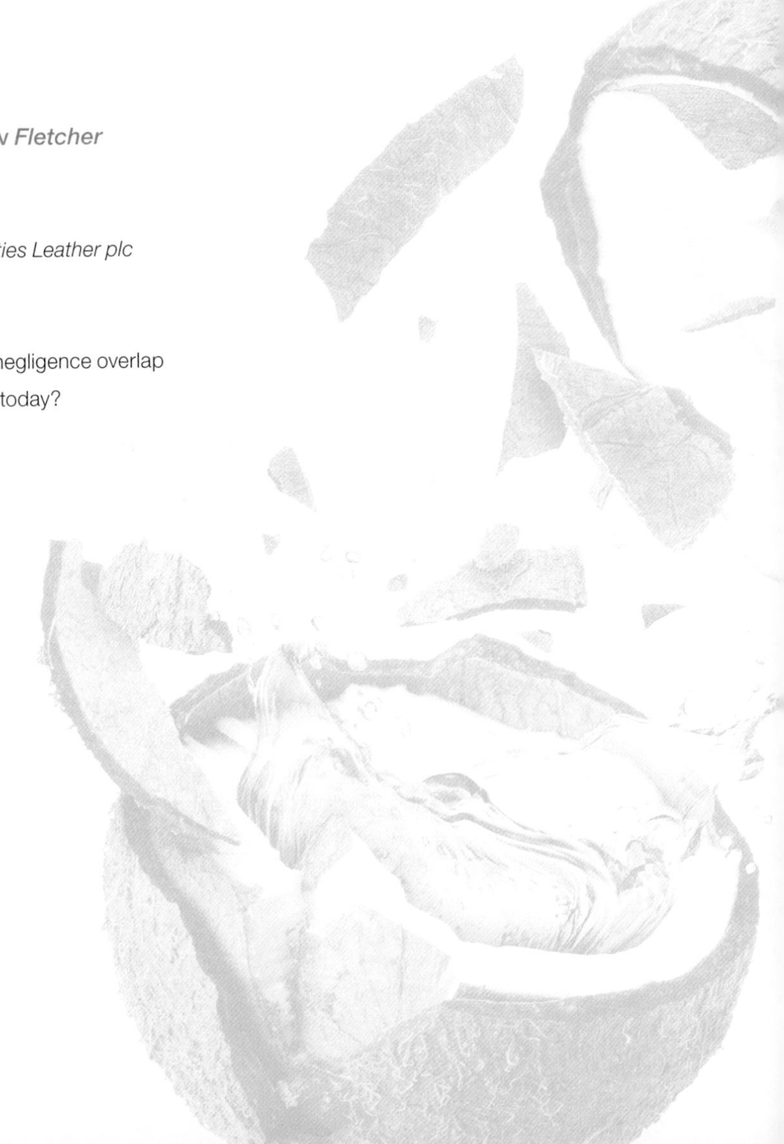

Introduction to Part IV

1. In this Part we consider the role of the 'land torts'—the torts of trespass to land, private nuisance and the rule in *Rylands* v *Fletcher*—in the regulation of the use of land.

2. In **Chapter 18**, we focus on trespass to land and nuisance. Trespass is concerned with intentional and direct interferences with property. Like the trespass to the person torts (**Chapter 15**), it is actionable per se (without proof of harm).

3. Private nuisance is concerned with *indirect* and unreasonable interferences with property interests and, as such, often involves less tangible harms. Unlike in trespass, harm must be shown. While private nuisance can be concerned with actual physical damage, it is more often used to protect claimants' 'amenity' interests. That is, claims are usually based on the loss of *enjoyment* of land. Private nuisance seeks to regulate the relationship between neighbours, defines mutual rights and obligations with respect to property use and protects claimants' ability to use and enjoy their land without unreasonable interference from others. The governing concept is one of 'reasonable use of land' and, in deciding whether a defendant is a reasonable user, many factors are taken into account. Unlike negligence, the *conduct* of the defendant is not (usually) relevant. A defendant can take all manner of precautions yet still be an unreasonable land user.

4. Some elements of private nuisance have been affected by human rights law. In particular, there have been human rights challenges to the requirement that only those with a proprietary interest in the property alleged to be affected by a nuisance can sue in relation to violations of Article 8 of the European Convention on Human Rights with respect to the right to home, private and family life.

5. Public nuisance is a crime, which may, in certain circumstances, also lead to a civil claim. Its role has largely been overtaken by statute and here we simply provide a short overview. Individuals may claim in public nuisance only if they suffer additional harm arising from a nuisance that otherwise materially affects the reasonable comfort and convenience of life of a sufficiently large number of citizens.

6. The 'tort' of *Rylands* v *Fletcher* is considered in **Chapter 19**. This contrasts with nuisance in that it involves the consequences of one-off 'escapes' of things accumulated on land (as opposed to ongoing states of affairs) and imposes 'strict liability' for these. Essentially, this action has been shaped over time by three key cases: *Rylands* v *Fletcher* [1868], *Cambridge Water Co Ltd* v *Eastern Counties Leather plc* [1994] and *Transco* v *Stockport Metropolitan Borough Council* [2003]. The latter two decisions have placed significant limitations on the application of the rule.

7. The development of the *Rylands* rule has led to an increased overlap with ideas from private nuisance and, importantly, negligence. A particular category of cases—where a state of affairs is 'continued' or 'adopted' and where there is later an escape—could seemingly now be defined in any of the three torts. Other jurisdictions have completely subsumed the rule within negligence. Without doubt, this action is now very limited in scope and application—perhaps having more historical interest than practical application in the twenty-first century.

Trespass to land and nuisance

18

Problem question

Read this problem question carefully, and keep it in mind while you are working through the chapter that follows. At the end of the chapter, you will be able to apply what you have learnt to the problem question and advise the relevant parties.

Lekan owns a large country estate in Buckhampton. He wants to develop it as an environmentally friendly residential adventure centre catering for stressed-out city executives. To this end, he has constructed a network of ropes, ladders and bridges in the canopy of his woodland for them to come and 'Swing High' from tree to tree. Unfortunately, misplaced marketing has led to the majority of his customers being large, noisy groups of young people on stag and hen weekends. Lekan also provides facilities for paintballing and a quad-bike cross-country course. In line with his stated environmental policy, he has recently begun to use large volumes of seaweed, collected from nearby beaches, as fertiliser for his large organic vegetable patch. He has been encouraged to do so by his local council's recycling officer, who is keen to stop waste material going to landfill sites.

Lekan receives the following complaints:

(a) Sarah, who lives downwind of Lekan's estate, complains that the smell of the rotting seaweed makes her physically sick.

(b) Sandy, a 14-year-old, lives on a neighbouring farm. He complains that the noise from the quad bikes is causing his guinea pigs to miscarry their young.

(c) Jess who, when she walks her dogs, parks her car next to Lekan's boundary fence, complains that her car has, on a few occasions, been hit by stray paintballs.

(d) Ailsa complains that the 'Swing High' centre 'lowers the tone of the neighbourhood' and that her back garden can be seen from the platforms in the trees.

18.1 Introduction

Consider the following examples:

- ***Christine does not like her neighbour's overhanging tree, as it causes too much shade to fall on her garden. As the neighbour refuses to prune it, Christine retaliates by having frequent late-night garden parties through the summer months.***
- ***Barry runs a relaxation and meditation centre and complains that the noise from the dance studio on the floor above him stops his customers relaxing properly.***
- ***Juliet lives near an industrial estate which has grown in size since she moved there. She complains that the noise of lorries delivering goods overnight keeps her awake.***
- ***Dev, who grows organic roses, complains that his flowers are wilting due to toxic smoke being emitted from a nearby factory.***
- ***Laura complains that rats, which have infested the compost heap in her neighbour's garden, keep coming onto her property.***
- ***Antony's neighbour sweeps up leaves in his garden and piles them up near the adjoining fence. The pile of leaves topples over and touches the fence. Some leaves are carried over the fence by a strong gust of wind.***
- ***Ameera has a dinner party. Upon going upstairs to get a cardigan, she finds one of the guests in her bedroom, looking in her wardrobe.***

These scenarios indicate situations where tort law might protect the interests of the land users involved. This chapter considers the part the torts of trespass and nuisance play in the regulation of land use and touches on the possible contribution that these torts could make to the protection of the environment. Specifically, we will look in this chapter at trespass to land, private nuisance and—briefly—at public nuisance.[1] The subsequent chapter outlines what is known as the 'tort' or the rule in ***Rylands* v *Fletcher* [1868]**. All these torts predate the tort of negligence, which was not 'created' until the twentieth century. They are used to protect the claimant's ability to use and enjoy their land freely without unwanted and unwarranted interference by the defendant. This idea is distinct from negligence, which seeks only to protect the individual from harm (including to land) that is inflicted carelessly. Negligence is a *conduct*-based tort, but the land torts are primarily *consequence*-based (though in some circumstances the courts take the conduct of the defendant into consideration). Fault plays a very limited role; land torts are not organised in the 'duty–breach–damage' formulation that we are familiar with from

1. Note, however, that various statutory nuisances also exist, which give wider public law protection of interests in land. Councils are obliged to investigate complaints about issues that might be a 'statutory nuisance' (nuisances covered by the Environmental Protection Act 1990) and, should they agree that this is happening, has happened or will happen in the future, must serve an abatement notice (which can lead to penalties if not adhered to). Examples include noise from premises, machinery or vehicles; insect infestations or smells arising from trade/industrial premises; accumulations of rubbish, etc.

negligence and, as we shall see, nor has their exact relationship and/or overlap with the tort of negligence ever been properly established.

18.2 Trespass to land

Trespass to land, like trespass to the person (**Chapter 15**), is concerned with *direct* harm. Its primary importance is in the protection of property rights. When we refer to harm in this context, actual *damage* to the land concerned is not necessary: as with trespass to the person, trespass to land is actionable per se (i.e. without proof of damage). The harm lies in the fact that land owned by one party has been unjustifiably interfered with by another.[2] What constitutes unjust interference is a matter of debate. The most obvious is where someone enters someone else's land or property (or remains there) without permission, but there are other, less clear, interferences, as we shall see.

When we refer to land in this context, we mean not only what is commonly understood as land, but also things under it, built on it and even the airspace above it. To claim in trespass, the claimant must either own or otherwise be in possession of the land (e.g. by being a tenant)—it is the fact of possession of the land in question that is the legal interest protected. The interference must be direct—it must also be *physical*, in the sense that something must have happened. A commonly used example is that of neighbouring home owners and overhanging plants. If I pruned a tree growing in my garden and threw the branches into yours, I would commit trespass, as this is a direct action with a physical consequence (the branches land in your garden). However, if you were unhappy simply because I did *not* prune the branches, so much so that they grew out over your garden, this would be only an indirect and non-physical consequence, so would not usually be trespass (although it may be trespass into airspace or otherwise actionable in private nuisance—see **section 18.3**).

What is physical interference? This can be broken down into four categories, as in **Table 18.1**. As you will see from the examples in the table, more things can be a trespass

TABLE 18.1 Types of physical interference with land

Nature of the interference	Examples
Crossing a boundary on to land	Walking across a field or garden without permission Entering someone's house or other premises without permission Putting an arm through a window or door without permission Machines, cranes or signs overhanging someone else's property
Remaining on land	Not leaving property when asked to do so by the owner or occupier

2. Despite common misperception, trespass is not usually criminal in nature, though there are some statutory criminal trespasses, such as under the Criminal Justice and Public Order Act 1994.

TABLE 18.1 *Continued*

Nature of the interference	Examples
Going beyond what is permitted while on someone's land	Dinner guests take a peek into the bedrooms without permission A shopper goes past a 'no entry' sign at the back of a supermarket
Putting or placing objects on someone's land	Deliberately throwing items from one property onto another Cattle straying from one person's land to another's Allowing a dog to run across a private field Leaning a bicycle against the wall or window of someone's property

than you might have originally thought—and possibly you have done many of these things without thinking.

18.2.1 **Intention**

A key element of trespass is intention—the act that constitutes the trespass must be intentional. However, it is not the trespass that must be intended, merely the direct action (e.g. entry into a property) that resulted in it. Put another way, it does not matter that you did not deliberately trespass on someone else's property—if you voluntarily took yourself there, you will have trespassed.[3] In *League Against Cruel Sports* v *Scott* [1985] hunting dogs strayed onto the claimant's land (areas of Exmoor where there were wild deer sanctuaries)—this amounted to a trespass.[4] Here, the court avoided the fact that there was no actual intention to allow the dogs onto the land by saying that persistently and frequently holding hunts alongside the land, when there was no means of preventing the dogs from straying, could be seen as an implied intention to trespass. Therefore, because it is the act that must be intentional, rather than the actual trespass, some trespasses can be committed accidentally, or make what would otherwise seem to be innocent use of land a trespass.

This is evident in 'airspace' trespass cases. When does something entering the space *above* one's land amount to a trespass to land owned or occupied by the claimant? In *Laiqat* v *Majid* [2005], an extractor fan on the defendant's land was found to be a trespass—it protruded over the claimant's land by 75 centimetres at a height of 4.5 metres. Similarly, in *Kelsen* v *Imperial Tobacco Co* [1957], the defendant's advertisement sign that

3. If your actions were *involuntary*—e.g. you were pushed onto the land by someone else—you would not have trespassed. What is considered to be a 'voluntary action' is not always straightforward. Compare *Smith* v *Stone* [1647] with *Gilbert* v *Stone* [1647]: in *Smith*, a man who was carried onto the claimant's land was held to have acted involuntarily, thus was not liable in trespass. In *Gilbert*, a man entered another's premises under duress (he was being threatened)—this was still trespass as the act of entering the land had been deliberate and intentional, even if not 'voluntary'.

4. In fact it seems that this trespass was deliberately crafted by the claimants, see **section 1.3.4**.

jutted out eight inches into the area above the claimant's shop was a trespass. In a less permanent sense, if the arm of a crane swings through airspace above one's property then this too can be a trespass (see *Anchor Brewhouse Developments Ltd* v *Berkley House (Docklands Developments) Ltd* [1987]).[5]

Pause for reflection

How far up can a trespass occur in the airspace above someone's property? In *Lord Bernstein of Leigh* v *Skyviews & General Ltd* [1978], the claimant sued in respect of a light aircraft flying above his property to take aerial photographs. His claim was rejected, as the activity being carried out by the defendant took place above the level of an ordinary user of land. The Civil Aviation Act 1982 specifically states that a trespass is not committed if an aircraft flies above property at a 'reasonable height' having regard to the prevailing conditions (s 76(1)).

While this decision helps us to determine where a trespass might stop (how high up), it raises further questions: is flying aircraft not an 'ordinary' activity in the twenty-first century?[6] If not, why is the use of an industrial crane (*Anchor Brewhouse*) to be regarded as 'ordinary'? Do you think the cases are helpful? Or should there be another way of deciding whether something in the airspace above land is a trespass, such as whether it blocks out light? Think about *Laiqat* and *Kelsen* again—do these *really* seem like trespasses to you?

Trespass in the other direction—below the claimant's property—has been considered by the Supreme Court.

***Star Energy Weald Basin Ltd and another (Respondents)* v *Bocardo SA (Appellant)* [2010] SC**

Bocardo owned land in Surrey, under which part of an oilfield lies. Star Energy had a licence granted by the Crown allowing it to bore for and obtain petroleum from the oil field from neighbouring land vested in the Crown. Without acquiring a licence from Bocardo to do so, Star Energy drilled three wells from the Crown land, which travelled diagonally downwards and entered Bocardo's land below ground level (at depths between about 800ft and 1,300ft) and ran for between about 250m and 700m. No material physical harm was done to the estate by the drilling and installation of the wells and there was no interference with Bocardo's use or enjoyment of its land. Bocardo also had no right to the petroleum. Nevertheless, when Bocardo became aware of the wells, it commenced an action in trespass.

→

5. So might the overhanging branches that annoy Christine, in the earlier scenario, also be a trespass?
6. Consider the potential impact of recreational drones on this area of law and particularly how this area of law may interact with the development of the law on invasion of privacy.

→

The High Court held that the wells constituted an actionable trespass and this decision was affirmed by the Court of Appeal. The Supreme Court considered how far below ground ownership rights extend. Lord Hope said:

> There must obviously be some stopping point, as one reaches the point at which physical features such as pressure and temperature render the concept of the strata belonging to anybody so absurd as to be not worth arguing about. But the wells that are at issue in this case, extending from about 800 feet to 2,800 feet below the surface, are far from being so deep as to reach the point of absurdity. Indeed the fact that the strata can be worked upon at those depths points to the opposite conclusion. (at [27])

Thus, Star Energy had trespassed on Bocardo's land. On a secondary issue relating to the appropriate measure of damages, the Supreme Court affirmed the Court of Appeal's decision that damages were only available for the amenity loss caused by the technical trespass. This sum was measured at £1,000.[7]

18.2.2 **Defences**

Lack of permission is a necessary ingredient of trespass. Correspondingly, permission (express or implied)—or a 'licence'—to enter or remain on land constitutes a valid defence, subject to the person with that permission (the licensee) not exceeding the boundaries of the permission (e.g. the dinner guest looking in Ameera's wardrobe in the earlier scenario).[8] Licences can be revoked, although the manner in which this can be done often depends on what type of licence was initially granted—for example, whether it was one given under a contract.

Legal justification is a defence to a claim in trespass (e.g. where the police are authorised by law to enter premises to carry out an arrest under the Police and Criminal Evidence Act 1984). However, exceeding the boundaries of such authority carries severe consequences and, if this happens, the trespass alleged is deemed to have begun at the moment the defendant entered the property (even though at that time, legal justification to be there existed). This is known as trespass *ab initio*, and is discussed further shortly.

7. The High Court had awarded Bocardo 9 per cent of the proceeds from the field since 2000 (£621,180 plus interest), and the same percentage of future income. Newspaper reports suggested the case was to be taken to the ECtHR (see e.g. Paul Cheston 'Mohamed Al Fayed's dream of becoming an oil baron is capped by court' *London Evening Standard* 28 July 2010). Compare the government's plan to prevent householders from suing in trespass in relation to shale gas and oil drilling under their land taking place without their permission (Damian Carrington 'Queen's speech: fracking to get boost from trespass law changes' *The Guardian* 4 June 2014).

8. This has notable similarities with the duty owed under the Occupiers' Liability Act 1957 to only those visitors that have been expressly invited or have been (or are treated as having been) given permission to enter or use the premises (s 1(2)) for a particular purpose: 'When you invite a person into your house to use the staircase, you do not invite him to slide down the banisters' (Scrutton LJ, *The Carlgarth* [1927] at 110). See **section 11.2.1.2**.

Another defence is necessity.[9] What is meant by this is that the action claimed as trespass might be deemed a necessary one for the defendant to have taken in order to protect either a public interest (e.g. to prevent floodwaters spreading by going on to someone's land to lay sand bags)[10] or a private interest (e.g. to prevent the defendant themselves from personal injury or property damage). In *Esso Petroleum* v *Southport Corporation* [1956], the necessity defence was successfully used by a ship's captain who discharged oil into the sea, polluting the shoreline. While there was some debate about whether this action amounted to a trespass or to nuisance, it was found to have been a necessary action in order to prevent the ship breaking up at sea and endangering the lives of the crew.

Counterpoint

What is necessary in a given situation often depends on the viewpoint of the person asked—the court may or may not agree with the defendant's viewpoint, as necessity in many situations is subjective. In particular, it seems that for the defence to be successful, a sufficient degree of 'peril' is required. In *Southwark London Borough Council* v *Williams* [1971], for example, squatters occupying a number of the council's empty properties claimed necessity in defence. Lord Denning MR thought differently, saying that 'if homelessness were once admitted as a defence to trespass, no-one's house would be safe' (at 744). He relied on the 'floodgates' policy argument, saying that if the defence were used once it 'would open a door that no man could shut'. He also invoked a fear of lawlessness, stating that the:

> courts must, for the sake of law and order, take a firm stand. They must refuse to admit the plea of necessity to the hungry and the homeless; and trust that their distress will be relieved by the charitable and the good. (at 744)

Thus, he was arguing that there may be better means to address the problem of homelessness, rather than for the courts to be seen to condone squatting.[11]

In *Monsanto plc* v *Tilly* [2000], protesters entered land belonging to Monsanto, a company (in)famous for developing and growing genetically modified (GM) crops. The protesters, including →

9. As it is in a trespass to the person claim, see **section 15.5.2**.

10. In *Dewey* v *White* [1827] the necessity defence was allowed where firemen deliberately destroyed the claimant's chimney to prevent the spread of fire to neighbouring properties.

11. Nothing much has changed. The Legal Aid, Sentencing and Punishment of Offenders Act (LASPO) 2012 (s 144) made it an offence to squat in a residential building. In relation to the defence of necessity, consider Daniel Gauntlett, who died in February 2013 having slept rough on a freezing cold night on the doorstep of a bungalow he had previously squatted. His inquest was asked to consider whether he 'had died obeying the law' and whether the government, in failing to put into place measures to protect the vulnerable when passing LASPO, s 144, had violated his Art 2 right to life. In December 2014, the coroner recorded a verdict of death by natural causes exacerbated by self-neglect. See also Layla Moran MP 'Homeless people are vulnerable, not criminal. The law is 200 years out of date' *The Guardian* 29 January 2019.

→

the defendant, believed that GM crops have harmful environmental and societal effects and, as part of their campaign, argued it was *necessary* to enter land owned by Monsanto to uproot the crops, in order to protect both public and environmental health. This was rejected by the Court of Appeal—though the court recognised that there might be some occasions when the destruction of one crop might be necessary in order to save others. In this instance, the court viewed the crop destruction as a symbolic gesture, designed to attract media attention: the necessity argument failed. Furthermore, the fact that there is public law protection offered to 'the public interest' in relation to GM crops clearly influenced the court—as in the squatters' case, it was perceived that there were better ways to achieve the intended goals than trespassing.

18.2.3 **Trespass *ab initio***

If a party is permitted to be on land by statute or common law (as opposed to by licence only), but commits a wrongful act while there ('oversteps the boundaries'), then their original entry onto the land becomes a trespass. Essentially, their permission to be there is cancelled retrospectively. This is a historical concept, first defined in *The Six Carpenters* [1610]. Six carpenters went to an inn, where they ordered and paid for bread and wine. Later, they ordered more wine but refused to pay for it. The court held that a wrongful act committed after lawful entry onto someone's premises could make the original entry a trespass (however, the carpenters were not liable as they had not committed a wrongful act, only an omission). There is little difference between the principle and that which operates when a person is on someone else's premises under licence (e.g. a guest at a dinner party) but proceeds to do something that they should not do (e.g. look in the bedroom wardrobes). However, a distinction is made in terms of remedy. While peeking in the wardrobes may turn someone into a trespasser, there is little harm that can be compensated, so damages are likely to be nominal. By contrast, had the six carpenters been found liable, the innkeeper could have recovered damages for the wine not paid for, as well as for the fact that a trespass had occurred.

In *Elias* v *Pasmore* [1934], police officers (legally) entered a man's premises to arrest him. While there, they seized some of his belongings—some items were seized lawfully but others were not. The court found that a trespass was committed only in respect of the unlawfully seized items; it did not render the original entry illegal. Thus, it seems that trespass *ab initio* will occur only where the later wrongful act contravenes the entire basis for the original entry. As the original basis of entry was to make an arrest, the court found that this purpose had not been disturbed by the wrongful act.

Counterpoint

On the basis of *Pasmore*, it may seem that the doctrine of trespass *ab initio* has little muscle. To us, a doctrine that can protect people against abuses of authority while on their land seems useful, particularly given the limited scope that exists for suing organisations such as the police in negligence.[12]

→

12. See **section 6.5.3**.

→

In *Chic Fashions (West Wales) Ltd* v *Jones* [1967], the doctrine's existence was criticised. The police searched the claimant's premises for stolen goods, seizing goods that they wrongly believed were stolen. While the wrongful seizure itself was held to be lawful (as the police warrant gave them the authority to remove any goods that they considered to have been stolen), Lord Denning MR (*obiter*) suggested that the trespass *ab initio* doctrine was antiquated and failed to recognise the simple fact that a lawful act should *not* be rendered unlawful by subsequent events (at 313, 317 and 320). However, he later went on to make use of the doctrine in *Cinnamond* v *British Airports Authority* [1980], finding taxi drivers who were unlawfully touting for business to have trespassed from the moment they entered the airport premises. Perhaps this tells us that the decisions in *Pasmore* and *Chic Fashions* say more about the judicial attitude to claims against the police (in a similar vein to within the tort of negligence) than about the trespass *ab initio* doctrine itself.

18.2.4 **Remedies**

Claimants in trespass usually seek damages and/or an injunction. Damages compensate the claimant for harm already suffered due to the direct interference with their property. An injunction may be used to prevent a continuing trespass.[13] However, other remedies are available in appropriate situations, such as re-entry (when the rightful owner/occupier of land has been excluded from it). This 'self-help' remedy may be used only if 'reasonable force' is all that is required to assert the right to re-enter. Conversely, where an owner or occupier of land has lost possession, an action for the recovery of land might be taken, allowing (if successful) the defendant to be ejected by court order. Further, an action for mesne[14] profits may be brought to claim money from anyone who has wrongfully occupied the land and made a profit or saved expenditure in the process of doing so (e.g. a tenant who outstays the terms of their tenancy agreement and does not pay rent for the extended time spent in the property). It also covers the costs associated with putting right any deterioration to the fabric of the property as well as any (reasonable) costs associated with repossession.

18.3 **Private nuisance**

Whereas trespass is concerned with *direct* interferences to land, private nuisance deals with *indirect* and *unreasonable* interferences to land, including what might be called consequential interferences resulting from a direct action (*Southport Corporation* v *Esso Petroleum Co Ltd* [1954]). Private nuisance is located squarely within the relationship between neighbours; that is, the people living nearby rather than the 'neighbour' we

13. Though interesting issues arise in the context of protestors, in the sense that preventing protests may amount to a violation of the right to freedom of expression given by Art 10, or of private life under Art 8 ECHR. See *Mayor of London* v *Hall* [2010]; *Manchester Ship Canal Developments* v *Persons Unknown* [2014].

14. Pronounced 'mean'.

meet in negligence (***Donoghue* v *Stevenson*** [1932]). In short, private nuisance regulates relationships (and, in particular, conflicts) between neighbours, defining their mutual rights and obligations with respect to land use by striking a fair and reasonable balance between them. It seeks to protect the claimant's ability to use and enjoy their land without unreasonable interference by the defendant. In this way, *Conaghan & Mansell* suggest, nuisance is often viewed as a 'minor' tort with minimal implications or impact beyond the cosy world of neighbourly squabbles or 'ordinary people' against industry (p 124). This means that references to its potential role in environmental protection are to a large extent downplayed; they become a 'pale green' aside its traditional concerns.[15]

Counterpoint

Behind the usual accounts of private nuisance, which manage to give the tort the appearance of coherence, is a more nuanced picture of a tort developed piecemeal over time to protect particular interests of particular sections of society. It should not be thought that the ordering of nuisance into particular categories in a textbook serves to make it coherent. Nuisance has been described as a tort of 'mongrel origins',[16] uncertain and lacking definition or any coherent goals or purpose.[17]

Conaghan & Mansell argue that traditional accounts of nuisance conceal a more sinister subtext extending well beyond neighbours engaging in garden-fence disputes. There are many examples of this when the cases themselves—not just the principles the judgments leave behind—are deconstructed. Behind, for example, the 'seemingly innocuous conflict between a cricket club and a house owner who objected, reasonably, to the showering of cricket balls in her back garden' (*Miller* v *Jackson* [1977]), appears the 'elusive and potentially dictatorial character of the Public Interest' (*Conaghan & Mansell* p 124). Similarly, 'hovering on the sidelines of a dispute between the occupant of a "good class residential street" and his next-door neighbours, who were engaged in an activity . . . which allegedly threatened the values of property and the character of the street' (they ran a brothel (*Thompson-Schwab* v *Costaki* [1956])), is 'the dark and rather ominous shadow of Civilised Society' (p 124).

So viewed, nuisance tells of more than just un-neighbourly behaviour. In its tales of polluted shrubs and rivers and disrupted TV signals, its narratives of anti-social boat-racing, cricket and piano playing, it reveals its social, historical and ideological contexts. Its case law is at times also indicative of the struggle between the 'haves and have-nots', the cosy privileged classes of London's Belgravia and those living in the one-time slums of Bermondsey.[18] Our point is this: there is more going on in nuisance than neighbourly squabbles that can be resolved

→

15. *Conaghan & Mansell* Ch 6.

16. FH Newark 'The Boundaries of Nuisance' (1949) 65 LQR 480.

17. Conor Gearty 'The Place of Private Nuisance in a Modern Law of Torts' [1989] CLJ 214, 215. Maria Lee also argues that the '"boundaries" of private nuisance remain somewhat "blurred"' (2003, p 298).

18. See ***Sturges* v *Bridgman*, section 18.3.3.2**. Also see, in a wholly different context, but making the same point, Dayna Nadine Scott '"Gender-Benders": Sex and Law in the Constitution of Polluted Bodies' (2009) 17 Feminist Legal Studies 241.

→

with a simple application of legal principles. Traditional expositions of nuisance—its textbook appearance—are not only an excellent example of the ability of judges and legal academics to rationalise and synthesise the irrational and fluid,[19] but also can be seen to clothe, subdue, constrain and ultimately obscure its political underpinnings, history and environmental potential. It could be argued that nuisance has failed to achieve its potential to develop into a real environmental tort—perhaps because of the balancing acts undertaken and the 'privileging' of the already privileged.

18.3.1 What is private nuisance?

Private nuisance is 'any unlawful interference with a person's use or enjoyment of land or some right over it'.[20] It is primarily concerned with conflicts arising over neighbours' respective uses of land and seeks to protect the claimant's use and enjoyment of land from an activity or state of affairs which the defendant has caused. Unlike trespass, it is concerned with *indirect* interferences (e.g. smells, noise or vibrations) and is actionable only on proof of some *damage* (including the subjective damage of 'amenity' interests as well as physical damage: see **Table 18.2**). In seeking to protect ownership rights, nuisance encourages people to be 'good neighbours' (though, as we shall see, this really extends only to those neighbours with a proprietary interest in land—mere 'users' of land are not necessarily protected). At the heart of nuisance is a balancing act—using one's land freely, while not harming the land-based interests of others.

TABLE 18.2 Basic differences between nuisance and trespass

	The legal harm	When actionable	Example
Trespass	Direct interference with land.	Actionable per se (i.e. without proof of damage).	I dump some waste on your land. As well as, most likely, this amounting to various waste offences, I have committed a trespass. I have directly interfered with your land and even if you tell me to move it and I do; that is, even if there is no continuing harm, I will still have committed the trespass. The most obvious example of a trespass is walking (without permission) across someone's land; this is also a direct interference. →

19. *Conaghan & Mansell* p 125.
20. Percy H Winfield 'Nuisance as a Tort' [1931] CLJ 189, 190. Note, however, that he prefaced this with the comment that 'nuisance' is not a term capable of exact definition.

TABLE 18.2 *Continued*

	The legal harm	When actionable	Example
Nuisance	Indirect interference with use and enjoyment of land.	Actionable upon proof of damage (to the interest in the land).	Instead of dumping the waste on your land, I simply leave it on my land to putrefy. It begins to smell, and flies gather—possibly there are rats that may go onto your land. This would give rise to an action in nuisance, as an indirect harm arising on one person's land and spreading to another's (though compare *Gregory* v *Piper* [1829], a trespass case).[21]

Things that may be included in an action for private nuisance are:

- actual (physical) damage to land (e.g. by flooding, noxious fumes or vibrations);
- interference with 'amenity' interests—the use and enjoyment of land (e.g. by the creation of smells, dust or noise);
- encroachment (e.g. by tree roots or overhanging branches).

Private nuisance came into its own during the Industrial Revolution when courts faced new and pressing problems arising out of extremely polluting industrial land use, which were not compatible with how neighbours wanted to use their parcels of land. One case that highlights well the problems of industrialisation is ***St Helen's Smelting Co* v *Tipping*** [1865].

St Helen's Smelting Co v *Tipping* [1865] HL

Poisonous vapours from the defendant's smelting works damaged trees and shrubs on Mr Tipping's 1,300-acre Lancashire estate one and a half miles away. He brought a claim in nuisance. The defendant contended that, as almost the whole neighbourhood was devoted to smelting or similar manufacturing activities, he could continue his activities with impunity.

The House of Lords disagreed. Lord Westbury distinguished between nuisances producing what he called 'material injury to property' or 'sensible injury to the value of the property' and that which merely leads to 'personal discomfort' (lost amenity). He held that the former category may never arise from a reasonable use of land—that is, it will always amount to a nuisance.[22] The injury to the claimant's trees and shrubs gave rise to an action in nuisance irrespective of whether the pollution from the defendant's works was normal for the locality.

21. Laura, in the scenarios outlined previously, would seem only to have an action in private nuisance. Antony may have a trespass claim in respect of his neighbour's leaves touching his fence—though only a claim in nuisance (subject to the principles outlined later) in respect of the leaves that blow over.

22. So it seems that Dev, in the scenarios outlined at the beginning of the chapter, will have a successful claim in nuisance, despite the argument that his use of land was 'sensitive'—see **section 18.3.3.3**.

Lord Westbury's reasoning, about the difference between damage to property and personal discomfort, later developed into the so-called 'locality' rule—which simply means that the locality in which the nuisance takes place will be taken into account where there is interference with amenity interests (i.e. use and enjoyment of the land), but not where actual physical damage occurs.

Counterpoint

The consequence of this distinction is that physical damage is viewed as a graver form of injury than 'mere' discomfort or inconvenience. Or, put simply, that 'actual' damage to land (including drop in value) is worse than damage to people's subjective interests in it. 'Mere' personal discomfort is treated with more latitude, unless the intrusion is such that it 'materially interferes with the ordinary comfort physically of human existence, not simply elegant or dainty modes or habits of living' (Knight-Bruce V-C, *Walter* v *Selfe* [1851] at 852). A recent example illustrating this point can be seen in *Fearn and others* v *The Board of Trustees of the Tate Gallery* [2019].[23] On this basis, loss of a view from one's property is loss of 'elegant' living (amenity) and not interference with the ordinary comfort of human existence. There is no remedy in nuisance against a neighbour whose new greenhouse blocks your beautiful view because 'the law does not give an action for such things of delight' (Wray CJ, *Bland* v *Moseley* [1587]). Whilst it might be easy to say that noxious fumes that destroy every plant in my garden should be actionable in nuisance, it is far more difficult to weigh up the complaints of a resident in an industrial area who says that lorries travelling to a factory nearby cause noise and dust that affect her amenity interests, for example by making her unable to sleep and worsening her asthma.

This distinction is, however, perhaps easier to articulate in theory than in practice—there are definite grey areas between lost amenity and damage to property. Moreover, what is the locality? It is the court that determines whether an area is, for example, industrial, rural or commercial. We must therefore be careful not to approach the locality rule too narrowly. This is not to suggest, however, that there are, in essence, two torts: one concerning physical damage and the other discomfort or inconvenience. In fact, the idea that two divergent torts had been created by ***St Helen's Smelting*** was ruled out by the House of Lords in ***Hunter* v *Canary Wharf Ltd*** [1997]. Instead, the distinction between amenity interests and physical damage is best seen as a question of degree. Interferences resulting in physical damage are more likely to be regarded as unreasonable than less tangible amenity losses (disturbance, feeling sick, worsened asthma, inability to sleep and so on), which usually require the courts to engage in a more intricate balancing exercise, taking into account a number of factors, before deciding whether an alleged interference is a nuisance.

The difference between physical damage and lost amenity retains a somewhat uneasy presence in modern nuisance law. A recent example can be seen in *Network Rail Infrastructure Ltd* v *Williams and another* [2018], a case about Japanese knotweed, in which the Court of Appeal had to determine whether the presence of the knotweed in the soil (which lessened the sale value of the property) damaged the claimants' amenity interests and, if so, how. They were,

→

23. Though the decision of the High Court in that case, where the nuisance claim failed on locality, was later rendered obsolete by the Court of Appeal that the claim was not one in nuisance at all (*Fearn and others* v *The Board of Trustees of the Tate Gallery* [2020]).

→

the defendants argued, merely 'worried' that their property would be damaged in the future. It could, however, have been argued that the presence of the knotweed rhizomes in the soil (which the claimants would need to spend time and money getting rid of) was in fact physical damage to their property, notwithstanding the fact that the plant had not (yet) caused any physical damage to their homes. However, the Court of Appeal found that what had happened was a 'classic example' of the interference with amenity interests in land (at [55]). Sir Terence Etherton MR said that the presence of the rhizomes:

> imposes an immediate burden on the owner of the land in terms of an increased difficulty in the ability to develop, and in the cost of developing, the land, should the owner wish to do so . . . [A]ny improvement or alteration of the property requiring the removal of contaminated soil would require disposal of the soil either on site or, more likely, off site by special, and probably expensive, procedures.

As we can see, it is not always easy to distinguish between 'sensible injury to property' and 'personal discomfort': surely if your land becomes uncomfortable to live on, then its value (to you) is similarly diminished? Both interference with amenity and damage to property can cause 'sensible injury to the value of property'. The House of Lords in ***Hunter*** affirmed that both material physical damage and loss of amenity amounted to interference with property interests. This would suggest that, in deciding whether conduct amounts to a nuisance, the same factors should be considered for each. If both are property interests, why should lengthy exposure to horrible smells be treated differently from material damage to property?

18.3.2 **Who can sue?**

A claimant must first establish that they have legal 'standing'—that is, the right to sue. Nuisance is not the only place in tort law where standing is an issue and where what seem like potentially legitimate claims can fail even before they begin.[24] In private nuisance, *Malone* v *Laskey* [1907] set the initial boundaries. A woman was injured while using the toilet when its cistern fell on top of her. It had been dislodged by vibrations emanating from the electricity generator on the neighbouring defendant's property. Despite her injuries, the Court of Appeal held that she had no cause of action in nuisance against the defendant, because she had no proprietary interest in the premises—the house belonged to her husband's employer. She was 'merely present in the house'.

As the aim of private nuisance is to protect the claimant's use and enjoyment of land, it is perhaps obvious that the claimant must have an interest in the land that has been unreasonably interfered with. However, what link or interest must the claimant have? Is this an interest in land as defined by property law or simply a substantial link with the land?

24. In a claim under the Consumer Protection Act 1987 in relation to a defective product that has caused consequential property damage, a claimant must first establish that the *value* of that property damage exceeds £275 (see **section 12.3.1**). Further, strictly speaking, in negligence a claimant can sue only if they have suffered a recognisable *harm* (***Rothwell* v *Chemical and Insulating Co Ltd*** [2007], *Dryden and others* v *Johnson Matthey plc* [2018]; cf *Rees* v *Darlington Memorial Hospital NHS Trust* [2002]).

This traditional view of nuisance—the 'interest in land' requirement—was challenged in *Khorasandjian*. Miss Khorasandjian was subjected to a campaign of harassment by a former boyfriend.[25] She sought an injunction to prevent him 'harassing, pestering or communicating' with her, especially by means of persistent and unwanted telephone calls to her mother's home, where she lived. Like Mrs Malone, she had no proprietary interest: she merely lived in the house with her mother. Nevertheless, Dillon LJ in the Court of Appeal allowed her claim in nuisance stating that 'the court has at times to reconsider an earlier decision in light of changed social conditions . . . If the wife of the owner is entitled to sue in respect of harassing telephone calls, then I do not see why that should not also apply to a child living at home with her parents' (at 735). This innovative approach was subsequently followed by a differently constituted Court of Appeal in *Hunter* v *Canary Wharf Ltd* [1996]. Here, Pill LJ found that it was enough for the claimant to demonstrate a 'substantial link' to the property in question (the occupation of a property as a home was sufficient to enable the occupiers to sue). However, the House of Lords disagreed.

Hunter v *Canary Wharf Ltd* [1997] HL

A number of local residents, including home owners, their families and other licensees, complained about the erection of the Canary Wharf tower in the London Docklands development. The tower—which stands nearly 250 metres high, is over 50 metres square and has a metallic surface—interfered with the television reception of nearby homes. Two initial questions arose: first, could an actionable nuisance exist in respect of interference with television reception? Secondly, if this was possible, who of those affected could sue?

The House of Lords held that interference with the television reception was *not* capable of amounting to a nuisance. There was no 'emanation' from the Canary Wharf tower which, according to Lord Hope at least, was viewed as a requirement of nuisance.[26] The tower was simply stopping something going onto the property of its neighbours. It was held, by analogy to cases that refused liability for blocking a view, that the defendants were free to build what they wanted to on their land, subject to planning permissions and other restrictions such as easements. Hence, complaints could be made only at the planning stage and not by means of private nuisance.

When addressing the second question, the law lords reasserted the traditional view from *Malone*. Defining nuisance as a 'tort directed against the plaintiff's enjoyment of his rights over land' (at 688),[27] Lord Goff held that claims in nuisance can be brought only by claimants with an interest in land—that is, landowners, tenants, grantees of an easement or *profit à prendre*, or those with exclusive possession.

25. Of course, should the same facts arise today the claimant should be able to rely on the Protection from Harassment Act 1997; see further **section 15.6.2**.

26. See also, on the question of what emanates (and from where), *Hussain and another* v *Lancaster City Council* [1999].

27. In reference to Newark (**n 16**).

Hunter meant that someone cannot claim in nuisance if they are merely a member of the landowner's family (as in *Khorasandjian*), a guest (long or short term), a lodger or an employee (including live-in employees, such as au pairs). Recognising such people's claims, the law lords suggested, would be to effect a fundamental change in the nature and scope of nuisance and give rise to a number of practical difficulties. They believed that to extend nuisance in this way would transform it into a tort *to the person*, rendering redundant what they viewed as sensible restrictions on the right to sue for personal injury in negligence, for example by allowing liability for mere discomfort without damage (lost amenity). Put simply, the House of Lords was keen to reinforce nuisance as a tort to land, not to people. The idea that the planning system is a 'more appropriate form of control' was recently restated by the Court of Appeal in *Fearn and others* v *The Board of Trustees of the Tate Gallery* [2020].[28]

Pause for reflection

see online resources

To what extent is the standing requirement an unnecessary restriction reflecting a return to the historical roots of private nuisance at the expense of its potential role in protecting the environment and/or protecting people from harassment? Do you think the requirement is (a) necessary and (b) logical? Consider *Khorasandjian* v *Bush* [1993]. Do you agree that what she suffered should not be considered a nuisance?

Counterpoint

It is unclear the extent to which ***Hunter*** is compatible with Article 8(1) of the European Convention on Human Rights (ECHR) (as incorporated into domestic law by the Human Rights Act (HRA) 1998), which establishes that 'everyone has the right to respect for his private and family life, his home and his correspondence'. The 'interest in land' requirement might need to be reconsidered in order to secure fuller protection of the right to respect for private and family life, and possibly also the right not to be discriminated against (Art 14). As we see in **section 18.4.3**, Article 8(1) has already been interpreted broadly by the European Court of Human Rights (ECtHR), permitting parties without rights in the home to sue.

In *Khatun* v *UK* [1998]—an appeal to the European Commission of Human Rights on part of the ***Hunter*** decision—it was found that the distinction made in ***Hunter*** between those with a proprietary interest in land and those without was not applicable for the purposes of Article 8(1) (although it was felt that the defendant's activities (building the tower) could be justified under Art 8(2) as pursuing a legitimate and important aim

28. Sir Terence Etherton MR at [82].

given the public interest in developing the once run-down Docklands area of London and the limited interference to the applicant's home). The decision in *Khatun* suggests that, should a suitable case arise, a court would be able to challenge the ***Hunter*** limitations. Indeed, to an extent this may already have happened.

McKenna v British Aluminium Ltd [2002] Ch D

Claims in private nuisance and in *Rylands* v *Fletcher* (Chapter 19) were brought by over 30 children from a number of households alleging that emissions and noise from the defendant's neighbouring factory were an invasion of privacy and had caused them mental distress and physical harm. The defendants argued that following *Hunter* the claims should be struck out unless each of the claimants could point to a proprietary right—that is, show they had standing to take their claim.

In the High Court, Neuberger J rejected the defendant's argument and refused to strike out the claims, saying that:

> there is obviously a powerful case for saying that effect has not been properly given to Article 8(1) if a person with no interest in the home, but *who has lived in the house for some time* and had his enjoyment of the home interfered with, is at the mercy of the person who owns the home, as the only person who can bring proceedings. (at [53])

Pause for reflection

The way the law currently stands—as identified by counsel for the claimants in *McKenna*—excludes one very large group in particular from ever being able to claim in private nuisance: children. Children are never likely to have the required proprietary interest in a property to be able to sue. Do you think this should be the case?

18.3.3 The concept of the 'reasonable user'

As we have indicated, nuisance is a consequence-based tort: liability does not depend on whether the defendant acted reasonably or whether they did all they could to prevent the nuisance occurring. Put another way, taking reasonable care does not prevent liability.[29] Instead, the court must consider a range of factors in order to determine nuisance.

The factors that the court can take into account can be split into three categories:

(1) always considered (intensity—including duration, frequency and timing of the interference);

29. Including adhering to terms of an environmental permit: *Barr and others* v *Biffa Waste Services Ltd* [2012].

(2) sometimes considered, dependent on the *type* of claim (the nature of the locality); and

(3) sometimes considered, if *relevant* on the facts (sensitivity of the claimant; bad intention of the defendant).

As we will see, many of these factors are also important in relation to the question of remedies. We will look at each category in turn. Essentially, each of the (relevant) factors must be weighed against the others. It is helpful to imagine a set of simple balancing scales, mentally placing each factor onto the scales on the relevant side, working out in whose favour the scales will tip. If the scales ultimately tip towards the claimant then their claim will be successful—if towards the defendant then the claim fails.[30] ***Coventry*** now assists us in many of these considerations.

Coventry v *Lawrence* [2014] SC

Katherine Lawrence and Raymond Shields moved into 'Fenland' in January 2006, a bungalow situated less than one kilometre from a speedway stadium in an otherwise rural area. The stadium was constructed with the necessary planning permission (lasting ten years) in 1975. Permission was renewed on a permanent basis in 1985. Stock car and banger racing started at the stadium in 1984 and a 'Certificate of Lawfulness of Existing Use or Development' was issued in respect of this in 1994. Behind the stadium a motocross track initially operated under temporary planning permission which later became permanent.

In 2008, the couple initiated proceedings against the owners and operators of the stadium and track, seeking an injunction to stop the activities taking place there, which they claimed amounted to a noise nuisance. At first instance, the claimants succeeded and an injunction limiting the activities (and thus the noise) of the defendants was granted (though the injunction was stayed while the claimants had to rebuild their house, which had in the meantime been severely damaged by fire). The Court of Appeal reversed the decision, finding that the claimants had failed to establish a nuisance. Largely, this was because of the planning permissions that the stadium and track operated under, which, according to Jackson LJ, had changed the character of the locality.

The Supreme Court reinstated the trial judge's decision. The noise from the stadium and track, notwithstanding the planning permission, amounted to a nuisance. The fact of planning permission may have relevance to the remedy to be awarded, and the precise terms of it may sometimes have a bearing on whether or not a nuisance exists at all (see e.g. Lord Neuberger at [96]). The injunction (though still stayed) was restored, though the court seemed to suggest that judges are too ready to grant injunctions without considering whether to award damages instead and that if/when the case goes back before the judge a consideration of whether to discharge the injunction and substitute damages could be undertaken.[31]

30. A good—if long—example of this in practice can be seen in *Stephen Anslow and others* v *Norton Aluminium Ltd* [2012].

31. Note *Peires* v *Bickerton's Aerodromes Ltd* [2016], which indicates courts will still more readily favour an injunction where that is the most appropriate remedy in the circumstances. As Peter Smith J acknowledged, there must be some give and take—he found that 'the Claimant's approach has been one of reasonable restraint; the Defendant's approach regrettably has not been the same' (at [120]).

18.3.3.1 Factors that are always considered

The intensity of the interference

Unlike trespass to land where any interference to property can amount to a trespass, in private nuisance a threshold exists—everyone has to put up with some interference from their neighbours at some time (*Southwark LBC* v *Mills* [2001]). However, interferences can become unreasonable when they occur frequently or for long periods of time, as the earlier pop music example indicates. The idea is best explained by Lawton LJ in ***Kennaway* v *Thompson*** **[1981]**:

> [N]early all of us living in these islands have to put up with a certain amount of annoyance from our neighbours. Those living in towns may be irritated by their neighbours' noisy radios or incompetent playing of musical instruments; and they in turn may be inconvenienced by the noise caused by our guests slamming car doors and chattering after a late party. Even in the country the lowing of a sick cow or the early morning crowing of a farmyard cock may interfere with sleep and comfort. *Intervention by injunction is only justified when the irritating noise causes inconvenience beyond what other occupiers in the neighbourhood can be expected to bear.* The question is whether the neighbour is using his property reasonably, having regard to the fact that he has a neighbour. The neighbour who is complaining must remember, too, that the other man can use his property in a reasonable way and there must be a measure of give and take, live and let live. (at 94, emphasis added)

If any interference could be a nuisance, the tort simply would not work. The interference must be substantial, in the sense that, for example, it continues for a long time or takes place at an unreasonable time of day (or night). That said, while ordinary everyday living cannot be an unreasonable use of land, an action for physical damage to property, even if caused by a temporary or short-lived activity, is likely to succeed—though in such cases the court will award damages rather than an injunction (this makes sense: as the nuisance has finished, there is nothing on which to base injunctive relief).[32] In *Crown River Cruises Ltd* v *Kimbolton Fireworks Ltd* [1996], a 15–20-minute firework display at the end of the fiftieth anniversary of the Battle of Britain celebrations was held to be a nuisance to a Thames boat owner whose boat suffered substantial fire damage.

18.3.3.2 A factor that is sometimes considered, dependent on the type of claim

The nature of the locality

The reasonableness of land use can depend on, alongside other considerations, the character or nature of the area it is in—its 'locality'. Courts are more likely to find that noise from a local factory is a nuisance to local residents if the factory is in a residential area rather than an industrial one. Similarly, farmyard smells and noises are less likely to be a nuisance in an overwhelmingly rural area.[33] However, as we have already indicated, following ***St Helen's Smelting***, the 'locality principle' applies only in cases where the claimant has suffered lost amenity. It is not a relevant consideration where the claim

32. As in *Stephen Anslow and others* v *Norton Aluminium Ltd* [2012].

33. A good example of the idea is found in *Hirose Electrical UK Ltd* v *Peak Ingredients Ltd* [2011]. An electrical manufacturer complained about strong odours including garlic and curry coming from neighbouring premises. The High Court found that such odours had to be tolerated on a light industrial estate. The claimant appealed, arguing that the area had been mischaracterised as a light industrial estate rather than a business park—which might have led to a different conclusion—but was unsuccessful.

is about material physical damage (e.g. plants killed by poisonous fumes), which in law can never arise from a reasonable use of land.[34]

In ***Coventry***, Lord Neuberger described the claimants' property as follows:

> Across open fields, about 560 metres from the Stadium and about 860 metres from the Track, is a bungalow called 'Fenland' . . . It stands in about 0.35 hectares of garden, and is otherwise surrounded by agricultural land. The nearest residential property to Fenland appears to be about half a mile away, and the small village of West Row is about 1.5 miles to the south-east of Fenland (and about one mile to the south east of the Stadium). (at [12])

Given the idyllic and overwhelmingly rural nature of this description, it becomes easier to see how noise from a motocross and speedway stadium might constitute nuisance.

A classic quote summing up the 'nature of the locality' idea comes from ***Sturges* v *Bridgman*** [1879]. There, Thesiger LJ said that 'what would be a nuisance in Belgrave Square would not necessarily be so in Bermondsey' (at 865). Clearly he meant that the character of the neighbourhood in question must be considered when determining whether a nuisance has or has not happened—put another way, people in some (poorer?) areas should be expected to put up with more than (affluent?) people in others.

Counterpoint

This supports the idea that nuisance is highly subjective and contextual. By this, we mean that for an activity to be a nuisance, someone must have complained about it—and this depends on their own subjective interpretation of the context in which the activity is taking place.

The locality rule therefore accentuates and mirrors inequalities already existing within society. Those who live in what the court considers to be economically and socially poorer areas are expected to have to cope with more interference from others, more environmental pollution and so on.[35] *Conaghan & Mansell* point out that, historically, the compromise 'distinction drawn in ***St Helen's Smelting Co* v *Tipping*** [1865] between inflicting material damage to property and producing "sensible personal discomfort"', and the so-called locality rule, were of 'crucial significance in limiting the liability of industrialists for nuisance' (p 133). They point to an observation made by Cornish and Clark that in the 'period immediately after 1865, it was almost impossible to sue for amenity damage (smells, noise, vibrations) if one lived in an industrial area'[36] and conclude that 'inevitably the distinction had a disproportionate class impact by protecting the primary interests of residential landowners (in the physical integrity of their property) while denying any redress to those who simply wish to live in an environment free from the stench and clamour of industrial activity' (p 133). Ironically, it seems those who suffer most from the ravages of pollution are deemed the least worthy of protection.

→

34. Though even where there is substantial material damage to land, claimants must initiate their claims within the six-year limitation period, as the Court of Appeal has recently reminded us in *Jalla* v *Shell International Trading and Shipping Company* [2021].

35. See the article referred to in **n 18**.

36. *Law and Society in England: 1750–1950* (Sweet & Maxwell, 1989), p 157.

→

It seems that things have not moved very far in this respect. In *Baxter* v *Camden LBC (No 2)* [2001], the tenant of a first-floor flat within an old converted house complained of continuing noise from the flats above and below her to the council that had converted the property (with inadequate soundproofing) in 1975. Dismissing her claim, Tuckey LJ in the Court of Appeal returned to a familiar concept, saying that 'occupiers of low cost, high density housing must be expected to tolerate higher levels of noise from their neighbours than others in more substantial and spacious premises' (at [10]).

The nature or character of a locality may change. For example, over a period of time the primary use of land may evolve from industrial to residential (or vice versa) or from green fields to commercial. Such evolution might be gradual or it may be faster and deliberately calculated to change the area, such as the development of the east end of London in preparation for the 2012 Olympic Games. Therefore, when considering a claim, the courts have to consider the locality as it is, not how it once was. When there is deliberate development or quick, radical change to the nature of an area, it is likely that planning permission will have been sought and received. So, is it the granting of permission or the actions taken on the back of the permission, once granted, that change the nature of a locality?

Gillingham Borough Council v _Medway (Chatham) Dock Co Ltd_ [1993] QBD

In 1982, a disused navy dockyard in Chatham, Kent, was closed by the government. The area was subsequently divided into three parts, one of which was taken over by the Medway Ports Authority to be used as a 24-hour commercial port. Many residents complained about the level of traffic passing their properties, particularly throughout the evening and night. At one point it was recorded that a lorry was passing every 1.5 minutes in the early hours of the morning. Residents complained of interrupted sleep and general disturbance to their manner of living—for example, few of them could ever open the windows at the front of their houses because of the heavy volume of passing traffic. As a substantial group of residents was affected, the local council took an action in (public) nuisance on their behalf, asking for an injunction to prevent the movement of the lorries, particularly at night. The same council had granted the planning permission to the defendants allowing them to develop the port, even though it had been aware of the likely disturbance this would cause to local residents. When the planning application was made, local residents had been given the opportunity (as is usually the case) to voice their opinions.

Buckley J held that the granting of planning permission had in this instance changed the nature of the locality, which was now wholly commercial in its character. Local residents therefore could not complain about the serious disruption caused to them by commercial operations.

Gillingham does not mean that every time planning permission is granted the nature of a locality will change. It is a question of fact to be decided in each case. In this respect, ***Gillingham*** should be contrasted with ***Wheeler* v *JJ Saunders Ltd*** [1996], and the comments of the Supreme Court in ***Coventry*** should be considered.

Wheeler v *JJ Saunders Ltd* [1996] CA

Between two neighbours a house, with outbuildings and an adjacent farm, were in common ownership. Wheeler bought the house and the outbuildings and obtained planning permission to convert the outbuildings into holiday cottages. The farm was let to the defendants, who also obtained planning permission (despite the claimants' opposition), to extend the capacity of their pig farm and build two new sheds, each capable of housing 400 pigs, with openings for ventilation, slatted floors and channels underneath to contain excrement. One shed was 11 metres from Wheeler's house. On occasion, strong smells emanated from the farm to the claimant's property, affecting them and also visitors to the holiday cottages. Wheeler claimed in nuisance in respect of the smells emanating from the pig farm. At first instance, an injunction was granted preventing the defendants using the sheds and the claimant was awarded £2,820 in general damages.

The Court of Appeal held that the smell emanating from the defendants' farm was an actionable nuisance. Planning permission was not the same as statutory authority and was not a defence to a claim in nuisance. Although planning permission *could* alter the nature of a locality (*Gillingham*), it had not done so in this instance—the nature of the locality remained the same.

In distinguishing the effect of planning permission in ***Gillingham***, the court found that this had been 'strategic' in nature—that is, it was a deliberate attempt to change the nature of the locality for the good of the community. In ***Wheeler*** the planning permission was merely 'expansive'—it allowed an already existing pig farm to become bigger. This difference meant the planning permission did not change the *nature* of the entire locality and so did not prevent a nuisance being caused to the claimants by the smell.[37] In *Watson* v *Croft Promosport Ltd* [2009], the Court of Appeal ruled that despite planning permission being given for a motor-racing circuit on the basis that it was reasonable for the locality, the activity still amounted to an actionable nuisance (the nature of the locality was viewed as predominantly rural) and an injunction was granted to prevent racing on more than 40 days per year. This view was confirmed in ***Coventry*** in similar circumstances. Despite the (multiple) planning permissions granted to the defendants, it was found to be 'wrong in principle that, through the grant of a planning permission, a planning authority should be able to deprive a property-owner of a right to object to what would otherwise be a nuisance' (at [90]). Lord Neuberger doubted the distinction

37. Juliet is unlikely to be able to claim in private nuisance if the locality was already industrial when she moved there, even if the industrial operations have increased over time. However, as locality is only one factor to be taken into account, the outcome of her claim may depend on the intensity of the disturbance.

previously drawn between strategic and other permissions, regarding this as 'a recipe for uncertainty' (at [91]).[38] Thus, it seems that though planning permission *may* still change the nature of a locality, this will be a matter of fact to be assessed on a case-by-case basis. In fact, Lord Neuberger continued:

> the mere fact that the activity which is said to give rise to the nuisance has the benefit of a planning permission is normally of no assistance to the defendant in a claim brought by a neighbour who contends that the activity cause a nuisance to her land in the form of noise or other loss of amenity. (at [94])

However, the tests relating to planning permission are now beginning to appear rather circular in nature. In *Fearn* [2019], in which occupants of the Neo Bankside block of apartments next to the Tate Modern claimed in nuisance because their flats were regularly looked into by people accessing the Tate's external viewing gallery, planning permission had allowed both developments to take place at the same time. The defendants submitted that 'the planning approval of the viewing gallery, in the context of the largely parallel application for Neo Bankside, was evidence capable of supporting the submission that there was no nuisance' (at [185]). This was rejected by Mann J as nothing indicated that the planning authorities had specifically considered the impact of the viewing platform. He considered the 'character of the locality' more important—defined by Mann J as 'a part of urban south London used for a mixture of residential, cultural, tourist and commercial purposes' (at [190]). Concluding on this point, he said that 'the significant factor is that it is an inner city urban environment, with a significant amount of tourist activity. An occupier in that environment can expect rather less privacy than perhaps a rural occupier might. Anyone who lives in an inner city can expect to live quite cheek by jowl with neighbours' (at [190]).[39]

18.3.3.3 Other factors that are sometimes considered, if relevant on the facts

The sensitivity of the claimant

To be a nuisance, a court must find that the defendant's use of land is potentially unreasonable to *anyone*. This implies that the claim of someone affected because of their own sensitivities (where an 'ordinary' person would not be so affected) will fail. For example, in *Heath* v *Mayor of Brighton* [1908], the vicar and trustees of a church sought to stop noise emanating from the defendant's power station as the vicar complained that it disturbed his deliberations over his sermons but, as no one else appeared to be disturbed by it, an injunction was refused.

The idea is better explained by *Robinson* v *Kilvert* [1889]. The claimant rented premises from the defendant, which he used as a paper warehouse. The defendant then started a manufacturing business in the cellar of his building for which he needed the air to be both hot and dry. Heating the cellar to achieve this caused the temperature of the

38. Though Lord Carnwath supported the idea in 'exceptional cases' (at [223]).

39. Note that the claimants also failed in the Court of Appeal, because it was found that 'overlooking' could not lead to an action in nuisance at all—thus even the nature of the locality had no relevance (*Fearn and others* v *The Board of Trustees of the Tate Gallery* [2020]). It is interesting to consider whether nuisance analysis should always be considered inappropriate as related to questions of privacy, as it is clearly arguable that privacy is an amenity interest and that interference with privacy *in one's home* amounts to an interference with enjoyment of property.

floor of the claimant's warehouse above to rise to 80° Fahrenheit. This, while it would not have damaged ordinary paper or caused anyone using the building any physical discomfort,[40] dried out the specialist brown paper that the claimant was storing (and, as the value of the paper was affected by its weight, it lost value). The claimant sought an injunction preventing the defendant from heating the cellar. The Court of Appeal rejected his claim, holding that 'a man who carries on an exceptionally delicate trade cannot complain because it is injured by his neighbour doing something lawful on his property, if it is something which would not injure anything but an exceptionally delicate trade' (Lopes LJ at 97).

However, despite the fact that a claimant's sensitivity may sometimes render a claim in nuisance ineffective, it is clear that after an actionable nuisance *is* established, a claimant will receive damages for all of their losses even if these are the result of interference with what may be considered a sensitive use of land. In *McKinnon Industries Ltd* v *Walker* [1951], for example, the claimant was able to recover the cost of damage to his orchids (as well as lost profits on them), even though the defendant contended that orchid growing was a sensitive activity.[41]

Counterpoint

It is often difficult to determine what is 'unduly sensitive', particularly as this relates to the claimant's use of land and not to the claimant themselves.[42] If the storage of a particular type of paper is unduly sensitive (*Robinson*), but the growing of orchids is not (*McKinnon*), would the idea of sensitivity extend, for example, to the transmission of a signal to television viewers?

In *Bridlington Relay* v *Yorkshire Electricity Board* [1965], a company providing a residential relay system of sound and television broadcasts claimed in nuisance alleging that its business would be affected by electromagnetic interference from two electricity pylons erected between 200 and 250 feet from its mast and wiring that passed, at its nearest point, 169 feet away. Buckley J refused to grant an injunction, pointing to the sensitive nature of the business, saying that interference with purely 'recreational' facilities (e.g. television reception) was not actionable in nuisance.

As with many cases in private nuisance, *Bridlington Relay* may be a product of its time. Perhaps recognising this, Buckley J referred to the electrical interference not being actionable 'at present', meaning that as times change, so might the question about 'recreational' facilities. Indeed, *Bridlington Relay* was ruled 'out of date' in the Canadian case *Nor-Video Services* v *Ontario Hydro* [1978]. Despite the House of Lords' reluctance in ***Hunter*** to answer how the case would be decided in 1997, it is hoped that the ability to receive an adequate television signal (a 'recreational' activity enjoyed by the vast majority of people) *would* in fact now be regarded as an ordinary and natural use of land.

40. As noted by Cotton LJ at 94.

41. Barry, in the examples at the start of the chapter, may therefore have difficulty in taking his claim, unless he can show that the noise from the dance studio would also affect someone with a less delicate trade.

42. Though see *Pusey* v *Somerset County Council* [2012].

In fact, the position on 'abnormal sensitivity' has since moved on. It must now be considered alongside (or as part of) the issue of foreseeability.

Network Rail Infrastructure Ltd v *Morris (t/a Soundstar Studio)* [2004] CA

Network Rail appealed against a finding that they were liable for nuisance caused by electromagnetic interference emitting from a signalling system, which affected the sound of electric guitars in Morris's recording studio. They submitted that Morris's use of the studio was abnormally sensitive to the magnetic waves and was not protected by the law of nuisance as he was involved in an extraordinary commercial activity, rather than the ordinary use of equipment in an ordinary way. Additionally, Network Rail argued that it could not have reasonably foreseen the problem, taking into account the distance between the signalling system and the studio, where the magnetic field was much weaker. Morris contended that they should have foreseen the nuisance as they had inherited a report from British Rail which detailed similar complaints from third parties who had musical rehearsal studios either in or near the affected area.

Allowing the appeal, the Court of Appeal found that the modern law of tort had discarded some established detailed rules and instead required a broad approach. To establish liability in nuisance, the test was not that of foreseeability alone, but of foreseeability as an aspect of reasonableness. The concept of abnormal sensitivity was thought outmoded and, whether Morris's use of his studio was a sensitive use of premises was irrelevant. The correct test was whether it was *foreseeable* that specific damage would be caused to a specific claimant. However, even though the use of electronic equipment was a feature of modern-day life in the ordinary use and enjoyment of property, it was not reasonable to expect Network Rail to foresee the interference caused based on a report compiled several years prior to them taking over the maintenance of the rail track and which contained observations that were not specific enough to have reasonably expected them to have taken preventative action.[43]

Unlike negligence, nuisance is not supposed to be based on the defendant's fault. The defendant can take as much care as possible, but if the way they use their land has the *effect* of causing nuisance to a neighbour they can be liable. Nuisance is (at least in theory) supposed to be consequence-based—perhaps in this sense the concept of foreseeability is misplaced. In *Fearn* [2019], Mann J appeared to agree, refusing to find that the concept of sensitivity had been overruled by ***Network Rail***.

43. In relation to the beginning of chapter scenarios, would it be reasonably foreseeable to the owners of a dance studio that noise emanating from it could cause others nuisance?

Counterpoint

Some elements of private nuisance do seem to have changed over time, making it appear closer to negligence in terms of the factors that may be considered. The question is always whether what the law considers to be an unreasonable use of land on the part of the defendant also amounts to them being 'at fault' for the way they use their land. In ***The Wagon Mound (No 2)*** [1967], which we considered in the chapter on breach in negligence (**section 8.5**), Lord Reid pointed out that while the level of fault may not be such as to amount to a breach of duty in negligence, some level of fault is almost always necessary in nuisance (at 639). But what did he mean by 'fault'? As we will see, since ***Cambridge Water Co Ltd* v *Eastern Counties Leather plc*** [1994] (discussed in **Chapter 19**), *foreseeability* in the ***Wagon Mound*** sense is now relevant in the land torts as well as in negligence. As ***Network Rail*** indicates, it has already become 'dominant' over some of the more traditional concerns in nuisance cases. An activity on land can be a nuisance only if it is reasonably foreseeable to the defendant that the activity might be a nuisance to someone else—so where does this leave fault?

Bad intention of the defendant

In assessing whether the defendant is a reasonable user of land, their motive may be taken into account. This is only an issue where actions by the defendant are undertaken in bad faith or with malice towards the claimant.

Christie v *Davey* [1893] Ch D

Christie was a music teacher who occasionally worked from home. Her children also played musical instruments. The claimant had lived in her home for three years with no problems with her neighbours until, on 30 September 1892, the defendant wrote to her saying:

> During this week we have been much disturbed by what I at first thought were the howlings of your dog, and, knowing from experience that this sort of thing could not be helped, I put up with the annoyance. But, the noise recurring at a comparatively early hour this morning, I find I have been quite mistaken, and that it is the frantic effort of someone trying to sing with piano accompaniment, and during the day we are treated by way of variety to dreadful scrapings on a violin, with accompaniments. If the accompaniments are intended to drown the vocal shrieks or teased catgut vibrations, I can assure you it is a failure, for they do not. I am at last compelled to complain, for I cannot carry on my profession with this constant thump, thump, scrape, scrape, and shriek, shriek, constantly in my ears. It may be a pleasure or source of profit to you, but to me and mine it is a confounded nuisance and pecuniary loss, and, if allowed to continue, it must most seriously affect our health and comfort. We cannot use the back part of our house without feeling great inconvenience through this constant playing, sometimes up to midnight and even beyond. Allow me to remind you of one fact, which must most

→

→

surely have escaped you—that these houses are only semi-detached, so that you yourself may see how annoying it must be to your unfortunate next-door neighbour. If it is not discontinued I shall be compelled to take very serious notice of it. It may be fine sport to you, but it is almost death to yours truly. (at 317–18)

Taking offence at the letter, the claimant did not reply. Instead of writing again, the defendant chose to create his own disturbances: banging on the wall, clattering metal trays together, whistling and shouting each time he heard music emanating from the claimant's house. In response, the claimant sued in private nuisance—unsurprisingly the claim was met by a counterclaim from the defendant.

The claimant won an injunction against the defendant, but his counterclaim was not allowed. Giving judgment, North J commented that the defendant had acted 'only for the purpose of annoyance', adding 'in my opinion, it was not a legitimate use of the defendant's house' (at 327).

It can be seen from this case that—with reference to the scales analogy—both claims may have been equally weighted until the defendant's malicious motive was added to the equation. This firmly tipped the scales in favour of the claimant.[44]

Pause for reflection

What do you think would have happened if, instead of writing the letter, the defendant had sued the claimant in nuisance, alleging that the music was 'to me and mine . . . a confounded nuisance and [causes] pecuniary loss, and, if allowed to continue, it must most seriously affect our health and comfort. We cannot use the back part of our house without feeling great inconvenience through this constant playing, sometimes up to midnight and even beyond'? Do you think the outcome of this case was correct? Would the decision have bettered the relationship between the neighbouring families?

see online resources

Having said that the defendant's bad intention tipped the balance in favour of the claimant in ***Christie***, it does not do so in all cases where malicious behaviour is exhibited. In *Bradford Corporation* v *Pickles* [1895], the defendant deliberately drained his land with the intention of decreasing the water supplied to his neighbour, in the hope that this would force the neighbour to buy his land. However, the House of Lords rejected the claim for an injunction, refusing to take the defendant's alleged malice into account.

44. So, Christine's bad intention in holding frequent late-night garden parties as retaliation for overhanging branches may amount to a nuisance and allow her neighbour to make a claim against *her*!

Counterpoint

Bradford is distinguishable from ***Christie*** in various ways. In *Bradford*, the claimant had no *right* to receive the water supply and therefore no right had been interfered with on which to base the alleged nuisance. As the case involved so-called 'natural rights' (water rights) and it was already well established that a land owner has the absolute right to do as he wishes with water filtering through his land even if his behaviour appears utterly unreasonable to others, the motive of the defendant was 'irrelevant'. That said, a laissez-faire attitude prevailed when *Bradford* was decided and a lenient approach was taken to people who wanted to better themselves—in fact this was seen as largely commendable. Pickles had done no more than try to get a good deal on the sale of his land—his behaviour was not malicious, but sensible. Perhaps what has caused this case to be included in textbook sections on malice or bad motive is the fact that the case speaks of Mr Pickles as being an unpleasant character—possibly, whether this was true or not, the claimants wanted to portray him as such to make his behaviour look all the more malicious and encourage the court to follow ***Christie***.

Malice was, however, present in *Hollywood Silver Fox Farm Ltd* v *Emmett* [1936]. Here, the defendant deliberately fired guns near his land's boundary with the claimant's fox farm, knowing this would distress the foxes and probably stop them breeding. An injunction was granted to stop him, even though the claimant's use of the land for the specific purpose of breeding foxes could be said to be abnormally sensitive. Had noise been made by the defendant *without* malice (e.g. if noise was a natural consequence of his use of land), the claim would likely have failed.

Pause for reflection

Does taking malice into account, where relevant, seem to make private nuisance at least in part based on *conduct*? If the defendant's conduct is to be taken into account, can it truly be said that nuisance is a consequence-based tort?

18.3.4 **Defences to nuisance**

A number of defences can be raised against actions in private nuisance. The general defences of contributory negligence and *volenti non fit injuria* (**Chapter 10**) may apply. Additionally, defences specific to nuisance claims (including public nuisance) exist. The most important of these are dealt with here,[45] before we consider some things that are *not* valid defences. Many of these issues were also considered in ***Coventry***.

45. There are others not considered here, such as 'inevitable accident', 'act of God' or an (unforeseeable) act of a stranger.

18.3.4.1 Statutory authority

If the defendant's activities are authorised by statute or, more specifically, a statute provides that the defendant *must* use their land in a particular way, which then inevitably causes a nuisance to a neighbouring land user, the defendant has a total defence to nuisance claims (*Manchester Corporation* v *Farnworth* [1930]). So, although nuisance may be established on the facts, the claimant will have no remedy. In a sense, this illustrates the idea of separation of powers—courts cannot challenge or undermine what Parliament has determined the situation should/will be. Convention suggests that Parliament will have considered what best suits the area and its occupants, including the various conflicting uses of land. Statute may also authorise whether, when and how much compensation is to be paid to those affected by the defendant's activities.

Statutory authority, then, is exactly that. The defendant has the authority, created by statute, to use their land in a particular way, with particular consequences. This must be distinguished from planning permission, which we discussed when looking at the nature of the locality in private nuisance claims (**section 18.3.3.2**). Similarly, environmental permits have been found neither to be equivalent to statutory authority nor to change the nature of a locality (*Barr and others* v *Biffa Waste Services Ltd* [2012]).

The effect of statutory authority is clearly illustrated in *Allen* v *Gulf Oil Refining Ltd* [1981]. The expansion of the Gulf Oil company in part of Wales was expressly authorised by the Gulf Oil Refinement Act 1965. The statute stipulated that an oil refinery should be built but was silent on the way it should operate once in use. In a test case, local residents claimed in nuisance, alleging that noise and vibrations emanating from the refinery caused them unreasonable levels of disturbance and asking that its operations cease. The House of Lords viewed the issue as hinging upon statutory interpretation and considered whether the nuisance was impliedly or expressly authorised by the statute. However, it also placed the burden of establishing this on the defendant, meaning that the test for the defence has a high threshold. A bare majority held that the refinery's operations were implicitly authorised by statute, meaning that the nuisance caused by its operation was inevitable, raising a full defence to the claim.

Pause for reflection

It is interesting to note that the claimants in *Allen* would potentially have been successful in *negligence*, had the nuisance created exceeded that which was impliedly authorised by the statute. That said, in order to be able to sue in negligence, each claimant would have needed to establish a tangible harm on which to found their claim. What was the 'harm' here and could a claim in negligence be based on this?

While statutory authority remains an available defence to a nuisance claim, it must now be considered alongside the HRA. Section 3(1) of the HRA requires legislation to be interpreted compatibly with people's fundamental rights under the ECHR. Clearly, in nuisance, the most apparent of these rights is that from Article 8(1) which guarantees respect for one's private, home and family life. The inclusion of the word 'home' seems to suggest that nuisance-type claims suffered by 'ordinary' people may have a human rights dimension. In the context of statutory authority, this means that courts must be careful in the way they interpret statutes giving a defence to a claim in nuisance, particularly when 'implying' an authorisation rather than it being expressly written. It should also be remembered that Article 8(2) allows derogation from the right where this satisfies a legitimate aim, is in accordance with the law and is *necessary* in a democratic society. While this does not necessarily provide an escape clause for the creators of nuisance under statute, the fact that Parliament has authorised an activity suggests that individual claimants trying to rely on human rights arguments might face an uphill struggle.

Hatton v *UK* [2003] ECtHR

The claimant lived near Heathrow Airport. In 1993, a new system for controlling night flights was introduced, relying on a 'noise quota' as opposed to a restriction on the number of flights that could come into or out of the airport. Hatton and other nearby residents claimed that the pattern of night flights from the airport was an unreasonable use of land in that there was too much noise, which caused lack of sleep and other symptoms, in violation of their right to respect for private, home and family life under Article 8(1). Although the claimants could seek judicial review of the night flights operation, they argued that they had not received (and could not receive) an effective remedy for this violation, in breach of Article 13.[46]

The lower chamber of the ECtHR agreed that there was a violation of Article 8(1) and that any derogation from this under Article 8(2) had to be proven, rather than assumed. Modest damages of around £4,000 were awarded.[47] However, on appeal by the UK Government, the Grand Chamber overturned the Article 8(1) finding, based on the exceptions permitted by Article 8(2). In particular, the Grand Chamber noted that night flights would reasonably contribute to the economic wellbeing of the country and that affected residents could easily move from the area if they wished.[48] However, the Article 13 finding was upheld, so the claimants received the compensation: although the decision could be judicially reviewed, this could not provide the claimants with an effective remedy as the merits of their case could not be considered.

18.3.4.2 Twenty years' prescription and coming to nuisance

An otherwise unreasonable user of land has a defence if they can show that they have been using their land in the way complained of for more than 20 years in which the claimant had been able to claim. The time starts from the point at which the claimant becomes aware of the nuisance-causing activity.

46. Under the Civil Aviation Act 1982, s 76, private law claims in the domestic courts had not been possible.

47. Though it should be noted that the cost of compensating everyone similarly affected was estimated at approximately £2 billion.

48. Similar justifications had been used in a previous case relating to noise from Heathrow (generally, rather than specifically night flights) in *Powell and Rayner* v *UK* [1990]. In ***Hatton***, a strong dissenting judgment thought this approach was too conservative, and argued that Convention rights should be interpreted in a way that would expand protection against environmental pollution.

Sturges v Bridgman [1879] CA

The defendant had operated as a confectioner for more than 20 years in premises adjoining the garden of premises where a doctor practised. The confectioner used grinding equipment in the rear of his premises. The doctor built a consulting room in his garden and then found that noise and vibrations emanating from the confectioner's work interfered with his work. He sued in nuisance for an injunction to prevent the grinding from continuing. The confectioner argued that this should not be granted on the grounds that (a) he had operated in the same way for such a long time and (b) the doctor, in building his consulting room where he did, had 'come to the nuisance'.

The injunction was granted even though the confectioner had operated in the same way from those premises for more than 20 years—and the doctor knew this and had made no prior complaints. The time ran only from the point that this began to be a nuisance, and this was after the consulting room had been built by the doctor. The court also viewed 'coming to the nuisance' as an ineffective defence, so this could not be relied upon by the confectioner.

This decision seems somewhat harsh. The doctor, knowing who his neighbour was, had built his consulting room right by the site of the activity that would—perhaps inevitably—become a nuisance to him. However, it has long been the case that 'coming to the nuisance' is not a defence, and the defence of 20 years' prescription did not apply as the claimant was able to argue that he only became *aware of the nuisance* once his surgery was extended.[49] Put another way, nuisance law protects people even if their actions (e.g. moving closer to a boundary fence) result in those of their neighbour becoming a nuisance. This is increasingly an issue as cities and towns expand, as residential areas are built ever closer to things such as tanneries, sewage works and factories that were once on the outskirts. Despite the fact that it might be argued that people should choose carefully where they move to, or research an area more thoroughly, it is no defence for these industries to say they were there first.

Miller v *Jackson* [1977] is a classic example. The defendant cricket club had played on its ground for more than 70 years when adjacent land was sold to developers who subsequently built a housing estate there. The claimants bought one of the houses and claimed in nuisance alleging that cricket balls were frequently hit into their garden. The fence around the cricket ground had already been raised when the houses were built; a recognition of the fact that the club should do its best to prevent stray balls. A majority of the Court of Appeal (Lord Denning MR dissenting) reluctantly found the club's activities actionable in nuisance. ***Sturges*** was affirmed as good law—the fact that the claimants had 'come to the nuisance' was not a defence. In so deciding, the majority prioritised the personal right of claimants freely to enjoy their land, even where this may have negative effects on established enterprises or community interests. However, had

49. Similarly, in ***Coventry***, the defendants had no prescriptive right to continue their activities—though they had been *operating* for 31 years by the time the claimants moved in, the *nuisance* only began at that point, as that was when the claimants became affected by it (at [142]–[143]). Lord Neuberger also confirmed that 'coming to the nuisance', as the claimants had, was no defence (at [51]).

an injunction been awarded, it would effectively enable people who had chosen to move into the houses overlooking the cricket ground to stop it from being played. In *Miller*, a different majority (Lord Denning MR and Cumming-Bruce LJ) refused the claimants an injunction, awarding damages instead, on the ground that community interests outweighed the personal interests of the claimants.

Counterpoint

Miller, particularly Lord Denning's judgment, warrants closer scrutiny, as it further illustrates the subjective nature of the tort of nuisance. While textbook accounts of nuisance deal with concepts and tests which seem to exist in and of themselves and assume some kind of rational form, Lord Denning's judgment shows that, actually, a particular legal outcome is preferred which subsumes nuisance almost entirely within personal judicial preferences. Indeed, arguably the only significant constraint on judges is the linguistic one that they must justify their decisions using the language of these concepts, tests and standards, rather than by reference to the subjective preferences that in fact underlie them. It is judges, for example, who decide what kind of inconvenience claimants should have to tolerate. They do this by reference to what is required of the ordinary reasonable person (taking into account what they feel their expectations ought to be as a resident of the area in which they live—e.g. Bermondsey or Belgrave Square). This, particularly when allied with the locality rule, has operated as an excellent vehicle for judicial prejudices while at the same time disguising the essentially class-based nature of the exercise being carried out. The whole balancing exercise undertaken in the test of 'reasonableness' is a means by which judges can offer their intuitive sense of the justice of the case as a legal solution. Our fascination with learning 'rules', principles and concepts arguably, therefore, distracts us from what is really going on.

Conaghan & Mansell argue that textbook emphasis on the minority status of Lord Denning's judgment in *Miller* downplays its subversive aspects (p 138). After all, if he failed to persuade the rest of the Court of Appeal, why should we look at his judgment? The important point is that Denning 'felt free to deny liability', to fail to find an actionable nuisance, taking into account the nature of the locality and the value of the defendant's activity. As *Conaghan & Mansell* point out, however, 'at the same time, to impose liability as the majority held, emphasising the degree of inconvenience experienced by the plaintiffs in the enjoyment of their property (including the threat of physical danger) was also neither inappropriate nor incorrect. *Either outcome* could be considered consistent with legal doctrine. The difference between the majority and minority on the question of liability is explicable largely in terms of the weight attributable to the social value of cricket' (p 138, emphasis added).

They continue:

> For Lord Denning cricket is a game, which in the summertime 'is the delight of everyone'. It is a game where 'the young men play and the old men watch', a game which, in this instance, has gone on for 70 years on a green which until recently was adjoined by 'a field where cattle grazed'. This field has now become a housing estate occupied by, among others, the plaintiff, 'a newcomer who is no lover of cricket'. Lord Denning views the closure of the cricket club as a potentially disastrous calamity. The cricket ground

→

→

> might be replaced by 'more houses or a factory. The young men will turn to other things instead of cricket. The whole village will be much the poorer. And all this because of a newcomer who has just bought a house there next to the cricket ground' (p 341). In this passage, Denning is appealing to a quaint and charming picture of English country life. He conjures up images of green fields, sleepy sunny afternoons, the quiet sounds of a cricket match on a summer's day. His head is populated with old men, young men and grazing cattle. His characters are white, male and English. Threatening this bucolic vision of English men at play is a newcomer, the sort of person who lives on a housing estate, who does not appreciate the finer points of cricket, who might even be female and who brings in her wake the threat of social degeneration as young men are forced to abandon cricket and go to work in factories. (pp 138–9)

Lord Denning's imagery is deliberate. Its purpose is to persuade the court that there was *no nuisance* (rather than merely refusing the injunction, as the majority held). However, his description of rural England borders on overstatement. As William Twining notes:

> Lord Denning missed an important trick as an advocate. By innuendo (or confabulation) he suggests a romantic picture of rural life in the South of England—a nostalgic evocation of village cricket in Hampshire between the Wars, almost straight out of *England Their England*. But Lintz was a depressed mining village in the North of England, where cricket is a serious matter. Would not a picture of an impoverished community dependent on an activity that seriously engaged young males be a much stronger argument for saying that this was a reasonable use of land?[50]

Though public benefit or the 'utility' of the defendant's activity was once a factor that had some bearing on whether that activity would be regarded as a nuisance, these days the utility value (e.g. the overall benefit to society) of the defendant's use of their land is generally not taken into consideration (or not explicitly) when asking whether it is unreasonable.[51] That said—except, perhaps, for Lord Denning—it was never a factor that carried heavy weight (see e.g. *Adams* v *Ursell* [1913]). However, utility is apparently still considered by courts when determining what *remedy* should be awarded to the claimant. Claimants seeking a cessation of nuisance-causing activities require an injunction. As we will see, courts have considerable discretion in deciding *whether* an injunction should be granted and, if so, to what *extent* the defendant's activities should be prevented. Where the defendant's activity has high social utility, an injunction is less likely to be awarded as the court may deem it appropriate that the activity should continue (see ***Dennis* v *Ministry of Defence* [2003]**).

50. William Twining *Rethinking Evidence* (CUP, 2006), pp 303–5.

51. Acknowledged by the Court of Appeal most recently in *Barr and others* v *Biffa Waste Services Ltd* [2012].

18.4 Remedies and the human rights dimension

Although it makes sense for us to consider remedies for private nuisance here, it is important to note that the remedies we detail can also be sought in relation to claims in public nuisance and under the rule in ***Rylands* v *Fletcher*** (**Chapter 19**).

There are two main remedies in nuisance: injunctions (which seek to prevent or stop a nuisance) and damages (compensation). In basic terms, the primary remedy for nuisance is an injunction. As we shall see, it is also possible for a claimant to recover under the HRA.

18.4.1 Injunctions

A claimant seeking an injunction is asking the court to prevent the part of the defendant's activity that amounts to a nuisance, rather than to prevent the activity from continuing in its entirety (though sometimes the two may be indistinct). As an injunction is an equitable remedy it is discretionary. A court can therefore decide to award an injunction in whole or in part (e.g. injunctive relief might be temporary or partial—that is, it may operate for a specific period of time or may restrict particular activities at certain times of the day). As seen in *Miller*, courts are generally willing to award an injunction unless there are specific reasons that indicate damages would be more suitable (*Shelfer* v *City of London Electric Lighting Co* [1894]; *Regan* v *Paul Properties Ltd* [2006], *Anslow* v *Norton Aluminium* [2012]).[52] It was confirmed in ***Coventry*** that the prima facie position is that an injunction should be granted, unless the defendant can convince the court why it should not be (at [121]).

In *Shelfer*, a pub landlord complained that vibrations and noise caused by the defendant were a nuisance and he was granted an injunction, even though doing so would inevitably deprive many people in the London area of electricity. Smith LJ laid down four conditions that a court must take into account when deciding whether to grant damages in lieu (in place of) of an injunction: whether the injury to the claimant is small, can be estimated in money terms and compensated by a small monetary payment, and whether the granting of an injunction would be oppressive for the defendant (at 322–3).

Whilst not saying that damages can never be awarded, the implication was that damages will (or should) be a 'rare' outcome. If a defendant has already been judged to be an unreasonable user of land, it hardly seems appropriate that the harm suffered by the claimant would be characterised as 'small' and 'adequately compensated' by money. It is the nature of the harm itself—particularly when claims are made in respect of amenity interest—that makes injunctions more appropriate. In *Shelfer*, the court was concerned to prevent defendants (who would often have more legal presence and strength than those who claimed against them) from 'buying the right' to commit nuisance by paying damages to those affected. Lord Neuberger reviewed the authorities in ***Coventry***, concluding that each of the *Shelfer* criteria was in some way flawed and:

> (i) an almost mechanical application of A L Smith LJ's four tests, and (ii) an approach which involves damages being awarded only in 'very exceptional circumstances', are each simply wrong in principle, and give rise to a serious risk of going wrong in practice. (at [119])

52. See also the Senior Courts Act 1981, s 50.

Instead he found that the decision whether or not to award damages in lieu of an injunction was a matter of discretion, which would depend on the facts of each case, and 'should not . . . be fettered' (at [120]).

As we have already discussed, the appropriateness of an injunction was examined by the Court of Appeal in *Miller* where the majority held that an injunction should not be granted, despite the cricket club's activities being a nuisance. The decision to award damages in lieu was in part justified on the basis that village cricket was an activity that held much 'public interest'. This issue was raised again in ***Kennaway***.

Kennaway v *Thompson* [1981] CA

The claimant complained that noise caused by power-boat racing in a lake close to her home was a nuisance. The defendants contended that she had chosen to build her house near the lake in the knowledge that some racing took place, thus she should not be entitled to an injunction.

In the Court of Appeal, Lawton LJ was critical of the judgment in *Miller*, finding that the relevant authority was *Shelfer*, in light of which the claimant should be awarded an injunction *despite* the fact she may have been aware of the power-boat racing or any public interest that might be involved in allowing the activity to continue. Exercising its discretion, the court awarded only a partial injunction, requiring the racing organisers to adhere to a planned timetable of events.

Essentially, the partial injunction awarded in ***Kennaway*** was used to create a compromise between neighbouring users of land. As we have highlighted, being reasonable neighbours requires some give and take—in such a situation the claimant might be expected to have to put up with *some* noise; the Court of Appeal was simply establishing how much was reasonable.[53]

More recent case law—as well as the enactment of the HRA—seems to indicate that a different approach to remedies may be required if the activity complained of is carried out by a public authority in the public interest. In such cases, even when an activity amounts to a nuisance, it may be felt that the public interest in the continuation of the activity outweighs the claimant's right to an injunction and that damages might be more appropriate.[54] This idea is explored further later.

18.4.2 Abatement and damages

Abatement is a 'self-help' remedy where the claimant takes it upon themselves to do something to stop the nuisance continuing. Clearly, this is a risky strategy—by taking action in this way, one might become a trespasser. As such, it has limited application to most nuisances, though might apply in situations where the problem complained of is

53. A similar exercise was undertaken in *Watson* v *Croft Promosport Ltd* [2009].
54. As in ***Hatton***. Though cf *Barr and others* v *Biffa Waste Services Ltd* [2012].

one of encroachment. That is where, for example, tree roots or branches from one property grow so that they encroach (intrude) into a neighbouring property. Often in such cases, instead of issuing nuisance proceedings, a potential claimant may avail themselves legitimately of the remedy, as long as they do no more than is necessary to abate the nuisance.[55]

Aside from where damages are awarded in lieu of an injunction, damages (perhaps *as well as* an injunction) may be considered appropriate in other nuisance claims. In *Raymond* v *Young* [2015], the claimants suffered multiple trespasses and persistent harassment and nuisance from their neighbours for nearly 40 years. The Court of Appeal found that it could be appropriate to award damages for the loss of value to a property, even where a full injunction had been granted. However, courts should not award damages for loss of amenity *in addition* to the damages for lost value, as that would constitute double recovery.

With the exception of trespass, the land torts become actionable only with proof of harm. Damages awards are subject to the foreseeability test set out in ***The Wagon Mound (No 1)*** **[1961]**, namely that the liability can arise only for damage of a *type* that can be reasonably foreseen. As these are *land* torts, however, the question of if and when damages for *personal injury* should be awarded is a difficult and contentious one. Put simply, if the harm must be categorised as a harm to the land (or an interest in it), then how can personal injury fall into that category?

In private nuisance (and under the rule in ***Rylands*** **v** ***Fletcher***), it is technically not possible to claim damages for personal injury: the torts protect the claimant's interest in land only. Therefore, damages for private nuisance are awarded only where the value of the land concerned (in sale or rent) has decreased, or for the effect a nuisance has on the claimant's use and enjoyment of the land (their 'amenity' interest).[56] Consequently, one effect of damages compensating injury to land and not the person is that the award will not increase even if many people are affected on the same piece of land (***Hunter***).

However, 'personal injury' (for which the appropriate claim would be in negligence), is not the same as 'personal discomfort'. The latter is more properly regarded as *part of* a diminished enjoyment of the land in question (lost amenity), for which damages *are* recoverable. In *Bone* v *Seale* [1975], for example, the claimant recovered damages for the personal discomfort they suffered as a result of the unpleasant smell emanating from a neighbouring pig farm. While the monetary value of the claimant's land could not be shown to have decreased, the damages reflected the claimant's lost enjoyment of the land while affected by the smell (this has to be the case, otherwise smell could never be a nuisance).

55. Confirmed in *Delaware Mansions Ltd* v *Westminster City Council* [2001]. In the scenarios outlined at the beginning of the chapter, Christine may have been able to trim back her neighbour's branches, as long as she did so reasonably. This may have removed her perceived need for retaliation.

56. This was confirmed by the House of Lords in ***Hunter***. Similarly, in ***Transco*** **v** ***Stockport Metropolitan Borough Council*** **[2003]**, the House of Lords confirmed the same in relation to claims under ***Rylands*** **v** ***Fletcher***.

Pause for reflection

Do you find this argument convincing? In claims of this type, is it the *land* that suffers (because there are smells that come over it) or the *claimant* (who complains about the smell)? If it is truly the land that suffers, it must follow that *all* neighbours would be equally affected. However, as people have different sensitivity to smells, not all would consider the same smell to be a nuisance—how can it be the land that is affected? Would the argument carry more or less weight if the people complaining were actually made physically sick by the smells? Would it be better simply to acknowledge that personal injury *is* recoverable in private nuisance?[57]

Because of the nature of the harm (to land), economic losses such as lost profits can be recovered only where they are a consequence of the claimant's inability to use their land to make those profits. Put another way, economic loss consequential upon damage to a proprietary interest may be recoverable, but 'pure' economic loss is not. For example, in *Andreae* v *Selfridge & Co Ltd* [1938] a hotel owner received damages for lost profits when her hotel suffered a drop in custom while the defendants carried out construction work nearby. It is far easier to claim for damage to property. Damages for this type of harm are readily recoverable and their quantification is straightforwardly assessed according to normal principles. In *Halsey* v *Esso Petroleum Co Ltd* [1961], damages were even awarded for damage to clothes hung on a washing line in the claimant's garden.

Pause for reflection

Does the fact that a claimant could recover damages for something as 'unimportant' as laundry seem surprising to you? Damage to any kind of property owned by the claimant is compensable—in practical terms this means that while a claimant would be unable to recover for their own broken leg, they would be able to recover damages for the broken leg of any animal on the land owned by them![58] Can this be a correct distinction?

That said, it seems that damage to property must be allowed, even though damages for personal injury remain unavailable. What would happen if a farmer complained that poisonous fumes which emanated from the defendant's factory subsequently ruined not only his crops but also caused some of his cattle to die? If he could recover only for damage to his land then the farmer would be awarded only damages for his crops (which would be treated as part of the land in question). Yet both of these are simply alternative means of farming one's land—so there would seem to be no reason why the law should protect one and not the other.[59]

57. As is the case in *public* nuisance, as we shall see later.
58. Newark (**n 16**), p 490.
59. As pointed out by Paula Giliker, *Tort* (Sweet & Maxwell, 2020), p 405.

18.4.3 **Under the Human Rights Act 1998**

There have been tensions within the ECtHR about human rights claims based on environmental issues that result in nuisance. The ECtHR has held that forms of environmental pollution nuisances may fall within the scope of the right to respect for the home and private life provided for in Article 8(1).[60] For example, in *Powell and Rayner* v *UK* [1990], a case about noise from Heathrow Airport, the ECtHR held that the rights of Mr Rayner, who owned land just over a mile away from a major runway, were clearly at stake because of the noise levels (although it ultimately found that running the airport was a modern economic necessity which justified the violation under Art 8(2)).[61] In comparison, in *López Ostra* v *Spain* [1995], the claimant's Article 8 rights *were* found to have been violated by exceptionally severe pollution coming from a factory 12 metres away from her home. This was the first time that what might be termed an 'environmental' case had succeeded.[62]

***Marcic* v *Thames Water Utilities plc* [2003] HL**

Mr Marcic sued in private nuisance and for a violation of his Article 8 rights following frequent sewage floods at his home. The sewage flooded his garden and lapped at his back step but never entered his house. Thames, the sewerage undertaker, prioritised renovation work to combat internal flooding. The cause of the flooding was the overloading of the sewer network which, although originally adequate, by then had too many properties connected to it (under statute, new properties are given a right to discharge into the existing sewerage network). Marcic asked for damages and an injunction compelling Thames to make improvements.

The Court of Appeal relied on *Powell and Rayner* and *S* v *France* [1990]—a case about interference with property from a nearby nuclear plant—finding that if a 'fair balance' was to be struck between claimants whose rights have been breached and the public interest, then even though states have a margin of appreciation, they must still compensate those whose rights are necessarily breached. In *S* v *France* the Commission said that: 'when a state is authorised to restrict rights or freedoms guaranteed by the Convention, the proportionality rule may well require it to ensure that these restrictions do not oblige the person concerned to bear an unreasonable burden' (at 263). Thus, the Court of Appeal awarded Mr Marcic compensation.[63]

The House of Lords rejected the nuisance action, holding that Thames had not acted unreasonably. The law lords stressed the particular position that Thames was in; that is, it was a company which funded improvements to, inter alia, the sewerage network under a formula

→

60. The other main applicable right is Art 1 of Protocol 1, the right to peaceful enjoyment of possessions.

61. As was the case in ***Hatton***, discussed earlier. See also *Khatun* v *UK* [1998].

62. Though it can be noted that part of the reason for her success was 'domestic irregularity' in the sense that Mrs López Ostra had clearly been let down by a culpable failure on the part of the Spanish regulatory authorities. Thus, it seems that in comparable cases, such 'domestic irregularity' will need to be shown in order for a claim to be successful.

63. Note that ***Dennis*** (discussed later) was decided after the Court of Appeal decision in ***Marcic*** but before the House of Lords' decision.

→

derived from legislation (Water Industry Act 1991) and operated by the economic regulator for the water industry (Ofwat). This was the downfall for the human rights claim: the law lords considered that Parliament had already provided statutory remedies (enforcement orders), which Ofwat could serve on sewerage companies where it felt that they should do more to protect the interests of their customers. So, the issue was whether this *statutory scheme* violated Mr Marcic's human rights. The law lords held that it struck the right balance between the different interests involved (e.g. the interests of those affected by flooding and all customers who ultimately pay for systematic improvements through their bills). Lord Nicholls found that 'the malfunctioning of the statutory scheme on this occasion does not cast doubt on its overall fairness' (at [53]). Essentially, Marcic lost because he had not asked Ofwat to make an enforcement order and instead took a private law action in the courts. That is, he had not established that there was the type of 'domestic irregularity' that seems to be required post-***Hatton***. Had Marcic's claim succeeded, it was estimated that the cost to Thames alone would have been in the region of £1 billion.

Pause for reflection

Lord Nicholls went on to say (echoing the Court of Appeal judgment) that 'the minority who suffer damage and disturbance as a consequence of the inadequacy of the sewerage system ought not to be required to bear an unreasonable burden' (at [45]), but did not expand on this. Lord Hope addressed this point, finding that by compensating those whose properties are flooded internally, offering a free clean-up service in the case of external flooding and bearing in mind Thames's obligation to allow domestic connections and the funding formula, a fair balance was struck.

Do you think the decision in ***Marcic*** protects sewerage companies at the expense of customers? Because a scheme for making enforcement orders under the Water Industry Act 1991 exists, water and sewerage companies—who often operate at considerable profit—will rarely have to compensate those who, like Mr Marcic, suffer because of their inaction. A second issue here is the extent to which public law controls are actually used by public regulators, for example the enforcement orders, so relied on by the House of Lords in ***Marcic***, had at the time *never been used* by Ofwat. Is a 'fair balance' between competing interests really being struck?

In *Dobson* v *Thames Water Utilities Ltd* [2008] a large number of claimants, some occupying properties as owners or lessees and some with no legal interests (including children), sued in respect of a sewage treatment works operated by Thames. They complained that odours and mosquitoes from the sewage works caused them a nuisance as a result of Thames's negligence. Unlike in ***Marcic***, Thames should therefore be liable for damages for nuisance, negligence and under the HRA (based upon alleged violations of Art 8 and Art 1 of Protocol 1 to the ECHR). Thames countered that complaints about odour or mosquitoes from the sewage works were about a failure of its duty to 'effectually deal' with the contents of sewers at the sewage works under section 94 of the Water Industry Act 1991 and/or a failure properly to treat waste water received and discharged by the sewage works in accordance with the Urban Waste Water Treatment (England and Wales) Regulations 1994. Further, as such failures were enforceable under section 18 of the 1991 Act by Ofwat, following ***Marcic***, no common law remedy or remedy under the HRA arose towards individual claimants. Ruling on preliminary issues in the High Court, Ramsey J agreed that the ***Marcic*** principle would preclude a nuisance claim, absent negligence. However, where the allegation related to a nuisance *caused by* negligence, a claim would lie.[64] He said:

> Whilst the principle in *Marcic* precludes the claimants from bringing claims which require the court to embark on a process which is inconsistent and conflicts with the statutory process under the [1991 Act], it does not preclude the claimants from bringing a claim in nuisance involving allegations of negligence where, as a matter of fact and degree, the exercise of adjudicating on that cause of action is not inconsistent and does not involve conflicts with the statutory process. (at [148])

Similarly, a claim under the HRA would be allowed to proceed. Appealing the High Court's decision, the 'negligent nuisance' finding was not disputed, but the appropriateness of the available remedies was.[65]

Two issues in particular were considered on appeal. First, had the child claimants in *Dobson* received 'just satisfaction'?[66] Ramsey J had concluded that they had, in the damages that were awarded to their parents for the nuisance to the *household* (at [209]). The Court of Appeal refused to say so as bluntly, instead preferring to be directed by comments from ***Hunter*** to the effect that the impact on all occupiers of the land in question may have been taken into account when assessing damages in nuisance. According to Waller LJ, the essential question was:

> whether it is *necessary* to award *damages* to another member of the household or whether the remedy of a declaration that Article 8 rights have been infringed suffices, alongside the award to the landowner, especially where no pecuniary loss has been suffered. (at [45], original emphasis)

This issue would have to be readdressed at a new trial and accordingly Ramsey J's decision was reversed on this point (at [46]). The second issue was similar: could those with proprietary interests, who *had* already received damages for nuisance, claim *additional* damages under the HRA (i.e. for their own personal damages rather than damage to the 'land')? Predictably, given their comments quoted earlier, the Court of Appeal found that this would be 'highly improbable, if not inconceivable' (at [50] and [52]). Unsurprisingly, therefore, in *Dobson and others* v *Thames Water Utilities Ltd (No 2)* [2011], Ramsey J found that no additional damages under the HRA were justified: damages already given for the nuisance constituted 'sufficient just satisfaction'.

The HRA does not provide for a new tort of 'breach of the Convention' which one individual can rely on against another. But, as we have seen, when deciding cases involving

64. It is notable that Ofwat intervened in *Dobson*, submitting that it was reasonable to assume that their lordships in ***Marcic*** intended to preserve scope for claims to be brought arising out of allegations of negligence in the physical operation of sewers or sewerage treatment works. In ***Marcic***, Thames was not accused of having failed to operate its sewerage system properly. Ofwat also submitted that such allegations are unlikely to raise the issues of regulatory balancing and infrastructure investment which were the focus of the decision in ***Marcic*** (at [103]–[112]).

65. *Dobson* v *Thames Water Utilities Ltd* [2009].

66. HRA, s 8(3).

human rights, courts must consider whether a claimant receives 'just satisfaction' for violations of those rights. If domestic law does not provide a sufficient remedy then additional remedies may become necessary. There is no reason, however, why these must be remedies in tort law.

Further, despite what we have said in relation to *Miller*, the role played by the social or public interest in an activity has become part of the consideration of the *appropriate remedies* for a proven nuisance.[67] This overlaps with the impact of the HRA, as can be seen in ***Dennis***.

Dennis v *Ministry of Defence* [2003] QBD

Dennis was the owner of a large estate near Stamford in Cambridgeshire, situated about two miles from RAF Wittering, a site owned by the Ministry of Defence (MOD) and used as an operational and training base for Harrier jump jets. Frequent noise (there were, on average, 70 occurrences each day) from the planes, which were often flown at low altitude, caused Dennis and his family disturbance. They argued that this caused diminution in the capital value of the property and that they had been unable to develop the commercial potential of the estate, consequently losing profit. Dennis sought an injunction and damages or damages in lieu amounting to £10 million.

The MOD accepted that flying the aircraft caused noise and disturbance to the claimant but not that it was an actionable nuisance. It countered the claim with a number of arguments, including that the use of RAF Wittering for training pilots was an 'ordinary use' of land in the modern era and that the training exercises were undertaken for the public benefit. Furthermore, the MOD contended that the claimants had 'come to the nuisance' and/or that it had gained a prescriptive right to use the land for training Harrier pilots; and that the claimants' land was not capable of generating the commercial profit they had estimated.

The court refused to award an injunction and instead awarded Dennis damages of £950,000. This sum was meant to represent any loss of capital value, and reflect past and future loss of use and amenity in the land. Buckley J held that (a) the noise from the Harrier jets was highly intrusive, frightening, persistent and unpredictable and accordingly constituted a very serious interference with the claimant's amenity interests; (b) the training of Harrier pilots could not be regarded as an 'ordinary use' of land even where the use was justifiable on other grounds. The level of noise and disturbance had increased considerably since the introduction of Harriers in 1969. The use was now so extreme that it could not be regarded as a feature of the area. In any event, even if such a use were to be considered 'ordinary', it had to be conducted in a manner which did not maximise the disturbance to the claimant. And (c) a public benefit might excuse an otherwise actionable nuisance provided no more damage was done than was reasonably necessary (following ***Marcic***). A defence based upon public benefit should not, however, be allowed to succeed where a human rights claim (in this case Art 8(1) ECHR) would succeed.

67. This was explicitly argued by the claimants in *Watson* v *Croft Promosport Ltd*, though the Court of Appeal found that only in 'a marginal case where the damage to the claimant is minimal . . . consistent with the principles of *Shelfer*, the effect on the public of the grant of an injunction is properly to be taken into account' (Richards LJ at [51]). Following ***Coventry***, it now seems clear that this is not precisely the approach that should be taken.

In essence, Buckley J reached his decision by balancing the orthodox elements of nuisance with a rights-based approach. The 'public benefit' of training Harrier pilots was not considered when determining whether the training was a nuisance, but became relevant in determining the appropriate remedy. When public benefit was factored in, Buckley J awarded the claimant damages in lieu of an injunction.[68] Therefore, the noise from the flights, which the court had *agreed* was a nuisance, was allowed to continue. The award of damages in effect allowed the RAF to 'buy' the right to continue the nuisance (exactly the position that the court in *Shelfer* said should be avoided). So, while 'public benefit' (as defined by the court) cannot prevent something being a nuisance, it can have a significant impact on the remedy awarded, even where human rights are affected.[69]

One further point to note regarding potential human rights claims in relation to nuisance is that Article 14 ECHR provides that other Convention rights must be enjoyed without discrimination. This might be thought to have the potential to affect the refusal of claims based on standing after ***Hunter*** (i.e. who has standing to sue and who does not). However, in *Khatun* v *UK* [1998], the European Commission on Human Rights found no violation of Article 14 because everyone in the locality was treated in the same way, meaning there was no discrimination. Put another way, the rich and poor of the London Docklands area were treated alike. That said, Article 14 may affect the locality rule, as judging the reasonableness of a polluting activity (alleged nuisance) differentially according to whether it interferes with a 'run down' or 'high class' location may well be discriminatory.[70]

18.5 **Public nuisance**

Public nuisance is a crime, which, in some circumstances, where the harm is suffered by a section of the community or the community as a whole, may also lead to a civil action, including where the harm is personal injury.[71] Although courts frequently draw comparisons between private and public nuisance they are in reality very different and

68. Compare the recent similar case of *Peires* v *Bickerton's Aerodromes Ltd* [2016] where there was no public interest element and—post-***Coventry***—a partial injunction was granted (with *obiter* judgment on what damages for diminution in value would amount to should the case be decided in that way in the event of an appeal).

69. In ***Dennis***, Buckley J held that because the award of loss of amenity was based on loss of enjoyment of the estate which envisaged enjoyment by a family as opposed to one individual, it was not appropriate to award further sums to Mrs Dennis based on a violation of *her* human rights. In *Dobson*, Ramsey J said that this was 'a finding which depended on the facts and was not a finding that, as a matter of law, an award of damages in nuisance would provide just satisfaction to all those in the same household' (at [206]). Note how this contrasts with his opinion on child claimants.

70. That said, the justification tests still have to be applied, as does the judicially constructed test of 'domestic irregularity', and the circumstances where amenity damage will be so excessive as to be a human rights violation will undoubtedly be rare.

71. In *Corby Group Litigation* v *Corby Borough Council* [2008] the Court of Appeal confirmed that *obiter* comments in ***Hunter*** and ***Transco*** had not impliedly reversed this principle and that the essence of the right protected by the tort of public nuisance is the right not to be adversely affected by an unlawful act or omission whose effect is to endanger the life or health of the public.

each seeks to protect very different interests;[72] we therefore do not discuss public nuisance in much detail here. Public nuisance is distinct from private nuisance in that its object is the recognition and protection of publicly held rights and not the protection of private property interests. In this sense, claimants do not necessarily claim in respect of some harm done to their interest in land, but in respect of community-based activities.

An individual may claim in public nuisance only where they have suffered particular harm arising from activity that has materially affected the reasonable comfort and convenience of life of a sufficiently large number of citizens.[73] This is because the essential characteristic of public nuisance is the infringement of a *public* right, an interference with the interest of a community rather than an individual:

> [A]ny nuisance is 'public' which materially affects the reasonable comfort and convenience of life of a class of Her Majesty's subjects. The sphere of the nuisance may be described generally as 'the neighbourhood'; but the question whether the local community within that sphere comprises a sufficient number of persons to constitute a class of the public is a question of fact in every case. It is not necessary . . . to prove that every member of the class has been injuriously affected; it is sufficient to show that a representative cross-section of the class has been so affected . . . (Romer LJ, *Attorney General* v *PYA Quarries Ltd* [1957] at 184)

In the same case, Denning LJ also did not say how many people must be affected in order for a nuisance to be public. Instead, he described a public nuisance as 'a nuisance which is so widespread in its range or so indiscriminate in its effect that it would not be reasonable to expect one person to take proceedings on his own responsibility to put a stop to it' (at 191).

A commonly used example of a public nuisance is an obstruction of the highway, but it covers more than this. As *Conaghan & Mansell* point out, it has also 'been held to include quarry-blasting . . . an ill-organised pop festival, and engineering a hoax bomb scare' (pp 127–8, but see *R* v *Rimmington; R* v *Goldstein* [2005]). A recent case illustrates the potential breadth of public nuisance, extending one claim to cover, inter alia, 'organising, attending or participating in . . . raves', 'playing loud music', 'urinating and/or defecating other than when making use of toilet facilities', 'lighting fires, fireworks, stoves, barbeques and/or naked flames', 'consuming or selling of nitrous oxide (laughing gas)' and 'bringing vehicles, including any engine or generator, onto any part of the prescribed area'.[74] In *Corby Group Litigation* v *Corby District Council* [2009], a local authority was liable in public nuisance for 'causing, allowing or permitting the dispersal

72. Reaffirmed by Akenhead J in *Corby Group Litigation* v *Corby District Council* [2009], though the damages claim was later settled out of court.

73. For an interesting (if long) judgment on a claim made on behalf of nearly 16,000 claimants, which ultimately failed on the science, and the uncertainty caused by lack of evidence of actionable harms suffered caused by the alleged nuisance (a fire at a wood processing plant)—as well as some pointed comments about 'claims farming' practices—see *Saunderson and others* v *Sonae Industria (UK) Ltd* [2016].

74. The 'prescribed area' in question was London Fields, in Hackney, and the claim was a response to behaviour seen in reaction to the relaxation of some of the Covid-19 restrictions in the summer of 2020: *London Borough of Hackney* v *Persons Unknown In London Fields, Hackney (The 'prescribed area')* [2020].

of dangerous or noxious contaminants' from land reclamation sites, which had caused birth defects in many children born in the area.[75]

What constitutes a 'class' of Her Majesty's subjects is a question of fact for the court. We know that it is not necessary to show that every member of that section of the community has been affected, as long as the nuisance can be shown to have affected a representative cross-section of that group of people.[76] That said, it is not enough for an individual who wants to claim to show merely that they are a member of the affected group—they must show that they have suffered 'special' or 'particular' damage in excess of that suffered by the public at large. This can include personal injury (unlike private nuisance), property damage and loss of custom, profit or business. In *Castle* v *St Augustine's Links* [1922], for example, a car driver on the road next to the defendant's golf course was struck by a golf ball hit from the thirteenth tee. Evidence showed that balls from the golf course frequently went over the highway and the court ruled that the positioning of the thirteenth tee amounted to a public nuisance. The class of persons affected were highway users and among them the claimant had suffered special damage. In *Tate & Lyle Industries Ltd* v *GLC* [1983], parts of the riverbed of the Thames silted up because of ferry terminals erected by the defendants. Large vessels were unable to access a jetty and the claimants incurred expense in carrying out their own dredging operations. Their claim in public nuisance was successful because the building of the ferry terminals had interfered with the public right of navigation enjoyed by all users of the river and special damage had been suffered by the claimant (the cost of the dredging). In *R* v *Rimmington; R* v *Goldstein*, both cases concerning the sending of malicious items through the post, neither defendant was found guilty (these were criminal cases) of public nuisance. Rimmington sent 538 racially offensive items to people across the country. Goldstein had, as a joke, sent some salt through the post to a friend. When the envelope leaked in the sorting office, an anthrax scare ensued. Neither incident, however, affected what their lordships thought to be a 'class' of Her Majesty's subjects in the required way, but only 'individuals' (Lord Rodger at [47]).

18.6 **Conclusion**

In this chapter we have started to look at the 'land torts'. These are distinct, in particular from negligence, in that they are supposedly based on establishing liability without fault. *Trespass to land* involves the direct and intentional act (it must be the act that is deliberate, not the trespass) of entering land upon which you have no permission (express or implied) to be. It is actionable per se, in that no damage needs to have been caused—the (legal) harm is the trespass itself.

Private nuisance differs in that it governs the relationship between neighbours, producing liability when one neighbour (in the literal sense) interferes with the rights of another to use and enjoy their land. As it is a tort to the land, not to the person, a proprietary interest

75. Abandoning an appeal to the findings of public nuisance (and negligence in the clean-up operation), Corby Borough Council instead agreed to settle the claims with an undisclosed sum of money, while not admitting liability. See BBC News 'Birth defect children in Northamptonshire agree payout' 16 April 2010.

76. An example is *East Dorset District Council* v *Eaglebeam Ltd* [2006].

in the land affected is required in order to be able to sue (***Hunter***). Essentially, the rules of nuisance require a certain amount of give and take between neighbours—the tort is committed only when one becomes an 'unreasonable user' of land. What makes someone an unreasonable land user is the central question—it has to do with the nature of the locality or neighbourhood, and, in respect of the act complained of, its intensity, frequency and duration. A factor that may prevent successful claims—even before defences are considered—is 'sensitive' use of the claimant's land, though this now seems to be subsumed into the more familiar (from negligence) notion of foreseeability (***Network Rail***).

Public nuisance differs in its scope and application, not only because it is primarily a crime, but also because it seeks to recognise and protect publicly held rights rather than an individual's property rights. That said, many things that are public nuisances could also be a private nuisance if an individual's interest in land was affected.

What may impact most on nuisance law in the future is the development of rights-based claims, particularly with respect to Article 8(1) ECHR. Activities carried out in the 'public interest' (though potentially human rights violations) may, however, affect the available remedy. Whereas an injunction would often seem more appropriate, as it stops the nuisance continuing (or limits it), damages may be awarded in lieu where the defendant can show that what is a nuisance to one person (or even many) has a broader benefit for society.

End-of-chapter questions

After reading the chapter carefully, try answering the questions which follow.

1 What is the nature of the harm controlled by private nuisance?

2 In negligence, duty of care (and in some cases, the standard of care) is used as a means of restricting claims. Where are such limitations to be found in nuisance?

3 Do the land torts appropriately weigh the interests of the individual against those of wider society?

4 Do the land torts protect landowners' interests too much, or not enough?

If you would like to know what we think visit the **online resources**. www.oup.com/he/horsey7e

Answering the problem question

Consider again the problem question at the start of this chapter. Now having read about the topic, **what would be your advice to the various parties?**

Here are some pointers to get you started

→ Lekan, as the creator of all the problems, will be the defendant. The claimants are Sarah, Sandy, Jess and Ailsa.

→

→

→ Sarah is complaining that the smell of the seaweed is a nuisance as it makes her feel physically sick. The first question, however, would be whether she has 'standing' to sue (*Hunter*). If she has, though she cannot claim for physical harm, she may be able to claim that this affects her use and enjoyment of land, but whether she succeeds would depend on the factors to be weighed for and against her claim, including the nature of the locality (*Coventry*).

→ Sandy is claiming in respect of noise, which has a long history in nuisance claims. However, he is 14, meaning that it is unlikely he has standing.

→ Jess's car has been hit. Is the claim best made in nuisance or trespass? Might it be public nuisance?

→ Has a harm been suffered by Ailsa?

If you need some more guidance

→ An **annotated version of the problem with issues and cases to consider** can be found in the Appendix.

see online resources

→ A **suggested outline answer** to check your ideas against can be found in the online resources that accompany the book.

Further reading

A good place to start your reading is with Maria Lee's 2003 article as it shows not only how the tort of private nuisance is not based on constant and clearly definable principles but also on value judgements. For a look at the interaction between public regulation (including planning permission) and private nuisance, Lee's 2011 article is also worth reading. Steel's analysis of the locality rule, after ***Coventry***, is also helpful, as is Nolan's chapter.

Campbell, David 'Of Coase and Corn: A (Sort of) Defence of Private Nuisance' (2000) 63 MLR 197

Lee, Maria 'What is Private Nuisance?' (2003) 119 LQR 298

Lee, Maria '*Hunter v Canary Wharf Ltd* (1997)' in Charles Mitchell and Paul Mitchell (eds) *Landmark Cases in the Law of Tort* (Hart, 2010)

Lee, Maria 'Tort Law and Regulation: Planning and Nuisance' [2011] JPEL 986

Nolan, Donal 'The Essence of Private Nuisance' in Ben McFarlane and Sinéad Agnew (eds) *Modern Studies in Property Law, Volume 10* (Hart, 2019), Ch 5

Simpson, AW Brian 'Victorian Judges and the Problem of Social Cost: *Tipping v St Helen's Smelting Company* (1895)' in *Leading Cases in the Common Law* (OUP, 1995)

Steel, Sandy 'The Locality Principle in Private Nuisance' [2017] CLJ 145

Wightman, John 'Nuisance—The Environmental Tort? *Hunter v Canary Wharf* in the House of Lords' (1998) 61 MLR 870

Actions under the rule of *Rylands* v *Fletcher* 19

Problem question

Read this problem question carefully, and keep it in mind while you are working through the chapter that follows. At the end of the chapter, you will be able to apply what you have learnt to the problem question and advise the relevant parties.

Grab-and-Buy supermarket owns land on which it has built a huge two-storey metal-framed customer car park. One day, after extremely stormy weather with strong winds and heavy rain, the top level of the car park buckles; some of the metal railing breaks free and falls onto the neighbouring petrol station owned by Low-Price-Pumps. The impact damages the pumps and injures one of Low-Price-Pumps' customers. Furthermore, water that had collected on the upper level of the car park due to an inadequate drainage system pours on to Low-Price-Pumps, flooding the forecourt of the petrol station. The station has had to close for two days, causing £10,000 loss of profit.

Low-Price-Pumps spends £50,000 having the forecourt cleaned and making safe the pumps. Grab-and-Buy argues that damage to the pumps caused by high winds is something that Low-Price-Pumps could and should have insured against.

Advise the parties.

19.1 Introduction

Consider the following examples:

- *Townbury Council's outdoor swimming pool has to be closed after an adjacent ornamental lake bursts its banks after heavy rainfall and lake water floods into the pool, making it unsafe.*
- *A gas pipe owned by Racksco and supplying gas for domestic use is exposed after a tap is left on accidentally by an old lady living in a warden-assisted flat provided for her by Townbury Council. Over time, water seeps from her premises to an embankment supporting the pipe, causing it to weaken and eventually crumble.*

→ ***A large pile of wood and other materials is collected on land belonging to Townbury Fire Service, in preparation for its annual bonfire party on 5 November, to which all residents of the town are invited. A group of youths is caught trying to set the pile of wood alight, and fire officers dampen the wood down until they are ready to light it themselves. However, wind transports some still smouldering pieces of wood to the neighbouring property, where they burn down a garden shed.***

We have already considered the way in which trespass, private nuisance and, to a lesser extent, public nuisance protect people's ability to exercise their rights to enjoy land without undue or unreasonable interference. In this chapter we consider a particular cause of action, a variation on the nuisance theme—the rule from ***Rylands* v *Fletcher* [1868]**. This protects an occupier against interference due to an *isolated escape* from (as opposed to an *ongoing interference with*) neighbouring land. This action is rare. It has been shaped over time by three key cases: ***Rylands* v *Fletcher*, *Cambridge Water Co Ltd* v *Eastern Counties Leather plc* [1994]** and ***Transco* v *Stockport Metropolitan Borough Council* [2003]**.

The ***Rylands*** rule is another method for regulating land use. It emerged out of the Industrial Revolution's widespread impact on society, beginning in the eighteenth century, changing the face of the country by the mid-nineteenth century—to far less agricultural and increasingly industrial. With industry came increased risk of harm from things such as water, noxious chemicals and so on 'escaping' from factories, reservoirs and the like. ***Rylands*** was a direct legal response to some of these risks. It created so-called 'strict liability' for such escapes—that is, liability without fault.[1] Owners of factories, reservoirs and so on would be liable even if they had taken all reasonable care to ensure that escapes did not occur. As in the previous chapter, we will also look here at the contribution the ***Rylands*** rule makes, or could make, to the protection of the environment—given its very nature it perhaps has a clearer role to play in this respect than nuisance. However, we will see not only that the rule appears to have limited use in the modern day,[2] but also that the strictness of liability under it appears to have become somewhat diluted.

19.2 The rule in *Rylands* v *Fletcher*

The rule in ***Rylands*** holds that where there has been an escape of a dangerous thing in the course of a non-natural use of land, the occupier of that land is liable for the damage to another caused as a result of the escape, irrespective of fault. A strict liability rule seems somewhat incongruous against the increasing incidence of fault-based considerations in modern nuisance cases.[3] That said, liability under the rule, while strict, is not absolute. There are defences to the action and latterly the courts have decided

1. We have previously encountered the idea of strict liability in relation to defective products in **Chapter 12**.
2. That is not to say it is not argued—see e.g. *Jalla* v *Shell International Trading and Shipping Co* [2021].

that defendants should be liable only for *foreseeable* consequences of escapes. In fact, until relatively recently, the rule was largely considered to be of little real significance—an interesting relic of legal history. As we shall see, the action has been rarely used. Though the decision in ***Cambridge Water*** reawakened interest (particularly academic), any enthusiastic revival of the rule seems overly ambitious given that ***Cambridge Water*** actually further *limits* the scope of ***Rylands*** actions and arguably, therefore, its usefulness. In ***Transco***, Lord Hoffmann remarked that 'it is perhaps not surprising that counsel could not find a reported case since the Second World War in which anyone had succeeded in a claim under the rule' (at [39]). The rarity of success in a ***Rylands*** claim seems unlikely to change following further limitations from ***Transco***.

Rylands v *Fletcher* [1868] HL

The defendant mill owner employed independent contractors to build a reservoir on his land to provide water for his mill. During construction, the contractors discovered disused shafts from an old coal mine on the defendant's land, which they assumed had been blocked up. However, when the reservoir was filled, the water in it burst through the old shafts, flooding the claimant's operating mine. The claimant sought compensation from the mill owner for the damage caused.

The independent contractors had clearly been negligent in failing to ensure that the mine-shafts were properly blocked up, but the claimant's action was against his neighbour and he had not (and could not reasonably have) known of the existence of the shafts on his land and so could not be shown to be negligent (nor was he vicariously liable for the contractors' negligence). The court also doubted whether an isolated escape of something from one area of land to another (as opposed to an ongoing emanation) could found an action in nuisance. Nevertheless, the claim succeeded.

Although the case went to the House of Lords, it was Blackburn J in the Court of Exchequer Chamber (*Fletcher* v *Rylands and another* [1866]) who has long been considered to have given the classic statement of principle, finding that:

> the true rule of law is that the person who for his own purposes brings on his land and collects and keeps there anything likely to do mischief if it escapes, must keep it in at his peril, and, if he does not do so, is *prima facie* answerable for all the damage which is the natural consequence of its escape.

The House of Lords approved this principle (at 339–40), Lord Cairns adding the stipulation that the defendant must also be engaged in a 'non-natural' use of land (at 338).

In ***Rylands***, the defendant was strictly liable for all the damage caused by the escape of the water from the reservoir, even though he was in no way to blame for it.[4] While

3. See e.g. ***Network Rail Infrastructure Ltd* v *Morris (t/a Soundstar Studio)*** [2004] discussed in **section 18.3.3.3**.

4. So, would the owner of the ornamental lake in the first scenario at the beginning of this chapter be liable to Townbury Council? The question now will be whether the modern requirements of a claim under ***Rylands*** have been met—have they?

this may not, at first glance, seem very 'fair', like many cases it is a product of its time. It was decided in a climate of rising social and political concern about the dangers of reservoirs and other processes of industrialisation at a time when another serious reservoir incident had recently occurred.[5] This may have persuaded the courts that strict liability in such circumstances was necessary in order to ensure 'social justice' in the sense of protecting people against the ravages of industrialisation.[6]

There are four requirements that claimants must establish to succeed under the rule. The first three derive from ***Rylands*** itself; the first two from Blackburn J's often-quoted statement in the Court of Exchequer and the third added by Lord Cairns in the House of Lords. The fourth requirement was not added until much later and comes from the leading opinion of Lord Goff in ***Cambridge Water***.

(1) The defendant brings on his land for his own purposes something likely to do mischief . . .

(2) . . . if it escapes . . .

(3) . . . which represents a non-natural use of land . . .

(4) and which causes foreseeable damage of the relevant type.

We will look at each of the requirements in turn.

19.2.1 'The defendant brings on his land for his own purposes something likely to do mischief . . . '

This requires a voluntary act of bringing something on the land, and is perhaps the natural result of concern about industrial practices. Blackburn J justified his rule by explaining that it could deal with the effect of industry on those who had no control over it, saying:

> the person whose grass or corn is eaten down by the escaping cattle of his neighbour, or whose mine is flooded by the water from his neighbour's reservoir, or whose cellar is invaded by the filth of his neighbour's privy, or whose habitation is made unhealthy by the fumes and noisome vapours of his neighbour's alkali works, is damnified without any fault of his own. (at 280)

The interesting question, however, is what constitutes things that can be brought onto land that are 'likely to do mischief'—though 'brought onto' in this sense probably means 'kept on'. Notably, most of the things the cases have been concerned with would be perfectly harmless in and of themselves, if they were not allowed to escape.

5. With severe loss of life. See AW Brian Simpson 'Legal Liability for Bursting Reservoirs: The Historical Context of *Rylands* v *Fletcher*' (1984) 13 LS 209, 219.

6. Though it is interesting to note that the reservoir bursting in ***Rylands***—essentially an accident, albeit large-scale, causing only property damage—convinced the courts to act to create a strict liability rule. This stands in stark comparison to other 'large-scale' accidents and personal tragedies we have seen in tort (e.g. the Hillsborough Stadium disaster, see further **section 5.6**), following which the courts have sought to restrict liability.

In ***Rylands***, water (collected in large volume in one area) was obviously within the 'likely to do mischief' category and, since then, other cases have determined that electricity (*National Telephone Co* v *Baker* [1893]), gas (*Batchellor* v *Tunbridge Wells Gas Co* [1901]), noxious fumes (*West* v *Bristol Tramways Co* [1908]) and even a flagpole (*Shiffman* v *Order of St John* [1936]) or a part of a fairground ride (*Hale* v *Jennings* [1938]) also fit the description. Put simply, the thing or substance brought onto land need not be ultra-hazardous, but must be capable of causing damage—and therefore be dangerous—*if* it escapes.

This requirement seems to have been reinforced and made harder to satisfy by the House of Lords in ***Transco***.

Transco v *Stockport Metropolitan Borough Council* [2003] HL

The defendant owned a block of flats next to a disused railway embankment, which it also owned. A pipe carrying water to the flats from the water main leaked and a large quantity of water travelled through a crack in the ground to the embankment, over time saturating it and causing it to collapse. There was no evidence that the leak was due to any carelessness on the part of the defendant. When the embankment collapsed it exposed and left unsupported a high-pressure gas pipeline owned by Transco (formerly part of British Gas), who had to act promptly in order to prevent the pipe fracturing. Their preventative actions cost about £94,000.

The first question for the court was whether the defendant had 'brought something on to his land likely to do mischief'. In answering, Lord Bingham said:

> I do not think that the mischief or danger test should be at all easily satisfied. It must be shown that the defendant has done something which he recognised, or judged by the standards appropriate at the relevant place and time, he ought reasonably to have recognised, as giving rise to an exceptionally high risk of danger or mischief if there should be an escape however unlikely an escape may have been thought of. (at [10])

This set a very high threshold, which the law lords found was not satisfied in *Transco*. In addition, Lord Scott stated that Transco's claim should fail because there had been no 'escape' from the defendant's land (see **section 19.2.2**)—the water from the leaking pipe had simply moved from one part of the defendant's land to another; it had not exited the land or gone over any boundary.

This means that the test as to what is 'likely to do mischief if it escapes' is in fact quite strict. Only when it can be shown that the defendant recognised (or should have recognised) that an *exceptionally* high risk of danger arose if the thing or substance accumulated on their land was able to escape will there be any possibility of liability arising. This would not change even if the risk of an escape taking place was low.[7]

7. Have you now changed your mind about whether Townbury Council would be able to recover damages from the owner of the ornamental lake? Similarly, would Racksco have any claim since the ***Transco*** decision?

Counterpoint

Essentially, the 'likely to do mischief' test has been transformed by the *Transco* decision into a foreseeability test. A defendant will not now incur liability if they could not have foreseen an exceptionally high risk of danger should whatever was brought onto their land escape. As we indicated in our discussion of private nuisance (**section 18.3.3.3**), foreseeability, as a requirement in land torts (traditionally understood as distinct from the tort of negligence and stemming from the trespass torts), seems rather misplaced—it hints at there being a requirement of fault. This is particularly troubling in relation to *Rylands* liability, which is supposed to be strict. So, it should not matter whether the defendant could or should have 'recognised' (foreseen) that a thing would give rise to an exceptionally high risk of danger if it escaped.

19.2.2 **'. . . if it escapes . . .'**

The ***Rylands*** rule was established to deal with isolated escapes from land and therefore proof of an actual escape of a 'thing likely to do mischief' is vital to a claim. In *Read* v *Lyons* [1947], a munitions inspector was injured while visiting a munitions factory when an artillery shell exploded during the manufacturing process. As there was no indication that the manufacturers had been negligent, the claimant brought an action in ***Rylands***. The House of Lords rejected her claim. There had been no 'escape'—the shell had not left the defendant's premises. Crucially, the claimant was still on the property when she was injured: had she stepped over the threshold, she would have succeeded. The law lords held that an escape occurs only when the substance or item causing damage actually moves from the defendant's premises to a place outside the defendant's occupation or control. This was confirmed by the Court of Appeal in *Stannard (t/a Wyvern Tyres)* v *Gore* [2012]. Tyres stored on the defendant's land caught fire, subsequently destroying both the claimant's and the defendant's premises. While agreeing that it would be possible for ***Rylands*** liability to be based on fire, the court found that this would be rare, as it would need to be the fire itself that was brought onto land and then escaped. As the tyres themselves had not escaped, there could be no liability.[8]

Pause for reflection

Lord Macmillan held (*obiter*) in *Read* v *Lyons* that he was not prepared to allow personal injury claims under *Rylands*. He said that 'as the law now stands an allegation of negligence is in general essential to the relevancy of an action of reparation for personal injuries' (at 16–17).[9] Do you agree? Should liability be confined to property damage or do you think that when people keep 'dangerous' things or substances on their land which injure someone if they escape, they should pay compensation?

8. Note also that the storage of tyres in this case was held to be a 'natural use' of land, meaning no liability could have arisen even if there had been an escape. See, however, *LMS International Ltd and others* v *Styrene Packaging and Insulation Ltd and others* [2005], especially [26]–[33].

9. Confirmation that personal injury claims can also be made in public nuisance was given in *Corby Group Litigation* v *Corby Borough Council* [2008], discussed in **section 18.5**.

There has been some debate as to whether *intentionally* releasing something from one's land is capable of being viewed as an 'escape' and therefore falling within the ***Rylands*** sphere of liability. In *Rigby* v *Chief Constable of Northamptonshire* [1985], police officers, in an attempt to catch a criminal hiding in a shop, fired CS gas into the premises to 'flush' the man out. This resulted in a fire which damaged the shop. The court held that where direct harm had been caused by an intentional act, trespass would be the correct action. However, in *Crown River Cruises Ltd* v *Kimbolton Fireworks Ltd* [1996], Potter J suggested that intentional releases (in this case fireworks) *could* be deemed to be 'escapes' if not deliberately aimed in the direction of the claimant or their property.

19.2.3 **'. . . which represents a non-natural use of land . . .'**

As we have seen, the third requirement that there be a 'non-natural' use of land was added by Lord Cairns in the House of Lords in ***Rylands***. This was his interpretation of the original formulation from Blackburn J in the lower court, who referred to the defendant bringing onto or accumulating on the property something 'which was not naturally there'. This means that the rule does not apply to things that are naturally to be found on a particular area of land. However, what is naturally on land—or what is 'non-natural use'—has been variously interpreted over time.

It appears clear, for example, that no liability can arise in respect of trees, shrubs or other plants that are naturally found on the defendant's land, even if some part of these 'escapes' onto the claimant's property (*Giles* v *Walker* [1890]).[10] It might be different, however, if the trees or plants in question were *introduced* by the defendant. The classic definition of 'non-natural use' is found in *Rickards* v *Lothian* [1913]:

> It is not every use to which land is put that brings into play [the] principle. It must be some special use bringing with it increased danger to others, and must not merely be the ordinary use of land or such use as is proper for the general benefit of the community. (Lord Moulton at 280)

In *Rickards*, a tap was left running by an unknown party in the part of a building leased by the defendant. This caused a flood, damaging the claimant's goods stored on the floor below. Despite there being an escape, no liability was found as the defendant was found to have been using the premises in an ordinary way.

Counterpoint

'Non-natural' use appears to have become 'non-ordinary' use—a much narrower definition, as many things that are not 'natural' on land will in fact be quite ordinary. Further, what is 'ordinary' will depend on the time, place and context of the use of the land in question. This definition begins to make the test look a little like negligence (or like the reasonable user test in nuisance)

→

10. Though this might be trespass.

→

and has allowed the courts to decide that various industrial activities are in fact 'natural' uses of land. This not only goes against the rule's strict liability origins but would seemingly water down any impact that the rule from ***Rylands*** could have on environmental protection.

In *British Celanese* v *Hunt* [1969], strips of metal escaped from a factory where the defendants manufactured electrical components. These hit overhead power lines, causing a power failure to the claimant's factory. However, because the area in which both factories were sited was given over to an industrial estate, the defendants escaped liability under ***Rylands*** (although they were on other grounds found liable in both negligence and nuisance). The substance in question was certainly not 'naturally' on the land: it had been brought there by the defendants and had escaped—but the use of the land was 'ordinary' in the context of industry, as well as being beneficial to the community (in the sense of providing a necessary commodity, creating employment, etc). Similarly, in *Read* v *Lyons*, the manufacture of artillery shells in wartime was found to be a natural use of land given the political/social context (although it should be noted that the *Read* decision was later doubted in ***Transco***). The most recent interpretations of 'non-natural' use come from the Court of Appeal. In *Stannard (t/a Wyvern Tyres)* v *Gore* the storage of around 3,000 vehicle tyres on land was deemed natural use, despite them igniting and the fire escaping, destroying the neighbouring premises, and even though the capacity of a typical storage facility was exceeded and the stacking of the tyres was done 'haphazardly and untidily'.[11] In *Northumbrian Water Ltd* v *McAlpine Ltd* [2014], in the context of large quantities of wet concrete escaping into a water drain (later setting, causing extensive damage), Moore-Bick LJ stated that 'redevelopment of land in an urban setting cannot in my view be regarded as other than normal and reasonable, unless it involves the use of unusual methods of working' (at [19]).

The definition of 'ordinary' use of land will inevitably change with time (for example, keeping a car was 'non-natural' in 1919, but would not be regarded as so today) and context. Having such a broadly interpretable rule allows the courts considerable flexibility when deciding whether to apply the rule in a new case. Overall, in our view, this had a negative effect on the use of the rule in ***Rylands*** as it means that a claimant is far less likely to succeed in any claim taken against general industrialised activity, which, of course, are the very activities likely to do the most damage (and the very activities from which the strict liability principle arose). There is no real explanation why the courts felt that this change of direction was necessary. Perhaps it was to limit the number of claims in a similar way to the duty of care in negligence, which may in turn be a consequence of changed emphasis in the law of tort and whose interests it is used to protect.

19.3 ***Cambridge Water* v *Eastern Counties Leather plc***

A major case that substantially changed the meaning of 'non-natural use' (or 'non-ordinary use') of land was ***Cambridge Water***. In the background to this case sit a number of common law decisions (e.g. *Ballard* v *Tomlinson* [1885]) which recognised that

11. cf *Harooni and another* v *Rustins Ltd* [2011].

downstream landowners hold a 'natural right' to receive water in its 'natural quality and quantity'.[12]

Cambridge Water Co Ltd v Eastern Counties Leather plc [1994] HL

The defendants owned and operated a tannery and, in the process of degreasing leather pelts, used a particular chemical solvent—perchloroethylene (PCE)—for many years, ceasing its use in 1976. In the tanning process, large quantities of PCE had been spilled onto the concrete floor of the tannery. Over time, this seeped through the concrete and into the soil below, from where it 'travelled', eventually entering the watercourse and polluting a well situated 1.3 miles away and owned by the claimants for extracting drinking water for the city of Cambridge. The PCE pollution in the water was only discovered in 1983 when the water company became obliged by a European Directive to test for certain chemicals, including PCE. Cambridge Water was forced to move its well, at a cost of more than £1 million, and sued the defendants for the costs associated with the relocation in negligence, nuisance and under the rule in *Rylands*.

By the time the case reached the House of Lords, the claims in negligence and nuisance had failed, largely because the harm that had occurred had been unforeseeable to the defendants. This left only the *Rylands* action. Giving the leading opinion in the House of Lords, Lord Goff felt bound to say that 'the storage of substantial quantities of chemicals on industrial premises should be regarded as an almost classic case of non-natural use' (at 309), notwithstanding any benefit to the community that is served by the industry or the fact that this might be seen (especially in a tannery) to be an 'ordinary use' of the land in question. He also found that the PCE entering the watercourse could be viewed as an isolated escape, despite the fact it had happened over a period of time and was caused by many separate spillages. However, despite these liberal interpretations, the claimants could not recover because the damage was ultimately too remote.

19.3.1 '. . . and which causes foreseeable damage of the relevant type'

Lord Goff's view on the 'escape' and the issue of 'non-natural' use of land appears to contradict the direction taken by the courts in the mid-twentieth century. While this may be viewed as a good thing, in that courts would subsequently be more able and therefore more likely to find 'non-natural' uses of land (a triumph for environmentalists),[13] the *reason* for the changed approach shows that this is not indeed the case. As we mentioned earlier, a *fourth* requirement to the ***Rylands*** test was added in ***Cambridge Water***—what prevented the claimant's recovery of damages was the fact that the harm suffered was regarded as too remote. Lord Goff added the requirement that any damage caused by

12. Though note that the decision in *Ballard* was not about the reasonableness or otherwise of upstream use but was more a policy decision reflecting the fact that people downstream tend to suffer more from pollution.

13. Though the trend may now be back in the other direction: see *Stannard (t/a Wyvern Tyres)* v *Gore* [2012] and *Northumbrian Water Ltd* v *McAlpine Ltd* [2014].

the escape must be *foreseeable* and, in considering this, held that it was not foreseeable even to the skilled person that quantities of chemical spilt on concrete would ultimately cause damage to the claimant's water. Although some damage from the spillage of the PCE might be imagined, the damage to the claimant's well could not be, particularly given that the European Directive had not been in force.

Lord Goff justified his findings by analogy to nuisance (which, as discussed in **section 18.3.3.3**, also has a foreseeability requirement) and by allusion to Blackburn J's original formulation in ***Rylands***, in which he referred to 'anything *likely* to do mischief if it escapes'. In fact, it is said that as a student at Oxford Lord Goff had read and been very impressed by an article by FH Newark which argued against the separation of ***Rylands*** liability and private nuisance.[14] The ***Cambridge Water*** situation provided him with an opportunity to put this into practice. He closed the gap between ***Rylands*** and nuisance in two ways. First, by equating non-natural use with reasonable use he essentially established the rule *as an application of nuisance* to one-off escapes (a position later confirmed by the House of Lords in ***Transco***). Secondly, he introduced the remoteness principle from ***The Wagon Mound (No 1)*** [1961].[15]

As we have already indicated, 'non-natural use' had come to be interpreted so as to *limit* liability under ***Rylands*** where the courts felt it necessary or appropriate to do so. However, Lord Goff recognised that the addition of the foreseeability requirement would sufficiently limit the scope of liability, so there remained no need to do so with the 'ordinary use' test.

Pause for reflection

Why do you think the courts felt it necessary to try and rein in liability under the rule in *Rylands*? If the objective was originally to protect claimants (or society as a whole) from the negative environmental and other effects of industry, do such limitations seem appropriate? And for whose benefit do these limitations exist?

There has been some discussion as to how far the foreseeability test extends and about what exactly must be foreseeable—the harm alone or also the escape in the first place? Lord Goff's opinion is not entirely clear on these points (perhaps a reflection of his priorities at the time), but the commonly held view is that it is not the *escape* that must be foreseeable, merely the *damage* resulting from the escape. As *Conaghan & Mansell* point out:

> authority for this position can be derived from the *Rylands* decision itself: Blackburn J's allusion, for example, to 'anything likely to do mischief' suggests that the defendant must reasonably recognise the dangerous nature of the substance under his control but, having done so, he 'must keep it at his peril', implying liability regardless of whether or not he could reasonably have foreseen and/or guarded against an escape. (p 144)

14. FH Newark 'The Boundaries of Nuisance' (1949) 65 LQR 480.
15. **Section 9.3.1.**

Therefore, the correct question is: *once there has been an escape, is the damage suffered by the claimant of a type or kind that was a reasonably foreseeable consequence of such an escape?*[16]

Lord Goff also considered the ongoing position. There was still clearly PCE pollution affecting the particular well—once the testing of the water had included tests for PCE, the problem was known. On this point, Cambridge Water argued that, even though the damage (pollution by PCE) may have been unforeseeable *when it was spilt*, it had clearly *become* foreseeable by the time the case reached the court, *and* the PCE was still escaping. Could the defendant therefore be liable for *continuing* escapes? Lord Goff dismissed this argument, holding that because the defendants could not possibly have foreseen the fact that the well would become polluted at the date of the spillages, strict liability for the damage (which became foreseeable at a later date, but by which time nothing could be done to prevent the escapes continuing) should not be imposed upon them. The PCE had escaped beyond the defendants' control (even though it would have been possible—but expensive—for them to clean up the water).[17]

Counterpoint

Before leaving ***Cambridge Water***, consider the following passage from *Conaghan & Mansell*:

> [T]he interesting question is not whether ***Cambridge Water*** was correctly decided but rather *why* the Law Lords chose to decide the case as they did. To some extent, the result can be attributed to good housekeeping instincts—Lord Goff considered that the application of a foreseeability criterion to the determination of liability in ***Rylands*** would lead to 'a more coherent body of common law principles' (at 76) . . . More generally, however, it is instructive to consider the broader social and political context within which ***Cambridge Water*** was decided. [Eastern Counties Leather] is judicially perceived as a model company which excites the admiration of right-thinking people. Mann LJ notes that it is of 'high repute' locally, taking a proper 'pride in its history' as a business which was first incorporated in 1879 (at 56). Lord Goff commends the company's 'good standard of housekeeping' and its 'modern and spacious' accommodation (at 63). Into this idyllic scene of industrial industriousness comes a European regulation which, for no demonstrable health reason, renders water from the Sawston borehole no longer 'wholesome' and thereby threatens the whole future of this well-established business with a damages bill of almost £1,000,000. Anyone could be forgiven for thinking that this offends justice and common sense, particularly in circumstances where the alleged polluters couldn't possibly have known that their activities would have such expensive consequences . . . However the effect of placing the cost of pollution on Cambridge

→

16. Might it be argued, therefore, that the factory owners, in the scenarios outlined at the beginning of the chapter would, unlike Eastern Counties Leather, be liable, as such pollution is foreseeable since ***Cambridge Water*** itself?

17. Note, then, that the decision goes against the environmental principle that the 'polluter should pay'. See also *Jalla* v *Shell International Trading and Shipping Co* [2021].

→

> Water is equally disquieting—they will inevitably recoup their loss through raised water rates, but in what sense is it more just to require the residents of Cambridge to foot the bill? (pp 146–7)

In economic and environmental terms, then, the ***Cambridge Water*** decision favours industry over society (and distributive rather than corrective justice); the losses or costs are spread among the citizens who pay for their water. The question is whether this is a better solution than one requiring polluters to pay. An environmental perspective may reflect an entirely different outcome—making polluters pay is surely preferable to making society pay for both the environmental and social cost of industry, and may operate as a deterrent against future polluting practices. Lord Goff considered the environmental question—and whether this should be a policy consideration that weighed heavily against Eastern Counties Leather—but thought that the creation of mechanisms for protecting society from pollution was more properly the role of Parliament, not the judiciary through the development of one small rule in tort. Put simply, he believed that pollution should be regulated by public, not private, law.

It is also questionable just how much 'development' of the tort the imposition of liability on Eastern Counties Leather would involve. In ***Rylands***, the defendant landowner could not possibly have foreseen that one potential consequence of his erection of a reservoir would be the flooding of his neighbour's mine. The point was that despite the unforeseeable nature of the harm, he should be held strictly liable for it happening, as by building the reservoir he had *assumed the risk* of all harms that might be caused by the water escaping, whether foreseeable to him or not. Why should this be any different when we are faced with a modern 'model company'?

Pause for reflection

Do you think that the ***Cambridge Water*** decision was correct? Could it have been decided differently? Remember that the House of Lords found major disagreements on some points thought to be determinative by the Court of Appeal (which had found in favour of Cambridge Water). Does this mean the House of Lords was necessarily right and the Court of Appeal was necessarily wrong? You may like to take into consideration the fact that although PCE was not known to have any deleterious health consequences to humans, it had, by the time ***Cambridge Water*** was decided, been found to cause liver cancer in mice.

Also consider what the damages claim in ***Cambridge Water*** was *for*. The costs incurred related to the finding of a new site for a water borehole and the sinking of a new well. What this means is that the *old well was never cleaned up*. Should there have been an obligation on one of the parties to clean up the PCE from the old well? If so, which party, and why?

see online resources

19.4 *Transco v Stockport MBC*

The final requirement of ***Rylands*** comes from the House of Lords in ***Transco***, which approved and expanded upon Lord Goff's opinion in ***Cambridge Water***. Dealing with what could be considered to be 'non-natural' land use, the law lords found that the provision of a piped water supply from the mains to a block of flats was a totally natural use of land. ***Transco*** now makes it even harder for claimants to establish a defendant's liability. Not only will the 'mischief test' be harder to satisfy, the 'non-natural use' test will also be. The House of Lords noted the link between these two concepts and all five law lords thought that a correct redefinition or re-interpretation of 'non-natural use' should require there to be some use that is 'extraordinary and unusual' according to the standards of the day.[18] Piping water to a block of flats in an urban area clearly does not fit this definition, therefore there would have been no liability in ***Transco*** on this point.[19] Typically, Lord Hoffmann reverted to economic analysis, suggesting that the role of insurance in cases of this type was also relevant, saying that 'a useful guide in deciding whether the risk has been created by a "non-natural" user of land is to ask whether the damage which eventuated was something against which the occupier could reasonably be expected to have insured himself' (at [46]).

Pause for reflection

Should it matter whether the party was—or is considered by the court to ought to have been—insured? The question, when it comes down to economic analysis, is about which party is better placed to bear the costs. If Transco had to bear the cost, it could then redistribute this cost by increasing the prices paid by all its customers. Similarly, if Stockport MBC had to pay, an increase in council tax for local residents would cover the cost. Similar points arise if we consider payment 'in advance', via the payment of insurance premiums. Do you think it should be councils who insure themselves against eventualities of this type, or the companies who provide the services (e.g. gas), usually in the interests of making profit? Or, more accurately, should citizens in a particular area bear the costs, or the customers of a profit-making enterprise?

Lord Hoffmann seems to suggest that if an occupier of land could have foreseen such an eventuality, they should (a) have insurance and (b) the use of land would be classified as 'ordinary' so the ***Rylands*** test would not be satisfied. This puts the insurance burden firmly upon occupiers (potential claimants). Put simply, on this view a claimant cannot say that they thought that there might be a risk of harm occurring, but they chose not to insure, and then go to court seeking damages under the rule in ***Rylands***. Lord Hoffmann's approach, however, was not favoured by the other law lords and was in fact explicitly rejected by Lord Hobhouse (at [60]).

18. Lord Bingham at [11]. Lord Walker agreed, also adding the word 'special' to the requirement (at [106]).

19. See also Ward LJ in *Stannard (t/a Wyvern Tyres)* v *Gore* who found that tyres are not 'exceptionally dangerous or mischievous' things and use of land as a tyre-fitting business neither 'extraordinary' nor 'unusual' (at [50]), and Moore-Bick LJ in *Northumbrian Water Ltd* v *McAlpine Ltd* at [19].

19.5 **Standing and defences**

19.5.1 **Who can sue?**

Cambridge Water seemed to move the ***Rylands*** rule closer to nuisance, with the addition of the foreseeability requirement. Indeed, this was Lord Goff's intention. Only a few years later, the House of Lords' decision in ***Hunter* v *Canary Wharf Ltd*** [1997] made having a proprietary interest in land a prerequisite to a claim in nuisance. This meant that the question arose as to whether this would extend to those taking claims in ***Rylands***. It is clear that others have successfully claimed under the rule in the past (*Perry* v *Kendrick's Transport Ltd* [1956]), though this was criticised in *Read* v *Lyons*. However, if the focus of both actions is the same, namely the protection of rights to and over land, as Lord Goff suggested, it would seem logical that the right to be able to take a claim would be the same for each. This position was confirmed by the House of Lords in ***Transco***;[20] therefore only parties with ownership or exclusive possession of the land concerned have standing to claim under ***Rylands***.

Counterpoint

Following *Transco* it is clearly no longer possible to claim for personal injury under the rule in *Rylands* (in the same way that it is not technically possible in nuisance).[21] This limitation has, however, been criticised by some scholars as being at odds with the House of Lords' belief that there may be 'a category of case, however small . . . in which it seems just to impose liability even in the absence of fault' (Lord Bingham, *Transco* at [6]).

Roderick Bagshaw argues that it is strange to limit the rule to damage to real property especially given that one of the reasons for the rule in the first place was as a response to a loss of life in a number of disasters. For example, Lord Walker in his speech in *Transco* refers to the Aberfan tragedy in which 144 people (including 116 school children) were killed when on 21 October 1966 thousands of tons of colliery waste from the Merthyr Vale Colliery slid down a mountain side above the village of Aberfan in south Wales, destroying 20 houses and the village school. To suggest (in the absence of negligence) there would only have been good reason to compensate the property owners and not for the deaths and personal injuries of those involved seems extraordinary. This, however, is the result of subsuming *Rylands* within nuisance.

see online resources

It also appears that other losses are excluded from the rule, now it has been subsumed into private nuisance and (see **section 19.6**) more closely aligned with negligence. In *D Pride & Partners (A Firm)* v *Institute for Animal Health* [2009],[22] for example, Tugendhat J excluded claims for pure economic loss from both nuisance and ***Rylands*** actions.

20. See e.g. Lord Hoffmann (at [46]), in the context of who is best placed to insure against property damage, Lord Hobhouse (at [52]) who indicates that 'other parts of the law of torts' cover personal injuries and, perhaps most conclusively, Lord Bingham (at [9]).

21. In the past personal injury claims had been included without question: *Hale* v *Jennings* [1938]; *Perry* v *Kendrick's Transport Ltd* [1956].

22. Discussed in **section 7.2**. Also see *Colour Quest* v *Total Downstream UK plc* [2010].

19.5.2 **Defences**

The initial defences available under the rule in ***Rylands*** come from Blackburn J's original judgment. He indicated that there should be only three defences to the (strict) liability. These are outlined in **Table 19.1**.

TABLE 19.1 Defences to a claim under the rule in *Rylands* v *Fletcher*

Defence	**Examples**
Fault of the claimant or express or implied consent	*Ponting* v *Noakes* [1894] The claimant's horse died after it reached over a fence to eat poisonous leaves from a tree on the defendant's land. The defendant was not liable as the harm suffered was due to the horse's own intrusion
Escape caused by the unforeseeable act of a stranger	*Box* v *Jubb* [1879] A reservoir overflowed onto the claimant's land, but this was the result of another neighbouring reservoir owner's actions, over which the defendant had no control and of which he had no knowledge; the defendant was therefore not liable *Rickards* v *Lothian* [1913] The claimant's premises were flooded due to a continuous overflow of water from a sink on the top floor of the building. This was caused by a tap being turned on full and the wastepipe plugged by the deliberate act of a third party. The defendant was not liable as he could not reasonably have known of the act so as to do anything to prevent the harm
	Perry v *Kendricks Transport Ltd* [1956] A disused motor-coach in the defendant's car park was set alight by young boys, causing injury to a 10-year-old. However, it had not been left in such a condition by the defendant that it was reasonable to expect that children might meddle with it and cause the fire. The act of the third party must be unforeseeable. If the defendant should have foreseen the intervention, the defence will not be established
	Northwestern Utilities Ltd v *London Guarantee Co* [1936] The claimant's hotel was destroyed by fire after a gas leak ignited. It was foreseeable that works undertaken by a third party near the defendant's gas mains might cause damage and require remedial work. It was therefore no defence to argue that the fire was caused by the acts of a third party

Defence	Examples
Escape caused by an 'act of God'	*Nichols* v *Marsland* [1876] The defendant had ornamental pools on his land, which contained large quantities of water and which had been formed by damming up a stream that ran through his property. Extraordinarily high rainfall caused the banks of the pools to collapse and the escaping water destroyed four bridges on the claimant's land. The court ruled that the defendant should not be found liable for an extraordinary act of nature, which he could not have reasonably foreseen
	Greenock Corporation v *Caledonian Railway* [1917] A concrete paddling pool for children had been constructed by the local authority in the bed of a stream, requiring an alteration of its natural course. An extraordinary level of rainfall caused the pool to overflow. Due to its construction, water which would have ordinarily flowed downstream flowed down a public street. The House of Lords held that such an event did not qualify as an 'act of God'

Pause for reflection

The defendant will not be liable where an escape happens solely because of natural causes, in circumstances where no human foresight or prudence could reasonably recognise the possibility of such an occurrence and take preventative measures. Arguably, however, modern technological and scientific advances render this defence largely defunct. Do you think that exceptionally heavy rains or violent winds would be unforeseeable today? What kind of exceptional situations would now be considered (after *Greenock*) an 'act of God'?

Blackburn J's defences are not the only ones applicable to ***Rylands*** claims, others more familiar from nuisance can also arise. Statutory authority is the primary example and the approach to this is the same as is taken in nuisance.[23] Contributory negligence and *volenti non fit injuria* are also applicable.[24] The fact that defences are available at all is somewhat controversial—they essentially suggest that an element of fault resides in an area of tort that is supposed to have created strict liability. This, in our opinion, weakens the action's potential use in environmental protection. The subsuming of the action into nuisance has also created doubt about its usefulness in the modern day and, as we

23. **Section 18.3.4.1.**

24. As was indicated in *Colour Quest* v *Total Downstream UK plc* [2010]. *Steele* argues that 'consent' in this form must mean something closer to 'shared benefit' if it is to be consistent with the purpose of the rule (p 689). See further **Chapter 10.**

shall see in the following section, it appears that to some extent any residual application of ***Rylands*** is edging closer and closer in some circumstances to a fault-based land tort.

19.6 The nuisance/*Rylands* v *Fletcher*/negligence overlap

Lord Walker, in ***Transco***, suggested that liability in nuisance (and presumably, therefore, under ***Rylands***) 'overlaps with (indeed, is a sort of condominium with) that of negligence' (at [96]). A series of cases supports this—that is, cases in which there is clearly fault on the part of the defendant, but where the harm is to the claimant's interest in land and liability has been found in nuisance or ***Rylands***.[25] These cases started within a category known as 'continuing or adopting a nuisance', and refer to those situations where a pre-existing nuisance (created usually by a third party) was allowed to continue by the defendant, sometimes resulting in the 'escape' of something from the defendant's land. Furthermore, in *Burnie Port Authority* v *General Jones Pty Ltd* [1994], the Australian High Court expressly incorporated the ***Rylands*** rule into negligence. In ***Cambridge Water*** a foreseeability requirement—more familiar from negligence and considerations of fault—was added to both claims in private nuisance and under ***Rylands***. Lord Walker, in ***Transco***, thought that the scope of the action had been restricted by developments in negligence (at [99]). Thus, it seems that questions must now be asked about the role of fault within these types of claim, particularly in those cases that seem, on their facts, to straddle private nuisance and ***Rylands***.

Sedleigh-Denfield v *O'Callaghan* [1940] HL

A drainage pipe on the defendants' land had been constructed by the local authority without the defendants' knowledge. When it was built, its end should have been covered with a grille or grate to stop debris blocking it and causing flooding. A grate had been provided but was put in the wrong place, rendering it useless. The claimant's land was flooded and damaged on more than one occasion when the pipe became blocked following heavy rainfall.

The House of Lords held the defendants (an order of monks) liable on the ground that they had 'continued or adopted' an existing nuisance. While it was clear that the nuisance itself—that is, the problem—had been *created* by the local authority in its negligent construction of the pipe, the defendants had done nothing to rectify the problem. Because at least one of the monks was found to have known about the existence of the pipe, and the fact that the problem would have been easy to rectify, it was held that the defendants had not taken reasonable steps to stop the nuisance continuing.

25. *Steele* states that ***Rylands*** 'provides a direct alternative to negligence in some circumstances', adding: 'In terms of long-term survival, that has been its problem' (p 679).

This clearly illustrates what we mean by a claim 'straddling' the tort of private nuisance and an action under ***Rylands***. The applicability of a particular action turns on what is categorised as the 'nuisance' or problem in the first place. If it is the pipe, this is an ongoing situation (at least, the risk created would be) and would fall in the private nuisance category. However, if it is the flooding of the claimant's land then it could be viewed that the water, once *accumulated* behind the blockage in the pipe, had 'escaped', making this a ***Rylands*** situation. However, it also seems eminently possible that this is, in fact, negligence—the defendants did not act reasonably or failed to take reasonable steps to do something about the grate and the potential problem that the pipe could become blocked. This is clearly a fault-based consideration and shows how the three different tort actions overlap. Is what is actually being said that there is a *duty* to do something about a known and existing state of affairs, if it could pose a potential problem?[26] If so, this is clearly *breached* by not doing so, and is what *causes* the damage complained of, subject to any foreseeability considerations. Conor Gearty argues that '[t]his was negligence pure and simple, confused by an ill-fitting and woolly disguise of nuisance'.[27]

The harm in ***Sedleigh-Denfield*** originated from a third party's actions, but similar effects arise in situations caused by acts of nature. In *Goldman* v *Hargrave* [1967], a gum tree on the defendant's property was struck by lightning. The defendant took what turned out to be inadequate steps to alleviate the risk that the tree would catch fire. The tree continued to smoulder, eventually igniting, the fire travelling to the neighbouring property and causing damage. The Privy Council followed ***Sedleigh-Denfield***, finding the defendant liable for the damage, based on his knowledge of the foreseeable danger.[28] Again, this seems both like an escape (of fire) and a fault-based consideration, aligning it more closely with negligence, and indeed the Privy Council treated it as such, though it refused to state whether the case could also be decided under nuisance.

19.6.1 The 'measured duty of care'

The cases in this area seem to involve an escape of one sort or another and without the added limitations to the ***Rylands*** rule would appear to be almost classic examples of the type of harm that Blackburn J imagined would attract strict liability. In relation to them a new term of art emerged: a 'measured duty of care' in nuisance, in which *positive* duties are owed by landowners to act to prevent damage to others.[29]

In *Leakey* v *National Trust* [1980], a portion of a large mound of earth on the defendant's ground collapsed (as exposure to weather conditions had weakened it over time), damaging two houses owned by the claimant which were situated at the bottom of the mound. As the defendants had long been aware of the effect of the weathering on the earth, they were found liable. Here, again, the Court of Appeal explicitly considered the relationship between nuisance and negligence in claims of this type, essentially coming to the point

26. In negligence this would be dealt with as a question of duty regarding the actions of a third party which then cause damage to the claimant—see, for an example of a case with no real discernible difference, *Smith* v *Littlewoods* [1987], **section 4.5.4**.

27. Conor Gearty 'The Place of Private Nuisance in a Modern Law of Torts' [1989] CLJ 214, 237.

28. Thus it seems that Townbury Fire Service, in the scenarios outlined earlier, could also be liable.

29. *Steele* points out that the notion of 'duty' is alien to nuisance, but also that the analysis of these cases is not typical of negligence, either, due to their subjective rather than objective standard (p 620).

that the two actions were one and the same in these situations. We would add that given the 'type' of nuisance being considered, ***Rylands*** is subsumed in these claims as well, by virtue of the 'escapes' that cause the damage in all of them. The result of *Leakey* is that a claim can now be taken in nuisance or negligence, but cases since have tended to rely on nuisance, possibly because it is easier to do so than to go back to 'duty, breach, cause' formulations. It is also perhaps arguable that where the only harm is to amenity interests, the claim must by its very nature be framed in nuisance and, therefore, all claims of this type might as well be.[30] However, at least where there is actual damage to property, the claims seem as though they would equally as easily succeed in negligence if framed in that way (see e.g. *Holbeck Hall Hotel Ltd* v *Scarborough Borough Council* [2000]; *Lippiatt* v *South Gloucestershire Council* [2000]; *Bybrook Barn Centre Ltd* v *Kent County Council* [2001]; *Delaware Mansions Ltd* v *Westminster City Council* [2002]; *Vernon Knight Associates* v *Cornwall Council* [2013]), yet all are considered nuisance actions. Indeed, in *Delaware Mansions*, Lord Cooke went as far as to say that the nuisance/negligence distinction in these cases 'is treated as of no real significance' (at [31]).

That said, in *Lambert and others* v *Barratt Homes Ltd and another* [2010], a local authority succeeded in its appeal against a finding that it should have prevented the flooding of the claimant's land from surface water that accumulated on its own land by constructing a catch pit and drainage system for the water at considerable cost. This indicates that the *scope* of the duty may be used to limit claims even where a measured duty of care seems appropriate. As the accumulation of the surface water had in fact been caused by Barratt (by blocking a drainage ditch and culvert on land adjacent to the local authority's)—and because Lambert could recover the entire cost of drainage work from Barratt in nuisance—the scope of the authority's 'measured duty' extended only to cooperation and to allowing others to facilitate the drainage of water from its land.[31]

Pause for reflection

Given the arguments made earlier, and the cases cited there, do you think there is any continuing role for the action in *Rylands*, or would it be better to do as Australia has done and completely subsume the action into the tort of negligence?

19.7 Where does *Rylands* v *Fletcher* fit today?

In ***Cambridge Water***, Lord Goff questioned whether ***Rylands*** was best seen as analytically distinct from nuisance or if they should be viewed as two parts of the same thing. Even though the ***Rylands*** rule had developed out of a desire to protect landowners from the risks of isolated escapes from industry and other risky activities, he held that 'it would . . . lead to a more coherent body of common law principles if the rule were to be regarded as essentially an extension of the law of nuisance to isolated escapes from land' (at 306). In ***Transco***,

30. Though as we have seen, to claim for personal injury, a claim would have to be formulated in negligence.

31. cf *Vernon Knight Associates* v *Cornwall Council* [2013].

the House of Lords confirmed that ***Rylands*** actions should be viewed as a sub-species of private nuisance. This, to a large extent, brought to an end a long period of uncertainty and academic speculation on the matter. Their lordships also reviewed the scope, relevance and application of the rule in the modern day and provided guidance as to its future application.

In particular the House of Lords in ***Transco***:

- rejected the suggestion that the rule should be absorbed into negligence as in Australia and Scotland;
- rejected the suggestion that the rule should be more generously applied, confining it to 'exceptional' circumstances where the occupier has brought something onto his land which poses an 'exceptionally high risk' to neighbouring property should it escape and which amounts to an 'extraordinary and unusual use of land' given the place and time in which it occurs; *and*
- clarified that only those with rights to land could sue, bringing the action into line with private nuisance, following ***Hunter***, and confirming that no claim for personal injury could be brought under it.

Transco limits the rule in ***Rylands*** to a role in the protection of interests in land (as in nuisance). In so doing it prevents it from taking on a broader role in ensuring that those who wish to indulge in ultra-hazardous (but socially beneficial) activities make appropriate provision for absorbing the inevitable costs of occasional catastrophes and environmental harms. In this respect, the function or purpose of this area of tort law as a regulatory system—if it ever had one—is lost.

It is clear that the ***Rylands*** rule has always been difficult to rationalise, and particularly so in the modern day, where it seems largely unnecessary to hold on to it. It was judicially created to deal with dangers caused by large-scale building of reservoirs and other rapid industrial development, making it seem like an exception to nuisance through its dealing with one-off events via the imposition of strict liability. However, by the mid-1990s, as ***Cambridge Water*** shows, its impact and potential as a tool for environmental protection was constrained—again, a product of the time in which a Conservative government prioritised business concerns. Furthermore, many of the practices on which it may have impacted had, by this time, been regulated in other ways—reservoirs, for example, by then coming under the Reservoirs Act 1975. Sadly, things have not really improved following the reconsideration of the action by the House of Lords in ***Transco***, as to all intents and purposes ***Rylands*** is now merely a form of nuisance and, as we argued in the previous section, potentially more accurately viewed as a sub-species of *negligence*. As a result, its deliberate differences from nuisance, including the ability to recover for personal injury and 'wrongful' conduct—as well as most of its environmental potential—have either been lost or become (unintentional) inconsistencies. Bagshaw contends that:

> [i]t is often asserted that 'hard cases make bad law', but ***Transco*** confirms that bad law is also easily made when a case is too straightforward. Perhaps it was because it was so clear to their Lordships that the claim should not succeed (the defendant's activity being too commonplace, insufficiently risky, there being no escape and the claimant's loss being easily insurable) that they allowed inconsistencies and controversial propositions to stray into their speeches. But given that very few claims rely on the rule in ***Rylands*** v ***Fletcher*** and ***Transco*** did nothing to encourage greater use of the rule, the main effect of these imperfections will probably be to challenge law students and textbook writers. (2004, at 392)

19.8 **Conclusion**

In this chapter we considered the rule from ***Rylands***, a judicially created action allowing claims against those who allow substances to escape from their land and cause damage to others' property. This rule was completely a product of the time—there were societal concerns about the effects of mass industrialisation, including, as in the case itself, the building of artificial reservoirs.

Due to its historical context, the rule has been (and can be) used only in limited circumstances and the primary bulk of case law comes from the late nineteenth and early twentieth century. But it should be remembered that the tort of nuisance was already in existence before ***Rylands***, and this would allow people to sue for uses of land that interfered with their own interests on a more frequent or ongoing basis. It should also be noted that the tort of negligence emerged as a separate entity in the early twentieth century, and many of the cases brought under ***Rylands*** could, in some ways, be construed as negligence actions. These days, it is only those situations where a completely accidental escape occurs that could be said to fall outside the bounds of negligence.

The rule today is best understood through a trilogy of cases: ***Rylands*** itself, then ***Cambridge Water*** in the mid-1990s, followed by ***Transco*** early this century. These three House of Lords' decisions have in their own way shaped the way the rule can be used, either by adding new requirements (***Cambridge Water***), or redefining the way the existing requirements should be interpreted (***Transco***). That said, there is potential—subject to its now stringent requirements—to use the rule to help to protect the environment from one-off catastrophes, not in a preventative sense but perhaps with more regard to clean-up measures when things go wrong. Whether this was what was intended when the rule was created is debatable—it was more likely intended as a vehicle to compensate (wealthy) land*owners* than to protect the land itself.

The usefulness of the rule is certainly questionable in the modern day—it appears from ***Cambridge Water*** and, also, the nuisance case of ***Hunter***, that its scope (particularly as a tool for environmentalists) has been severely restricted. The rule has moved closer to nuisance (and negligence), with all that that entails, including requirements of foreseeability and proprietary interest in land in order to be able to claim. In other jurisdictions, the rule has been swallowed by negligence. Without doubt, this is a rule now very limited in scope and application—potentially having more historical interest than practical application in the twenty-first century.

End-of-chapter questions

After reading the chapter carefully, try answering the questions which follow.

1. How could the action under *Rylands* be used to help to solve environmental problems?
2. Does the action under *Rylands* serve any useful purpose in the modern day?
3. Should we follow the Australian High Court and formally view the action under *Rylands* as a species of negligence?

If you would like to know what we think visit the **online resources**. www.oup.com/he/horsey7e 

Answering the problem question

Consider again the problem question at the start of this chapter. Now having read about the topic, **what would be your advice to Low-Price-Pumps?**

Here are some pointers to get you started

- → The first issue is whether Low-Price-Pumps has standing to take a claim (*Transco*).
- → Their first claim is for property damage to the pumps and the economic loss suffered as a result of the closure.
- → They would need to satisfy the four criteria for a successful claim under *Rylands*, as modified by *Transco*, including establishing whether each harm is damage 'of the relevant type' and whether it was foreseeable (*Cambridge Water*), as well as whether Grab-and-Buy brought onto or accumulated something on its land that carried with it 'exceptional' danger.
- → Consider also whether, should the claim be otherwise successful, Grab-and-Buy might be able to avail itself of one of the defences to the *Rylands* claim.

If you need some more guidance

see online resources

- → An **annotated version of the problem with issues and cases to consider** can be found in the Appendix.
- → **A suggested outline answer** to check your ideas against can be found in the online resources that accompany the book.

Further reading

A good place to start your further reading is the chapter by AW Brian Simpson, which helps to contextualise the ***Rylands*** litigation. More up-to-date and insightful interpretations are provided in numerous other articles, particularly by Bagshaw and Nolan, and an interesting discussion of the potential usefulness of the claim in relation to fracking is provided by Costello.

Amirthalingam, Kumaralingam '*Rylands* Lives' [2004] CLJ 273

Bagshaw, Roderick '*Rylands* Confined' (2004) 120 LQR 388

Costello, Roisin 'Reviving *Rylands*: How the Doctrine Could Be Used to Claim Compensation for Environmental Damages Caused by Fracking' (2014) available at http://dx.doi.org/10.2139/ssrn.3058635

Nolan, Donal 'The Distinctiveness of *Rylands v Fletcher*' (2005) 121 LQR 421

Simpson, AW Brian 'Bursting Reservoirs and Victorian Tort Law: *Rylands and Horrocks v Fletcher* (1868)' in *Leading Cases in the Common Law* (OUP, 1995)

Wightman, John 'Liability for Landslips' [2000] Env L Rev 285

Liability, damages and limitations

PART V

20 Vicarious liability

20.1 Introduction

20.2 Stage 1: a relationship of, or akin to, employment

20.3 Stage 2: a tortious act . . .

20.4 . . . committed 'in the course of employment'

20.5 Conclusion

End-of-chapter questions

Further reading

21 Damages for death and personal injuries

21.1 Introduction

21.2 What are damages for?

21.3 Calculating damages

21.4 Independent, joint and several concurrent liabilities

21.5 Time limitations on claims

21.6 The problem with damages

21.7 Debunking the compensation myth

21.8 Conclusion

End-of-chapter questions

Further reading

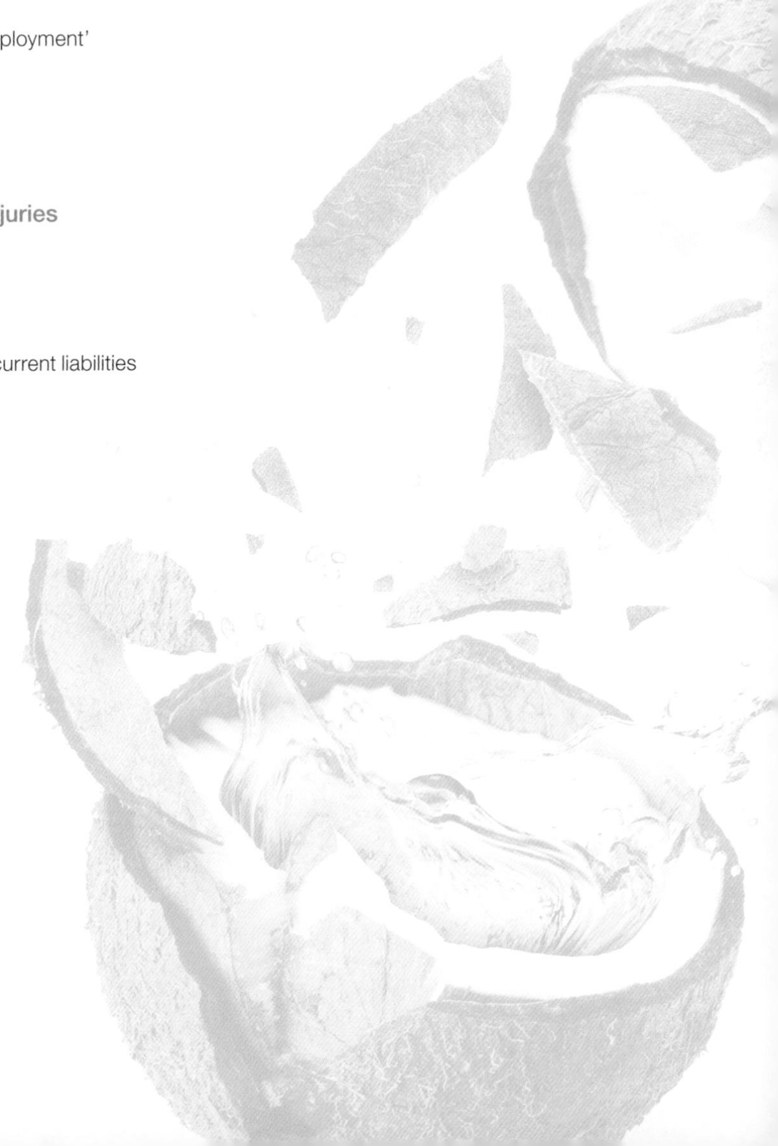

Introduction to Part V

1. In this Part of the book we turn to various issues in relation to the award of damages in tort, as well as *who* might pay in some situations. In practice, damages dominate tort law, yet the substantive rules governing *liability* are the focus of most teaching.

2. In **Chapter 20**, we look at the principle of *vicarious liability*, a form of secondary liability, arising in the context of employment relations and, increasingly, other relationships akin to employment, through which employers may, in certain circumstances, be liable for the torts of their employees, even though the employer themselves may be entirely blameless.

3. The imposition of vicarious liability depends on the level of connection between the employee's tortious activity and the job they are employed to do. The imposition of vicarious liability is one of the most important exceptions to the general approach of the common law whereby liability for any wrongdoing is imposed on, and only on, the wrongdoer(s).

4. In **Chapter 21** we consider the principles that lie behind *damages* awards, finding that the primary object of the law is to compensate those who have been harmed by another's wrongdoing. This is done by making an award that seeks to put the claimant into the position that they would have been in had the harm not occurred and can encompass pecuniary (financial) and non-pecuniary losses, such as pain, suffering and loss of amenity. Special (quantifiable at the time of trial) and general damages (including future losses, not quantifiable at the time of trial) are awarded. These are calculated using multiplicands (the sum to be multiplied) and multipliers (the number of years the loss should be multiplied by). In the past, damages tended to be awarded as a lump sum. More recently there has been some movement towards structured damages settlements.

5. Multiple defendants can incur liability independently, jointly or severally. Either the court will apportion damages between them or one defendant can seek a contribution from another via the Civil Liability (Contribution) Act 1978.

6. We then look at limitation periods that exist in respect of all damages claims—not uncontroversially. Subsequently, we consider a number of further critiques that can be (and have been) made of the damages system as well as some proposed alternative systems.

7. Finally, we return to the idea of 'compensation culture', analysing whether, in fact, we do live in such a culture and, if so, what response would be appropriate.

Vicarious liability

20

Problem question

Read this problem question carefully, and keep it in mind while you are working through the chapter that follows. At the end of the chapter, you will be able to apply what you have learnt to the problem question and advise the relevant parties.

Harry Lock Eyes is a popular restaurant and bar. Mario, its owner, prides himself on its mellow atmosphere and friendly staff. However, behind the scenes it is a different story.

Bert, the restaurant's sommelier, and Dillon, the head chef, have fallen out over Bert's wine choices for his signature dish. Eventually Dillon's quick temper gets the better of him—he grabs an empty wine bottle and hits Bert across the back of the head. Meanwhile, Cadbury Blacker, the local librarian, is setting up for her regular evening set singing chilled out versions of indie classics. As Dillon storms out from the kitchen he trips over a lead she has failed to tape down, and twists his ankle. Clem, the restaurant manager, phones Dougal at home to see if he can come in to cover Bert's shift. Dougal had been expecting to have the night off and had just settled down to watch TV. Though Clem makes it clear he does not have to come in, Dougal is irritated by her request. He cycles to the restaurant and when he gets there he punches her.

Meanwhile, Biggles is walking around the bar talking to the customers. He is employed as a host to make the guests feel comfortable, and so is a well-known figure at the bar. For convenience, Mario employs Biggles through an agency, which pays Biggles's wages. Bella has been coming to the bar for a few weeks and Biggles has been particularly welcoming. He often encourages her to stay late to help him tidy up and then gives her a lift home in his sports car. After one such occasion Bella complains that Biggles has sexually assaulted her. A subsequent criminal investigation upholds her claim.

Advise the parties.

20.1 Introduction

Consider the following situations:

→ ***A school teacher sexually assaults a pupil over several nights during a school trip.***

→ ***A young girl is injured when she falls out of a recycling van when the driver negligently speeds round a corner. She was helping the refuse workers on their rounds, against the wishes of their employer.***

→ ***An office worker is subjected to a sustained period of homophobic harassment and intimidation by her supervisor.***

Consider the examples above. There are a number of potential civil and criminal claims. Most obviously, the injured girl may wish to sue the driver of the recycling van in negligence, the office worker might bring a claim against his supervisor under the Protection from Harassment Act 1997 or for breach of contract, while, alongside a criminal prosecution, the school pupil might bring a claim against his teacher in the tort of battery. In each case, the defendant is the tortfeasor, that is the person who committed the tort. But what of the tortfeasors' employers? Might they also be liable? Certainly if they've been negligent—for example, in failing to provide a safe place of work—the claimants may argue that they are *personally* liable for their injuries.[1] However, they may also be liable *vicariously* for their employees' actions.

Vicarious liability is a mechanism by which one person (the defendant) is held liable to a claimant for a tort committed by someone else (the tortfeasor). Its main application is in employment relationships: an employer is vicariously liable for torts committed by their employees in the course of their employment. Recent years have, however, seen a significant expansion of vicarious liability beyond employment relationships to other relationships which are, in the relevant sense, akin to employment. Nonetheless, for simplicity, we will often refer to the defendant as the employer and the tortfeasor as the employee.

As a form of secondary liability, the imposition of vicarious liability is not predicated on any wrongdoing by the employer—they may well be, and often are, entirely blameless. Rather liability is imposed vicariously on the employer for the tortious actions of their employee (who remains primarily liable for their actions, though is typically not worth pursuing for financial reasons). The idea of vicarious liability is then at odds with the general approach of the common law and the principle of corrective justice whereby liability for any wrongdoing is imposed on, and only on, the wrongdoer(s). And as such, its imposition of strict, no-fault liability requires clear and principled justification.

Unfortunately, such guidance has, until recently, been unforthcoming.[2] At its most basic, vicarious liability is a mechanism that ensures a just and practical remedy for harm, while

1. See further **Chapter 13**.

2. See e.g. Longmore LJ in *Maga* v *Birmingham Roman Catholic Archdiocese Trustees* [2010] who commented that '[t]here is by no means universal agreement . . . Is it that the law should impose liability on someone who can pay rather than someone who cannot? Or is it to encourage employers to be even more vigilant than they would be pursuant to a duty of care? Or is it just a weapon of distributive justice? Academic writers disagree and the House of Lords in ***Lister***'s case did not give any definitive guidance to lower courts' (at [81]).

seeking to deter future wrongdoing.[3] Its development has typically been seen as the result not of 'any very clear, logical or legal principle, but [of] social convenience and rough justice' (*Imperial Chemical Industries Ltd* v *Shatwell* [1965] at 685). Over the years a number of policy objectives or justifications have been offered for the imposition of vicarious liability—see, for example, Lord Phillips in ***Various Claimants* v *Catholic Child Welfare Society and others*** **[2012]** at [34]–[35] and Lord Reed in *Cox* v *Ministry of Justice* [2016] at [19]–[24].

Justifications for the imposition of vicarious liability

(1) The employer is likely to be in a position to compensate the claimant. They not only have, to use Glanville Williams's description, 'a purse worth opening' or 'deeper pockets' than the employee (Williams 1956, p 232), but can also be expected to insure against such liability. The presence of liability insurance, in turn, means that vicarious liability acts as 'a loss-distribution device' whereby the financial loss arising from the wrongdoing can be spread more widely across the community through insurance premiums and/or higher prices.

(2) The tort will been committed as a result of activity untaken by the employee on behalf of the employer or as part of the business of the employer—the so-called 'enterprise liability' or 'delegation of task' arguments.[4] These suggest that as employers derive an economic benefit from their employees' work, they should bear any related burdens: 'a person who employs others to advance his own economic interest should in fairness be placed under a corresponding liability for losses incurred in the course of the enterprise'.[5]

(3) The employer by employing the employee has taken the risk of harm occurring and so, as they either gain a benefit from that risk or because of their role in creating it, they should bear responsibility should the risk materialise.[6]

(4) The employee will have been under the 'control' of their employers. The imposition of vicarious liability therefore acts as an incentive ensuring that employers not only maintain standards of 'good practice' and take care when making appointments, but explore ways of going beyond those set by the standard of the 'reasonable person'.

Pause for reflection

Courts and commentators tend to argue that vicarious liability can be justified, if at all, on the basis of a combination of various policy considerations: the desire to spread losses or shift them on to those best positioned to meet them, to encourage greater supervision of workers

→

3. See e.g. Lord Nicholls in ***Majrowski* v *Guy's and St Thomas' NHS Trust*** [2006] at [9].
4. John Bell 'The Basis of Vicarious Liability' [2013] CLJ 17, 18.
5. John Fleming *The Law of Torts* (9th edn, LBC Information Services, 1998), p 410.
6. Lord Phillips in ***Christian Brothers*** combined the second and third justifications to suggest that '[v]icarious liability is imposed where a defendant, whose relationship with the abuser put it in a position to use the abuser to carry on its business or to further its own interests, has done so in a manner which has created or significantly enhanced the risk that the victim or victims would suffer the relevant abuse' (at [86]) (see further Bell (**n 4**)).

→

and so reduce future wrongdoing, and a feeling (which may or may not stand up to close scrutiny) that employers should take the rough with the smooth and so bear the costs as well as enjoying the benefits of the employees' actions. Yet, while all these provide reasons for requiring the employer to meet their employees' liabilities, the problem is that if we were *really* committed to furthering these particular policies, the law would look very different.

First, these policy considerations cannot explain the particular rules on vicarious liability that the courts have in fact developed. For example, as we will see, vicarious liability depends on the employee actually having committed a tort. But the concern to shift or spread losses applies irrespective of whether the employee acted wrongfully. So, if we really were motivated to impose liability because this would see the losses spread, we would have no reason for limiting vicarious liability to those cases where the employee has caused loss by committing a tort. Instead, we would make the employer liable wherever their employee causes others loss while doing their job. The same goes for the benefit and burden argument. By contrast, the argument that vicarious liability exists to encourage greater supervision by employers of their employees' conduct suggests that liability should be imposed on the employer only where this really would be likely to lead to greater supervision and so a reduction of future harms. Given the practical limitations on an employer to 'control' their employee in the modern-day employment context *and* that most cases of negligence arise from isolated and unpredictable acts of carelessness, which the employer could have done nothing to prevent, it is hard to argue that this policy supports the present practice of imposing vicarious liability in respect of *all* torts committed in the course of employment.

Secondly, these policy considerations extend beyond the employment context. For example, the argument that losses should be spread applies *wherever and however someone is injured* and so is not uniquely applicable when the injury is caused by an employee acting in the course of their employment. Again, if we *really* believed that the law of tort should be concerned with spreading losses, then we would have no reason for making liability in general dependent on a breach of duty or for having a general rule that liability depends on the defendant having caused the relevant loss. If our motivation is to spread losses, it should be irrelevant whether the defendant acted carelessly or whether they were in any way responsible for the loss that was suffered. Instead we should impose liability on whomever we can find who carries insurance, since this is the best way of seeing the loss spread amongst society. That the law generally attaches liability only to those who actually caused the claimant's loss, and then, again as a general rule, only where their conduct has fallen below a particular standard, tells us that, at root, the law of torts is not designed to spread losses (though it may sometimes have this effect).

The same is true when we look at the other policies set out earlier. In each case, a real commitment to furthering these policies would lead not only to changes in the law of vicarious liability but a radically different law of tort—indeed, they would require us to view tort law as fundamentally misconceived. But if these policies cannot account for the law of tort *generally*, then we should be suspicious of any attempt to justify particular parts of tort law on this basis. We would be saying that, though generally these are not the policies which justify tort law as a whole, they do justify (some of) the rules of tort in the employment context. But why here and not elsewhere? We are left with a distinction that appears entirely arbitrary.

see online resources

Counterpoint

Of course, we should feel uncomfortable with the conclusion that an important and long-standing aspect of tort law is arbitrary and unprincipled. As such, lawyers have sought to find an explanation for vicarious liability which is consistent with the basic aims and structure of tort law generally. Perhaps the most important example of this is an argument made by Robert Stevens.[7]

His suggestion is that we should not view vicarious liability as an instrument for the law to impose on one person liability for torts committed by another. Rather it is just one particular example of the law on the attribution *of conduct*. What does this mean? The best example of this comes in relation to companies. Companies, as artificial legal constructs, can only 'act' (enter contracts, acquire property, commit torts) through natural persons (i.e. human beings). Accordingly the law needs a set of rules determining whose actions 'count' as the actions of the company; for instance, whose consent is needed for the company to enter into a contract. Stevens argues that we should understand the rules of vicarious liability in the same way. When the law holds an employer vicariously liable it is because the actions of the employee are attributed to the employer. The employee's actions are treated as the actions of the employer, and so torts committed by the employee are regarded as torts committed by the employer.

This suggests that, contrary to appearances, vicarious liability is not an exception to the general rule that the law of tort imposes liability only where the defendant has caused and is responsible for the loss suffered by the claimant. If the employee's actions are treated in law as the employer's actions, then any harms done by the employee are, at the same time, harms done by the employer. When the employer is held liable, they are accordingly being held liable for *their own* actions.

Unfortunately, this argument does not solve the problems posed by the law on vicarious liability. Even if we accept (and it is not clear why we should) that the law does indeed require, outside the context of companies, rules for the attribution of conduct, the question is why has the law chosen this set of rules rather than some other? Why should, in the context of employment, the actions of the employee be attributed to (and be regarded as the actions of) the employer? This question is particularly important given that the effect of such rules is that the employer is held legally liable for losses which most of us would regard as caused by, and the responsibility of, someone else.

This question just takes us back to where we started, needing a justification for the rules we have. Stevens's argument, if correct, tells us only what sort of rules these are: namely, rules of attribution. It does not tell us why we have or should embrace this particular set of rules. Unless we are content for the law to be and to appear arbitrary, these questions require an answer. As such, Stevens's argument ultimately fails to take us beyond the unpersuasive combination of policies set out earlier.

7. *Torts and Rights* (OUP, 2007), pp 257–74.

A defendant will be vicariously liable where the following conditions are met:

- there is an employer–employee relationship, or one akin to employment,[8] between the defendant and the tortfeasor (stage 1);
- the tortfeasor committed the tortious act while acting in the course of their employment (stage 2).

20.2 Stage 1: a relationship of, or akin to, employment

In order for a defendant to be held vicariously liable for another's act, the two must be in a relationship of employment or one which is regarded as akin to employment. However, identifying when two parties are in such a relationship is not as straightforward as one might expect.[9] Traditionally, the problem has been to determine which workers count as employees. Clearly not everyone you pay to do work for you becomes your employee. So, for instance, if you hire a plumber to mend your toilet or you take an Uber home, though the plumber and Uber driver are, in a sense, doing work for you, we would not, and the law does not, call them your employees. While the notion of who is and is not an employee is clear at the extremes, things become more indistinct at the borders particularly in relation to 'atypical' workers—for example, agency workers, homeworkers, part-time workers, the self-employed and 'regular' casual workers.[10]

Counterpoint

The law distinguishes employees from independent contractors (the general term applied to those who do work for us but who are not our employees). Historically this division has been key to the law of vicarious liability: a defendant would be vicariously liable for torts committed by their employees in the course of their employment, but not for torts committed by independent contractors.[11] Nonetheless, a defendant may be *personally* liable for harms resulting from the actions of an independent contractor where the defendant owes what is called a non-delegable duty of care. A non-delegable duty is, in simple terms, a duty not (simply) to take care but to see that care is taken. What this means is that, in cases of non-delegable duties of care, the defendant is unable to discharge their duty by (carefully) entrusting—delegating—responsibility for the discharge of the duty to another. This means that should the person to whom the duty is owed be injured as a result

→

8. e.g. between partners of a firm of solicitors (*Dubai Aluminium Co Ltd* v *Salaam* [2003]), a police chief constable and officers, and members of unincorporated organisations (see ***Various Claimants***).

9. For an example of the court's determination of employment status, see *Pimlico Plumbers Ltd* v *Smith* [2018].

10. McKendrick 1990, p 770.

11. The Supreme Court has recently confirmed the rule that there is no vicarious liability for the torts of independent contractors in *Barclays Bank* v *Various Claimants* [2020].

→

of the carelessness of the person to whom the relevant task has been entrusted, the *defendant* will be in breach of their duty, notwithstanding that they have exercised reasonable care in the selection of their delegate. Non-delegable duties are owed by employers to their employees (discussed in **Chapter 13**), however they also arise in other contexts.

In *Woodland* v *Essex County Council* [2013], the claimant, then aged 10, suffered a serious brain injury following an incident during a swimming lesson at a local pool, provided by professional swimming instructors employed by the school as independent contractors. Unable to rely on vicarious liability (the swimming instructors were not the school's employees) and/or occupier's liability (the school did not control the premises), it was argued that the school owed the claimant a non-delegable duty of care to ensure that reasonable care was taken of her not only by the school and its employees, but also by any third party with which the school contracted to perform its educational functions. The Supreme Court unanimously agreed. Lord Sumption gave the leading judgment, in which he set out the circumstances in which a non-delegable duty will arise (at [22]–[23]) and justifications for the imposition of such duties (at [25]). Lady Hale gave a concurring judgment in which she drew the following analogy:

> Consider the cases of three 10-year-old children, Amelia, Belinda and Clara. Amelia's parents send her to a well-known and very expensive independent school. Swimming lessons are among the services offered and the school contracts with another school which has its own swimming pool to provide these. Belinda's parents send her to a large school run by a local education authority which employs a large sports staff to service its schools, including swimming teachers and life-guards. Clara's parents send her to a small state-funded faith school which contracts with an independent service provider to provide swimming lessons and life-guards for its pupils. All three children are injured during a swimming lesson as a result (it must be assumed) of the carelessness either of the swimming teachers or of the life-guards or of both. Would the man on the underground be perplexed to learn that Amelia and Belinda can each sue their own school for compensation but Clara cannot? . . .
>
> As lawyers, we know that the three girls fall into three different legal categories. Amelia (we will assume) has the benefit of a contractual obligation of the school to secure that care be taken for her safety. Belinda has the benefit of the rule which makes an employer vicariously liable for the negligence of its employees. Clara has the benefit of neither and can only succeed if the school has an obligation to secure that care be taken for her safety . . .
>
> The reason why the . . . school is liable is that . . . the school has undertaken to teach the pupil, and that responsibility is not discharged simply by choosing apparently competent people to do it. The . . . school remains personally responsible to see that care is taken in doing it. (at [30], [32], [34])

The parties in *Woodland* returned to court in February 2015, almost 15 years after the accident, to determine the primary facts on which the negligence claim depended (*Woodland* v *Maxwell and Essex County Council* [2015]). The court held that both the swimming teacher and lifeguard had fallen below the standard of care expected of them and that, following the Supreme Court's ruling, Essex County Council was, as a result, in breach of their non-delegable

→

→

duty of care towards the claimant. Damages had reportedly been assessed earlier at £3 million. A later judgment found the lifeguard should contribute one-third to the third defendant's liabilities to the claimant both in respect of damage and legal costs. Essex County Council did not seek a contribution from the swimming teacher, who was uninsured at the time of the accident (*Woodland* v *Maxwell and Essex County Council (No 2)* [2015]).[12]

So, how does a court determine who is an employee?[13] Traditionally, the courts looked to the level of 'control' the employer exercised, not only over what the potential employee did but over *how* they did it as a way of determining employment status (*Stephenson Jordan & Harrison Ltd* v *McDonall & Evans* [1952]). However, in a climate where employees are increasingly expected to show—and are rewarded to the extent to which they do show—initiative and exercise discretion, this reflects an outdated view of the workplace. Accordingly, the courts have now taken the view that control is just one of a number of factors considered by the courts when determining a worker's status. Other factors include the extent to which the worker is 'managed' or 'accountable' to the employer, the centrality of their activates to the enterprise of the employer and the integration of their activities to the employer's business (*JGE* v *The Trustees of the Portsmouth Roman Catholic Diocesan Trust* [2012] at [72]). The key case here is ***Various Claimants* v *Catholic Child Welfare Society and others*** [2012] (also known as the ***Christian Brothers*** case).

Various Claimants v *Catholic Child Welfare Society and others* [2012] SC

The case was brought by 170 men who had been sexually and physically abused by members ('the brothers') of a Catholic group—the Brothers of the Christian Schools ('the Institute')—who were employed as teachers at a residential school for children in local authority care attended by the claimants. The abuse was alleged to have taken place over a 40-year period.[14]

→

12. In *Armes* v *Nottinghamshire County Council* [2017] the Supreme Court refused to find that a local authority owed a non-delegable duty of care to the claimant, who was physically and emotionally abused by two sets of foster parents, with whom the authority placed her. The court concluded that such a duty would come into conflict with the authority's duty to act in the best interests of children in its care. The child's best interests would sometimes require allowing them to stay with their families or friends. Yet, if the authority was to be liable for the tortious acts of those family members and friends, its own interest in avoiding liability would steer it away from allowing the children to stay with them. However, as we shall see, the court held that the authority was vicariously liable for the foster parents' actions, on the basis that its relationship to the foster parents was 'akin' to employment.

13. An individual may be an employee for some circumstances and not others. An employer may agree not to call someone an 'employee' (e.g. in order to avoid the payment of tax or National Insurance) but may nonetheless be vicariously liable for the 'non-employee's' actions, if in all other respects they act as an employee (*Ferguson* v *Dawson* [1976]).

14. In 1990, the school's headmaster, Brother James, was expelled from the Institute after it was discovered that he had systematically sexually abused boys in his care over a 20-year period. He was later convicted of numerous serious sexual offences against the boys at the school. The school closed in 1994.

→

The first question for the court was whether the relationship between the Institute and the brothers teaching at the school was one that was capable of giving rise to vicarious liability (stage 1). In the Court of Appeal it had been held that, since the brothers were at the time employed by the school, only the school (or, rather, the body managing it)—and so not the Institute—could be vicariously liable. The Supreme Court disagreed, however, holding that *both* the school *and* the Institute were vicariously liable for the abuse the brothers had committed.[15] In reaching this conclusion, the court held that, though the brothers were not employed by the Institute, the relationship between them was nonetheless sufficiently 'akin to' employment as to justify the imposition of vicarious liability (an approach adopted by the Court of Appeal in *JGE* v *The Trustees of the Portsmouth Roman Catholic Diocesan Trust*[16]). In coming to this conclusion, Lord Phillips identified five 'policy reasons' which support vicarious liability in the context of employment relationships:

> (i) the employer is more likely to have the means to compensate the victim than the employer and can be expected to have insured against that liability; (ii) the tort will have been committed as a result of activity being taken by the employee on behalf of the employer; (iii) the employee's activity is likely to be part of the business activity of the employer; (iv) the employer, by employing the employee to carry on the activity, will have created the risk of the tort committed by the employee; (v) the employee will, to a greater or lesser degree, have been under the control of the employer. (at [35])

It is by reference to these five incidents that certain non-employment relationships might nonetheless be treated as *akin* to employment:

> Where the defendant and the tortfeasor are not bound by a contract of employment, but their relationship has the same incidents, that relationship can properly give rise to vicarious liability on the ground that it is 'akin to that between an employer and an employee'. (at [47])

It was on this basis that the relationship between the Institute and the brothers was held to be akin to employment: though no contract existed between the Institute and the brothers, the vows the brothers gave to the Institute operated in much the same way, and the work the brothers did at the school was at the Institute's direction and done in furtherance of the Institute's mission and in accordance with its rules (at [56]–[60]):

> Provided that a brother was acting for the common purpose of the brothers as an unincorporated association, the relationship between them would be sufficient . . . just as in the case of the action of a member of a partnership. Had one of the brothers injured a pedestrian when negligently driving a vehicle owned by the Institute in order to collect

→

15. Historically, dual vicarious liability was not permitted: an employee 'is the servant of one or the other, but not the servant of one and the other; the law does not recognise several liability in two principals who are unconnected' (*Laugher* v *Pointer* [1826]).

16. This case was the first to consider the essential elements of the employer–employee relationship (stage 1) in the context of allegations of sexual abuse against Roman Catholic priests. This had been conceded in previous cases. See further Janet O'Sullivan 'The Sins of the Father—Vicarious Liability Extended' [2012] CLJ 485.

→

> groceries for the community few would question that the Institute was vicariously liable for his tort. (at [61])

Lord Phillips went on to address the second stage of the vicarious liability test: whether there was a sufficiently 'close connection' between the acts of abuse and the brothers' employment such as to justify holding the Institute liable for these acts. In finding that the necessary connection had been made out, he continued:

> Living cloistered on the school premises were vulnerable boys. They were triply vulnerable. They were vulnerable because they were children in a school; they were vulnerable because they were virtually prisoners in the school; and they were vulnerable because their personal histories made it even less likely that if they attempted to disclose what was happening to them they would be believed. The brother teachers were placed in the school to care for the educational and religious needs of these pupils. Abusing the boys in their care was diametrically opposed to those objectives but, paradoxically, that very fact was one of the factors that provided the necessary close connection between the abuse and the relationship between the brothers and the Institute that gives rise to vicarious liability on the part of the latter. There was a very close connection between the brother teachers' employment in the school and the sexual abuse that they committed, or must for present purposes be assumed to have committed. (at [92]–[93])

see online resources

Pause for reflection

The impact of the *Christian Brothers* case is far-reaching. John Bell notes:

> [T]he Supreme Court has rightly side-stepped argument that the peculiar employment situation of a particular helper, such as a celebrity presenting a show for a broadcaster or a repair mechanic sent out under a service contract who is engaged technically on a self-employed basis, can lead the enterprise to evade vicarious liability for the actions of the celebrity or repairman. What weighed with the courts in [the ***Christian Brothers*** case] and *JGE* is that the abusers were placed by the enterprise, as part of their mission, in a position from which the tortfeasor happened to cause a harm which was a risk inherent in the activity in question. (2013, p 20)

Might we soon see broadcasting companies defending vicarious liability claims?[17]

The 'akin to employment' approach was confirmed by the Supreme Court in *Cox* v *Ministry of Justice* [2016]. In this case the Ministry of Justice was held variously liable for the injuries of the catering manager (Cox) at HM Prison Swansea, who was negligently injured by a prisoner (Inder), who was carrying out paid work under supervision in the kitchen, when he dropped a large bag of rice on her upper back. The prisoner's activity in unloading

17. See further Morgan 2013, pp 143–4; Giliker 2013, pp 312–13.

supplies was 'akin to employment' even though his relationship to the prison was not voluntary. The ***Christian Brothers*** case developed 'a modern theory of vicarious liability':

> The result of this approach is that a relationship other than one of employment is in principle capable of giving rise to vicarious liability where harm is wrongfully done by an individual who carries on activities as an integral part of the business activities carried on by the defendant and for its benefit (rather than his activities being entirely attributable to the conduct of a recognisably independent business of his own or of a third party), and where the commission of the wrongful act is a risk created by the defendant by assigning those activities to the individual in question. (Lord Reed at [24])

The court concluded that this approach was satisfied on the facts:

> Prisoners working in the prison kitchens, such as Mr Inder, are integrated into the operation of the prison, so that the activities assigned to them by the prison service form an integral part of the activities which it carries on in the furtherance of its aims: in particular, the activity of providing meals for prisoners. They are placed by the prison service in a position where there is a risk that they may commit a variety of negligent acts within the field of activities assigned to them. That is recognised by the health and safety training which they receive. Furthermore, they work under the direction of prison staff. Mrs Cox was injured as a result of negligence by Mr Inder in carrying on the activities assigned to him. The prison service is therefore vicariously liable to her. (Lord Reed at [32])

A further application of this approach by the Supreme Court came in *Armes* v *Nottinghamshire County Council* [2017]. Here the court held that the relationship between a local authority, responsible for children put into its care, and foster parents, into whose homes those children were placed, was akin to employment, such as to make the authority vicariously liable for abuse carried out by the foster parents. The court came to its decision by appealing to the five incidents identified in the ***Christian Brothers*** case and concluding that they were all present in the relationship between the authority and the foster parents. In particular, it held that the fact that the child was placed into a foster home in fulfilment of the authority's duty towards children in its care, and that the authority recruited and trained foster carers and paid them allowances, meant that the foster parents played an 'integral part of the local authority's organisation of its child care services' (at [60]). Moreover, while the authority did not micro-manage how the foster parents cared for the children, it nonetheless 'exercised powers of approval, inspection, supervision and removal', which gave it 'a significant degree of control over both what the foster parents did and how they did it' (at [62]).[18]

Most recently, the Supreme Court in *Barclays Bank* v *Various Claimants* [2020] used this approach to explain why there is *no* vicarious liability for the torts of independent contractors. The claimants were employees or prospective employees of Barclays and Barclays had arranged for them to have medical examinations with a Dr Bates. It was alleged that the doctor had, during these examinations, sexually assaulted the claimants, who sought to hold Barclays vicariously liable for those assaults. It was accepted that the doctor was not himself a Barclays employee but was instead an independent

18. See further Simon Deakin 'Organisational Torts: Vicarious Liability versus Non-Delegable Duty' [2018] CLJ 15.

contractor. Nonetheless, the Court of Appeal had held that Barclays could be vicariously liable for his torts. The Supreme Court allowed Barclays' appeal. As Lord Reed had held in ***Cox***, vicarious liability would attach where the tortfeasor's activities were an integral part of the business activities carried on by the defendant but not where their activities were attributable to the conduct of a recognisably independent business of their own or of a third party. An independent contractor is, necessarily, one acting in the course of an independent business of their own. The court also stressed that if it was clear that the tortfeasor was engaged in an independent business of their own, there was no need to consider the five incidents listed in the ***Christian Brothers*** case.

20.3 **Stage 2: a tortious act . . .**

An employer cannot be vicariously liable unless their employee did indeed commit a tort. If they did not, there is nothing for their employer to be vicariously liable for.[19] Over the years, most cases have tended to involve the tort of negligence, however it is clear that an employer may also be vicariously liable for an employee's intentional acts including battery (*Mattis* v *Pollock (t/a Flamingos Nightclub)* [2003]), sexual assaults (***Lister* v *Hesley Hall Ltd* [2002]**), stealing (*Morris* v *CW Martin* [1966]; *Brink's Global Services Inc* v *Igrox Ltd* [2009]), harassment (***Majrowski* v *Guy's and St Thomas' NHS Trust* [2006]**) and misuse of private information (*WM Morrison Supermarkets plc* v *Various Claimants* [2018]).

***Majrowski* v *Guy's and St Thomas' NHS Trust* [2006] HL**

The claimant, Majrowski, brought a claim against his employer in respect of harassing, bullying and intimidating treatment by his departmental supervisor in breach of the Protection from Harassment Act 1997. He claimed that she had singled him out, and was excessively critical about his work and time-keeping in front of other members of staff. Majrowski claimed that his supervisor's behaviour was fuelled by homophobia: he is a gay man. An internal investigation (following a formal complaint from the claimant) established that harassment had occurred. The question for the court was therefore whether the supervisor's employer was vicariously liable.

Finding for the claimant, the House of Lords held:

> [I]t is difficult to see a coherent basis for confining the common law principle of vicarious liability to common law wrongs . . . the rationale also holds good for a wrong comprising a breach of statutory duty or prohibition which gives rise to civil liability, provided always the statute does not expressly or impliedly indicate otherwise. (at [10])

After all, Lord Nicholls continued: 'why should an employer have special dispensation in respect of the newly-created wrong and not be liable if an employee commits this wrong in the course of his employment? The contemporary rationale of employer's liability is as applicable to this new wrong as it is to common law torts' (at [27]).

19. Although see Robert Stevens 'Vicarious Liability or Vicarious Actions' (2007) 123 LQR 30.

Pause for reflection

Lord Nicholls in ***Majrowski*** posed the following question:

> Take a case where an employee, in the course of their employment, harasses a non-employee, such as a customer of the employer. In such case the employer would be liable if his employee had assaulted the customer. Why should this not equally be so in respect of harassment? In principle, harassing arising from a dispute between two employees stands on the same footing. If, acting in the course of his employment, one employee assaults another, the employer is liable. Why should harassment be treated differently? (at [28])

Do you think harassment should be treated differently from physical assaults? Is there a danger of disgruntled employees, suffering from stress as a result of what is expected of them by their immediate superiors, deciding to bring (perhaps fraudulent) claims for harassment?[20]

More recently, Maurice Kay LJ in the Court of Appeal expressed doubts over the number of workplace harassment cases:

> it is doubtful whether the legislature had the workplace in mind when passing an Act that was principally directed at 'stalking' and similar cases . . . I do not expect that many workplace cases will give rise to this liability. It is far more likely that, in the great majority of cases, the remedy for high-handed or discriminatory misconduct by or on behalf of an employer will be more fittingly in the Employment Tribunal. (*Veakins* v *Kier Islington* [2009] at [17])

20.4 . . . committed 'in the course of employment'

An employer will be vicariously liable for torts committed by an employee only if the tort is committed 'in the course of their employment'. Of course, this simply prompts another question: when is an employee acting in the course of their employment? Traditionally when making these assessments, the courts relied on the 'Salmond test' which asked whether the employee's act was 'a wrongful and unauthorised mode of doing some act authorised by the master'.[21] This test was rejected by the House of Lords in ***Lister*** in favour of a 'close connection' test.

20. See Lord Nicholls's response to these fears (at [30]) and Baroness Hale's rather reluctant application of the principles of vicarious liability in her concurring opinion (at [64]–[74]).

21. JW Salmond *Law of Torts* (1907); now in the last edition of *Salmond & Heuston on the Law of Torts* (21st edn, Sweet & Maxwell, 1996), p 443. See e.g. the Court of Appeal decision in *Trotman* v *North Yorkshire County Council* [1999] in which the court refused to find the employers of a school teacher who sexually abused a pupil vicariously liable because the abuse was not an unauthorised mode of carrying out an authorised act. *Trotman* was overruled by the House of Lords in ***Lister***.

Lister v *Hesley Hall Ltd* [2002] HL

Mr Grain was employed by Hesley Hall Ltd as the warden of a residential facility attached to a school, which specialised in teaching children with emotional and behavioural difficulties. Its purpose was to provide the children with a homely and caring setting—beyond and distinct from their school environment—in which to adjust to everyday living. The warden was responsible for the discipline and day-to-day running of the house. Over the course of four years he systematically sexually abused a number of boys, including the claimants.[22] The claim that the defendants, the warden's employers, were personally negligent in their care, selection and control of the warden was rejected at first instance and was not pursued further. The question for the House of Lords was whether they were vicariously liable for the warden's acts of abuse.

A unanimous House of Lords held that the warden's actions were 'so closely connected' with his employment that it would be fair and just to hold the employers vicariously liable. Though 'sexual abuse is a particularly offensive and criminal act of personal gratification on the part of its perpetrator and therefore could be easily described as the paradigm of those acts which an employee could not conceivably be employed to do' (at [53]), the sexual abuse in this case 'was inextricably interwoven with the carrying out by the warden of his duties' (Lord Steyn at [28]).

Pause for reflection

It has been suggested that 'the facts in *Lister* shouted vicarious liability so loudly the outcome was obvious the moment the Lords freed themselves from the wooden reading of the Salmond test'.[23] Do you agree? Would your answer differ if the defendant was a non-profit organisation or religious community rather than a commercial enterprise? Think again about the justifications for the imposition of vicarious liability, particularly in relation to the allocation of risk. Is there a difference between a charity (which is not seeking to make a profit) and a company (which derives an economic benefit from their employee's work and is more easily able to spread the loss through liability insurance or higher prices) bearing the risk of an employee's deliberate wrongdoing?

The 'close connection' test in ***Lister*** is both practically and theoretically problematic. It is easier to state than apply. As Paula Giliker notes, it simply prompts further question: how closely connected to their employment do the employee's actions need to be?[24] The courts have been grabbling with its application for over a decade. Lord Phillips in the ***Christian Brothers*** case opined that the 'test of "close connection" approved by all tells one nothing about the nature of the connection' (at [74]).[25] And so, unsurprisingly, the

22. He was subsequently sentenced to seven years' imprisonment for multiple offences involving sexual abuse.

23. Bruce Feldthusen 'Vicarious Liability for Sexual Abuse' (2001) 9 Tort L Rev 173, 177.

24. 'Rough Justice in an Unjust World' (2002) 65 MLR 269.

25. Compare e.g. *Weir* v *Chief Constable of Merseyside Police* [2003]—in which an off-duty police officer was found to be acting in the course of his employment when he assaulted a young man he found rummaging through his girlfriend's things by throwing him down some stairs and locking him

question as to what precisely amounts to a sufficiently close connection to make it just for the employer to be held vicariously liable returned again to the Supreme Court in ***Mohamud* v *WM Morrison Supermarkets plc*** [2016].[26]

Mohamud v *WM Morrison Supermarkets plc* [2016] SC

A petrol station attendant assaulted the claimant (who was of Somali origin) in a brutal and unprovoked attack while at work. Finding his employer vicariously liable for his attack, Lord Toulson was 'not persuaded that there is anything wrong with the ***Lister*** approach as such. It has been affirmed many times and I do not see that the law would now be improved by a change of vocabulary' (at [46]). The court therefore had to consider two matters. First, the nature of the employee's job, that is the 'functions or "field of activities" [that] have been entrusted by the employer to the employee' (at [44]) and, secondly, 'whether there was sufficient connection between the position in which he was employed and his wrongful conduct to make it right for the employer to be held liable under the principle of social justice' (at [45]). He concluded:

> In the present case it was Mr Khan's [the employee's] job to attend to customers and to respond to their inquiries. His conduct in answering the claimant's request in a foul mouthed way and ordering him to leave was inexcusable but within the 'field of activities' assigned to him. What happened thereafter was an unbroken sequence of events. It was argued by the respondent and accepted by the [trial] judge that there ceased to be any significant connection between Mr Khan's employment and his behaviour towards the claimant when he came out from behind the counter and followed the claimant onto the forecourt. I disagree for two reasons. First, I do not consider that it is right to regard him as having metaphorically taken off his uniform the moment he stepped from behind the counter. He was following up on what he had said to the claimant. It was a seamless episode. Secondly, when Mr Khan followed the claimant back to his car and opened the front passenger door, he again told the claimant in threatening words that he was never to come back to the petrol station. This was not something personal between them; it was an order to keep away from his employer's premises, which he reinforced by violence. In giving such an order he was purporting to act about his employer's business. It was a gross abuse of his position, but it was in connection with the business in which he was employed to serve customers. His employers entrusted him with that position and it is just that as between them and the claimant, they should be held responsible for their employee's abuse of it. Mr Khan's motive is irrelevant. It looks obvious that he was motivated by personal racism rather than a desire to benefit his employer's business, but that is neither here nor there. (at [47]–[48]).

in the police van which he had borrowed to help his girlfriend move flat—with *N* v *Chief Constable of Merseyside Police* [2006], in which a police officer who wore his police uniform to go 'on the prowl' for vulnerable young women, who he later raped and indecently assaulted, was held not to be acting in the course of his employment.

26. This case was heard alongside *Cox* v *Ministry of Justice*. As Lord Reed explains: 'The judgments are separate because the claims and issues are separate, but they are intended to be complementary to each other in their legal analysis' (at [1]).

Lord Toulson's reference to Mr Khan's actions as 'an unbroken sequence of events' has now been glossed and qualified by the Supreme Court in *WM Morrison Supermarkets plc* v *Various Claimants* [2020]. There, Skelton, a disgruntled Morrison's employee, had been entrusted with payroll data which he was to submit to Morrison's auditor. He did this, but also made a copy of the data which he then made publicly available on a file-sharing website, in breach of s 4(4) of the Data Protection Act 1998. While Skelton's leak of the data could be said to have been the culmination of a sequence of events starting with his receiving this data in his capacity as a Morrison's employee, the court considered that his torts were nonetheless not committed in the course of that employment. The key question, adopting a test first set out by Lord Nicholls in *Dubai Aluminium Co Ltd* v *Salaam* [2003], was whether Skelton's disclosure of the date 'was so closely connected with acts he was authorised to do that, for the purposes of the liability of his employer to third parties, [it] may fairly and properly be regarded as done by him while acting in the ordinary course of his employment' (at [32]). In answering this question, and contrary to the suggestion of Lord Toulson, the tortfeasor's motives—in the sense of whether he was doing his employer's business or acting for his own personal reasons—was an important consideration.

Pause for reflection

As *Morrison* v *Various Claimants* makes clear, however, the fact than an employee is engaged in intentional wrongdoing will not necessarily mean they are acting outside the course of their employment.

> It is no answer to say that the employee was guilty of intentional wrongdoing, or that his act was not merely tortious but criminal, or that he was acting exclusively for his own benefit, or that he was acting contrary to express instructions, or that his conduct was the very negation of his employer's duty. (Lord Millett, ***Lister*** at [79])

An employer may instruct their employee to take reasonable care or not to do a specific intentional act, but if the employee nonetheless goes on to do the very thing they have been told not to do (and this amounts to a tort), the employer cannot rely on the argument that, far from doing their job, the employee was doing the very thing they had been instructed not to do. In *Rose* v *Plenty* [1976], for example, despite strict instructions to the contrary, a milkman allowed a boy to help him deliver the milk and to accompany him on his rounds. The milkman's employer was held vicariously liable for injuries the boy suffered when he fell from the milk float as a result of the milkman's negligent driving. More recently in *Wendall* v *Barchester Healthcare Ltd* [2012] and *Wallbank* v *Wallbank Fox Designs Ltd* [2012] the employer was held vicariously liable for an employee's unprovoked, very violent—and criminal—reaction to a colleague's perfectly reasonable query as to whether he might work an extra shift.[27]

Do you think this is fair on employers? While it would clearly defeat the purpose of vicarious liability if the fact that conduct was prohibited by the employer meant that the employee's action would automatically fall outside the course of their employment—few employers explicitly authorise the commission of torts by their employees, in fact most do quite the opposite—if an employer has done all they could reasonably be expected to do, is making them vicariously liable for their employee's (prohibited) actions justified?

27. He was subsequently sentenced to 15 months' imprisonment.

Counterpoint

It has been suggested that cases such as ***Lister*** and ***Christian Brothers*** would be better dealt with through the imposition of a non-delegable duty of care on the defendant.[28] This has the advantage of recognising the particular social need—that is, increasing the protection of vulnerable parties in institutional care—without getting distracted by the various policy rationales of vicarious liability. However, as Giliker notes, existing precedent imposing vicarious liability for intentional torts and a reluctance to extend existing non-delegable duties mean that such a development is unlikely (2009, p 44).

> The real obstacle in this context, however, is in fact the *nature* of liability sought to be imposed . . . the non-delegable duty proposed would be to ensure that no harm is suffered by a victim due to the negligent or intentional actions of the person to whom the duty is delegated . . . It is one thing for an employer to accept responsibility for its employees' . . . negligent failure to operate a safe system of work, but quite another to take responsibility for deliberate and criminal actions in the workplace. (2009, p 46)

20.5 **Conclusion**

An employer will be vicariously liable for the actions of their employee or, to use *Weir*'s description, a 'helper' that is a representative of the enterprise where the harm is caused (p 105) where there is an employer–employee relationship, or a relationship 'akin' to employment, and the employee has committed a tort in the course of their employment. The doctrine of vicarious liability imposes liability on the employer *without fault* on the part of the employer and as such requires adequate justification. This can be found not only in the employer's deep pockets and their ability to spread the loss through, for example, liability insurance or higher prices but also in their role in the creation of the risk of injury.

End-of-chapter questions

After reading the chapter carefully, try answering the questions which follow.

1 In what circumstances will an employer be liable for the actions of an employee? How far, if at all, should this extend to cover things that the employee has been expressly forbidden by the employer to do?

2 How, if at all, can the imposition of vicarious liability on a blameless employer be justified?

If you would like to know what we think visit the **online resources**. www.oup.com/he/horsey7e

28. See e.g. Paula Giliker 'Making the Right Connection: Vicarious Liability and Institutional Responsibility' (2009) 17 Torts LJ 35, 42–8; Stevens 2007 and John Murphy 'Juridical Foundations of Common Law Non-Delegable Duties' in Jason Neyers, Erika Chamberlain and Stephen Pitel (eds) *Emerging Issues in Tort Law* (Hart, 2007).

Answering the problem question

Consider again the problem question at the start of this chapter. Now having read about the topic, **what would be your advice to the various parties?**

Here are some pointers to get you started in thinking about how to answer this question

- In order for Mario to be liable for Dillon's actions you should establish that he is an employee (you are told his), that he has committed a tort (hitting Bert over the head is a battery) and this is in the course of his employment. This latter aspect is the most controversial but is likely—on recent case law—to be established.
- In contrast, the claim in respect of Cadbury Blacker's actions will turn on whether she is a) an employee or in a relationship akin to employment and whether she has committed a tort (i.e. has she been negligent in failing to tape the lead down).

If you need more guidance

- An **annotated version of the problem with issues and cases to consider** can be found in the Appendix.

see online resources

- A **suggested outline answer** to check your ideas against can be found in the online resources that accompany the book.

Further reading

The best place to start your further reading is with Paula Giliker's 2013 article which considers the decision in the *Christian Brothers* case.

Giliker, Paula 'Vicarious Liability "On the Move": The English Supreme Court and Enterprise Liability' (2013) 4 JETL 306 and follow-up blog 'Vicarious Liability in the Supreme Court: Can we finally say it is no longer on the move?' University of Bristol Law School blog, 7 April 2020

Giliker, Paula 'Analysing Institutional Liability for Child Sexual Abuse in England and Wales and Australia: Vicarious Liability, Non-Delegable Duties and Statutory Intervention' [2018] CLJ 506

McIvor, Claire 'The Use and Abuse of the Doctrine of Vicarious Liability' (2006) 35 CLWR 268

McKendrick, Ewan 'Vicarious Liability and Independent Contractors—A Re-Examination' (1990) 53 MLR 770

Morgan, Phillip 'Vicarious Liability on the Move' (2013) 129 LQR 139

Morgan, Phillip 'Certainty in Vicarious Liability: A Quest for a Chimaera?' [2016] CLJ 202

Nolan, Donal 'Reining in Vicarious Liability' [2020] Industrial LJ 609

Stevens, Robert 'Non-Delegable Duties and Vicarious Liability' in Jason Neyers, Erika Chamberlain and Stephen Pitel (eds) *Emerging Issues in Tort Law* (Hart, 2007)

Williams, Glanville 'Liability for Independent Contractors' [1956] CLJ 180

Damages for death and personal injuries

21

Problem question

Read this problem question carefully, and keep it in mind while you are working through the chapter that follows. At the end of the chapter, you will be asked to apply what you have learnt to the problem question and advise the relevant parties.

Emma is a 45-year-old London-based consultant paediatrician. Because of her increasingly high profile and the fact that she is held in high respect by her peers, she has in recent years also fronted a number of popular television series that delve into various aspects of children's medicine. In the last year alone, she was paid over £50,000 for this. She also does a lot of work, including fundraising, for various children's charities: last year she was sponsored to cycle the Great Wall of China and raised over £15,000. She enjoys time with her two teenage children (she is divorced from their father) and in particular loves weekends away with them sailing or waterskiing, although also enjoys sharing more simple activities with them, such as taking their dog for long walks in the park. She is an avid cook and attends a cookery class every Thursday evening, followed by a meal out with her friends.

Emma is seriously injured in a multiple car accident, for which she was in no way to blame. She is rendered paraplegic, confined to a wheelchair and suffers constant pain. She has to give up her job, but continues to try and do some of the voluntary work for the charities she is involved with. She, along with her two children, has to move out of her three-storey house in north London and into a specially adapted ground-floor flat. Her boyfriend, Clive, who has a career in advertising, agrees to move in with her and be her carer; he gives up his job. She loses interest in sex and is unable to carry on with the majority of her leisure pursuits.

It is established that a combination of two other drivers' negligence caused the accident in which Emma was injured.

Advise Emma.

21.1 Introduction

Consider the following examples:

- ***A pedestrian is knocked down and killed by a speeding motorist.***
- ***An office worker suffers psychiatric injury after being subjected to a campaign of transphobic bullying by her supervisor.***
- ***A runner trips over a loose paving slab on her morning run, breaking her ankle.***
- ***A school fails to diagnose a student's dyslexia, believing the student's poor performance is simply down to laziness. The student fails their GCSEs.***
- ***A house burns down as a result of an explosion at a nearby oil refinery.***
- ***A prisoner is kept in their cell for over 24 hours after prison guards walk out on an unofficial strike.***
- ***A group of ramblers take a shortcut over a field without the farmer's permission.***
- ***A student collapses unconscious after an evening of heavy drinking. His housemates lock him in the bathroom overnight while he sobers up.***
- ***A first-time buyer buys a house on the basis of an inaccurate survey. As a result the property is worth significantly less than they paid for it.***
- ***A professional footballer wants to prevent a national newspaper publishing allegations about his private life.***
- ***The lead singer of a Smiths tribute band is branded as a 'meat-eating wannabe who can't hold a note' on their former management's website.***

As we explained in the introduction to this book, one of the primary functions of the tort system is to provide compensation for those 'wronged' by someone else. Despite the majority of tort textbooks (including this one) focusing more on the principles of *establishing liability*, suing in tort is central to its operation, rather than secondary, as in contract law. This is often expressed by saying that in tort, the wrongs come first, and these define the right; whereas in contract, the rights come first and define the wrong.[1] In all the situations just outlined (many of which are based on cases you may now have come across) a legal wrong, for which the law provides a remedy, may have occurred. Damages (monetary compensation) are the primary remedy available in the tort of negligence, but the same is true of, for example, trespass (to land and to the person), defamation and claims against manufacturers for defective products.[2] Other torts attract damages less often, due to the nature of the harm(s) involved. In privacy claims, for example, claimants

1. i.e. it is the contract that one enters into that defines one's rights in contract law and a wrong can occur only if those rights are breached. In tort, there must be a wrong (e.g. negligence) for the right to claim damages to accrue.

2. Other remedies, more appropriate to the particular torts to which they apply, have been discussed in the relevant chapters.

seeking to prevent publication of private information will most likely seek injunctive relief. This is because injunctions, in a sense, come *before* a harm and operate to prevent it from materialising (or at least to its worst potential). However, if private information has *already* been published, the only possible remedy is compensation.[3] Once harm has occurred, it is hard to imagine how it can be 'rectified' other than by the payment of compensation. In all these situations, subject to a tort being established according to the substantive rules set out elsewhere in this book, damages could become payable.

This chapter focuses on damages: who gets them, who pays, how they are calculated and how well the system works. The focus will, in the main, be on negligence claims. We will also return to some of the larger themes and ideas that have permeated previous chapters.

As we have noted, tort texts give far more emphasis to the rules and principles governing the imposition of liability than to those governing damages awards. This is because they tend to concentrate on the substance of the law, rather than its underlying procedural aspects. In a vast number of cases, liability is not contested (therefore there are considerably more cases in the *background* of tort, in addition to those (disputed) claims we have encountered in earlier chapters, and especially where damages were awarded—we represent here only the 'tip of the iceberg'). Damages are the bread and butter of the civil lawyer in practice. As Richard Lewis points out:

> It is extraordinary how much attention is focused upon issues of liability as opposed to the quantum of damages. Practitioners are bemused by the pre-occupation of academics with the rules on fault: they are aware that liability is infrequently challenged by insurers—being raised as a preliminary issue in only about 20 per cent of their cases—whereas the amount of compensation is almost always open to some negotiation.[4]

Everything that follows should be considered in this context. A very small proportion of tort claims reach the higher courts and the pages of textbooks.[5] Many claims are settled or dismissed before proceeding to trial.

Much of the problem has been (decreasing) access to justice and the increasing cost of claims, particularly escalating and disproportionate fees.[6] Lord Justice Jackson's extensive review of civil litigation costs, designed to find ways to reduce the cost of

3. *Mosley* v *News Group Newspapers Ltd* [2008], discussed at **section 16.6**, provides a good example, especially when the follow-up actions taken by Mosley are considered—see *Mosley* v *Google* [2015].

4. Richard Lewis 'The Politics and Economics of Tort Law: Judicially Imposed Periodical Payments of Damages' (2006) 69 MLR 418.

5. In its first year (2009), only four tort claims were dealt with by the Supreme Court, compared with a total number of claims made in the same year (for personal injury) in the county court and Queen's Bench Division of the High Court of over 180,000. In the county court, more than half the claims were for less than £5,000 (Ministry of Justice *Annual Judicial and Court Statistics 2009* (published September 2010)).

6. In *Motto and others* v *Trafigura Ltd and another* [2011] the 30,000 claimants received a £30 million settlement but the fees in the case amounted to nearly £105 million (at [26]). The judgment shows that without the success fees and after the event (ATE) premium, the costs would have been only £40 million (at [35]–[36]). See also *MGN Ltd* v *UK* [2011] where the conditional fee arrangement (CFA) used in ***Campbell* v *MGN* [2004]** was found to violate the right to freedom of expression. In *Coventry* v *Lawrence* [2015] the Supreme Court rejected the idea by 5:2 that the CFA and uplift which made the defendants liable for 60 per cent of the costs (about £640,000) was a violation of the defendant's Art 6 rights.

civil litigation (mainly to defendants) while at the same time maintaining access to justice, was published in January 2010.[7] Some of his main recommendations included the abolition of recoverable success fees and after the event (ATE) insurance from the losing side in conditional fee arrangements (CFAs—usually 'no win, no fee'), and permitting damages-based arrangements (DBAs—a contingency fee arrangement previously only available in some employment cases).[8] To assist claimants with the inevitable financial implications of these changes he proposed a 10 per cent increase in general non-pecuniary damages to help towards paying the fees for which they would be liable as well as 'qualified one-way cost shifting' (QOCS).[9] Despite opposition, mainly from claimant groups and ATE insurers,[10] Jackson's proposed reforms were implemented in 2013.[11] Many are contained in the Legal Aid, Sentencing and Punishment of Offenders (LASPO) Act 2012 (Part 2), affecting agreements and insurance policies entered into after the relevant sections of the Act came into force on 1 April 2013.[12] LASPO also made serious cuts to Legal Aid for civil (and other) litigants (Part 1). LASPO, therefore, has serious implications for access to justice, seemingly shifting both power and funding to the benefit of insurers and away from those who are injured. In February 2019, the Ministry of Justice published a (long-awaited) review of the impact of LASPO Part 2,[13] which concluded (unsurprisingly) that the civil justice reforms had achieved their aims (of reducing costs in personal injury litigation and preventing unmeritorious claims).[14]

7. Lord Justice Jackson *Review of Civil Litigation Costs: Final Report* (TSO, 2010).

8. The Damages-Based Agreements Regulations 2013 came into force on 1 April 2013. The Regulations preclude partial or 'hybrid' damages-based agreements (DBAs) (under which lawyers can be paid at a reduced rate as the case proceeds—payable win or lose—plus a (lower) contingency fee in the event of success). In other words, lawyers agreeing to act under a DBA must do so as a full 'no win, no fee' agreement (receiving no fee if the client recovers no damages).

9. Ministry of Justice *Proposals for reform of civil litigation funding and costs in England and Wales* Consultation Paper CP 13/10 (November 2010): 'QOCS would offer costs protection to the vast majority of personal injury claimants, with their only having to pay a winning defendant's costs where it is reasonable to do so based on the claimant's own wealth or their unreasonable behaviour during the case' (at [7]).

10. See Owen Boycott '"No-win, no-fee" brought down News of the World, says hacking victims' lawyer' *The Guardian* 19 July 2011.

11. Not without criticism (John Hyde 'Jackson reforms a "serious risk" to justice, says Law Society' *Law Society Gazette* 13 March 2014).

12. In *Simmons* v *Castle* [2012] the Court of Appeal ruled that general damages in civil cases (including breach of contract) would rise by 10 per cent for all judgments handed down after 1 April 2013 where the case involves either pain, suffering and loss of amenity in respect of personal injury, nuisance, defamation or 'any other tort that causes suffering, inconvenience or distress to individuals'. The court felt compelled to enact this particular aspect of the Jackson reforms ahead of the 1 April 2013 implementation date so parties could plan their litigation strategies accordingly.

13. Ministry of Justice 'Post-Implementation Review of Part 2 of LASPO' 7 February 2019. A review of LASPO Part 1 (on Legal Aid) was published on the same day, with less acclaim, and some proposals for ways to 'fill the gaps in access to justice' the cuts to Legal Aid created.

14. This conclusion was not accepted uncritically—see John Hyde 'LASPO Part 2: MoJ content that civil reforms have driven down costs' *Law Society Gazette* 7 February 2019.

21.2 What are damages for?

While the primary focus of damages is compensatory, other types of damages exist; though these are very limited in scope. These 'non-compensatory damages' include:

- *exemplary damages*—a higher than usual sum must be paid, in part as a 'punishment' or to set an example to other potential defendants when there has been 'outrageous' conduct;[15]
- *aggravated damages*—a higher sum than is usual is awarded to a particular claimant in recognition of the fact that they have suffered to a greater degree than would be expected, as a result of the defendant's actions;[16]
- *contemptuous damages*—a claimant receives a lesser sum than might be usual, in recognition that a legal wrong has been committed, but showing the court's displeasure that such a claim was brought;[17] and
- *nominal damages*—a legal wrong has been committed but no actual (recognised) loss has been suffered by the claimant.[18]

Many of these link directly back to some of the other functions of tort—deterrence, retribution and so on.[19]

Making a defendant pay (compensatory) damages is often about more than simply compensating the claimant for the wrong that was done to them. The fear of having to pay damages may influence behaviour and in this sense may have a deterrent effect.[20]

15. The justifications for exemplary damages were classically stated by Lord Devlin in *Rookes* v *Barnard* [1964]. They are rare and limited to certain categories of case—for an example in the context of false imprisonment, see *Muuse* v *Secretary of State for the Home Department* [2010] at [71]–[77], and for an impressive lower court judgment concerning deliberate damage to a prisoner's personal property, see *Thakrar* v *Secretary of State for Justice* [2015]. Lord Justice Leveson's *Report into the Culture, Practices and Ethics of the Press* (see **section 16.3**) suggested that exemplary damages might become more commonplace for media invasions of privacy, and this was introduced by the Crime and Courts Act 2013, s 34. Recent consideration has been given to exemplary damages in the context of a psychiatric harm claim in relation to witnessing the Omagh bombing, with the conclusion being that extending the situations in which they might be provided is for 'Parliament or the higher courts, and probably the Supreme Court' (*Young* v *Downey* [2020] at [38]).

16. See e.g. *Johnson* v *Steele and others* [2014]; *Richard* v *BBC and another* [2018].

17. See ***Grobbelaar* v *News Group Newspapers Ltd* [2002]**. The claimant may also have costs awarded against them, so although they technically 'win', they may be worse off.

18. See *Walker* v *The Commissioner of the Police of the Metropolis* [2014]. For an interesting case, leading to a split nine-member Supreme Court, see ***R (on the application of Lumba)* v *Secretary of State for the Home Department* [2011]** discussed at **section 15.4.3**. Exemplary damages were refused despite the behaviour of the officials involved. 'Vindicatory' damages were preferred by three of the nine Justices hearing the appeal, though the six majority judges ruled that no such head of damages exists.

19. Of interest here is also the notion of the 'conventional award' (set at £15,000), created in *Rees* v *Darlington Memorial Hospital NHS Trust* [2003], supposedly for lost autonomy and which is now available in all cases where the birth of a healthy but unwanted child occurs as a result of negligence (see **section 7.5.2**).

20. On this point, consider Joanne Conaghan's contention that allowing liability in negligence cases against the police (and other public authorities) might result in 'change[d] institutional behaviour', Joanne Conaghan, 'Civil liability: addressing failures in the context of rape, domestic and sexual abuse' Inaugural Lecture, University of Bristol, 19 February 2015. The full lecture is available to view at **www.youtube.com/watch?v=y1bawCpPr30&app=desktop**.

For example, once one employer pays compensation for having poor safety conditions in the workplace, it can only be hoped that other (similar) employers will take note and alter their safety conditions in a manner that both protects their employees from suffering harm and avoids the necessity for them to have to pay compensation in the future. The idea is that people learn from their mistakes, and the mistakes of others.

In another sense, compensatory damages can operate as a type of retribution. Whatever the size of the award, successful claimants are more likely to feel vindicated—that the law was on their side—than those who receive nothing. Put another way, when someone is to blame for the harm you suffered, it is quite natural to want to 'make them pay'. Similarly, compensation payments may be seen as an acknowledgement of the wrong that was done—or even as an apology for it.

Counterpoint

Though it can be said that tort claims are brought for a variety of (often intertwining) reasons,[21] for most people, in most claims, monetary compensation is probably the ultimate aim. The reasons for this can be seen to stem from as far back as the Industrial Revolution, which inevitably increased the number of serious accidents suffered, particularly in the workplace. Similarly, the introduction of motorised transport clearly had an effect on the number (and type) of injuries people sustain. These things (among others) led, over time, to the gradual emergence of claims for damages for personal injury as the 'dominant' tort action.[22] The problem with this is that it leads to a perception of tort as being *purely* a vehicle for accident compensation, when that is not its sole function, nor the reason it was created. Primarily, tort was a system for righting wrongs (corrective justice), coupled with the notion of individual responsibility, in that people (wrongdoers) were held responsible for their harmful actions. If tort *is* (realistically?) primarily a mechanism for accident compensation (more akin to distributive justice), then it will inevitably be compared with other forms of accident compensation and, when this happens, we see that tort performs incredibly badly. If the aim is to achieve compensation for as many people as deserve it, then the tort accident compensation system has a surprising number of flaws—which largely stem from the fact that the system is based on fault, blame and culpability.

Many questions are raised by having a tort system that is both fault-based and centred around compensation. This becomes particularly apparent when we look at who actually pays the majority of compensation that is awarded (insurers, employers, etc) and how the costs of this are then spread among other ('innocent') members of society. Moreover, there may be perhaps other, *better* ways of ensuring that those who *need* money (e.g. to pay healthcare costs, or because they are unable to live the way they did before they were harmed) actually receive it and not merely those few who are able to find someone to (legally) blame for the harms they suffered. One problem with the tort system being based on *fault* is that other justifications for compensation are largely overlooked.

→

21. See **Chapter 1**.

22. Remember that negligence—the primary vehicle for personal injury claims—did not really 'emerge' until 1932.

→

Furthermore, in most cases, the *degree* of fault is not considered—a worse act of negligence, for example, does not lead to a higher damages award. In essence, there is a fixed sum given for a particular harm, or at least fixed parameters for calculating it, as long as it can be shown (in negligence at least) that this is someone else's fault (see further **section 21.3**).

The realities of what the tort system is about are often lost when trawling through textbooks, cases, actuarial tables (see **section 21.3.1**) and so on. Cases are brought on the basis of injury, loss and disability, but these aspects are sanitised from the version we, as lawyers, see—we deal in legal principles, costs and awards, rather than stepping back and remembering who it is we are talking about, the injuries they have suffered and the disabilities (physical and societal) that they face.

Pause for reflection

Should it be the purpose of tort law to do anything *other* than attempt to compensate victims of harm? Is punishment or retribution more suited to the mechanisms of public or criminal law than private law suits taken by individuals? Does making a defendant pay damages work as a deterrent from committing further wrongs? Consider the fact that many 'torts' committed (especially within negligence) are *accidental*—how can you deter someone from having another accident in the future? Should we punish someone because they did?

From another perspective, even 'simple' accidents, such as those caused by a momentary lapse of concentration while driving, may be deterred by making the 'wrongdoer' pay compensation—the driver may be more likely to be more careful in future. But is this really what happens? Who actually pays in these situations (see e.g. the comments of Lord Denning in *Nettleship* v *Weston* [1971])?

Compensatory damages in tort are designed, as far as money can do so, to provide *restitutio in integrum*,[23] defined as:

> the sum of money which will put the party who has been injured, or who has suffered, in the same position he would have been in if he had not sustained the wrong for which he is now getting compensation or reparation. (Lord Blackburn, *Livingstone* v *Raywards Coal Co* [1880] at 39)

Tort damages are meant to return the claimant (as far as money can) to their pre-tort position: the position they were in before injury occurred. This may include both general and special damages (see **section 21.3.2**) covering pecuniary (financial) and non-pecuniary (emotional, social, amenity and so on) losses.

This principle contrasts with the way damages are awarded for breaches of contract, where the aim is to put the claimant into the position they *expected to be in* if the contract

23. Literally, from Latin, restoration to the original position.

was perfectly executed. While it is usually relatively easy to envision this (e.g. a contract may have been entered into with expected profits already calculated), it is often quite difficult to imagine what money compensates for in tort. Say, for example, a pedestrian was hit by a negligent driver and rendered permanently paraplegic. How does money compensate for the loss of the ability to walk, run or dance? How can damages put that person back to the position they were in before the tort occurred? Furthermore, if the same claimant also suffered depression as a result of their injuries, how should this be compensated? These are the primary difficulties we face when looking at damages in tort—the calculation does not work according to how *deserving* someone is or even necessarily according to their *need*, but is based purely on what economic worth is put on a particular harm.

Pause for reflection

Now that you have looked in more detail at the law(s) of tort(s) and, with an awareness that the financial implications are not comparable:

(1) Rank, on a scale of 1–10 (10 high), how deserving of compensation are those who suffer the following harms *due to the wrong of another*:
   (a) A broken leg.
   (b) A mental breakdown resulting from stress.
   (c) Trauma after witnessing the death of a child in an accident.
   (d) The burning down of a home.
   (e) The loss of life savings.
   (f) The publication of intimate details in a national newspaper.
   (g) The birth of a child following a failed sterilisation.
   (h) Failure to recognise a child's special educational needs.
   (i) Disturbance by constant noise from a nearby factory.

(2) How much do you think each claimant should be awarded for the harms listed?

see online resources

Take time to consider why you ranked the harms the way you did, and why you awarded more money to some claimants than others—what do the monetary sums reflect?

The question of damages is subject to all the substantive rules that we have discussed in the earlier sections of this book and which *limit liability* and, consequently, the *availability* of compensation. A claimant in negligence, for example, must still overcome the technical hurdles: establishing a duty of care, breach of that duty and harm caused by that breach which is not too remote a consequence—and we should remember that these 'hurdles' are judicially created obstacles placed *in the way of* recovery. Exclusionary rules on duty, for example, are clearly devices used to *control and limit* liability and keep it within what the courts insubstantially define as 'reasonable bounds'—claimants who are seriously harmed by clearly negligent actions on the part of a public body, for example, will find it hard to establish that a duty was owed to them.[24] Similarly, where the harm

24. See **Chapter 6**.

suffered is 'purely' economic, or psychiatric, or was caused by an omission or the actions of a third party, a claimant unable to establish that a duty was owed will not recover damages for their injury *no matter how serious it is* and *however clearly negligent the defendant was*.[25] Additional problems, as we have seen, come with establishing breach and causation in fact and law, and even then the defendant may have a defence. Thus, from the outset, it should be clear that not all those who *deserve* compensation can receive it.

21.3 **Calculating damages**

21.3.1 **Forms of damages payments**

Damages in tort have traditionally been awarded on a 'one-shot, lump sum' basis. This means that the court assesses, at the date of trial, the amount of compensation required by the claimant to meet their needs, considering investment returns, for the rest of their life. Such an award is final.[26] Understandably, despite the attraction of a 'clean break' between claimant and defendant, this method attracted much criticism, even the judiciary noting that 'there is really only one certainty: the future will prove the award to be either too high or too low' (Lord Scarman, *Lim Poh Choo* v *Camden & Islington Area Health Authority* [1980] at 183).

As explained earlier, damages in tort represent restoring the claimant, as far as money can, to their pre-tort position. This means that if, for example, someone becomes unable to work as a result of physical injuries caused by someone else's negligence, their compensation will include a sum that reflects *what they would have earned* had they not been injured.[27] Similarly, where costs are incurred by the claimant *as a result of the injury*, compensation will include these as, without the tort occurring, money would not have been spent in that way.

Lump sum damages are calculated using 'multiplicands' and 'multipliers'.[28] A multiplicand is the sum that must be multiplied (e.g. a sum of £20,000 lost earnings per year) and the multiplier is the number of years this must be multiplied by. Various multipliers may be applied to different multiplicands—for example, a person would only be expected to *work* until retirement, so this will help determine how many years any lost earnings should be multiplied by, but they would be expected to *live* longer than this, so medical costs incurred for the rest of someone's life would have a greater multiplier than their lost earnings. That said, the calculations are not as simple as it might seem—working out the multiplier requires more than simply an assessment of how much

25. See **Chapters 4**, **5** and **7**.

26. Awards were traditionally based on a high rate of return—4.5 per cent. It has latterly been realised that this is not realistic and changes have been made with the aim of protecting claimants against lower rates of return. How this has been done, and the effectiveness of such changes, is beyond the scope of this chapter.

27. For an extreme example, consider *Collett* v *Smith* [2009]. In this case, an 18-year-old reserve player for Manchester United was injured by a negligent tackle and was awarded £4,577,323—£3,854,328 of this for future lost earnings.

28. 'Multiplicands' obviously still have a place in periodic payments (see later in this section)—it is the *method* of paying them that differs.

longer a person had to work until retirement. There is no longer a default retirement age (previously 65)—when retirement is expected to occur might depend on a number of different factors. Even if there was a default age, the salary multiplier for a 40-year-old would not be as much as 25 years when there is a lump sum payment. Reduced multipliers are used for two main reasons: first, when lump sum payments are made, the fact that this sum can be invested means that to award the full number of years could *overcompensate* someone. Secondly, the court considers the 'vicissitudes of life'—the fact that illness, disease or other circumstances might anyway have prevented that person working until retirement age.

Multipliers are calculated by reference to an annual assumed interest rate after tax and inflation, known as the 'discount rate'.[29] For a 45-year-old woman expected to retire at 67 the multiplier is approximately 20 years, based on a –0.25 per cent discount rate. The figures are not plucked from thin air: the courts look at complicated actuarial tables (compiled by a group including actuaries, lawyers and insurers), known as the 'Ogden Tables' to help them.[30] The use of these tables in assessing damages claims was formally approved by the House of Lords in *Wells* v *Wells* [1999]. Different tables exist depending on at what age retirement was expected, when a pension would have started to pay out and a person's life expectancy. The tables are different for males and females (to take into account differences in expected mortality, among other things).[31]

In terms of particular injuries, guidelines issued by the Judicial College detail a range of 'prices', according to a tariff, that may be attached to various injuries when a judge calculates damages. For example, for the complete loss of sight in one eye, awards are currently in the range of £46,240–51,460. For tetraplegia (also known as quadriplegia) it would be £304,630–379,100. For 'severe' post-traumatic stress disorder it is £56,180–94,470, and for 'moderate' knee injuries £13,920–24,580. More 'prices' from the judicial guidelines are shown in **Figure 21.1**.[32]

29. At the time of writing, the applicable discount rate is –0.25% in England and Wales.

30. Currently the 8th edition (2020). The tables can be viewed on the Government Actuarial Department website at **www.gov.uk/government/publications/ogden-tables-actuarial-compensation-tables-for-injury-and-death**. They are updated to take into account factors such as changes in mortality rates, the current financial situation and the effect of various decided cases. In some cases, judges have highlighted the need not to adhere too rigidly to the tables: see e.g. *Kennedy* v *London Ambulance Service NHS Trust* [2016]. That said, in *Cadet's Car Rentals* v *Pinder* [2019], the Privy Council clarified how to use the Ogden Tables in calculating future loss of earnings, stating that a two-stage approach must be adopted. First, work out what the pre-accident income would have been going forward and then work out what the residual earning capacity is going forward, deducting this from the first number.

31. Note that though the tables are used in most cases, there are some situations which render them inappropriate, e.g. for some freelance/periodic work patterns: see *Blamire* v *South Cumbria Health Authority* [1993]; *Ward* v *Allies & Morrison Architects* [2012].

32. Figures are taken from the Judicial College *Guidelines for the Assessment of General Damages in Personal Injury Cases* (15th edn, OUP, 2019). The figures here take into account the effect of the Court of Appeal decision in *Simmons* v *Castle* [2012] (at [20]), introduced by LASPO (see **section 21.1**). Alternative figures without the 10 per cent uplift are also given in the *Guidelines*, for injuries suffered before the uplift came into force on 1 April 2013.

FIGURE 21.1 Judicial guidelines for damages in personal injury cases

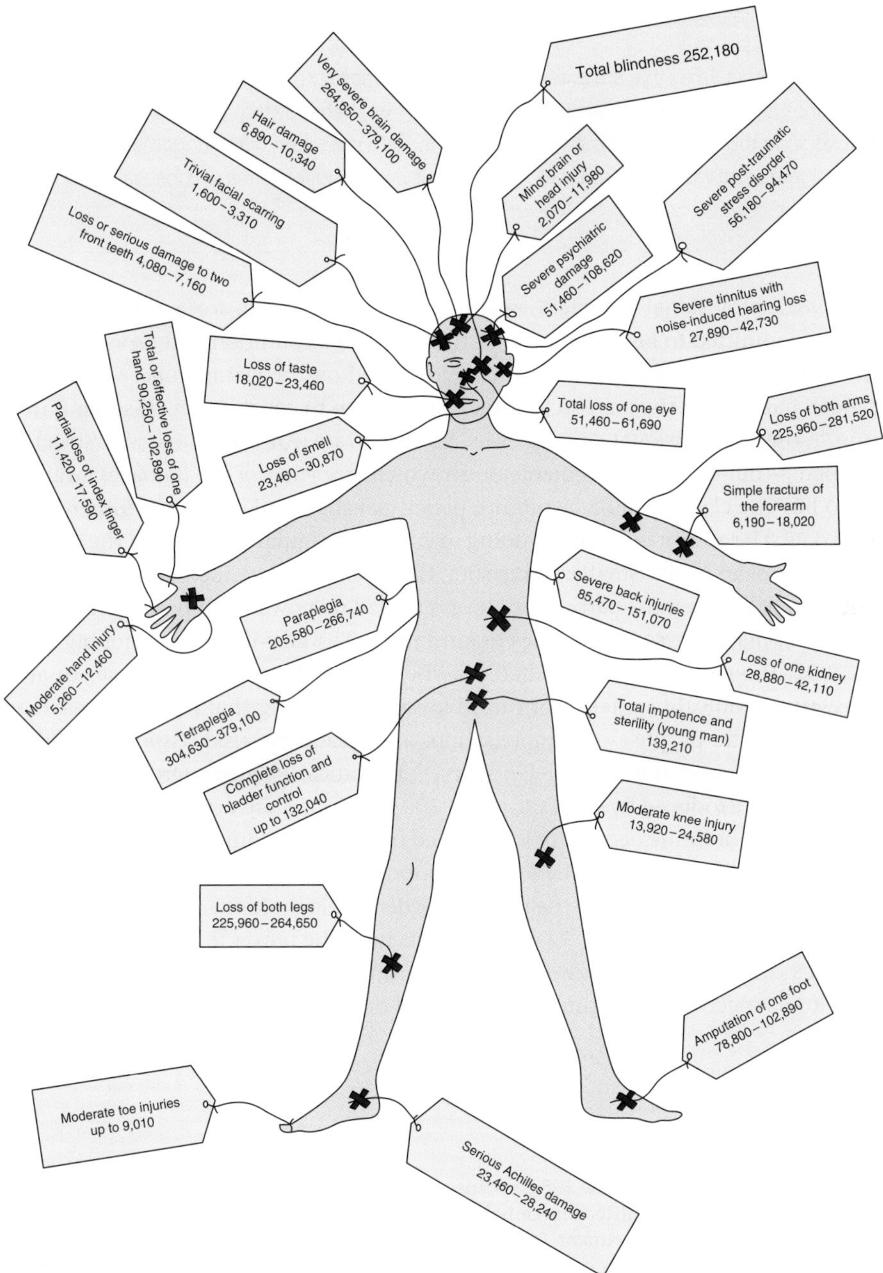

Source: Artwork © David Eaton/Oxford University Press; statistics reproduced with kind permission of Oxford University Press and the Judicial College (*Guidelines for the Assessment of General Damages in Personal Injury Cases* (15th edn, 2019)).

Pause for reflection

Do you find the awards that are available for various injuries surprising (remember that these will be injuries caused by someone else's negligence)? Are there any that you think are quite high, in relation to the injury itself or, conversely, any that do not seem high enough? Who decides these figures and what are they based on? Should we consider injuries and losses in monetary terms?

Since 1982, 'provisional' damages awards have been allowed, for actions where it is 'proved or admitted to be a chance' that the claimant's condition will seriously worsen in the future.[33] Damages awarded initially are based on the claimant *not* suffering this extended harm, with the proviso that they may return to court if they *do* suffer it in the future.[34] Use of provisional damages was, however, rare. An alternative was 'structured settlement'—out-of-court agreements under which a portion of the damages award was used to buy the claimant a life assurance policy, payable until death or another (earlier) agreed date. The advantage was that doing so ensured a regular 'income' for the claimant, often on top of an initial (smaller) lump sum. However, structured settlements were based on agreement between the parties and the courts had no power to impose them, however sensible this may have seemed in the circumstances. The take-up rate was not high.

In 2002, the government consulted on whether to give courts the power to award *compulsory* periodical payments for future losses, concluding that periodical payments 'better reflect the purpose of compensation' and 'place the risks associated with life expectancy and investment on defendants'.[35] Periodical Payment Orders (PPOs) were subsequently introduced by the Courts Act 2003.[36] Courts are now *required* to consider PPOs in respect of future pecuniary loss derived from personal injury, and may order that damages wholly or partly take the form of periodical payments based on the claimant's annual future needs,[37] without the need for Ogden Table multipliers or discounts taking into account future life events.[38] Further, courts have the power to vary PPOs where the claimant's condition seriously worsens—or considerably improves—at a later date, but only if it was specified at the time of the original order that it was to be variable.[39] PPOs

33. Administration of Justice Act 1982, s 6, inserting s 32A into the Senior Courts Act 1981.

34. Only *one* return is permitted and only for the injury/disease specified in the original claim.

35. Lord Chancellor's Department *Damages for Future Loss: Giving the Courts the Power to Order Periodical Payments for Future Loss and Care Costs in Personal Injury Cases* (March 2002), [22].

36. Amending s 2 of the Damages Act 1996 (in force April 2005).

37. Whether this is what the claimant wishes or not: *Thompstone* v *Tameside & Glossop Acute Services NHS Trust* [2008] (see e.g. Waller LJ at [108]).

38. For a concise explanation of how damages can be calculated in these awards, see Richard Lewis 'The Indexation of Periodical Payments of Damages in Tort: The Future Assured?' (2010) 30 LS 391, especially 395–6.

39. Damages (Variation of Periodical Payments) Order 2005, SI 2005/841.

are not without their critics and some commentators have indicated that even where PPOs would be more appropriate lump sums will still be preferred by many claimants.[40]

21.3.2 Special and general damages

Special damages are awarded for costs that are quantifiable at the time of trial, such as the loss of earnings or pension *already suffered* by the claimant or money *already spent* on care, medical treatments, special equipment (e.g. a wheelchair), transport and household costs (including adaptations), plus interest accrued on these sums. Essentially, these are pecuniary (financial) losses only.

General damages are those that cannot be quantified at the time of trial and are designed to compensate a claimant for the losses they suffer more generally arising from the harm they have incurred as a result of a tort being committed. These are often more problematic, and include *future* pecuniary losses such as (inter alia) loss of net future earnings and future medical, care and social costs, as well as future expenditure, such as any specialist equipment that might be needed, transport and household costs (including adaptations). Importantly, general damages can also include sums for non-pecuniary losses, such as pain, suffering and lost amenity (PSLA) incurred as the result of injury.[41]

The cost of future care is recoverable, as long as it is necessary or reasonably incurred. It is not necessary for a carer to be a professional. If a partner or close relative, for example, gives up work to care for an injured person, the law provides that they should be paid for doing so. In *Hunt* v *Severs* [1994], a woman injured in a motorcycle accident required long-term care. The claimant later married the defendant motorcyclist, and he became her carer. The House of Lords held that the claimant could claim the cost of a carer from the defendant and that this part of her damages award would be held in trust for the carer. Because of the specific situation in this case, however, the damages were not paid as their lordships found that public policy did not justify the payment of a damages award by the defendant simply for them to be given back to him. However, it should be noted that it would not have been the *defendant* who paid but his insurers, therefore the decision seems somewhat strange. Following *Hunt*, it would seem that claimants will be left worse off if the person who cares for them is also the defendant. Where this is not the case, a full sum for the cost of (past and future) care can be awarded.[42]

40. See e.g. Lewis (**n 4**) and Lewis (**n 38**) 406–7.

41. Not without controversy, particularly when the claimant's condition is such that they will not know they have lost amenity (*Lim Poh Choo* v *Camden and Islington Area Health Authority* [1980]).

42. The Law Commission recommended in 1999 that this position (in respect of past but not future care costs) be legislatively reversed (Law Com No 262). In May 2007, a government consultation *The Law on Damages* proposed that the law be amended to make the claimant personally obliged to account for the money to the carer and that this should also apply to future care services 'gratuitously provided' (at [115]–[116]). A clause was included in the government's draft Civil Law Reform Bill (2009) to this effect. Following public consultation on the Bill, the government decided not to proceed, as it would 'not contribute to the delivery of the government's priorities' (Ministry of Justice 'Civil Law Reform Bill: Response to Consultation', 10 January 2011).

21.3.3 **Death and damages**

When a claimant dies, any claim that they might have had against a defendant survives them.[43] That is, their estate is able to bring the claim and, if damages become payable, they are paid to the estate (thus can be passed on in inheritance, etc).[44]

Death is also dealt with under the Fatal Accidents Act 1976, which establishes a mechanism whereby dependants of the deceased can make a claim for *their* losses (e.g. the loss of the main income into a household) and for bereavement.[45] Dependants, for the purposes of the Act, include the spouse or civil partner, children (under the age of 18) or parent of the deceased as well as any de facto dependants.[46] Non-married partners are also included, provided that they had lived with the deceased 'as husband or wife' for at least two years prior to their death.[47] This was different for bereavement claims until 2020, but cohabiting partners of the deceased may now also claim bereavement damages.[48] However, it is only possible for a dependant to claim *if the deceased party would have been able to bring a claim had they lived*—that is, a proven tort must have been committed, without a suitable defence being available, and subject to limitation provisions (see **section 21.5**).[49] Dependants can claim all financial losses incurred by them due to the death, such as the proportion of the deceased's earnings that would have been spent on them (ongoing or in the form of savings for the future, and including 'non-essentials' such as annual holidays). They can also claim the 'value' of the 'service' of the deceased—for example, if they were the main childcare provider, the value of the time of childcare could be claimed by the spouse or partner in order that the child was able to attend nursery or similar, meaning that the surviving spouse would not have to give up work, etc. Such losses are either assessed by the multiplier/multiplicand[50] method as before (though clearly involving even more complicated calculations) or by periodical payments.

In *Knauer* v *Ministry of Justice* [2016], a seven-member panel of the Supreme Court held unanimously that the correct date from which to assess the multiplier when assessing

43. Since the Law Reform (Miscellaneous Provisions) Act 1934 (s 1), with the exception of defamation claims and claims for bereavement under the Fatal Accidents Act 1976.

44. Further, the Law Reform (Miscellaneous Provisions) Act 1934, s 1(4), provides that if the defendant dies and there was a time period before the *defendant's* death in which the claimant would have been able to claim damages (if, e.g., they were injured as a result of negligence then the defendant died before the claim came to court), the claim can still be brought against the defendant's estate.

45. Sections 1 and 1A respectively.

46. The full list is given in s 1(3).

47. Section 1(3)(b).

48. The Fatal Accidents Act 1976 (Remedial) Order 2020, SI 2020/1023 added s 1A(2)(aa) into the legislation. The High Court called for this change in 2016—though finding that cohabitees were unable to claim for bereavement did not directly engage Art 8, it said that there was no legal justification for treating them differently: *Smith* v *Lancashire Teaching Hospitals NHS Trust and another* [2016]. The Court of Appeal later found that there were violations of both Arts 8 and 14 and therefore that the bereavement award should be given to anyone who has been in a relationship for at least two years at the point of death (*Smith* v *Lancashire Teaching Hospitals NHS Foundation Trust and others* [2017]).

49. Section 1(1).

50. Which would be the annual value of the dependency, net of deductions.

damages for future loss in claims under the Act should be the date of trial and not the date of death. In doing so, it refused to follow two older House of Lords' decisions (*Cookson* v *Knowles* [1978] and *Graham* v *Dodds* [1983]) which had held the relevant time to be the date of death. The Law Commission had recommended this be changed,[51] as in most cases calculating from the date of death leads to under-compensation and therefore is contrary to the *restitutio in integrum* principle. Lord Neuberger and Lady Hale, in a jointly written judgment, explained that '[c]alculating damages for loss of dependency upon the deceased from the date of death, rather than from the date of trial, means that the claimant is suffering a discount for early receipt of the money when in fact that money will not be received until after trial' (at [7]).

When claiming for bereavement itself, the Act provides for damages of £15,120,[52] a sum meant in some way to compensate for the 'other' (non-pecuniary) losses associated with a person's death. This sum cannot be claimed by children of the deceased, only by a spouse or partner or, if the deceased was a minor, the parents—there are more limitations here than for dependency claims (and if the sum is awarded to two parents, it is divided between them). Therefore, if a 19-year-old child was killed, no compensation for the parents' bereavement would be available and, in the reverse situation, children who lose a parent may receive compensation for pecuniary dependency losses they suffer, but not for non-pecuniary bereavement and grief.

Pause for reflection

Is the death of a loved one (caused by the 'fault' of someone else) adequately compensated by £15,120? How can such an arbitrary line be drawn? Comparing the guidance figures for claimants who suffer personal injury, evidently it is often much cheaper to kill your victim than it is to 'merely' injure them. Because the effects of many injuries last a lifetime, the compensation which can be awarded for them does too. Doesn't the effect of someone's death last a lifetime? Is this properly taken into account by the Fatal Accidents Act?

Patrick Atiyah called bereavement damages 'highly objectionable'.[53] His reasons were twofold. First, the 'motives of relatives in seeking such awards may be questionable' and, more importantly, 'it seems arbitrary to select the death of a close relative as the criterion for paying what is still to many people a substantial sum of money . . . the relatives of a person who is very severely injured (but not killed) in an accident may well suffer much greater mental suffering than the relatives of someone who is killed'. Secondly, he argued that a statutory award fails to take into account the differences in the actual relationships covered—regardless of the

→

51. *Claims for Wrongful Death* (Law Com No 263, 1999).

52. Damages for Bereavement (Variation of Sum) (England and Wales) Order 2020, SI 2020/316. This figure was increased from £12,980 for all deaths before 1 May 2020 (itself an increase from £11,800 in 2013, £10,000 in 2008 and £7,500 in 2002). Note that a different scheme operates in Scotland—one that many think is fairer (see Association of Personal Injury Lawyers 'Damages for bereavement a "postcode lottery" say lawyers' 24 September 2013).

53. Peter Cane *Atiyah's Accidents, Compensation and the Law* (7th edn, CUP, 2006), p 90.

→

actual closeness of the parties or, for example, the state of the deceased party's health. Do you agree? Compare the availability of damages for psychiatric harm suffered through witnessing a negligently caused accident and what has to be proved before one can bring a claim as a secondary victim.[54]

21.4 Independent, joint and several concurrent liabilities

It is, of course, possible that there is more than one wrongdoer in a single tort claim, in that there may be multiple parties whose actions are partly or wholly the cause of the claimant's harm. When this occurs, the law delineates which party or parties can be sued by an individual claimant, by establishing the categories of independent, joint and several and concurrent defendants (see **Table 21.1**).

TABLE 21.1 Multiple defendants: what type of liability?

Description	Example	Type of liability	Who pays what?
Two or more parties cause different harms to the claimant	A car is hit by one negligent driver, causing property damage, then later by another negligent driver, causing injury to the claimant	Independent	Each co-defendant pays for the actual harm they caused (but only one case needs to be brought by the claimant)
Two parties being sued were acting with the same common goal and caused the same damage	An employee commits a tort in the course of employment, for which the employer would be vicariously liable	Joint	Either party (or both) can be sued for the entirety of the damage
The actions of two or more separate defendants happened independently but contributed to the same harm	A claimant suffers whiplash after their car is crashed into by two negligently driven cars at the same time	Several concurrent [55]	Either party (or both) can be sued for the entirety of the damage. Where only one is sued, they can recover an appropriate portion of the damages paid via the Civil Liability (Contribution) Act 1978

54. See **section 5.6**.

55. Note that in both joint and several concurrent liability, where an employer/employee or insurer/insuree are held liable, recovery of some of the costs from the actual wrongdoer (e.g. employee) is technically possible through the principle of 'subrogation'.

Where two or more parties cause different harms to the claimant at different times (although there may be only minutes between them), who pays (and what for) is often a question of causation (i.e. whether the latter defendant broke the chain of causation back to the harm caused by the original defendant). When we say that harms are different in this context, we might mean for example that they are different *types* of harm entirely (e.g. personal injury and property damage) or that they are essentially the same *type* of harm but operate at different *levels* (e.g. the difference between a leg injury suffered in a car accident followed by death after being treated at hospital). Each defendant in such circumstances is potentially liable *independently* of the other. In *Rahman* v *Arearose Ltd* [2000], a man was attacked in his workplace, a fast-food restaurant—his employer was held vicariously liable for the violent attack, which left him needing hospital treatment. In hospital, he received negligent treatment to his right eye, leaving it blinded. He subsequently developed various psychiatric complaints, which his psychiatrist was able to attribute, to various extents, to the initial attack and to his loss of sight.[56] The Court of Appeal apportioned damages respectively between the employer and the health authority—each defendant was clearly negligent and therefore liable to pay some compensation—the question was what proportion of the total each should pay.

However, there are instances where it can be said either that two (or more) parties being sued were acting with a common goal and caused the same damage, or that the actions of two or more separate defendants happened independently but all contributed to the same harm (a common example is where a claimant suffers whiplash after their car collides with two negligently driven cars at the same time). In such cases, the law makes it easier for the claimant to receive the total sum of damages that is deemed appropriate for the harm: the claimant may claim against one of the defendants for the whole of the damages.[57]

In the former example, where two or more defendants act with a commonly held goal, each is held jointly liable.[58] The claimant can sue either, both or all defendants together for the entirety of the damage (but the whole sum can be recovered only once).[59] This mechanism (and legal fiction) ensures that the claimant can receive the whole sum, without having to locate multiple defendants. It also means, for example in the employer/employee situation, that there is someone joined to the action—and liable—who has sufficient funds to pay (and backed by insurance). The claimant may have other entirely practical reasons for suing one rather than the other, for example if both defendants were companies and one has become bankrupt.

56. Note, however, that the 'divisibility' of psychiatric harm has since been doubted in *Dickins* v *O2 plc* [2008].

57. And that defendant may later take proceedings against any other defendant who was equally liable, via the Civil Liability (Contribution) Act 1978. Section 2 states that apportionment shall be calculated to a degree that is 'just and equitable having regard to the extent of that person's responsibility for the damage in question'.

58. Joint liability also applies to employers and employees, where the employee commits the tort and the employer becomes liable for it via the principle of vicarious liability, and also in various other contexts such as principals and agents, employers and independent contractors, where a non-delegable duty of care exists, etc—see **Chapters 13** and **20**.

59. See e.g. ***Fairchild*** **v** ***Glenhaven Funeral Services*** [2002], discussed at **section 9.2.2.2**.

In the second example, the liability would be several and concurrent (see *Fitzgerald* v *Lane* [1988]; *Vision Golf* v *Weightmans* [2005]). As with joint liability, the claimant can choose to sue either defendant for the entirety of the damages (although can recover only once). Again, this is a mechanism used to ensure that further barriers are not put in the way of the claimant receiving compensation. It is not as unfair as it might seem—whichever defendant pays is then able to seek a contribution to the damages paid out (via the Civil Liability (Contribution) Act 1978). That is, unless, as in the bankruptcy example, the co-defendant is unable to pay or, where the amount is disputed, a separate court action may ensue where the amount to be paid by each will be judicially apportioned. The benefit is that the claimant in the original action is not affected by any arguments between co-defendants, on whom the burden of apportionment of damages (and therefore 'blameworthiness'?) squarely falls.[60] Apportionment is based on each defendant's proportion of responsibility for the injury that occurred (and of course will be subject to a reduction if the claimant was also in part responsible (contributorily negligent) for their own harm, as in *Fitzgerald* v *Lane*).

21.5 Time limitations on claims

Section 2 of the Limitation Act 1980 provides that tort actions, including those for trespass to the person, must be brought within six years of the tort being committed (the main exception being for minors, where the time period runs from when they reach the age of 18), otherwise they are 'time-barred'. Sections 11–14 make exceptions for actions for 'damages for negligence, nuisance or breach of duty', where the claim is in respect of personal injury. In these cases, the limitation period is *three* years from either the date when the cause of action accrued or the 'date of knowledge',[61] whichever is the later.[62] Importantly, this applies in situations where a negligent act causes what is known as 'latent damage'—damage that only arises (or is recognised) later, not as an immediate consequence of the tort, though still a result of it—here the limitation period runs from the time that damage or harm *begins to be suffered*.

The question whether a claimant could claim in negligence for what were in fact *intentional* acts (which technically involve no 'breach of duty'), where the harm suffered was latent, arose in *Stubbings* v *Webb* [1993]. Here, a woman claimed damages from her adopted father and step-brother for sexual abuse and rape, which had occurred between 16 and 28 years before, when she was a child. She sought to use the exception created

60. Though cf ***Barker* v *Corus UK Ltd*** [2006], also discussed at **section 9.2.2.2**.

61. Defined in s 14. This includes constructive knowledge: *Collins* v *Secretary of State for Business, Innovation and Skills and another* [2014]. A good recent illustration of the question about when the cause of action accrues can be seen in *Balls* v *Reeve and another* [2021] in relation to a claim for asbestosis, resulting from exposure between 1953 and 1983.

62. Three years is also the period within which claims in defamation or under Part 1 of the Consumer Protection Act 1987 must be brought.

under section 11 of the 1980 Act because although she clearly knew that she had been abused (and had not sued at the time, when she would have had an action in trespass), she did not realise until 1984 that she had suffered psychological injuries as a result of the abuse. Given the timing, her claim was novel, seeking to make use of the extended limitation period for latent damage caused by negligence. Put simply, she claimed that the abuse had been *negligent* because the law would have prevented her claim in trespass, but it did not do so in negligence as the 1980 Act dealt with the possibility that *harm* could be suffered later than when the tort was committed. Her claim was made one month from the end of the extended limitation period under section 11: she had become 'aware' of the psychological harm almost exactly three years previously. Unsurprisingly, the defendants argued that she was time-barred as hers was simply a trespass claim, and thus subject to a six-year limitation period which had long since expired.

The Court of Appeal allowed her claim. However, the House of Lords unanimously overturned the decision, turning to technical interpretation of the statute and the precise meaning of the words 'negligence, nuisance or breach of duty' and what the law lords perceived the intentions of Parliament to be. Lord Griffiths held that he could not construe the words 'breach of duty' as including deliberate acts and also that Parliament could not have intended the phrase to include abuse and rape. In discussing the difference between breach of duty and infringing rights—which is how he saw deliberate acts—he asked '[i]f I invite a lady to my house one would naturally think of a duty to take care that the house is safe but would one really be thinking of a duty not to rape her?' (at 508). Predictably, the case was decided in favour of the defendants. The decision meant that section 11 could not apply to a case of deliberate assault, including sexual assault or abuse, and that actions for such harms are not actions for 'negligence, nuisance or breach of duty'. Subsequently, the European Court of Human Rights agreed (in *Stubbings* v *UK* [1996]). However, this position was remedied by the House of Lords in ***A* v *Hoare* [2008]**.

A v *Hoare, C* v *Middlesbrough Council, X* v *Wandsworth LBC, H* v *Suffolk County Council, Young* v *Catholic Care (Diocese of Leeds)* [2008] HL

Hoare was a conjoined appeal in which a number of claimants sued a number of different institutional defendants, both private and public bodies (including local councils and a Catholic Church care organisation) and, in one case, a private individual. This was *A* v *Hoare* itself, where the claimant, who was raped by the defendant, had not sued him earlier (for it is rarely worth claiming compensation from someone without the means to pay), but decided to do so when she later learnt that he had won £7 million on the lottery while in prison.

The claimants—all victims of sexual assaults and/or abuse—framed their claims in negligence to circumvent the limitation period problem. To avoid the *Stubbings* obstacle, the cases against institutions alleged 'systemic abuse' so as to show that the *organisation* was *negligent in allowing the abuse to continue*, rather than that each individual act was negligent in itself. The lower courts in *Hoare* followed *Stubbings*, but the claimants appealed further, submitting that *Stubbings* was wrongly decided and that the House of Lords should overturn it.

→

→

Lord Hoffmann, giving the leading judgment, summarised the claimants' position:

> The general rule is that the period of limitation for an action in tort is six years from the date on which the cause of action accrues. This period derives from the Limitation Act 1623 and is now contained in section 2 of the 1980 Act. All the claimants started proceedings well after the six years had expired. It follows that, if section 2 applies, their claims are barred. But sections 11 to 14 contain provisions, first introduced by the Limitation Act 1975, which create a different regime for actions for 'damages for negligence, nuisance or breach of duty', where the damages are in respect of personal injuries. In such cases the limitation period is three years from either the date when the cause of action accrued or the 'date of knowledge' as defined in section 14, whichever is the later. In addition, section 33 gives the court a discretion to extend the period when it appears that it would be equitable to do so. The chief question in these appeals is whether the claimants come within section 2 or section 11. In the latter case, the claimants say either that the date of knowledge was less than three years before the commencement of proceedings or that the discretion under section 33 should be exercised in their favour. (at [1])

The House of Lords held that *Stubbings* had indeed been wrongly decided and, in respect of ***A*** v ***Hoare***, allowed the woman's appeal, referring the case back to the High Court for assessment of whether the section 33 discretion could be exercised. In the other cases, the claims were either upheld (with the damages that the lower courts said they would have awarded had they been able to) or referred back to see whether the section 33 discretion should be applied—the implication being that it would (see Lord Hoffmann at [49]), given the nature of the injuries suffered.

Technically, the House of Lords can depart from precedent (i.e. say that a previous case decided by them was wrongly decided) only when the decision in the former case can be thought to be 'impeding the proper development of the law or to have led to results which were unjust or contrary to public policy' (Lord Hoffmann at [20]). This was exactly the effect of *Stubbings* and the reason the law lords felt they could overturn that decision. The development of the law relating to vicarious liability[63] weighed heavily on them, as did decisions in cases that seemed to defy all logical principles and which could clearly be described as 'impeding the proper development of the law' or having an 'unjust' result. As Baroness Hale acknowledged:

> the abuse itself is the reason why so many victims do not come forward until years after the event. This presents a challenge to a legal system which resists stale claims. Six years, let alone three, from reaching the age of majority is not long enough . . . (at [54])

63. Where it has been recognised that organisations or institutions may be vicariously liable for acts of sexual abuse committed by an employee during the course of their employment (or akin to employment) (see ***Lister*** v ***Hesley Hall Ltd*** **[2002]** (discussed at **section 20.4**) and *JGE* v *The Portsmouth Roman Catholic Diocesan Trust* [2012], ***Various Claimants*** v ***Catholic Child Welfare Society and others*** **[2012]**, *Armes* v *Nottinghamshire County Council* [2017] (discussed at **section 20.2**), *JXJ* v *The Province of Great Britain of the Institute of Brothers of the Christian Schools* [2020] and *Barry Congregation of Jehovah's Witnesses* v *BXB* [2021]).

One such case was *KR* v *Bryn Alyn Community (Holdings) Ltd* [2003]. Here, the Court of Appeal said that the need to frame a claim in artificial ways (e.g. the 'systemic abuse' negligence claims in ***Hoare***) when the real cause of complaint was deliberate sexual abuse for which the employer ought to be vicariously liable was causing 'arid and highly wasteful litigation turning on a distinction of no apparent principle or other merit' (Auld LJ at [100]). In *S* v *W (Child abuse: damages)* [1995], a girl sued her parents in respect of sexual abuse conducted by her father: her father in trespass and her mother in negligence, for not preventing the abuse. As her action was brought nearly ten years after the last intentional act, she was time-barred from taking the claim against her father but the claim against her mother fell under section 11 of the 1980 Act and also section 33, where a discretional extension to the limitation period could be granted. Put simply, the girl could sue her mother but not her father; the person who actually abused her and caused her harm. Sir Ralph Gibson, in the Court of Appeal, viewed the outcome as both 'illogical and surprising' and recommended that the Law Commission should review the situation. Subsequently, the Law Commission reviewed the law of limitation of actions, presenting its findings to Parliament in 2001.[64] Its report described the legal effects of *Stubbings* as 'anomalous', with particular reference to *S* v *W* (at [1.5]). Partly on this basis, the Law Commission recommended a uniform regime for personal injuries, whether claims were brought in negligence or trespass (at [1.14]). No action on this had been taken by Parliament prior to ***Hoare***.

Counterpoint

The decision in *Stubbings* was seemingly quite out of date with modern thinking about rape and abuse. The problem in such cases is that victims of child abuse often do not acknowledge or understand the harm they have suffered until much later and may not tell anyone or seek advice until later still. So, in terms of bringing claims, those abused as children may be well into adulthood by the time they realise that they have suffered harm. However, the law then stood in their way, as abusive behaviour is not negligent but intentional. This meant that claimants had to attempt to distort and bend the law in order to frame their claims in negligence, where they might have been able to take advantage of the exception created by sections 11 and 14 of the 1980 Act and the discretion available to judges under section 33. This made some arguments tenuous, as can be seen from the claims of 'systemic negligence' made in *Hoare* and, because it meant people who had suffered serious and deliberately inflicted harms would have no option but to do this to achieve justice, discredited the law in the process. The House of Lords did no more than acknowledge this in *Hoare*, but the decision is significant as it removed the legal barrier faced by future claimants in similar situations; claimants who may already face serious and considerable personal problems in identifying and acknowledging the harm done to them—precisely the reason that the limitation period issue arises. In this sense, this is a good example of judges adapting law where Parliament has failed to act on either previous judicial prompting or even advice from its own advisory body, the Law Commission.

→

64. *Limitation of Actions* (Law Com No 270, 2001).

→

The situation following ***Hoare*** has been described as follows:

> [A]s their Lordships observed, the situation as it stood was bringing the law into disrepute, both by forcing the distortion of legal arguments and failing to do justice to tort victims. Many difficulties remain for abuse victims seeking civil redress. And there are still issues to be debated about whether litigation is really the best way to address these kinds of social ills. However, at the individual level, the injustice wrought by the harshness of *Stubbings* appears for the time being to have been alleviated.[65]

This appears correct. The decision in ***Hoare*** opened the door to numerous other similar claims (see e.g. *Pierce* v *Doncaster MBC* [2007]; *AB* v *Nugent Care Society, GR* v *Wirral Metropolitan Borough Council* [2009]; *Raggett* v *Society of Jesus Trust of 1929* [2010]; *Durham County Council* v *Dunn* [2012]).[66]

The Limitation Act 1980 also provides that actions where contribution is sought between several concurrent defendants must usually be started within two years of the original date of settlement or award. A limitation period of three years exists in relation to the Fatal Accidents Act 1976; the time period runs from the date of death, not the date of the tort, if this came earlier. Claims under the Human Rights Act (HRA) 1998 are the most significantly limited—section 7(5)(a) states that they must be initiated before the end of one year after the act complained of took place.[67]

21.6 **The problem with damages**

***Tomlinson* v *Congleton Borough Council* [2003] HL**

We previously encountered this case in the chapter on occupiers' liability (**section 11.4.1**). Tomlinson was a teenager who dived badly, against the rules, into the shallow part of a lake, ending up tetraplegic (paralysis of all four limbs). He sued the local council which controlled the lake

→

65. Peter Cane and Joanne Conaghan *The New Oxford Companion to Law* (OUP, 2008), p 7. See also Nicola Godden 'Sexual Abuse and Claims in Tort: Limitation Periods after *A v Hoare (and other appeals)* [2008] and *AB and others v Nugent Care Society; GR v Wirral MBC* [2009]' (2010) 18 Fem LS 179.

66. Though not all claims have been successful, e.g. *TCD* v *Harrow and others* [2008], *obiter* comments in *EL* v *The Children's Society* [2012] and *Archbishop Bowen and another* v *JL* [2017]. In different contexts, see *Whiston* v *London Strategic Health Authority (successor body in law for the Queen Charlotte's Maternity Hospital)* [2010] (an adult claiming in respect of brain injuries suffered at birth); cf *Ministry of Defence* v *AB and others* [2012] (injuries arising from nuclear testing in the 1950s).

67. Though this can be extended if the court thinks it 'equitable having regard to all the circumstances' (s 7(5)(b)). See *A* v *Essex County Council* [2010] for an example where the Supreme Court declined to extend the limitation period in an action against an education authority as it would not be 'equitable' to do so.

→

and its surroundings. Had the case not been appealed to the House of Lords, Tomlinson would have received a large damages award, as the Court of Appeal believed his claim should succeed. Because of the ruling of the majority of the House of Lords, however, Tomlinson received *nothing*.

Such a case clearly illustrates the dilemma where two demands of 'justice' collide. On the one hand, we can argue that Tomlinson should be compensated in order to make his life more bearable (in terms of pain, suffering, quality of ongoing care and so on). On the other hand, the defendant has an equally valid claim that it should not be made to pay for things which were not (wholly) caused by its own fault and, especially, when having to pay would put demands on a budget that would mean money could end up being diverted from public services and amenities.

The many reasons for claiming damages in tort can be highlighted here, though two in particular stand out.

(1) Corrective justice—justice can be seen to be about fairness and correcting the situation (by putting the claimant back into the position he would have been in had the accident not occurred) is one way of doing this. But in cases of death, or where there is injury to such a serious extent as that suffered by Tomlinson, this simply is not possible, although compensation can play a role in holding people accountable for their (negligent) actions.

(2) Compensation—as we have already indicated, an action in tort is often simply about getting the money required in order to live life to an acceptable standard. Given that Tomlinson could not be cured, what he needed was enough money to be able to live comfortably and not to worry about the future. But the question also has to focus on who is being asked to pay, and whether they should—was the council really to *blame* in any way for Tomlinson's injuries? Often, the answer to the 'who pays?' question is that it will be insurance companies who pay (in ***Tomlinson*** the council would have had insurance)—in which case, should we be concerned about who was to blame?

There are many limitations to the system within which damages are awarded in tort. The primary reason for most of these is that *legal* fault (negligence) does not always equate with *moral* blame. If we say that a fault-based system is justified then it often does not seem fair that those who are truly to blame are not the ones who pay—the principles of vicarious liability and the increased prevalence of insurance, particularly compulsory insurance, shift the focus of the system to ask who *can* pay rather than who *should* pay, as a system truly based on fault (and the idea of corrective justice and individual responsibility) would do.[68] Given that this is the case, we should perhaps ask whether fault and blame are the correct framework around which to base compensation. There are alternative ways to determine it, one of these being need. To ask who *needs* damages, however, is more closely aligned to asking who *can* pay; both are underpinned by ideas of collective rather than individual responsibility, and focus on the fact that the primary aim of tort is (or has become) compensation. It is only when need is separated from fault that

68. See Patrick Atiyah 'Personal Injuries in the 21st Century: Thinking the Unthinkable' in P Birks (ed) *Wrongs and Remedies in the 21st Century* (OUP, 1996).

any kind of equitable distribution of compensation can be envisaged—that is, if everyone who needed it (whether there was someone else to blame *or not*) received adequate compensation for the injuries they suffered, we truly would live in a fairer society.[69] Furthermore, it is not self-evident why judges are the arbiters of who gets compensation, from whom, in what circumstances and how much.

To date, fault-based liability has been heavily undermined by the growth of the insurance industry and the expansion of the principle of vicarious liability. If the system was truly fault-based, it would be far easier to see the principles of retribution, deterrence, justice, etc playing a part—but as it is not the wrongdoer (legal *or* moral) who usually pays, it could be argued that all of these other aspects and functions of tort no longer hold true—compensation alone has become the true focus.[70] In part, this must be what led to the claims that we now live in a 'compensation culture' (see box at **section 1.3.2**). This is hardly surprising given that the legal system itself seems to focus on compensation rather than justice. We shall look more closely at the idea of a compensation culture later in the chapter.

Pause for reflection

Why do you think the emphasis of the tort system changed? Various things are factors in this. On the one hand, there was the inevitable increase in accidents attributable to employers and other parties who made suitable targets for tort actions following the Industrial Revolution. Similarly, the rise of the car—and of the tort of negligence itself—helped to contribute to the gradual emergence of damages claims for personal injury caused by negligence as the predominant actions in tort. A growing number of car accidents (and, therefore, injuries) led to the passage of the Road Traffic Act 1930, which introduced compulsory liability insurance for motorists (the first example of this type of insurance in the UK), as well as the establishment of the Motor Insurers' Bureau in 1936. These were later followed by the Employers' Liability Act 1969, another compulsory insurance scheme meaning that employers would be *able* to pay, via insurance, when someone was injured in the course of employment. In addition, the rise of the largely unjustified (except in the sense that someone would be able to pay) spectre of vicarious liability has helped to change the focus from ensuring that the defendant pays to ensuring that the claimant *gets paid*.

Moreover, when looking at whether the loss has actually been shifted from the innocent victim to the wrongdoer, we encounter further issues. We can ask again, with the principle of vicarious liability and the fact that the whole tort system operates under the shadow of the insurance industry, is loss-shifting really what is happening? Given that when, for example, employers, drivers, goods manufacturers or NHS trusts become liable, they are likely to be insured against the loss, the question of who actually bears the costs of the wrongs committed inevitably arises. If manufacturers have to keep paying out, the price of consumables will

→

69. See e.g. the Government Workers' Compensation Scheme, introduced in the late nineteenth century—a no-fault scheme; everyone injured was entitled to compensation.

70. See Sumption, Lord 'Abolishing Personal Injuries Law—A Project' Personal Injuries Bar Association Annual Lecture, London, 16 November 2017, discussed in **section 1.3.2**.

→
rise—*society* ends up paying for the harms incurred by individuals and therefore the risks associated with manufacturing. If employers (or their insurance companies) pay for the torts of their employees, the price of insurance goes up, and society as a whole ends up paying. If a driver's insurance company pays damages following an accident, not only will the individual driver's insurance premiums rise, but so will the premiums paid by other drivers insured by the same company, or at least those within the same insurance bracket (based on age, gender, experience and so on). If an NHS trust pays out, not only could it be said that we are taking money away from an already stretched health service, thereby potentially depriving others of quality care, but taxpayers will ultimately pay. In all these examples (and more), there is no instance of the wrongdoer paying, thus it cannot truly be said that the tort system is a loss-shifting system. If anything, it operates as a system of loss-distribution, and society at large bears the costs of all harms and all risk.

While it may be said that suing regulates conduct by the deterrent effect of liability avoidance, and therefore has implications for the future, the fact that we have deviated from a moral towards a purely legal notion of blame has some potentially undesirable social consequences.[71] A growth in litigation and 'litigation consciousness' perhaps inevitably brings with it an increase in the number of 'frivolous' claims. Society, and the organisations within it (including public bodies, employers, etc), in realising this, may adopt a 'safety' culture and defensive practices. Similarly, a blame culture may grow, where few accept that there can be such things as 'accidents' and even fewer are prepared to take risks—which may once have been seen as necessary and vital, for example in terms of innovation and improvement. On this issue, sociologist Frank Furedi argues that '[r]isk avoidance has become an important theme in political debate and social action'.[72] He highlights the precautionary approach seemingly adopted by today's society, which views 'risk' negatively. As an example of the negative effect of this, in the context of tort/regulation and school trips, he says:

> [T]he tragic death of a child on a school outing invariably turns into a major national story about the risks involved in such activities. Such tragedies are usually followed by calls for tighter regulation of school outings. Another response is to seek someone to blame. Not surprisingly, many teachers have become reluctant to organise such events. (pp 7–8)

Responding to the *British Medical Journal*'s 2001 declaration that it was to ban the word 'accident' from its pages, stating that 'most injuries and their precipitating events are predictable and preventable', Furedi argues that:

> cleansing the term accident from our cultural narrative inexorably leads to a relentless search for someone to blame. This is where the legal profession takes over and provides the injured with an obvious target for a compensation claim . . . Educating people to discover

71. See Frank Furedi and Jennie Bristow *The Social Cost of Litigation* (Centre for Policy Studies, September 2012).
72. Frank Furedi *The Culture of Fear* (2nd edn, Continuum Press, 2002), p 2.

> that what they thought was their fault can actually be blamed on someone else seems to be part of the project of purging the idea of an accident from the English language . . . Like the BMJ censors, [claims management companies] believe that behind every injury lurks an act of negligence. (p 11)

Furedi contends that almost all accidents, with hindsight, can be reinterpreted so as to show 'culpable negligence' was involved. Further, he argues that the implication of all this is a restrained society, identified by lowered expectations and a 'dissipation of the human potential'[73]—he describes this as 'a society that celebrates victimhood'. Furedi's interpretation is hyperbolic—but he is correct in one respect: a move towards compensation rather than fault does result in a different type of blame.

Making Amends, a government report published in 2003, said that the system provides little incentive to report incidences of medical negligence or to learn from them.[74] Focusing on the immediate cause (the negligence of the doctor) rather than how things can more generally be improved (e.g. in the Health Service as a whole) hinders the deterrent function of tort. The courts can also be seen, on occasion, to turn their focus to achieving compensation for claimants, rather than any other principles of justice, sometimes distorting the law to achieve this aim.[75]

Pause for reflection

It is quite likely that the majority of those who suffer injury do want money—this is both necessary and enabling. However, as we discussed in the introduction, often claimants seek other things too: an explanation or apology, reassurances that some action will be taken to prevent the same harm happening to someone else in the future and so on.[76] The tort system seemingly fails to provide these things—do you think its focus should change? Do you think that tort (private litigation through the courts) is the appropriate vehicle to address these issues? What is the alternative?

That tort should be a vehicle for accident compensation is not a view shared by everyone, and the tort system was not designed to function in this way—distributive justice (for that surely is the end result, even if unintended, of an accident compensation system) simply was not part of the agenda. When compensation *is* based on fault in the way that it currently seems to be, all kinds of questions are raised about who gets it, and

73. Ibid, p 13.

74. Sir Liam Donaldson, Chief Medical Officer *Making Amends: a consultation paper setting out proposals for reforming the approach to clinical negligence in the NHS* (2003), p 55.

75. An example of this is ***Nettleship* v *Weston*** (discussed at **section 8.3**) where it can clearly be argued that the young and, crucially, inexperienced driver was not at (moral) fault, yet the court held her to the standard of a competent driver so that she necessarily fell below the standard required (i.e. she would be in breach) and the instructor could therefore be compensated through her insurance for her 'negligence'). Unusually, this is openly acknowledged in the judgment itself—perhaps due only to the typical candidness of Lord Denning.

76. Note that the Compensation Act 2006, passed following an inquiry of the Constitutional Affairs Select Committee into 'compensation culture' and contingency fees, contains a provision to the effect that in claims for negligence or breach of statutory duty, an apology, offer of treatment or other redress shall not of itself amount to an admission of liability (s 2).

whether they are more deserving than anyone else suffering the same type of harms. A study of the tort system also shows that it is, when compared with other avenues of 'compensation' such as social security, actually very generous, in terms of the sums awarded. One of the obvious reasons for this is the difference in the way compensation is paid—usually in a lump sum, rather than on a weekly or monthly basis, and not as dependent on an individual's financial circumstances (a person injured by the fault of someone else would still be able to claim from them even if they had large sums of money in savings, but many benefits are means-tested).

However, this 'generosity' of tort should not be misunderstood; only a select few (those who overcome all the 'hurdles') get compensation at all. In 1972 the Pearson Committee surveyed all accident compensation in England and Wales. Reporting in 1978, it showed that only 6.5 per cent of people injured or killed in accidents actually received damages. When we consider that accident victims (those potentially able to frame their claim in tort) make up only about 10 per cent of those disabled in society, the true figure of those who will receive damages for disabling injuries is closer to 1 per cent. This figure clearly stands in stark contrast to the 'compensation culture' claim that too much is being paid out to too many!

Furthermore, our tort system, based as it is on the payment of damages where fault can be established, is expensive to operate and largely inefficient. This is not in itself a criticism of the decisions of any particular case or cases, or of government failure to amend the system in a particular way. It is a case of the figures speaking for themselves. The Pearson Committee calculated that the cost to run the tort system (in the 1970s) amounted to 85 per cent of the sums paid out. Put simply, this means that for every pound paid in compensation, 85 pence had to be spent to achieve that result. Or, for every £10,000 paid out, £8,500 had to be put in. In comparison, the running costs of the New Zealand system discussed later are estimated at about 7 per cent. To summarise, tort as accident compensation is expensive to run, compared with social security, for example, but relatively high awards of compensation can be achieved. The 6.5 per cent of accident victims who *do* achieve compensation through the tort system are therefore estimated to consume about 40 per cent of the total actually paid out to all accident victims. Bearing in mind that some of those victims will get nothing, the tort system appears heavily skewed towards those who can successfully jump through hoops and it seems little wonder that it has been described as a 'damages lottery'.[77]

Pause for reflection

Consider *Tomlinson* again. Why should his future have depended solely on the fact that (overall) five senior judges voted one way, and four voted the other? Does this give at least an element of doubt as to the correctness of the final outcome? If he did deserve compensation, what does this say about other incapacitated people who are unable to obtain a remedy? For example, what about people born with spinal defects, who cannot 'blame' anyone—are

→

77. Patrick Atiyah *The Damages Lottery* (Hart, 1997).

→

they more, less or equally deserving of compensation than John Tomlinson? Is litigation the appropriate mechanism in this kind of situation or, as a society, ought we to be doing more for *everyone* with disability, no matter how caused?

On the other hand, consider the effect that ***Tomlinson*** might have had if the House of Lords had *not* reversed the Court of Appeal's decision. While tort law can be said to be useful in terms of its potential deterrent effects, this is positive only where the activity being deterred is wrongful or does not have social value—that is, the idea is not to deter socially valuable activities. In a similar vein, Frank Furedi opines that 'some local councils are worried that children might get injured through conkering—the age old custom of playing with horse-chestnuts. Consequently, local councils have implemented the policy of "tree management"—cutting down trees—to make horse-chestnut trees less accessible to children.'[78] What would have been the practical effect of the Court of Appeal's decision in ***Tomlinson*** had it been allowed to stand—that is, what would the council have had to do?[79]

21.6.1 **Alternative sources of compensation**

A study of tort law, dominated as it tends to be by negligence and considerations of fault and blame, means that the fact that compensation could be achieved in other ways is often under-considered or even overlooked. Particularly where the harm is personal injury or property damage, other mechanisms of compensation—or other types of compensation scheme—would perhaps better serve the needs of claimants. Despite the textbook perception, in reality tort plays only a very minor role in compensating those who suffer such harms. The Pearson Committee's figure showing that only 6.5 per cent of people injured in accidents receive damages indicates that the bulk of 'compensation' for physical harms must be derived from other sources—or is simply not present at all (i.e. some people must receive nothing). These other sources might include payments from employers, insurance and other schemes (e.g. the Criminal Injuries Compensation Scheme or Motor Insurers' Bureau) and social security. What should be noted, however, is that claimants pursuing these alternatives are likely to receive less than they would in a damages award. Because of the *restitutio in integrum* principle, tort damages seek to compensate victims for the whole of the harm they have suffered, including future losses and costs.

78. Furedi (**n 72**) p 4.

79. See also *Simonds* v *Isle of Wight Council* [2003]. Note, however, that s 1 of the Compensation Act 2006 requires courts considering the *standard* of care in a claim for negligence or breach of statutory duty to take into account whether requiring particular steps to be taken to meet the standard would prevent or impede a 'desirable activity' from taking place. This provision was designed to improve awareness of this aspect of the law and to help to ensure that 'normal' activities are not prevented because of a fear of litigation and excessively risk-averse behaviour and essentially enshrines the House of Lords' position in ***Tomlinson*** into statute. According to the Explanatory Notes to the Act, the provision was also designed to address the misperception that there is a compensation culture following the 2004 report of the Better Regulation Task Force.

The Pearson Committee made a number of other reform proposals, the main one being the retention of a 'mixed' system of tort and social security, with greater emphasis on social security and more finesse in how the two systems worked alongside each other. Outside this, it was recommended, a separate scheme for victims of road accidents should exist, however they were caused. Even the limited reforms proposed were, however, never adopted—perhaps one reason for this was simply due to bad timing, and the change of government in 1979. Under Mrs Thatcher, it was never likely that we would see an expansion of state-funded or collective schemes and far more likely that emphasis on individuals would be retained.[80] Now, it seems that the question is not what the tort system could be replaced with (or whether it should be replaced), but what improvements or reforms we can make to the existing system. Some procedural reforms and other changes have already taken place. Whether these changes can be viewed positively is debatable and, indeed, the focus seems to have changed again, including judicially, to looking at how the availability of the tort system can be constricted. Perhaps this is a reaction to the 'compensation culture' perception and, in particular, to more and more claims arising against public bodies, especially post-HRA. With such constriction in mind, the question can again be asked whether the tort system is the right place for these issues to be addressed (injuries, disability, the responsibilities of public bodies, etc) and, if not, where they *should* be addressed, and who by?

Counterpoint

Many accident victims who would in theory be able to claim in tort do not do so, meaning that (a) even fewer people receive full compensation than ought to (if that is the principle we adhere to), and (b) more people rely on other systems such as social security, funded by taxpayers, than ought to. While this may not be problematic if one believes that society should shoulder the costs of risk and injury, it is still worth considering why this may be—why do people who may have potentially 'winnable' claims in tort *not* claim, given that they will receive full compensation if they win?

One of the problems here is built into the system itself—litigation is not only costly for most people (in that the claimant must be able to fund their action and risks losing two sets of costs if the claim fails)[81] but is also incredibly time-consuming. Some cases take years to come to court. Moreover, because the rules and hurdles of tort have become so well established and familiar, there will be greater pressure from defendants and legal advisors acting for either party to settle out of court. Why risk losing everything (full compensation) if what you consider to be a fair (or almost fair) proportion of it is guaranteed? Furthermore, despite numerous claims suggesting that there is a litigation explosion based on the existence of a 'compensation culture', it remains more difficult than would be expected, not only in terms of money, for laypeople to access the legal system.[82]

→

80. Similar things can be said about the current Conservative Government and the general political climate post-Brexit.

81. Subject to the increased prevalence of DBAs and ATE insurance schemes.

82. Note that claims management companies are now statutorily regulated under the Compensation Act 2006, Part II.

→

Access to the system (and thus access to justice) is a topical issue, with further proposed reforms to the system continuing post-Jackson[83]—including a fixed-costs system for claims up to £250,000, a proposed increase in the level of claim that can be dealt with on the fast track, low-value system (therefore without legal representation for claimants) from £1,000 to £5,000, and cuts to damages for low-value soft-tissue injuries as part of a commitment to 'tackling' the number and cost of whiplash claims (the Ministry of Justice consulted between November 2016 and January 2017 on reforms to the procedure for whiplash and low-value injury claims). Relatedly, the Civil Liability Act 2018 was passed into law on 20 December 2018. Section 3 deals with damages for whiplash, stating that '[t]he amount of damages for pain, suffering and loss of amenity payable in respect of the whiplash injury or injuries, taken together, is to be an amount specified in regulations made by the Lord Chancellor' (s 3(2)). This gives the Lord Chancellor the power to limit damages for whiplash injuries to fixed amounts. Draft Regulations (for approval in Parliament before implementation 31 May 2021) were published in early 2021, setting an upper limit of £4,345 for whiplash claims.

21.6.1.1 'No-fault' liability and simple compensation schemes

The principle of 'no-fault' liability is a radical one—support for it is based on the idea that if the aim is primarily to ensure that people harmed receive compensation, the current system is inefficient, expensive, arbitrary and inadequate. Put another way, creating liability without having to first find fault would enable more people to receive compensation for their injuries, whether or not they could legally attach blame to someone. Such a system would be more closely aligned with need than blame. Another likely benefit of a no-fault system is that it would be cheaper (and therefore also more cost-effective) to run. Such systems are not without precedent. In New Zealand, a no-fault compensation scheme has been in operation since 1974 and tort actions have been significantly reduced. The costs are met by premiums paid by, for example, road users, industry and employers (therefore inevitably passed on in some way to individuals). While it is true to say that the scheme has since become more restrictive (rather than expanded, as may have been hoped) due to rising costs, it remains cheaper than a fault-based system with the added benefit that more people can more easily access compensation.[84]

Pause for reflection

What does the fact that we have chosen fault as the primary consideration in determining who gets compensation say about our societal values?

83. In fact, in November 2016, the then Lord Chancellor, Liz Truss, announced that Lord Justice Jackson had been commissioned to undertake a further review of costs in civil litigation.

84. See Nicholas Mullany, who says the New Zealand system is 'not as expansive as many have assumed' ('Accidents and Actions for Damages to the Mind—Kiwi Style' (1999) 115 LQR 596).

In *Making Amends*, the government proposed reform of the approach to clinical negligence in the NHS. One proposal was the creation of a no-fault scheme in relation to certain ('lower value') types of clinical negligence, in response to rising compensation costs for the NHS. This was rejected, largely due to the expense of implementing such a scheme, though the report also identified that awards might be lower and that there would not necessarily be any deterrent or learning effects if it were to be put in place (pp 14–15).[85]

A further recommendation was for 'an NHS Redress Scheme [to] be introduced to provide investigations when things go wrong; remedial treatment, rehabilitation and care when needed; explanations and apologies; and financial compensation in certain circumstances' (p 1). The idea was not only to provide compensation more easily to those in need, but also to lessen the NHS's costs when defending claims, in terms of both money and staff time, as well as to improve morale, restore public confidence and prevent increase in 'defensive practices' and litigation avoidance. The rationale was based on reported figures from the NHS Litigation Authority (now renamed 'NHS Resolution').[86] These showed that 60–70 per cent of medical negligence claims did not proceed beyond initial contact with a solicitor or disclosure of medical records, 30 per cent of claims formally pursued were abandoned by the claimant and 95 per cent reached out-of-court settlement. Further, the adversarial nature of the tort system was considered, as was the ineffectiveness and expense of continuing to operate the existing system.

The consultation resulted in the NHS Redress Act 2006, designed to provide a simpler route to compensation, without recourse to litigation, for 'lower value' (up to £25,000) medical negligence where the harm could have been avoided. Section 3 provides for full investigation; provision of an explanation to the patient and of the action proposed to prevent future incidents; and development and delivery of a package of care providing remedial treatment, therapy and arrangements for continuing care. In addition, payments for pain and suffering, out-of-pocket expenses and care or treatment which the NHS cannot supply are provided for. This tallies with responses given to a government-commissioned survey before *Making Amends* was published, which asked respondents what they felt the most appropriate response from the NHS would be to negligently inflicted injuries. The responses are summarised in **Table 21.2**.

TABLE 21.2 Response considered most appropriate for negligently inflicted injuries

Response considered most appropriate to the event[87]		
Response	Frequency	Per cent
An apology or explanation	134	33.9
An inquiry into the causes	92	23.3
Disciplinary action	23	5.8

85. Interestingly, as a result of its devolved powers, in 2012 the Scottish Government publicly consulted on a no-fault compensation scheme for medical accidents (recommended by the McLean Committee Report 2011) which, should it happen, would almost entirely remove medical cases from the civil courts. Nothing has been heard of the idea for a long time, it perhaps having been shelved when the 2014 Scottish independence referendum took place.

86. *NHS Redress Act 2006 Regulatory Impact Assessment*, p 3.

87. **Section 1.2.1**.

TABLE 21.2 *Continued*

Response considered most appropriate to the event		
Financial compensation	44	11.1
Support in coping with the consequences	65	16.5
Don't know	11	2.8
Not stated	0	0
Other	89	22.5
Total	395	100

Source: © Crown Copyright (2006).

Overall, the government predicted that the NHS Redress Scheme would:

> provide a real alternative to litigation for the less severe cases, removing the lottery and risks of litigation, whilst reducing the general burden of unnecessary legal costs. It will provide a fair, equitable and appropriate response to people who have been harmed in the course of their health care. In this respect, the scheme will be consistent with wider Government policy on improving access to justice.[88]

In a similar vein, following a 2007 public consultation, in March 2010 the Ministry of Justice proposed a 'quick and simple compensation scheme for road traffic accidents', which would 'apply to road traffic accident personal injury claims valued between £1,000 and £10,000, which in the past have formed the vast majority of claims'.[89] The scheme came into effect for all personal injury claims arising from road traffic accidents from 30 April 2010. The Prime Minister announced in January 2012 that the threshold of low-value traffic claims would increase to £25,000 and, following further consultation in 2012, also extended the scheme 'horizontally' from the end of July 2013 to include employers' liability and public bodies.[90]

More recently, in February 2021 health minister Nadine Dorries announced that a wholesale review of the 'outdated' system of clinical negligence compensation was in progress. Speaking in an evidence session before Parliament's Health and Social Care Committee, she said:

> we are looking at, in the round, across the NHS, not just in maternity, about how those issues of no blame, no-fault compensation, clinical negligence, how they are treated and how they are dealt with and how we look at them, and we administer them.

88. **n 86**, p 5.

89. The Young Report described this as a 'model of how an effective system should work' and recommended extension of a similar system to low-value clinical negligence claims (p 22). It also said that raising the threshold of low-value car accident claims to £25,000 should be considered, as should the introduction of a 'good Samaritan clause' (see Ch 4, p 77).

90. Ministry of Justice 'Extension of the Road Traffic Accident scheme to include employers' and public liability claims up to the value of £25,000' (2012), **https://consult.justice.gov.uk/digital-communications/extension-rta-scheme**; Ministry of Justice, 'Extension of the Road Traffic Accident Personal Injury Scheme: proposals on fixed recoverable costs' (2013), **https://consult.justice.gov.uk/digital-communications/extension-rta-scheme/results/rta-costs-response.pdf**.

21.6.1.2 First-party insurance

Given that we all accept risks (e.g. crossing a road), and understand the limitations of compensation through the tort system, first-party insurance might be a better means of ensuring that everyone receives the compensation they need when they are injured. If we insured *ourselves* against damage (some people already do, for example Daniel Craig was reported to have taken out a £5 million insurance policy in case he suffered injury performing his own stunts in the *Bond* films, and others reportedly include David Beckham's legs, insured for £100 million in 2006, Taylor Swift's legs, Mariah Carey's voice, Jennifer Lopez's body, Dolly Parton's chest and so on) then we would be more or less guaranteed compensation that meets our needs when injury occurs. More importantly, recovery would not be based on the requirement to show fault. Crucially, also, a high degree of personal autonomy, individual responsibility and choice would be recognised, for example in the types or amount of excess chosen (the amount you must pay yourself before the insurer starts paying), upper limits for claims or what types of harm are covered. This would let individuals, to a large extent, set their own premiums and decide what they were willing to pay and what risks they were willing to accept by not paying for them. People would assume responsibility for their own misfortunes before they happened and there would be quick and easy payments when injuries occur, rather than having to sue someone *after* the event (if they could be found).

There are further practical reasons for at least contemplating personal insurance as an alternative to compensation via litigation (not only because you are protected even if no one is at fault). As we have seen in many of the previous chapters, whether the judiciary is explicit about it or not, insurance considerations play a large part in the development of the law and the success or otherwise of many claims (see, as just some of the many examples, Lord Hoffmann in ***Transco* v *Stockport Metropolitan Borough Council*** [2003], Lord Denning in ***Nettleship* v *Weston*** [1971], etc). How far insurance considerations have so far influenced the law is, however, disputed. Some argue that it should not matter whether parties are insured, as the primary focus should be on the claimant and compensating them if the 'rules' show that we should. Others view insurance as a relevant consideration when deciding liability.

Atiyah was a strong advocate for first-party insurance over fault-based compensation. He argued that the decline of the welfare state, coupled with the recognition of new types of harm, alongside the inadequacies of the tort system mean that litigation on an individual basis is no longer the answer—if it ever was. He argued that we should recognise that the majority of compensation can already be said, in the long run, to be paid by insurance companies, thus we should move towards first-party insurance. Wedded to this is the fact that insurance (via tort) currently does not cover certain kinds of injury or certain ways in which injuries were caused—a first-party insurance system would rectify this. He proposed such a scheme for road traffic accidents (replacing the current compulsory third-party insurance scheme) advocating its relative simplicity and cost-effectiveness, as well as fairness in terms of who pays in and out. Indeed, he went further, recommending also that for all other accidents, injuries and disabilities, however they are caused, 'the action for damages for personal injuries should simply be abolished, and first-party insurance should be left to the free market' (p 189).

Pause for reflection

Consider *Tomlinson* again. Had he known that he was the kind of person who liked to take risks and had the foresight to insure himself, there would have been no tort action and his insurance company *would have paid out*, probably without argument. Does this show the potential value of first-party insurance?

Counterpoint

The idea of first-party insurance is attractive but suffers from the problem that people are not equal—some could afford more cover than others. Though *Atiyah* contended that the wealthy would pay more (as their premiums to protect their earnings or any valuable assets would be higher than those of the ordinary person) there is no real solution for those at the opposite end of the scale. While he acknowledged that with *third*-party insurance schemes, higher earners are favoured and the lower paid, retired and unemployed may be discriminated against, he did not acknowledge that the same might be true of *first*-party insurance. Even if it were compulsory, if someone is poor they may be tempted to pay lower/minimum premiums, thereby insuring themselves and their family for less. This is all very well when it comes to abstract notions of personal autonomy and individual responsibility: it would be their choice. But it has to be questioned, we think, how autonomous such a choice would be. Someone may insure themselves for less because they believe they cannot afford more, yet be in more 'risky' employment. If first-party insurance became compulsory (in a similar way to comprehensive motor insurance) then we agree that this would increase competition on the free market and prices may be kept down—but, as another thing to pay for each month, many people would find themselves substantially worse off. Furthermore, it is undeniable that insurance companies would be the main beneficiaries of such a scheme and this casts further doubt on its value for the truly poor. *Atiyah* merely brushed over these issues in his concluding paragraph, saying that:

> the answer is that almost everybody will actually save more money by abolishing the present system than they will need to pay for their new first-party insurance. The poorest people, especially, will actually save on their motor insurance policies . . . Of course some state social security safety net will still be needed for those not otherwise covered at all. (p 193)

Interestingly, the Jackson Report recommended increased availability and use of 'Before the Event' (BTE) insurance, encouraging people to take out legal expenses insurance, for example as part of household insurance.[91] This is not the same as insuring oneself *against losses caused by injuries* as first-party insurance would be, but is an example of a way claimants can take responsibility and protect themselves against the *cost of litigation* should this become necessary.

91. Lord Justice Jackson *Review of Civil Litigation Costs: Final Report* (TSO, 2010), Ch 8.

21.7 Debunking the compensation myth

The phrase 'compensation culture' is a pejorative and politically loaded term used to describe a society in which it is acceptable for anyone suffering personal injury to seek damages through litigation, even when injury is minimal or the argument that the defendant was at fault is tenuous.[92] As Quill and Friel contend, 'a central concern of the public and political perception of personal injuries claims . . . is the high cost of tort claims to society, reflected in insurance premiums . . . often accompanied by an assumption that tort law and practice is flawed and improperly raising such costs and is further accompanied by a depiction of both claimants and their lawyers as motivated more by greed than justice' (p 3). The term has been applied to the tort system, particularly since the late 1990s, with the growth in CFAs and the increased pervasiveness of claims management companies.[93] In ***Tomlinson***, Lord Hobhouse said that the 'pursuit of an unrestrained culture of blame and compensation has many evil consequences' (at [81]). Similarly, recent governments have fixated on the idea that we live in a 'compensation culture'.[94] Former Prime Minister David Cameron said that:

> [a] damaging compensation culture has arisen, as if people can absolve themselves from any personal responsibility for their own actions, with the spectre of lawyers only too willing to pounce with a claim for damages on the slightest pretext.[95]

But is this true? Are too many claims being made (particularly frivolous or fraudulent ones) and, more importantly, if they *are* being taken, are they being won? In other words, are defendants paying out when they should not be?

In May 2004, the *Better Routes to Redress* report showed that UK expenditure on tort claims was 0.6 per cent of GDP (in comparison with 1 per cent cited by the Institute of Actuaries in 2002). Comparatively, this was found to be less than in ten other industrialised countries and only Denmark was found to spend less (p 15).[96] Similarly, it showed that the overall number of personal injury claims was declining (p 11) and concluded that the existence of a compensation culture was more self-perpetuating myth than reality.[97] That is, many people believed there was such a culture, and behaviours changed in reaction to this. In the first paragraph of its response to the report, the government said that it was:

> determined to scotch any suggestion of a developing 'compensation culture' where people believe that they can seek compensation for any misfortune that befalls them, even if no-one else is to blame. This misperception undermines personal responsibility and respect for the law and creates unnecessary burdens through an exaggerated fear of litigation.[98]

92. See box at **section 1.3.2**.
93. *Atiyah* said 'complaints are often heard that we are "going down the American road" without, very often, explaining what the American road is, or what is wrong with it' (p 2).
94. See e.g. Lord Young *Common Sense, Common Safety* (Cabinet Office, 2010), described as a 'Whitehall-wide review of the operation of health and safety laws and the growth of the compensation culture' (in particular p 19). See also our discussion in **section 14.2**, particularly of the Enterprise and Regulatory Reform Act 2013.
95. Young Report, 'Foreword by the Prime Minister', p 5.
96. The figure for the United States was 1.9 per cent.
97. See also APIL and TUC's joint report 'The Compensation Myth: Seven myths about the "compensation culture"' (March 2014) which includes more up-to-date figures on many relevant points.
98. 'Tackling the "Compensation Culture": Government Response to the Better Regulation Task Force Report: "Better Routes to Redress"' (10 November 2004).

The Association of Personal Injury Lawyers (APIL), in its 2020–23 strategic plan, claims that:

> Many PI lawyers have practiced for several years in a hostile environment where misconceptions have been bred from misinformation . . . This has led to deeply entrenched public views that too many claimants are fraudsters and too many PI lawyers are greedy ambulance chasers. A government focus on whiplash has undermined the work of the sector and public support. The 'compensation culture' has never really existed. It is a misconception. (p 5)

We should also debate whether seeking compensation—or encouraging people to do so—should necessarily be viewed negatively. While some may try to 'play the system' there are, as should by now be apparent, many hurdles in place before a claimant can be successful. It is possible that increased awareness of rights encourages more people to claim, and even that this results in more settlements out of court but, largely, any organisation, business, company, public body or other defendant who settles will have been advised to do so by their lawyers, either because it is cheaper to do so in terms of both finances and reputation or, crucially, because there is already existing precedent that suggests that the claimant might in fact win. None of these so-called frivolous claimants are able to evade the law. It should be remembered that, for example, in ***Tomlinson***, a case often cited as an example of the 'have-a-go' culture and the types of frivolous claim that might be made, his injuries were incredibly severe and there was at least the *potential* that the council concerned had not done all it could to prevent such injuries occurring—as the Court of Appeal recognised.

Better Routes to Redress found that 'the compensation culture is a myth; but the cost of this belief is very real' (p 3). The idea that we live in a compensation culture is in the main a myth perpetuated by sensationalist media coverage of a small number of cases, which often does not go as far as reporting on the *outcome* of unusual claims being made (which may never reach court, let alone succeed—but *will* sell papers) or give any idea of the context in which the claim arose. The Young Report said that 'the problem of the compensation culture prevalent in society today is . . . one of perception rather than reality',[99] and went to some effort to explode the pervasive myths behind 'health and safety hysteria in the media'.[100] Lord Dyson, speaking in 2013, said 'there was, and still is . . . a perception that there is a compensation culture, and that perception has real, and negative, consequences. That perception is not however as grounded in reality as had been suggested.'[101] Encouragingly, however, a media analysis undertaken by APIL found 85 per cent fewer references to 'compensation culture' in the media since 2009 (p 8).

The effects of such myths may be positive (e.g. resulting in easier access to compensation for the majority of those affected by medical negligence) or negative (in the sense of

99. At p 19—seemingly contradicting the then Prime Minister's statement in the foreword.

100. See Annex D, pp 49–50.

101. Lord Dyson MR 'Compensation Culture: Fact or Fantasy?' Holdsworth Club Lecture, 15 March 2013, at [10]. Also see Richard Lewis 'Compensation Culture Reviewed: Incentives to Claim and Damages Levels' [2014] JPIL 209 and the *government* statistics provided by the Department for Work and Pensions' Compensation Recovery Unit (updated 23 April 2018) on the number of claims per year, available at **www.gov.uk/government/publications/compensation-recovery-unit-performance-data/compensation-recovery-unit-performance-data**.

encouraging 'defensive' practices or the removal of services in order to avoid being faced with litigation). Perhaps this is the problem we actually face—the *idea* that a compensation culture exists has become so prevalent that its effects are felt in a multitude of ways, often with negative consequences. In 2004, the then government said 'we need to take action: both to tackle practices that help spread the misperceptions and false expectations; and to improve the effectiveness and efficiency of the system for those who have a genuine claim to compensation'.[102] The current government's view is that much of the problem can be tackled by reforming access to justice, as indicated by a continuing commitment to Lord Justice Jackson's recommendations (discussed at **section 21.1**). It remains to be seen whether the system will improve and, if so, whether this tackles the perception of the 'compensation culture'.

In fact, because of the many changes to the tort litigation system in recent years, and because ATE insurance premiums and solicitors' uplifts on costs in no win, no fee CFAs are no longer recoverable from the losing party, the practical effect is that claimants will receive less damages, as a higher proportion will have to be paid to their lawyers. This renders lower value cases commercially unviable—further limiting access to justice.[103]

21.8 Conclusion

In this chapter, we looked at how damages are awarded following tort claims. We started by considering the principles lying behind damages awards, finding the primary object of the law to be to compensate those who are harmed by another's wrongdoing. This is done by making an award that seeks to put the claimant into the position that they would have been in had the harm not occurred. Damages awards can encompass pecuniary (financial) and non-pecuniary losses. Future losses (those not quantifiable at the time of trial) are calculated using multiplicands (the sum to be multiplied) and multipliers (the number of years the loss should be multiplied by). In the main, damages are awarded as a lump sum.

Multiple defendants can incur liability independently, jointly or severally. Either a court will apportion damages between them or one defendant can seek contribution from another. However, there are time limits placed on all damages claims—not uncontroversially. Many further critiques of the way damages can be and are awarded can be (and have been) made, not least the need to establish fault and blame in order to achieve compensation, and the fact that this means that many people go without. The tort system, viewed in this way, seems to benefit very few people and other ways of achieving fairer compensation for more people have been proposed.

102. **n 98**, pp 2–3.

103. Thankfully, empirical work which will hopefully help us begin to understand how the 'real world' of tort law has been affected by the recent reforms has begun and the new litigation and negotiation 'tactics' being used (see Richard Lewis 'Tort Tactics: An Empirical Study of Personal Injury Litigation Strategies' (2017) 37 LS 162.

End-of-chapter questions

After reading the chapter carefully, try answering the questions which follow.

1. Should the focus of the tort system be based on fault, or on other considerations such as need, equality or deterrence?
2. Is it right that society as a whole largely shoulders the burden of higher compensation payouts, through principles of insurance, higher prices for goods and services, and tax?
3. Do we (as a society) blame and claim too much?
4. Is the tension between achieving justice for claimants and doing justice by defendants simply irreconcilable?
5. Should any time limitations be put on tort claims?
6. Should the tort system be more concerned with distributive than corrective justice?

If you would like to know what we think visit the **online resources**. www.oup.com/he/horsey7e

Answering the problem question

Consider again the problem question at the start of this chapter. Now having read about the topic, **what compensation would Emma receive from the two negligent drivers?**

Here are some pointers to get you started

→ Negligence is not disputed, so you do not need to establish the defendants' liability.

→ Damages should be thought of in terms of special and general damages (see **section 21.3.2**). What losses can be quantified by the time of trial? For the physical injuries suffered, **Figure 21.1** may be helpful.

→ General damages are more problematic—here they may include future lost earnings (both regular and special earnings from the TV work) and pension (calculated using a multiplier/multiplicand method), future medical treatment and equipment, the cost of care, continued pain, suffering and loss of amenity (her social activities will be relevant here).

If you need some more guidance

→ An **annotated version of the problem with issues and cases to consider** can be found in the Appendix.

see online resources

→ A **suggested outline answer** to check your ideas against can be found in the online resources that accompany the book.

Further reading

The further reading outlined here is primarily related to critiques of the damages system. Many of the books, articles and other reading below have already been directly cited or mentioned in the text but, for reasons of space and conciseness, we have not been able to treat each of these in full. Therefore, we would recommend at least browsing through all those listed here, to better understand how the law on damages currently operates, as well as the critiques of the system.

Association of Personal Injury Lawyers, *Our Strategic Plan 2020–23 and beyond* (2020)

Atiyah, Patrick *The Damages Lottery* (Hart, 1997)

British Medical Journal 'BMJ Bans "Accidents"' (2001) 322 BMJ 1320 (2 June)

Cane, Peter *Atiyah's Accidents, Compensation and the Law* (7th edn, CUP, 2006)

Conaghan, Joanne 'Tort Litigation in the Context of Intra-familial Abuse' (1998) 61 MLR 132

Donaldson, Liam (Chief Medical Officer) Making Amends: A Consultation Paper Setting Out Proposals for Reforming the Approach to Clinical Negligence in the NHS (HMSO, 2003)

Furedi, Frank *The Culture of Fear* (2nd edn, Continuum Press, 2002)

Hand, James 'The Compensation Culture: Cliché or Cause for Concern?' (2010) 37 J L & Soc 569

House of Commons Constitutional Affairs Committee 'Compensation Culture', Third Report of Session 2005–06, vol I

Lewis, Richard, 'The Politics and Economics of Tort Law: Judicially Imposed Periodical Payments of Damages' (2006) 69 MLR 418

Lewis, Richard, Annette Morris and Ken Oliphant 'Tort Personal Injuries Claims Statistics: Is There a Compensation Culture in the United Kingdom?' (2006) 14 Torts LJ 158

Morris, Annette 'Spiralling or Stabilising? The Compensation Culture and our Propensity to Claim Damages for Personal Injury' (2007) 70 MLR 349

Murphy, John 'The Nature and Domain of Aggravated Damages' [2010] CLJ 353

Oliphant, Ken 'Beyond Misadventure: Compensation for Medical Injuries in New Zealand' (2007) 15 Med L Rev 357

Quill, Eoin and Raymond J Friel (eds), *Damages and Compensation Culture: Comparative Perspectives* (Hart, 2019)

Tilbury, Michael 'Aggravated Damages' (2018) 71 CLP 215

Williams, Kevin 'State of Fear: Britain's Compensation Culture Reviewed' (2005) 25 LS 499

Appendix: annotated problem questions

The purpose of these annotations is to suggest some of the things you should consider when answering the problem questions at the beginning of each chapter. We have tried to 'contain' each question as far as possible within the context of the chapter in which it appears. Inevitably, however, there is overlap between issues in the various chapters, which we have highlighted in the annotations. As you become more familiar with answering problem questions in tort law you will begin to recognise the issues more easily. Remember that although problem questions usually focus on one or two issues, you need to make sure that you consider *all* aspects of the claims so that your answer is as detailed as possible. So, for example, in relation to a negligence problem question which primarily raises issues relating to 'breach', you should also address those relating to duty, causation and defences (even if only very briefly). Sometimes the same issue will arise at different points in the question; where this happens we will only point it out once. More detailed outline answers to many of the problem questions (as well as downloadable versions of the annotated answers in this Appendix) are available on the **online resources** (www.oup.com/he/horsey7e). These are not 'model' answers, but rather more targeted guidance that breaks each question down into more manageable pieces and points you in the right direction(s). To get the most out of the problem questions, you should try to draft your own answer to them before looking on the **online resources**.

see online resources

When answering a problem question you should:

(1) Use the 'story' or facts to help you—what are the relevant facts? Why has the examiner included that information? What else would it be helpful to know?

(2) Answer the question. Where the facts are unclear or some relevant fact appears to be missing, don't be tempted to make up alternative facts—just explain what difference the factual uncertainty would make to the legal outcome.

(3) Clearly identify the potential claimants, defendants and claims—who will be bringing the claim(s)? Who will the defendant(s) be and, importantly, *what* will the claims be for (e.g. personal injury or property damage, etc)?

(4) Distinguish unproblematic issues (to be dealt with very briefly) from the legally difficult ones (to be discussed and analysed in more detail).

(5) Incorporate intelligent *argument* on the difficult legal issues—typically 'the answer' will not be straightforward and so you should present the various arguments supported by 'evidence' (usually case law) that might be put forward and highlight the one you think is the strongest and why.

(6) Come to a conclusion—how you think the court would decide the point, even if it is only fairly tentative.

(7) Use case law appropriately. Don't get distracted by the facts of a case; it is the point of law—or principle—that a case establishes that is important.

Special duty problems: omissions and acts of third parties annotated problem question

Margaret, who is 75, is in the supermarket on a busy Saturday afternoon when she feels pains in her chest. It transpires she is having a heart attack and she collapses to the floor. Although the supermarket is crowded, no one comes to help her.

Brian, the store manager, puts a call out over the PA system asking if there is a doctor present, but otherwise offers no assistance. Hearing the announcement, Karen, a nurse, comes forward and tries to help Margaret, but fails to put her in the recovery position. Margaret later dies.

Meanwhile, some youths see Margaret's car, which was left unlocked and with the key still in the ignition in the supermarket car park as she did not want to spend time looking for a parking space. The youths drive off in the car, failing to stop at a pedestrian crossing, hitting Jill and her daughter Heather who were crossing the road. Both are injured, Heather seriously. One of the youths, Luke, who was not wearing a seat belt, suffers a serious head injury.

Advise the parties.

The central question here is whether these are all 'callous bystanders' (Lord Nicholls, ***Stovin v Wise* [1996]**) or whether anyone owed M a *duty* to come to her aid.

Does the action B has taken mean that he has 'assumed responsibility' for M in any way? See ***Barrett v MOD* [1995]**. If he has, he will owe her a duty of care. If he has not, there is no duty and M's claim against him will end here.

At the outset it is important to note what claims will be made, by whom, for what and against whom. Here, we have M v B (and the supermarket vicariously?), M v K, J & H v M, L v M.

This indicates negligence on M's part. Can she be sued even though she is dead? (See **Chapter 21.**) Who would sue her and what for? Would this also make her contributorily negligent (see **Chapter 10**) in relation to her own claims, should any succeed?

This is definitely assumption of responsibility by K—is a duty then owed? If so, what is the *content* of the duty? Working out how far the duty extends allows you to consider whether or not there is a *breach*.

Here, L is another potential claimant. However, the question is whether M should owe him a duty of care, even though he, as the third party, was (at least. in part) responsible in some way for his own injuries. See also **Chapter 9** on causation points (quite tricky here), including whether he may have broken the chain of causation in his own claim.

Even if L can establish a claim against M should he be found contributorily negligent? See **Chapter 10.**

The alleged negligence (whether K fell below the standard of care expected) would have to be established. Failing to do something is an omission (which is why it is first important to establish whether K owed M a duty of care in respect of omissions).

So who would actually be taking this action, and what for? See **Chapter 21**.

Therefore, J and H have been harmed by the actions of the youths, who become the third party in relation to a claim against M. The question is whether M should be held to owe J and H a duty of care in respect of the actions taken by third parties as a result of her own negligence (leaving the car unlocked). Compare ***Home Office v Dorset Yacht* [1970]** and *Topp v London Country Bus* [1993].

Special duty problems: psychiatric harm annotated problem question

Following months of speculation the legendary indie guitar band—*Blinking Idiot*—are about to embark on a reunion tour of the UK. They are performing a warm-up gig at a small intimate venue when a spotlight falls onto the stage causing a massive explosion killing the band members: Madeleine, Amish and Dave. Unfortunately, the lighting rig (onto which the spotlight was fitted) had been negligently maintained by Rack & Horse Lighting. The sight is particularly gruesome.

Hannah, Amish's wife, is watching the gig from the VIP area of the venue. She is physically unharmed, but later suffers nightmares and depression. This is particularly traumatic for her as she had previously suffered from depression, but had sought help and recovered.

Pete, Madeleine's brother, is listening to the live radio broadcast of the gig from his hotel room in Paris. He hears the explosion and thinks he can hear Madeleine screaming. He rushes to the airport, managing to catch a flight that is just leaving, and arrives at the hospital three hours after the accident. Unfortunately, Madeleine's body has not yet been moved to the morgue and is still covered in blood and grime from the explosion. He develops post-traumatic shock disorder.

Lucy has attended every *Blinking Idiot* gig in the UK and has travelled to a number of their overseas concerts. She is a founder member of their fan club and regularly contributes to their fan magazine. She always tries to stand as close as possible to the stage. Miraculously she was not hurt by the explosion but has since been overcome with grief.

Tim was one of the first on the scene. He is a trainee ambulance man and this was his first major incident. He rushes to the stage but quickly sees that there is little he can do. He spends the next two hours comforting distraught fans. He later suffers from recurring nightmares and panic attacks.

Stuart, one of the roadies, is overcome with feelings of guilt and depression. It was his job to fix the lighting and he feels the explosion was his fault. A subsequent investigation completely exonerates him.

Advise the parties.

Rack and Horse Lighting will be the defendants in all the claims.

Hannah is likely to be too far away to be a primary victim (although this depends on how far away the VIP area is—if it was near to the stage she could be in the zone of danger as in ***Page* [1996]**). If she is not a primary victim, she would therefore need to show that she meets the criteria set out in ***Alcock* [1992]**. Note that her previous depression will not defeat her claim as a secondary victim if a person of 'ordinary phlegm and fortitude' would have suffered some sort of psychiatric harm. Assuming this is the case, the 'egg shell skull' principle will allow her to recover for the full extent of her injury (even if it goes beyond what is reasonably foreseeable).

Pete will need to satisfy the secondary victim criteria as set down in ***Alcock***. The key issue here is proximity in time and space—could hearing Madeleine on the radio be akin to seeing her on TV? Given what the law lords said in ***Alcock*** about TV images, this is unlikely to be successful. He will also need to establish a close tie of love and affection with his sister. You should apply and distinguish ***Alcock, McLoughlin* [1982]** and *Galli-Atkinson* [2003].

Tim is a rescuer. Following ***White* [1998]** he will need to establish that he meets either the primary or secondary victim requirements.

Stuart would be considered an involuntary participant as in ***Dooley* [1951]**. He may also be a primary victim depending on how close he is standing to the stage.

Although Lucy may be a primary victim (on the basis of ***Page***), she has not suffered a recognisable psychiatric illness—mere grief is not recoverable.

Special duty problems: public bodies annotated problem question

PC Plod and PC Bill both work for the Countyshire Constabulary. They are involved in investigating a high-profile criminal case involving a bank robbery.

One night, PCs Plod and Bill are on motorway patrol when a car passes them at a fairly high speed. PC Plod, who is driving the patrol car, recognises the car as belonging to one of his neighbours, Mr Smith, with whom he has had a long-standing feud since Mr Smith had an affair with his wife. Determined to get his own back on Mr Smith, PC Plod, despite PC Bill's objection, decides to give chase. As the cars approach 110 mph, PC Plod loses control and the two cars collide. Mr Smith's car turns over several times before eventually coming to a stop. PC Bill is injured.

PC Plod calls an ambulance from the Countyshire Ambulance Service. This takes 30 minutes to arrive and, even then, because of staff shortages, the paramedic on board is an unqualified trainee. He examines Mr Smith and concludes that he is dead, so devotes his attention to a fairly minor leg wound suffered by PC Bill. Half an hour later a doctor arrives at the scene. When he examines Mr Smith he realises he is actually alive, but deeply unconscious. Despite the doctor's best efforts, Mr Smith dies on the way to hospital.

Meanwhile, the criminal gang under investigation take part in another bank robbery in a nearby town, during which a hostage is killed. Witnesses seeing the hostages being dragged into the bank at gunpoint had called the police and been assured that they were on their way. In fact, the call had gone to PC Plod, who had ignored it because he was more interested in chasing Mr Smith. Bruce, the husband of the hostage who died, believes the police could have done more to prevent her death. The owner of the bank believes the police were negligent in failing to prevent the robbery.

Advise the families of Mr Smith and the hostage as to any potential claims in negligence.

This is your starting point. Who are the people who will be suing? Who will the defendants be? What is the negligence alleged? Note there may be quite a number of different claims here.

Should either of the officers be found to have committed a tort, the Chief Constable of Countyshire Constabulary may also be a defendant through the principle of vicarious liability **(Chapter 20)**. They may also be sued directly if there was any indication of the force's negligence in the facts.

You should note that it is often important to look out for 'red herrings' or facts that simply aren't relevant to the claims you are dealing with. Here, e.g., there is no question about whether this car was 'speeding' or whether the driver of the car was negligent, as the driver is not a defendant.

This might be relevant to any defences raised by PC Plod.

This suggests potential negligence on PC Plod's part, indicating that he will be a defendant.

So there is (at least) a claim for personal injury stemming from the collision, though you are not asked at the end to advise PC Bill—watch out for things like this and don't get distracted!

Consider the points on assumption of responsibility made in ***Michael* v *Chief Constable of South Wales Police* [2015]**.

Again, this relates to any potential claim that may be taken against the ambulance service. Is it 'negligent' to have an unqualified trainee on board an ambulance? If so, this might be a claim against the ambulance service *directly*, for failing to provide an adequate service. However, you should be aware of the policy/operational distinctions that operate in these types of claims.

A claim is likely to be made by the family of Mr Smith (e.g. either acting on behalf of his estate or even directly, if there are dependants—see **Chapter 21**). The allegation is that the car chase caused him to suffer his injuries, then an unqualified paramedic was negligent in his assessment of Mr Smith, leading to the delay that subsequently may have caused his death (note there may be a factual causation issue here, see **Chapter 9**). This means that there are two defendants to this claim, and the duty, breach, causation formula must be followed in respect of each (note, however, that this claim against PC Plod is not one related to the investigation or suppression of a crime and so will not invoke the ***Hill* [1989]** line of authorities: see ***Robinson* v *Chief Constable of West Yorkshire* [2018]**). Either, both or neither may end up being liable. Either way, this is still going to be a claim against a public body, however, because if found to be negligent, the ambulance service will be responsible for the tort of the paramedic through the principle of vicarious liability (see **Chapter 20**). The ambulance service may also be sued directly here, for sending an unqualified trainee (although breach would not be self-evident in them doing this). NOTE: this is therefore a different claim from the one made directly against the ambulance service (for arriving late), earlier.

The claim here is that the police were negligent in their efforts to prevent a crime. Can the police be sued in this respect (and who sues, when the person who is injured dies? See **Chapter 21**). See e.g. ***Hill*, *Smith* v *Chief Constable of Sussex Police* [2008]** and ***Michael* v *Chief Constable of South Wales Police* [2015]**. Also see *Van Colle* [2008] (and ***Michael***) in relation to a claim under the HRA—can this case be distinguished?

This raises similar issues to those in the claim above, although that was about personal injury (death) and this is about a financial loss. Does that make a difference here? Note, however, you are not asked to advise the owner of the bank.

This relates to any claim made against the ambulance service and the question here will be whether they had a duty to arrive promptly and, if they did, whether they have breached it by taking 30 minutes to arrive. See ***Kent* v *Griffiths* [2001]**. The breach issue might depend on exactly why they took so long and if this could be considered reasonable in the circumstances—see **Chapter 8**.

Special duty problems: economic loss annotated problem question

Rachael and Chris invested £600,000 in Read-Sing-Sign, a children's charity bookshop, after speaking to Amanda, a personal friend who is also an auditor. Amanda had prepared a financial report for the trustees of the shop, but showed it to Rachael and Chris 'off the record'. This showed that the bookshop was doing well and made good annual profits. It later transpired that the audit was inaccurate as Amanda failed to include some unpaid debts in the figures. The shop was in fact worthless.

Meanwhile, Rachael, who was relying on a £200,000 inheritance from her grandfather in order to be able to pay for her share of the shop, was told by the solicitors dealing with her grandfather's will that it is invalid and the terms of his previous will, which left everything to a local cats' home, would have to be followed. This is because he failed to sign both copies of the latest version of the will. The solicitor's copy was filed without checking the signature was present.

Advise Rachael and Chris as to the likelihood of success of any claims in negligence that they may take.

It should be noted at the outset that there is generally no duty of care owed in respect of claims for pure economic loss and that their only potential route would be to rely on ***Hedley Byrne* v *Heller* [1963]** and any later derivations of this rule.

Would this invoke a relationship of 'trust and confidence'?

A has clearly been negligent in her preparation of the report. The question is whether she would owe R & C a duty of care in respect of the economic loss they have suffered. As indicated in **Chapter 7**, this depends on whether their claim can be said to fall within the exception to the general exclusionary rule created in ***Hedley Byrne***, including whether it was reasonable for the claimant to rely on the advice given.

This brings into question whether any reliance on the part of R & C would be 'reasonable'.

This is a negligent act—again, the question is whether the solicitors would owe a duty of care to Rachael. A duty of care would clearly be owed to the grandfather but he (and his estate) has suffered no loss. See ***White* v *Jones* [1995]**. Note, however, this is not a question of the negligent drafting of a will, but negligent administration. Would the outcome be any different?

Compare ***Caparo* [1990]** and *Cramaso LLP (Appellant) v Ogilvie-Grant, Earl of Seafield and others (Respondents) (Scotland)* [2014]. Is this a similar situation?

This is, therefore, Rachael's loss.

Breach of duty: the standard of care annotated problem question

Kate and Iris have spent the afternoon looking at wedding dresses. Before heading home they go to a new champagne bar to celebrate finding 'the one'. Iris offers Kate a lift home in her car, assuring Kate that she's alright to drive as she's 'probably only just over the drink-drive limit'. On the journey home Iris loses control of the car and crashes into a lamp post. Kate suffers minor cuts and bruises and is taken to hospital for a check-up. At the hospital Kate contracts an infection in a cut to her right arm. The doctor on duty decides not to treat the infection with antibiotics immediately as he has recently read a report in a little-known medical journal which suggested that it is better to allow the body 'time to heal' following a trauma. Kate's right arm is partially paralysed.

Advise Kate.

Iris clearly owes Kate a duty of care (though you should still establish this), and has caused her injuries so the question you need to consider is whether Iris is acting as a reasonable driver. You need to work through the factors which the courts consider when setting the standard of care.

Kate also has a claim against the doctor. Again duty is straightforward. The issue here is one of 'informed consent'. There is no suggestion that the doctor has had a conversation with Kate above the risks relating to treatment vs non-treatment. Compare and contrast the decisions and reasoning in ***Bolam*** **[1957]**, *Bolitho* [1998] and ***Montgomery*** **[2015]**. The doctor's actions also raise issues relating to causation (**Chapter 9**).

You should also consider whether Kate was contributorily negligent when she got into the car with Iris knowing that Iris had been drinking (**Chapter 10**).

Causation and remoteness of damage annotated problem question

Stefaan and Gavin spend the evening drinking in the pub. Stefaan offers Gavin a lift home in his car, assuring Gavin that this will be fine as he is 'probably only just over the limit'. Driving home, Stefaan swerves to avoid a fox and crashes the car. The paramedics who arrive at the scene find that Gavin has broken his arm but otherwise only has minor cuts and bruises. Gavin is taken to hospital to be checked by a doctor.

At the hospital Gavin is seen by Cheryl, the doctor on duty. Cheryl disagrees with the paramedics' opinion and, deciding Gavin's arm is not broken but only sprained, puts it in a sling, without setting it in a cast. As she was so busy that evening, she decided not to bother sending him for an X-ray first. Gavin returns to hospital the following month with pain in his arm. It transpires that his arm *was* in fact broken and, because it was not set in the proper cast, the bones have fused together wrongly, resulting in a permanent disability. An expert witness says that there was a chance this might have happened anyway, even if Cheryl had not been negligent. Gavin has to have an operation to try and re-set the bones, but this will not improve his arm to the condition it was in before the accident.

A week later Gavin is knocked down by a speeding motorist who fails to stop and cannot be traced. His right arm is so badly injured that it has to be amputated.

Advise Gavin in relation to the claims in negligence he may bring.

There is no problem establishing duty here and it seems likely that breach is easily established. Can we say that 'but for' S's negligence, G would not have suffered these injuries? See ***Barnett*** **[1969]**.

All this raises the question whether any of these actions fell below the standard of care expected by a doctor and, as such, analysis will be guided by the ***Bolam*** **[1957]** and *Bolitho* [1998] tests, as now supplemented by ***Montgomery v Lanarkshire Health Board*** **[2015]**.

Is this harm a foreseeable consequence of (a) a car accident and (b) negligent treatment for a broken arm? *What* has to be foreseeable (see ***The Wagon Mound (No 1)*** **[1961]**)?

This raises a causation question about what would have happened had she not acted negligently. See *Bolitho* [1998] for similar points.

Whatever the outcome of G's claims, will any of the defendants be able to raise a defence? (See **Chapter 10**.) Should he have got into the car?

The question, in trying to establish factual causation, is 'how much chance'? If it was more than 50 per cent likely that the permanent disability would have originated from the original break, then C is not the 'but for' cause of this harm (see ***Barnett*** **[1969]** and ***Hotson*** **[1987]**). However, unlike in these cases, there is a previous act of negligence: does this mean that S will remain the 'but for' cause, even for these 'extended' injuries? What happens if it was less than 50 per cent likely that this injury would have resulted from the original accident? Could C's actions (if negligent) break the chain of causation back to S?

How does this affect the claims to be made against (a) S and (b) C? The motorist cannot be sued as he is untraceable. See ***Baker*** **[1970]** and ***Jobling*** **[1982]**.

Defences to negligence annotated problem question

Ben, Graeme and Andy are old school friends. Every year they go camping together in Snowdonia National Park. After they arrive on the Friday night, they decide to go to the pub where Ben and Graeme spend several hours reminiscing and by the time they leave they are both over the legal driving limit. Andy has not been drinking. On their way back to the campsite they pass a farm and notice a tractor with its keys in the ignition. Graeme gets in and starts the engine. Ben and Andy quickly jump in beside him. None of them wear a seat belt. At first, Graeme drives slowly around the farmyard but when Ben says 'Is that the best you can do?' he decides to go 'off-road' and drives it into a field. Unfortunately, on the rough ground Graeme loses control of the tractor and it overturns. Ben and Andy are thrown out onto the field. Ben is seriously injured. Though Andy escapes with only minor physical injuries, he later develops post-traumatic stress disorder (PTSD) as a result of the incident. One day while walking home from work Andy 'snaps' lashing out at an innocent passer-by and causing them serious injury. Though it is recognised that his actions were as a result of his PTSD, he is jailed for six months and loses his job.

Advise the parties (you should assume that, in the absence of applicable defences, Ben and Andy would have a good claim in negligence).

This is an important detail. It means the Road Traffic Act 1988 would not apply and so the defence of *volenti* is arguable.

Will Andy's claim against Graeme be defeated by the defence of illegality? You should consider the application of ***Gray* v *Thames Trains* [2009]** here.

You need to address this point both in relation to *volenti* (is Ben too drunk to consent to the risk?) and contributory negligence (has Ben failed to exercise reasonable care for his own safety?).

Can Ben's failure to wear a seat belt (together with his jumping in quickly alongside Graeme) be used to argue that he accepted the nature and extent of the risk he was exposed to? The cases to consider here are ***Morris* v *Murray* [1991]** and ***Dann* v *Hamilton* [1939]**—which one is close to the facts you have been given? What about Andy? As he *hadn't* been drinking, is *volenti* more likely to be made out?

Consider why this piece of information is included here—can Ben's active encouragement be used to argue that Ben and Graeme are engaging in a joint criminal enterprise (as in *Pitts* v *Hunt* [1991])? It may also be helpful in arguments relating to contributory negligence.

You should consider each defence in turn. Remember when considering contributory negligence you should work through each of the three requirements: (1) failure to exercise reasonable care for his own safety; (2) whether his actions contributed to his damage; and (3) what would be a just and equitable reduction? Consider the guidelines in ***Froom* v *Butcher* [1976]**.

Occupiers' liability annotated problem question

'Camden Cool', an after-school youth club run by the local authority, is holding an open day to raise funds for the club. One of the main attractions is a large bouncy castle supplied, erected and supervised by Elsinore Castles, a small local company. Joseph and Harry are the first to try it out. They both suffer minor cuts and bruises when the castle breaks free from its moorings and lifts into the air. It later turns out that it had not been appropriately tethered to the ground. Unfortunately, despite assuring Jake, the club's youth worker, when he phoned to book the castle, that they had the necessary documentation, Elsinore's public liability insurance had expired two months before the accident.

In the chaos that follows, Iris (Joseph's sister) wanders off alone. She is too young to be a member of the club and so doesn't know her way around the buildings. She is seriously injured when she falls down a flight of stairs after going through a door marked 'Private: No Unauthorised Entry'.

Meanwhile Frank and Bill (who are members of the club) have sneaked off to play football. After a particularly poor shot at goal their ball lands on a flat roof. Although they know the roof is 'out of bounds', as everyone is busy at the open day, they decide to climb onto the roof to retrieve it. As they do so one of the skylights breaks. Bill falls through the roof hitting his head hard, causing him to lose his hearing.

Advise the parties of any claims they may have under the Occupiers' Liability Acts 1957 and 1984.

Although usually an occupier will not be liable for the negligence of an independent contractor, the facts here are very similar to those in ***Gwilliam* [2002]**. In that case it was held that there was a duty to check that the independent contractors had appropriate liability insurance but, on the facts, it had not been breached. Cf *Naylor v Payling* [2004] and *Glaister v Appleby-in-Westmoreland Town Council* [2009].

It is likely that Joseph and Harry are visitors—however, you need to establish why this is and not just assume it. This means an action will be brought against the local authority under the OLA 1957.

Here you are told that Frank and Bill are members of the club and so should be treated as visitors under the 1957 Act—but an occupier can restrict their duty as has been done here (by making the roof 'out of bounds') and ***Tomlinson* [2003]** would suggest that when they are on the roof they are trespassers. You therefore need to assess whether the local authority owes them a duty of care by working through the subsections of s 1(3). Remember after doing so you also need to consider issues relating to breach and causation. Finally, it is likely that Bill would be found to be contributorily negligent (see **Chapter 10** and, in particular, the case of *Young v Kent County Council* [2005]).

Note that here you need only to consider a claim under the OLAs. If neither of the Acts is applicable there may also be a claim in negligence—as this is harder to establish you should go to the OLAs first.

It is crucial to establish here whether Iris is a visitor or a non-visitor—the 1957 and 1984 Acts say different things about 'warnings'. If Iris is a trespasser (assuming a duty can be established) all the occupier needs to have done is to take 'reasonable steps' to bring the risk to her attention (the 1984 Act, unlike the 1957 Act, does not make special allowances for children). You should also consider the position if Iris is a visitor, and her position under the 1957 Act.

Product liability annotated problem question

After many years of research, Rack and Horse Pharmaceuticals (RHP) develop a drug to treat breast cancer. After only 18 months of clinical trials, it received a licence and went on the market in the UK in March 2016. Although the drug itself is completely pure, it is now known that in less than 0.5 per cent of patients (those who carry a particular gene) it can produce an undesirable side effect known as Tort Syndrome. This side effect is not widely publicised as both RHP and the government are keen to encourage widespread uptake of the drug in the relevant groups of women.

In 2021, 20 claimants who were given the drug between 2016 and 2018 and who contracted Tort Syndrome begin an action against RHP alleging both negligence and liability under the Consumer Protection Act 1987. RHP argues against liability because up until 2019, there was no genetic test that could determine which individuals carried the gene in question.

The claimants bring evidence to show there was an article in an Outer Mongolian scientific journal, published both in hard copy and on the Internet in 2017, which suggested a test to determine whether individual women carried the specific gene for the reaction to the drug that causes Tort Syndrome. Had RHP conducted clinical trials for longer, the company would have been able to identify the characteristics of the women likely to react badly to the drug and to issue appropriate warnings and advice.

Advise the parties.

In a claim under the Consumer Protection Act, Rack and Horse Pharmaceuticals would be the 'producer' and should be identified as such, using the relevant section of the statute.

The drug is clearly a 'product' for the purposes of the Consumer Protection Act and should be identified as such, using the relevant section of the statute.

Under the Consumer Protection Act the test for liability is different and producers will be strictly liable for any harm caused by defects in their products.

But is the reaction to the vaccine the only potential cause, or might there be multiple potential causes? If so, cause in fact might be difficult to establish (see **Chapter 9**).

The claimants here have suffered physical harm (and there may be some consequential losses). Note that not all harms which may be caused by products are recoverable under the Act.

This suggests negligence and so the claimants may wish to claim in the tort of negligence as well. They would need to establish liability using the normal principles of duty, breach and causation—could they?

To succeed in a negligence claim the claimants must establish duty, breach and causation. There is no problem with duty (***Donoghue***) **[1932]**, and possibly not breach—but causation is likely to prove tricky unless the drug is the only potential cause of Tort Syndrome.

Should this risk have been made public? Is it negligent not to have done so (this may be an alternative claim)?

Does this make the vaccine 'defective' for the purposes of the Consumer Protection Act (s 3)? Consider the cases **A v *National Blood Authority*** **[2001]** and *Gee and others v Depuy International Ltd* [2018].

The criterion is that such knowledge should be 'accessible'—is this? See ***EC* v *UK*** **[1997]**. Can RHP rely on the 'development risks' defence?

Employers' liability annotated problem question

Every Tuesday, Thursday and Friday evening there is a drop-in centre for young people between the ages of 11 and 16 at Kings Wharf, a local community centre. It is run by a team of youth workers employed by James.

Harry is youth counsellor at the centre. He is busy setting up the hall for the evening's activities when he slips on a puddle of greasy water from a leaking radiator and breaks his wrist. He had reported the leak to his supervisor, Dougie, over a week earlier and it had not been fixed. Tom, a youth worker at the centre and Harry's partner, sees him fall. Frustrated by Dougie's lack of action, Tom punches him on the nose.

Danny works in the centre kitchen, making snacks and drinks for the young people. He is using a food processor to make some cookies when a fragment of metal is thrown off by the machine and enters his eye. The food processor had been serviced two weeks earlier in accordance with the provisions of the Kitchens Safety Act 2003 [a fictitious statute] which states that 'all moving parts on food-mixers must be maintained'.

Advise the parties.

All the claims will be brought against James—you should establish this at the outset.

Perhaps a classic case of a non-delegable duty of care—James owes Harry a duty to ensure a safe system of working—see further ***Latimer* v *AEC Ltd*** **[1953]**.

Might Danny also have a claim for breach of statutory duty? You should work through the following questions stating clearly what more information you need in order to answer them fully: (1) Does the statute give rise to a claim in tort law? (2) Is a duty owed to the claimant? (3) Has the defendant breached their duty? (4) Does the claimant's loss or injury fall within the scope of the duty? (see **Chapter 14**).

James will be vicariously liable for Tom's actions if the following conditions are satisfied: Tom is an employee of James (this is likely to be straightforward); Tom has committed a tort 'in the course of his employment' (see **section 20.4**).

An employer also has a duty to take reasonable care to provide all necessary equipment (including safety equipment), as well as instructions on how to use it and to maintain it in a reasonable condition. See common law and the Employers' Liability (Defective Equipment) Act 1969.

Intentional interferences with the person annotated problem question

Henry, Mark, Mary and Anne are sitting in the students' union bar discussing their outfits for the forthcoming 'Law Society Spring Ball'.

Thomas, Mary's ex-boyfriend, walks by and says quietly to Henry, 'I'll get you! No one steals my girl and gets away with it'. Although Henry is not particularly upset by this, he decides to teach Thomas a lesson. When no one is looking, he deliberately trips Thomas up. Thomas falls over but is not hurt. He quickly jumps up and runs after Henry. Thomas hits Henry and pushes him away and Henry falls awkwardly and hits his head. As Mary rushes to get a doctor, Thomas corners her and whispers, 'I miss you, let's try again'. She pushes him away.

Meanwhile Mark and Anne have sneaked into the bar's storeroom for some time alone. On seeing this, Thomas locks the storeroom door. It remains locked until Rafe, the barman, comes on duty some time later and unlocks it.

Later that evening, Thomas calls Catherine, Henry's pregnant ex-girlfriend, who lives some distance away, and tells her Henry has been badly hurt. She takes the news very badly. Thomas then calls Mary's mobile; as she is still at the hospital with Henry she does not answer it. By the time she checks her phone she has 12 missed calls.

Advise the parties.

It will be easier to answer this problem question chronologically by claim rather than by party.

You need to consider here whether Thomas's whispered comment is an assault—also remember to address the point raised by the following sentence—it does not matter that Henry is not upset by Thomas's threat (see ***Stephens* v *Myers* (1830)**).

Could Thomas's comment be an assault? If so, is Mary's action in pushing him away self-defence? If not, then Mary's actions will amount to a battery.

Be careful here—the facts are not the same as *Wilkinson v Downton* [1897]. Does it apply to true statements? If not, could there be a claim in negligence (for communication of shocking news) (see **Chapter 5**)?

The point to emphasise here is the one raised in *Williams v Humphrey* [1975]—i.e. that Thomas will be liable for the full extent of Henry's injuries (even though he did not intend to hurt him to this extent). Also remember to address any relevant defences here.

This will be a battery (and, possibly, if Thomas noticed what Henry was doing, an assault). You need to work through the requirements for each of these torts. Remember there is still an actionable battery even though Thomas is not physically hurt, you need to say why this is.

A clear case of false imprisonment—as with the other torts you need to work through the elements of this tort emphasising that it makes no difference to the existence of the tort that they were unaware of their 'imprisonment' (although this will affect the amount of damages awarded)—remember to cite the appropriate case law.

Here you need to discuss whether Thomas's actions amount to harassment under the Protection from Harassment Act 1997.

Invasion of privacy annotated problem question

Elizabeth is the fiancée of a Premiership footballer, Alessandro Talentti. She has always been happy to be photographed with Alessandro at awards evenings, film premieres and charity events and also while out with her girlfriends shopping or lunching, or with other footballers' wives and girlfriends watching football matches.

Recently, as she has started to organise her wedding, which she wants to be intimate and private, Elizabeth has found the media attention intrusive and has had several arguments with photographers wanting to take her picture whilst out shopping or in small, quiet restaurants. One photographer, Chris, is particularly persistent and takes photographs when she is leaving a hospital after visiting her mother who is very ill. He also photographed her (using a long-range lens) going to a small London bridal boutique when she was shopping for bridesmaids' dresses with her young sister and niece.

On the wedding day—the press having been successfully excluded from the venue —one of the caterers secretly takes some pictures of the wedding ceremony and the reception, where there were many famous guests. He sells these pictures to *Peachy!*, a well-known celebrity glossy magazine; the pictures are published in the following week's issue and online as an 'exclusive'. Meanwhile, a journalist contacts Alessandro saying he has found out that he had a brief affair the previous year while away at a football tournament and that this information is going to be published the following day.

Advise Elizabeth and Alessandro as to any legal actions they might be able to pursue.

In the past E has not minded publicity—will this affect any of her claims?

Do her wishes add anything to her claims? Consider ***Douglas* v *Hello!* [2005]**.

Is the fact that she has made public her desire for her wedding to stay private relevant? See ***Murray* v *Express Newspapers* [2008]**.

Is this comparable with ***Campbell* [2004]**? Does it make her claim stronger that another person is involved? Does E have a 'reasonable expectation of privacy' in this situation? If a court has to weigh up the right to privacy (Art 8 ECHR) with the right to freedom of expression (Art 10 ECHR), who do you think will win here?

Is there any 'harm' done by these pictures? Compare e.g. ***Campbell* v *MGN***. Does E have a 'reasonable expectation of privacy' in this situation? If a court has to weigh up the right to privacy (Art 8 ECHR) against the right to freedom of expression (Art 10 ECHR), who do you think will win here? See also *Mosley* v *News Group Newspapers* [2008].

Following ***Douglas* v *Hello!*** would this be actionable? Is there a difference in this case in that there was no existing arrangement to sell pictures to another magazine? If so, would that go in E's favour or against her?

Does this suggest that it is a 'private' wedding? Leading to the couple having a legitimate or 'reasonable expectation of privacy' with all relating to it?

Would this fall foul of the (current) IPSO Editors' Code? If so, would any remedy the IPSO could provide be acceptable?

Does the fact that there are children being photographed help her claim? See ***Murray* v *Express Newspapers*** and *Weller* v *Associated Newspapers Ltd* [2015], but compare *AAA* v *Associated Newspapers Ltd* [2013]. Does E have a 'reasonable expectation of privacy' in this situation? If a court has to weigh up the right to privacy (Art 8 ECHR) against the right to freedom of expression (Art 10 ECHR), who do you think will win here?

This would suggest that Alessandro would seek an injunction to prevent the publication of the story. Consider the purpose of injunctions and the implications for freedom of expression if the story is not published, as well as the public's 'right to know'. Consider the opinion of the court in *Mosley*—in the context of publication of information about private sexual relationships—but also the question of AT being a 'role model' and cases where footballers and other famous people have had this kind of information published on this basis. Recent cases have focused on the balance of the Art 8 right to a private life against Art 10's freedom of expression—each must be carefully weighed against the other—what do you think the outcome would be here, and why?

Defamation annotated problem question

In the Hood, a weekly fashion and TV magazine, is famous for its celebrity 'scoops'. This week's issue includes the following stories:

'TV CHEF IN JUNK FOOD SHAME!'—a two-page story about a TV chef, who prides herself on her healthy recipes, and who has been spotted buying an unhealthy snack in her local supermarket. In fact, she was accompanied by a film crew and was buying it for the new series of her show. The article does not mention this.

'EXPLOITED FOR THE SAKE OF FASHION'—a four-page feature in which claims are made about Rack and Horse Design, a designer clothing company. The article suggests that the company is:

- exploiting its shop workers in the UK by paying below minimum wages;
- destroying the environment through its continued use of highly toxic dyes;
- forcing workers in the developing world to work in 'inhumane and degrading' conditions.

'BOOZED-UP & KICKED OUT'—a photo spread (accompanied by brief captions) of 'celebrities' appearing worse for wear after a night out. Underneath the headline—but in much smaller print—there is an explanation that these are staged photos using celebrity look-a-likes.

Advise *In the Hood's* editor as to the magazine's potential liability in the tort of defamation.

What is it that is defamatory here? Think about why the magazine does not mention why the chef is buying the unhealthy snack. Remember that s 1 of the Defamation Act 2013 requires the statement to reach a 'seriousness' threshold.

Will *In the Hood* have to establish the truth of all these claims in order to rely on the defence of truth (Defamation Act 2013, s 2)? Could the defence of honest opinion apply here (Defamation Act 2013, s 3)?

You should first consider whether each of the claims is capable of being defamatory before considering any applicable defences, if necessary.

Compare *Charleston v News Group Newspapers Ltd* [1995]—do you think the reasoning in this case is likely to be applied? Is *O'Shea* [2001] a closer analogy? If not, why not?

Trespass to land and nuisance annotated problem question

Lekan owns a large country estate in Buckhampton. He wants to develop it as an environmentally friendly residential adventure centre catering for stressed-out city executives. To this end, he has constructed a network of ropes, ladders and bridges in the canopy of his woodland for them to come and 'Swing High' from tree to tree. Unfortunately, misplaced marketing has led to the majority of his customers being large, noisy groups of young people on stag and hen weekends. Lekan also provides facilities for paintballing and a quad-bike cross-country course. In line with his stated environmental policy, he has recently begun to use large volumes of seaweed, collected from nearby beaches, as fertiliser for his large organic vegetable patch. He has been encouraged to do so by his local council's recycling officer, who is keen to stop waste material going to landfill sites.

Lekan receives the following complaints:

(a) Sarah, who lives downwind of Lekan's estate, complains that the smell of the rotting seaweed makes her physically sick.

(b) Sandy, a 14-year-old, lives on a neighbouring farm. He complains that the noise from the quad bikes is causing his guinea pigs to miscarry their young.

(c) Jess who, when she walks her dogs, parks her car next to Lekan's boundary fence, complains that her car has, on a few occasions, been hit by stray paintballs.

(d) Ailsa complains that the 'Swing High' centre 'lowers the tone of the neighbourhood' and that her back garden can be seen from the platforms in the trees.

Lekan, the 'creator' of the alleged nuisances, will be the defendant.

The first question, following ***Hunter*****, [1997]** would be to ask whether Sarah has 'standing' to sue.

Sarah is complaining that the smell of the seaweed is a nuisance. What remedy would she require? Might the 'nature of the locality' affect her claim?

Physical sickness cannot be claimed in private nuisance—although it might be part of 'lost amenity'. Is there a potential claim in public nuisance? What would she have to show? Does she have a human rights-based claim?

Will Jess be able to claim? Does she have standing to sue in nuisance? If there is physical damage to her car, the locality rule would not need to be applied (***St Helen's Smelting*** [1865]).

Would a child of this age have 'standing'? What issues does this raise?

The alleged nuisance. What might be the remedy sought for this? Consider whether the 'nature of the locality' might affect either the success of the claim or, if successful, the remedy (see ***Coventry* v *Lawrence*** [2014]).

Can this be construed in any way as a harm to the land affected? Is Sandy 'abnormally sensitive' in his use of land? Or would the harm be 'foreseeable' (***Network Rail*** [2004]).

What kind of claim is this? Is it one based on human rights? Or is it trespass?

Is this a nuisance claim? Possibly public nuisance if this affects a class of Her Majesty's subjects. On the visibility of her back garden, see *Fearn and others v The Board of Trustees of the Tate Gallery* [2019].

Is this trespass? If so, the standing issue may not be a problem—but her car is not 'land', nor is she on her own land.

Actions under the rule of *Rylands* v *Fletcher* annotated problem question

Grab-and-Buy supermarket owns land on which it has built a huge two-storey metal-framed customer car park. One day, after extremely stormy weather with strong winds and heavy rain, the top level of the car park buckles; some of the metal railing breaks free and falls onto the neighbouring petrol station, owned by Low-Price-Pumps. The impact damages the pumps and injures one of Low-Price-Pumps' customers. Furthermore, water that had collected on the upper level of the car park due to an inadequate drainage system pours on to Low-Price-Pumps, flooding the forecourt of the petrol station. The station has to close two days, causing £10,000 loss of profit.

Low-Price-Pumps spends £50,000 having the forecourt cleaned and making safe the pumps. Grab-and-Buy argues that damage to the pumps caused by high winds is something that Low-Price-Pumps could and should have insured against.

Advise the parties.

In the ***Rylands* v *Fletcher* [1868]** claim for the property damage suffered by LPP, LPP would need to establish liability using the four criteria, as modified by ***Transco* [2003]**: (1) The defendant brings on his land for his own purposes something likely to do mischief ...(2) ... if it escapes ... (*Read* v *Lyons* [1947]) (3) ... which represents a non-natural use of land (***Transco***; *Stannard* v *Gore* [2012]; *Northumbrian Water Ltd* v *McAlpine Ltd* [2014]) use of land ... (4) ... and which causes foreseeable damage of the relevant type. (See *Stannard* v *Gore* for a 'list' of what needs to be considered in each claim.) Note that since ***Transco*** the substance brought or accumulated on land must bring with it an 'exceptional' danger.

LPP is the claimant here. The first question to ask is whether they have standing to take a claim (***Transco*** confirmed that this is a requirement in ***Rylands* v *Fletcher*** claims) as it is in nuisance (following ***Hunter***).

These are the losses LPP will be claiming (possibly in addition to a claim representing the cost of compensating their customer for personal injury).

LPP's first claim is for property damage.

Does this suggest an alternative action in negligence?

If there is a possibility that liability can be established, can GAB use the stormy weather as a defence?

Do this—and any of the other harms—meet the foreseeability requirement from ***Cambridge Water* [1994]**?

Would the customer be able to sue for their personal injuries under ***Rylands* v *Fletcher***? If not, is there any other route they could take? Negligence is usually the best chance for personal injury claims but is there any evidence of negligence on the part of GAB here? The claimant would need to establish duty, breach and causation—would there be a problem doing so? Alternatively, if LPP has to pay the customer compensation, would it be able to claim this from GAB in its ***Rylands* v *Fletcher*** claim?

Is this a relevant argument? See discussion of the role of insurance in ***Transco***.

Vicarious liability annotated problem question

Harry Lock Eyes is a popular restaurant and bar. Mario, its owner, prides himself on its mellow atmosphere and friendly staff. However, behind the scenes it is a different story.

Bert, the restaurant's sommelier, and Dillon, the head chef, have fallen out over Bert's wine choices for his signature dish. Eventually Dillon's quick temper gets the better of him—he grabs an empty wine bottle and hits Bert across the back of the head. Meanwhile, Cadbury Blacker, the local librarian, is setting up for her regular evening set singing chilled out versions of indie classics. As Dillon storms out from the kitchen he trips over a lead she has failed to tape down, and twists his ankle. Clem, the restaurant manager, phones Dougal at home to see if he can come in to cover Bert's shift. Dougal had been expecting to have the night off and had just settled down to watch TV. Though Clem makes it clear he does not have to come in, Dougal is irritated by her request. He cycles to the restaurant and when he gets there he punches her.

Meanwhile, Biggles is walking around the bar talking to the customers. He is employed as a host to make the guests feel comfortable, and so is a well-known figure at the bar. For convenience, Mario employs Biggles through an agency, which pays Biggles's wages. Bella has been coming to the bar for a few weeks and Biggles has been particularly welcoming. He often encourages her to stay late to help him tidy up and then gives her a lift home in his sports car. After one such occasion Bella complains that Biggles has sexually assaulted her. A subsequent criminal investigation upholds her claim.

Advise the parties.

In order for Mario to be vicariously liable you will also need to establish that Cadbury Blacker is an employee and that the battery has happened in the 'course of her employment'. See ***Lister*** **[2002]** and compare *Wendall Barchester Healthcare Ltd* [2012] and *Wallbank v Wallbank Fox Designs Ltd* [2012].

Dillon will want to argue that Mario is vicariously liable for Cadbury Blacker's actions but is she an employee? See *JGE* [2012] and ***Various Claimants*** **[2012]**.

In absence of any other information, potential claims will be brought against Mario.

Dillon has therefore committed a battery against Bert. You should work through the relevant stages of this tort, to clearly establish this (see **section 20.2**). Remember it is essential that the employee commits a tort (for which they will be *personally* liable), otherwise there is nothing for the employer to be *vicariously* liable for. When doing this you should also consider any defences—is Bert contributorily negligent?

Has Cadbury Blacker committed a tort? You should consider whether she owes Dillon a duty of care, that she has breached this duty (i.e. that she has fallen below the standard of care expected) and that this has caused Dillon's injuries. Could Dillon also be contributorily negligent? What would you need to know in order to establish this?

So are Mario or the agency liable for his actions? Or both? See *Viasystems (Tyneside) Ltd v Thermal Transfer (Northern) Ltd and others* [2005] and ***Various Claimants.***

Biggles has clearly committed a tort (battery) against Bella but has he done so in the 'course of his employment'?

Like Dillon, Dougal has committed a battery against Clem. There is no need to repeat your discussion of the relevant law here, you can simply refer to your discussion of Bert's claim against Dillon, pointing out any factual/legal differences. This should remind you of the facts of *Wendall v Barchester Healthcare Ltd* [2012]. Often examiners will use or adapt the facts of cases in a problem question. Be careful not to fall into the trap of assuming that just because the facts of the problem question look similar to a real case that the outcome will be the same. Your examiner may have 'tweaked the facts' in order to test your knowledge and application of the law.

Unless you are told otherwise, usually you should not discuss matters relating to criminal law when answering a tort problem question.

Damages for death and personal injuries annotated problem question

Emma is a 45-year-old London-based consultant paediatrician. Because of her increasingly high profile and the fact that she is held in high respect by her peers, she has in recent years also fronted a number of popular television series that delve into various aspects of children's medicine. In the last year alone, she was paid over £50,000 for this. She also does a lot of work, including fundraising, for various children's charities: last year she was sponsored to cycle the Great Wall of China and raised over £15,000. She enjoys time with her two teenage children (she is divorced from their father) and in particular loves weekends away with them sailing or waterskiing, although also enjoys sharing more simple activities with them, such as taking their dog for long walks in the park. She is an avid cook and attends a cookery class every Thursday evening, followed by a meal out with her friends.

Emma is seriously injured in a multiple car accident, for which she was in no way to blame. She is rendered paraplegic, confined to a wheelchair and suffers constant pain. She has to give up her job, but continues to try and do some of the voluntary work for the charities she is involved with. She, along with her two children, has to move out of her three-storey house in north London and into a specially adapted ground-floor flat. Her boyfriend, Clive, who has a career in advertising, agrees to move in with her and be her carer; he gives up his job. She loses interest in sex and is unable to carry on with the majority of her leisure pursuits.

It is established that a combination of two other drivers' negligence caused the accident in which Emma was injured.

Advise Emma.

These are all physical activities that E may not now be able to enjoy. While she can still spend time with her children, the non-pecuniary losses here will have to be compensated.

Can she still do this? If not, it adds to her non-pecuniary loss.

This also goes to her non-pecuniary losses.

We are not told what her precise salary is, so the multiplicand figure here (as we know that she has to give up her job) will largely be guesswork. However, it is fairly safe to say that a consultant paediatrician working in London will be on quite a high salary! You could investigate roughly how much this might be and start your calculations from there. Remember that the multiplicand will also take into account future prospects of promotion etc (as well as the inevitable 'vicissitudes' of life). What would the multiplier be on her lost earnings?

How does liability split between them? See e.g. *Fitzgerald* v *Lane* [1988].

Is this anything that is claimable by E? Or not a loss that she has suffered? Does it merely add to her non-pecuniary losses? Could she continue to fundraise in other ways?

Would E be able to claim damages for the cost of care provided by him? See *Hunt* v *Severs* [1994].

Does this *save* her money or is it a loss? If she had to pay to alter the flat in any way to make it suitable for her to live in, these costs may be claimable as special damages.

Physical injuries may be more easy to quantify than non-pecuniary losses. What can she claim for here? If she gets a lump sum, what would the multiplier be for her continued need for medical treatment?

These are additional earnings. A claim may be based on these, but unlike her other job, this may be less permanent—how long could someone like E expect to have a high profile on TV?

The object of a question like this is to get you to work out (roughly) how much compensation E will be able to claim. Negligence is not disputed so you need not talk about duty, breach, causation etc. Obviously, the amount of damages you end up with might not be the same as a court would award—the idea is for you to identify and discuss the various principles that apply to the different parts of the claim, not to get an exact figure. On the physical injuries, you may find **Figure 21.1** helpful. Consider also whether this is the kind of situation where the court might exercise its power to insist that the parties create a Periodical Payment Order to cover the future losses. If so, how would this work?

Index

A

Abatement 90, 97–8, 100, 571–3
Access to justice 653–4, 660
Acts of God 598
Admissions of responsibility 19–20
Adversarial tort system 175, 655
Aggravated damages 524, 629
Aims of tort law 8–20, 22
Airspace, trespass into 539, 540–2
Alcohol *see* **Drunkenness**
Allocation of loss 11–12, 22
Alternative sources of compensation 14–15, 652–8
- adversarial tort system 655
- criminal injuries compensation 14
- insurance 11–12, 14, 18
- no-fault liability 18, 651, 654, 656
- road traffic accidents, proposal for no-fault scheme in relation to 656
- social security 14, 18, 40, 651–3, 657

Ambulance services 158–60
- calls, duty to respond to emergency 158–60
- duty of care 158–60, 184
- fire service 159
- policy/operational distinction 159

Analogy, reasoning by 50, 52, 68, 70–1, 74–5, 212, 215, 338
Anonymity orders 478–80
Apportionment of damages 259, 263–6, 272, 284–5, 641–2, 661
Armed forces 155, 171–3, 174
- combat immunity 172–3
- Crown immunity 172
- defensive practices 171
- duty of care 171–3, 174
- friendly fire incidents 171–2
- life, right to 172–3

Asbestos/mesothelioma 110, 238–9, 258–9, 261–9, 271–2, 308
Assault 411, 418–21, 446
- actionable per se, as 412
- apprehension of force 418–21
- battery 418
- consent 431
- definition 411
- direct and immediate force 412, 418–21, 446
- arassment 420–1
- immediacy 418–21
- intention 412, 436
- justification or excuse 418, 421
- reasonable apprehension of force 418–19
- recklessness 414
- threatening gestures 420
- *Wilkinson* v *Downton*, tort in 421
- words 420–1

Assumption of responsibility/risk *see also* ***Volenti non fit injuria***
- armed forces 171
- economic loss 167, 189, 198, 203–6, 209, 214
- education-based claims 181
- fire services 156
- negligence 49, 51
- omissions 81, 84–8, 89
- police 166–9
- psychiatric harm 134–6
- public bodies 145–6, 177–8, 184
- references 214
- third parties 93–6, 100
- vulnerable adults, local authorities' duty to 48–9
- wills, drafting 212

B

Battery 411, 414–17, 446
- actionable per se, as 412
- assault 418
- consent 431–4
- definition 411, 414
- direct and immediate force 412, 414, 417, 446
- false imprisonment 424
- feminist critique 416–17
- generally acceptable conduct 416–17
- hostile intent 416
- intention 412–15, 436
- justification or excuse 414, 417, 431
- medical treatment, consent to 432–4
- recklessness 414, 415
- touching 414, 415–17, 436
- transferred intent 415

Bereavement damages 638, 639–40
Blame culture 14–15, 630, 649–50
Blood products, infection with contaminated 372–4, 377
Bodily integrity 3–4, 231, 411
***Bolam* test** 181, 226–36, 277, 376
Breach of confidence 459–69
- celebrities/public figures 459–69
- commercial secrets 459
- freedom of expression 464–5, 468
- Human Rights Act 1998 461
- injunctions 459–63
- life, right of 459–60
- marital relationships 459
- misuse of private information 464–5
- non-disclosure agreements (NDAs) 461–3
- photographs 460–1, 463–8
- pre-existing relationships 459, 464
- privacy 450–3, 473–82
- public interest 460, 462–3

Breach of duty 42–56, 58, 217–50, 358–60 *see also* **Breach of statutory duty; Standard of care**
Breach of statutory duty 397–406
- benefit, whom statute is intended to 402–3
- breached, whether duty had been 404–5
- claimant, whether a duty is owed to the 403–4
- claims in tort, whether statute gives rise to 398–403
- common employment, doctrine of 397, 401
- course of employment 401
- employers' liability 387, 391, 400–5
- harassment 398
- health and safety 401–2
- insurance 403
- negligence 398, 401, 403
- Parliament, intention of 398–9, 402–3, 405
- reasonable care 404
- standard of care 246, 404
- statutory interpretation 398

Bullying 183, 390–1, 445, 462, 618
Burden of proof
causation 255, 272
false imprisonment 431
product liability 364, 370, 377–8
road traffic accidents 247
standard of care 247–9
But for test (factual causation) 252–79, 287, 307

C

Capacity 423, 428, 433–5
***Caparo* test** *see* **Three-stage test**
Care and skill 33, 221, 389–90
Care, costs of 637
Carelessness
but for test 254–5
contributory negligence 305, 306–7
duty of care 29, 36, 42, 58, 67
economic loss 189
product liability 33, 358–9
Rylands v *Fletcher*, actions under 587
standard of care 248
three-stage test 69
Causation 42, 252–87 *see also* **Intervening acts**
allocation of responsibility 252
apportionment of damages 259, 263–6, 272
asbestos, exposure to 258–9, 261–9, 271–2
balance of probabilities 252
burden of proof 255, 272
but for test (factual causation) 252–79, 287, 307
explaining the test 254–5
multiple sufficient causes 277–9
problems with the test 256–7
clinical negligence 232, 255, 259–61, 270–7, 287
but for test 255, 259–61, 271
informed consent 270–1
loss of a chance 273–6, 287
Compensation Act 2006 265–8
contribution/joint and several liability 262–6
contributory negligence 263, 266, 310
corrective justice 10–11, 13
damages 633, 641
duty of care 58, 62–3
employers' liability 39, 389, 392
factual causation 44, 252–79, 287
Fairchild exception 261–9, 272
fault 44, 254
foreseeability 287
indeterminate causes 271–2
inform, failure to 270–1
legal causation 44, 252–4, 279–87, 374
loss of a chance 273–6, 287
material contribution to harm 257–61, 266
material increase in risk 260–1, 267–8
mesothelioma exception 261–9, 271–2
multiple/cumulative causes 256–65, 269, 272
problem question 671
product liability 354, 358–60, 374–5, 384
psychiatric harm 130
real or operative causes 279
remoteness 252, 279, 280–3
self-employment 266
standard of care 45, 254
standard of proof 252, 255, 271, 287
superseding events 277–9
third parties 90, 95, 98
uncertain actions 277
unjust results 261–71
Celebrities/public figures
breach of confidence 459–69
defamation 486, 491–2, 494–6, 498, 508–9
injunctions 451–3, 460–1, 467–8, 475, 478–80
misuse of private information 463–8, 480
private and family life, right to respect for 471–2, 474–5
social media 450, 467
super-injunctions 408, 451, 478–80, 494, 524–5
Children
abuse 642–6
allurements 330
care, children in 182–3, 617
contributory negligence 306–7, 312
damages 642–6
education-based claims 179–82, 184–5
foster children 183, 617
harassment and bullying, campaign of 93–4, 145–6, 183–4
occupiers' liability 329–31, 339–42
omissions 84–5, 86, 100
parents, omissions of 84–5, 86, 100
privacy 475–7
public bodies 143–4, 152–4, 177, 182–3
road traffic accidents 306, 310–12
standard of care 225–6
trespass 330, 339–40
Chilling effect 440, 488–9, 506
Claimants and plaintiffs, terminology of 22
Clapham omnibus, man on the 220
Clinical negligence
best interests of patients 435
Bolam test 181, 226–36, 277, 376
but for test 255, 259–61, 271
capacity 433–4
causation 232, 255, 259–61, 270–7, 287
consent to medical treatment 230–4, 270–1, 432–5
costs 628, 655–6
damages 650, 655–6
deterrence 650
hospital waiting times 73
informed consent 230–4, 270–1
loss of a chance 273–6, 287
NHS Redress Scheme 655–6
NHS Resolution 655
no-fault scheme, proposal for 656
psychiatric harm 120–5
responsible body of medical opinion 226–36
reporting incidences 650
special skills 227–36
standard of care 226–36, 238–9
warn, failure to 231, 234–5
Coastguard 173–4
Combat immunity 172–3
Compensation *see also* **Compensation culture; Damages**
aims of tort law 8, 11–18
alternative sources of compensation 11–12, 14–15, 18, 40, 652–8
Compensation Act 2006 19–20, 245–6, 265–8
corrective justice 11–13, 15
deterrence 40
fault over need, prioritising 14
insurance 11–12, 14, 18
lottery, tort law as a 14
no-fault liability 18, 651, 654, 656

social security 14, 18, 40, 651–3, 657
Compensation culture 14–16, 22, 648, 659–61
access to justice 653–4, 660
blame culture 14–15, 630, 649–50
claims management companies (CMCs) 659
conditional fee agreements (CFAs) 659, 661
costs 661
defensive practices 660–1
deterrence 17, 660–1
duty of care 36–7
frivolous claims 660
have-a-go culture 660
individual responsibility 14–15, 659
insurance
after the event 661
lobbying by insurance companies 15–16
premiums 659
Jackson Report 661
media sensationalism 14–15, 660
myth, as 15–17, 659–61
occupiers' liability 321, 335
over-deterrence 17
product liability 368–9
Social Action Responsibility and Heroism Act (SARAH) 2015 17, 83, 246
tort claims, UK expenditure on 659
whiplash claims 16
Complex structure theory 200–1, 357
Concurrent liability 42, 640–2
Conditional fee agreements (CFAs) 628, 659, 661
Confidentiality *see* **Breach of confidence**
Consent 3, 431–4 *see also* **Volenti non fit injuria**
assault 431
battery 431–4
informed consent 230–4, 270–1
intoxication 432
medical treatment 432–5
Mental Capacity Act 2005 433–4
Rylands v *Fletcher*, actions under 597
Consumer protection *see* **Product liability**
Contempt of court 525
Contemptuous damages 629
Contract
breach of contract 631–2
comparison with tort 2–3
damages 631–2
disclaimers 196, 203, 209
duty of care 33–5
economic loss 194–5, 198–9, 202, 204, 209
exclusion of liability 196, 203, 209, 292, 333–4
omissions 86
privity of contract 33, 35, 355, 383–4
product liability 33–44, 354–5, 383–4
third parties 22, 33, 35, 90–4, 355, 383–4
unfair contract terms 209, 292, 333–4
Contribution 262–6, 284–5, 641–2, 646, 661
Contributory negligence 304–13
but for test 307
carelessness 305, 306–7
causation 263, 266, 310
children 306–7, 312
contributing to damage, failure to exercise care as 304, 306–7
damages, reduction in 263, 304–5, 307–12
drink driving 309
employers' liability 387–8, 389
failed to exercise reasonable care, whether claimant 304, 305–6, 313
helmet, failure to wear a 309
Law Reform (Contributory Negligence) Act 1945 40, 304, 307–8
nuisance 564
occupiers' liability 331–2, 336
product liability 368–9
road traffic accidents 305–12
Rylands v *Fletcher*, actions under 598
seat belts 307, 308–10
smoking 308
volenti non fit injuria 294–6
Copyright 450
Corrective justice 8, 9–11
allocation of loss 11–12
causation 10–11, 13
damages/compensation 11–13, 15
distributive justice 130–1
fault 10–12, 13
individual responsibility 10, 12–13, 647
insurance 12–13
psychiatric harm 115, 130–1
public bodies 179
vicarious liability 608
Costs
after the event insurance 628
clinical negligence 655–6
compensation culture 661
conditional fee agreements 628
damages 627–8
defamation 486, 494
fixed costs 654
Jackson Review 627–8, 661
legal aid cuts 628
qualified one-way cost shifting (QOCS) 628
success fees 628
Criminal offences
Criminal Injuries Compensation Scheme 14
harassment 441, 446
illegality 296–303
intentional interferences with the person 411–12, 414, 444
rape myths 167
road traffic accidents 4
stalking 440, 445
Crown immunity 141, 172

D

Damages 625–63 *see also* **Compensation; Compensation culture**
aggravated damages 524, 629
alternative sources of compensation 652–8
apportionment of liability 259, 263–6, 272, 284–5, 641–2, 661
bereavement damages 638, 639–40
blame culture 630, 649–50
breach of contract 631–2
calculation of damages 632, 633–40
care, costs of 637
causation 633, 641
child sexual abuse and time limitations 642–6
clean breaks 633
clinical negligence
costs 655–6
NHS Redress Scheme 655–6
no-fault scheme, proposal for 656
reform 655
reporting incidences of 650
compensatory damages 629–30
concurrent liability 640–2
contemptuous damages 629
contribution 641–2, 646, 661
contributory negligence 263, 304–5, 307–12

Damages (*Continued*)
corrective justice 630, 647–8
costs 627–8
after the event insurance 628
clinical negligence 655–6
conditional fee arrangements (CFAs) 628
fixed costs 654
Jackson 627–8
legal aid cuts 628
qualified one-way cost shifting (QOCS) 628
success fees 628
damages-based arrangements (DBAs) 628
death 638–40
defamation 524–5, 531
dependants, claims by 638–9
deterrence 629–30, 648–9, 652
discount rate 634, 639
distributive justice 650–1
economic loss 191–5, 198–9, 273
employers' liability 648–9
exclusionary rules 632–3
exemplary damages 524, 629
fatal accidents 638–40
fault 11–12, 630–1, 647–51, 654, 657, 661
forms of payments 633–7
frivolous claims 649
future losses 637, 639, 652, 661
general damages 631, 637
harassment 441
independent liability 640–2
individual responsibility 40, 647, 657, 658
injunctions 441, 443, 545, 568–72, 577–8, 581, 627
insurance 16, 637, 648–9, 652, 657–8
joint and several liability 640–2, 661
Judicial College guidelines 634–5
juries, assessment by 525
just satisfaction 576–7
Law Commission 639, 645–6
loss of a chance 273–6
loss of amenity 637
loss of earnings 31, 190–3, 278, 297, 633, 637–8
loss of profits 191–4, 198, 573
lump sums 633–4, 637
mixed system of social security and tort law 653
multiplicands and multipliers 633–4, 636, 638–9
negligence 631, 633, 642–3, 648, 652
no-fault compensation 656
nominal damages 427, 430, 629
non-compensatory damages 629
non-pecuniary losses 190, 628, 631, 639, 661
nuisance 555, 560, 568–78, 581
occupiers' liability 646–7
Ogden Tables 634, 636
pain and suffering 637
pecuniary losses 190, 562–3, 576, 631, 636–7, 639, 661
Periodical Payment Orders (PPOs) 636–7, 638
personal injury 31–2, 189, 625–63
precautionary approach 649–50
pre-tort position, return to 631, 633
problem question 682
problem with damages 646–58
provisional damages 636
purpose of damages 629–33
reform 652–8
restitutio in integrum 631, 639, 652
retribution 629–31, 648
road traffic accidents 654, 656
Rylands v *Fletcher*, actions under 591–2, 594
settlements 627–8, 653, 655
social security 651–3, 657
special damages 631, 637
structured settlements 636
success fees 628
time limitations on claim 642–6, 661
trespass to land 544
vicarious liability 644–5, 648
vindication 525
vicissitudes of life 634
whiplash 654
Danger, creation of a source of 88, 90, 96–7, 100
Deaths
custody, deaths in 85–6, 100, 168–9, 286–7
defamation claims 488
dependants, claims by 638
fatal accidents 3, 638–40, 646
product liability 362–3
suicide 85–6, 100, 134, 168–9, 386–7, 481
Defamation 485–533
absolute privilege 509, 510
abuse of power 494
apologies 501, 506, 523–4
balancing exercise 503
celebrities/public figures 486, 491–2, 494–6, 498, 508–9
chilling effect 488–9, 506
common law 486, 493, 505–7, 512–14, 521
communication to a third party 504–5
companies 486–9, 499
contempt of court 525
costs 486, 494
court proceedings 510
damages 524–5, 531
aggravated 524
exemplary 524
juries, assessment by 525
vindication 525
death 488
Defamation Act 2013 486–90, 492, 505–6, 507, 509–17, 525–31
defamatory statements, meaning of 490–8
defences 488, 497, 506–24, 531
deterrence 525
distributors 522–3
establishing claims 488–90
European Convention on Human Rights 486, 506
fair comment 518, 519, 520
foreseeability 504–6
freedom of expression 486, 494, 502, 509, 517
balancing exercise 504
chilling effect 488–9, 506
European Convention on Human Rights 486, 506
internet 523
parliamentary proceedings 510
restrictions 486
government bodies 488–9
groups or classes of people, references to 503–4
honest opinion defence 487, 506, 510, 518–21, 523
basis of opinion 520–1
facts, opinions not 518–19, 521
Human Rights Act 1998 486
hypothetical reasonable reader 500–1
immunity 517
injunctions 524–5
innocent defamation 522–3
innuendo 498–501
false or popular 499
true or legal 499
intention 498, 501–2, 504
judicial proceedings, contemporaneous reports of 510
jurisdiction 489, 522
jury trials 525
justification defence 487, 497, 518, 523

legal aid, unavailability of 486
libel and slander, distinction between 490
libel tourism 489
limitation periods 505–6
local authorities 488–9
malice 509, 510–12, 523
mere abuse 498
multiple publication rule 487
newspaper archives 506
offer of amends 523–4
parliamentary proceedings 510
percolation phenomenon 525
photographs 496, 502–3
political parties 489
politicians 486, 489, 500–1
potentially defamatory statements 496–7
privilege 509–15
absolute 509, 510
qualified 506, 509, 510–14
Reynolds defence 510, 512–17
problem question 678
public interest defence 506, 507, 511, 512–17
public opinion 518
publication 488, 504–6, 515, 521, 531
newspaper archives 506
public interest 512–17
republication 505–6
secondary publishers 506, 522
single publication rule 505–6
stale publications 506
whether statement had been published 504–6
qualified privilege 506, 509, 510–14
reasonableness 491, 502, 504, 522
references 510–11
refers to claimant, whether statement 501–4
remedies 501, 506, 523–5, 531
republication 505–6
reputation 3–4, 486–8, 491–2, 498–9, 504, 509, 511, 517
responsible journalism test 513
Reynolds defence 510, 512–17
ridicule 498
right-thinking people 490–2, 499, 506–7
serious harm requirement 486, 488, 492–3, 504, 516
single publication rule 505–6
slander 490
social media 489, 495–7, 500–1, 504, 522, 524–5
sting of the defamation 507–8
strict liability 503
truth 506–11, 515, 518
vindication 525
websites/internet 443, 522–3
percolation phenomenon 525
social media 489, 495–7, 500–1, 504, 522, 524–5
whether statements are defamatory 490–501
who can sue 488–9
women, violence and abuse against 492–4, 508–9
Defective premises 197–200, 208–9, 324–5
Defective products *see* **Product liability**
Defences 290–314 *see also* **Contributory negligence; Illegality; *Volenti non fit injuria***
defamation 488, 497, 506–24, 531
harassment 443–5
intentional interferences with the person 431–5
nuisance 564–9
occupiers' liability 335–6
problem question 672
product liability 363, 375–7
Rylands v *Fletcher*, actions under 597–9
self-defence 435
statutory authority 565–6, 598
trespass to land 542–3
Defendants as tortfeasors 22
Defensive practices 141, 143, 162–4, 171, 660–1
Dependants, claims by 638–9
Design defects 360–2, 369–70, 378
Detention *see* **False imprisonment**
Deterrence 8, 18–19, 22, 648–50
clinical negligence 650
compensation culture 17, 660–1
damages 40, 629–30, 648–9, 652
defamation 525
duty of care 59–60
insurance 18–19
negligence 40
no-claim bonuses 19
occupiers' liability 335
over-deterrence 16
product liability 358
socially valuable activities 652
standard of care 246
Disclaimers 196, 203, 209
Discrimination 169, 299, 578
Distributive justice 130–1, 141, 223, 342, 650–1
Drunkenness
consent 432
drink driving 295, 309
omissions 87–8
Duty of care 42–55, 58–101 *see also* **Fair, just and reasonable test; Three-stage test**
analogy, reasoning by 69–70, 74–5
Anns, retreat from 64–7, 70, 113
armed forces 171–3, 174
breach of duty 42, 43–55, 58
Caparo v *Dickman* 65–76, 356
carelessness 29, 36, 42, 58, 67
case example 48–55
causation 58, 62–3
compensation culture 36–7
contractual relationships 33–5
control mechanism, as 42–3, 59
crushing liability 59–60
deterrence 59–60
Donoghue v *Stevenson* 29, 33–6, 43, 56, 61–6, 70, 73–6
economic loss 188–216
education-based claims 179–82, 184–5
emergency services 155–6, 158–60, 184
employers' liability 386–96
establishment of a duty 65–74
expansion of liability 64
floodgates argument 59–60
foreseeability 35–6, 58–9, 61–9, 73
historical background 32–3, 56, 61–5
incremental approach 69–76
legally recognised harm 31
neighbour principle 33–6, 56, 61–2, 74
non-delegable duty of care 387, 388–91, 393, 395
novel situations 59, 70–4, 356
occupiers' liability 321–36
omissions 59, 78–88
police 146–52, 160–71
policy 60, 63–4, 67, 69, 76
precedent 59, 74
product liability 33, 356–8, 360–1
psychiatric harm 43, 58–9, 102–37
public bodies 138–87
reasonableness 29, 34–6, 61–4, 66–7, 73–4

Duty of care (*Continued*)
recognition of duty 32–3, 59, 70
remoteness 58, 62–3
road traffic accidents 58–9
Rylands v *Fletcher* 600–1
vulnerable adults, local authorities' duty to 48–55

E

Economic loss 3, 188–216
analogy, reasoning by 211–12, 213
assumption of responsibility/risk 189, 198, 203–6, 209, 214
bad bargains 198
carelessness 189
complex structure theory 200–1, 357
consequential economic loss 189–92, 203
contract law 194–5, 198–9, 202, 204, 209
crushing liability, burden of 193, 215
damages 191–5, 198–9, 273
defective buildings 197–200, 208–9
duty of care 188–216
egg shell skull rule 283
exclusionary rule 195–7, 206, 215
exceptions to exclusion 195–7
fair, just and reasonable test 72, 215
fiduciary relationships 196–7, 201, 212, 215
flexible approach 210–14
floodgates argument 193–4
foreseeability 193–4, 208, 215
Hedley Byrne principle 195–8, 206
beyond *Hedley Byrne* 210–14
disclaimers 196
extension of *Hedley Byrne* principle 201–9
negligent misstatements 195–8
references 213–14
incremental principle 206, 212, 215
insurance 194, 211
loss of a chance 273
loss of earnings 191
loss of profits 191–4, 573
material physical damage 198–200
negligent misstatements 195–8, 206, 215
non-pecuniary loss 190
nuisance 573
pecuniary loss 190
police 167
policy 192–3, 205–6, 215
problem question 669
product liability 198, 355, 357
pure economic loss 189–205, 210–15, 357, 573
references for employment 213–14
relational economic loss 194
reliance 193, 196–7, 201–2, 206–9, 212, 214
Rylands v *Fletcher* 596
special relationships 201–3, 206–7, 211
statements and activities, difference between 197
surveys 209
trust and confidence, relationships of 196, 201, 203, 211
types of loss 190
voluntary assumption of risk 203–6
wills, drafting 210–14
Editors' Code of Practice (IPSO) 457–8
Education-based claims 179–82
assessment of needs 180–1
assumption of responsibility 181
duty of care 179–82, 184–5
dyslexia, failure to diagnose 180–1
Human Rights Act 1998 181–2
messed up lives, claims relating to 179–80
policy 180
vicarious liability 181
Effective remedy, right to an 149, 153, 184, 566
Eggshell skull rule 112, 282–3
Emergency services 142, 155–60, 174 *see also* **Fire service; Police**
ambulance services 158–60
armed forces 155, 171–3, 174
coastguard 173–4
heat of the moment 241–2
standard of care 241–2
Employers' liability 386–96
adequate materials and equipment 390, 391–2, 393
asbestos/mesothelioma 110, 238–9, 258–9, 261–9, 271–2, 308
breach of statutory duty 387, 391, 390–1, 396, 400–5
bullying, victimisation or harassment 390–1, 445, 462
but for test 257–8, 260–72, 277
care and skill 389–90
causation 39, 389, 392
common employment doctrine 39–40, 387–8, 391, 397, 401
competent workforce 388–91
contributory negligence 387–8, 389
control 86
course of employment 388, 401, 612, 619–23
damages 648–9
employees, injuries caused by 387–8, 390–1
false imprisonment 425–6
fault 391
harassment 446
hearing loss 240–1
individual responsibility 387
industrialisation 39, 56
insurance 19, 39, 388, 403, 648
intervening acts 285–6
loss, shifting of 39
non-delegable duty of care 387, 388–95, 612–13, 623
omissions 86–7
personal liability 387
precautions 236–7, 240, 393–4
problem question 675
proper system of work 392–4
psychiatric harm 129–32, 134–6, 394
reasonable care 388–9
references 394
safe systems of work 389–90, 392–5
safe workplaces 390, 395
standard of care 239–40
stress at work 134–6, 394, 446
supervision, effective 389–90, 392–4
vicarious liability 87, 387–8, 608–24
volenti non fit injuria 387–8
Employment *see also* **Employers' liability**
loss of earnings 31, 190–3, 278, 297, 633, 637–8
references 213–14, 394, 510–11
Encroachment 548, 571–2
Escapes *see* ***Rylands* v *Fletcher*, rule in**
EU law

Product Liability Directive 362–3, 373
Rylands v *Fletcher*, actions under 592
European Convention on Human Rights (ECHR) *see also* **Freedom of expression; Private and family life, right to respect for**
defamation 486, 506
discrimination 578
effective remedy, right to an 149, 153, 184, 566
fair trial, right to a 149–51, 153–5, 182
Human Rights Act 1998 20–1, 469, 486, 574
inhuman or degrading treatment 20, 148, 153
liberty and security, right to 20, 428–9
life, right to 20, 146–52, 172–3, 459–60
margin of appreciation 148
positive obligations 172
European Union see **EU law**
Ex turpi causa rule 297
Exclusion of liability 196, 203, 209, 292, 333–4
Excuse *see* **Justification or excuse**
Exemplary damages 524, 629
Expenditure on tort claims by UK 659

F

Fair, just and reasonable test 65–73 *see also* **Three-stage test**
economic loss 72, 215
hospital waiting times 73
police 161
policy 67
proximity 71–2
public bodies 177, 178, 182
Fair trial, right to a 149–51, 153–5, 182
False imprisonment 411, 421–31, 446
actionable per se, as 412
authorisation, without legal 428–9
battery 424
burden of proof 431
definition 411, 421–2
direct and immediate harm 412, 426, 446
duration 424
employers' liability 425–6
escape, reasonable means of 424
freedom of movement, restrictions on 421–31
Human Rights Act 1998 428
intention 412–14, 422–3, 436
justification or excuse 421–2, 428–9
knowledge 427–8
liberty and security, right to 428–9
Mental Capacity Act 2005 423, 428
Mental Health Act patients, compulsory detention of 427–8
necessity 428
omissions 426
police
cordons 428–9
detention without arrest 430–1
potential deprivation of liberty 427–8
prisoners 423, 426–7
recklessness 423
total restraint 421, 423–5, 428
Fatal accidents 3, 638–40, 646
Fault
causation 44, 254
corrective justice 10–12, 13
damages 11–12, 630–1, 647–51, 654, 657, 661
employers' liability 391
individualism 38
insurance 657
land-based torts 538–9
negligence 38, 39, 41
no-fault liability 18, 651, 654, 656
nuisance 562
occupiers' liability 342–3, 351
product liability 361–3, 365, 375, 377
Rylands v *Fletcher*, actions under 584, 597
standard of care 43–4
Feminist critique 220–1, 416–17
Fiduciary relationships 196–7, 201, 212, 215
Financial loss *see* **Economic loss**
Fire service 155–8
ambulance services 159
assumption of responsibility 156
duty of care 155–8
emergency calls, response to 155–6
insurance 158
omissions 88, 158
policy 158
positive acts 156–7
proximity 156
standard of care 157, 241
Floodgates argument
duty of care 59–60
economic loss 193–4
privacy 454
product liability 355–6
psychiatric harm 125
Foreseeability *see also* **Three-stage test**
abatement 98
causation 287
defamation 504–6
duty of care 35–6, 58–9, 61–9, 73
economic loss 193, 208, 215
egg shell skull rule 282–3
harassment 444
intervening acts 284
negligence 35–6, 45
nuisance 32, 561–2, 572, 581, 585–6
omissions 84
police 160–1, 163, 166, 169, 184
product liability 361
proximity 66
psychiatric harm 107–10, 112–13, 118, 128, 133–6
public bodies 175
reasonableness 61–4, 66–7
remoteness 62, 280–3
Rylands v *Fletcher*, actions under 585, 591–5, 597, 599–600
standard of care 237–9, 243
third parties 90–1, 93, 98
Freedom of expression
balancing exercise 469–73, 481–2, 504
breach of confidence 464–5, 468
chilling effect 440, 489
defamation 486, 494, 502, 509–10, 517, 523
internet 523
misuse of private information 464–5, 468–9
parliamentary proceedings 510
privacy 450–1, 453–4, 469–73, 479–82
public interest 471
qualified right, as 471
Frivolous or vexatious claims 141, 179, 649, 660
Future losses 637, 639, 652, 661

G

Gender *see* **Women**

H

Harassment 411–12, 440–6
alarm or distress 441–2
assault 420–1
breach of statutory duty 398
children 93–4, 145–6, 183–4
civil remedies 441, 446
course of conduct 441–5, 446
criminal offences 441, 446
damages 441
defences 443–5
definition 441–2
employers' liability 390–1, 446
foreseeability 444
injunctions 441, 551
knowledge, actual or constructive 444
nuisance 551–2
online campaigns or trolling 443
police 168–9
press intrusion 440
privacy 478
Protection from Harassment Act 1997 440–6
psychiatric harm 420
revenge pornography 468
sexual harassment 6, 443, 462–3
social media 421, 443
stalking 440, 445
telephone calls 420–1, 551
vicarious liability 618–19
Wilkinson v *Downton*, tort in 411, 437–8, 446
workplace, bullying in the 445
Health and safety at work *see* **Employers' liability**
***Hedley Byrne* principle** 195–8, 206, 201–14
Helmet, failure to wear a motorcycle 309
Highways
highways authorities 174, 176
obstruction 579–80
Hillsborough Stadium disaster 105, 107–8, 114–18, 128–9, 132–3
Horseplay 225–6, 242 *see also* **Practical jokes**
Human rights *see* **European Convention on Human Rights (ECHR); Human Rights Act 1998**
Human Rights Act 1998 3–4, 20–1, 22 *see also* **Freedom of expression**
breach of confidence 461
defamation 486
discrimination 578
education-based claims 181–2
European Convention on Human Rights 20–1, 469, 486, 574
false imprisonment 428
horizontal effect 21
individuals, claims by 20–1
margin of appreciation 113, 148, 574
misuse of private information 21, 464
nuisance 552, 565–6, 570, 574–8
police 163–4
privacy 21, 450, 469–73, 478, 481–2
public bodies 21, 139, 143, 142–3, 184
time limitations 646
vertical effect 20

I

Illegality 297–303, 312–13
arrest, resisting 312
causation 299
criminal offences 297–303
damages 297
discrimination 299
ex turpi causa rule 297
Law Commission 298
policy 297, 299–301, 303
range of factors approach 300–2
Immunity
combat immunity 172–3
Crown immunity 141, 172
defamation 517
omissions 83
police 71–2, 149–52, 166–9
public bodies 141, 154–5
Imprisonment *see* **False imprisonment**
Incremental approach 37, 69–76, 206, 212, 215
Independent contractors 334–5, 585, 612–13, 617–18
Individual responsibility
aims of tort law 12–13
collective responsibility 12–13
compensation culture 14–15, 659
corrective justice 10, 12–13, 647
damages 40, 647, 657, 658
employers' liability 387
insurance 657–8
occupiers' liability 321, 342, 351
omissions 80
standard of care 248
volenti non fit injuria 295
Industrialisation 39, 56, 400, 548, 556, 586, 590, 603
Inform, failure to 270–1
Informants, identity of 168
Inhuman or degrading treatment 20, 148, 153–4, 184
Injunctions
breach of confidence 456–63
celebrities/public figures 451–3, 460–1, 467–8, 475, 478–80
contempt of court 525
contra mundum (against whole world) 459
damages 441, 443, 545, 568–72, 577–8, 581, 627
defamation 524–5
harassment 441, 551
nuisance 551, 555, 557, 560, 563–4, 567–71, 577–8
privacy 451, 478–9
super-injunctions 408, 451, 478–80, 494, 524–5
trespass to land 545
Insurance
alternative to tort system, as 11–12, 14, 18
ATE (after the event) insurance 628, 661
breach of statutory duty 403
BTE (before the event) insurance 658
compensation culture 15–16, 659, 661
compulsory insurance 223, 388, 403, 647–8, 657–8
corrective justice 12–13, 22
costs of insurance 649
damages 16, 637, 648–9, 652, 657–8
deterrence 18–19
economic loss 194, 211
employers' liability 19, 388, 402, 648
equality, lack of 658
fault 657
first-party insurance 657–8
individual responsibility 658
legal expenses insurance 658, 661
lobbying by insurance companies 15–16
loss-spreading 22, 40, 223, 335, 609
negligence 40–1
occupiers' liability 19, 328, 335
policy 91
premiums 659
product liability 362
psychiatric harm 106

road traffic accidents 223, 648–9, 657
Rylands v *Fletcher*, actions under 595
standard of care 224
third parties 91, 658
vicarious liability 648
welfare state, decline of 657
wills, drafting of 209
Intention *see also* **Intentional interferences with the person**
defamation 498, 501–2, 504
false imprisonment 412–14, 422–3, 436
limitation periods 642–3
nuisance 554, 562–4
Rylands v *Fletcher*, actions under 589
transferred intent 415
trespass to land 540–2, 580
vicarious liability 622
Wilkinson v *Downton*, tort in 436–9
Intentional interferences with the person 410–48 *see also* **Harassment**
assault 411–12, 418–21, 436, 446
battery 411, 414–17, 446
consent 431–4
criminal offences 411–12, 414, 444
defences 431–5
false imprisonment 411, 421–31, 446
hostile intent 416
lawful justification or excuse 431–5
necessity 434–5
physical harm or distress, intentional infliction of 436–46
problem question 676
recklessness 414
self-defence 435
trespass to the person 411–21, 444, 446
Wilkinson v *Downton*, tort in 411, 436–40, 446
Interests protected by tort law 3–8, 22
Internet *see* **Websites/Internet**
Intervening acts 283–7
acts of the claimant 285–7
apportionment of damages 284–5
but for test 278–9
contribution 284–5
contributory negligence 285–6
criminal acts 286–7
employers' liability 285–6
foreseeability 284
later negligent acts 283–5
legal causation 279–80, 283–7
suicide 286–7
third parties 90, 95
Intoxication *see* **Drunkenness**
Invasion of privacy *see* **Privacy**

J

Joint and several liability 42, 262–6, 272, 640–2, 661
Justification or excuse
assault 418, 421
battery 414, 417, 431
defamation 487, 497, 518, 523
false imprisonment 421–2, 428–9
intentional interferences with the person 414, 417–18, 421–2, 431–5
vicarious liability 609
Justiciability 142, 172, 175–9, 181

L

Land *see* **Defective premises; Occupiers' liability; Private nuisance; *Rylands* v *Fletcher*, rule in; Trespass to land**
Latent damage 642–3
Law Commission
breach of statutory duty 403
damages 639, 645–6
illegality 298
limitation periods 645
psychiatric harm 106, 120
public bodies 178–9
Lawrence, Stephen, murder of 20, 161–2, 170
Leveson Inquiry 450–1, 455–6
Liberty and security, right to 20, 428–9
Life, right to 20, 146–52, 172–3, 459–60
Limitation periods 642–6, 661
Local authorities 37, 47–56, 174–5, 184–5, 488–9
Loss of a chance 273–6, 287
Loss of amenity 637
Loss of earnings 31, 190–3, 278, 297, 633, 637–8
Loss of profits 191–4, 573
Loss-shifting
corrective justice 11–12
distributive justice 223
employers' liability 39
insurance 22, 40, 223, 335, 609
occupiers' liability 335
vicarious liability 609

M

McGregor Commission 451
Macpherson Report 170
Malice
defamation 509, 510–12, 523
malicious falsehood 450, 453
nuisance 563–4
Margin of appreciation 113, 148, 574
Material contribution to harm 257–61, 266
Material increase in risk 260–1, 267–8, 272–3
Media
compensation culture 15–17, 659–61
Editors' Code of Practice (IPSO) 457–8
harassment 440
IMPRESS (Independent Monitor for the Press) 458
Independent Press Standards Organisation (IPSO) 456–8
Leveson Inquiry 450–1, 455–6
Press Complaints Commission 451–2, 455–7
Press Recognition Panel 456
privacy 449–58, 469–81
responsible journalism 513
sensationalism 133, 660
women, reporting in media of violence and abuse against 492–4
Medical negligence *see* **Clinical negligence; Medical treatment, consent to**
Medical treatment, consent to 230–4, 270–1, 432–5
Mental Capacity Act 2005 423, 428, 433–5
Mental harm *see* **Psychiatric harm**
Mental Health Act patients 85–6, 427–8
***Mesne* profits** 545
Mesothelioma/asbestos 110, 238–9, 258–9, 261–9, 271–2, 308
Messed up lives, claims relating to 37, 179–84
Minors *see* **Children**
Misuse of private information 21, 451, 463–9, 473, 480–2
breach of confidence 464–5
celebrities 463–8, 480
freedom of expression 464–5, 468–9
Human Rights Act 1998 464

Misuse of private information (*Continued*)
photographs 463–8
pre-existing relationships 464
private and family life, right to respect for 464
public interest 468
reasonable expectation of privacy 465–9
revenge pornography 468
Motor accidents *see* **Road traffic accidents (RTAs)**
Multiplicands and multipliers 633–4, 636, 638–9, 661

N

Necessity
false imprisonment 428
intentional interferences with the person 434–5
medical treatment, capacity to consent to 434–5
Mental Capacity Act 2005 434–5
trespass to land 543–4
Negligence 29–57 *see also* **Clinical negligence; Contributory negligence; Duty of care; Negligent misstatements; Standard of care**
assumption of responsibility 49, 51
breach of statutory duty 398, 401, 403
causation 44, 45, 47
conduct-based, as 538
contract 196, 203, 209, 292, 333–4
damages 631, 633, 642–3, 648, 652
defences 44, 46
definition 41–2
deterrence 40
elements of tort 41–55
expansion of liability 35, 37, 39, 64, 125, 179, 196–7, 215
fair, just and reasonable test 65–73, 215
fault 38, 39, 41
foreseeability 35–6, 45
historical development 32–40
infant industries, supporting 39–40
joint and several liability 42
limitation periods 642–6
loss-shifting 40
modern law, role of 40–1
negligent misstatements 195–8, 206, 215
neighbour principle 33–6, 47, 61–2, 74, 219
nuisance 576
political context 37
principles 38
privity of contract 35
product liability 355–61, 363, 384
reasonableness 29, 37–8
remoteness 42
Rylands v *Fletcher*, actions under 538, 599–601, 603
scope 4
social and political thinking, influence of 38
strict liability 38–9
trespass to land 544–5
vulnerable adults, local authorities' duty to 47–56
Wilkinson v *Downton*, tort in 436
Neighbour principle 33–6, 47, 61–2, 74, 219
Nervous shock *see* **Psychiatric harm**
New Zealand no-fault system 651, 654
No-fault liability 18, 651, 654, 656
Noise 554, 557, 564, 566, 570–1, 574
Non-disclosure agreements (NDAs) 461–3
Notices
exclusion of liability 333–4
negligence 332–4, 341–4
occupiers' liability 292
trespass 344
unfair contract terms 333–4
warnings 292, 344
Novel situations 37, 59, 69–74, 98, 179–84, 356
Novus actus interveniens *see* **Intervening acts**
Nuisance *see* **Private nuisance; Public nuisance**

O

Obstruction of the highway 579–80
Occupiers' liability 319–51
activity duty 322–3
allurements 330
calling, persons in exercise of a 331, 333–4
children 329–31, 339–42
compensation culture 321, 335
contributory negligence 331–2, 336
control of premises 323–5
damages 646–7
danger, knowledge of presence of non-visitors in vicinity of 345
Defective Premises Act 1972 324–5
defences 335–6
deterrence 335
disabilities, persons with 327
duty of care 321–36
establishment of a duty 340–6
exclude liability, notices which 333–4
fault 342–3, 351
faulty execution of work 334–5
fixed or moveable structures, premises as 327
independent contractors 334–5
individual responsibility 321, 342, 351
insurance 19, 328
invitees 321, 325–7
knowledge/awareness of danger 340, 344–5
licensees 320–1, 327
notices 292, 332–4, 341–4
occupancy duty 322–3
occupier, definition of 323–5, 340
Occupiers' Liability Act 1957 320–36, 343–4, 346, 349–50
Occupiers' Liability Act 1984 320–1, 339–50
personal injuries 319–51
positive obligations 327
premises, definition of 327, 340
problem question 673
property damage 321
reasonable care 327–36
reasonable expectations of protection against risk 341, 345–6
recklessness 320–1
resources of occupier to make premises safe 328–9
risks willingly accepted by non-visitors 346
standard of care 320, 324, 327–36, 346
third parties 335
trespassers 320–1, 326, 330, 339–40, 344
vicinity of risk, reasonable grounds to believe someone will come into 340
visitors
invitation or permission only, by 321, 325–7
lawful 321–36, 343–4
other visitors, harm caused by 323

skilled visitors 331
unlawful 321, 339–50
vulnerabilities 327
volenti non fit injuria 292, 331, 336
vulnerable adults 327
warnings 331–3, 346
duty to warn 332
notices 292, 332–4, 341–4
when duty is owed 322–7
Ogden Tables 634, 636
Omissions 78–88
acts and omissions 79–84
ambulance services 158
assumption of responsibility 81, 84–8, 89
control over person harmed 84–8, 89, 100
creation or adoption of risks 84, 88, 89
dangerous situations, creation of 88
deaths in custody 85–6
drunken people, watching out for 87–8
duty of care 59, 78–88
employers' liability 86–7
false imprisonment 426
fire services 88, 158
foreseeability 84
immunity from suit 83
individual responsibility 80
MHA patients, suicide after absconding of 85–6
parents and children 84–5, 86, 100
police 85–6, 87, 100
political, moral and economic reasons 81
positive obligations to act 79–86, 88, 100
pre-tort relationships 79–81
problem question 666
proximity 82
public bodies 143, 184
pure omissions 80–2, 88
reasonableness 84
relationships, context of 80–1, 84–6, 100
rescue, duty to 12, 78–80, 82–5
third parties 79, 89, 94–5, 100
vicarious liability 87, 88
Overhanging plants and trees 539, 548

P

Pain and suffering, damages for 637
Pearson Commission 651, 652–3
Periodical Payment Orders (PPOs) 636–7, 638
Personal injury
damages 31–2, 189, 625–63
interests protected by tort law 3–5
limitation periods 642–6
loss of a chance 273–6, 287
loss of amenity 637
loss of earnings 31, 190–3, 278, 297, 633, 637–8
loss of profits 191–4, 573
nuisance 572–3
occupiers' liability 319–51
police 160–71
probability of injury 236, 248
product liability 362–3
psychiatric harm 103–4, 106, 108–12, 127–31, 136
public bodies 140–1
Rylands v *Fletcher*, actions under 588, 596, 602
seriousness of injury 236, 239–40, 243–5, 248
Personal responsibility *see* **Individual responsibility**
Phone hacking scandal 451, 455–6
Photographs
breach of confidence 460–1, 463–8
defamation 496, 502–3
fake photos 496
misuse of private information 463–8
privacy 452–3, 471, 473–7
Physical injuries 3, 103–4, 106, 108–12, 127–31, 136, 282
Plaintiffs and claimants 22
Planning permission 554, 557–9, 565
Police 140, 160–71
arrest 71–2, 160–3, 424
assumption of responsibility 166–9
conflicts of interest 167
cordons 428–9
deaths in custody 85–6, 100, 168–9, 286–7
defensive practices 162–4
detention without arrest 430–1
domestic violence 162–5
duty of care 160–71
economic loss 167
effective remedy, right to an 149–51
fair, just and reasonable test 161
fair trial, right to a 149–51
false imprisonment 428–31
foreseeability 160–1, 163, 166, 169, 184
harassment within police service 168–9
immunity 71–2, 149–52, 166–9
informants, identity of 168
inhuman or degrading treatment 148
institutional racism 161
investigative duty 147–8, 150, 164
liability principle 164–6
liberty and security, right to 428
life, right to 146–52
margin of appreciation 148
messed up lives, claims relating to 179
omissions 85–6, 87, 100
Osman case 91, 93, 146–54, 161, 167, 178–80
policy 146, 149–54, 161–5, 168–70
policy/operational distinction 160, 167–70
private and family life, right to respect for 151
proximity 148–52, 161, 168
psychiatric harm 105–8, 114–16, 119, 128–30, 168
racist stereotyping 162
rape myths 167
rape of fellow officers 169–70
safety of police 169
standard of care 164
striking out 151–4
suicides in custody 85–6, 100, 168–9
third parties 91, 94–6
Policy 6–8 *see also* **Public interest**
ambulance services 159
armed forces 171, 173
definition 6–8
democratic argument 8
duty of care 60, 63–4, 67, 69, 76
economic loss 192–3, 205–6, 215
education-based claims 180
fair, just and reasonable test 67
fire services 158
illegality 297, 299–301, 303
insurance 91
judicial creativity 6–7
operational/policy distinction 159, 160, 167–70
police 146, 149–54, 161–5, 168–70
principle distinguished 6–7
product liability 367
psychiatric harm 4, 103–5, 112, 133–4
third parties 91, 93
three-stage test 69,
vicarious liability 610, 615, 623

Political context 37, 38, 81
Pollution 546–9, 556, 574, 578, 594
Post-traumatic stress disorder (PTSD) 104, 117–18, 131, 297
Practical jokes 391, 414, 436–40 *see also* **Horseplay**
Precautions
costs of precautions 236–7, 240–1, 243–5
damages 649
employers' liability 236–7, 393–4
standard of care 236–8, 240–5
Pregnancy and childbirth 112–13, 124, 203, 232–3, 271, 360–1, 367
Prescription 566–9
Press Complaints Commission (PCC) 451–2, 455–7
Press Recognition Panel (PRP) 456
Prisoners
breach of statutory duty 402
completion of sentence, detention after 430
deaths 134, 168–9, 241
false imprisonment 423, 426–7
prison officers, strike of 427
Prison Rules 402
psychiatric harm 134
segregation 429
strip searches of prison visitors 437–8, 480–1
suicide 134, 241, 286
Privacy 3, 449–84 *see also* **Misuse of private information; Private and family life, right to respect**
anonymity orders 478–80
breach of confidence 451, 459–69, 481–2
Calcutt Committee 451–2
celebrities/public figures 450–3, 473–82
children 475–7
definition 452, 453, 482
Editors' Code of Practice (IPSO) 457–8
existence of tort of invasion of privacy 451–4
floodgates argument 454
freedom of expression 450–1, 453–4, 473, 479–80
harassment 21, 450, 469–73, 478, 481–2
how privacy has been protected 454–8
Human Rights Act 1998 21, 450, 469–73, 481
IMPRESS (Independent Monitor for the Press) 458
Independent Press Standards Organisation (IPSO) 456–8
information, public's right to 451
iniquity 477–80
injunctions 451, 478–9
Leveson Inquiry 450–1, 455–6
limits to current protection 480–1
malicious falsehood 453
media 449–55, 473–80
Parliament, role of 451–4, 482
phone hacking scandal 451, 455–6
photographs 452–3, 473–7
precedent 453, 454
Press Complaints Commission 451–2, 455–7
Press Recognition Panel 456
problem question 677
public interest 457–8, 475, 478–9
publish, right to 455
reasonableness 455, 465–9, 474–7, 482
self-regulation 451–2, 454–5
sexual activity 460, 467, 474–5, 477–8, 486
social media 450–1
strip searches of prison visitors 435–6, 480–1
super-injunctions 451, 478–80
telephone tapping 453
Younger Committee 454
Private and family life, right to respect for, 469–73
balancing exercise 469–73, 481–2
celebrities 471–2, 474–5
commercially sensitive information 474
definition 472
freedom of expression 450, 469–73, 481–2
balancing exercise 469–73, 481–2
public interest 471
qualified right, as 471
Human Rights Act 1998 450, 469–73, 482
journalistic, literary or artistic material 470
media 469–73, 481
misuse of private information 464
nuisance 552–3, 565–6, 574–8, 581
photographs 471
police 151
prior notification, right to 475
public bodies 142–3, 145–53, 470
qualified right, as 471
strip-searches of prison visitors 480–1
suicide attempts, broadcasting of 481
Private nuisance 545–78
abatement 571–3
self-help 571–3
trespass 571–2
amenity interests, interference with 547–50, 552, 555–6, 572
bad intention 562–4
balancing of interests 546, 547, 554
coming to nuisance 567–9
continuing or adopting a nuisance 599–600
contributory negligence 564
damages 555, 560, 568–78, 581
defences 564–9
definition 547–50
discrimination 578
economic loss 573
encroachment 451, 548
factors to be considered 553–64
fault 562
foreseeability 32, 561–2, 572
harassment 551–2
Human Rights Act 1998 552, 574–8
indirect and unreasonable interferences 545–7
industrialisation 548–9
injunctions 551, 550, 555, 557, 560, 563–4, 567–71, 577–8
intensity of interference 553, 555, 581
intention 554, 562–4
interests in land 550–2
locality rule 549, 554, 555–7, 581
malice 563–4
negligence 576
neighbours 545–7, 562–3, 571, 580–1
noise 554, 557, 564, 565, 566, 570–1, 574
ownership rights 547
personal injuries, damages for 572–3
physical damage 547–50
planning permission 554, 557–9, 565
pollution 546–9, 556, 574, 578
prescription (20 years) 566–9

private and family life, right to respect for 552–3, 565–6, 574–8, 581
problem question 679
proof of damage 547
public benefit of activities 568–9, 578
public interest 546, 571, 574
public nuisance 578–9, 581
reasonable user of land 553–64, 569, 581
Rylands v *Fletcher*, actions under 592, 596, 598–603
sensitivity of the claimant 554, 559–62, 581
sewerage undertakers 574–6
smell 547–50, 555–6, 558, 572–3, 575
statutory authority, defence of 565–6
television reception, interference with 551–2, 560
tree roots or branches, encroachment of 572
trespass distinguished 547–8, 571–2
volenti non fit injuria 564
who can sue 550–3, 581

Privity of contract 33, 35, 355, 383–4

Problem questions 665–82

Product liability 353–84
blood products, infection with contaminated 372–4, 377
breach of duty 358–60
burden of proof 364, 370, 377–8
carelessness 33, 358–9
causation 354, 358–60, 374–5, 384
cigarettes and alcohol 365–6
claims, bringing 363–4
compensation culture 368–9
complex structure theory 357
consumer expectation test 364, 368–72
Consumer Protection Act 1987 Part 1 354, 362–84
contractual relationships 33–4, 354–5, 383–4
contributory negligence 368–9
damages 357–8, 363, 367–9
defect, definition of 364–74
defences 363, 375–7
design defects 360–2, 369–70, 378
deterrence 358
development risks defence/state of the art defence 375–8, 384
Donoghue v *Stevenson* 354–60, 384
duty of care 33, 356–8, 360–1
economic loss 194, 198, 355, 357
fault 361–3, 365, 375, 377
floodgates argument 355–6
foreseeability 361
goods, definition of 364
harmful characteristics of products 373
instructions 367
insurance 362
intermediate examination 359–60
legitimate expectations 368, 373
limitations 374–5, 384
limits of negligent liability 360–2
manufacturers 33, 36, 354, 355–65, 369–70, 374–8, 384
negligence, claims in 355–61, 363, 384
non-standard and standard products 373
personal injury and death 362–3
policy 367
privity of contract 33, 355, 383–4
problem question 674
producers 363, 374–5, 377–8
Product Liability Directive 362–3, 373
product, definition of 364
property damage 362–4
recalls 358
replacements 357
scope of liability 356–60
smoking 365–6
standard of care 355, 365, 376
strict liability 354, 361–3, 369–70, 372–3, 375, 377–8, 384
suppliers 363
Thalidomide tragedy 360–1, 375, 378
toxic shock syndrome 366–7
ultimate consumers 34–5, 356
warnings 355, 366–7, 371–2
wrongful birth 367

Property damage 3, 140, 321, 362–4, 547–50

Proximity 68, 69–70 *see also* **Three-stage test**
armed forces 171
fair, just and reasonable test 71–2
fire services 156
foreseeability 66
neighbour principle 33–6, 47, 61–2, 74, 219
omissions 82
police 148–52, 161, 168
psychiatric harm 106–7, 116, 118–20, 123, 129, 133
public bodies 175–6
third parties 90–3, 95–6, 100
vulnerable adults, local authorities' duty to 47–56

Psychiatric harm 3–4, 102–37
Alcock control mechanisms 116–17, 120–6, 128–33, 136
anxiety and distress, ordinary feelings of 104
asbestos, exposure to 110
assumption of responsibility 134–6
bystanders 118, 127
causation 130
childbirth 111
clinical negligence 120–5
close ties of love and affection 116–17, 123
closeness to accident 116
communication of shocking news 126, 132–3
control mechanisms 105, 112, 116–21, 126, 131
corrective justice 115, 130–1
definition 103–5
distributive justice 130–1
duty of care 43, 58–9, 102–37
egg shell skull rule 112
employers' liability 129–32, 134–6, 394
exaggerated or fraudulent claims 136
exclusionary rule 105–6
false claims, fear of 136
floodgates argument 125
foreseeability 107–10 112–13, 118, 128, 133–6
grief 104, 113
harassment 420
Hillsborough Stadium disaster 105, 107–8, 114–18, 128–9, 132–3
immediate aftermath of accidents 36, 113, 118–20, 126, 132–4
involuntary participants/unwitting participants 131–2
Law Commission 106, 120
means by which shock is caused 119–27
physical injuries 103–4, 106, 108–12, 127–31, 136
police 105–8, 114–16, 119, 128–30, 168

Psychiatric harm (*Continued*)
policy 4, 103–5, 112, 133–4
post-traumatic stress disorder (PTSD) 104, 117–18, 131
primary victims 107–12, 115, 124, 126–32
prisoners, suicide of 134
problem question 667
proximity 106–7, 116, 118–20, 123, 129, 133
recognised psychiatric illnesses 104, 113, 116
relationships with immediate victims 116–18
rescuers 107, 127–31
restrictions 106
secondary victims 107–8, 112–28, 130
self-harm by defendants 133–4
stress at work 134–6, 394
sudden shocking events 119–20, 124–5
televised events 115, 125–6, 132–3
time and space, proximity in 118–20, 123
whiplash 106
Wilkinson v *Downton*, tort in 436–40
witnesses 105, 107, 115–29, 133–5
Public bodies, private law duties of 138–87 *see also* **Emergency services; Police**
alternative claims 146–7
armed forces 155, 171–3, 174
assumption of responsibility 145–6, 177–8, 184
child protection 143–4, 152–4, 177, 182–3
conflicts of interest 143–4
corrective justice 179
Crown immunity from suit 141
defensive practices 141
district councils 174–5
distributive justice 141
duty of care 138–87
education-based claims 179–82, 184–5
assessment of needs 180–1
assumption of responsibility 181
dyslexia, failure to diagnose 180–1
European Convention on Human Rights (ECHR) 181–2
messed up lives, claims relating to 179–80
policy 180
vicarious liability 181
effective remedy, right to an 184
exclusionary rule 140–2
fair, just and reasonable test 177, 178, 182
fair trial, right to a 153–5, 184
foreseeability 175
foster care 183
gross incompetence 140
Human Rights Act 1998 21, 139, 143, 184
immunity/exemption 154–5
inhuman or degrading treatment 153–4, 184
judicial reluctance to allow recovery 140–2
justiciability of claims 142, 175–9, 181
Law Commission 178–9
local authorities 37, 174–5, 177, 184–5
messed up lives, claims relating to 37, 179–84
neglect 140
novel claims, recognition of 37, 179–84
omissions 140, 142, 184
parliamentary sovereignty 140
personal injuries 140, 142
policy 139, 143, 180, 183
powers and duties distinction 175–7
precedent 154
private and family life, right to respect for 143, 184, 470
problem question 668
property damage 140
proximity 175–6
public/private divide 141, 175
resources 175–6
separation of powers 140
social claims 180–1, 182–5
standard of care 178, 181
striking out 153–4
third parties 142, 184
vexatious claims 141
vicarious liability 181, 183–4
vulnerable tenants, campaign of harassment and bullying against 145–6, 183–4
when public bodies owe a duty of care 142–6
Public figures see **Celebrities/ public figures**
Public interest
breach of confidence 460, 462–3
defamation 506, 507, 511, 512–17
freedom of expression 471
misuse of private information 468
nuisance 546, 571, 574
privacy 457–8, 475, 478–9
Public nuisance 578–80
class, definition of a 580
obstruction of the highway 579–80
private nuisance 578–9, 581
Publicity 8, 20, 22

R

Rape myths 167
Reasonableness *see also* **Fair, just and reasonable test**
assault 418–19
breach of statutory duty 404
Clapham omnibus, man on the 220
contributory negligence 304, 305–6, 313
defamation 491, 502, 504, 522
duty of care 29, 34–6, 61–4, 66–7, 73–4
employers' liability 388–9
feminist critique 220–1
foreseeability 61–4, 66–7
negligence 29, 37–8, 327–36, 341, 345–6
nuisance 553–64, 569, 581
omissions 84
precautions 240
privacy 455, 465–9, 474–7, 482
reliance 206–9, 214
standard of care 43, 219–24, 236–7, 240, 248
Recklessness 237, 320, 414, 415, 423
Re-entry, right of 545
References 213–14, 394, 510–11
Reliance 193, 196–7, 201–2, 206–9, 212, 214
Remoteness 280–3
causation 252, 279, 280–3
duty of care 58, 62–3
egg shell skull rule 282–3
extent of damage 281
foreseeability 280–3
negligence 42
physical damage 282
problem question 671
reasonableness 62
Rylands v *Fletcher*, actions under 591–2
type of damage 281–2
Res ipsa loquitur 247–8, 249
Rescue, duty to 78–80, 82–5, 107, 127–31, 241–2
Retribution 629–31, 648
Revenge pornography 468

Road traffic accidents (RTAs)
burden of proof 247
children 306, 310–12
contributory negligence 305–12
criminal offences 4
damages 654, 656
drink driving 295, 309
duty of care 58–9
helmet, failure to wear a motorcycle 309
Highway Code, breach of 247
illegality 302
insurance 223, 648–9, 657
intervening acts 284–5
learner drivers 222
no-fault scheme, proposal for 656
seatbelts 307, 308–10
standard of care 222, 224–5, 236, 247
volenti non fit injuria 293–4
whiplash 16, 42, 106, 641, 654, 660
***Rylands* v *Fletcher*, rule in** 2, 538, 583–604
Acts of God 598
Cambridge Water case 585, 590–3, 596, 599, 601, 603
consent 597
contributory negligence 598
damages 591–2, 594
danger test 587
defences 597–9
duty of care 600–1
economic loss 596
escapes of dangerous things onto land 587, 588–9, 591–2, 597–8, 601
EU law 592
fault 584, 597
foreseeability 585, 591–5, 597, 599–600
industrialisation 584, 586, 603
insurance 595
intention 589
mischief test 586–8, 595
natural causes 598
negligence 538, 599–601, 603
non-natural use of land 585, 589–95
polluter pays 594
private nuisance 592, 596, 598–603
problem question 680
remoteness 591–2
social justice 586
statutory authority 598
strangers, acts of 597
strict liability 584–6, 590, 598, 600, 602
Transco v *Stockport MBC* 584–90, 592, 594–6
trespass 589
volenti non fit injuria 597–8
who can sue 596–7

S

Seatbelts 307, 308–10
Self-defence 435
Self-help 545, 571–3
Self-regulation 451–2, 454–5
Separation of powers 140
Sexual harassment 6, 443, 462–3
Single interest torts 4
Skill and care 33, 221, 389–90
Smoking 308, 365–6
Social Action Responsibility and Heroism Act (SARAH) 2015 17, 83, 246
Social claims 145, 180–1, 182–5
Social media
defamation 489, 495–7, 500–1, 504, 522, 524–5
privacy 450–1
Social security and welfare state 14, 18, 40, 651–3, 657
Sporting events
spectators 292–3
standard of care 242–3, 246
volenti non fit injuria 292–3, 296–7
Squatting 543
Stalking 440, 445
Standard of care 29, 46, 217–50
asbestos, exposure to 238–9
balance of factors 243–4, 248
Bolam test 226–36
breach of duty 217–50
breach of statutory duty 246, 404
burden of proof 247–9
carelessness 248
causation 45, 254
children 225–6
Clapham omnibus, man on the 220
clinical negligence 226–36, 238–9
Bolam test 226–36
causation 232
respectable body of medical opinion 226–36
warn, failure to 231, 234–5
common practice 226–36
Compensation Act 2006 245–6
deterrence 246
Donoghue v *Stevenson* 32
emergency services 157, 241–2
employers' liability 239–40
entertainment events 218–19
errors and mistakes 219–20
establishing breach of duty 247–8
fault 43–4
foreseeability 237–9, 243
heat of the moment 241–2
historical development 32
horseplay 225–6, 242
individual responsibility 248
insurance 224
Learned Hand test 245
negligence 320, 324, 327–36, 346
neighbour principle 219
objective standard 220–5
police 164
precautions 239–43, 248
probability of injury 237–9, 243–4
problem question 670
product liability 355, 365, 376
public bodies 178, 181
reasonableness 43, 219–24, 236–7, 240, 248
recklessness 237
res ipsa loquitur 247–8, 249
rescuers 241–2
resources 241
road traffic accidents 222, 224–5, 236, 247
school trips 218–19
seriousness of injury 239–40, 243–4, 248
setting the standard of care 236–43
Social Action, Responsibility and Heroism Act 2015 245–6
social value of activities 241–3, 246, 248
special skills 226–36
sporting events 242–3, 246
Stress at work 134–6, 394, 446
Strict liability
defamation 503
negligence 38–9
product liability 354, 361–3, 369–70, 372–3, 375, 377–8, 384
Rylands v *Fletcher*, actions under 584–6, 590, 598, 600, 602
vicarious liability 608
Striking out 149, 151–4, 169
Subsoil, trespass into 541
Suicide 85–6, 100, 134, 168–9, 286–7, 481
Super-injunctions 408, 451, 478–80, 494, 525
Supervision 90, 95, 389–90, 392–4
Surveys 209

T

Telephones
harassment 420
phone hacking scandal 451, 455–6
tapping 453
Television reception, interference with 551–2, 560
Thalidomide tragedy 360–1, 375, 378
Thin skull rule 282–3
Third parties 79, 89–99, 100
abate danger, failure to 90, 97–8, 100
assumption of responsibility 93–6, 100
causation 90, 95, 98
contract 22, 33, 35, 90–4, 355, 383–4
control third party, duty to 89–90, 94, 100
danger, creation of a source of 90, 96–7, 100
foreseeability 90–1, 93, 98
insurance 91
intervening acts 90, 95
negligence 335
novel category, as 98
omissions 79, 89, 94–5, 100
police duty to victims of crime 91, 94–6
policy 91, 93
positive duty to act 93
problem question 666
proximity 90–3, 95–6, 100
public bodies 142, 184
Rylands v *Fletcher* 597
special relationships 90–6, 100
defendants and claimants 90–5, 96
third parties and defendants 95–6
supervision, relationships of 90, 95
trespass to land 98
warn, duty to 93, 96
Three-stage test 68–71, 74–6 *see also* **Fair, just and reasonable test; Foreseeability; Proximity**
Anns, retreat from 69
analogy, reasoning from 68, 74–5
Caparo test 68–71, 74–6
carelessness 69
debunking the test 68–9
novel situations 69–71
policy 69
Time limitations 642–6, 661
Tort law, definition of 2–3, 22
Tree roots or branches, encroachment of 572
Trespass to land 539–45
ab initio trespass 542, 544–5
abatement 571–2
actionable per se, as 30, 539
activism and publicity 30
airspace 539, 540–2
children 330, 339–40
damages 544
defences 542–3
direct interference 539–40, 545, 580
injunctions 545
intention 540–2, 580
legal justification 542
licences 542, 544
mesne profits, actions for 545
necessity 543–4
negligence 320–1, 326, 330, 339–40, 344, 544–5
nuisance 547–8, 571–2
overhanging plants 539
ownership or possession of land 539
physical interference 539–40
problem question 679
re-entry, right of 545
remedies 544–5
Rylands v *Fletcher*, actions under 589
self-help 545
squatting 543
subsoil 541
third parties 98
warning notices 344
Trespass to the person 30, 411–21
Trust and confidence, relationships of 194, 203
Two hunters problem 272

U

Unfair contract terms 209, 292, 333–4

V

Vicarious liability 22, 608–24
akin to employment test 612–18, 623
attribution of conduct 611
atypical workers 612
child abuse 614–16, 617, 620, 644–5
close connection test 616, 619–22
common employment doctrine 391
common law 608
control test 609, 614
corrective justice 608
course of employment 388, 612, 619–23
damages 644–5, 648
education-based claims 181
employment relationships 87, 387–8, 608–24
foster parents 617
harassment 618–19
independent contractors 612–13, 617–18
insurance 648
integral part of business activities test 618
intention 622
justifications for imposition of duty 609–12
loss-spreading 609
non-delegable duties 612–14, 623
omissions 87, 88
policy 610, 615, 623
problem question 681
public bodies 181, 183–4
Salmond test 619–20
strict liability 608
tortious acts 618–19
wrongful and unauthorised mode of doing acts 619–22
Victimisation 390–1
Vindication 9, 19–20, 525
Visitors 321–36, 339–40, 343–4
Volenti non fit injuria 291–7, 312–13
contributory negligence 294–6
drink driving 295
employers' liability 387–8
establishment of defence 293–7
exclusion clauses 292
individual responsibility 295
intoxication 291–2
knowledge 292–6
nuisance 564
occupiers' liability 292
Rylands v *Fletcher*, actions under 598
spectators 292–3
sport 292–3, 296–7
warning notices 292
Vulnerable adults, local authorities' duty to 48–55, 145–6, 183–4

W

Warnings
clinical negligence 231, 234–5
failure to warn 231, 234–5
notices 292, 334

occupiers' liability 292
product liability 355, 366–7, 371–2
third parties 93, 96
trespass 344
Websites/Internet *see also* **Social media**
defamation 522–3, 525
harassment 443
online campaigns or trolling 443
percolation phenomenon 525
pseudonyms 523
Welfare state and social security 14, 18, 40, 651–3, 657
Whiplash claims 16, 42, 106, 641, 654, 660
***Wilkinson* v *Downton*, tort in** 2, 411, 420–1, 436–40, 446
damages 654
harassment 411, 437–8, 446
intention 436–9
negligence 436
practical jokes 436–40
psychiatric harm 411, 436–40
strip searches of prison visitors 437
Wills, drafting of 210–14
Women
battery 416–17
feminist critique 220–1, 416–17
pregnancy and childbirth 112–13, 124, 203, 232–3, 271, 360–1, 367
sexual harassment 6, 443, 462–3
violence and abuse against women, reporting in media of 490–1
***Woodroffe-Hedley* v *Cuthbertson*, case study on** 8–20
Workplace injuries *see* **Employers' liability**
Wrongful birth claims 367
Wrongs 1–2, 22

Young Report 660